Detroit Studies in Music Bibliography, No. 81

Editors
J. Bunker and Marilyn S. Clark
University of Kansas

PRIVATE MUSIC COLLECTIONS

CATALOGS
AND
COGNATE
LITERATURE

James B. Coover

HARMONIE PARK PRESS
WARREN, MICHIGAN 2001

Copyright 2001 by Harmonie Park Press

Printed and bound in the United States of America
Published by
Harmonie Park Press
23630 Pinewood
Warren, Michigan 48091

Editors, J. Bunker Clark and Elaine Gorzelski
Cover design, Mitchell Groters
Typographer, Kristin Bernacchi

Library of Congress Cataloging-in-Publication Data

Coover, James, 1925-
 Private music collections : catalogs and cognate literature / James B. Coover.
  p. cm. -- (Detroit studies in music bibliography ; no. 81)
  Includes bibliographical references and index.
  ISBN 0-89990-099-2 (alk. paper)
   1. Music libraries--Catalogs--Bibliography. 2. Private
libraries--Catalogs--Bibliography. I. Title. II. Series.

ML111.C64 2001
026.78--dc21   2001020417

Dedicated with profound gratitude and affection to

Mrs. Eulalia Chapman
Director, Bibliographical Center for Research
Denver, Colorado
1943-61

Miss Eileen Thornton
Director, Vassar College Library
Poughkeepsie, New York
1945-56

Dr. Carol June Bradley
Music Library, Vassar College, 1960-67;
since then,
Associate Director of the Music Library and
Adjunct Professor of Music at the
State University of New York at Buffalo

Contents

Foreword

Our first music collectors were presumably bards, out after new repertory. The best collectors would likely also have been the most venerable bards, but their collections survived only as they were passed on to other bardic collectors. The emergence of musical notation, mostly over the late middle ages, and the printing press in the Renaissance, mark the turning points in the story of music collecting. And almost at once the story must have begun to get nasty as collectors, with the evidence on paper, confronted the bards, who may never have known or may have forgotten what was now on paper, but who also knew that the music itself was really somewhere else. However strongly one sides with the bards, one also welcomes the collectors, even if they were also the first known music critics, and even as their efforts anticipate the textual study of modern musicologists. The passion of music, along with the search for its meaning, thus comes to be shared, both by those who perform it and listen to it, and by those who love it so deeply as to want to confess their love by collecting its documentary evidence. Not surprisingly, the chemistries of music lovers and of bibliophiles blend together to produce potent legendry.

The census is exotic and vast. Behind the solemn entries cited here lies a deep passion, often an eccentricity, that recalls Holbrook Jackson's *The Anatomy of Bibliomania* (1932). Many of Jackson's rubrics are clearly exemplified in the pages that follow. "Poverty no Hindrance, Riches no Help" (Jackson's part 3, section 4): might he have in mind Walter N. H. Harding? "The Book Thief " (part 17, section 3): is he not thinking of the scoundrels in Berlin who haunted the Deutsche Staatsbibliothek just after World War II? "Of Book-Hunting" (part 21): this was said to be Alfred Cortot's favorite pastime in the afternoon to take his mind off his evening concert.

As for the vast range of music collectors, this compendium naturally raises questions of scope. What is a music collector? Do those who collect in other areas, and find the odd music book that they want, thereby become music collectors? Do composers (like Beethoven, Gershwin, or Mozart) become collectors merely because they fail to throw or give away their manuscripts? Does this apply to performers and their working scores? How about the bardic collectors of oral artifacts (like Millman Parry) or our burgeoning population of discophiles? If the answers to these questions are yes, readers can argue for countless addenda. If no, some of the most fascinating entries would need to go. The answer could also be maybe. Some, but not all, composers and performers were also serious bibliophiles, from Johannes Brahms (see frontispiece), Camille Saint-Saëns, and Jerome Kern, to Boris Christoff and Fritz Kreisler. Were their bibliophilic tastes reflected in the music they made? One can conjecture endlessly, and with as much delight, or agony, as one might wish. As for the folk music field workers, the collecting lineage requires even more problematical definitions, if it is not to end in Homer himself (or themselves), not to mention King David collecting his psalms from angelic performances on high.

This book chronicles those among them whose names are recorded, and in an array of sources that James Coover has been turning up over the years. If the list is long, it is partly because the years in question are now approaching fifty, also because good librarians are by definition those who know how to scare out the unusual sources. He has not chased down every personal source, partly because verifying particulars is problematic, partly because there are so many possible sources. The record, as this book tells us, is vast. Its list can not possibly be complete—at most it can survey the dimensions and guide the reader to the evidence. Its debts are recorded (to cite some of the landmarks singled out in the introduction) in A. Hyatt King's elegant scholarly insights and Lenore Coral's antiquarian diligence, and thanks to Otto Albrecht's journalistic curiosity and Siegrun Folter's vigorous fascination with great landmarks. (See "Sources and Related Readings" for citations, pp. xxv-xxxviii.) Coover seems well aware of the challenge. Rather than working to surpass any of these in their particular strength, he has been satisfied with the strength of the earlier major source he uses extensively, Marie Bobillier. Her 1913 survey is remembered as one that attempts, through a bibliographic list, to call attention to a topic that needs to be recognized in its own right. Her section on "Bibliothèques privées" (pp. 124-39) includes a total of 134 titles; Coover lists between twenty and thirty times as many—ample evidence that she had a good idea, as well as a topic that will be with us longer than some today may wish us to believe. Music is a demanding art, and this long and fascinating list attests to that.

D. W. KRUMMEL

University of Illinois, Urbana
June 2000

Acknowledgments

This work has been in progress for almost forty years, putting me profoundly in debt to literally dozens of friends and colleagues—too many to thank appropriately. For what is right about the book, of course, they share responsibility; for its flaws, none.

I cannot avoid repeating words of gratitude offered to many persons acknowledged in my earlier works, *Music at Auction* (1988), *Antiquarian Catalogues of Musical Interest* (1988), and *Musical Instrument Collections* (1981). But I shall try to abbreviate.

I am particularly indebted to a number of libraries, especially the British Library, its Trustees; the assistants in the Reading Room and the North Library, the heads of the Music Division, A. Hyatt King, Oliver Neighbour, and Hugh Cobbe; and the head of music in the manuscript division, Arthur Searle. The remarkable collections of the Grolier Club in New York City were thrown open to me over a period of years by its then librarian, Robert Nikirk. The Music Division of the New York Public Library under Frank Campbell and, at that time, the head of Rare Books, Susan Sommer, assisted constantly. David McKitterick at Cambridge University granted me stack privileges to solve some knotty problems. The Rare Book Section of the Regenstein Library at the University of Chicago, and the Reference Divison of the Newberry Library in Chicago were equally helpful.

Most rewarding, too, was a chance to spend a week working in the vast collections at the Vereeniging ter Bervordering van de Belangen des Boekhandels in Amsterdam, administered by Dr. G. J. Brouwer and his colleague Dr. F. van den Bosch. A remarkable resource! The Sibley Library at the Eastman School of Music and its then associate director, Charles Lindahl, were very generous during a number of visits, giving me unobstructed access to the collections I needed. Dr. C. J. J. von Gleich and his staff of the Music Department at the Gemeentemuseum in Den Haag made my week-long stay there unusually productive.

The venerable firm of Christie's in London gave me access to its muniments room and its early catalogs. A number of antiquarian music dealers considerately opened their collections to me and volunteered good advice. Among them were William Reeves, H. Baron, Albi Rosenthal, Theodore Front, Nigel Simeone, J. & J. Lubrano, and Richard Macnutt.

Important counsel, lists, and background information were graciously and frequently furnished by Lenore Coral, music librarian at Cornell University and one of the pioneer investigators of music auction sales. Her University of London dissertation remains a pivotal work in studies of the retail music trade.

Over many years I have admired and learned from the many articles and books by my friend Dr. D. W. Krummel, who has graciously supplied his own introduction to this work. The bibliographical world will be indebted to his many and varied scholarly writings for a long time to come.

To the many others whose contributions of verifications, copies of title pages, and other knowledge cannot be fully specified, my sincere gratitude. Their help came mostly by mail, and to repeat an earlier acknowledgment: each problem they helped to solve was, without that help, probably insoluble, and each solution was important.

> Hugh Amory, Houghton Library, Harvard University
> Dr. Alf Annegarn, librarian, Instituut voor Muziekwetenschap, Rijksuniversitet, Utrecht
> Dr. Otto Biba, Gesellschaft der Musikfreunde, Vienna
> Anne J. Blankert, librarian, Rijksbureau voor Kunsthistorische Documentatie, Den Haag
> Ruth Bleeker, curator of music, Boston Public Library
> Dr. Blom, Oberbibliotheksrat, Universitäts- und Stadtbibliothek, Köln
> Evan Bonds, then music librarian, University of Virginia
> Jean Bowen, head, Reference Division, New York Public Library
> The librarians at the Civico museo bibliografico musicale, Bologna
> Susan Clement, music specialist, Library of Congress
> Conservateur en chef, Bibliothèque Royal Albert Ier
> A. B. Craven, director of Library Services, Central Library, Leeds
> Margaret Crum, assistant librarian, Department of Western Manuscripts, Bodleian Library, Oxford University
> Mrs. Susan Dean, Special Collections, Newberry Library, Chicago
> Rudolf Elvers, Musikabteilung, Staatsbibliothek, Berlin
> Stephen Fry, then head of the Music Library, University of California at Los Angeles
> Laila Garpe, Lending Department, Kungliga Biblioteket, Stockholm
> Dr. R. Heilinger, Katalogabteilung, Österreichische Nationalbibliothek, Vienna

Jacques Lethève and Simone Wallon, Bibliothèque nationale, Paris

Rene de Maeyer, curator, Koninklijk Muziekconservatorium, Brussels

A. Märker, Bibliothek, Historisches Museum, Frankfurt a.M.

Ralph Malbon, City Librarian, Liverpool

João Oliveira da Costa, Biblioteca Nacional de Lisboa

Paul Raspe, Library of the Conservatoire Royal de Musique, Brussels

Ellen Roeser, Leiter, Musikbibliothek der Stadt, Leipzig

Leanne Langley Scruton, editor, Macmillan, London

Caroline T. Spicer, Reference Department, Olin Library, Cornell University, Ithaca

E. Stollar, Phillips (firm), auctioneers, London

Dr. Magda Strebl, Leiterin der Katalogabteilung, Österreichische Nationalbibliothek, Vienna

E. Thys, librarian, Staadsbibliotheek, Antwerp

Toonkunst Bibliotheek, Amsterdam

Rigbie Turner, Music Department, Pierpont Morgan Library, New York City

Dr. F. Vandenhole, head of the Documentation Department, Centrale Bibliotheek,
    Rijksuniversiteit, Ghent

Barbara F. Veloz, reference librarian, Smithsonian Institution Libraries, Washington, D.C.

Dott.ssa Angela Vinay, Istituto centrale per il catalogo unico delle biblioteche italiane, Rome

Diane Parr Walker, music librarian, University of Virginia

Simone Wallon, conservateur, Bibliothèque nationale, Paris

Prof. Emilia Zanetti, librarian, Biblioteca musicale governativa del Conservatorio di Musica
    "S. Cecilia," Rome

Lengthy working trips to Britain, Holland, and many libraries in the U.S. were made possible by two grants from the Research Foundation of the State University of New York, and another from the American Council of Learned Societies. Earlier awards were received from the Salmon Fund at Vassar College. The Buffalo campus of the State University has always been supportive of my work in sometimes mundane but invariably critical ways.

I am immeasurably indebted to Christopher R. Coover of the Book and Manuscript Division of Christie's, New York, for sharing with me his insights into the book trade, collectors, and collecting. Dr. Carol June Bradley, who read portions of the typescript and offered timely advice, played a significant role in the work's completion. I am also profoundly grateful for the care lavished on the production of the book by Prof. J. Bunker Clark, the editor of the series, and by Elaine Gorzelski and Kristin Bernacchi of Harmonie Park Press.

Introduction

*If printing is the art preservative of all arts, then book
collecting is the preservative of that preservative.*[1]

This work, first, identifies the most important literature relating to private music collections—that is, books and descriptive articles (both published and unpublished), manuscript lists, household inventories, sale catalogs, and the like. It is intended as a specific complement to my earlier book on musical instrument collections.[2] Its second goal is to indicate the present whereabouts of those collections, both those with literature and those without.

The earliest list here is dated 1467, the latest 1995. There are no geographical or language limitations. I hope it appeals to music researchers, bibliophiles, students of collectors and collecting, and to those interested in provenance and taste. (For amplification of the scope and the various treatments of the information included, see the Table of Contents.)

COLLECTORS

Most people are, to varying degrees, collectors of one thing or another, often for inscrutable reasons. One reason is fairly common, however: we like possessions—especially if they are unique or the best of their kind—that permit us to feel part of something that has been going on for a long time.[3]

"Private Libraries," pp. 44-67 of my book *Music at Auction*, a summary of the music sales of the London auction firm of Puttick and Simpson from 1794 to 1971. Listed in the section "Sources" as **Coover 2**. This and subsequent sigla, are from "Sources and Related Readings," pp. xxv-xxxviii.

[1] John T. Winterich, *The Grolier Club, 1884-1967* (New York: Grolier Club, 1967), 49.

[2] *Musical Instrument Collections: Catalogues and Cognate Literature,* this series, 47 (this publisher, 1981).

[3] John T. Winterich and David Randall, *A Primer of Book Collecting* (New York: Crown, 1966), 179-80.

Excitement often flavors the collecting process, and for some the chase becomes transcendent. Though modest the initial impulse, "the bump of acquisitiveness,"[4] as the celebrated bookseller Dr. Rosenbach called it, is apt to develop. The afflicted then collect for the sake of collecting; the pursuit grows more intoxicating than its outcome—ownership. "Bibliomania"[5] fuels a few contests among collectors in the auction and antiquarian trade. But what may seem to be unsuitable avarice often turns out to be Carter's "scholarly motive."[6]

Knowledge, taste, energy, a competitive spirit, skilled buying techniques, good advice, and an abundance of money brought together such extraordinary music collections as those of Hirsch, Fétis, Heyer, Matthew, Cortot, Scheurleer, Wolffheim, and other true bibliophiles.[7] To those so driven, and to many of lesser zeal (or smaller purses), we owe incalculable debts. We would be poor without such great collections.

LITERATURE

We have not as energetically studied and appreciated a number of lesser but worthwhile collections. Fortunately, that is changing. The literature is rapidly expanding, encouraging additional investigations. Notable among recent studies are A. Hyatt King's book on British collectors (1963);[8] Lenore Coral's dissertation on music in early British auction (1974);[9] Otto Albrecht's article on private music collections in *New Grove*;[10] James T. Fuld and David Hunter's "Collectors and Music Bibliography";[11] Siegrund Folter's 1987 *Private Libraries*;[12] the series of directories of music libraries in various countries prepared by Rita Benton;[13] directories of American music collections by Carol June Bradley;[14] and *RAMH*.[15] All of these include information about private libraries absorbed into institutions. And to them, this book is immensely indebted.

Some of this expanding literature has focused on composers' libraries. In this bibliography, for example, at least 24 citations concern J. S. Bach's library, including reprints, translations, reprints of reprints, and

[4] Abraham Simon Wolf Rosenbach, *Books and Bidders* (Boston: Little, Brown & Co., 1927), 254.

[5] A term used by, among others, Joseph Rosenblum in his article "John Allan: Methodical Bibliomaniac," *American Book Collector* 7 (February 1987): 3-11. It has been labelled by others as *Biblioholism*, the title of Tom Raabe's book (Golden, Colorado: Fulcrum, 1991); "Collectomania"; *An Unruly Passion*, the subtitle of Werner Meunsterberger's book *Collecting* (Princeton University Press, 1994); or *A Gentle Madness*, the title Nicholas Basbanes chose for his splendid 1995 book (New York: Holt).

[6] John Carter, "Definition of a Book-Collector," *Bouillabaisse for Bibliophiles*, ed. William Targ (Cleveland and New York: World Publishing Co., 1955), 23.

[7] Perhaps nowhere more epitomized than the agitation of the Scheide family, as described by Basbanes (p. 271) when John, the son of the founder, feuded with Dr. Rosenbach over 5/8 of an inch having been trimmed from the side margins of an Icelandic Bible. The good Dr. won!

[8] **King**, 254.

[9] **Coral**.

[10] **Albrecht**.

[11] In *Music Publishing and Collecting: Essays in Honor of Donald W. Krummel*, ed. David Hunter (Urbana-Champaign: University of Illinois, 1994).

[12] **Folter**.

[13] **Benton**.

[14] **Bradley**.

[15] *RAMH*.

studies of contents. For his son C. P. E. Bach, there are 10 such citations; for Beethoven, 14; and for Brahms, 21. Perhaps more interesting are the numbers for some non-composers: for Fuchs, an astonishing 36; for Santini and Toulouse/Philidor, 29 each; for Hirsch, 20; for Scheurleer, 14; for Heyer, 13; and for Zweig, 17.

Equally interesting but discomfiting are the few references to women's collections. The rich libraries formed by Mary Flagler Cary, Mary Louise Bok, and Nadia Boulanger, for example, have drawn less attention than they may deserve. Several sales of music instruments by Puttick & Simpson from 1891 to 1903 included the properties of "A Lady." Only three collections indexed in a book listing nearly 6,000 music antiquarian catalogues[16] are identified as those of women. In the following list, only the twelve citations relating to the library of Anna Amalia, Princess of Prussia, begin to match the number of citations for men's libraries noted above.

Ephemera

Wise collectors usually can distinguish the significant from the commonplace, but not everything they gather is routinely bibliophilic. Commonplace items creep in, and ephemera is hard to avoid. Nevertheless, good collectors form coherent collections and preserve the essential tools for future scholarship.

At the time of acquisition, some of that may be ephemera, but the trifles of one generation are frequently the treasures of the next. The huge collections amassed by the legendary, "obsessed" Sir Thomas Phillipps, the greatest book and manuscript collector of all time, serve as lessons. Among the thousands of extraordinary bibliophilic treasures were vast quantities of manuscript material, much of it considered worthless by most of his contemporaries, much of it, in fact, dredged from dustbins where it was destined for pulping. Among these seemingly insignificant scraps were documents today considered priceless.[17]

He fulfilled what John Carter calls one of a collector's most significant functions: "to anticipate the scholar and historian, to find some interest where none was recognized before, to rescue books from obscurity, to pioneer a subject or an author by seeking out and assembling the raw material for study."[18]

Institutional Libraries

Whole or in part, by gift or purchase, many collections ineluctably end up in institutions. Institutions actively collect, too. The materials they gather remain preserved and available to the world, and while this flow comforts scholars it elicits lamentation from collectors, auctioneers, and antiquarians. Their "life

---

[16] **Coover**.

[17] Sir Thomas was not a collector of music, but musicians will nevertheless be fascinated and informed by the story of this extraordinary person in Nicolas Barker's *Portrait of an Obsession* (London: Constable, 1967), a condensation of A. N. L. Munby's magnificent *Phillipps Studies* (Cambridge, 1951-60; reprint, London: Sotheby Parke Bernet Publications, 1971).

[18] **Carter**, 25.

blood," as Frank Herrmann notes,[19] is the recirculation of coveted materials. But there is an ongoing redefinition of that to be coveted, the commonplace of one century becoming the desired rarity of the next. A steady supply of materials for sale seems assured. And Landon's remarks about institutional obligations should be of some comfort to those who lament.[20]

SALES

This is not to say that we will ever again see libraries at sale rivalling those of Harley, Sunderland, Ashburnham, Phillipps, Heber, Turner, Spencer, Rosburghe, Huth, and the rest, for we will not. Nor will we ever again see as many important music collections at sale as were dispersed by the antiquarians and auctioneers listed below in section 5.

The number of music collections they dispersed was massive. Puttick & Simpson alone sold 233; Sotheby's, 130; Liepmannssohn, 63; others, one to several dozen. Accurate counts are impossible, for many sales included the properties of several consignors (often unnamed) or portions of several libraries. Individual collections were often brought up a few items at a time in several sales,[21] sometimes years apart.[22] Nor is it always possible to distinguish what may have been the stock of an antiquarian dealer from a library consigned anonymously by a private collector. It may have been an accumulation from a real "collector," as the dealer advertised, or only an accumulation swept off the shelves in the dealer's shop.[23]

IDENTIFYING SELLERS

Whether libraries of Hirschian grandeur or others less imposing, their owners' names appear in alphabetical order in the major section of this work. The following section is arranged chronologically. It includes literature about collections whose owners chose anonymity or disguise as, e.g., "A Gentleman, Deceased," or, in a late 19th-century Liepmannssohn sale, a "wohlbekannten Sammler." Edward Harris faced

---

[19] **Herrmann**. See also John Carter's sometimes caustic remarks on "Collecting by Libraries," part of an address to the Bibliographical Society in 1969, reprinted, pp. 217-24, in the "Epilogue" to the third and subsequent editions of his masterful *Taste and Technique in Book Collecting* (Cambridge: Cambridge University Press, 1949): ". . . the most menacing figures are the professed rare book librarians, the men whose business it is to take books and manuscripts out of private hands and immure them forever behind steel doors and glass." Carter does find some redeeming virtues in the whole process, however. Many private collections are formed by owners who, in fact, anticipate the eventual institutionalization of their creations.

[20] Richard Landon, "The Collector and the Library," in *Celebrating*, notes that in response to the generosity of private collectors, "the institution assumes a responsibility and a commitment of no mean order. Collections must be nourished or they will die; the valleys between and the peaks must be populated; they must be preserved and they must be made available to the international scholarly community."

[21] It is not always possible, even upon first-hand examination, to determine if the properties of any of three or four persons in a single catalog are true collections, libraries, or mere accumulations.

[22] Alfred Bovet's properties appeared in four sales, the earliest in March 1901, the last in November 1911.

[23] The concept of "Accumulators," in contrast to "Collectors," is expounded in **Carter 2**, 2, and entertainingly elaborated upon by Harrison Hayford in his essay in *Celebrating*. **Thaw** agrees with Carter: "Sheer accumulation is not true collecting; the activity must be driven by the desire to impose a kind of order on the materials at hand." While I believe a collection must evidence a measure of coherence, Carter's and Thaw's definitions have not been followed strictly in this book.

many such dilemmas while compiling an index to Hodgson's sale catalogs in the British Museum. He notes that the names of owners were attached to only 1,219 of 3,905 sales, 2,687 remaining "anonymous."[24]

Even when the consignor is known, dilemmas persist. Pollard points out that collections do not always come up for sale immediately upon the death of the collector.[25] This is demonstrated in section 1. Among Puttick's sales, the library of the composer John Wall Callcott, who died in 1821, was sold by his grandson 65 years later, 5 July 1886. Sales of William Crotch's library began in 1873, 26 years after his death; James Hook's not until 47 years after he died; Joah Bates's collection was sold 68 years after his demise by his heir, Edward Bates. In these cases, the identity of the original collector was recorded or specified. If, however, the name of the heir is not the same as the collector's, and the collection is sold in the heir's name, misattribution is likely.

COLLECTIONS FOR FUTURE STUDY

Despite King's near-heroic, ground-breaking work,[26] other collections dispersed by Puttick's stand worthy of closer attention: the Gauntlett sales in 1847 and 1849; Ayrton's four sales beginning in 1848; Bishop's five sales, which began in 1855; Callcott's in 1862 and 1888; the three Oliphant sales in 1873; the many Warren sales, curiously stretched out over thirty-one years; the apparently unnoticed sale of numerous Aloys Fuchs manuscripts and autographs in 1852; the 1917 sales, consignors unnamed, of more items from the Fuchs collection with added selections from the famous Meyer-Cohn cabinet; and finally, the noteworthy collection of Charles Letts sold in 1912.

And there are the collections listed below—some sales, some not—which remain fascinating and may warrant greater study.[27] Until such study is completed, we cannot be certain.

- Robert Eitner's list, here under Artaria & Co. (1), though only ten pages long, includes extraordinary materials.
- The sales of Joseph Warren's properties (1) in 1841, 1864, 1872, and 1881—an amazing string. The fourth, in 1872, contained in lot 118 "Purcell. The works entirely . . . autograph. . . . In all 42 compositions, many of them now unknown. 1680."[28]

---

[24] Edward B. Harris, "Messrs. Hodgson & Co. List of Sales by Auction from 9 September 1807 to 12 December 1901. Compiled from the Original Catalogs, with Index and Notes," Ms. in British Library, pressmark S.C. Hodgson(a). In his index Harris used the word "Miscellaneous" instead of "Anonymous." He also observes that the adjective used for unnamed consignors up to 5 November 1852 was "Respectable"; after that they were characterized as "Eminent."

[25] **Pollard/Munby**, 15.

[26] Except for the Fuchs and Letts sales mentioned here, most of these collections and those in the preceding paragraph are described to a greater or lesser extent in **King**. See his index.

[27] The siglum "(1)" after an item in this list indicates that there is literature about the collection in section 1. The others have no catalogs or articles written about them and are cited here from secondary sources such as *RAMH*, **Benton**, and **Bradley**.

[28] There are sometimes sound business reasons for not offering a great volume of material—all of Warren's collection, for example—at a single sale; the market's capacity to absorb it at any one time is limited.

- Carvalhaes's collection of 21,000 librettos (1)
- The vast riches in Donebauer's autograph collection (1)
- Edberg's 5,900 concert programs covering 1895 to 1950, with card indexes, as well as a seemingly unique collection of 840 drawings describing orchestral seating positions! (1)
- Ernst Henschel's collection of concert programs now at the British Library (1)
- In a single lot in Sotheby's sale of 16 September 1960, more than 1,000 musicians' ALS. Under **Lane** (1)
- 460 autographs of 19th-century composers in lot 341 in a sale by Labitte, 30 June 1881, under **F***** in (1)
- Lester Levy's collection of 30,000 pieces of sheet music (1)
- Meredith Willson's gift of over 250,000 pieces of sheet music, with 78 rpm and cylinder recordings to the University of California at Los Angeles
- Under **Niles** (1), Bella Landauer's splendid collection of 24,000 items of sheet music
- Brahms's own library containing 162 holographs of works by other composers (1)
- Ulderico Rolandi's gift of 35,000 librettos to the Venetian Biblioteca e istituto di lettere (1)
- Santini's curious collection of Ms. and printed music, 16th to 18th centuries—over 1,000 works by more than 700 composers
- Stainer's rich collections partly purchased by Harding; see under both in (1)
- Anna Amalia's magnificent library noted earlier (1)
- Gotthold's 55,000 volumes of hymnology and other 16th to 18th-century music now at the former USSR-KA; Oblastnaja biblioteka (1)
- Wilhelm Heyer's collection of 1,700 holographs of 700 composers and 20,000 letters (1)
- Bertarelli's collection of 11,000 illustrations of musicians and theater personages now at Milan's Biblioteca Trivulziana (1)
- The twenty-five volumes of manuscripts, "Arie di diversi autori," sold as a single lot in the Edward Taylor sale in 1863; in that same sale, thirteen other lots of undescribed "manuscript part books"
- Seventy-seven volumes of Italian manuscripts collected by the Duke of Cambridge comprising a single lot in the sale of his library, 28 November 1850
- Oesterlein's library of Wagner materials, 10,180 lots filling a 4-volume catalog which took 13 years to publish, 1882-95 (1)
- And finally, the collections of music materials put together by non-musicians—for example, van Gogh, Heine, Lenin, Pepys, Madame Pompadour, Wallace Stevens, Carl van Vechten, and others. Literature about some of these appears in (1).

If located, a number of these could be the basis of interesting and useful studies like those by Krummel, Einstein, Haar, Schaal, Knapp, Monterosso, "Dotted Crochet," and Leaver.[29]

---

[29] Donald W. Krummel, "A Musical Bibliomaniac," *MT* 115 (1974): 301 (about the Harding collection, now in the Bodleian); Alfred Einstein, "Die Sammlung Speyer," *Philobiblon* 8 (1935): 155-60; James Haar, "The *Libraria* of Antonfrancesco Doni," *Musica disciplina* 24 (1970): 101-33; Richard Schaal, "Die Musikbibliothek von Raimund Fugger, d.j.," *Acta musicologica* 29 (1957): 126-37; J. Merrill Knapp, "The Hall Handel Collection," *Princeton University Library Chronicle* 36 (1974-75): 3-18; Raffaelo Monterosso, "Guida alla biblioteca di G. Cesari, musicologo cremonese," *Annali della Biblioteca Governativa* 1 (1948): 35-42; Dotted Crochet, "The Musical Library of Thomas William Taphouse," *MT* 45 (1904): 629-36; Robin A. Leaver, *Bach's Theological Library* (Neuhausen-Stuttgart: Hänssler, 1983). These are just a few examples of the many descriptive essays included in the annotations in the Benton directories of music libraries mentioned earlier.

Handeliana and Some Curiosa

King[30] notes that in England Handeliana was a "begetter of specialised collections."[31] Bearing this out, some 23 Puttick & Simpson sales alone included sizeable portions of Dr. Arnold's edition. Other editions by Walsh, Randall, Wright, and Cluer were almost as popular. And they still appear in catalogs.

Sales of Handeliana also contained some curiosities—for example, his will, watch, pitchpipe, and the anvil dubiously associated in the catalog with the famed chorus. Curiosa crops up in many sales. In that of Stumpff's properties in 1847 (1), lot 64, contained "the initials of Mozart and his wife worked in their own hair," and lot 29, a "chased silver snuff box, with a lock of Beethoven's hair set in a locket outside." In another Puttick sale, 12 February 1878 (1), the theatrical wardrobe of Frank Bodda and Madame Bodda-Pyne included a collection of "Stage Jewellry (sold with all faults and errors of description)," and among the bracelets and tiaras was lot 74, "The original Lurline wreath worn by Miss Pyne." 90 lots of cigars were appended to the firm's sale of 30 June 1869 ("15,000 genuine Havana cigars . . . in fine condition, fit for immediate use")![32] In the printed catalog of Fétis's library these odd (i.e., weird) instruments appear:

> Paddon, John. *The Cheirochema*. London: Bridgewater printer [n.d.] 1 p. (item no. 6322)
>
> *Das Semeimelodion (Noten-Klanginstrument) in seiner Bedeutung . . .* , von Armin Früh. Halle: Kamrodt, 1859. (item no. 5663)

Edward Rimbault, who was "honored" by a satirical hoax catalog of his library (see nos. 2239-41) was also, according to a 1939 suggestion in the *London Times*, suspected of purloining seventeen early works missing from Christ Church (see item 24 in the bibliography). An even grander hoax, "The Shipton Hoard," is described in fascinating detail by **King** (pp. 39-42). The two big sales, not of James Bartleman's library, but of "duplicate books [and music]" from his collection nos. 178 and 179, [1807] and 1815 (in the bibliography) tantalizingly preceded the sale of his library in 1822.

Genesis

This book has been over forty years in the making, but in that time it has generated many articles, papers, and other books. (In the slang of the TV world, they would be called "spin-offs.") The preparation of *Musical Instrument Collections*—a complement to this present work—provoked a consuming interest in the activities of the London auction house Puttick & Simpson.[33] The study of that firm effectively postponed work on this bibliography for seven years. The interest in Puttick's fired a still-unquenched curiosity about the British music trade, resulting in several other publications: a chronicle of publishers and pirates in Victorian times,[34] an investigation of the publishing antiquarian firm of William Reeves,[35]

---

[30] **King**, 161. He notes prices paid for several editions on p. 95.
[31] As confirmed recently by publication of a collection of essays by Handel experts in **Best**.
[32] Miss D. K. Kleinfeldt, a cataloger at Puttick & Simpson from 1914 to 1936, told the author during a discussion of curious collections that some of the more clamorous sales she attended featured pot lids and tea cozies.
[33] **Coover 2**.
[34] *Music Publishing, Copyright and Piracy in Victorian England* (London: Mansell, 1985).
[35] "William Reeves, Booksellers/Publishers, 1825-," in *Music Publishing and Collecting: Essays in Honor of Donald W. Krummel,* 39-67.

and a list of nearly 6,000 music antiquarian catalogs, many gathered by myself beginning in the early 1950s, others run to earth and examined in numerous dealers' and libraries' collections.[36] During that time, work on this book was limited, to say the least.

At the outset, the focus of this study was catalogs of eighteenth-century private collections. Interest quickly shifted to the contents of composers' libraries, an effort intrinsically more interesting and more musicologically worthwhile. (Grants from Vassar College supported both of these ventures.) Several years later, however—even with the late A. Hyatt King's help and sage advice—deciding which collectors were worthy of the appellation "composer," and which not, became too difficult. This irked both King in his innovative book *Some British Collectors of Music*[37] (note: not composers), and much later, Siegrun Folter in her list of catalogs of musicians' libraries.[38] (Even they were hard to classify.) Otto Albrecht, in his magnificent article for the *New Grove*,[39] did not wrestle with the problem; any libraries worth mentioning, to whomever they belonged, he nestled under the rubric "Collections, private."

THIS BOOK'S TITLE

The words raise some questions; separately and joined, they resist perfect definition. What is a "private" music collection, anyway? Decades ago, when I told my distinguished colleague Donald Krummel that, for the purposes of this book, court and chapel libraries would be considered "private," he doubted they should be called that. As he pointed out, documentation on them was meager—at that time certainly true. Today, however, though a lot of work still beckons, careful studies and distinguished publications about them have been proliferating. Many of those studies are cited here in the section "Sources and Related Readings," and they made my proposed inclusion of those "suspect" collections more feasible than when I discussed them with Dr. Krummel.

I have taken the second word, "Music," to be a blanket term including all types of materials, not just music scores. And so, other materials are here—books, recordings, and graphic materials, as well as scores.

Then what are the criteria determining a true "collection"? How rich must an assemblage be to warrant that designation? How considered must have been its assemblage? Do casual "accumulations" (noted earlier) count, even if they are not rich resources? What measure of calculated coherence ought the word "collection" imply? Must items in the collection feature, e.g., some period, school of composition, musical style, an eminent composer, a music medium, a particular format (manuscripts, prints, duodecimo, fancy binding), or a special provenance? How big does an "accumulation" have to be, or how significant, to qualify? How interesting its contents?

---

[36] **Coover**.
[37] **King**.
[38] **Folter**.
[39] **Albrecht**.

Such worries, perhaps unnecessary, have but slightly diminished the number of citations set out here. Inevitably, a number of less than rich, perhaps even mediocre, collections have been embraced. Though tempted to omit them if described as "collection" or "library" by their owners, by their colleagues, by firms responsible for their dispersal, or in journal articles, I went along with that perception.

MECHANICS

1. An effort has been made to provide locations for each item cited.[40] The sigla used are almost all from RISM. A few are not. Some come from Lugt's bibliography (see Sources and Related Readings) others are made-up RISM-like codes—for example, GB-Rosenthal for the collection of the venerable Albi Rosenthal. For books and journals which are widely available, I have simply used the siglum "g.a." to indicate "generally available."

2. Buyers of sales items are noted if their own libraries were later put up for sale. See, for example, 27 November 1882 in section 2.

3. Literature about collections known by family name only—no first name—precede the same family name if a first name is known.

4. There are numerous references to dealers' catalogs as sources—Haas, Rosenthal, and Baron, to mention just three. They are all indexed in section 5.

5. "Literature" has been used to separate literature from catalogs of collections. If "Literature" does not appear, users should assume the citations which follow are for "Catalogs."

6. There are birth and/or death dates for all important collectors but not for lesser, more obscure collectors and "accumulators."

ABBREVIATIONS

n&p   indicates that the sale catalog contains, usually in manuscript, the names of buyers and prices paid for lots. It does not imply that every lot in the catalog bears such information.

Ms.   Manuscript

ALS   Autograph Letter Signed

C.-P.   Commissionaire-Priseur

Exp.   Expert

g.a.   Item is generally available (point 1, above)

NE   "Not examined" means I was unable to find a copy in the collection I visited, nor a person or institution from which a microfilm copy could be secured.

---

[40] This, however, is not a comprehensive union catalog. Users of the bibliography must be careful to distinguish between locations of *collections* and those for the literature about those collections.

Sources and Related Readings

Sigla in the left column are used throughout the book to indicate sources of information included in the entries. The other works contributed in added ways to this bibliography.

Acta *Acta musicologica*. Vol. 1- (1928-). (Imprint varies.)

Albrecht Albrecht, Otto E. "Collections, private." *NG* 4:536-58.

> Near the top alphabetically, and perhaps appropriately, for it ranks high among the many sources on which this book depends.

Atlick, Richard D. *The English Common Reader: A Social History of the Mass Reading Public, 1800-1900*. Chicago: University of Chicago Press, 1957.

> Especially relevant here are chapters 12 and 13, "The Book Trade," 1800-50 and 1850-1900.

Amerigrove *The New Grove Dictionary of American Music*. Ed. H. Wiley Hitchcock and Stanley Sadie. 4 vols. London: Macmillan; New York: Grove's Dictionaries of Music, 1986.

> "Libraries and Collections," by Mary Wallace Davidson, D. W. Krummel, with Donald Thompson.

AMw *Archiv für Musikwissenschaft*. Vol. 1-. Wiesbaden: Franz Steiner, 1918-.

AMZ *Allgemeine Musikzeitung*. Vol. 1-. Berlin: Luckhardt'sche Verlagshandlung, 1874-1943.

Auction Catalogues of Music: A Series of Facsimiles. Introductions by A. Hyatt King. Amsterdam: Frits Knuf, 1973-.

Barandoni Barandoni, Stefano. *L'archivio musicale della chiesa conventuale dei Cavalieri di Santo Stefano di Pisa: storia e catalogo*. Ed. Stefano Barandoni and Paolo Raffaelli. [Firenze]: Libreria musicale Italiana, 1994.

Barblan   Conservatorio di Musica Giuseppe Verdi, Milan. *Catalogo della biblioteca, diretto da Guglielmo Barblan letteratura musicale e opere teoriche.* Vol. 1. Milano, 1969.

Barnes, James J. *Free Trade in Books: A Study of the London Book Trade since 1800.* Oxford: Clarendon Press, 1964.

Barthélémy   Liège, Conservatoire Royal de Musique. *Catalogue des imprimés musicaux anciens . . .* [by] *M. B.* Liège: Mardaga, 1992.

Basbanes, Nicholas A. *A Gentle Madness: Bibliophiles, Bibliomaniacs, and the Eternal Passion for Books.* New York: Henry Holt, 1995.

    A massive (628 pp.) survey of "collecting," it synthesizes a vast array of literature on the topic.

BdMS   *Bibliographie des Musikschrifftums.* Frankfurt a.M.: F. Hofmeister, 1936-.

Becker   Becker, Carl Ferdinand. *Systematisch-chronologische Darstellung der musikalischen Literatur von der frühesten bis auf die neueste Zeit.* Leipzig: R. Friese, 1836. *Anhang* and *Nachtrag*, 1839.

Beisswenger   Beisswenger, Kirsten. *Johann Sebastian Bachs Notenbibliothek.* Kassel: Bärenreiter, 1992.

Benton 1-5   *Directory of Music Research Libraries, Including Contributors to the International Inventory of Musical Sources (RISM).* Comp. Rita Benton. Iowa City: University of Iowa Press, 1970-72; Kassel: Bärenreiter, 1979-.

    The existing 5 volumes are cited here as, e.g., **Benton 1**, **Benton 2**, etc.

Bertini   Roma, Biblioteca Corsiniana e dell'Accademia nazionale dei Lincei. *Catalogo dei fondi musicali Chiti r Corsiniano.* Ed. Argia Bertini. Bibliotheca musicae: collana di cataloghi e bibliografie, 2. Milano: Istituto editoriale italiano, 1964.

Bertini 2   Congregazione dell'oratorio di Roma. *Inventario del fondo musicale dell'Oratorio.* Ed. Argia Bertini. 4 vols. Roma, 1968-71.

Best   *Handel Collections and Their History.* Ed. Terence Best. Oxford: Clarendon Press; New York: Oxford University Press, 1993.

BdZL   *Bibliographie der deutschen Zeitschriften-Literatur.* Leipzig: Fr. Andra's Nachfolger [etc.], 1896-.

    And its various Abteilungen.

"Biblioteche italiane in possesso di fondi musicali." *Fontes* 18 (1971): 107-57.

BiBB   *Internationale Bibliographie des Buch- und Bibliothekswesens.* Leipzig: Harrassowitz, 1904-12, 1922-39.

Block, Andrew. *Book Collectors' Vade mecum.* London: Dennis Archer, 1932.

_____. *A Short History of the Principal London Antiquarian Booksellers and Book-Auctioneers.* London: Dennis Archer, 1933.

Blogie Blogie, Jeanne. *Répertoire des catalogues de ventes de livres imprimés.* Collection du Centre national d'archéologie et de l'histoire du livre, 4. Bruxelles: Fl. Tulkens, 1982-.

> Catalogs to date in the Bibliothèque Albert Ier: 1. Belge, 2. Français, 3. Britanniques.

Boalch Boalch, Ronald H. *Makers of the Harpsichord and Clavichord, 1440-1840.* 2nd ed. Oxford: Clarendon Press, 1974. 3rd ed., ed. Charles Mould, 1995.

Bobillier Bobillier, Marie (pseud., Michel Brenet). "Bibliographie des bibliographies musicale." *L'Année musicale* 3 (1913): 1-152.

> Also published separately; then reprinted, New York: Da Capo, 1971.

Bohatta, Hanns. "Die Bedeutung der Antiquariats- und Auktionskataloge für den Bibliographen." *Archiv für Bibliographie, Buch- und Bibliothekswesen*, 2. Jg., Heft 2 (1928): 72-79.

Book Collecting and Scholarship: Essays by Theodore C. Blegen, James Ford Bell, Stanley Pargellis, Colton Storm, and Louis B. Wright. Minneapolis: University of Minnesota Press, 1954.

Borren Borren, Charles van den. "Inventaire des MSS de musique polyphonique qui se trouvent en Belgique." *Acta 5* (1933): 66, 120, 177; 6 (1934): 23, 65, 116.

Bozarth, George. "The First Generation of Brahms Manuscript Collections." *Notes* 40 (1983): 239-62

Bradley Bradley, Carol June. *Music Collections in American Libraries: A Chronology.* This series, 46. This publisher, 1981.

Braun, Werner. "Die Music in deutschen Gelehrten-bibliotheken des 17. und 18. Jahrhunderts." *Mf* 10 (1967): 241-50.

British Music Yearbook. Vol. 1-. London: Macmillan; New York: St. Martin's Press, 1972/73-.

Brook Brook, Barry S. *Thematic Catalogues in Music: An Annotated Bibliography.* Hillsdale, N.Y.: Pendragon, 1972. 2nd ed. Stuyvesant, N.Y.: Pendragon, 1997.

Brown Brown, James Duff, and Stephen Samuel Stratton. *British Musical Biography: A Dictionary of Musical Artists Authors and Composers.* Derby: Chadfield, 1897.

Bruno, Guido. *Adventures in American Bookshops, Antique Stores and Auction Rooms.* Detroit: Douglas Book Shop, 1922.

BS   Johnson, Douglas, Alan Tyson, and Robert Winter. *The Beethoven Sketchbooks.* Berkeley: University of California Press, 1985.

> "A Survey of the Principal Collections" by Johnson, pp. 13-43, discusses the auction of Beethoven's *Nachlass*, listing some of the autographs found in various copies. Reprints of the *Nachlass* itself are listed, described, and concorded in "The *Nachlass* Catalogue," also by Johnson, in Appendix B. It is based in part on his article about the Artaria collection, here under **Johnson** (below).

Carter   Carter, John. *Books and Book-Collectors.* Cleveland and New York: World, 1957.

Carter 2   _____. *Taste and Technique in Book Collecting.* New York: R. R. Bowker, 1948.

Cataloghi   Società italiana di musicologia. *Cataloghi di fondi musicali italiani . . . in collaborazione con il R.I.S.M.* Padova: CLEUP, 1989.

Celebrating   *Celebrating the Acquisition of the Two Millionth of the State University of New York at Buffalo Libraries: Proceedings.* Buffalo: University Libraries, State University of New York, 1983. (Unpaged.)

> Contains "The Collector and the Library," by Richard Landon; "An Apology for Book Accumulation," by Harrison Hayford; "The Heritage of Book Collecting," by Robert Nikirk; "Rare Book Collectors and the University Libraries," by Samuel Streit.

Coover   Coover, James B. *Antiquarian Catalogues of Musical Interest.* London: Mansell, 1988.

Coover 2   _____. *Music at Auction: Puttick and Simpson (of London), 1794-1971, Being an Annotated, Chronological List of Sales of Musical Material.* This series, 60. This publisher, 1988.

Coral, Lenore. "Music in Auctions: Dissemination as a Factor of Taste." In *Source Materials and the Interpretation of Music: A Memorial Volume to Thurston Dart*, ed. Ian Bent, 383-401. London: Stainer & Bell, 1981.

Coral   _____. "Music in English Auction Sales, 1675-1750." Ph.D. diss., University of London, 1974.

> *See also* entry under **Munby/Coral**.

Coussemaker, Charles Edmond Henri de. *Notice sur les collections musicales de la bibliothèque de Cambrai et des autres villes du département du nord.* Paris: Techener, 1843. Reprint, Utrecht: Joachimsthal, 1972.

DaSML   Davidsson, Åke. *Svensk Musiklitteratur: En förteckning.* [Stockholm?, 1946.]

> With supplements.

Davidsson   _____. "Cultural Background to Collections of Old Music in Swedish Libraries." *Fontes* 3 (1964):21-28.

Davies   Davies, J. H. *Musicalia: Sources of Information in Music*. 2nd ed., rev. and enl. Oxford and New York: Pergamon, 1969.

        "Principal Music Collections in Private Hands and Now to Be Found in Institutions and Libraries of Great Britain."

Downs   Downs, Robert Bingham. *American Library Resources: A Bibliography and Guide*. Chicago: American Library Association, 1951.

        Supplements: 1950-61, 1962, 1961-71, 1972.

Edling, Anders. "The Music Collections of the Uppsala University Library." *Fontes* 34 (1987): 114-17.

Eitner   Eitner, Robert. *Biographisch-bibliographisches Quellen-Lexikon*. 10 vols. Leipzig: Breitkopf & Härtel, 1898-1904. Reprint, New York, Musurgia, 1947. "Neuaufl.," Wiesbaden: Breitkopf & Härtel, 1959-60. "2. verb. Aufl.," Graz: Akademische Druck- und Verlagsanstalt, 1959-60.

Farrenc, Aristide. *Les Livres rares et leur destinée*. Rennes: H. Vatar, 1856.

        Annotation in **Krummel 3**.

Fédorov   Fédorov, Vladimir. "V. V. Stasov chez l'abb F. Santini à Rome." In *Anthony van Hoboken: Festschrift zum 75. Geburtstag*, ed. Joseph Schmidt-Görg, 55-62. Mainz: B. Schott's Söhne, 1962.

Fétis   Fétis, François Joseph. *Biographie universelle des musiciens et bibliographie générale de la musique*. 2nd ed., 1873. 10 vols. Reprint, with supplement by Arthur Pougin, Bruxelles: Editions Culture et Civilisation, 1963.

Field, Eugene. "The Malady Called 'Catalogitis'." In William Targ, *Bouillabaisse for Bibliophiles*, 329-35. Cleveland and New York: World, 1955.

Folter   Folter, Siegrun H. *Private Libraries of Musicians and Musicologists: A Bibliography of Catalogues*. Buren: Frits Knuf, 1987.

        Annotation in **Krummel 3**.

Folter 2   Folter, Roland. *Deutsche Dichter- und Germainisten-Bibliotheken: Eine kritische Bibliographie*. Stuttgart: Fritz Eggert, 1975.

Fontes   *Fontes artis musicae*. Paris: International Association of Music Libraries, 1954-.

Franklin, Colin. "Collecting Printed Music: A Neglected Pleasure." *Biblio* 2, no. 1 (1997): 38-41.

Frati   Frati, Carlo. *Dizionario bio-bibliografico del bibliotecari e bibliofili italiani dal sec. XIV al XIX*. Firenze: L. S. Olschki, 1933.

Fuld, James J., and David Hunter. "Collectors and Music Bibliography: A Preliminary Survey." In *Music Publishing and Collecting: Essays in Honor of Donald W. Krummel*, ed. Hunter, 215-33. Urbana-Champaign: University of Illinois, 1994.

Gaspari   Bologna. Conservatorio di musica "G. B. Martini." *Catalogo della biblioteca musicale.* Comp. Gaetano Gaspari et al. Bologna: Libreria Romagnoli dall'Acqua, 1890-1943. Reprint, Bologna: A. Forni, 1961.

Gerboth   Gerboth, Walter. *An Index to Musical Festschriften.* New York: Norton, 1969.

Gleich   Gleich, Clemens von. "Niederländische Musikalien in Holland: Wege und Umwege." In *Beiträge zur Musikdokumentation: Franz Grasberger zum 60. Geburtstag,* ed. Gunter Brosche, 93-99. Tutzing: Schneider, 1975.

Gmeinwieser   Gmeinwieser, Siegfried. *Die Musikhandschriften in der Theatinerkirche St. Kajetan in München: Thematischer Katalog.* München: Henle, 1979.

_____. "Die Musikaliensammlung des Johann Michael Hauber." *KmJ* 60 (1976): 77-79.

Grove 3   *Grove's Dictionary of Music and Musicians.* 3rd ed., ed. H. C. Colles. 5 vols. New York: Macmillan, 1927-28. American supplement, 1928; supplementary volume, 1940.

"Libraries and Collections of Music," by Carl Engel, 3:152-90.

Grove 5   _____. 5th ed., ed. Eric Blom. 5 vols. London: Macmillan; New York, St. Martin's Press, 1954. Supplement, 1961.

"Collections, private," by Otto Eric Deutsch, 1:373-75; "Libraries and Collections," by Charles Cudworth, 5:160-223. For latest editions, see below under *NG*.

Grumbacher, Rudolf. "Öffentliches interesse und private Sammeltätigkeit." In *Festschrift Rudolf Elvers zum 60. Geburtstag,* ed. Ernst Herttrich and Hans Schneider, 223-28. Tutzing: Schneider, 1985.

Albi Rosenthal, in a review in *M&L* 67 (1986): 406, says "a thoughtful and challenging essay on the merits and mutual responsibilities of private music collectors vis-à-vis public institutions and scholars."

Haberkamp   Haberkamp, Gertraut. *Die ehemaligen Musikhandschriftensammlungen der königlichen Hofkapelle und der Kurfürstin Maria Anna in München.* München: G. Henle, 1982.

See her list of sources.

_____. *Thematischer Katalog der Musikhandschriften der Fürstlich Wallerstein'schen Bibliothek Schloss Harburg.* Kataloge bayerische Musiksammlung, 3. München: Henle, 1976.

Hamilton, Sinclair. "Collecting Tastes of a Century Ago." *Colophon* 3 (1950): 271-78.

Handbuch der Musikbibliotheken in Deutschland: Öffentliche und wissenschaftliche Musikbibliotheken sowie Spezialsammlung. Ed. Marion Sommerfeld. Berlin: Deutsches Bibliotheksinstitut, 1994.

Hawkins, Sir John. *A General History of the Science and Practice of Music*. 5 vols. London: Payne and Son, 1776. New ed., London: Novello, 1853. Reprints of 1853 edition, New York: Dover, 1963, and Graz: Akademische Druck- und Verlagsanstalt, 1969.

Hermann   Hermann, Frank. *Sotheby's: Portrait of an Auction House*. London: Chatto & Windus, 1980.

Hirsch, Paul. *Katalog der Musikbibliothek Paul Hirsch, Frankfurt am Main*. Ed. Kathi Meyer and Paul Hirsch. 4 vols. Berlin/Frankfurt am Main: Martin Breslauer, 1928-47. (Vol. 4 has imprint Cambridge: University Press.)

    Collectors' catalogs, 4:423-33.

Hirsch   British Museum, Department of Printed Books, Hirsch Music Library. *Books in the Hirsch Library, with Supplementary List of Music*. London: British Museum, 1959.

Hunter, Michael. "Auction Catalogues and Eminent Libraries." *Book Collector* 21 (1972): 471-88.

IBAK   Loh, Gerhard. *Internationale Bibliographie der Antiquariats-, Auktions-und Kunst-Kataloge, "IBAK."* Leipzig: Universitäts-Bibliothek, 1960-.

Irwin, Raymond. *Origins of the English Library*. London: Unwin, 1958.

Jackson, Holbrook. *Anatomy of Bibliomania*. London: Soncino Press, 1932.

JAMS   *Journal of the American Musiological Society*. Vol. 1- (1948-).

JbP   *Jahrbuch der Musikbibliothek Peters*. Vols. 1-47. Leipzig: C. F. Peters, 1894-1940. Reprint, Vaduz: Kraus, 1965.

Jayne, Sears Reynolds. *Library Catalogues of the English Renaissance*. Berkeley: University of California Press, 1956.

Johansson   Johansson, Cari. "Något om de äldre samlingarna i Kungl. Musikaliska akademiens bibliotek." In *Svenska musikperspektiv*, ed. Gustav Hillström, 88-114. Publikationer utg. av Kungl. Musikaliske Akademiens, 9. Stockholm: Nordiska Musikförlaget, 1971.

Johnson   Johnson, Douglas. "The Artaria Collection of Beethoven Manuscripts: A New Source." In **BS**, 174-89.

Kahl   Kahl, Willi. "Öffentliche und private Musik-Sammlungen in ihrer Bedeutung für die Renaissancebewegung des 19. Jahrhunderts in Deutschland." In Gesellschaft für Musikforschung Internationaler Musikwissenschaftlicher Kongress, Bamberg, 1953, *Bericht*, 289-94. Kassel: Bärenreiter, 1954.

King   King, A. Hyatt. *Some British Collectors of Music, c. 1600-1960*. Cambridge: Cambridge University Press, 1963.

KmJ
Kirchenmusikalisches Jahrbuch. Regensburg, New York, Cincinnati: Friedrich Pustet, 1886-.

Koltypina
Koltypina, G. B., and L. N. Podgug. *Bibliografiia muzkal'noi bibliografii*. Moscow: Publichnaia biblioteka, 1963.

Kouba
Kouba, Jan. *Pruvodce po pramènech k dejinám hudby: Fondby a sbirky uložené v Čechách*. Praha: Academia, 1969.

Krummel
Krummel, Donald W. "American Music Bibliophiles and Their Collections." *AB Bookman's Weekly* 76, no. 24 (1985): 4292-99.

Krummel 2
_____. *Bibliographical Handbook of American Music*. Urbana: University of Illinois Press, 1987.

Krummel 3
_____. *The Literature of Music Bibliography: Writings on the History of Music Printing and Publishing*. Berkeley, Calif.: Fallen Leaf Press, 1992.

> See the annotated bibliographies, "The History of Music Libraries" (pp. 327-30); "Musical Antiquarians and Collectors," in chapter 7, entitled "The Custodial Setting." *See also* entry under *RAMH*.

Krummel 4
_____. "The Beginnings of Current National Bibliography for German Music." In *Richard S. Hill: Tributes from Friends*, ed. Carol June Bradley and James B. Coover, 307-29. This series, 58. This publisher, 1987.

_____. "Music Libraries." In *Encyclopedia of Library History*, ed. Wayne A. Wiegand and Donald G. Davis, Jr. Garland Reference Library of Social Sciences, 503. New York: Garland, 1993.

Lambertini
Lambertini, Michel'angelo. *Bibliophilie musicale*. Edition abrégée. Viseu: Andrade & Ca., 1924.

Lancour
Lancour, Harold. *American Art Auction Catalogues, 1785-1942: Union List*. New York: New York Public Library, 1944.

> Reprint, with revisions and additions, in *Bulletin of the New York Public Library*, January 1943-February 1944.

Landon
Landon, Howard Chandler Robbins. *Haydn: Chronicle and Works*. 5 vols. Bloomington: Indiana University Press, 1976-80.

Learmont, Brian. *A History of the Auction*. N.p.: Barnard & Learmont, 1985.

Levy
Levy, Lester. "Sheet Music Buffs and Their Collections: A Personal Memoir." *American Music* 1, no. 4 (winter 1983): 90-99.

Lewis
Lewis, Mary S. "Response: Manuscripts and Printed Music in the World of Patrons and Collectors." In *Atti del XIV Congresso della Società internazionale di musicologia: Trasmissione e recezione delle forme di cultura musicale, Bologna, 27 agosto-1° settembre 1987, Ferrara-Parma, 30 agosto 1987,* vol. 1: *Round Tables*, ed. Angelo Pompilio et al., 319-25. Turin: E. D. T. Edizione, 1990.

L&PMTR   *London and Provincial Music Trades Review*. Vols. 1-38. London: G. D. Ernest & Co., 1877/78-1915.

Lugt   Lugt, Frits. *Répertoire des catalogues de ventes publiques intéressant l'art ou la curiosité*. La Haye: Martinus Nijhoff, 1938.

MA   *Musical America*. Vol. 1-. New York, 1898-.

M&L   *Music & Letters*. Vol. 1-. London, 1920-.

McCredie, Andrew. "Music Libraries in Australia." *Australian Journal of Music Education* 15 (July 1974): 61-64.

McKay   McKay, George Leslie. *American Book Auction Catalogues, 1713-1934: A Union List*. New York: New York Public Library, 1937. Supplements 1-2, 1946-48.

Mecklenberg   Mecklenberg, Günther. *Vom Autographensammeln*. Marburg: J. A. Stargardt, 1963.

Mf   *Die Musikforschung*. Vol. 1-. Kassel: Bärenreiter, 1948-.

MfM   *Monatshefte für Musikgeschichte*. Vols. 1-37. Berlin: Trautwein; Leipzig: Breitkopf & Härtel, 1869-1905.

MGG   *Die Musik in Geschichte und Gegenwart*. Ed. Friedrich Blume. 17 vols. Kassel: Bärenreiter, 1949-86.

New edition in progress.

Milson   Milson, John. "The Nonesuch Music Library." In *Sundry Sorts of Music Books: Essays Presented to O. W. Neighbour*, ed. Chris Banks, Arthur Searle, and Malcolm Turner, 146-82. London: British Library, 1993.

MMR   *Monthly Musical Record*. Vol. 1-. London: Augener & Co., 1871-.

MO&MTR   *Musical Opinion and Music Trade Review*. Vol. 1-. London, 1877/78-.

Mornet, David. "Les Enseignements des bibliothèques privées (1750-1780)." *Revue d'histoire litteraire de la France* 17 (1910): 449-96.

Little or nothing to say about music, but an interesting study of private collectors, their collections, their origins and destinies.

MQ   *Music Quarterly*. Vol. 1-. New York: G. Schirmer [etc.], 1915-.

MR   *Music Review*. Vol. 1-. Cambridge: W. Heffer, 1940-.

Münster   Münster, Robert. "Die handschriftlichen Nachlässe in der Musiksammlung der Bayerischen Staatsbibliothek." In *Beiträge zur Musikdokumentation Franz Grasberger zum 60. Geburtstag*, ed. Günter Brosche, 259-72. Tutzing: Schneider, 1975.

Muensterberger   Muensterberger, Werner, *Collecting, an Unruly Passion: Psychological Perspectives*. Princeton: Princeton University Press, 1994.

Review: **Thaw**.

Munby/Coral   Munby, A. N. L., and Lenore Coral. *British Book Sale Catalogues, 1676-1800: A Union List*. London: Mansell, 1977.

Music Index   *The Music Index*. This publisher, 1949-.

MT   *Musical Times*. Vol. 1-. London: Novello, 1844-. To vol. 45, 1904, as *Musical Times and Singing Class Circular*.

Myers   Myers, Robin. *The British Book Trade from Caxton to the Present Day*. London: André Deutsch, 1973.

NG   *The New Grove Dictionary of Music and Musicians*. Ed. Stanley Sadie. 20 vols. London: Macmillan; New York: Grove's Dictionaries, 1980. Rev. ed., 2001, appeared too late for use in this book.

NG-L   _____. "Libraries," 10:719-821.

NUC   *National Union Catalog: Pre-1956 Imprints* [and supplements]. London: Mansell, 1968-.

Notes   Music Library Association. *Notes*. New series, vol. 1-. Canton, Mass.: Music Library Association, 1943-. *Supplement for Members*. Vol. 1-, 1947-.

NzfM   *Neue Zeitschrift für Musik*. [Various places and publishers], 1834-1943, 1950-. Reprint of vols. 1-91, 1834-1924, Scarsdale, N.Y.: Annamarie Schnase, 1963-65.

Ongaro   Ongaro, Giulio M. "The Library of a Sixteenth-Century Music Teacher." *Journal of Musicology* 11 (1994): 357-75.

ÖmZ   *Österreichische Musikzeitschrift*. Vol. 1. Wien: H. Bauer-Verlag [etc.], 1946-.

Pag   Pagliaini, Attilio. *Catalogo generale della libreria italiana, 1847-99*. Milano: Assoc. Typ.- Libr. Ital., 1901-22. *Supplemento* 1-4, 1912-58.

Penney 3   Penney, Barbara. *Music in British Libraries: A Directory of Resources*. 3rd ed. London: Library Association, 1981.

Penney 4   _____. 4th ed. London: Library Association, 1992.

Pettersen   Pettersen, Hjalmar. *Bibliotheca norvegica*. Christiana: Cammeyer, 1899-1924.

    Vol. 1: *Nordisk Boglexikon, 1643-1813*.

Petzholdt, Julius. *Bibliotheca bibliographica: Kritische Verzeichnis*. Leipzig: Engelmann, 1866.

Plant, Marjorie. *The English Book Trade: An Economic History*. London: G. Allen & Unwin, 1939.

Pollard/Munby   British Museum, Department of Printed Books. *List of Catalogues of English Book Sales, 1676-1900, Now in the British Museum*. Ed. A[lfred] W. Pollard. London: British Museum, 1915.

The edition cited here is Pollard's, expanded with voluminous manuscript additions by A. N. L. Munby. A number of copies are available in both England and the U.S.

Pollard, Graham, and Albert Ehrman. *The Distribution of Books by Catalogue.* Cambridge: Roxburghe Club, 1965.

Preibish   Preibish, André, Helmut Kallmann, and Maria Calderisi. "Music Resources in Canadian Collections/Resources musicales des bibliothèques canadiennes." In *Research Collections in Canadian Libraries/Collections de recherche es bibliothèques canadiennes.* 2 vols. Ottawa: National Library of Canada, 1980.

Pritchard, Brian W. "A Brief Survey of the Collections and Function of Music Archives in Czechoslovakia." *Continuo* 7 (1977): 18-24.

Prod'homme   Prod'homme, Jacques Gabriel. "Les Institutions musicales (bibliothèques et archives) en Belgique et en Hollande." *SiMG* 15 (1913-14): 458-88.

P&S   Puttick & Simpson, auctioneer, London. "List of Sales [1846-1870]."

Typescript in the British Library, pressmark 11906.f.6.

Quinze Annés de ventes publiques, 1898-1913: Répertoire chronologique de 1700 catalogues. Paris: Schemint, 1914.

Raabe, Tom. *Biblioholism: The Literary Addiction.* Golden, Colo.: Fulcrum, 1991.

RAMH   Krummel, Donald W., Jean Geil, Doris J. Dyen, and Deane L. Root, comps. *Resources of American Music History: A Directory of Source Materials from Colonial Times to World War II.* Urbana: University of Illinois Press, 1981.

Reitlinger, Gerald. *The Economics of Taste.* London: Barrie and Rockliff, 1961-63.

RILM   *RILM Abstracts of Music Literature.* [Flushing, N.Y.], 1967-.

International Repertory of Music Literature.

Rklitskaya, A. D., ed. G. P. Koltypina. *Muzykal'nye biblioteki i muzykal'nye fondy y bibliotekakh SSSR: spravochnik* (Music libraries and music holdings in the libraries of the USSR: a guide). Moskva: Gos. Biblioteka SSSR imeni Lenina, Otdel Notnkh Izdanii i Zvkozapisei, 1972.

Review by Barbara Krader, *Notes* 30 (1974): 529-30.

RMI   *Rivista musicale italiana.* Vol. 1-. Firenze: Fratelli Bocca, 1894-.

Rosenthal   Rosenthal, Albi. "The Music Antiquarian." *Fontes* 5 (1958): 180-90. Reprinted in Carol June Bradley, *Reader in Music Librarianship* (microcard, 1973), 81-89, and in **Coover**, xv-xxiv.

Samuel   Samuel, Harold. "The Yale Music Library: Some Recent Acquisitions." *Music at Yale* 20 (May 1991): 13-15.

Sartori   Sartori, Claudio, ed. "La biblioteche italiane: La situazione generale; Biblioteche italiane in possesso di fondo musicale." *Fontes* 18 (1971): 107-57.

Schaal   Schaal, Richard. *Führer durch deutsche Musik-bibliotheken*. Taschenbücher zur Musikwissenschaft, 7. Wilhelmshaven: Heinrichshofen, 1971.

Scheurleer   Scheurleer, Daniel François. *Catalogus der muziekbibliothek*. 3 vols. 's-Gravenhage: [Gebr. Giunta d'Albani], 1893-1910.

Scheurleer 2   _____. *Catalogus van de muziekwerken en de boeken over muziek*. 2 vols. 's-Gravenhage: M. Nijhoff, 1923-25.

Seaton, Douglass, ed. "Important Library Holdings at Forty-one North American Universities." *Current Musicology* 17 (1974): 7-68.

Shaylor, Joseph. *Fascination of Books*. New York: G. P. Putnam's Sons, 1912.

SiMG   *Sammelbände der internationalen Musik-Gesellschaft*. Vols. 1-15. Leipzig: Breitkopf & Härtel, 1899-1914. Reprint, Hildesheim: Olms, 1970.

Sims, George. *More of the Rare Book Games*. Philadelphia: Holmes, 1988.

_____. *The Rare Book Game*. Philadelphia: Holmes, 1985.

Sotheby & Co., auctioneer, London. *Catalogue of Sales: A Guide to the Microfilm Collection, Parts I-IV*. Ed. Lenore Coral. Ann Arbor: Xerox University Microfilms, 1973-76.

_____. *A List of the Original Catalogues of Principal Libraries Which Have Been Sold*. London: Compton and Ritchie, 1828.

Squire   Squire, William Barclay. "Musical Libraries." [Grove's] *Dictionary of Music and Musicians*, 1st ed., 4 vols. (1879-90), 2:417-27.

Startsev   Startsev, Ivan Ivanovich. *Sovetskaia literature o muzyke, 1918-1947: Bibliograficheski ukazatel knig*. Ed. S. D. Uspenskaia. Moskva: Sovetskii kompozitor, 1963.

Stevens, Alfred Arthur. *The Recollections of a Bookman: A Record of Thirty-three Years with Three Famous Book Houses*. London: H. F. & G. Witherby, 1933.

Straeten   Straeten, Edmond van der. *Musique aux Pays-bas*. 8 vols. Bruxelles, 1867-88. Reprint, in 4 vols., New York: Dover, 1969.

STMf   *Svensk tidskrift för musikforskning*. Vol. 1-. Stockholm, 1896-.

Tanselle, G. Thomas. *Libraries, Museums, and Readings: The Sixth Solomon M. Malkin Lecture*. New York: Columbia University, 1991.

Targ, William. *Bouillabaisse for Bibliophiles*. Cleveland and New York: World, 1955.

_____. *Carousel for Bibliophiles*. New York: Philip C. Duchesnes, 1947.

Thacker, Martin. "Single Composer Collections: Libraries, Archives or Documentation Centres." *Fontes* 37 (1996): 296-98.

Thaw   Thaw, E. V. Review of Werner Muensterberger, *Collecting: An Unruly Passion* (Princeton University Press, 1994). *New Republic* 11 (April 1994).

Tilmouth   Tilmouth, Michael. "Calendar of References to Music in Newspapers Published in London and the Provinces (1600-1719)." *Research Chronicle of the Royal Musical Association* 1 (1961).

Tuksar, Stanislav. "New Musical Sources in Croatia (Yugoslavia)." *Acta* 57 (1985): 121-38.

Valdrighi   Valdrighi, Luigi Francesco, Conte. *Musurgiana*. Bibliotheca musica Bononiensis, ser. 3, no. 14. Modena: Cesare Olivari, 1879. Reprint, Bologna: Forni, 1970.

Vereeniging   Vereeniging ter bervordering van de balangen des Boekhandels, Amsterdam. *Catalogus der Bibliotheek*. Vol. 1-. Amsterdam: P. N. Van Kampen & Zoon, 1885-.

> Vol. 4, 1934, and Vol. 8 (*Supplement-catalogus*), 1932-73, published in 1979, each contain immense listings of auction and antiquarian catalogs, and many sales of music collections.

VfMW   *Vierteljahrsschrift für Musikwissenschaft*. Vols. 1 (1885)-10 (1894). Leipzig: Breitkopf & Härtel, 1885-98. Reprint, Hildesheim: Olms, 1966.

Walters, Gwynn. "Early Sale Catalogues: Problems and Perspectives." In *Sale and Distribution of Books from 1700*, ed. Robin Myers and Michael Harris, 106-25. Oxford: Polytechnic Press, 1982.

Weckerlin   Weckerlin, Jean Baptiste. *Katalog der Musik-bibliothek: Musik - Tans - Theater, Versteigerung, 10. bis 12. März 1910*. Leipzig: C. G. Boerner, 1910.

Wendt, Bernhard. "Das Auktionswesen." *Der deutsche Buchhandlungsgehilfe* 3, no. 4 (1935): 110-16.

_____. "Zur Geschichte des deutschen Antiquariatsbuchhandels." *Zeitschrift für Bücherfreund*, no. 38, 3. Folge, 5 (1934): 103-08.

_____. *Der Versteigerungs- und Antiquariats-Katalog in Wandel dreier Jahrhunderten*. Leipzig: Liebisch, 1937.

Wheatley, Henry B. *The Prices of Books*. New York: Harper; London: George Allen, 1898.

Winks, Robin, ed. *The Historian as Detective: Essays on Evidence*. New York: Harper & Row, 1969.

Wolffheim   Wolffheim, Werne Joachim. *Versteigerung der Musikbibliothek . . . durch die Firmen, Martin Breslauer & Leo Liepmannssohn, Berlin*. 2 vols. Berlin, 1928-29.

Wroth, Lawrence C. "The Chief End of Book Madness." *Library of Congress Quarterly Journal of Current Acquisitions* 3 (October 1945): 69-77.

> The "end" is the enrichment of libraries: "What would these libraries have been without the book collector?" (quoted in Basbanes, *A Gentle Madness*).

ZiMG   *Zeitschrift der internationalen Musikgesellschaft.* Vols. 1 (1899/1900)-15 (1913/14). Leipzig: Breitkopf & Härtel, 1899-1914. Reprint, New York: Johnson Reprint, 1970.

ZfMW   *Zeitschrift für Musikwissenschaft.* Vol. 1-. Leipzig: Breitkopf & Härtel, 1918-.

Section 1

Catalogs and Literature

Catalogs of collections whose owners are unnamed are gathered chronologically in section 2. Boldface numbers within parenthesis refer to entries in this catalog.

1   Abel, Carl Friedrich, 1723-87

MR. GREENWOOD, AUCTIONEER, LONDON

A Catalogue of the Capital Collection of Manuscript and Other Music. An Exceedingly Valuable and Fine-toned Viol de Gamba . . . &c. of Charles Frederick Abel. Musician to Her Majesty . . . Sold . . . the 12th of December, 1787 and Following Day. . . . [London, 1787.] 8 p. 92+101 lots. Music, lots 1-38 (Mss. 22-38, mostly by Abel). [US-NY Frick]

Lugt, no. 4232.

2   Aber, Adolf, 1893-1960

HODGSON & CO., AUCTIONEER, LONDON

A Catalogue of Books from Various Sources, Comprising a Collection of 16th and 17th Century Breviaries and Missals, Property of Rev. F. E. P. S. Langton . . . Books on Music, the Property of Dr. Adolf Aber (decd.) . . . Sold October 20th, 1960 and Following Day. London, 1960. 40 p. 661 lots. Aber's lots, 245-330. [US-NYgr]

3   Aberdeen Musical Society

Johnson, David Charles. "An Eighteenth-Century Scottish Music Library." *RMA Research Chronicle* 9 (1971): 90-95. [g.a.]

A transcript of the Society's library catalog of ca. 1755.

4   Abraham, Burggraf zu Dohna (Saxony), 1579-?

LITERATURE

Mies, Otto Heinrich. "Elizabethan Music Prints in an East-Prussian Castle [of Schlobitten]." *Musica disciplina* 3 (1949): 170-72. [g.a.]

A note about the collection formed by Abraham.

5   [Abramson, Axel]
Broberg, C. J., comp. *En större och sällsynt samling af Svensk dramatik, balletter, oratorier m. m. som kommer att forsaljas paa Stockholms bokauktionekammare. . . .* Stockholm: K. L. Beckmans boktrykeri, 1897. 247 p.   [US-CA (priced)]
>   An auction catalog.

6   [Adamson, Lovell, et al.]
SOUTHGATE & SON, AUCTIONEER, LONDON   CAT. NO. 65
Catalogue of a Miscellaneous Collection of Books in Various Departments of Literature, Among Which Are . . . Also, an Extensive Collection of Music, by the Most Eminent Native and Foreign Composers . . . Sold . . . March the 14th, 1842, and Following Day. . . . [London, 1842.] 24 p. 655+ lots. Music, lots 161-251.   [GB-Lbl]
>   **Lugt**, no. 16501.

Adamson, Mr., a Music Seller. *See under* **Cerutti**

7   **Adler, Guido,** 1855-1941
Means, Mary Gail. *A Catalogue of Printed Books and Music in the Guido Adler Collection.* Athens: University of Georgia Photoduplication Service, 1972.   [US-BUu]
>   Microfilm copy of thesis, Georgia, 1968. Library and papers purchased by
>   US-ATS, 1948-52. **Bradley.**

8   _____
Reilly, Edward R. *The Papers of Guido Adler at the University of Georgia: A Provisional Inventory.* [N.p.], 1975. vii, 270 leaves.   [US-Wc, -CU]

9   **Adolphus Frederick, Duke of Cambridge,** 1774-1858
PUTTICK & SIMPSON, AUCTIONEER, LONDON   CAT. NO. 185
Catalogue of the Musical Collections of . . . Including . . . Also Two Violins by Stradivarius [&c.] to Which Is Added Another Musical Library and Numerous Valuable Musical Instruments . . . Will Be Sold by Auction . . . November 18, 1850. [London], 1850. 22 p. 564 lots. Instruments, lots 489-564.   [GB-Lbl]
>   Lot 250 is a catalog with incipits of all the Duke's instrumental music. **King.**

10   [Adolphus Frederick], Duke of Cambridge; Well-Known Collector [i.e., W. Morris]
PUTTICK & SIMPSON, AUCTIONEER, LONDON   CAT. NO. 680
Musical Library of a Well-Known Collector . . . Curious and Rare Masses and Motetts . . . Early Theoretical Works . . . Sold . . . June 10 and Following Day. . . . London, 1861. 801 lots.
                                                                            [GB-Lbl]
>   Lot 718: 77 volumes from the sale of Adolphus Frederick's 18 November
>   1850 (above) sale.

11   **Aerde, R. van [Archiviste de la Ville de Malines]**
[Catalogue de la vente des bibliothèque . . . juin 1945.] N.p., n.d.
>   Not located; cited from Les Amis de la Musique catalog no. 319, lot 32: 400
>   items, principally music.

12   **Agosti, Arrigo** and **Egle**
Gozzi, Susanna, and Alessandro Roccatagliati. *Catalogo della discoteca storica Arrigo ed Egle Agosti di Reggio Emilia. I. Opere complete e selezione.* Biblioteca degli historiae musicae cultores, 42. Firenze: L. Olschki, 1985. 103 p.   [g.a.]
> Donated to the Teatro Municipale di Reggio Emilia; contains about 5000 recordings.

13   **Aign, Walter**
HANS SCHNEIDER, ANTIQUARIAT   CAT. NO. 218
Musikliteratur, darunter die Wagner-Sammlung Walter Aign, Bayreuth. . . . Tutzing, [1978]. 84 p.   1130 lots.   [g.a.]
> Wagner items, lots 728-966.

14   **Aiguillon, ducs d'**
Bobillier, Marie. "Une Bibliothèque musicale. . . ." *Revue de l'Agenais et des anciennes provinces du sudouest, Bulletin*, 1899.   [US-Wc, -AA, -COL, -Cjc]
> Cited from **Benton 3**:60, no. 2, but is incorrect. The *Bulletin* for 1899 does not contain the article.

15   _____
Tholin, Georges, and M. M. Bosvieux. "Bibliothèque d'ouvrages de musique provenant du château des ducs d'Aiguillon." In *Inventaire sommaire des archives communales antérieures à 1790*, sér. 2, suppl. Paris: Paul Dupont, 1884.   26 p.
> Not located. **Albrecht** says 352 items, including 195 Mss., now in F-AG. **Benton 3**:60, no. 2.

16   _____
LITERATURE
Robert, Jean. "La Bibliothèque musicale du château d'Aiguillon." *Recherches sur la musique française classique* 13 (1973): 56-63.   [g.a.]

17   **Airson, Rev. Mr.**
FLACKTON, MARRABLE & CLARIS, AUCTIONEER, CANTERBURY?
Library . . . Musical Library. Canterbury, November 1789.
> An addendum by A. N. L. Munby in Ms. to the *List of English Sale Catalogues* (facing p. 92). Sale catalog not located.

Akerlken, D. von.   *See under* **Berg, P. J. W. van den**

18   **Alba, House of (Berwick, Jacobo Maria del Pilar Carlos Manuel Stuart Fitzjames, 10. duque de, 1878-19?)**
LITERATURE
Subirá, José. "La Musique de chambre espagnole et française du 18ᵉ s. dans la bibliothèque du Duc d'Albe." *Revue de musicologie* 7 (1926): 78-82.   [g.a.]

19   _____
Subirá, José. *La música en la casa de Alba: Estudios históricos biográficos.* Madrid: [Establecimiento tip. "Successores de Rivadeneyr"], 1927. xxii, 374 p., 60 plates.   [g.a.]

20   Alberdingk Thijm, J. A.
FREDERICK MULLER, AUCTIONEER?, AMSTERDAM
Collections scientifique & artistiques, formées par feu . . . Professeur d'esthétique à l'Académie royale des Beaux-Arts à Amsterdam . . . La vente 10 . . . avril [-29] Mai 1890. 4 vols. A'dam: Muller, 1890. 5316 lots.   [NL-Avb]

> "Hymnologie chrétienne," lots 1313-53. "Théâtre," lots 3304-24. "Chansonniers," lots 4313-49. "Musique," lots 5226-316.

Albert, Duke of Prussia, 1490-1568. *See section 3*

21   d'Albert, Eugen, 1864-1932
HUG & CO., ANTIQUARIAN, ZÜRICH   CAT. NO. 1
Musik-bibliothek Eugen d'Albert. Zürich, n.d. 8 p. 254 lots (many more items).
[Mimeo at GB-Lbl (Hirsch)]

> Prices fixed.

Albert, Friedrich August, King of Saxony, 1828-1902. *See section 3*

22   Albrecht, Henry F., d. 1875
Alphabetisch geordnetes Verzeichniss einer Sammlung musikalischer Schriften. Catalogue of H. Albrecht's Collection of Musical Writings. Newport, R.I., 1854. 32 p. 477 titles.
[Cat. in Ms. US-NYp]

> Collection purchased by Joseph W. Drexel and was the nucleus of his library. See Susan T. Sommer, "Joseph W. Drexel and His Musical Library," in *Music and Civilization: Essays in Honor of Paul Henry Lang,* ed. Edmond Strainchamp et al., 270-78. New York: Norton, 1984.

Albrecht V, Duke of Bavaria, 1528-79. *See works by* **Otto Hartig** *and* **Bertha Wallner** *under* **Fugger Family**

23   Alcock, Thomas
MR. WHEATLEY, AUCTIONEER, LONDON
A Catalogue of the Miscellaneous and Medical Library of the Late . . . [Including] *Several Pieces of Music by Handel, Arne, Corri, Pleyel, &c. A Few Lots of Prints . . . Sold . . . 12th November 1823 and Four Following Days. . . .* [London], 1833. 2, 48 p. 1408 lots. Music, lots 834-59.   [GB-Lbl (with buyers and prices)]

> **Lugt,** no. 11435.

24   Aldrich, Henry, Dean of Oxford, 1647-1710
Malchair, J. B. *Catalogue of the Printed and Manuscript Music Given by Dean Aldrich to the Library of Christ Church College, Oxford* [1787].

> Ms. 2125 in Royal College of Music Library. **King,** pp. 13-14. Microfilm copy at US-IO. **Albrecht** says 8000 vols., printed and Ms.

> See also W. G. Hiscock's article "Bibliographical Notes: Christ Church missing books, II. Printed music," in *London Times Literary Supplement,* Saturday, 11 February 1939, 96, in which the author speculates about the possibility that E. F. Rimbault (1816-76) may have purloined some, if not all, of 17 early works missing from the Christ Church Library, including works by Campion, Dowland, Morley, Purcell, et al.

25 **Aldrich, Richard,** 1863-1937
A Catalogue of Books Relating to Music in the Library of. . . . New York: Plimpton Press, 1931. viii, 435 p. ca. 2500 numbers.   [Copies US-Bp, -CA, -NYp, -Pc, -Wc]
     Albrecht says given to US-CA in 1986.

Alexander, Lesley. *See in* "Anonymous" *section 2 under* **A Well-Known Conductor**

26 **Alexander Ferdinand, Fürst,** 1704-73
"Catalog sämtlicher Hochfürstlicher Thurn und Taxischer Sinpfonien [*sic*]." [ca. 1782-95.]
                                          [Unpaged Ms.   D-Rtt]
     Thematic. Cited below by Haberkamp (**30**).

27 _____
"Catalogus Aller-Balleten Music. Verfasst Anno 1786, in Theatre und Musik Catalogen."
                                              [Ms. D-Rtt]
     Cited by Haberkamp (**30**).

28 _____
"Inventarium über sämmtliche vorhandene F. Musicalien. Aufgenommen am 12. Mai 1838 (von Haertel). [Inside title:] Catalog sämtl. Hochfürstl. Thurn und Taxischen Ballets Melodram, Prologen, Opern Kirchen-und Harmonie Musick."   [Ms. D-Rtt]
     Cited by Haberkamp (**30**).

29 _____
Färber, S. *Das Regensburger Fürstlich Thurn und Taxissche Hoftheater und seine Opera 1760-1780.* Regensburg, 1936.   [g.a.]
     Catalog of operatic works in the Hofbibliothek, pp. 1-154.

30 _____
Haberkamp, Gertraut. *Die Handschriften der Fürst Thurn und Taxis Hofbibliothek Regensburg. Thematischer Katalog.* . . . . Kataloge Bayerischer Musiksammlungen, 6. München: Henle, 1981. xxxii, 500 p.   [g.a.]
     Haberkamp reprints as "Beilagen" the following manuscript catalogs:

     • Beilage 1: "Verzeichnis der beim französischer Hoftheater verfügbaren Musikalien 1772: Liste des musiques appartenantes à S:A:S: Monsignor Le Prince de la Tour et Tassis." (FZA, HFS-Akten 2441)

     • Beilage 2: "Verzeichnis der bei der deutschen Schaubühne verfügbaren Theatermusikalien 1784 . . . die mit * gezeihnete sind von Hr. Schopff." (FZA, HFS-Akten 2440)

     • Beilage 3: "Verzeichnis der italienischen Opern aus dem Katalog des Musikintendanten Baron von Schacht 1786. Catalogo Le Opere Italiane appartenenti a S:A:S:"

     • Beilage 4: "Verzeichnis der Kirchenmusik aus dem katalog der Musikintendanten Baron von Schacht 1790."

     • Beilage 5: "Übersicht des Domtenaristen Sebastian Obermeier über die Neurodnung der f. Musikalienbibliothek 1875." (FZA, DK Aktenabgabe)

31 _____

LITERATURE

Barbour, James Murray. "Pokorny Vindicated." *Musical Quarterly* 49 (1963): 35-58.   [g.a.]

About Baron Schacht's appropriation of Pokorny's symphonies listed in his "Schacht-Katalog."

32 _____

Barbour, James Murray. "Pokorny und der 'Schacht'-Katalog" [Deutsche Fassung von Hugo Angerer]. In *Beiträge zur Kunst und Kulturpflege im Hause Thurn und Taxis,* ed. Max Piendl, 269-98. Kallmünz: Lassleben, 1963.

A longer version of the preceding.

33 _____

Angerer, Hugo. "Die Musiksammlung der Fürst Thurn und Taxis Hof-Bibliothek in Regensburg." In *Oberpfälzer Dokumente der Musikgeschichte,* ed. H. Beck, 31-48. Regensburger Beiträge zur Musikwissenschaft, 1. Regensburg, 1976.   [g.a.]

Alexandrine, Princess of Prussia, 1803-92. *See under* **Auguste Friederike**

34 **Alfonso de Bourgon y Braganza**

Madrid. Ayuntamiento Biblioteca Musical Circulante. *Catálogo. Ed. ilus.* Madrid: Ayuntamiento Seccion de Cultura e Información, 1946. xv, 610 p.

_____. *Apéndice.* . . . 2 vols. Madrid, 1956-72.   [Catalog US-Wc, -NYp, -Cu]

Cited by **Benton 3**:25, no. 52. Kinsky says US-Wc bought items from the collection.

35 **Alizard, Adolph Joseph Louis,** 1814-?

Notice d'un choix d'ouvrages rares et importants sur la musique, la littérature et l'histoire et d'une collection nombreuse de mémoires sur divers sujets de mathématique, provenant de la bibliothèque de feu S. F. Lacroix [les livres sur la musique provenant de feu Alizard] . . . *vente . . . 13 février 1845 et jours suivants.* . . . Paris: Cretaine, 1845. 32 p. Music, lots 1-157.

[US-Wc (entered under Lacroix)]

Noted by **Eitner, Fétis, Scheurleer.**

36 **Allott, Rev. Richard; [Col. Borton];** et al.

PUTTICK & SIMPSON, AUCTIONEER, LONDON   CAT. NO. 550

Catalogue of the Musical Library of the Late . . . Cathedral and Other Sacred Music, Rare Works in Music Literature . . . Curious Manuscript Scores, Valuable Instrumental Music [&c.] *. . . Sold . . . July 31st, and Monday, August 2nd, 1858.* 25 p. 568 lots. Music, lots 1-492.

[US-NYp (Drexel 832)]

37 Almeria, Countess of Esterhazy

L. AND A. BRECHER, FIRM, BRNO   CAT. NO. 34

Music. Children's and Other Illustrated Books, with Portions from the Property of Almeria, Countess Esterhazy, Later Countess Murray of Melgum. . . . Brno, [ca. 1935]. 477 lots.

[GB-Lbl, US-NYgr, -R, NL-Avb]

38 Alsager, Thomas Massa, 1779-1846

LITERATURE

Levy, David. "Thomas Massa Alsager, Esq. (1779-1846): A London Musical Life."

Not examined. A paper read before the Southeast Chapter of the American Musicological Society, 20 September 1984.

→ *See also* **Boscawen, George Henry** (sale of 26-28 May 1853)

39 Alsbach, Johan Adam, 1873-1961

CHR. J. BALLE, AUCTIONEER, AMSTERDAM

. . . *Muziekbibliothek van wijlen . . . Joh. Alsbach* [auction, 20-22 March 1962]. Amsterdam, 1962. 40 p. 2363 lots.

Not examined; cited in *IBAK* 62/63. Collection now in NL-Add.

40 Alströmer, Patrick A., Baron, 1733-1804

LITERATURE

Fagraeus, Jona Theodor. "Berättelse, om Alströmerska Biblioteket uti Alingsås." In Stockholm. Königl. Biblioteket, *Tidningar*, 1768.

Albrecht says some of the collection given to S-Skma in 1772. Johannson (**43**), says the family's collection also went there in 1949.

41 _____

Brolén, Carl Axel. *Om Alströmerska brevsamlingen i Uppsala universitets bibliotek.* Uppsala: Akad. Bokh., 1917. 47 p.

Not examined; cited from *Svenskt Bogkatalog.*

42 _____

Tegen, M. "Svenska Manuskript i Alströmer-samlingen i K. Musikaliska Akademiens Bibliotek." *STMF* 36 (1954): [140]. [g.a.]

43 _____

Johansson, Cari. "Studier kring Patrik Alströmers musiksamling." *STMf* 43 (1961): 195-207. [g.a.]

Whole issue devoted to *Studier tillägnade Carl-Allen Moberg 5 juni 1961.*

44 Alter, Georg

LITERATURE

Adler, Osrael, and Beatrix Schulz-Raanan. "Das Georg-Alter-Archiv: Dokumente zur Geschichte des Vereins für musikalische Privatausfführungen in Prag und des Kolisch-Quartetts." In *Ars iocundissima: Festschrift für Kurt Dorfmüller zum 60. Geburtstag*, ed. Horst Leuchtmann and Robert Münster, 1-13. Tutzing: Schneider, 1984. [g.a.]

45 Altieri, Paolo
Noto, Italy, Biblioteca communale
. . . *Indice alfabetico delle opere a della reccolta musicale del.* . . . Noto: Tipografia popolare, 1913. 19 leaves.   [US-NYp only]

Amalia, Princess, 1732-75. *See under* **Anna Amalia** *and* **Auguste Friederike**

46 Ambros, August Wilhelm, 1816-76
Alphabetischer-catalog der Sammlung von Compositionen alter Meister italiaener, niederländer aus dem Nachlasse des Dr. A. W.

> Lot 162 in Liepmannssohn's catalog no. 172 (the sale of James Mathews's library). Both the Ms. catalog (unpaged, fol.) and the collection are now at US-Wc. **Albrecht** says now at A-Wn!

47 Ambrosini, Raimondo, d. 1914
Raccolta di opere riguardanti Bologna nella Biblioteca di. . . . Rome: Garagnani, 1906.
                                                                                                      [US-Cn, -Lau]

> **Albrecht** says collection now in I-Bam.

48 Amersfoordt, Jacob Paulus, 1817-95
G. Theod. Bom & Zoon, auctioneer, Amsterdam
Notitie van Teekeningen, Historie- en Topgraphische Prenten . . . Fraaie en kostbare oude Violen, violoncels . . . eeinige muziek, enz., nagelaten door . . . Publieke verkooping . . . 23 Maart 1886 en volgende dagen. Amsterdam, 1886. 46 p. 929 lots. Music, lots 861-904.
                                                                                                      [NL-Ka, -Pk, -Avb]

> **Lugt,** no. 45549.

Amersfoordt-Dijk de Vries, Mrs. R. W. P. *See under* **Berg, P. J. W. van den**

49 Ammann, Dr. Robert, 1886-1960
J. A. Stargardt, firm, Marburg
Autographensammlung. . . . Marburg, 1963. 335 p. 131 plates & facs.

> "III. Musik," pp. 201-58, lots 949-1189. Published in 3 vols. at time of sale, 16 November 1961 (I. Teil "Musik," pp. 7-63, lots 1-237), but brought out in one vol. in 1963. Grolier Club copy of I. Teil, 1961, is priced, no buyers. A J. S. Bach letter fetched 35,000 DM. **Albrecht.**

50 Ammon, Fr. August von (of Dresden)
T. O. Weigel, auctioneer, Leipzig
Verzeichniss der hinterlassenen Bibliothek des Herrn Dr. . . . *nebst mehreren anderen Bibliotheken, sowie einem Anhange von Musikalien und Bücher über Musik an 4. December 1861.* . . . Leipzig, 1861. 187 p. 5442 lots. Music, lots 5169-442.   [US-NYgr]

51 Amplonius da Berka, fl. 1400
Erfurt, Stadtbücherei
Beschreibendes Verzeichniss der Amplonianischen Handschriften Sammlung zur Erfurt . . . hrsg. mit einem Vorworte . . . und die Geschichte seiner Sammlung von Dr. Wilhelm Schum. . . . Berlin: Weidmann, 1887. lviii, 1010 p.   [Film at US-NYcu; collection D-EF]

52 Anderson, Emily, 1891-1937; **E. G. Millar;** et al.

SOTHEBY & CO., LONDON, FIRM

Catalogue of Valuable Printed Books, Music, Autograph Letters, and Historical Documents, Comprising . . . Works on Music and Musicians; Music by Grétry, Haydn, Mozart . . . Autograph Letters of Bartok, Chopin, Berlioz, Debussy, Richard Strauss and Wagner, and Autograph Music of Delius . . . [&c.] . . . Sold . . . 22nd July, 1963, and the Following Day. London, 1963. 98 p. 525 lots. [g.a.]

Anderson's, 386-406 (contains many more items); Millar's, 447-54 (mostly ALS). **Folter 2.**

53 ──────────

HANS SCHNEIDER, ANTIQUARIAT, TUTZING   CAT. NO. 101

Musikbücher und Musikdrucke aus fünf Jahrhunderten [darunter Bestände aus der Bibliothek Emily Anderson, London]. Tutzing, [1964]. 58 p. 815 lots. [g.a.]

54 André, Jean Baptiste, 1823-82

Thematisches Verzeichnis werthvoller meist noch ungedruckter original-Handschriften W. A. Mozart's. Berlin: Franz Stage, [1856]. 15 p. 38 nos. [US-NYp, -Wc, -GB-Lbl]

Folter, no. 3.

55 André, Johann Anton, 1755-1842

In 1799 Johann Anton received the Mozart *Nachlass* from Costanze (531 compositions). At his death the collection was divided among his 5 sons. Many items were later auctioned in the famous Stumpff sale in London in 1847 (q.v.). The shares belonging to Johann August and Gustave were bought by D-Bds.

See **Albrecht.** Johann prepared 2 thematic catalogs of Mozart's works–published Offenbach a.M., [1805, 1828], and another in 1841 matching the sale catalogs (**56, 57**).

56 ──────────

ANDRÉ, FIRM, PUBLISHERS, OFFENBACH A.M.

Verzeichniss derjenigen Musikwerke von W. A. Mozart . . . von welchen die Originalhandschriften im Besitze des Hofrath André in Offenbach a.M. sind. . . . Offenbach a.M.: [André], 1841. 77 p. 280 lots. [US-NH, GB-LBL (Hirsch IV:1064)]

Folter, no. 4.

57 ──────────

ANDRÉ, FIRM, PUBLISHERS, OFFENBACH A.M.

Thematisches Verzeichniss derjenigen Originalhandschriften von W. A. Mozart, . . . welche Hofrath André in Offenbach a.M. besitzt. Offenbach a.M.: [J. André], 1841. 77 p. 280 lots. [US-Wc, -NYp, -Bp, -R, GB-Lbl]

Lots 277-90, "Authentische Abschriften," with notes in Mozart's hand.

58 Andrews, Henry C.

BANGS & CO., AUCTIONEER, NEW YORK

Catalogue of the Library of the Late . . . Comprising Miscellaneous Works in General Literature and a Special Collection of Music and the Literature of Music. To Be Sold by Auction . . . May 1st and 2nd, 1899 by Bangs & Co. . . . New York, 1899. 43 p. [US-Wc]

59   Angel, Alfred, 1816-76
PUTTICK & SIMPSON, AUCTIONEER, LONDON
Catalogue of the Valuable Musical Library of the Late . . . Also of Some Interesting and Rare Autograph Letters. . . . A Few Handelian Relics, etc. Which Will Be Sold . . . November 24th, 1876. [London], 1876. 21 p. 343 lots.   [US-Lau, -CHua, GB-Lbl]

Anhalt Zerbst, Princes of. *See* **Johann IV, Fürst zu Anhalt-Zerbst**

Anna Amalia, Duchess of Saxe-Weimar, 1739-1807. *See section 3*

60   Anna Amalia, Princess of Prussia, 1723-87
Contained holographs of the Bach Brandenburg Concertos, St. Matthew Passion, B-Minor Mass, cantatas, motets, etc. **Albrecht**: After her death, collection acquired by Joachimsthal, then transferred to Royal Library. After WW II, most went to D-Bim; 266 vols. back in D-B, some not accounted for. See long article in **Albrecht**. *See also section 3.*

61   _____
"Catalogus über der Durchtauchtigsten königlichten Prinzessin Amalia von Preussen Königl. Hoheit Musicalien bestehend in denen drey Styli nemlich der Kirche, Theater- und Cammer-Styl."
The Ms. in Staatsarchiv, Dresden is a copy of an older, now lost, catalog, according to *Bach-Dokumente* 3 (1972): 386.   [g.a.]

62   _____
"Abschriften von Werken Johann Sebastian Bachs im Besitz der Prinzessin Anna Amalie von Preussen, Berlin, 1783(?)." Reprinted in *Bach-Dokumente* 3 (1972): 382-87.   [g.a.]
See also in same vol., pp. 354, 447-48.

63   _____
"Catalogue des livres qui composent la bibliothèque de son altesse Roiale Madame la Princesse Amalie de Prusse, Soeur du Roi [i.e., Friedrich der Grosse], 1783." 90 p.
A Ms. in the Brandenburgische Landeshauptarchiv, Potsdam. In 3 parts: "Livres françois"; "English books"; "Teutsche Bücher."

_____. "Supplement. Zum Catalogo derer von der höchstseeligen Prinzessin Amalia Königl. Hoheit dem Joachismthalischen Gymnasio legirten Bücher."

64   _____
"Inventariums des zu Berlin befindlichen Nachlasses der am 30ten Maerz 1787 höchsteelig verstorbenen Prinzessin Anna Amalia . . . aufgenommen von der zur Regulierung des Nachlasses verorodneten Commission."
A copy of the Potsdam (**63**),1783 item. The Ms. is in the Deutsche Zentralarchiv, Abt. Merseburger, H. A. Rep. 46 W.133.

65 _____

Zelter, Carl Friedrich. "Verzeichnis Sämtlicher Musicalien welche der Bibliothek des Königl. Joachimsthalschen Gymnasii, durch des Vermächtniss Ihre Königl. Hoheit der Prinzessin . . . angehören Aufgennomen im Jahre 1800 durch Carl Friedrich Zelter."

The Ms. is in the Deutsche Staatsbibliothek, Mus. Ms. theor. catalog 76.
Cited in *Bach-Dokumente* 3 (1972): 386. [g.a.]

66 _____

BERLIN, JOACHIMSTHALSCHES GYMNASIUM, BIBLIOTHEK
Katalog der musikalien-Sammlung des . . . Gymnasium. Verfasst von Robert Eitner. Berlin: T. Trautwein, 1884. iv, 106p. 627 nos. [g.a.]
MfM, Jahrg. 1884, *Beilage.* **Folter**, no. 6.

67 _____

Münnich, R. "Aus der Musikaliensammlung der Weimarer Landesbibliothek, besonders dem Nachlass der Anna Amalie." In Hermann Blumenthal, *Aus der Geschichte der Landesbibliothek zu Weimar und ihrer Sammlungen: Festschrift . . . ,* 168-?. Jena: G. Fischer, 1941.

[US-ICarbs, -CU]

68 _____

Blechschmidt, E. R. *Die Amalien-Bibliothek. Musik-bibliothek der Prinzessin. . . . Historische Einordnung und Katalog. . . .* Berlin: Merseburger, 1965. 346 p. 680 items. [g.a.]
Main part of the book is a catalog. **Folter**, no. 7.

69 _____

Sachs, Curt. "Prinzessin Amalie von Preussen als Musikerin." *Hohenzollern-Jahrbuch* 14 (1910): 181-91.

70 _____

Kirchner, Joachim. "Die Einbänder der Amalienbibliothek." *Die Heftlade* 1 (1922/24): 17-20.

71 _____

Wutta, Eva Renate. *Die Bach-Tradition in der Berliner Amalien-Bibliothek. Mit zahlreichen Abbildungen von Handschriften nebst Briefen der Anna . . . (1723-1787).* Tutzing: H. Schneider, 1989. 321 p. [g.a.]

72 **Anrooy, Hijmans van; Dr. de Ramitz; H. D. J. Kellevink**
G. THEOD. BOM & ZOON, AUCTIONEER, AMSTERDAM
Notitie van Musikstuhlen, Violen . . . [etc.] en afkonstig van een geliquideerde muziekhandel en een instrumentwinkel beiden te Amsterdam. Publieke verkooping . . . 25 april 1913 en volgende dagen. . . . A'dam, 1913. 29 p. 722 lots. Music, lots 1-258. [NL-Avb]

73 **Antoine I, Prince of Hanover,** 1661-1731
Labande, Leon Honoré. *La Bibliothèque musicale du Prince . . . de Monaco.* Paris, 1925.
Not located; in Otto Haas catalog no. 13, lot 481.

74   **Apel, Willi,** 1893-1988
INDIANA UNIVERSITY, MUSIC LIBRARY
The Apel Collection of Early Keyboard Sources. . . . [Bloomington, 195?]. [22] leaves.
[US-BLu, -WTU]

75   **Appunn, Anton (of Hanau); Edward Bernsdorf (Leipzig); Edward J. Hopkins (London)**
LIST & FRANCKE, FIRM, LEIPZIG   ANT.-VERZ. NO. 335
Geschichte und Theorie der Musik. Aeltere praktischer Musik, aus dem Nachlasse der. . . .
Leipzig, 1902. 90 p. 2533 lots.   [US-Wc (with printed prices)]

76   **Arbon, J. O.** [probably Jan George, book publisher]
J. VAN BAALEN & ZOON, AUCTIONEER, ROTTERDAM
Catalogus van een uitgebreide verzameling boeken . . . eeinige fraaije Prenten, eenige goede
Muzijk en fraaije Muzijk-Instrumente, verkocht . . . 18 November 1857 en volgende dagen.
Rotterdam, 1857. 105 p. 3907 lots. Music, 57 lots, pp. 99-200.   [NL-DHrk]
        Lugt, no. 23816.

77   **Archibald, Mary Mellish**
RALPH PACKARD BELL LIBRARY
Catalogue of Canadian Folk Music in the Mary Mellish Archibald Library and Other
Special Collections . . . Mount Allison University [compiled by Eleanor E. Magee and
Margaret Fancy]. [Sackville, N.B.]: Ralph Packard Bell Library, Mount Allison University Library,
[1974]. 88 p.   [g.a.]

78   _____
        Creelman, Gwendolyn, et al. *Canadian Music Scores and Recordings: Classified Catalogue of*
        the Holdings of Mount Allison University Libraries Compiled by. . . . Publication in Music, 3.
        Sackville, N.B.: Ralph Packard Bell Library, Mount Allison University Library, 1978. viii, 192 p.
[g.a.]
            "A list of all Canadian music in the . . . Library and the Alfred Whitehead
            Memorial Music Library."

        Arena, D. Pasquale Caracciolo, Marchese de. *See under* **Caracciolo, D. Pasquale, Marchesa**
            di Arena

79   **Areu, Manuel**
        Montaño, Mary Caroline. "The Manuel Areu Collection of 19th-Century Zarzuelas [An Index]."
        Master's thesis, University of New Mexico, 1976. xii, 329 leaves.

80   **Arkwright, Godfrey E. P.,** 1864-1944
SOTHEBY & CO., AUCTIONEER, LONDON
Catalogue of a Selected Portion of the Well-Known Collection of Old and Rare Music and
Books on Music, the Property of . . . Sold . . . 13th February 1939, and Following Day.
[London], 1939. 64 p. 301 lots.   [Film at CRL; compiler]
            Albrecht: Includes " . . . a notable series of first or contemporary editions of
            Handel's works" (lots 104-54), mostly Walsh. See also **King**, pp. 74-75.
            → *See also under* **Dale, B.** (Hodgson sale in 1945)

81 Arkwright, Godfrey E. P.; Lord Basing; A. R. Wood; et al.

SOTHEBY & CO., AUCTIONEER, LONDON

Catalogue of Valuable Printed Books, Autograph Letters, Illuminated & Other Manuscripts etc. . . . Works on Music and Art, the Property of the Late . . . Sold . . . 4th December, 1944, and Two Following Days. [London], 1944. 64 p. 774 lots. [g.a.]

Arkwright properties, lots 372-448. Lot 449, J. C. Smith's Ms. copy of Handel's *Belshazzer*.

82 Armytage, Sir George; "A Lady"

PUTTICK & SIMPSON, AUCTIONEER, LONDON

Catalogue of Valuable Music Properties . . . Including Valuable Old Violins (Property of a Lady) . . . and the Extensive Library of Music Formed by the Late Sir George Armytage . . . Sold . . . February 24th, 1903, and Following Day. . . . London, 1903. 27 p. 590 lots. [GB-Lbl]

Armytage's library, lots 462-590.

83 Arnold, Franck Thomas, 1861-1940

Cudworth, Charles L. [A complete list of the collection given to GB-CU in 1945.] *Cambridge University Reporter*, 6 February 1945, pp. 411-16.

Cited from **King**, p. 84.

84 _____

LITERATURE

Wakeling, D. R. "An Interesting Music Collection." *ML* 26 (1945): 159-61. [g.a.]

Albrecht: 486 vols. to GB-CU, 1945; some now at GB-CDu. See also **King**, p. 84.

85 Arnold, Hubert

"The Musical Library of the Late Hubert Arnold (solo violinist)." N.p., n.d. [compiler]

Typewritten, 8.5″x 11″.

86 Arnold, Samuel, 1740-1802

MR. WHITE, AUCTIONEER, LONDON

A Catalogue of the Extensive and Entire Musical Library of the Late Dr. Arnold, Deceased. . . . Several Original Mss. . . . Also, Many Thousands of Engraved Plates, Copyrights, Published and Unpublished Works, the Remaining Copies of His Edition of Handel's Works. . . . A Large Quantity of Musical Types, a Few Books, Original Pictures of Handel . . . a Large and Unique Collection of 4 Portraits of Distinguished Musical Characters . . . Sold . . . May the 24th, 1803, and Three Following Days. London, 1803. 24 p. 499, 167 (4th day) lots.

[US-R, -Wc, -CN (photo of DLC copy)]

Folter, no. 8; **Albrecht**; **Wolffheim** 1:339. Arnold's Handel ed., 4th day, lots 47-106; "Plates and copies of Dr. Arnold's works," lots 107-32. Lot 153 (4th day), "All the plates of Dr. Arnold's edition of Handel's works, in Number upwards of eight Thousand, a particular account of which will be produced at the sale." Lot 137, "The plates of Dr. Arnold's continuation of the Cathedral Musick, all perfect, in Number Twelve Hundred and One." Copy at US-R, days 1-2, mostly priced.

87   Arnold, Samuel, Dr., and **J. T. (or S.T.?)**
PUTTICK & SIMPSON, AUCTIONEER, LONDON   CAT. NO. 1122
Books and Music from Libraries (Catalog of a Large Collection of Miscellaneous Books, &c.) . . . Sold . . . April 14 and Three Following Days, 1869. London, 1869.   [GB-Lbl]
> **King**, p. 137, says only lots 1513-31 comprise music.

88   Arrigoni, Luigi
Organografia, ossia Descrizione degli istrumenti musicali antichi. Autografia e bibliografia musicale della collezione Arrigoni Luigi, bibliofilo antiquario in Milano. . . . Milano: [Stb. tip. F. Pagnoni], 1881. 118 p.   [US-NYp, -Wc]
> Music library, pp. 57-94 (267 items); ALS, pp. 1-56; instruments, pp. 95-118 (172 items).

89   Artaria, Karl August, 1855-1919
Katalog der Privat-Sammlung August Artaria. Wien: Artaria, 1896. 104 p.   [US-PHlc]
> Not examined.

90   _____
[Eitner, Robert]. *Neue Erwerbungen der Königlichen Bibliothek zu Berlin. Beilage zu Nr. 11, MFM, 1901.* Leipzig: Breitkopf & Härtel, 1901. 10 p.   [g.a.]
> Lists 29 Mss. (more titles, mostly autograph) by Haydn, 5 by Mozart, 68 by Beethoven, 6 by Schubert, as well as printed works. Collection was purchased from Artaria by Erich Prieger for 200,000 marks, later sold to the German government for the royal library.

91   _____
Johnson, Douglas. "The Artaria Collection of Beethoven Mss.: A New Source." In *Beethoven Studies,* ed. Alan Tyson, 174-236. New York: Norton, 1973.   [g.a.]

92   Artaria & Co., Wien
Verzeichnis von musikalischen Autographen, revidirten Abschrift und einigen seltenen gedruckten original-Ausgaben, vornemlich der reichen Bestände aus dem Nachlasse Joseph Haydn's und Ludwig van Beethoven's, ferner der Manuscripte von Mozart, Schubert, Rossini . . . im Besitze von August Artaria in Wien. Wien: Im Selbstverlag des Besitzers, 1893. 26 p. 224 lots.   [US-NYp, -CHH, GB-Lbl, compiler (photo)]

Arundel, 12th Earl of, d.1580 [i.e., **Fitzalon, Henry**]. *See under* **Lumley, Lord**

93   Arundell, Dennis, et al.
SOTHEBY & CO., AUCTIONEER, LONDON
Catalogue of Medical and Other Valuable Printed Books, Music, Autograph Letters and Historical Documents . . . Sold . . . the 24th of July, 1961, and the Following Day. . . . [London], 1961. 98 p. 510 lots.
> Music, lots 366-437; Arundell's, 366-72; Mrs. A. L. Snapper's, 425-37. Hardly coherent libraries!

94   Arx, Cesar von
SCHUMANN, FIRM, ZÜRICH   ANT.-CAT. NO. 430
[Katalog: Literatur, Theater, Musik, enthält u. a. Teile der Sammlung Cesar von Arx.] Zürich,
[1951]. 62 p. 1236 lots

> Not examined; cited from **Folter 2**, no. 13.

95   Asenjo y Barbieri, Francisco, 1823-94
Subirá, José. "Mss. de Barbieri existente en la Biblioteca Nacional [Madrid]." *Las ciencias*
(Madrid) 3, no. 2 (1936): 385-96. Lists, pp. 391-95.   [compiler (photocopy)]
> **Albrecht**: ca. 4000 vols. now in E-Mn.

96   Ashbrook, Viscountess; et al.
SOTHEBY & CO., AUCTIONEER, LONDON
*Catalogue of Valuable Printed Books, Music, Autograph Letters, etc. . . . Music and Books on
Music and Musicians. Autograph Music of Berlioz, Debussy, Chopin . . . Autograph Letters or
Documents of J. S. Bach, Leopold Mozart, Wagner . . . Sold . . . 16th of June, 1958, and the
Following Day. . . .* [London], 1958. 86 p. 544 lots.   [g.a.]

> Music, lots 275-432; Ashbrook's, 275-386; other music Mss. and ALS, 387-
> 426. "Collection of autograph music of Sir William Herschel, Property of
> Mrs. C. D. Shorland, 427-32."

97   Asher, A., & Co.
LEO LIEPMANNSSOHN, FIRM, BERLIN   CAT. NO. 103
Catalogue de livres rare et curieux faisant partie de la libraire A. Asher & Co. Berlin, 1873.
48 p. 453 lots. Music, lots 261-449.   [GB-LRosenthal]

98   Ashfield, Frederick; "A Gentleman"
[Heath, J.] *A Catalogue of a Small but Very Curious Library of the Books and MSS. of . . . ;
Who Lately Deceased in His Return from Italy; a Gentleman Distinguished for His Elegant
Taste in Alchymy, Philosophy . . . and Musick. . . . With Several Compleat Setts of Concerto's,
Solo's and Sonata's by the Most Celebrated Italian Masters and Others . . . Together with
[Instruments] . . . Sold . . . the 24th of This Instant March . . . Next Door to the Golden Ball Near
St. James'-House, Pall-Mall. . . .* [London, 1729.] 43 p. various lottings.   [GB-Lbl]

> "Music and musical instruments," pp. 40-43 (46 lots, but dozens of items!).
> 91 lots are indexed in Lenore Coral's dissertation, p. 161, and discussed, pp.
> 63-64. **Coral**.

99   Atchley, Dr. E. G. C. F.
MESSRS. GEORGES, FIRM, BRISTOL   CAT. NO. 547
*Theology, Including Liturgy, Ecclesiology, Church Music, etc., from the Library of the Late.
. . .* Bristol, 1962. 52 p. 1658 lots (more items). Liturgy and church music, etc., lots 876-1172
(more items).   [US-NYgr]

100   Atkinson, John William
SOTHEBY, WILKINSON & HODGE, AUCTIONEER, LONDON
Catalogue of the Library of . . . Comprising Topographical Works . . . [etc.] *A Small Collection
of Music . . . Sold . . . 10th Day of July, 1888.* [London, 1888.] 21 p. 394 lots. Music, lots 291-
340, et passim.   [Film at CRL]

> Particularly heavy buyers were Liepmannssohn and William Cummings.

101   Attwood, G. Carew Reynell; Sir Isaac Heard
SOTHEBY & CO., AUCTIONEER, LONDON
Catalogue of Autograph Letters and Historical Documents, Including Specimens of . . .
Mendelssohn, Schubert, Weber, Strauss, Beethoven, Schiller, Haydn [etc.] *. . . Will Be Sold . . .*
23rd Day of November, 1900 and Following Day. London: Dryden Press, 1900. [Film at CRL]

> Letters of composers addressed to Thomas Attwood, his father, pp. 9-11,
> lots 72-86. Heard's collection, lots 567-81. An excellent sale; some
> holographs, including one by Wagner.

102   [Auberlen, Ad   ]
MORITZ EDELMANN, FIRM, NUREMBERG   ANT.-CAT. NO. 4
Minnesang und Meistersang. Volks- und Kirchenlied. Alte und neue Musik. Theater. Nürnberg,
n.d., 189-?, or 1901? 86 p. 2122 lots.   [NL-Avb, US-NYgr]

> Did not comprise all of Auberlen's collection.

Aubry, Pierre, 1874-1910. *See section 3*

August II, Duke of Braunschweig-Lüneburg, 1579-1666. *See section 3*

103   Auguste Friederike, Consort of Friedrich Ludwig, Archduke of Mecklenburg-Schwerin,
       1776-1871
"Verzeichniss der von dem Vice-Canzler von Both angekauften Musikalien" ([17—]). 17
leaves. 340 nos.

> Cited from Kade (**107**).

104   _____
"Catalogus musicalium, ([17—]). 67 leaves. 131 numbers.

> Cited from Kade (**107**).

105   _____
A. W. C. SAAL
"Verzeichniss der Musicalien der Durchlauchtigsten Frau Erbprinzessin Helena Paulowna,
Kaiserl. Hoheit, zusammengetragen von. . . . " 51 p. Ms.?

> Cited from Kade (**107**).

106   _____
"Verzeichnis Sämtlicher Musikstücke welche in dene Hof-Concerte, Kirchen etc., aufgeführt
worden sind von 1803." 44 leaves, Ms.

> Cited from Kade (**107**).

107   _____
OTTO KADE
Die Musikalien-Sammlung des grossherzoglich Mecklenburg-Schweriner fürstenhauses aus
den letzten zwei Jahrhunderten. Auf allerhöchsten befehl Seiner Königlichen Hoheit des
grossherzogs Friedrich Franz III. alphabetisch-thematisch verzeichnet und ausgearbeit von
Otto Kade . . . . 2 vols. Schwerin: Sandmeyerschen Hofbuchdruckerei, 1893.   [US-BE, -Wc]

Reprinted, Olms, 1974.   [g.a.]

1. "Musicalien der Seeligen Schwester Amalia [i.e., Princess, 1732-75]," 2:73-76.
2. "Nachlass der hochseligen Frau Grossherzogin Mutter Alexandrine, Prinzessin von Preussen [1803-92]," 2:78-83.
3. "Nachlass des Prinzen Gustav [1781-1851]," 2:333-48.
4. "Nachlass weiland Ihrer Kaiserlichen Hoheit der Frau Erbprinzessin Helen Pawlowna (1784-1803)."

[Nachtrag.] *Der musikalische Nachlass weiland Ihrer Königliche Hoheit der verwittweten Prinzessin Frau Erbherzogin Auguste . . . geboren Prinzessin von Hessen-Hamburg* [1776-1871]. . . . Schwerin: Sandmeyerschen Hofbuchdruckerei, 1899. 142 p.   [US-BE, -Wc]

Thematic. Also issued separately.

108   Augustus Frederick, Duke of Sussex, 1773-1843

MESSRS. EVANS, AUCTIONEERS, LONDON

Bibliotheca Sussexiana. The Extensive and Valuable Library of . . . Which Will Be Sold by Auction by . . . Monday, July 1st, and Twenty-Three Following Days [and] *January 30, and Ten Following Days.* 6 vols. [London: W. Nicol], 1844-45. [US-BLu, -Wc, -CA, -BE, -Cu, -NYp, Bp]

Vol. 1: theology, includes missals, psalters, graduals, etc.; vol. 2: Mss.; vol. 4: includes fine arts; vol. 5: includes drama, biography, bibliography; vol. 6: [residue]. A few good music items (Petrucci, a Kircher treatise, etc.) and some psalters, missals, and breviaries, *inter alia.*

109   Augustus Frederick; Dr. Southey

Catalogue of the Most Splendid . . . Collection of Books . . . from the Library of . . . and the Library of the Late English Poet Laureate Dr. Southey . . . Sold at Auction . . . November [1845]. New York: Gunley & Hill, [1845?]. 77 p. Music? Not examined.   [US-NYp, -PRu]

110   ———

CHRISTIE & MANSON, AUCTIONEERS, LONDON

Catalogue of the Valuable Collection of Manuscript and Printed Music of . . . the Duke of Sussex . . . Which Will Be Sold by Auction . . . 20 April, 1846 . . . by . . . Christie & Manson. . . . London, [1846]. 13 p. 210 lots.   [GB-Lbl, with buyers and prices]

King: ". . . reveal[s] a rather pedestrian taste."

111   Avé-Lallement, Luise

CHR. HELLMUNDT AND W. ORF

Die musikalischen Albumblätter der . . . zu Leipzig. Eine Autographen-sammlung a. d. Leipziger Universitätsbibliothek. Faks.-Ausg. Einführung u. Kommentar von. . . . Leipzig, 1981. 29 p. (facs.), 26 p. (commentary).

Not examined; cited from Dan Føg, *Catalogue,* 357:22.

Aylesford, Earl of. *See* **Finch, Heneage**

[Ayrton,   **].** *See* Reade catalog of 26 July 1848 and the Hingston sale of 23 June 1859

112 [Ayrton, probably **William]**
Mr. W. P. Musgrave, auctioneer, London
Catalogue of a Choice Collection of Modern Vocal and Instrumental Music by the Most
Favorite Composers, Together with [Instruments] *. . . and a Few Plates with Copyrights . . .*
Sold . . . 1st of April, and Following Day. [London, 1830.] 19 p. 250 lots. Music, lots 1-186,
218-50.   [US-NYp]

> On title page of US-NYp copy in Ms.: "The best books in this catalogue
> were the property of W. Ayrton."

113 [Ayrton, probably **William]; Thomas Kennedy**
Puttick & Simpson, auctioneer, London   Cat. no. 120
Extensive, Rare and Valuable Library of a Distinguished Professor [Ayrton] *. . . Rare and*
Early Editions of Madrigals, Antiquarian and Ecclesiastical Music, History, and Theory
Treatises, Including Some Very Rare Works; Handel's Works in Full Score by Dr. Arnold, Fine
and Perfect [lot 287] *Another the Same* [lot 422] *a Unique Collection of Handel's Operas*
[Walsh ed., lot 423] *Curious MSS. of Early Composers; Further Portion of Kennedy's Instrument*
Stock . . . Sold June 23rd, 1849 and Following Day. London, 1849. 718 lots. [US-NYp, -Bp]

> In **Coover 2**, a lengthy annotation, "an outstanding group of materials."

114 _____
Puttick & Simpson, auctioneer, London   Cat. no. 545
Catalog of the Interesting, Rare and Valuable Musical Library of the Late . . . Including
Manuscripts of Mozart, Locke, Haydn, and Others . . . To Be Sold . . . July 3, 1858. London,
1858. 478 lots.   [US-NYp, GB-Lbl]

> Lengthy annotation in **Coover 2** with details of contents. See also **King**
> and **Albrecht**.

115 BMI/HAVERLIN Archives
Literature
Roy, James G., Jr. "The BMI/Haverlin Archives Go Abroad." *Fontes* 24 (1977): 76-79.   [g.a.]

> Founded by Carl Haverlin; owned by BMI.

116 Bach, August Wilhelm, 1796-1869
List & Francke, firm, Leipzig   Cat. no. 56
Verzeichniss einer werthvollen Sammlung theoretischer Werke über Musik, sowie älterer
praktischer Musik und neuerer Musikalien. (Theilweis aus dem Nachlasse des Herrn Prof. A.
W. Bach in Berlin.) Leipzig, 1869. *MAC* dates 1870! 60 p. 2277 lots + 52 lots.   [US-Wc]

> Compositions by A. W. Bach. **Folter**, no. 10.

117 _____
J. A. Stargardt, auctioneer, Berlin
Verzeichniss einer werthvollen musikalischen und hymnologischen Sammlung u. Autographen
(auch die vom Direktor A. W. Bach hinterlassene) deren Versteigerung . . . 9. November 1869.
. . . Berlin, 1869. 34 p. 666 lots.   [GB-Lbl Hirsch 492 (5)]

> "Manuscripten-Sammlung des verstorbenen . . . A. W. Bach," lots 1-32; his
> autograph collection, lots 33-111. **Folter**, no. 9.

118 _____

List & Francke, firm, Leipzig
Verzeichnis der hinterlassenen Bibliothek des Herrn Dr. jur. Adolph des Arts in Hamburg, welche nebst . . . einer Sammlung des Herrn Prof. A. W. Bach in Berlin versteigert. . . . Leipzig, 1870. 162 p. 4200 + lots.

    Music, lots 3455-4200; more details in **Folter**, no. 11. Not examined.

119   **Bach, Carl Philipp Emanuel**

Hinrich Jürgen Köster, auctioneer, Hamburg
Verzeichniss auserlesener theologischer, juristischer . . . Bücher in allerley Sprachen, nebst einigen Musikalien und Kupferstischen, welche am 11 August und folgende Tage, Morgens . . . auf dem Eimbeckischen Hause öffentlich verkauft werden sollen. Hamburg: Wörner, 1789.
[g.a.]

    Music sections, pp. 61-80, are reprinted in facsimile, with a supplied index, in Ulrich Leisinger's article "Die 'Bachsche Auction' von 1789," *Bach Jahrbuch* 77 (1991): 97-126.

120 _____

Verzeichnis des musikalischen Nachlasses des verstorbenen Capellmeisters. . . . Leibhaber, welche etwas zu kaufen wünschen, können sich an die verwittwete Frau Capellmeisterin Bach in Hamburg verwenden. Hamburg: Gedruckt bey Gottlieb Friedrich Schniebes, 1790. 142 p. ca. 1200 lots.   [US-Wc, -NYp, -CU (film), -CHH (Xerox)]

    Folter, no. 12: reprinted in *Bach-Jahrbuch* 35 (1938): 103-36; 36 (1939): 81-112; 37 (1940-48): 161-81. For a "Nachwort," see Miesner (**126**).   [g.a.]

121 _____

    "Bach-Handschriften [i.e., J.S.] und -Bildnisse im Nachlass [C.P.E.], Hamburg, 1790." In *Bach-Dokumente*, 3:490-504. Kassel: Bärenreiter, 1972.   [g.a.]

122 _____

Verzeichniss von auserlesenen . . . meistens Neuen Büchern und Kostbaren Werke . . . welche nebst den Musikalien aus dem Nachlass des seel. Kapellmeisters C. P. E. Bach . . . Montags, den 4ten März 1805 in Hamburg im Eimbeckischen Hause öffentlicht verkauft werden sollen. Hamburg: Gedruckt in der Börsen-Halle von Conrad Müller, 1805. 34 p. [1293] lots.

_____. *Dritter Anhang. Verzeichnis von Musikalien aus dem Nachlass des seel. Hrn. Kapellmeisters C. P. E. Bach, grösstentheils ungedruckte Manuscripte von C. P. Emanuel Bach und J. Sebastian Bach. . . .*   [Folter, one location, D-B]

    According to **Folter**, no. 13, the catalog was issued after the death of Anna Caroline Philippina Bach (1747-1804), who had owned the collection. Not all from C. P. E. Bach's estate.

123 _____

    Bach, Johanna Maria. "Musikalien Johann Sebastian Bachs im Nachlasskatalog Carl Philipp Emanuel Bachs." Reprint in *Bach-Dokumente*, 3:449. Kassel: Bärenreiter, 1962.   [g.a.]

124 _____

Wade, Rachel W. *The Catalogue of Carl Philip Emanuel Bach's Estate: A Facsimile of the Edition by Schniebes, Hamburg, 1790.* Annotated, with a preface by Rachel W. Wade. Garland Reference Library of the Humanities, 240. New York and London: Garland, 1981. xxiii, 194 p. [g.a.]

> "Verzeichnis," pp. [1-142]. Wade cites 10 Ms. copies of the *Nachlassverzeichnis.* Eight were cited by Miesner (**126**), some of which are now lost; but some unknown to Miesner have turned up. Wade describes the following:
>
> 1. B-Br, Fétis 5217A (the catalog Wade reprints); 2. B-Bc, TT 16615; 3. DK-Kk; 4. GB-Lbl (Hirsch I.679); 5. D-Mbs, Mus. Th. 3885; 6. US-Wc, ML 134.B15A1; 7. D-Bds, Db312; 8. A-Wgm, 349/4; 9. D-Ha, A539/3; 10. D-Ha, Ms. 1137/1.

125 _____

Bach, Carl Philipp Emanuel. *Autobiography, Verzeichniss des musikalischen Nachlasses.* Annotations in English and German by William S. Newman. Facsimiles of Early Biographies, 4. Buren: Frits Knuf, 1991. 142 p. [g.a.]

126 _____

Literature

Miesner, Heinrich. "Philip Emanuel Bachs musikalisches Nachlass." *Bach-Jahrbuch* 36 (1939): 81-112; 37 (1940-48): 161-81. [g.a.]

127 Bach, Johann Sebastian

"Spezifikation der Hinterlassenschaft Johann Sebastian Bachs, Leipzig, Herbst, 1750." In *Bach-Dokumente,* 2:490-512. Kassel: Barenreiter, 1969.

> "Cap. VI, An Instrumenten," pp. 492-93 (19 items). "Cap. XII, An geistlichen Büchern," pp. 494-96, 505-08.
>
> Ms. in Staatsarchiv, Leipzig. A reprint of the theological library list is in vol. 2, pp. 747-51 and 956-78, of Philipp Spitta, *Johann Sebastian Bach* (Leipzig: Breitkopf & Härtel, 1873-80 ; reprint, Wiesbaden, 1962; trans. Clara Bell and J. A. Fuller-Maitland, London: Novello, Ewer & Co., 1884-85; reprint, 2 vols. New York; Dover, 1952, reissue, 3 vols., 1992); in Charles Sanford Terry, *Bach: A Biography* (London: Oxford University Press, 1928; rev. ed., 1933; reprint, 1962), pp. 269-75; Arthur Mendel and Hans T. David, eds., *The Bach Reader*, 2nd ed. (New York: Norton, 1966), pp. 191-97; and Robin A. Leaver, *Bachs theologische Bibliothek* (Neuhausen-Stuttgart: Hännsler, 1983), pp. 30-41. For more literature about the list see the bibliography in *Bach-Dokumente*, 3:498.

128 _____

Scheide, William H. "Johann Sebastian Bachs Sammlung von Kantaten seines Vetters Johann Ludwig Bach." *Bach-Jahrbuch* 46 (1959): 52-94. [g.a.]

> With thematic incipits and musical examples.

129 _____

Trautmann, Christoph. *"Ex libris Bachianis* [I]*": Eine Kantate Johann Sebastian Bachs im Spiegel seiner Bibliothek,* [Katalog]. Zürich: Musikverlag zum Pelikan, 1969.

Folter, no. 14: to accompany a recording of BWV 84; in fact, a catalog of an international exhibit for the 44th German Bachfest, 25-30 June 1969 in Heidelberg.

130 _____

Leaver, Robin A. "The Valuation of Bach's Library." *Bach: Quarterly Journal of the Riemenschneider Bach Institute* 9, no. 2 (April 1978): 28-32.   [g.a.]

Includes a short title (and correct) list of contents, pp. 29-30.

131 _____

Ex libris Bachianis II: Das Weltbild Johann Sebastian Bachs im Spiegel seiner theologischen Bibliothek. Austellung zum Heidelberger Bachfest 1985. Heidelberg: Kurpfälzisches Museum, 1985. 48 p.   [g.a.]

See "Ex libris I" catalog, 1969, Trautmann (**129**).

132 _____

Beisswenger, Kirsten. *Johann Sebastian Bachs Notenbibliothek.* Kassel: Bärenreiter, [1992]. 451 p.

Catalog, pp. 44-400, heavily thematic.

133 _____

Literature

"Quittung: Buchauktion, Leipzig, September 1742." In *Bach-Dokumente*, 1:199. Kassel: Barenreiter, 1963.   [g.a.]

A note in Bach's hand about prices paid for some additions to his Nachlass sold at the auction of Andreas Winckler's library, 3 September 1742, in Leipzig. Ms. in D-Dbs (Mus. ep. Bach, Joh. Seb., Varia I).

Reprinted in Leaver (**142**), 1975; facs. reprint in Besch (**139**), 1963. See also Schulze (**138**), 1961, pp. 95-99.

134 _____

Preuss, Hans. *Bachs Bibliothek. Sonderabdruck aus der Zahn-Festgabe.* Leipzig: A. Deichert, 1928.   [US-Wc]

Description of books in the "Spezifikation." From pp. 105-29 in the *Festgabe für Theodor Zahn* (Leipzig: Deichert, 1928).

135 _____

Hamel, Frederick. *Johann Sebastian Bach: Geistige Welt.* Göttingen: Vanderhoeck & Ruprecht, 1951.   [g.a.]

2nd through 4th eds. without subtitle. An analysis of Bach's library, pp. 94-112.

136 _____

Godman, Stanley. "Bach's Bibliothek: Die noch vorhandenen Handexemplare." *Musica* 10 (1956): 756-61; 11 (1957): 363.   [g.a.]

137 _____

Frick, M. "Three Volumes of Bach's Library Featured [in the Calov Bible]." *Quad* 10, no. 9 (16 November 1961).   [g.a.]

Not examined.

138 _____

Schulze, Hans-Joachim. "Marginalien zur Einigen Bach-Dokumentation." *Bach-Jahrbuch* 48 (1961): 79-99.   [g.a.]

"Eine Buch-Auktion im September 1741," pp. 95- .

139 _____

Besch, Hans. "Eine Auktionsquittung J. S. Bachs." In *Festschrift für Friedrich Smend zum 70. Geburtstag*, 74-79. Berlin: Verlage Merseburger, [1963].   [g.a.]

140 _____

Trautmann, Christoph. "Calovii Schrifften, 3. Bände aus Johann Sebastian Bachs Nachlass und ihre Bedeutung für das Bild des Lutherischen Kantors Bach." *Musik und Kirche* 39 (1969): 144-60.   [g.a.]

141 _____

Geck, Martin. "Bachs Schriftenverständnis." *Musik und Kirche* 40 (1970): 9-17.   [g.a.]

142 _____

Leaver, Robin A. "Bach und die Lutherschriften seiner Bibliothek." *Bach-Jahrbuch* 61 (1975): 124-32.   [g.a.]

143 _____

Wilhelmi, Thomas. "Bachs-Bibliothek: Eine Weiterführung der Arbeit von Hans Preuss." *Bach-Jahrbuch* 65 (1979): 107-29.   [g.a.]

Additional identification and description of items in Preuss's (**134**) "Bachs-Bibliothek," 1928.

144 _____

Oswald, Hilton C. "'Bach's Bible' in the Concordia Seminary Library." *Notes* 39 (1982): 172-75.
                                                                                                                                          [g.a.]

145 _____

Leaver, Robin A. *J. S. Bach and Scripture: Glosses from the Calov Bible Commentary.* St. Louis: Concordia, 1985. 191 p.   [g.a.]

Facsimiles of marginal comments and corrections in Bach's hand, etc.

146 Bachmann, Edwin

LITERATURE

Clinton, Ronald D. "The Edwin Bachmann Collection: Perspectives on Early Editions of Solo and Chamber Music with Keyboard." *Library Chronicle of the University of Texas at Austin* 25, no. 36 (1984): 11-23.   [g.a.]

Almost entirely about Beethoven, very little about the Bachmann collection.
Derives from Clinton's D.M.A. thesis (vii, 72 leaves) at the University of Texas, 1983.   (film copy at US-NYp)

147 Bacon, John

MR. WHITE, AUCTIONEER, LONDON

A Catalogue of the Collection of Music Books and Instruments, the Property of . . . Which Will

Be Sold by Auction by Mr. White . . . Westminster, on Wednesday, June 26th, 1816. . . .
[Westminster, 1816.] 8 p. 157 lots.   [US-Wc (priced), -Cn]
    Folter, no. 15. Not in **King**.

148   **Bacon, Montague; Rev. Dr. Baker; Rev. Mr. Holden; Dr. Tyron; John Shipton; Thomas Davie**
THOMAS OSBORNE, AUCTIONEER, LONDON
*A Catalogue of Books of the Libraries of the Several Gentlemen Undermentioned, Deceased;
the Whole Being Above Thirty Thousand Volumes . . . with Several Other Considerable Libraries
. . . Sold (for Ready Money Only) . . . the 10th of May 1750 . . . Till the First of April. . . .* London:
T. Osborne, 1750. 392, 8 p. 14,844 + 324 lots.   [only US-NYgr and F-Pn]
    About 40 musical items indexed in Lenore Coral's dissertation, p. 189. **Coral**.

149   **Baden, J[ac]**
*Fortegnelse over en deel af afg. Professor J. Badens Bogsamling, som tilligemed en udsøgt
Samling af Musikalier for Claveret og Sangen, bortsaelges andagen den 7de Januarii 1805
ved offentlig Auction i Professor-Gaarden pass Hiernet af store Kannicke-og lille Fiolstroedet
No. 250. . . .* Kiøbenhavn, 1804. 118 p. Music, pp. 108-18 (58 lots but many more items).
    Not examined; citation furnished by Dk-Kk.

150   **Baermann, Heinrich,** 1794-1847; **Karl Baermann,** 1811-85; **Bernhard Rudolf Abeken**
KARL ERNST HENRICI, AUCTIONEER, BERLIN   CAT. NO. 80
*Autographen-Sammlung, enthaltend die Autographen aus dem Nachlass der Clarinettisten
. . . sowie aus dem Archiv einer bedeutenden Musikalienhandlung. . . . Verst. . . . 29 [-30]
November 1922.* Berlin, 1922. 156 p. 1107 lots. Music and theater, lots 149-672, with illus.;
Weber, 604-58; Loewe, 352-85; etc.   [US-NYgr (priced), NL-Avb]
    Folter, no. 16.

151   **Bäumker, Wilhelm,** 1842-1905
Härtig, Michael. "Die Sammlung Bäumker der Universitäts- und Stadtbibliothek Köln, mit
verzeichnis des Erkelenzer Landes im 19. Jahrhundert." In *Beiträge zur Musikgeschichte der
Stadt und des Kreises Erkelenz,* 91-106. Beiträge zur rheinischen Musikgeschichte, 73. Köln:
Arno Volk Verlag, 1968.   [g.a.]

152   **Bagford, John,** 1650 or 51-1716
Pollard, A. W. "A Rough List of the Contents of the Bagford Collection." *Bibliographical
Society Transactions* 7 (1904): 143-59.   [g.a.]

153   _____

LITERATURE
Fletcher, W. Y. "John Bagford and His Collections." *Bibliographical Society Transactions* 4
(1898): 105-201.   [g.a.]

154   _____

Steele, Robert. "John Bagford's Own Account of His Collection of Titlepages." *Library,* ser. 2,
8 (1907): 223-24.   [g.a.]

155 —————

King, A. Hyatt. "Fragments of Early Printed Music in the Bagford Collection [in Harley 5836]." *M&L* 11 (1959): 269-73.   [g.a.]

156 **Baker, James (of Coleman Street)**
Sotheby & Wilkinson, auctioneer, London
Catalogue of the . . . Library Formed by the Late . . . Which Will Be Sold by Auction by S. Leigh Sotheby and John Wilkinson at Their House . . . on Thursday, the 24th Day of May, 1855 and Following Day. . . . [London]: J. Davy and Sons, Printers, 1855. 42 p.
[GB-Lbl, US-CA, -NYp, -Cn]

157 **Baker, Rev. James; William Cramer; [E. Bligh; T. C. Knight]**
Puttick & Simpson, auctioneer, London   Cat. no. 405
Catalogue of a Large Collection of Music from Several Private Libraries, Including Those of the Late Rev. James Baker . . . the Late William Cramer . . . Also Musical Instruments [belonging to Bligh] *. . . Will Be Sold by Auction . . . April 30th, 1855.* [London], 1855. 42 p. Music, lots 1-1014.   [GB-Lbl US-NYp, -Wc]

Annotations in **Coover 2**.

158 **Baker, Thomas,** d. 1773
Richard Macnutt and Burnett & Simeone, firms, Tunbridge Wells
The Music Collection of an Eighteenth-Century Gentleman. Royal Tunbridge Wells, 1985. [8] p. 19 lots.   [g.a.]

Offered *en bloc* for £900.

Baker, W. H. *See under* **Lucas, Charles** (sale, 1869)

159 **Balaton, ?**
Berlász, J., and B. Varga, *A keszthely Helikon Könyvtár Balaton Gyújtménye.* Budapest, 1965.
With a supplement, a title list. 19th century composers' signatures and dedications. Now at H-KE. Not examined; cited from **Benton 5**:95, no. 43.

160 **[Balham, Mr.]**
Leigh, Sotheby and Son, auctioneer, London
A Catalogue of a Small, But Very Valuable Collection of Books, Coins, Medals, and Music of a Gentleman Lately Deceased . . . Sold . . . March 9, 1802. 15 p. 509 lots.   [Film at CRL]
Music, lots 384-90 plus a number *inter alia*, but not an important group.

161 **Balle [Nic Edinger]**
Beeken, auctioneer, Copenhagen
Fortegnelse over en berndelig Samling Boger . . . og en Deel Musikalier . . . tildeels tilhorende . . . Hr. Bishop Balle . . . den 16 April 1811 . . . og folgende Dage bortsoelges ved Auccion. . . . København, 1811. 142, 54, 88, 63 p. Music, pp. 51-59 (162 lots).   [DK-Kh]

162 **Bamberg, Eduard von**
Katalog der Professor Dr. von Bamberg'schen Bibliothek, bestehend aus Werken deutscher und ausländischer Literatur über Kunst, Musik, Geschichte, Bellestristik, etc. Glogau, 1907. 297 p. 16,043+76 lots.

Not examined; cited from **Folter 2**, no. 26.

163 _____

*Die Oper / Musikwissenschaft / Philosophie / Atheismus / Mystik. . . . Teil IV der Bibliothek
. . . [wie oben] . . . Braunshardt. Friedrich Meyer . . . (25.2.1929).* 33 p. Lots 3719-4333.

Not examined; cited from **Folter 2**, no. 30.

164   B[ancel, E   M   ]

*Catalogue des livres précieux et des manuscrits avec miniatures composant la bibliothèque
de. . . .* Paris: Labitte, 1882. xxxii, 303 p. 882 lots.   [US-Wc, -NH, -CA]

Sold 8 May 1882 and following days. ". . . contenait une magnifique série de
vieux chansonniers et cantiques," according to Weckerlin.

_____. *Table alphabétique des noms d'auteurs et des ouvrages anonymes. . . .* Paris:
Labitte, 1882.   [US-CA only]

165   Banér, Gustaf Adam, 1624-81

Davidsson, Aake. "Dulle Banerens' Musiksamling." *STMf* 35 (1953):152-57.   [g.a.]

Includes a Ms. inventory of Uppsala Universitetsbibliotek Cod. W 1710:
"Catalogus librorum Domini Comitus et Gubernatoris Generalus Gustavi
Adami Banerii iam pie defuncti, Fol. 210v, Libri musici."

Bang, Maria, 1879-1940. *See under* **Paganini**

166   Barb, H. A.

Brockhausen & Bräuer, firm, Vienna   Cat. no. 9

Bibliographie des Hofraths. . . . I. Abth., Musikwissenschaft. Musikalien. Seltenheiten. Wien,
n.d. 19 p. 477 lots.   [US-NYp only]

167   Barber, Stephen Nicholson

Puttick & Simpson, auctioneer, London   Cat. no. 2214

*Catalogue of the Extensive Library of Music of the Late. . . . Organ Music . . . Instrumental
Works, a Few Curious Old MSS. Works on the History and Theory of Music . . . Sold November
27th, 1883.* [London], 1883. 15 p. 426 lots.   [GB-Lbl]

Barbirolli, Sir John, 1899-1970. *See under* **Oldman, Cecil Bernard**

168   Barbosa Machado, Diego, 1682-1772

His collection of printed scores was taken to Rio de Janeiro by João VI.
Now in BR-Rn. See Robert Stevenson, *Renaissance and Baroque Music
Sources in the Americas*, 259-300. Washington: General Secretariat,
Organization of American States, 1970.

169 _____

Horch, Rosemarie Erika. *Villancicos da coleçao . . . Catalogo. . . .* Rio de Janeiro: Biblioteca
nacional, 1969. 192 p.   [US-BUu]

→ *See also* **Horch** *under* **João IV**

Baring, Mrs. Edward Charles (Lady Revelstoke). *See under* **Revelstoke**

Barlow, Alan. *See under* **White, Eric W.**

Barnard, Sir Andrew Barnard. *See under* **Smart, Sir George Thomas**
>British Library catalog says Sir Andrew Bernard. US-NYp and US-Wc both
>say Sir G. Bernard.

170   Barnouw, N   ; R. H. Broers
Bom, AUCTIONEER, AMSTERDAM
[A Catalog of Instruments and Volumes Sold Mar. 21-28, 1874.] Amsterdam, 1874. 116 p. 2647
lots.   [NL-Avb, NL-DHrk]
>Not examined; cited from **Lugt**, no. 34669.

171   Barons, Krišjanis, 1835-1925
Berzkalne, Anna. *Typenverzeichnis lettischer Volksromanzen in der Sammlung Kr. Barons'*
Latvju Dainas. FF Communications, 123. Helsinki: Suomalainen Tiedeakatemia, Academia
Scientiarum Fennica, 1938. 58 p.   [US-CA]

172   Barrett, William Alexander, 1834-91; **Francis E. H. J. Barrett,** 1869-1925
MESSRS. HODGSON & CO., AUCTIONEER, LONDON
A Catalogue of Valuable and Rare Books, Including a Selection from an Old Country Library
. . . Issues from the Kelmscott Press . . . to Which Is Added the Extensive Collection of Books on
Music Formed Mainly by the Late . . . Sold . . . June 25th, 1925, and Following Day. . . .
[London], 1925. 50 p. 631 lots.   [GB-Lbl]
>Lots 321-631, "The music library formed by the late William Alexander
>Barret . . . and added to by the late F. E. H. J. Barrett, formerly musical editor
>of the *Morning Post*." Early printed books and Mss., lots 381-494. **King**,
>p. 73.

173   _____

>*LITERATURE*
>Griffin, Ralph Hare. *An Account of Two Volumes of Manuscript Anthems Once in the Barrett*
>*Collection.* [London, 1929]. 11 p.   [GB-Lbl (Hirsch no. 994)]

Barrett-Lennard Collection.   *See under* **Lennard, Henry Barrett,** 1818-99

174   Barrow, William
SOTHEBY & CO., AUCTIONEER, LONDON
Catalogue of Music, Musical Manuscripts [etc.] *Including Autograph Music of Lennox*
Berkeley, Handel, Mahler [etc.], *the "Sterndale Bennett" Manuscript of "Messiah"; Important*
Series of [108] *Letters of Puccini* [the Property of William Barrow and Several Others Unnamed]
. . . Sold . . . 11th-12th March, 1974. London, 1974. 103 p. 377 lots.   [g.a.]
>Barrow's properties, lots 1-21; music from various owners, lots 22-179.
>Exceptional.

175   Barry, Smith
MR. CHRISTIE, AUCTIONEER, LONDON
A Catalogue of the . . . Library of [chiefly Ms.] *Music of the Late Hon. S. Barry, Dec., Also a*

Few Musical Instruments . . . Sold by Auction . . . June . . . 1803. London: Christie, 1803. 11 p.

[US-NYp]

Bartenstein, Schloss. *See* **Hohenlohe-Bartenstein, Fürst zu**

176   Barth, ?

Prussia, General-intendantur der K. Schauspiele in Berlin, Bibliothek

Abtheilung II. des Kataloges. Textbücher der Barth'schen Sammlung, zusammengestellt von Carl Schäffer. Berlin: Günther & Sohn, 1892. 100 p.   [US-Wc only, but reported lost]

Partial contents, according to US-Wc card: Opern, Operetten, Musik-dramen, Schauspiele und Trauerspiele mit Musik, Ballets und Pantomimen.

177   Barthélemon, François Hippolyte, 1741-1808

Mr. H. Phillips, auctioneer, London

A Catalogue of the Genuine and Valuable Assemblage of Musical Instruments, Manuscript and Printed Music, a Few Select Pictures . . . Property of That Eminent Performer . . . Deceased . . . Among Which Are His Unique Straduarius . . . Stainer . . . Amati . . . Original Manuscript Compositions, Handel's Works, Theoretic Works [etc.] *Sold . . . the 31st of January, 1809.* 7 p. 65 lots.

The catalog is not, as **King** says, among the Warren sales catalogs now in the Harding collection but, in fact, in a volume of catalogs at US-R (ML 138/H815), partly priced.

Bartholomew, W. *See under* **Edwards, F. G.**

178   Bartleman, James, 1769-1821; **Richard Guise**

Mr. White, auctioneer, London

A Catalogue of the Duplicate Books or Mr. Bartleman's Collection of Music, Amongst Which Are . . . a Large Collection of Harpsichord Music . . . Dr. Arnold's Edition of Handel's Works, Complete in 37 Volumes . . . a Very Excellent Violoncello, Several Violins . . . Also the Reserved Part of Mr. Guise's Collection, &c. . . . Sold . . . June 7, and Following Day. London, [1807]. 20 p. 387 lots.   [US-R]

"The reserved part of the late Mr. Guise's Collection, &c.," lots 250-387.

179   Bartleman, James; Robert Cooke, 1768-1814

Mr. White, auctioneer, London

A Catalogue of the Duplicate Books and Articles of Mr. Bartleman's Collection of Music. Also Part of the Collection of Mr. Robert Cooke, Deceased . . . Comprising Many Scarce and Curious Articles. And the Collections and Instruments of Several Other Eminent Professors and Amateurs . . . Sold . . . February 19, 1816. [London, 1816?] 29 p. 1015 lots.

Not in **Albrecht** or **King**. Original at US-Wc includes buyers and prices; US-CN and compiler also have copies. Many manuscripts (Durante, Galuppi, Lully, etc.).

Another sale by Mr. White, 26-27 June 1821, contained mostly musical instruments and only a few items of music, *inter alia.* Copy at US-R.

180   _____

Mr. White, auctioneer, London

A Catalogue of the Very Valuable and Celebrated Library of Music Books . . . a Very

Extensive and Matchless Assemblage of the Most Choice and Scarce Productions and Works of All the Great Masters Ancient and Modern, Rich in Every Class but Particularly Church Music, Masses, Motetts and Madrigals . . . [Including] *Marcello's Psalms in MSS., Contained in Thirty-Two Cases . . . Sold . . . 20th of February, 1822, and 8 Following Days.* [Westminster: Printed by J. Hayes, 1822.] 45 p. 1477 lots.

[US-CHua, -Wc, -U, -R, GB-Lbl (Hirsch no. 1078) US-CN; compiler (copy, n & p)]

"Italian songs in score, MSS. . . ," day 4, lots 584-651. **Albrecht** and **King**, pp. 34-35.

181 **Bartók, Béla,** 1881-1945

Lampert, Vera. "Zeitgenössische Musik in Bartóks Notensammlung." In *Documenta bartókiana*, ed. László Somfai, 5:142-68. Mainz: Schott, 1977. [g.a.]

182 **Basevi, Abramo,** 1818-85

FLORENCE, CONSERVATORIO DI MUSICA "LUIGI CHERUBINI," BIBLIOTECA

Catalogo del Fondo Basevi nella Biblioteca . . . [by] *Antonio Addamiano* [and] *Jania Sarno . . . Musica vocale; Opere teatrali, manoscritte e a stampa.* Cataloghi di fondi musicali italiani . . . , 16. Roma: Ed. Torre d'Orfeo, 1994. lxxxix, 491 p. 593 items. [g.a.]

183 ———

LITERATURE

Trivisonno, Anna Maria. "The Basevi Collection in the Library of the Cherubini Conservatory, Florence (Italy)." *Fontes* 23 (1985): 114-17. [g.a.]

Albrecht.

184 [**Bashford, Mrs. E. M.; A. S. Newson;** et al.]

SOTHEBY & CO., AUCTIONEER, LONDON

Catalogue of Valuable Printed Books, Music, Autograph Letters, and Historical Documents, Comprising Autograph Music of Sir Arthur Sullivan, Including Full Scores of Cox and Box, Trial by Jury, H. M. S. Pinafore, the Pirates of Penzance . . . Autograph Diaries from 1881 to 1900 . . . Letters of Berlioz, Brahms, Gounod [etc.] *. . . Sold 17th of June, 1966.* London, 1966. 66 p. 270 lots. [US-NYgr, GB-Lbl, film at CRL]

Bashford's Sullivan scores, lots 168-200 (many more items). The unpublished holograph full score of *Pinafore* fetched $16,800. Sullivan items, property of Newson, lots 203-11. Other Sullivan items, various properties, *inter alia.*

185 **Bastiaans, Johannes,** 1812-75

Balabrega, A. F. *Catalogus van eene verzameling Boeken, over verschillende vakken van wetenschap, kund en letteren . . . werken over Toonkunst, en de Toonwerken van de voornaanste Componisten . . . nagelaten door . . . Organist aan het grande Orgel in de Groote Kerk te Haarlem . . . verkooping . . . 6, 7 en 8 september 1875. . . .* Haarlem, 1875. 28 p. 864+ lots. Music, lots 639-864. [NL-Avb]

186 **Bates, Edward**

PUTTICK & SIMPSON, AUCTIONEER, LONDON   CAT. NO. 1023

Catalogue of the . . . Musical Library of the Late . . . Comprising Many Works Formerly in the Possession of Joah Bates . . . Together with . . . Musical Instruments . . . To Be Sold . . . Dec. 20, 1867. [London, 1867]. 20 p. 487 lots. Music, lots 1-371. [US-NYp, GB-Lbl]

King, p. 56.

187 **Bates, F. W.; R. Underwood**
PUTTICK & SIMPSON, AUCTIONEER, LONDON   CAT. NO. 1333
Catalogue of a Collection of Music, Including the Libraries of F. W. Bates and R. Underwood.
. . . Also Musical Instruments . . . Will Be Sold . . . July 25-26, 1872. [London, 1872.] 20 p. 539
lots. Music, lots 1-433.   [US-NYp, GB-Lbl]

Bates, Joah, 1741-99. *See under* **Bates, Edward**
Albrecht: library sold by Edward in 1867 contained Handel editions later
acquired by A. H. Mann. See under sales of James Hook's and Mann's
properties.

Bath Harmonic Society. *See under* **Plumb, J. B.**

188 **Baughman, Roland**
LITERATURE
Barzun, Jacques. "The Latest Berlioz Finds." *Columbia Library Columns* 17, no. 3 (May 1968):
8-12.   [g.a.]
Describes some of the notable items.

189 **Baumgart, Expedit Friedrich (in Breslau),** 1817-74; **Ludwig Friedrich Hetsch,** 1806-72
LIST & FRANCKE, FIRM, LEIPZIG   ANTIQ. CAT. NO. 83
Verzeichniss der werthvollen Sammlung theoretischer Werke über Musik, sowie älterer
praktischer und neuer Musikalien, aus den Nachlasses von . . . Antiquarisches Verzeichniss
Nr. 83. Leipzig, 1873. 37 p. 1313 lots.   [NL-Avb]
Folter, no. 133, under Hetsch. Properties are not differentiated.

Bax, Mrs. Barbara. *See under* **White, Eric Walter**

190 **Bayley, E. A.; "A Well-Known Amateur"**
PUTTICK & SIMPSON, AUCTIONEER, LONDON   CAT. NO. 720
Catalogue of a Large Collection of Valuable Music, Comprising Various Antiquarian Works
. . . Also Numerous Musical Instruments . . . from Several Private Collections . . . Sold . . . May
19th, and Following Day. . . . London, 1862. 32 p. 899 lots. Music, lots 1-733.   [GB-Lbl]

191 **Bayrhoffer, Wilhelm**
Catalogs found under his name are not of his private library but of his
commercial lending library, issued 1850-57, with supplements, accounting
for 19,252 numbers.

192 **Beauchesne, Alfred de**
CHARAVAY, AUCTIONEER, PARIS
Catalogue des autographes de musiciens, chanteurs, etc., composant le cabinet de M. . . .
vente April 3, 1877. Paris: Charavay, 1877. 17 p. 209 lots.   [Not located]
Cited by **Lugt**, no. 37298ᵃ, **Weckerlin**, no. 93, **Wolffheim** 1:345.

193 **Bech, Terence R.**
INDIANA UNIVERSITY, BLOOMINGTON, ARCHIVES OF TRADITIONAL MUSIC
Catalogue of the Terence R. Bech Nepal Music Research Collection, Compiled by Anne Helen
Ross . . . ; Project Director, Frank J. Gillis. Bloomington, 1978. 435 p.   [g.a.]

194 **Bêche** ; **Alexandre Étienne Choron**
LEBLANC, AUCTIONEER (ET LIBRAIRE), PARIS
Catalogue de livres et oeuvres de musique autographes, manuscrits, imprimés ou gravés,
provenant du cabinet de M. Bêche, ancien Director de la Chapelle du Roi, à Versailles; et
. . . M. Choron, Directeur de l'école spéciale de chant . . . vente . . . lundi 4 janvier 1836, et
jours suivants. Paris: Leblanc, 1836. 65 p. 834 lots (many more items).

[GB-Lbl (Hirsch), US-NYp, NL-DHgm]

Folter, no. 20. **Albrecht** and US-NYp date [1835]. **Bobillier** says 36 p.;
US-NYp, 48!

195 **Becher, Wilhelm, Rev.** (the friend of Lord Byron)
FRANK MURRAY, FIRM, DERBY
Catalogue of the Greater Portion of the Musical Library of the Rev. Becher of Southwell,
Offered at the Affixed Prices. . . . Derby, 1866. 15, iii p. 140 lots.

Not in **King**. Copies at US-Bp and US-Wc. That at US-Wc is a large paper
copy, one of 25, from the James E. Matthew collection. In Liepmannssohn's
sale of that library (catalog no. 172) at lot 166, the annotation says Becher's
catalog "contains 140 numbers of mostly old practical music of the 18th
century."

→ *See also under* **Reay, Samuel** (sale of 1907)

196 **Becker, Carl Ferdinand,** 1804-77
Alphabetisch und chronologisch geordnetes Verzeichniss einer Sammlung von musikalischen
Schriften. Ein Beitrag zur Literaturgeschichte der Musik und auf Verlangen einiger Freunde
zum Drucke befördert von dem Besitzer der Sammlung Carl Ferdinand Becker. Leipzig: Breitkopf
& Härtel, 1843. 22 p. 1014 lots. [US-Cn, -MSu, -PO]

Folter, no. 21, a lengthy description. Also **Albrecht**. Collection now at
Leipzig Stradtbücherei.

197 _____
. . . 2. verm. ausg. Leipzig: Breitkopf & Härtel, 1846. 26 p. 1120 lots.

[US-Wc, GB-Lbl (Hirsch IV:1080)]

"Nachträge," pp. 1015-120. An author, short title, place, and date list of
works (mostly theory) dealing with music divided by sections (e.g., 1600-
699), with indications of where in Becker's *Darstellung* (Leipzig, 1836 and
1839) biographical information about each author can be found.

198 **Becker, Georg,** 1834-1928
"Georg Becker's Musikalienbibliothek in Lancy bei Genf." *MfM* 4 (1872): 55-56; "Aus meiner
bibliothek," *MfM* 8 (1876): 155-57; 9 (1877): 4-7; 10 (1878): 100-04; 11 (1879): 61-62; 12 (1880):
13-14; 13 (1881): 161-64. [g.a.]

Albrecht: library now at F-LYm.

199 _____
"Petit Extrait du catalogue des ouvrages . . . du seizième et dix-septième siècle de la bibliothèque de G. Becker." In his *La Musique en Suisse . . . jusqu'à la fin du dix-huitième siècle,*
87-190. Genève: F. Richard, 1874. [US-Nyp]

A supposed *nouvelle éd.* of only 102 p. was published by Éd Henn in Geneva in 1923, but has not been located.

200   Becker, Hans, 1860-1917
> LIST & FRANCKE, FIRM, LEIPZIG   ANT.-VERZ. NO. 470
> *Musikliterature - Musikalien. Nachtrag zum unserm Katalog Nr. 466. Aus dem Besitze des Herrn. . . .* Leipzig, 1918. 24 p. 691 lots.
>> **Folter**, no. 22.

201   Becker, J
> H. HOTTER, FIRM, REGENSBURG   CAT. NO. 17
> *Musik . . . , bibliothek von J. Becker, gemischten Inhaltes.* Regensburg, 1889.
>> Not examined or located; cited from *VfMW* 5 (1889): 640.

202   Becker, Karl E.
> Schroeder, Adolf E. "The Karl Becker Manuscripts: A German Folk Song Collection in the Library of Congress." *Jahrbuch der Volksliedforschung* 21 (1976): 178-82.   [g.a.]
>> Cited from *RILM* 10, no. 2 (1976): 4592.

Bedel, Laure. *See* **Jacquard, Laure (Bedel)**

203   Beecke, Ignaz Franz von, 1733-1803
> "Aus dem Nachlassinventar des Musik-Intendentan Ignaz v. Beecke [deceased], 2. Januar 1803."   [g.a.]
>> Ms. in Archiv-Wallerstein. Reprinted in **Haberkamp** (see Sources, pp. xxx-xxxi).

204   Beethoven, Ludwig van, 1770-1827
> The inventories of Beethoven's properties at the time of his death contained in the so-called *Nachlass* catalogs have been something of a bibliographical muddle until recently. Chapter 1, "A Survey of the Principal Collections," and Appendix B, both supplied by Douglas Johnson to the splendid compilation by himself, Alan Tyson, and Robert Winter (*The Beethoven Sketchbooks*, "**BS**" in Sources) clears away much of the disarray. As Johnson points out, "the documents relating to the auction of 5 November 1827 have not been adequately described or accurately transcribed by scholars in the past" (p. 571).
>
> It at least straightens out, fully describes, and compares the five separate extant manuscript *Nachlass* catalogs and some of their reprintings. In Appendix B they are assigned codes as follow:
>
> O₁ By Anton Gräffer, now in the Stadt- und Landesarchiv, Vienna, signed by witnesses and principals at the appraisal, but no buyers listed. Ends with lot 252.
>
> S   By Gräffer, also in the Vienna archive, with a cover added by Ignaz Sauer, along with his *Nöthige Anmerkung*, with names of buyers and sale prices for some lots. The copy is sometimes associated with Artaria (see **210**).
>
> Ho A copy prepared by Gräffer for Jakob Hotschevar, which includes the *fremdes*

Eigenthum, annotations by Hotschevar, as well as buyers and prices. Copy in Beethovenhaus, Bonn.

Ha Copy by Tobias Haslinger, it abbreviates Sauer's title page, and the *fremdes Eigenthum* (which he calls *Angesprochene Werke*) and notes prices—Haslinger's own purchases included. Copy at Eastman School of Music, Rochester, N.Y.

F Copy made by Aloys Fuchs *after* the auction, includes buyers' names and prices, the *fremdes Eigenthum*. According to Johnson (and a concordance which he furnishes), catalog entries differ from those in the Gräffer copies, "sometimes providing more precise descriptions" (p. 569). Fuchs supplied the following title page to his copy: "Vollständiges Verzeichniss: des am 5. November 1827 zu Wien am Kohlmarkt No. 1149 öffentlich versteigerten musik. Nachlasses des Tonsetzers Ludwig van Beethoven . . . [etc.]."

The copies vary greatly, as Johnson points out, even the three done by Gräffer. Haslinger and Fuchs both altered the text of original entries.

Various transcriptions of the *Nachlass* catalogs have appeared in many places, as the following citations attempt to show. But as Johnson is at pains to emphasize, "no one—not even Thayer—has sought to reproduce the text of any of the catalogs exactly." In the following, a chronological arrangement has been attempted.

205 _____

Seyfried, Ignaz von. "Gerichtliche Inventur und Schätzung d. d. 16 August 1827 der zur Verlassenschaft gehörige Musikalien und Bücher des am 26 März 1827 in Wien im Schwarzspanierhause Nr. 200 verstorbenen Tonsetzers Ludwig van Beethoven." In his *Ludwig van Beethoven's Studien im Generalbasse . . . Anhang*, 41-45. Wein: Haslinger, [1832].

Based, not surprisingly, on Haslinger's Manuscript *Nachlass* catalog (Ha, **204**). It does not include prices and buyers, and many entries appear only in abbreviated form. **Folter**, no. 23, describes contents, but additional information she gives about other reprints is not entirely dependable.

206 _____

[Another edition.] Wien: T. Haslinger, 1852; reprint, Hildesheim: Olms, 1967.   [US-BUu]

207 _____

[Another reprint in] *Ludwig von Beethoven's Studies in Thorough Bass, Counterpoint and the Art of Scientific Composition* . . . , trans. H. H. Pierson. Leipzig: Schuberth & Co., 1853.
[US-NYp, -PO]

Schuberth also published a 2nd rev. ed. in German organized by Pierson in 1853.   [US-NYp]

208 _____

Thayer, Alexander Wheelock. *Chronologisches Verzeichnis der Werke Ludwig van Beethovens*. Berlin: Schneider, 1865.   [g.a.]

209 _____

Frimmel, Theodor von. "Gerichtliche Inventur und Schätzung. . . ." In his *Beethoven-Studien*, 2:185-97. Munchen: G. Müller, 1906.

Johnson says it is an exact reprint of that in Thayer's 1865 book (**208**), though leaving the impression that it derives from O$_1$. **Folter**, no. 23, incorrectly calls it a copy of a *Nachlass* catalog supposedly executed by Domenico Artaria, but it is, in fact, one of those made up by Gräffer. Domenico turned out to be a "greedy buyer" at the November auction, according to Johnson in his article "The Artaria Collection" (**217**).

210 _____

ARTARIA & CO., FIRM, WIEN

Verzeichniss der musikalischen Autographe von Ludwig van Beethoven . . . im Besitze von A. Artaria in Wien. Auf grundlage einer Aufnahme Gustave Nottebohm's neuerlich durchgesehen von Prof. Dr. Guido Adler. Diese Sammlung bildet . . . aus den musikalischen Nachlasse Beethoven's . . . versteigering in Wien, Winter 1827/28. . . . Wien: Selbstverlag, 1890. 22 p. 96 lots. [US-Wc]

> A number of items from the Beethoven *Nachlass* in this catalog eventually became the property of Joseph Fischoff (1804-57). A handwritten catalog of that collection, according to Johnson (**217**), is now in the Deutsche Staatsbibliothek with the title "Ein beschriebenes Verzeichnis Beethoven'scher Werke in Autographien u. Copien, anscheinend aus Fischoff's Besitz" (see Johnson, p. 179).

211 _____

ARTARIA & CO., FIRM, WIEN

Verzeichniss von musikalischen Autographen, revidirten Abschriften und einigen seltenen gedruckten Originalausgaben, vornemlich der reichen Bestände aus dem Nachlasse Joseph Haydn's und Ludwig van Beethoven's ferner der Manuscripte von Mozart, Schubert, Rossini und anderen namentlich Wiener Tonsetzern im Besitze von August Artaria in Wien. . . . Wien: Im Selbstverlag, 1893. 26 p. [US-Wc, -CHH, compiler (Xerox)]

> Notes the presence of more than just Beethoven manuscripts.

212 _____

Hajdecki, A. "Nachlass Beethoven's Bibliothek, Garderobe und sonstige Mobiliar." *Wiener Fremdenblatt,* 15 November 1903.

> Not located; cited from *BdZL.*

213 _____

La Laurencie, Jean de. *Le Dernier Logement de Beethoven (Notre-Dame de Montserrat).* Paris: Schola Cantorum, 1908. 59 p. [g.a.]

> [Inventory of B's library and music at his death.]

214 _____

Kinsky, Georg. "Zur Versteigerung von Beethovens musikalischem Nachlass." *Neues Beethoven-Jahrbuch* 6 (1935): 66-68. [g.a.]

> **Folter**, no. 23. Though the text of the catalog is not complete, this was, according to Johnson, the first attempt to publish a complete list of the buyers, somewhat rearranged from the copy made by Fuchs.

215 _____

Kinsky, Georg. *Manuskripte, Briefe, Dokumente von Scarlatti bis Stravinsky. Katalog der Musikautographen-Sammlung Louis Koch, beschrieben und erläutert von Dr. Georg Kinsky.*

Stuttgart, 1953.

> **Folter**, no. 23. Beethoven *Nachlass*, pp. 136-37.

216 _____

Thayer, Alexander Wheelock. *The Life of Beethoven.* Rev. and ed. by Elliot Forbes. Princeton: Princeton University Press, 1964. [g.a.]

> The "Gerichtliche Inventur . . ." in English, 2:1061-76. **Folter**, no. 23.

217 _____

Johnson, Douglas. "The Artaria Collection of Beethoven Manuscripts: A New Source." In *Beethoven Studies*, ed. Alan Tyson, 174-89. New York: Norton, 1973. [g.a.]

> → *See also under* **Bernard, Joseph Karl**, the sale catalog by Malota of his library, which includes "Die Beethovenautographe aus Bernards Nachlass: ein Geleitwort von Dr. Th. v. Frimmel," pp. 1-4.

218 **Behagel, Johann Georg,** 1797-1828

Ehmann, Wilhelm. "Musikalischer nachlass — Johann Georg Behagel." *AmF* 3 (1938): 435-57. [g.a.]

> Catalog by composer, mainly Mss., pp. 436-45.

219 **Beijers, J L (Libraire à Utrecht)**

Martinus Nijhoff, firm, Den Haag

Catalogue des livres modernes: Geographie, histoire, belles lettres, théâtre, musique, beaux-arts, provenant en grande partie de feu. . . . La Haye, 1901. 430 p. 4471 lots. Music, lots 3689-707; Théâtre, lots 3620-88. [NL-Avb]

220 **Beke, Leendert van; G. Greni; A. Grossi**

Catalogus van zeer Fraije ende rare Bederduitse Boeken, als meede van uytnemde Partyen-Muzycq, Muzycq-Instrumenten, Pren-Konst. . . . Nagelaten by Leendert van Beke, in zyn Castelein in't Gemeen-Lanshuys, van Delfland. Welke verkogt zullen wersen . . . 20 February 1708. . . . Delft: Gedruckt by Andries Voorstad, 1708. 20 p. 613 lots. [NL-Pka, compiler (film)]

> "Catalogus van de Musyk-Boeken . . . ," pp. 11-13 (154 lots, more items, e.g., no. 23, G. Greni, 7 Boeken; no. 24, A Grossi, 5 Boeken).

221 **Bellamy, Rev. Dr.**

Literature

"Music Library Is to Be Instituted at Oxford [its nucleus, the collection of Rev. Dr. Bellamy]." *MT* 51 (1910): 709. [g.a.]

Bellamy, Thomas Ludford. *See under* **[Binfield, ? (of Reading)]**

222 **Benavente, S B**

G. Theodore Bom & Zoon, auctioneer, Amsterdam

Notitie eener uitgebreide en belangrijke verzameling Muziek voor Piano, Viol, Violoncel . . . Violen, Fluiten, Cithers [etc.] . . . Verkooping . . . van den Notaris L. H. J. Mirani . . . 23 tot . . . 25 Mei 1905. Amsterdam, 1905. 31 p. 875 lots. Music, lots 1-782. [NL-Avb]

223 **Bender, Augusta**
Pommer, J. "Augusta Benders Volkslieder-sammlung." *Das deutsche Volkslied* 2 (1900):107-08.
Not examined; cited in *BdZL* (1900).

224 **Benincasa, Luciano,** 1607-71, and **Family**
ANCONA, BIBLIOTECA COMUNALE "LUCIANO BENINCASA"
Catalogo della opere musicali della Biblioteca . . . [by] *Marco Salvarini.* Roma: Ed. Torre
d'Orfeo, 1988. 272 p. 684 items.   [g.a.]

225 **Bennett, Rev. W. J. E.; Rev. W. G. Cookesley**
PUTTICK & SIMPSON, AUCTIONEER, LONDON   CAT. NO. 2473
Catalogue of the Theological Library of the Late . . . Classical Library [of Cookesley] *and
Other Private Libraries. . . . Works on the Liturgy and Ritual. . . . Album of Musical Autographs,
Antique and Other Music (Including the Histories of Burney and Hawkins) . . . Sold . . .
February 2nd, 1887 and Two Following Days. . . .* London, 1887. 63 p. 1140 lots.   [GB-Lbl]
Music, lots 990-1056 (many more items). Owner of music not identified.

226 **Bennett, Sir William Sterndale,** 1816-75
PUTTICK & SIMPSON, AUCTIONEER, LONDON
*Catalogue of the Important and Interesting Collection of Books and Music Forming the
Library of the Late. . . . The Music Includes Compositions of Auber, Bach, Beethoven* [etc.] *Also
Interesting Autographs & Manuscripts, Including Examples of Beethoven, Goethe, Handel.
. . . Correspondence of Dr. Wesley Relative to the Publication of Bach's Works . . . Sold . . . April
26th, 1875.* [London], 1875. 32 p. 475 lots.   [GB-Lbl, US-Bp, -NYp, -CHua (priced)]
An important sale, including the 25 ALS of Dr. Wesley, the holograph of
Mendelssohn's *Fingal's Cave Overture,* holograph of his *Quartetto,* 12
ALS from him to C. Coventry, etc. The sale was described in a lengthy
article about items in the sale in the *Musical Standard* 8 (1875): 276-77.
King, pp. 61-62. See also annotation in **Coover 2**.

227 **Bennett, Sir William Sterndale; James King; Musical Society of Oxford**
PUTTICK & SIMPSON, AUCTIONEER, LONDON   CAT. NO. 1772
*Catalogue of a Valuable Collection of Ancient and Modern Music . . . from the Libraries of the
Late Sir . . . the Late Mr. James King . . . and the Musical Society of Oxford . . . Sold October 15,
1878.* [London], 1878. 16 p. 431 p.   [GB-Lbl]
Bennett's, lots 217-336; **King's,** pp. 1-80; the **Oxford Society,** pp. 153-216.

228 **Benson, George; Messrs. Sprague & Co.**
PUTTICK & SIMPSON, AUCTIONEER, LONDON   CAT. NO. 2297
*Catalogue of the Valuable Library of Music of the Late . . . Lay Vicar of Westminster Abbey
. . . Comprising Works on Musical History and Theory, Oratorios, Operas, Masses, etc. . . .
Original & Other MSS. Some Bearing Autographs, etc., Also a Collection of Scarce Portraits
& Prints, Relating to Music. . . . Residue of the Stock of Printed Music and . . . Plates of Messrs.
Sprague & Co. . . . Sold . . . November 25, 1884.* [London], 1884. 22 p. 499 lots.   [GB-Lbl]
Benson's properties, lots 1-199; another's, 200-316; the rest, various owners.

Benson, George (1885 sale). *See under* **Goss, Sir J.**

229   Bentheim-Tecklenburg, Graf zu
Thurman, Erich. [Thematic catalog of extant manuscripts, 1968/69.]
> Manuscript **Brook**, no. 1046b. Material on loan to D-MÜu since 1966.

230   _____
Thurman, Erich. [Thematic catalog of the manuscripts in the Fürst zu Bentheimschen Musikaliensammlung Burgsteinfurt, 1970.]
> Manuscript **Brook**, no. 205. Materials on loan to D-MÜu.

231   Bentz, René Louis, 1904-53
Ulbrich-Sandreuter, Hermann.*Über den musikalischen Nachlass von. . . .* Bern: E. Bentz, 1954.
> Not examined; cited from *Mitteilungen* of the *Schweizerische musikforschende Gesellschaft.*

232   Beretta [probably **Giovanni Battista,** 1819-76]
H. F. Münster (C. Kayser), firm, Verona and Leipzig
Catalogo della libreria musicale del M. G. B. Beretta, già direttore del R. Conservatorio di Bologna . . . [Sold by]. . . . [Verona?], 1878.
> Not examined or located; cited from *MfM* (1878), which indicates it contained 724 theoretical and practical works.

233   Berg, P. J. W. van den; D. van Akerlaken; P. H. Witkamp; W. Smit; Mrs. Amersfoordt-Dijk
R. W. P. de Vries, auctioneer, Amsterdam
Catalogus van de zeer belangrijke bibliotheken . . . rechtsgeleerdheid en staatswetenschappen. . . . Taal- en Letterkunde . . . Tooneel en muziek, schoone kunsten en plaatwerken . . . nagelaten door. . . . Verkooping . . . 12 December 1892 en volgende dagen. . . . A'dam, 1892. 244 p. 3913 lots. Music, lots 3323-612.   [NL-Avb]
> Ca. 200 lots are from van den Berg; ca. 40 from Mrs. Amersfoordt-Dijk.

Berger, S [i.e., F. sale of 1910]. *See under* **Edwards, F. G.**

234   Berggreen, Andreas Peter, 1801-80
Literature
Holzapfel, Otto. "Sammlung Berggreen im Deutschen Volksliedarchiv." *Jahrbuch für Volksliedforschung* 16 (1971): 179-81.

235   Berlijn, Anton W., 1817-70
Catalog van Manuscripten des verstorbenen Tonsetzers. . . . [Amsterdam: Harms & Co., 187-.]
16 p. 335 items.   [US-CIhc]
> US-CIhc only: supplied on the title page "A[ron] W[olf]."

236   Berlin [**Royal Library**]
Puttick & Simpson, auctioneer, London   Cat. no. 903
Catalogue of an Extremely Interesting Collection of Antiquarian Music . . . Comprising the Works of . . . Ahle . . . [et al.] *. . . Which Will Be Sold . . . March 2, 1866.* [London, 1866.] 32 p. 351 lots.
                                                              [GB-Lbl, US-NYpNN]

237 **Bernadotte Family** (the Swedish Royal Family)
Lomnås, Erling. "Något om musikalierna i Bernadotte-biblioteket på Stockholm slott." *STMf* 61,
no. 2 (1974): 171-78. [g.a.]
Not examined; cited from *RILM*.

238 **Bernard, Jean**
De Vries, Jeronimo, Alberto Brondgeest, Engelbert Michael Engelberts, and Cornelis François
Roos. *Catalogue van eene verzameling fraaije schilderijen. . . . Teekeningen . . . Prenten . . .*
nagelaten door . . . benevens eene uitmuntende Verzameling van . . . Muzijk-Instrumenten en
Muzijk-Werken verkocht . . . 24 November 1834 en volgende dagen. . . . Amsterdam, 1834.
78 p. 1732 + 43 lots. [D-Bk, NL-Apk, US-Bp, F-Pe]
At end: "Catalogus van uitmuntende Muzijk-Instrumenten en Muzijk-
Werken . . . 26ˢᵗᵉⁿ November 1834 . . . verkocht werden . . . ," pp. [75-78].
Music, pp. 77-78, 85 lots but many more items.

239 **Bernard, Joseph Karl**
FRANZ MALOTA, FIRM, VIENNA   CAT. NO. 60
Autographen-Katalog, enthaltend 25 Briefe sowie eine eigenhändige Denkschrift von Ludwig
van Beethoven, nebst einer kleinen Sammlung Autographe von. . . . Vorrätig bei Franz Malota.
. . . Wien, [n.d.]. 43 p. 300 lots. [US-Wc]
"Die Beethovenautographe aus Bernards Nachlass," by Dr. Th. v. Frimmel,
pp. 1-4.

Bernsdorf, Edward. *See under* **Appunn, A.**

240 **Bernstein,   , Dr.; Dr. Elsster; C. L. von Stieglitz**
T. O. WEIGEL, AUCTIONEER, LEIPZIG
Verzeichnis der Bibliotheken des Herrn . . . , welche nebst einem bedeutenden Anhange von
Musikalien am 17 September 1855 . . . versteigert werden sollen. . . . Leipzig, 1855.
368 p. 8928 + 1110 lots (of music scores and parts; many items in most lots). [US-NYgr]
Consignments undifferentiated.

241 **Bernstein, Carl**
LIEPMANNSSOHN, AUCTIONEER, BERLIN   AUK.-CAT. NO. 14
Katalog der von den verstorbenen Dr. [as in preceding?] . . . Klassischen deutschen Literatur-
periode . . . versteigert 14 Okt. und folgenden Tage. . . . Berlin, 1895. 63 p. 719 lots.
[GB-LRosenthal]

Berri, Dr. Pietro. *See under* **Dannreuther, Edward**

242 **Berstett, [August?], Freiherr von** [1769-1837?]
HAUS DER BÜCHER, AUCTIONEER, BASEL   AUKTION NO. 228
Bibliothek Freiherr von Berstett. Bibliothek eines Musikgelehrten und andere Beiträge.
Autographen. . . . Alte Drucke [etc.]. *Versteigerung . . . 11 [-12] April 1957.* Basel: Haus der
Bücher; Zürich: L'Art ancien, 1957. 127 p. 1172 lots. Music, lots 1-221. [NY-NYgr, compiler]

243 **Bertarelli, Achille**
Arrigoni, Paolo, and Achille Bertarelli. *Ritratti di musicisti et artisti di teatro conservati nella*
[Civica] *raccolta delle stampe e dei disegni. Catalogo. . . .* [Milano]: Tip. del "Popolo d'Italia,"

1934. x, 454p., xxx plates. 5626 titles.   [g.a.]

    "Achilles Bertarelli, raccoglitore e donatore," p. vi. Now at I-Mt, 11,000 illustrations of musicians and theater personages.

Berwick, Jacobo . . . , duque de. *See under* **Alba, House of**

244   Best, C. W.
Oberlin College, Conservatory of Music, Library
Mr. and Mrs. C. W. Best Collection of Autographs, in the Mary M. Vial Music Library. . . .
Oberlin, Ohio: Oberlin College Library, 1967. 55 p.   [g.a.]

245   Beständig, Otto; Adolf Merkens
Anton J. Benjamin, firm, Hamburg
Katalog antiquarischer Musikalien. Vokalmusik, zum Teil aus dem Bibliotheken von. . . .
Hamburg: A. Benjamin, 1900.
    Not located; cited from **Bobillier** and *ZiMG* (1900/01).

246   Betti, Adolfo, 1873-1950
Jones, D. B. "The Adolfo Betti Music Collection at the University of Texas." Thesis, University of Texas, 1956.
    Not examined; cited from *Amerigrove*.

247   Bever, Thomas, 1725-91
Mr. White, auctioneer, London
        King, pp. 22-23, notes that the sale took place 7 and 8 June 1798 and says it was described in the *Gentleman's Magazine* 68 (1798): 517, but it was not found after a search of both vol. 68 and the year 1798. No copy of White's catalog is known to exist, according to **Albrecht**.

248   Beyer, Konrad, Hofrat, 1834-1906
Liepmannssohn, auctioneer, Berlin   Autogr.-Verst. no. 36
Katalog einer wertvollen Autographensammlung aus dem Nachlass . . . Conrad Beyer in Wiesbaden, sowie aus dem Besitz eines hervorragenden Sammlers. Versteigerung am 19. und 20. November 1906. Berlin, 1906. 177 p. 1322 lots.   [US-NH, -Bp, -NYpNN]
    Music, section 6, lots 1044-322, include the autograph of Brahms's, "Paganini Variations," etc.

249   Bianchi, Francesco (1752-1810?); **Patrick Blake**
Mr. Phillips, auctioneer, London
The Musical Compositions of the Late Celebrated Signior Francesco Bianchi; and the Valuable Musical Instruments and Music of the Late Sir Patrick Blake. A Catalogue . . . Sold . . . the 25th Day of March, 1819. [London], 1819. 12 p. 148 lots. Music, 95 lots.
    [GB-Lbl, compiler (copy of that catalog, with interleaves showing buyers and prices)]

250   Biber, Albert
Henkel, Robert C. *Rare and Scarce Sheet Music* [lists nos. 300 and 600]*; Psalms and Sacred Songs; Music.* Jersey City, N.J.: Henkel, [1974?]. 4 lists unpaged. Lots: 330, 190, 41, 77.
                                                                           [compiler]
    Predominantly sheet music.

251 Bibliopholus, Docteur
"La Bibliothèque musicale: Essai sur l'origine, les progrès, les transformations, les révolutions et la décadense de ma bibliothèque." *La France musicale* 7 (12, 19, 26 mai; 2, 9, 23 30 juin; 7 juillet, and continuing, 1844). [F-Pc, F-Pn, NL-DHgm only]
    Complete series not examined.

252 Bickford, Vahdah Olcott, 1885-1980
Purcell, Ronald C. *Guitar Music Collection of Vahdah Olcott-Bickford, Compiled by. . . .* Northridge, Music Library, California State University, International Guitar Research Archive, 1991-. [g.a.]
    To be published in 2 vols.

253 _____
    LITERATURE
"The Gentle Art of Collecting." *Cadenza* 28, no. 4 (April 1921): 44-45.
    Not examined.

254 Bie, Oscar, 1864-1938
PERL, AUCTIONEER, BERLIN   AUKTION NO. 185
Bücher des 15.-20. Jahrhunderts [darunter ein Prof. Oscar Bei] *. . . versteigert . . . 28 May, 1934.* Berlin: Perl, 1934. 64 p. 1007 lots. Bie's properties, pp. 1-45.
    Not examined; cited from **Folter**, no. 26.

255 Bieber, Albert A.
AMERICAN ART ASSOCIATION, FIRM
. . . American Plays, Poetry and Songsters. A Most Unusual Gathering of Early and Modern American Literature. . . . Illustrated . . . with Original Notes by the Owner. . . . New York, [1923]. Unpaged. 708 lots. [NL-Avb]
    "Songsters, etc.": lots 161-265.

256 [Biltz, Karl, 1830-1901]
J. A. STARGARDT, AUCTIONEER, BERLIN
Neuer deutscher Bücherschatz. Verzeichnis einer . . . reichen Sammlung von Werken der deutschen Litteratur des XV. bis XXIX. Jahrhunderts. Mit bibliographischen Bemerkungen. . . . Versteigerung 18-21 Mai, 1896. Berlin: Imberg & Lefson, 1895. 246 p. 1000 lots.
[US-BApi only]

257 _____
MARTIN BRESLAUER, COMPILER   CAT. NO. 3
Das deutsche Lied, geistlich und weltlich, bis zum 18ᵗᵉⁿ Jahrhundert. Documente frühen deutschen Lebens, 1. Berlin: M. Breslauer, 1908. xi, [277]-581 p. [g.a.]
    Based on the Biltz collection. Cf. p. [iii].

258 [Binfield, (of Reading)]; **Thomas Ludford Bellamy**
PUTTICK & SIMPSON, AUCTIONEER, LONDON   CAT. NO. 13
Catalogue of an Extensive and Valuable Musical Library . . . and Musical Instruments . . . Sold . . . Jan. 12th, and Following Day. . . . [London], 1847. 19 p. 411+ lots. Music, lots 1-340.
[GB-Lbl]

259   **[Binfield   (of Reading); Newton]**
PUTTICK & SIMPSON, AUCTIONEER, LONDON   CAT. NO. 572
Catalogue of a Collection of Music of Various Kinds. . . . Popular Works of Handel, Mozart,
Mendelssohn, etc., in Scores and Parts . . . Sold . . . April 16th, 1859. 15 p. 332 lots. Music,
lots 1-273.   [GB-Lbl]

Binns, C. W. *See under* **Caraman-Chimay** (sale, 14 June 1976)

260   **Birch-Reynardson, H   F**
IFAN KYRLE FLETCHER, FIRM, LONDON   CAT. NO. 10
Old Music, Principally of Theoretical Interest . . . and a Small but Choice Collection of
Seventeenth Century Vocal Music, from the Library of. . . . London, 1939. 35 p. 703 lots.
    [US-NYgr]

Birket-Smith, Frederik, 1880-1952.   *See under* **Rischel, Thorvald,** 1861-1939

261   **Birnbaum, Eduard,** 1855-1920
Werner, Eric. *Manuscripts of Jewish Music in the . . . Collection.* Cincinnati, 1944. 32 p.
    [g.a.]
       Offprint from the *Hebrew Union College Annual* 18 (1944): 420-28.
       → *See also under* **Mandell, Eric**

262   **Bischoff, Ferdinand,** 1826-1915
Federhofer, Hellmut. "Mozartiana im Musikalien-Nachlass von . . . ." *Mozart-Jahrbuch* (1965/
66), 15-38.   [g.a.]
       Collection now in Akademie für Musik und darstellende Kunst und
       Landesmusikschule, Graz. See **Benton 2**:3, no. 6.

263   **Bishop, Sir Henry Rowley,** 1768-1855**; "A Distinguished Amateur"; The Hon. Mrs. Bruce:**
       T. Lea; et al.
PUTTICK & SIMPSON, AUCTIONEER, LONDON   CAT. NO. 413
Catalogue of a Valuable Collection of Music, Including the Library of the Late . . . and of a
Distinguished Amateur; Also the Very Extensive and Highly Valued Assemblage of Musical
Instruments . . . Which Will Be Sold . . . June 14th, and Two Following Days. . . . [London],
1855. 36 p. 877 lots. Bishop's collection, lots 132-385; Amateur's, lots 386-692; T. Lea's, lots
732-88.   [GB-Lbl, US-NYp]
       Albrecht; **King**, pp. 51-52; **Coral**. This was first Bishop sale; another with
       John Blockley et al. (**275**,1883); another under Greatheed (**1112**, 1888).

264   **Bishop, John (of Cheltenham),** 1817-90
Descriptive Catalogue of Rare Musical Works in the Library of. . . . Cheltenham: John T.
Norman, [ca. 1890].   [GB-Lbl (Hirsch no. 425)]
       No lot numbers; items were not for sale. Issued about 1885 according to
       King, p. 92. Noted by **Barclay-Squire** in *Grove*.

265   —————
ELLIS & ELVEY, FIRM, LONDON
Catalogue of Rare and Valuable Books Relating to Music, Comprising the Library of. . . .
Winter Catalogue . . . Part II. Rare Books on Music. London, 1897. 69 p.
    [US-PHf, -PHu, -Wc, -NYgr (priced)]

Bishop's properties, lots 529-1195, with separate title page but without pagination, that followed by another [48] p.

266 _____

<small>LITERATURE</small>
Hadden, J. Cuthbert. "A Catalogue of Rare Music Books." *MO&MTR* 21 (1898): 241-42.

[GB-Lbl]

267 Bisschopinck, Ludwig, 1895-1959
Dreimüller, Karl. "Musikerbriefe an einen rheinischen Musikliebhaber: Aus der Sammlung Ludwig Bisschopinck in Mönchengladbach." In *Anthony von Hoboken: Festschrift zum 75. Geburtstag,* ed. Joseph Schmidt-Georg, 29-48. Mainz: B. Schott's Söhne, [1962].   [g.a.]

268 Black, Frank J.
<small>PIERRE BERÈS, NEW YORK</small>   <small>CAT. NO. 24</small>
Music: The Exceptional Collection of Music Scores, Mainly in First and Early Editions and Books About Music Formed by Dr. Frank J. Black. New York: Pierre Berès, [195?]. 15 p. 168 nos.   [US-NYgr, compiler]

269 Blake, Sir Patrick
<small>MR. PHILLIPS, AUCTIONEER, LONDON</small>
The Musical Compositions of the Late Celebrated Signior [Francesco Bianchi], *and the Valuable Musical Instruments and Music of the Late Sir Patrick . . . Sold . . . the 25th day of March, 1819. . . .* [London], 1819. 12 p. 148+ lots. Music, lots 56-77, 94-111, 134-148.

[GB-Lbl, compiler]

Also entered under Bianchi (**249**).

270 Blancheton, Pierre Philibert, d. 1756
Paris, Conservatoire National de Musique et de Déclamation, Bibliothèque, Fonds Blancheton. *. . . Inventaire critique du fonds Blancheton. . . .* 2 vols. Paris: E. Droz, 1930-31.

[US-NH, -BP, -CHH, -Wc]

Compiler: Lionel de La Laurencie. Blancheton's collection of manuscript music of symphonies was formed between 1740 and 1744, according to the Library of Congress note. The Mss. are copies by Estien (probably Charles Estien).

271 _____

<small>LITERATURE</small>
Hirschberg, Jehoash. "The Formation and Destruction of the Fonds Blancheton." *Current Musicology* 27 (1979): 36-44.   [g.a.]

272 [Blaubeen, M P ; J. van Andel; A. J. van Prehn]
<small>H. G. BOM, AUCTIONEER, AMSTERDAM</small>
Catalogus eener uitgebreide verzameling Boeken over Rechtswetenschap . . . Muziek . . . Kantoorbehoeften . . . verkooping . . . 21 Juni 1880 . . . en tien volgende dagen. Amsterdam, 1880. 179 p. 4800+ lots. Music, lots 1250-482.   [NL-Avb, -Apk]

Before imprint: ". . . De Instrumenten, Muziek Verscheidenheiten op Zaturday 26 Juni." **Lugt**, no. 40309.

273   **Bliss, Francis Edward**
Sᴏᴛʜᴇʙʏ, Wɪʟᴋɪɴsᴏɴ & Hᴏᴅɢᴇ, ᴀᴜᴄᴛɪᴏɴᴇᴇʀ, Lᴏɴᴅᴏɴ
Catalogue of the Valuable Library of . . . Comprising . . . a Long Series of Extremely Rare
Songs & Ballads . . . Sold . . . 18th Day of April, 1898, and Following Day. . . . [London,
1898.] 34 p. 511 lots. Songs, lots 271-435.   [Film at CRL]

274   **Bliss, Mildred**
Liszt, Franz. *The Letters of Franz Liszt to Olga von Meyendorff, 1871-1886, in the Mildred*
Bliss Collection at Dumbarton Oaks. Trans. William R. Tyler, introduction and notes by Edward
N. Waters. Washington and Cambridge: Harvard University Press, 1979. xxi, 532 p.
[g.a.]

  Bequeathed to US-CA in 1969.

275   **Blockley, John,** 1800-82; **Sir Henry Rowley Bishop; Henry Phillips; William Crotch**
Pᴜᴛᴛɪᴄᴋ & Sɪᴍᴘsᴏɴ, ᴀᴜᴄᴛɪᴏɴᴇᴇʀ, Lᴏɴᴅᴏɴ
Catalogue of a Collection of Books and Music, Including the Private Library of the Late. . . .
Also Numerous Works on the History and Theory of Music . . . Important Autograph Manuscripts
. . . Collections of the Late Sir Henry Rowley Bishop, Henry Phillips, Dr. Crotch, etc. . . . Sold
May 29th, 1883, and Following Day. [London, 1883.] 116, 7 p. 1407 lots. Music, lots 523-695.
[GB-Lbl]

276   **Blunt, Janet Heatley,** 1859-1950
  Lɪᴛᴇʀᴀᴛᴜʀᴇ
  Pickering, Michael. *Village Song & Culture: A Study Based on the Blunt Collection of Song*
  from Adderbury, North Oxfordshire. London: Croom Helm, 1982. 187 p.   [g.a.]
    Collection now at GB-Lcs.

  Boag, Mrs. Mary Ann.   *See under* **Hodges, Edward**

277   **Bodda, Frank,** 1823-92; **Louisa F. Bodda (Pyne),** 1832-?
Pᴜᴛᴛɪᴄᴋ & Sɪᴍᴘsᴏɴ, ᴀᴜᴄᴛɪᴏɴᴇᴇʀ, Lᴏɴᴅᴏɴ   Cᴀᴛ. ɴᴏ. 1723
Catalogue of the Legal Rights of Representation of Various Operas & Other Popular
Compositions, Belonging to, and Being the Property of. . . . Also . . . the Very Useful Library of
Music . . . Used by Bodda in "Vocal Classes" . . . Sold . . . 12th February 1878. [London,
1878]. 17 p. 79 lots.   [GB-Lbl]

278   **Boddaert-Van Cutsem, Gustave**
Vɪᴄᴛᴏʀ Mɪᴄʜɪᴇʟs, ɴᴏᴛᴀɪʀᴇ, Gᴀɴᴅ
Catalogue des livres ancienne et modernes, partitions, musique théatrale . . . composant la
bibliothèque. . . . Gand: Imp. I. Vanderpoorten, 1888. 90 p. 1201 lots. Music, pp. 8-81, 1119
lots, then to end, *inter alia.*   [B-Br, compiler (film)]
    Blogie, col. 240.

279   **Bodmer, Hans Conrad Ferdinand,** 1891-1956
  "Beethoven-sammlung H. C. Bodmer, Zürich." In *Luzern/Lucerne. Internationale Musik-*
  ausstellung . . . 16. Juli-1. September 1938 im Rathaus, nos. 373-478. [Luzern]: Buchdruckerei
  C. J. Bunker, 1938.   [US-NH, -Cn, -NYp, -Wc, -Chh, -IO]
    Albrecht: bequeathed to Beethovenhaus, Bonn. Included autograph of
    "Waldstein" sonata, and others, and 415 letters.

280 _____

Unger, M. *Eine Schweizer Beethovensammlung. Katalog.* Schriften der Corona, 24. Zürich: [n.p., 1939]. 239 p. 16 tables.

Not located; cited from Hans Schneider antiquarian catalog no. 222, lot 23.

281 _____

Beethovenhaus, Bonn. *Sonderausstellung aus der Beethoven-Sammlung H. C. Bodmer, Zürich. Exposition spéciale de la collection Beethoven . . . Special Exhibition Arranged from the Beethoven Collection of. . . .* [Deutscher Text von Joseph Schmidt-Görg; traduction française par Henri Perrin; translation into English by E. Wolff.] Bonn: Verlag des Beethoven-Hauses, 1953. 19 p.   [US-PO]

282 _____

LITERATURE
Schmidt, Hans. "Das Bonner Beethoven-Archiv." *ÖMZ* 25, no. 2 (December 1970): 769-74. [g.a.]

283 Bodmer, Martin, 1899-1971
Rau, Arthur. "Bibliotheca Bodmeriana, I: Manuscripts; II: Printed Books." *Book Collector* 7 (1958): 386-95; 8 (1959): 31-45.   [g.a.]

Music manuscripts, pp. 393-94; printed music and books, vol. 8, p. 39.
Albrecht.

284 Böhm, Karl, 1894-1981; **Ludwig Kusche,** 1901-
HANS SCHNEIDER, FIRM, TUTZING   CAT. NO. 273
Sammelsarium musicalem, darunter Bestände aus dem Besitz von Karl Böhm und Ludwig Kusche. Tutzing: Schneider, 1983. 92 p. 1600 lots.   [g.a.]

Böhm's properties identified, lots 1356-531; Kusche's properties are not.
Folter, no. 27.

285 Böhme, Franz Magnus, 1827-98
LIST & FRANCKE, FIRM, LEIPZIG   CAT. NO. 311
Geschichte und Theorie der Musik. Praktische, geistliche und weltliche Musik. Kirchen- und Volkslied. Schriften über das Theater. Autographen . . . aus dem Nachlasse des Herrn . . . und anderer. . . . Leipzig, 1899. 82 p. 2320 lots. Autographs, lots 2048-320.   [US-NYp, NL-Avb]

Some of the collection, according to *NG-L* now at D-WRh. **Folter,** no. 28.

286 _____

LITERATURE
Stockmann, Erich. "Zum Nachlass Franz Magnus Böhmes." *Deutsches Jahrbuch für Volkskunde* 8 (1962): 180.

A catalog? Not examined; cited from **Folter,** no. 28.

287 Boer, S M
BRONDGEEST, DE VRIES, ENGELBERTS, EN ROOS, AUCTIONEERS, AMSTERDAM
Catalogus van eene verzameling fraije schilderijen, meest door Hedendaagsche Nederlandsche Meesters. Alsmeded von eeinige coortreffelijke muzijk instrumenten, en van de meest gezochtste Musijkwerken . . . Nagelaten . . . verkocht . . . 15ᵈᵉⁿ April 1840. . . . [Amsterdam, 1840.] 2, 19 p. 142 + 52 lots. Music, lots 9-52.   [US-Bp, -DHrk, -Apk, US-NYFrick (buyers & prices)]

Folter, no. 65, under De Boer. **Lugt,** no. 15769.

288 Boers, Jan Conradus, 1812-96
Catalogus van werken over muziek van wylen den Heer J. C. Boers. [Delft, ca.1900.]
Manuscript. 5 vols. in 1 (186 fols., paged continuously). 1787 + 10 lots.　　　[US-NYp only]

>In Liepmannssohn catalog no. 223, lot 288. **Albrecht** does not mention
>catalog; collection now at NL-DHgm.

289 ──────
Burgersdijk & Niermans, auctioneer, Leiden
Catalogue de la bibliothèque linguistique de feu M. le Dr. P. J. Cosijn et de la bibliothèque musicale de feu M. J. C. Boers, professeur en musique à Delft. Vente du 2. au 7. mai 1900.
Leyden: Burgerdijk & Niermans, 1900. 132 p. 2304 + lots. Music, lots 1798-935.　　[NL-Avb]
>**Folter**, no. 29.

290 Boers, Jan Conradus; S. Kummerle (in Samaden); A. H. Th. Pfeil (in Leipzig)
List & Francke, firm, Leipzig　　Cat. no. 324
Geschichte und Theorie der Musik. Praktische, geistliche und weltliche Musik. Schriften über das Theater. Autographen. Aus dem Nachlasse. . . . Leipzig, 1901. 90 p. 2519 lots.

　　　　　　　　　　　　　　　　　　　[US-Wc, -NYp, NL-Avb]
>**Folter**, no. 30.

291 Bogoras, Waldmar; Waldemar Jochelson
Literature
Spear, Louise S. "The Bogoras and Jochelson Siberian Collection." *Resound* 1, no. 1 (January 1982): 2-4.　　　　　　　　　　　　　　　　　　　　　　　　　　　　　　[g.a.]

292 Boissière, P. de la
>[Catalog containing a "Section musicale," noted in Pincherle's catalog
>(**2125**), but not verified. He says Paris?: Davidts, 1763.]

293 Boisteaux (of Nantes)
(C. P.) Hunault, auctioneer, Nantes
[Catalog. Sale, 18-20 January 1875.] Nantes, 1875. 23 p.
>Not examined; cited from **Blogie**, no. 2: music, including manuscripts.

294 Bokemeyer, Heinrich, 1679-1751
Kümmerling, Harald. *Katalog der Sammlung Bokemeyer.* Kieler Schriften zur Musikwissenschaft, 18. Kassel: Bärenreiter, [1970]. 423 p. 1839 lots.　　　　　　　　　　　　　　[g.a.]
>A remarkable catalog: thematic incipits for all 1839 works, pp. 21-59;
>facsimiles of the holographs, pp. 155-279; watermarks reproduced, pp. 305-
>423. According to **Folter**, no. 31, most of the library came from Georg
>Österreich (1664-1735), passed to Bokemeyer who enriched it. Later it was
>acquired by Forkel, still later by the Berlin State Library. Now divided between
>DDR-B and D-Bds.

295 **Bonamici, Diomede,** 1823-1912
Lustig, R. "Saggio di catalogo della collezione di melodrammi della R. Marcelliana." *La bibliofilia*
35 (1923-24): 305; 36 (1924): 67.   [g.a.]

    RILM lists 17th- and early 18th-century librettos in B's collection.

Bonaventure, Jules.   *See under* **Laurens, Jean-Joseph**

296 **Bonjour, Abel**
GAND ET BERNARDEL (EXP.); ESCRIBE (C.-P.)
*Vente du . . . 5 février 1887, Hotel Drouot . . . succession de M. Abel Bonjour . . . Neuf
violoncelles . . . Archets de Tourte . . . Pianos et musique.* Paris, 1887. 15 p. 116 lots (mainly
instruments).   [F-Pn, B-BC]

    Lugt, no. 46239.

297 **Boogard, F.**
H. G. BOM, AUCTIONEER, AMSTERDAM
*Catalogus eener zeer belangrijke verzameling Boeken . . . Plaatwerken . . . Muziek . . . [enz.
. . . nagelaten door] . . . Verkooping . . . 17 Juni 1878, en vijf volgende dagen. . . .* Amsterdam,
1878. 74 p. 2314 + 7 lots. Music, pp. 51-52 (70 lots).   [NL-Avb]
    Lugt, no. 38518.

298 **Border, Richard George,** et al.
SOTHEBY & CO., AUCTIONEER, LONDON
*Catalogue of Music, Valuable Printed Books and Autograph Letters . . . the Property of . . .
and Including Letters of Arne, Bellini, Berlioz, Brahms* [et al.] *Sold . . . 9th [-10th] April 1962.*
112 p. 534 lots. Music, lots 1-327.   [US-Cn, film at CRL]

    Border properties, lots 1-108; other music owners not identified.

299 **Borghese, Paolo, Principe,** 1845-1920
"Catalogue of the Principal Part of the Collection of Music in the Library of H. E. D. Paolo
Borghese. . . ." Rome, 1891. 217 leaves.   [Ms. US-Cn]

300 _____
VINCENZO MENOZZI, BOOKSELLER, ROME
*Catalogue de la bibliothèque de s.e.d. Paolo Borghese, prince de Sulmona . . . vente aura
lieu: 1. ptie, le 16 mai au 7 juin 1892; 2 ptie., le 6 au 28 février 1893.* 2 vols. In vol. 1, music,
inter alia. Rome: V. Menozzi, 1892-93.

    See extract of "troisième partie–musique" (**301**).

    Albrecht notes that the library of Italian vocal music began with Camillo
    Borghese, Pope Paul VI, 1552-1621. Many items went to F-Pc, I-Rac, and
    GB-Lbl.

_____. *Liste des prix d'adjudication des livres composant la bibliothèque. . . .* Rome,
1892. 62 p. [Complete sets   US-BE, -Cn, -Cu, -Bp, -NYp, -COu, -Wc, GB-Lbl (Hirsch, priced)]

    This list of prices is summarized and various lots are described in *MT* 33
    (1892): 658.

301 _____

VINCENZO MENOZZI, BOOKSELLER, ROME

. . . Bibliotheca Burghesiana: catalogue des livres composant la bibliothèque de S. E. Don Paolo Borghese. . . . Extrait du catalogue (troisième partie - musique). Rome: V. Menozzi, 1892. 64 p. Lots 4194-493.

> According to an announcement of the sale by Menozzi, the music in the "Extract comprises the important collection of music belonging to the XVIth centuries, formed by Cardinal Scipione Borghese." It consists of treatises and superb sets of printed part books.

302 _____

Vogel, Emil. "Schicksal der Borghese-Sammlung." *Peters Jahrbuch* 2 (1896): 73-74.

> Lists items in the sale of 1892 that were purchased by GB-Lbl, F-Pn, the dealers Liepmannssohn and Olschki.

303 _____

LITERATURE

"Nota è la sorte della biblioteca del Borghese di cui è recente la vendita, che andò dispersa in massima parte per l'Europe e per l'America." *La bibliofilia* 9 (1907-08): 309.

> Not examined. Cited in **Frati**, *Dizionario* (Firenze, 1933) under Borghese.

304 _____

Zanetti, Emilia. "Una biblioteca dispersa e un catalogo provido di ottanta anni fa (Vicende della Biblioteca Borghese)." *Almanacco dei bibliotecari it.* (1973), 137-45.

> Not examined. Cited from *RILM* (1973).

305 **Borremans, Joseph,** 1775-1858

Catalogue des musiques sacrées et des opéras délaissés par feu . . . , ex-maître de chapelle de l'église Saint-Gudule, ex-sous-chef d'orchestre au Théâtre Royal de la Monnaier. [Bruxelles, 1858.] 16 p.

> **Albrecht** says an auction catalog. Cited also in **Bobillier**, Edmond van der Straeten's *La Musique aux Pays-Bas* (reprint, New York: Dover, 1969), and **Folter**, no. 32, with incorrect imprint and incomplete title. Not located.

[Borton,   ] (sale of 31 July 1858). *See under* **Allot, Rev. Richard**

306 **Boscawen, George Henry, 3rd Earl of Falmouth; Thomas Massa Alsager**

PUTTICK & SIMPSON, AUCTIONEER, LONDON

Catalogue of the Important Musical Collections of the Earl of Falmouth, in Which Is Comprised the Musical Library of . . . T. M. Alsager . . . To Be Sold by Auction May 26 [-28] 1853. [London, 1853]. 43 p. 873 lots. Music, lots 1-720.   [GB-Lbl]

> **Albrecht** notes only the sale of the properties of the 2nd Earl in 1871. **King**, p. 48.

307 _____

LITERATURE

Levy, David. "Thomas Massa Alsager, Esq. (1779-1846): A Musical Life." A paper read before the Southeast Chapter of the American Musicological Society, 29 September 1984.

Bosch te Goes, R. B. van den. *See under* **Musis Sacrum**

308   Bosius, D. Gottfried Christian, 1619-71

Literature

Braun, Werner. "Eine Musikaliensammlung des 17. Jahrhunderts Bibliotheca Bosiana. . . . Lipsiae . . . 1699." In Braun's "Musik in deutschen gelehrten Gelehrtenbibliotheken," *Mf* 10 (1957): 242-43.   [g.a.]

Twenty nine titles described from auction catalogs.

309   [Bottini,   ]

"Collezione Bottini." In Associazione dei musicologi italiani. . . . *Catalogo generale delle opere musicali. Serie XIII. Città di Pisa. Collezione Private . . .* , 67-73. Parma: Freschig, 1935.   [g.a.]

310   Boulanger, Nadia, 1887-1979

Nadia Boulanger, révélateur de la musique [exhibit]. Compiled by Josiane Bran-Ricci. Paris: Musée instrumental, 1987.

Not examined. Cited by Jeanice Brooks (**314**).

311   _____

Literature

Lesure, François. "A travers la correspondance de Nadia Boulanger." *Revue de la Bibliothèque nationale* 5 (September 1982): 16-23.

Offers a discussion of Boulanger's bequest.

312   _____

Chailley, Nadia. "Nadia Boulanger au Conservatoire Supérieur de Musique au Lyon." *Revue musicale* 353-54 (1982): 95-96.   [g.a.]

Ca. 15,000 scores, 1000 volumes of books and journals.

313   _____

Hommage à Lili Boulanger, 1893-1918: Exposition du 5 au 25 novembre 1993, Conservatoire Niedermeyer, Issy-les Moulineaux. Issy-les-Moulineaux: Délégation des affaires culturelle et partenariat avec l'Association amis de Nadia & Lili Boulanger et l'ADIAM 92, 1993. 66 p.

[g.a.]

314   _____

Brooks, Jeanice. "The Fonds Boulanger at the Bibliothèque Nationale." *Notes* 51 (1995): 1227-37.   [g.a.]

Mainly scores, including autograph manuscripts. About 2000 items.

315   Bourblanc, Saturnin de

Le Moigne-Mussat, Marie-Claire. "Rameau et le gout nouveau dans les bibliothèques à Rennes au XVIII siècle." *Bulletin et mémories de la Société Archéologique du Départment d'Ille-et-Vilaine, France* 138 (1986): 81-89.

Discusses holdings in the 18th century of the municipal library in Rennes and the private libraries of Saturnin de Bourblanc and Christoph Paul Robien. Cited from *RILM*.

316 Bournonville, August
Fryklund, D. August. *Bournonville.* [Katalog över en samling handlingaroch föremäl rörande B. utställd i Hälsinborg 1929.] Hälsingborg, 1929.
> Not located; cited from *DaSML.*

317 Bourret,   (Neuchâtel)
Boudot, Jean, and Jacques Guerin. *Catalogue de la bibliothèque de feu M. Bourret, ancien intendant de la principauté de Neuchastel et de Valengin, en Suisse, dont la vente . . . 18 juillet 1735 et jours suivants . . . à l'Hôtel de Luynes. . . .* Paris, 1735. 523 p. 6496 lots.

[US-NH]

> Not examined.

318 _____

Farrenc, Aristide. "Extrait du catalogue de vente de la bibliothèque de M. Bourret, faite a Paris, en 1735." In *Revue de musique ancienne et moderne,* 554-63. Paris/Rennes, 1856.
> Lists some of the music items purchased with prices fetched.

319 _____

. . . Livres de philologie grecque et latine, ouvrages anglais [etc.], *collection de traités sur la musique, etc. de la bibliothèque de feu M. Bourret . . . dont la vente se fera le lundi 14 juin et jours suivans . . . par le ministère de M. Hocart. . . .* Paris: B. Duprat, 1841. 47 p.   [US-NYp]
> At head of title: "Par continuation."

320 Boutroux de Ferrà, Anne-Marie
Adamczyk-Schmid, Bozena. "Warianty tekstu w rekopisach muzycznych Fryderyka Chopina z kolekcji. . . ." *Rocznik chopinowski* 19 (1987): 135-44.
> Not examined; cited from *RILM* (1988), p. 18.

321 Bover, Felix
LITERATURE
Bonhôte, J. M. "La Collection de psautiers de la bibliothèque [publique de la ville Neuchâtel]." *Jahrbuch für Liturgik und Hymnologie* 7 (1962): 182-85.   [g.a.]

322 Bovet, Alfred
LEO LIEPMANNSSOHN, AUCTIONEER, BERLIN   AUTOGR.-VERST. NO. 28
Katalog einer hervorragend schönen grössten Sammlung von Musiker-autographen . . . zum grössten Theil aus dem Besitze des verstorbenen Herrn A. Bovet. . . . Versteigerung zu Berlin . . . den 7 März, 1901. . . . [Berlin, 1901.] 37 p. 370 lots.   [US-Bp, NL-Avb]

323 _____

LEO LIEPMANNSSOHN, AUCTIONEER, BERLIN.   VERST. NO. 31
Katalog einer hervorragen schönen Sammlung von Büchern zur Geschichte, Theorie, u.s.w. der Musik des verstorbenen Alfred Bovet (Valentigney). Versteigerung . . . 7. und 8. April 1902. Berlin, 1902. 26 p. 375 lots.   [NL-Avb and US-NYp (wanting last 2 pp.)]
> Noted (in French) in *ZiMG* 3 (1901/02): 302.

324 _____

LEO LIEPMANNSSOHN, AUCTIONEER, BERLIN   AUTOGR-VERST. NO. 32
Katalog. . . . Musiker-autographen (Musikmanuskripte, Briefe und sonstige Schriftstücke. . .

aus dem Besitze . . . Alfred Bovet). Erste Abtheilung: Komponisten und Virtuosen . . . 24. November 1902. 100 p. 1241 lots.   [GB-LRosenthal]

325 _____

LEO LIEPMANNSSOHN, AUCTIONEER, BERLIN   AUTOGR.-VERST. NO. 33
Katalog einer schönen Autographen-sammlung . . . aus dem Besitze Alfred Bovet (Zweite Abtheilung) . . . 27. Mai 1903, und folgenden Tage. . . . Berlin, 1903. 94 p. 1189 lots.
                                                                    [GB-LRosenthal]

326   Bovet, Alfred; Ignaz Moscheles, 1794-1870
LEO LIEPMANNSSOHN, AUCTIONEER, BERLIN   AUTOGR-VERST. NO. 39
Autographen-Sammlungen von Ignaz Moscheles und Reserve Alfred Bovet, bestehend zum grössten Teil aus wertvollen Musik-Manuskripten und Musikerbriefen. Versteigering am 17. und 18. November 1911. Berlin, 1911. 197 p. 864 lots.   [NL-Avb, US-NYp, -Wc]

> Moscheles, lots 1-178; Bovet, lots 179-864. His Wagner-Sammlung, lots 664-792, pp. 128-83. **Folter**, no. 242, under Moscheles.

327 _____

LEO LIEPMANNSSOHN, AUCTIONEER, BERLIN   ANT. CAT. NO. 158
Autographen: Fürsten. Staatsmänner . . . Zum grossen Teil aus der Sammlung . . . Alfred Bovet und aus Nachlasse des . . . Friedrich Förster, nebst . . . Portraits. . . . Berlin, 1905. 2141 lots.
                                                                    [US-Wc, NL-Avb]

328   Bowen, Mrs. Vera; [Mona Inglesby]; et al.
SOTHEBY & CO., AUCTIONEER, LONDON
Catalogue Principally of Diaghilev Ballet Material: Costumes, Costume Designs and Portraits [and Scores], the Property of . . . Sold . . . 13th of June 1967. . . . London, 1967. i-xx, 117 p.
                                                                    [g.a.]

> Bowen's properties, lots 1-20, 56-79, 99-105, 147-52. Music scores, lots 107-14, the property of Inglesby, "forming part of the Anna Pavlova music collection which was purchased from her husband on her death by Messrs. Novello." Acquired by Inglesby from Novello in 1943.

329   Bowman, Martin J. (Gouda); et al.
G. THEODORE BOM & ZOON, AUCTIONEERS, AMSTERDAM
Catalogus der muziek-verzameling, waarlij liedboeken, oude en nieuwe muziek, nagelaten door . . . en der boeken en praktwerken. Woordenboeken, technische werken [etc.]. Deels afkomstig van de geliquideerden Boekhandel der Firma Blom & Olivierse . . . verkooping . . . 26 November en volgende dagen. . . . A'dam, 1901. 94 p. 1942+ lots. Music, lots 1-238.
                                                                    [NL-Avb (with names and prices)]

330   Boyce, William, the Elder, 1710-79
MESSRS. CHRISTIE AND ANSELL, AUCTIONEER, LONDON
A Catalogue of the Truly Valuable and Curious Library of Music, Late in the Possession of Dr. William Boyce . . . Consisting of All Dr. Green's Curious and Valuable Manuscripts . . . Will Be Sold by Auction . . . Pall Mall . . . April 14, 1779, and the Two Following Days. . . . London, 1779. 32 p. 267 lots (more items).   [GB-LEc (film), compiler (Xerox)]

> **King**, pp. 20, 116-17. **Albrecht** says R 1977. Author has not managed to locate the reprint.

331 _____

Mr. Musgrave, auctioneer, London

A Catalogue of a Very Extensive & Extremely Valuable Collection of Vocal & Instrumental Music, Comprising the Duplicates of a Professor, the Libraries of a Distinguished Amateur, & of the Late William Boyce, Including the Choicest Portion of the Property Which Formerly Belonged to the Celebrated Doctor Boyce . . . Which Will Be Sold . . . the 29th March 1824, and 2 Following Days. . . . London, 1824. 19 p. 366 lots (large 4⁰).   [GB-Lbl, US-R]

King, p. 28.

332 _____

Literature

King, A. Hyatt. "Frederick Nicolay, Chrysander and the Royal Music Library." *MMR* 89 (1959): 13-24.   [g.a.]

> Nicolay, probably on the advice of Hawkins, bought some Mss. at the Boyce sale of 1779 (previous citation). He was Queen Charlotte's librarian. His own library was sold by Sotheby 29 November 1809. (The nucleus of the Royal Library was a purchase by King George III in 1762.) **King** and **Benton 2**:178.

333 **Brachthuizer, Jan Daniel,** 1803-83

R. W. P. de Vries, auctioneer, Amsterdam

Catalogus van de belangrijke Bibliotheek over Muziekgeschiedenis, Anthropologie, Naturwisschappen . . . nagelaten door . . . te Amsterdam. . . . Verkooping . . . 6 Februari 1886, en volgende dagen. Amsterdam, 1886. 120 p. 2029 + lots + A-R. Music, lots 1-821.

[NL-Avb (with names & prices)]

334 **Brahms, Johannes,** 1833-97

V. A. Heck, firm, Vienna   Liste no. 46

Johannes Brahms. Briefe, Manuskripte und Reliquien, grösstenteils aus seinem Nachlass. Wien, [n.d.]. 8 p. 33 lots.   [GB-Lbl (Hirsch), US-Wc]

> Bequeathed to A-Wgm. **Albrecht**.

335 _____

Orel, Alfred. "Johannes Brahms' Musikbibliothek." *Simrock Jahrbuch* 3 (1930-34): 18-47.

[g.a.]

> The catalog is reprinted in Kurt Hoffmann's *Die Bibliothek von Johannes Brahms*, 1974 (**338**). **Folter**, no. 33.

336 _____

Hans Schneider, firm, Tutzing   no. 100

Johannes Brahms, Leben und Werke, seine Fremde und seine Zeit. Tutzing, 1964. 229 p. 16 plates, 1750 lots.   [g.a.]

> "Bücher und Noten aus dem Besitz von Johannes Brahms," pp. 64-86.

337 _____

Geiringer, Karl. "Schumanniana in der Bibliothek von Johannes Brahms." In *Conviviorum musicorum: Festschrift Wolfgang Boetticher,* 79-82. Berlin: Merseburger, 1974.   [g.a.]

338 _____

Hoffmann, Kurt. *Die Bibliothek von Johannes Brahms Bücher und Musikalienverzeichnis.* Schriftenreihe zur Musik. Hamburg: Karl Dieter Wagnerm, 1974. xxxiv, 171 p. 872 lots.   [g.a.]

> "Johannes Brahms' Musikbibliothek von Prof. Dr. Alfred Orel," pp. 193-96.
> Includes citations for 16 items not previously noted. **Folter**, no. 34.

339 _____

Hancock, Virgina Lee Oglesby. "Brahms and His Library of Early Music." D.M.A. diss., University of Oregon, 1977.

> Not examined; see following entry.

340 _____

Hancock, Virgina Lee Oglesby. *Brahms Choral Compositions and His Library of Early Music.* Studies in Musicology, 76. Ann Arbor: UMI Research Press, 1983. vi, 229 p.   [g.a.]

> "Early Music in Brahms' Library," pp. 9-101.

341 _____

Bozarth, George S. "The First Generation of Brahms Manuscript Collections." *Notes* (1983): 239-62.   [g.a.]

> Lists Brahms holographs once in the collections of Rieter-Biedermann, Simrock, Senff, Clara Schumann, Levi, Joachim, Kalbeck, Grimm, and others, and the manuscripts' present locations.

342 _____

Bozarth, George S. "Brahms Lieder-Inventory of 1859-60 and Other Documents of His Life and Work." *Fontes* 30 (1983): 98-116.   [g.a.]

> From an autograph copy "recently discovered" in the Gesellschaft der Musikfreunde. Bozarth includes as "C. Catalogue of Brahms's library of books and music," no. 1, "The 'Rough Catalogue' (formerly Private Collection, Vienna since 1936, A-Wst, Ia.85.172)," with a list of non-music titles; and no. 2, "The 'Fair-Copy' Catalogue (formerly WBC, now AS-Wst, IA.67.338)," the music portion of which was published by Orel (**335**) and reprinted by Hofmann (**338**).

343 _____

LITERATURE

Mandyczewski, Eusebius. "Die Bibliothek Brahms." *Musikbuch aus Österreich* 1 (1904): 7-17.

> [US-Bp, -Wc, compiler]

> **Folter**, no. 35.

344 _____

Geiringer, Karl. "Brahms als Musikhistoriker." *Die Musik* 25 (Mai 1933): 571-78.   [g.a.]

> Also in *Johannes Brahms Festschrift,* 11-18. Berlin: Max Hesse, 1933. **Folter**, no. 35.   [g.a.]

345 _____

J. A. Stargardt, firm, Berlin   Cat. no. 388
"Brahms als Autographensammler von Georg Kinsky." *Der Autographen Sammler* 2 (Berlin, 1937/38).

> Not examined; cited in part from **Folter**, no. 35, and Kinsky bibliography in *MGG*.

346 _____

Mecklenburg, Günther. "Johannes Brahms." In his *Von Autographensammeln,* 55-59. Marburg, 1963.

347 _____

Geiringer, Karl and Irene. "The Brahms Library in the 'Gesellschaft der Musikfreunde'." *Notes* 30 (1973): 6-14.   [g.a.]
> **Folter**, no. 35.

348 _____

Geiringer, Karl and Irene. "Die Bibliothek von Johannes Brahms, anlässlich ihrer Neuaufstellung in Wien." *Neue Zürcher-Zeituing*, no. 154 (8 April 1973): 51-52.
> **Folter**, no. 35. .

349 _____

Hancock, Virginia Lee Oglesby. "Sources of Brahms Manuscript Copies of Early Music in the Archiv der Gesellschaft der Musikfreunde in Wien." *Fontes* 24 (1977): 113-21.

> [g.a.]

> **Folter**, no. 35.

350 _____

Bozarth, George S. "Johannes Brahms und die Liedersammlungen D. G. Corners, K. S. Meisters, und F. W. Arnolds." *Mf* 36 (1983): 177-211.   [g.a.]

351 _____

McKay, Elizabeth. "Brahms and Scarlatti." *MT* 130 (1989): 586-88.   [g.a.]
> About copies of Scarlatti's keyboard works in Brahms's library.

352 **[Brand,]**
Puttick & Simpson, auctioneer, London   Cat. no. 648
Catalogue of a Large Collection of Ancient and Modern Music in All Classes, Works of Handel, Operas in Score . . . a Few Music Plates, and Numerous Musical Instruments . . . Sold . . . September 1st, and Monday September 3, 1860. London, 1860. 34 p. 906 lots. Music, lots 1-819.   [GB-Lbl]

353   Brandenburg-Preussische Herrscherhaus
LEO LIEPMANNSSOHN, AUCTIONEER, BERLIN   AUTOGR.-VERZ. NO. [15]
Katalog einer hervorragend schönen Autographen-Sammlung . . . namentlich das
Brandenburg-Preussische Herrscherhaus . . . Ausserdem Dichter und Schriftsteller . . . Musiker
(Briefe und Komponisten, etc.) . . . 18. November 1895 und folgenden Tage. Berlin, 1895.
112 p. 1262 lots. Music, lots 1189-245.   [GB-LRosenthal]
        "Schauspieler," lots 1246-61.

354   Brandt, R E
ELLIS, FIRM, LONDON
Playford's Brief Introduction to the Skill of Musick. An Account, with Bibliographical Notes,
of a Unique Collection Comprising All the Editions from 1654 to 1730. In the Possession of
Messrs. Ellis, London. London: Ellis, 1926. [19] p.   [US-Wc]

355   [Brandt-Buys, Henri F R]; et al.
R. W. DE VRIES, AUCTIONEER, AMSTERDAM
Catalogue d'une belle collection de livres. Droit et jurisprudence . . . [etc.] *provenant des*
bibliothèques de feu M. M. D. Lopes de Leao Laguna [et al.]. *Vente . . . 17 juin et jours*
suivantes, 1907. . . . A'dam, 1907.

_____ . *Veiling zaterdagavond 22 juni. . . . Catalogus der Muziekbibliotheek, van*
wijlenden heer. . . . A'dam, 1907. 155, 8 p. 2204 lots in this separate supplement.   [NL-Avb]
        Music, lots 2073-204.

356   Brassin, Louis
RUDOLPH LEPKE, AUCTIONEER, BERLIN   No. 1065
Verzeichnis der Musik-Bibliothek und Autographen-Sammlung . . . des . . . Klaviervirtuosen
Professor. . . . Versteigerung . . . den 16. November 1896 und am folg. Tage. . . . Berlin, [1896].
25 p. 608 lots (more items).   [GB-Lbl (Hirsch)]
        Autographs, lots 278-608.

357   Breazul, George
Brancusi, Petre. *George Breazul si istoria a muzicii romanesti.* [Bucuresti]: Ed. Muzicala, 1976.
478 p.   [g.a.]
        Library catalog, pp. 466-77.

358   [Bree, Johann Bernard van, 1801-57]
C. F. ROOS; G. DE VRIES [AND] W. ENGELBERTS, AUCTIONEERS, AMSTERDAM
Catalogus van eene Verzameling Antiquiteiten, Rariteiten . . . voorts eenige Muzijk-
Instrumenten en Kasten. . . . Welke verkocht . . . den 10ᵈᵉⁿ April 1862. . . . Amsterdam, 1862.
16 p.
        "Muzijk-Instrumenten en Muzijkwerken . . . nagelaten door . . . J. B. van
        Bree," pp. 14-16 (13 instruments, 48 scores and books).

_____ . *Vervolg op den Catalogus der Muzijkwerken . . . J. B. van Bree. . . .* Amsterdam,
1862. 4 p. 108 lots.   [NL-Apk only, interleaved with names and prices]

359   Breitkopf, Johann Gottlieb Immanuel, 1719-94

Bibliothecae Joh. Gottl. Imman. Breitkopf nuper defvnti. Pars prior in classes digesta et quod monvmenta typographica. . . . Publica avctione in rvbri collegii Vaporario, A.D. XIX Oct. [1795?]. Lipsiae: Ex Typographeo Breitkoffio, [1795?].

Not located; discussed in Bernhard Wendt's *Der Versteigerungs-und Antiquariats-Katalog . . . ,* 26. Leipzig: Liebisch, 1937.

360   _____

Hitzig, Wilhelm. *Katalog des Archivs von. . . . I. Musik-Autographe . . . II. Briefe.* 2 vols. Leipzig: Breitkopf & Härtel, 1925-26. 50, 50 p.   [US-Wc]

348 lots in vol. 1; large quantities of items in vol. 2 are not numbered.

361   _____

J. A. Stargardt, auctioneer, Eutin in Holstein   no. 498

Auktion: Musik-Autographen . . . versteigerung . . . 10. Oktober in den Räumen Stuttgarter Kunst-kabinett, Stuttgart. . . . Katalog 498 der Firma . . . [Beschriebendes Verzeichnis: Wolfgang Schmieder]. Eutin in Holstein, [1951]. 78 p. 68 lots, plates.   [g.a. (prices fixed)]

Contains Schmieder's descriptive list of the music autographs, pp. 323-27 now in D-DS. An unsigned note on the cover of the copy at US-NYgr says "The sale was cancelled a few days before October 10th."

362   _____

Literature

Schmieder, Wolfgang. "Johann Gottlob Immanuel Breitkopfs Privatbibliothek. Werden und Vergehen." In *Otto Glaunig zum 60. Geburtstag,* 2:73-87. Leipzig: Hadl, 1938.

[compiler (Xerox)]

363   _____

Schmieder, Wolfgang. "Das Archiv des Hauses Breitkopf & Härtel." *AmZ* 65 (1938): 122-23.

[g.a.]

364   Brentano, Franz Domenico Marie Josef and **Antonia,** 1765-1844

Joseph Baer, auctioneer, Frankfurt a.M.

Zwölf ungedruckte Briefe Beethovens. Briefe Goethes. . . . Briefe von [others]. *Urkunden und Briefe der Familie Brentano von Birkenstock . . . Öffentliche Versteigerung . . . 9. April 1896. . . .* Frankfurt a.M., 1896. 47 p. 107 lots.   [US-NYgr, -NH, -Bp]

365   Breslauer, Martin

Das deutsche Lied: Geistlich und weltlich bis zum 18ten Jahrhunder. *Dokumente frühen deutschen Lebens, 1, "Katalog III."* Berlin: M. Breslauer, 1908. 314 p. 556 lots. Reprint, Hildesheim: Olms, 1966.   [g.a.]

Much of the collection originated with Biltz, and this catalog is also under him in this list (**256**).

366   Breyer,   (organist in Torgau)

List & Francke, firm, Leipzig

Verzeichniss der von dem Astrologem Herrn Karl Vogt in München, sowie Herrn Joh. Friedr. Ilzig hinterlassenen Bibliotheken, welche nebst mehreren Anderen Büchersammlungen und

*einer bedeutenden Sammlung von Musikalien aus dem Nachlasse des Herrn Organist Breyer
. . . am 11. April 1864 . . . versteigert werden soll.* Leipzig: O. Wigand, 1864. 202 p. 4071 + 675
lots (of music).   [US-NYgr, -Cn]

367   Breyner, Dr. Charles
PARKE-BERNET GALLERIES, INC., AUCTIONEER, NEW YORK CITY
*French Books, Literature - Art - Music. Collection of . . . Public Auction, Tuesday and Wednesday,
March 5 and 6. . . .* New York, 1963. 91 p. 503 lots.   [US-NYgr]

> Music in First Session, Tuesday, lots 1-248, and *inter alia* (many items,
> e.g., lot 200 = 200 vocal scores, lot 207, 14 biographies).

368   Bridge, Sir Frederick, 1844-1924
MESSRS. HODGSON & CO., AUCTIONEER, LONDON
*A Catalogue of Valuable Books and Manuscripts, Comprising Modern Books from the Berens
Collection* [i.e., Randolph Berens] *. . . Musical Books and Manuscripts of the Late . . . Including
an Interesting MS. of Exercises in Composition by Thomas Attwood (1765-1838) with
Comments and Improvements in the Hand of Mozart . . .* [etc.] *July 2nd, 1924, and 2 Following
Days.* London, 1924. 68 p. 948 lots.   [GB-Lbl]

> Music portion of the Bridge collection, lots 530-622. The Attwood studies
> fetched £110. Noted by both **King**, pp. 72-73, and **Albrecht**.

369   Bright, Benjamin Heywood
S. LEIGH SOTHEBY & CO., AUCTIONEER, LONDON
*A Catalogue of the Curious and Valuable Collection of Manuscripts Formed by the Late . . .
Sold . . . June 18th, 1844. . . .* [London, 1844]. 35 p. 290 lots.   [GB-Lbl, US-CA, -I; film at CRL]

370   —————
S. LEIGH SOTHEBY & CO., AUCTIONEER, LONDON
*A Catalogue of the Valuable Library of the Late . . . Containing a Most Extensive Collection
of Valuable Rare, and Curious Books . . . Sold . . . March 3, 1845, and Eleven Following Days.
. . .* [London], 1845. viii, 388 p. 6197 lots. Music, lots 3983-87 but contains 33 valuable items.
   [GB-Lbl; US-Wc, -CLp, -MAu; film at CRL]

371   Britton, Thomas, 1651-1714
MR. WARD, AUCTIONEER, LONDON
*A Catalogue of Extraordinary Musical Instruments . . . Also Valuable Compositions, Ancient
and Modern, by the Best Masters in Music . . . Being the Entire Collection of Mr. Thomas
Britton of Clerkenwell, Small Coal-Man, Lately Deceased, Who at His Own Charge Kept Up
So Excellent a Consort Forty Odd Years at His Dwelling House, That the Best Masters Were at
All Times Proud to Exert Themselves Therein . . . Sold by Auction at Mr. Ward's House in Red
Bull-Yard . . .* 1714.   [Reprints g.a.]

> The original no longer exists but was reprinted in Sir John Hawkins, *A
> General History of the Science and Practice of Music,* 2:792-93. London:
> Payne and Sons, 1776. **King**, pp. 11-12, and **Albrecht**. Often reprinted; for
> a list see Duckles/Keller, no. 560.

372   [Broadhurst,   ]
PUTTICK & SIMPSON, AUCTIONEER, LONDON   CAT. NO. 1013
Catalogue of a Large and Interesting Collection of Antiquarian and Modern Music . . .

Including Flute and Violin Music, Also Musical Instruments . . . Sold November 18th, 1867, and Following Day. London, 1867. 44 p. 1267 lots Music, lots 1-1178.   [GB-Lbl]

> In **King** as Anon.

373   **Broadwood, John,** and **Sons**
Catalogue of Books in the Library of John Broadwood & Sons' Manufactory. London: Witherly & Co., 1874. 116 p.   [GB-Lbl]

> Not examined. Not in **King**.

374   **Brodsky, Adolph,** 1851-1929
Thomason, Geoffrey. "The Brodsky Archive at the RNCM [Royal Northern College of Music]." *Brio* 22, no. 2 (1985): 46-49.   [g.a.]

375   **Broedelet, H. W.; J. P. Felperlaan**
J. H. DUNK, AUCTIONEER, ROTTERDAM
Catalogus van eene belangrijke verzameling boeken . . . taal- en letterkunde en godgeleerdheid. Plattwerken en muziek . . . nagelaten door . . . en een voornam predikant . . . verkooping . . . 23 mei 1872 en volgende dagen. . . . Rotterdam, 1872. 135 p. 2549 lots Music, pp. 128-34 (119 + lots).   [NL-Avb]

376   **Broek, (Cornelis van den) Cornelisz**
H. GARTMAN AND W. VERMANDEL, AUCTIONEER, AMSTERDAM
Catalogus van een schoon kabinet Printkonst . . . twee verzamelingen Printen en Pourtretten. . . . En laastelyk Muziek en Muziek-Instrumenten . . . nagelaten door Cornelis van den Broek Cornelisz. Verkocht . . . 15 Maart 1790. . . . Amsterdam, 1790. 275 p. 2500 lots. Music, pp. 71-73 (44 lots).   [NL-Avb]

> **Lugt**, no. 4547.

377   **Broekhuijzen, G. H., Jr.**
G. THEOD BOM, AUCTIONEER, AMSTERDAM
Catalogus eener uitgelreide verzameling . . . Boeken kostbare Pracht- en Plaatwerken, oude Gravuren [etc.]. *Een verzameling Muziek en Muziekwerken van wijlen den heer . . . verkocht . . . 3 November 1875 en volgende dagen.* Amsterdam, 1875. 203 + n. p.1 (autré ed. 843 p.).
                                                    [NL-DHrk, -Rbm, -Apk]

> Section 2, "Muziek," pp. 31-40 (222 lots). **Lugt**, no. 35875.

378   **Bronsart von Schellendorf, Hans August Alexander,** 1830-1913
LEO LIEPMANNSSOHM, FIRM, BERLIN   AUTOGR.-VERST. NO. 44
. . . Versteigerung der Autographen des musikalischen Nachlasses von Hans von Bronsart. . . . Berlin, 1919. 50 p. 406 lots.   [NL-Avb]

> **Folter**, no. 36.

379   **Brook, John**
SOTHEBY & CO., AUCTIONEER, LONDON
Catalogue of Valuable Printed Books, Important Autograph Letters, Literary Manuscripts and Historical Documents . . . [and] *the Important Collection of Musical Manuscripts, the Property of . . . Sold . . . 4th of May 1936, and Two Following Days.* [London, 1936.] 116 p. 817 lots.   [Film at CRL]

Music ALS, "Property of a gentleman," lots 464-86. Brook properties, lots 487-522, autograph Mss., including lot 460, a Paër holograph.

380   Brooke, John, of Leicester
MR. GREENWOOD, AUCTIONEER, LONDON
A Catalogue of a Genuine and Exceedingly Valuable Collection of Prints, Books of Prints, and a Well Chosen Library, Select Music . . . Musical Instruments . . . Collected with Great Care and at a Considerable Expense By the Late . . . Sold . . . the 1st of March, 1796 and Three Following Days. London, 1796. 20 p. various lottings.
[Priced copy at Courtauld Library, London]
"Music and instruments," pp. 18-19, lots 45-78 (but many more items).

Brooke, W. T. *See under* **Vaughan, W. A.**

381   Broome, Arthur [Maj.-General]
SOTHEBY, WILKINSON & HODGE, AUCTIONEER, LONDON
Catalogue of Important and Valuable Works from Various Private Collections, Including a Portion of the Library of the Late Major General . . . and a Small Library of Elementary & Classical Music [Broome's?] *. . . Sold 14th of August, 1872.* 125 p. 2232 lots.   [Film at CRL]

382   Brossard, Sebastian de, 1655-1730
Catalogue des livres de musique théorique et pratique vocale et instrumentale, tant imprimée que manuscrite, qui sont dans le cabinet du . . . et dont il supplie très humblement Sa Majesté d'accepter le don, pour ètre mis en conservez dans sa bibliothèque. Fait et escrit en l'année 1724.   [compiler (film)]
Ms.: library given to Louis XV, basis of collection in Bibliothèque nationale, Paris. Original Mss. at F-Pn, Rés.VMA8.20. **Albrecht.**

383   _____
LITERATURE
[Marie Bobillier], "Sebastian de Brossard prêtre, compositeur, écrivain et bibliophile (1655-1730) d'après ses papiers inédits." *Mémoires de la Société de l'histoire de Paris et de l'Ile-de-France* 23 (1896): 72-124.

384   _____
Lebeau, Elizabeth. "L'Entrée de la collections musicale de Sebastian de Brossard à la bibliothèque du Roi, d'après des documents inédits." *Revue de musicologie* 32 (1950): 77-93; 23 (1951): 20-43.   [g.a.]
Reprints selections from Brossard's correspondence about the collection.

385   Brown, Allen Augustus, 1835-1916
BOSTON, PUBLIC LIBRARY, ALLEN A. BROWN COLLECTION
Catalogue of the Allen A. Brown Collection of Music in the. . . . Boston: The Trustees, 1910-16. 4 vols. Issued in 13 parts, 1908-16.   [g.a.]
Albrecht: given to US-Bp in 1894; consists of 6990 volumes, some 50,000 pieces.

386   _____

C. F. Libbie & Co., auctioneer, Boston

Catalogue - Part II, of the Valuable Private Library of the Late . . . Comprising Works on Drama and Music. Large Collection of Magazine Excerpts . . . Scores, Librettos . . . Periodicals, Newspaper Clippings . . . Photograph Album . . . Auction Sale: Thursday, June 21, 1917. . . . Boston, 1917. 25 p. 369 lots (many more items in bundles).[US-Bp (priced), -NYp, -Wc, -Woa]

McKay, no. 7855.

387   **Brown, J. C. (of Philadelphia)**

Stan V. Henkels, auctioneer, Philadelphia   Cat. no. 1219

Views . . . Lincolniana . . . Music . . . Military Buttons To Be Sold . . . October 16, 1918. Philadelphia, 1918. 46 p. 686 lots. Music, lots 658-80.   [US-NYp, -WOaMWA, -AA]

Lancour, no. 3766.

388   **Brown, W. J., Jr. (of Old Bond St.)**

Puttick & Simpson, auctioneer, London   Cat. no. 608

Catalogue of [His] *Library of Music and Musical Literature. . . . Will Be Sold . . . January 12, 1860.* [London, 1860.] 42 p. 882 lots.   [GB-Lbl, US-NYp (Drexel no. 845)]

Psalm tune books, lots 294-437; versions of the Psalms, lots 438-513. **King**.

389   **Browne, John,** 1608-91

Ashbee, Andrew. "Instrumental Music from the Library of . . . , Clerk of the Parliaments." *M&L* 58 (1977): 43-59.

RILM: collections of viol music of 17th century now dispersed (Christ Church, Oxford; King's College, Cambridge; various individuals).

390   **Brugman, Johann B. H.; R. L. Schotten;** et al.

R. W. P. de Vries, auctioneer, Amsterdam

Catalogue des bibliothèques juridiques, literaires, scientifiques et musicales de feu . . . vente le 18 juin et les hours suivants. . . . Amsterdam, 1913. 168 p. 2549 lots. Music, lots 1884-2029, Theater, lots 1852-83.

Consignors are recorded in margins of NL-Avb copy; approximately 120 lots from Brugman.

391   **Brunnings, Florence E.**

Folk Song Index: A Comprehensive Guide to the Florence E. Brunnings Collection. Garland Reference Library of the Humanities, 252. New York: Garland, 1981. lxxxi, 357 p.   [g.a.]

392   **Brunsvik, Franz von,** fl. early 19th c.

Hornyák, Maria. *A Brunszvik család marton-Vásári - és kottatára.* Martonvásár: Mezögazdasági Kutatóintézet, 1991. 214 p. 561 pieces.

Cited from *RILM* 25, no. 109 (1991).

393   **Brunswick (family); Esterhazy (family); Keglevich (family)**

Literature

Novácek, Zdenko. "Angaben über Beethovens Schaffen in den Archiven von Bratislava." In *Bericht über den internationalen Beethoven-Kongress, 10-12 Dezember 1970 in Berlin,* ed. Heinz Alfred Brockhaus and Konrad Niemann, 495-98. Berlin: Verlag für neue Musik, 1971.

> *RILM:* Brunswick archives now in the Zentrales Staats-Archiv, Bratislava; Esterhazy group in the Zentrales Slowakisches Staatsarchivs; the Keglevich collection remains in Budapest.

394   **Brydges, James, 1st Duke of Chandos,** 1674-1744

"A Shortened and Modernized Catalog of Music Belonging to His Grace, James, Duke of Chandos, from the Original in the Handwriting of Mr. Noland, Subscribed by Dr. Pepusch in 1720." Reprinted in Baker, Charles Henry Collins, and Muriel I. Baker, *The Life and Circumstances of James Brydges . . . Patron of the Liberal Arts*, 134-40. Oxford: Clarendon Press, 1949. Music, 127 items, pp. 134-39.   [g.a.]

> **Coral**, p. 67: "We shall never know how it was dispersed." **King**, p. 16. Some 17 items from this collection appeared in a Christie's sale of 18 November 1981 (see *Early Music*, October 1982, pp. 525-26).

395   _____

Idem. "Supplemented by another catalog in Pepusch's own hand dated 23 October 1721" [no longer extant], appears as appendix to Beek's essay (**397**).

396   _____

COCK, AUCTIONEER, LONDON

[Sale of a "large and valuable" library . . . 12 March 1747. London]: Exeter Exchange in the Strand, 1747.

> From Beek's essay (**397**), and also listed in vol. 4 of Pollard/Munby *List*. Copy of the Cock catalog is at GB-Ob.

397   _____

Beeks, Grayson. "The Chandos Collection." In *Handel Collections and Their History*, ed. Terence Best, 137-57. Oxford: Clarendon Press, 1993.

> "Appendix 1: Handel in the Cannons Music Library," pp. 154-55. "Appendix 2: Contents of the Cannons Music-Library, items 23-25," p. 157.

398   **Buchanan, Annabel Morris**

> [Collection at US-CHH; Ms. on ILL]

399   **Bückens, Ernst**

Kahl, Willi. "Musikhandschriften aus dem Nachlass Ernst Bückens in der Kölner Universitäts- und Stadtbibliothek." In *Aus der Welt des Bibliothekars: Juchoff Festschrift*, 159-71. Köln: Greven, 1961.

> Not examined. Cited in **Gerboth** and in **Benton 2**:81.

400   **Bull, Ove Schjeldberg,** d. 1790

Fortegnelse over Praesten Hr. Owe Bulls efterladte Bøger og Musikalien, som ved offentlig Auction blive bortsolgte, i S. T. Frue Bulls Huus, den [?] *Septembr.* Trondheim, 1791. 16 p. "Musikalier" (40 lots), pp. 14-15.

> Examined only title page. Cited in **Pettersen**'s *Nordisk Boglexikon*, p. 128.

Bull, P.   *See under* **Caraman-Chimay** (sale, 14 June 1976)

401   Bumpus, John S., 1861-1913
"Sacred Music with English Words." British Library, Add. Ms. 50202.

> A ten-page list in his hand but not the whole of his collection, according to **King**, p. 77.

402   Bunting, Edward, 1773-1843
BELFAST, QUEEN'S UNIVERSITY, LIBRARY
The Bunting Collection of Irish Folk Music and Songs. Edited from the Original Manuscripts by D. J. O'Sullivan. . . . 6 vols. *Journal of the Irish Folk Song Society* 22/23-28-29 ([Dublin], 1927-29).   [g.a.]

403   Burdett-Coutts, Angela, Baroness
SOTHEBY, WILKINSON & HODGE
Catalogue of the Valuable Library, the Property of the Late Baroness . . . Sold . . . 15-17 May 1922. . . . London, 1922.   [Film at CRL]

Burghersh, Lord.   *See under* **Fane, John**

Burgis, Peter.   *See section 3*

404   Burney, Charles, 1726-1814
"Catalog of the Books, Tracts and Treatises of All the Original Authors, Ancient and Modern, in Greek, Latin, German, French, Italian, Spanish and English, on the Particular Faculty of Music . . . of the Late. . . ." [ca. 1814.]   [GB-Lbl Add.Mss.18191]

> The collection was offered to the British Museum but not purchased (see **405**). The Mss. catalog was acquired in 1850.

405   _____

MR. WHITE, AUCTIONEER, LONDON
The Late Dr. Burney's Musical Library. A Catalogue of the Valuable and Very Fine Collection of Music, Printed and MS., of the Late . . . Which Will Be Sold by Auction by Mr. White, at His Rooms, Storey's Gate, Great George Street, Westminster, on Monday, the 8th of August, 1814, and Following Days, at Twelve o'clock (Pursuant to His Will). . . . [London, 1814.] 42 p. 822 lots.
                                                                                    [US-Wc]

> Rimbault's copy, interleaved, with his notes. Lacks the Addenda, which brings it to 1080 lots (film - compiler). See Grant's review noted in item **407**. Also **King**, pp. 31-32. **Folter**, no. 37, cites only the sale of Burney's non-music library. Music books and treatises not in White's sale eventually sold to GB-Lbl. Rare Chinese instruments owned by Burney were offered to the Museum but declined. See 1973 reprint (**407**) and **Albrecht**.
>   [compiler copy)]
>
> → *See also under* **Taylor, Edward**

406   _____

Piano generale per una storia della musica di Charles Burney con un catalogo della sua biblioteca musicale. Monumenta Bononiensia, 21. Bologna: A.M.I.S., 1972. ix, [18] p.   [g.a.]

> Giovanni Battista Martini's account of his meeting with Burney. Includes a facsimile with preface and transcription of the catalog by Vincent Duckles. Not in **Folter**.

407 _____

[Burney, Charles.] *Catalogue of the Music Library of Charles Burney, Sold in London, 8 August 1814.* Reprint, with an introduction by A. Hyatt King. Auction Catalogues of Music, 2. Amsterdam: Frits Knuf, 1973. ix, 2 p.

> Lacks the Addenda. Missing lots set out in review by Kerry Grant in *Notes* 31 (1974): 45-48.

408 _____

LITERATURE

Duckles, Vincent. "A General Plan for a History of Music of Dr. Charles Burney with a Catalogue of His Music Library." In *Festschrift Albi Rosenthal*, ed. Rudolf Elvers, 131-38. Tutzing: Hans Schneider, 1984.   [g.a.]

> The "Catalogue" is of Burney's still-forming collection as copied by Padre Martini when he met Burney in 1770. It is presently Mss.1.F.62 at I-Bc.

409   Burrell, Mary (Banks)

Catalogue of the Burrell Collection of Wagner. Documents, Letters, and Other Biographical Material. London: Nonpareil Press, 1929. xi, 99 p. 518 lots.   [g.a.]

> **Hirsch**, catalog no. 427, says it was compiled by Peter E. Wright.

410 _____

LITERATURE

Stefan, Paul. "The Burrell Collection of Wagneriana Comes to America . . . Acquired by Mrs. Bok: Old Controversies May Be Settled by Documents Now in Philadelphia Bank Vaults." *MA* 52, no. 2 (25 January 1932): 7.

411 _____

Kaprowski, Richard. "The Selling of the Burrell Collection: An Editorial Report." *Current Musicology* 27 (1979): 7-9.   [g.a.]

412   Busch, Fritz, 1890-1951

Lerma, Dominique-Réne de. *The Fritz Busch Collection; An Acquisition of Indiana University.* Lilly Library Publication, 15. Bloomington: Indiana University Library, 1972. 52 p.

[g.a.]

> **Folter**, no. 38.

413 _____

LITERATURE

Anderson, David E. "Fritz Busch and Richard Strauss: The Strauss Scores in the Busch Nachlass." *Music Review* 49 (1988): 289-94.   [g.a.]

414   Busoni, Ferruccio, 1866-1924

Mayer, Anton. "Die Bibliothek Ferruccio Busonis." *Das Sammelkabinet* 3, no. 4 (1924): 1-4; Beilage zu *Faust* 3, no. 4 (1924).

> Not examined; cited from **Folter**, no. 39.

415 _____

MAX PERL, AUCTIONEER, BERLIN   AUKTION 96

Bibliothek Ferruccio Busoni. Werke der Weltliteratur . . . illustrierte Bücher. . . . Eine hervorragenda Cervantes- und E. T. A. Hoffman-Sammlung. Bücher mit handschriftlichen Dedikationen. Musik. Verst . . . 30 [-]31 März 1925. Berlin, 1925. 111 p. 1421 lots. (Not many music lots.)   [US-PRu, -CA, -NYgr, NL-Avb]

    Folter, no. 39.

416 _____

LITERATURE

Beaumont, Antony. "Ferruccio Busoni: Composer and Bibliophile." *Librarium* 26 (1983): 119-34.

    Not examined; cited from **Folter**, no. 39.

417 _____

Triebels, Hans. "De vijfduizend banden van Busoni's bibliotheek: De stad der boeken." *Mens en melodie* 46 (1991): 594-99.   [g.a.]

    Cited from *RILM*.

Butler, Rev. George (Dean Peterborough).   *See* **Moore, Thomas** (sale of 25, 27-28 June 1853)

C***, Baron von.   *See under* **Golterman** (Ant. -Verz. by Leipmannssohn, no. 38)

C****, Sammlung.   *See under* **Ulex**

418 Caccamisi-Marchesi, André Anzon, Baron

LEO LIEPMANNSSOHN, FIRM, BERLIN   ANT-VERZ. NO. 43

Autographen-Sammlung zum Teil aus dem Nachlass des. . . . Shakespeareforschers Prof. Friedrich August Leo, und kostbare Musik-Autographen und Manuskripte z. T. aus dem Besitz des Herrn Baron André Anzon Caccamisi-Marchesi. Versteigerung vom 21. bia 22. November 1913. Berlin, 1913. 111 p. 871 lots. Music, lots 566-871.   [US-Wc]

    Folter 2:486.

419 Callcott, John Wall, 1766-1821

["Rough catalog of the library of . . . including (f. 10b) treatises of music, about 1796, and (f. 20b) 'Music Books, October 25, 1805'," etc.] British Library, Add. Ms. 27692.

        [GB-Lbl; compiler (film)]

    From **Barclay-Squire** 3:384.

420 _____

MR. WHITE, AUCTIONEER, LONDON

A Catalogue of the Very Fine Collection and Extensive Collection of Musical and Literary Works, Printed and Manuscript . . . Which Will Be Sold . . . on April 15th, 1819, and Five Following Days. [London: G. Sidney, 1819.] 31 p. 1121 lots. [US-Wc; US-Cn (copy of -Wc)]

    Albrecht. King, pp. 26, 43. *See also* **421**.

421 Callcott, Robert S.; A Gentleman, Retiring

PUTTICK & SIMPSON, AUCTIONEER, LONDON   CAT. NO. 2431

Effects of the Late Callcott Consisting of the Library of Music from the Libraries of John Wall Callcott, William Crotch, and Henry Smart, and Others . . . Sold . . . July 5th. 1886. London, 1886. 250 lots.   [GB-Lbl]

422   [**Callcott, William Hutchins,** 1807-82]

PUTTICK & SIMPSON, AUCTIONEER, LONDON   CAT. NO. 771

Catalogue of a Collection of Music . . . Also Musical Instruments . . . Properties of Amateurs . . . Sold June 13th and June 15th, 1863. . . . London, 1863. 27 p. 724 lots. Music, lots 1-606.

[GB-Lbl]

→ *See also under* [**Euing**] (sale of 29 May 1876)

423   **Callcott, William Hutchins; William Crotch,** 1775-1847; **William Horsley,** 1774-1858; **Henry Smart,** 1813-79; **John Wall Callcott; Musical Society**

PUTTICK & SIMPSON, AUCTIONEER, LONDON   CAT. NO. 2431

Catalogue of the Effects of the Late . . . Consisting of the Library of Music, from the Collections of . . . and Others, Many Having Valuable Autograph Notes Attached . . . Sold July 5th, 1886. London, 1886. 13 p. 250 lots. Music, lots 39-250.   [GB-Lbl]

Lugt, no. 45909.

424   [**Calvert,**   ]

MR. FLETCHER, AUCTIONEER, LONDON

Catalogue of the Collection of Music, Ancient and Modern, Comprising Ornithoparcus' Micrologus 1609 . . . Arnold's Cathedral Music. . . . Musical Instruments . . . Sold . . . April 29th, 1844, and Following Day. [London, 1844.] 18 p. 379 lots. Music, lots 1-342.   [GB-Ob]

In pencil above title in GB-Ob copy: "Calvert's Library."

425   **Calvocoressi, Michel Dimitri,** 1877-1944

FIRST EDITION BOOKSHOP, FIRM, LONDON   CAT. NOS. 48 & 49

Songs and Chamber Music from the Library of. . . . Kingston-on-Thames, 1964.   [g.a.]

In no. 48, songs, lots 392-446; in no. 49, chamber music, lots 642-68.

426   **Calvör, Casper,** 1650-1725

LITERATURE

Burose, H. "Die Calvörsche Bibliothek zu Lebzeiten ihres Gebrüders." *Harz-Zeitschrift* 18 (1966): 1-16.

Not examined. (**Benton 2**:54, no. 53, says at D-CZ.)

427   **The "Cambio" Collection**

LA SCALA AUTOGRAPHS, INC., FIRM, HOPEWELL, N.J.

Signed Italian Opera Photos - Rare Signed and Unsigned German Programs - Signed Cinema Photos Section One: The "Cambio" Collection - Rare Signed Italian Opera Photos. Hopewell, N.J.: La Scala, 1992. 4 p. 358 lots. "Cambio" collection, lots 1-284.   [g.a.]

Cambridge, Duke of (sale of November 1850).   *See* **Adolphus Frederick**

428   **Camidge, Dr. ; ? Snaith**

PUTTICK & SIMPSON, AUCTIONEER, LONDON   CAT. NO. 870

Catalogue of a Collection of Music . . . Vocal and Instrumental Works . . . Valuable Full Scores . . . Also Musical Instruments . . . Sold June 29th, 1865. [London, 1865]. 18 p. 515 lots. Music, lots 1-391.   [GB-Lbl]

429   Camm, John B. M.

LITERATURE

Riddle, Charles. "Music in Public Libraries, with Special Notes on the 'John B. M. Camm Music Reference Library' and a Comparison of the Classification of Music." *Library Association Record* 16 (1914): 1-10.   [g.a.]

> Presented by Camm to the Borough of Bournemouth in 1912. Originally ca. 4000 volumes. Cited from *Grove*, 3rd ed.

430   Campori, Giuseppe, Marchese, 1821-87

Lodi, Luigi. *Catalogo dei manoscritti posseduti dal Marchese Campori. Appendice comp. da Raimondo Vandini*. Modena: n.p., 1875-84. 2 vols. in 1.

> **Albrecht**: now at I-MOe.

431   _____

LITERATURE

Kast, Paul. "Die Autographensammlung Campori und ihr musikalischen Schätze [now in the Biblioteca Estense, Modena]." *Bericht über den internationalen musikwissenschaftlichen Kongress, Kassel, 1962*, 226-28. Kassel: Bärenreiter, 1963.   [g.a.]

432   Canal, Pietro, 1807-83

Biblioteca musicale del Prof. P. Canal in Crespano Veneto. Bassano: Prem. stabn. tip. Sante Pozzato, 1885. 104 p. 1152 titles.   [US-Cn, -NYp, -Wc]

> **Albrecht**: 1000 works on music theory, 118 prints, and more than 400 Mss.
> Now in Biblioteca nazionale Marciana, Venice. **Folter**, no. 40.

433   _____

LITERATURE

[There is a notice of the purchase of his collection of 20,000 volumes for 250.000 lire in *ZfMW* 10 (1927/1928): 255. Frati's *Dizionario*, Firenze 1933, p. 130, mentions a note about the collection in pt. 2, pp 12-13 of *All'Insegna del Libro* 1, no. 1 (gennaio 1928).]

434   _____

Ferrari, L. "La collezione musicale Canal alla Marciana di Venezia." *Accademie e bibliotech* 1 (1927/28): 140-43; 3 (1929/30): 279-80.

> Cited in Frati *Dizionario* (**433**) and in **Benton 3**:280, no. 403.

435   Cantzler, G.

Verzeichnis der hinterlassenen Musikalien und theoretischen Werke über Musik aus der Sammlung des Herrn . . . welche am 30. October 1873 und den folgenden Tage . . . versteigert werden sollen. Aufträge zu dieser Auction nehmen alle Buch-Antiquariats- und Musikalien-Handlung entgegen, in Greifswald die Herren: Ludwig Bamberg, Julius Bindewald. . . . Greifsawald, [1873?]. 18 p. 787 lots.   [GB-Lbl (Hirsch no. 492(8)), ex-Jos. Müller]

> Imprint covered by a pasted-up lot 856 from another sale.

436   Capdevilla Roviro, Felipe

Olivar, Alexandre. "Notas sobre manuscritos, v.: El fondo particular Capdevilla Roviro di Barcelona." *Hispaniae sacra* 8 (1955): 439-.

437   Capel, General T. E.
CHRISTIE'S, AUCTIONEER, LONDON
Catalogue of the Library of General the Honorable . . . Comprising Works in General Literature, Books of Prints . . . and a Large Collection of Music, for the Violin and Piano, and Quartets . . . Sold . . . May 3, 1855. London, 1855. 14 p. 304 lots. Music, lots 227-88 (many more items); manuscript music, lots 269-75.   [Christie's, London]
        Lugt, no. 22405.

438   Capel, John
MESSRS. WINSTANLEY, AUCTIONEER, LONDON
A Catalogue of Nearly the Whole of the Excellent Furniture . . . and Other Articles of Taste. . . . The Valuable Library of Music. . . . A Fine Copy of Marcello's Psalms . . . Sold . . . 26th of April, 1847 and Three Following Days. [London], 1847. 40 p. 637 lots. Music, lots 81-174 only.   [GB-Lbl]
        Lugt, no. 18591.

439   [Capes,   ]
PUTTICK & SIMPSON, AUCTIONEER, LONDON   CAT. NO. 555
Catalogue of a Large Collection of Music, Including Theatrical and Historical Works, Scores and Arrangements of Operas and Oratorios . . . Also a Very Curious Collection of Manuscript Full Scores, of the Works of Celebrated Italian Writers, Chiefly Sacred . . . Sold . . . November 4th, 1858 and Following Day. London, 1858. 23 p. 647 lots. Music, lots 1-611.   [GB-Lbl]

440   Capes, S. J.
Moore, J. N. "The Capes-Openhym Collection of Pianoforte Recordings." *Yale University Library Gazette* 40 (1965): 104-12.   [g.a.]

441   Caracciolo, D. Pasquale, Marchese di Arena
Catalogo di musica instrumentale e vocale che esiste nell'archivio musicale del Signor Marchese . . . formato nel mese di Febbrajo dell'anno 1814. [n.p., 1814]. 19 leaves. 8°.
        Not examined; cited from **Wolffheim** 1:265 and Ganley antiquarian catalog no. 31.

Caraman-Chimay, Thérèse de, Princesse.   *See* **Chimay, Thérèsè Cabarus, Countess de Caraman and Princesse de**

442   Carbonel, Joseph François Narcisse, 1733-1955
Catalogue de livres rares et curieux, partitions d'opéras, recueils de chant, etc., provenant de la bibliothèque de feu M. Carbonel, ancien directeur de la musique de la reine Hortense . . . vente . . . 30 mai 1856, et jours suivants. . . . Paris: L. Potier, 1856. 52 p. 413, 82 lots. Music books, lots 69-78; scores, the final 82 lots.   [NL-DHgm]
        Folter, no. 41; **Scheurleer 2** 1 (1923):10; **Weckerlin 1**; **Albrecht**; **Wolffheim** 1:341, etc.

443   Card, Edward J., d. 1877
PUTTICK & SIMPSON, AUCTIONEER, LONDON
Catalogue of a Large and Valuable Collection of Music . . . Capital Selection of Flute Music (the Library of the Late . . . , the Eminent Flautist) . . . Rare Tracts and Treatises, Original

Editions of Scarce Operas . . . Rare Engraved Portraits . . . Important Musical Autographs . . . Also Musical Instruments . . . Sold . . . August 22nd, 1877. [London, 1877.] 21 p. 476 lots. Music, lots 1-403.   [GB-Lbl]

Card's consignments, *inter alia.* Many Walsh editions.

444   Carey, Clive (Francis Clive Savill)
LITERATURE
Frampton, George E. "Clive Carey, Dorothy Marshall and the West Sussex Tradition." *English Dance and Song* 48 (1986): 7-8.

445   Carlo, Alberto, King of Sardinia, 1798-1849
Pertz, G. H. "Handschrift der privat Bibliothek der König in Turin." *Archiv der deutsche Geschichtskunde (Hannover)* 9 (1847): 599-611.

Collection now at I-Tr, according to **Benton 3**:269-369.

446   Carminati, Costantino and Alessandro
ASSOCIAZIONE DEI MUSICOLOGI ITALIANI
"Catalogo delle musiche donati dai Nob. Frat. Cost. ed. Alessandro Carminati [in the Museo Correr]." In *Catalogo generale delle opere musicali. . . . ,* ser. 6, vol. 1., *Città di Venezia,* [53]-65. Venezia, 1912-13.   [g.a.]

Carmouche, Pierre F. A. [sale of 14 June 1887].   *See under* **Vadé**

447   Carnaby, J ; J. Harvey
SOTHEBY, WILKINSON & HODGE, AUCTIONEER, LONDON
Catalogue of the First Portion of the Important and Valuable Collection of Ancient & Modern Music of the Late . . . Comprising . . . Important Original and Autograph Manuscripts of Eminent Musicians, &c. . . . Sold . . . 6th Day of July, 1885. [London, 1885]. 31 p. 383 lots.
                                                                                      [Film at CRL]

448   Caroline Amelia Elizabeth, Consort of George IV, 1768-1821, called **Queen Caroline**
GALLERIA SANGIORGI, AUCTIONEER, ROME   ANNO V, N.57
Catalogo della biblioteca particolare Regina Carolina d'Inghilterra. Romanzi - Storie - Poesie - Musica. Vendita dal giorno 2 al 5 Aprile. Roma: Tip. dell Unione Cooperativa Editrice, 1895. 39 p. 455 lots. Music, lots 431-55 include some manuscripts.

449   Carr, R P (of Wandsworth)
SOTHEBY, WILKINSON & HODGE, AUCTIONEER, LONDON
Catalogue of the Important, Curious & Valuable Collection of Musical Works, Rare Treatises and Works on Music, Its History and Theory, Harmony and Composition, from the Library of . . . and Other Collections; Including Some Very Rare and Early Printed Music . . . Sold . . . the 27th Day of May, 1878. [London, 1878]. 32 p. 406 lots.   [Film at CRL]

450   Carreras y Dagas, Juan (d. 1870)
Catalogo de la biblioteca musical y museo instrumental propriedad de. . . . Barcelona: Manuel Miro y D. Mars'a, 1870. 70 p. ca. 3000 items.   [US-R]

Folter, no. 42, **Barblan**, and **Bobillier**. Collection now at E-Bc.

Carrodus, John Tiplady, 1836-95 [sale of 1910].   *See under* **Sawyer, Dr.**

451   **Carter, John**
MR. SOTHEBY, AUCTIONEER, LONDON
A Catalogue of the Valuable Collection of Antiquities, Music, Drawings and Prints of the Late . . . Will Be Sold by Auction . . . on Monday, February 23, and Two Following Days. London: Wright and Murphy, [1818]. 9 p. 234 lots of books and Mss. Music, lots 179-218, 219-234 (Carter's works in Ms.).

> Not examined; cited in Quaritch catalog no. 1026, 1982.

452   **Carter, Robert**
LITERATURE
Maurer, Maurer. "A Musical Family in Colonial Virginia." *MQ* 34 (1948): 358-64.   [g.a.]

> The library noted pp. 361-62.

Carter, Thomas. *See under* **Scholfield, Dr.**

453   **[Cartier, Jean Baptiste,** 1765-1841]
LIEPMANNSSOHN & DUFOUR, FIRM, PARIS   CAT. NO. 33
Catalogue des livres relatifs à la Musique de grandes partitions et d'une riche collection d'ancienne music de chambre, en partie de la plus grand rareté. Paris, 1870. ? p. 1141 lots.
                                                                                                        [g.a.]

> Not examined; cited by **Folter**, no. 43, **Bobillier**, and in **Rosenthal's** article on Liepmannssohn's catalogs in the *Festschrift Hans Schneider zum 60. Geburtstag*, 193-216. Munich: Verlag Ernst Vögel, [1981].
>
> *See* two other catalogs *under* **Picquot**. **Folter**, nos. 44-46, puts all three under Cartier!

454   **Cartwright, S.**
PUTTICK & SIMPSON, AUCTIONEER, LONDON
A Collection of Musical Works, Including the Library of the Late . . . Operas and Oratorios . . . Scarce Early Editions . . . Theoretical and Practical Works . . . Sold . . . February 24. . . . London, 1892. 351 lots.   [Not GB-Lbl; GB-Cu]

455   **Caruso, Enrico,** 1873-1921
AMERICAN ART GALLERIES, NEW YORK
The Enrico Caruso Collection of Books. On Exhibition from February 28, 1923, Until Day of Sale. New York, 1923. [40] p. Music, lots 1138-350.   [US-NYgr]

> Not examined; cited from Ganley catalog no. 20, 1955. **Folter**, no. 47, says published by American Art Association.

456   **Carvalhaes, Manoel Pereira Peixoto d'Almeida,** 1856-1922
LIVRARIA SÁ DA COSTA, AUCTIONEER, LISBON
Catalogo da importante biblioteca que pertenceu so falecido escritor e musicógrafo erudito e bibliófilo illustre . . . organisado por Augusta Sá da Costa, que será vendida em leilão so a direccào da Livraria Sá da Costa no dia 4 do próximo mès de Junho e dias seguintes [1928]. . . . Lisboa: Livraria Sá da Costa, 1928. 311 p.   [Cat. US-NYp, -CHua]

> Not examined; **Albrecht** says a collection of more than 21,000 librettos of operas, oratorios, and cantatas, purchased by the Italian government, now in I-Rsc.

457   **Carvalho Monteiro, Antonio Augusto de**

The collection is described by Lambertini in his *La bibliofilia* 21 (1919): 22 and was said to contain theoretical works of 15-16th centuries. **Albrecht** could not trace.

458   **Cary, Mary Flagler,** 1901-67

PIERPONT MORGAN LIBRARY, NEW YORK

The Mary Flagler Cary Music Collection; Printed Books and Music, Manuscripts, Autograph Letters, Documents, Portraits. [Comp. by O. E. Albrecht, H. Cahoon, and D. Ewing.] New York, [1970]. xii, 108 p., xlix plates.   [g.a.]

459   _____

LITERATURE

Albrecht, Otto E. "Musical Treasures in the Morgan Library." *Notes* 28 (1972): 643-51.   [g.a.]

460   _____

Burrows, Donald. "The Autographs and Early Copies of 'Messiah': Some Further Thoughts." *ML* 66 (1985): 201-19.

The so-called "Goldschmidt Messiah" Ms. was among these now at US-NYpm. It was lot 108 in Puttick's sale 4 May 1850.

→ *See also* an article by Baker *under* **Koch, Fred R.**

461   **Castell, William**

PUTTICK & SIMPSON, AUCTIONEER, LONDON

Large Collection of Ancient and Modern Music, Including the Library of the Late . . . with Others Comprising String and Wind Solos, Duets, Operas, Oratorios . . . Manuscript Orchestral Sets . . . Treatises, Sheet Music, &cc. . . . Sold . . . May 10. . . . London, 1889. 374 lots.

[Not GB-Lbl; GB-Cu]

462   **Castell, William; Mr. Earle (of Tiverton)**

PUTTICK & SIMPSON, AUCTIONEER, LONDON

Extensive Collection of Musical Property . . . Pianofortes [etc., Property of Tiverton]. *The Collection of Musical Portraits in Oil, etc., of the Late Castell . . . Sold . . . May 21 . . .* London, 1889. 298 lots.   [Not GB-Lbl; GB-Cu]

463   **Castellane, Cordelia (Greffulhe), Comtesse de,** 1796-1847

Catalogue des principaux livres et music (partitions), composant la bibliothèque de feue Mme la comtesse de Castellane, dont la vente aura lieu . . . le lundi 2 août, et les trois jours suivants . . . par le ministère de Me Grandidier. . . . Paris: Chimont, 1847. 35 p.   [US-NYp]

Not examined.

464   **Catelani, Angelo,** 1811-66

Cataloghi della musica di composizione e proprietà del M.° Angelo Catalani, preceduti dalle sue Memorie autobiografiche. Luigi Francesco Valdrighi, *Musurgiana,* ser. 2, no. 1. Modena: Societa tipografica, 1893. viii, 134 p. Music, pp. 85-124.   [US-NYp, -Wc]

Folter, no. 48. **Bobillier.**

465 **Cecil, Robert, 1st Earl of Salisbury,** 1563-1612
Hulse, Lynn. "The Musical Patronage of . . . ." *Journal of the RMA* 116 (1991): 24-40.

> The article notes a catalog of the library compiled 26 January 1614/15: "Salisbury MSS bills 14/1. and box 'Library catalogue' (two copies, ff. 26ᵛ and 27ᵛ)," p. 29.

466 **Cernkovic, Rudolph**
"The Museum That Music Built." *Pittsburgh Press,* Roto section, 15 June 1975.   [US-Pct]

467 **Cerutti, Signor; T. Pymer; Clayton Pymer; Joseph Gwilt,** 1784-1863; **Mr. Damson, a Musicseller**
Puttick & Simpson, auctioneer, London   Cat. no. 379
Catalogue of a . . . Collection of Music from Several Private Collections, Including Those of the Late Signor Cerutti [et al.]. . . . Also Numerous and Important Musical Instruments . . . Sold . . . July 19, 1864, and Two Following Days. [London, 1854.] 39 p. 1113 lots. Music, lots 1-891.   [GN-Lbl and US-NYp (Drexel 850)]

468 **Cesari, Gaetano,** 1870-1934
Monterosso, Raffaelo. "Guida all biblioteca di G. Cesari, musicologo cremonense." *Annali dell Biblioteca governativa* 1 (1948): 35-47.

> Not examined. Bequeathed to I-CR, according to **Benton 3**:171-72, no. 103.

469 **Chabrier, Emmanuel,** 1841-94
Durand-Ruel, M. (Expert); (C.P.) [= Chevallier]. *Catalogue de tableaux, pastels, aquarelles* [etc.] *. . . vente . . . 26 mars 1896. . . .* Paris, 1896. 24 p. 38 lots.   [g.a.]

> No music. All art, including Monet and Manet. **Lugt**, no. 54240.

470 **Challoner, Neville Butler,** b. 1784
Puttick & Simpson, auctioneer, London   Cat. no. 20
Collection of Music . . . Preceptive and Other Works for the Harp and Pianoforte . . . To Be Sold . . . April 1847 . . . London, 1847. 236 lots.   [GB-Lbl]

> Above lot no. 1 is printed "Monday, March 29th, 1847"! *See* **Coover 2**.

> → *See also* under **Ganz, L.** (sale of August 1849)

471 **Champagne, Claude,** 1891-1965
Duchow, Marvin. "A Selective List of Correspondents from the Personal Documents of Claude Champagne." *CAUSM/ACEUM Journal* 2 (fall 1972): 67-82; 3 (fall 1973): 71-79.   [g.a.]

> Now in the National Library in Ottawa.

Champfleury, pseudo. *See under* **Fleury, Jules,** 1821-99

Chandos, Duke of. *See* **Brydges, James, 1st Duke of Chandos,** 1674-1744

Chapman, Mrs. R. W. *See under* **Gresnirere**

472   Chappell, William, 1809-88

Bernard Quaritch, firm, London

The Miscellaneous and the Musical Library . . . To Be Sold by B. Quaritch. London: G. Norman and Son, 1887. 128 p. Music, lots 143-535.   [Also US-NYp]

> A bit confusing. There seem to have been two issues of this catalog with the same title but different pagination. This issue is **Folter**, no. 49, copy at US-NYp (*MCP). Quaritch's catalog no. 86 cites a "2d issue," same date containing 112p., 557 lots, and is **Folter**, no. 50.

473   Charles, Louis de Bourbon, Duke of Parma, 1799-1883

Alès, Anatole. *Bibliothèque liturgique: Descriptions des livres liturgies imprimés au XVe et XVIe siècles, faisant partie de la bibliothèque de S. A. R. Mgr. Charles-Louis de Bourbon (Comte de Villafranca).* Paris: Hennuyer, 1878. vi, 558 p.

—————————. Supplement, ibid., 1884. viii, 42, [4] p.

[US-Ic, -NH, -PHU, -Wc, GB-Lbl (Hirsch no. 428)]

Albrecht: inherited by his grandson, Robert de Bourbon.

474   —————————.

Literature

Galbiati, G. "La biblioteca liturgia dei Duchi di Parma all' Ambrosiana." *La bibliofilia* 37 (1935).

[g.a.]

> Not examined.

475   Charles XIII, King of Sweden and Norway, 1748-1818

Literature

Mörner, C. G. Stellan. "Carl XIII's notsamling." *STMf* 31 (1949): 182-200.   [g.a.]

476   Châteaugiron, René Charles Hippolyte Le Prestre, Marquis de, 1776?-1848

P. Jannet, auctioneer, Paris   Cat. no. 2596?

Catalogue de livres, musique, etc., provenant de la bibliothèque de feu M. le marquis H. de Châteaugiron dont la vente aura lieu les . . . 19 et . . . 20 décembre 1849. . . . Paris: P. Jannet, 1849. 25 p. 227 lots.   [US-Wc, -NYgr]

Blogie.

477   Chichester, J. H. R.; Richard Randell

Puttick & Simpson, auctioneer, London   Cat. no. 753

Catalogue of the Musical Library of J. H. R. Chichester, Esq., and . . . Mr. R. Randell (Pupil of Handel) . . . Including . . . Musical Instruments . . . Will Be Sold . . . March 4, 1863, and the Following Day. . . . [London, 1863.]   [GB-Lbl and US-NYp]

478   Chigi Family

> Frati says the library passed through the following family hands: Fabio, 1599-1667 (Pope Alessandro VII); Flavio snr., 17th century; Flavio jnr. (Chigi-zondadari), 1714-?

479 _____.

ROME, BIBLIOTECA CHIGIANA
*Catalogo della Biblioteca a Chigiana giusta i cognomi degli autori ed i titoli degli anonimi
. . . disposto salto gli auspicy . . . Flavio Chigi. . . .* Roma: F. Bizzarrini Komarek, 1764. xi, 637 p.
[US-Ic, -NYcu, -Cn]

480 _____.

"Indice dei libri stampati e manoscritti che sono nella libreria de' nobili signori Marchesi Flavio
e Angelo Chigi (Zondadari) compilato nell'anno 1795. Nota estratta. . . ." Reprinted by Raeli in
Rivista musicale italiana 26 (1919): 132-39.   [g.a.]

     This group of materials donated to Biblioteca Civica, Siena, 1847.

481 _____.

     Baronci, G. "Catalogo generale dei manoscritti in musica esistenti nella biblioteca Chigiana."

         A 1930 manuscript, Bibl. Vat., Sala di Consultazione dei Mss., Cat. 191,
         according to the following article.

482 _____.

     Lincoln, Harry B. "I manoscritti chigiana di musica organo cembalistica delle biblioteca
Apostolica Vaticana." *L'organo* 5 (1967): 63-82.   [g.a.]

         Inventories Mss. Q.IV.24-29 and Q.VIII.205-6. Bought by the government;
         given to the Vatican in 1923.

483 _____.

     LITERATURE
Lefevre, Renato. "Il principe Agostino Chigi e la sua libraria di campagna." In *Ariccia: Fine sec.
XVII*. Selci-Lama: Pliniana, 1990. 115 p.

         Acquired by Commune di Ariccia (Rome) in 1988 with the Chigi Palace
         (I-Rvat). Ca. 400 vols. with 700 works, including 400 theater librettos, 230
         operas. Cited from *RILM* 25/122 (1991).

484 **Chimay, Thérèse Cabarus, Countess de Caraman and Princesse de** (1775-1835)
SOTHEBY & CO., AUCTIONEER, LONDON
*Catalogue of Printed & Manuscript Music, Autograph Letters of Musicians, & Books on Music
& the Theatre, Comprising the Property of Madame la Princesse . . . R. F. Wolfe, Esq., . . . C. W.
Binns, Esq., . . . P. Bull, Esq., . . . and Other Properties. Day of Sale: Mon. 14th June, 1976.* [g.a.]
     Not examined.

485 **Chippindale, Edward**
PUTTICK & SIMPSON, AUCTIONEER, LONDON
*Catalogue of the Select and Valuable Musical Library of the Late. . . . Folio Editions of
Operas and Oratorios . . . Some Interesting Old Manuscripts . . . Musical Instruments . . . Sold
. . . July 26, and Following Day, 1875.* [London, 1875.] 34 p. 693 lots. Music, lots 1-603.
[GB-Lbl and US-NYp]

486 **Chiti, Girolamo,** 1681-1759 [**Albrecht** says 1679]
     He gave his collection to Cardinal Corsini. *See under* Corsini Collection
     (**573**).

487   Choral Harmonists Society
PUTTICK & SIMPSON, AUCTIONEER, LONDON   CAT. NO. 932
Catalogue of a Large and Interesting Collection of Music of Varied Character . . . the Musical Library of the "Choral Harmonists" . . . and Remaining Stock of Moore's Musical Works . . . Musical Instruments . . . Sold . . . June 22, 1866, and Following Day. [London, 1866.] 32 p. 954 lots. Music, lots 1-864.   [GB-Lbl]

488   Chorley, Henry Fothergill, 1808-72
PUTTICK & SIMPSON, AUCTIONEER, LONDON   CAT. NO. 1327
Catalogue of Valuable Books, Rare French and English Poetry . . . Illuminated Missals and Books of Hours . . . Works on the Theory and Composition of Music, Many Containing Manuscript Remarks by the Late . . . Sold . . . July 1 [-4], 1872. [London], 1872. 82 p. 1269 lots.
[GB-Lbl and US-Chua]

489   Choron, Alexandre Etienne, 1771-1834
For joint sale of 4 January 1836, *see under* Bêche (**194**).

490   _____.

LIEPMANNSSOHN & DUFOUR, FIRM, PARIS   CAT. NO. 29
Catalogue d'une belle collection de livres anciens & modernes relatifs à la musique et de partitions provenant en grande partie de la bibliothèque de A. Choron. Paris. Liepmannssohn et Dufour, 1869. 79 p. 1360 lots.   [NL-DHgm and US-NYp]
Scheurleer 2 1 (1923): 12 incorrectly dates 1889. **Folter**, no. 51.

491   Chotek, Count Jan Rudolph, 1749-1824
Catalogo. [A thematic catalog, in manuscript compiled about 1809. 151 p., some blank.]
Brook, nos. 990-93. **Albrecht**: his library at Kačina Castle, Kutna Hora, is no longer extant; only the catalog exists.

492   Christian, Jan
Kolbuszewska, Aniela. "Zbiory muzyczne ksiecia brzeskiego Jana Christiana." In *Tradycje ślaskiej kultury muzycznej*, 85-115. Wroclaw: Akademia Muzyczna, 1987.
Not examined; cited from *RILM*.

493   Christian Ludwig II, Herzog von Mecklenburg-Schwerin, 1683?-
LITERATURE
"Die Musiksammlung besitzt ausser den schon vermekten Kompositionen." In Clemens Meyer, *Geschichte der Mecklenburg-Schwerin Hofkapelle*, 81-84. Schwerin i. M., 1913.

494   Christie-Miller, Sydney Richardson, 1874-1931
Alphabetical List of Black Letter Ballads & Broadsides, Known As the Heber Collection, in the Possession of . . . Britwell Bucks. London, 1872. 15 p.   [US-Wc]

495   _____.

Collmann, Herbert Leonard. *Ballads & Broadsides, Chiefly of the Elizabethan Period and Printed in Black-Letter, Most of Which Were Formerly in the Heber Collection and Are Now in the Library at Britwell Court, Buckinghamshire. . . .* Oxford: University Press, 1912. xiii, 287 p.   [Film at US-Wc]

496 _____.

S<small>OTHEBY AND</small> C<small>O</small>., <small>AUCTIONEER</small>, L<small>ONDON</small>
Catalogue . . . of the Renowned Library Formerly at Britwell Court, Burnham Bucks . . . , the Property of . . . Which Will Be Sold by Auction by . . . 1916-17. [London, 1916-27.]   [US-NH]
> "Early English Music" was offered in the sale of 15 and 20 December 1919.
> 166 lots. See **497**.

497 _____.

S<small>OTHEBY</small>, W<small>ILKINSON</small> & H<small>ODGE</small>, <small>AUCTIONEER</small>, L<small>ONDON</small>
Catalogue of a Very Important, Interesting & Valuable Collection of Books of Airs, Ballads, Catches, Madrigals, Songs & Other Music from the Renowned Library, Britwell Court, Burnham Bucks . . . Including Many of the Scarcest Song Books of the Elizabethan and Jacobean Periods . . . Sold . . . 15th of December 1919. [London, 1919.] 23 p. 166 lots.
> [US-NYp, -Wc and compiler (names and prices)]
> This is one of 21 sales of the properties which took place from 1916 to 1927.

498 _____.

The Britwell Handlist: Short-title Catalogue of the Principal Volumes from the Time of Caxton to the Year 1800 Formerly in the Library of Britwell Court, Buckinghamshire. 2 vols. London: Quaritch, 1933. (xiv, 1067 p., [65] leaves of plates.)
> Compiled from the catalogs of sales between 1900 and 1927. Ca. 160 items
> in 1919 sale, especially English madrigals, acquired by US-SM.

Christopher, S. W.   *See under* **Vaughan, W. A.**

499   **Chrysander, Karl Franz Friedrich,** 1826-1901
Clausen, Hans Dieter. *Händels Direktionspartituren ("Handexemplare").* Hamburger Beiträge zur Musikwissenschaft, 7. Hamburg: Karle Dieter Wagner, 1972. 281 p.   [now at D-Hs]
> From Chrysander's *Nachlass* catalog, pp. 91-250.

500   **Cianchettini, Pio,** 1799-1851
S<small>OUTHGATE</small>, G<small>RIMSTON</small> & W<small>ELLS</small>, <small>AUCTIONEER</small>, L<small>ONDON</small>
Catalogue of a Very Extensive Collection of Original Italian Music (in Score) . . . Handel, Paer, Blasis, Rossini, Bianchi, Sacchini, Haydn [etc.] *Consisting of Arie, Duetti, Terzetti . . . Opere Serie e Buffe, Collected by Mr. . . . During a Four-Years Residence at Naples; Together with Copyrights of Several Pieces of Music, in MS., for the Pianoforte by Paul Wineburger of Hamburgh; and Pio Cianchettini . . . Sold . . . June 17th, 1833.* [London, 1833.] 15 p. 215 lots (many more items).   [GB-Lbl]
> "Miscellaneous MSS.," lots 130-59; "MSS. opere," lots 160-200.

501   **Cicogna, Emanuele Antonio,** 1759-1868
V<small>ENICE</small>, M<small>USEO</small> C<small>ORRER</small>
"Fondo primitivo Correr e provienze seguenti: Ospetale dell Pietà (desposita), lascito Emanuele Cicogna, lascito Gabriele Pantoni." In *Associazione dei musicologi italiani,* ser. VI, Puntata I: *Venezia, Museo Correr,* [67]-161. Parma: Freschig, 1913.   [g.a.]

502   _____.

LITERATURE

Fulin, R. "Saggio del catalogo dei codici de Emanuele Antonio Cicogna." *Archivio Veneto* 4 (?): 59-132, 337-98.   [NIC (not for loan or copy)]

     Not examined; cited from **Frati**.

503   **Cicogna, Giuseppe**

Catalogo della pubblicazione musicali di proprietà del conte Gius. Cicogna. . . . Milano: Galli, 1885. 37 p.

     Not examined; cited from **Pagliaini**.

504   **Cini, Giorgio (Fondazione), Venice**

LITERATURE

"Die grösste private Stiftung seit dem Nobel-Preis: Der italienische Mäzen Graf Cini fördert die schönen Künste." *Neue Zeitschrift für Musik* 118 (1957): 354-55.   [g.a.]

505   **Claesz, Cornelis**

Vanhulst, Henri. "La Musique dans le catalogue des livres françois de Cornelis Claesz (Amsterdam, 1609)." *Revue belge de musicologie* 44 (1990): 57-77.   [g.a.]

     "Annexe," a diplomatic reproduction of the original catalog, pp. 68-77.

506   _____.

LITERATURE

Schelvan, A. A. van. "Een catalogus van den amsterdamschen boekverkooper Cornelis Claesz." *Het Boek* 11 (1922): 330-31.

     Cited from Vanhulst (**505**).

507   **Clam-Gallas, Count Christian,** 1771-1839**; Countess Carolina**

Speer, ?. "Catalogo delle carte di musica appartementi al Sig. Conte Cristiano Clam e Gallas. . . . Da me per conservare Speer, Maestro di musica."

     Mss. compiled ca. 1810. **Brook**, no. 987. **Albrecht**: library formerly at Friedland, now at CS-Pnm, includes Beethoven's WoO 44.

508   **Clarence, O. B.**

IFAN KYRLE FLETCHER, FIRM, LONDON   CAT. NO. 190

The History of Entertainment. . . . Books, Drawings, Prints, Statuettes, Autograph Letters and Documents, from the Famous Collections of O. B. Clarence, M. Willson Disher, Richard Northcott and Harold Rubin, Offered for Sale. . . . London, [1959]. 58 p. 503 lots (illus.).

                        [GB-Lbl and US-BUu]

     "Opere" & "Ballet," lots 214-443.

509   **Clark, Richard,** 1780-1856

PUTTICK & SIMPSON, AUCTIONEER, LONDON   CAT. NO. 329

Catalogue of Several Important Musical Properties, Amongst Which Are I. The Copyright Works of the Late Thomas Moore in Original Mss. and Engraved Plates. II. The Very Interesting Literary and Musical Collections of Richard Clark . . . V. A Miscellaneous Collection of Musical Instruments . . . Sold . . . June 25 [27 and 28] *1853.* [London, 1853.] 42 p. 680 lots. Music, lots 1-615.   [GB-Lbl and US-NYp]

510 _____

PUTTICK & SIMPSON, AUCTIONEER, LONDON   CAT. NO. 431
A Catalogue of a Large and Valuable Collection of Music from Several Private Libraries . . .
Also the Engraved Plates and Copyrights of Several Valuable Modern Compositions . . .
Sold . . . November 16th, 1855, and Following Day. [London, 1855.] 615 lots. Music, lots
1-470.   [GB-Lbl]

511 _____

PUTTICK & SIMPSON, AUCTIONEER, LONDON   CAT. NO. 487
Catalogue of a . . . Collection of Music . . . from the Library of. . . . Some Instrumental and
Miscellaneous Music from the Library of a Late Distinguished Professor . . . Sold by Auction
. . . May 2, 1857. [London, 1857.] 20 p. 530 lots. Music, lots 1-409.   [GB-Lbl, -NYp (Drexel)]
→ *See also under* [**Taylor, Edward**]

512   Clarke, Herbert L.

LITERATURE
"Memorabilia from the Herbert L. Clarke Library, Department of Bands, University of Illinois."
International Trumpet Guild Newsletter 6, no. 2 (1980): 8-14.   [g.a.]

Clarke, Mary (Cowden) and **Charles (Cowden).**   *See under* **Novello, Vincent**

513   Clementi, Muzio, 1752-1832

MR. WATSON, AUCTIONEER, LONDON
A Catalogue of an Assemblage of Vocal and Instrumental Music, Including a Select Portion
of the Library of the Late Celebrated . . . [Including] *Valuable Manuscripts in Score and Parts,*
Treatises . . . Sold . . . December 19, 1832, and Following Days. [London, 1832.] 19 p. 416
lots. Music, manuscripts and musical instruments interspersed throughout.   [GB-Lbl]

Clerque de Wissocq de Sousberghe.   *See* **Sousberghe, Clerque de Wissocq, Vicomte de**

514   [Clive,   Miss]

PUTTICK & SIMPSON, AUCTIONEER, LONDON   CAT. NO. 384
Catalogue of a Small Musical Library and Several Valuable Musical Instruments . . . Sold
. . . September 13th, 1854. [London], 1854. 13 p. 326 lots. Music, lots 1-161.   [GB-Lbl]

515   Clive Family [Lord Robert Clive, 1725-74]

A. ROSENTHAL, FIRM, OXFORD   CAT. NO. 10
The Music Collection of Lord Clive of India . . . and His Family. Oxford: A. Rosenthal, 1948.
60 p. 186 lots.   [US-R]
> **King,** p. 17: the collection, remarkably, remained intact until this date.
> **Albrecht** says some 50 vols. went to US-BE.

Cockburn, D.   *See under* **Hodges, Edward**

516   Coe, Sadie Knowland

EVANSTON, ILL., PUBLIC LIBRARY
Catalogue of the Sadie Knowland Coe Music Collection and Other Musical Literature. . . .
Compiled by Gertrude L. Brown. . . . Evanston, Ill., 1916. 126 p.   [US-Cn, -Cj, -NYp]
> According to **Downs:** 1600 scores, 400 pieces of sheet music, 572 pianola
> rolls. **Folter,** no. 52.

517   Coers Frzn, F R
[Collection of songbooks, sold in Utrecht by ?, 25 November-2 December 1935. Catalog at NL-VBBA.]

518   Coggins, J. (late of Piccadilly), 1780-?
MR. WHEATLEY, AUCTIONEER, LONDON
A Collection of Books in History, Biography, Voyages and Travels. . . . A Small Collection of Books on Music, and the Copyrights and Copperplates of Several Popular Music Publications, the Property of . . . July 1st, 1831, and Four Following Days (Sunday Excepted). [London, 1831]. 39 p. 1179 lots. Music, lots 953-1070.   [GB-Lbl (names & prices)]

519   Cohen, Harriet
Foreman, Ronald Lewis Edmund. "A Catalogue of Autograph Manuscript Sources of Music by Sir Arnold Bax [in Her Bequest to the British Library]." *RMA Research Chronicle* 12 (1974): 91-105.   [g.a.]
> *RILM* locates and dates Mss. of 166 works, etc.

520   Cohn, Al, 1925-88
EAST STROUDSBERG UNIVERSITY, EAST STROUDSBERG, PENN.
Al Cohn Memorial Collection. Ed. Ralph Hughes. The Jazz Family, album 3. East Stroudsberg: University, [1995]. 63 p. (2-62, photos)

521   Cohn, Alexander Meyer, 1853-1904
CHISWICK PRESS
Catalogue of a Unique and Extremely Important Collection of Autograph Letters and Manuscripts of the World's Greatest Composers [A Collection Based upon the Purchase Made at the Dispersal of the Famous Meyer-Cohn Cabinet and the Collections of Duprey, Thayer, and Stargardt Have Also Contributed to It]. London: Chiswick Press, [n.d., 1905?]. Unpaged, [ca. 130 p.].   [GB-Lbl, US-Cn (priced)]
> Magnificent folio, letter press, with facsimiles. Us-Cn dates 1911. **Albrecht** says now at D-Bim.

522   _____
J. PEARSON & CO., FIRM, LONDON
A Unique and Extremely Important Collection of Autograph Letters and Manuscripts of the World's Greatest Composers. . . [cf. above citation!]. London, [n.d., between 1895-1910]. 33 p. 75 lots.   [US-Eu, -Wc, compiler]
> "This noble collection is principally based upon the famous Meyer-Cohn cabinet. The collections of Duprey, Bailly, Fuchs, Lonsdale, and Thayer have also contributed notably to it." Some of those items reappeared in a Puttick & Simpson sale, 29 November 1917. See lengthy annotation in **Coover 2**.

523   _____
J. A. STARGARDT, FIRM, BERLIN
Die Autographen-Sammlung . . . mit einem Vorwort von Erich Schmidt. 2 vols. Berlin: J. A. Stargardt, 1905/06. (316 p.) 3437 lots.   [US-NYp, -Bp, -NYcu, -NH, -CA, -R (priced)]
> "Musiker," 2:262-89 (lots 3009-227). "Schauspieler u. Sänger," pp. 289-99.

524 _____

LITERATURE

[Notes on the second sale of autographs sold by Stargardt.] *MT* (1906): 102. [g.a.]

525 Coirault, Patrice

LITERATURE

Wallon, Simone. "Le Fond Coirault de la Bibliothèque nationale." *Revue de musicologie* 49 (1963): 108-11. [g.a.]

526 Coke, Gerald, 1907-90

The Gerald Coke Handel Collection, 21st July to 27th July, 1985. [Exhibition, Jenkyn Place, Bentley, Hampshire. Lowestoft: Creasy Flood, 1985.] 63 p. [g.a.]

> Incorporates some of William Smith's Handel collection.

> → *See also under* **Smith, William C.**

527 _____

Music Manuscripts in Major Private Collections: The Gerald Coke Handel Collection - A Listing and Guide to Parts One, Two and Three of the Harvester Microfilm Collection. Unpublished Music Manuscripts from the Great English Collections, 8. [Brighton: Harvester Microfilm, 1988.] Index, 50 p. [g.a.]

528 _____

LITERATURE

"Collecting Handel [ed. by Donald Burrows from a typescript prepared by Gerald Coke in 1988]." In *Handel Collections and Their History,* ed. Terence Best, 1-9. Oxford: Clarendon Press, 1993. [g.a.]

> → *See also under* **Smith, William C.**

529 Coke, Sir Thomas, Vice Chamberlain, 1674-1727

PUTTICK & SIMPSON, AUCTIONEER, LONDON   CAT. NO. 1617

Library of the Classical Harmonists' Society [lots 256-86] . . . *Theoretical and Practical Treatises . . . Vice Chamberlain Coke's Unique and Remarkable Collection of Original Documents About the Opera in England, 1706-15 . . . with Rare Autograph Letters of Numerous Operatic Celebrities . . . Sold . . . August 21 and Following Day, 1876.* 541 lots. [GB-Lbl]

> Lengthy annotation in **Coover 2**. The provenance of Coke's papers is described by Judith Milhouse and Robert D. Hume in their important book *Vice Chamberlain Coke's Theatrical Papers, 1706-15, Edited from Manuscripts in the Harvard Theatre Collection and Elsewhere*, pp. xxix-xxxix. Carbondale: Southern Illinois University Press, 1982. [g.a.]

530 Colard, Hector

GALERIES GEORGES GIROUX, AUCTIONEER, BRUSSELS

Catalogue de la bibliothèque de feu Hector Colard. 1ʳᵉ partie: musicologie & partitions modernes . . . vendue . . . 5 mai et jours suivants [1924]. Bruxelles: Galeries Georges Giroux, 1924. 144 p. 802, 447 lots. [GB-Lbl (Hirsch), US-NYgr, -BE, -NH, -WC, -NYp]

> The contents are described in some detail in **Folter**, no. 53. An announced second sale, "Le partitions anciennes seront vendues en octobre 1924," was apparently never held.

531   Cole, Mrs. Helen; Charles Ramsden; N. Hudson; Mrs. F. Highfield Jones
SOTHEBY & CO., AUCTIONEER, LONDON
Catalogue of Valuable Printed Books, Fine Bindings, Autograph Letters and Historical Documents . . . [Which] *Include Letters or Holograph Music of Berlioz, Liszt, Mendelssohn, Richard Strauss and Elgar . . . Sold . . . November 22nd, 1954.* [London], 1954. 36 p. 257 lots.
[Film at CRL]

> Musicians' ALS or Mss., "Various Properties," lots 205-22. Owners not specified.

532   Cole, Jack
SOTHEBY PARKE BERNET & CO., AUCTIONEER, NEW YORK
Catalogue of the Jack Cole Collection of Books and Pictures on the Dance. Part 1: *The Property of John David Gray . . . Sold . . . 16th* [and] *17th July 1979.* New York, 1979. 125 p. 542 lots. Much music throughout.   [US-BUu]

533   _____

LITERATURE
King, A. Hyatt. "In the Sale Room." *MT,* no. 1639 (1979): 741.   [g.a.]

534   Colin, Eugène, 1879-1965
LITERATURE
Linden, Albert van der. "Eugène Colin et la musicologie." In *Volkskunde Huldeschrift Paul Collaer* 77, nos. 3-4 (1976): 246-56.   [g.a.]

> *RILM*: discusses the collection now in B-Bc.

535   Colizzi, J   H   [pour A]; Dr. ? K[auclitz]
[Sale of 14 and 28 November 1808 at La Haye by Scheurleer noted in **Lugt**, no. 7479.] 2, 22 p. 836 lots, 67 of them music.
> **Lugt** says at NL-RKDH only, but it is lost.

536   Collalto Family (Count Thomas Viciguerra Collalto, 1741-69)
Straková, Theodora. "Hudba u brtnických Collaltu v 17. a 18. století" [Music in Pirnitz, the residence of the family]. 2 vols. Diss., Brno, 1967.
> Not examined; cited from *RILM* 68:1999, and **Albrecht**.

537   Collegium Musicum "Audi et Tace," Leeuwarden
The Important Collection of 18th Century Orchestral Material from the Archive of. . . . [Utrecht, Joachimsthal, n.d.] [21] p.   [NL-DHgm only]

> All verso pages are illus., facs. Noted, a manuscript catalog made for the Collegium's leader, Jean des Comunes (1760-1843) in the 1790s.

538   Colles, Henry Cope, 1879-1943
HODGSON & CO., AUCTIONEER, LONDON
A Catalogue of the Valuable Music Library of the Late . . . with Other Properties . . . Sold . . . November 25th, 1943, and Following Day. London, 1943. 41 p. 641 lots.
[US-NYgr, GB-Lbl (Hirsch no. 429, priced)]
> Colles's properties, lots 97-226 (many more items).

539   **Colloredo Family**

[A manuscript thematic catalog at CS-Bm that includes incipits for the "Leichtensteinsche Sammlung," the "Colloredsche Sammlung," etc. The collections are still at CS-KRa, the catalog at CS-Bm.]

     Brook, no. 699, and **Albrecht**.

540   **Colón, Fernando,** 1488-1539

Huntington, Archer M. *Catalogue of the Library of Ferdinand Columbus, Reproduced in Facsimile from the Unique Manuscript in the Columbus Library of Seville.* New York: [Edward Bierstadt], 1950. [260] p.   [US-Npv, -CLp, -CLwr]

     Includes music, *inter alia.* **Albrecht**: surviving portion of the collection now at E-Sco.

541   _____

SEVILLE, BIBLIOTECA COLUMBINA

La Bibliothèque française de Fernand Colomb [par Jean Babelon].   Revue des bibliothèques, suppl. 10. Paris: E. Champion, 1913. xliv, 341 p.

     Noted by **Frati,** p. 175.

542   _____

Plamenac, Dragan. "Excerpts Columbiniana: Items of Musical Interest in Fernando Colon's 'Registrum'." In *Miscelánea en homenaje a Mons. H. Angles,* 2:663-87. Barcelona, 1958-61.

         [g.a.]

543   _____

LITERATURE

Chapman, Catherine Weeks. "Printed Collections of Polyphonic Music Owned by Ferdinand Columbus." *JAMS* 21 (1968): 34-84.   [g.a.]

544   **Comarque, Rev. David**

THOMAS OSBORNE, AUCTIONEER, LONDON

A Catalogue of Some Tracts and Pamphlets Collected by the Late Earl of Oxford . . . Number IV . . . to Which Is Added the Entire Collection of Musick of the Reverend Mr. Comerque, of Putney. . . . Printed for T. Osborne in Grays-Inn, Where the Libraries of the Late Mr. Comerque . . . and Mr. Johnson, &c Is Now Selling [1 October 1747] *and Will Continue Till Lady Day Next. . . .* London, 1747. 62 p. 3188, 60 lots. Comarque's, lots 1-60, ca. 80 music lots indexed by **Coral,** pp. 185-66, discussed, pp. 66-67.   [GB-Lbl, US-NYgr, -CA]

545   **Comarque, Rev. David; Rev. Mr. Johnson; Rev. Mr. Hodgson; Charles Leadbetter**

THOMAS OSBORNE, AUCTIONEER, LONDON

A Catalogue of the Libraries of. . . . The Whole Consisting of Near Thirty Thousand Volumes, Relating to the History, Antiquities, and Constitution of All the State in Europe . . . the 14th of December, and Will Continue Selling Till Lady-Day. . . . [London, T. Osborne, 1747.] 16 music lots indexed by **Coral,** p. 186; discussed, pp. 66-67.   [GB-Olc, US-Wc]

546   **Commer, Franz,** 1813-87

LEO LIEPMANNSSOHN, FIRM, BERLIN   ANT.-VERZ. NO. 65

Katalog 65, enthaltend die Musik- und hymnologische Bibliothek des verstorbenen Professor Franz Commer. Berlin, 1888. 46 p. 680 lots.   [GB-Lbl, NL-VBBA, US-Wc]

     Folter, no. 54, and **Scheurleer** 1 (1923): 12. **Albrecht**: now at D-Bds.

547 _____

LEO LIEPMANNSSOHN, FIRM, BERLIN   ANT.-VERZ. NO. 66
Katalog 66. Musikalische Literatur und Musikalien. Letzte Erwerbungen sowie Nachträge zur Commer'schen Bibliothek. Berlin, 1888. 34 p. 555 items.   [GB-Lbl, NL-VBBA, US-Wc]

> **Folter**, no. 55.

> → *See also* two Liepmannssohn sales, nos. 75 and 76 in 1889, *under* **Grell, Edward A.**, which contained Commer properties.

548   **[Compton, ? , Marquess of Northampton; Hannah Gluck George Rolleston]**
CHRISTIE, MANSON & WOODS, AUCTIONEER, LONDON
Important Literary and Musical Manuscripts and Autograph Letters . . . Sold . . . July 5, 1878. [London], 1978. 57 p. 104 lots.   [US-NYgr]

> A very good collection.

549   **Compton, Henry,** d. 1824?
LEIGH AND SOTHEBY, AUCTIONEER, LONDON
A Catalogue of the Entire Library of the Late . . . of St. James's Palace. Likewise His Valuable Collection of Music . . . Sold . . . May 8, 1811 . . . and Five Following Days. [London, 1811.] 41 p. 1480 lots. Music, lots 948-86, 1195-234, 1445-80.   [GB-Lbl, compiler]

Condell, [**Henry**]. *See under* **Sharpe** (sale of 30 March 1825)

550   **Conrad, Johann Gottlieb**
LITERATURE
Werner, Anne. "Ein sächsischer Landschulmeister . . . und sein Musikbücherei." In *Festschrift Arnold Schering*, 250-58. Berlin, 1937.   [g.a.]

551   **Constapel, H.**
Catalogue des livres nouveaux et autres qu'on trouve chez H. Constapel, libraire à la Haye, 1760. 16 leaves.

> Noted in **Scheurleer** 1 (1923): 12. Private collection, publisher's, or vendor's? Not examined.

552 _____

POOTEN, FIRM, THE HAGUE
Catalogue général de pièces de théâtre detachées imprimés, ou que l'on trouve en nombre chez . . . , libraire, à Côte du Parlement d'Angleterre, dans le Pooten à la Haye, 1771. 16 leaves. small 8°.

> Noted in **Scheurleer** 1 (1923): 12. As above, a private collection, publisher's, or vendor's? Not examined.

553 _____

Catalogue de pièces de théâtre, qu'on peut avoir séparément chez H. Constapel, libraire à la Haye. [La Haye, 1759]. ? leaves. small 8°.

> Noted in **Scheurleer** 1 (1923): 12. Not examined.

554   Contarini, Marco, 1631-89

Weil, Taddeo. *I codici musicali Contariniani . . . nella Biblioteca di San Marco in Venezia.* Venezia: Ongania, 1888. xxx, 121 p. 956 Mss., 4673 printed scores.   [g.a.]

> **Albrecht**: rich in 17th-century Venetian opera scores (autographs and copies) willed by descendent to I-Vnm in 1839. Reprint, Biblioteca musica Bononiensis, ser. 1, no. 4 (Bologna: Forni, 1969).

555   Conti Castelli, Sebastiano, Marchese

Parisini, Federico. [A note about his collection in the preface to *Catalogo* of the Bologna, Liceo Musicale, compiled by Gaetano Gaspari . . . , 1 (Bologna, 1890): xxxii-xxx.]   [g.a.]

> Reprint of Gaspari catalog (Bologna: Forni, 1961).

556   Contin di Castelseprio

Venice, Conservatorio di Musica Benedetto Marcello

Il Fondo Contin di Castelseprio del Conservatorio . . . , [by] Gigliola Bianchini. [In preparation.]

> Noted in Bianchini and Manfredi's catalog of the Fondo Pascalato, n. 32 (Firenze: Olschki, 1992).

557   Cooke, Benjamin, 1734-93?

Mr. Fletcher, auctioneer, London

Catalogue of the Extensive, Rare and Valuable Musical Library of the Late . . . Numerous Full Scores . . . Handel's Works . . . Dr. Cooke's Manuscript Works . . . Sold August 5th, and . . . 6th, 1845. . . . [London, 1845.] 18 p. 450 lots. Music, lots 1-417, includes a Bull Ms.

                    [GB-Ob, US-NYp (Drexel)]

558   Cooke, Mathew; B. Jacobs

> **King**, p. 92, notes brief articles in the *Harmonicon* for 1830, pp. 136 and 179, about this sale: The musical libraries "of Mr. Jacob and his master Mathew Cooke are, by a curious coincidence, united in one sale. . . ."

559   _____

Mr. W. P. Musgrave, auctioneer, London

Catalogue of the Very Select and Valuable Musical Library of Those Eminent Professors (both deceased) . . . Vocal and Instrumental Works . . . Treatises . . . Sold 2nd of March, 1830 and Following Days. [London, 1830.] 27 p. 331 lots. Music, lots 10283.

                    [GB-Lbl, US-NYp (Gauntlett's copy priced), compiler]

Cooke, Robert, 1768-1814.   *See* **Bartleman** (sale of 1816)

Cooke, T.   *See under* **Robinson, James** (sale of 11 November 1861)

560   Cooper, A. Davis

Puttick & Simpson, auctioneer, London

Catalogue of Musical Instruments . . . [etc.] *Also the Library of Music Belonging to the Late . . . Including a Small Collection of Rare Manuscripts . . . Sold . . . June 25th* [-26th] *1895.* [London, 1895.] 24 p. 456 lots. Music, lots 212-456. Mss., lots 303-53 (more items). [GB-Lbl]

561   Cooper, Anthony Ashley, 4th Earl of Shaftesbury, 1711-71
[Ms. inventory of Handel collection made in 1861 now at GB-Lbl, Add. Ms. 29864, ff. 98-102.]
Noted by Winton Dean in *Handel Celebration*, ed. Jacob Simon, 22-24. London: National
Portrait Gallery, 1985.   [g.a.]

> Collection is now at GB-Lbl. There is another Ms. catalog of Shaftesbury's
> library, dated 1709, in London, Public Record Office, Ms. 30/24/23.

562   _____

Hicks, Anthony. "The Shaftesbury Collection." In *Handel Collections and Their History*, ed.
Terence Best, 86-107. Oxford: Clarendon Press, 1993.   [g.a.]

> "Appendix 1: Catalogue of Handel scores at St. Giles's house (1761)," pp.
> 98-102 (19th-century copies of this now at GB-Lbl and GB-Lcm). "Appendix
> 2: The Shaftesbury Handel Collection," pp. 102-07. In 1987, most of the
> manuscript volumes were acquired by Gerald Coke (**527**).

563   Cooper, Gerald Melbourne, 1892-1947; **Ernest Augustus Kellner;** [**John**] **Fawcett**
Mr. Fletcher, auctioneer, London
*Catalogue of the Extensive and Valuable Musical Collections of the Late Mr. . . . , Organist of
St. Paul's Cathedral, and of Her Majesty's Chapel Royal; Also of Mr. . . . Kellner, Deceased,
Teacher of Music to His Late Majesty George IV; and of the Late Mr. Fawcett, Formerly of the
Theatre Royal, Covent Garden, Comprising a Most Extensive Assortment of Classical Music,
Sacred and Secular; Valuable Scores, Printed and Manuscript of the Works of the Great
Masters; Early Treatises . . . Together with . . . the Well-Known Cremona Violins of the Late
Richard Chase Sidney . . . Sold December 9th, 1844, and Three Following Days.* [London,
1844.] 31 p. 863 lots. Music, lots 1-590.   [GB-Ob]

> First days unexceptional; 4th day, valuable. **King** notes another Kellner
> sale, 9 December 1844. Some of Cooper's library was given to E. J. Dent, by
> him to GB-Lwcm, 1947.

564   _____

Dean, Winton. "The Malmesbury Collection." In *Handel Collection and Their History*, ed.
Terence Best, 29-38. Oxford: Clarendon Press, 1993.   [g.a.]
> Contents: pp. 37-38.

565   Cooper, Joseph Thomas, 1819-79
Puttick & Simpson, auctioneer, London   Cat. no. 1913
*Catalogue of the Valuable Musical Library of the Late . . . Classical Works for the Pianoforte
. . . Anthems and Services . . . Works on Music History and Theory . . . Sold April 19, 1880.*
London, 1880. 18 p. 361 lots.   [GB-Lbl]

566   Coover, James B., b. 1925
Coover, James B. *Antiquarian Catalogues of Musical Interest.* Compiled by. . . . London and
New York: Mansell, 1988. 371 p.   [g.a.]

> Incorporates citations to some 6000 antiquarian catalogs, most of which
> were then in the compiler's collection but are now at US-BUu.

567   Corbett, William, d. 1748
> [**King**, p. 15, says collection sold about 1750 but "no sales catalogue has
> come to light."] See also Hawkins, *History*, 283.

568   **Corfe, Joseph,** 1740-1820

> **King**, p. 134, notes a sale of his collection by an unknown dealer in 1826. Catalog is lot 287 in the Finch sale of 1873 (Hirsch no.492 (7)), but not otherwise located. Six volumes of Italian vocal music in manuscript appeared in the 12 April 1848 sale of Hatchett's library (**1193**).

569   **Cornelius, Peter,** 1824-74

LITERATURE

Stephenson, G. "Zeugnisse . . . der Peter Cornelius Nachlass der Stadtbibliothek Mainz." *Mainzer Zeitschrift* 59 (1964).

> Not examined; cited from **Benton 2**:85, no. 177. Bequeathed to D-MZs.

570   **Cornewall Family (Moscas Court, Hampshire)**

> [**King**, p. 17, says a manuscript catalog of the collection now owned by Albi Rosenthal contains about 2000 items. A special section dated 1795 lists properties of a Miss Cornewall.]

571   **Coronini von Cromberg, Sophie (Fagan), Gräfin,** 1792-1857

Marinis, Tammaro de. . . . *I libri di musica della contessa Sofia Coronini Fagan, salvati a Gorizia nel settembre 1916.* Milano: tipi di Bertieri e Vanzetti, 1919. xv, 59p.

> [US-Cn, -NYp, -WC]

572   **Corsby, George (of Princes St.)**

PUTTICK & SIMPSON, AUCTIONEER, LONDON   CAT. NO. 1255

Catalogue of a Collection of Miscellaneous Music . . . Scores . . . Scarce Music Treatises . . . Also Numerous and Valuable Musical Instruments . . . , Including a Portion of the Stock of Mr. G. Corsby . . . Sold June 26th, and Following Day. [London, 1871.] 21 p. 637 lots. Music, lots 1-441.   [GB-Lbl]

573   **Corsini Collection**

> Collection formed by Girolamo Chiti, given to Neri Corsini, 1624-79, expanded by Lorenzo, 1652-1740 (Pope Clement XII, by Neri Maria, Cardinal, 1685-1770), given to the R. Accademia dei Lincei, now Accademia nazionale dei Lincei e Corsiniana (I-Rli) by Corsini in 1883.

574   ————

ROME, SAN GIOVANNI IN LATERANO, ARCHIVIO MUSICAL LATERANENSE
"Inventario generale di tutti i libri e carte di musica [by F. Mattei and Girolamo Chiti], 1748."

> Ms. in the Vatican, no. AAA15. Cited from **Benton** and **Gmeinwieser**.

575   ————

ROME, SAN GIOVANNI IN LATERANO, ARCHIVIO MUSICAL LATERANENSE
"Inventario di tutte le opere musicali raccolta di G. Chiti, 1751."

> Ms., in Biblioteca Corsiniana, Rome, Musica 1:1. Cited from **Benton**.

576   ————

Mattei, Francesco, and Girolamo Chiti. "Catalogo, 1754."

> Ms., Vatican no. AAA12a and 12b. Cited from **Benton** and **Gmeinwieser**.

577 _____

> Chiti, Girolamo. [another list, 1756]
>> Biblioteca Corsiniana Ms. C8. Cited from **Benton**.

578 _____

> Querci, G. "Lettera al sig. dott. Giovanni Lami contenente la descrizione della Biblioteca del Sig. Principe Corsini, fatta già pubblica . . . ." *Novelle letterarie pubblicate in Firenze l'anno 1755*, 16, no. 10 (7 marzo); no. 11 (14 marzo); no. 12 (21 marzo).
>> Not examined; cited from **Frati**.

579 _____

> Chiti, Girolamo. "Inventario di tutte le materie musicali raccolte in passa(ti) cinquantanni Comprate cambiate, o ri-cercate del dal R^do sig. D. Goralamo Chiti Primo Cappel/lano Custode dell'Insigne Capella Corsini posta . . . à primiera fondatione dell'anno 1735 al Presente 1757. . . ." In Vito Raeli, "La Collezione Corsini . . . ," *RMI* 25 (1918): 345-76; 26 (1919): 112-39; 27 (1920): 60-84.   [g.a.]
>> Discusses and reprints parts of various inventories and catalogs, e.g., that of 1757.

580 _____

> Mattei, Lorenzo, and Giuseppe Lorenzini. "Inventario musicale della Sacrosancta Archibasilica Lateranense Scanzia II."
>> Ms. 1776, located ? Not examined; noted by Gmeinwieser (**584**).

581 _____

> Bertini, Argia. *Biblioteca Corsiniana e dell' Accademia dei Lincei, Fondo Chiti e Corsiniana. Catalogo*. Bibliotheca musicae, 2. Milano: Istituto Ed. Italiano, 1964. 109 p.   [g.a.]

582 _____

LITERATURE
> Raeli, Vito. "La biblioteca Corsini dei Lincei e l'annessavi collezione musicale." *Accademie e biblioteche d'Italia* 3 (1930): 427-44.   [g.a.]
>> Not examined; cited in **Bertini**, *Catalogo dei fondi musicale* (1964), p. 9.

583 _____

> Smeriglio, Panfilia Orzi. *I Corsini a Toma e le origine della Biblioteca Corsiniana*. Roma: Accademia Nazionale dei Lincei, 1958.

584 _____

> Gmeinwieser, Siegfried. *Girolamo Chiti: Eine Untersuchung zur Kirchenmusik in S. Giovanni in Laterano*. Ratisbona: Bosse Verlag, 1968. 194 p.   [g.a.]
>> Portion appeared in an Italian translation by G. Pestelli in *Nuovo rivista musicale italiano* 4 (1970): 665-77.

585 _____

> Duckles, Vincent. ". . . Observations of the Correspondence between Girolamo Chiti and Padre Giambattista Martini." *Revue belge de musicologie* 26/27 (1972/73): 16-17.   [g.a.]

586   Corte-Callier, Gaetano La
"La collezione La Corte-Callier della B[iblioteca] U[niversitaria] di Messina." *Accademie e biblioteche d'Italia* 1, no. 3 (1927): 111-13.

587   Cortot, Alfred, 1877-1962
Bibliothèque Alfred Cortot . . . Catalogue établi par Alfred Cortot et rédigé par Frederick Goldbeck, avec la collaboration de A. Fehr. Préface de Henry Prunières. Première partie, Théorie de la musique. Argenteuil: R. Coulouma, 1936. 212 p. ca. 800 nos.   [g.a.]

> **Folter**, no. 56, and **Albrecht**. Portions now in US-NYp, -BE, -Cn, and -LEX; see long note in **Albrecht**.

588   _____
King, A. Hyatt, and O. W. Neighbour. "Printed Music from the Collection of Alfred Cortot." *British Museum Quarterly* 31 (1966): 8-16.   [g.a.]

589   _____
Traficante, Frank. "The Alfred Cortot Collection at the University of Kentucky Libraries." *University of Kentucky Library Notes* 1, no. 3 (spring 1970) [whole issue]. 19 p. Catalog, pp. 15-19.   [g.a.]

> **Folter**, no. 57.

590   _____
Traficante, Frank. "Dispersal of the Cortot Collection: 290 Treatises in Lexington." *Notes* 26 (1970): 713-17.   [g.a.]

591   _____
Hollingsworth, Dell. "Sacred Vocal Music from the Collection of Alfred Cortot." *Library Chronicle of the University of Texas at Austin* 25/26 (1984): 25-49.   [g.a.]

> "Short-title list," pp. 43-49.

592   _____
Bowling, Lewis P. "The Alfred Cortot Collection, University of Kentucky Libraries: A Bibliography." *Midwest Note-book: Publication of the Midwest Chapter of the MLA* 2, no. 3 (January 1994): 2-6.   [g.a.]

593   _____

LITERATURE
Herreid, R., "Die Bibliothek Cortot in Paris." *Anbruch* 19 (1937): 155-57.   [g.a.]

594   _____
Rosenthal, Albi. "Alfred Cortot as Collector of Music." In *Essays in Honour of Alec Hyatt King*, ed. O. W. Neighbour, 206-14. New York [etc.]: K. G. Saur, [1980].   [g.a.]

Cosijns, P. J.   *See under* **Boers, Jan Conradus**

595   Costa, Francisco Edoardo da, 1818-54; et al.
PUTTICK & SIMPSON, AUCTIONEER, LONDON   CAT. NO. 425
Catalogue of a Large Collection of Music, Consisting of Selections from Several Libraries

. . . Sacred Music, Scores of Operas, etc., Instrumental Music . . . Nearly 10,000 Pieces of Modern Music . . . Sold August 10, and Following Day. [London, 1855.] 21 p. 586 lots. Music, lots 1-438. [GB-Lbl]

596   **Costa, Sir Michael,** 1808-84

SOTHEBY, WILKINSON & HODGE, AUCTIONEER, LONDON
Catalogue of the Library of the Late . . . Including Many Valuable Musical Scores by Various Composers. . . . Important Books and Manuscripts, the Properties of Other Collectors . . . Sold . . . the 11th Day of August, 1884. [London, 1884.] 27 p. 397 lots. Music, lots 76-131.

[Film at CRL]

There is a note about the sale in the *London and Provincial Trades Review* 84 (15 September 1884): 29; another in the *Musical Times*, 1 August 1884, with a list of items and prices: "An interesting sale of presentation rings, ivory batons, and other pieces of bijouterie." The same issue, pp. 451-52, notes "The Costa Bequest" for scholarships to students at the Royal Academy, "the first bequest of equal significance" to Handel's bequest to the Royal Society of Music.

597   —————

PUTTICK & SIMPSON, AUCTIONEER, LONDON   CAT. NO. 2819
Valuable Musical Property . . . Pianofortes . . . [etc., and music from the library of Sir Michael Costa, lots 222-82] *. . . Sold . . . June 23 1891.* London, 1891. [g.a.]

598   —————

WILLIAM REEVES, FIRM, LONDON   CAT. NO. 44
Catalogue of a Large Collection of Musical Literature . . . Unpublished from Sir Michael Costa's Library; Programs. . . . London, 1891. [GB-LReeves]

599   **Coüet, Jules**

CH. BOSSE AND L. GIRAUD-BADIN, LIBRAIRE, PARIS
Catalogue de la bibliothèque de feu M. Jules Coüet, bibliothecaire-archiviste de la Comédie-Française (un vieux bibliophile). Huitième partie, ouvrages sur la musique . . . théâtre . . . ouvrages relatifs au théâtre. . . . ev vente 7-9 November, 1938. Paris, 1938. 125 p. Lots 3813-4496. Music, lots 3813-914. [NL-VBBA]

Not examined; cited from **Blogie 2**.

600   **Coupland, Leslie Downes**

SOTHEBY & CO., AUCTIONEER, LONDON
Catalogue of Printed Books and a Few Manuscripts . . . Property of [Various Collectors]. *. . . Music, Including XVIIIth Century Compositions, the Property of the Late . . . Coupland . . . Sold . . . 2nd February 1931, and 3 Following Days.* [London, 1931.] 152 p. 1321 lots. Music, lots 473-517; Coupland's, lots 499-517; Anon., lots 473-98. [NL-VBBA; film at CRL]

601   **Courcy, Frédéric de**

J. -F. DELION, FIRM, PARIS
Catalogue d'une collection de livres . . . composant la bibliothèque de feu M. . . . Paris: J.-F. Delion, 1862. viii, 66 p. [US-CN and NL-DHgm]

"Chansons," lots 223-44 (collections, not individual pieces). Cited in **Scheurleer** 1 (1923): 12.

602 Coussemaker, Edmond de, 1805-76
Catalogue de la bibliothèque et des instruments de musique de feu m. Ch. Edm. H. de Coussemaker. . . . Bruxelles: F. J. Olivier, 1877. iv, 208 p. 1618, 36 nos.[US-NH, -Nyp, and -Wc]

> Sale dates, 17-20 April 1877, but the collection now resides in the Bibliothèque Royale Abert Ier in Brussels (**Albrecht**). **Folter**, no. 58. Reprint: **603**.

603 _____
Catalogue of the Music Library of Charles Edmond Henri de Coussemaker, Sold at Brussels 1877. Introduction by A. Hyatt King. Auction Catalogues of Music, 7. Amsterdam: Knuf, 1978. 224 p.   [g.a.]

> Reprint of (**602**).

604 Coward, James, 1824-80
Puttick & Simpson, auctioneer, London   Cat. no. 2051
Catalogue of a Valuable Assemblage of Musical Properties Comprising the Library of the Late . . . in Beautiful Condition and in Elegant Bindings . . . Also Musical Instruments . . . Sold October 18, 1881. [London, 1881.] 14 p. 362 lots. Music, lots 1-202.   [GB-Lbl]

> The collection must have been earlier purchased by the firm of Metzler & Co., for a brief note in the *MO&MTR* 4 (August 1881): 420 says that "Messrs. Metzler & Co. have for sale the musical library of the late Mr. James Coward, which comprises 129 volumes of glees, madrigals, canons, and cathedral music . . . ," etc. Metzler may well have consigned the materials to Puttick's, an auction house, better suited than Metzler, a retailer and publisher, to disperse them.   [GB-Lbl]

605 Cramer, C.; et al.
Puttick & Simpson, auctioneer, London   Cat. no. 158
Collection of Music, Including the Library of the "Glee Club" . . . Sold . . . February 28 and Following Day, 1876. London, 1876.

> Lot 88: "an extensive collection of C. Cramer's MS. scores, collected from celebrated composers, mostly autograph."

Cramer, Francis.   *See under* **Penson, G.** (sale of 9 March 1847)

606 Cramer, François
Mr. McCalla, auctioneer, London
A Catalogue of Classical Music, Valuable Instruments, Works of Art, &c., by Order of the Proprietor . . . Retiring from Public Life. . . . Small Library of Choice Books . . . Engravings . . . Sold by Auction by . . . July 23, and Following Day [1844]. [London, 1844.] 16 p. 69 lots.
[compiler]

607 Cramer, Johann Baptist, 1711-1858
Mr. White, auctioneer, London
A Catalogue of the Mr. J. B. Cramer's Select, Valuable, and Entire Collection of MS. and Prints, Vocal and Instrumental Music, of Both Modern and Ancient Authors . . . Also Some Compositions by John Sebastian Bach . . . and Some Printed Books . . . Sold . . . May 21st, 1816, and Following Day. [London, 1816.] 15 p. 327 lots.
[GB-Lbl, US-Wc and compiler, all with n & p. US-Can has copy of US-Wc]

> **King**, pp. 25-26.

608 _____

Mr. Watson, auctioneer, London
Catalogue of a Valuable Collection of Vocal & Instrumental Music, Including the Library of the Late . . . Who Is About to Reside on the Continent; Five Portraits . . . Manuscript in the Hand-writing of Haydn, &c. &c. . . Sold by Auction by . . . at the Mart . . . 23rd of May, 1835. 9 p. 158 lots. [compiler]

Cramer, William. *See under* **Baker, James** (sale of 10 April 1855)

Crandall, Marjorie Lyle. *See under* **Harwell, Richard Braksdale**

609 **Craufurd, C H , Rev.**
Sotheby, Wilkinson & Hodge, auctioneer, London
Catalogue of a Selected Portion of the Choice Library of. . . . Also, Some Scarce Early Works on Music . . . Sold . . . the 20th Day of April, 1864. [London, 1864.] 38 p. 333 lots. Music, lots 163-64, 225-44. [Film at CRL]

610 **Crawford, Alexander William Ludwig, 25th Earl of,** 1793-1878
Sotheby, Wilkinson & Hodge, auctioneer, London
Bibliotheca Lindesiana. Catalogue of the Library of the Right Honorable the Earl of Crawford. First Portion . . . Sold . . . 13th Day of June, 1887, and Nine Following Days. . . . [London, 1887.] 220 p. 2148 lots. Music, lots 1464-516. [Film at CRL]

611 **Crawford, J. R.**
Crawford, Dorothy. "The Crawford Theatre Collection." *Yale University Library Gazette* 41 (1967): 131-35. [g.a.]

612 **[Crewe, Lady]**
Puttick & Simpson, auctioneer, London
Catalogue of a Collection of Music . . . Vocal and Instrumental Works . . . Valuable Full Scores . . . Sold . . . September 8th, 1865, and Following Day. [London, 1865.] 32 p. 862 lots. Music, lots 1-781. [GB-Lbl]

613 **Crofts, Thomas, Rev. (of Peterborough)**
Mr. Paterson, auctioneer, London
A Catalogue of the Curious and Distinguished Library of the Late . . . Sold by Auction by . . . Covent-Garden . . . April 7, 1783 and Forty-two [sic!] *Days.* [London, S. Paterson, 1783.] 420 p. 8360 + lots. "Musica," lots 5686-731. [NL-Avb]

> The sale took place from April 7 through May 18. It was rich in early prints, Gardanos, etc., and there were many more items than lots, e.g., lot 5708 comprised 8 titles.

614 **Cronheim, Paul; Rudolf Mengelberg; Max Vreedenburg**
Frits Knuf, firm, Buren   Cat. nos. 119 and 121
Musicology: The Libraries of Dr. Paul Cronheim, Dr. Rudolf Mengelberg and Max Vreedenburg. 2 vols. Buren: Knuf, 1976-77. 46 and [28] p. 872 and 373 lots. [g.a.]

> **Folter**, nos. 59 and 60.

Crosby Brown, Mary.   *See under* **Brown, Mary Elizabeth** (**Adams**), *section 3* (**3324**)

615   Crotch, William, 1775-1847
PUTTICK & SIMPSON, FIRM, LONDON   CAT. NO. 1374
Catalogue of the Musical Library of the Late . . . Which Will Be Sold by Auction by . . . on February 20th, 1873, and Following Day. [London, 1873.] 30 p. 275 lots. [GB-Lbl, US-Wc]
> **King**, p. 60.

616 _____
PUTTICK & SIMPSON, FIRM, LONDON   CAT. NO. 1678
Catalogue of a Collection of Music, Including the Library of the Late . . . , Music. Doc. . . . Sets of the Handel Society, Musical Antiquarian Society's Publications . . . Sold . . . June 28, 1877. [London, 1877.] 16 p. 319 lots. Music, lots 1-182. Crotch's materials, lots 146-88 (but not identified as such).   [GB-Lbl]
> **King**, p. 60. Some of Crotch's scores, manuscripts and sketchbooks were donated by members of the family of Arthur Henry Mann (d. 1929) to GB-NW in 1941.
> → *See also under* **Callcott, William Hutchins** (sale of 13 and 15 June 1863)

617   Crozat, Joseph Antoine, Marquis de Tugny, 1696-1740
THIBOUST, AUCTIONEER, PARIS
Catalogue des livres de Monsieur le President Crozat de Tugny. Dont la vent . . . du mois d'août 1751. . . . Paris: Chez Thiboust, imp. du roi, 1751. xvi, 472 p.
[US-Wc, -Cn, -NYp, -NYgr]
> Not examined; cited from Hans Schneider catalog no. 237, lot 93; Liepmannssohn's no. 223, lot 308. Pincherle sale catalog, lot no. 438 (says "section musicale").

618   [Cummings, William Hayman, 1831-1915]
PUTTICK & SIMPSON, AUCTIONEER, LONDON   CAT. NO. 706
Catalogue of the Music Library of a Well-Known Collector, Together with the Modest Stock of a Provincial Music Seller . . . Also Musical Instruments . . . Stock . . . Sold January 6th, 1862, and Following Day. . . . [London, 1862.] 25 p. 699 lots. Music, lots 1-587.   [GB-Lbl]
> Lots 313-30, manuscripts, including Handel's *Athalia* in J. C. Smith's hand. Cummings is not mentioned in the catalog, only the index of Puttick's sales (see Introduction).

619   Cummings, William Hayman, 1831-1915
Cummings, Norman P., comp. *The Music Library of Dr. William H. Cummings.* London: printed by C. Jacques & Son, 1910. 106 p. 1257 lots (A-B only!).
> *MT* 39 (1898): 81 notes his extensive library and mentions his son Norman's catalog, hoping "it will be published." It has not been located. Citation for this edition from US-CHua.

620 _____
SOTHEBY, WILKINSON & HODGE, AUCTIONEER, LONDON
Catalogue of the Famous Musical Library of Books, Manuscripts, Autograph Letters, Musical Scores, etc. . . . Sold by Auction . . . Thursday, 17th of May, 1917, and Following Day, and on Monday, 21st of May and Three Following Days. . . . [London]: Dryden Press, [1917].

161 p. 1744 lots. All music. Lots 1-280, manuscripts and ALS.
> [US-Wc (with names & prices), -NYp, -CHua, -Bp and GB-Lb (Hirsch no. 433); film at CRL]
>> **King**, pp. 71-72; not **Folter**! Comments and a list of some items with prices fetched appeared in *MT* 58 (1 August 1917): 373.

621 _____

> There was considerable residue from the 1917 sale, apparently, for some 400 pieces were sold to Marquis Tokugawa, which then went to the Nanki Library. After WW II, ownership was once again transferred to Kyubei Okhi (*see* **2026** and also under **Okhi** elsewhere in the bibliography). Items purchased by various dealers at the sale were in turn sold by them over a number of years in bits and pieces, as follow:

622 _____

> P. S. & A. E. DOBELL, FIRM, LONDON   CAT. NO. 264
>> [In this catalog from July 1917, not located, lots 493-519 were reputedly from the Cummings collection.]

623 Cummings, William Hayman; T. L. Southgate
> HAROLD REEVES, FIRM, CLAYGATE, SURREY   CAT. NO. 8
> *A Catalogue of Books on Music and Musicians. Old and Rare, Second-hand and New . . . Including Many Interesting Items from the Libraries of. . . .* Claygate, Surrey: Harold Reeves, 1917. 32 p. 839 lots.   [NL-Dhgm]

624 _____

> MESSRS. ELLIS, FIRM, LONDON   CAT. NO. 21
> *Ellis's Catalogue of Rare Books and Manuscripts of and Relating to Music, Selected from the Famous Library of the Late . . . on Sale. . . .* London, 1918. 65 p. 619 lots.   [US-NYgr]

625 Cummings, William Hayman; A. Huth; A. H. Littleton; Sir John Stainer; et al.
> BERNARD QUARITCH, FIRM, LONDON   CAT. NO. 355
> *A Catalogue of Manuscripts and Books Relating to Music from the Libraries of . . . Offered . . .* [Oct.]. . . . London: Quaritch, 1919. 80 p. 763 lots.   [US-Cn, -Wc]
>> **Folter**, no. 61.

626 _____

> Nanki Ongaku Bunko. *Catalogue of the W. H. Cummings' Collection in the Nanki Music Library.* [Tokyo]: The Library, 1925. 70 p. Ca. 500 nos.   [US-AUS, -BE, -NYcu, -Wc]
>> **Folter**, no. 62.

627 Cummings, William Hayman; Max Freidlander, 1852-1934; **Joseph Hollmann**
> Tokyo. Nanki Music Library. *Zosho Mokuroku Kicho shiryo* [the Okhi Music Collection]. Tokyo: The Library, 1970. 60 p. 809 lots. Summaries in English.   [g.a.]
>> **Folter**, no. 62.

628 Curran, Elma Hege
> LITERATURE
> "A Gift to the Moravian Music Foundation: The Elma Hege Curran Collection." *Moravian Music Journal* 37 (1992): 5.

629   **Curzon, Sir Clifford,** 1907-82

     LITERATURE

Neighbour, Oliver W. "The Curzon Collection." *British Library Journal* 11 (1985): 60-66. [g.a.]

630   **D , Comtesse**

     J. A. STARGARDT, FIRM, BERLIN

Catalogue d'une collection choise [sic] *de livres et de monuments la plupart provenant de la bibliothèque de Mme. la Comtesse D. . . .* Berlin, 1875.

         Auction took place January 4 and following days. "Werke über Musik": lots 2185-289. Not examined; information from *MfM* 6 (1874): 162.

631   **Daehne, J C W de**

     P. VAN DAALEN WETTERS, AUCTIONEER, DEN HAAG

Catalogue d'une très belle bibliothèque. . . . Une partie de musique & des instrumens de musique & diverses curiosités précieuses . . . vendues publiquement . . . 10 septembre 1804 & jours suivans. . . . La Haye, 1804. 4, 291 p. 7215 lots. Music, pp. 280-84, 113 lots.

                                                    [NL-Avb, US-CA]

     Not examined; cited from **Lugt,** no. 6851.

632   **Dale, Benjamin J.,** 1885-1943**; Godfrey E. P. Arkwright,** 1864-1944

     HODGSON & CO., FIRM, LONDON

A Catalogue of Music Books Comprising. . . . Together with the Music Library of the Late, . . . and the Remaining Portion of That of the Late G. E. P. Arkwright . . . Sold . . . August 2nd, 1945, and Following Day. London, 1945. 42 p. 648 lots.   [US-NYgr, compiler (priced copy)]

     King, pp. 74-75.

633   **Dalley-Scarlett, Robert,** 1887-1959

Brown, Patricia. *Early Published Handel Scores in the Dalley-Scarlett Collection, Fisher Library, University of Sydney: A Descriptive Bibliography.* Music Monograph, 1. Nedlands: University of Western Australia Press, [1971]. 53 p.   [US-Wc]

     Supplement to Studies in Music 5 (1971). Collection at AUS-Sml.

634   _____

Kinnear, Betty, and Robert Illing. *An Illustrated Catalogue of Early Editions of Handel in Australia.* Adelaide: [n.p.], 1977. 255 p.   [US-Wc]

     In the Fisher Library, University of Sydney.

635   _____

     LITERATURE

Illing, Robert. "Dalley-Scarlett Collection of Music and Books About Music." *Australian Library Journal* 19 (1930): 459-67.   [g.a.]

636   _____

Brown, Patricia. "Introduction to Robert Dalley-Scarlett and His Collection." *Studies in Music* 5 (1971): 87-89.   [g.a.]

     Albrecht.

637   Danckert, Werner, 1900-1970
Hans Schneider, firm, Tutzing   Cat. no. 182
Musikbibliothek Werner Danckert . . . sowie einige andere Beiträge [mit Nachtrag]. Tutzing: Schneider, [1974]. 72, 8 p., illus. 915 lots.   [g.a.]
    Folter, no. 63.

638   Dandeleu, Jean-Baptiste, d. 1667
"Libri musici." In Edmond vander Straeten, *Musique aux Pays-Bas*, 1:21-30. Bruxelles: Murquardt, 1867. Reprint, New York: Dover, 1968.   [Reprint g.a.]
    A catalog of D's music library reprinted by Straeten from the complete catalog of D's library (all fields) entitled *Cathalagus librorum Joannis Dandeleu.* Copy is preserved in the "Archives de Royaume," according to Straeten. **Albrecht**.

639   _____
"Inventaire des instruments et livres de musique de feu le sieur . . . , vivant premier commissaire ordinaire des monstres des gens de guerres du Roy, retrouvez en la maison mortuaire d'iceluy, à Bruxelles, avec les nombres d'iceux et le spécification de leurs auteurs, mis en marge, comme s'ensuit [1667]. . . ." In Edmond vander Straeten, *Musique aux Pays-Bas*, 1:31-37.
    [g.a.]
    See imprint in **638**.

Dando, Joseph Haydon Bourne, 1806-94.   *See under* **Westbrook, Dr. W. J.** (sale of 31 October 1894)

Danican, François André.   *See under* **Toulouse, Louis Alexandre**

640   Danilov, Kirsha
Beljaev, Viktor M. *Sbornik Kirshi Danilova: opyt restavratsii pesen.* Moskva: Sovetskij kompozitor, 1969. 227 p.
    Not examined; cited from *RILM.*

641   Danjou, [Jean Louis] F[élix], 1812-66
Catalogue des livres et manuscrits relatifs à la musique faisant partie de la bibliothèque de M. F. Danjou. Montpellier, 1850. 12 p.
    Not examined. Cited in **Fétis**, *Catalogue*, no. 5190; **Gaspari**, *Catalogo* of the Bologna Civico Museo; and **Blogie 2**, who says, "après 1844"!

642   Danneley, John Feltham, 1786-1836
Mr. W. P. Musgrave, firm, London
Catalogue of Musical Properties, Including the Very Choice Library of. . . . Portion of the Stock in Trade of a Dealer . . . Sold . . . the 21st of September, 1830, and Following Days. [London, 1830.] 32 p. 479 p. Music, lots 1-312, 351-442.
    A fine collection of rare items. US-NYp has Gauntlett's copy with some names and prices.

643   Dannreuther, Edward, 1844-1905; **Dr. Pietro Berri,** 1901-79
HERMAN BARON, FIRM, LONDON   CATALOG NO. 115
Musical Literature, Including Books from the Libraries of. . . . London, 1979. 40 p. 950 lots.
[US-CHua; compiler]

> Much of Dannreuther's collection is now at GB-Lcm; chamber music parts
> at US-PO.

Danz, Carl. *See* **Anon.** sale of 9 November 1863.   [g.a.]
> **Folter,** no. 64.

644   D'Arminy, Le Gendre
PRAULT, FIRM, PARIS
*Catalogue des livres de la bibliothèque de M. Le Gendre d'Arminy. Dont la vente . . . à l'Hôtel
de Longuiville . . . de lundi vingt-cinq Avril 1740, lendermain de Ouasimodo, & jours suivans.
. . .* Paris: Chez Prault, Quay de Conty, vis-à-vis la descente du Pont-Neuf, à la Charité, 1740. 166
p. 1739+ lots.   [US-NYgr]

> Music, section 7, lots 692-858. "Ballets & Opera suivant l'ordre chor-
> nologique de leurs représentations," lots 698-796 (Lully to Monteclair).

645   David, Ferdinand, 1810-73
RICHARD HATCHWELL, FIRM, LITTLE SOMERFORD
*Maalmesburg Miscellany No. 5: A Miscellaneous Collection of Engraved and Manuscript
Music of the 18th and 19th Century, Including a Series of First Editions of Mendelssohn from
the Library of. . . .* Little Somerford, Wiltshire: Richard Hatchwell, [ca. 1963]. Unpaged. 167 lots.

[US-CHua]

> David's Mendelssohn items, lots 91-107. The strange venue for the sale
> results from the fact that part of Ferdinand David's library went to his son,
> Peter Julius Paul David, who died in Oxford in 1932 (from a note in the
> catalog). Examined copy belonging to Herman Baron, antiquariat.

646   David, Hans Theodore, 1902-67
"Library of the Late . . . Acquired [by Baldwin-Wallace College]." *Bach* 1 (2 November 1970): 25.
[Collection US-BER]

Davis J C . *See under* **Warren-Horne, E. T.** (sale of January 1810)

647   Dean, H W
MR. WHITE, FIRM, LONDON
*Collection of Music, and Library of Books. A Catalogue of a Fine Collection of Music . . . Also
the Library of Books . . . Sold . . . July 17th, 1816.* [London, 1816.] 17 p. 198 lots.
[US-Wc, photocopy at US-Cn]

> Not in **King**!

Dean of Peterborough (**Rev. George Butler**).   *See under* **Moore, Thomas** (sale of 25, 27-
28 June 1853)

DeBas, W A F H. *See under* **Koning, David**

648 **DeBellis, Frank V.**
LITERATURE
Van de Moortell, Raymond. "The Frank V. De Bellis Collection: A Treasury of Italian Civilization."
California State Library Foundation Bulletin 34 (January 1991): 8-15.   [g.a.]
    Albrecht: now at US-SFsc.

Debroux, Joseph.   *See under* **Terry, Leonard** (Liège. Conservatoire Collection)

649 **Debussy, Claude,** 1862-1918; **Jules Huret**
GEORGES ANDRIEUX, FIRM, PARIS
Catalogue de vent des livres précieux anciens, romantiques, modernes, manuscrits, documents
et letters autographes; collection Jules Huret et Claude Debussy. Vente le 30 novembre [et]
les [1-8] *décembre 1933.* [Paris: G. Andrieux, 1933.] 170 p. Debussy, lots 174-224 (mainly
Debussy holographs).   [US-CN, film copy at US-BUu]
    Folter, no. 66.

650 **Decroix, J J M**
LITERATURE
Lebeau, E. "J. J. Decroix et sa collection Rameau." In *Mélange d'histoire . . . offerts à P.-M.*
Masson, 2:81-91. Paris: Masse, 1955.   [US-Cn; film copy at US-NBuU]
    Cited in **Benton 3**:108, no. 113. Collection now in F-Pbn. **Folter**, no. 66.

651 **de Deney, A. R.**
PHILLIPS, AUCTIONEER, LONDON   SALE NO. 28,780
Musical Instruments, Books on Music, Musical Manuscripts Including . . . Reference Books,
at One Time the Property of W. E. Hill & Sons . . . Private Library of Scholarly Music Books, the
Property of the Late A. R. de Deney . . . Sold . . . 24 October 1991. . . . London, 1991. 53 p. 525
lots (de Deney's, 303-525).   [compiler]

652 **De Geer, Charles,** 1730-78
LITERATURE
Dunning, Albert. "Die de Geer'schen Musikalien in [Schloss] Leufsta. Musikalische Schwedisch-
Niederländische Beziehungen im 18. Jh." *STMf* 48 (1966): 187-210.   [g.a.]
        "Verzeichnis," pp. 187-210. Now at S-N; acquired by the city, 1904. **Albrecht**
        lists under Louis de Geer (1622-95), and adds that part of the Leufsta
        collection is still there, S-LB.

653 _____
LITERATURE
Vretblad, Äke. "Charles De Geers samling av musikalier i Leufstra Bruk." *STMf* (1955), 156-60.
                                              [g.a.]

        Article notes: "Catalogue des livres de musique redigé par Charles De Geer
        le Jeune, 1763," a Ms. in photocopy.   [S-Sma]

De Glimes,   , Prof., 1814-81. Collection bequeathed to B-Lc and B-Bc. *See under* **Terry, Léonard**

654   Dehn, Siegried Wilhelm, 1799-1858
J. A. STARGARDT, FIRM, BERLIN   CAT. NO. 45
Verzeichniss einer werthvollen Sammlung von musikalischen und hymnologischen Werken, Liedern, Opern, Comödien, Autographen und Manuscripten, zum Theil aus dem Nachlasse des Herrn Prof. Dehn in Berlin. Berlin: Weinberg, 1860. i, 30 p. 604, 12 lots.

> Not examined; cited from **Folter**, no. 67, **Bobillier, Petzholdt,** and **Albrecht,** who say many items now at D-Bds. Some theoretical works acquired by Lowell Mason (**1808**), now at US-NH.

655   _____

LITERATURE
Riedel, Friedrich W. "Siegfried Wilhelm Dehns Besuche in Wien 1841 bis 1846." In *Grasberger Festschrift*, 391-404. Tutzing: Schneider, 1975.   [g.a.]

656   Deketh, A   and Z. Reipers
W. P. VAN STOCKUM, FIRM, DEN HAAG
Catalogus van Boeken . . . benevens Landkarten, Handschriften. Brieven en onderteelende Stukken; Muziek en Muziek-instrumenten, waaronder Klassieke en nieuwe Muziek voor Zang en verschill . . . verkocht . . . 7 December 1857 en volgende dagen. . . . 's-Gravenhage, 1857. 164 p. 5029 + 24 lots. Music, pp. 150-91.   [NL-Avb]
> **Lugt,** no. 23858.

De Landau. *See* **Landau, Horace de**

De Liz, Francisco Lopez de. *See* **Duliz, Francisco de**

657   [Denielle,   ]
G. MARTIN, FIRM, AUCTIONEER, PARIS
Catalogue des livres de feu M. D***. [Paris: Chez G. Martin, 1749.] 72, [2] p. Music, lots 1248-64, include Couperin Mss.

> "A la fin: La vente des livres de feu M. D*** se fera en détail lundi 4 août 1749 & jours suivans . . . Recens quelques estampes et livres de musique."
> Not examined; cited from Toulouse, *Catalogue*, p. 32, FA no. 15165 (a).

658   Densmore, Frances, 1867-1957
Howard, Helen Addison. "A Survey of the Densmore Collection of American Indian Music." *Journal of the West* 13, no. 2 (April 1974): 83-96.   [g.a.]

659   _____

LITERATURE
Parthum, Paul. "A Special Collection: Frances Densmore Ethnomusicological Library." *Student Musicologists at Minnesota* 4 (1970/71): 76-79.   [g.a.]
> Donated to Macalester College, St. Paul, Minnesota; later transferred to US-Wc. Over 100 volumes.

660   Den Tex, C   A
FREDERICK MULLER, AUCTIONEER?, AMSTERDAM
Verkooping van eene fraaije verzameling muziekwerken, nagelaten door . . . Te Amsterdam . . . den 26 januarij. . . . Amsterdam, 1856. 6 p. 171 lots.   [NL-Avb]

661   Dent, Edward Joseph, 1856-1957

> Dent received the library of Gerald Cooper, later passed it on to GB-Lwcm.
> *See under* **Cooper, Gerald**.

662   Dent, Edward Joseph; J[ohn] B[rand] Trend, 1887-1958

SOTHEBY & CO., FIRM, LONDON
Catalogue of Printed Books and Music, Comprising Music and Books on Music and Musicians, with Some Manuscripts, the Property of . . . [with Various Other Properties] . . . Sold . . . January 20th, 1958, and Two Following Days. [London], 1958. 116 p. 903 lots. Music, lots 312-458, 488-531. Dent's properties, lots 312-487 (many more items); Trend's, lots 506-31. [Film at CRL]

> **King**, no. 78.

663   ——————

HERMAN BARON, FIRM, LONDON   CAT. NO. 40
Catalogue of Music Literature, Including Books from . . . Dent's Library. London, 1958. 430 lots.   [GB-LReeves]

664   ——————

HERMAN BARON, FIRM, LONDON   CAT. NO. 40
Catalogue of Vocal and Instrumental Music, Including Scores from . . . Dent's Library. London, 1958. 400 lots.   [US-NYp]

665   Dermota, Anton, 1910

Ziffer, Agnes. *Musiksammlung der Österreichischen Nationalbibliothek. Sonderausstellung 11. Juni-31. 1971. Sammlung Anton Dermota.* Wien: Österreichischen Nationalbibliothek, 1971. 31 p. ca. 170 items.

> Not examined; cited from *RILM*.

666   ——————

Zeman, Herbert. "Literarische Autographen aus der Sammlung von Anton Dermota." *Jahrbuch des Wiener Goethe-Vereins* 86-87 (1982-84, publ. 1986): 387-572.

> Not examined; cited from *RILM* and **Folter**, no. 2.

667   ——————

Leibnitz, Thomas, and Agnes Ziffer. *Katalog der Sammlung . . . . : Musikhandschriften und Musikerbriefe, bearb. von. . . .* Publikationen des Instituts für Österreichische Musikdokummentation, 12. Tutzing: H. Schneider, 1988. 190 p. 612 lots.   [g.a.]

668   ——————

LITERATURE
Ziffer, Agnes. "Sammlung Anton Dermota." In *Musik und Dichtung: Anton Dermota zum 70. Geburtstag,* ed. Herbert Zeman, 36-40. Wien: Österreichischen Nationalbibliothek, 1980.
                                                                        [g.a.]

669   ——————

Zeman, Herbert. *Autographen aus drei Jahrhunderten. Literatur, Theater, bildende Kunst, Wissenschaft. Eine Dokumentation der Sammlung Dermota.* Veröffentlichung des Ludwig Boltamann; Instituts für Österr. Literaturforschung und des Wiener Goethe-Vereins. Graz, Wien, Köln: Styria, 1987. 242 p.   [g.a.]

> Not examined; cited from **Folter**, no. 2.

Des Arts, Adolph.   *See under* **Bach, A. W.** (sale of 1870)

670   Dèsiré, M   (Amable Courtecuisses, *dit*), 1822-73
Notice d'une jolie collection de livres d'amateur, ouvrages sur le théâtre, partitions de musique, etc., composant la bibliothèque de M. Dèsiré. Paris: Chasles, 1874.   [F-Pn]
    Not examined; cited from **Bobillier**.

671   Despois, E [probably **Eugene André**, 1818-76, writer on theater and drama]
Catalogue des livres de la bibliothèque de feu. . . . Paris, 1876.
    Not examined; cited from **Scheurleer,** *Catalogue* 1 (1923): 12.

672   Dessauer, J   H   [or H. J.? (see **674)**]; et al.
    G. THEOD. BOM, & ZOON, FIRM, AMSTERDAM
Notitie van de muziekbibliotheek van de . . . muziekleerar en componist te Amsterdam. . . . Verkooping . . . 19 [-24] October 1906. . . . A'dam: Bom, 1906.   [NL-Avb (NV 3396)]
    Not examined.

673   Dessauer, J   H; D[aniel] F[rançois] Scheurleer; et al.
    G. THEOD. BOM & ZOON, FIRM, AMSTERDAM
Catalogue van belangrijke Bibliotheken afkonstig van de Heeren H. J. Dessauer te Amsterdam . . . D. F. . . . 16 November 1908 en volgende dagen. . . . A'dam: Bom, 1908. 136 p. + 2 suppls. 2699 lots. Music, lots 2073-134, 2505-20.   [NL-Avb (Nv 3459, interleaved with n & p)]

674   Dessauer, Joseph, 1798-1876; **Dr. E. von K . . .**
    GILHOFER & RANSCHBURG, FIRM, VIENNA   AUKTION 12
Autographensammlung des Komponisten Joseph Dessauer . . . und Sr. E. von K. Musik-ms. von Beethoven [u.a.]. *Versteigerung in Luzern . . . Nov. 1933.* Luzern: Gilhofer & Ranschburg, 1932. 48 p. 470 lots, undifferentiated.   [US-Wc and -CHua]

675   Destinn, Emmy, 1878-1930
Pysvejc, O. Knihkupec. *Biblioteka Emmy Destinnové, I. Cást . . . Knetna 1934. . . .* Praha, 1934. 89 p. 882 lots.   [NL-Avb]
    Little music but some related works. Bequeathed to CS-Pu.

676   Deutsch, Otto Erich, 1883-1967
    SANDERS & CO., FIRM, OXFORD   LIST M.2
Franz Schubert 1797-1839 [!] *Comprising: (1) Works by Schubert, (2) Arrangements of Schubert's Works by Contemporaries and Others, (3) Works by Schubert's Friends and Contemporaries.* Oxford, 1953. 16 p. [21] nos. Mimeographed.
    Not examined; cited from **Folter,** no. 69. **Albrecht** says now at A-Smi.

677   De Vincent, Sam, b. 1918
    NATIONAL MUSEUM OF AMERICAN HISTORY (U.S.), ARCHIVES CENTER
Register of the Sam DeVincent Collection of Illustrated American Sheet Music, ca. 1790-1980. Series 3: *African-American Music, ca. 1828-1980,* by Karen Linn, with an introduction by John Edward Hasse. Washington D.C.: Archives Center, Smithsonian Institution, 1989.   [g.a.]

678   [**Devonshire, Mrs.**   ]
PUTTICK & SIMPSON, FIRM, LONDON
Catalogue of a Collection of Music . . . Important Music Copyrights and Engraved Plates,
Also Musical Instruments . . . Sold August 24th, 1870. London, 1870. 18 p. 460 lots Music,
lots 1-285.   [GB-Lbl]

679   **Diaghileff, Serge,** 1872-1929
SCRIBNER, FIRM, NEW YORK CITY
"Collection of Scores, Orchestral Parts and MS. Material from the Library of. . . ." [New York,
1938.] 42 Ms. leaves.   [US-NYp only]

680   **Diaghileff, Serge; Raymond Grigorakis; Serge Lifar**
HANS SCHNEIDER, FIRM, TUTZING   CAT. NO. 209
Opernpartituren, darunter Bestände der Sammlungen. . . . Tutzing, [1977]. 13 p. 600
lots. Properties not differentiated.   [g.a.]

681   **Díaz de Luco, Juan Bernal,** 1495-1556
LITERATURE
Marín, Tomás. "La biblioteca del obispo Juan Bernal Díaz de Luco." *Hispania sacra* 5, no. 10
(1952): 263-326.   [g.a.]

682   **Dickinson, Mrs. June M.,** and **Edward**
Locke, Ralph P., and Jurgen Thym. "New Schumann Materials in Upstate New York: A First
Report on the Dickinson Collection, with Catalogues of Its Manuscript Holdings." *Fontes* 27,
nos. 3-4 (1980): 137-61.   [g.a.]

683   _____
LITERATURE
"The Dickinson Collection of Clara and Robert Schumann Materials: A Report." *Abstracts of*
Papers Read at the 46th Annual Meeting of the American Musicological Society and the
Society for Music Theory, Denver, Colorado, 6-9 November, 1980, 31-32.   [g.a.]

684   **Diehl, Katherine S.**
"Diehl Collection Given to the University of Texas." *Hymn* 28 (1977): 153.   [g.a.]
              Brief notice and description of 77 hymnals.

685   **Dielman, Louis H.**
Upton, William Treat. "18th Century American Imprints in the Society's Dielman Collection of
Music." *Maryland Historical Magazine* 35 (1940): 374-81.   [g.a.]
              Presented by Caroline R. Hollyday. It was first at the Musical Fund Society
              of Philadelphia.

686   **Dieren, Bernard J. van,** 1884-1936; **Vera Hollander; Mary Fraser**
SOTHEBY & CO., FIRM, LONDON
Catalogue of Valuable Printed Books, Music, Autograph Letters . . . the Property of Bernard
J. van Dieren . . . [Vera Hollander's Puccini A.L.S., etc., etc.] . . . Sold . . . 15th of December, 1964.
. . . London, 1964. 195 p. 954 lots. Music, lots 365-481.   [Film at CRL]

To Dieren, over 100 letters and postcards from Delius, lots 382-407; Mss., property of Mary Fraser, lots 365-82; Puccini materials, property of Vera Hollander, lots 428-455.

→ *See also under* **Powis**

Dietrich, Albert. *See under* **Golterman** (Liepmannssohn sale of 21-22 May 1909; **Albrecht** does not mention Golterman)

Dietrichstein'sche, Fürstlich, Fidelcommiss-Bibliothek, Marburg. *See under* **Heymann, A.**

687 Dietsch, Pierre, 1808-65
Lavigne, Exp.-Libraire, Paris
Catalogue d'une collection de musique vocale et instrumentale . . . composant la bibliothèque de feu Dietsch . . . vente . . . novembre 15. . . . [Paris, 1866.] 16 p. 151 lots (many more items).
[NL-DHgm]

Not examined. **Folter**, no. 70. **Scheurleer** 1 (1923): 13.

Disher, M. Willson. *See under* **Clarence, O. B.**

688 Ditfurth, Franz Wilhelm, Freiherr von, 1801-80
Schwinn, Willi. *Studien zur Sammlung Fränkischer volkslieder von. . . .* Beiträge zur Volksliedforschung, 4. München: Neuer Filser-Verlag, 1939. vi, 154 p.   [US-Wc]
Originally a dissertation, Würzburg, 1939.

689 ⸻

Literature
Liebleitner, K. "Aus dem Nachlass des Volksliedforschers. . . ." *Das deutsche Volkslied* 33 (1931): 90-95.
Cited from *MGG*.

690 Dixon, J   H
Sotheby, Wilkinson & Hodge, firm, London
Catalogue of a Valuable Collection of Books, Including the Library of the Late . . . Sold . . . 6th of August, 1866, and Three Following Days. [London, 1866.] 96 p. 1858 lots. Music, lots 866-912.   [Film at CRL (n & p)]

691 Dobrée, Thomas, 1810-95
Musée Dobrée, Bibliothèque
Catalogue de la bibliothèque du Musée. . . . 2 vols. Nantes, 1903-04.   [F-Nd]
Includes music in items *inter alia*.

692 Dobson, John, 1814-88
Sotheby, Wilkinson & Hodge, firm, London
Catalogue of the Library of the Late . . . Consisting of Early and Rare Theology, an Extensive & Valuable Collection of Psalmody and Hymnology, Music & Musical Treatises . . . Sold . . . 22nd Day of November, 1889. 36 p. 492 lots.   [Film at CRL (n & p)]
King, p. 68.

→ *See also under* **Vaughan, W. A.** (sale of 1890)

693 Dörffel, Alfred, 1821-1905

Verzeichniss der in der Leihenanstalt für musikalischen Literatur von . . . in Leipzig enthaltenen Bücher, Schriftwerke und Musikalien. Zweite Abth.: Partituren, Orchesterstimmen und Klavierauszüge mit Text. Leipzig, [1896?].   [US-Wc]

694 Doflein, Erich, 1900-1977

DR. HENNING MÜLLER-BUSCHER, FIRM, LAABER   CAT. NO. 28

Musikbibliothek Prof. Dr. Erich Doflein. Laaber: Laaber-Verlag, [198-]. No pagination. 946 lots.   [compiler]

Folter, no. 71.

695 Dolmetsch, Arnold, 1858-1940

Poulton, Diana. "The Dolmetsch Library, Haslemere, MS II.B.1: A Preliminary Study." *Consort* 35 (1979): 327-41.   [g.a.]

Dom Pedro II, Kaiser of Brazil. *See* **Pedro II, Emperor of Brazil**

696 Donebauer, Fritz

Batka, Richard. *Aus der Musik und Theater-welt. Beschreibendes Verzeichnis der Autographen-sammlung . . . in Prag.* Prag: Buchdruckerei Löwit & Lamberg, Selbstverlag, 1894. lxxx, 150 p. No lot numbers. 1200 autographs.   [US-Wc, -Bp, GB-Lbl (Hirsch 434)]

Folter, no. 72.

697 _____

Batka, Richard. *Aus der Musik- und Theater-welt . . . II. Ausg.* Prag: Löwit & Lamberg, 1900. xvi, 326 p.

Folter, no. 72, says ca. 3000 nos. Also in Leipmannssohn catalog no. 218, lot 183. Not examined. A note in *SiMG* 5 (1903/04): 253 says that there were 260 letters to Spohr in the Donebauer collection.

698 _____

J. A. STARGARDT, FIRM, BERLIN

Sammlung Fritz Donebauer . . . Briefe, Musikmanuskripte, Portraits zur Geschichte der Musik und des Theaters. Versteigerung vom 6. bis 8. April 1908. Berlin: Stargardt, 1908. iv, 123 p. 1054 lots.   [US-NH, -Cn, -BE, -Bp, -GB-Lbl (Hirsch 5786)]

Geleitwort: Richard Batka. **Folter**, no. 73; **Scheurleer** 1 (1923) :12.

699 _____

LITERATURE

Rychnovsky, E. "Die Mozartiana der Autographensammlung Fritz Donebauer in Prag." *Deutsche Arbeit* (Prague) 5, no. 5 (1905/06).

Not examined; cited from *BiBB* (1906).

700 _____

Freiherr von Röslerstamm, E. "Die Autographen Donebauer." *Zeitschrift für Bücherfreunde* 12 (1908): 119-25.

701 Doorn, J   van; Antoni van Heurn
PIETER VAN OS, FIRM, DEN HAAG
*Catalogus van een zeer fraaye Bibliothek . . . Boeken in all Facultyten . . . Nagelaten door
. . . van Heurn. Voorts een meenigte Muziek-werken en Instrumenten . . . nagelaten door . . .
van Doorn . . . verkogt . . . I. Maart 1762, en 7. volgende Daagen.* 's-Gravenhage, 1762. 271 p.
[NL-Avb (Nv234)]

"Verzameling van Uytmuntende Geschreven en Gedrukte Muziek werken,"
pp. 255-66 (392 interesting lots).

702 Doorslaer, Georges van [de Malines], 1864-1940
[*Catalogue de la vente des bibliothèque . . .* Novembre 1945.]
Not located; cited from Les Amis de la Musique, *Catalogue* no. 319, lot 32.

703 Doppler, Adolf, 1850-1906
LITERATURE
Federhofer, Hellmut. "Mozartiana in Steiermark." *Mozart-Jahrbuch* (1958 [publ. 1959]), 109-114.
[g.a.]

Doria-Pamphilj, Don Frank, Count and **Donna Orietta.** *See under* **Pamphilj, Benedetto,
Cardinal,** 1653-1730

704 Douglas, Charles Winfred
Ellinwood, Leonard Webster, and Anne Woodward Douglas. *To Praise God: The Life and
Works of. . . . Together with a Check-List of the Douglas Collection in the Washington Cathedral
Library.* New York: Hymn Society of America, 1958. 75 p. [g.a.]

(Papers of the Hymn Society, 23.) **Albrecht**: library is now at
US-Wca.

705 Douglas [or Duglas?], Duchess
"Elenco di tutta la musica appartenente à S. E. La Duchessa Duglas. Aprile, 1819."
Ms., 12.5 pp., 4°. Not located; cited from Otto Haas, *Catalogue*, no. 27, lot
23.

Dow,   . *See* Oakland Free Library *under* **Vesper, Oliver Morse**

706 Dowding, William
W. P. MUSGRAVE, FIRM, LONDON
*A Catalogue of the Entire Collection of Music, Instruments, and a Portion of the Library of
Books, Late the Property of . . . Sold . . . February 12th, 1823, and Following Day. . . .* London,
1823. 14 p. 262 lots. Music, lots 1-42, 59-215. [GB-Lbl and US-R]
King, p. 27.

707 Dragonetti, Domenico, 1763-1846
GEORGE ROBINS, FIRM, LONDON
*A Catalogue of the Extraordinary Assemblage of Bijouterie and Articles of Taste, the Property
of the Late Signor . . . Music, Coins and Knick Knacks . . . At His Auction Room, in Covent
Garden . . . the 15th Day of July, 1846, and Two Following Days. . . .* London, 1846. 23 p. 179
+ 137 lots. Music, 2nd day, lots 1-92. [GB-Lbl]

King, pp. 43-44, says his library was never sold in toto. He gave Mss. to Novello (in Novello sale; see **708**) and over 180 volumes to the British Museum (see **709**). Other items that went to Sir F. A. G. Ouseley are now at GB-T.

708 _____

PUTTICK & SIMPSON, AUCTIONEER, LONDON   CAT. NO. 277
A Portion of the Musical Library of Vincent Novello, Including Inedited Manuscripts from the Library of Signor Dragonetti (Bequeathed to Mr. Novello) . . . Sold . . . June 25th, 1852. London, 1852. 367 lots.

See lengthy annotation in **Coover 2**. The sale catalog was reprinted by A. Hyatt King in the series *Auction Catalogues of Music*, published by Frits Knuf, 1975.

709 _____

Catalogue of Additions to the Manuscripts in the British Museum in the Years MDCCCXLVI-MDCCCXLVII. London: Woodfall and Kinder, 1864.   [GB-Lbl]

At pages 147-53, nos. 25,979-26,160: volumes bequeathed by Dragonetti in 1846. **King** says this is a full list of the bequest.

710 **Drexel, Joseph Wilhelm,** 1833-88
Catalogue of Jos. W. Drexel's Musical Library, Consisting of Musical Writings, Autographs of Celebrated Musicians, Prints Relating to Music . . . and Music for the Church, Theatre, etc. Part I: Musical Writings. Philadelphia: King & Baird Printers, 1869. xxi, 48p. 1536 lots. [g.a.]

Copy at US-Wc: "Library formed by the union of the libraries of H. F. Albrecht and Dr. R. A. LaRoche. . . . Mr. Albrecht spent over 13 years in different countries in the formation of his Collection. . . ." Preface is signed "J.W.D." Comprises "1536 works in 2245 volumes &c. . . . and is to be followed by a 2d, 3d and 4th catalogue."

US-NYp has interleaved copy extending it to 484 leaves with a title page which reads: "Jos. W. Drexel. Catalogue. Musical Library," and bears the date 1882!

711 _____

"Catalogue of a Collection of Autograph Letters, Documents and Music. . . ." [Part 2 of "Catalog of his Musical Library." N.p., n.d.] 19 leaves.

Ms. in US-NYp (Drexel no. 960).

712 _____

"Catalog of Music for the Church, Theatre, Concert Room & Chamber. Part 3 of the Catalogue of J. W. Drexel's Musical Library." Philadelphia, 1871. 51 p.

Ms. in US-NYp (Drexel no. 964).

713 _____

LUDWIG ROSENTHAL, FIRM, MUNICH   CAT. NO. 26
Bibliotheca musica, theatralis, saltatorio . . . de la librarie ancienne de Ludwig Rosenthal. . . . München: [E. Huber, 1880]. 248 p.   [US-NYgr and -NYp]

Apparently the catalog from which Drexel made his last large purchases, some 50 items for a total cost of $392.97, over half of them rare books on music. (See Susan Sommer articles, below.)

714 _____

Catalog of . . . Musical Library. . . . Philadelphia, 1882. 336 leaves.

Ms. in US-NYp.

715 _____

NEW YORK, PUBLIC LIBRARY, LENOX LIBRARY
Short-title List. [New York, 1887-99.]   [US-NYp only]

12 parts. Parts 11-12, the Drexel collection.

716 _____

Palsits, N. H. "Books on Music [the Drexel Collection in the Lenox Branch of the New York Public Library]." *New York Times,* Saturday Supplement, 30 April 1898, p. 286, cols. 3-4.

717 _____

Sommer, Susan T. "Drexel Collection." *MGG* 15 (1973), cols. 1846-49.   [g.a.]

718 _____

Sommer, Susan T. "Joseph W. Drexel and His Musical Library." In *Music and Civilization: Essays in Honor of Paul Henry Lang,* ed. Edmond Strainchamps and Maria Rika Maniates, 270-78. New York: Norton, 1984.

719 **Dreyer, Otto**
"Verzeichnis der Bücher aus dem Nachlass von. . . ." *Glareana* 23 (1974), leaves 7-9.

720 **Drinker, Henry Sandwith,** 1880-1945
Circulating Library of Choral Music. University of Pennsylvania Choral Series. Presented to the Association by Henry S. Drinker. [Philadelphia, 1940.] 44 p.   [US-NPv]

721 _____

. . . Drinker Library of Choral Music Presented to the Association of American Colleges . . . Under the Supervision and in the Custody of Westminster Choir College. [Princeton, N.J., 1943.] vii, 53 p. Ca. 200 nos.   [g.a.]

Folter, no. 74.

722 _____

Drinker Library of Choral Music, Prepared, Pub. and Donated to the Association. . . . Princeton, N.J.: Assn. of American Choruses, [1947]. 5, xiv, 81 p. ca. 250 nos.   [g.a.]

Folter, no. 75.

723 _____

Idem. [Philadelphia: Assn. of American Choruses, 1957.] 116 p. ca. 400 nos.   [g.a.]

Folter, no. 76.

724 Driscoll, James Francis, 1875-1965
LITERATURE
Floyd, Samuel, Jr. "Black Music in the Driscoll Collection." *Black Perspectives in Music* 2 (1974): 158-72. ca. 84,000 titles.   [g.a.]
    Albrecht: now at US-Cn.

725 Dubrunfaut, A[ugustin] P[ierre], 1797-1881
ÉTIENNE CHARAVAY, (EXPERT), FIRM, PARIS
Catalogue de la precieuse collection d'autographes composant le cabinet de feu. . . . Deuxième série. Compositeurs de musique, artistes dramatiques. La vente . . . des 23 wet 24 Mai 1883. . . . Paris, 1883. 49 p. 394 lots. Music, lots 1-165.   [US-NYgr (with p in Ms.) and at NL-Avb]
    Many more items than lots, e.g., lot 164 comprises 120 items.

726 Du Bus, François [1669-1710?]
Bergmans, Paul. "Une Collection de livrets d'opéras italiens (1669-1710), à la bibliothèque de l'Université de Gand." *SiMG* 12 (1910-11): 221-34.   [g.a.]
    32 items fully described from a sale in Gand in 1875.

727 Düben, Freiherr Anders von, 1673-1738
    According to *MGG*, the Düben family was a musical dynasty from 1590 to 1738. The Düben-Sammlung was given to S-Uu in 1732. Long, detailed article in **Albrecht**.

728 _____
Lindberg, Folke. "Katalog över Dübensamlingen i Uppsala Universitetsbibliotek. Vokalmusik i handsckrift."
    Unpublished Mss. according to *MGG*; available on film.

729 _____
Stiehl, C. "Die Familie Düben und die Buxtehude'schen Manuskripte auf der Bibliothek zu Upsala." *MfM* 21 (1889): 2-9.   [g.a.]
    "Verzeichnis," pp. 4-9.

730 _____
Grusnick, Bruno. "Die Dübensammlung. Ein Versuch ihrer chronologischen Ordnung." *STMf* 46 (1964): 27-82; 48 (1966): 63-186.   [g.a.]
    Includes a catalog of 525 ordered and numbered items by Gustav, plus paleographic studies of watermarks, etc.

731 _____
LITERATURE
    See "C. G. Von Dübens Memorial [1744]" in *STMf* 3 (1921): 96-97; and "Carl Vilhelm von Dübens Memorial . . . 1760," ibid., 122-24.   [g.a.]

732 _____
UPSALA, UNIVERSITET, BIBLIOTEK
"Meddelanden och aktstycken ett nyfunnst komplement till Dübensamling av Jan Olof Rudén." *STMf* 47 (1965): 51-58   [g.a.]

733 —————

Davidsson, Aake. "Die Dübensammlung in der Musikforschung." In *Festschrift für Bruno Grusnick zum 80. Geburtstag,* ed. Rolf Saltzwedel and Klaus-Dietrich Koch, 42-50. Neuhausen/ Stuttgart: Hänssler, 1981. [g.a.]

    Not examined; cited from *RILM.*

734 —————

Snyder, Kerala J. "Cataloguing Sweden's Düben Collection." *Computing in Musicology* 8 (1992): 27-28.

735 —————

Edling, Anders. "The Music Collections of the Uppsala University Library." *Fontes* 34 (1987): 114-17.

736 **Dürniz, Thaddäus, Freiherr von,** 1756-1807

Scharnagl, August. *Freiherr . . . von Dürniz und seine Musikaliensammlung, mit Wiedergabe des handschriftlichen Katalogs.* Musikalische Arbeiten, 12. Tutzing: H. Schneider, 1992. 185 p. [g.a]

    A facsimile of a manuscript thematic catalog from the late 18th century.

737 —————

LaRue, Jan, and Amy Daken. "The Dürniz Thematic Catalogue: A Document of Country Taste." *Notes* 50 (1994): 1321-28. [g.a.]

    "Appendix: Alphabetical Index to the Dürniz Catalogue [Scharnagl's edition, see above]," pp. 1323-28.

738 **[Duff-Gordon, Lucie (Austin), Lady,** 1821-69]

PUTTICK & SIMPSON, AUCTIONEER, LONDON   CAT. NO. 445

Catalogue of a Large and Valuable Collection of Music. . . . Fine MS. Full Score of Bellini's La Somnambula. . . . Also Musical Instruments . . . Sold March 28th, 1856. London, 1856. 19 p. 496 p. Music, lots 1-456. [GB-Lbl]

Dukas, Paul, 1865-1935. *See under* **Viñes**

Duke of Cambridge. *See* **Adolphus Frederick**

Duke of Sussex. *See* **Augustus Frederick**

Duke of York. *See* **Frederick Augustus**

739 **Duliz [De Liz], Francisco Lopez**

FREDERIC, BOUCQUET, AUCTIONEER, DEN HAAG

Catalogue d'une partie . . . de livres François . . . avec . . . un grand nombre de livres de musique: Collection faite à grand frais, & depuis longues années par un amateur (M. Duliz). Laquelle se vendra à La Haye, Lundi le 20 May 1743. . . . La Haye: Frederic Boucquet, [1743]. 68, 20 p. 1027, 16, 24, 364 lots. [NL-DHgm (with p in Ms.)]

    "Catalogue des livres de musique," 20 pp. at end, 364 lots. First section rich in opera scores.

740 _____

Scheurleer, Daniel François. "Een Haagsche Muziekliefhebber uit de 18e eeuw. [Francisco Lopez de Liz, with a Catalog of His Musical Library]." In *Tidskrift der Vereiniging voor Muziekgeschiedenis* 9 (1910): 41-64.   [g.a.]

"Catalogue des livres de musique," pp. 48-64. 364 lots.

741 Duncker [family?]; J. van Reidel; ? Wagner
KARL ERNEST HENRICI, FIRM, BERLIN   AUK. CAT. NO. 112
Autographen, enthaltend die Sammlung Duncker, Wagner, von Riedel, u.a.m. . . . Versteigerung . . . 30. September [-] 2. Oktober 1926. Berlin, 1926. 202 p. 1514 lots. Music, lots 960-1143.
[US-NYgr]

Not examined. A note in *ZfMW* 9 (1926/27): 64 repeats citation but cites the name Reichel and adds: *II. Musik Theater, Bildende Kunst*, and dates 1927.

742 Dunwalt, Gottfried
Commer, Franz. "Catalogus musicalium Godefridi Dunwalt Canonici Collegiatae Ecclesiae B. Mariae V. ad Gradus Coloniae. 1770." 3 Bl., 84 Gez. BL.   [compiler (film)]

A Ms. thematic catalog in Hirsch Collection at GB-Lbl.

743 Duodo, Amalia Astori
H. BARON, FIRM, LONDON   UNNUMBERED OFFER
"Music from the Collection of. . . . London, [n.d., 199-?]. 6 leaves, typescript. 209 lots.

Bound with: "All by Rossini" (typed citations superimposed on facsimiles of copyists' Ms. pp. in xerox). 18 leaves. 18 items.

744 Duyse, Florimond van
CAMILLE VYT, LIBRAIRE
Catalogue de la bibliothèque de feu. . . . Gand, 1913. 16 p. 716 lots.
[compiler (ex-Scheurleer copy)]

E , G . *See* **E[ckl], G[eorge]** (sale of 22 February 1922)

Eagles, Rev. John. *See under* **Rivers, Sir Henry** (sale of 1856)

Earl of Aylesford, 6th. *See* **Finch, Heneage**

Earl of Aylesford, 8th. *See* **Finch, Charles Wightwick**

Earl of Falmouth. *See* **Boscawen, George Henry**

Earl of Westmoreland. *See* **Fane, John**

745 Ebeling, Christoph Daniel, ca. 1791-1817
Versuch einer auserlesenen musikalischen Bibliothek mit Rücksicht auf Herrn Stockhausens Bibliothek abgefasst. [Hambourg . . . , 1770.]

Not examined, not located; cited from **Bobillier** and **Fétis**.

746 Ebergs, P[eder]
Fortegnelse over afdøde Stadsmusicus P[eder] Ebergs efterladte Musikalier, Instrumenter of Bøger. [Trondheim, 18**.] 1 leaf. F°.

> Not examined; cited from Pettersen's *Nordisk Boglexikon*, p. 145.

747 Eberhard III, 1628-57
"Katalog der Bibliothek der Hofkapelle von 1569. Verzeichnis der Gesangbüecher [*sic*], so der Capellmaister beyhanden." Transcribed by G. Bossert in his "Die Hofkapelle unter Eberhard III, 1628-57." *Würtembergische Vierteljahrshefte für Landesgeschichte* 20, no. 2 (1911): 128-33.

748 Ebers, Georg
HENRICI, FIRM, BERLIN   VERST. 109
Autographen, Musik, Theater, bildende Kunst. Der Sammlungen Georg Ebers, Auguste Pattberg, Wottge, Diersberg zweiter Teil sowie einer grossen mitteldeutschen Sammlung erster Teil u. a . . . Versteigerung 1.-2., 6, 1926. [Berlin]: Henrici, 1926. 86 p. 777 lots.

> Not examined; cited from **Folter 2**, no. 159.

749 Eckard, Johann Gottfried, 1735-1809
LITERATURE
Reeser, Eduard. "De Nalatenschap van Johann Gottfried Eckard." In *Anthony van Hoboken: zum 75. Geburtstag,* ed. Joseph Schmidt-Görg, 122-30. Mainz: B. Schott's Söhne, [1962].   [g.a.]

750 Eckhardt, J H
Verzeichnis von Musikalien welche bey ihm vorräthig und für dabey gesetzten Preis zu haben sind. Greifswald, [probably 1903]. 16 p.

> Not located; cited from Haas catalog no. 11, lot 125.

751 E[ckl?], G[eorg?], et al.
DOROTHEUMS-VERSTEIGERUNGSAMT, FIRM, VIENNA
I. Autographen-Versteigerung. Musiker, Dichter, Gelehrte [et al]. *Aus der Sammlung G. E., und aus anderen Wiener Besitze. Vom 22. bis 25. Februar 1922 . . . Wien.* [Wien?, 1922.] 75 p. 1152 lots. "Musiker," lots 1-490.   [US-NYgr, with prices fetched laid in]

752 Eckl, Georg
DR. IGNAZ SCHWARZ, FIRM, VIENNA   VERST. NO. 14
Sammlung Georg Eckl. I. Teil, Theater - Musik. [Foreword by Gustav Gugitz.] *Versteigerung* [17. Mai 1926 und die folgenden Tage]. . . . Wien, 1926. 115 p. 1343 lots. Music, lots 690-901 (many more items).   [compiler, US-NYgr, -Wc, VBBA]

753 _____
BÜCHER-AUKTIONSSAAL DES DOROTHEUMS, VIENNA   AUK. NO. 296
Nachlass Georg Eckl. I. Teil. Austriaca - Viennensia. . . . anrichten van Ziegler und Janscha . . . Lanner-Schubert-Strauss, Erst- und Frühausgaben. Notenmanuskripte, Autographen, usw. [Auktionstag . . . 3. April 1930.] Vienna, 1930. 32 p. 690 lots. Music, lots 623-90 (many more items).   [US-NYgr]

754   **Écorcheville, Jules Armand Joseph,** 1872-1915
Catalogue des livres rares et precieux composant la collection musicale de feu . . . avec une introduction de M. Henry Prunières . . . vente du 26 au 29 mai 1920. Paris: E. Paul, 1920. 82 p. 611 lots (many more items).   [compiler (priced), US-NYgr, -NYp, -Wc]
Folter, no. 80; **Hirsch**, no. 435; **Albrecht**.

755   **Edberg, Albert**
LITERATURE
Helmer, Axel. "Edberska samlingen." *Svenskt Musikhistoriskt Arkiv Bull* 20 (1985): 18-20. [g.a.]
        According to *RILM*: 5900 concert programs, 1895-1950 with card-indexes
        . . . and 840 drawings of orchestral seating plans, lists of players and photos.

756   **Edinburgh Philharmonic Society**
PUTTICK & SIMPSON, AUCTIONEER, LONDON   CAT. NO. 1226
Catalogue of a Collection of Miscellaneous Music, Including the Musical Library of the Edinburgh Philharmonic Society. . . . Also Valuable Musical Instruments . . . Sold January 26th, 1871. London, 1871. 18 p. 605 lots. Music, lots 1-501.   [GB-Lbl]

757   **Edwards, Frederick George,** 1853-1909; **S.** [i.e., **F.**] **Berger;** [**W. Bartholomew**]
PUTTICK & SIMPSON, AUCTIONEER, LONDON   CAT. No. 4411
Catalogue of the Musical Library and Collection of Autograph Letters of the Late F. G. Edwards, Esq., Editor of the "Musical Times." Also a Portion of the Library of S. [i.e., *F.*] *Berger, Secretary to the Philharmonic Society . . . Sold April 18th, 1910.* London, 1910. 21 p. 266 lots. Edward's, lots 1-82 and autograph letters, lots 222-40. Property of W. Bartholomew, lots 83-221; Berger's, lots 241-66.   [GB-Lbl]

Edwards, Mrs. Harry (née **Elis. Sauret**).   *See* **Sauret**

758   **Edwards, Julian**
"Catalogue of the Library of the Late. . . . " [New York, ca. 1910.] 49 fols., Ms. typed.
[US-Wc only]
        Worthless, poor catalog, though sizeable, good library.

759   **Edwards, William, of Spaulding**
PUTTICK & SIMPSON, AUCTIONEER, LONDON
Catalogue of a Collection of Ancient & Modern Music . . . Also Musical Instruments, Including the Collection of William Edwards . . . Will Be Sold . . . April 29, 1875. . . . [London, 1875.] 12 p. 278 lots. Music, lots 1-182.   [GB-Lbl, US-NYp (Drexel 860)]

760   **Egelund**
HENRICI, AUCTIONEER, BERLIN   VERST. 100
Autograph Sammlung Egelund, u.a.m. historische Autographen. . . . Musik - Theater - bildende Kunst, Literatur und Wissenschaft . . . Versteigerung . . . 16. [-] *17. Februar 1925.* Berlin, 1925. 91 p. 737 lots. Music, lots 357-464 (includes good Brahms and Wagner items).   [US-NYgr]

761   **Eggenberg Family**
Záloha, J. "Dilla ceských skladatelu v dodatcich ceskokrumlovské hudebni sbirky." *Hudebni veda* 5 (1968): 458 f.
        Not located; cited by **Albrecht**.

762   Egk, Leopold, Bishop of Olomouc
Literature
Sehmal, Jíři. "Das Musikinventar des Olmützer Bischofs Leopold Egk aus dem Jahre 1760 als Quelle vorklassiker Instrumentalmusik." *AMw* 29 (1972): 285-317.   [g.a.]
> **Albrecht**: now lost.

Ehreshoven, Schloss.   *See under* **Nesselrode Family**

763   Einstein, Alfred, 1880-1952
Literature
Roberts, James. "Works with Trombone in the Alfred Einstein Collection of 16th and 17th-Century Instrumental Music." *International Trombone Association Journal,* October 1984.
                                                                                                   [g.a.]
> Collection now at US-Nsc.

764   Eitner, Robert, 1822-1905; **Heinrich Reimann**
Leo Leipmannssohn, firm, Berlin   Cat. no. 162
Musikgeschichte und- bibliographie aus [!] *den Sammlungen des Professors Robert Eitner und Dr. Heinrich Reimann.* Berlin, [1906]. 54 p. 757 lots.   [g.a.]
> **Folter**, no. 81. Properties are not differentiated.

> → **Eitner, Robert**. *See also under* **Rust** (Liepmannssohn catalog no. 165, sale of 1907)

765   Elgar, Sir Edward, 1857-1934
Harold Reeves, firm, London   Cat. no. 34
Music and Musical Literature. . . . A Large Collection of Books on Music and Musicians. . . . Many Rare and Out of Print Works, Volumes from the Library of . . . and Other Recent Purchases. London, 1922. 24 p. No lotting.
> **Folter**, no. 82, notes only the Sotheby, Wilkinson & Hodge sale of non-music materials, 20 February 1922.

766   Ellerton, John Lodge, 1801-73
Puttick & Simpson, auctioneer, London
Catalogue of the Musical Library of the Late . . . with Other Collections, Comprising Full Scores . . . Scarce Early English and Italian MSS. . . . Works on the History and Theory of Music. . . . Music Plates and Copyrights of Works by Joseph Warren and Henry Phillips; Also Musical Instruments . . . Sold . . . December 1st, 1893, and Following Day. London, 1873. 37 p. 831 lots. Music, lots 1-717 (many more items). Lot no. 193, a "collection of music catalogs from 1797 to 1853—a total of 84 catalogs in 5 volumes." Bought by Laidlaw for £1/1.
                                                               [GB-Lbl, US-WYnp; film at US-NBuU]

767   Ellingson, Ter
Literature
"The Ellingson Collection of Asian Music." *Resound* 1, no. 3 (July 1982): 1-2.
> Collection of field tapes recorded 1973-74 now at the Archive of Traditional Music at Indiana University.

768 **Elphinstone, Lord;** et al.
SOTHEBY & CO., AUCTIONEER, LONDON
Catalogue of Valuable Printed Books, Music, Oriental Manuscripts, Autograph Letters and Historical Documents. . . . The Property of Reginald Francis . . . Col. C. H. Wilkison [and others]. *First and Early Editions of Lully . . . Property of the Right Hon. Lord Elphinstone . . . Sold . . . 21st July, 1958, and the Two Following Days.* [London], 1958. 104 p. 779 lots. Music, lots 639-56; Lully items, lots 639-49.   [Film at CRL]

769 **Elson, Louis Charles,** 1848-1920
LITERATURE
"The Unequalled Elson Library." *Musical Courier* 53, no. 3 (1906): 26.   [g.a.]

[**Elwin,**]. *See* **Grant,** **Miss**

770 **Ely, Edith,** 1886-1961
J. B. MUNS, FIRM, BERKELEY, CAL.   LIST 85-1
The Musical Autographs, Photographs, Programs, Letters, Handbills, Manuscripts, News Clippings, etc. Collection of Madame Edith de Lys, Dramatic Soprano, 1886-1961. . . . Berkeley, 1985. Unpaged. 146 lots.   [g.a.]

771 **Émeric-David, Toussaint Bernard,** 1755-1839
J. TECHENER, AUCTIONEER, PARIS (C.P. = CHARLES PILLET)
Catalogues des livres anciens et modernes composant la bibliothèque de feu . . . vente . . . 20 mars et les jours suivants. . . . Paris: Chez J. Techener, 1862. 553 p. Music, lots 945-59 (more items).   [US-Cn]

772 **Enfield Musical Society**
PUTTICK & SIMPSON, AUCTIONEER, LONDON   CAT. NO. 2238
Catalogue of a Valuable Assemblage of Musical Properties, Including Full Compass Pianofortes. . . . Also a Quantity of Music, Library of the Enfield Musical Society . . . Sold February 19th, 1884. London, 1884. 9 p. 223 lots.   [GB-Lbl]

773 **Engel, Carl; Charles Goodban,** 1784-1863
PUTTICK & SIMPSON, AUCTIONEER, LONDON   CAT. NO. 2097
Catalogue of the Extremely Interesting and Valuable Library of Music, Musical Treatises and Collection of Folk Lore, Formed by Carl Engel. . . . Also, the Musical Library of the Late. . . . A Few Curious Musical Instruments . . . Sold May 4 [1882] *and Following Day.* London, 1882. 34 p. 633 lots.   [GB-Lbl]

774 _____
BERNARD QUARITCH, FIRM, LONDON   CAT. NO. 343
Catalogue of Works on Music, Songs, Games, Sports . . . [etc.] *Offered for Cash at the Affixed Net Prices by . . . London, August 1882.* London, 1882.   [US-NYgr and NL-Avb]

> Pp. 785-864, lots 8394-9472, "History of music, works on sacred, instru-
> mental, and popular music; national songs, Christmas carols, ballads, &
> books of dance music" (Engel's).
> → *See also* under **Steed, A. O.**

775 _____
WILLIAM REEVES, FIRM, LONDON   CAT. NO. 10 (PART 1)
Catalogue of Music & Musical Literature, Ancient and Modern. . . . Music from Several

Libraries (Carl Engel, John Hullah et al.) *All Recently Purchased.* . . . London, 1883. Pp. 86-116. No lots.   [compiler]

776   **Engel, Carl; Joseph Warren,** 1804-81
PUTTICK & SIMPSON, AUCTIONEER, LONDON   CAT. NO. 2034
Catalogue of the Extensive Collection of Books on Musical History, Theory and Practice of. *. . . Also Various Musical Compositions. . . . Also the Residue of the Library of the Late Joseph Warren . . . Sold July 7th, 1881.* London, 1881. 26 p. 433 lots. Engel's, lots 1-344; Warren's, lots 345-433.   [GB-Lbl]
       King, p. 64.

777   **Engel, Franz**
HEINRICH KERLER, FIRM, ULM   CAT. NO. 278
Geschichte und Technik des Theaters, Theater der alten Zeiten, Opern, Operetten, etc., mit Partitur, Orchester- und Solo-Stimmen, Partituren, Klavierauszüge und einzelne Teile, Scenarien, Entr'acte-Musik für Streichorchester mit Stimmen, vollständige Blechmusik mit Stimmen, Schau-Lustspiele mit Rollen und Soufflierbuch. Zum grössten Teil Bibliothek von. . . . Ulm, 1900.
       Not located; cited from *ZiMG* (1900).

778   **Engel, Hans,** 1894-1970
HANS SCHNEIDER, FIRM, TUTZING   CAT. NO. 229
Musikbibliothek Prof. Dr. Hans Engel nebst einigen anderen Beiträgen. Tutzing: Schneider, [1979]. 75 p. 1208 lots. Engel's, lots 1-864.   [g.a.]
       Folter, no. 83.

779   **Engelmann, Theodor**
HENNING OPPERMAN (VORMALS R. GEERING), AUCTIONEER, BASEL
Illustrierte Bücher des 18. und 19. Jahrhunderts . . . Deutsche und Schweizer Literatur . . . Bibliothek von . . . Versteigerung . . . 26. [-] 28. April 1932. . . . Basel, 1932. 123 p. 1336 lots. Music, ca. 50 lots, *inter alia.*   [US-Wc]

780   **English Opera Company**
PUTTICK & SIMPSON, AUCTIONEER, LONDON   CAT. NO. 910
The Entire, Very Complete and Expensive Theatrical Wardrobe . . . For Mounting Various Operas . . . Also the Extensive Musical Library in Scores and Parts. . . . London, 1866. 523 lots. Operas, scores, parts, libretti, lots 454-520.   [GB-Lbl]

781   **Enschedé, Jan Willem,** 1865-1926
VAN STOCKUM ANTIQUARIAAT, AUCTIONEER, DEN HAAG
Catalogue de la bibliothèque de feu M. J. W. Enschedé. [Vente publique du 12-21 mars 1927. . . .] La Haye: Van Stockums Antiquariaat, 1927. 239 p.   [C-Tp, US-CA]

782   **Erben, André**
LEO LIEPMANNSSOHN, AUCTIONEER, BERLIN   CAT. NO. 55
Versteigerung von Musikmanuskripten Wolfgang Amadeus Mozarts aus dem Besitz von . . . den 12. Oktober 1929 . . . durch Leo Liepmannssohn [und] *Karl Henrici. Beschreibendes Verzeichnis von Georg Kinsky.* Berlin, [1929]. 44 p., 28 plates. 26 lots.
       [US-Wc, -CHH, -IO, -NYcu; compiler]

783 _____

LEO LIEPMANNSSOHN, AUCTIONEER, BERLIN   CAT. NO. 62
*Musikmanuskripte Wolfgang Amadeus Mozarts. Aus dem Besitz von. . . . 2ᵉʳ und letzter Teil
. . . 9. Dezember 1932. . . .* Berlin, 1932. 34 p., 9 plates. 32 lots.   [US-NYp; compiler]

784 **Erdmann, Eduard,** 1896-1958
HANS SCHNEIDER, FIRM, TUTZING   CAT. NO. 75
Musikbibliothek Eduard Erdmann und andere Beiträge. Tutzing, [1960]. 48 p. 1000 lots.
[g.a.]

   Properties not differentiated. **Folter,** no. 85.

785 **Erlebach, Philipp Heinrich,** 1667-1714
"Die Musik in Rudolstadt zu Erlebachs Zeiten . . . Inventarium Ueber die, zur Hochgräffl.
Rudolstädtischen Hoff Capell gebörigen musicalischen Sachen. . . ." In *Denmäler deutscher
Tonkunst,* Bd. 46/47, ed. Otto Kinkeldey, xxii-xxix. Leipzig: Breitkopf & Härtel, 1914.
[g.a.]

786 _____

  LITERATURE
  Baselt, Bernard. "Die Musiksammlung der Schwarzburg-Rudolfstädtischen Hofkapelle unter
  Philipp Heinrich Erlebach." In Martin-Luther-Universität, Halle-Wittenberg, *Tradition und
  Aufgaben der Hallischen Musikwissenschaft,* pp. ? Wissenschaftliche Zeitschrift der Martin-
  Luther-Universität Halle-Wittenburg, Sonderabend. Halle, 1963.   [US-NH, -CHH. -U, -IO]
    Not examined.

787 _____

  Tzschöckell, Helmut. "Die Notenbestände der ehemaligen Hofkapellen Rudolstadt und
  Sondershausen im Staatsarchiv in der [Schloss] Heidecksburg." *Rudolstädter Heimathefte* 12
  (1966): 6-9.
    Not located; cited from **Benton 2**:144, no. 117.

  Erwein, Franz, 1776-1840.   *See under* **Schönbrun-Wiesentheid**

  Erwein, Hugo Damien, Graf, 1738-1817.   *See under* **Schönborn-Wiesentheid**

788 **Esser, Mej. Cateau**
  R. W. P. DE VRIES, AUCTIONEER, AMSTERDAM
  *Catalogus van eene fraaie verzameling muziekwerken opera-, operette- en orkest-materiaal
  enz . . . uit de nalatenschap . . . Veiling: Dinsdag 5 april 1927. . . .* A'dam: de Vries, 1927.
  32 p. 258 lots.   [NL-Avb]

  Essers, C   W   A.   *See under* **Plugge** (sale of 30 June 1914)

789 **Essex, Tim,** 1764-1847
  PUTTICK & SIMPSON, AUCTIONEER, LONDON   CAT. NO. 54
  *Catalogue of a Valuable Collection of Music, Including the Library of the Late . . . Comprising
  Sacred and Organ Music, Vocal Music, Glees. . . . An Extensive Assemblage of Instrumental
  Music, in Scores and in Parts . . . and a Choice Collection of Musical Literature . . . Sold . . .
  January 27, 1848, and Following Day.* London, 1848. 16 p. 427 lots. Music, lots 1-394.
  [GB-Lbl]

790   **Este, House of** (9th-19th century)
"Inventario degl'instromenti e libri grandi di musica che havea in custodia il gia. D. Nicolò 1625." Reprinted in E. van der Straeten, *La Musique aux Pays-Bas*, vol. 6, p. 120; and in Valdrighi's *Musurgiana*, no. 11 (1884): 68-71.   [g.a.]

791   _____
Cittadella, Luigi Napoleone. *Il castello di Ferrara: descrizione storico artistica*. Ferrara: Taddei e Figli, 1875. 107 p.   [US-NYcu, -Wc]

> Appendix 1, pp. 63-85, "La libreria di Borso d'Este" (an inventory of manuscripts owned by the family in 1467). Not examined; cited from Frati. **Albrecht**: library now at I-MOe.

792   _____
Spinelli, Alessandro Giuseppe. "Della raccolta musicale estense." *Memorie della R. Accademia di scienze, lettere ed arti in Modena*, ser. 2, 9 (1893): xii-xxxiv.   [g.a.]

> Also published separately.

793   _____
Finzi, Vittorio. "Bibliografia delle stampe musicali della R. Biblioteca Estense." *Rivista delle biblioteche* 3 (1892): 77-89, 107-14, 162-76; 4 (1893): 16-26, 174-186; 5 (1895): 48-64, 89-142.   [g.a.]

794   _____
Bertoni, G. "La biblioteca de Borso d'Este." *Atti della R. accademia delle scienze di Torino* 61 (1925-26): 706-28.

> Not examined; cited from **Frati**, p. 210. Includes (?) the inventory of 1467.

795   _____
Haas, Robert Maria. . . . *Die Estensischen Musikalien: Thematisches Verzeichnis mit Einleitung. Mit Unterstützung der Deutschen Gesellschaft für Wissenschaft und Kunst in Prag*. Regensburg: G. Bosse, 1927. 232 p.

> Not examined; cited from **Benton 2**:15, no. 55.

796   _____
Luin, Elisabeth Jeannette. . . . *Repertorio dei libri musicali di S. A. S. Francesco d'Este nell'Archivio di stato di Modena*. Firenze: L. S. Olschki, 1936. Reprinted from *Bibliofilia* 38 (1936): [419]-45.   [g.a.]

797   _____
Lodi, Pio. *Citta di Modena: Raccolta musicale Estense*. Boll. dell'Associazione dei musicologi italiani, ser. 8. Parma: Officina Grafica Fresching, [1916-24]. 561 p. Reprint, Forni, 1967.
[Reprint, g.a.]

798   _____
Gianturco, Carolyn. "Catelani rivisitato" (Angelo Catelani's 1865 thematic catalog of Alessandro Stradella's music in the Estense Collection). In *Alessandro Stradella e Modena*, 11-16. Modena: COPTIP, 1985.

799 _____

Crowther, Victor. *Oratorio in Modena* [A survey of the collection of Francesco II d'Este, Duke of Modena, 1674-94]. Oxford: Clarendon Press, 1992. x, 215 p.

800 _____

LITERATURE
Roncaglia, Gino. "Gli splendori dell'Estense." *La Scala* (giugno 1952): 15-18.   [g.a.]

801 _____

Chiarelli, Alessandra. "La collezione estense di musica stradelliana sulla sua formazione." In *Alessandro Stradella e Modena,* ed. Carolyn Gianturco, 116-24. Modena: COPTIP, 1985.

See another article from this work, no. **798**.

802   **Esterházy Family**

The foundation was laid by Nikolaus, 1583-1645. It was first enlarged by Pál, 1635-1713, then by Prince Paul Anton, 1711-62.

803 _____

Harich, James. "Opera — és színdárab szövegkönyvek [librettos and play books]; Szöveg — könyvgyüjtemény [textbook collection]." Typescript, 1941.   [H-Bn.Ms.mus.th.112]

804 _____

Harich, James. "Inventare der Esterházy-Hofmusik-kapelle in Eisenstadt." *Haydn Yearbook* 9 (1975): 5-125.

Harich reprints 6 manuscript inventories of different dates by different compilers:

I.   "Inventar 1721," pp. 11-21

II.   "Werners Katalog, 1737-1738: Catalogus über die dermalig Brauchbare Chor oder Kirchen Musicalien."

III.   "Thematisches Verzeichnis von 1740," pp. 31-36, lists 386 compositions; reprinted with incipits.

IV.   "Katalog von 1759," pp. 67-88.

IV.   [*sic*]. "Haydns Opernliste 1784," pp. 89-95. In fact, it is no. V; there are two no. IV's.

V.   "Hummels [Johann Nepomuk] Katalog 1806: Inventorium des Hochfürstlich Esterhazyschen Kammer und Theatermusicalien wie auch Musicalischen Instrumente von 1806."

Harich notes an inventory of 1858, as well, p. 116, with 3000 works listed. This 1858 inventory (according to Sas, **808**), based on a list prepared in the 1820s, is now at H-Bn and titled: "Inventar Nr. 42. Inventarium über die hochfürstlich Esterházyschen Kammer- und Theater Musicalien zu Eisenstadt von Jahre 1858."

→ *See also* entries in **Benton** directory, part 2, about the Eisenstadt archives

805 _____

Bartha, Dénes, and László Somfai.

VI.   "Musikalische Quellen (Catalogue raisonné der Esterházy-Opernsammlung, in chronologischer Ordnung dere Premièren.)" In *Haydn als Opernkapellmeister: Die Haydn-Dokumente der Esterházy-Opernsammlung,* 177-391. Mainz: B. Schott's Söhne, 1960.   [g.a.]

> Chapter 2: Die Esterházy-Opernsammlung, pp. 32-43, reviews early catalogs of the collection, including most of those reprinted by Harich (**804**), but adding what they call a "Champée" of 1756 to that of the 1759. Chapter 9, pp. 404-34: Die Kopisten der Opernsammlung.

806 _____

Bárdos, Kornel. *A tatai Esterházyak zebéje 1727-1846.* Budapest: Akadémiai Kiadó, 1978. 259 p. VI. "A müvek tematikus jegyzéke," pp. 78-248.

807 _____

Catalog no. V., Hummel's 1806 catalog.

> Ms. in the Goethe Museum in Düsseldorf (**804**) was also reprinted, with a transliteration and commentary by Else Radant, in "A Facsimile of Hummel's Catalog of the Princely Music Library in Eisenstadt," *Haydn Yearbook* 11 (1980): 5-182.

808 _____

Sas, Ágnes. "Rediscovered Documents from the Esterházy Collection. . . ." *Studia musicologica academicae scientiarum hungaricae* 34 (1992): 167-85.   [g.a.]

809 _____

". . . Documents from the Esterházy Archives in Eisenstadt and Forchtenstein," ed. János Harich II; commentary by Else Radant and H. C. Robbins Landon. *Haydn Yearbook* 19 (1994): [whole issue]. 359 p. 265 items.   [g.a.]

810 _____

LITERATURE

Bakács, I. "Az Esterházy család hercegi ágának levéltára [The archives of the princely branch of the Esterházy family]." *Levétári Levéltárak* 2 (1956): 4.

811 **Eudel, Paul,** 1837-1911
Catalogue de la bibliothèque de musique. . . . Paris, 1898.

> Cited in **Scheurleer** 1 (1923): 12. Not otherwise verified or located.

812 [**Euing, William,** 1788-1874]
[Brown, James D.] According to Brown & Stratton, *British Musical Biography* (1887), a notice of the library and its contents appeared anonymously in Mason's *Public and Private Libraries in Glasgow* (1885).

813 _____

PUTTICK & SIMPSON, AUCTIONEER, LONDON   CAT. NO. 1598
Catalogue of a Collection of Music, a Portion of the Library of a Well-Known Professor. . . . History and Theory of Music with Interesting MS. Notes. . . . Rare Autographs and MSS. Seventeen Letters to Kallman Addressed to Dr. [William Hutchins] *Callcott* [etc.]. *Unpublished Manuscripts of George Barker . . . Sold May 29, 1876, and Following Days.* London, 1876. 37 p. 650 lots. Music, lots 1-559. Callcott Mss., lots 436-44 ; Barker's, lots 445-79c. [GB-Lbl]

> **King**, p. 61: ". . . the notorious anonymous catalogue, which nevertheless gives a fair idea of his wonderful judgment. . . ."

814 _____

ANDERSON'S COLLEGE, GLASGOW, LIBRARY, EUING COLLECTION
The Euing Musical Library. Catalogue of the Musical Library of the Late Wm. Euing, Esq.,
Bequeathed to. . . . Glasgow: printed by W. M. Ferguson, 1878. 4, 256 p.   [US-CA, -NYp, -Wc]

> **King**, p. 61. **Albrecht**. **Penney**: 2500 early editions on music theory, psalm
> books, letters containing biographies and autobiographies used in
> Sainsbury's *Dictionary* (1824) sold in two Puttick & Simpson sales, 17
> August 1853 and a Warren sale, 8 April 1881. Also included, a set of part
> books by John Playford, notebook and manuscripts of John Stafford Smith.

815 _____

[James Ludovic Lindsay Crawford, 26th Earl of], 1847-1913. *Bibliotheca Lindesiana.*
Catalogue of a Collection of English Ballads of the XVIIth and XVIIIth Centuries Printed
for the Most Part in Black Letter. [Aberdeen: University Press], 1890. xiii, 686 p.

[US-
Wc, -CHua, -CLp]

> "Appendix B. First lines and titles of the ballads in the Huth and Euing
> Collections," pp. [663]-86.

816 _____

Hubens, Arthur. "La Bibliothèque Euing à Glasgow, divulgée pour la première fois par un
catalogue descriptif de quelques-uns de ses ouvrages les plus rares et plus précieux." *Rivista*
musicale italiana 23 (1916): 243-72.   [g.a.]

> A select list of holdings.

817 _____

Farmer, Henry George. "The Euing Musical Collection." *MR* 8 (1947): 197-203.   [g.a.]

> Notes the poor quality of the 1878 catalog of the collection (now at the
> University of Glasgow) and how others have characterized it (*Grove,* 2nd
> ed., 2:703, "altogether inadequate"), etc. and proceeds to note important, early,
> and rare works inadequately treated there.

818 _____

GLASGOW, UNIVERSITY OF GLASGOW
The Euing Collection of English Broadside Ballads in the Library of. . . . Glasgow: University
Publications, 1971. 686, xxiv p., illus.   [US-NYp, -MWA]

> Collection formed by J. O. Halliwell [i.e., James Orchard Halliwell-Phillips,
> 1820-89].

819 _____

LITERATURE
"The Euing Musical Library." *Musical News and Herald* 7 (11 August 1894): 117-18.
[journal is available on film]

820 **Euler, J   F**

H. & G. BACKHUYSEN AND J. P. WYNANTS, AUCTIONEERS, DEN HAAG
Catalogue d'une belle collection de livres & oeuvres d'estampes . . . dessins & estampes . . .
des curiosités très rares & precieuses . . . vendus . . . 23 fevrier 1801 & jours suivants. . . . La
Haye, 1801. 4, 91 p. 1935 lots.   [NL-DHmw]

> **Lugt**, no. 6203^a, says with 65 lots of music. Not examined.

Evans, Edwin.   *See under* **Revelstoke, Lady**

821   [**Evans, Sir John,** 1823-1908]
SOTHEBY, WILKINSON & HODGE, AUCTIONEER, LONDON
Catalogue of Valuable & Rare Books, Illuminated Horae and Antiphonaries . . . Sold . . . 15th of March 1911. . . . [London, 1911.] 80 p. 621 lots.   [Film at CRL]
"Another Property," consists of music, lots 128-42, including early prints.

822   **Evelyn, John,** 1620-1706
According to **King**, p. 10, there is a Ms. catalog of Evelyn's collection at Christ Church ("Catalogus Evelynianus 1687," Ms. 20ᵃ, p. 190). Also noted by **Albrecht**. Collection now at GB-Och.

823   **Fabbrini, Paolo**
Catalogo di musica di vari autori, posti con ordine alfabetico, che si trova vendibile in Pisa, appresso Antonio Gastone Tarocchi esecutare, testementario del Gia' Signor Paolo Fabbrini, all'eredita' del quale detta musica appartiene. Livorno, 1789. 64 p.
[GB-Lbl]
Bound in an 8° volume labeled "Catalogues" and shelved as the last (the latest date) on the shelves of English book trade catalogs before 1801. All other catalogs in the volume are English auctions by Stewart, etc.

824   **Fabricius, Johann Albert,** 1668-1736
Braun, Werner. "Die Musikalien in einer norddeutschen Gelehrtenbibliothek der Bachzeit: Bibliothecae beati Jo. Alb. Fabricii Pars I, 1738." *Mf* 10 (1957): 243-46.   [g.a.]
Approximately 80 titles are set out.

Fagan, Sofia Coronini.   *See* **Coronini**

825   **Fairbank, Janet,** 1903-47
Borroff, Edith. "The Fairbank Collection." (Including a list of the contents.) *College Music Symposium* 16 (spring 1976): 105-22.   [g.a.]
Mainly contemporary American songs given to US-Cn.

826   **Falkenstein, Constantin Karl,** 1801-55
THEODORE OSWALD WEIGEL, FIRM, LEIPZIG
Catalogue de la riche collection de lettres autographes de feu. . . . La vente publique . . . le 7. avril 1856, Maison Weigel . . . 1ʳᵉ partie. Leipzig, 1856. 156 p. 5160 lots (many more items).
[US-NYgr]
Musicians, lots 4292-764.

Falmouth, Earl of.   *See* **Boscawen, Edward**

827   **Fanan, Giorgio**
Ciancio, Laura. *Libretti per musica manoscritti e a stampa del Shapiro nella collezione Giorgio Fanan: Catalogo e indici.* Ancilla musicae, 2. Lucca: Libreria musicale italiana, 1992. xx, 381p.   [g.a.]

828   [**Fane, John, 11th Earl of Westmoreland,** known as **Lord Burghesh,** 1784-1859]
Puttick & Simpson, auctioneer, London   ˙Cat. no. 2477
Catalogue of an Assemblage of Valuable Musical Properties. . . . Also the Library of the Late . . . Printed and Manuscripts, Autographs of Haydn and Beethoven . . . Sold . . . February, the 22nd, 1887. London, 1887. 17 p. 359 lots. Music, lots 198-359.   [GB-Lbl]

> Some of his collection went to GB-Lam before this sale.

829   **Fantoni, Gabriel,** 1833-1900 (?)
Vicenza, Civico Museo
Catalogo della raccolta Fantoni nel Museo Civico. . . . Vicenza, 1893. viii, 413, xxiii.

> Fedele Lampertico's preface is summarized in *Bollettino delle pubblicazioni italiani* (1893), p. 297. Catalog not examined.

830   _____
Venice, Museo Correr
Fondo primitivo Correr e provenienze seguenti . . . lascito Gabriel Fantoni, in Associazione dei musicologi italiani, *Catalogo generale,* ser. 6, vol. 1, *Città di Venezia,* [67]-161. Parma: Freschig, 1913.   [g.a.]

831   **Farrenc, A**[ristide], i.e., **Jacques Hippolyte Aristide,** 1794-1865
(C.-P.) Delbergue-Cormont. *Catalogue de la bibliothèque musicale théorique et pratique de feu. . . . La vente aura* [lieu] *le lundi 16 avril et jours suivants. . . .* Paris: J. F. Delion, 1866. 131 p. 1622 nos.   [US-CHmu (priced), -Cn, -Cu, -Wc]

> **Folter,** no. 86. **Albrecht:** "included more than 100 autographs."

_____. *Supplement.* Paris, [1866]. 4 p.   [GB-Lbl, Hirsch no. 492(1) only]

832   **Fatio, Henry**
Henri Darel, auctioneer, Paris?
Catalogue de la precieuse collection de lettres autographes composant le cabinet de feu M. Henry Fatio. Deuxième vente . . . 15-17 juin 1932. [Paris?, 1932.] Music, lots 590-1185.

> Not examined. Cited from note in *ZfMw* 14 (1931-32): 464.

833   **Favart, Charles Simon,** 1710-92
Tross, auctioneer, Paris
Catalogue des livres de la bibliothèque de Favart: Musique, ouvrages sur les arts, poésie, théâtre dont la vente aura lieu le lundi 21 novembre 1864, et jours suivants. Paris: Tross, 1864. xi, 149 p. 1912 lots.   [NL-DHgm, Us-NYp, -Cn, -PRu, -R]

834   **Favresse, Felicién,** 1898-1960
Emile Relecom, auctioneer, Brussels
Bibliothèque de feu . . . d'un compositeur de musique . . . autographes . . . vente [26-27 January 1962]. [Bruxelles, 1962.] 28 p. 787 lots.

> Not located; cited from *IBAK* (1962-63).

Fawcett, [**John**], 1768-1837.   *See under* **Cooper, Gerald** (Fletcher sale of 9 December 1844)

835   Feininger, Laurence Karl Johann, 1909-76
Repertorium cantus pleni, I-III. Tridenti: Societas Universalis Sanctae Ceciliae, 1969, 1971, 1975.
[g.a.]

I.   Antiphonaria. 245 p. ca. 6000 nos.

II.   Gradualia. 271 p. ca. 6000 nos.

III.   Antiphonaria, prelo, excusa. xxiii, 390 p. ca. 10,000 nos.

Folter, no. 87 a,b,c.

836 _____

LITERATURE
La biblioteca musicale Laurence K. J. Feininger. Edited by Danilo Curti and Fabrizio Leonardelli.
Trento: Provincia Autonoma di Trento, 1985. 179 p.   [g.a.]

Essays by many authors on Feininger's collections.

837   Feith,
FELIX DÖRFFEL, FIRM, DARMSTADT   LISTE [NO. 32]
Sammlung Feith, Prag. Abth. 2., Musik und Theater. [Darmstadt], 1963. 3 leaves.   ? lots.

Not located; cited from *IBAK* (1962-63).

Ferdinand II, Erzherzog von Innerösterreich 1578-1637.   *See under* **Karl von Steiermark,**
Erzherzog von Innerösterreich, 1540-90

838   Ferraioli, Gaetano, Marchese, 1839-90 and **Alessandro, Marchese,** 1846-1919
Mori, Elisabetta. *Libretti di melodrami e balli del secolo XVIII, Fondo Ferraioli della Biblioteca
Apostolica Vaticana.* Biblioteconomica e bibliografia, 19. Firenze: Olschki, 1984. 226 p.
[US-BUu]

839 _____

Gialdroni, Guiliana and Teresa M. *Libretti per musica del fondo Ferrajoli della Biblioteca
Apostolica Vaticana.* Ancilla musicae, 4. Lucca: Libreria musical italiane . . . , 1933. xviii, 540 p.
[US-BUu, -AA]

840   Ferrier, Kathleen, 1912-53
LEONARD HYMAN, FIRM, LONDON   CAT. NO. 74
Vocal Music . . . Scores . . . Songs . . . Together with Some Music Formerly Belonging to. . . .
London, 1957. 15 p. 342 lots (Ferrier's, lots 288-313).

841   Fétis, François Joseph, 1784-1871
BRUSSELS, BIBLIOTHÈQUE ROYALE DE BELGIQUE
. . . Catalogue de la bibliothèque de F. J. Fétis, acquise par l'État belge. Bruxelles: C. Muquardt,
1877. xi, 946 p. 7325 nos. Music, lots 1158-871.   [g.a.]

Catalog printed from the collector's own manuscript. **Folter,** no. 88, **Albrecht.**

Reprint, Bibliotheca musica bononiensis, ser. 1, no. 7 (Bologna: Forni,
1969). **Folter,** no. 88.

842 _____

NOEL CHARAVAY, FIRM, PARIS
Catalogue d'une interessante réunion de lettre autographes provenant de la correspondence de F. -J. Fétis . . . comprenant entre autres des lettres de C.-Ph.-E. Bach, Berlioz, F. Liszt [etc.]. Paris, 1910. 40 p. 118 lots.

Not examined. **Folter**, no. 89.

843 _____

LITERATURE
[Eitner, Robert.] "Catalogue de la Bibliothèque de F. J. Fétis." *MfM* 9 (1877): 175-79.   [g.a.]
   Folter, no. 88.

844 _____

Becquart, Paul. "La Bibliothèque d'un artiste et d'un savant." *Revue belge de musicologie* 26-27 (1972-73): 145-56.   [g.a.]

845 _____

Huglo, Michel. "Les Anciens Manuscrits du fonds Fétis." *Revue belge de musicologie* 32-33 (1978-79): 35-39.   [g.a.]

846 _____

Huys, Bernard. "François-Joseph Fétis." *Fontes* 30 (1983): 29-30.   [g.a.]
   Fétis bought portions of the libraries of François Perne (1834), Libri (1858), Gaspari and La Fage (1862), and Farrenc (1866). **Folter**, no. 88.

   → *See* literature *under* each collector's name at appropriate places in this bibliography.

847 **Fetzer, Johann Nicolas Friedrich,** fl. 1842
FRIEDRICH BERTRAM, FIRM, SONDERSHAUSEN   ANTIQ. CAT. NO. 5
Verzeichnis einer sehr guten Sammlung guter Werke der theoretischen und praktischen Musik, theilweise aus dem Nachlass des Herrn Kammermusikus und Hoforganist Fetzer. . . . Sondershausen, 1863. 18 p. 697 lots.
   Cited from **Folter**, no. 90.

848 **Fibich, Zdenko**
LAVIGNE (EXP.), CHARLES PILLET (C.P.), PARIS
Catalogue de musique instrumentale . . . Livres modernes provenant de la collection de M. Fibich . . . vente . . . Rue Drouot . . . 28 mai 1868. . . . Paris: Lavigne, 1868. 14 p. 5123 lots. Music, lots 1-51.   [NL-DHgm]
   Cited from **Blogie**, no. 2.

849 **Fibiger, August**
LITERATURE
Mikanová, Eva Tomandlová. "Horcickuv seznam hudebnin z pozustalosti bakovského ucitele Aug. Fibigera" (and Inventory). *Miscellanea musicologica* 5 (1958): 5-131.   [g.a.]

850   **Fiers, F   ; Hyacinthe de Grave** [et al.]
C. J. FERNAND, AUCTIONEER (COMMISSIONAIR = E. C. LAVAUT), GHENT
*Catalogue d'une belle collection de tableaux, livres, musique et estampes, délaissés par . . .
vente . . . 4 mai 1802 et jours suivants. . . .* A Gand: C. J. Fernand, 1802. 26 p. 455 lots. Music,
lots 1-62.   [NL-BG]

> **Lugt**, no. 6423.

851   **Figus-Bystrý, Viliam**
Muntág, E. *Viliam Figus-Bystrý, hudobná pozostalost'* [The musical bequest of . . .]. Martin, 1964.

> Not examined; cited from *RILM*. Same article appeared in *Hudobný archiv*
> 2 (1977): 245-58.

852   **Filippi, Joseph de**
AUGUSTE AUBRY (LIBRAIRE), PARIS
Catalogue de la bibliothèque théâtrale de . . . vente . . . 27 mai 1861, et jours suivants [i.e., 4 juin].
. . . Paris, 1861. 3 vols. (184, 114, 41 p). 1162, 1608, 523 lots.
[NL-DHgm, US-NYgr, -Bp, -NYp, -Cn, -NYcu]

> "Sur la musique et les théâtres lyriques," vol. 1: lots 511-705; "Sur la danse
> et les ballets," vol. 1, lots 706-25; "Opéra comique," vol. 2, lots 1275-83
> (hundreds of items in cartoons); "Théâtre musical italien," vol. 2, lots 1494-
> 1543 (many more items); "Opéras allemandes," vol. 2, lots 1590-92 (but over
> a hundred items). Vol. 3, sets and costumes.

853   _____

*Essai d'un bibliographie générale du théâtre, ou catalogue raisonné de la bibliothèque d'un
amateur. Complétant le catalogue Soleinne.* Paris: Aubry, 1861. vii, 223 p.
[US-NYp, -Su, -CA, -MAu, etc.]

> Not examined; cited in Filippi's own sale catalog (without named author),
> p. 121.
>
> → *See also under* **Soleinne**

854   **Fillon, Benjamin,** 1819-81
CHARAVAY FRÈRES, PARIS
Inventaire des autographes et des documents historiques composant la collection de. . . .
Paris: E. Charavay, 1877- [83]. 15 series in 6 vols.   [US-CA, -Su, -MAu, -NYcu]

> Sale catalog. Sér. 10 = "Musiciens." According to **Schaal**, contains many items
> once property of Aloys Fuchs.

855   _____

Idem. Paris: Charavay Frères [etc.], 1878-1900. 3 vols. (15 series).

> Another edition. Again, Sér. 10 = "Musiciens."

856   _____

LITERATURE
[Poligny, Germaine de.] *Autographes d'artistes et des musiciens réunis par Benjamin Fillon, décrits
par Étienne Charavay.* La Roche-sur Yon: Imp. V. Cochard-Tremblay, 1879. 19 p.

[US-NYcu only]

857   Filmer Family, Baronetcy

Shepherd, Brooks, Jr. "A Repertory of 17th Century English House Music." *JAMS* 9 (1956): 61.

[g.a.]

> Abstract of a paper read at an AMS chapter meeting, April 1956. **Albrecht**: collection sold to US-NH.

858 _____

Ford, Robert. "The Filmer Manuscripts: A Handlist." *Notes* 33 (1978): 814-25.   [g.a.]

859   Filz   ; Th   Jerres

J. M. (H. LEMPERTZ) HEBERLE, AUCTIONEER, COLOGNE

Katalog der nachgelassenen Bibliothek des Herrn Domcapitulars und Dompfarrers Dr. Filz, des Weltgeistlichen Herrn Th. Jerres, und mehrer Andern, welche nebst einer Sammlung von Musikwerken und Musikalien, am 18. Februar 1856 und an den folgenden Tagen [-22.] . . . öffentlich versteigert . . . werden. . . . Köln, 1856. Unpaged, 1522 + 3027 + 49 lots. Music, lots 2344-750 (II. Abth.).   [US-NYgr]

860   Finch, Charles Wightwick, 8th Earl of Aylesford

SOTHEBY, WILKINSON & HODGE, AUCTIONEER, LONDON

Catalogue of the Valuable Books and MSS. First Day's Sale: Valuable Books and MSS., Mainly Relating to MUSIC, the Property of the Late A. H. Littleton . . . Rare and Valuable Books Illustrating the History of Music Printing. . . . Also the Properties of the Rt. Hon. the Earl of Aylesford, Including . . . Manuscript Scores (Many Unpublished) of Handel and Other Composers, Formerly in the Possession of Mr. Charles Jennens, the Friend of Handel [etc.]. . . . [London, 1918.] 147 p. 1241 lots. Finch properties, lots 201-326c. Sale day, May 13. [compiler (copy)]

> **Albrecht** and **King**, p. 72. Many of the works in J. C. Smith's manuscript copies were bequeathed to the 3rd Earl of Aylesford by Jennens in 1773, according to Roberts (**866**). In Sotheby's sale (see earlier sales under entries for the 6th Earl, **865**), most were bought by Harold Reeves, others by Barclay Squire for the King's Music Library in GB-Lbl. Reeves's purchases were acquired by Sir Newman Flower in Reeves's 1932 sale (**861**; see other entries for Flower's library, 1922, under his name). Most of Flower's Handel items eventually went to the Manchester Public Library.

> Though the 5th and 6th Earls of Aylesford had little to do with building the collection, the first sale of the riches collected by previous Earls, especially the 3rd and 4th, took place two years after the death of the 6th. In this Sotheby sale, 35 years later, most of the rest of the collection was auctioned.

> Roberts's essay (**866**) discusses the Handeliana in this and a number of antiquarians' catalogs, several of which follow.

861 _____

HAROLD REEVES, FIRM, LONDON   CAT. NO. 102

Old, Rare and Interesting Musical Works, Including a Collection of Old English Song Books . . . An Original Haydn-Solomon Manuscript. Some Rare and Unknown Operas from the Library of the Earl of Aylesford. . . . A Copy of the Newly Discovered Earliest Known Pianoforte Music. . . . London, 1932. 36 p. Aylesford lots, 12,678-13,592.   [GB-Lbl]

862 _____

First Edition Bookshop, Firm, London   Cat. no. 26
George Frederic Handel, 1685-1759: An Original MS. of Great Importance and a Few First Editions. Addenda to Catalogue 25. [London, 1937.]   [US-R]

>   Contains items from the Aylesford collection according to Dr. John Roberts.

863 _____

Duck, Leonard. *The Aylesford Handel Manuscripts: A Preliminary Checklist.* [Manchester: Public Free Library, 1965.] 5 p.   [US-NYp]

>   Reproduced from *Manchester Review* (autumn 1965), pp. 228-32.

864 _____

Leamington Book Shop, firm, Fredericksburg, Va.   Cat. no. 32
Music, Notable for Importance, Rarity and Condition, 1500-1960. . . . There Are Many Other Items from the Library of Lord Aylesford (see table of contents). . . . Fredericksburg, Va., 1968. 64 p., 6 plates. 250 lots (46 from Aylesford).   [compiler]

865   **Finch, Heneage, 6th Earl of Aylesford,** 1824-71

Puttick & Simpson, auctioneer, London   No cat. no.
Catalogue of a Collection of Music, Including the Valuable Library of the Late. . . . Rare Instrumental Works, Sonatas, Symphonies, Concertos . . . Scarce Treatises . . . Old Manuscript Part-Books of Madrigals, Motets, etc. Valuable Autograph MS. Compositions, etc. . . . Sold . . . August 25, 1873. London, 1873. 23 p. 430 lots. Music, lots 1-386.   [GB-Lbl, US-NYp]

>   British Museum catalog says the 4th Earl; Hirsch no. 492(7) and **King,**
>   p. 58, say 6th! **Albrecht** notes this catalog only.

866 _____

Roberts, John. "The Aylesford Collection." In *Handel Collections and Their History,* ed. Terence Best, 39-85. Oxford: Clarendon Press, 1993.   [g.a.]

>   "Appendix: Handlist of manuscripts in the Jennens and Aylesford collections," pp. 65-85.
>
>   → *See also* under **Jennens**

867   **Findeisen,**

Schultze (Auktions-Secretaire), Schwerin?
*Verzeichniss der von dem herrn Hofrath Findeisen hinterlassenen, grösstentheils juristischen Bücher, Land-charten und Musikalien, welche den 31*sten *März 1807 in dem Hause des Herrn Koch Dehn zu Schwerin . . . versteigert werden sollen.* [N.p.], 1807. 82 p. Music, pp. 60-82. 473 lots.   [compiler]

868   **Finger, Gottfried,** probably 1685-1717

Banister & Playford, firm, London
A Choice Collection of Vocal and Instrumental Musick in Italian, French, and English Composed by Several Grand Masters . . . the Collection of a Great Master, Who Has Left the Land . . . [to Be Sold November 25, 1704. London, 1704?].

>   Not located; cited from the announcement of the sale appearing in Tilmouth.
>   Compare with following advertisement (of the same sale?).

869 _____

HENRY PLAYFORD, FIRM, LONDON

A Choice Collection of Vocal and Instrumental Musick in Italian, French, and English, Composed by Several Great Masters . . . Being the Collection of a Great Master, Who Has Left the Land [2 December 1704 and 17 February 1705]. [London, 1705?]

> Not located; quoted from an advertisement noted by Tilmouth. The advertisement adds that the "Collection was consigned here by a Mr. Banister and a Mr. Keller who had bought it from Finger."

870 **Fink, G[ottfried] W[ilhelm]**, 1783-1846

BREITKOPF & HÄRTEL, FIRM, LEIPZIG

Verzeichnis eines Theiles der von Dr. G. W. Fink in Leipzig hinterlassenen Bibliothek. Leipzig: Breitkopf & Härtel, [1846]. 16 p. ca. 425 lots.   [US-CHua]

> Not examined; cited from *NUC* 172:563 and **Wolffheim** 1:341.

871 **Finzi, Gerald,** 1901-56

Davie, Cedric Thorpe. *Catalogue of the Finzi Collection in St. Andrews University Library.* St. Andrews, Scotland: University Library, 1982. 71 p.   [g.a.]

> **Albrecht**; **King**, p. 80; *NG*-L, p. 767, describes as chiefly 18th-century music.

872 **Fischer,   (Dr. in Grossottersleben); Franz Hartenstein**

LIST & FRANCKE, FIRM, LEIPZIG   ANT.-CAT. NO. 292

Geschichte und Theorie der Musik. Praktische geistliche und weltliche Musik. Hymnologie. Liturgik. Schriften über das Theater. Aus dem Nachlasse der Herren. . . . Leipzig, 1895. 66 p. 1902 lots.   [US-Cn]

873 **Fischoff, Joseph,** 1804-57

Berlin. Deutsche Staatsbibliothek, Ms. Mus. 81. [An inventory of Fischoff's collection acquired by D-Bds in 1859.]

> Cited from **Schaal** (1966): 109.

874 _____

T. O. WEIGEL, AUCTIONEER, LEIPZIG

Catalog der musikalische Bibliothek des verstorbenen Prof. Joseph Fischhof in Wien. Leipzig, 1860. ? p. 540 lots.

> **Folter**, no. 91 (not seen); also in Leipmannssohn catalog no. 172, lot 184, and in **Schaal** (1967), who says [Wien, 1858]. **Albrecht**. Often cited but not located!

875 _____

LITERATURE

Fuchs, Aloys. "Die Sammlung des Hon. Prof. Jos. Fischhof." *Cäcilia* 23 (1844): 50-51.   [g.a.]

876 _____

Schaal, Richard. "Dokumente zur Wiener Musiksammlung von Joseph Fischoff: Ihre Erwerbung durch die Berliner Staatsbibliothek." *Mozart-Jahrbuch* 15 (1967): 339-47.   [g.a.]

> Acquired by G-Dbs in 1859.

877 **[Fiscowich,   ]**
El teatro. Collection de obras dramaticos y liricas. Obras musicales. Madrid: Fiscowich, 1897.
200 p.

> Not located; cited from **Bobillier** and *JbP* (1897).

878 **Fitzalan, Henry, 12th Earl of Arundel,** d. 1580

> Began the famed Nonesuch Library. *See here under* **Lumley, John, Baron**,
> 1534?-1609.

879 **Fitzgerald, Gerald, Lord**
King, Alec Hyatt. "The Wandering Minstrels and Their Archive." In *Ars iocundissima: Festschrift für
Kurt Dorfmüller zum 60. Geburtstag*, 169-77. Tutzing: Hans Schneider, 1984.   [g.a.]

> "Inventory," pp. 174-77.

880 **Fitzwilliam, Richard, 7th Viscount,** 1745-1816
Cambridge University
*A Schedule or Inventory of 1. The Printed Books and Manuscripts . . . , and of 4. The Musick,
Bound and Unbound, of the Right Honorable Richard, Late Viscount Fitzwilliam, Bequeathed
to . . . the University of Cambridge. . . .* [Cambridge, 1816.] Various pagings.

> [In manuscript at GB-Cfm]

> **King**, pp. 36-37; **Albrecht**.

881 _____

> Literature
> Cudworth, Charles. "Richard, Viscount Fitzwilliam, and the French Baroque Music in the
> Fitzwilliam Museum, Cambridge." *Fontes* 13 (1966): 27-31.

> > Collection went to Cambridge in 1816.

882 **Flack, J   G**
Mr. White (Storeys' Gate, Great George St.), auctioneer, London
*A Catalogue of All the Valuable Musical Instruments, Books, &c., the Property of. . . . The
Book's Comprise "Boyce's Cathedral Music"* [etc.] *Sold . . . June 24th, 1813 and Following
Day. . . .* London, 1813.

> > **King**, p. 93, but he puts under 1816 in the Appendix. King believes it was
> > included among the Warren sales catalogs in the Harding collection (**1177**)
> > now at GB-Ob, but the volume of catalogs in which this is found is, in fact,
> > at US-R.

883 **Flanders, Helen Hartness,** 1898-1972
Quinn, Jennifer Post. *An Index to the Field Recordings in the Flanders Ballad Collection at
Middlebury College, Middlebury, Vermont . . . with Computer Assistance by James Krupp.*
[Middlebury, Vt.]: Middlebury College, 1983. 242 p.   [g.a.]

884 _____

> Literature
> Cockrell, Dale. "The Helen Hartness Flanders Ballad Collection, Middlebury College." *Notes*
> 39, no. 1 (1982): 31-42.   [g.a.]

885 **Flaxman, John**
CHRISTIE, MANSON & WOODS, AUCTIONEER, LONDON
A Catalogue of a Valuable Assemblage of Engravings and a Fine Collection of Vocal Italian Music . . . Sold . . . July 1, 1828 . . . London, 1828. 12 p. 182 lots.   [GB-Lbl]
>   Not located. Noted in **Pollard/Munby**, opposite 173.

886 **Fleischer, Oskar** 1856-1933
DÜNNEBEIL, MUSIKALIENHANDLUNG HAUS, ?
[A group of 25 tissue pages, 8.5 x 11 inches with Fleischer's books and music, purpled, estimated at 800-900 Items, but not lotted. Prices fixed and printed.]
>   Some fragments of manuscripts from the collection are now at US-R, but no catalog
>   has been located.

887 **Fleisher, Edwin Adler,** 1877-1959
PHILADELPHIA, FREE LIBRARY, EDWIN A. FLEISHER MUSIC COLLECTION
Check List of Chamber Music Presented by. . . . [Philadelphia], 1932. 1 vol., unpaged.
                                                                            [US-NYp (film)]
_____. *Supplement.* [Philadelphia], 1934. 1 vol., unpaged.

888 _____
PHILADELPHIA, FREE LIBRARY, EDWIN A. FLEISHER MUSIC COLLECTION
The Edwin A. Fleisher Music Collection in the Free Library [a descriptive catalog]. 2 vols. Philadelphia, 1933-45. Ca. 6000 nos.   [g.a.]
>   Vol. 1, privately printed; vol. 2, Innes Press. **Folter**, no. 92; **Albrecht**.
>   Information for the majority of the works was provided by Karl Geiringer.

_____. . . . *Supplementary List, 1945-55.* [Philadelphia: Privately printed, 1956.] 33 p. **Folter,** no. 92.

889 _____
The Edwin A. Fleisher Orchestral Music Collection in the Free Library of Philadelphia: A Descriptive Catalogue. [Rev. ed.] Philadelphia: Free Library of Philadelphia, 1965. 91 p.
                                                                            [g.a.]
_____. *Supplementary List, 1945-66.* [Philadelphia, 1966?] **Folter**, no. 92.

890 _____
PHILADELPHIA, FREE LIBRARY, EDWIN A. FLEISHER MUSIC COLLECTION
The Edwin A. Fleisher Orchestral Music Collection in the Free Library: A Cumulative Catalogue, 1929-77. Boston: G. K. Hall, 1979. 956 p.   [g.a.]
>   **Folter**, no. 92.

891 _____
LITERATURE
Bradley, Carol June. "A History of the Edwin A. Fleisher Music Collection of the Free Library of Philadelphia." Philadelphia, 1957. 41 leaves, typescript.   [US-BUu (photo)]

892 _____
Bronson, Arthur. "The World's Greatest Music Library." *American Mercury* 62 (1946): 444-77.

893 Fleury [pseudo., **Champfleury**], **Jules**, 1821-99
LÉON SAPIN, FIRM, PARIS
Catalogue des livres rares et curieux composant la bibliothèque . . . avec un préface de Paul Eudel. Paris: Léon Sapin, 1890. xxi, 106 p. 967 lots.　　　　[US-NYgr, NL-Avb]
　　　"Chansons populaires," lots 191-234.

Flörsheim, G. (Basle), present owner of the autograph collection of Louis Koch, 1862-1930.
See **1546**

894 Flower, Sir (Walter) Newman, 1879-1964
Catalogue of a Handel Collection Formed by . . . , Idlehurst, Sevenoaks, Kent. [London: printed by Cassell & Co., 1922.] 32 p.　　　　[US-Wc]
　　　Albrecht: acquired by GB-Mp.

895 _____
SUNDAY TIMES, LONDON
The Second Sunday Times Book Exhibition, November 12-26, 1934. Catalogue of the Loan Collection. In the Great Hall at Grosvenor House. . . . [London: St. Clements Press, 1934.]
[US-NYcu]
　　　Section 2: "George Frederic Handel: The Newman Flower Collection," pp. 7-9 (lots 55-84). The exhibition also included items from the Speyer Collection (**2531**).

896 _____
MANCHESTER, ENG., PUBLIC LIBRARIES, HENRY WATSON MUSIC LIBRARY
George Frederic Handel: The Newman Flower Collection. [Manchester]: Manchester Public Library, 1972. xiii, 134 p.　　　　[US-NYp, -BUu]
　　　Some of the Mss. under "The Aylesford Manuscripts" have, in fact, no connection with the Aylesford collection. See *Handel: A Celebration*, ed. J. Simon (London: National Portrait Gallery, 1986), p. 24, note 17. **Albrecht**.

897 _____
Hall, James S. "The Aylesford Manuscripts in the Possession of Sir Newman Flower."
　　　A Ms. copy cited by Hans Dieter Clausen, in his *Händels Direktionspartituren* (Hamburg, 1972), 278.

898 _____
Talbot, M. "Some Overlooked Mss. in Manchester." *MT* 115 (1974): 942-44.　　　[g.a.]
　　　Finding list of 17 manuscripts, pp. 942-43. Describes 18th-century Italian music in the Flower collection derived from Charles Jennens through Heneage Finch (**865**), until auctioned by Puttick & Simpson in 1918, some going to Sotheby's, where a quantity were bought by Flower.

899 _____
LITERATURE
Straeten, Edmund van der. "A Remarkable Handel Collection: Christopher Smith's Transcripts of Handel's Works." *MT* 63 (1922): 322-24.　　　[g.a.]

Smith's transcripts went to his son who gave them to a relative, Heneage Finch, Earl of Aylesford (**865**), ca. 1774. Some were then sold to the music antiquarian Harold Reeves about 1920, who resold them to Flower.

900   [**Flowers** (maybe **George French**), 1811-72]
PUTTICK & SIMPSON, AUCTIONEER, LONDON   CAT. NO. 391
Catalogue of a Musical Library of Works in All Classes . . . Rare Old Motetts . . . Sold . . . December 16, 1854. London, 1854. 15 p. 356 lots. Music, lots 1-321.   [GB-Lbl]

901   [**Flowers**]; **William Hawes**
PUTTICK & SIMPSON, AUCTIONEER, LONDON   CAT. NO. 1351
Catalogue of a Large Collection of Miscellaneous Music, Comprising the Libraries of Dr. George French Flowers [lots 114-54] *and Professor Hawes . . . Sold . . . November 15, 1872.* [London], 1872. 17 p. 485 lots. Music, lots 1-435.   [US-NYp, GB-Lbl]

"Compositions in the autograph of celebrated composers," lots 175-206. Hawes's consignments not identified.

902   **Foà, Mauro**
LITERATURE
Gentili, Alberto. "La raccolta di raritá musicali 'Mauro Foà' alla Biblioteca Nazionale di Torino." *Accademie e biblioteche di Italia* 1 (1927-28): 36-50.   [US-Cou]

Albrecht: partly the collection of the Durazzo family. Collection given in 1927 to I-Tn.

→ *See also under* **Giordano**

903   _____
Gentili, Alberto. "La raccolta Mauro Foà nella Biblioteca Nazionale di Torino." *RMI* 34 (1927): 356-68.   [g.a.]

It also appeared in a German translation by Roslin Charlemont in *Italien* 2 (1929).   [g.a.]

904   _____
Verona, Gabriella Gentili. "La collezione Foà e Giordano." *Vivaldiana* 1 (1969): 31-56.   [g.a.]
Benton 3:268-368, no. 368, and **Albrecht**.

905   _____
Dunham, Mary Meneve. "The Secular Cantatas of Antonio Vivaldi in the Foà Collection." Ph.D. diss., University of Michigan, 1969. U.-M. no. 70-4066.   [g.a.]

906   _____
TORINO, BIBLIOTECA NAZIONALE DI UNIVERSITARIA
Raccolta Mauro Foà; Raccolta Renzo Giordano . . . [by] *Isabella Fragalà Data* [and] *Annarita Colturato . . . I.* Roma: Ed. Torre d'Orfeo, 1987. lxxxvii, 613 p. 143 + 310 (some thematic) items; 143 = Foà's; 310 = Giordano's (pp. 247-566).

907   Focques d'Ernonville (?) of Albeville
GAND ET BERNARDEL (EXP.), PARIS
[Vente après dècés de M . . .] *du 8 juin 1881 . . . collection de musique.* Paris, 1881. 8 p. 58
lots. Music, lots 20-40 (parcels). [GB-Lbl (Hirsch)]
      Hirsch copy has some prices and marginal descriptions.

Förster, Friedrich, 1791-1869. *See under* **Bovet, Alfred** (Liepmannssohn catalog no. 58, 1905)

908   Fokker, A   D
DEKKER & NORDEMANN, FIRM, AMSTERDAM   LIST NO. 11
Musical Theory and Musical History [from the collection of . . .]. Amsterdam, 1974. 4 p. 35
lots. [compiler]

909   Foley, Patrick K.
*A Catalogue of Choice and Rare Books, Consisting of First Editions of American and English
Authors . . . Dramatic and Musical Literature. . . .* Boston, 1900. 34 p. 642 lots. Music, lots
355-567. [US-Bp]

910   Fonscolombe-Lamotte
Catalogue de la bibliothèque musicale de M. de Fonscolombe-Lamotte. Paris, 1861.
      Not located; cited from **Bobillier** and **Scheurleer** 1 (1923): 12.

911   Foote, Alexander
SOTHEBY, WILKINSON & HODGE, AUCTIONEER, LONDON
*Catalogue of Valuable Books & Manuscripts, Including the Musical Library of . . . and
Various Other Properties, Comprising Autograph Manuscripts and Numerous Rare Works
. . . Sold . . . the 17th of February, 1890 and Following Day. . . .* London, 1890. 52 p. 657
lots. Foote's library, lots 1-119. [US-NYp, GB-Lbl and on CRL film]

912   Forbes, Henry, 1804-59
PUTTICK & SIMPSON, AUCTIONEER, LONDON   CAT. NO. 621
*Catalogue of Several Valuable Musical Properties, Including the Library of . . . Will Be Sold
. . . April 24, 1860, and Two Following Days.* [London, 1860.] 39 p. 1029 lots. Forbes's
library, lots 1-649. [GB-Lbl, US-NYgr]

913   Forkel, Johann Nikolaus, 1749-1818
      According to **Folter**, no. 31, the collection was acquired from Heinrich
Bokemeyer (**294**), most of which had previously come from that of Georg
Österreich, 1664-1735. *See* annotation here *under* **Bokemeyer.** Forkel's
library eventually passed to the Kgl. Institut für Kirchenmusik in Berlin,
later to D-B and D-Bds.

914   _____
*Verzeichniss der von dem verstorbenen Doctor und Musikdirector Forkel in Göttingen
nachgelassenen Bücher und Musikalien welche den 10ten May 1819 und an den folgenden
Tagen . . . in der Wohnung des Univ. Gerichts-Procur. und Notars Fr. Justus Schepeler an der
Judenstrasse in Göttingen meistbietend verkauft werden.* Göttingen: F. G. Huth, 1819. 200 p.
[compiler (Xerox) of 1819 ed.]

First 2201 nos. are books; next 546, pictures, silhouettes; next 1592, music; 52 Ms.; and a supplement to the books, 15 nos. **Albrecht** cites a reprint, 1977-78, but it has not been located. **Folter**, no. 93.

915 Formosa, Santa Maria
LITERATURE
Cisilino, Siro. "Il fondo musicale di. . . ." *Ateneo veneto*, 2nd ser., no. 2 (1964).
> Not verified.

916 Fornerod, Aloys, 1890-1965
Musée de Pully. *Hommage à Aloys Fornerod . . . exposition organisée pour commérorer le dixième anniversaire de la mort du musicien . . . 19 avril-30 août 1975* [catalog]. Pully: La Musée, [1975]. [39] p. [US-Wc]

917 Fortún, Julia Elena
Antologia de Navidad. La Paz, 1956.
> According to **Albrecht**, the anthology includes her collection of ca. 300 17th- and 18th-century Ms. villancicos.

918 Fouw (C. de) L   F
W. K. MANDEMAKER, FIRM, THE HAGUE
Catalogus eener Boekverzameling (Waaronder vele Zeldzame- en een aantal Muzijk-werken.) . . . nagelaten door . . . C. de Fouw, L. F. . . . verkooping 16 December en volgende dagen. . . . s'Gravenhage, 1829. 87 p. 2509 + 2 lots. Music, pp. 61-67, 151 lots. **Lugt**, no. 12,189. [NL-Avb]

Francesco II, d'Este, Duke of Modena, 1660-94.   *See* Elizabeth Luin's *Repertorio* (1936) *under* **Este Family**

919 Francisci, Miloslav
Muntág, E. *Miloslav Francisci, hudobná pozostalost* [the musical bequest of . . .]. Martin, 1965. (*Edicia Fondy LAMS,* 32.)
> Not examined; cited from *RILM*. Collection went to CS-Mms.

920 Franck, César, Family
SOTHEBY, PARKE BERNET & CO., AUCTIONEER, LONDON
Continental Autograph Letters and Manuscripts, with a Section by Musicians and Composers, and with Some Printed Music, Including a Highly Important Collection of Musical Manuscripts by César Franck; Musical Manuscripts by Brahms, Britten, Boyce, Gounod and Glazunov; Domestic Accounts by Beethoven . . . Sold by Auction . . . 26th- [27th] November, 1980. London, 1980. 169 p. 412 lots. Music, lots 212-331. [GB-Lbl; film at CRL]
> "Property of Newnham College, Cambridge," lots 213, 310-28; "Property of the descendents of César Franck," lots 241-68.

Frank, Edmund. *See under* **Proelss**

921   **Frank, Ernst,** 1847-89

Münster, Robert. "Verzeichnis." In *Musik und Musiker am Oberrhein,* 1:55. Mainz, 1974.

[g.a.]

> Catalog not located; cited in *Beiträge zur Musik-dokumentation: Franz Grasberger Festschrift* (Tutzing: H. Schneider, 1975), 264. Collection now at D-Mbn.

922   **Franz II,** 1768-1835; **Franz Joseph,** 1848-1916, **Emperors of Austria**

LITERATURE

Schmid, Ernst Fritz. "Die Privatmusikaliensammlung des Kaisers Franz II und ihre Wiederentdeckung in Graz im Jahre 1933." *ÖMZ* 25 (1970): 596-99.   [g.a.]

> **Albrecht** provides a short history of the collection of over 10,000 volumes discovered by Schmid in 1933 in the Musikverein für Steiermark, to whom Franz Joseph gave it in 1879. The library was eventually sold to A-Wn in 1936.

Franz Ludwig, Graf von Oettingen-Wallerstein.   *See here under* **Kraft, Ernst, Prince of Oettingen-Wallerstein**

923   **Franz von Paula, Clemens,** 1722-70

Terri, Salli Critchlow. "The Instrumental Music Collection of . . . ."

> Paper presented at the Northern California Chapter of the American Musicological Society, Berkeley, 11 March 1989.

924   **Fraser, Elyza,** 1734-1884; **Mary Bristow**

Williams, Roger B. *Catalogue of the Castle Fraser Music Collection.* [Aberdeen: Aberdeen University and Roger B. Williams, 1994.] xxx, 296 p.   [g.a.]

> "over 2000 items."

925   **Fredenheim, Carl Fredric, 1748-1803**

LITERATURE

Johansson, Cari. "Carl Fredric Fredenheim and His Collection of Eighteenth-Century Music." *Fontes* 13 (1966): 46-49.   [g.a.]

926   **Frederick Augustus, Duke of York,** 1763-1827

MR. SOTHEBY, AUCTIONEER, LONDON

Catalogue of the Most Extensive and Invaluable Selection of Maps and Charts, the Property of . . . To Which Is Added, the Remaining Portion of the Library . . . Sold . . . July 4, 1827, and Three Following Days. . . . [London], 1827. 36 p. 825 lots. Music, lots 784-825.

[GB-Lbl; film at CRL]

927   **Frederik IX, King,** 1899-1927

LITERATURE

Schiødt, Nanna. "The Private Music Collection of King Frederik IX: Views on Music Documentation from the Cataloguing Process." In *Musikdokumentation gestern, Heute und Morgen: Harald Heckmann zum 60. Geburtstag,* ed. Wolfgang Rehm, 71-76. London/Kassel: Bärenreiter, 1984.   [g.a.]

928 **Freeling, Clayton; Signor Cerutti; T. Pymer; Joseph Gwilt**
PUTTICK & SIMPSON, AUCTIONEER, LONDON   CAT. NO. 379
Catalogue of a Collection of Music from Several Private Collections: Cerutti [lots 677-779];
Pymer [lots 188-309]; *Gwilt* [lots 385-440]; *Freeling* [lots 780-841] . . . *Sold . . . July 19 and Two*
Following Days. . . . London, 1854. 1113 lots.   [GB-Lbl]

929 **Friedländer, Max,** 1852-1934
LENGFELD'SCHE BUCHHANDLUNG, FIRM, COLOGNE   CAT. NO. 36
Musik, Geschichte und Theorie, praktische Musik, Bücher aus den Hauptgebieten des
musikalischen Schrifttums. Eine umfangreiche Sammlung "Das deutsche Lied im 18. Jahrh."
in Originalausg.[etc.]. Köln, [1929]. 119 p. 1851 lots. Friedländer's, 1276-565.   [compiler]
Folter, no. 94. **Albrecht**.

930 **Friedländer, Max; Leopold Hirschberg**
M. LENGFELD, FIRM, COLOGNE   CAT. NO. 37
Praktische Musik. Erst- und Frühdrucke van Werken Franz Schuberts und anderer Meister
der Romantik und Neuromantik. . . . Köln, [1930]. 100 p. 1363 lots.
                                                        [US-Wc, -NYp, -R, NL-Avb; compiler]
Folter, no. 95.

"Geleitwort" by Georg Kinsky. Most of the Schubert lots (1-307) were from
Friedländer's collection. Hirschberg's properties included "Alten Notendrucke von
Berlioz, Brahms, Chopin, Liszt" (et al.).

Interesting comments about the Lengfeld firm, its owner, and this catalog are in
Percy Muir's "An Open Letter to Paul Hirsch," *MR* 12 (1951): 3-6.

931 **Friedländer, Max; Werner Wolffheim,** 1877-1930
LEO LIEPMANNSSOHN, FIRM, BERLIN   CAT. NO. 237
Seltenheiten aus allen Gebieten der Musikliteratur vom 14. bis zur Mitte des 19. Jahrhunderts,
z.T aus dem Sammlungen von . . . Max Friedländer und Dr. Werner Wolffheim. Berlin:
Liepmannssohn, [1934]. 95 p. 1107 lots.   [US-R, -PV, GB-Lbl, NL-Avb, compiler]
Folter, no. 96. **Albrecht**. Properties not differentiated.

932 _____
LEO LIEPMANNSSOHN, FIRM, BERLIN   CAT. NO. 238
Musiktheorie. z. T. aus dem Sammlungen von. . . . Berlin: Liepmannssohn, 1935. 96 p. 2200
lots.   [US-Wc, -PV, GB-Lbl, NL-Avb, compiler]
Folter, no. 97.

→ **Friedländer, Max**. *See also under* **Tokugawa**

933 **Friedrich II, Herzog von Sachsen-Gotha,** 1732-72
Baselt, Bernhard. "Verzeichnis der Privatmusikalien Herzog Friedrichs II. von Sachsen-Gotha."
In his *Der Rudolstädter Hofkapellmeister Ph. H. Erlebach.* Diss., University of Halle, 1964.
Albrecht; *BdMS* (1964), no. 2789. Not examined. Collection now at D-GO1.

934 **Frimmel, Theodor von,** 1853-1928
LEO LIEPMANNSSOHN, FIRM, BERLIN   CAT. NO. 222
Musiker-Biographien. Berlin, [1930]. 125 p. 2167 lots.   [GB-Lbl, NL-Avb]
Folter, no. 98.

935   Frisk, Lars Göran
LITERATURE
Böckman, Sten. "Radions schlagerexpert: Han har 50,000 plattor hemma i vardagsgrummet."
Musikern 10 (1986): 10-12.   [g.a.]

936 _____
Östergren, Frank. "I Lars-Göran Frisks källare: Stenkakor till tusen." *Hifi & Musik* 3 (1986): 4-7.
                                                                                               [g.a.]

937   Fryklund, Lars Axel Daniel, 1879-1965
. . . *Collection Fryklund. Musica.* Hälsingborg: Schmidts boktr., 1929. 109 p.   [US-CA only]

Contents: [Instruments] – Autografer – Böcker – Bilder – Henriette Nissen
– August Bournonville.

Not examined; cited from *JbP* (1929) and *DaSML.*

DaSML also cites a 29-page catalog, August Bournonville, *[Katalog över
en samling handlingar och föremäl rörande B. utställd i Hälsingborg
1929]* (Hälsingborg, 1929). Not located.

938 _____
Fryklund, Daniel. *Collection Fryklund 1949.* Hälsingborg: ASktiebolaget boktryck, 1949.
50 p.   [US-AA]

Comprises both instruments and musical library, which, according to **Albrecht**,
includes several thousand items related to the *Marseillaise*, most of which
are now in S-Sm. Some items at S-Skma.

939 _____
LITERATURE
Fryklund, Daniel. "Eine schwedische Sammlung von Briefen von und an Fétis." In International
Society of Musicology, 1st Congress, Liège, *Compte rendu* . . . , 113-17. Guilford: Billings, 1930.
                                                                                    [compiler (copy)]

Fuchs, Albert. *See under* **Liliencron, Rochus Wilhelm Traugott** (Liepmannssohn catalog no. 181)

940   Fuchs, Aloys, 1799-1853
Many of the following citations derive from Richard Schaal's magnificent
study of Fuchs' library: *Quellen und Forschungen zur Wiener
Musiksammlung von Aloys Fuchs* . . . . (Wien: Böhlaus Nachf., 1966). 156 p.
*(Oesterreichische Akademie der Wissenschaften, Philosophisch-
historische Klasse, Sitzungsberichte, 251. Band, 1. Abhandlung).* See
especially the sections "Standrots-Repertorium über die Sammlung des A.
Fuchs [an outline of the collection's organization]," pp. 65-69; and "Auswahl-
Verzeichnis der von Fuchs angelegten Kataloge der Sammlung [listing 26
manuscript catalogs in 8 different libraries]," pp. 70-72. **Albrecht**: most of
the library survives in A-GÖ.

The arrangement here is as chronological as possible.

→ *See also under* **Fillon** and **Thalberg**

941 _____

Fuchs, Aloys. "Alphabetisches Verzeichnis derjenigen Componisten, von welche sich Original-Handschriften in der Sammlung des Aloys Fuchs vorfinden". Wien, 1829. 3 leaves.

In A-Wn., Ms. S.m.2470.

942 _____

Fuchs, Aloys. "Alphabetisches Namens-Katalog über die Tonkünstler-Portrait-Sammlung des Aloys Fuchs in Wien 1841."

Ms. in D-Bds, catalog Mus. Ms. 321, nebst Abschrift, catalog Mus. Ms. 321a.

943 _____

Fuchs, Aloys. "Catalog über die Musikalien-Sammlung des Aloys Fuchs in Wien. Enthalt grösstentheils Partituren." 27 sheets.

In D-Bds, catalog Mus. Ms. 311.

944 _____

Fuchs, Aloys. [Introduction by Fuchs.] "Mitglied der K. K. Hofkapelle in Wien" (to his music catalog of 1848, followed by a list of the composers named in it).

Ms. in GB-Lbl, Add. Ms. 32438, ff. 2-4b.

945 _____

Fuchs, Aloys. "Alphabetisches Namens-verzeicniss jener Komponisten, von denen sich die eigenhändige Noten und Textschrift in der Sammlung . . . in Wien vorfindet."

Ms. in D-Lem, I.2° 36.

946 _____

[Fuchs, Aloys?] "Autoren von denen mehreres oder komplettes enthalten ist, und Aufzählung der Kompositionen in ganzen Sammlungen. Ferner die nach Autoren geordnetes Faszikel. . . ."

Ms. in D-Bds, catalog Mus. Ms. 309.

947 _____

Fuchs, Aloys. "Vocal-Quartetten, ernshafter und komischer Gattung. . . . "

Ms. in D-Bds, catalog Mus. Ms. 309.

948 _____

Fuchs, Aloys. "Verzeichnis einer Parthie italienischer Opern-Musikstücke in geschriebenen Partituren von berühmten Autoren."

Ms. in D-Bds, catalog Mus. Ms. 309.

949 _____

Fuchs, Aloys. "Äeltere Kirchenmusik und neuere geistliche Musik" [1850].

Ms. in D-Bds, catalog Mus. Ms. 309.

950 _____

Fuchs, Aloys. "Äeltere Clavier- und Orgel-Compositionen dann moderne Clavier-Musik [1850]."

Ms. in D-Bds, catalog Mus. Ms. 309.

951 _____

Fuchs, Aloys. "Namens-Katalog [über die Tonkünstler-Portrait-Sammlung des Aloys Fuchs in Wien. 1853]."

>Ms. in D-Bds, catalog Mus. Ms. 317. Discussed at some length by Schaal
>in his study noted above (**940**).

952 _____

BUTSCH, FIDELIS [i.e., BIRETT'SCHE ANTIQUARIATS-BUCHHANDLUNG F. BUTSCH], FIRM, AUGSBURG
Catalog einer ausgewählten Sammlung von Incunabeln, literarischen Curiositäten und Seltenheiten . . . im June 1851. Augsburg, 1851.   [D-As]

>"Musikwerke berühmter Meister in Originalhandschriften," pp. 126-29
>(some from the Fuchs collection).

953 _____

PUTTICK & SIMPSON, AUCTIONEER, LONDON   CAT. NO. 1828
Catalogue of a Most Interesting and Valuable Collection of Autograph Letters, Chiefly Musical and Literary. Also Original Manuscript Compositions, Mostly from the Celebrated Collection of . . . , Including Beethoven's Pastoral Symphony . . . Sold . . . April 23rd, 1878. 25 p. 302 lots. Music, lots 1-111.   [GB-Lbl]

>Holograph sketches for the pastoral symphony (and other works), lot 110,
>bought by Marshall (**1790**) for £55-0-0.

954 _____

BERTLING, RICH., FIRM, DRESDEN   LAGER-CAT. NO. 34
Autographen. Dichter, Schriftsteller, Gelehrte, Musiker. . . . Das in seiner Reichhaltigkeit und Kostbarkeit an Musikhandschriften einzig bestehende Album Fuchs. Ein anderes werthvolles Stammbuch aus neuerer Zeit. . . . Dresden, 1899. 38 p. 481 lots.

>**Folter**, no. 99, who says this is one of four such albums Fuchs gave to
>Sigismond Thalberg during his lifetime. She provides references for further
>reading.

955 _____

GILHOFER & RANSCHBURG, FIRM, VIENNA   AUKTION-CAT. NO. 8
[Katalog der bedeutenden und werthvollen] Autographen-Sammlung Angelini-Rossi (Rom), II. Theil . . . Collection Aloys Fuchs, Musik-Manuskripte und Briefe von Musikern. Versteigerung zu Wien . . . 11.- [16.] März 1901. Wien, 1901. 109 pp. 1121 lots.   [NL-Avb]

>"Musiker," lots 786-954, letters of Aron, Bach, Beethoven, et al.

956 _____

Riedel, Friedrich W. "Aloys Fuchs als Sammler Bachscher Werke." *Bach-Jahrbuch* 47 (1960): 83-99.   [g.a.]

>"Verzeichnis der im Stift Göttweig verwahrten Bach-quellen aus dem
>Nachlass von Aloys Fuchs," pp. 91-99. **Folter**, no. 103.

957 _____

Riedel, Friedrich W. "Die Bibliothek des Aloys Fuchs." In *Hans Albrecht in Memoriam: Gedenkschrift . . .*, 207-24. Kassel: Bärenreiter, 1962. ca. 400 nos.   [g.a.]

>"Zur Bibliothek Aloys Fuchs. Ergänzungen und Berichtigungen," *MF* 16 (1963):
>270-75.

958 _____

Svobodová, Marie. "Das 'Denkmal Wolfgang Amadeus Mozarts' in der Prague Universitats-Bibliothek." *Mozart-Jahrbuch* 15 (1967): 353-87.   [g.a.]

Description of the collection founded in 1837, enlarged in 1845 by Fuchs.

959 _____

Schaal, Richard. "Die Autographen der Wiener Musik-sammlung Aloys Fuchs." *Haydn-Jahrbuch* 6 (1969): 5-191.   [g.a.]

Catalog, pp. 18-191, ca. 1500 nos. Based on Fuchs's own catalogs.

960 _____

Schaal, Richard. "Handschrift-Kopien aus der Wiener Musiksammlung von Aloys Fuchs unter Benutzung der Originalkatalog." *Haydn-Jahrbuch* 7 (1970): 255-80. Ca. 100 nos.   [g.a.]

Folter, no. 103.

961 _____

Schaal, Richard. *Die Tonkünstler-Porträts der Wiener Musiksammlung von Aloys Fuchs.* Quellenkatalog der Musikgeschichte, 3. Wilhelmshaven: Heinrichshofen, 1970. 108 p.   [g.a.]

About 2000 portraits, most now in D-Bds, though earlier sold to F. A. Grasnick (**1098**). See also Schaal's article "Die Berliner Mozart-Abschriften der Sammlung Fuchs-Grasnick," *Mozart-Jahrbuch* (1971-72 [publ. 1973]): 415-18.

962 _____

Literature

[Kiesewetter, Raphael Georg, according to Schaal.] "Autographen Sammlung des Tonsetzer älterer und neuer Zeit des Hrn. Aloys Fuchs in Wien." *AmZ* 34 (1832), cols. 743-47.

963 _____

Fischof, Joseph. "Die Heroen der Tonkunst in der Autographensammlung des Herrn Aloys Fuchs in Wien." *Monatsschrift: Mittheilungen aus Wien* (1835), 1-27.

Not examined; cited from **Becker**.

964 _____

Fuchs, Aloys. ". . . aus meiner eigenen musikalischen Sammlung." *Cäcilia* 23 (1844): 52-53.
                    [g.a.]

965 _____

Fischer von Röslerstamm, E. "Felix Mendelssohn und Aloys Fuchs." *Mitteilungen für Autographen-sammler* 5 (1888): 85.

Not examined; cited from **Schaal**.

966 _____

Gräffler, Franz. "Mozartsammlung des Herrn Fuchs." In his *Kleiner Wiener Memoiren und Wiener Dosenstücke,* ed. A. Schlosser und G. Gugitz, 117-20. Denkwürdigkeiten aus Alt-Oesterreich, 13/14. 2 vols. München: G. Müller, 1918, 1922.

Reprinted in Schaal, pp. 58-60; summarized in Lewicki's article (**967**).

967 _____

[Lewicki, R.] "Die Mozart-Sammlung des Alois Fuchs." *Mozarteums-Mitteilungen* 2 (1920): 36-37.   [g.a.]

    Folter, no. 103.

968 _____

Schaal, Richard. "Bemerkungen zur Musiksammlung von Aloys Fuchs." *Mozart-Jahrbuch* (1960/61): 233-35.   [g.a.]

    Folter, no. 103.

969 _____

Riedel, Friedrich Wilhelm. "Über der Auftheilung der Musiksammlung von A. Fuchs." *Mf* 15 (1962): 374-79.   [g.a.]

    Folter, no. 103.

970 _____

Schaal, Richard. "Zur Musiksammlung Aloys Fuchs." *Mf* 15 (1962): 49-52.   [g.a.]

    Folter, no. 103.

971 _____

Riedel, Friedrich Wilhelm. "Der Wiener Musiksammler Aloys Fuchs und seine Beziehungen zum Stift Göttweig." *Aus der Heimat I, Kulturbeilage des Amtblatts der Bezirkshauptmannschaft Krems/Donau* (1962), 28, 30-32.

    Not examined; cited from **Folter**, no. 103.

972 _____

Riedel, Friedrich Wilhelm. "Musikpflege im Benediktinerstift Göttweig um 1600." *Kirchenmusikalisches Jahrbuch* 46 (1962): 83-98.   [g.a.]

973 _____

Schaal, Richard. "Quellen zur Musiksammlung Aloys Fuchs." *Mf* 16 (1963): 67-72.   [g.a.]

    Folter, no. 103.

974 _____

Schaal, Richard. "A. Fuchs als Handschriften-Vermittler." *Mf* 18 (1968): 304-07.   [g.a.]

    Folter, no. 103.

975 _____

Riedel, Friedrich Wilhelm. "Die Libretto-Sammlung in Benediktinerstift Göttweig." *Fontes* 13 (1966): 105-11.   [g.a.]

976 _____

Schaal, Richard. "Die Handschrift Aloys Unterreiters: Neues zum Hauptkopisten der Sammlung Aloys Fuchs." *Mozart Jahrbuch* (1980-83), 392-98.   [g.a.]

977   **Fuchs zu Pucheim und Mittelberg, Ignaz Joseph, Graf,** 1760-1838

Schenck, Erich. "Eine Wiener Musiksammlung des Beethoven-Zeit." In *Festschrift Heinrich Besseler zum sechzigsten Geburtstag*, 377-88. Leipzig: Universität, Musikwissenschaftliches Institut, 1961.   [US-NYp]

978   **Fürall, Franz Xaver**

"Nachlassinventar des Musicus Franz Xaver Fürall anlässlich der Versteigerung 1780."

Ms. in Archiv-Wallerstein, Dienerakten 1:18, 16. Reprinted in **Haberkamp** (see Sources and Related Readings, p. xxx).

979   **Fürstenberg, Clemens Lothar, Reichsführer von (zu Herdringen-Adolfsburg)**

[A discussion of "Fürstenbergiana" and a Ms. catalog appear in Domp's *Studien zur Geschichte der Musik an Westfälischen Adelshöfen*, 122-27 (Düsseldorf: Krumbiegel, 1934).] Collection also under care of Joachim Egon, Fürst zu Fürstenberg, 1923-.

980   _____

Haberkamp, Getraut. "Autographe Musikhandschriften des 19. und 20. Jahrhunderts in Der Fürstlich Fürstenbergischen Hofbibliothek Donaueschingen." In *Ars iocundissima: Festschrift für Kurt Dorfmüller zum 60. Geburtstag . . .* , ed. Horst Leuchtmann and Robert Münster, 97-113. Tutzing: H. Schneider, 1984.   [g.a.]

981   _____

Johne, E. "Die Fürstlich Fürstenbergische Hofbibliothek und ihre Musikbestände." *Badische Heimat* 8 (1921): 55-82.

Not located or examined.

982   _____

Johne, E. "Aus der Fürstliche Fürstenberg Hofbibliothek in Donaueschingen." *NMZ* 43 (1922).

Not examined; cited from *ZfMW* 6 (1923/24), "Zeitschriftenschau."

983   _____

"Die Musikalien der Bibliotheca Fürstenbergiana zu Herdringen." In Deutsches Musikgeschichtliches Archiv, Kassel, zusammengestellt und bearb. von Jürgen Kindermann, Bd. IV, Nrn. 2-3, *Katalog Nr. 20/21 der Filmsammlung*, 1-141. Kassel: Bärenreiter, 1987/88.

[g.a.]

_____. *Addenda et corrigenda*. Bd. IV, Nr. 6. Katalog Nr. 24, 297. Kassel: Bärenreiter, 1992.

Fürstlich Oettingen-Wallerstein'sche Bibliothek.   *See under* **Kraft, Ernst, Prince of Oettingen-Wallerstein**

Fugger, Marcus.   *See* **Oettingen-Wallerstein'sche Bibliothek**

Fugger Family.   *See under* **Wilhelm, Herzog von Beyern,** 1752-1837

984   Fugger Family Library

Library was begun by Johann Jakob Fugger (1516-75) and Raimund (1528-69). According to **Albrecht**, most survive in D-Mbs, A-Wn, and D-Af, and contain most of Petrucci's output.

985 _____

LITERATURE

"Verzaichnuss Rayd. Fuggers Instrument vnd Musica 1566." Reprinted by A. Sandberger in "Bemerkungen zur Musikgeschichte der Städte Nürnberg und Augsburg." In *Denkmäler der Tonkunst in Bayern* 5, no. 1 (1904): l-li.

Original is in the Münchener Reichsarchiv, *Libri antiquitatum*, 1:70-73.

986 _____

"Inventari der erkaufften von Her: Huldrick Fugger, gleichwol noch nit bezalten musica per fl. 4000 so, in 11. eingemachten zue Brandenburgm im Schloss ligt."

A 1580 Ms. in Archiv der Fürstl. und Gräfl. Fuggerschen Stiftungsminitration Augsburg 7,2.

987 _____

Mauchter, Matthaeus. ". . . Bibliothecae celeberrimae Alberti Fuggeri. Catalogus constans ex melioribus diversarum facultatum et linguorum uctoribus: 17046, libris: 13828 . . . Anno a partu Virginis 1655."

Albert Fugger (1624-92) sold the inherited library to the Holy Roman Emperor Ferdinand III in 1655. Mauchter was Imperial Librarian of the Hofkammerarchiv in Vienna.

988 _____

Hartig, Otto. *Die Gründung der Münchener Bibliothek, durch Albert V und Johann Jakob Fugger.* München: Verlag der Königlich bayerischen Akademie der Wissenschaften, 1917. xiv, 412 p.   [US-MSu, -Ate]

989 _____

Kroyer, Theodor. "Musikalische Handschriften in der Fürstl. Fuggerschen Domanialkanzlei in Augsburg. Nach dem Stand vom Herbst 1918."

Ms. in D-Mbs.

990 _____

Nowak, Leopold. "Die Musikhandschriften aus Fuggerschem Besitz." In *Die Oesterreichische Nationalbibliothek: Festschrift Josef Bick,* ed. Josef Stummvoll, 119-38. Wien: H. Bauer-Verlag, 1948.   [US-NYp]

991 _____

Schaal, Richard. "Die Musikbibliothek von Raimund Fugger D. J." *Acta* 29 (1957): 126-37.   [g.a.]

Schaal reprints list of Mss. (only), but mentions the instruments in the collection.

992 _____

Rowell, Lois Irene. "The Music Collection of . . . : A Bibliographical Study." *Journal of the Graduate Students at the Ohio State University* 7 (1978): 36-85.   [g.a.]

"Inventory of the Fugger Music Library: printed books [i.e. scores]," pp. 49-85. "The Collection of Raymond Fugger the Elder," pp. 49-52; ". . . of Raymond Fugger, the Younger," pp. 53-85.

993 _____

Die Fugger und die Musik: Lautenschlagen Llernen und Leben: Anton Fugger zum 500. Geburtstag: Ausstellung in den historischen Badstuben im Fuggerhaus, 10 Juni bis 8. August 1993, ed. Renate Eikelmann. Augsburg: Hofmann-Verlag, 1993. 224 p.

> An exhibition catalog.

994 _____

LITERATURE

Wallner, Bertha Antonia. "Die Gründung der Münchener Hofbibliothek durch Albert V. und Johann Jakob Fugger." *ZfMW* 2 (1919/20): 299-305.   [g.a.]

> Comments on the music materials included in Otto Hartig's monograph of
> the same title (see above, Albrecht V, Duke of Bavaria, 1528-1579).

995 _____

The Fugger News-Letter . . . , ed. Victor von Klarwill, trans. Pauline de Chary. . . . New York and London: Putnam's, 1925. 284 p.   [g.a.]

> About the sale of the library to Emperor Ferdinand III and its contents, pp. viii-xiv.

996 _____

Strieder, J. "Die älteste Bibliotheksstiftung der Fugger." *Zentralblatt für Bibliothekswesen* 50 (1933).   [g.a.]

997 _____

Lehmann, Paul. *Eine Geschichte des alten Fuggerbibliotheken.* 2 vols. Tübingen, 1956-60.

> See especially vol. 1, chapters 1 and 2. Lehmann reconstructs the various
> Fugger collections.

998 _____

Winter, Paul. "Die Fugger-Mäzene der Musik." *NMZ* 120 (1959): 301-03.

999 _____

Kellman, Herbert. "Josquin and the Courts of the Netherlands and France: The Evidence of the Sources." In *Josquin des Prez: Proceedings of the International Josquin Festival-Conference . . . 1971 . . . ,* ed. Edward E. Lowinsky and Bonnie Blackburn, 201-03. London: Oxford University Press, 1976.   [g.a.]

1000 **Fuld, James Jeffrey,** b. 1916-
LITERATURE
"Surrounded by One's Friends." *Notes* 32 (1975/76): 479-90.   [g.a.]

1001 _____

"A Collection of Music Autographs." *Manuscripts* 32 (1980): 13-.

> Not examined.

1002 _____

    "Music Posters and Programs: The Need for an Inventory." *Notes* 37 (1981): 520-32.   [g.a.]

1003 _____

    "The Fuld Collection: Fifty Years of Music Collecting." *Sheet Music Exchange* 3 (April 1985): 16-21.   [g.a.]

1004   Fulda, Fürchtegott Christian
    Katalog der hymnologischen Bibliothek des Herrn Fürchtegott Christian Fulda . . . in Halle. Halle: Johann Friedrich Lippert, 1985. iv, 51 p. 2789 nos.

        "Verkauf en bloc" to D-Bds, according to **Folter 2**, no. 204. Not examined.

1005   Gaehler, Caspar Siegfried
    [Verzeichnis seiner Büchersammlung], 1826.

        Not located; cited in **Wolffheim** 1, item no. 341.

1006   Gallini, Natale
    Parke-Bernet Galleries, auctioneer, New York, Sale no. 1065
    Sixty-Six XVII-XX Century Italian Musical Manuscripts, from the Natale Gallini Collection, by Order of the Present Italian Owner. Public Auction Sale, May 3 [1949]. New York: Parke-Bernet Galleries, 1949. 34 p. 66 lots.   [US-NYp, -Wc, compiler]

        That "Present Italian owner," was someone named "Garzanti," according to a Ms. notation on the compiler's copy.

1007 _____

    Literature
    Ferrari, Luigi. *La collezione Gallini: Gusto, usanze, modi del teatro musicale italiano nel secondo Ottocento; con saggi di Giampiero Tintori* [e] *Mietta Corli*. Milano: Electa, 1982. 207 p.   [US-BUu]

1008   Gallo, Vincenzo and **Antonio**
    Literature
    Fabris, Dinko. *Il fondo musicale Gallo della Biblioteca Comunale di Barletta*. Barletta: Comunale di Barletta, 1983. 232 p.

        Not examined; cited from *RILM*.

1009   Galluzzi, Giuseppe (of Milan)
    List & Francke, firm, Leipzig   Cat. No. 37?
    Verzeichnis mehrerer Bücher- und Autographen-Sammlung welche am 13. März 1905 und folgende Tage . . . zum Teil aus der Bibliothek des Grafen. . . . Leipzig, 1905. 99 p. 3479 lots.
        [US-Wc]

1010   Galpin, Francis William, 1858-1945; [**Ernest Mauer**]
    Hodgson & Co., auctioneer, London
    A Catalogue of Books from Various Sources . . . The Collection of Books on Music and Musical Instruments Formed by the Late Canon F. W. Galpin . . . An Extensive Collection of Scores for Small Orchestras . . . Over 1100 Pieces . . . 21000 Band Parts . . . [etc.] *. . . Sold July 18th, 1946.* 43 p. 654 lots. Galpin's, 530-86; M's, lots 617-18 (many more items).
        [GB-Lbl, US-Nygr]

1011   Galston, Gottfried, 1879-1950
UNIVERSITY OF TENNESSEE, LIBRARY
Bayne, Pauline Shaw. *The Gottfried Galston Music Collection and the Galston-Busoni Archive.*
Knoxville, 1978. xix, 297 p.   [g.a.]

> Galston Music Collection, pp. 1-277. Galston-Busoni Archive, pp. 281-97.
> **Folter**, no. 104.

1012   Ganche, Édouard, 1880-1945
HEINRICH HINTERBERGER, FIRM, VIENNA
*Musée Frédéric Chopin de Mr. Édouard Ganche à Lyon. Mis en vente . . . par . . . Heinrich
Hinterberger. (Catalogue du Musée Frédéric Chopin . . . Bibliothèque archives. Objets ayant
appartenu à . . . Chopin.)* [Vienna, 1937?]

> Not examined. The collection was offered for sale before World War II,
> according to the preface of a Chopin *Barcarolle* which was part of that
> sale. Hirsch copy at GB-Lbl says "reproduced from typewriting."

1013   _____

> *LITERATURE*
> Nectoux, Jean-Michel, and Jean-Jacques Eigeldinger. "Edouard Ganche et sa collection Chopin."
> *Revue de la Bibliothèque Nationale* 3, no. 7 (1983): 10-21.
>
> > Not examined; cited from *RILM*.

1014   _____

> Nectoux, Jean-Michel, and Jean-Jacques Eigeldinger. "Edouard Ganche i jego kolekcja
> Chopinowska." *Rocznik Chopinowski* 17 (1985): 235-51.
>
> > Translation of previous article.

1015   Gantter, Louis
PUTTICK & SIMPSON, AUCTIONEER, LONDON   CAT. NO. 3
*Catalogue of the Musical Library of . . . Also Musical Instruments . . . Will Be Sold . . . August
10, 1846.* [London, 1846.] 13 p. 230 lots. Music, lots 1-194.   [GB-Lbl]

> Heading on p. 3, "Monday, August 12, 1846."

1016   _____

PUTTICK & SIMPSON, AUCTIONEER, LONDON   CAT. NO. 3
*Catalogue of a Valuable Collection of Music, Comprising Numerous Choice Works . . . Vocal,
Piano Forte and Instrumental Music, Sacred Music, Anthems . . . Theoretical, Historical, and
Perceptive Works, Early and Rare Treatises, &c. . . . Sold . . . October 26th, 1847.* London,
1847. 15 p. 295 lots. Music, lots 1-249.   [GB-Lbl]

1017   [Ganz, L   ]
PUTTICK & SIMPSON, AUCTIONEER, LONDON   CAT. NO. 130
*Catalogue of a Select and Valuable Music Library, Including Many Esteemed Works of the
Best Masters . . . Miscellaneous Musical Literature . . . Musical Instruments . . . to Which Is
Added the Remaining Portion of Printed Music, of Mr. Challoner . . . Sold August 31, 1849
and Following Day.* London, 1849. 18 p. 504 lots. Music, lots 1-187.   [GB-Lbl]

1018   Garcia,

LITERATURE

Hare, Maud Cuney. "Texas Library Sheds Light on Early Spanish Music." *Musical America* 36, no. 12 (1922): 31.   [g.a.]

1019   Gardiner, George

LITERATURE

Purslow, George. "The George Gardiner Folk Song Collection." *Folkmusic Journal* 1, no. 3 (1967): 129-57.   [g.a.]

> Now in the Vaughan Williams Memorial Library (*né* English Folk Dance & Song Society) at GB-Lcs. Some items at GB-Gm.

1020   Garms, Johann Hendrik, Jr., et al.

VON STOCKUM ANTIQUARIAAT, AMSTERDAM

Catalogue d'une importante collection de livres, provenant des bibliothèques de feu M. M. J. Th. de Visser . . . [et al]. Une partie de la bibliothèque musicale de M.-J. H. Garms Jr., Amsterdam . . . vente . . . du 22 Avril am Mai 1933. . . . A'dam, 1933.   [NL-DHgm]

> Music, pp. 209-24, lots 3220-661.

Garzanti.   *See* **Gallini**

1021   Gaspari, Gaetano, 1807-81

L. POTIER, AUCTIONEER, PARIS

Catalogue des livres rares, en partie de XVe et XVIe siècles, composant la bibliothèque musicale de . . . suivie d'un catalogue de livres choises en divers genres, vente . . . 29 janvier 1862 et les deux jours suivants. Paris: Potier, 1862. vii, 55 p. 515 lots.

                                                                        [US-Wc (priced), -NH, -BE, -U, -NYgr]

> **Folter**, no. 15; **Albrecht**.

1022   _____

Parasini, F. [A note regarding Gaspari's collection in the preface to] Bologna, Liceo musicale, *Catalogo della Biblioteca . . . ,* i-xxxix. Bologna, 1890.   [g.a.]

> Reprint, Bologna: Forni, 1961. Some rarities are noted by Parasini, pp. xxvii-xxx.

1023   _____

LITERATURE

Vatielli, F. [A note about Gaspari's collection]. In "Una mostra bibliografica nella Biblioteca del Liceo musicale di Bologna." *Bibliofilia* 10 (1908-09): 189.   [g.a.]

1024   Gast, Gideon de

PAULUS NIJHOFF, AUCTIONEER, ARNHEM

Catalogus van een groot [?] gebonden Boeken in all [?] en Talen Kerk en Schoolgoed . . . en fraaie Collectie Muzyk en Muzijk-Instrumenten . . . &c. alles nagelaten door Gideon de Gast, Boekverkoper te Arnhem waarachter een 2de Catalogus van Boeken, Muzijk en Muzijk Instrumenten, daar ander beste . . . en anderen . . . [8 April 1783]. Arnhem, 1783.

                                                                                              [NL-Avb (only?)]

> P. Nijhoff's first catalog. See "Boekenveilingen van Paulus Nijhoff,

1783-1831," pp. [77]-106, in *De Arnhemsche Boekverkoopers . . . Nijhoff.* *'s-Gravenhage, 1934. 2 vols. in 1 (178 p.; 2nd catalog begins, p. 161), "Muziek," pp. 133-40 (180 lots); pp. 166-68 (66 lots). For title of second catalog, see below.

1025 _____

PAULUS NIJHOFF, AUCTIONEER, ARNHEM
Catalogus van een [verzameling] . . . Boeken . . . een fraaije Collectie Muzijk en Muzijk-Instrumenten, Billard . . . nagelaten door . . . te Arnhem, waar achter een 2ᵈᵉ Catalogus van Boeken, Muzijk en Muzijk-Instrumenten . . . verkogt . . . 7 April 1783, en volgende dagen. Arnhem, 1783. 160 p. 3154 lots (including 180 lots of music). [NL-Avb]

1026 [Gauntlett, Henry John, 1805-76], A Gentleman
PUTTICK & SIMPSON, AUCTIONEER, LONDON   CAT. NO. 51
Catalogue of the Very Extensive, Rare and Valuable Musical Library of a Distinguished Gentleman Comprising the Most Esteemed Works . . . the Rarest Works of the Old Masters . . . Handel's Works in Full Score and an Extraordinary Assemblage of Stringed Instruments . . . Sold December 17th, 1847, and Following Day. London, 1847. 24 p. 524 lots. Music, lots 1-152, 217-524. **King**, pp. 45-46.   [NL-Avb]

1027 _____

PUTTICK & SIMPSON, AUCTIONEER, LONDON   CAT. NO. 103
Catalogue of an Extensive, Rare and Valuable Musical Library Comprising Valuable Music in All Classes [etc.] with Musical Instruments . . . Sold . . . February 19th, 1849 and Two Following Days. London, 1849. 32 p. 656 lots. Music, lots 1-331, 429-656.
[GB-Lbl, US-NYp (with Rimbault's markings)]
This catalog not in **King's** list.

1028 Gautier, Louis, Jr.
P. WYNANTS, AUCTIONEER, DEN HAAG
Catalogus eener fraaye verzameling boeken, in verscheiden faculteyten en taalen . . . Als meede een Appendix van rechtsgeleerden, en andere boeken; Eeen collectie van muziek-werken, dito instrumenten . . . nagelaten door . . . Verkogt . . . 10 February 1794, en volgende dagen. . . .'s-Gravenhage, 1794. 4, 106 p. 2134 lots (including 63, music). [NL-DHga]

Geer, Charles de.   *See* **De Geer, Charles**

1029 Gehring, Franz Edward, 1838-84
ALBERT COHN, AUCTIONEER, BERLIN
Katalog der musikalischen Bibliothek des Herrn Dr. F. Gehring, nebst Beiträgen aus einigen anderen Sammlungen. Berlin: Cohn, 1880. viii, 143 p. 1671 lots.
[US-R, -Wc, -NYp, GB-Lbl (Hirsch 439)]
Sale: November 29 and following days. **Folter**, no. 106. Some items now at D-Mbs and D-BN, according to *NG-L*, p. 750.

1030 _____

Verzeichniss der Bücher und musikalien Sammlung aus dem Nachlasse des Herrn Franz Gehring. Wien, 1884.
Not located; cited by **Bobillier** only.

1031   **Geibel, Carl; Carl Herz von Hertenried**
C. G. BOERNER, AUCTIONEER, LEIPZIG
[Katalog der] *Autographen Sammlungen Dr. Carl Geibel und Carl Herz von Hertenried, Wien . . . Versteigerung vom 3. bis 6. Mai.* Leipzig: C. G. Boerner, 1911. 226 p. 1211 lots.
[US-NYp, -Wc, -Bau, NL-DHgm]
Vol. 7, "Musik," lots 920-1211, includes ALS and fine holographs.

1032   **Geigy-Hagenbach, Karl,** d. 1949
J. A. STARGARDT, MARBURG AND HAUS DER BÜCHER, BASEL   CAT. NO. 552
Autographen aus der Sammlung . . . und anderen Besitz. Auktion. . . . Basel & Marburg, 1961.
180 p. 1081 lots, 54 plates. Music, lots 818-962.   [US-NYgr (price sheet laid in)]
Albrecht notes two earlier sales, 1929 and 1939. Not located.

1033   _____
LITERATURE
"Karl Geigy-Hagenbach und seine [Handschriften-] Sammlung. Zum siebzigsten Geburtstag."
Philobiblon 9 (1936): 125-28.   [g.a.]
Now at CH-Bu.

1034   **Georg V, King of Hanover,** 1819-78
HANS SCHNEIDER, FIRM, TUTZING   CAT. NO. 160
Musikalische Erst- und Frühdrucke [zum Teil aus der Bibliothek]. . . . Tutzing: Hans Schneider,
1971. 49 p. 321 lots.   [g.a.]

1035   _____
HANS SCHNEIDER, FIRM, TUTZING
Musikliteratur, darunter ein grösserer Bestand aus der Bibliothek des Königs Georg V. von Hannover. Tutzing: Schneider, [1971]. 88 p. 948 lots.   [g.a.]

1036   **George, Robert Olney**
LITERATURE
Novick, Amy E. "The Robert O. George Collection [of jazz recordings donated to the Indiana Archives of Traditional Music]." *Resound* 1, no. 3 (July 1982): 2-3. 2376 recordings.   [g.a.]

George III, King of England.   *See* **Great Britain - Kings and Rulers**

1037   **Gerber, Ernst Ludwig,** 1746-1819
Wissenschaftlich geordnetes Verzeichniss einer Sammlung von musikalischen Schriften, nebst einer Anzahl von Bildnissen berühmter Tonkünstler und musikalischer Schriftsteller, wie auch von verschiedenen Orgelprospecten, als Beitrag zur Literaturgeschichte der Musik, und auf Verlangen einer Freunde zum Druck befördert von dem Besitzer derselben. . . .
Sondershausen: Gedruckt mit Fleckschen Schriften, 1804. 48 p. ca. 1000 items.
[US-NY, -Wc, compiler]
Not a sale catalog. Divisions listed in **Folter**, no. 107. Collection now in A-Wgm, but not all of it, according to Plath's essay (**1038**), which says portions were acquired by Johann Anton André and with André's library auctioned by Joseph Baer on 10 February 1854 (*see here under* **André**).

1038 _____

Plath, Wolfgang. "Zum Schicksal der André-Gerberschen Musikbibliothek." In *Bachiana et alia musicologica: Festschrift Alfred Dürr zum 65. Geburtstag . . .* , ed. Wolfgang Rehm, 209-25. Kassel: Bärenreiter, 1983.   [g.a.]

1039   Gerdes, H., et al.

G. THEOD. BOM, AUCTIONEER, AMSTERDAM

Boekverkooping 11-13 September 1945. Bibliotheken: Prof. Dr. G. Schaake [et al.]. *Publieke verkooping. . . .* A'dam, 1945. 17 p. 190, 226 lots.   [NL-Avb]

"Muziekbibliotheek uit Haagsche bezit [i.e., Gerde's]," pp. 10-17. 226 lots.

1040   Gerlach, Carl Gotthelf; Gottlob Harrer

Glöckner, Andreas. "Handschriftlichte Musikalien aus dem Nachlassen von . . . in den Verlags-angeboten des Hauses Breitkopf 1761 bis 1791." *Bach-Jahrbuch* 70 (1984): 107-16.   [g.a.]

Gershwin, George, 1898-1937.   *See under* **Van Vechten**

1041   Gevaert, François Auguste, 1828-1908

CAMILLE VYT, AUCTIONEER, GHENT

Catalogue de la bibliothèque de feu M. le baron Fr. Aug. Gevaert . . . La vente aura lieu . . . 18-19 mai 1909. . . . Gand: Vyt, 1909. 40 p. Music, lots 1-416.   [US-NYp, -IO]

Divisions listed in **Folter,** no.108.

1042   [Gibson, B   H   ]

PUTTICK & SIMPSON, AUCTIONEER, LONDON   CAT. NO. 158

Catalogue of the Very Select Musical Library of a Professional Gentleman, Including an Extensive Collection of Glees and Other Vocal Music . . . Handel's Messiah, MS. Score, Containing Some Passages in the Autograph of the Immortal Composer . . . Autograph Scores by Dr. Boyce . . . Theoretical Works . . . Sold . . . May 4th, 1850. . . . London, 1850. 13 p. 290 lots. Music, lots 1-174, 183-290.   [GB-Lbl]

Messiah, in Christopher Smith's hand, went to Southey for £3.

1043   Gibsone, Burford George Henry, d. 1868?

ALEXANDER REED, LONDON

Catalogue of Books, Prints, Maps, Music, and Coins, the Property of . . . Sold by Auction . . . East Side of Pilgrim-Street . . . 25th April, 1831, and Following Days. . . . London, 1831. 11 p. 112, 170, 124 lots.   [US-NYgr]

Music, first day, lots 1-25 (but many more items).

1044   Giedde, Wilhelm Hans Rudolph Rosenkrantz, 1756-1816

COPENHAGEN, KONGELIGE BIBLIOTEK

Catalogue of Giedde's Music Collection in the Royal Library of Copenhagen. Compiled by Inge Bittmann. [Egtved]: Ed. Egtved, 1976. 198 p.   [g.a.]

Mss. and anon. works provided with incipits.

1045 _____

LITERATURE

Krabbe, Niels. "Simoni dall Croubelis 'compositeur ved musiquen'–København 1787."
Musikforskning 3 (1977): 11-25. [g.a.]

> Discusses relationship of Croubelis's Mss. in the Royal Library to Giedde's
> collection.

1046 Gieysztora, Jakuba Kazimierza, 1827-97

Brzezinska, Barbara. "Muzykalia w Warzawskim antykwariacie Jakuba Kazimierza Gieysztora."
In Warsaw, Biblioteca Narodowa, *Rocznik biblioteki narodowy* 11 (1975): 181-214.

[compiler (Xerox)]

> An index, pp. 190-213, of musical items included in 17 issues of G's
> antiquarian catalogs, 1882-96.

1047 Gilchrist, Anne Geddes

LITERATURE

Dean-Smith, Margaret. "The Gilchrist Bequest." *Journal of the English Folk Dance and Song
Society* 7 (1955): 218-27. [g.a.]

1048 _____

Dean-Smith, Margaret. "The Work of Anne Geddes Gilchrist." *Proceedings of the American
Musicological Society* 84 (1958): 43-53. [g.a.]

Gimo House and Collection.   *See under* **Lefebure, Jean**

1049 Giordano, Renzo

LITERATURE

Gentili, Alberti. "La musica di antiche musiche 'Renzo Giordano' alla Biblioteca Nazionale di
Torino." *Accademie e biblioteche d'Italia* 4 (1930): 117-25. [compiler (Xerox)]

> → *See also under* **Foà**. (The combined Foà-Giordano collection is in I-Tn.
> **Albrecht**.)

1050 Giustiniani, Alvise, Conte, 1909-62

Miggiani, Maria Giovanna. *Il Fondo Giustiniani del Conservatorio Benedetto Marcello:
Catalogo dei manoscritti e delle stampe.* Firenze: Olschki, 1990. 56, 613 p. 832 items, thematic.

[g.a.]

> **Benton 2**:405 cites a work by Mario Messinis, *Biblioteca del Conservatorio
> di Musica B. Marcello di Venezia: Catalogo del Fondo Musicale
> Giustiniani* (Venezia, 1960), but it could not be located, nor is it mentioned
> in Miggiani's thorough work.

1051 Glazebrook, Percy

SOTHEBY & CO., AUCTIONEER, LONDON
*Catalogue of Valuable Printed Books, Autograph Letters & Historical Documents, etc.,
Comprising the Well-Known Musical Library Formed by . . . Will Be Sold by Auction . . . 17th
of December, 1951, and Following Day. . . .* [London, 1951]. [US-Lbl]

> The music collection, pp. 8-19, lots 46-156.

1052   Gleason, Frederick Grant, 1848-1903
Peters, Aileen M. "Analysis of [His] Collections of Music, Scrapbooks and Diaries." M.Ed.
thesis, Library Science, Chicago Teachers College South, August 1965. Not examined.

> **Krummel 2** says collection now at US-Cn.

1053   Glee Club, London
Puttick & Simpson, auctioneer, London
*Catalogue of a . . . Collection of Music . . . Including the Library of . . . the "Glee Club"; Also
. . . Music Plates and Copyrights . . . [and] Musical Instruments . . . Sold . . . February 28, 1876,
and Following Day. . . .* [London, 1876]. 42 p. 1024 lots. Music, lots 1-875. [US-NYp, GB-Lbl]

> Some lots contain many items, e.g., lot 88: "An extensive collection of J. B.
> Cramer's MS. scores collected from celebrated composers, mostly
> autograph."

1054   Glen, John, 1833-1904
Glen, John. *Early Scottish Melodies, Including Examples from MSS. and Early Printed Works.
. . .* Edinburgh: J. & R. Glen, 1900. xvi, 271 p., illus.   [US-B, -NH, -NYp, etc.]

> At Glen's death in 1904, the collection was purchased by Lady Dorothea
> Ruggles-Brise, who gave it to the National Library of Scotland. Most of its
> contents were listed in Glen's *Early Scottish Melodies* (1900).

1055   Goddard, Edward, Rev.
Sotehby, Wilkinson & Hodge, auctioneer, London
*Catalogue of the Important and Valuable Collection of Ancient & Modern Music (Theoretical
& Practical) Formed by . . . A Few Other Musical Instruments . . . Sold by Auction by . . . the
4th of February, 1878.* [London], 1878. 33 p. 498 lots.   [US-Wc; film at CRL]

1056   Goedeke, Karl, 1814-87
F. A. Brockhaus, auctioneer, Leipzig
*Verzeichniss der aus dem Nachlasse der Herren Professor . . . in Göttingen und Pastor Erhard
Schultz . . . stammenden Bibliotheken . . . Litteratur . . . Philosophie, Musikalien und Schriften
über Musik und Theater, welche am 27. Juni 1888 und den folgenden Tagen . . . versteigert
werden sollen. . . .* [Leipzig: Leipziger Bücher-Auction, 1888.] 185 p. 5720 lots.

> Not examined; cited from **Folter 2**.

1057   Göpel [Johann Andreas], 1776-1823
*Verzeichnis der von dem verstorbenen academ. Musiklehrer, Organisten Göpel in Rostock
nachgelassenen Musikalien, musikalischen Instrumente und Bücher, welche am 1ˢᵗᵉⁿ
Sept^{br}. 1824 und folgenden Tagen . . . verkauft werden sollen durch der Auctions-Secretaire
Uebele. . . .* Rostock: Adlers Erben, 1824. 52 p. Music, pp. 1-38. Sections separately lotted.
[compiler]

1058   Goetz, Mrs. Angelina (Levy)
London, Royal Academy of Music, Angelina Goetz Library
A Catalogue of the . . . Library, Presented to the Royal Academy of Music, London, 1904. . . .
Compiled and edited by A. Rosenkranz. [London: Novello & Co., 1904.] 4, 224 p.   [US-Wc]

> Mainly full scores, according to **Davies**.

1059 **Götz [Hermann], Freiherr von,** 1840-76; **C. F. Gutwasser; C. C. Hille; Prof. Dr. Meineke; Consul G. Meusel**

G. Salomon, auctioneer, Dresden

Katalog der reichhaltigen Bibliotheken aus dem Nachlasse der . . . den 5. November 1877 und die folgenden Tage . . . versteigert werden. Dresden, 1877. 80 p. 2676 lots.   [US-NYp]

1060 **Gogh, Vincent van,** 1853-90

R. W. P. de Vries, auctioneer, Amsterdam

Catalogue de la bibliothèque privée de feu . . . Manuscrits - reliures - livres à gravures des 15e et 16e siècles . . . chansonniers [etc.] La vente . . . 15 [-16] janvier 1918. . . . Amsterdam, 1918. 102 p.   [NL-Avb]

"Theatre et musique," lots 1852-2029.

1061 **Goldmark, Rubin,** 1872-1936

Autographs, Letters and Memorabilia of Musicians Bequeathed to the Music Library of the Circulation Department New York Public Library by Rubin Goldmark. [New York?, n.d.] 29 items in 1 vol.   [US-NYp only]

1062 **[Goldschmidt, Otto],** 1829-1907

Sotheby, Wilkinson & Hodge, auctioneer, London

Catalogue of Books & Autograph Letters and Musical & Other Manuscripts. Handel's Score of the Messiah Written by J. C. Smith (the Celebrated Goldschmidt Manuscript). Autograph Letters & Music & Musical Compositions of Beethoven [etc.] . . . Sold . . . 18th of July. . . . [London, 1907].   [Film at CRL]

Lot 475, "The Property of the late Otto Goldschmidt, Esq.," Handel's score of *Messiah*, went to Read for £100. There is more about the "Goldschmidt Messiah" in an article by Burrows here under Cary (**460**). The Ms. is now at US-NYpm.

1063 _____

Literature

[A notice of the sale of 19 July 1907 and some of the Mss. included.] *MT* 48 (1907): 529-30.

1064 **Golterman, Georg Eduard,** 1824-98; **Albert [Herman] Dietrich,** 1829-1908?; **Baron von C***

Leo Liepmannssohn, firm, Berlin   Ant.-Cat. no. 38

*Katalog einer Autographen-Sammlung bestehend aus . . . Musik-Manuskripten und Musikerbriefen . . . aus den Nachlässen des Kapellmeisters Georg Eduard Golterman . . . Albert Dietrich . . . Sr. Excellenz, des Barons von C***. Versteigerung . . . 21. und 22. Mai 1909.* Berlin, 1909. 111 p. 937 lots.   [US-NYp]

Folter, no. 109-a.

Goltz, Doure **van der, Comtesse; M   C   Philippe; D   J   van Stegeren; C   P   Pous Kolhaas.**
See under **Heyblom**

1065 **Gonzaga Family**

Chambers, David, and Jane Martineau. *Splendours of the Gonzaga.* London: Victoria and Albert Museum, 1982. 248 p.   [g.a.]

Cited from *RILM*.

Goodban, Charles, 1812-81. *See under* **Engel** (sale of 1882)

1066 Goodkind, Herbert K

Druesedow, Elaine, Laura Snyder, and Alan Boyd. *H. K. Goodkind Collection: A Preliminary Checklist*. Oberlin, Ohio: Oberlin College Library, 1992. 203 p. [g.a.]

1067 _____

LITERATURE

Boe, David, S. Frederick Starr, William A. Moffett, Rachel Goodkind, and Hans E. Tausig. "Dedication of the Herbert K. Goodkind Collection at Oberlin College, February 21, 1987." *Journal of the Violin Society of America* 9 (1988): 187-200. [g.a.]

1068 [Goodman,   ]

PUTTICK & SIMPSON, AUCTIONEER, LONDON   CAT. NO. 1164
Catalogue of a Large and Interesting Collection of Music . . . Full and Vocal Music . . . Concerted Music . . . Musical Instruments . . . Sold December 22nd, 1869. London, 1869. 24 p. 883 lots. Music, lots 1-801. [GB-Lbl]

1069 Goodson, Richard, 1655-1718

Goodson, Richard, Jr. "Catalogue of the Books [in the Music School at Oxford] . . . " copied "from the Riting of My Father's," as attested at the end by Dr. Philip Hayes.

[GB-Lbl Add. Ms. 33965, ff. 44-46]

1070 _____

Goodson, Richard. "Transcript of the Two Papers Cattalougs [*sic*] of the Instruments and Books Belonging to the Musick School [at Oxford]," in the hand of Richard Goodson, Jr., copied from one in the hand of his father, followed by "A Coppie of Another and Smaller Cattalogue . . . wch I guess might be wrote before the former." [GB-Lbl Add. Ms. 30493, ff. 9-]

1071 _____

Malchair, J. B. "Catalogues of Richard Goodson's and Dean Aldrich's Collections of Manuscript and Printed Music, Bequeathed by Them to the Library of Christ Church College, Oxon."

> **King**, pp. 13-14, 145, says now Ms. 2125 in the Royal College of Music Library. He dates it 1787. See note under Aldrich, Henry (**24**).

Gordon, Lady Duff. *See* **Duff-Gordon, Lucie (Austin), Lady**

1072 Gordon, Jacques, 1899-1948

LITERATURE

Watanabe, Ruth. "The Gordon Collection of String Music." *University of Rochester Library Bulletin* 7 (1952): 25-27. [g.a.]

> A bequest.

1073 Gorke, Manfred, 1897-1956

LEIPZIG, MUSIKBIBLIOTHEK

Katalog der Sammlung Manfred Gorke: Bachiana u. andere Handschr. u. Drucke d. 18. u. frühen 19. Jh., [bearb. von Hans-Joachim Schulze]. Bibliographische Veröffentlichungen der Musikbibliothek der Stadt Leipzig, 8. Leipzig: Musikbibliothek d. Stadt Leipzig, 1977. 168 p. 702 items, mostly Bach items. [g.a.]

> **Folter**, no. 110-a.

1074   Goss, Sir John, 1800-80; **Arthur Robert Ward, Rev.**
PUTTICK & SIMPSON, AUCTIONEER, LONDON   CAT. NO. 2313
Catalogue of the Valuable Libraries of Music and Musical Literature of the Late . . . and of the Late . . . Fine Collection of Musical Portraits . . . Sold January 29, 1885. London, 1885. 17 p. 385 lots.   [GB-Lbl]

> Ward's portraits, lots 328-38 (46 in 1 lot!) and lots 218-327. Remainder of properties, Goss's.

1075   Goss, Sir John; Arthur Robert Ward, Rev.; Julian Marshall; George Benson
PUTTICK & SIMPSON, AUCTIONEER, LONDON   CAT. NO. 2329
Catalogue of Music and Musical Literature, Including the Residue of the Goss Library . . . A Selection of Works in Fine Bindings from the Marshall Sale . . . Treatises, Autographs and Manuscripts, Musical Portraits and Engravings, Including Those the Late Benson [lots 317-82] *. . . Sold April 8th and Following Day. . . .* London, 1885. 828 lots.   [GB-Lbl]

> Difficult to differentiate the consignors of most of the lots.

1076   Gostling, William, ca. 1652-1733
MESSRS. LANGFORD, AUCTIONEER, LONDON
Bibliotheca musicae reconditae eximiaeque locuples. A Catalogue of the Scarce, Valuable, and Curious Collection of Music, Manuscript and Printed of the Reverend and Learned . . . Consisting of a Great Variety of Vocal and Instrumental Music of All Kinds, Commencing at the Reformation, and Continued to Nearly the Present Time . . . Many of Them in Manuscript, and Some in the Handwriting of the Respective Authors. In This Sale are Three Volumes of Anthems by Mr. Handel . . . in Manuscript . . . Sold by Auction . . . the 26th of This Instant May 1777 and the Following Day. . . . London, 1777. 20 p. 84 and 89 lots (many more items, e.g.: lot 2, second day, consisted of 40 volumes, mostly manuscript). [GB-Lbl (Hirsch), compiler (film)]

> **King**, pp. 19-20: **Albrecht**. According to **Davies**, many 17th-century choirbooks in the collection ended up at York Minster.

1077   Gostling, William, and son, **William**
LITERATURE
Ford, Robert. "Music and Musicians at Canterbury Cathedral, 1660 to 1700." Ph.D. diss., University of California, Berkeley, 1983.

> Information on "their lives, collections, and milieu."

1078   Gotthold, Friedrich August, 1778-1858
KÖNIGSBERG, PRUSSIA, STAATS-BIBLIOTHECA GOTTHOLDIANA
Die musikalischen Schätze der königlichen und universitäts-Bibliothek zu Königsberg in Preussen, aus dem Nachlasse . . . Nebst Mitteilungen aus dessen musicalischen Tagebüchern. Ein Beitrag zur Geschichte und Theorie der Tonkunst, von Joseph Müller. Bonn: Marcus, 1870. 431 p.   [US-NY, -Wc, -NYp]

> **Folter**, no. 111; **Albrecht**. See the lengthy description of the collection by Robert Eitner in *MfM* 2 (1870): 146-48.

1079   _____
LITERATURE
Killer, H. "Zur Musik des deutschen Ostens im 18. Jahrhundert (aus der Sammlung Gotthold der Staats- und Universitäts-bibliothek Königsberg, Prussia)." *Königsberger Beiträge* (1929), 228-42.

1080 _____

Braun, Werner. "Mitteldeutsche Quellen der Musiksammlung Gotthold in Königsberg." *Musik des Ostens* 5 (1969): [84] - 96. [US-NYp]

> Discusses an inventory by Joseph Müller (1870), which throws light on two collections, one that of Joseph Kötschau (**1556**), and Andreas Unger's (d.1657) (**2739**), the older of the two. Noted in *RILM*.

1081 _____

Garber, Klaus. "Eine Bibliotheksreise durch die Sowjetunion: Alte deutsche Literatur zwischen Leningrad, dem Baltikum und Lemberg." *Neue Rundschau* 100 (1989): 5-38.

> Describes partial survival of the Gotthold collection through World War II.

Gottschalg, Alexander Wilhelm, 1827-1908. *See under* **Mottl** (Liepmannssohn sale no. 41)

1082 **Graan, J de** [et al.]

 C. EN ZOON VAN DOORN, AUCTIONEER, DEN HAAG

Catalogus eener goed geconditioneerde verzameling Boeken . . . nagelaten door . . . J. de Bas . . . [en] J. Verhoeven . . . benevens de muziek-bibliotheek, nagelaten door J. de Graan, beroemd violist te 's Gravenhage . . . verkooping . . . 28 April 1874 en volgende dagen . . . 's Gravenhage, 1874. 45 p. 1363 + 59 lots. Music, lots 488-795+. [NL-Avb]

Grabau, Johann A. *See under* **Ritter, August Gottfried**

1083 **Graf, Ernst,** 1886-1937

Wissler, Elisabeth. *Verzeichnis der handschriftlichen Musikalien* [aus dem] *legat Prof. Ernst Graf. Aufgenommen von E. W.* Bern: Schweizerische Landesbibliothek, 1938. ii, 30 leaves (typescript).

> Not located, cited from *Peters Jahrbuch*, 1938.

1084 **Graham, Richard,** d. ca. 1750; **Thomas Day; Thomas Cawley; Charles d'Orléans, Rothelin**

THOMAS OSBORNE, AUCTIONEER, LONDON

A Catalogue of the Libraries of . . . to Which Is Added an Appendix . . . Sold . . . the 11th of December, and Will Continue Selling till Lady-Day, 1750. [London: Osborne, 1750.] 320, 31 p. [US-Cn, F-Pn]

> Approximately 70 lots of music are indexed in **Coral**.

1085 **Grainger, Percy Aldridge,** 1892-1961

O'Brien, Jane. *The Grainger English Folk Song Collection. . . .* Nedlands: University of Western Australia, Dept. of Music . . . , 1985. xv, 158 p. [g.a.]

> A discography.

1086 _____

Percy Grainger's Personal Library, with an Introduction by Bruce Clunies Ross. Melbourne, Australia: Grainger Museum of the University of Melbourne, 1990. [g.a.]

> 4 microfiche, 14.5 x 10 cm. Reproduces the card catalog of shelf list with an introduction.

1087 _____

LITERATURE

Dreyfus, Kay. "The Adelaide Grainger Collection Transferred to the Grainger Museum, University of Melbourne." *Miscellanea musicologica (Adelaide Studies)* 9 (1977): 49-71.

[g.a.]

1088 _____

Clifford, Phil. "Grainger's Collection of Music by Other Composers." *Delius Society Journal* 84 (October 1984): 18-19.

Cited from *Music Index*.

1089 **[Grant,   Miss; Mr. Elvin; Mr. Taylor]**

SOTHEBY, WILKINSON & HODGE, AUCTIONEER, LONDON

Catalogue of Autograph Letters and Historical Documents . . . Manuscript Music & Letters of Celebrated Composers . . . Sold . . . the 22nd of July 1909. . . . [London, 1909.] 26 p. 269 lots.

[Film at CRL]

1090 **[Grant, Albert]**

PUTTICK & SIMPSON, AUCTIONEER, LONDON   CAT. NO. 1751

Catalogue of Unpublished Compositions of Giacchino Rossini, Each MS. "Signed by the Master" . . . Sold . . . May 30, 1878. London, 1878. 16 p. 121 leaves.   [GB-Lbl]

A note in the *London and Provincial Music Trades Review* 6 (15 April 1878): 12, says "G gave 4000 pounds for them. The sale will certainly bring . . . representations of publishers all over the world."

1091 **Granville Family**

The collection was begun by Bernard Granville (1709-75), added to by his nephew and heir John (Dewes) Granville, then by Capt. Bernard Granville. It was first offered at auction in 1858. The volumes were purchased by a "G," quite possibly the consignor (McLean, **1096**, says "probably bought by his eldest son"). The collection, in any event, remained in the family until the next auction in 1912. In 1915, GB-Lbl somehow acquired 37 Ms. copies of works by Handel that appeared in that sale. (See annotation to the following.)

1092 **Granville Family; John Christopher Smith; et al.**

PUTTICK & SIMPSON, AUCTIONEER, LONDON   CAT. NO. 526

Catalogue of a Very Important and Interesting Collection of Distinguished Amateur; and Important Series of Handel's Works Written by J. C. Smith for Bernard Granville [lot 183]. *A Trio in Handel's Autograph* [lot 184 from another collection] . . . *Other Interesting Manuscripts from the Library of J. C. Smith . . . Sold . . . January 29th and Following Day. . . .* London, 1858. 477 lots.   [GB-Lbl]

All of the contents of lots 183-85 and J. C. Smith's Handel manuscripts, lots 187-89 are set out in facsimile in **Coover 2**, pp. 166-69. The 37 volumes in lot 183 were eventually purchased by the British Museum in 1915. See the lengthy commentary about the sale in McLean's article (**1096**), pp. 664-65.

1093 _____

SOTHEBY WILKINSON & HODGE, AUCTIONEER, LONDON

Catalogue of Valuable & Rare Books and Splendid Illuminated & Other Manuscripts . . . the Famous Collection of Handel Manuscripts Known as the "Granville Collection," Comprising Numerous Scores of His Works, Including the Messiah and Autograph Score of a Vocal Trio . . . Sold . . . 28th of March, 1912, and Following Day. [London, 1912.]   [Film at CRL]

> Lots 459-61 comprise the "Granville Collection," bought by Attwood. They had been sold in the earlier Puttick & Simpson sale, 1 January 1858 (**1092**).
>
> This sale was announced in the *Musical News* 42 (23 March 1912): 173, in a lead article which says with some surprise that the collection "has remained in the family until now [i.e., 1912]."

1094 _____

Burrows, Donald. "The 'Granville' and 'Smith' Collections of Handel Manuscripts." In *Sundry Sorts of Music Books . . . Essays Presented to O. W. Neighbour,* 231-47. London: British Library, 1993.   [g.a.]

> Catalog, pp. 242-44.

1095 _____

LITERATURE

Streatfield, R. A. "The Granville Collection of Handel Manuscripts." *Musical Antiquary* 2 (1910/11): 208-24.   [g.a.]

1096 _____

McLean, Hugh. "Bernard Granville, Handel and the Rembrandts." *MT* 126 (1986): 593-601. [g.a.]

> Notes both the Puttick and the Sotheby sales and also reprints the contents of the auction of Handel's private art collection (67 lots) in 1760. See complete citation for the sale catalog under **Handel**.

1097 _____

McLean, Hugh. "Granville, Handel and 'Some Golden Rules'." *MT* 126 (1985): 662-65.

> Refers at length to the 1858 offering of the Granville collection, that which was apparently bought in. Handel's "Golden Rules" was bought by Cummings, sold when his library was dispersed in May 1917, now resides in the Nanki Music Library (see under **Ohki**).

1098   **Grasnick, Friedrich August**

> Grasnick purchased most of the Aloys Fuchs collection. See citations listed here under **Fuchs**, a few of which provide information about what was in Grasnick's collection. Because they went to D-Bds in 1879, they are, therefore, repeated below.

1099 _____

"Inventar [of the Grasnick-Fuchs collection]."

> Ms. in G-Bds, catalog Ms. 119.

1100 _____

VOTKE , FRAU PROFESSOR

"Verzeichniss der von Frau Professor Votke für dir Königl. Bibliothek angekauften Autographe, musikalien Bücher [etc.], 1879." 10 leaves.

> Ms. in D-Bds, catalog Mus. Ms. 119. Identical to previous citation? Summarized by Richard Schaal in his *Quellen und Forschungen zur Wiener Musiksammlung von Aloys Fuchs* (Wien: Böhlaus Nachf., 1966), 80-82, and in *Bach-Jahrbuch* 1960 (Berlin, 1961), 87.

1101 _____

LITERATURE

Schaal, Richard. "Die Berliner Mozart-Abschriften der Sammlung Fuchs-Grasnick." *Mozart Jahrbuch* (1971-72 [publ. 1973]): 415-18.   [g.a.]

1102 Gratiano, Dr. (of San Marco)

SILVISTRE, AUCTIONEER, PARIS

Catalogue de la bibliothèque du Docteur Gratiano . . . La vente se fera 22 février [-2 Mars], 1844. Paris, 1844. 176 p. 1250 lots. Music books, lots 143-436.   [US-NYgr]

1103 Graumann, Dorothea

"Catalogue de musique pour Mad[emoise]lle D[orothea] Graumann / 1797." 88, [2] p. Ms. at A-Gu. Thematic.

> Cited from **Brook**, no. 475.

1104 _____

LITERATURE

Federhofer, Hellmut. "Ein thematischer Katalog der Dorothea Graumann (Freiin von Ertmann)." In *Festschrift Joseph Schmidt-Görg zum 60. Geburtstag*, 100-10. Bonn, 1957.   [g.a.]

1105 Gray, Thomas, 1716-71

SOTHEBY, S. LEIGH, & JOHN WILKINSON

Catalogue of a Most Interesting Collection of Music and Books of the Poet Gray . . . Various Editions of His Works . . . Sold . . . August 28th, 1851. 31 p. 170 lots.

                    [US-CA (with n & p), -NYp; film at CRL]

> Lot 95, "The 'valuable collection' of MS. music [Italian operatic arias, for the most part] made while Gray was in Italy . . . Selections from the best masters . . . " (ten volumes). Lot 96, various Ms. compositions.
>
> The music was bought by Hamilton for £12, who later consigned it to Puttick & Simpson's sale no. 1185 in 1870, where it was purchased by Pickering for £4. Pickering resold it to the American collector Charles W. Frederickson. In the 1887 sale of his library by Bangs, Bangs bought it, later presented it to Mrs. C. M. Raymond (Annie Louise Cary), from whose possession the volumes somehow came into Krehbiel's (see **1107**). Subsequently they became the property of Wilmarth S. Lewis of Connecticut. See **Coover 2**, pp. 207-08.
>
> **King**, p. 49.
>
> **Albrecht** notes another sale catalog dated 1921, saying it was reprinted in 1975, but neither has been located.

1106 _____

Sotheby, S. Leigh, & John Wilkinson
Catalogue, Briefly Descriptive, of Various Books and Original Manuscripts of. . . . [London.]
Printed by W. Niol, [1851]. 1, 4, 27 p. 14 copies only printed.

[US-Wc, -CA, -NYp, -LAuc (photostat)]

1107 _____

Literature
Krehbiel, Henry. "Gray's Musical Collection." In his *Music & Manners of the Classical Period,*
3-39. New York, 1898. [g.a.]

1108 _____

Cudworth, Charles. "Thomas Gray and Music." *MT* 112 (1971): 646-48. [g.a.]

1109 Great Britain - Kings and Rulers

Burney, Charles. "Chronological List of Handel's Works: Original Manuscripts in the Possession
of His Majesty [King George III]." In his *An Account of the Musical Performances in Westminster
Abbey and the Pantheon . . . ,* 42-46. London: Printed for the Benefit of the Musical
Fund . . . , 1785. Reprint, Amsterdam: Knuf, 1964. [R, g.a.]

1110 _____

British Museum, Department of Printed Books, King's Music Library
Barclay Squire, William. *Catalogue of the King's Music Library.* London: Sold at the British
Museum and by B. Quaritch, 1927-29. 3 vols., illus. [g.a.]

> Deposited by His Majesty, King George V in the Museum in 1911. Originally
> formed by King George III and Queen Charlotte, added to by subsequent
> purchases and gifts.

1111 _____

Literature
King, A. Hyatt. "English Royal Music-Lovers and Their Library, 1600-1900." *MT* 99 (1958):
311-13. [g.a.]

> Contributions by ten generations of the royal family.

1112 Greatheed, Samuel Stephenson, 1812 or 1813-87; **Sir Henry Rowley Bishop,** 1786-1855

Puttick & Simpson, auctioneer, London   Cat. no. 2548
*Catalogue of an Extensive Collection of Music, Including the Miscellaneous Library, Together
with the Published Compositions, Engraved and Stereotype Music Plates, and Copyrights
of the Late . . . Also a Useful Collection of Theoretical Works, the Property of an Amateur.
Scarce Operas, etc, of Sir H. R. Bishop . . . Sold January the 23rd, 1888.* London, 1888.
17 p. 335 lots. [GB-Lbl]

1113 Greatorex, Thomas, 1758-1831

> 67 volumes of Handel Mss. from Greatorex's collection (later John Ireland's)
> were presented to GB-Cfm by Henry Barrett-Lennard (**1667**), in 1902. They
> were lot 252 in the following sale.

1114 _____

MR. WATSON, AUCTIONEER, LONDON

Bibliotheca musica. A Catalogue of the Valuable Musical Library of the Late . . . (Organist of Westminster Abbey), Including a Portion of the Library of the Pretender . . . In the Collection . . . Portraits of Musicians, &c. The Handel Bookcase . . . Copies of His Compositions in the Handwriting of . . . Smith . . . [etc.] . . . Sold . . . April 3rd, 1832 and [3] *Following Days.* London, 1832. 32 p., 429 lots. Music lots 1-393.   [GB-Lbl]

> Lot 252: the "famous collection of 67 volumes of J. C. Smith copies of Händel," known as the Lennard collection, now in the Fitzwilliam (**King,** pp. 37-38).

1115 _____

MR. WATSON, AUCTIONEER, LONDON

A Catalogue of a Valuable Assemblage of Vocal + Instrumental Music, Comprising the Library of the Remainder of the Collection Formed by T. Greatorex . . . [etc.] *. . . Sold . . . June 26, 1832, and* [4] *Following Days.* . . . London, 1832. 30 p. 636 lots. Music, lots 1-319, 344-429, 437-566. Mss., lots 454-76.   [GB-Lbl, compiler (film)]

> A fuller citation is included here under **Groombridge, Stephen,** et al.

1116 _____

LITERATURE

Hogg, James. "The Sale of the Music Library of the Late Mr. Greatorex." *Harmonicon* 10 (1832): 118.

> A brief note that describes some of the items in the sale.

1117   Green, Towneley

SOTHEBY, WILKINSON & HODGE, AUCTIONEER, LONDON

Catalogue of Valuable Autograph Letters and Documents Including the Collection of . . . Inherited from His Aunt . . . Miss Charlotte Reynolds . . . Letters of Celebrated Music Composers . . . the Autograph Scores . . . of an Unknown Cantata by Haydn . . . Will Be Sold by Auction . . . 13th Day of May, 1901. [London], 1901. 38 p. 25 scattered lots of ALS or Mss.
[Film at CRL]

1118   Gregar, Joseph, Hofrat

ALOIS REICHMANN, AUCTIONEER?, VIENNA

Bibliothek . . . Theater - Musik - Literature, Bibliographie. . . . Vienna, 1962. 40 p. 614 lots.

> Not located; cited from *IBAK.*

1119   Greggiati, Giuseppe, Canon, 1793-1866

Descrizione e stima delle opere musicali raccolte nel gabinetto di casa Greggiati che formano parte della sostanza caduta in credità al commune di Ostiglia. Rovere, 1874.

> Not located.

1120 _____

OSTIGLIA, BIBLIOTECA MUSICALE GREGGIATA

Ostiglia, biblioteca dell'opera Pia Greggiati: Catalogo del fondo musicale: a cura di Claudio Sartori. Milano: Nuovo istituto editoriale italiano, 1983.   [g.a.]

> Vol. 1, *Le edizione.* Bibliotheca musicae: Collana di cataloghi e bibliografie, 7.

1121 _____

LITERATURE

Knud, Jeppesen. "P. da Palestrina, Herzog Guglielmo Gonzaga und die neugefunden Mantover-Messen Palestrinas." *Acta* 25 (1953): 132-79.   [g.a.]

> Describes the transfer of music from the Capitolo di S. Barbara di Mantova by sale in 1850 to Canon Greggiati.

1122   Greissle, Felix, 1894-1982

Wayne, Shoaf R. "From the Archives: The Felix Greissle Collection." *Journal of the Arnold Schoenberg Institute* 10, no. 1 (June 1987): 65-82.   [g.a.]

> Describes more than 500 items: 374 letters, 36 scores, G's arrangements, books, etc.

1123   Grell, Eduard August, 1800-1886

ALBERT COHN, FIRM, BERLIN   CAT. NO. 182

. . . Katalog des antiquarischen Bücherlagers von Albert Cohn in Berlin . . . Musikalische Bibliothek des verstorbenen Herrn Eduard Grell . . . Nebst einigen Beiträgen aus anderen Sammlungen. Berlin: A Cohn, 1887. 68 p. 773 lots.   [US-NYp (priced), NL-DHgm]

> **Folter,** no. 112.

1124 _____

LEO LIEPMANNSSOHN, FIRM, BERLIN   ANT.-CAT. NO. 56

Aeltere instrumental- und vokal-Musik zum grössten Theile aus der Sammlung des Professor. . . . Berlin: Liepmannssohn, 1887. 53 p. 894 lots.   [D-Bds]

> **Folter,** no. 113.

1125   Grell, Eduard August; Graf Wilhelm von Redern

LEO LIEPMANNSSOHN, FIRM, BERLIN   ANT.-CAT. NO. 58

Opern in Partitur oder Klavierauszug, im Druck oder Ms., von italienischen, französischen, belgischen, deutschen, englischen und schwedischen Komponisten: Eine wertvolle und verstorbenen Grell und Grafen von Redern. Berlin: Liepmannssohn, 1887. 20, 26 p. 259, 554 lots.   [NL-Avb]

> **Folter,** no. 113.
>
> → *See also under* **Redern, Graf Wilhelm** (Liepmannssohn sale of his materials, catalog no. 58, 1887)

1126   Grell, Eduard August; Graf Wilhelm von Redern; Franz Commer, 1813-87

LEO LIEPMANNSSOHN, FIRM, BERLIN   ANT.-CAT. NO. 75

Musik-Manuskripte, vorwiegend älteren Datums, zum grössten Theil aus dem Nachlässen von professor Eduard Grell . . . Graf Wilhelm von Redern . . . Franz Commer. . . . Berlin, 1889. 29, 33 p. 694, 634 lots.   [US-Wc, -NYp, NL-Avb]

> Vol. 1: Instrumental music; vol. 2: *Vokalmusik aller Art.* **Folter,** no. 115-16.

1127   [Gresham,   ?]

PUTTICK & SIMPSON, AUCTIONEER, LONDON   CAT. NO. 340

Catalogue of an Interesting and Valuable Musical Library . . . Some Works on the History and Theory of Music, etc. The Musical Instruments Included . . . Sold . . . October 20th, 1853, and Following Day. London, 1853. 20 p. 433 lots. Music, lots 1-397.   [GB-Lbl]

1128   **Gresnirere, Juan B.; Mrs. Richard A. Northcott; C. B. Oldman; Mrs. R. W. Chapman; Dr. Hendrik Otto Raimund, Baron van Tuyll van Serooskerken**

SOTHEBY & CO., AUCTIONEER, LONDON

Catalogue of Valuable Holographs, Printed and Engraved Music, Books About Music and Musicians, and Autographed Letters of Composers, Comprising Letters of [Musicians] *the Property of* [Gresnirere and Mrs. Northcott] . . . *First Editions of Mozart, the Property of C. B. Oldman. An Important Collection of Holograph Music of Mendelssohn . . . the Property of Mrs. R. W. Chapman . . . A Very Fine Collection of Rare First Editions of . . . Bach . . . the Property of . . . Tuyll van Serooskerken . . . Six Holograph Organ Church Preludes by . . . Bach, the Property of . . . Tuyll van Serooskerken, and Other Properties . . . Sold . . . the 11th May, 1959, and the Following Day. . . .* London, 1859. 67 p. 413 lots.   [Film at CRL]

> Gresnirere's properties, lots 1-34, 280-86; Northcott's, 112-204; Oldman's, 205-69 (more items); Chapman's, 335-64 (and magnificent!); the Baron's, 365-413. Chapman's collection "belonged to Mrs. Dorothea Wach, granddaughter of Mendelssohn, and was bequeathed to her adopted daughter, Mrs. Chapman. **Folter**, no. 275, puts under Oldman!
>
> Rossini holographs and ALS, lots 52-71; Verdi holographs and ALS, lots 76-111.   [Film at CRL]

1129   **Greville, Charles; Sir Robert Smith**

LEIGH & S. SOTHEBY, AUCTIONEER, LONDON

A Catalogue of a Very Good Collection of Books Containing Those Purchased by the Late Hon. Charles Greville, from the Library of . . . Smith . . . A Good Collection of Music Among Which Is a Complete Collection of Catch Club Prize Music, in Manuscript, 31 Vol. . . . Sold June 11, 1810. [London, 1810.] 9 p. Music, pp. 8-9, lots 204-39.

>   [US-R in the "lost" Warren volume of catalogs]

1130   **Gridjani,   ?**

Papajanopoulos. "Die Musik-Bibliothek von Gridjani." *Mousika Chronika* (Athens), no. 29 (1931).

> Not located; cited from "Zeitschriftenschau" in *ZfMW*.

1131   **Grieg, Edvard Hagerup,** 1843-1907

LITERATURE

Röntgen, J. "Edvard Grieg's musikalischer Nachlass." *Die Musik* 7, no. 5 (1908): 288-300.

>   [g.a.]

> Mostly music.

1132   _____

McKinnon, Lise. "The Grieg Archives in the Bergen Public Library." *Fontes* 34 (1987): 117-20.

>   [g.a.]

1133   **Grieg, Gavin,** 1856-1914

[Shuldham-Shaw, Patrick.] [Index of the Gavin Grieg manuscript collection of folk music. 195-?] 9 vols. Typewritten.

>   [US-Wc ("Obtained from the English Folk Dance and Song Society")]

1134 **Griffith, George Edward,** d. 1829
MR. WHEATLEY, AUCTIONEER, LONDON
Catalogue of the Valuable and Extensive Library of the Late . . . Together with the Books of Portraits. Library of Music, Collection of Casts and Pictures, the Property of a Well-Known Amateur of Fine Arts . . . August 3, 1831, and Eight Following Days (Sunday Excepted). London, 1831. 66 p. Sections are separately lotted.

Music, 9th day, pp. 61-62, 25 lots (but many items, 5-7 per lot).

Grigoraki, Raymond. *See under* **Diaghileff, Sergei** (Schneider catalog no. 209)

1135 **Grillparzer, Franz,** 1791-1872
Racek, Fritz. "Die Musiksammlung der Wiener Stadtbibliothek." *ÖmZ* 10 (1955): 171-74. [g.a.]
G's collection went to the Stadtbibliothek.

1136 **Grolier, Jean, Vicomte d'Aguisy,** 1479-1565
LEVIN & MUNKSGAARD, FIRM, COPENHAGEN
Et hundrede og halvtreds gamle boger og manuskripter vanskelige at finde. . . . Copenhagen, 1929.

Not located; cited from "Zeitschriftenschau," in *ZfMW*.

1137 **Groombridge, Stephen; Thomas Greatorex; John Sidney Hawkins,** 1719-89; **Mr. Eley**
MR. WATSON, AUCTIONEER, LONDON
A Catalogue of a Valuable Assemblage of Vocal and Instrumental Music, Comprising the Library of . . . , the Remainder of the Collection Formed by T. Greatorex . . . Together with a Portion of the Library of John Sidney Hawkins . . . Many of the Works Are from the Libraries of the Pretender and of the Margravine of Anspach . . . [Musical Instruments] *. . . Sold . . . June 26, 1832, and Following* [4] *Days . . .* London, 1832. 30 p. 636 lots. Music, lots 1-219, 344-429, 437-566. Mss., lots 454-76.   [GB-Lbl (some n & p)]

1138 **Groosen, A   J   , Mrs.**
SOTHEBY PARKE BERNET, AUCTIONEER, LONDON
Catalogue of Important Musical Manuscripts, Autograph Letters of Composers and Musicians' . . . Printed Music and Books on Music and Musical Instruments . . . Will Be Sold . . . 23rd November 1977 . . . London, 1977. 61 p. 300 lots.   [Film at CRL]

1139 **G[ross], A   G**
Catalogue de livres anciens et modernes sur la musique composant la bibliothèque de M. A. G. Paris: Martin, 1883. 104 + 94 nos.

Not located; cited from **Bobillier** and **Weckerlin**, nos. 93 and 86(2).
Wolffheim 1:345.

Grüters, August. *See under* **Liliencron** (Liepmannssohn catalog no. 181)

1140 **Grundmann, Herbert**
Schmidt, Anna-Maria. *Die älteren Musikalien der Sammlung Herbert Grundmann im Beethoven-Archiv Bonn.* Bonn: Bouvier, 1983. 154 p.

Not located; cited from *RILM*.

1141   Gruneisen, Charles Lewis, 1806-79
STORR & SONS DEBENHAM, AUCTIONEER, LONDON
His library offered for sale 3 June 1880 according to notices in *London & Provincial Music Trades Review* 32 (15 June 1880): 17, and in *Musical Opinion and Music Trade Review* (1 July 1880), p. 33. Sale catalog not located.

1142 _____
"Descriptive list of an interesting collection of autograph letters [for the most part belonging to the late Mr. Gruneisen]." In William Reeves, bookseller, *Musical Catalogue* 10, part 2 (London, 1883): 139-42. London, 1883.
Bought at auction by Debenham et al. (**1141**). Sizeable collections as single lots. Advertised by Reeves as early as his catalog no. 7, 1881 as a catalog for 6p "in press." "Now ready" in catalog no. 8, 1881.

1143   Guglielmo, P   D   , Signor, Prof. of Singing
S. LEIGH SOTHEBY & JOHN WILKINSON, AUCTIONEER, LONDON
Catalogue of Instrumental Music and Popular Songs by Eminent Composers, Together with the Engraved Plates and Copyrights of . . . Sold by Auction . . . the 29th of November, 1854. [London], 1854. 11 p. 147 lots.   [Film at CRL]
Coral dates 16 November 1855, but *see here under* **Clark, R.** for that sale.

Guildhall School of Music and Dance.   *See* **London Guildhall School of Music** *under* **Hopkinson, Cecil**

Guise, Richard.   *See* **Bartleman** (sale of 8-9 June 1807)

1144   Guitry, Sacha, 1885-1957
E. & A. ADER, J.-L. PICARD AND J. TALAN (C.-P.); CASTAING, M. (EXP.), PARIS
Autographs et documents historiques dont la vente . . . Hotel Drouot Sall no. 10 . . . 21 novembre 1974 . . . par. . . . Paris, 1974. 102 lots. Music lots, *inter alia.*   [compiler]

1145   Gullen, J   A   , et al.
H. G. BOM, AUCTIONEER, AMSTERDAM
Catalogus van de belangrijke en kostbare Bibliotheken, nagelaten door . . . D. P. Beets . . . A. F. de Boer . . . [8 others] en J. A. Gullen, Organist te Amsterdam . . . Verkooping . . . 1 October 1901, en twaalf volgende dagen. . . . Amsterdam, 1901. 235 p. 26,437 + 985 lots. Music, lots 147-374.   [NL-Avb]
The music was Gullen's.

1146   Gunn, John, 1765?-ca. 1824
W. P. MUSGRAVE, AUCTIONEER, LONDON
A Catalogue of the Select and Entire Musical Library of the Late . . . Likewise Excellent [Instruments] . . . Will Be Sold by Auction by Mr. W. P. Musgrave . . . June 1 & 2, 1824. [London], 1824. 22 p. 257 lots. Music, lots 36-257.   [GB-Lbl, compiler (film)]

Gustav, Prince, 1781-1851.   *See* **Auguste Friederike**

1147   Gwilt, Joseph, 1784-1863; **Giuseppe Naldi,** 1770-1820
W. P. MUSGRAVE, AUCTIONEER, LONDON
A Catalogue of a Very Choice Collection of Modern Instrumental Music by the Most Eminent Masters [and Instruments], *Property of Joseph Gwilt, Also . . . A Portion of the Signor Naldi's Collection* [Instruments] *. . . Sold . . . 10th July 1820.* [London, 1828?] 15 p. 165 lots. Music, lots 1-120, 139-65.   [compiler (film)]
→ *See also under* **Cerutti** (Puttick & Simpson sale of 19-20 July 1854)

1148   _____
PUTTICK & SIMPSON, AUCTIONEER, LONDON
Catalogue of the Furniture and Other Effects of the Late . . . 300 Volumes of Choice and Rare Books, Musical Instruments . . . Scarce and Valuable Music [etc.] *. . . Sold . . . October 14th and Two Following Days. . . .* London, 1856. 188 lots.   [GB-Lbl (Hirsch 565, vol. 2{15})]

1149   [Gyrowetz, Adalbert, 1763-1850?]
D. WEBER, AUCTIONEER, VIENNA
Verzeichniss einer . . . Sammlung van Oehlgemählden . . . nebst sehr guten classischen Musikalien und Partituren, welche am, 23. und 24. März 1840 . . . versteigert werden . . . Das gedruckte Verzeichniss ist zu haben bei Herrn D. Weber. . . . Wien: gedruckt bei J. B. Wallishausser, 1840.   [A-Wak, -Wal]
Not examined; cited from **Lugt,** no. 15728.

1150   Haas, Robert Maria, 1886-1960
HANS SCHNEIDER, FIRM, TUTZING   CAT. NO. 83
Musikliteratur, darunter die Bibliothek. . . . Tutzing, [1962]. 40 p. 634 lots.   [g.a.]
Haas properties not differentiated.

1151   Hackett, Charles Danvers
PUTTICK & SIMPSON, AUCTIONEER, LONDON   CAT. NO. 564
Catalogue of a Collection of Miscellaneous Music, Including a Selection from the Library of [lots 564-633, 658-734] *. . . Sold . . . February 23rd and Two Following Days. . . .* London, 1859.
[GB-Lbl]

1152   Hackley, Emma Azalia
DETROIT, PUBLIC LIBRARY
Catalog of the E. Azalia Hackley Memorial Collection of Negro Music, of Dance, and Drama. Boston: G. K. Hall, 1979. iv, 510 p.   [g.a.]

1153   Haeberlein, Carl
FELIX DÖRFFEL, FIRM, DARMSTADT
Autographen . . . [including Musiker] *. . . Sammlung Dr. C. Haeberlein.* Darmstadt, 1964. 4 leaves. 52 lots.
Not examined; cited from *IBAK.*

1154 **Hagen, Sophus Albert Emil,** 1842-1929
KONGELIGE BIBLIOTEK (DENMARK), HANDSKRIFTAFDELNINGEN
Hagens samling i det Kongelige Biblioteks Hanskriftafdeling, kilder til dansk musikhistorie samlet af S.A.E. Hagen. Registrant udarbej det af Nanna Schiodt, Dan Fog, Hans Danelund.
Kobenhavn: Kongelige Bibliotek, 1981. 167 p. illus.   [US-NBu]

1155 **Hale, Philip,** 1854-1934
BOSTON, PUBLIC LIBRARY, MUSIC DEPT.
"A list of a part of the library of Philip Hale, and the original acknowledgments to Mrs. Hale of gifts from his library to various colleges, libraries, etc.," compiled by the Music Dept. Boston, 1942. 32 numbered leaves, 22 leaves.   [US-Bp]
> A scrapbook.

1156 **Hall, James S.,** 1899-1973
Knapp, J. Merrill. "The Hall Handel Collection." *Princeton University Library Chronicle* 36, no. 1 (autumn 1974): 3-18.   [g.a.]

1157 _____
Knapp, J. Merrill. "The Hall Collection." In *Handel Collections and Their History,* 171-83. Oxford: Clarendon Press, 1993.   [g.a.]
> Now at Us-PRu.

1158 **Halle, Philip,** 1656-1742
Harman, R. Alec. *A Catalogue of the Printed Music and Books on Music in Durham Cathedral Library.* London: Oxford University Press, 1968. 151 p. 682 items.   [g.a.]
> Principally from Halle's collection and that of the Sharp family of Bamburgh Castle.

1159 **Halliwell-Phillipps, James Orchard,** 1820-89
An Account of the European Manuscripts in the Chetham Library, Manchester. . . . Manchester: Simms and Dinham, 1842. ca. 26 p.   [GB-Mch]

1160 _____
A Catalogue of Proclamations, Broadside Ballads, and Poems. Presented to the Chetham Library, Manchester, by. . . . London: printed for private circulation only [by C. and J. Adlard], 1851. xx, 272p. 3100 "entries."   [US-Wc, -NH, -Bp, -NYp, -CLp, -AA]

1161 _____
A Catalogue of a Unique Collection of Ancient English Broadside Ballads, Printed Entirely in Black Letter. On Sale by John Russell Smith. . . . [London: Chiswick Press, C. Whittingham], 1856. vii, 141 p.   [US-Wc, -AA, -PHu, -CLp]

1162 **Halm, [? Anton,** 1789-1872]
[A notice of a public sale a "few weeks ago," with a brief list of important lots sold.] *MMR* 13 (1883): 144.   [g.a.]

1163 **Halm, Hans,** b. 1887
LITERATURE
"Schubert-Funde eines Münchener Bibliothekars." *NMZ* (1947), 24-26.   [g.a.]

1164   Hamel, Fred, 1903-57

J. L. BEIJERS, AUCTIONEER, UTRECHT

*Book Auction Sale, 3rd April 1963. Books on Music and Musicology, Collected by the Late
. . . , Hamburg.* Utrecht: J. L. Beijers, 1963. 109 p. 1308 + lots. Music, lots 800-1219.

[NL DHgm, -Avb (n & p)]

>   **Folter,** no. 119.

1165   _____

HANS SCHNEIDER, FIRM, TUTZING   CAT. NO. 96

Musikliteratur, darunter grössere Bestände der Bibliothek Fred Hamel. . . . [Tutzing: Schneider,
1963.] 68 p. 890 lots.   [g.a.]

>   **Folter,** no. 120.

1166   Hamelsveld, Ijsbrand van, 1743-1812

GARTMAN, VAN DER HEY EN SCHMIDT, FIRM, AMSTERDAM

*Catalogus van twee Verzamelingen . . . Boeken, in alle Faculteiten . . . Eene collectie
Teekeningen en Printen . . . Muzyk en Muzykinstrumenten . . . nagelaten door. . . .* Amsterdam,
1812. 4, 109 p. 3299 lots. Music, pp. 101-02 and lots 11-42.   [NL-Avb only]

1167   Hammer, Carl Joseph, 17-?

"Musicaliensammlung des Carl Joseph Hammer . . . , 1827."

>   Ms. at US-Wc. Volumes 12 and 13 are catalogs of the collection, the latter
>   thematic.

1168   Hammond, Thomas, d. 1662

Crum, Margaret. "A Seventeenth Century Collection of Music Belonging to Thomas Hammond,
a Suffolk Landowner." *Bodleian Library Record* 6 (1957): 378-86.   [g.a.]

>   Most items at GB-Ob, some at GB-Lbl and GB-Och.

1169   Hammond Jones, W   H   ; A Prof. [Thomas Tallis Trimnell, 1850-97?**; J Thomas]**

PUTTICK & SIMPSON, AUCTIONEER, LONDON

*Catalogue of Musical Instruments . . . and Several Libraries of Music, Including the Property
of the Late . . . Sold . . . September 27th . . . and Following Day. . . .* [London, 1898.] 31 p. 608
lots. Music, lots 311-610.   [GB-Lbl]

>   "Library of a Prof. leaving England for Health," lots 361-459 [Trimnell?];
>   Hammond Jones, lots 460-524; [J. Thomas], lots 525-608.

1170   Handel, George Frideric, 1685-1759

MR. LANGFORD, AUCTIONEER, LONDON

*A Catalogue of the Genuine and Entire Collections of . . . Pictures, of John Ellys, Esq.; and
George Frederick Handel . . . Both Lately Deceased . . . Sold by Auction . . . the 27th and 18th
of This Instant, February, 1760.* [London, 1760.]

>   "Second day's sale, Mr. Handel's collection." 67 lots. Not examined.

1171 _____

Simon, Jacob. "Handel's Collection of Paintings." In *Handel: A Celebration of His Life and Times* [catalog of an exhibit], 289-90. London: National Portrait Gallery, 1985.

"The dispersal of Handel's collections," p. 290.

1172 _____

Simon, Jacob. "Handel's Library: The Evidence of Book Subscription Lists." In *ibid.*, 286-88.

1173 **Hanfstaengel, Edgar,** 1842-1910

GALERIE HUGO HELBING, AUCTIONEER, MUNICH

Sammlung des Herrn Hofrat . . . , ölgemälde alter und moderner Meister; fünfundzwanzig eigenhändige Briefe Richard Wagners . . . [etc.] . . . den 11 Mai 1909. . . . München, 1909. 50 p. 75 plates.   [US-Wc]

Not examined.

1174 **Hanslick, Edward,** 1825-1904

V. A. HECK, FIRM, VIENNA   CAT. NO. 24

Musik und Theater: Bücher und Autographen zum Teil aus dem Nachlasse des Herrn Hofrat Dr. . . . Wien, [ca. 1925]. 57 p. 1046 lots. Autographs, lots 1-628.   [US-Cn, NL-Avb]

Folter, no. 121.

1175 **Hansson, Per Wilhelm**

"Enskilda arkiv. Per Wilhelms Hanssons brevsamling." *Svenskt Musik Historisk Arkiv Bull.* 7 (1971): 24-37.   [g.a.]

1176 **Haraszti, Emil,** 1885-1959

HANS SCHNEIDER, FIRM, TUTZING   CAT. NO. 105

Musikliteratur, grösstenteils aus der Bibliothek des ungarischen Musikwissenschaftlers. . . . Tutzing, 1964. 67 p. 992 lots.   [g.a.]

Folter, no. 122 (with a different title!). Liszt biographical material went to F-Pim, 1965.

1177 **Harding, Walter N. H.,** 1883-1973

LITERATURE

"Contemporary Collectors XXXIII: British Song Books and Kindred Subjects." *Book Collector* 11 (1962): 448-59.   [g.a.]

Given to GB-Ob.

1178 _____

Krummel, Donald W. "A Musical Bibliomaniac." *MT* 115, no. 1574 (April 1974): 301-02.   [g.a.]

1179 **Harington, Henry, Dr. (of Bath)**; 1727-1816

LEIGH & SOTHEBY, AUCTIONEER, LONDON

A Catalogue of the Musical Collection (Printed and in Manuscript) *of the Late . . . Together with Some Very Curious Manuscripts and Missals . . . Sold by Auction . . July 2, 1816.* 9 p. 157 lots. Music, lots 1-69.   [US-R; film at CRL]

H was author of "Drink to me only."

Harksen, G   C   R.   *See* **Konig, David**

1180   **Harley, Edward, 2nd Earl of Oxford,** 1689-1741
Cooke, Matthew. "Catalogue of the Collection of Cathedral Music Made by Dr. Thomas Tudway, for Edward, Lord Harley, now in the British Museum, Harleian MSS. 7337-42. In the Autograph of Thomas Matthew."   [GB-Lbl]
Lady Oxford sold the Mss. to GB-Lbl in 1753 (7,639 volumes).

1181   **Harmsworth, Robert Leicester, Sir,** 1870-1937
SOTHEBY & CO., AUCTIONEER, LONDON
Catalogue of the Unrivalled Collection of English Prayer Books and of Psalters, Forming Part of the Renowned Library of . . . Which Will Be Sold by . . . 28th of January, 1946. London, 1946. 36 p.   [US-BEm]

Harrer, Gottlob.   *See* **Gerlach, Carl Gotthelf**

1182   **Harris, Caleb Fiske,** 1818-81
LITERATURE
Damon, S. Foster. "The Harris Collection of Sheet Music." *Books at Brown* [University] (1951), 1-4.   [g.a.]

1183   **Harris, George W.**
Gilman, Sander L. "German Hymnals in the Harris Hymnal Collection: A Short-Title Checklist." *Cornell Library Journal* 10 (1970): 40-48.   [g.a.]

Harrison, Samuel, 1760-1812.   *See* **Malchair, John Baptist** (sale of 18 May 1814)

1184   **Hart, George** [1839-91?]
"Catalogue of Musical Literature Collected by Him, 1903."
Not examined. Ms. at GB-Lbl, Add. Ms. 54177.

1185   **Hartenstein, Franz**
LIST & FRANCKE, AUCTIONEER, LEIPZIG
Verzeichnis mehrerer Bücher- und Musikalien-Sammlungen . . . Aus der Bibliotheken . . . Musikdirektor Franz Hartenstein in Halle . . . Versteigerung . . . 22 November [and Following Day], *1897.* Leipzig, 1897. 113 p. 3996 lots. Music, lots 2179-507.   [US-NYp]
Folter, no. 123.
→ *See also* sale in 1898 under **Fischer**

1186   **Hartog, Jacques,** 1837-1917; **Hugo Suringar** [et al.]
R. W. P. DE VRIES, AUCTIONEER, AMSTERDAM
Catalogue d'une belle collection de livres sur la théologie, jurisprudence, economie, politique . . . [etc.] *provenant de feu . . . P. C. F. Frowein . . . Hartog, Leerar in de muziekgeschiedenis aan het Conservatorium te Amsterdam . . . Hugo Suringar, Uitgever te Leeuwarden . . . vente le 8 juillet et les jours suivants. . . .* Amsterdam: de Vries, 1918. 375 p. 5306 + lots. Theater and music, lots 3969-4155.   [NL-DHgm]

1187 Hartzler, J   D

Luper, Albert T. "A Partial Check List of Printed Collections of Church Music with American Imprints in the Private Library of. . . ." Iowa City: University of Iowa, 1961. 10 p.

[US-IO]

A collection of 2750 volumes of early American church and instructional music.

1188 _____

LITERATURE

Fouts, Gordon E. "Music Instruction in America to Around 1830 as Suggested by the Hartzler Collection of Early Protestant American Tune Books." Ph.D diss., University of Iowa, 1968. viii, 342 p.   [g.a. on film]

Collection is at US-GO.

Harvey, J.   *See* **Carnaby, J.**

1189 [Harvey, W   J   ]

SOTHEBY, WILKINSON & HODGE, AUCTIONEER, LONDON

Catalogue of Autograph Letters and Historical Documents . . . Musical Scores & Autographs . . . Sold . . . 19th of May, 1906. London, 1906. 39 p. 332 lots.   [Film at CRL]

Lots 135-36, many Mss. by Arne, Cooke et al.; lots 202-45, music Mss. of Harvey; lots 237-45, Mss. by Santini.

1190 Harwell, Richard Barksdale

Confederate Imprints, 1861-65 [microform] *Based on Confederate Imprints, a Check List, 1955* [and] *Richard B. Harwell, More Confederate Imprints, 1957.* New Haven, Connecticut: Research Publications, [1974]. 144 reels.   [g.a.]

Harwell's sheet music now at US-U.

1191 Hase, Henry

FLETCHER & WHEATLEY, AUCTIONEER, LONDON

A Catalogue of the Library of the Late Henry Hase . . . Also His Valuable Collection of Sacred and Other Music, Printed and in Manuscript, Chiefly in Score, Including [etc.] *Sold . . . Messrs. Fletcher & Wheatley . . . 191 Piccadilly . . . July 10th and 11th, 1840.* 21 p. 512 lots. Music, lots 370-505.   [GB-Lbl]

1192 [Haswell, P   ] et al.

SOTHEBY & CO., AUCTIONEER, LONDON

Catalogue of Valuable Printed Books, Fine Bindings, Autograph Letters and Historical Documents . . . Property of [the Earl of Cork, R. A. de C. Eastwood, J. E. Pullinger, G. R. B. Conway, P. Haswell] *Including . . . Holograph Music of Liszt and Beethoven . . . Sold . . . December 20th, 1954.* 39 p. 227 lots.   [Film at CRL]

Musicians' ALS and Mss., property of Haswell, lots 158-65; no. 160, Beethoven Sketch; no. 158, Liszt corrections.

1193 Hatchett, Charles, 1765?-1847
Puttick & Simpson, auctioneer, London   Cat. no. 64
Catalogue of a Portion of the Very Extensive, Rare and Valuable Library of the Late . . . of Battersea . . . Sacred Music, Masses, Motetts, Anthems, Organ and Piano Forte Music . . . Antiquarian and Ecclesiastical Music, Many Choice Works on the History and Theory of Music . . . Original Manuscripts . . . Sold April 12th, 1848. 15 p. 313 lots. Music, lots 1-308.
[GB-Lbl]

1194 [_____]
Messrs. Hodgson & Co., auctioneer, London
A Catalogue of the Birch Hall Library . . . to Which Are Added Miscellaneous Books . . . Also a Small Collection of 18th Century Music, Including an Interesting Volume of MS. Songs by Henry Purcell, and MSS. of Franco Uria and Giuseppe Schuster . . . July 9th, 1925, and Following Day. London, 1925. 48 p. 657 lots.   [GB-Lbl]

> "A collection of 18th century music, mostly with the autographs or stamp of Charles Hatchett," lots 623-57.

1195 Hatzfeld, Adolphe
Chantavoine, Jean. "A travers une collection d'autographes." *Le Ménestrel* 94 (1932): 346-47, 354-56, 362-64, 371-72, 379-80, 386-87.   [g.a.]

> An album of composers' ALS reprinted.

1196 Hauber, Johann Michael, 1778-1843
"Hauber Collec[tionis] Music[ae] Catalogus, Tom[us] I, Tom[us] II." 2 vols. 205, 243 lots.

> Ms. thematic catalog in Archiv für Theatinerkirche, München. Not examined; cited by Gmeinweiser (**1197**) in *KmJ* 60 (1976): 89.

1197 _____
Gmeinwieser, Siegfried. "Die Musikaliensammlung des Johann Michael Hauber, Stiftpropst von St. Kajetan in München." *KmJ* 60 (1976): 89-91.   [g.a.]

> A large portion went to D-Mds in 1821, another, smaller group to D-Rp in 1824.

1198 Hauff, Johann Christian, 1811-91
Joseph Baer & Co., firm, Frankfurt   Lager-Cat. no. 295
Geschichte des Theaters. Theoretische und praktische Musik . . . enthaltend die Bibliothek und Musikalien des verstorbenen Musikdirektors J. C. Hauff . . . Nebst einer Sammlung, Werke über das Theater, und einer kleinen Auswahl von Autographen von Musikers und Bühnenkünstlern. Frankfurt a.M., 1892. 80 p. 1399 lots. Autographs, lots 1363-99.   [NL-DHgm]

1199 Hauser, Franz, 1794-1870
C. G. Boerner, firm, Leipzig   Cat. no. 80
Katalog der Bibliothek Hauser, Karlsruhe. Werthvolle Musiksammlung; kostbare Stammbucher des XVI. und XVII. Jahrhunderts. . . . Leipzig: C. G. Boerner, [1905]. 156 p. 1082 lots. Music, lots 1-438.   [US-NYp, -Bp, GB-Lbl]

> **Folter**, no. 125. Now in D-DS.

1200 _____

LITERATURE
Fuchs, Aloys. [Notes on Hauser's collection.] *Cäcilia* 23 (1844): 51-52. [g.a.]

1201 _____

Lehmann, Karen. "Neues zur Vorgeschichte des Bach-Sammlung Franz Hausers." *BzB* 6 (1988): 65-81. [g.a.]
    Bach literature acquired in 1904 by D-Bds; other items are at D-DS.

1202 Hausmann, Valentin Bartholomäus, b. 1678
" . . . Verzeichniss seiner musikalischen Bücher und Schriften, welches, wegen der vielen Mss., mitgenommen zu werden veredient." In Johann Mattheson's *Grundlage einer Ehren-Pforte* . . . , 106-08. Berlin: Kommissionsverlag Leo Liepmannssohn, 1910. Reprint, Kassel: Bärenreiter, 1969. [Reprint g.a.]
    81 items.

Haverlin, Carl. *See under* **BMI/Haverlin**

1203 Hawes, John Mullinex
PUTTICK & SIMPSON, AUCTIONEER, LONDON   CAT. NO. 2811
Catalogue of the Collection of Music, Pictures and Engravings, of the Late . . . Comprising Operas and Oratorios . . . Instrumental Music . . . Church Music, Old Psalmodies . . . Early Violin Sonatas & Concertos . . . Works on Musical History and . . . Portraits . . . Sold . . . May the 25th, 1891. 13 p. 239 lots. [GB-Lbl]

1204 Hawes, William, 1785-1846; **A Distinguished Amateur**
MR. WATSON, AUCTIONEER, LONDON
A Catalogue of a Choice Collection of Vocal and Instrumental Music, Comprising a Portion of the Library of . . . and the Library and Instruments of a Distinguished Amateur . . . An Extremely Fine Collection of Italian Songs . . . Illuminated Missal of the Thirteenth Century. &c. . . . Sold June 18th, 1833, and [3] *Following Days.* London, 1833. 28 p. 514 lots.
                                                                    [US-NYp, compiler]
    Lots 221-27, autograph copies of Italian songs in the hands of Haydn and Boccherini.

1205 Hawkins, Enoch (of H. M. Chapel Royal, St. James)
S. LEIGH, SOTHEBY AND CO., AUCTIONEER, LONDON
Catalogue of [His] *. . . Musical Library, and Miscellaneous Books . . . Collection of Cathedral Music . . . Books of Prints . . . Will Be Sold . . . on Monday, the 14th of June, 1847, and Following Day.* [London, 1847.] 31 p. 650 lots. Music, lots 1-307 and *inter alia.* [US-NYp]
    King, p. 45.

1206 Hawkins, James, 1682-1739
Dickson, William Edward. *A Catalogue of Ancient Choral Services and Anthems, Preserved Among the Manuscript Scores and Part-Books in the Cathedral Church of Ely. . . .* Cambridge: University Press, 1861. 55 p. [g.a. on microfilm]

1207   **Hawkins, John Sidney,** 1758-1842 (inheritor of Sir John Hawkins's Collection) [1st sale]
Mr. Wheatley, auctioneer, London
Catalogue of a Large and Valuable Collection of Musical Instruments the Property of . . . (Son of the Celebrated Writer . . .) Also, an Exceedingly Curious Collection of Treatises on Music . . . Sold, the 26th Day of June, 1832. . . . London, 1832. 11 p. 204 lots.   [GB-Lbl (n & p)]

> **King** notes 154 lots of music. Madrigal collection bequeathed to GB-Lbl.

1208   _____ [2nd sale].   *See under* **Groombridge** (sale, 26-30 June 1832).

> A "3rd sale" by Mr. Fletcher, 8-17 May 1843, contains no music materials.

1209   _____ [4th sale]
Mr. Fletcher, auctioneer, London
Valuable Music and Musical Instruments. Catalogue of the Extensive and Valuable Collection of Music & Musical Instruments of the Late . . . , Comprising Early Treatises by Zarlino, Galilei, Salinas [et al.]. *Also the Engraved Plates to Sir John Hawkins 'History of Music,' and . . . Musical Instruments . . . Sold 29th May 1843, and Following Day.* London, 1843. 28 p. 668 lots. Music, lots 1-620.   [GB-Ob, compiler (Gauntlett's copy)]

> **King** says, incorrectly, that sale was by Evans.

1210   **Hawkins, Thomas**
Novello, Vincent. "Lists in the Hand of Novello, 1849, of Two Collections of Organ and Pianoforte Music, Then in the Possession of Thomas Hawkins, of 18 Bedford Place, Islington."
[Ms. at GB-Lbl, Add. Ms., ff. 41, 41b]

1211   **Haydn, Joseph,** 1732-1809
Elssler, Johann. "J. Haydn's. Verzeichniss musicalischer Werken theils eigner, theils fremder Comp[o]sition." [ca. 1804-05.] 72 p. F°
[Ms. at GB-Lbl, Add. Ms. 32070 (ff.40). Copies at US-R, -Wc, compiler]

> I. Gestochene Musicalien. II. Verzeichniss geschriebener Musicalien.
> III. Compositions=Bücher. IV. Haydn's Verzeichniss eigener Manuscripten.
> Reprinted in full in Landon *Chronicle*, 5:299-320.

1212   _____
["Haydn's Catalogue of his Libretto Collection."] "In allen 207 Büchel/davon sind 62 duplirt," at end. [between ca. 1799 and ca. 1804. Landon.]   [g.a.]

> Ms. in the Museum der Stadt Wien according to Landon *Chronicle*, 5; elsewhere cited as Vienna, Staats- und Landesbibliothek, Handschriften-sammlung Ia 121, 329. Reprinted in full with commentary in Landon *Chronicle,* 5:320-25.

1213   _____
Artaria & Co., publisher, Vienna
Verzeichnis von musikalischen Autographen, revidirten Abschriften und einigen seltenen gedruckten Originalausgaben, vornemlich der reichen Bestände aus dem Nachlasse Joseph Haydn's und Ludwig van Beethoven's, ferner der manuscripte von Mozart, Schubert, Rossini und anderen namentlich Wiener Tonsetzern im Besitze von August Artaria in Wien. . . . Wien: Im Selbstverlage, 1893. 26 p.   [compiler]

1214 _____

LITERATURE

Deutsch, Otto Erich. "Haydn als Sammler." *Österreichische Muzikzeitschrift* 14 (1959): 188-93.

[g.a.]

Describes various catalogs of Haydn's collection.

1215 Hayes, William, 1707-77; **Philip Hayes,** 1738-97

SMART'S MUSIC WAREHOUSE

A Catalogue of a Very Curious and Valuable Musical Library of Ancient and Modern Composers by the Most Eminent Masters . . . Collected Through a Series of Years with Infinite Care and Judgment, by the Late. . . . Lot No. 377, Is a Choice and Valuable Collection of Songs of Henry Lawes, Written by Himself. . . . This Capital Collection Is Deposited at Smart's Music Warehouse. London, 1798. 30 p. 544 lots.   [GB-Lbl]

1216 Haym, Nicolai Francesco, 1679-1730 (Handel's librettist)

C. COCK, AUCTIONEER, LONDON

Catalogue of the Large and Valuable Library of Books . . . Relating to Divinity, Philosophy, History and Philology . . . with a Large Collection of the Most Valuable Italian Poets . . . Sold . . . the 9th of March 1729-30 [at Cock's Auction-Room, Poland Street]. [N.p., n.d.]

[US-BE, GB-Lbl]

36 lots of music are indexed by **Coral**, p. 163, and discussed, pp. 55-57.

1217 Hazard, ?

LARNAUDIE, AUCTIONEER, PARIS

Notice . . . de la bibliothèque musicale de M. Hazard, dont la vente se fera le 30 octobre 1854. . . . Paris, [1854]. 8 p. 133 lots.   [US-NYgr]

1218 Hazen, Margaret Hindle

NATIONAL MUSEUM OF AMERICAN HISTORY, ARCHIVES CENTER

Register of the Hazen Collection of Band Photographs and Ephemera, ca. 1818-1931. . . . Washington, D.C.: Archives Center, 1990.   [g.a.]

Heard, Sir Isaac, 1730-1822. *See* **Attwood**

1219 [Heath,   ; et al.]

MR. EDWARD FOSTER, AUCTIONEER, LONDON

Greet Street, Soho Square. A Catalogue of the Household Furniture . . . Music & Musical Instruments . . . Sold . . . the 28th of May, 1831. . . . [London], 1831. 12 p. 259 + 14 lots.

[GB-Lva]

Lugt, no. 12681.

1220 Heath, John Benjamin

Nathan, Hans. "Autograph Letters of Musicians at Harvard [the Heath Collection]." *Notes* 5 (1948): 461-87. Facsimiles, pp. 471-78.   [g.a.]

1221 **Heather, William,** ca. 1563-1627
"A Catalogue of All the Books wch belong now to y^{e} Musick Schoole 1682."

> Ms. Mus. Sch. C.204*, reprinted in Margaret Crum, "Early Lists of the Oxford Music School Collection," *M&L* 48 (1967): 28-32. Collection bequeathed to GB-Ouf in 1627, deposited in 1885 in GB-Ob.

1222 _____
"A Catalogue of So Many Setts of Bookes as Were Given by Doctor Heather to the Universitie of Oxford, at the Tyme of His First-Founding the Practise of Musick There."

> Ms. Mus. Sch. C.103*, Oxford. Reprinted in Crum; see preceding citation.

1223 _____
Goodson, Richard (the Younger). "A Transcript of y^{e} Instrument[s] and Books Belonging to y^{e} Musick School - Intending to Compare y^{e} Cattalogue with y^{e} Books. . . . "

> 1690 Ms. at GB-Lbl, Add. Ms. 30493 and 33965. Goodson's transcripts of his father's lists which were reprinted by Wyn K. Ford, pp. 198-203 in *JAMS* 17 (1964).

1224 _____
Bergsagel, John. "The Date and Provenance of the Forrest-Heyther Collection." *M&L* 44 (1963): 240-48.

> On his death, William Forrest's collection went to Heather, who gave it to GB-O.

1225 **Heather, William Edward,** 1784-ca. 1835
Mr. W. P. Musgrave, auctioneer, london
Catalogue of Vocal and Instrumental Music, Including the Library of . . . Sold . . . the 20th of May, 1830, and [2] *Following Days . . .* London, 1830. 22 p. 325 lots. Music, lots 1-109, 149-76, 199-213, 233-325.   [US-NYp (Gauntlett's copy)]

1226 **Hefner, O[tto] T[itan] van**
G. Th. Bom en Zoon, auctioneer, amsterdam
[A sale including a collection of songbooks, 20-21 June 1944.] Amsterdam, 1944.   [NL-Avb]
> Not examined.

1227 **Hegar, Friedrich,** 1841-1927
Literature
Erismann, Hans. "Friedrich Hegars Korrespondenznachlass." *Neue Zürcher Zeitung* (May 1977): 123-24.   [g.a.]
> Approximately 280 composers' letters.

1228 **Heger, Robert,** 1886-1978, et al.
Hans Schneider, firm, Tutzing   Cat. no. 262
Musikdrücke - Musikbücher, darunter Bestände der Bibliothek Robert Heger, Heinrich Kaminski und Richard Kraus. Tutzing, 1982. 101 p. 1173 lots. Lots not differentiated. [g.a.]
> **Folter,** no. 127.

1229 Heimsoeth, Prof. Dr. (in Bonn)
J. M. Heberle, (H. Lempertz' Söhne), auctioneer, Cologne
Catalog der nachgelassenen musikalischen Bibliothek des Herrn . . . welche nebst einigen alten Drücken . . . sowie einem Nachträge von Musikalien . . . den 15. . . . 16. November 1878 . . . Köln, 1878. 30 p. 928 lots (many more items). [NL-Avb]

1230 Heine, Heinrich, 1797-1856
C. G. Boerner, firm, Leipzig
Musik-Manuskripte Heinrich Heines. Nachlass. Leipzig, [1908?]. Unpaged ([13] p.). 17 lots. [NL-DHgm]

> **Folter**, no. 2863, says 1908.

1231 Heineman, Dannie H., 1872-1962
Pierpont Morgan Library, New York
Books and Manuscripts from the Heinemann Collection [Catalog]. New York, 1963. [US-BUu]

> "Autograph manuscripts and letters of musicians," pp. 80-91.

1232 _____
Pierpont Morgan Library, New York
The Dannie and Hettie Heineman Collection. New York: The Library, 1978. 109 p., illus. [US-PHu]

1233 _____
Literature
Waters, Edward N. "The Music Collection of the Heinemann Foundation." *Notes* 7 (1949-50): 181-216.

> On deposit at US-Wc.

1234 Hellier, Samuel, 1737-84
Literature
Young, Percy M. "The Shaw-Hellier Collection." *Brio* 23 (1986): 65-69. [g.a.]

1235 _____
"The Shaw-Hellier Collection in the University of Birmingham." *Newsletter of the American Handel Society* 1 no. 3 (December 1986): 1-2. [g.a.]

1236 _____
"Samuel Hellier: A Collector with a Purpose." *Book Collector* 39 (1990): 350-61. illus. [g.a.]

1237 _____
"The Shaw-Hellier Collection." In *Handel Collections and Their History,* 158-70. Oxford: Clarendon Press, 1993. [g.a.]

> Estate bequeathed to Thomas Shaw.
>
> "Appendix: Handel items in the . . . collection," pp. 167-70.

1238   Helminger, Eon

Catalogue de la bibliothèque musicale, théorique et pratique de feu M. E. Helminger, dont la vente aura lieu à Nice . . . dans le courant de janvier 1898 pour tous renseignements s'adresser à M. Eon, bouquiniste . . . à Nice. . . . Nice, 1897. 71 p. No lot nos. Music, pp. 1-51, ca. 250 lots.

[NL-DHgm, B-Br]

Folter, no. 128.

1239   Helmore, Thomas, 1811-90

PLAINSONG AND MEDIEVAL MUSIC SOCIETY, BURNHAM

Catalogue of the Society's Library. . . . Burnham: Nashdom Abbey, 1928. 39 p., facs.

Includes the liturgical and musical books from Helmore's library, according to van Kuik's catalog no. 8, lot 80. Not examined.

1240   Hemett, Jacob

MR. CHRISTIE, AUCTIONEER, LONDON

A Catalogue of the Valuable and Extensive Library of Manuscript and Printed Music, Capital Cremona Violins . . . Sold . . . the 18th of June 1791. . . . London, 1791. 4 p. 87 lots. Music, lots 57-75 (many more items). [GB-Lc]

Lugt, no. 4758.

1241   Henkel, Heinrich, 1822-99

The collection was begun by Johann Michael Henkel, 1780-1851, passed to his son Georg Andreas Henkel, 1805-71, was then left to his younger brother, Heinrich. Much was bequeathed by his daughter to the Landesbibliothek Fulda in 1932. Other portions went to D-F (according to Wolf, no. **1246**). US-Wc purchased most of the instrumental music from Liepmannssohn in 1910, a collection he calls "The Henkel Collection," but I find no record of such a Leipmannssohn sale or auction around that time. Nevertheless, see Wolf's splendid article!

1242   _____

"Zur Geschichte der fürstbischöflichen Hofkapelle in Fulda im 18. Jahrhundert." *Fuldaer Geschichtsblätter* 35 (1959): 82-96.

Reprints a non-thematic inventory from 1788 of instruments and music owned by the Hofkapelle.

Not examined; cited from Wolf (**1246**).

1243   _____

LITERATURE

Theele, Joseph. "Die Sammlung Henkel in der Landesbibliothek Fulda." *Fuldaer Geschichtsblätter* 27 (1934): 89-93.

Not examined; cited from Plath article (**1245**).

1244   _____

Gottron, Adam. "'Capella Fuldensis' und die Fuldaer Dommusik im 19. Jahrhundert." *Musicae sacrae ministerium . . . Festgabe für Karl Gustav Fellerer . . . seines 60. Lebensjahre,* ed. Johann Overath, 139-45. Köln, 1962. [g.a.]

1245 _____

Plath, Wolfgang. "Mozartiana in Fulda and Frankfurt: New Material about Heinrich Henkel and His Estate." *Mozart Jahrbuch*, 1968-70 (1970): 333-86.   [g.a.]

    Albrecht puts under Henkel, Johann Michael.

1246 _____

Wolf, Eugene K. "Fulda, Frankfurt, and the Library of Congress: A Recent Discovery." *JAMS* 24 (1971): 286-91.   [g.a.]

    An excellent description of the complex destination and provenance of various parts of these collections.

1247 **[Henkel, (Michael,** 1780-1851?)]

PUTTICK & SIMPSON, AUCTIONEER, LONDON   CAT. NO. 457

Catalogue of a Large Collection of Music, Including Works on History and Theory, About 5000 Recently Published Pieces . . . Also Musical Instruments . . . Sold . . . August 5th, 1856. London, 1856. 13 p. 350 lots. Music, lots 1-280.   [GB-Lbl]

1248 **Henschel, Ernst**

King, A. Hyatt. "A Collection of Musical Programmes [formed by E. H.]." *British Museum Quarterly* 33 (1969): 91-92.   [g.a.]

1249 **Henschel, George,** 1850-1934

PUTTICK & SIMPSON, AUCTIONEER, LONDON   CAT. NO. 3837

Catalogue of Valuable Music Property, Including Pianofortes [etc.] *and the Greater Part of the Select Library of Music of . . . and a Few Etched Portraits . . . Sold May 31st, 1904.* London, 1904. 17 p. 330 lots. Music, lots 199-330.   [GB-Lbl]

    Henschel's lots 235-329.

1250 **Hentschel, Erich**

VENATOR KG, AUCTIONEER, COLOGNE

Auktion 45. Theater - Tanz - Musik [im Bild]. *Sammlung Erich Hentschel, 24. Juni 1977.* Köln: Venator Kg, 1977. 57 p. + 17 plates. 3686 lots. Music, *inter alia.*   [US-NYgr]

1251 **Herbeck, Johann, Ritter von,** 1831-77, et al.

CHRISTIAN M. NEBEHAY, FIRM, VIENNA   LIST 51

. . . Music - Theatre - Fête-books, from the Estate of. . . . Vienna, [1951?]. 50 p. 305 lots. Music, lots 2-124.   [US-NYgr]

    Folter, no. 130.

1252 **Herbert, Edward Robert Henry, 5th Earl of Powis;** et al.

SOTHEBY & CO., AUCTIONEER, LONDON

Catalogue of a Valuable Collection of Printed Books, Music, Autograph Letters and Historical Documents, Comprising . . . the Autograph Manuscript of Schubert's 'Morgenlied' and 'Abendlied'; Music of Benjamin Britten, Kodaly [et al.]*; A Collection of Music and Letters of Béla Bártok. Letters, and a Shopping List of Beethoven, and Letters of Berlioz, Brahms* [et al.] *. . . Sold . . . 15th*[-16th] *May, 1967.* London, 1967. 138 p. 483 lots (many more items).

[Film at CRL]

    Herbert's lots 283-308; A Lady, 385-414 (Bártok items); Bernard van Dieren, 433-38 (Heseltine scores); lot 434 (120 letters & card from H. to Delius); Mrs. Mudnay, 470-83 (excellent!).

1253 **Herbert, G** ; et al.
PUTTICK & SIMPSON, AUCTIONEER, LONDON   CAT. NO. 4154
Catalogue of Valuable [Instruments] . . . *the Property of the Late F. G. Allwood . . . the Large Library of the Late G. Herbert . . . Sold . . . October 29, 1907.* London, 1907. 19 p. 383 lots. Music, lots 1-177, Herbert's, 244-98.   [GB-Lbl]

1254 **Herbst, Johannes**
Gombosi, Marilyn, ed. *Catalogue of the . . . Collection.* Chapel Hill: University of North Carolina Press, 1970. 255 p. 1040 lots.   [g.a.]

> **Folter**, no. 131.
>
> The music in the collection "over 1000 anthems in 473 numbered manuscripts," was issued on microfiche by University Music Editions, New York. 2 vols. 11,676 p.
>
> See below. The collection is now at US-WS.

1255 _____

> *LITERATURE*
>
> "Herbst Collection on Microfiche." *Music: The AGO & RCCO Magazine* 10 (November 1976).

1256 **Hermann, Theodore** (conductor, Haymarket Theatre)
MESSRS. THOMASON & CO., LONDON

> Notice of a sale, 21 September 1881, of "a large quantity of copyright music, property of the late . . . band parts, operatic, and other musical scores," appeared in *Music Trades Review* 5 (November 1881).

1257 **Heron-Allen, Edward,** 1861-1943
De fidiculis bibliographia: Being an Attempt Towards a Bibliography of the Violin and All Other Instruments Played with a Bow in Ancient and Modern Times. London: Griffith, Farran & Co., 1890-94. 2 vols., paged continuously. 60 copies printed.   [g.a.]

> Collection acquired by GB-Lcm, some items by GB-Ouf (see below).

1258 _____

Libri desiderati: An Appendix to "Fidiculis bibliographica." New York: printed for the Postulant, 1888. 8, iv p.   [US-CA, -PRu]

_____. *First Supplement.* London, 1889. 4 p.   [US-CA]

_____. *Second Supplement. Periodical Publications.* London, 1889. 4 p.   [US-CA]

_____. *Third Supplement. Periodical Publications and Reference Books.* London, 1890. 8 p.

_____. *Fourth Supplement. Instruction Books.* London, 1891. 4 p.

> Collection now at GB-Lcm.

For 5th and 6th *Supplements,* see **1261**.

1259 _____

Libri desiderati: Prolegomena to "De Fidiculis bibliographia." 3rd ed. London: printed for the author by Mitchell & Hughes, 1890.　　　　　　　　　　　[US-Wc, -BP, NYp]

> Revised up to 1890 from the original edition (1888), 1st and 2nd *Supplements* (1889), 2nd edition (1890) and 3rd *Supplement* (1890). 2nd edition and 3rd *Supplement* (his *Fidiculis opuscule, Opusculum III*).

1260 _____

The Violin. Duplicate Books for Sale or Exchange from the Collection of . . . Prolegomena to "De fidiculis bibliographia." London, 1892.

> Not located; cited from **Bobillier** and **Scheurleer** 1 (1923): 15.

1261 _____

Libri desiderati: Postscriptum to "Fidiculis bibliographia." His *De fidiculis opuscula. Opusculum V.* London: printed for the author by Mitchell & Hughes, 1893. 14 p.

> Revised up to 1893 from the original (1888), the 3rd *Supplement* (1890), 4th *Supplement* (1891), 5th and 6th *Supplements* (London, 1892).

1262 _____

> **King**, p. 86, also notes a typescript catalog, dated 1900, of some 530 volumes, which the collector gave to the Music School at Oxford.

1263　Hertel, Erwin
J. B. Muns, firm, Berkeley, Cal.
Music Books. Berkeley, 1984. 140 lots.　　　　　　　　　　　　　[US-BUu]
> "Violin books mainly from the collection of . . . ," lots 66-90.

1264　Hertzberg, Harry
San Antonio, Public Library
A Bibliography of 19th Century Clown Songsters of the Harry Hertzberg Circus Collection of the . . . Library. San Antonio: Carleton Print Co., [preface dated 1962]. [4] p.　　[US-Wc]

1265　Hertzmann, Erich, 1782-1963
University of California, Berkeley, Music Library
Partial Table of Contents for a Collection of Beethoven Autograph Manuscripts on Microfilm and a List of Manuscripts. [Berkeley], 1965. 6 leaves.　　　　[US-BEu, -NYcu]
> "The Erich Hertzmann Collection."

1266　Hervey, Arthur, 1855-1922
John Walker, firm, London　　　Cat. no. 5
A Catalogue of Books and Pamphlets . . . Music in Score and Musical Criticism from the Library of. . . . London, [1923]. 36 p. 1031 lots. Music, lots 530-813.　　　[US-NYp, -Wc]
> **Folter**, no. 132.

1267   Herwart Family

> The collection belonged to Hans Heinrich Herwart. It was sold by Johann Heinrich Herwart (1520-83) to the Duke Wilhelm V of Bavaria in 1586. The Ms. catalog (first citation) was prepared in 1858 after Herwart's death by Wolfgang Prommer, secretary to the Duke. According to Taricani's 1993 article, below (p. 1363n) the catalog is a compilation of "numerous indices" to items in the Herwart collection, surviving portions of which exist in D-Mbs Mss. Cbc 120a-f, Cbc 115 (printed vocal music), and Clm 271.

1268   _____

> Ms. in Bayerische Staatsbibliothek, Munich, Cod. Bav. catalog no. 115.

1269   _____

Martinez-Göllner, Marie Louise. "Die Augsburger Bibliothek Herwart und ihre Lautentabulaturen: Ein Musikbestand der Bayerische Staatsbibliothek aus dem 16. Jahrhundert." *Fontes* 16 (1969): 29-48.   [g.a.]

> A catalog of instrumental music. For vocal music in the catalog, see no. **1270**.

1270   _____

Slim, H. Colin. "The Music Library of the Augsburg Patrician Hans Heinrich Herwart (1520-83)." *Annales musicologiques* 7 (1977): 68-109.   [g.a.]

> Mainly vocal music.

1271   _____

Ness, Arthur. "The Herwart Lute Manuscripts at the Bavarian State Library, Munich: A Bibliographical Study. . . ." 2 vols. Ph.D. diss., New York University, 1984.   [g.a.]

1272   _____

Literature

Taricani, JoAnn. "The Music Manuscripts of the Herwart Library: The Use of Paleographical Evidence to Define and Reunite a Renaissance Collection." Abstract in American Musicological Society - Society for Music Theory, *Abstracts of Papers Read at the 46th Annual Meeting . . . Denver, Colorado, 6-9 November 1980*, 13-14.

1273   _____

Taricani, JoAnn. "A Renaissance Bibliophile as Musical Patron: The Evidence of the Herwart Sketchbooks." *Notes* 49 (1993): 1357-89.   [g.a.]

Herz von Hertenreid, Carl.   *See under* **Geibel, Carl** (sale of 3-6 May 1911)

1274   Herzog, George
Literature
Graf, Marilyn. "The Papers of George Herzog." *Resound* 5, no. 1 (January 1986): 5-6.   [g.a.]

1275 **Hesse-Darmstadt (Landgraviate), Grafen und Erzherzog,** 1567-1918

Kaiser, Fritz. "Zur Geschichte der Darmstädter Musiksammlung." In *Durch der Jahrhunderte Strom. Beitrag zur Geschichte der Hessischen Landes und Hochschulbibliothek Darmstadt,* 108-40. Frankfurt A.M.: Klostermann, 1967.   [g.a.]

Hetsch, Ludwig Friedrich (in Mannheim).   *See under* **Baumgart, E. F.** (1873 sale)

1276 **Heuss, Alfred Valentin,** 1877-1934; **M. Seydel; Bernhard Friedrich Richter**

KARL MAX POPPE, FIRM, LEIPZIG   CAT. NO. 50

Zum jubiläum Bach-Händel-Schütz. Musik - Theater. Enthaltend die Musik-bibliotheken der Herren Dtr. . . . und Prof. M. Seydel, Leipzig. Sowie eine wertvollen Sammlung von Werken von und über J. S. Bach und die Thomaskantoren von S. Calvius bis K. Straube aus dem Besitz des Herrn Prof. Bernhard Friedrich Richter, Leipzig. Leipzig: K. M. Poppe, 1935. 132 p. 3619 lots.
[compiler]

Folter, no. 134.

1277 **Hevingham-Root, Laurie**

LITERATURE

"National Library Acquires Important Operatic Collection [1551 recordings from 1898 to 1912 and more than 200 Scores]." *Continuo: Newsletter of the IAML, Australia and New Zealand Branch* 7 (1977): 26.   [g.a.]

1278 **Heyer, Wilhelm,** 1849-1913

Wit, Paul de. *Katalog des Musikhistorischen Museums von Paul de Wit, Leipzig . . . mit zahlreichen Abbildungen nach photographischen Originalaufnahmen. . . .* Leipzig: P. de Wit, 1903. 207 p.   [g.a.]

In 1905 the collection passed to Heyer in Cologne. Included was a large collection of musicians' portraits. See **Albrecht** for detailed description.

1279 _____

Kinsky, Georg. *Musikhistorisches Museum von . . . in Cöln.* Leipzig: Breitkopf & Härtel, 1910-16. 4 vols. (vol. 3 never published). Vol. 4, Musik-Autographen, ed. Frau Wilhelm Heyer (1916). xxxi, 870, 2, 32 p.   [US-Wc, -AA, -CLwr, -CHus, -BUu]

See excellent long review by A. Einstein in *ZfMW* 2 (1919/20): 246-48.

1280 _____

K. E. HENRICI & LEO LIEPMANNSSOHN, AUCTIONEERS, BERLIN

Versteigerung von Musiker-Autographen aus dem Nachlasse des . . . 6. [-] 7. Dezember 1926. Beschreibendes Verzeichnis von Dr. Georg Kinsky. Berlin, 1926. 120 p., 6 plates. 613 lots.
[US-Wc; compiler]

1281 _____

K. E. HENRICI & LEO LIEPMANNSSOHN, AUCTIONEERS, BERLIN

[Zweiter Teil.] *Versteigerung von Musikbüchern, praktischer Musik und Musiker-Autographen des 16. bis 18. Jahrhunderts, aus dem Nachlass . . . 9. [-10] Mai 1927.* Berlin, 1927. 114 p., 18 plates. 577 lots.   [compiler]

1282 _____

K. E. Henrici & Leo Liepmannssohn, auctioneers, Berlin
[Dritter Teil.] *Versteigerung von Musiker-Autographen aus dem Nachlass des . . . den 29.*
September 1927 . . . Beschreibendes Verzeichnis von Dr. Georg Kinsky. Berlin, 1927. 74 p.,
9 plates. 442 lots.   [compiler]

1283 _____

K. E. Henrici & Leo Liepmannssohn, auctioneers, Berlin
[Vierter und letzter Teil.] *Versteigerung von Musiker-Autographen aus dem Nachlass des . . .*
den 23. Februar 1928 . . . Beschreibendes Verzeichnis von Dr. Georg Kinsky. Berlin, 1928.
67 p. 405 lots.   [compiler]

1284 _____

K. E. Henrici & Leo Liepmannssohn, auctioneers, Berlin
Verzeichnis von Musikerbildnissen sowie Darstellungen mit Musikinstrumenten aus dem
Nachlass . . . Versteigerung 12. [-13] September 1927. Berlin, 1927. 58 p. 729 lots. [US-NYp]

1285 _____

Karl Ernst Henrici, auctioneer, Berlin   Verst. 132
Autographen. Musik und Kunst . . . Aus einem Nachlass und anderem Besitz [343 Nrn. z. T.
auserlesene Stücke noch aus der Heyerschen Sammlung] *. . . 27. und 28. April 1928.* Berlin,
1928.

Not examined; noted in *ZfMW* 10 (1927/28): 512.

1286   Heyer, Wilhelm, 1849-1913; Edward Speyer

Unger, Max. *Eine Schweizer Beethovensammlung* [Mss]. *Katalog.* Schriften der Corona, 24.
Zürich: Verlag der Corona, [1939]. 235 p.   [US-Wc]

1287 _____

Literature

Kinsky, Georg. "Die Autographensammlung des Heyer-Museums in Köln." *Rheinische Musik*
und Theaterzeitung 14 (19-?): 43.

Not examined.

1288 _____

Kinsky, Georg. [A discussion of the sale of Mss. from the Heyer Museum by the firm K. E.
Henrici, 6-7 December 1926.] In *ZfMW* 9 (1926/27): 314-16.   [g.a.]

[Another discussion of the sale, 9-10 May 1927, with citations, prices, and names of buyers for
many items], ibid.: 656-57.

[Yet another about the 29 September 1927 sale of Mss., with buyers' names and prices], ibid. 11
(1927/28): 126-27.

1289 _____

Closson, Ernest. "Le Musée Heyer de Cologne cédé à Leipzig." *Revue musicale* 8 (July 1927):
64-66.   [g.a.]

1290 _____

Kahn, Johann. "Die Versteigerung des Musikhistorischen Museums Heyer-Köln." *Allgemeine Musikzeitung* 54 (1927): 559.

[g.a.]

1291   **Heyman, August; Alexander Fürst Dietrichstein**
GILHOFER & RANSCHBURG, AUCTIONEER, VIENNA   AUK. CAT. NO. 61
Öesterreich und die Nachfolgestaaten. Sammlung Dr August Heymann, Wien, Theater und Musik . . . Versteigerung 27 Februar-März 1934. Wien, 1934. 75 p. 827 lots. 16 tables.

[US-NYp, -Wc, -NYgr]

Heyther, William, 1563-1627. *See here under* **Heather, William**

Hickson, Thomas. *See* **Husk, William Henry**

1292   **Hientzsch, Johann Gottfried,** 1787-1856
MÜLLER, AUCTIONEER, BERLIN
Verzeichniss der vom verstorbenen Direktor Hientzsch nachgelassenen musikalischen Bibliothek . . . welche am 2. Februar 1887 und folgenden Tagen . . . versteigert werden. Berlin: Müller, 1857.

[US-Wc]

     Folter, no. 135.

Hiles, John, 1810-82. *See* **Steed, A. O.**

1293   **Hill, Arthur Frederick,** 1860-1940
SOTHEBY & CO.
Catalogue of the Well-Known Collection of Musical Books, Autograph Letters and Manuscripts, Formed by . . . Sold . . . 16th of June 1947, and Following Day. London, 1947. 46 p. 330 lots. 17 plates.

[US-Wc]

     Lots 241-323, autographs; lots 235-50, visiting cards. Hill: 75. **Albrecht** notes another sale in 1972-73, but I cannot verify that. Some items were acquired by GB-Lbl. A few choice items from this 1947 sale appeared in a Sotheby's sale in London, 10 May 1984, according to Arthur Searle in his "Salerooms," *Early Music* 12 (1984): 529.

1294   **Hill, Thomas** [prob. 1760-1840]
MESSRS. EVANS, AUCTIONEER, LONDON
Catalogue of the Valuable Library, Prints, Autographs and Manuscripts of the Late . . . Including a Letter of Mozart's of Extraordinary Interest Relative to the Composition of His Requiem, Dated 1791 . . . Sold . . . March 10, and Six Following Days, 1841. [London], 1841. 80 p. 1654 lots. Music items, *inter alia.* Mozart letter, lot 1610.

[US-NYgr]

1295   **Hiller, Ferdinand von,** 1811-85
J. M. HEBERLE (H. LEMPERTZ' SÖHNE), AUCTIONEER, COLOGNE
Katalog der Autographen, Bildnisse, Musik-Compositionen etc., nachgelassen von dem . . . verstorbenen Herrn . . . am 28. bis 30 September 1887 . . . versteigert werden. Köln, 1887. 64 p. 1297 lots. Music, lots 898-1067, 1258-97.

[D-KNu]

     Folter, no. 136.

1296 Hiller, Johann Adam, 1728-1804
BUREAU DE MUSIQUE DE HOFFMEISTER ET KÜHNEL, LEIPZIG
Erste Fortsetzung des Catalogs geschriebener, meist seltener Musikalien auch theoretischer Werke welche im Bureau de Musique . . . zu haben sind. NB: Grösstenteils aus J. A. Hiller's Nachlass. Leipzig: Fr. Schödel, [1905 or 1906]. 50 p.   [US-Wc]
    Folter, no. 137, says ca. 1300 entries.

1297 Hinckley, Henry; A Gentleman Returning to the Continent
W. P. MUSGRAVE, AUCTIONEER, LONDON
A Catalogue of an Extensive and Valuable Library of Music, Late the Property of . . . with the Collection of a Gentleman . . . Comprising Together the Most Esteemed Instrumental & Piano-forte Compositions . . . Operas . . . Treatises [Also Musical Instruments] . . . Sold . . . November 20th, 1822. [London, 1822.] 14 p. 164 lots. Music, lots 1-53, 68-164.   [compiler]
    King, p. 27.

1298 Hindemith, Paul, 1895-1963
Briner, Andres. "Paul Hindemiths Privatbibliothek (Musikalien)." *Schweizer Jahrbuch für Musikwissenschaft,* n.F., 13/14 (1993/94): 275-330.
    A very curious numbering system provides only 127 numbers for several
    hundred titles.

1299 [Hingston, John]
PUTTICK & SIMPSON, AUCTIONEER, LONDON   CAT. NO. 202
Catalogue of a Valuable Musical Library, Including the Works of Ancient and Modern Writers . . . Instrumental Music, etc.; Also Musical Instruments . . . Sold April 9th, 1851. [London], 1851. 8 p. 196 lots. Music, lots 1-138.   [GB-Lbl]

1300 [Hingston, John; William Ayrton; Thomas Kennedy; G. F. Jarman]
PUTTICK & SIMPSON, AUCTIONEER, LONDON   CAT. NO. 584
Catalogue of an Interesting Collection of Miscellaneous Music, Operas, Oratorios, Instrumental Works . . . and Numerous Very Important Music Instruments . . . Sold . . . June 23, 1859. [London], 1859. 14 p. 304 lots. Music, lots 1-160.   [GB-Lbl]

1301 [Hingston, John]; Well-Known Collector; Thomas Attwood Walmisley
PUTTICK & SIMPSON, AUCTIONEER, LONDON   CAT. NO. 812
Catalogue of the Library of the Late Walmisley, and the Library of Musical History, Theory, etc., of a Well-Known Collector [i.e., Hingston] *. . . Sold . . . May 18th and Following Day. . . .* London, 1864. 584 lots.   [GB-Lbl]

1302 Hipkins, Alfred James, 1826-1903
SOTHEBY & CO., AUCTIONEER, LONDON
Catalogue of Valuable Books and Manuscripts . . . [etc]. A Portion of the Musical Library of . . . Sold . . . 4th Day of April, and Two Following Days. . . . [London], 1898. 68 p. 860 lots. Hipkins, lots 575-632.   [Film at CRL]

1303 _____

PUTTICK & SIMPSON, AUCTIONEER, LONDON   CAT. NO. 3918
Catalogue of Valuable Books Composing the Library of the Late . . . [and] *a Portion of the Library of the Late Mackenzie Walcott . . . Books on Music and Musicians . . . Sold April 17th, and Following Day.* [London], 1905. 37 p. 538 lots. Music, *inter alia.*   [GB-Lbl]

1304   Hirsch, Paul, 1881-1951

Many of the following catalogs are set out in Sigrun Folter's bibliography (nos. are given) with considerable useful detail about the contents of each. See also lengthy paragraph in **Albrecht** who says the Hirsch collection contained "almost the entire library of the British scholar James E. Matthew." The Hirsch library was acquired by GB-Lbm in 1946.

1305 _____

Katalog einer Mozart-Bibliothek. Zu W. A. Mozarts 150. Geburtstag 27. Januar 1906. Frankfurt A.M.: Druck von Wüsten & Schönfeld, 1906. 5, 75 p. ca. 480 items.
                                                                             [US-NH, -Wc]

Folter, no. 138.

1306 _____

FRANKFURT AM MAIN, KUNSTGEWERBEMUSEUM
Ausstellung: Schmuck und Illustration von Musikwerken in ihrer Entwicklung vom Mittelalter bis in die neueste Zeit. 23. Dezember 1908 bis 24. Januar 1909. [Frankfurt am Main?, 1908?] 46 p. 279 items.   [US-Cn]

The greater part of the exhibition consisted of materials from the Hirsch collection.

1307 _____

LEIPZIG, MUSIK-FACHAUSSTELLUNG, 1909
Zweite Musik-Fachausstellung in Krystallpalast zu Leipzig, 3, bis 15. Juni 1909. Katalog der Sonderausstellung aus der Musik-Bibliothek Paul Hirsch. Frankfurt a.M., [1909]. "Sonderausstellung," [32] p. 40 lots.   [GB-Lbl]

Folter, no. 139.

1308 _____

. . . Eine kleine Bücherschau . . . Veranstaltet im Hause Paul Hirsch, Oktober 1920. Führer durch die Ausstellung. . . . [Frankfurt a.M.: privately printed, 1920.] 42 p. 214 items. Music items, nos. 1-52.   [US-MSu]

Folter, no. 141.

1309 _____

. . . Goethe und die Musik. Auswahl von Schriften Goethes und seines Kreises sowie von Kompositionen seiner Werke, überreicht von der Musikbibliothek. . . . Frankfurt a.M.: [privately printed], 1920. 12 p. 57 lots.   [US-NH, GB-Lbl]

Folter, no. 140.

1310 _____

Katalog der Musikbibliothek Paul Hirsch, Frankfurt am Main, ed. Kathi Meyer und Paul Hirsch. Berlin: M. Breslauer, 1928-47.   [g.a.]

> 4 vols. (vol. 4 has imprint Cambridge University Press). Vol. 1: *Theoretische Drucke bis 1800* (299 p., 650, 50 nos.); vol. 2: *Opern-Partiturn* (335 p., 976 nos.); vol. 3: *Instrumental- und Vokalmusik bis etwa 1830* (362 p., 1193 nos., 31 pls.); vol. 4: *Erstausgaben, Chorweke, Gesamtausgaben, Nach-schlagwerke* [etc.] (xxiii, 695 p., 1706 nos., 36 pls.). Vol. 1[-4?] reprinted, Morsum/Sylt: Cicero Press, 1993.
> **Folter**, no. 142.

1311 _____

BRITISH MUSEUM, DEPT. OF PRINTED BOOKS, HIRSCH LIBRARY
Music in the Hirsch Library. London: British Museum, 1951. 438 p. Ca. 8700 nos.
                                                                                     [US-NYp, -BU]

> Preface by C. B. Oldman. **Folter**, no. 143.

1312 _____

SOTHEBY & CO., AUCTIONEER, LONDON
Catalogue of Valuable Printed Books, Music, Autograph Letters, Literary Manuscripts and Historical Documents . . . Property of Sydney A. Spencer . . . Music, the Property of the Late . . . [etc.] . . . May 24th, 1954 and Following Day. [London], 1954. 68 p. 353 lots. Music, lots 122-89, Paul Hirsch properties, lots 172-89.   [Film at CRL]

1313 _____

BRITISH MUSEUM, DEPT. OF PRINTED BOOKS
Books in the Hirsch Library. With Supplementary List of Music. (Accessions, Third Series, Part 291B.) London: Trustees of the British Museum, 1959. 542 p. Ca. 12,000 nos.   [g.a.]
> **Folter**, no. 145.

1314 _____

LITERATURE
Hirsch, Paul. "Musik-Bibliophile, aus dem Erfahrungen eines Musik-Sammlers." In *Von Büchern und Menschen: Festschrift Fedor von Zobelitz . . . ,* 247-54. Weimar: Gesellschaft der Bibliophile, 1927.   [US-CA, -CLp, -NYgr, compiler]

1315 _____

Meyer, Kathi. "Die Musikbibliothek Paul Hirsch in Frankfurt am Main." *Taschenbuch für Büchersammler* (1927 [1926]): 10-14.
> Not located.

1316 _____

Epstein, Peter. "Die Musikbibliothek Paul Hirsch in Frankfurt." *Zeitschrift für Bücherfreunde,* 20 (1928): 80-89.   [US-NYp]
> **Folter**, no. 147.

1317   _____

Lanckorónska, Maria Gräfen. "Die Bibliothek Paul und Olga Hirsch." *Philobiblon* 3, no. 10 (1930): 434-45.   [g.a.]

1318   _____

Peppercorn, Lisa M. "Una nova biblioteca musical na Inglaterra." *Revista brasiliera de musica* 6 (1939): 38-42.   [g.a.]

1319   _____

King, A. Hyatt. "The Hirsch Music Library." *MT* 87 (1946): 265-67.   [g.a.]

1320   _____

Muir, P. H. "The Hirsch Catalogue." *MR* 9 (1948): 102-07.   [g.a.]
    Folter, no. 147.

1321   _____

King, A. Hyatt. "The Hirsch Library, Retrospect and Conclusion." *Notes* 9 (1952): 381-87.   [g.a.]

1322   _____

Niderlechner, Max. "Der Sammler Paul Hirsch." *Imprimateur* 11 (1952/53): 134-38.   [g.a.]
    Folter, no. 147.

1323   _____

"Private Libraries XVI: A Working Library of Music—Mr. Paul Hirsch." *Times Literary Supplement,* 15 April 1939, p. 224.   [g.a.]

1324   _____

King, A. Hyatt. "Paul Hirsch and His Music Library." *British Library Journal* 7, no. 1 (1981): 1-11.   [g.a.]

1325   **Hirschberg, Leopold,** 1867-1929
Katalog der Büchersammlung . . . ; eine Ergänzung zu dessen Erinnerungen eines Bibliophilen. . . . Berlin: Wilmersdorf, O. Goldschmidt-Ganrielli, 1920. 246 p. Music items, *inter alia.*
                                                     [US-Wc, -Cu, -Cj]

        → *See also under* **Friedländer, Max** (1930 sale)

His, M.   *See* **Schlotter, V.**

1326   **Hobler, Paul** [perhaps **John Paul**, writer on music]
A Catalogue of Music, Bound and Unbound, Late the Property of . . . , Deceased. Which Will Be Exposed to Sale, at His House, No. 26, Berwick-Street, Soho, on Monday and Tuesday, May 18 and 19, 1875, from Ten Till Five o'Clock Each Day, and No Longer. [London]: J. Peck, Printer, 1795. 8 p. 113 lots.

        King, p. 93: one of the "lost" collectors revealed only by the list of names Warren wrote in his personal catalog. King records as "Stobler," not Hobler, and opines that this catalog is in the lost vol. 1 of Warren's collection, but as noted earlier, that volume is located at US-R (Vault/ML138/H815/no. 2).

1327   **Hoboken, Anthony van,** 1887-1983

Hoboken, Anthony van. "Erster Bericht des Meisterarchivs." *ZfMw* 11 (1928/29): 577-81.   [g.a.]

Ca. 6000 volumes with an emphasis on Haydn, supplemented by a large collection of photocopies. Given to A-Wn. See the following.

1328   _____

Haas, Robert. "Die Händelaufnahmen im Wiener Meisterarchiv." *Händel-Jahrbuch* 4 (1931): 117-26.

1329   _____

ÖSTERREICHISCHE NATIONALBIBLIOTHEK, VIENNA
Katalog des Archivs für Photogramme Musikalisches Meisterhandschriften, Widmung Anthony van Hoboken. Ed. Agnes Ziffer. Wien: G. Prachner, 1967.   [g.a.]

Vol. 1: *Muesion: Veröffentlichungen der Österreichischen National-bibliothek*, n.F., Reihe 3, Bd. 3.

1330   _____

Ziffer, Agnes. "Katalog des Archivs für Photogramme musikalischer Meisterhandschriften. In *Beiträge zur Musikdokumentation: Franz Grasberger zum 60. Geburtstag*, 505-20. Tutzing: Schneider, 1975.   [g.a.]

1331   _____

ÖSTERREICHISCHE NATIONALBIBLIOTHEK, VIENNA
Das Hoboken-Archiv der Musiksammlung der . . . ; eine Ausstellung zum 90. Geburtstag v. Anthony van Hoboken, 23. März bis 14. Mai 1977 [Gestaltung u. Red. Franz Grasberger; Katalogtexte, Rosemary Hilmar]. Wien: Österreichischen. Nationalbibliothek, 1977. 66 p.   [g.a.]

1332   _____

VIENNA, NATIONALBIBLIOTHEK, MUSIKSAMMLUNG
Katalog der Sammlung Anthony van Hoboken in der Musiksammlung der . . . Musikalische Erst- und Frühdrucke. Hrsg. vom Institut für österreichische Musikdokumentation unter Leitung von Günther Brosche. Tutzing: Schneider, 1982-83.   [g.a.]

Vol. 1: *Johann Sebastian Bach und seine Söhne*, rev. Thomas Leibnitz. (xviii, 180 p.) Vol. 2: *Ludwig van Beethoven, Werke mit Opuszahl*, rev. Karin Breitner und Leibnitz (viii, 238 p.) Vol. 3: *Ludwig van Beethoven, Werke ohne Opuszahl und Sammelausgaben*, rev. Thomas Leibnitz. Vol. 4: *Johannes Brahms/Frederic Chopin*, rev. Karin Breitner and Thomas Leibnitz. Vol. 5: *Christoph Willibald Gluck/Georg Friedrich Händel*, rev. Karin Breitner. Vol. 6: *Joseph Haydn, Symphonien* (Hob. I, Ia). Vols. 7 & 8. Hob II bis XI; XIV-XX/1. Vol. 9: *Joseph Haydn, Vokalmusik* (Hob. XX/2-XXXI), rev. Karin Breitner. Vol. 11: *Wolfgang Amadeus Mozart, Werke KV 6-581*, rev. Karin Breitner. Vol. 12: *Mozart.*

Acquired by A-Wn in 1974.

1333   _____

Leibnitz, Thomas. "Anthony van Hoboken und Joseph Haydn. Anlässlich des 95. Geburtstages des bedeutenden Haydn-Forschers." In *Festakt zum 250. Geburtstag Joseph Haydns*, ed. Günter Brosche, 15-21. Wien: Österreichischen Nationalbibliothek, 1982.   [g.a.]

Contains a list of Haydn prints from the Hoboken collection, now in A-Wn.
Albrecht notes.

1334 _____

Literature
VIENNA, NATIONALBIBLIOTHEK, MUSIKSAMMLUNG
Das Archiv für Photogramme musikalischer Meisterhandschriften in der Musiksammlung.
. . . Biblos-Schriften, 18. Wien, 1958. 39 p., illus.   [g.a.]

1335 _____

Hoboken, Anthony van. "Zur Enstehung meiner Sammlung musikalischer Erstund Frühdrucke."
In *Beiträge zur Musikdokumentation: Franz Grasberger zum 60. Geburtstag*, 101-06. Tutzing:
Schneider, 1975.   [g.a.]

1336 Hodges, Charles
PUTTICK & SIMPSON, AUCTIONEER, LONDON   CAT. NO. 97
Catalogue of a Valuable Collection of Autograph Letters Formed by the Late . . . [including 36
letters of musicians—Beethoven, Haydn, Mozart et al.] . . . *Sold 18th December and Three
Following Days.* . . . [London], 1848. 902 lots.   [GB-Lbl]

1337 Hodges, Edward, 1796-1867
PUTTICK & SIMPSON, AUCTIONEER, LONDON   CAT. NO. 825
*Catalogue of Music and Instruments, Including Sections from the Libraries of E. Hodges, Mrs.
Mary Ann Boag, the Late W. Hopwood, D. Cockburn* [et al.] . . . *Will Be Sold* . . . *July 4.* [London,
1864.] 33 p. 866 lots. Music, lots 1-696. Hodges's books and music, lots 697-840.
                         [US-NYp (Drexel), GB-Lbl]

1338 _____

Kaufman, Charles H. "The Hodges and Newland Collections in the Library of Congress."
Current Musicology 18 (1974): 78-79.   [g.a.]

1339 Hoffmann von Fallersleben, Heinrich August, 1798-1874
KARL ERNST HENRICI, AUCTIONEER, BERLIN   CAT. NO. 156
. . . *am 10. Aug. 1929* . . . *Handschriftliches, Bücher, Schriften, Gelegenheitsdrucke aus seinem
Nachlass.* Berlin, 1919. 4, 61 p. 17 nos. (more items). Music in nos. 170-72, 176-77.   [compiler]
        Folter, no. 154. Other sales of the collector's properties in 1843, 1846, 1852,
        1855, and 1880 cited by Folter contain very little of musical interest.

1340 [Hofmann,   Baron (Generalintendant)]
GILHOFER & RANSCHBURG, AUCTIONEER, VIENNA
*Katalog einer werthvollen Sammlung von Autographen und historische Documenten, zum
Theil aus dem Nachlasse eines hervorragenden Sammlers. Versteigerung* . . . *21.* [-23.] *Februar
1898.* . . . Wien, 1898. 72 p. 653 lots.   [US-NYgr]
        Music throughout, including excellent letters.

1341 Hoheneck Family
Gottron, Adam. "Die Musikbibliothek des Frh. Karl Anton von Hoheneck zu Mainz (d.1771)."
In *Zu 70. Geburtstag von Joseph Müller-Blattau . . . ,* 89-96. Saarbrücker Studien zur
Musikwissenschaft, 1. Kassel: Bärenreiter, 1966.   [g.a.]

1342   Hohenlohe-Bartenstein, Fürst zu
"Catallago delle opere, sinfonie, cantate, ariette, duetti, terzetti . . . ed altre musicaglie appartenenti all orchestra della Corte di Halbergstetten, nell' anno 1807."
Manuscript at D-HL? Copy at City University of New York.

1343   Hohenzollern, House of
Wernhammer, Georg. [Thematic catalog in manuscript, D-SI: Hausarchiv Hohenz. Sigmaringen 23, 4. Mikroaufnahme Nr. 50.] 177 p., including 136 blanks.
Compiled 1768. **Brook**, p. 1217.

1344   _____
Schindele, Johann Michael. "Catalogus über die Sämtliche Musicalische Werck, und derselben Authorn, nach Alphabetischer Ordnung: Welche von ihro Hochfürstl. Durchlaucht dem . . . Fürsten und Herrn, Herrn Carl Friedrich Erbprinzen zu Hohenzollern angeschafft worden seynd. 1766." (D SI: Hausarchiv Hohenz. Sigmaringen, 23, 3. Mikroaufnahme Nr. 52-58.) 189 p., including 92 blanks. Manuscript.
Brook, p. 1216: "An inventory of 570 works from a collection, now lost once located at Hohenzollern Castle in Sigmaringen."

1345   _____
Lehner, F. A. *Verzeichniss der Handschriften.* . . . Sigmaringen: Druck der P. Liehner'schen Buchdr., 1872. iv, 119 p.   [US-PHu]

1346   _____
Schüler, Annelise. "Zwei thematische Musikkataloge aus Sigmaringen. Ein Beitrag zur Geschichte der Musik am Hofe zu Sigmaringen im 18, Jahrhundert."
Unpublished *Examensarbeit*, Freiburg i Br., 1957. **Brook**, p. 1218.

1347   _____
LITERATURE
Schmid, Ernst Fritz. *Musik an den Schwäbischen Zollernhöfen der Renaissance.* Kassel: Bärenreiter, 1962. xxviii, 730 p.   [g.a.]

1348   Hohn, Maia Bang
LITERATURE
U.S. Library of Congress. Gertrude Clarke Whittall Foundation. *Paganiniana* [by Harold Spivacke]. Washington, D.C.: [Government Printing Office], 1945. 19 p.   [g.a.]
Offprint from the Library of Congress *Quarterly Journal of Current Acquisitions* 2 (October/December 1944): 49-67.

1349   Hol, Richard; L. J. Groot; Dr. Nieboer; J. Zelling
Van Huffel, A. J., Boekhandel, Utrecht. *Catalogus der Bibliotheken van wijlen de heeren L. J. Groot . . . [et al.] benevens der gedeeltetuke Bibliotheek van wijlen den heer Richard Hol, toonkunstenaar te Utrecht . . . Verkooping 12-17 Maart 1906.* Utrecht, 1906. 89 p. 2255 + lots. Music, lots 2061-255.   [NL-DHgm]

1350   Holbrooke,   ; [et al.]
MESSRS. CHRISTIE AND MANSON, AUCTIONEER, LONDON
A Catalogue of a Genuine Collection of the Works of Hogarth . . . and an Assemblage of Printed Music, the Property of a Gentleman . . . Sold . . . March the 27th, 1832. London, 1832. 8 p. 107 lots.   [Film at CRL]

> H's music, lots 63-74 (many items); other music, lots 84-101.

1351   [Hole, Captain A   ]
PUTTICK & SIMPSON, AUCTIONEER, LONDON   CAT. NO. 453
Catalogue of the Interesting and Valuable Library of a Distinguished Collector . . . Theoretical and Historical Treatises . . . Stock . . . Also Instruments . . . Sold . . . June 25th, 1856. [London], 1856. 27 p. 772 lots. Music, lots 1-711.   [GB-Lbl]

Holland, Wilhelm Ludwig, [1822-91?].   *See* **Jähns, F. W.**

1352   [Hollander,   ]
PUTTICK & SIMPSON, AUCTIONEER, LONDON   CAT. NO. 655
A Large Collection of Miscellaneous Music, Scores of Operas, Oratorios . . . Also Musical Instruments . . . Sold . . . December 6, 1860. London, 1860. 30 p. 807 lots. Music, lots 1-672.
                                                                                                [GB-Lbl]

> Hollander's properties not identified.

Holleben Sammlung.   *See under* **Ulex** (sale of 27 May 1927)

1353   Hollenfeltz,
Borren, Charles van den. [A description of his collection now in the Brussels Conservatoire.] *Annuaire du Conservatoire* (1947).   [g.a.]

1354   Hollier, Laetitia, d. 1871
GRESHAM COLLEGE, LONDON, LIBRARY
Catalogue of Books, Pictures, Prints, etc., Presented by . . . to, and Also of Books and Music in the Library of Gresham College. London, 1872. 2 vols. in 1. Music in vol. 2.   [US-Wc]

Hollmann, Joseph.   *See under* **Tokugawa**

1355   Holloway, W. Williams
SOTHEBY, WILKINSON & HODGE, AUCTIONEER, LONDON
Catalogue of the Libraries of the Late W. Williams Holloway, Esq. [and others] . . . *Comprising Excessively Rare Collections of Madrigals and Other Musical Works . . . Sold . . . 13th of August, 1879, and Three Following Days.* [London, 1879.] 101 p. 1524 lots.   [Film at CRL]

> Holloway's, lots 172-208.

1356   Holmes, Augusta Mary Anne, 1847-1903
LITERATURE
DuPage, René Pichard. "Une Musicien versaillaise, Augusta Holmes." *Rev. de l'histoire de Versailles et de Seine-et-Oise* 20 (1920). 52 p.

> Separately published, Paris: Fischbacher, 1921.

1357   **Holmes, Edward,** 1797-1859

Hodgson & Co., auctioneer, London

A Catalogue of Books and Music, Comprising Books and Autograph Letters . . . Also the Important Music Collection Formed by Edward Holmes (Dec'd.) of the Firm of Walsh, Holmes & Co., Ltd., Including . . . a Collection of Music . . . Published by James Walsh . . . Books . . . Collections of Song Books . . . Interesting Manuscripts and Autograph Letters, etc. . . . Sold . . . March 23 [-24] 1961. London, 1961. 44 p. 585 lots (many more items). Holmes' lots 326-585. Mss. and ALS, 566-81.   [compiler (priced copy)]

1358   **Honywood, Michael**

Fenlon, Iain. "Michael Honywood's Music Books." In *Sundry Sorts of Music Books . . . Essays Presented to O. W. Neighbour,* 183-200. London: British Library, 1993.   [g.a.]

    Appendix: ". . . music books indentifiable as being from Michael Honywood's Collection," pp. 191-98 (54 nos.).

1359   _____

Literature

Lincoln Cathedral Library. *Catalogue of the Wren Library of Lincoln Cathedral: Books Printed Before 1801,* compiled by Clive Hunt. New York: Cambridge University Press, 1982. xiv, 599 p.   [g.a.]

    See Introduction.

1360   _____

Linell, N. "Michael Honywood and Lincoln Cathedral Library." *The Library,* ser. 6, vol. 6 (1983): 126-39.   [g.a.]

1361   **Hook, James,** 1746-1827

Mr. Fletcher, auctioneer, London

A Catalogue of a Choice Collection of Valuable Music, Manuscript and Printed; Consisting of the Manuscript Scores, Many . . . Unpublished, Together with . . . Printed Songs . . . Property of the Late Celebrated Melodist . . . Also . . . Musical Instruments . . . Sold . . . July 5th, 1842. [London], 1842. 9 p. 177 lots. Music, lots 1-127.   [GB-Ob; compiler (film)]

1362   _____

Puttick & Simpson, auctioneer, London

Ancient and Modern Music, Including Selections from the Library of . . . Full and Vocal Scores, Instrumental Music, Original MSS. of Scarce Works, Theoretical and Practical Treatises, Old Psalmodies . . . Sold . . . January 30, 1874. [London, 1874.] 21 p. 475 lots. Music, lots 1-424.   [GB-Lbl]

    King, pp. 57, 59-60, 84 calls this a "mixed" sale with Hook's properties not identified. **Albrecht**: some of the Mss. acquired by A. H. Mann (**1757**) are now at GB-Cu.

1363   **Hopkins, Dr. Edward John,** 1818-1901

Puttick & Simpson, auctioneer, London   Cat. no. 3536

Catalogue of the Music Library Formed by the Late . . . Sold . . . May 7th, 1901. [London], 1901. 16 p. 257 lots.   [GB-Lbl]

    → *See also under* **Appunn, A.**

1364 Hopkins, John Larkin, 1819-73; **Jozef Poniatowski,** 1816-73

PUTTICK & SIMPSON, AUCTIONEER, LONDON

Large and Varied Collection of Music, Including the Library of the Late Hopkins, and a Selection from the Library of Prince Poniatowski [lots 79-109]; *a Canon for Two Voices in the Autograph of Mendelssohn . . . Scarce and Valuable Treatises . . . Sold . . . October 30, 1873.* [London], 1873. 16 p. 437 lots. Music, lots 1-392.   [GB-Lbl]

Lot 241, 19 volumes of word books for the Concerts of Ancient Music, 1786-1846 (incomplete). Mendelssohn holograph, lot 277.

1365 Hopkinson, Cecil

NATIONAL LIBRARY, EDINBURGH

Hector Berlioz, 1803-69. Edinburgh: National Library, 1969. 22 p. (Catalog no. 10.)
[US-I, -Cu, -Cn, -BApi]

Some of the over 700 Berlioz items donated by C. H. to the library. See **King,** pp. 87-88. **Albrecht.**

A gift in 1969 consisted principally of Verdi materials.

1366 Hopkinson, Cecil; Guildhall School of Music and Drama

SOTHEBY, PARKE BERNET & CO., AUCTIONEER, LONDON

Catalogue of Printed and Manuscript Music, Autograph Letters of Musicians, and Books on Music, Dance and the Theatre . . . Sold . . . 12th December 1979. [London], 1979. 64 p. 256 lots.   [g.a.]

Lots 1-41, "a portion of the reference library of the late Cecil Hopkinson." Guildhall properties, lots 59-87.

1367 Hopkinson, Francis, 1737-91

Richard, C. "An Eighteenth-Century Music Collection." Thesis, University of Pennsylvania, 1968.

Not examined.

1368 Hopwood, William

PUTTICK & SIMPSON, AUCTIONEER, LONDON   CAT. NO. 824

Catalogue of [His] *Musical Library . . . Will Be Sold . . . July 2, 1864.* [London, 1864.] 13 p. 329 lots.   [GB-Lbl, US-NYp]

Second sale of Hopwood's properties with Hodges (**1337**), 4-5 July 1864.

Horne, Edmund Thomas Warren.   *See* **Warren-Horne, Edmund Thomas**

1369 Horsfall, James

JOHN WHITE, AUCTIONEER, LONDON

A Catalogue of an Extremely Valuable and Rare Collection of Manuscript Scores . . . Which Will Be Sold by Mr. White . . . on Tuesday, July 23rd, 1816. . . . [London, 1816.] 4 p.
[US-Wc]

1370 _____

JOHN WHITE, AUCTIONEER, LONDON

[Catalog of the Musical Library of James Horsfall, sold by auction by John White, 20-23 August 1817.] [London, 1817.] 12, 8 p. (2nd and 4th days' sales, only.)

[US-Wc (August 21 and 23 only)]

No Horsfall sales in King. Other days not located.

1371 Horsley, Charles Edward, 1822-76

PUTTICK & SIMPSON, AUCTIONEER, LONDON   CAT. NO. 716

Catalogue of the Valuable . . . Musical Library of . . . Also Musical Instruments . . . Sold . . . April 16, and the Following Day. [London, 1862.] 25 p. 601 lots. Music, lots 1-429.

[GB-Lbl, US-NYp]

→ *See also* **Callcott, W. H.**

1372 Houten, Theodore van

Silent Cinema Music in the Netherlands: The Eyl/Van Houten Collection of Film and Cinema Music in the Nederlands Filmmuseum. Buren: Frits Knuf, 1992. 328 p.   [g.a.]

1373 Howard, Dr. Samuel, 1710-82

MR. WHITE, AUCTIONEER, LONDON

Collection of Old Music. A Catalogue of the Greater Part of the Valuable Collection of Vocal and Instrumental Music, Late the Property of . . . , Deceased; Consisting of Services and Anthems by the Most Esteemed Authors of the Last Two Centuries . . . Among the Scores are Several Original Copies . . . Sold . . . at His Rooms, Storey's Gate, Great George Street, Westminster . . . June 25, 1799. . . . London, 1799. 11 p.   [US-R, GB-Lbl, compiler (film)]

King, p. 23. **Albrecht.**

1374 Howe, Earl

CHRISTIE, MANSON & WOODS, AUCTIONEER, LONDON

Autograph Letters of George Frideric Handel and Charles Jennens, the Property of the Late Earl Howe . . . Sold . . . July 4, 1973. [London], 1973. 28 p. 3 lots. [Film at CRL and compiler]

Lot 1, 9 surviving ALS to Jennens, Handel's librettist. Lot 2, testimonial from the Bishop of Elphin about Handel. Lot 3, 40 ALS, Jennens correspondence to Edward Holdsworth chiefly about Handel and their deteriorating relationship.

1375 _____

Hicks, Anthony. "An Auction of Handeliana." *MT* 114 (1973): 892-93.   [g.a.]

1376 Hueber, Peter, 1766-1843

Wagner, Renata. [Kurzverzeichnis of his Nachlass in the Bayerische Staatsbibliothek, in its *Kleine Ausstellungsführer* 20 (1973).]

Not located; cited in *Grasberger Festschrift.*

Hülls, Elias. *See under* **L'Arronge**

1377   **Hughes-Hughes, Augustus,** 1857-1942
PUTTICK & SIMPSON, AUCTIONEER, LONDON   CAT. NO. 6067
Catalogue of Books and Manuscripts, Including the Musical Library of . . . and from Various Sources . . . Sold . . . February 4th, 1925. . . . [London], 1925. 23 p. 309 lots.   [GB-Lbl]

> Hughes-Hughes's lots 46-69 (more items), but not a very impressive collection.

1378   **Hullah, John Pyke,** 1812-84
CHRISTIE, MANSON & WOODS, AUCTIONEER, LONDON
Catalogue of the . . . Library of Printed and Manuscript Matter . . . &c., of Mr. J. Hullah . . . Sold . . . December 20, 1860. London: W. Clowes & Sons, 1860. 32 p. 868 lots.

[GB-Lbl, US-NYp]

> **King,** p. 54.

1379   **[Hullah, John Pyke]; Michael Rophino Lacy,** 1795-1867; **Mr. Bretell**
PUTTICK & SIMPSON, AUCTIONEER, LONDON   CAT. NO. 1004
Catalogue of a Large and Valuable Collection of Antiquarian and Modern Music . . . Mr. Rophino's Dramatic and Musical Copyrights. The Late Mr. Bretell's Copyrights and Printed Stock . . . Sold . . . August 8th, 1867, and Two Following Days. London, 1867. 50 p. 1413 lots. Music, lots 1-1312.   [GB-Lbl]

> Not in **King**.

1380   [_____]
PUTTICK & SIMPSON, AUCTIONEER, LONDON   CAT. NO. 1100
Catalogue of a Large Collection of Ancient and Modern Music . . . Full Scores . . . Rare Antiquarian Music, Theoretical Treatises, etc. . . . Sold . . . January 13th, 1869, and Following Day. [London], 1869. 34 p. 997 lots. Music, lots 1-776.   [GB-Lbl]

> Not in **King**.
>
> → *See under* **Engel, Carl** (sale by Reeves)

1381   _____
PUTTICK & SIMPSON, AUCTIONEER, LONDON   CAT. NO. 2273
Catalogue of the Valuable Collection of Music and Library of Works on Musical Literature Formed by the Late Dr. . . . Operas & Oratorios in Full & Vocal Score, Theoretical and Practical Treatises, Works on the History of Music. Manuscripts . . . Also . . . Library of a Well-Known Amateur, Among Which Will Be Found an Extensive Collection of Ancient and Modern Musical Works . . . Sold . . . June 25th, 1884. [London], 1884. 23 p. 423 lots. Hullah's, 1-249a, 423.   [GB-Lbl]

> **King** says it is the second Hullah sale, but it must be at least the third.

1382   **Hulthem, Charles van,** 1764-1832
Bibliotheca Hulthemiana, ou, Catalogue méthodique de la riche collection de livres et des manuscrits délaissés. . . . Gand: Impr. de J. Poelman, 1836-37. 6 vols., illus.

> Catalog compiled by August Voisin. The collection purchased by the Belgian government as the basis for the national library (B-Br). Music, *inter alia,* vols. 1-2, 4.

1383   **Hummel, Johann Nepomuk,** 1778-1837; **Hermann Zopf**
LIST & FRANCKE, ANTIQUARIAN, LEIPZIG   CAT. NO. 164
Verzeichniss von theoretischen Werken über musik sowie seltenen älteren praktischen Musikstücken und neueren Musikalien nebst Schriften über das Theater aus den nachgelassenen Sammlungen der Herrn J. N. Hummel und Dr. Hermann Zepf in Leipzig. Leipzig, 1884. 61 p. 2271 lots.   [US-Wc]

> **Folter,** no. 156. Properties not differentiated. "Autographen von Beethoven und Fr. Liszt," lots 2265-71.

1384   **Humperdinck, Engelbert,** 1854-1921
LITERATURE
Sch[uchter], G[ilbert]. "Der Humperdinck-Nachlass in Frankfurt." *ZfM* 112 (1951): 189.   [g.a.]

1385   **Hunt, Arthur Billings,** 1890-1967
Roe, C. H. *The Hunt Library of Music.* New York: A. B. Hunt, [1946]. [33] p., illus.

[US-BP, -NYp]

> Collection now at US-NYcu.

1386   _____
Lord-Wood, J. "Musical Americana in the Hunt-Berol Collection at the Columbia University Libraries." Thesis, Columbia University, 1975.

> Not examined. A bequest to Columbia. Hunt also gave hymnology materials to Macalester College, St. Paul, Minnesota.

1387   **Huntington, Archer Milton,** 1870-1955
SOTHEBY & CO., AUCTIONEER, LONDON
Catalogue of the . . . Collection of American and European Autograph Letters, Manuscripts, Documents and Music, the Property of the American Academy of Arts and Letters . . . Sold . . . 12th November, 1963. London, 1963. 80 p. 180 lots.   [Film at CRL]

> Musicians' ALS throughout. Collection given to the Academy; Academy withdrew it to put on sale in 1963.

1388   **Huntington, Henry Edwards,** 1859-1927
HENRY E. HUNTINGTON LIBRARY AND ART GALLERY, SAN MARINO, CALIFORNIA
Early English Music, 1540-1640. Huntington Library Photostats, List no. 7. [San Marino, 1940.] 7 leaves.   [g.a.]

1389   _____
HENRY E. HUNTINGTON LIBRARY AND ART GALLERY, SAN MARINO, CALIFORNIA
Backus, Edythe N. *Catalogue of Music in the Huntington Library Printed Before 1801.* Huntington Library, List no. 6. San Marino, California, 1949. ix, 773 p.   [g.a.]

1390   _____
LITERATURE
Backus, Edythe N. "The Music Resources of the Huntington Library." *Notes,* 1st ser., 14 (1942): leaves 27-35.   [g.a.]

1391 **Husk, William Henry,** 1814-87; **Thomas Hickson;** et al.
PUTTICK & SIMPSON, AUCTIONEER, LONDON   CAT. NO. 2527
Catalogue of an Extensive Collection of Music, Including the Libraries of the Late . . . the Late . . . and [others]. *Scarce and Useful Theoretical & Practical Treatises . . . A Few MSS., etc. . . . Sold November the 7th, 1887.* [London], 1887. 20 p. 428 lots.   [GB-Lbl]

> Husk's, lots 1-105; Hickson's [et al.], 106-428.

1392 **Huth, Henry,** 1815-78
Huth, Henry. *The Huth Library: A Catalogue of the Printed Books, Manuscripts, Autograph Letters, and Engravings . . . with Collations* [etc.]. London: Ellis and White, 1880. 5 vols., paged continuously.   [US-NYp, -STu]

> → *See also under* **Euing, William** (the Bibliotheca Lindesiana catalog of 1890)

1393 _____
SOTHEBY, WILKINSON & HODGE, AUCTIONEER, LONDON
Catalogue of the Famous Library of Printed Books, Illuminated Manuscripts, Autograph Letters, and Engravings Collected by Henry Huth, and Since Maintained and Augmented by His Son Alfred H. Huth, Fosbury Manor, Wiltshire . . . To Be Sold . . . June 12-13, 1911. London, 1911. 43 p.   [US-NH, -NYp, -Eu, etc.]

1394 _____
BRITISH MUSEUM
Catalogue of the Fifty Manuscripts and Printed Books Bequeathed to the British Museum by Alfred H. Huth. London, 1912. xvi, 130 p.   [US-STu, -BUu, -Wc, etc.]

> ". . . the ballads have been catalogued by Mr. Arundell Esdaile. . . . "

1395 _____
SOTHEBY, WILKINSON & HODGE, AUCTIONEER, LONDON
Catalogue of the Famous Library . . . [as in no. **1393**] *. . . Sold by Auction by . . . 1911-20.* London: Dryden Press, [1911-20]. 9 vols., illus., paged continuously.   [US-Wc, -NH]

1396 _____
Catalogue of the Famous Library of. . . . London: Dryden Press, [1922]. 54 p.
    [US-Wc, -MSu]

> → *See also under* **Cummings, W. H.** (Quaritch catalog no. 365, 1919)

1397 **Huygens, Constantin, heer van Zuilichem,** 1596-1687
"Myn Bibliotheque, Instrumenten, Printhorst en diergelijcke, sullen mijne Drij Sonen onder haar deelen by Lotinge . . . Wat aengaet mijne menighvuldige Composition in allerhande Soorte van Musique. ende wat ich van die materie van anderen hebbe vergaedert. . . . " Mss. in Leiden, Universitets-Bibliotek, Cod. Hug. 46, n° I blz. 8.   [US-BE, -Cj]

> Reprinted in Adrianus David Schinkel's *Nodere bijzonderheden betrekkelijk Constantin Huygens en zijn familie . . .* ('s-Gravenhage: Schinkel, 1851).

1398 _____

TROYEL, ABRAHAM, AUCTIONEER, DEN HAAG

Catalogue variorum & insignium in omni Facultae & Lingua. Librorum, Bibliothecae . . . Ouorum auctio habebitur Hagae-Comitis in Officina Abrahami Troyel, Bibliopolae op de grotte Zael ban't Hof. Ad diem Lunae 15 Martius 1688. Hagae-Comitis . . . , 1688. 56, [2] p.

"Musyck-boeken [80 items]," last [2] pp. Reprint, see next item.

1399 _____

W. P. VAN STOCKUM & ZOON, FIRM, DEN HAAG

Catalogus der bibliothek van . . . , verkocht op de groote zaal van het hof te 's-Gravenhage, 1688. Opnieuw uitgegeven door W. P. van Stockum Jr, naar het eenig overgebleven exemplaar. 's-Gravenhage . . . , 1903. x, 65 p.   [US-Wc, -BE, -CHua, -NYp, -Cj, NL-DHgm]

Reprint of no. **1398**.

1400 _____

LITERATURE

Leendertz, P., Jr.. "En merkwaardige Catalogus." *Tijdschriften voor Nederl. Taal- en Letterkunde* 24 (1904): 197-207.

1401 _____

Vries, Henry. "De 'Muszyck-boecken' in het bezit van Const. Huygens." *Maatschappij der Nederlandsche letterkunde te Leiden, Handelingen en mededeelingen* (1899/1900), 36-44.

[US-Cu]

Also appeared in *Vereeniging voor Nederlandse Muziekgeschiedenis, Tijdschrift* 6 (1900): 253-60, which reprints some pages from the 1688 catalog (no. **1398**).

1402 Iddesleigh, Lady Rosalind Lucy, Countess of, d. 1950

SOTHEBY & CO., AUCTIONEER, LONDON

Catalogue of the Valuable Printed Books . . . [etc.] the Property of [Several Owners]. Letters or Holograph Music of Berlioz, Liszt, Mendelssohn, Richard Strauss and Elgar . . . the Property of the Rt. Honble. The Countess of Iddesleigh . . . Sold . . . November 22nd, 1954. . . . [London], 1954. 36 p. 257 lots. Music, lots 202-22.   [Film at CRL]

Musicians' ALS, lots 205-22.

1403 Idelsohn, Abraham Zebi, 1882-1938

Adler, Israel, and Judith Cohen. *A. Z. Idelsohn Archives at the Jewish National and University Library. Catalogue.* Yuval Monograph Ser., 4. Jerusalem: Magness Press, Hebrew University, 1976. 134 p.   [g.a.]

1404 Indy, Vincent d', 1851-1931

Catalogue des partitions et livres provenant de la bibliothèque . . . nombreuses . . . partitions d'orchestre ou de piano des maitres . . . dont beaucoup annotées par V. d'Indy ou à lui dedicacées . . . Autographes. Dont la vente, par suite de décès, aura lieu hôtel des Ventes à Paris . . . les 20 et 21 janvier 1933. . . . Paris, 1933. vi, 58 p. 372 lots.   [US-NYp, GB-Lbl]

Folter, no. 157. **Hirsch. Blogie 2**.

1405 —————

Tiersot, Julian. "La Bibliothèque musicale de Vincent d'Indy." *Bulletin du bibliophile et du bibliothécaire* 12 (1933): 247-55, 322-27.   [g.a.]

Islington Musical Society.   *See under* **Stanford, John Frederick** (sale, 22 June 1881)

1406   **Ives, Elam, Jr.,** 1802-64

LYMEN AND RAWDEN, NEW YORK

The Entire Professional Library of E. Ives, Jr., Embracing a Large and Valuable Collection . . . on the Science, Theory, and Practice of Music . . . Sold . . . 377 and 379 Broadway, Corner of White Street . . . March 12-13, 1852. New York, [1852]. 15 p. 543 lots. Music, *inter alia.*

[US-NYp]

1407   **Ivogün, Maria,** and **Michael Raucheisen**

HANS SCHNEIDER, firm, TUTZING   CAT. NO. 164

Das deutsche Lied, Erstausgaben und Frühdrucke, darunter die Sammlung Marie Ivogün und. . . . Tutzing: Schneider, [1971]. 152 p. 888 lots.   [g.a.]

Edited by Jürgen Fischer. **Folter**, no. 158.

1408   **Jackson, George Pullen,** 1874-1953

UNIVERSITY OF CALIFORNIA, LOS ANGELES, LIBRARY

Revitt, Paul J., comp. *The George Pullen Jackson Collection of Southern Hymnody. . . .* Los Angeles: University of California, Library, 1964. 126 p. 112 nos.   [g.a.]

Folter, no. 159. **Albrecht**: purchased by US-LAuc ca. 1955.

1409   **Jacobi, Erwin Ruben,** 1909-78

Bircher, Martin. "Von Boethius bis Hindemith: Eine Zürcher Sammlung von Erstausgaben zur Geschichte der Musiktheorie." *Librarium* 13 (1970): 134-61.   [g.a.]

Folter, no. 161. **Albrecht**.

1410 —————

[HUG & CO., ZÜRICH?]

Seltene Originalausgaben von Musica practica und Musica theoretica aus dem 13.-20 Jahrhundert, sowie einige Autographen und Manuskripte in der Bibliothek von . . . , 2. erg. Ausg. [Zürich], Juli 1970. 41, [2] leaves, typescript.   [US-Wc (photocopy)]

1411 —————

HUG & CO., FIRM, ZÜRICH

Musikbibliothek Erwin R. Jacobi. Seltene Ausgaben und Manuskripte. Katalog. Dritte, erg. und rev. Aufl. Zusammengestellt von Regula Puskás. Zürich: Verlag Hug & Co., 1973. 84 p. 514 lots (more items).   [US-Wc, -R]

Folter, no. 160: "acquired by Zentralbibliothek, Zürich in 1975."

1412 —————

HANS SCHNEIDER, FIRM, TUTZING   CAT. NO. 269

Musiklitertaur, darunter Bestände Dr. Erwin R. Jacobi. Tutzing, 1982. 70 p. 1025 lots. [g.a.]

Jacobi's not identified.

1413   **Jacobi, Samuel**

Krummacher, Freidhelm. "Zur Sammlung Jacobi der ehemaligen Fürstenschule Grimma." *Mf* 16 (1963): 324-47.   [g.a.]

    Now in D-Dlb.

Jacobs, Benjamin.   *See under* **Cooke, Matthew**

1414   **Jacobsthal, Gustav,** 1845-1912

AKADEMISCHER GESANGS-VEREIN, STRASSBURG

Die älteren Musikwerke der von . . . begründeten Bibliothek des "Akademischen Gesangs-vereins," Strassburg, von Friedrich Ludwig. Strassburg: Druck von J. H. E. Heitz, 1913. 14 p. No lotting.   [US-Wc]

    Albrecht: library is now at F-Sim.

1415   **Jacquard, Laure (Bedel)**

MAURICE DELESTRE, (C.-P.), PARIS

Vente aux enchères publiques . . . après décès de Mme veuve Jacquard, née Laura Bedel. Mobilier, bronzes d'art . . . Musique: Partitions pour piano, violon, violoncelle . . . 16 [-17] juin 1897. [Paris], 1897. 4 p. Music, pp. 1-3.   [F-Paa, -Pe]

1416   **Jähns, Friedrich Wilhelm,** 1809-88; **Wilhelm Ludwig Holland**

KARL ERNST HENRICI, AUCTIONEER, BERLIN   CAT. NO. 125

Autographen aus verschiedenem Besitz darunter Sammlung . . . Deutsche. Kaiser. Haus Brandenburg. Allgemeine Geschichte. Musik und Kunst. . . . Versteigerung . . . 24. [-25.] November 1927. . . . Berlin, 1927. 138 p. 917 lots.   [NL-Avb]

    "Musik, Theater und bildende Kunst," lots 418-545. **Folter**, no. 162.

1417   **Jähns, Friedrich Wilhelm; Wilhelm Ludwig Holland; Josef Liebeskind**

KARL ERNST HENRICI, AUCTIONEER, BERLIN   CAT. NO. 126

Musiker-Autographen in der Hauptsache aus den Sammlungen . . . Versteigerung . . . 15. Dezember 1927. . . . Berlin, 1927. 36 p. 206 lots, all music.   [NL-Avb; compiler]

    Folter, no. 163.

1418   **Jähns, Friedrich Wilhelm; Wilhelm Ludwig Holland; Josef Liebeskind;** et al.

KARL ERNST HENRICI, AUCTIONEER, BERLIN   NO. 135

Autographen. Literatur und Wissenschaft. Musik. Theater. Bildende Kunst. Aus den Sammlungen Elias, Hülle, L'Arronge, Fr. Wilhelm Jähns, u. a. . . . Versteigerung 25 July 1928. . . . Berlin, 1927. 66 p. 477 lots.   [NL-Avb]

    Folter, no. 2. Not in **Folter 2** who does cite Henrici's Versteigerung no. 136, 25 July 1928, but that sale did not include any music items.

1419   _____

"Die Sammlung Weberiana von . . . (erworben 1881)." In Deutsche Staatsbibliothek, *Carl Maria von Weber, Autographen Verzeichnis,* ed. Eveline Bartlitz, 12-56. Deutsche Staatsbibliothek, *Handschrifteninventare,* 9. Berlin, 1986.   [g.a.]

    "Verkaufsangebot," in Ms. was 205 pp. in length. **Albrecht**.

1420   Jaëll, Marie, 1846-1925
Lang, Madeleine. *Collection Marie Jaëll, pianiste, compositeur, auteur, 1846-1925.* Strasbourg: Bibliothèque Nationale et Universitaire, 1980. 86 p.   [g.a.]

> Collection is at F-Sn.

1421   Jahant, Charles
"1001 Nights at the Opera." *Quarterly Journal of the Library of Congress* (spring 1982), 102-15.

> A collection of signed photos of opera stars in US-Wc.

1422   Jahn, Otto, 1813-69

> First portion of Jahn's collections auctioned by Joseph Baer on 7 February 1870. Following days contained no music. The same is true for another sale by Baer 13 June 1870. **Folter,** nos. 165 and 166, but should not have been included.

1423   _____

JOSEPH BAER, AUCTIONEER, BONN
Otto Jahn's musikalische Bibliothek und Musikalien-Sammlung. Versteigerung in Bonn am 4. April 1870 und an den folgenden Tagen . . . unter Leitung Joseph Baer. . . . [Bonn: C. Georgi, 1870.] vi, 106 p. 2884 lots.   [US-Wc (priced), NL-DHgm]

> "Ludwig van Beethoven's Briefe [263] in authentischen Abschriften . . . ," lot 186. "Joseph Haydn's Briefe," lot 280: (63 Briefe und Billete in authentischer Abschrift). "Autographen . . . Bach . . . Beethoven . . . Haydn . . . [etc.]," lots 935-38. **Folter,** no. 166. **Hirsch. Wolffheim. Albrecht.** Collection went to D-Bds and D-BNu.

1424   _____

JOSEPH BAER AND M. LEMPERTZ, AUCTIONEER, BONN
Otto Jahn's Bibliothek. Deutsche Litteratur und Kunst (Goethe-Sammlung). Versteigerung in Bonn am 23. Mai 1870, und an den folgenden Tagen. . . . Bonn, 1870. 86 p. 2670 lots.
                                    [NL-DHgm]

> "Theater- und Operntexte," lots 1474-899. **Folter,** no. 167.

1425   _____

JOSEPH BAER ET AL., AUCTIONEER, BONN
Otto Jahn's Bibliothek. Fünfte Abtheilung. Bonn, 1870. 114 p. 3328 lots.   [NL-DHgm]

> "Musik, Tanz und Theaterwesen," lots 577-678. Sizeable portions of Jahn's collections were bought by Kyllmann of Bonn whose library was later sold by the firm Lengfeld in 1928, catalog no. 34 (**1591**).
>
> **Folter,** no. 169.

1426   Jahnn, Hans Henry, 1894-1959
Hans Henry Jahnn, Schriftsteller, Orgelbauer, 1894-1959: Eine Ausstellung. Katalog. Wiesbaden: Steiner, 1973.

> Not examined; rev. in *NZfM* 12 (1973): 827-28.

1427   Jameson,   , Dr. (of Cheltenham)
Mr. W. P. Musgrave, auctioneer, London
. . . A Catalogue of the Musical Library and Instruments of the Late . . . Will Be Sold . . . by Mr. W. P. Musgrave . . . June 7, 1825. [London], 1825. 14 p. 154 lots. Music, lots 1-104.

[GB-Lbl]

1428   [Janes, Ely]
Puttick & Simpson, auctioneer, London   Cat. no. 741
Catalogue of a Collection of Music, Including the Library of a Professor . . . Works of Eminent Composers . . . Works on Music History and Literature . . . Also Musical Instruments . . . Sold . . . November 20th, 1862, and Following Day. . . . [London], 1862. 23 p. 627 lots. Music, lots 1-542.

[GB-Lbl]

1429   Jansson, Daniels Anders, 1891-1958
Literature
Helenius, Eva. "Riksspelmannen Daniels Anders Janssons i Hillersboda (Svärdsjö)." *Svenskt Musikhistorisk Archiv, Bulletin* 10 (1973): 28-29.

[g.a.]

1430   Jarrett, W   E   (of Cheltenham); et al.
Puttick & Simpson, auctioneer, London   Cat. no. 2978
Catalogue of a Collection of Miscellaneous Music, the Property of . . . and Others. Also Valuable Musical Properties . . . Pianofortes . . . Violins . . . [etc.] *. . . Sold January 22nd* [-23rd], *1894.* [London], 1894. 21 p. 434 lots. Music, lots 1-150.

[GB-Lbl]

Jarrett's properties, lots 26-150.

1431   Jasen, David A.
Literature
Recorded Ragtime. Hamden, Conn.: Archon Books, 1973.

This and the following based on his collection of recordings.

1432   Jasen, David A.; Trebor Jay Tichenor
Rags and Ragtime: A Musical History. New York: Seabury Press, 1978.

1433   Jefferson, Thomas, 1743-1826
Sowerby, E. Millicent. *Catalogue of the Library of Thomas Jefferson.* 5 vols. Washington: Government Printing Office, 1955.

[g.a.]

1434 _____
Nolan, Carolyn Galbraith. "Thomas Jefferson: Gentleman Musician." M.A. thesis, University of Virginia, 1967.

[US-CHua]

Jefferson's catalog of 1783; transcription of the music section, pp. 112-19.

1435 _____
Cripe, Helen. *Thomas Jefferson and Music.* Charlottesville: University Press of Virginia, 1974. xi, 157 p.

[g.a.]

"The Monticello Family's music collection," pp. 77-87; "Jefferson's catalog of 1783 . . . ," pp. 97-104; "Collections of Jefferson family music," pp. 105-28.

1436 _____

LITERATURE

Peden, William. "Thomas Jefferson: Book Collector." Ph.D. diss., University of Virginia, 1942.

1437 _____

Kidd, Thomas. "Thomas Jefferson as Collector and Bibliographer of Music." Paper read at meeting of the Capital Chapter of the American Musicological Society, University of Virginia, 3 April 1993.

Jelinek, F X . *See* **Warren, Joseph** (8 April 1881)

1438 **Jellard, Paul D.**

J. & J. LUBRANO, FIRM, GREAT BARRINGTON, MASS.

The Paul D. Jellard Dance Library . . . from Australia. South Lee, Mass., 1986. 24 p. 575 lots.
[g.a.]

1439 **Jennens, Charles,** d. 1773

Smith, Ruth. "Making Use of Handel: Charles Jennens (1700-1772)." In *Atti del XIV congresso della Societa internazionale di musicologia . . .* , vol. 3, *Free Papers,* 221-31. Torino: EDT, 1990.
[US-BUu]

→ *See also* **Finch, Heneage, 6th Earl of Aylesford**

1440 _____

LITERATURE

Hicks, A. "An Auction of Handeliana." *MT* 104 (1973): 892-93.

> A brief but important notice about Christie's sale July 4 which included 9 ALS from Handel to Jennens and another 111 from and to Jennens and Edward Holdsworth (1684-1746). All had been the property of Earl Howe; his family inherited them from Jennen's niece. The Handel ALS were bought jointly by Breslauer and Otto Haas for £35,000. Gerald Coke purchased many other Handel items.

1441 **Jennings, James**

MR. WHEATLEY, AUCTIONEER, LONDON

Miscellaneous Collection of Books, Prints, and Music, Including the Library of the Late . . . Sold . . . February 6th, 1834, and Four Following Days. . . . London, 1834. 44 p. 1280 lots. Music, lots 1247-69 (many more items, e.g., lot 1269 encompasses 18 volumes of Handel's works). [GB-Lbl]

Jensch, Georg. *See* **Mittmann, Paul**

1442 **Jensen, Adolf,** 1837-79

Salomon, Gustav. *Katalog einer Sammlung guter Bücher und Musikalien aus verschiedenen Nachlässen, u. a. . . . Herrn Adolf Jensen . . . den 17. November 1879 und folgenden Tage . . . versteigert werden.* Dresden, 1879. 73 p. 2293 lots. Music, lots 114-411. [US-NYp]

Folter, no. 171.

1443   Jeppesen, Knud, 1892-1974

Christoffersen, Peter Woetmann. "Knud Jeppesen's Collection in the State and University Library (Aarhus, Denmark): A Preliminary Catalogue." *Dansk Aarbog for Musikforskning* 7 (1973-76): 21-49.   [g.a.]

1444   Jerkowitz, Joseph

"Thematisches Verzeichniss der den unterzeichneten angehörenden Musikalien Jos. Jerkowitz./ Schlasslowitz den 1. Juli 1832."

Manuscript thematic catalog of a collection at D-Mbs. Ca. 500 incipits. **Brook**, no. 632.

1445   Jessye, Eva A.

Blanding, M. C. "A Catalogue of the Eva A. Jessye Afro-American Music Collection." Thesis, University of Michigan, 1974.

Not examined.

1446   Joachim, Joseph, 1831-1907

J. A. Stargardt, firm, Berlin   Cat. no. 489
Autographen aus allen Gebieten, dabei eine Sammlung von Briefen bedeutender Musiker, Dichter, Gelehrter und Maler an Joseph Joachim. Eutin in Holstein, [1950]. 47 p. 251 lots. Joachim's, lots 184-251.

Not located; cited from **Folter**, no. 172.

1447   Joachim, Joseph; Philipp Spitta, 1841-94**; Hedwig von Holstein;** [**Max Kalbeck,** 1855-1921]

C. G. Boerner, auctioneer, Leipzig   Cat. no. 92
Katalog einer kostbaren Autographen-Sammlung aus Wiener Privatbesitz. Wertvolle Autographen und Manuskripte aus den Nachlass von . . . Versteigerung . . . 8.-[9.] Mai 1908. . . . Leipzig, 1908. 70 p. xvi plates. Music, lots 1-202.   [US-NYgr,-NH]

Notice of the sale by Richard Neustadt, "Interessante Dokumente aus einer Musiker-Autographen-Versteigerung" in *Neue Musikzeitung* 29 (1908).

Folter, no. 181, under **Kalbeck**, with brief description.

1448   Joachim II., Heklar (ruled 1535-71)

"1557. Inventar der handschriftlichen Musikalien." Ms. in Kgl. Hausarchiv, R.XIX.s.v.Wesalius. Reprinted in Curt Sach's *Musik und Oper*, [199]-201. Berlin: Bard, 1910.   [g.a.]

1449   João IV, King of Portugal, 1604-56

Craesbek, Paulo. *Primeira parte do index da livraria de musica do muyto alto, e poderoso Rey Dom Ioão o IV. Nosso Senhor.* Lisboa: per ordem de sua Mag. por Paulo Craesbek, 1649. [15], 521, [525] p. 951 lots.

Folter, no. 173, provides a good history, a description, and a list of cognate articles about this fine library destroyed in the Lisbon earthquake of 1755.

The catalog was republished by Vasconcellos in 1875 (see **1450**) and in facsimile in Ribeiro's study, 1967 (**1456**).

1450 _____

Vasconcellos, Joaquim Antonio da Fonseca e. *Ensaio critico sobre o Catalogo d'el-rey D. João IV, por Joaquim de Vasconcellos.* . . . Archeologia artistica [anno 1, vol. 1, fasc. 1]. Porto: Imprensa Portugueza, 1875. xv, 102 p.   [US-NYp, -NH, -Wc]

1451 _____

Primeria part do index da livraria de mvsica do mvyto alto, e poderoso rey Dom Ioão o IV. nosso senhor. Por ordem de Sua Mag., por Paulo Craesbeck. Anno 1649. [Lisboa, 1874.] 10, 525 p.   [US-NBu, -Wc]

    Folter, no. 173.

1452 _____

[Vasconcellos, Joaquim Antonio da Fonseca e.] *El-rey D. João o 4.ᵗᵒ Biographia—a politica do monarcha. Vm ervdito no paço de Uilla Uiçosa. Cartas & controuersias. Svas composições . . . O bibliophilo consvmmado.* Porto: [Typographia Universaal], 1900. 4, xxxi, 368 p.

    [US-Wc, -CA]

    Partial contents: Fontes bibliographicas.—Lista de nomes de artistas do Catalogo . . . de 1873.—La bibliothèque musicale de D. Jean IV de Portugal.—Eratas do Catalogo d'el-Rei na ed. de 1649. **Folter**, no. 173.

1453 _____

[Vasconcellos, Joaquim Antonio da Fonseca e.] Idem. Porto: [Typographia Universal], 1905. xxxi, 368 p.   [US-NYp, -Wc, -NH, -Cl, -Bp]

    Contents follow those in preceding citation with the addition of a critical study of the catalog by Ernest David reproduced (pp. 247-74) from *Revue et gazette musicale* 41 (1874).

1454 _____

Joaquim, Manuel. "A propósito dos livros de polifonia existentes no Paço Ducal de Vila Viçosa." *Anuario musical* 2 (1947): 69-77.   [g.a.]

1455 _____

Joaquim, Manuel. *Vinte livros de música polifónica do paço ducal de Vila Viçosa catalogados, descritos e anotados.* . . . Lisboa: Fundaçao da Casa de Bragança, 1953. xxxi, 300 p.

    [US-NYp, -BUu]

1456 _____

Sampaio Riberio, Mário de. *Livraria de música de el-rei D. João IV: estudo musical, histórico e bibliográfico.* 2 vols. Lisboa: Academia Portuguesa da História, 1967-.   [g.a.]

    Includes the 1649 catalog in facsimile, an analysis by D. Peres, "Nótulas de bibliografia musical," etc.

1457 _____

    LITERATURE

Sousa Viterbo, Francisco Marques de. "A livraria de musica de D. João IV: e o seu index." In *Academia das ciancias de Lisboa. Memorias. Classe de sciencias moraes, politicas e bellas-lettras*, new ser., t. 9, part 1, 55 (1902). 19 p.   [US-NYp]

1458 _____

Sampaio Ribeiro, Mário de. *Damião de Goes na livraria real da música*. Lisboa: [Imprenza Beleza], 1935. 3, 46 p., facs.

> "Para o meu trabalho estribo - me na Primeira parte do index da livraria do muyto altoe poderoso rey dom João o IV nosso senhor, no redição felta pelo sr. Joaquim de Vasconcellos," p. 14. Not examined; cited from **Folter**, no. 173.

1459 _____

Coelho, Ruy. "D. João IV, a sua' livraria de musica' e o colegio dos reis, de Vila Viçosa." *Revista dos centenarios* 1, no. 12 (1939): 21-35.

> Not examined; cited from **Folter**, no. 173.

1460 _____

Branco, Luiz de Freitas. *D. João IV, músico*. [Lisboa]: Fundaçao da Casa Bragança, 1956. xvi, 257 p.

Jochelsen, Waldemar.   *See* **Bogoras**

1461   Johann George, von Brandenburg (ruled 1571-98)
"1582. Musikalienventar." Ms. in Kg. Hausarchiv, Rep. XIX Pers. Spec. Reprinted by Curt Sachs in his *Musik und Oper*, 203-05. Berlin: Bard, 1910.   [g.a.]

1462   Johann IV, Fürst zu anhalt-Zerbst
Werner, Th. W. "Die im herzoglichen Hausarchiv zu Zerbst augefundenen Musikalien aus der zweite Hälfte des 16. Jahrhunderts." *ZfMW* 2 (1919/20): 681-724.   [g.a.]

1463   Johnson, Eldridge Reeves, 1867-1945
Molleck, Mary. *The Guide to Eldridge Reeves Johnson* [exhibition]. Dover: Delaware State Museum, 1973.
> Not located.

1464   Johnson, Harold E.
IRWIN LIBRARY, RARE BOOKS & SPECIAL COLLECTIONS
The Harold E. Johnson Jean Sibelius Collection: A Complete Catalogue. Compiled by Gisela Schlüter Terrell. Indianapolis: Irwin Library, Butler University, 1993. xii, 101 p.   [g.a.]

1465   Johnson, James Weldon
Brown, Rae Linda. *Music, Printed and Manuscript, in the James Weldon Johnson Memorial Collection of Negro Arts and Letters: An Annotated Catalog*. New York: Garland, 1982. xxiii, 322 p.   [g.a.]

1466   Johnson, William F
C. F. LIBBIE & CO., AUCTIONEER, BOSTON
Catalogue of an Important Collection . . . Together with the Dramatic and Musical Collection of . . . , an Old-Time Boston Actor, Comprising Old Plays, Music and Manuscripts . . . [Sold November 26th and 27th, 1918]. Boston, 1918. 132 p. 1661 lots. Music, lots 1042-58 (but many more items).   [US-NYp, -NYgr]

1467 Jolles, Henri, 1902-65
 Hans Schneider, firm, Tutzing Cat. no. 126
 Bibliothek Henri Jolles. . . . Tutzing: Hans Schneider, [1967]. 112 p. 1950 lots.   [g.a.]
  Folter, no. 174.

1468 Jonas, Fritz
 Leo Liepmannssohn, firm, Leipzig Verst.-Cat. no. 50
 Autographen. Literarische Autographen. Historische Autographen. Musiker, Schauspieler
 und bildende Künstler, Stammbücher, z. T. aus der Sammlung des Herrn Dr. . . . Versteigerung
 . . . 10. Juni [und 11. Juni] 1927. Leipzig, 1927. 68 p. 697 lots.   [US-Wc, GB--Lbl]
  "Musiker, Schauspieler und bildende Künstler," lots 509-684. **Folter 2,** no.
  384.

1469 Jonas, Oswald, 1897-1978
 Kunselman, Joan. *The Oswald Jonas Memorial Collection, Including Correspondence and*
 Working Documents of Heinrich Schenker and Oswald Jonas. Riverside: University Library,
 University of California, 1979. [13] p., illus.   [g.a.]

1470 _____
 University of California, Riverside, Library
 Lang, Robert, and Joan Kunselman. *Heinrich Schenker, Oswald Jonas, Moriz Violin: A Checklist*
 of Manuscripts and Other Papers in the Oswald Jonas Memorial Collection. University of
 California Publications. Catalogs and Bibliographies, 10. Berkeley: University of California Press,
 1994. xxvi, 227 p.   [g.a.]

1471 _____
 Literature
 Kunselman, Joan D. "University of California, Riverside: The Oswald Jonas Memorial Collection."
 Current Musicology 28 (1979): 7-8.   [g.a.]

1472 _____
 Federhofer, Hellmut. *Heinrich Schenker nach Tagebüchern und Briefen in der Oswald Jonas*
 Memorial Collection, University of California, Riverside. Studien zur Musikwissenschaft, 3.
 Hildesheim: G. Olms, 1985. ix, 380 p.   [g.a.]

1473 Jones, , Dr.
 William Lord, auctioneer, Shipston-on-Stour
 A Catalogue of Musical Instruments, Music, Electrical Apparatus and Machines . . . [etc.] . . .
 Sold by Auction . . . at the Museum in Shipston-on-Stour, on . . . the 2nd and 3rd Days of
 January 1828. . . . [Shipston-on-Stour: "White, Printer," 1828.]
  Cited from Quaritch catalog no. 1026. Not examined. Quaritch says "very
  scarce . . . printed music (151 lots)."

1474   Jones, Edward, Bard y hrenin, 1752-1824
Mr. Sotheby, auctioneer, London
A Catalogue of a Portion of the Curious Library of . . . Comprising an Extraordinary and Rare Collection of Old Poetry, Songs, Old Ballads, and Works Relative to Music . . . Sold . . . February 9, 1824, and Five Following Days. . . . [London], 1824. 50 p. 1832 lots. Jones's music, 1st & 2nd day, lots 1-588.   [US-R, film at CRL]
>   His general library was sold in 1823. **Albrecht**.

1475   _____

Mr. Sotheby, auctioneer, London
A Catalogue of the Interesting and Remaining Library of . . . Containing an Extremely Rare Collection of Music, and Works on Music . . . Musical Instruments &c. . . . Sold . . . February 7th, 1825. [London, 1825.] 34 p.   [Film at CRL]
>   **King**, pp. 35-36.

1476   Jones, G   N   ; [Thomas Oliphant?]
Puttick & Simpson, auctioneer, London   Cat. no. 516
Catalogue of a Large and Interesting Assemblage of Music and Instruments, Including the Collections of G. N. Jones . . . Also Musical Instruments . . . Sold . . . November 28, 1857. [London, 1857.] 16 p. 372 lots. Music, lots 1-300.   [GB-Lbl]
>   Unpublished Mss. of Charles Chaulieu, lots 293-300.

1477   Jones, T   (of Nottingham)
W. P. Musgrave, auctioneer, London
Musical Property. A Catalogue of [His] *Musical Library . . . Sold . . . February* [13-15] *1826. . . .* [London, 1826.] 31 p. 390 lots.   [US-NYp (with buyers' names), GB-Lbl]

1478   [Jorge, John]
Puttick & Simpson, auctioneer, London   Cat. no. 241
Catalogue of the Musical Library of a Professor, Deceased, Including Works in All Classes . . . Also Musical Instruments of Various Kinds . . . Sold . . . January 8th, 1852. [London], 1852. 11 p. 272 lots. Music, lots 1-145.   [GB-Lbl]

1479   Joseffy, Rafael, 1852-1915
Musical Library Owned by . . . (1853 [sic]*-1915). Piano Compositions, Orchestral Parts and Scores. Catalog No. 1.* [New York: Carl Joseffy, 1941.] 8, [1] p. 220 lots.   [US-Wc, -Bp]
>   **Folter**, no. 175, says published 1949! The collection went to US-U.

1480   _____

Musical Library Owned by . . . 1853 [sic]*-1915. Piano Compositions, Orchestral Parts and Scores, Chamber Music, Vocal Scores.* [*Catalogue.* New York: Rafael Joseffy Memorial, 1942.] 61, [3] p. ca. 1500 lots.   [US-Wc, -Bp, compiler]
>   **Folter**, no. 176.

1481   Joyce, Patrick Weston, 1827-1914
Literature
Eigeartaigh, Caitlin Ui. "Patrick Weston Joyce: The Collector as Editor." *Irish Folk Music* 2 (1974-75): 5-14.

1482   Juana, Princess of Austria, 1535-73
A Ms. inventory of her collection of music and musical instruments conserved at the Biblioteca de la Real Academica de la Historia (Ms. 9-24-4-5543) was reprinted by Perez Pastor in *Memorias de la Real Academica Espanola* 11 (1914): 315-80.

1483 _____
Roqueta, Jaime Moll. "La Princesa Juana de Austria y la música." *Anuario musical* 19 (1964): 119-22.   [g.a.]

1484 _____
LITERATURE
Roqueta, Jaime Moll. "Libros de música e instrumentos musicales de la Princessa Juana de Austria." *Anuario de la Real Academia de Historia* (Madrid) 20 (1965): 11-23.   [g.a.]

1485   Juell, Frederik, Baron
Reventlow, Sybille. *Musik på Fyn blandt kendere og liebhavere.* Kobenhavn: Gad, 1983. 396 p.   [US-Nyp]
   See especially pp. 35-41 and 77-101.

1486   Jullien, Adolphe, 1845-1932
GIRAUD-BADIN, AUCTIONEER, PARIS
Bibliothèque de M. . . . Éditions originales d'auteurs de l'époque romantique. . . . [La vente aura lieu les 6 et 8 mai 1933.] Paris, 1933. 62 p. 244 lots (more items).
                                                                              [GB-LBl (Hirsch no. 5792)]
   Folter, no. 177, but mistakenly, for there are few music items in this catalog.
   See **1487**.

1487 _____
COUTURIER, ANDRÉ (= C.P.), AND ROBERT LEGOUIX (= EXP.)
Catalogue des livres sur la musique et partitions provenant de la bibliothèque de . . . La plupart avec documents ajoutés et annotés . . . Nombreuses partitions avec intéressantes dédicaces autographes de: C. Cui - Debussy - Delibes - [etc.] vente 23 juin 1933. . . . Paris, 1933. 52 p. 217 lots.   [GB-LBl, US-NYp, -Wc, -CHua, compiler]
   Folter, no. 178.

1488   Kafka, Johann Nepomuk, 1819-86
GABRIEL, CHARAVAY, AUCTIONEER, PARIS
Catalogue d'une précieuse collection de musique manuscrits originaux et letters autographes, partitions, morceaux de musique . . . provenant du cabinet de M. Johann Kafka . . . vente . . . 14 mai, 1881. 24 p. 90 lots.   [US-Wc, -Bp, GB-Lbl (all priced)]
   Rich in Beethoven and Mozart items. **Folter**, no. 179. **Albrecht.**

1489   Kaiser, Georg Felix;   ? Wallerstein
OSWALD WEIGEL, AUCTIONEER, LEIPZIG   AUK.-CAT. N.F. NO. 81
Theoretische und praktische Musik. Theater. Bibliothek des verstorbenen . . . , sowie die Mozart-Sammlung des Herrn Redakteur Wallerstein. Versteigerung . . . 16. [-18] Dez. 1918. . . . Leipzig, 1918. 64 p. 877 lots. Properties not differentiated.   [NL-Avb]
   Folter, no 180.

1490 _____ [only]

Oswald Weigel, auctioneer, Leipzig   Auk.-Cat. N.F. no. 83
Weltliteratur. Musik. Buchschmuck . . . Bibliothek Dr. Georg Kaiser. Versteigerungstage 3.-6.
März 1919. Leipzig, 1919. 81 p. 1087 lots. Music, lots 639-737.   [NL-Avb]
        Not in **Folter**. Noted in *ZfMW* 1 (1918/19): 568.

1491 **Kalbeck, Max,** 1850-1921

C. G. Boerner, auctioneer, Leipzig   Auk. no. 92
Katalog einer kostbaren Autographen-sammlung aus Wiener Privatbesitz [Max Kalbeck],
werthvolle Autographen und Manuskripte aus den Nachlass von Josef Joachim, Philipp
Spitta, Hedwig von Holstein . . . Versteigerung . . . 8.-9., 1908. Leipzig, 1908. 70 p., 15 plates. 477
lots. Music, lots 1-202.

        Folter, no. 181.

        → *See* article by Neustadt here *under* **Joachim**

1492 _____

Christian M. Nebehay, firm, Vienna   Liste no. 18
Musikbibliothek Max Kalbeck. . . . Vienna, [n.d., 1949?] 33 p. 344 lots. Mimeographed.
                                                                              [US-NYgr]

        Folter, no. 182.

1493 **Kaldeck, G   (of Vienna)**

Catalogue of the Collection of First and Early Editions of Mozart's Compositions and Works
of Some Contemporary Composers, Vienna, October 1928. [Vienna, 1928.] 3 p., 38 leaves. 616
lots.   [US-Wc]

        420 lots are Mozart items. With price list: "prices to be understood in dollars."
        Not in **Folter**.

1494 **Kalergi, John**

Sotheby, auctioneer, London
Catalogue of the Valuable Library of the Late . . . A Valuable Collection of Theoretical,
Classical and Other Music, by the Best Composers . . . Sold . . .7th of August, 1863. [London,
1863.] 92 p. 1397 lots. Music, lots 447-590.   [Film at CRL]

1495 **Kallir, Rudolf F.**

Literature
. . . Autographensammler - lebenslänglich. Geleitwort Gottfried v. Einem. [Zürich: Atlantis
Musikbuch-Verlag, 1977.] 119 p. Many facsimiles.   [compiler]
        A discussion of music holographs in his library.

Kaminski, Heinrich.   *See* **Heger, Robert** (1982 sale)

1496 **Kamler, Heinz-Georg**

Ottner, Carmen. "Briefe und Kompositionen Franz Schmidts im Privatbesitz: Die
Autographensammlung Dr. Heinz-Georg Kamler." *Studien zur Musikwissenschaft* 38 (1987):
215-65.   [g.a.]

1497   **Kapp, Jack**

"Cartoons for the Record [recording industry]: The Jack Kapp Collection [in the Library of Congress]." *Quarterly Journal of the Library of Congress* 38 (summer 1981): 180-95.   [g.a.]

1498   **Karl von Neisse, Erzherzog von Hapsburg, Bischof von Breslau und Brixen,** d. 1624

"Inventarium oder verzaichnis aller posidifn, regaln, fliegeln oder clavizimbelen . . . sowoll aller und jeder bücher, gross und klein, geschriebener und gedruckter, Lateinisch und Wälschen concerten . . . Item von alten und neuen authoribus allerlai pücher von Motetten, messen . . . so alle von dem Antonio Cifra mit einem ordentlichen inventario eingeantwort, welches inventaria verlohren und jetzigem capellmaister Stephano Bernardo nichts eingeantwortet auch sich nichts darumb wil annembern."   [g.a.]

Ms., ca. 1625, reprinted in *Jahrbuch des kunsthistorischen Sammlungen des Kaiserhauses* 33 (1915): 126-27.

1499   **Karl von Steiermark, Erzherzog von Innerösterreich,** 1540-90; **Ferdinand II, Erzherzog,** 1578-1637

"Verzaichnus Irer Frl. Dur: etc. Instrumenten, Trometten vnnd Gesanng Püecher, auch was darzue gehörig, so ich durch Merten Cammerlander den vierten Juni im siebenundsiebenzigisten Jar, auch aines Thayls hernach, höchsternenter Irer Frl.: Drht: Öbristen Musico Siman Gatto einanworten vnd übergegen hab lassen."   [g.a.]

Ms. in Vienna, Haus-, Hof- und Staats-archiv. Hofakten des Ministeriums des Innern, I C 4, Kart. 7, ff. 20-21. Reprinted in Hellmut Federhofer's *Musikpflege und Musiker am Grazer Habsburgerhof der Erzherzöge Karl und Ferdinand von Innerösterreich (1564-1619)*, 281-82. Mainz: B. Schott's Söhne, [1967].

1500   —————

"Catalogvs / Librorvm / Bibliothecae Avlicae / Graecensis / ex mandato / Augustissimi Imperatoris / Leopoldi I. A.A. [etc.] Anno MDCLXXII."

Ms. in Graz, Steiermärkisches Landesarchiv, Handschrift I,10. Reprinted in Hellmut Federhofer's *Musikpflege und Musiker . . .* [see **1499**], pp. 289-95.

1501   —————

"Catalogus librorum Bibliothecae Avlicae Graecensis ex Mandato Augustissimi Imperatoris Leopoldi I. A.A. etc. in novvm ordinem redactorum et conscriptorum, Anno MDCLXXII."

Ms. in Graz, Steirmärkisches Landesarchiv, Handschrift I. Reprinted in Hellmut Federhofer's *Musikpflege und Musiker . . .* [see **1499**], pp. 289-95.

1502   —————

Literature

Federhofer, Hellmut. "Musik am Grazer Habsburgerhof der Erzherzöge Karl II und Ferdinand (1564-1619)." *ÖMZ* 25 (1970): 585-95.

1503   **Katzman, Henry M[anners,** b. 1912]

Freuh, Donald. "The Henry M. Katzman Collection: Gershwin Materials."   [US-Lu] Typescript, 1972.

Kearns, W   D   .   *See under* **Rookwood** (Sotheby sale, 20-21 November 1978)

1504   Keating, George T.
STANFORD UNIVERSITY, MEMORIAL LIBRARY OF MUSIC
Catalogue of the . . . Library . . . by Nathan van Patten. Stanford, Calif.: Stanford University Press, 1950. 310 p. 1226 nos.   [g.a.]
   Albrecht: based on Keating's collection.

1505   Keller, Max, 1770-1855
Münster, Robert. "Übersicht [of his collection]." *Mozart-Jahrbuch* (1971/72), 162-64.
   A list of 106 *Musikhandschriften und Musikdrucken* from Keller's collection, sold by Jakob Oberdorfer, Munich antiquarian, November 1859. Much of Keller's collection now at D-Mbn. Sale catalog not located.

1506   Keller, Otto, 1838-1927
Bührer, Karl Wilhelm. . . . *Das Brückenarchiv I: Allgemeine Gesichtspunkte; Das Keller'sche Musikarchiv.* Schriften über "Die Brücke," Nr. 3. Ansbach: F. Seybold, 1911. 15 p.
                                                                    [US-NYp, -I]

1507 _____
   "Mein Musikarchiv. Vorschläge zu einer allgemeinen Musikbibliographie." *Allgemeine Musikzeitung* 36, no. 14 (1909).
      Not located; cited from **Bobillier**, but citation may be faulty.

Kellner, Ernest August, 1792-1839.   *See under* **Cooper, George** (sale of 9 December 1844)

1508   Kelner, Ephraim
PETERSON, AUCTIONEER, ESSEX ST., LONDON
      [**King** cites from Hawkins: 908, a sale, 26 March 1763, but the catalog is apparently no longer extant.]

1509   [Kelso, Mrs.   ]
PUTTICK & SIMPSON, AUCTIONEER, LONDON   CAT. NO. 531
A Catalogue of a Large Collection of Valuable Miscellaneous Music, Including Cathedral and Sacred Music, Operas, Vocal and Instrumental Music, Works in Musical Literature . . . Engraved Plates . . . Also Instruments . . . Sold March 17, 1858. . . . [London], 1858. 16 p. 425 lots. Music, lots 1-357.

1510   Kent, James, 1700-76; **Vincent Novello,** 1781-1861
MR. WATSON, AUCTIONEER, LONDON
. . . Catalogue of a Valuable Collection of Vocal & Instrumental Music, Including the Library of the Late James Kent, and a Portion from the Library of Mr. V. Novello . . . Sold by Auction . . . at the Mart . . . 22nd of May, 1835. [London, 1835.] 11 p. 170 lots.   [compiler]
   King, pp. 47, 91, 94, and 148, but does not mention this catalog.

1511 Kern, Jerome David, 1895-1945
Anderson Galleries, auctioneer, New York   Sale nos. 2307 and 2311
The Library of Jerome Kern, New York City. To Be Sold . . . January 7-10. . . . 2 vols. New York:
Anderson Galleries, 1929. 1482 lots.   [US-Bp]

> **Folter,** no. 184. An earlier Anderson sale, 11 February 1927. (**Folter,** no. 183,
> contains no music items.)

1512 _____
Parke-Bernet Galleries, auctioneer, New York   Sale no. 2131
*The Later Library of . . . Important Literary Manuscripts and First Editions . . . Personal
Copies, Songs from His Musical Comedies; Orchestral Settings, Music Reference Books. . . .*
New York, 1962. 72 p. 288 lots.   [g.a.]

> **Folter,** no. 185.

1513 Kestner, Hermann & August
Werner, Th   W. "Die Musikhandschriften des Kestnerschen Nachlasses im Stadtarchiv zu
Hannover." *ZfMW* 1 (1918/19): [441]- 66.

> In this article Werner refers to another article with the same title in
> *Hannoverschen Geschichtsblättern*, with no vol. or date indicated.
> Collection at D-HVsa.

1514 _____
Fecher, Adolf. "Die Beethoven-Handschriften des Kestner-Museums in Hannover, I, II." *ÖMZ*
26 (1971): 366-68, 639-41.   [g.a.]

> Collection at D-HVkm.

1515 Kew, Alfred
Puttick & Simpson, auctioneer, London   Cat. no. 2518
*Catalogue of a Collection of Musical Instruments . . . Also the Library of Music, Chiefly for the
Violoncello Belonging to the Late Alfred Kew . . . Autograph MS. of Ludwig van Beethoven, etc.
. . . Sold August the 17th, 1887.* [London], 1887. 9 p. 207 lots. Music, lots 154-207.   [GB-Lbl]

> Kew's library, lots 157-207; Mss., 191-207.

1516 Keyaerts, R.
Paul van der Perre, auctioneer, Brussels
*Important bibliothèque. Musique et musicologie . . . Livres illustrés . . . vente March 22-24,
1962.* Brussels, 1962. 142 p. 1338 lots.

> Not examined; cited from *IBAK* (1962/63).

1517 Khylberg, Bengt, 1915-
Literature
Kjellberg, Erik. "'Lämma sina excerpter i ett sådant skick': Om Bengt Khylberg samling vid
SMA." *Svenskt musikhistorisk arkiv, Bulletin* 19 (1985): 14-18.   [g.a.]

1518 Kick, Jakob Friedrich, 1795-1882
"Katalog der ehemals Kick'schen Notensammlung." In August Bopp's *Das Musikleben in der
Freien Reichsstadt Biberach . . . ,* 100-79. Kassel: Bärenreiter, 1930.

> [US-NYp, -CHua, -Wc]

1519   Kidson, Frank, 1855-1926

Farmer, Henry George. "The Kidson Collection." *Consort* 7 (1950): 12-17.   [g.a.]

> Collection is now at GB-Gm. Some volumes were given to GB-LE in 1926.
> **King**, p. 73: "a collection of about 4000 items, including his vast index of
> airs in 57 volumes." **Albrecht.** Penney (no. 237) says 9000 items of early
> English music and folksongs.

1520   Kieber,

LIST & FRANCKE, AUCTIONEER

[A catalog noted by Rosenthal but not located.]

1521   Kiesewetter, Raphael Georg, 1773-1850

Catalog der Sammlung alter Musik des K. K. Hofrathes . . . edlen von Wiesenbrunn. . . . [Wien:]
Gedruckt bei den P. P. Mechitharisten, 1847. xxvii, 96 p. ca. 1500 nos.   [US-NH, -Wc]

> Most of the collection was left to A-Wn, but some ended up at D-Ds. This
> catalog is supplemented by the following. **Folter**, no. 186.

1522   _____

*Galerie der alten Contrapunctisten; eine Auswahl aus ihren Werken, nach der Zeitfolge
geordnet zu deutlicher Anschauung des fortschreitens der Kunst . . . Alles in verständlichen
Partituren aus dem Archiv alter Musik des k. k. Hofrathes . . . von ihm Eigens zusammengestellt.
Eine Zugabe zu seinem Haupt-catalog.* Wien: [Gedruckt bei den P. P. Mechitharisten], 1847. xvi,
28 p. ca. 220 nos.   [US-NYp, -Wc, -NH]

> **Folter**, no. 187.

1523   _____

LITERATURE

Fuchs, Aloys. "Die musikalische Bibliothek praktischer Werke im Besitze des k. k. Hofraths,
Herrn R. G. Kiesewetter von Wiesenbrunn." *Cäcilia* 23 (1844): 47-49.   [g.a.]

King, James. *See* **Bennett, Sir William** (sale of 15 October 1878)

Kingsley, George, 1811-84. *See under* **Moffat, Alfred**

1524   Kipke, Carl, 1850-1923; **Eugene Segnitz,** 1862-1927

RUDOLPH HÖNISCH, FIRM, LEIPZIG   ANTIQ. CAT. NO. 70

*Musik und Theater. Musikalische Seltenheiten. Aus den Bibliotheken der verstorbenen
Musikschriftsteller . . . , Leipzig und Professor Eugene Segnitz. . . .* Leipzig, 1928. 98 p. 2124
lots.   [NL-DHgm, compiler]

> **Folter**, no. 188. Also a notice in *ZfMW* 10 (1927/28): 448.

1525   Kippenberg, Anton and **Katharina**

Katalog der Sammlung Kippenberg. . . . [Zweite Ausg.] 3 vols. Leipzig: Insel-Verlag, 1928.
                [US-NH, -COL]

> **Albrecht**: collection included large number of musical settings of Goethe's works.
> Collection now at D-DÜK.

1526 _____

Katalog der Musikalien [des] *Goethe-Museum*[s] *Düsseldorf, Anton-und-Katherina-Kippenberg-Stiftung,* comp. Ingen Kähmer, ed. Jörn Göres. Düsseldorf: Goethe-Museum, 1987. 621 p. illus.

1527 _____

LITERATURE
Jahrbuch der Sammlung Kippenberg. Vols. 1-10. Leipzig: Insel-Verlag, 1921-35.   [g.a.]

_____. Neue Folge, Ibid., 1963.

1528   Kirby, Percival Robson; P. E. Previte
SOTHEBY & CO., AUCTIONEER LONDON
Catalogue of Music, Printed Books, Theatrical Posters, Musical Manuscripts, Continental Autograph Letters, and Historical Documents [Including] *Properties of the Late . . . Sold . . . 8th* [-9th] *May 1972.* London, 1972. 123 p. 584 lots.   [compiler; film at CRL]
   Kirby's, lots 1-13; Previte's (mainly Mendelssohn Mss.), lots 259-68.

1529   Kirby, Percival Robson; Mrs. Diana Napier Tauber
SOTHEBY, AUCTIONEER, LONDON
Catalogue of Music, Musical Manuscripts, and Autograph Letters, Comprising the Property of. . . . [London]: Sotheby, 1975. 45 p. 207 lots.   [US-Wc]
   Day of sale, 16 April 1975. **Folter**, no. 189.

1530   Kirkpatrick, Ralph, 1911-84
Strohm, Reinhard. "Scarlattiana at Yale." In *Händel e gli Scarlatti a Roma,* 113-52. Firenze: Olschki, 1987.
   With a list of works.

1531   Kitchiner, William, 1775-1827
LEIGH & S. SOTHEBY, AUCTIONEER, LONDON
Musical Library: A Catalogue of the Very Extraordinary Assemblage of Manuscript and Printed Music . . . the Complete Works of the Best Composers . . . Sold . . . February 6, 1809 and Four Following Days. . . . [London, 1809.] 39 p. 980 lots.   [US-R, compiler, film at CRL]
   King, pp. 25, 38.

1532 _____

MR. SOTHEBY, AUCTIONEER, LONDON
A Catalogue of the Unreserved Portion of the Musical and Miscellaneous Library of the Late . . . Containing Some Curious Tracts . . . Songs, Vocal Music, and Rare Facetiae . . . Sold . . . July 10th, 1827, and Two Following Days. [London, 1827.] 27 p. 882 lots. Music, lots 746-882.   [Film at CRL]

1533 _____

S. LEIGH SOTHEBY, AUCTIONEER, LONDON
Catalogue of the Very Curious and Choice Musical Library Formed by the Late . . . Sold . . . December 14th [1838]. [London, 1838.] 11 p. 195 lots.   [Film at CRL]

1534   [Kite, J   C]
SOTHEBY & CO., AUCTIONEER, LONDON
Catalogue of Valuable Printed Books, Music, Autograph Letters and Historical Documents,
Comprising . . . Music and Books on Music and Musicians, the Autograph Score of Beethoven's
"Schottische Liede [sic]*", and Autograph Music of Boccherini, Cherubini, Granados, Mozart*
[et al.] *Sold . . . 29th* [-30th] *June 1964.* London, 1964. 103 p. 515 lots.   [Film at CRL]

> Kite's lots 343-431 (but hundreds of items; e.g., lot 343 comprised 8 Walsh
> editions); lots 378-431, ALS; Karl Heller's ALS, lots 444-47; Beethoven
> holographs, property of Louis Koch, lots 448-51A; 451-57, Wagner ALS.

1535   **Kittel, Johann Christian,** 1732-1809
[Strigelius.] *Verzeichniss derjenigen Musikalien und musikalischen Schriften aus dem*
Nachlasse des verstorbenen Hrn. Organist Kittel in erfurt, welche in dem Strigeliussischen
Hause auf der Pilse . . . versteigert werden sollen. Erfurt, 1809. 40 p. 889 lots.

> Not examined; cited from **Folter**, no. 190, and **Beisswenger**.

1536   **Klein, Christian Benjamin,** 1754-1825
Virneisel, W. "Christian Benjamin Klein und seine Sammlung musikalischer Handschriften."
Diss., Bonn, 1924.

> Not located. Collection now in D-BNms and D-BNu.

1537   _____

BONN, RHEINISCHE FRIEDRICH-WILHELMS-UNIVERSITÄT, BIBLIOTHEK
"Die Sammlung Klein." In *Katalog der Musikhandschriften im Besitz des*
Musikwissenschaftlichen Seminars der . . . Universität, viii-xiii, 1-129. Beiträge zur Rheinischen
Friedrich-Wilhelms-Universität, 89. Köln: Arno Volk Verlag, 1971. 595 nos.

> [US-CHua, -Bu]

> Compiled by Magda Marx-Weber. **Folter**, no. 191. **Albrecht**.

1538   **Klemm, Heinrich**
Beschreibender Catalog des Bibliographischen Museums von . . . Manuskripte und
Druckwerke des 15. und 16. Jahrhunderts. . . . Dresden: H. Klemm, 1884. viii, 509 p.
> [US-Wc, -U, -PROu]

> Collection purchased by Saxony in 1886. Reissued with accessions to mid-
> 1885 as *Katalog des Museums Klemm, erste und zweite Abth. . . .* Dresden
> & Leipzig, 1885. viii, 534 p. Not examined; cited from Lengfeld Antiq.-Cat.
> no. 36, lot 134: ". . . zahlreiche liturgische und musik-theoretische Drucke
> des 15. u. 16 Jahrhunderts."

1539   **Klengel, Paul**
M. LENGFELD, FIRM, COLOGNE   CAT. NO. 50
Musik. Praktische Musik des 17.-20. Jahrhundert. Musikbücher - Musikerportraits. Köln,
1935. 89 p.

> Not examined. According to *Jahrbuch Peters*, 1935, it contains part of
> Klengel's library.

1540   **[Klingemann, Karl]**

J. A. Stargardt, firm, Marburg   Cat. no. 560
Autographen aus verschiedenem Besitz . . . versteigert . . . 28. November 1962. . . . Marburg, 1962. Not located.

> A portion of the Klingemann collection, according to Staehelin in *Festschrift Rudolf Elvers*, 490 (see **1541**).

1541   _____

Staehelin, Martin. "Musikalien aus dem Besitz von Mendelssohns Freund Karl Klingemann." In *Festschrift Rudolf Elvers,* ed. Ernst Herttrich & Hans Schneider, 483-90. Tutzing: Schneider, 1985.

[g.a.]

> A list of items now in D-BNba.

1542   **Knapton, Philip**

Mr. Watson, at the Town's Room, auctioneer, London
Assemblage of Music, Including the Library of Philip Knapton (deceased) . . . Remaining Stock in Trade . . . Sold February 19, and Two Following Days, 1884. London, 1884. 23 p. 548 lots. Music, lots 1-525.

[GB-Lbl]

[Knight, T C .]   *See* **Baker, Rev. James** (sale of 30 April 1855)

1543   **Knorring, Baron Karl von,** 1810-70; **Paul Kristeller** (1863-1931)

Hoepli, firm, Milan; Henning Opperman, Basel   Auk. Cat. no. 437
Autographen-Sammlung des kammerherrn und russischen gesandten Baron . . . ; der schriftliche Nachlass von Prof. Dr. Paul Kristeller . . . Stammbücher in geschäftslokal der Firma Henning Opperman . . . Montag, den 28. bis Mittwoch, den 30 Mai 1934. Mailand: U. Hoepli, [1934]. 121 p. 1170 lots. Music, *inter alia.*

[US-Wc; compiler]

1544   **Knyvett, William,** 1779-1856

W. P. Musgrave, auctioneer, London
. . . A Catalogue of a Very Valuable and Celebrated Collection of Music, the Whole Being Actually the Property of . . . Which Will Be Sold by Auction by . . . on the 30th of June, and 1st of July, 1825. [London]: W. Watson, [1825]. 26 p. 274 lots.

[US-Wc, -NYp, -Cn (copy of US-Wc)]

1545   **Koch, Fred R.**

Baker, Evan. "Lettere di Giuseppe Verdi a Francesco Maria Piave (1843-65): Documenti della Frederick R. Koch Collection e della Mary Flagler Cary Collection presso la Pierpont Morgan Library di New York." *Studi Verdiani* 4 (1986-87): 136-66.

[g.a.]

> A catalog with a critical introduction.

1546   **Koch, Louis,** 1862-1930

Manuskripte, Briefe, Dokumente, von Scarlatti bis Stravinsky: Katalog der Musikautographen-Sammlung . . . Beschrieben und erläutert von Georg Kinsky. Stuttgart: Hoffmansche Buchdruckerei F. Krais, 1953. xxii, 360 p.

[US-Wc, -NYp, -Bp, -NBu]

1547   **Kochno. Boris; Serge Lifar**

Dane, Marie-Claude. *Hommage à Diaghilew: Collections Boris Kochno et Serge Lifar.* Paris: Musée Galliéra, 1872. 1 vol., unpaged.

[US-NYp]

1548   Koehler, Ernst (organist, Breslau)
HEINRICH LESSER, FIRM, BRESLAU
Bibliothek Ernst Koehler. (Theoretische und praktische Musik.) Verzeichniss des antiquarischen Bücherlagers von Heinrich Lesser, no. 3. Breslau, 1873. 16 p. 370 lots.
[GB-Lbl (Hirsch 597.(4))]

1549   Koen, Ger.
VAN THOL, FIRM, THE HAGUE
Catalogus excellentissimorum librorum. Onder dez. een partye muzyk-boeken en muzyk-instrumenten. Nachgelassen door Ger. Koen, J. v. B. en K. v. K. 's-Gravenhage: van Thol, 1741.
Not located; cited from **Bobillier**. Impossible to otherwise verify or locate.

1550   Koenig, Robert
ANTIQUARISCHEN BÜCHERLAGERS, FIRM, BERLIN   CAT. NO. 101
Deutsche Litteratur und Sprache. Musikwissenschaft. Enthält auch die Bibliothek des verstorbenen Prof. . . . Berlin, 1901. 95, 94 p. 3562 lots.
Not located; cited from **Folter 2**, no. 438.

1551   Könnecke, Gustav, 1845-1920; et al.
KARL ERNST HENRICI, AUCTIONEER, BERLIN   AUK. CAT. 107
. . . Versteigerung von Autographen aus den Gebieten der Literatur, Wissenschaft und Kunst. Nachlass des . . . 22. und 23. Febr. 1926. Berlin, 1926. 91 p. 738 lots.   [NL-Avb]
Musik, Theater und bildende Kunst, lots 612-738. See also *ZfMW* 8 (1925/26): 384.

1552   Koester, K [probably **Karl,** 1843-   ]
J. F. CARTHAUS, FIRM, BONN
Systematisches Verzeichnis der Musikalien-bibliothek des verstorbenen Geh. Medizinalrates Prof. Dr. Koester in Bonn. Bonn: J. F. Carthaus, 1905. 36 p.
Not located; cited from *BiBB, 1906.*

1553   ——————
KARL MAX POPPE, FIRM, LEIPZIG   LAGER-CAT. NO. 6
Praktische Musik. . . . Leipzig, 1913. 102 p. 2806 lots.   [US-NYgr]

1554   Köstlin, Heirnich Adolf, 1846-1907; **Adolf Zumsteeg**
HEINRICH KERLER, FIRM, ULM A.D.   ANT.-CAT. NO. 375
Geistlich und profane Musik. Theater. Hierin die musikalischen Bibliotheken von. . . . Ulm a.D., [n.d., 1908?]. 57 p. 1785 lots.   [US-Wc, GB-Lbl]
Properties not differentiated. **Folter**, no. 192. Eleven later sales of Köstlin's theological library cited by **Folter** contain no music. This catalog noted in *ZfMW* 10 (1908/09): 126.

1555   Kötschau, Johann Nicolas Julius
KLASSENBACHSCHEN BUCHDRUCKEREI?, NAUMBURG
Verzeichniss der Musikalien und Bücher aus dem Nachlasse des verstorbenen Musikdirektors . . . versteigert werden sollen. . . . Naumburg: Gedruckt in der Klassenbachschen Buchdruckerei, 1845.
Not located; cited from **Beisswenger**.

1556   Kötschau, Julius, 1788-1845
Braun, Werner. "Mitteldeutsche Quellen der Musiksammlung Gotthold in Königsberg." *Musik des Ostens* 5 (1969): 84-86.   [g.a.]

  → *See also* entry no. **1080** under **Gotthold**

1557   Kofler, Leo, 1837-1908
MERWIN-CLAYTON SALES CO., AUCTIONEER, NEW YORK
Catalogue of Interesting and Scarce Works on Natural History . . . Together with a Valuable Collection of English and German Books on Music, Singing and Voice Culture, Formerly Belonging to Prof. Kofler . . . Sold May 25, 26 and 27, 1908. . . . New York, 1908. 117 p. 1206 lots. Music, lots 719-64 (but many more items).   [US-NYp, -NYgr, -NH]

1558   Kolisch, Rudolf, 1896-1978
Busch, Regina. "Der Nachlass von Rudolf Kolisch." *Mitteilungen der internationalen Schönberg-Gesellschaft* 2 (October 1987): 7-8.   [g.a.]

  Collection at US-CA.

  → *See also under* **Moldenhauer, Hans** (exhibit catalog of 1988)

1559   Kollmann, August Friedrich Christoph, 1756-1829
PUTTICK & SIMPSON, AUCTIONEER, LONDON   CAT. NO. 1642
. . . Catalogue of a Valuable Collection of Music, Including an Important Selection from the Library of the Eminent Theorist A. F. C. Kollmann . . . Which Will Be Sold . . . January 30, 1877, and Following Day. . . . [London, 1877.] 22 p. 603 lots. Music, lots 1-515.
                                                                                                                          [US-Wc, GB-Lbl]

  King, pp. 60-61.

1560   Kolovrat-Krakovsky [family?]
Rutová, Milada. "Instrumentalní koncerty kolovratské hudební sbírky ze zámku radenínskéha [Instrumental concerts of the Kolovrat music collection from the Radenin Castle]." *Casopis Moravského muzea* 25/26 (1973).

  Not located; cited from **Benton 5**:54.

1561   Koning, David, 1820-76; **G. C. R. Harksen; W. A. F. H. De Bas;** et al.
H. G. BOM, AUCTIONEER, AMSTERDAM
Catalogus der belangrijke Bibliotheken, nagelaten door wijlen de heeren Dr. G. J. Vinke . . . [et al.] *en der Muziekversamelingen van wijlen de heeren David Koning* [etc.] *Verkooping . . . 22 maart 1882 en negen volgende dagen. . . .* Amsterdam, 1882. 168 p. 3159 + 1074 lots. Music, pp. 143-55 (720 lots + 8 instruments).   [NL-Avb]

1562   Koppel, Franz
OSWALD WEIGEL, AUCTIONEER, LEIPZIG. AUK. CAT., N.F. NO. 105
Theater - Musik . . . Aus der Bücherei des verstorbenen Geh. Rats Dr. Franz Koppel, Ellfeld. Versteigerungstage, 15. und 16. Dezember, 1920. Leipzig, 1920.

  Not located; cited from notice in *ZfMW* 3 (1920/21): 192.

1563   **Kossmaly, Carl,** 1812-93; **Jean F. Schucht,** 1832-94
LIST & FRANCKE, FIRM, LEIPZIG   CAT. NO. 272
Schriften über das Theater. Theoretische und praktische Musik aus dem Nachlasse des Herren.
. . . Leipzig, 1896. 85 p. 2655 lots. Properties not differentiated.   [NL-AVb, -DHgm; compiler]
Folter, no. 205.

1564   **Koster, Albert**
HENRICI, FIRM, BERLIN   VERST. NO. 97
Autographen in der Hauptsache aus dem Nachlasse der verstorbenen Geheimrats . . . , vol. 2:
Musik - Theater - bildende Kunst. Berlin, 1924. 54 p. 379 lots.
        Sale, 20 November 1924. Not examined; cited from **Folter 2,** no. 443.

1565   **Koudelka, Joseph, Freiherr von,** 1773-1850
R. FRIEDLÄNDER & SOHN, AUCTIONEER, BERLIN
*Catalogue des livres de musique rares, surtout du XV. et XVI. siècle, provenant de la
bibliothèque de feu . . . qui seront vendue . . . le janvier 1859. . . .* Berlin: Impr. de Guthschmidt
* Comp, [1859]. 16 p. 193 lots.   [US-Bp, -NBu (film), GB-Lbl (Hirsch)]
        Folter, no. 206. **Albrecht:** acquired by A. W. Thayer and with his library
        then presented by Joshua Bates to US-Bp.

1566   _____

        LITERATURE
        Fuchs, Aloys. "Die musikalische Bibliothek des Hrn. Feldmarschall-Lieutenants Freiherrn von
        Koudelka in Wien." *Cäcilia* 23 (1844): 50.   [g.a.]

1567   **Kraft, Ernst, Prince Graf von Oettingen-Wallerstein**
        The library, now in Schloss Harburg, was built up with material from nearby
        monastery libraries and "libraries of the neighboring Öttingen-Wallerstein
        line," from Count Balden, and from Augsburg and Mannheim antiquarians
        and publishers (Piersol, p. 55).

1568   _____

        Schmid, Ferdinand. "Verzeichnis der gedruckten Musikalien, die sich 1745 auf dem Kirchenchor
        der Wallersteiner Pfarrkirche befanden, aufgestellt von Chor-regenten Ferdinand Schmid."
        Ms. reprinted by Haberkamp in no. **1574,** from Paulus Weissenberger's
        Geschichte der katholischen Pfarrei Wallerstein . . . vol. 2: *Kulturgeschichte*
        (1946), p. 37.

1569   _____

        Schreiber, Ig. "Catalogus, meiner sowohl bey Hof, als Pfarkirche in das 25.ste Jahr gebrauchten
        Musicalien, Wallerstein den 10ten May 1765, Fr: Ig: Schreiber, Reg: Chori."
        Ms. in Archiv-Wallerstein, reprinted in Haberkamp (**1574**).

1570   _____

        "Aus dem Nachlassinventar des Grafen Franz Ludwig zu Oettingen-Wallerstein, d. Wallerstein,
        7. September 1791."
        Ms. in Archiv-Wallerstein [P.A. Franz Ludwig no. 13], reprinted in
        Haberkamp (**1574**).

1571 _____

Grupp, G. *Oettingen-Wallersteinsche Sammlungen in Maihingen. Handschriften-verzeichnis. 1. Hälfte,* ed. G. Grupp. Nordlingen: Th. Reische, 1897. 36 p.   [Film at US-U]

Music Mss., 11th-15th centuries, lots 713-804.

1572 _____

KARL & FABER, AUCTIONEER, MUNICH   AUK. NO. 9

Bibliophile Kostbarkeiten aus der Fürstl. Öttingen-Wallerstein'sche Bibliothek . . . und aus der Bibliothek des . . . Marcus Fugger (III. Teil) und Beiträge aus anderen Besitz. . . . Manuskripte . . . Einbände . . . Inkunabeln . . . Musik . . . Geschichte . . . [etc.] *Versteigerung 11. Mai 1934.* Munich, 1934. 93 p., 20 plates. 492 lots. Music, *inter alia.*   [US-Wc]

→ *See* other entries for the **Fugger** collection under that name.

1573 _____

Piersol, Jon Ross. "The Oettingen-Wallerstein Hofkapelle and Its Music." 2 vols. Thesis, University of Iowa, 1972. 844 leaves.   [g.a. on film]

"Description and incipits of the wind ensemble music, wind concertos and chamber music [in the Fürstlich Oettingen-Wallerstein'sche Bibliothek]," vol. 2, leaves 507-821.

1574 _____

Haberkamp, Gertraut. *Thematischer Katalog der Musikhandschriften des Fürstlich Oettingen-Wallerstein'schen Bibliothek Schloss Harburg . . . mit e. Geschichte d. Musikalienbestandes von Volker von Volckamer.* Kataloge Bayerischer Musiksammlungen. München: Henle, 1976. xxxv, 298 p.   [g.a.]

In his review of this catalog in *JAMS* 32 (1979): 555, Barry Brook added a "sad Postscript . . . Recent press accounts state that both the music collection and the general library are to be sold . . . should the state of Bavaria not be able to purchase and maintain the collection *in situ*, the Harburg holdings will be sold at auction. . . . "

→ *See also under* **Misligowski, Carl**; **Schaden, Fr. Michael von**; **Beecke, Ignaz von**; **Zwierzing**

1575   **Krall, ?**

MUSICANA UNLIMITED, FIRM, CHICAGO   CAT. NO. 9

"Lot 164, The Krall Collection of First Editions of the Pianoforte Music of Robert Schumann." In *Catalogue No. 9: Musical Materials, Rare and Scarce, Including . . . ,* [10-11]. Chicago, [1950].   [US-NBu]

26 opus numbers . . . the "largest single collection of these works [in first editions] ever to be offered in America."

Kraus, Richard.   *See* **Heger, Robert** (sale of 1982)

1576   **Krauss, Clemens,** 1893-1954

HANS SCHNEIDER, FIRM, TUTZING   CAT. NO. 52

Dirigierpartituren, überwiegand aus dem Nachlass von Clemens Krauss. [Tutzing über München, 1956.] 13 p. 725 lots. Krauss's lots not identified.   [US-NBu]

Folter, no. 207.

1577 _____

LITERATURE

Kende, Götz Klaus. "Ein Clemens-Krauss-Archiv in Wien." *ÖmZ* 11 (1956): 188-90.   [g.a.]

Krauss, Clemens; Viorica Ursuleac.   *See under* **Schmidt, Franz**

1578   Kreisler, Fritz, 1875-1962
PARKE-BERNET GALLERIES, AUCTIONEER, NEW YORK
Valuable and Important Incunabula and Other Rare Early Printed Books and Illuminated Manuscripts, Together with Notable Specimens of Later Periods, Collected by. . . . New York: Parke-Bernet, 1949. 127 p. 174 lots.   [Film at CRL]

   Folter, no. 208. But no music items!

1579 _____

LITERATURE

Spivacke, Harold. "The Brahms and Chausson Manuscripts Presented by Mr. Fritz Kreisler." *Library of Congress Journal of Current Acquisitions* 6 (May 1949): 57-62.   [g.a.]

1580 _____

Lochner, Louis P. *Fritz Kreisler.* New York: Macmillan, 1950. xv, 450 p.

   Not examined; cited from **Folter,** no. 208. See pp. 381-89.

1581   Kretzschmar, Hermann, 1848-1924; **Emil Vogel,** 1848-1924
LEO LIEPMANNSSOHN, FIRM, LEIPZIG   CAT. NO. 213
. . . *Musikerbiographien, zum Teil aus den Bücherein der Herren Geh.-R. Prof. Dr.* . . . Leipzig, [n.d., 1925?]. 97 p. 2084 lots.   [US-Wc, NL-Avb]

   Properties not differentiated. **Folter,** no. 209. Noted also in *ZfMW* 8 (1925/26): 64.

1582 _____

LEO LIEPMANNSSOHN, FIRM, LEIPZIG   CAT. NO. 214
Musik-Geschichte, z. T. aus den Bücherein der Herren . . . Musikbibliographie. Kataloge . . . Gesamtausgaben . . . Verlagswerke. . . . Berlin, [n.d., 1925?]. 21 p. 334 + 30 lots.
          [NL-Avb; compiler]

   Properties not differentiated. **Folter,** no. 210.

1583   Kristeller, Hans, b. 1890-
[Katalog der] *Offenbach-Sammlung des Dr. Hans Kristeller, Porto-Ronco, Schweiz.* [N.p., n.d., 193_?] 53 numbered leaves. 1205 items.   [US-Wc, -NYp]
   Mimeographed.

Kristeller, P.   *See* **Knorring, Karl von, Baron**

1584   Krohn, Ernst C., 1888-1975
Keck, George Russell. "Pre-1875 American Imprint Sheet Music in the Ernst C. Krohn Special Collections, Gaylord Music Library, Washington University, St. Louis, Mo.: A Catalog and Descriptive Study." Ph.D. diss., University of Iowa, 1982. 973 p.   [US-NBu]

1585 Kroyer, Theodor, 1873-1945
WALTER RICKE, FIRM, MUNICH   CAT. NO. 37
[Musikliteratur aus Nachlass. . . .] Munich, [1962].

> Not located; cited from *IBAK* 1966/67. No response by the seller to a request, March 1993, for a complete citation.

1586 Kruijs, M. van't
H. G. BOM, AUCTIONEER, AMSTERDAM
Catalogus der muziekbibliotheek en van eene collectie werken over spelen, nagelaten door . . . M. van't Kruijs, organist te Amsterdam . . . verkooping . . . 1ᵉⁿ Februari 1886. . . . Amsterdam, 1886. 23 p. 350 lots. Music, lots 1-308.   [NL-Avb]

Kümmerle, Salomon, 1832-96.   *See* **Boers, Jan Conradus**

1587 Kürschner, Joseph, 1853-1902
ROSSBERG'SCHEN BUCHHANDLUNG, LEIPZIG   ANT. CAT. NO. 4
Bibliothek Jos. Kürschner. Theater und Musik. Leipzig, [n.d., 1905?]. 98 p. 3024 lots.
[US-R]
> **Folter 2**, no. 455.

1588 Kufferath, Maurice, 1852-1919
FIEVEZ, F. (= EXPERT), BRUSSELS
Catalogue d'une belle collection de livres anciens et modernes . . . Édition originales et illustrés. Musique, partitions . . . avec dédicaces des auteurs . . . Autographes, provenant de la collection de feu [Berlioz, Brahms, Caruso, Delibes, etc.] . . . vente publique . . . 15 [-17] Février 1932. . . . Bruxelles, 1932. 54 p. 950 lots. Music, lots 301-600.   [NL-Avb]

> Autographs, including some music, 601-739 (but many more items).

1589 Kuhnle, Wesley, 1898-1962
LITERATURE
Rayner, Clare G. "The Wesley Kuhnle Repository at California State University, Long Beach." *Notes* 33 (1976): 16-26.
[g.a.]

1590 Kurtz, Andrew George (of Liverpool), d. 1895
SOTHEBY, WILKINSON & HODGE, AUCTIONEER, LONDON
Catalogue of Important and Valuable Autograph Letters and Historical Documents from Various Collections; Also a Most Interesting Collection of Musical Scores, &c., the Collections of the Late A. G. Kurtz . . . Sold . . . 5th Day of July, 1895, and Following Day. [London, 1895.] 44 p. 510 lots. ALS and Music, lots 1-120.   [Film at CRL]

> Brief notice with some contents in *MO & MTR* 18 (1 September 1895): 800.
> **Albrecht**: some materials bequeathed to GB-Lbl.

Kuschem Ludwig Walter Helmüth, b. 1901- .   *See under* **Böhm** (sale by Schneider, 1983)

1591 Kyllmann,   ?   (of Bonn)
LENGFELD'SCHE BUCHHANDLUNG, FIRM, COLOGNE   CAT. NO. 34
Musiksammlung Kyllmann. Praktische Musik von ca. 1150-1860 in Erst- und Original-Ausgaben. Musikhandschriften. Köln, [n.d., 1928?]. 34 p. 590 lots. Mss., lots 366-94.
[NL-Avb, GB-Lbl (Hirsch)]

> Noted in *ZfMW* 11 (1928/29): 64.

1592   Laborde, Léon Emmanuel Simon Joseph, Marquis de, d. 1869
SOTHEBY & CO., AUCTIONEER, LONDON
Catalogue of Valuable Printed Books and Manuscripts, Autograph Letters and Historical Documents . . . Property of [Various Collectors], *and the Chansonnier de Laborde . . . Property of the Marquis . . . 14th of November, 1932, and Following Day.* London, 1932. 65 p. 494 lots.
[Film at CRL]

> The Chansonnier, lot 222 (pp. 26-28) was bought by Quaritch for £500; subsequently became the property of E. P. Goldschmidt & Co.; finally, US-Wc. See correlated studies of the Chansonnier by Helen E. Bush, "The Laborde Chansonnier," *Papers of the American Musicological Society* (1940), 565-79.   [g.a.]

Lacroix, S   F .   *See* **Alizard, Adolf Joseph Louis**

1593   LaFage, Juste Adrien Lenoir de, 1805-62
"Extraits du catalogue critique et raisonné d'une petite bibliothèque musicale." *Revue de la musique ancienne et moderne* (1856), 252-59, 356-64, 442-53.   [g.a.]

> See **Albrecht**.

1594   _____
Extraits du catalogue critique et raisonné d'une petite bibliothèque musicale. Rennes: Impr. de H. Vatar; [Paris: Chez Tardif, 1857]. 120, 40 p. ca. 100 items.
[US-Wc, -Bp, -Cn, -CA (lacks Appendix)]

> Part published earlier (**1593**). Otto Haas antiquarian catalog 27:30 says very scarce—copies with the music appendix (40 pp.) "are hardly to be found at all." **Folter**, no. 211.

1595   _____
Catalogue de la bibliothèque musicale de feu . . . Traité généraux et spéciaux sur la théorie de la musique et la compositions; historique, biographie, oeuvres de musique pratique de divers genres, etc. . . . [vente . . . 15 décembre 1862 et les 12 jours suivants . . .]. Paris: L Potier, 1862. iv, 200 p. 2300 lots. Music, lots 1-1935.   [US-Wc, -Cu, -NYp, -NYgr, NL-Avb (some n & p)]
> **Folter**, no. 212.

1596   _____
Staehelin, Martin. "Zum Schicksal des altes Musikalien-Fonds von San Luigi dei Francesci in Rom." *Fontes* 3 (1970): 120-27.   [g.a.]
> Traces items from 16th and 17th century inventories of the church through LaFage's collection, who must have acquired them in Rome in 1849.

1597   LaFragua, Jose Maria
LITERATURE
Chapa, M. "Musica en la coleccion Jose Ma. Lafragua." *Heterofonia* 14 (1981): 64-66.

1598   Lago,   , Dr.
Bustamente y Urrutia, José María de. *Catalogo general alfabético de autores de la Biblioteca del "Doctor Lago."* Santiago: "El eco fraciscano," 1929. xvi, 527, 22 p.   [US-Wc, -BE, -AA]
> Not examined; cited from **Benton 3**:41, no. 88.

1599   LaGrange, Henry-Louis

Zychowicz, James L. "Music Manuscripts in the Bibliothèque Musicale Gustav Mahler, Paris." *Fontes* 41 (1994): 279-95.

> The Mahler library based on LaGrange's library with additions from Sylvain Dupuis, 1856-1931; Frederick Goldbeck, 1902-81; Yvonne Lefébure, 1898-1986; Maurice Fleuret, 1932-90; Antonio de Almeida, b. 1928; and Alfred Cortot.

1600   Laidlaw, William (of Liverpool)

PUTTICK & SIMPSON, AUCTIONEER, LONDON   CAT. NO. 2201

Catalogue of the Very Extensive Library of Music of the Late . . . (of Liverpool), Comprising Full and Vocal Scores of Operas, Oratorios . . . Handel's Works by Arnold . . . Theoretical Treatises, Original and Other Manuscripts . . . Sold . . . August 17th, 1883. [London], 1883. 22 p. 403 leaves (more items).   [GB-Lbl]

> **King**, p. 64.

1601   Laidlaw, William; William Lemare 1839-1917?

PUTTICK & SIMPSON, AUCTIONEER, LONDON   CAT. NO. 2202

Catalogue of an Extensive Collection of Musical Properties [Instruments] *. . . Also the Remainder of the Library of Music of the Late . . . Chiefly Comprising Manuscript Scores and Parts (Many Being Original and Bearing Autographs) . . . Also That of William Lemare . . . Sold August 22nd, 1883.* 17 p. 417 lots. Music, lots 153-417.   [GB-Lbl]

> Laidlaw's properties, lots 154-255; Lemare's, 319-417.

1602   Lambertini, Michel'angelo, 1862-1920

Bibliophilie musicale. Les bibliothèques portugaises. Essais de classification: les livres d'un amateur: Cabinet iconographique. [Lisboa: Typ. do Annuaire commercial], 1918. 302 p. 2339 nos.   [US-NYp, -Wc, -NH, -CA, compiler]

> Works for the study of musical instruments, forming a natural complement of the museum founded by the author, later acquired by A. A. Carvalho Monteiro and now in Conservatorio Nacional in Lisbon. **Folter**, no. 213.

1603   _____

Idem. *Éd. abregée* [!] Viseu: Tip. Andrade & Cie, 1924. 247 p.   [US-Wc, Cu]

> **Folter**, no. 213.

1604   Landau, Emil

HENRICI, AUCTIONEER, BERLIN   AUK. CAT. NO. 34

Autographen aus den Gebieten der Literatur und Wissenschaft sowie der Musik, aus den Nachlass des . . . Versteigerung . . . 12. Juni 1928. Berlin, 1928. 53 p. 297 leaves, illus. Music, lots 212-97.   [US-NYgr]

> **Albrecht** says music occupies 92 pages!

1605   Landau, Horace de, Baron, 1824-1903

Roediger, Francesco. *Catalogue des livres manuscrits et imprimés composant la bibliothèque de M. Horace de Landau-Finaly. . . .* 2 vols. Florence, 1885-90.   [US-Wc, GB-Lbl (Hirsch 453)]

> The Horace Landau Memorial collection was bequeathed by Horace Finaly to I-Fn in 1945.

1606 _____

SOTHEBY & CO., AUCTIONEER, LONDON
Catalogue of the Renowned Library of the Late . . . The Second Portion: The Famous Musical Collection Which Will Be Sold . . . the 17th of October, 1949 and Following Day. . . . [London: Sotheby, 1949.] 88-157, 22 facs. Music, lots 130-446. [Film at CRL]

> Some went to US-WC (see **1610**), some to the dealer Otto Haas.

1607 _____

Pashby, John. "The Landau Music Collections." *MT* 90 (1949): 305-07. [g.a.]

> About the Sotheby auction (**1606**).

1608 _____

LEONARD HYMAN, FIRM, LONDON   CAT. NO. 45
Music and Music Literature, Including Italian Music and Music Theory from the Landau Library, Florence. London, 1949/50. 16 p. 232 lots. [compiler]

1609 _____

HANS P. KRAUS, FIRM, NEW YORK CITY   CAT. NO. 140
Early Music (Including Choice Items from the Library of Baron Horace Landau). . . . New York, [1950]. 24 lots. [US-CHua]

1610 _____

LITERATURE
"Music from the Collection of Baron Horace de Landau." *Library of Congress Quarterly Journal of Current Acquisitions* 7 (August 1950): 11-21. [g.a.]

1611 _____

Mondolfo, Anita. "La biblioteca Landau-Finaly." *Studi di bibliografia . . . in memorie di Luigi De Gregori*, 265-85. Roma: Palombi, 1949.

> Not examined; cited from **Benton 3**:180-81, no. 127.

1612 **Landauer, Mrs. Bella Clara,** 1874-1968
Some Aeronautical Music from the Collection of. . . . Paris: privately printed, 1933. [9], 11 p. 23 facs. [US-Wc, -Bp, -CA, etc.]

1613 _____

"Some Music Sheets from the. . . . Tradecard Collection at the New York Historical Society. . . ." [New York], 1940. [27] p. facs. Typewritten.

> "No copies for sale."

1614 _____

Leaves of Music by Walt Whitman from the Collection of. . . . [New York]: privately printed, 1937. [84] p., illus. [US-Wc, -BUu, CLp]

> Lists 244 pieces based on Whitman poems.

1615 _____

My City, 'Tis of Thee; New York City on Sheet-Music Covers. Selected from the Music Collection of. . . . New York: New York Historical Society, [1951]. 25 p., [69] p. of facsimiles.

[g.a.]

1616 Lande, Lawrence M.

A Checklist of Early Music Relating to Canada, Collected, Compiled and Annotated by . . . *From His Private Library.* Lawrence Landau Foundation for Canadian Historical Research, 8. Montreal: McGill University, 1973. 23 p.   [US-BUu]

1617 Landsberg, Ludwig, 1805-58

[An inventory of his collection in D-Bds, Ms. catalog Mus. Ms. 95/96.]

Cited by **Schaal** (1966), p. 109.

1618 _____

[A complete catalog of his collection in Ms. in the Fétis collection in B-Br.]

Cited by **Schaal** (1966), pp. 45-46.

1619 _____

LIST & FRANCKE, FIRM, BERLIN

Catalogue de la bibliothèque du Professeur Landsberg à Rome. Musique ancienne. Berlin: Impr. chez Kühn, 1859. 29 p. Ca. 600 nos.   [US-Wc, GB-Lbl, NL-DHgm]

Large collection of Mss. and early prints. In Ms. on title page of US-Wc copy: "In Besitz der Kg. Bibliothek z. [Berlin]," i.e., D-Bds. **Folter**, no. 214.

1620 _____

Autographen aus dem Nachlasse des Prof. Landsberg zu Rom. Berlin: Ernst Kühn, 1859. 8 p. 149 nos.

Not examined; cited from **Folter**, no. 215.

1621 _____

LITERATURE

[A description of the Beethoven sketchbooks in the Landsberg Collection.] In Douglas Johnson and Alan Tyson, *The Beethoven Sketchbooks*, 31-33. Berkeley: University of California Press, 1985.

[g.a.]

1622 Lane, Capt. J J

SOTHEBY & CO., AUCTIONEER, LONDON

Catalogue of Valuable Printed Books, Music, Drawings, Autograph Letters, etc., Comprising a Collection of Music and Books on Music . . . *the Property of* . . . *Sold* . . . *June 15th, 1957.* [London], 1957. 88 p. 480 lots. Music, lots 1-90.   [Film at CRL]

Lane's properties, lots 1-76.

1623 [Lane, Capt. J J ; Mrs. E. H. Wilkins; Harold Reeves; Charles Loeser]

SOTHEBY & CO., AUCTIONEER, LONDON

Catalogue of Valuable Printed Books, Fine Bindings, Music, Autograph Letters and Portraits, Including . . . *the Autograph Full Score of Part of Wagner's "Rienzi" and the Corrected Proofs of "Tristan und Isolde" the Property of the Late Mrs. E. H. Wilkins. Autograph Letters or*

Music of Berlioz . . . Debussy, Donizetti [etc.] *Sold . . . the 19th of September, 1960, and the* [Two] *Following Days. . . .* [London], 1960. 135 p. 798 lots. Music, lots 978-248a (many more items).   [Film at CRL]

> Lane's properties, lots 98-106; Wilkin's, 135-36, 245-48; Reeves's, 137-210 (mostly ALS; lot 178 alone, over 1000 ALS!); Loeser's, 229-41 (ALS). Lot 225, 26 unpublished Puccini letters. Lot 248a, Beethoven's pencil corrections on proof copy of the Archduke Trio.

1624   Lang, François, 1908-44

Herlin, Denis. *Collection musicale François Lang.* Domaine musicologique, 13. Paris: Klincksieck, 1993. 301 p. 1354 items.

> About two-thirds of the library came from the collection of Gustave Legouix, mainly in the 1930s during Legouix's activities as an antiquarian dealer.

1625   Lang, Nikolaus, 1772-1837

LITERATURE

Münster, Robert. "Nikolaus Lang und seine Michael-Haydn-Kopien in der Bayerischen Staatsbibliothek." *ÖmZ* 27 (1972): 25-29.   [g.a.]

1626   Langenbach, Wilhelm; Max Plock

OSWALD WEIGEL, AUCTIONEER, LEIPZIG   AUK. CAT. N.F. 50

Theater- Musik, hierin u. a. die Sammlungen des . . . [Versteigerung] *15* [-17] *Dezember, 1915.* [Leipzig], 1915. 81 p. 1153 lots. Music, lots 652-1083.   [NL-Avb, -DHgm]

> Theater, lots 1-651.

1627   Langhans, Wilhelm, 1832-1902

B. LIEBISCH, FIRM, LEIPZIG   ANT. CAT. NO. 180

Antiquariats-Katalog Nr. 180 [zum Teil aus der Bibliothek von . . .] *Musik. 1. Geschichte und Theorie. Opern. Zeitschriften. Tanz. 2. Lied und Gesang. 3. Kirchenlied und Kirchenmusik.* Leipzig, 1910.   [US-NYp, GB-Lbl (Hirsch), NL-Avb]

> Noted in *ZiMG* 11 (1909/10): 202.

1628   Langton, F   E   P   S   ; George Kitchin; Adolf Aber

HODGSON & CO., AUCTIONEER, LONDON

A Catalogue of Books from Various Sources Comprising the Properties of. . . . [Music, etc.]

> Not located. Sale date, 20-21 October 1960. Cited from *IBAK* (1960/61).

1629   Lannoy, Heinrich Edouard Joseph, Freiherr von, 1787-1853

Bischoff, Ferdinand. "Verzeichnis der in der Lannoy-Sammlung enthalten Musikalien."

> Ms. in the library of the Steirmärkische Landeskonservatoriums in Graz (no. 38,410).

1630   ——————

Suppan, Wolfgang. "Die Musiksammlung des Freiherrn von Lannoy." *Fontes* 12 (1965): 9-22.
                                                                                                            [g.a.]

> **Folter**, no. 216, says a total of 1256 items; Suppan notes only about 340! Collection now at A-Gk(h), but **Albrecht** says "bulk of the collection acquired in 1935 by A-Wn!"

1631 _____

Becker-Glauch, Irmgard. "Die Haydniana der Lannoy-Sammlung: Eine archivalische Studie." *Haydn-Studien* 3 (1973): 46-52.   [g.a.]

La Roche, R.   *See under* **Drexel, Joseph**

1632   Larpent, John, 1741-1824

HENRY E. HUNTINGTON LIBRARY AND ART GALLERY
Catalogue of the Larpent Plays in the . . . Library. Compiled by Dougald MacMillan. Huntington Library lists, 4. San Marino, Calif., 1939. xv, 442 p.

Larpent collection includes librettos.

1633   L'Arronge, Adolf, 1838-1908**; Elias Hülle; Friedrich Wilhelm Jähns;** et al.

KARL ERNST HENRICI, FIRM, BERLIN   CAT. NO. 135
Autographen, Literatur und Wissenschaft, Musik, Theater, bildende Kunst. Aus dem Sammlungen von . . . [Versteigerung June 25 . . .]. Berlin, 1928. 66 p. 477 lots. L'Arronge's, lots 248-333.   [NL-Avb]

Folter, no. 217.

1634   L * * [i.e., **Lassabatthie, Théodore**, 1800-1871]

Notice d'une collection d'ouvrages sur l'art dramatique et autres composant la bibliothèque de M. L* *. Paris, 1851.

Not located; cited from **Scheurleer** 1 (1923): 16.

1635   Lasserre, V

LEO LIEPMANNSSOHN, FIRM, BERLIN   CAT. NO. 89
Catalogue d'une belle collection de musique instrumentale, spécialement de musique ancienne pour instruments à cordes, suivie de quelques ouvrages de musique vocale et de livres relatifs à la musique, provenant de la bibliothèque musicale de M. V. Lasserre, à Châtellerault. En vente aux prix marqués. Berlin, 1891. 33 p. 550 lots.   [NL-Avb]

1636   Latrobe, Christian Ignatius, Rev., 1758-1836

MR. FLETCHER, AUCTIONEER, LONDON
Catalogue of a Collection of the Valuable Musical Library of the Late . . . Valuable Works in Musical Literature . . . Handel's Complete Works, Best Edition . . . Several Old, Rare and Valuable Musical Treatises . . . A Fine Portrait of Handel, etc. etc. . . . Sold . . . May 2nd, 1842. London, 1842. 9 p. 201 lots.   [GB-Ob]

Mss. of Hasse, Jomelli, Naumann, Graun, lots 86-91; part books, 16th-17th centuries, lots 143-68. **King**, pp. 42-43, but did not see catalog.

1637   Laufer, Berthold

LITERATURE
Graf, Marilyn B. "The Chinese Collection of Dr. Berthold Laufer." *Resound* 1, no. 2 (April 1982): 3-4.   [g.a.]

1638   Laufer, H   J   , d. 1856

King, p. 76, says Laufer's collection of over 1000 items are scattered, some in H. Baron catalogs, but not identified.

1639 **Laurens, Jean-Joseph Bonaventure,** 1801-90; **Jules Bonaventure**
Caillet, Robert. *Catalogue de la collection musicale . . . donnée à la ville de Carpentras pour la bibliothèque d'Inguimbert.* Carpentras: Impr. Seguin, 1901. xxii, 25-151 p. Ca. 1000 nos. Collection at F-C.   [US-NYp, -CHua, GB-Lbl (Hirsch)]
       Folter, no. 218.

1640 _____
          LITERATURE
          Caillet, Robert. "Une Importante Collection musicale à la Bibliothèque Inguimbertine de Carpentras." *Marseilles, Institut historique de Provence, Compte rendus et memoires (du Congrès)* 3 (1929): 203-05.   [compiler (copy)]

1641 _____
          Caillet, Robert. "Les Portraits de musiciens, por Bonaventure Laurens, à la bibliothèque de Carpentras." In Richard Cantinelli and E. Dacier, *Les Trésors des bibliothèques de France,* 3:64-70. Paris, 1930.   [US-NYp]

1642 **Lavallée, Ad**
          A. V̲ANDERHOEVEN, A̲UCTIONEER, B̲RUSSELS
          Blogie, col. 240, notes a 33 p. sale catalog of music, at B-Br (VI.87.350 A 102[b]).
               Not examined; cited from **Blogie**.

1643 **Lavoisier, Marie Anne Pierretee Paulze,** 1758-1836
          Catalogue des livres de bibliothèque de Madame la comtesse de Rumford. . . . 2 vols. [Paris?], 1830.   [US-I (film)]
               Manuscript in cataloger's hand, with many titles crossed out, probably items sold at auction in 1836. The remainder of the library is at US-I.

1644 **Lean, Vincent Stuckey**
          B̲RISTOL, M̲UNICIPAL P̲UBLIC L̲IBRARIES
          The Stuckey Lean Collection, ed. Morris Mathews. . . . Bristol, 1903. viii, 265 p.
                                   [US-NYp, -Wc, -BApi, -CLp]
               Music, section 5, pp. 231-38 (unnumbered), but a *very* ordinary collection at GB-BRp.

1645 **Le Beau, Luise Adolpha,** 1850-1927
          Bispo, Antonio Alexandre. "Um manuscritos de modinhas da Biblioteca Estatal Bávara de Munique." *Boletim da Sociedade Brasileira de Musicologia* 3 (1987): 133-53.   [g.a.]
               Manuscript list of modinhas at D-Mbs bequeathed by the pianist.

1646 **Le Blanc-Duvernoy**
          Collection Le Blanc Duvernoy: Musique instrumentale musicale. Catalogue. Auxerre, 1907.
               Collection now at F-AU. Catalog not located. Cited from *NG*-L.

1647   Leborne, Aimé-Ambroise-Simon, 1797-1866
DUTARTE (C.-P.); EDOUARD VERT (EXP.)
Catalogue de morceaux de musique et fragments de partitions, autographes . . . de lettres autographes de compositeurs & musiciens, et de nombreuses partitions . . . formant la bibliothèque musicale de feu . . . 29 [-30] avril 1867. . . . Paris, 1867. 16 p. No lot nos.
[NL-Avb, -DHgm, B-Br]

> **Folter,** no. 219 (incomplete citation).

1648   Leduc, August, firm [its library]
Catalogue des ouvrages qui composant la Bibliothèque de l'Abonnement de Lecture musicale d'Augus^{te} Leduc & Cie. Paris, [1807]. 46 p.

> On p. 1, a Ms. copy of Tinctoris's *Terminorum musicae diffinitorium* is offered!

Leeuwarden, J. *See here under* **Merkman, J.** (sale of 21 September 1773)

1649   Leeuwen Boomkamp
Musizieren in 3 Jahrhunderts: Graphische Blätter aus der Sammlung van Leeuwen Boomkamp . . . 6. Juli bis 7. September 1969 in Ansbach. Ansbach, 1969. 15 p. 30 items.   [NL-DHgm]

1650   Lefebure, Jean, 1736-1805
UPSALA, UNIVERSITET, BIBLIOTEK
Davidsson, Aake. *Catalogue of the Gimo Collection of Italian Manuscript Music in the University Library. . . .* Acta Bibliothecae R. universitatis upsaliensis, 14. Uppsala, 1963. 101 p.
[US-NYp, -NBu]

> The Gimo collection was brought together by Lefebure ca. 1758-63. Given to S-Uu in 1951 by Gustaf Brun.

1651   _____
Davidsson, Aake. "A Collection of Italian Manuscript Music in the University Library of Uppsala." *An. Academiae Regiae Scientiarum Upsaliensis* 14 (1970): 7-29.

> Not examined.

1652   [Lefebvre, Charles Édouard, 1843-1917]
Catalogue de la bibliothèque théâtrale, musicale et poétique d'un vieil amateur. Paris: Menu, 1877.

> Not located; cited from **Bobillier** and by **Weckerlin,** who says it contains 450 nos. Also in Lengfeld's *Catalogue,* no. 36 (lot 112).

1653   _____
Catalogue d'une collection de livres rares et d'ouvrages sur la musique en vente chez Ch. Lefebvre. Bordeaux, 1879. 19 p. 189 lots.   [Copy NL-DHgm]

> Not located; cited from **Scheurleer** 1 (1923): 18. Also in Liepmannssohn's *Katalog,* no. 214, lot 189. Part 2 of a Paris auction, 20-21 June 1934, of Lefebvre properties contained 32 lots of chamber music scores.

1654 Legh, Elizabeth, 1695-1734
Dean, Winton. "The Malmesbury Collection." In *Handel Collection and Their History,* ed. Terence Best, 29-38. Oxford: Clarendon Press, 1993.   [g.a.]
> "Appendix: The Contents of the . . . Collection," pp. 37-38.

1655 Legouix, Isidore Édouard
Hardou, firm, Paris
Catalogue de musique et d'ouvrages et écrits sur la musique en vente chez Hardou. Fin de la liquidation de la maison Legouix. Paris: Impr. Seringe Frères, 1874. 94 p. 3367 lots.
[US-NYp, -Wc]

1656 Lehman, Robert Owen
"R O L F." *Notes* 21 (1963): 83-93.   [g.a.]
> Ca. 80 manuscripts are listed but the article is out-of-date because many others have been added to the collection, some removed.

1657 Leibl, Carl, 1764-1870
Göller, Gottfried. *Die Leiblische Sammlung: Katalog des Musiklien des Kölner Domcapelle. . . .* Beiträge zur Rheinischen Musikgeschichte, 57. Köln: Arno Volk-Verlag, 1964. viii, 133 p.   [g.a.]

Leiburg, L.   *See under* **Lutgendorff**

1658 Leicester, Sir Peter
Halcrow, Elizabeth M. *Sir Peter Leicester: Charges to the Grand Jury at Quarter Sessions.* Remains, Historical and Literary, Connected with the Palatine Counties of Lancaster and Chester, ser. 3, vol. 5. Manchester: Chester Society, 1953. xxxv, 168 p.   [GB-Lbl]
> **King**, p. 147, says a list of his music and instruments, pp. 151-52.

1659 Leichtentritt, Hugo, 1874-1951
Utah, University, Library
A Catalogue of Books and Music Acquired from Library of Dr. . . . Ed. Carol E. Selby. Bulletin of the University of Utah, vol. 45, no. 10. Salt Lake City: University of Utah, 1954. 106 p. Ca. 100 nos.   [g.a.]

1660 Leigh, Arthur George
Puttick & Simpson, auctioneer, London   Cat. no. 4440
Catalogue of Musical Instruments . . . and the Musical Library Formed by . . . Including MSS., Books and Music and Autograph Letters . . . Sold . . . June 28th. . . . London, 1910. 19 p. 315 lots.   [GB-Lbl]
> Leigh's books and music, lots 143-315, include some manuscripts and ALS.

1661 Leigh, Francis
Thomas Ballard, at the Rising-Sun in Little Britain
Bibliotheca Leighiana: or, A Catalogue of the Entire Library of the Late Learned Dr. . . . with One of the Best Collections of MUSICK . . . That Was Ever Offer'd to Sale . . . the 19th of February 1719/20 at Paul's Coffeehouse . . . Till All Are Sold. . . . [London]: T. Ballard, 1719/20. 44 p. 1099 lots.   [GB-Lbl]

"A curious collection of MUSICK . . . ," pp. 43-44 (26 lots). Lots are indexed in **Coral**, p. 150, discussed pp. 59-60.

1662 Leining, House of

Valentin, Caroline Pichler. *Theater und Musik am fürstlich Leiningischen Hofe, Dürkheim 1780-92. Amorbach 1803-14.* Neujahrsblätter, Gesellschaft für frankische Geschichte, 15. Würzburg: Kabitzsch & Mönnich, 1921. 168 p., illus.   [US-TA]

    Collection at D-AB. Catalog not examined.

1663 Lemaire, Théophile, b. 1820

Catalogue de la bibliothèque de . . . Ouvrages sur la musique: théorie, histoire et critique. Sur les musiciens, les chanteurs, les instruments de musique, la danse. Ouvrages relatif au théâtre et à Molière. Musique pour l'orchestre et le piano . . . Ouvrages divers, principalement sur la langue française. Dessins et estampes . . . vente aura lieu Salle Sylvestre . . . 20. mardi 21, mercredi 22 et jeudi 23. avril 1896. Paris: E. Sagot, 1896. 112 p. 840 lots. Music, lots 1-660.
                                                                                    [US-NYp, -R, -Bp, -Wc]

    Folter, no. 221.

1664 Lemann, H B (of Eltham)

PUTTICK & SIMPSON, AUCTIONEER, LONDON   CAT. NO. 2336
Catalogue of a Very Comprehensive & Almost Unique Collection of the Pianoforte Works of the Most Eminent Composers . . . Property of the Late . . . Also of Several Musical Instruments . . . Also (the Property of a Collector) Ancient and Modern Music, Theoretical and Practical Works . . . Sold . . . May 8th and . . . May 11th, 1885. [London], 1885. 32 p. 672 lots.   [GB-Lbl]

    Lemare, W. *See under* **Laidlaw, William** (Puttick & Simpson sale no. 2202)

1665 [Lemon,   ]

PUTTICK & SIMPSON, AUCTIONEER, LONDON   CAT. NO. 503
Catalogue of a Large Collection of Miscellaneous Music, Consisting of Sacred Music, Operas, Instrumental Music, in Score and Parts, Vocal Music, Glees, Songs . . . Also Musical Instruments . . . Sold . . . July 24th, 1857. [London], 1857. 22 p. 648 lots. Music, lots 1-562.   [GB-Lbl]

1666 Lenin, Vladimir Il'ich, 1870-1924

Kunetskaia, Liudmilla Ivanova. *Notnaia biblioteka sem'i Ul'ianovykh. Katalogspravochnik.* Moskva: "Soc. kompozitor," 1970. 67 p.   [US-Wc]

1667 Lennard, Henry Barrett, 1818-99

Smith, John Christopher. "Collection of the Works of Handel, Copied by J. C. Smith, Esq., His Amanuensis, Now in the Possession of. . . ."

    Mentioned in the bibliography of Victor Schoelcher's *Life of Handel*, ix.
    Not located.

1668 _____

Mann, A. H. "Catalogue of the Barrett-Lennard Collection." Ms., Keeper's Room, Fitzwilliam Museum, according to Burrows (**1670**).

1669 ─────────

Rockstro, William Smythe. *The Life of George Frederick Handel.* London: Macmillan, 1883. xv, 451 p.

> Items in Lennard's collection identified ("Catalogue of Handel's works"), pp. 432-39.

1670 ─────────

Burrows, Donald. "The Barret Lennard Collection." In *Handel Collections and Their History,* ed. Terence Best, 108-35. Oxford: Clarendon Press, 1993.

> 67 Handel manuscripts now at GB-Cfm. Previously owned by Thomas Greatorex and sold in the sale of his library April 1832. Bought by Dr. John Ireland, went to John Leman Brownsmith, then bought by Lennard. Ultimately the property of A. H. Mann (**1668**).
>
> "Appendix 1: Binding styles in the . . . collection," pp. 128-33.
> "Appendix 2: Serial numbers and evidence of provenance," pp. 134-35.
> "Appendix 3: Other manuscripts of Handel's works from Lennard's library," p. 136.

1671   Lenshoek, C P

NIJHOFF, MARTINUS & J. L. BEIJERS, AUCTIONEER, DEN HAAG
Catalogue de la bibliothèque de feu . . . Dont la vente . . . 21 [i.e. 28] *janvier 1884 et jours suivants. . . .* La Haye: M. Nijhoff [etc.], 1884. 3, 171 p.   [US-Wc, NL-DHgm]

> Not examined.

1672   Leroi, Pierre

VIDAL-MÉGRET, J. (EXP.); M. RHEINS, R. LAURIN, P. RHEIMS (C.P.)
Bibliothèque musicale de Pierre Leroi . . . vente . . . 15 octobre 1965. Paris, 1965. 4 unnumbered pages.

> Not located; cited from *IBAK* (1966/67).

Leslie, Henry, Choir. *See under* **"A Gentleman"** (anonymous sale of 3 April 1882) *and also under* **Mapleson, James** (sale of 28 May 1888)

Leslie, Serge. *See under* **Niles, Doris**

1673   Letts, Charles

PUTTICK & SIMPSON, AUCTIONEER, LONDON   CAT. NO. 4605
Catalogue of Books, Comprising the Musical Library of the Late . . . Antiquarian Music, Works and Treatises on Music . . . Collection of Autograph Letters and Manuscripts, Including Original Scores of Beethoven and Mozart . . . Sold . . . January 25th, and Following Day. [London], 1912. 48 p. 684 lots. Music, lots 301-684. ALS, lots 624-84.   [GB-Lbl]

1674   Levy, Lester Stern, 1896-1989

Levy, Lester. *Picture the Songs: Lithographs from the Sheet Music of Nineteenth-Century America.* Baltimore: Johns Hopkins University Press, 1976. x, 213 p.   [g.a.]

1675 ─────────

"Some Pre-1801 Imprints in the . . . Collection of American Sheet Music: A Thematic Catalogue and Subject Index."

> Typescript, 264 entries at US-BApi. **Brook,** no. 731.

1676 _____

Milton S. Eisenhower Library
Guide to the Lester S. Levy Collection of Sheet Music. Baltimore: Library, Johns Hopkins University, 1984. viii, 40 p., illus. [US-Wc, -BAue, -NBu]

1677 _____

Literature
Milton S. Eisenhower Library
"Recollections of a Sheet Music Collector." *Notes* 32 (1976): 491-502. illus. [g.a.]

> *See* additional literature in D. W. Krummel's *Bibliographical Handbook of American Music* (University of Illinois Press, 1987).

Liano, Chevalier de. *See* **Sanafe, Comte de**

1678 Libau, J F
Straeten, Edmond vander. "Liste de musique d'église appartenant a J, -F. Libau, Prêtre de Sainte-Gudule; Achetée." In his *Musique aux Pays-Bas*, 1:85-90. Bruxelles: Muquardt [etc.], 1867-88. Reprint, New York: Dover, 1969. [g.a.]

1679 Libri, Guillaume [i.e., **Guglielmo**]
Vincent Tillaird, auctioneer, Paris
Catalogue d'une collection extraordinaire de livres, principalement sur les sciences mathématiques, la musique, littérature italienne, etc. provenant de la bibliothèque de M. Libri, dont le vente aura lieu à Paris . . . 14. October, 1858 et jours suivants. . . . Paris: V. Tillard, 1858. xii, 396 p. 5608 lots. Music, *inter alia.* [US-NYp, -NYgr]

1680 _____

S. Leigh Sotheby & John Wilkinson, auctioneer, London
Catalogue of the Reserves and Most Valuable Collection of the Libri Collection, Containing One of the Most Extraordinary Assemblage of Ancient Manuscripts and Printed Books . . . Sold . . . the 25th of July, 1862, and Three Following Days. [London, 1862.] 185 p. 713 lots. Music, lots 370-407. [Film at CRL]

1681 Liebeskind, Josef, 1860-1916
Karl Ernst Henrici, firm, Berlin   Cat. no. 122
Musiker-Autographen, Sammlung Josef Liebeskind; Besichtigung: Mittwoch 28. September 1927 . . . Versteigerung . . . 29. September 1927. . . . Berlin: K. E. Henrici, 1927. 11 p. 67 lots. [US-Wc, NL-Avb, compiler]

> **Folter**, no. 222.
> → *See also under* **Jähns, F. W.** (sale of 15 December 1927)

1682 _____

Literature
Unger, Max. "Josef Liebeskinds Musikbibliothek [Schweizerische Landesbibliothek]." *Schweizerische Musikzeitung* 76 (1936): 521-25. [g.a.]

1683 Liebmann, Otto
J. A. Stargardt, firm, Marburg   Cat. no. 508
Autographen und Kunstblätter. Nachlass . . . und anderer Besitz. Auktion am 5. Mai 1953. Marburg, 1953. 68 p. 216 lots. [US-NYgr]

1684   Liechtenstein-Kastelkorn, Karl, Prince Bishop of Olomouc, 1624-95
[Seventeenth-century music from Kroměříž, Czechoslovakia: A catalog of the Liechtenstein music collection.]

> Collection now at CS-KRa. Microfilm copy of the catalog at US-SY. **Albrecht** says a new catalog is in preparation by Donald L. Smithers.

Lifar, Serge.   *See under* **Kochno, Boris** (sale in 1972)

1685   Liliencron, Rochus Wilhelm Traugott, 1820-1912; **Albert Fuchs; August Grüters**
LEO LIEPMANNSSOHN, FIRM, BERLIN   CAT. NO. 181
Musiktheorie. Musikaesthetik und -Philosophie, Musik-Paedagogik, Instrumentation, Musik-Lexika, . . . z. T. aus den Bibliotheken . . . Rochus von Liliencron [et al.]. Berlin [n.d., 1913?]. 146 p. 2003 items.   [US-Wc, NL-Avb, -DHgm]

> **Folter**, no. 181, and *ZiMG* 14 (1912/13): 34. Both say 2093 lots.

1686   Linden, Albert van der, 1913-77
HERMAN BARON, FIRM, LONDON   CAT. NO. 114
Catalogue . . . Musical Literature, Including Books from the Library of. . . . London: H. Baron, [1978]. 44 p. 1076 lots.   [compiler]

"Lindesiana, Bibliotheca."   *See* **Crawford, Alexander William Ludwig**

1687   Lindner, Ernst Otto Timotheus, 1820-67
LEO LIEPMANNSSOHN, FIRM, BERLIN   CAT. NO. 15
Verzeichniss der von Dr. . . . hinterlassenen musikalischen Bibliothek, nebst Sammlung älterer und neuerer Musikalien. [Berlin], 1879. 98 p. No lot nos., ca. 2000 lots.   [US-NYp, -Wc]

> **Folter**, no. 223.

1688   Lindsen, J F A ; et al.
J. L. BEIJERS, AUCTIONEER, UTRECHT
Catalogus der Bibliotheken van wijlen de . . . Heeren Dr. H. J. Polak [and 9 others] . . . *en de muziek-bibliothekeek van den Wel Ed. Heer J. F. A. Lindsen. Verkoping 9-18 November 1908.* Utrecht, 1908. 186 p. 3975 + lots. Music, lots 2720-3130.   [NL-Avb]

> Lot 3130 is a collection of ca. 500 portraits of musicians.

1689   Linley, Rev. Osias Thurston; Rev. George King; Benjamin Blake (all deceased)
MR. WATSON, AUCTIONEER, LONDON
Catalogue of the Valuable Musical Library of. . . . An Extremely Curious Collection of Manuscripts, Some in the Handwriting of Haydn . . . An Assemblage of . . . Music . . . As Has Not Appeared Before the Public for Many Years, Together with Musical Instruments . . . Sold . . . the 14th of June, 1831, and Three Following Days. . . . [London], 1831. 14, 30 p. 266, 530 lots. Music, lots 1-111, 117-252. Mss., lots 195-213.   [US-NYp]

1690   Liszt, Franz, 1811-86
Liszt Ferenc hagyatéka a Budapesti zeneműveszéti föiskolán. I. Könyvek. Franz Liszt's Estate at the Budapest Academy of Music. I. Books. Ed. and comp. on the Basis of Mária Prahács Uncompleted Work by Eckhardt Mária. Acta Academiae artis musicae de Francisco Liszt Nominatae, 1. Budapest: The Academy, 1986-. Vol. 1, 270 lots.   [g.a.]

1691 _____

LITERATURE

Gábry, György. "Franz Liszt-Reliquien in National-Museum, Budapest." *Studia musicologia Academiae scientiarum hungarica* 17 (1975): 408-23, with plates. [g.a.]

1692 _____

["Aus Liszt's Nachlass. . . . "] A note in *ZfI* 7 (1886/87): 320, about its transfer to the Vienna Historisches Museum.

1693 Littleton, Alfred Henry, 1845-1914

Catalogue of One Hundred Works Illustrating the History of Music Printing from the Fifteenth to the End of the Seventeenth Century, in the Library of. . . . London: Novello and Co., 1911. 38 p., illus. no lot nos. [US-Wc, -NH, -Bp, -AA]

> Davies says early music treatises are now at GB-Lu, sold in the Sotheby sale noted in cross-reference below. For more about the library see D. W. Krummel's article "An Edwardian Gentlemen's Music Exhibition," *Notes* 32 (1976): 711-18.

1694 _____

Pulver, Jeffrey. "Illustrations of the History of Music Printing in the Library of. . . ." *MT* 55 (1914): 650-51; 56 (1915): 21-22, 84-86. [g.a.]

> → *See also under* **Finch**, **Charles Wightwick** (sale, 13-16 May 1918) and **Cummings**, **W. H.** (sale, October 1919)

1695 Littleton, Edward

"[Catalog of the] Littleton Collection. Purchased by Private Treaty from Lord Hatherton of Teddesley Park, Staffordshire, with Bookplate of His Ancestor, Sir Edward Littleton, Bt. . . ." [N.p.: n.d., ca. 193-?] Typescript, 27 leaves. Mss., leaves 1-9. [US-Wc]

Liverpool Festival Choral Society.   *See under* **Taylor, John Bianchi** (sale of 23 January 1882)

1696 Livius, Barhan J

MR. FLETCHER, AUCTIONEER, LONDON

Catalogue of a Portion of the Musical Library of . . . Comprising Numerous Italian, German, and Other Manuscript Full Scores, Unpublished, Collected on the Continent During the Last Twenty Years, with the Assistance of Signors Rossini and Saliva; Also Valuable Full Scores of Italian [etc.] *Operas, Many of Which Are Presentation Copies with the Autographs of the Composers . . . Theoretic* [sic] *Works, &c., &c. . . . Sold . . . February 5th, 1845. . . .* 16 p. 267 leaves, Music, lots 1-155. [GB-Ob]

1697 Llewellyn, Henry

MR. WATSON, AUCTIONEER, LONDON

Catalogue of a Valuable Collection of Modern Vocal & Instrumental Music, Including the Library of the Late . . . Sold . . . 13th of July, 1831, and Friday the 15th. . . . [London, 1831.] 7, 7, p. 253, 50 lots. Music, lots 1-99, 125-230. [US-NYp]

1698   Lobkowitz, Prince Joseph Franz (Maximilian), 1772-1816
"Musicalia der Fürstlich Lobkowitzschen Bibliothek in Raudnitz." In Paul Nettl, *Beiträge zur böhmischen und mährischen Musikgeschichte,* 60-70. Brünn: R. M. Rohrer, 1927.
[US-Wc]

>   Mss. pp. 65-70. Collection now at CS-Pnm.

1699 _____
>   *LITERATURE*
>   Nettl, Paul. "Excerpta aus der Raudnitzer Textbücher-Sammlung." *Studien zur Musikwissenschaft* 7 (1920): 143-44.   [g.a.]

1700   Lobkowitz, Prince Joseph Franz (Maximilian); Tomislav Volek
Fojtíková, Jana. "Die Beethoveniana der Lobkowitz-Musiksammlung und ihre Kopisten." In *Beethoven und Böhmen: Beiträge zur Biographie . . . ,* 219-58. Bonn: Beethoveniana, 1988.
[g.a.]

1701   Locatelli, Pietro Antonio, 1695-1764
THEODORUS CRAJENSCHOT, AUCTIONEER, AMSTERDAM
Catalogus van een uitmuntende Verzameling van de raarste en zeidzaamste italiansche en eenige fransche boeken . . . manuscripten . . . Portraiten . . . Muziekwerken . . . nagelaten door . . . Verkogt . . . den 21 august en volgende dagen/1765. . . . Amsterdam, 1765. 53 p. Music, 39-45 (115 lots).   [NL-Au]

>   Reprinted in Albert Dunning, *Pietro G. Locatelli,* 141-95. Buren: F. Knuf, 1981.

1702   Locke, Robinson
LITERATURE
"Robinson Locke's Wonderful Collection of Clippings in the Toledo-Blade Office [About Musical and Dramatic Artists]." *Musical America* 13, no. 1 (1910): 21.
>   Now housed at US-NYp.

1703   Locker-Lampson, Frederick, 1821-95
ROWFANT LIBRARY
The Locker Library: A Catalogue of the Printed Books, Manuscripts Autograph Letters, Drawings and Pictures Collected by. . . . London: Locker-Lampson, 1886. xii, 232 p., illus.
[US-Wc]

>   Some autographs now at US-NYp.

1704 _____
ROWFANT LIBRARY
[Another ed.]: *An Appendix to the Rowfant Library. A Catalogue. . . .* London: Quaritch, 1886. xvi, 181 p., illus.   [US-NYp, -NH, -MSu]

1705 _____
ROWFANT LIBRARY
The Rowfant Library . . . Collected Since the Printing of the First Catalogue in 1886. . . . London: Chiswick Press, 1900. xvi, 181 p., illus. [cf. preceding!]   [US-NYcu]

Compiled by Godfrey Locker-Lampson; preface by Augustine Birrell. Half-title: *An Appendix to the Catalogue of Mr. Locker-Lampson.*

1706 _____

ROWFANT LIBRARY
The Rowfant Books: A Selection of One Hundred Titles from the Collection of. . . . New York: Dodd, Mead, [1906]. 87 p.

1707 Lockwood, Normand, b. 1906

LITERATURE
Norton, Kay. "The Normand Lockwood Archive. . . . " *American Music Research Center Journal* 1 (1991): 73-74.   [g.a.]

Collection at US-BO.

Löser, Charles.   *See* **Lane, Capt. J. J.** (sale, 19 December 1960)

1708 Löwenstein-Wertheim-Freudenberg, Hubertus, Graf zu, b. 1906
Schmid, Ernst Fritz. *Musik am Hofe der Fürsten von . . . (1720-50).* Mainfränkischer Hefte, 16. Würzburg: Freunde Mainfränkischer Kunst und Geschichte, 1953. 69 p., illus.
[US-BE, -I]

Collection now at D-WERl.

1709 Löwis, August von; Karl Vollmöller
OTTO HARRASSOWITZ, FIRM, LEIPZIG   BÜCHER-CAT. NO. 438
Volkskunde und Kulturgeschichte. Musik-theater, enthaltend u. a. die Bibliothek . . . und Teile der Bibliothek [Vollmöller]. . . . Leipzig, 1932. 134 p. 2880 lots. Music, lots 2541-804.
[NL-DHgm]

Folter 2, no. 763.

1710 Lombardi, Vincenzo (conductor)
ASTA LIBRARIA ANTIQUARIA (DIR. DA ULISSE FRANCHI NEI GIORNI)   CAT. NO. 55
. . . Vendite all' Auzione pubblica della Libreria appartenuta al defunto Prof. . . . Periodico mensile. Anno XII, 1° Dicembre 1914. Firenze, 1914. 104 p. 1050 lots (more items).
[compiler]

London. Guildhall School of Music.   *See* **Hopkinson, Cecil**

1711 London, Covent Garden Theater
Catalogue of All the Music [in score] *of the . . . Operas and Plays Produced at the Theater Royal . . . from 1809 to . . . 1846 . . . Will Be Sold . . . July 3, 4, 1856.* [London, 1845]. 18 p.
[US-NYp]

1712 Longe, Francis, 1748-1812
"List of Librettos Contained in the Longe Collection, Vol. 1-323." 27 p. 533 items.
Ms. copy of the list, in the hand of O. G. T. Sonneck, as well as the collection, at US-Wc.

1713 Lonsdale, Christopher
Sotheby, Wilkinson & Hodge
Catalogue of the Curious, Valuable and Interesting Collection of . . . Comprising . . . Also Autograph Letters and Correspondence . . . etc. . . . Sold . . . 28th of March, 1878. [London], 1878. 45 p. 993 lots. Music, lots 1-524.   [US-CHua; compiler]
> Lots 14-59, "Scarce works of Sir H. R. Bishop"; lots 799-890 (magnificent!), Beethoven and Haydn. **King**, p. 63.

1714 Lonsdale, R
Lonsdale, Christopher. *A Catalogue of Unique, Rare and Interesting Books, Autographs and Music . . . Great Exhibition, Anno Domini MDCCCLXII.* London, 1862. 20 p. 1752 lots.
[US-NYp]

Lopez De Liz. *See* **Du Liz, Lopez**

1715 Lorenz, Edward Simon
"Lorenz Collection Donated." *Hymn* 28 (1977): 25.   [g.a.]
> Donated to US-BIRu—a hymnal library of over 2176 volumes.

Lothar, Clemens, Reichsführer von Fürstenberg. *See under* **Fürstenberg**

Love, R   H   . *See* **Vaughan, W. A.**

1716 Lozzi, Carlo
Leo Samuel Olschki, firm, Florence
Una visita alla collezione del Com. C. Lozzi di autografi e documenti reguardante la musica e il teatro in tutto loro appartenenze e ogni sorta di spettacolo. . . . [Firenze, 1902?] 31 p.
[GB-Lbl (Hirsch)]
> Extract from *Bibliofilia* 3 (1902): 231-59. With a list of the autographs and reproductions.   [GB-Lbl]

1717 Lubomirska, Izabella, 1736-1816
Biegánski, Krzysztof. *Biblioteca muzyczna Zamku w Láncucie: Katalog.* [Kraków: PWM, 1968]. 430 p. 2367 items.   [US-BUu]
> Collection begun in 1780, enlarged by Potocki family. Now at PL-LA.

1718 [Lucas, Charles, 1808-69; **Alfred Whittingham]**
Puttick & Simpson, auctioneer, London   Cat. no. 834
Catalogue of an Extensive and Interesting Library of Music, Including the Collection of a Professor [Lucas] *. . . Rare and Curious Antiquarian Works . . . Early English Madrigals . . . Musical Instruments . . . Sold . . . August 22nd, and Two Following Days.* [London], 1864. 42 p. 1042 lots. Music, lots 1-883.

1719 Lucas, Charles; W. H. Baker
Puttick & Simpson, auctioneer, London   Cat. no. 1137
Catalogue of a Collection of Miscellaneous Music from Several Private Libraries, Including Lucas' and Baker's . . . Also Musical Instruments . . . Sold . . . June 30, 1869, and the Following Day. . . . [London], 1869. 33 p. 987 lots. Music, lots.   [GB-Lbl, US-NYp]

1720   **Lucchesi-Palli, Eduardo, Count**

LITERATURE

"Contratto stipulato dal conte Eduardo Lucchesi-Palli de' principi di Campofranco e il Ministero della Pubblica Istruzione per la conazione della sua biblioteca e archivio musicale da conservarsi in una sala della Biblioteca Nazionale di Napoli." *Bolletino ufficiale dell' istruzione* 14 (1888): 658-61.

1721   _____

Giacomo, Salvatore di. "La biblioteca Lucchesi-Palli." *Emporium: Rivista mensile illustrata d'arte e di cultura* 119 (1913): 193-203.

> Not examined. Cited from **Benton 3**:215, no. 212.

1722   _____

Guerrieri, G. "La mostra verdiana alla Nazionale." *Napoli: rivista municipale* (July/August 1952).

> Not located. Cited from **Benton 3**:215, no.212.

1723   _____

[Nobile, E.]. "Inediti verdiana nella Biblioteca Lucchesi-Palli." *Accademie e biblioteche d'Italia* 19 (1951): 111-17.

> Not examined.

1724   **Ludwig, Friedrich,** 1872-1930

"Katalog der musikwissenschaftliche Bibliothek von F. Ludwig, Göttingen." [Göttingen, ca. 1939.] 222 folios. Typescript.   [GB-Lbl (Hirsch)]

1725   **Ludwig V, Kurfürsten,** 1478-1544

"Aller meine gnedigen Herrn Gesang inventirt und Beschriben Anno XLIIII."

> Ms., Heidelberg, Univ.-Bibl., Pal.Germ.318. Discussed in Fritz Stein's *Geschichte des Musikwesens in Heidelberg*, 45-50. Heidelberg: Koester, 1921.

Lüstner, Louis.   *See under* **Stockhausen, Julius** (Liepmannssohn catalog no. 196, 1916?)

1726   **Lumley, John, Baron,** 1534?-1609

Jayne, Sears, and Francis Johnson. *The Lumley Library: The Catalog of 1609*. London: British Museum, 1956. xii, 371 p., illus.   [g.a.]

> Music listed, pp. 284-86. The catalog of 1609 is a copy of one made in 1596 which no longer exists. See Warren article (**1729**).

1727   _____

Milsom, John. "The Nonesuch Music Library." In *Sundry Sorts of Music Books . . . Essays Presented to O. W. Neighbour*, 146-82. London: British Library, 1993.

> "The Nonesuch music library: a revised catalog," pp. 151-71. Appendix A: "A chronological list of printed editions in the library," pp. 177-78. Appendix B: "A Burney source-book . . . and its Nonesuch sources," pp. 178-79.

1728 _____

LITERATURE

Cust, Lionel. "The Lumley Inventories." *Walpole Society* 6 (1917-18): 21-29.   [g.a.]

1729 _____

Warren, Charles W. "Music at Nonesuch." *MO* 54 (1968): 47-57.   [g.a.]

> Describes musical life at Nonesuch under Fitzalan, 12th Earl of Arundel and his inheritor, Lord Lumley. Much of the music itself has been edited and published in Judith Blezzard, *The Tudor Church Music of the Lumley Books,* Recent Researches in the Music of the Renaissance, 65 (Madison, Wisc.: A-R Editions, 1985).   [g.a.]

1730 Lumpkin, Ben Gray

Culwell, Gene Allen. "The English Language Songs in the . . . Lumpkin Collection of Colorado Folklore." 2 vols. Thesis, University of Colorado, 1976.   [US-BUu]

> Ca. 1500 folksongs.

1731 Lunn, H   C

PUTTICK & SIMPSON, AUCTIONEER, LONDON   CAT. NO. 3575

Catalogue of Musical Instruments . . . and the Library of Music of the Late H. C. Lunn . . . Sold November 26th, and Following Day. . . . [London], 1901. 24 p. 537 lots. Music, 438-537.

1732 Lunsford, Bascom Lamar

Beard, Anne Winsmore. "The Personal Folksong Collection of. . . . " 2 vols. Thesis, Miami University (Ohio), 1959. x, 741 p.   [Copy at US-Wc]

1733 Lutgendorff, ?

LEO LIEPMANNSSOHN, FIRM, BERLIN   CAT. NO. 184

Autographen . . . Bildende Künstler . . . Musiker . . . Stammbücher. . . . Berlin, 1913. 102 p. Music, lots 516-70.   [US-Wc]

1734 Lutgendorff, ?; L. Leiburg

LIPSIUS & TEICHER, FIRM, KIEL   CAT. NO. 153

[Catalog of L's collection.] Kiel, 1938. 1145 lots.   [NL-Avb]

Lynn Philharmonic Society.   *See under* **Stanford, John Frederick**

Lys, Edith de.   *See* **Ely, Edith**

1735 Maas [probably **Johann Gebhard Ehrenreich**, 1766-1823]**, Prof.**

> *. . . Büchern aus allen wissenschaftlichen Fächern, nebst Musikalien aller Art . . . versteigert . . . den 10. Okt. 1824.* 2 vols. Halle, 1824. (218, 37 p.) Music, 1:65-75.

> > Not located; cited by Naue in *Cäcilia: Intelligenz-Blatt* (Okto, 1824).

1736 MacBean, William Munro, 1852-1924

UNIVERSITY OF ABERDEEN, LIBRARY

Allardyce, Mabel D., comp. *MacBean Collection: A Catalogue of Books, Pamphlets, Broadsides, Portraits, etc. . . . in the Stuart and Jacobite Collection.* Aberdeen University

Studies, 126. Aberdeen: University Press, 1949. xxvi, 307 p., illus.   [US-I, -NYcu, -BE]

Includes Stuart and Jacobite songs, according to **Benton 2**:163, no. 1.

Mac Clellan, P. *See under* **Rockwood, Mrs. A.** (sale, 20 November 1978)

McConathy, Osbourne. *See under* **Mason, Luther Whiting**

1737   **McCutchan, Robert Guy,** 1877-1958

LITERATURE

Lindsey, Charles Edward. "An Important Tunebook Collection in California." *Notes* 29 (1973): 671-74.   [g.a.]

> Collection of hymnology given to Claremont College in 1957. **Albrecht** says 4450 items.

1738   **Mackinlay, Thomas** (publisher)

A Catalogue of Original Letters and Manuscripts, in the Autograph of Distinguished Musicians, Composers, Performers, and Vocalists. With Portraits. Collected by. . . . [N.p.]: for private circulation, 1846. 20 p. ca. 350 items.   [GB-Lbl]

> **King**, p. 44: "only thing of its kind published in the 19th century"; not a sales catalog. Library sold in 1866 (**1739**).

1739   —————

PUTTICK & SIMPSON, AUCTIONEER, LONDON   CAT. NO. 936

Catalogue of the Interesting and Valuable Library of the Late . . . A Good Selection of Works in the Standard Literature . . . Illustrated Books . . . Engraved Title Pages, Also . . . the Musical and Dramatic Autographs . . . Sold . . . July 12th, 1866. [London], 1866. 23 p. 439 lots.

[GB-Lbl]

> Autographs, chiefly music, lots 276-357.

1740   **Mackworth, Herbert, Sir,** 1737-91

Boyd, Malcolm. "Music Manuscripts in the Mackworth Collection at Cardiff." *M&L* 54, no. 2 (1973): 133-141.   [g.a.]

> Collection built by Mackworth at Gnoll Castle, 1766-90, later acquired by Bonner Morgan, still later to GB-CDp.

1741   **Macready, William Charles,** 1793-1873

CHRISTIE, MANSON & WOODS, AUCTIONEER, LONDON

Catalogue of the Library of . . . , Esq., Deceased . . . Also, the Collection of Bronzes [etc.] *. . . Sold . . . July 8, 1873, and Following Day. . . .* [London: printed by W. Clowes and Sons, 1873.] 30 p. 399 entries.   [US-Wc, -Bp]

> Principally about drama.

1742   **Madox, Erasmus**

S. LEIGH SOTHEBY & CO., AUCTIONEER, LONDON

Catalogue of the Select Library . . . of the Late . . . Together with an Admirable Selection of the Works of the Best Musical Composers . . . Sold . . . 14th of January, 1845, and Three Following Days. [London, 1845.] 64 p. 1307 lots. Music, lots 916-19.   [Film at CRL]

1743   **Maglione, Benedetto**
HUARD ET GUILLEMIN PAUL, AUCTIONEER, PARIS
Catalogue de la bibliothèque de feu M. . . . de Naples. . . . 2 vols. Paris: E. Paul, L. Huard et Guillemin, 1894. 2768 entries. Music, lots 182-225.   [US-NYp, -Bp, -Pc, -NYcu, -I]
    Premier part sold 22-27 January 1894.

1744   _____
LUIGI LUBRANO, AUCTIONEER, ROME
Libri di arte e musica, proveninenti dalla biblioteca di un noto bibliofilo napoletano . . . Vendita all'asta pubblica in Roma dal 6 all' 11 giugno 1935. . . . [Rome, 1935.] 106 p. 831 lots. Musica e teatro, lots 1-209.   [NL-Avb]

1745   **Magnis, Franz Anton, Count,** 1771-1848
LITERATURE
Klimesová, Eva. [A report on the music collection in the Count's chapel in Stráznice.] *OpusM* 1 (1969): 178-79.
    Not examined; cited from *RILM*.

1746   **Maine, Basil, Rev.,** 1894-1972
DAVID FERROW, FIRM
Catalogue of . . . Books on Music. . . . Great Yarmouth: Norfolk, 1984.
    Not examined; cited from *ACMI*.

1747   **Major, Emil, Dr.;** et al.
L'ART ANCIEN/HAUS DER BÜCHER, FIRMS, ZÜRICH/BASEL   VERST. CAT. NO. 11
. . . Musik und Musikbücher - Autographen von Musikern, Dichtern und Theaterleuten. Märchen und Sagen . . . [etc.]. *Aus dem Besitz des verstorbenen . . . Dr. Emil Major, eines Musikschriftstellers und einem Kunstfreundes . . . Versteigert . . . 7. und 8. Mai 1948. . . .* Zürich, 1948. 88 p. 1120 + lots. Music, lots 1-164.   [US-NYgr]
    Autographs, including music, lots 165-262.

1748   **Major, Ervin**
LITERATURE
Szepesi, Zsuzsanna. "Bártok-levelek az MTA Zenetudományi Intézet könyvtárának Major-gyüjteményeben." *Zenetudományi dolgozatok* (1988), 323-33.
    Not examined; cited from *RILM*.

1749   **Major, Joseph**
MR. SOUTHGATE, AUCTIONEER, LONDON
Catalogue of a Small Library of Books and Books of Prints . . . Drawings . . . Engravings . . . To Which Are Added, A Valuable Collection of Printed Music, by Handel, Haydn, Wesley [et al.] *. . . Various Treatises on Music . . . Sold . . . February 6th, 1829, and Following Day. . . .* [London], 1829. 15 p. 300 lots. Music, lots 80-176.   [GB-Lbl]

1750   **Malchair, John Baptist,** 1727-1812; **[Samuel] Harrison**
MR. WHITE, AUCTIONEER, LONDON
A Catalogue of a Valuable and Extensive Library of Music, Comprising the Several Collections of . . . and Other Eminent Professors . . . Works of All the Great Masters . . . Scarce Editions . . . [Also Musical Instruments, etc.] *. . . Sold . . . the 1st of March, 1814, and Three Following Days. . . .* London, 1814.   [GB-Lbl]

1751   [Maldeghem, Robert Julien, van, 1810-93]
Camille Vijt, firm, Ghent
Catalogue d'une belle et riche bibliothèque musicale . . . dont la vente aura lieu le 18 juin 1894. Gand: Vijt, 1894. 28 p. 290 lots.   [NL-DHgm (priced)]

1752 _____
Wallon, Simone. "Les Acquisitions de la bibliothèque du Conservatoire de Paris à la vente de la collection de Van Maldeghem." *Revue belge de musicologie* 9 (1955): 36-46.   [g.a]
With a list of items Weckerlin purchased for the Conservatoire (F-Pc), 27 lots.

1753   Malherbe, Charles Théodore, 1853-1911
"Autographiana: Albums musicaux et feuilles d'albums." *Revue internationale de musique* 1 (1898): 23-?
Not examined; cited from **Schaal** (1966), p. 125.

1754 _____
Literature
Lebeau, Elizabeth. "Un Mécène de la musique: Charles Malherbe, 1853-1911." In *Humanisme actif: Melanges d'art et de littérature offerts à Julien Cain*, 91-99. Paris: Hermann, 1968.
According to **Albrecht**, a bequest to F-Pc.

Malmesbury, Earls of.   *See* **Legh, Elizabeth,** 1695-1734

1755   Mandell, Eric, b.1902; **Arno Nadel,** 1878-1943; **Eduard Birnbaum,** 1855-1920
Literature
Mandell, Eric. "A Collector's Random Notes on the Bibliography of Jewish Music." *Fontes* 10 (1963): 34-39.   [g.a.]

1756 _____
Heskes, Irene. "A Duty of Preservation and Continuity: Collectors and Collections of Jewish Music in America." *Notes* 40 (1983): 263-70.   [g.a.]
Mandell collection is at Gratz College in Philadelphia (US-PHgc).

1757   Mann, Arthur Henry, 1850-1929
According to **King**, pp. 84-85, in 1930, King's College, Cambridge, received 590 volumes from Mann's library comprising Handel and Handeliana (fine libretti), 18th-century songbooks, choice early keyboard music. Mann bought some of those at sales of James Hook's properties by Fletcher (1842) and by Puttick & Simpson (1874) (**1362**). His collection of hymn books and psalm books went to Church House, Westminster. Mann's family presented ten volumes of autographs by James Hook (128 works) to GB-Cu. His Crotch collection and 54 portfolios of Ms. notes relating to East Anglian musicians were given to the Norwich Public Library. The residue was auctioned (**1760**).

1758 _____

Stephen, G. A. "Dr. Arthur Henry Mann: Memoir and Catalogue of His Manuscripts and Books." *Norwich Public Libraries Reader's Guide* 10, no. 2 (April/June 1930).

Not examined; cited from **King**, p. 84.

1759 _____

"The Crotch Collection, Presented by Bayford Stone, Esqre." *Norwich Public Libraries Reader's Guide* 12, no. 16 (October/December 1941).

Also cited from **King**; see preceding citation.

1760 _____

SOTHEBY & CO., AUCTIONEER, LONDON
Catalogue of Printed Books with a Few Autograph Letters and Manuscripts Comprising the Property of the Late Louis Napoleon Parker . . . Dr. A. H. Mann [and] *Others . . . Sold . . . the 25th of June, and Following Day. . . .* [London], 1945. 46 p. 617 lots.   [Film at CRL]

Lot 526, 400 detached numbers from ballets "in 2 suitcases." Lot 426, from the Parker Collection, "about 200 books and pamphlets," relating to Wagner.

1761   [Mann, J   Younie]

SOTHEBY & CO., AUCTIONEER, LONDON
Catalogue of Valuable Printed Books, Autograph Letters and Music, and Historical Documents . . . the Property of . . . J. C. Dundas . . . James Ford Bell [and others]. *Autograph Music of Beethoven, Haydn, Mendelssohn and J.-J. Rousseau, and the Autograph Manuscript of Weber's 'Oberon' . . . Sold . . . the 15th December, 1958 and the Following Day. . . .* [London], 1958. 104 p. 560 lots, illus.   [Film at CRL]

Music Mss. and ALS, lots 404-24, mostly the property of J. Younie Mann.

1762   Manning, Westley W

SOTHEBY & CO., AUCTIONEER, LONDON
Catalogue of Autograph Letters, Historical Documents and Holograph Music. First Portion: A-L . . . Sold . . . 11th of October, 1954 and Following Day. [London, 1954.] 52 p. 277 lots, illus.
[Film at CRL, US-BUu]

Excellent collection described by **King**, p. 78, included holographs of, e.g., Bach (lot 14); Beethoven (26-29); and an unrecorded song by Debussy in holograph, etc.

1763 _____

SOTHEBY & CO., AUCTIONEER, LONDON
Catalogue of Autograph Letters, Historical Documents and Holograph Music, the Property of . . . The Second Portion: M-Z, Including . . . Holograph Music of Scarlatti, Mozart, Schubert, Weber, Mendelssohn, Schumann and Hugo Wolf, etc. . . . Sold . . . the 24th January, 1955 and Following Day. . . . [London], 1955. 46 p. lots 278-502.   [Film at CRL]

Musicians' ALS and Mss., lots 278-502. Mozart sketches and holographs, lots 323-27. Holograph sketches for Schumann's *Frauenliebe*.

1764   Mansfeldt, Hugo

LITERATURE
"Hugo Mansfeldt Collection at the University of California, Berkeley Music Library." *Inter-American Music Review* 7 (1986): 85-87.   [g.a.]

1765   Manskopf, Friedrich Nicolas, 1869-1928

Very, Sarah C. "The Historical Museum of Mr. Manskopf." *Messenger* 4 (1903): 288-91.   [g.a.]

> The collection comprised 10,000 items—books and scores, including autographs. Now at D-F.

1766   _____

> *LITERATURE*
> Kersting, Ann Barbara. ". . . 3. Sammlung Freidrich Nicolas Manskopf . . . ca. 100.00 Stücke umfassende Sammlung von Konzertund Theaterprogrammen. . . . " *Forum Musikbibliothek* 2 (1994): 113-14.   [g.a.]

> A brief note about the collection at D-F.

1767   Mapleson, James Henry, 1830-1901

PUTTICK & SIMPSON, AUCTIONEER, LONDON   CAT. NO. 2561
Catalogue of the Very Extensive Ladies' and Gentlemens' Theatrical Wardrobe, Properties, Armour and Scenery, As Used at Her Majesty's Theatre, Haymarket, for the Operas of . . . Valuable, Extensive and Complete Library of Music, Consisting of Scores of the Various Operas, and Parts . . . Late the Property of . . . Sold . . . March the 14th, 1888, and Two Following Days. [London], 1888. 29 p. 654 lots.   [GB-Lbl]

> Mostly costumes.

1768   Mapleson, James Henry; Henry Leslie's Choir

PUTTICK & SIMPSON, AUCTIONEER, LONDON   CAT. NO. 2580
Catalogue of an Extensive and Valuable Collection of Music, Comprising the Library of Part Music Belonging to Mr. Henry Leslie's Choir; the Operatic Library, Late the Property of Mr. J. H. Mapleson . . . Sold . . . May the 28th, 1888. [London], 1888. 25 p. 386 lots. [GB-Lbl]

> Leslie's properties, lots 331-86; Mapleson's, 298-330. A brief note in *L&PMTR*, 15 July 1888, p. 25, remarks the purchase of the full score of *L'Africaine* with parts and a hundred chorus parts by Carl Rosa for a "perfectly ridiculous" price of £1 sterling.

1769   Mapleson, Mrs.; et al.

PUTTICK & SIMPSON, AUCTIONEER, LONDON   CAT. NO. 1994
Catalogue of a Valuable Library of Works on Musical History and Theory, the Musical Drama, etc. . . . the Extensive Collection of Full and Vocal Scores [etc.] *of the Late Mrs. Mapleson, Senior . . . Sold . . . February 21, 1881. . . .* [London], 1881. 21 p. 448 lots.   [GB-Lbl]

> Mrs. M.'s properties, lots 215-384.

Marchese of ***.   *See under* **Tessier, Andrea**

1770   Marchesi, Mathilde Graumann, 1821-1913; **Salvatore . . . Marchese della Rojata,** 1822-1908; **Blanche,** 1863-1940

CHRISTIE, MANSON & WOODS, AUCTIONEER, LONDON
The Marchesi Archive . . . Sale of Illuminated MSS., Continental and English Literature, ALS and Musical Manuscripts . . . 16 December, 1991. London, 1991. 38 p. No lotting.

[compiler]

> An extraordinary sale, including 1265 ALS. Splendid descriptions and an historical/biographical note, with illus., pp. 32-38.

1771   Margherita di Savoia, Queen
Elenco delle opere musicali donate alla Biblioteca a Regia Accademia di S. Cecilia da S. M. la Regina. Roma, 1896.

> Cited from **Benton** 3:252, no. 316, but not located, even by several librarian colleagues in Italy.

1772   Maria Anna, Electress, Consort of Maximilian III, Joseph, Elector of Bavaria, 1728-97
Schafhäutl, Karl Emil von. "Catalogo De Libri di Musica Di S.A.S.E. Maria Anna, Ellettore di Baviera. La prima colonna denota il Numero del Libro. La seconda le Arie l'Opere, Oratori, Serenata etc. La Terza gl' Autori. 1861."

> Munich, Kgl. Hof- und Staatsbibliothek, Mus. Ms. 1648. Collection at D-Mbs.

1773   _____

Haberkamp, Gertraut, and Robert Münster. *Die ehemaligen Musikhandschriftensammlungen der Königlichen Hofkapelle und der Kurfürstin Maria Anna von Bayern. Thematischer Katalog.* Kataloge Bayerischer Musiksammlungen, 9. München: Henle Verlag, 1982. xxxiv, 251 p.   [g.a.]

> "II. Die Musikaliensammlung der . . . Maria," pp. xxi-xxiii.

1774   Mario, Giovanni Matteo (Conte di Candia), 1810-83
Catalogue de la bibliothèque . . . de feu le Marquis . . . célèbre artiste de chant. Vente du 19 au 31 janvier 1903. Rome: Dario G. Rossi, 1902. 228 p. 1766 lots. illus.   [US-Wc]
> **Folter**, no. 225.

1775   _____

Antolini, Bianca Maria, and Annalisa Bini. "Johann Adolf Hasse nei manoscritti della biblioteca de S. Cecilia di Roma." *Analecta musicologica* 25 (1987): 495-511.   [g.a.]
> The Mss. once belonging to Mario.

Mark, W   H . *See* **Westbrook, W.   J**.

[Markey?], Distinguished Prof. of the Violoncello; John Christopher Smith, 1712-95; **Bernard Granville**. *See under* **Granville Family**

1776   Markgrafen zu Limpurg
HANS SCHNEIDER, FIRM, TUTZING   CAT. NO. 140
Musikalische Erstausgaben und Frühdrucke. Darunter . . . grösserer Bestände an Kammermusik aus dem Besitz des Markgrafen zu Limpurg. Tutzing: Schneider, [1969]. 56 p. 550 lots. illus.   [compiler]

1777   [Marquis of Blandford]
PUTTICK & SIMPSON, AUCTIONEER, LONDON   CAT. NO. 469
Catalogue of a Large Collection of Miscellaneous Music, Full Scores, Printed and MSS. . . . Also Musical Instruments . . . Sold . . . December 22. . . . London, 1856. 465 lots.   [GB-Lbl]

1778 **Marsh, John Fitchett,** d.1880

Puttick & Simpson, auctioneer, London   Cat. no. 1976

Catalogue of a Rare and Curious Collection of Music, Including the Valuable Library of the Late . . . Deposited by Him, by Way of Loan, in the Warrington Museum and Library [now withdrawn and offered for sale]. . . . *Original MSS., Works Bearing Interesting Autographs* [etc.] *Sold December 20, 1880.* [London], 1880. 22 p. 381 lots.   [GB-Lbl]

His art works, silver, etc., were sold in a separate auction by Sotheby's.

1779 **Marsh, Narcissus, Archbishop,** 1638-1713

Marsh's Library

Catalogue of the Manuscripts Remaining in Marsh's Library, Dublin. Dublin: printed by A. Thom and Co., [1913]. 137 p.   [US-BE, -MSu]

1780 _____

Charteris, Richard Colin. "Consort Music Manuscripts in the Marsh Library, Dublin." 2 vols. M.A. thesis, University of Canterbury, New Zealand, [1972]. 696 p.

Not examined; cited from *RILM* 6:1619. Collection given to EIR-Dm in 1713.

1781 _____

Charteris, Richard Colin. "Music Manuscripts and Books Missing from Archbishop Marsh's Library, Dublin." *M&L* 61 (1980): 310-17.   [g.a.]

Missing items determined by comparing present library with a catalog compiled by Elias Bouhéreau before 1719, added to between 1727 and 1761.

1782 _____

Charteris, Richard Colin. *A Catalogue of the Printed Books on Music, Printed Music, and Music Manuscripts in. . . .* Boethius Editions, 1. Clifden, Co. Kilkenny, Ireland: Boethius Press, 1982. xviii, 142 p.   [g.a.]

1783 _____

Literature

White, Newport John Davis, and Newport Benjamin. *An Account of Archbishop Marsh's Library, Dublin . . . With a Note on Autographs. . . .* Dublin: Hodges, Figgis & Co., 1926. 43 p.

1784 _____

Deedy, J. "An Account of Marsh's Library." *Library Review* 92 (1949): 219-.

Not examined; cited from **Benton 2**:159, no. 2.

Marshall, Dorothy Georgina Elizabeth. *See under* **Carey, Clive**

1785 **Marshall, Julian,** 1836-1903

King, pp. 56, 64-66, "one of the greatest of all British collectors." Besides music, Marshall collected printed and manuscript materials on a variety of subjects. Most of his prints and engravings were sold by Sotheby's in 1864. A collection of literature, with but a few items of music, was put up anonymously as the "library of a well-known amateur" in 1870. Some of his Handel manuscripts were purchased by Arthur J. Balfour in 1876, acquired 60 years later by GB-En. Hundreds of his other music manuscripts, including autographs of Beethoven, Haydn, Mozart, and others, plus printed books on music were purchased by the British Museum after tedious negotiations in 1880. A list of items acquired appeared in the Museum's *Catalogue of Additions to the Manuscripts*, 1881. For an engrossing essay about Marshall, his writings and collections, elements of those collections, and those tedious negotiations, see Arthur Searle's "Julian Marshall and the British Museum: Music Collecting in the Nineteenth Century," *British Library Journal* 11 (1985): 67-87. Much of the information above is based on that stellar report.

1786 _____

SOTHEBY, WILKINSON & HODGE, AUCTIONEER, LONDON
Catalogue of the Valuable Collection of Autograph Letters, Chiefly from or Relating to Eminent Musical Composers, Celebrated Singers and Actors . . . Including Holographs from . . . Bach . . . Clementi . . . Purcell . . . Rossini . . . Spontini [etc.] *. . . Sold . . . the 26th Day of June, 1884, and Following Day.* [London], 1884. 36 p. 297 lots. Music, lots 1-127.   [Film at CRL]

Documents relating to the Paris Conservatoire, a collection, lot 31. Lot 49, a remarkable scrap book of orders, payments, receipts, etc., relating to French minstrels, 14th-16th centuries.

1787 _____

SOTHEBY, WILKINSON & HODGE, AUCTIONEER, LONDON
Catalogue of the Musical Library of . . . Comprising Works of the Principal Composers, Including Many of Great Rarity . . . Sold . . . the 29th of July, 1884. [London], 1884. 76 p. 1339 lots.   [Film at CRL]

" . . . one of the finest music libraries ever sold by auction." *MT* 25 (1884): 529. William Reeves bought 496 of the total lots.

Marshall, Julian; Sir John Goss; George Benson. *See under* **Goss, John**

(Some items from the previous two sales of Marshall's library in 1884 appeared along with Goss's collections in this Puttick & Simpson 1885 sale.)

1788 _____

WILLIAM REEVES, FIRM, LONDON   CAT. NO. 17
Ancient and Modern Music, Treatises, Full Scores, Vocal Scores . . . Including a Portion of the Libraries of Julian Marshall and Hullah [including Bedford bindings]. . . . [London], 1886. 16 p.   [GB-LReeves only]

1789 _____

SOTHEBY, WILKINSON & HODGE, AUCTIONEER, LONDON
Catalogue of the Valuable and Interesting Library of . . . Original and Rare Editions of the Writings of the Early English Music-Masters . . . Sold . . . the 11th [and 12th] *Day of July, 1904.* [London], 1904. 55 p. 622 lots, of which ca. 90 are music.   [Film at CRL]

According to **Albrecht**, many items were acquired by William Hayman Cummings (**619**).

1790 Marshall, Julian; Thomas William Taphouse
ELLIS & ELVEY, FIRM, LONDON CAT. NO. 7
. . . *Part I, A-Powell, Including a Portion of Julian Marshall's Library.* . . . London, 1905. 868
lots. [US-NYgr, GB-LReeves]

The catalog was noted in *MT* 46 (1905): 802. "Strong in Arne (52 entries)."

1791 ⸻
HODGSON & CO., AUCTIONEER, LONDON
*A Catalogue of Rare and Valuable Books Comprising Fine Folio Illustrated Books . . . with
Other Properties . . . Musical Autographs and Printed Scores, from the Collection of the Late
Julian Marshall . . . Sold . . . 22 June and Following Day, 1922.* [London], 1922. 46 p.
[GB-Lbl, US-CA]

1792 ⸻
HAROLD REEVES, FIRM, LONDON CAT. NO. 60
*Music and Musical Literature . . . Original Editions of the Great Masters from the Julian
Marshall Collection.* . . . London, 1925. 40 p. No lotting. Marshall's lots, pp. 1-3.
[US-PV, -NYp, -R]

1793 Marshall-Hall, George William Lewis, 1862-1915
LITERATURE
Radic, Thérèse. *G. W. I. Marshall-Hall, Portrait of a Lost Crusader: An Introduction to the
Marshall-Hall Collection of the Grainger Museum, University of Melbourne.* . . . Music
Monograph, 5. Nedland: Dept. of Music, University of Western Australia, 1982. xii,
58 p., illus. [g.a.]

Martin, Hugo [pseud., **Martin Seydel**]. *See under* **Heuss, Alfred Valentin**

1794 Martin, [N], b. 1810
*Catalogue des livres anciens et modernes composant la bibliothèque musicale et théatrale
de feu . . . ancien directeur du Conservatoire de musique de la ville de Marseille.* . . . Paris: Ch.
Porquet, 1885. vi, 178 p. 2169 items. [US-Wc, -Bp, -R, NL-DHgm]
Folter, no. 226.

1795 ⸻
Catalogue de la bibliothèque de feu M. N. Martin. . . . [N.p., 188-.] 243 p.
[US-NYp, reproduced from Ms. copy]

Martin, William P. *See under* **Sellers, Ernest O.**

1796 Martin-Harvey, Sir John
IFAN KYRLE FLETCHER, FIRM, LONDON CAT. NO. 139
*Theater and Dance. Books, Manuscripts, Autograph Letters . . . etc., Including Many
Interesting Items from the Library of.* . . . London, [1950]. 40 p. 373 lots. Music, lots 1-327.
[compiler]

Catalog 139, "being a Supplement to Catalogs 123 & 134."

1797 Martinengo, Leopardo, Count

Concina, Giovanni. "Catalogo delle musiche donate dal. . . . " In Associazione dei musica italiana, *Pubblicazione, Serie VI, Puntata I, Venezia, Museo Correr*, 27-52. Parma: Freschig, 1913?   [US-Wc]

> Collection at I-Vc.

1798 Martini, Padre Giovanni Battista, 1706-84

Haberl, Franz Xavier. "Beiträge zur italienischen Litteratur des Oratorios im 17. und 18. Jahrhundert." *KmJ* 16 (1901): 49-64.   [g.a.]

> **Folter**, no. 227. A list of Ms. oratorios in Martini's library.

1799 _____

Schnoebelen, Anne. *Padre Martini's Collection of Letters in the Civico Museo Bibliografico Musicale in Bologna: An Annotated Index*. Annotated Reference Tools in Music, 2. New York: Pendragon Press, 1979. xix, 721 p.   [g.a.]

> 6000 letters from his contemporaries. Other portions of his library now at I-Bsf and A-Wn. Not in **Folter**.

1800 _____

LITERATURE

Parisini, F. "La biblioteca del Liceo musicale di Bologna." *Il bibliofilo* 4, no. 9/10 (1883): 129.   [g.a.]

1801 _____

Schnoebelen, Anne. "Padre Martini's Collection of Letters: An Overview." *Current Musicology* 19 (1975): 81-88.   [g.a.]

1802 _____

Schnoebelen, Anne. "The Growth of Padre Martini's Library as Revealed in His Correspondence." *M&L* 57 (October 1976): 379-97.   [g.a.]

1803 Martorell y Fivaller, Marquesas de

Catálogo de música perteneeciente á los Ex mos, os Tres Marquesas de Martorell. [N.p., n.d.] 48 p. Obl. 8°   [US-Wc]

> Accession mark at US-Wc dated 1923. Materials from the library exhibited at the Paris, Exposition Universelle, 1900, later bought by US-Wc. Before the title page, in Ms., are remarks about the condition of the contents and the rubber stamp of Leo Liepmannssohn, antiquarian, who perhaps offered the rich collection of operas to O. G. T. Sonneck.

1804 _____

LITERATURE

République française . . . Exposition universelle de 1900. Diplôme commemoratif, S. Exc. Madame de Martorell. Paris: Imp. A. Fereabeuf, 1900.

> An illustrated diploma awarded for her collection of music shown at the Exposition later purchased by US-Wc.

1805   Marx, Josef

J. & J. Lubrano, firm, Great Barrington, Mass.   Cat. no. 40

The Music Library of Josef Marx. Great Barrington, Mass., [1992]. 143 p. 1576 lots.   [g.a.]

Music and music literature, including periodicals, *Denkmäler* and *Gesamtausgaben.*

1806   Marx, Joseph, d. 1964

Literature

Gmeiner, Josef. "Der Nachlass Joseph Marx in der Musiksammlung der Österreichischen Nationalbibliothek." In *Zum 100. Geburtstag von Joseph Marx: Konzertabend und Austellung* . . . , ed. Günter Brosche, 23-28. Wien: Österreichischen Nationalbibliothek, 1982.   [g.a.]

1807   Maserer, William

Messrs. Christie and Ansell, auctioneer, London

A Catalogue of All the . . . Household Furniture, China, Linens. A Small Well-Chosen Library of Books. A Valuable Collection of Printed and Manuscript Music . . . Sold . . . December the 21st, 1781, and Following Day. [London], 1781. 15 p. Music, lots 142-49 (but many items).

[Film at CRL]

Lot 142, 5 vols. of Handel's songs; lot 147, 22 books of concertos; lot 149, "a large quantity of MS. and other music."

1808   Mason, Lowell, 1792-1872

Yale University, School of Music, Library

"Lowell Mason Library of Music. Catalogue of Authors. . . ." 3 vols. Ca. 10,300 pieces.

[US-NH]

Compiled by Joel Sumner Smith. Includes the library of J. C. H. Rinck, purchased by Mason in 1852; 50 volumes from the H. G. Nägeli, and theoretical works from the S. W. Dehn collections.

1809   _____

J. & J. Lubrano, firm, Great Barrington, Mass.   Cat. no. 28

"Duplicates from the Lowell Mason Collection of Music, Sold on Behalf of Yale University." In *Catalogue 28: Antiquarian Music and Musical Literature* . . . , 209-65. South Lee, Mass., 1987.

[g.a.]

1810   _____

O'Meara, Eva Judd. "The Lowell Mason Library." *Notes* 28 (1971): 197-208.   [g.a.]

1811   Mason, Luther Whiting, 1828-96**; Osbourne McConathy**

Hall, Bonlyn G. "Luther Whiting Mason's European Song Books [at the Library of Congress]." *Notes* 41 (1985): 482-91.   [g.a.]

The collection of ca. 700 books of school and folk songs published between 1850 and 1900 went from Mason to McConathy, then to Silver, Burdett Co., which gave it to US-Wc.

1812   Mason, William, 1829-1908
"Catalogue of Music, Wm. Mason." [N.p.], 1847.

> Holograph at US-NYp dated 25 January 1847. A catalog of Mason's library.

1813   Massanan, Antoni, 1890-1966
Crespi, Joanna. *Cataleg dels fons Antoni Massana de la Biblioteca de Catalunya.* . . . Seccio de musica, 38. Barcelona: La Biblioteca, 1992. 100 p. illus.   [US-Wc, -NYp, -CH, -BUu]

1814   Masseangeli, Masseangelo, 1809-78
R. Accademia filarmonia, Bologna
Catalogo della colezione d'autografi lasciata alla R. Accademia . . . dall'accademico Masseangelo Masseangeli . . . 1. Maestri di music, cantanti e suonatori. 2. Scrittori di cose musicali. 3. Fabbricatori di strumenti. 4. Coreografi e ballerini. 5. Editori di musica. 6. Autori . . . [etc.]. Bibliotheca musica bononiensis, ser. 1, no. 5. Bologna: Regia Tipogr., 1881. Reprint, Bologna: Forni, 1969. xv, 435 p.   [Reprint g.a.]

> A gift to I-Baf.

1815   _____

Literature
Dioli, Arrigo. "Origini e vicende dell'Accademia Filarmonica di Bologna." In *Festschrift Ferdinand Haberl zum 70. Geburtstag . . .* , ed. Franz Stein, 85-88. Regensburg: Bose, 1977.
    [g.a.]

1816   Massey, Edward Stocks
Burnley, England, Central Public Library
Catalogue of Music and of Literature Relating to Music in the. . . . Burnley?, 1929.

> _____. *Supplement . . .* 1932. Not located.

1817   Massimo, Leone, Fürst
Lippmann, Friedrich. "Musikhandschriften und -Drucke in der Bibliothek des Fürstenhauses Massimo, Rom." *Analecta musicologica* 17 (1976): 254-95; 19 (1979): 330-35.   [g.a.]

> Tl. I, Mss. (thematic catalog); Tl. II, "Autographe Briefe Rossinis und Donizettis in der Bibliothek Massimo, Rom."

1818   _____

Literature
Lippmann, Friedrich. "Eine unbekannte römische Musiksammlung: Bibliothek des Fürstenhauses Massimo." In Internationaler Musikwissenschaftlicher Kongress, Berlin, 1974, *Bericht*, 310-12. Kassel: Bärenreiter, [1980].   [g.a.]

1819   Masson, Elizabeth, d. 1865
Puttick & Simpson, auctioneer, London   Cat. no. 1612
Catalogue of the Valuable Musical Library of Miss . . . Musical Instruments . . . Sold . . . July 31, 1876. [London], 1876. 17 p. 379 lots. Music, lots 1-378.   [GB-Lbl]

1820   Matheson, William
Dichtung und Musik: Dokumente aus der Autographensammlung . . . Ausstellung, Museum Lindengut, Winterthur, 27. August - 26. September 1976. Winterthur, 1976. 50 p. facs.

"Musikerautographen," nos. 136-218. Not examined; cited from Otto Harrassowitz, *German Book Digest* 1 (1980): 28.

1821 **Mathieu [Jean Baptiste Charles,** 1762-1847?]
J. F. DELION, AUCTIONEER, PARIS
Catalogue de la collection musicale (littérature et oeuvres de musique pratique) qui composant le cabinet de feu . . . ancien maître de chapelle à Versailles . . . vente . . . 11 [-13] mai 1847. . . . Paris, 1847. 26 p. 302 lots (many more items).

[US-NTgr, NL-DHgm (with some Ms. prices)]

Mss., lots 296-300; lot 229, "Opéras de Philidor" (11 titles); lot 230, "Operas de Rameau" (13 items); lot 9, 23 tracts. **Folter**, no. 228.

1822 **Mattei, Stanislao,** 1750-1825
Parisini, F. [Preface to] Bologna. Liceo musicale. *Catalogo della biblioteca . . . compilata di Gaetano Gaspari . . .* , 1:i-xxxix. Bologna, 1890. Reprint, Bologna: Forni, 1961.

[Reprint, g.a.]

1823 **Mattheson, Johann,** 1681-1764
"Verzeichnis der Bücher und Schriften, welche der Herr Legationsrath Mattheson der öffentlichen Bibliothek vermacht und geschenkt hat." 1714.

Ms. in D-Hs, Bibliotheksarchiv VI, 4. See **1824**.

1824 _____
Marx, Hans Joachim. "Johann Matthesons Nachlass: Zum Schicksal der Musiksammlung der alten Stadtbibliothek Hamburg." *Acta* 55 (1983): 108-24.   [g.a.]

From *NG* 8 (1980), 8:68: "The most serious loss [WW II] was the virtually unexplained and irreplaceable collection of Johann Mattheson's MSS." Marx reprints the 1764 Ms. catalog cited above, pp. 117-21 (128 items).

1825 **Matthew, James E.,** d. 1910
Matthew, James E. *The Literature of Music.* London: Eliot Stock . . . , 1896. 281 p.

[g.a., compiler]

A narrative description of books mainly in his own library.

1826 _____
Matthew, James E. "Catalogue of a Library of Musical Literature and Music" [belonging to J. E. Matthew, compiled by the owner, 1906].

Typescript in the Hirsch collection at GB-Lbl. **King**, p. 71. In 1906, the library was sold to the dealer Liepmannssohn, subsequently offered in his catalogs, no. 170-73 (see **1828**). **Albrecht** says most of the collection ended up in the Paul Hirsch library, now at GB-Lbl.

1827 _____
Matthew, James E. "Catalogue of a Library of Musical Literature and Music [1907]." [2], 214, 197, 53 leaves (last 53, scores).

A ditto copy—purple, from typescript—owned in 1980 by Mr. deDeney, of London, now deceased. Identical with Hirsch copy above?

1828 _____

LEO LIEPMANNSSOHN, FIRM, BERLIN   CAT. NO. 170
*Catalogue . . . Containing Ancient Works Relating to Music, Liturgy and the Dance from
the 15th to the Beginning of the 19th Century, Chiefly from the Library of.* . . . Berlin, [n.d.,
1908?]. 108 p. 1204 lots. Prices fixed.   [US-Wc, -NYgr, -R, NL-Avb]
   Folter, no. 230.

1829 _____

LEO LIEPMANNSSOHN, FIRM, BERLIN   CAT. NO. 171
*Catalogue . . . Containing Musical Periodicals and Standard Works, with a Special Division
on Richard Wagner, Chiefly from the Library of.* . . . Berlin, [n.d., 1908?]. 79 p., illus. 1092
lots. Prices fixed.   [US-Wc, -NYp, -R, NL-Avb]
   Folter, no. 231.

1830 _____

LEO LIEPMANNSSOHN, FIRM, BERLIN   CAT. NO. 172
*Catalogue . . . Chiefly from the Library of . . . General Musical Bibliography. Music Catalogues
. . . General Musical History . . .* [etc.]. Berlin, [n.d., 1910?]. 115 p., illus. 1800 lots. Prices
fixed.   [US-Wc, -NYp, NL-Avb]
   Folter, no. 232. Sale noted in *ZiMG* 11 (1909/10): 98.

1831 _____

LEO LIEPMANNSSOHN, FIRM, BERLIN   CAT. NO. 173
*Musiker-Biogaphien. Schriften von Musikern. Briefwechsel und Memoiren. Thematisches
Verzeichnisse . . . meist aus der Sammlung des Herrn.* . . . Berlin, [n.d., 1910?]. 109 p. 2012
lots. Prices fixed.   [US-Wc, NL-Avb, GB-Lbl]
   Folter, no. 233.

1832 _____

LITERATURE
Matthew, James E. "Some Notes on Musical Libraries, and on That of the Writer in Particular."
Proceedings of the Musical Association 29 (1902/03): 139-68.   [g.a.]
   Library contained ca. 5500 pieces of music literature and about 1400 scores.
   Folter, no. 233.

1833 _____

Matthew, James E. "A Collection of Libretti." *MT* 49 (1908): 88-90.
   The author never does say whose collection he is discussing, but it is
   probably safe to assume that it was his own.
   → *See also under* **Cartier**, **Jean Baptiste**, 1765-1841; **Picquot**, **L.**
   (Liepmannssohn's catalog nos. 167 and 169); **Strickland**, **W. H.** (sale of
   30 April 1907).

1834 Matthews, C.

PUTTICK & SIMPSON, AUCTIONEER, LONDON   CAT. NO. 156
[Catalogue of His Musical Library . . . Also Musical Instruments . . . Sold . . . April 19th, 1850.]
[London], 1850. 14 p. 384 lots (more items). Music, lots 1-365.
   Title page missing from priced copy at GB-Lbl.

1835   Maule, James, 4th Earl of Panmure; Harie Maule
"Ane Catollogue of Books Left at Edr Agustt 1685."

Ms., Scottish Record Office, Dalhousie, GD 45/27/130. Noted by Cadell (**1836**).

1836   _____

Cadell, Patrick. "La Musique française classique dans la collection des Comtes de Panmure." *Recherches sur la musique française classique* 22 (1984): 50-58.   [g.a.]

Books and music collected by the two brothers while in France between 1678 and 1684. Collection now at GB-En. Cadell transcribes a list of Ms. ballets and operas from the Ms. in the Scottish Record Office cited above.

1837   Maximilian II, King of Bavaria, 1811-64
"Verzeichniss der von Sʳ M. dem Koenige Maximilian unter allerhochsten Eigenthums-Vorbehalte an die k. Hof- und Staats-Bibliothek abzegebenen Hand- und Druckschriften."

Ms. at D-Mbs, sign. Cod. bav. Catalog 97.

1838   _____

Wackernagel, Bettina. *Collectio musicalis Maximilianea.* Kataloge Bayerischer Musiksammlungen 5, no. 3. München: Henle Verlag, 1981. 112 p.   [g.a.]

1839   Maximilian III, Joseph, Elector of Bavaria, 1727-77
Ms. inventory, 1803, in Staatsarchiv für Oberbayern. München: Klosterliteralien (KL 1, Fasc. 685, Nr. 31), according to Münster (**1840**).

1840   _____

Münster, Robert. "Kurfürst Max III. Joseph von Bayern und die musizierenden Patres von Kloster Seeon." *Mozart-Jahrbuch* (1960/61), 195-206.   [g.a.]

1841   [May, G   , Rev.]
Pᴜᴛᴛɪᴄᴋ & Sɪᴍᴘsᴏɴ, ᴀᴜᴄᴛɪᴏɴᴇᴇʀ, Lᴏɴᴅᴏɴ   Cᴀᴛ. ɴᴏ. 246
Catalogue of a Collection of Music, Including Some of the Best Ancient and Modern Works . . . Sacred and Organ Music, etc. Also Musical Instruments . . . Sold . . . February 6th, 1852. [London], 1852. 11 p. 259 lots. Music, lots 1-222.   [GB-Lbl]

1842   Mayer-Reinach, Albert, 1876-1954
Oᴛᴛᴏ Hᴀʀʀᴀssᴏᴡɪᴛᴢ, ꜰɪʀᴍ, Wɪᴇsʙᴀᴅᴇɴ
Antiquarian Sale: Books and Scores. Wiesbaden: Harrassowitz, 198-? 38 p. Not lotted. Ca. 400 items.   [g.a.]

1843   Mazarin, Jules, Cardinal, 1602-61
Bernard, Madeleine. *Répertoire de MSS médiévaux contenant des notations musicales II: BMaz.* Paris: CNRS, 1966. 190 p., 16 plates 119 items.   [g.a.]

F-Pm, based on the Cardinal's personal library, opened in 1643 to the public, the oldest public library in France.

1844   Mazer, Johann, 1790-1847
STOCKHOLM. KGL. MUSIKALISKA AKADEMIENS BIBLIOTEK
"Catalogue thématique de musique." 7 vols. Manuscript thematic catalog
of ca. 4550 scores and parts at S-Skma.

1845   _____
Johansson, Cari. "Något om Mazers musiksamling i Kungl. Musikaliska akademiens bibliotek."
STMf 33 (1951): 142-46.   [g.a.]

1846   Mecklenburg-Schwerin, House of
Kade, Otto. *Die Musikalien-Sammlung des Grossherzoglichen Mecklenburg-Schweriner Fürstenhauses aus den letzten zwei Jahrhunderten.* 2 vols. Schwerin: Druck der Sanmeyerschen Hofbuchdruckerei, 1893.   [g.a.]
_____. *Nachtrag.* 1899. vii, 142 p.
Both reprinted, Hildesheim: Olms, 1974. According to **Albrecht**, the
ducal library was divided between D-ROu nd D-SWl.

1847   _____
LITERATURE
Meyer, Clemens. *Geschichte der Mecklenburg-Schweriner Hofkapelle.* . . . Schwerin: Davids,
1913. 4, 335 p., ports.   [US-Wc, -CA, -CHH]
Benton 2:146, no. 122, says it also lists music in the collections.

1848   Medinaceli, Duques de
Series de la mś importantes docvmentos del archivo y biblioteca del exmo. señor dvove de Medinaceli, celegidos por sv encargo y publicados a sus expensas por A. Paz y Mélia. [Madrid, 1915- .] 2. Ser.: Bibliographia, 1922.   [US-Mnu]
Albrecht says ". . . finest private collection of Spanish music, 16th-17th centuries."

1849   _____
Trend, John Brande. "Catalogue of the Music in the Biblioteca Medinaceli, Madrid." *Revue hispanique* 71 (1927): 485-554.   [g.a.]

1850   Meibom, Marcus, 1620-1719
HENRICI & VIDU & THEODORI BOOM, AUCTIONEERS, AMSTERDAM
Bibliotheca Marci Meibomii, Frederici tertii, Daniae Regis, olim consiliarii continens raros libros . . . Oui publica Auctioner Vendentur . . . 23. marti & seq. An. 1705. . . . Amstelodami
. . . , 1705. 464 p. 2388 [i.e., 3288] lots.   [US-NYgr]
Curiously, no music, but, because of the seminal importance of his book,
Antiquae musicae auctores septem, graece et latine (1652), included here.

1851   Meininger,
LITERATURE
Mühlfeld, Chr. "Die Meininger Musikbibliothek." *ZfM* 79, no. 16 (1912): 217-21.   [g.a.]

1852   Méjanes, Jean Baptiste Marie Piquet, Marquis de, 1729-86
Tessier, André. "Quelques sources de l'école française de luth au 17ᵉ s." In International Society of Musical Research, Congress (1st, 1930, Liège), *Compte rendu - Kongressbericht - Report*, 217-24. Burnham: Plainsong and Mediaeval Music Society, [1930].   [g.a.]

1853   Mellinet, Émile, 1798-1894
Catalogue des livres composant la bibliothèque militaire et musical de feu le général Mellinet dont la vente . . . 26 novembre [et] *. . . 6 décémbre 1894.* Paris: Champion, 1894. vi, 223 p. "Musique," 210-21.   [US-CHH]

1854   Meluzzi, Salvatore
Dario G. Rossi, firm, Rome
Catalogue des livres et manuscrits composant la bibliothèque de feu . . . , maître de la chapelle du Vatican, suivi du catalogue d'un choix de livres appartenant à un amateur. Roma: D. G. Rossi, 1906. 123 p., plates. 885 lots.   [US-Cn, -NYgr]

> Collection sold "mars 1906." Meluzzi properties, pp. 1-48, 329 lots.

1855   Mempell, Johann Nicolaus; Johann Gottlieb Preller
Schulze, Hans-Joachim. "Wie enstand die Bachsammlung Mempell-Preller?" *Bach-Jahrbuch* 60 (1974): 104-22.   [g.a.]

> Traces Mss. of the works of Bach and others now at D-LEm and D-B from Mempell and Preller through later collections of Daniel Friedrich Eduard Wilsing and Max Seiffert. (No catalogs or related literature about their collections discovered.)

1856   Mendel, Bernardo
Lilly Library, Indiana University
The Bernando Mendel Collection: An Exhibit . . . Descriptive Notes Written by Cecil K. Byrd and Others. [Bloomington, 1964.] 83 p.   [US-STu, -BUu (film)]

1857   —————
Lilly Library, Indiana University
An Exhibition of Books Presented to the Lilly Library. . . . Lilly Library, Publication, 11. Bloomington, 1970. 1 vol., unpaged.   [g.a.]

1858   Mendelssohn-Bartholdy, Ernst von (grandson of Felix)
"Überweisung der Autographensammlung . . . an die Kgl. Bibliothek Berlin." *ZiMG* 9 (1907/08): 426.   [g.a.]

> Brief paragraph. According to **Albrecht**, acquired by D-Bds in 1908. Ca. 700 family letters.

1859   Mendelssohn-Bartholdy, Felix, 1809-47
[Mendelssohn's inventory of his household goods in 1844.] Ms. at GB-Ob, Ms. M. Deneke Mendelssohn, c.29. Reprinted by Peter Ward Jones (**1862**).   [g.a.]

> Ff. 26-27 - books; ff. 29-30 - music. Another list of the collection made by Fanny Mendelssohn is at GB-Ob (Mss. M.Deneke Mendelssohn b.4), but was not reprinted by Jones.

1860   —————
Karl Ernst Henrici, auctioneer, Berlin   Verst Cat. 104
Autographen, Musik, Theater, bildende Kunst, Literatur und Wissenschaft, historische Autographen. . . . Berlin, 1925. 88 p. 603 lots. M's, 57-78.

> **Folter**, no. 235. Date of sale, 13 May 1925. Catalog not located.

1861 _____

Crum, Margaret. *Catalogue of the Mendelssohn Papers in the Bodleian . . .* Vol. 1: *Correspondence of . . . and Others* [Collected by F. M-B]. Vol. 2: *Music and Papers.* Musikbibliographische Arbeiten, 7-8. 2 vols. Tutzing: Hans Schneider, 1980-83.   [g.a.]
  Folter, no. 235.

1862 _____

Ward, Jones, Peter A. "The Library of. . . . " In *Festschrift Rudolf Elvers,* ed. Ernst Hettrich und Hans Schneider, 289-328. Tutzing: Schneider, 1985. 281 nos.   [g.a.]
  A catalog. Examines Mendelssohn's list of his and Cecile's library in 1844.

1863 _____

Walker, Ernest. "An Oxford Collection of Mendelssohniana." *M&L* 19 (1938): 426-28.   [g.a.]
  King, pp. 86-87.

1864 _____

Schneider, Max Friedrich. "Das Mendelssohn-Archiv in Berlin." *Jahrbuch der Stiftung Preussischer Kulturbesitz* (1964/65), 224-29.
  Folter, no. 235. Not located.

1865 **Mendelssohn-Bartholdy, Felix; Adolf Wach**

Richter, Brigitte. "Das Mendelssohn-Zimmer in Leipzig." *Musik und Gesellschaft* 22 (1972): 646-52.   [g.a.]
  " . . . memorabilia, such as furniture, paintings, and sculpture." Not examined.
  Cited from *RILM* 6:2773.

1866 _____

Elvers, Rudolf. "Felix Mendelssohn-Bartholdys Nachlass." In *Das Problem Musik,* ed. Carl Dahlhaus, 35-46. Regensburg, 1974.
  Not examined.

  → *See also* the following catalog of **Karl Mendelssohn-Bartholdy's** library

1867 **Mendelssohn-Bartholdy, Karl,** 1809-47
  LORENTZ, AUCTIONEER, LEIPZIG CAT. NO. 94
  Mittelalterliche und neue Geschichte nebst Hilfs. . . . Leipzig: Lorentz, 1897. ? p. 5570 lots.
                        [NL-Avb]
  Not examined. **Folter**, no. 234, says it contains Karl's library and part of Felix's.

1868 **Mendelssohn, Paul Victor Benecke,** 1868-1944
  LITERATURE
  Walker, Ernest. "An Oxford Collection of Mendelssohniana." *M&L* 19 (1938): 426-28.   [g.a.]
    King, pp. 86-87.

1869 _____

    Deneke, Margaret. *Paul Victor Mendelssohn Benecke, 1868-1944.* Oxford: [privately printed, 1954]. 60 p.   [GB-Lbl]

        King, p. 7, a privately printed booklet describing the origins of the collection. Begun by the composer's grandson, expanded after his death by Margaret, its inheritor.

Mengelberg, Rudolf. *See under* **Cronheim**

1870   **Mennicke, Carl,** 1880-1917

    Oswald Weigel, auctioneer, Leipzig   Aukt. Cat. N.F. 73
    Theater - Praktische und theoretischer Musik . . . [Nachlass von . . .]. Leipzig, 1918. 98 p. 1671 lots. Music, lots 371-1666.   [NL-Avb]

1871   **Menso, J E P E**

    Minerva. [Sale of songbooks, 7 September 1942.] s'Gravenhage, 1942.   [NL-Avb]

        Not examined. Cited from **Vereeniging** . . . *Catalogus* 8.

1872   **Menz, Anton Melchior von,** 1757-1801

        His collection served as the basis for that of the Toggenburg Family in Bolzano.

1873   **Mercer, Hon. Col. John; Nicholas Hawksmoor**

    Aaron Lambe, auctioneer, London
    A Catalogue of the Household Furniture and Effects of the . . . and . . . Both Deceased . . . Curious Collection of Musical Instruments . . . Sold . . . at Mr. Lambe's, Facing the Kings-Arms Tavern in Pall-Mall . . . the 15th Instant [of April] *and the Six Following Days. . . .* [London, 1740.] 31 p. various lottings.   [GB-Lbl]

        "Musical instruments and books of musick," pp. 13-14. 32 lots but many more items. 28 lots are indexed in **Coral**, p. 180, discussed p. 61.

1874   **Merkel, C L**

    List & Francke, firm, Leipzig   Cat. no. 107
    Verzeichniss von theoretischen und praktischen Musikwerken aus dem Nachlass des Prof. . . . Leipzig, 1876. 62 p. 2156 lots.   [US-NYgr, NL-DHgm]

Merkens. *See* **Beständig, Otto**

1875   **Merkmann, Vve P** [*née* **Leeuwarden, J**]

    Vincent van der Vinne, auctioneer, Haarlem
    Catalogus van een extra fraai Kabinetje Konstigeen plaisante schildergen . . . prenten en tekeningen . . . Fraaije muziek, tuincieraaden en rarietyten . . . verkogt . . . 21 September 1773. . . . Haarlem, [1773]. 22 p. 490 lots.   [F-Pe]

        Not examined; cited from **Lugt**, no. 2194, who says "Liv. mus. 129."

1876   **Merz, Karl,** [1836-90?]

    Pittsburgh, Carnegie Library
    Catalogue of the Karl Merz Musical Library Held by the Academy of Science and Art . . . for the Carnegie Free Library of Pittsburgh. Pittsburgh: Foster, 1892. 26 p.   [US-Pc]

        Folter, no. 236.

1877   Mettenleiter, Johann Georg, 1812-68

Some items bequeathed by him to Proske Bibliothek (D-Rp).

1878   Metternich, Rudolf

LITERATURE

Haas, Antonín. "Dopisy hudebních skladatelu v archivu Richards Metternich." *Acta regionalia 1970-1971, sbornik vlastivednych praci* (1972), 32-39.

Not located. Cited from *RILM*.

1879   Meyendorff, Alexander, Baron

SOTHEBY & CO., AUCTIONEER, LONDON

Catalogue of Valuable Autograph Letters, Historical Documents, Printed Books . . . [and] *An Important Collection of Letters and Musical manuscripts by Franz Liszt . . . Sold . . . 23rd of April, 1931, and Two Following Days.* [London, 1931.] 107 p. 674 lots.   [Film at CRL]

Meyendorff's properties, lots 218-31 (many more items).

1880   Meyer, André, b. 1898

Bridgman, Nanie, and François Lesure. *Collection musicale . . . : manuscrits autographes, musique imprimée, manuscrits, ouvrages théoriques, historiques et pédagogiques, librets, iconographie, instruments de musique.* Abbeville: Impr. F. Paillart, [1961]. 118, [295] p. 292 plates.   [US-Bp]

_____. *Supplement.* Abbeville: Impr. F. Paillart, [1963]. [16] p. facs. No lotting.   [g.a.]

1881   _____

LITERATURE

Berkofsky, Martin. "The André Meyer Collection—A Treasure in Jeopardy." *Hi Fidelity/Musical America* 31 (1981): MA30-33.   [g.a.]

1882   Meyer, Georg

ROBERT ALDER, FIRM, BERN   LIST NO. 65

[Catalog of his music collection.] 475 lots.

Not located; cited from *IBAK* 1960.

1883   Meyer, Hans

HELMUT & ERNST MEYER, AUCTIONEER, BERLIN   CAT. NO. 31

. . . Autographen-Sammlung Hans Meyer (Leipzig). I. Teil, sowie ausgewählte Stücke aus anderen Privatsammlungen. Musik - Literatur - Wissenschaft . . . 10. April 1933. Berlin, 1933. 88 p. 456 lots. Music, lots 1-42.   [US-NYgr]

1884   Meyerbeer, Giacomo, 1791-1864

Autographs from his collection were reportedly included among Schlesinger properties in a Liepmannssohn auction in 1907. **Benton 2**:118, no. 113, also notes a bequest to D-Bds.

→ *See also under* **Stockhausen, Julius**

1885   Meyerstein, Edward Henry William
SOTHEBY & CO., AUCTIONEER, LONDON
Catalogue of the Important Library of Classical, Musical, Literary [etc.] . . . *Formed by* . . . *Sold* . . . *15th of December, 1952, and Two Following Days.* . . . [London, 1952.] 53 p. 513 lots. Music, lots 279-378.   [Film at CRL]

> First editions of Beethoven, lots 283-333. **King**, p. 76, says the Beethoven editions "were almost the only focal point in an extraordinarily heterogeneous collection. . . . His autographs were distinguished." They must have been withdrawn, for they were given to GB-Lbl (**1886**). The bulk of the collection was auctioned, however.

1886   _____

LITERATURE
Schofield, B., and C. E. Wright. "The Meyerstein Bequest." *British Museum Quarterly* 18 (December 1953): 97-100.   [g.a.]

> See preceding annotation.

1887   Mies, Paul, 1889-1970
HANS SCHNEIDER, FIRM, TUTZING   CAT. NO. 207
Musikbibliothek Paul Mies . . . nebst einigen anderen Beiträgen. Tutzing, [1977]. 198 p. 2294 lots.   [g.a.]

> **Folter**, no. 238.

1888   [Milbourne,   ]
PUTTICK & SIMPSON, AUCTIONEER, LONDON   CAT. NO. 284
Catalogue of the Musical Library of an Eminent Professional Gentleman, Comprising Collections of Cathedral Music . . . English Songs . . . Theoretical and Historical Works, and Musical Instruments . . . Sold . . . July 15th, 1852. [London], 1852. 14 p. 290 lots. Music, lots 1-256.

1889   Millar, T F ; [Mrs. Stevens]
PUTTICK & SIMPSON, AUCTIONEER, LONDON   CAT. NO. 72
Catalogue of a Large Collection of Music, Being the Final Portion of the Stock of Mr. John Green . . . Also a Portion of the Music Library of Mr. T. F. Millar, of Bath . . . Sold June 9th, 1848. [London], 1848. 20 p. 266 lots. Music, lots 1-233.   [GB-Lbl]

> Millar's properties, lots 143-233.

1890   Miller, Dayton Clarence, 1866-1941
List of Works Relating to the Flute in the Library of . . . , with Annotations. Cleveland, Ohio: privately printed, 1922. 19 p.   [US-Wc, -Bp, -AA, -NYp]

> **Folter**, no. 239.

1891   _____

. . . Catalogue of Books and Literary Material Relating to the Flute and Other Musical Instruments, with Annotations. . . . The Dayton C. Miller Collections relating to the flute, 2. Cleveland: privately printed, 1935. 120 p.   [g.a.]

> The collection was given to US-Wc on Miller's death.

1892 _____

"A List of Books from the Dayton C. Miller Collection . . . from the Catalog . . . Compiled by Mr. Miller." In U.S. Library of Congress, Music Division, *Catalogue of Early Books on Music . . . Supplement . . .* by Hazel Bartlett, 136-43. Washington: Government Printing Office, 1944.

[g.a.]

1893   Miller zu Aichholz, Victor and **Olga, von**

Prillinger, Elfriede, ed. *Kammerhofmuseum der Stadt Gmunden. Sonderausstellung 1983. Johannes Brahms 1833-1897.* Gmunden: Eigenverlag des Kammerhofmuseums der Stadt, 1983. 43 p.

> Brahms items based on the Miller zu Aicholz collection donated to the museum. Not examined; cited from *RILM* 27 (1983): 17, 84.

1894   Misligowsky, Carl

"Beilage 3: Aus dem Nachlass inventar des Hofkaplans Carl Misligowsky, + Wallerstein, 8. Februar 1774." Ms. in Archiv Wallerstein. Reprinted in Gertraut Haberkamp, *Thematischer Katalog der Musikhandschriften der Fürstlichen Oettingen-Wallerstein'schen Bibliothek, Schloss Harburg.* München: Henle, 1976.   [g.a.]

1895   Mittmann, Paul; Georg Jensch

PREUSS & JÜNGER, FIRM, BRESLAU
Berichte Nr. 4: Musik (Literatur und Noten aus den Bibliotheken von . . .). Breslau, 1926. 2230 lots.

> Not located; cited in *ZfMW* 8 (1925/26): 608.

1896   Mlynarski, Doris Kenyon; James B. Pond

PARKE-BERNET GALLERIES, AUCTIONEER, NEW YORK
Autograph Letters, Manuscripts, Documents of Historical, Literary and Musical Interest . . . Including Rare XVI-XVIII Century Books on Music Belonging a New York Lady, Doris Kenyon Mlynarski, James B. Pond [et al.]. New York, 1954. 100 p. 349 lots.   [compiler (priced)]

> Extraordinary contents include ALS and holographs by Brahms (his op. 8), Delibes, Schumann, Mendelssohn, et al.

1897   Mlynarski, Emil

LITERATURE
Burokaite, J. "Archiwum Mlynarskiego na Litwie." *Ruch muzyczny* 16 (August 1969): 18.

> Not examined; cited from *RILM.*

1898   Mörike, Eduard, 1804-75

LEO LIEPMANNSSOHN, AUCTIONEER, BERLIN   NO. [9]
Katalog einer schönen Autographen-Sammlung zum Theile aus dem Nachlasse des Dichter's . . . 11. Mai 1891 und folgenden Tage. . . . Berlin, 1891. 85 p. 1118 lots Music, lots 457-600.

[GB-LRosenthal]

1899   Mörner, Marianne, 1895-1977

LITERATURE
Mörner, Aare Ruth. "Hovsångerskan Marianne Mörners notsamling." *Svenskt Musikhistorisk Arkiv Bulletin* 14 (1978): 22.   [g.a.]

1900   Moffat, Alfred Edward, 1866-1950
OTTO HAAS, FIRM, LONDON   CAT. NO. 20
*The Valuable Music Library Formed by . . . Chamber and Harpsichord Music, Mostly in
Editions of the 17th and 18th Centuries . . . with a Collection of Folk Songs and Some Opera
Scores.* . . . London: Haas, [1944]. 57 p. 700 lots.   [GB-Lbl, compiler]

> **King**, pp. 78, 148: much of it purchased by US-Wc. Other materials from
> Moffat's collection now at US-Nf.

1901   Moffat, Alfred Edward; George Kingsley, 1811-84
J. & J. LUBRANO, FIRM, GREAT BARRINGTON, MASS.   CAT. NO. 39
*Rare, Printed Music and Musical Literature from the Collection of the Forbes Library
in Northampton, Mass. . . . Including Items in the Possession of the Noted Scottish Music
Collector . . . and the American Psalmodist and Music Teacher, George Kingsley.* Great
Barrington, Mass., 1991. pp. unnumbered. 341 lots.   [g.a.]

> Moffat's properties, lots 1-69; Kingsley's, lots 70-341 (*inter alia*).

1902   _____

LITERATURE
Ingram, John E. "Collecting Colonial Music Materials." *AB Bookman's Weekly* 76, no. 24
(9 December 1985): 4315-19.   [g.a.]

> Many works in the collection derive from Moffat's library.

1903   Mohr, Ernst
Muikmanuskripte aus einer kleinen Privatsammlung." In *Totum me libris dedo: Festschrift . . .
Adolf Seebass*, 122-32. Basel: Haus der Bücher Ag, 1979.   [g.a.]

> 21 autographs fully described.

1904   Moirac, Edouard
Catalogue des livres . . . composant la bibliothèque de feu. . . . Paris, 1876.

> Not located. Cited from **Scheurleer** 1 (1923): 19.

1905   Moldenhauer, Hans, 1906-87
"A Webern Archive in America." In *Anton von Webern: Perspectives*, 117-66. Seattle: University
of Washington Press, 1966.   [g.a.]

1906   _____

"Excelsior! Die Genese des Webern-Archivs." In *Komponisten des 20. Jahrhunderts in der
Paul Sacher Stiftung*, 131-38. Basel: Paul Sacher Stiftung, 1986.   [g.a.]

1907   _____

BAYERISCHE STAATSBIBLIOTHEK/HOUGHTON LIBRARY
*Joint Exhibition: Sources for 20th-Century Music History. Alban Berg and the Second Viennese
School . . . Acquisitions from the Collection of Hans Moldenhauer* [and] *Rudolf Kolisch.* . . .
München/Köln, 1988. 138 p. 70 lots.   [g.a.]

> Catalog prepared by Helmut Hell, Sigrid von Moisy, and Barbara Wolff.

1908 _____

LITERATURE

"From My Autograph Collection: C. Ph. E. Bach - Dittersdorf - Mozart." In Internationaler Musikwissenschaftlicher Kongress, Vienna, 1956, *Bericht*, 412-15. Graz: Böhlaus Nachf., 1958.

[g.a.]

1909 _____

Nettl, Paul. "Hans Moldenhauer, Pionier der Musikwissenschaft: Seine Sammlung in Spokane. . . ." In *Festschrift Alfred Orel zum 70. Geburtstag* . . . , ed. Hellmut Federhofer, 133-37. Wien/ Wiesbaden: R. M. Rohrer, 1960.

[g.a.]

1910 _____

Szmolyan, Walter. "Die Wiener Stadtbibliothek erwarb Musikautographen aus der Moldenhauer-Sammlung." *ÖmZ* 36 (March 1981): 160.

[g.a.]

1911 _____

Hilmar, Ernst. "Versuch einer Bestandsaufnahme: Hans Moldenhauers 'Webern-Archiv'." *ÖmZ* 37 (October 1982): 574-75.

[g.a.]

1912 Molitor, Simon

LITERATURE

Fuchs, Aloys. "Die Musikalien-Sammlung des Herrn Simon von Molitor in Wien." *Cäcilia* 23 (1844): 49-50.

[g.a.]

Monk, Joseph Haydn Bourne.   *See under* **Westbrook, William Joseph** (Puttick & Simpson sale of 31 October 1894)

1913 Monkhouse, Rev. Dr.

W. P. MUSGRAVE, AUCTIONEER, LONDON

Music, Treatises, Instruments, Prints and Valuable Library of Books. A Catalogue of an Extensive and Curious Collection . . . Also a Patent Perpendicular Pedal Harp . . . Sold . . . December 10, 1823, and Two Following Days. [London, 1823.] 22 p. 248 lots. Music, lots 1-94, 108-248.   [GB-Lbl, US-NBu (film)]

>   **King**, pp. 27-28.

1914 Montabert, Germaine; et al.

PARKE-BERNET GALLERIES, AUCTIONEER, NEW YORK

Manuscripts and Autographs of the First Importance Including . . . Music Manuscripts by Mozart, Beethoven, Mendelssohn, Rubinstein and Others, Letters by Beethoven, Wagner, and Brahms . . . the Collection of the Late . . . in Addition to Material from a Westchester Private Collector . . . Auction, Tuesday, April 10. . . . New York, 1962. 85 p. 250 lots.   [g.a.]

>   Music Mss. and ALS, lots 13, 22-23, 29-32, 40, 118, 123, 156, 172-73, 182-83, 207-08, 210, 230-37 (Wagner), 222. Properties are not differentiated.

1915 Montbéliard, George, 16th century

Meyer, Christian. "Un Inventaire des livres et des instruments de musique de la chapelle des Comtes de Montbéliard (1555)." *Fontes* 25 (1991): 122-29.

>   Date of inventory, 1555. Collection now at? F-MD. Cited from *RILM* 25, no. 128 (1991).

Mooijen, H J . *See* **Plugge, P C.**

1916   Moore, Sampson (of Liverpool); Alfred J. Davis
PUTTICK & SIMPSON, AUCTIONEER, LONDON
*Catalogue of a Valuable Collection of Miscellaneous Music, Including the Library of the
Late . . . Also . . . Stock . . . Sold . . . August 16, 1875.* [London], 1875. 22 p. 535 lots (more
items). Music, lots 1-317. Moore's properties, lots 54-117+.   [US-NYp, GB-Lbl]

1917   Moore, Thomas, Sir, 1779-1852
PUTTICK & SIMPSON, AUCTIONEER, LONDON   CAT. NO. 328
*Catalogue of Upwards of One Thousand Autograph Letters, Addressed by Thomas Moore to
Mr. James Power, His Music Publisher . . . 1808-36 . . . Also Unpublished and Published
Autograph Manuscript Music, Corrected Proofs, &c. by Moore, Wade, Sir John Stevenson,
Sir Henry R. Bishop, Leigh Hunt, Novello, &c., Including a Large Portion of the Original
Manuscripts for the Irish Melodies, Sacred Songs, National Melodies . . . [etc.] . . . Sold . . .
June 23, 1853, and Following Day.* [London], 1853. 131 p. 501 lots.   [GB-Lbl, US-CA, -BE]

> This catalog was reprinted in *Notes from Thomas Moore to His Music
> Publisher, James Power (the Publication of Which Was Suppressed in London)*
> with an *Introductory Letter from Thomas Crofton Crocker.* New York: Redfield,
> [1854?]. Sizeable quotations from the letters are supplied.
>
> A fuller account of this catalog and the publication of Moore's letters and
> Irish melodies are furnished in the annotation to this catalog in **Coover 2**,
> pp. 153-55.

1918   Moore, Thomas, Sir; Richard Clark, 1750-1856
PUTTICK & SIMPSON, AUCTIONEER, LONDON   CAT. NO. 329
*Catalogue of Several Important Musical Properties, Amongst Which Are I. The Copyright
Musical Works of the Late Thomas Moore in Original MSS. and Engraved Plates. . . . II. The
Very Interesting Literary and Musical Collections of Richard Clark. . . . III. A Selection of
Music . . . from the Library of the Dean of Peterborough . . . V. A Miscellaneous Collection of
Musical Instruments . . . Sold June 25 . . . June 27 . . . June 28, 1853.* [London], 1853. 42 p. 676
[i.e., 680] lots.   [GB-Lbl]

> **King**, p. 61.

1919   _____
PUTTICK & SIMPSON, AUCTIONEER, LONDON
*Catalogue of a Collection of Books, Music and Engraved Portraits from the Library of . . .
Sold . . . April 20, 1874, and Two Following Day. . . .* [London, 1874.] 73 p.   [GB-Lbl]

> Only lots 164-96 are music items.

1920   Moreland, Samuel; A Very Ingenious Gentleman, Deceased
JOHN WILCOX, BOOKSELLER, LONDON
*. . . A Catalogue of the Libraries of . . . and a Very Ingenious Gentleman Deceased (Whose
Name I Am Not Allow'd to Mention). Being a Very Curious Collection of Books, in All Parts
of Polite Learning . . . Musick . . . Voyages, &c. . . . Sold at Davis's Coffee-House, in the Little
Piazza, Covent Garden . . . 7th of November, 1727. . . .* [London, 1727.]   [GB-Lbl, -Ob]

> 25 lots of music are indexed and disucssed by **Coral**, p. 62.

1921   Morris, W. ["A Well-Known Collector"]
PUTTICK & SIMPSON, AUCTIONEER, LONDON   CAT. NO. 680
*Catalogue of the Musical Library of a Well-Known Collector . . . Opera and Vocal Music,
Madrigals and Glees . . . Curious and Rare Masses and Motetts, Instrumental Music . . . Early
Theoretical Works . . . Important Collection of Manuscripts . . . Sold . . . June 10th, 1861, and
Following Day . . .* [London], 1861. 39 p. 801 lots.   [US-NYp, GB-Lbl]

> Lot 718 comprised Ms. scores, 77 vols. in number, "formed by the late Duke
> of Cambridge [i.e., Adolphus Frederick (**9**)] . . . sold by us in 1850."

1922   Moscheles, Felix
SOTHEBY, WILKINSON & HODGE, AUCTIONEER, LONDON
*Catalogue of Fine Books, Illuminated and Other Manuscripts . . . Letters from the Collection
of the Late . . . Left Him by His Father, Ignaz . . . Including Interesting Items of Mendelssohn,
Bach, Haydn, Beethoven, &c. . . . Sold . . . 22nd of July, 1918 and Three Following Days.*
[London, 1918.] 136 p. 1190 lots.   [Film at CRL]

> **Folter**, no. 243. Lot 636 includes "the most important series of Mendelssohn
> letters that has ever appeared in the market" (60 ALS in one lot!).

1923   Moscheles, Ignaz, 1794-1870
PUTTICK & SIMPSON, AUCTIONEER, LONDON   CAT. NO. 36
*Catalogue of an Extensive and Valuable Collection of Music, Including the Greater Portion
of the Library of . . . Curious Original Manuscripts; Handel's Works in Full and Vocal Scores
. . . Musical Instruments . . . Sold . . . July 23rd, 1847, and Following Day. . . .* London, 1847.
23 p. 617 lots. Music, lots 1-560.   [GB-Lbl]

> **King**, p. 6, says "mixed up with other properties . . . now no one can
> reconstruct its full extent and splendor."

1924   _____
LIST & FRANCKE, AUCTIONEER, LEIPZIG   AUK.-CAT. NO. ?
*Verzeichnis der hinterlassenen Bibliothek des Herrn Dr. Becker . . . welche nebst anderen
Bibliotheken, sowie einer Sammlung Musikalien aus dem Nachlasse des . . . Moscheles,
Ritter, etc. in Leipzig . . . versteigert werden soll.* Leipzig, 1871. 111 p. 3659 lots.   [NL-Avb]

> **Folter**, no. 241. M's properties, lots 2956-3437.

> → *See also under* **Bovet, Alfred** (for Liepmannssohn sale of November
> 1911)

1925   Mosewius, Johann Theodor, 1788-1858
L. F. MASKE, FIRM, BRESLAU   ANT.-CAT. NO. 44
*Musikalische Bibliothek, enthaltend die nachgelassenen Büchersammlung des . . . , sowie
eine Sammlung Musikalien, namentlich für Kirchenmusik.* Breslau: Druck von Nischkowsky,
[1859]. 26 p. 482 lots.   [GB-Lbl]

> **Folter**, no. 244.

1926   _____
SCHLETTER'SCHE BUCHHANDLUNG, AUCTIONEER, BRESLAU
*Verzeichnis von Musikalien aus dem Nachlasse des verstorbenen Dr. Johann Theodor
Mosewius, Musiklehrer und Lehrer der Tonkunst an d. Königl. Universität . . . zu Breslau . . .
versteigert 31. Mai [-Juni 3], 1859.* Breslau, 1859. 25 p. 852 lots.

> **Folter**, no. 245. Not examined.

1927   **Mottl, Felix,** 1856-1911

     KARL MAX POPPE, FIRM, LEIPZIG   CAT. NO. 3

     . . . Musikgeschichte. Bemerkt sei auch, das dieses Antiquariat die umfangrieiche Musikbibliothek . . . Mottl'e erworben hat, von der demnächst der Katalog erschienen wird. Leipzig, 1911?

         Not located; cited from *ZiMG* 13 (1911/12): 417.

1928   _____

     KARL MAX POPPE, FIRM, LEIPZIG   CAT. NO. 4

     Bibliothek Felix Mottl. Praktische Musik zum grossen Teil aus der Bibliothek des. . . . Leipzig, 1912. 66 p. 1600 lots.   [US-Wc, NL-DHgm]

         Folter, no. 246. Noted in *ZiMG* 14 (1912/13): 34.

1929   _____

     KARL MAX POPPE, FIRM, LEIPZIG   CAT. NO. 5

     Musikliteratur . . . Enthält u.a. den betr. Teil der Bibliotheken des Herrn. . . . Leipzig, 1913. 74 p. 1798 lots   [US-Wc, NL-DHgm]

         Folter, no. 247.

1930   **Mottl, Felix; A. W. Gottschalg; [Louis Spohr]**

     LEO LIEPMANNSSOHN, AUCTIONEER, BERLIN   AUK.-CAT. NO. 41

     Autographen-Sammlungen Nering-Boegel II. Teil, sowie Autographen aus dem Nachlass von Josef Viktor Widmann und eine kostbare Sammlung von Musik-Autographen und - Manuscripten z. T. aus dem Nachlässen des Kgl. Geh. Hofrats und Hofoperndirektors Felix Mottl und des Hoforganisten A. W. Gottschalg [sowie Louis Spohr]. Versteigerung 27. bis 29. März 1913. . . . Berlin, 1913. 135 p. 2250 lots. (Music = 300.)   [NL-Avb]

         Folter, no. 248. **Folter 2**, no. 874.

1931   **[Moulson, ?]; "An Amateur"**

     PUTTICK & SIMPSON, AUCTIONEER, LONDON   CAT. NO. 697

     Catalogue of a Large Collection of Music, Including the Library of an Amateur . . . Early English and Italian Vocal Music, . . . Valuable Full Scores . . . Historical and Theoretical Treatises . . . Musical Instruments . . . Sold . . . September 6th, 1861 and Following Day. . . . London, 1861. 29 p. 702 lots. Music, lots 1-642.   [US-NYp, GB-Lbl]

1932   **Mouravit, Gustave**

     Catalogue de la bibliothèque de . . . Deuxième partie. Livres anciens. (La vente aura lieu les 27 et 28 juin 1938.) Paris, 1938. 111 p. M's properties, lots 534-991.

         Not examined; cited in Hirsch catalog no. 5797 (no auctioneer noted), and only the "Deuxième partie."

1933   **Mozart, Felix Xaver Wolfgang,** 1791-1844

     Fuchs, Aloys. "Musikalischer Nachlass von W. A. Mozart (Sohn). Vermächtnis für das 'Mozarteum' in Salzburg. Wien am 1. Oktober 1844. In Gegenwart und unter Beihülfe der Frau Baroni verzeichnet und geordnet von Aloys Fuchs."

         Ms. in Salzburg, Mozarteum, Ms. 106.M21/267.

1934 _____

Hans Schneider, firm, Tutzing   Cat. no. 119
Musikalische Erst- und Frühdrucke (darunter grössere Bestände des Nachlasses von Wolfgang Amadeus Mozart Sohn). . . . Tutzing, [1966]. 44 p. 384 lots.   [g.a.]

> **Folter**, no. 249, relates that scores from Felix's estate were given by him to Mrs. Baroni- Cavacabo. He bequeathed them, in turn, to the Dommusikverein und Mozarteum in Salzburg from where they were later stolen, then sold to the antiquarian Hans Schneider. Items taken are listed by Hans Spatzenegger (**1935**).

1935 _____

Spatzenegger, Hans. "Entwendete Musikalien aus dem Besitz des Domchors in Salzburg." *Fontes* 25 (1978): 152-56.   [g.a.]

> "Aus dem Nachlass von W. A. Mozart Sohn [items missing from his bequest to the Dom Archiv]," pp. 153, ca. 16 items.

1936   **Mozart, Wolfgang Amadeus,** 1756-91
Schurig, Arthur. "Mozarts Nachlass an Büchern und Musikalien." In his *Wolfgang Amadeus Mozart* [2nd ed.], 2:453-59. Leipzig: Insel-Verlag, 1923.   [US-Wc, -NYp]

> **Folter**, no. 250.

1937 _____

Konrad, Ulrich, and Martin Staehelin. *Allzeit ein Buch: die Bibliothek Wolfgang Amadeus Mozarts. . . .* Weinheim: VCH Acta humaniora, 1991. Ausstellungskataloge der Herzog August Bibliothek, 66. 146 p., illus.   [g.a.]

> "Ausstellung . . . 5. Dezember 1991 bis 15. März 1992."

1938 _____

Literature
Babler, Otto F. "Mozart als Leser." *Philobiblon* 3 (1930): 62-65.   [g.a.]

1939 _____

Kinsky, Georg. "Mozarts handschriftlicher Nachlass." *Schweizer Musik-Zeitung* 76 (1936): 435-41.   [g.a.]

> Kinsky traces the provenance and (then, 1936) locations of many of M's Mss.

1940   **Müller, Adolf (Sr.),** 1801-86
Gilhofer & Ranschburg, auctioneer, Vienna   Auk. Cat. no. 9
Sammlung weiland des Herrn Capellmeisters am Hoftheater an der Wien Adolf Müllers sen. I. Abth. Theatralia. Musiker und Schauspieler-Porträts . . . Diverse Viennensia. Wien, 1901. 32 p. 514 lots.   [D-Bds]

> Not examined; cited from **Folter**, no. 253.

1941 _____

Gilhofer & Ranschburg, auctioneer, Vienna   Auk. Cat. no. 10
Katalog der bedeutenden und werthvollen Autographen-Sammlung weiland des Herrn . . . Adolf Müller, sen. Fortgesetzt von Adolf Müller, jun. Musik-manuscripte. Briefe von

Componisten, Sängern, Schauspielern . . . versteigerung zu Wien . . . 21.-25. October, 1901. Wien, 1901. vi, 78 p. 1007 lots. Music, lots 1-796.   [US-NYp, -Bp]

    Folter, no. 244.

1942 **Müller, Franz; Fritz Baedeker**

    KARL HENRICI, AUCTIONEER, BERLIN   AUK. CAT. NO. 137

    Autographen, Literatur und Wissenschaft, Kunst und Musik, aus dem Nachlass des Verlagsbuchhandlung Dr. Fritz Baedeker, nebst Beiträgen aus anderen Sammlungen. Versteigerung . . . 14. [-15.] August. Berlin, 1928. 110 p. 816 lots.   [NL-Avb]

    "Musik und Theater, Sammlungen Franz Müller," lots 641-816.

    Noted in *ZfMW* 10 (1927/28): 658.

1943 [_____] (only)

    KARL HENRICI, AUCTIONEER, BERLIN   VERST. 143

    Musiker-Autographen. . . . Berlin, 1928. 15 p. 129 lots.

    According to Mecklenburg, *Autographen-sammeln* (1962), 144, the properties belonged to Müller. Not located; cited from **Folter**, no. 255.

1944 **Müller, Joseph,** 1839-80

    LEO LIEPMANNSSOHN, FIRM, BERLIN   CAT. NO. 22?

    Katalog der musikalischen Bibliothek des verstorbenen Dr. Jos. Müller, Bibliothekar der Kgl. Hochschule für Musik zu Berlin . . . Die Versteigerung findet am Montag den 12. September 1881 . . . [und 4. Dezember 1882]. 2 vols. Berlin: Cohn, 1881-82. 92, 109 p. 1832 + 1713 lots.
        [US-Bp, -Wc; Pt. 1 at US-NYp, -NYgr, NL-Avb]

    I. Abth. "Theorie und Geschichte."

    II. Abth. "Hymnologie und praktisch Musik."

    Lot 657, Haydn thematic catalog in Mss.; lot 658, list of Haydn works and library in Ms.

    Folter, nos. 256 and 257.

1945 **Müller-Reutter, Theodor,** 1858-1919; **Hugo Riemann,** 1849-1919

    RUDOLPH HÖNISCH, FIRM, LEIPZIG   CAT. NO. 15

    Musik . . . enthaltend u. a. die wertvollen Bibliotheken der Musikprofessoren . . . Unfangreiche Bach-, Beethoven-, Liszt-, Mozart-, Schumann-, un Richard-Wagner-Sammlung. Leipzig, [n.d., 1921]. 98 p. 2028 lots.   [US-Wc, NL-Avb, compiler]

    Folter, no. 260. Noted in *ZfMW* 3 (1920/21): 256.

1946 _____

    RUDOLPH HÖNISCH, FIRM, LEIPZIG   ANT. CAT. NO. 16

    Musik / Theater / Theaterstücke / Deutsche Literatur [enthält dem zweiten Teil der Bibliotheken der . . .]. Leipzig: [n.p., 1921]. 98 p. 2584 lots.   [US-NYp, -NYgr, NL-Avb]

    Folter, no. 261. Noted in *ZfMW* 3 (1920/21): 448.

1947 **Müller-Reutter, Theodor** [only]

    RUDOLPH HÖNISCH, FIRM, LEIPZIG   ANT. CAT. NO. 29

    Musik. Musikalien. Bücher über Musik und Musiker. . . . Leipzig, [1923]. 98 p. 2227 lots.
        [GB-Lbl]

    Folter, no. 262.

1948   Müller von Asow, Erich Hermann, 1892-1964
V. A. HECK, FIRM, VIENNA   LISTE NO. 341
Musik. Bibliothek Müller von Asow. I. Teil. Wien, 1982. 82 p. 1312 lots.   [US-CHua]
    Erster Teil, music literature.

1949   _____
V. A. HECK, FIRM, VIENNA   LISTE NO. 346
Musik. Bibliothek Müller von Asow. II. Teil. Wien, 1983. 89 p., plates. 1390 lots.   [compiler]

1950   Muller, Joseph, 1877-1939
CHARLES SCRIBNER, SONS, FIRM, NEW YORK   CAT. NO. 105
First Editions of Famous American Songs. New York, [1936]. [72] p. 437 lots.   [g.a.]
    Folter, no. 263. Duplicates from M's collection.

1951   _____
Mell, Albert. "Paganiniana in the Muller Collection of the New York Public Library." *MO* 39
(1953): 1-25.   [g.a.]
    Muller's collection of "Star-Spangled Banner" items, ca. 200, was sold to
    US-Wc.

1952   Muoni, Damiano, 1820-94
*Libretti di melodrammi e balli, autografi di musicisti e chi altri artisti teatrali, presentati
all'esposizione musicale in Milano del cav. uff. Damiano Muoni.* Milano: Tip. Bartolotti,
1881. 112 p. 53 items.   [US-BApi, compiler (copy)]

1953   _____
L. BATTISTELLI, FIRM, MILAN   CAT. NO. 64
Collection d'autographes, manuscrits, parchemins [etc.] *en vente aux enchères publiques.*
Milan: L. Battistelli, [1907]. 26 p.   [US-U, -IO]

1954   Musical Institute of London
PUTTICK & SIMPSON, AUCTIONEER, LONDON   CAT. NO. 346
*Catalogue of the Valuable Library of the Musical Institute, Comprising Rare Treatises and
Works . . . of Music . . . Sold . . . December 15, 1853. . . .* [London], 1853. 17 p. 344 lots. Music,
lots 1-330.   [GB-Lbl]

1955   A Musical Society
SOTHEBY, S. LEIGH, AND JOHN WILKINSON
*Catalogue of a Valuable Collection of Handel's Oratorios, Consisting of Orchestral and
Single Vocal Parts, with Full and Vocal Scores, the Surplus Property of . . . Sold . . the 23rd
Day of June, 1859.* [London, 1859.] 9 p. 200 lots.   [Film at CRL]

1956   _____
PUTTICK & SIMPSON, AUCTIONEER, LONDON   CAT. NO. 1050
*Remaining Library of the Musical Society . . . Valuable and Rare Treatises and Works on the
History of Music . . . Sold . . . May 2nd* [and 4th] *1868. . . .* [London], 1868.
    Music from the Musical Society, lots 710-973. Includes stock of Thomas
    Holloway, also musical instruments. Copy missing at GB-Lbl; not examined.

Musical Society of Oxford. *See* **Bennett, Sir William Sterndale** (sale of 15 October 1878)

1957 Musiol, Robert Paul Johann, 1846-1903
LIST & FRANCKE, FIRM, LEIPZIG ANT.-CAT. NO. 372
Musikliteratur. Musikalien. Theater und Tanz. Autographen . . . z. T. aus dem Nachlasse des.
. . . Leipzig, 1905. 118 p. 3292 lots. [US-Wc, NL-Avb, GB-Lbl]
  Folter, no. 264. Noted in *ZiMG* 7 (1905/06): 82.

1958 Musis Sacrum te Leyden; R. B. van den Bosch te Goes
GEBROEDERS VAN DER HOEK, AUCTIONEER, LEYDEN
Catalogus eener belangrijke verzameling muzijk, zijnde orchest- , zang en instrumental muzijk
. . . Eerste afdeeling . . . afkomstig van het . . . Musis Sacrum . . . tweeded afdeeling, nagelaten
door . . . van den Bosch te Goes. Verkooping Dondersdag 19 Maart 1863. . . . Leyden, 1863.
22 p. 610 lots. [NL-Avb]
  Musis Sacrum's properties, lots 1-274; Bosch te Goes's lots 275-610.

1959 Mutzenbecker, Ludwig Samuel Dietrich, 1766-1838
HERRN AUKTIONSVERWALTER BEHRE, ALTONA
Verzeichnis der von dem Herrn . . . nachgelassenen musikalischen Bibliothek . . . reichen
Sammlung . . . welche den 11. Februar 1839 und folgende Tage. . . . Altona, 1839. 89 p. 1276
lots. [B-Br, compiler (copy)]

1960 Nachez, Tivadar
PUTTICK & SIMPSON, AUCTIONEER, LONDON CAT. NO. 6325
Catalogue of Books and Manuscripts, Including a Collection of Works on Music, Musicians
and Musical Instruments, the Property of . . . and Various Sources . . . Sold March 3rd, 1927.
[London], 1927. 26 p. 318 lots. [GB-Lbl]
  Nachez's properties, lots 201-07; many more items, but not a very
  distinguished collection.

1961 Nachod, Hans, 1885-1958
NORTH TEXAS STATE UNIVERSITY, DENTON
Kimmey, John A., Jr. *The Arnold Schoenberg-Hans Nachod Collection.* Detroit Studies in
Music Bibliography, 41. This publisher, 1979. 119 p. [115] leaves of plates. [g.a.]

1962 _____
  LITERATURE
  Steiner, Rudolf. "Der unbekannte Schönberg: Aus unveröffentlichten Briefen an Hans Nachod."
  Schweizerische Musik Zeitung 104/05 (1964): 284-86. [g.a.]

1963 _____
  Steiner, Eva and Rudolf. "Arnold Schönberg: An Unknown Correspondence." *Saturday Review,*
  27 March 1965, pp. 47-49. [g.a.]

1964 _____
  Newlin, Dika. "The Schoenberg-Nachod Collection: A Preliminary Report." *MO* 54 (1968):
  31-46. [g.a.]

Nadel, Arno, 1878-1943. *See under* **Mandell, Eric**

1965   **Nägeli, Hans Georg,** 1773-1836
Verzeichniss ungedruckter Compositionen grosser Tonsetzer der Vorzeit welche von Dr. Hans Georg Nägeli hinterlassen wurden und nunmehr in dessen, noch fortbestehender Musikalien-Handlung . . . käuflich zu haben sind. . . . Zürich, 1854. 6 p.   [D-Bds]

> **Albrecht** says "Catalogue by Brenet" [i.e., Bobillier], and that 50 volumes of the collection went to Lowell Mason (**1808**), thence to US-NH. Part of the library is at CH-Z. **Folter**, no. 266.

1966   _____
Walter, C. "Der musikalische Nachlass H. G. Nägelis." *Schweizerische Musik Zeitung* 76 (1936): 641-59.   [g.a.]

> **Folter**, no. 266; **Albrecht**.

1967   _____
Gojowsky, Detlef. "Wie enstand Hans Georg Nägelis Bach-Sammlung? Dokumente zur Bach-Renaissance im 19. Jhdt." *Bach-Jahrbuch* 56 (1970): 66-104.

1968   **Naldi, Giuseppe**
MR. OXENHAM, AUCTIONEER, LONDON
Catalogue of the Excellent Household Furniture, Modern Plate . . . Jewellery . . . Cellar of Wines . . . [Musical Instruments] . . . Collection of Music and Operas, in Score, of the Best Composers, the Property of . . . Dec'd . . . Sold . . . February 14 [-17] 1821. . . . London, 1821. 38 p. 456, 108 lots. Music, final 108 lots.   [US-R]

> **King**, p. 27. (Second sale, *see under* **Gwilt, Joseph.**)

1969   **Nan Kivell, Rex de Charambac**
Anderson, Gordon A., and Luther A. Dittmer. *Canberra, National Library of Australia, Ms. 4052/2 1-16* (The Musico-Liturgical Fragments from the Nan Kivel Collection). Publications of Mediaeval Music Manuscripts, 13. Henryville, Pa.: Institute of Mediaeval Music, [1981]. 19 p. 20 fol.   [g.a.]

1970   **Nanki Bunko, Tokyo (Nanki Music Library)**
> See long note about the collection's formation by Yorisada Tokugawa in the 1890s, and its present ownership by Kyubei Okhi *under* **Tokugawa**.

1971   **National Choral Society**
PUTTICK & SIMPSON, AUCTIONEER, LONDON
Catalogue of Extensive Stock of Popular Music Publications of Mr. G. W. Martin . . . Library of the . . . Society . . . Also Musical Instruments . . . Sold . . . December 16, 1875, and Following Day. [London], 1875. 32 p. 1012 lots.   [GB-Lbl]

> Society's properties, *inter alia.*

Naumann, E. W. R.   *See under* **Wenzel, E. F.**

1972   **Nedbal, Oskar,** 1874-1930
Buchner, Alexander. *Oskar Nedbal: Soupis pozustalosti.* Prague: Národni Muzeum, 1964.
[g.a.]

> Collection at CS-Pnm.

1973 Nejedlý, Zdenek

Postolka, Milan. "Hudební pamatky ze sbirky Zdenka Nejedlého." *Casopis Národniho muzea-rada historická* 150, no. 1/2 (1981): 37-55.   [g.a.]

> Collection now at CS-Pnm.

1974 Nesselrode (family), Schloss Ehreshoven

M. Lempertz, firm, Bonn

Bibliothek Schloss Ehreshoven . . . Versteigerung. . . . Aachen, 1925. 105 p. Lots 2709-3058, music, music literature, and autographs.

> G. Kinsky, in *ZfMW* 7 (1924-25): 446 says, the sale was 25 March 1924 in Bonn. The Aachen, 1925 citation is from the dealer Creyghton's catalog no. 50, lot 212.

Neuberger Hofkapelle.   *See under* **Ottheinrich, Kurfürsten von Neuberg**

"A New York Collector."   *See under* **Mlynarski, Doris Kenyon**

Newland, William A., 1813-1901.   *See* **Hodges, Edward,** 1796-1867

1975 Newman, Ernest, 1868-1959

Hodgson & Co., auctioneer, London

A Catalogue of the Music Library of . . . (Dec'd) Removed from Tadworth, Surrey . . . Sold . . . December 10th, 1959. [London: R. Stockwell, 1959.] 39 p. 578 lots.

[US-Cn, compiler (priced)]

1976 Newman, William Stein, 1912-2000

Literature

Newman, William S. "A Private Collector Takes Inventory." *Notes* 1 (1944): 24-32.   [g.a.]

1977 _____

Elliott, Patricia. "The William S. Newman Beethoven Collection at the Center for Beethoven Studies." *Beethoven Newsletter* 3, no. 2 (summer 1988): 32-35.   [g.a.]

1978 Newton, Richard; Ursula Fürstner

Sotheby & Co., auctioneer, London

Catalogue of Valuable Printed Books, Music, Autograph Letters, and Historical Documents, Comprising . . . Music and Books on Music, Including . . . Letters and Music of Berlioz, Brahms, Debussy [et al.], *Unpublished Letter of Beethoven; a Highly Important Collection of Autograph Music of Sibelius . . . Sold . . . 11th* [-12th] *May, 1970.* London, 1970. 168 p. 519 lots. Music, lots 237-519.   [Film at CRL]

> Newton's properties, lots 237-94 (many more items); Newton's ALS, lots 415-18; Fürstner's ALS, lots 500-519 (mainly Liszt).

1979 Ney, Elly, 1882-1968

Hans Schneider, firm, Tutzing   Cat. no. 137

Musikbestände Elly Ney. . . . Tutzing: Schneider, [1968]. 143 p., illus. 2216 lots.   [g.a.]

> **Folter,** no. 267.

1980   Ney, Michel, Prince of Moscow
AUG. AUBRY, LIBRAIRE, PARIS
Catalogue de livres & musique dépendant de la succession de feu M. le Prince de la Moskowa dont la vente aura lieu le vendredi 19 février 1858. . . . Paris, 1858. 8 p. 76 lots.
[GB-Lbl (Hirsch, from James Matthew Collection)]

1981   Niessen, Carl
"Collection of Works on the History of the Theatre, Principally in Germany." [N.p., 1933.] 38 leaves Ca. 570 items.

Original and carbon of typescript at US-Wc. "Received March 1933," according to the US-Wc card.

1982   Nieuwenhuijsen, Wilhelm Johan Frederik
J. L. BEIJERS, AUCTIONEER, UTRECHT
Catalogus van eene belangrijke verzameling muziek, boeken over muziek en muziekgeschiedenis benevens eenige fraaie muziekinstrumenten, nagelaten door . . . Organist de Domkerk . . . verkooping . . . van de notaris E. P. Temminck . . . 27 April en volgende dagen. . . . Utrecht: Beijers, [1870]. 88 p. 1940 + lots. Music, lots 1-1071. [NL-Avb, GB-Lbl (Hirsch)]

1983   Nieuwenhuyzen, J   J
FREDERICK MULLER, AUCTIONEER?, AMSTERDAM
Catalogus eener zeer belangrijke verzameling van Hollandsche boeken . . . dicht en letterunde . . . volksletterkunde, als: liedboeken, volksboeken, romans, voorts: psalmberijmingen, toneelspelen . . . nagelaten door . . . verkocht . . . 25 Maart 1861. . . . A'dam, 1861. [NL-Avb]

1984   Nightingale, J   C   ; J   O   Atkins
MR. WATSON, AUCTIONEER, LONDON
Catalogue of a Collection of Musical Property, Including the Libraries of the Late . . . Nightingale and . . . Atkins, a Bankrupt . . . Sold . . . December 23rd, 1833. London, 1833. 8 p. 150 leaves.   [US-NYp, compiler]

1985   Niles, Doris; Serge Leslie
Leslie, Serge. *A Bibliography of the Dance Collection of Doris Niles and Serge Leslie.* Annotated by Serge Leslie and edited by Cyril Beaumont. 4 vols. London: C. W. Beaumont, 1966-81.
[US-Wc, -BUu, -MSu]

1986   Nötzoldt, Fritz, b. 1908
LITERATURE
Brednich, Rolf Wilhelm. "Neuerwerbungen des Deutschen Volksliedarchivs: Die Bänkelsang-Sammlung Nötzoldt, Heidelberg." *Jahrbuch für Volksliedforschung* 25 (1980): 110-13.   [g.a.]

1987   Nohl, Karl Friedrich Ludwig, 1831-85
KIRCHOFF & WIGAND, FIRM, LEIPZIG   CAT. NO. 834
Musikwissenschaft. Geschichte der Musik. Theoretische Werke. Ältere praktische Musik. Ältere und neuere Opern und Oratorien, enthaltend einem Theil der Bibliothek des Professors . . . in Heidelerg. Leipzig, 1889. 41 p. 1267 lots.

Not located; cited from **Folter**, no. 271, who says Nohl properties are not differentiated.

1988 _____

LITERATURE

Staehelin, Martin. "Die Beethoven-Materialien im Nachlass von Ludwig Nohl." *Beethoven Jahrbuch* 10 (1978/81, publ. 1983): 201-19.   [g.a.]

1989   Nolthenius, Hugo (of Laren); et al.

A. J. VAN HUFFEL, AUCTIONEER, UTRECHT

Catalogus der bibliotheken van wijlen de Heeren J. Stibbe [etc.] *en van de muziekbibliotheek van wijlen den heer Hugo Nolthenius . . . Boekverkooping 25-29 nov. en 1-2 dec. 1930. . . .* Utrecht, 1930. 109 p. 2110 lots.   [NL-Avb]

> Nolthenius's properties, lots 1927-2110.

Nonsuch Library.   *See under* **Lumley, John, Baron**

Northcott, Richard, 1871-1931.   *See under* **Clarence O. B.**

> Author of books on Donizetti, Offenbach, Bishop, Covent Garden (where he was archivist from 1906 until his death), Gounod, and others. **King**, p. 80.

Northcott, Mrs. Richard A.   *See under* **Gresnirere, Juan B.**

1990   Noseda, Gustavo Adolfo, 1837-66

MILAN, ARCHIVIO MUSICALE NOSEDA

Indice generale dell' Archivio musicale Noseda, compilato dal Prof. Eugenio de' Guarinoni . . . con una breve biografia del fondatore e con alcuni cenni intorno all' archivio stesso ed all biblioteca del R. Conservatorio di musica di Milano. Milano: E. Reggiani, 1897. xiv, 419 p. 10,253 titles.   [US-NYp, -Wc, -BE]

> First published in the *Annuario* of the R. Conservatorio de Musica di Milano, 1889-96. Deposited in the Conservatorio in 1889. Includes 700 autographs.

1991 _____

Caraci, Maria. "Le cantate romane di Alessandro Scarlatti nel fondo Noseda." In *Händel, e gli Scarlatti a Roma,* ed. Nino Pirrotta & Agostino Zino, 93-111. Firenze: Olschki, 1987.   [g.a.]

1992 _____

LITERATURE

"L'Annuario del Conservatorio di Musica di Milano e l'Archivio musicale Noseda." *Il Teatro illustrato* 12 (1892): 75-76.   [US-BUu]

1993   Noske, Willem, 1918-

G. N. LANDRÉ, FIRM, AMSTERDAM   LIST NO. 31

Doubletten uit de vioolbibliotheek van Willem Noske. Deel I. Amsterdam, 1987. 117 lots.
                                           [g.a.]

1994 _____

PAUL VAN KUIK, ANTIQUARIAN, VOORSCHOTEN   CAT. NO. 15

3500 books on composers from the Willem Noske collection. Voorschoten, 1995. 101 p. 3455 lots.

> At least 5 other forthcoming catalogs of Noske's collection are announced on the back cover.

1995 _____

LITERATURE

Brieven en opdrachten van beroemde musici. . . . Letters and Dedications from Famous Musicians: Eight Autographs from the Willem Noske Collections. . . . Buren: F. Knuf, 1985. 96 p.   [US-Wc]

1996   Nostitz-Rhieneck, Erwin, Count

Simák, Josef Vitézslav. *Rukopisy Majorátní knihovny hrabat z Nostitz a Rhienecka v Praze, zprávu o nich podává J. V. Simák.* Prague: Nakl. Ceské akademie . . . , 1910. x, 165 p.

[US-STu]

Collection now at CS-Pdobrovského, according to **Albrecht**.

1997 _____

Ludvová, Jitka. "Hudba v rodu Nostitzu." *Hudební veda* 23/2 (1986): 144-64.

Not examined; cited from *RILM* which notes a 1781 inventory of stage decor and a list of operas and operettas copied for use in the Kotzen Theater in Prague.

1998   Novello, Vincent, 1781-1861

PUTTICK & SIMPSON, AUCTIONEER, LONDON   CAT. NO. 277

Catalogue of a Portion of [His] *Musical Library . . . in Which Will Be Found . . . Curious Early Printed Madrigals . . . from the Library of Signor Dragonetti . . . Sold . . . June 25, 1852.* [London, 1852.] 16 p. 367 lots. Music, lots 1-356.   [US-NYp, GB-Lbl]

1999 _____

PUTTICK & SIMPSON, AUCTIONEER, LONDON   CAT. NO. 739

Catalogue of a Portion of [His] *Remaining Musical Library . . . Also Musical Instruments . . . Sold . . . September 3* [-5]*, 1862.* [London], 1862. 46 p. 1277 lots. Music, lots 1-1030.

[US-NYp, GB-Lbl]

Both this catalog and the preceding one (1852) were reprinted with an introduction by A. Hyatt King (Buren: Knuf, 1975).   [Reprint g.a.]

2000   Novello, F. Vincent; Anon.

PUTTICK & SIMPSON, AUCTIONEER, LONDON   CAT. NO. 1359

Catalogue of a Collection of Music, Comprising . . . Autograph Compositions . . . A Few Copyrights . . . Sold December 20th, 1872. [London], 1872. 24 p. 474 lots. Music, lots 1-384.

[GB-Lbl]

Music "from Novello's Collection," lots 206-370.

2001 _____

LEEDS UNIVERSITY, BROTHERTON LIBRARY

The Novello Cowden Clarke Collection. [Leeds:] Brotherton Library, 1955. 19 p. [GB-LEbc]

Includes the collection of Mary Cowden Clarke, 1809-98, and Charles Cowden Clarke, 1787-1877.

→ *See also under* **Kent, James** (sale of 22 May 1835 by Mr. Watson)

2002   Novello & Co.
Sотневу & Co., auctioneer, London
Catalog of Valuable Printed Books, Music, Autograph Letters and Historical Documents,
Comprising . . . Music, Books on Music . . . Autograph Letters and Manuscripts
of Berlioz, Boito, Britten, Brahms, Busoni, Debussy [etc.] *. . . Sold 19th of July, 1965*
and the Two Following Days. London, 1965. 180 p. 849 lots.

[US-NYgr, -CN; film at CRL]

Novello's properties, lots 254-365 (*many* more items); property of A
Gentleman (Haydn items), lots 375-86 (more items); A Lady's, lots 395-401
(each lot contains dozens of items); B. van Dieren's, lots 403-36; Amedo de
Filippi of Hollywood's ALS and MS, lots 509-59 (hundreds of items!). An
impressive and important catalog.

2003   _____

Literature
Dibble, Jeremy. "The RCM Novello Library." *MT* 74 (February 1983): 99-101.   [g.a.]

2004   Nydahl, Rudolf; Otto Tausig, 1831-71
Orel, Alfred. "Schubertiana in Schweden." In *Musa - mens - musici. Im Gedenken an Walther
Vetter,* 297-307. Leipzig, 1969.

Nydahl's collection of autographs in the Stiftelsen Musikkulturens
Främhanden, Stockholm; Tausig's in Malmö. Not located. Cited from
RILM.

2005   _____

Holst, Gunnar. "Förteckning över musikhandskrifter, musikalier, brev och biografica." *Svenskt
musikkhistorisk arkiv, Bulletin* 8 (1972). 51 p. (whole issue).   [g.a.]

2006   _____

Rabenius, O. "Ett storartat musikarkiv. Märkliga original-manuskript av Mozart, Beethoven,
Wagner." *Svenska dagbladet,* 29 November 1942.

Not examined. Cited from *DASMl.*

2007   _____

Grahn, Göran. "Stiftelsen Musikkulturens främjande." *Fontes* 34 (1987): 112-14.   [g.a.]

2008   Obizzi Family

Albrecht: The collection formed by the children of Pio Enea II degli Obizzi,
near Padua, 1674-1727, was later taken to Vienna by the Duke of Modena,
Francesco d'Este. *See under* **Este.**

2009   Obreen, H   G   A
A. J. van Huffel, auctioneeer, Utrecht
[Sale of library of songbooks, 28 May ?]

Not examined. Cited from **Vereeniging.** . . . *Catalogus* 8:397.

2010 **Obrist, Aloys,** 1867-1910

R. LEVI, FIRM, STUTTGART   ANT. CAT. NO. 189

. . . *Musikbibliothek des Dr. A. Obrist. I. Bücher zur Geschichte und Theorie der Musik. II. Vokal- und Instrumentalmusik. III. Autographen und Portraits von Musikern.* Stuttgart: R. Levi, 1911. 106 p. 1976 lots.   [GB-Lbl (Hirsch 5861)]

    Folter, no. 272 (with a slightly different title).

2011 **O'Callaghan, George**

PUTTICK & SIMPSON, AUCTIONEER, LONDON   CAT. NO. 450

Catalogue of a . . . Collection of Music . . . Including a Portion of the Library of . . . Engraved Music Plates . . . Also Musical Instruments . . . Sold . . . May 26 [1856]. [London, 1856.] 28 p. 736 lots. Music, lots 1-413, 427-580.   [US-NYp, GB-Lbl]

2012 **Ochs, Siegfried,** 1858-1929

"Vom Schreibtisch und aus dem Atelier. Aus einer Autographensammlung. [Musikerautographen der Sammlung Siegfried Ochs in Berlin.]" *Velhagen und Klasings Monatshefte* 24 (November 1909): 369-80.

    Not located. Cited from *BiBB,* 1909.

2013 _____

C. G. BOERNER, FIRM, LEIPZIG   CAT. NO. 22?

Katalog einer berühmten Sammlung von Musikmanuskripten und Musikerbriefen welche . . . im ganzen Verkauf werden soll. . . . Leipzig: C. G. Boerner, [ca. 1910]. 79 p.

                                      [US-NYp, -Wc-, NYgr]

    Folter, no. 273.

2014 **Odoevski, Vladimir Federovich, Prince,** 1804-69

LITERATURE

Iagolin, Boris. "Bibliotheka Odoevskogo." *Sovetskaia Muzyka* 33, no. 6 (1969): 96-99.   [g.a.]

    Some items described. The collection was given by O's widow to the Moscow Conservatory in 1869.

    Albrecht notes a catalog of the collection by I. M. Kudriavtsev, Moskva, 1960, but it cannot be located.

    → *See also under* **Razumovsky, Dmitry Vasil'yevich**

2015 **Örtel, Friedrich Benedikt**

Braun, Werner. "Die Musikbibliothek des Sächsischen Hof -und Justizrates . . . (1751)." *Mf* 10 (1957): 247-50.   [g.a.]

2016 **Östergren, G A**

Förteckning öfver musikalier och böcker, kwilka utlånas uti G. A. Östergrens bibliothek. . . . Stockholm: Elmens och Granbergs Tryckeri, 1816. 88 p. 2356 lots. Music, *inter alia.*   [S-SK]

2017 **Oesterlein, Nikolaus,** 1841-98

Katalog einer Richard Wagner-bibliothek: Nach den vorliegenden Originalien zu einem authentischen Nachschlagebuch durch die gesamte, insbesondere deutsche Wagner-Litteratur. . . . 4 vols. Leipzig: Gebrüder Senf, 1882-95.   [g.a.]

Vol. 1. xxx, 321 p. 3373 lots

Vol. 2. xxviii, 352 p. Lots 3374-5567

Vol. 3. xxix, 517 p. Lots 5568-9 470

Vol. 4. xv, 172 p. Lots 9471-10, 180

Vols. 3-4 have special title pages: Beschreibendes Verzeichnis des Richard Wagners-Museums in Wien. Vols. 2-4 published by Breitkopf & Härtel. **Folter**, no. 274.

2018 _____

A. EINSLE, AUCTIONEER, VIENNA   AUK. CAT. NO. 74
Katalog einer Theiles der Bibliothek des Herrn . . . anderer, bestehend aus Doubletten des Richard . . . einer reichhaltigen Collection Beethoveniana, Autographen, Musik [u.s.w.] *Versteigerung . . . 18. November 1895 und folg. Tage. . . .* Wien, 1895. 38 p. 855 lots. Music, lots 590-855 (*many* more items).   [US-NYgr]

Österreich, Georg, 1664-1735.   *See under* **Bokemeyer, Heinrich,** 1679-1751

2019 Österreichisches Fürstenhaus

KARL & FABER, AUCTIONEER, MÜNCHEN   AUK. CAT. NO. 57
Bücher - Handschriften - Autographen . . . Versteigerung . . . 6. -7. Dez. 1956. München, 1956. 151 p., 12 plates. 1650 lots.

Music manuscripts "aus einem österreichischen Fürstenhaus und wurde 1700 und 1730 angelegt," lots 450-508; printed music, lots 509-64; autographs, including musicians', lots 565-632.

Oetting, C., d'. *See* **Philip Karl, Graf zu Oettingen-Wallerstein**

Öettingen-Wallerstein.   *See also under* **Misligowsky, Carl; Schaden, Fr. Michael von**

2020 Ogle, Cuthbert

Tyler, Lyon G. [article] *William & Mary Quarterly,* ser. 1, 3 (19-): 251-53.   [g.a.]

From York County, Virginia records.

2021 _____

Maurer, Maurer. "The Library of a Colonial Musician, 1755." *William & Mary Quarterly* 7 (1950): 39-52.   [g.a.]

2022 _____

Molnar, John W. "A Collection of Music in Colonial Virginia: The Ogle Inventory." *MQ* 49 (1963): 150-62.   [g.a.]

The inventory, pp. 158-61 (38 items). Unpublished Ms. of the inventory with more detailed report, 1962, in the Research Dept. of Colonial Williamsburg.

2023 _____

LITERATURE

Ingram, John E. "Collecting Colonial Music Material." *AB Bookman's Weekly* 76, no. 244 (9 December 1985): 4315-16.   [g.a.]

Brief paragraphs.

2024 Ogny, Comte d'
"Catalogue de la musique de Monsieur le Comte d'Ogny." Mss., 168 leaves, in Hirsch collection (4:1085).   [GB-Lbl; compiler (film and copyflo)]

2025 _____

"Catalogue de musique vocale." [Ca. 1780.]   [US-Wc; compiler (film and copyflo)]
US-Wc: "Copyist's Ms. (220 p.) thematic catalog of the author's collection."

2026 Okhi, Kyubei (present owner of Nanki Music Library)
See long note about the collection's formation by Yorisada Tokugawa in the 1890s, its history since then, until Okhi became owner in the late 1940s *under* **Tokugawa.**

2027 Oldman, Cecil Bernard, 1894-1969
Albrecht: much of his printed music was given to GB-Lbl. Other items were auctioned in May of 1959 (*see under* **Gresnirere**), some sold earlier to H. Baron and some 300 items appeared in Baron's catalog no. 53, 1961 (**2028**). A "collection of manuscripts, typescripts, notes, correspondence, printed music and items relating to articles written by Oldman about Mozart" (many items) were consigned by his widow, Mrs. S. J. M. Oldman, to Sotheby's for a sale 15 May 1979 (**2031**). She had earlier, in 1974, presented a number of items to A-Sm.

2028 _____

HERMAN BARON, FIRM, LONDON   CAT. NO. 53
[Mozartiana]. London, [1961]. 36 p. 332 leaves.   [compiler]
Folter, no. 276. **King**, p. 79.

2029 Oldman, Cecil Bernard; John Tobin; Sir John Barbirolli
SOTHEBY, PARK BERNET & CO., AUCTIONEER, LONDON
Catalogue of Valuable Printed Books, Autograph Letters and Historical Documents . . . Sold . . . March 15 [-16], 1971. London, 1971. 166 p. 646 lots. Music, lots 1-358.   [Film at CRL]
Oldman's properties, lots 1-30; Tobin's, 126-32; Barbirolli's, 263-84.

2030 _____

Eibl, J. H. "Zu den Autographen aus dem Nachlass von C. B. Oldman." *Mitteilungen der Internationaler Stiftung Mozarteum* 22 (1974): 16.   [g.a.]

2031 _____

Eibl, J. H. *Catalogue of Printed and Manuscript Music, Autograph Letters of Musicians and Books on Music and the Theatre, Playbills . . . Sold . . . May 15th, 1979. . . .* London, 1979. 64 p. 287 lots.
Oldman's properties, lots 1-3, 44-47, 146-47. **Folter**, no. 277.

2032 Oliphant, Thomas, 1799-1873
PUTTICK & SIMPSON, AUCTIONEER, LONDON   CAT. NO. 1387
Catalogue of the Important Musical Collection of . . . Comprising Printed Music, the Works of English and Italian Composers from the Sixteenth Century to the Present Time. . . . To Be Sold

. . . *April 24, 1873.* [London, 1873.] 44 p. 592 lots. All music.

[US-NYp, -Wc, GB-Lbl; compiler (priced)]

2033 _____

PUTTICK & SIMPSON, AUCTIONEER, LONDON   CAT. NO. 1388

Catalogue of the Valuable Music Plates and Copyrights of the Late . . . Vocal Music . . . . Songs and Ballads [etc.] *. . . Sold . . . April 2th, 1873.* [London], 1873. 19 p. 248 lots.   [GB-Lbl]

2034 [_____]

PUTTICK & SIMPSON, AUCTIONEER, LONDON   CAT. NO. 1396

Catalogue of a Large Collection of Music, Including Operas, Oratorios . . . Remainder of [Oliphant's?] *Music Library . . . A Few Music Plates and Copyrights; Copyright Manuscript Compositions of Mr. W. F. Taylor, Also Musical Instruments . . . Sold May 26th, 1873 and Following Day.* [London], 1873. 38 p. 1007 lots. Music and plates, lots 1-909.

[GB-Lbl]

2035 Olivier, François, 1907-48

LAUSANNE, BIBLIOTHÈQUE CANTONALE ET UNIVERSITAIRE, DEPT. DE LA MUSIQUE

Inventaire du fonds musical François Olivier. Lausanne, 1971. 69 p. 219 items.

[US-Wc, -BE, -NYcu]

      Folter, no. 279.

2036 Olmeda de San José, Federico, 1865-1909

KARL W. HIERSEMANN, FIRM, LEIPZIG   CAT. NO. 392

Musik und Liturgie, darunter, besonders alte original Manuscripte, seltene Drucke des 16. Jahrhunderts, eine Abteilung spanische Musik, original-Tonwerke von Beethoven und Wagner, etc. Zum Teil aus der Bibliothek des Don. Federico Olmeda . . . und einiger andere Sammlungen. . . . Leipzig: Karl W. Hiersemann, 1911. 74 p., illus., facs. 335 items.

[US-WYp, -CHua, NL-Dhgm; compiler]

      Magnificent collection, but properties are not differentiated. **Folter**, no. 278.

2037 Ommeren, C   van

A. J. VAN HUFFEL, AUCTIONEER, UTRECHT

[Sales including songbooks, 10-14 October 1935; 16-18 February 1937; 24 November 1937.]

[NL-Avb]

      In **Vereeniging** . . . *Catalogus* 8:397. Not examined.

2038 Oom, Adolphus Kent

PUTTICK & SIMPSON, AUCTIONEER, LONDON   CAT. NO. 612

Catalogue of a Collection of Music, Including the Remaining Library of . . . Also Numerous Valuable Musical Instruments . . . Sold . . . February 10, 1860. [London, 1860.] 19 p. 400 lots. Music, lots 1-343.   [US-NYp, GB-Lbl]

      First sale, 10 January 1860, contained no music. Several lots here comprise large collections, e.g.: lot 70, "Instrumental music," 46 volumes; lot 112, "Orchestral music," 283 works in 16 volumes; lot 203, "Flute music," 10 volumes.

2039   Oppel, Wigand
LUDOLPH ST. GOAR, AUCTIONEER, FRANKFURT A.M.
Verzeichnis von theoretischen Werken über Musik und Miscellanien, aus dem Nachlasse des Herrn Organisten . . . sowie neuerer Musikalien, welch bei Ludolph St. Goar . . . zu haben sind. Versteigert . . . Oktbr. 5, 1886. . . . Frankfurt A.M., 1886.   [GB-Lbl (Hirsch)]

Not examined.

2040   Opprel, A   , Dr.; et al.
J. L. BEIJERS, AUCTIONEER, UTRECHT
Catalogus van een belangrijke verzameling boeken en tijdschriften, afkomstig uit de bibliotheeken van wijlen de heeren . . . [and others] *. . . verkooping 2-12 mei 1938.* Utrecht, 1938. 196 p. 3497 lots. Music, 375 lots.   [NL-Avb]

Oranje-Nassau.   *See* William V, Prince of Orange

2041   Orme, Robert
The Famous Collection of Musical-Instruments, and Books. . . . Together with an Excellent Collection of Books of Musick, Containing the Choicest Sonatas, Motetts, Aires, &c. To Be Sold on 20th December 1711, at the New House Next the Wheat-Sheaf, in Henrietta-Street.

Not located. Cited from Michael Tilmouth's "Calendar of References to Music in Newspapers Published in London . . . 1660-1719," *RMA Research Chronicle* 1 (1961): 80. **King**, p. 12, notes an announcement of the sale in *The Daily Courant.* Auctioneer not identified.

2042   Ortigue, Joseph -Louis d', 1802-66
L. POTIER, AUCTIONEER, PARIS (C.P. = CHARLES PILLET)
Catalogue des livres rares et curieux composant la bibliothèque de M. J. d'O. Paris: Potier, 1862.   [US-NYgr]

Folter, no. 280, and **Albrecht** both note, but though Ortigue was a writer on music, the catalog contains no music items.

2043   _____
ADOLPHE LABITTE (LIBRAIRE), PARIS
Notice de livres sur la musique, partitions musicales, ouvrages bien conditionnés en maroquin . . . vente . . . 31 octobre 1871. . . . Paris, 1871. 16 p. 148 lots. Music, lots 1-51 only!   [NL-DHgm]

Folter, no. 281.

2044   Osborn, James Marshall, 1906-76
Witten, Laurence. "Contemporary Collectors XXIII: James Marshall Osborn." *Book Collector* 8 (1959): 383.   [g.a.]

Collection now at US-NH.

2045   Osborn, James Marshall; Marie-Louise Osborn
Boito, Diane. "Manuscript Music in the James Marshall and Marie-Louise Osborn Collection." *Notes* 27 (1970): 237-44.   [g.a.]

2046 _____

LITERATURE

Parks, Stephen. "The Osborn Collection: A Biennial Progress Report." *Yale University Library Gazette* 44 (1970): 114-36.   [g.a.]

> "Music manuscripts," pp. 134-36.

2047   Ossolinski, Jozef Maksymiljan, 1748-1826

Ketrzynski, Wojciech. *Katalog rekopisów biblioteken zakladu nar. im. Ossolinskich.* . . . Lwow: Nakl. Zakladu Nar im Ossolinskich, 1881-98.

> Collection in Wroclaw, P-WRzno. Cited from Wesseley (**2049**).

2048 _____

Mikulski, Tadeusz. *Zaklad imienia Ossolinskich 1817-1956. W dziesiecielecie dzialnósci we Wroclawiu.* Wroclaw, 1956.

> Cited from Wesseley (**2049**).

2049 _____

LITERATURE

"Anhang. Rkp. Bibl. Ossolinskich." In Othmar Wessely, *Zur Vorgeschichte des musikalischen Denkmalschutzes,* 425-28. Wien: Verlag der Österreichischen Akademie der Wissenschaften, 1976.

2050   Otho I, King of Greece, 1815-67

Themelis, Dimitris. "Die Musiksammlung aus der Privatbibliothek König Ottos I. von Griechenland." *Musik in Bayern* 18-19 (1979): 55-93.   [g.a.]

> Collection now at D-Mbs.

2051   Ottheinrich, Kurfürsten von Neuberg

"Aller meinz genedigen Herrn Gesang, inventirt und beschriben Anno XLIIII."

> Ms. at Heidelberg Universitätsbibliothek, Ms. Pal.Germ.318. Summarized in Hermelink's article (**2053**). A reported "Neudruck" in *Neues Archiv für die Geschichte der Stadt Heidelberg u. der Kurpfalz* 11 (1924): 45-50, proves to be only a summary, like Hermelink's.

2052 _____

["Inventar der von Kurfürst Ottheinrich von Neuberg nach Heidelberg mitgenommenen Kleinodien, Bücher, Kleidungsstücke usw. aus dem Jahr 1556."]

> According to Loyer (**2055**), a Ms. inventory in Bayerisches Staatsarchiv Neuberg, Depot Heimatverein Neuberg Nr. 52, pp. 133, 140, 150.

2053 _____

Hermelink, Siegfried. "Ein Musikalienverzeichnis der Heidelberger Hofkapelle aus dem Jahre 1544." In George Poensgen, ed., *Ottheinrich, Gedenkschrift zur vierhundert-Jährigen Wiederkehr* . . . , 247-60. Mitteilungen der Veereinigung der Fremde der Studentschaft der University Heidelberg, 5. [Heidelberg, 1956.]

> "Inhaltübersicht des Heidelberger Kapellinventars 1544," pp. 255-60. *MGG* discusses under Wittelsbach Family (**2880**).

2054 _____

Stein, Fritz Wilhelm. *Zur Geschichte des Musikwesens in Heidelberg bis zum Ende des 18. Jahrhunderts.* Heidelberg: G. Koester, 1921. 151 p.   [US-Wc, -CHua, -AA]

> Inaug.-diss., Heidelberg, 1912. Not examined; cited from *JbP*. Reported to contain a reprint of the 1544 inventory (**2053**).

2055 _____

LITERATURE
Loyer, Adolf. "Pfalzgraf Ottheinrich und die Musik." *AfMW* 15 (1958): 258-75.   [g.a.]

2056   **Ottley, William Young; An Eminent Professional Gentleman**
S. LEIGH SOTHEBY, AUCTIONEER, LONDON
Catalogue of the Valuable and Interesting Collections of Manuscript Music, the Property of the Late . . . and Also of an Eminent Professional Gentleman, Deceased, Many Years Attached to the Italian Opera . . . Including a MS. Copy of Handel's Messiah . . . Sold . . . 17th of August, 1838. [London, 1838.]   [GB-Lbl (Hirsch); film at CRL]
> **King**, pp. 38-39.

2057   **Ottoboni, Cardinal**
Everett, Paul. "Vivaldi Concerto Manuscripts in Manchester [i.e., the Central Library]." *Informazione e studi vivaldiana* 5 (1984): 23-52. Facs.   [g.a.]

> From *RILM*. In the Central Library, 24 Vivaldi, 81 other manuscripts which "were perhaps once part of the collection of Cardinal Ottoboni."

2058 _____

Everett, Paul. "A Roman Concerto Repertory: Ottoboni's 'What Not?'." *Proceedings of the Royal Musical Association* 105 (1983/84): 62-78.   [g.a.]

2059   **Oudijk van Putten, J   ; J   T   Grashius**
J. VAN BAALEN & ZONEN, AUCTIONEER, ROTTERDAM
Catalogus eener belangrijke verzameling Boeken, Pracht- en Plaatwerken, Muziek . . . nagelaten door . . . verkoping . . . 21 november 1870 en volgende dagen . . . ten overstaan van de notarissen van der Hoeven & Speelman. . . . Rotterdam, 1870. 96 p. 2676 + 31 lots. Music, lots 2438-595.   [NL-Avb, F-Pe]

2060   **Ouseley, Sir Frederick Arthur Gore,** Bart., 1825-89
"A Catalogue of the Musical Literature in the Library of F. A. G. O. Compiled by Sir Fred[k] Ouseley."

> Ms., St. Michael's College, Tenbury, no. 1259. Incomplete.

2061 _____

ST. MICHAEL'S COLLEGE, TENBURY
Fellowes, Edmund H., comp. *The Catalogue of Manuscripts in the Library. . . .* Paris: Éditions de l'Oiseau-Lyre, 1934. 319 p.   [g.a.]

> Includes manuscript copies made by Philidor for the Comte de Toulouse, later inherited by Louis Philippe, King of France (1773-1850), sold with his books in 1852, most passing into Ouseley's collection. See much material

on the Toulouse-Philidor and Ouseley collections here under **Toulouse-Philidor**. Note: the manuscript collection is now mostly in the Bodleian Library, Oxford.

"Printed books from the Toulouse Collection," pp. 34-39. "Extract from the Catalogue [by L. A. Potier] of the Louis-Philippe sale in Paris, December 1852," pp. 40-46.

2062 _____

LITERATURE
Ouseley, Sir Frederick Arthur Gore. "On the Early Italian and Spanish Treatises on Counterpoint and Harmony." *Proceedings of the Musical Association,* (1879), 76-99.   [g.a.]

> **King**, pp. 67-68, says based on Ouseley's collection. Also reprint, Vaduz: Kraus Reprint, 1966.

2063 _____

Ouseley, Sir Frederick Arthur Gore. "On Some Italian and Spanish Treatises on Music of the Seventeenth Century." *Proceedings of the Musical Association*, (1881-82), 83-98.   [g.a.]

> As above. Also reprint, Vaduz: Kraus Reprint, 1966.

2064 _____

Fellowes, Edmund H. [Describes Ouseley's collection.] In Montague Frederick Alderson, ed., and H. C. Colles, *History of St. Michael's College, Tenbury . . . ,* 78-101. London: Society for Promoting Christian Knowledge, 1943.   [US-NH, -Wc]

> Not examined.

2065 Ouvry, Fredric, 1814-81
Newton, Thomas W. *Catalogue of Old Ballads in the Possession of. . . .* London: privately printed [by T. Scott], 1877. xiv, 57 p. 194 entries.   [US-Wc, -Bp, -CLp]

2066 _____

SOTHEBY, WILKINSON & HODGE, AUCTIONEER, LONDON
Catalogue of Books, Including the First Part of the Oriental and Miscellaneous Library of Col. . . . Also Valuable Ancient Music . . . Sold July 24, 1877. [London, 1877.] 99 p. 1668 lots. Music, lots 1550-1625.   [Film at CRL]

2067 _____

SOTHEBY, WILKINSON & HODGE, AUCTIONEER, LONDON
Catalogue of the Important Library of Manuscripts and Printed Books of the Late . . . Comprising Autograph Letters, Musical and Dramatic, of Eminent English & Foreign Actors, Actresses & Musicians . . . Sold . . . 30th of March, 1882. [London, 1882.] 145 p. 1628 lots.

> Lots 264-65 include some 640 ALS, among them Meyerbeer, Paganini, Mendelssohn, etc.

2068 Ouwejan, R
INTERNATIONAL ANTIQUARIAAT, AUCTIONEER, AMSTERDAM
[Sales of songbooks, 16 June 1963 and 5 November 1963.]   [NL-Avb]

> Not examined; cited in **Vereeeniging** . . . *Catalogus* 8.

2069   **Paar, Ludwig Graf**
ALBERT COHN, AUCTIONEER, BERLIN
Katalog einer werthvollen Sammlung von Autographen und historischen Dokumente aus dem Besitz . . . Versteigerung . . . 20 [25] März 1893. . . . Berlin, 1893. 255 p. 2074 lots. Music, lots 1533-1648 (many more items).   [US-NYgr]

2070   **Paddon, James** (organist of Exeter Cathedral)
MR. WATSON, AUCTIONEER, LONDON
A Catalogue of a Collection of Vocal and Instrumental Music, Including the Library of the Late . . . Together with Upwards of Fifty Unpublished Compositions by the Celebrated Jackson. [Musical Instruments] . . . *Sold . . . at the Mart . . . 28th November 1835.* London, 1835. 12 p. 248 lots. Music, lots 1-131, 140-238.   [Compiler]

2071   **Paganini, Nicolò,** 1782-1840
The collection was put together by Paganini himself and remained in the family until 1910. The antiquarian firm of Joseph Baer acquired much of it at Battistelli's auction that year. V. A. Heck, another dealer in Vienna, later acquired it from Baer, then sold it in a sale in 1927 to "private hands," Mrs. Charles Hohn (Maia Bang). Eventually Whittall purchased it for the Library of Congress. For catalogs and literature about that Paganiniana, *see under* **Hohn, Maia Bang**.

Other Paganini properties appeared, *inter alia*, in sales by Leo Liepmannssohn: auction catalog 52, 16-17 November 1928; catalog 61, 20 May 1931; catalog 63, 9 December 1932; and in Otto Haas's catalog nos. 7, 8, and 10 (1938).

2072   _____
GEOFFREY (EXP.); ROUSSEAU (EXP.), AUCTION, PARIS
Collection de feu M. Paganini, le célèbre violiniste et du Baron Paganini, augmentée de la collection de M. H. J. M. B. Tableaux anciens et modernes . . . Ivoires, etc. . . . vente . . . 19 avril 1873. . . . Paris, 1873. 15 p. 111 lots.   [F-Pn]

No music; all artworks.

2073   _____
TURIN, ESPOSIZIONE GENERALE, 1898
Catalogo della collezione Nicolo Paganini per l'Esposizione di Torino [Esposizione industriale italiana, 1898]. Parma: Donti, 1898. 29 p.

Not located; cited from *PaG* 1:470, col. B.

2074   _____
Catalogo collezione "Niccolò Paganini." Parma: Tip. Operaia Adomi-Ugolotti, 1903.

Not located; cited from Chiesa, p. 482.

2075   _____
LUIGI BATTISTELLI, AUCTIONEER, FLORENCE   CAT. NO. 84
Collezione de celebre violinista . . . Musica inedita, doni regali e principeschi un grande mosaico . . . [etc.] *in vendite al publico incanto.* Firenze, 1910. 16 p. 233 lots.

Folter, no. 282.

2076 _____

V. A. HECK, FIRM, VIENNA
[Catalog of Paganini's Nachlass. . . .] Wien, 1927.

> Not located; cited in **Hirsch** catalog no. 5841.

2077 _____

HELMUT & ERNEST MEYER, AUCTIONEER, BERLIN
Sammlung von Original porträts und Studienblättern nach dem Leben aus dem Besitz des verstorbenen Geigenvirtuosen B. . . . Versteigerung den 19. Dez. 1931. Berlin, 1931. 56 p., plates. 28 lots.

> Not examined; cited from catalog no. 103 of the firm May & May, July 1982, lot 257, "with a loose interleaved sheet with estimated prices."

2078 _____

ROME BIBLIOTHECA CASANATENSE
Mostra di autografi e manoscritti di Niccolò Paganini, ed. Orchidea Salvati. . . . Roma: Roma Campo Marzio, 1972. 110 p.   [US-Dlc]

> Not examined; cited **Folter**, no. 282. Probably mostly Paganini Mss.

2079 Pagonkine,

CAMERLINCK (LIBRAIRE); JULES DELON (C.-P.), AUCTIONEER, PARIS
Catalogue d'une collection de livres + d'estampes (Théâtre, littérature, beaux-arts, linguistique, histoire, etc.) provenant du cabinet de . . . vente . . . les 5, 6 et 7 Décembre 1861. . . . Paris, 1861. 4, 60 p. 563 lots.   [F-Pn]

> Not examined; cited from **Lugt** (no. 26447) who says "Liv. musique," 485.

2080 Pamphilj, Benedetto, Cardinal, 1653-1730; later **Cardinal Giuseppe Doria**; now a private
library, I-Rdp (Archivo e Biblioteca Doria Pamphilj)
Holschneider, Andreas. "Die Musiksammlung der Fürsten Doria-Pamphilj in Rom." *AfMW* 18
(1961): 248-64.   [g.a.]

> With a complete index of holdings.

2081 _____

Lippmann, Friedrich. "Die Sinfonien-Manuscripts der Bibliothek Doria-Pamphilj." *Analecta musicologica* 5 (1968): 201-47.   [g.a.]

2082 _____

Lippmann, Friedrich, and Ludwig Finscher. "Die Streichquartette-Manuscripts der Bibliothek Doria-Pamphilj." *Analecta musicologica* 6 [i.e., 7] (1969): 120-44.   [g.a.]

2083 _____

Lippmann, Friedrich, and Ludwig Finscher. "Die Streichtrio-Manuscripts der Bibliothek Doria-Pamphilj." *Analecta musicologica* 9 (1970): 299-335.   [g.a.]

2084 _____

Rubrichi, R. Vignodelli. "Il fondo detto l'"Archhiviolo" dell'Archivio Doria Landi Pamphilj in Roma." *Miscellanea della Società Romana di Storia Patria* 12 (1972).   [US-BApi]

> Not available in U.S. for examination.

2085   _____

LITERATURE

Annibaldi, Claudio. "L'archivio musicale Doria Pamphilj: Saggio sulla cultura aristocratica a Roma fra il 16° e 19° secolo II." *Studi musicali* 11 (1982): 91-120, 277-344.

2086   **Paris, Pierre Adrien**

LITERATURE

Gazier, G. "Les Vrais Bibliophiles." *Trésors des bibliothèques de France* 5 (1933): 47-55. [g.a.]

2087   **Parker, Rev. John**

MR. WHITE, AUCTIONEER, LONDON

. . . A Catalogue of the Select and Entire Library of Music Books of . . . A Very Fine and Extensive Collection of Madrigals, Motetts, &c. (Including a Curious Folio Book of 1000 Pages, Copied from the Vatican Library) . . . An Ancient and Curious Manuscript Book on Vellum . . . Warren's Collections Catches and Glees . . . Scarce Italian Operas, MS. . . . Sold . . . the 16th of February 1813, & Following Day. . . . [London, 1813.] 16 p. 356 lots. Music, lots 1-256, 260-356.   [GB-Lbl (with names and prices)]

Parker, Louis Napoleon.   *See under* **Mann, A.**

Parys, Georges van.   *See* **Van Parys, Georges**

Parma, Robert de Bourbon, duca di.   *See* **Robert de Bourbon, Duke of Parma,** 1848-1907

2088   **Parr, Henry, Rev., Vicar of Yoxford**

PUTTICK & SIMPSON, AUCTIONEER, LONDON

Catalogue of a Collection of Books in Most Branches of Literature, and a Selection of Musical Treatises and Old Psalmodies from the Collection of . . . Sold . . . November 24 and Two Following Days. . . . London, 1890. 1007 lots. Parr's properties, lots 889-1007.   [GB-Cu]

2089   **Parry, Milman**

Serbocroatian Heroic Songs, Collected by. . . . Edited and translated by Albert Bates Lord. Vol. 1. Cambridge: Harvard University Press; Belgrade: Serbian Academy of Sciences, 1953-.   [US-BE]

"A digest of Serbocroatian epic songs in the . . . collection of Southslavic texts," 1: 21-45.

2090   **Pascolato, Alessandro,** 1841-1905

VENICE, CONSERVATORIO BENEDETTO MARCELLO, BIBLIOTECA

Il Fondo Pascolato del Conservatorio . . . [by] *Gigliola Bianchini* [and] *Caterina Manfredi. Catalogo dei manoscritti (Prima serie).* Historiae musicae cultores, Biblioteca, 52. Firenze: Leo S. Olschki, 1990. 421 p. 635 lots.   [g.a.]

Thematic incipits, pp. 301-85.

2091   **Pasdeloup, Jules Étienne,** 1819-87

Sibire (C. P.). *Bibliothèque musicale de . . . , créateurs des Concerts Populaires. Vente après décès de forts lots de musique des meilleurs auteurs et d'instruments de musique en l'hôtel Drouot, les 5 et 6 juin 1888.* Fontainebleu: Impr. Pouyé, 1888. 68 p. No lotting.   [US-R]

Folter, no. 283 (not seen).

2092 Pasta, Giuditta, 1797-1865

LITERATURE

"The New York Public Library Acquires Early English Manuscripts and the Giuditta Pasta Collection." *Fontes* 18 (1971): 81-82. [g.a.]

2093 Paston, Edward, 1550-1630

Brett, Philip. "Edward Paston (1550-1630): A Norfolk Gentleman and His Musical Collection." *Transactions of the Cambridge Bibliographical Society* 4 (1964-68): 51-. [g.a.]

2094 Pastrić, Ivan

Hrvoje, Morović. "Osnutak i uredenje Pastrićeve biblioteke splitskog sjemenista." *Vjesnik bibliotekara Hrvatske* 14 (1968): 128-35.

Collection at YU-Snb. Not examined; cited from *RILM*.

2095 Paul, Oskar, 1836-98; et al.

LIST & FRANCKE, AUCTIONEER, LEIPZIG

. . . Verzeichnis mehrerer Bücher- und Musikalien-Sammlung, welche am 21. [-24] November 1898 . . . versteigert werden sollen. Aus dem Nachlasse des Herrn Prof. Dr. . . . und anderer. . . . Leipzig, 1895. 68 p. 2604 lots. Music, lots 911-1705. [US-NYgr]

Properties not differentiated. **Folter**, no. 284.

2096 _____

LIST & FRANCKE, FIRM, LEIPZIG   ANT.-CAT. NO. 300

Geschichte und Theorie der Musik. Aeltere praktische Musik. Autographen. Aus dem Nachlasse des Herrn . . . Antiquarisches Verzeichnis Nr. 300. Leipzig, 1899. 63 p. 1787 lots.

[US-CN, NL-Avb]

Autographs, lots 1605-770. Properties are not differentiated. Prices fixed. **Folter**, no. 285. **Albrecht** notes this sale only.

2097 Payne, Alfred H.

HAROLD REEVES, FIRM, LONDON   CAT. NO. 54

Old, Rare and Interesting Musical Works . . . American Psalmody and Hymnody, 183 Scarce Volumes . . . Being a First Selection from the Alfred H. Payne Collection. . . . London, 1924-25. 32 p. 4210 lots. [US-BUu, -Wc, NL-Avb, NL-Dhgm]

Payne's properties, lots 4017-210. Reeves "has purchased the entire . . . Payne Collection of hymn and psalm-tune books."

2098 _____

HAROLD REEVES, FIRM, LONDON   CAT. NO. 63

All Kinds of Music . . . Including a Selection of the Works of . . . Arne . . . Recently Purchased from a Collector - a Further Portion of the Alfred Payne Library of Old Psalm and Hymn-Tune Books. . . . London, 1926. 32 p. [US-Wc, -BUu, -CHua, NL-Avb]

Payne's properties, pp. 8-9.

2099 Pearsall, Robert Lucas de (of Wartensee Castle), 1795-1856

[A Catalog of His Music Library.] British Museum Add. Ms. 38560.

Grove 3 says given by his heirs to CH-E.

2100 Pearse, John Barnard, 1842-1914
C. F. LIBBIE, & CO., AUCTIONEER, BOSTON
Catalogue of the Extensive Musical Library of the Late . . . Comprising . . . I. Musical History, Reference Books . . . II. The Violin, Its History, Antiquity [etc.] *. . . III. Bound and Sheet Music . . . Scores . . . Sale . . . April 4th and 5th, 1918.* Boston, 1918. 106 p. 1556 lots.
[US-NYp, -Wc (some prices)]

2101 Pedrell, Felipe, 1841-1922
INSTITUT D'ESTUDIS CATALANS, BARCELONA, BIBLIOTECA, DEPARTMENT DE MÚSICA
Catàleg dels manuscrits musicals de la Collecció Pedrell, per Mn. Higini Anglès. Biblioteca de Catalunya, Publicaciones del Department de música, 2. Barcelona, 1920 [i.e., 1921]. 138 p., illus. [US-NYp, -Wc]
Collection now at E-Bc.

2102 Penson, George
PUTTICK & SIMPSON, AUCTIONEER, LONDON   CAT. NO. 18
Catalogue of a Choice and Extensive Musical Library, Chiefly the Collection of the Late . . . Together with Musical Instruments, Comprising the Final Portion of the Well-Known Collection of Violins of Mr. Francois Cramer . . . Sold . . . March 9th, and Following Days. . . . [London], 1847. 18 p. 459 lots. Music, lots 1-425.
Title page missing at GB-Lbl; examined copy in private collection of Harrison Horblit (USA).

2103 Pepusch, John Christopher, 1667-1752
Cook, D. F. "J. C. Pepusch: An 18th-Century Musical Bibliophile." *Soundings: A Music Journal* 9 (1982): 11-28. [g.a.]

2104 Pepys, Samuel, 1633-1703
PEPYS LIBRARY
Bibliotheca Pepysiana: The Descriptive Catalogue of the Library of. . . . 4 vols. London: Sidwick & Jackson, 1914-40. illus. [US-Wc, -TA]
Vol. 2, "Early printed books to 1558." Vol. 3, "Medieval manuscripts."

2105 Perabo, Johann Ernst, 1845-1920
Scholfield, B. "The Perabo Collection of Musical Autographs Presented by Mrs. E. Perry Warren." *British Museum Quarterly* 3 (1928-29): 56-57. [g.a.]
Collection given to Mrs. Warren in 1904.

2106 Percheron, Achille Remy, 1797-1869
LIBRAIRIE BACHELIN-DEFLORENNE, AUCTIONEER, PARIS
Catalogue de la bibliothèque de feu . . . dont la vente aura lieu . . . 21 et . . . 22 november. . . . Paris, 1871. 58 p. [US-NYp]
Rich in chansonniers.

Perkins, Frederik.   *See under* **Rigby, Dr. Edward** (Puttick & Simpson sale, 17 July 1861)

Peyton, Richard.   *See under* **Rookwood, Mrs. A.**

Pfeil, A. H. T. (in Leipzig).   *See* **Boers, J. C.**

2107   **Pfitzner, Hans,** 1869-1949

LITERATURE

Nowak, Leopold. "Pfitzners Nachlass in der Musiksammlung der Österreichischen Nationalbibliothek." *ÖMZ* 24 (1969): 252-54.   [g.a.]

2108   _____

Brosche, Günter. "Der Pfitzner-Bestand der Musiksammlung der Österreichischen Nationalbibliothek. Der Nachlass und neue Erwerbungen. . . ." In *Festschrift Rudolf Elvers zum 60. Geburtstag,* ed. Ernst Herrtrich and Hans Schneider, 73-84. Tutzing: Hans Schneider, 1985.   [g.a.]

Philidor Collection.   *See under* **Toulouse, Louis Alexandre**

2109   **Philip Karl, Graf zu Oettingen-Wallerstein**

From *RILM*: "The collection was purchased between 1805 and 1808 by the prince-bishop Ernst von Schwarzenberg from Philip Karl, the count of Öttingen-Wallerstein." Now at CS-K and D-HR. For catalogs of and literature about that collection, *see here under* **Kraft Ernst, Prince of.** . . .

→ *See also* references under **Oetting, C.d'**, and **Oettingen-Wallerstein**

2110   **Philipp, Isadore**

LITERATURE

Timbrell, Charles. "The Isadore Philipp Archiv at the University of Louisville, Dwight Anderson Memorial Library." *Journal of the American Liszt Society* 35 (January-June 1994): 59-60.   [g.a.]

2111   **Philipp I, Duke of Pomerania-Wolgast,** 1515-60

Deutsch, J. *Die Bibliothek Herzogs Philipps I. von Pommern.* Aus den Schätzen der Universitäts-Bibliothek zu Greifswald, 6. Greifswald: L. Bamberg, 1931. 45 p.

Now at D-GRu.

2112   **Photiades, M**

BÈRES, PIERRE, FIRM, NEW YORK   SPECIAL LIST NO. 53

. . . *Music and Musical Literature* . . . *Partly from the Library of M. Photiades.* New York, [1949?]. [28] p. 324 items.   [US-NBu]

2113   **Piancastelli, Carlo**

Walker, Frank. "Rossiniana nella Raccolta Piancastelli." *Bolletino del Centro Rossiniano di studi* 5 (1959/60): 3, 41; (1960): 4, 62.   [g.a.]

In English in *MMR* 80 (1960): 138-47, 203-13.

2114   _____

COMITATO PERMANENTE PER LE ONORANZE AD ARCANGELO CORELLI

Catalogo della mostra dell edizione e mss Corelliani nelle raccolta Piancastelli della Biblioteca Comunale di Forli. Fusignano: Stamperia Cornacchia, 1967. 39 p.   [US-Wc]

Bequest to I-FOc in 1937.

2115 **Picart, Samuel; [Mrs. Denman]**

PUTTICK & SIMPSON, AUCTIONEER, LONDON   CAT. NO. 58

Catalogue of the Very Valuable Musical Library of Rev. Samuel Picart . . . Handel's Works . . . in Full Score by Dr. Arnold, Large Paper. An Opera, Unpublished and Autograph [i.e. Handel's Amadigi, with Ms. notes by Dr. Rimbault and T. M. Mudie]; A Collection of J. S. Bach, with an Unpublished and Autograph Work . . . the Second Contains the Canon Perpetuus, Both Unpublished . . . Numerous Works by Old Italian and Other Composers, Many Being Unpublished MSS. . . . A Curious Virginal Book, Formerly in the Possession of Queen Mary and Philip of Spain . . . Together with Musical Instruments . . . Sold . . . March 10, 1848. [London, 1848.] 16 p. 290 lots. Music, lots 1-147.   [GB-Lbl]

> **King**, pp. 95, 97, points out that the arms on the binding of the virginal book are *NOT* those of Queen Mary and King Philip. The putative autograph *Amadigi* Ms. turned up in many subsequent Puttick sales.

2116 **Pickering, Thomas**

SOTHEBY, WILKINSON & HODGE, AUCTIONEER, LONDON

Catalogue of the Valuable Collection of Choice Classical Music, Forming the Library of the Late . . . Comprising the Productions of the Most Eminent Musicians . . . Sold . . . 18th Day of December, 1876. [London, 1876.] 31 p. 438 lots (all music).   [Film at CRL]

> Some of this collection derived from large purchases made by Pickering at the sale of Thomas Oliphant's fine library 24-25 April 1873 (**2036**).

2117 **Picquot, L   ; Jean Baptiste Cartier,** 1768-1841

LEO LIEPMANNSSOHN, FIRM, BERLIN   CAT. NOS. 154 AND 157

Instrumental-musik von Anfänge des 16. bis zur Mitte des 19. Jahrhunderts . . . provenant des bibliothèque de. . . . 2 vols. Berlin, [n.d., ca. 1904]. 70, 87 p. 970, 1266 lots.

[US-Wc, NL-Avb]

> Cat. no. 154, 1. Abth., A-E; Cat. no. 157, 2. Abth., F-N, includes some properties of Friedrich Wilhelm Rust. **Folter,** nos. 44-45, under **Cartier**.

2118 **Picquot, L   ; Jean Baptiste Cartier; James E. Matthew; Friedrich Wilhelm Rust**

LEO LIEPMANNSSOHN, FIRM, BERLIN   CAT. NO. 167

Instrumental-musik vom Anfänge des 16. bis zur Mitte des 19. Jahrhunderts. 3. Abteilung: O-Z. . . . Berlin, [n.d., 1908]. 81 p. 1455 lots.   [US-Wc]

> Continues Liepmannssohn's catalog nos. 154 and 157, above. Properties are sometimes but not always differentiated. **Folter,** no. 46, again under **Cartier**.

2119 **Picquot, L   ; Jean Baptiste Cartier; James E. Matthew; Friedrich Wilhelm Rust**

LEO LIEPMANNSSOHN, FIRM, BERLIN   CAT. NO. 169

Instrumental-musik . . . 4. Abtheilung, Nachträge zur Kat. 154 u. 157 (A-N), nebst systematischer Uebersicht über sämtliche 4 Abteilungen . . . (154, 157, 167 u. 169) [aus den Bibliotheken von Picquot, Cartier, Rust, und Matthew]. Berlin, [n.d., 1909]. 54 p. 739 lots.

[US-Wc, NL-Avb]

> Not in **Folter**.

2120   Picquot, L   ; Jean Baptiste Cartier [only]

G. LEGOUIX, FIRM, PARIS   CAT. NO. 11

Musique instrumentale du 17ᵉ siècle au début du 19ᵉ siècle, . . . provenant la plupart des bibliothèques Picquot et Cartier. . . . Paris, [n.d.]. 26 p. 426 lots.

[GB-Lbl (Hirsch), NL-DHgm, US-NYp]

Not in **Folter**.

2121   Piguet, Paul, 1891-1981

BIBLIOTHÈQUE CANTONALE ET UNIVERSITAIRE (VAUD, SWITZERLAND), DÉPARTEMENT DES MANUSCRITS

Inventaire du fonds Paul Piguet, par Jocelyne Hefti. Inventaire . . . Département des manuscrits, 42. Lausanne: Bibliothèque . . . Lausanne Dorigny, 1993. 181 p.

2122   Pilkington, Charles Vere

LITERATURE

Pilkington, C. Vere. "A Collection of English 18th Century Harpsichord Music." *Royal Musical Association Proceedings* 83 (1956/57): 89-107.   [g.a.]

King, p. 82, "contains some considerable rarities."

2123   [Pincherle, Marc, 1888-1974]

LEFÈVRE L., & C. GÉRIN (EXPERTS), PARIS

Ouvrages sur la musique provenant de la bibliothèque d'un amateur. Paris: Hotel Drouot, 1964. [19] p. 126 lots.   [B-Br]

Folter, no. 286, and **Blogie 2**. Not examined.

2124   _____

CORNUAU (EXP.)

Cent raretés musicales . . . à Hôtel Drouot. . . . Paris, 1966. 24 p. 104 lots.   [D-Dl]

Folter, no. 287.

2125   _____

GUÉRIN, CLAUDE, AND MICHEL CASTAING (EXPERTS)

Collection musicale Marc Pincherle, dontla vente aux enchères publiques aura lieu Hotel Drouot - Salle N° 10 les 3, 4 et 5 mars 1975. . . . Paris: Girard-Badin, 1975. Unpaged [ca. 200 p.] 1047 lots (many more items).   [compiler]

Preface by G. Thibault, E. and A. Ader, J. L. Picard, and J. Tajan (C.-P). Abstract by François Lesure in *RILM*. The collection contained 239 ALS, 104 music Mss., 174 books on music, 473 volumes of scores. **Folter**, no. 288, **Blogie 2**, **Albrecht**.

2126   Piper, Edwin Ford, 1871-1939

Peterson, H. D. "Syllabus of the Ballad Collection of Edwin Ford Piper [at US-IO]." Ph.D. diss., University of Iowa, 1934.

Not examined; cited in *Amerigrove*.

2127   _____

LITERATURE

Oster, H. "The Edwin Ford Piper Collection of Folksongs." *Books at Iowa* 1 (1964): 28-33.

[g.a.]

2128   **Pisani, Pietro** and **Antonio**

Galici Candiloro, Antonina. *Lascito Pisani. Catalogo del fondo musicale.* Palermo: Officine Grafice I.R.E.S., 1972. 128 p.

> Lists, in alphabetical order, the Mss. in the Pisani collection now at I-PLcon. Not located; cited in *RILM*.

Pitti Palace.   *See* **Palazzo Pitti, Florence**

2129   **Pittman, Josiah,** 1816-86

PUTTICK & SIMPSON, AUCTIONEER, LONDON   CAT. NO. 2423

Catalogue of the Furniture and Effects and Library of Music, Books, etc. of . . . [Organist, Royal Italian Opera, etc., etc.] *. . . Also the Valuable Library of Music, Consisting Chiefly of Popular Editions of Operas and Oratorios, Treatises on Music, Interesting Manuscript Collections . . . Sold . . . June 10th, 1886.* [London, 1886.] 13 p. 243 lots. Mainly music.

[GB-Lbl]

2130   **Pixérecourt, René Charles Guilbert,** 1773-1844

J. CROZET, (EXP.?), PARIS

Catalogue des livres rares et précieux composant [sa] *bibliothèque . . . La vente aura lieu . . . 22 janvier 1839 et jours suivans* [i.e., -26 février]. *. . .* Paris, 1838. 4, 4, vii, 414 p. 2313 lots. Music, 484-91 lots (many more items).   [US-NYgr, -NYp, -BE, etc.]

> Lot 484, "MS. de la fin du XVᵉ siècle." "Révolution française. Poésies. Chansons [etc.]," pp. [343]-414.

2131   **Plamenac, Dragan,** 1895-1983

LITERATURE

Samuel, Harold E. "Zbirka Dragana Plamenca na Sveucilistu Yale." [Plamenac Festschrift.] *Spomenica u pocast Deraganu Plamencuisces,* 231-36. Arti musices, 17. Zagreb: Muzikolski Zavod Muzicke Akademije, 1986. 92 p.

> Collection acquired by US-NH in 1975. Catalog not located.

2132   **[Playford, John,** 1623-86]

HENRY PLAYFORD, FIRM, LONDON

A Curious Collection of Musick-Books, Both Vocal and Instrumental (and Several Rare Copies in Three and Four Parts, Fairly Prick'd) by the Best Masters . . . the Collection Is To Be Sold [11 June 1690] *. . . At His House at the Lower End of Arundel-Street in the Strand; Where the Collection May Be Viewed Four Days After the Publication in the Gazette.* [London, 1690?] [3] p. 121+6 lots.   [GB-Lbl, -Ob, US-NH, -BUu (copy)]

> Indexed in **Coral**, pp. 128-29, discussed, pp. 53-55, *et passim.* **King**, p. 94.

2133   —————

HENRY PLAYFORD, FIRM, LONDON

A Catalogue of Ancient and Modern Musick Books, Both Vocal and Instrumental, with Divers Treatises . . . and Several Musical Instruments . . . Sold at Dewing's Coffee-House in Pope's-Head Alley . . . December the 17th, 1691. [London, 1691.] 16 p.   [GB-Lbl]

> 201 + 105 lots indexed in **Coral**, pp. 131-33, and discussed, pp. 53-55.

Plock, Max. *See under* **Langenbach, Wilhelm** (sale December 1915)

2134   **Plowden, Charles Hood Chichele,** 1798-1866; **Charles Chichele,** 1825-78; **Harriet Chichele Plowden,** 1830-1907
King, A. Hyatt. "The Chichele Plowdens and the British Museum: Footnote to a Musical Bequest." In *Sundry Sorts of Music Books . . . Essays Presented to O. W. Neighbour,* 259-63. London: British Library, 1993.   [g.a.]

> Previously published in *Libraries, Diplomacy and the Performing Arts: Essays in Honor of Carleton Sprague Smith.* New York: Pendragon Press, 1991.
>
> The bequest included the holographs of the "Ten Great Mozart Quartets," sold in the Stumpff sale of 30-31 March 1847 (**2599**).

2135   **Plugge, P C ; Dr. Rombouts (of Scheveningen); Dr. C. W. A. Evans; Dr. H. J. Mooijen**
G. THEOD. BOM & ZOON, AUCTIONEER, DEN HAAG
Notitie van schilderijen, aquarellen . . . prenten en gravures . . . [etc.] Muziek voor piano, orgel, viool, zang en harmonie, afkomstig van . . . , van de voormalize Muziekkorpsen der dienst-doende Schulterijen van Amsterdam en 's-Gravenhage . . . verkooping 30 Juni tot 4 Juli 1914. . . . Amsterdam, 1914. 48 p. 1321 lots. Music, lots 900-1321.   [NL-Avb]

> It is not clear who consigned the music items.

2136   **Plumb, John Barker; Bath Harmonic Society; A Deceased Professor**
PUTTICK & SIMPSON, AUCTIONEER, LONDON   CAT. NO. 2109
Catalogue of the Extensive Music Library of the Late J. B. Plumb . . . String Duets, Trios, Quartetts, Quintetts . . . Also Scarce Works, Psalmodies, Autographs and Manuscripts, the Property of a Deceased Professor. A Lot of Modern Popular Sheet Music . . . Sold June 23, 1882. [London], 1882. 18 p. 433 lots (more items).   [GB-Lbl]

> Plumb's properties, lots 298-378; Professor's, 379-433; Bath Society, 73-100.

2137   **Podleská-Batková, Tekle**
LITERATURE
Holeček, J. "Hudebni akirky Tekly Podesk-Batkov."

> "Musical Collection from the Estate of. . . . " In preparation, according to *NG*-L, p. 731.

2138   **Pölchau, Georg Johann Daniel,** 1773-1836
"Katalog der Sammlung Pölchau. Bd. IV: Handschriften (praktische Musik). Berlin den 8. Mai 1832."

> Ms. at D-Bds, Mus. Ms. Theor. K41, Ms. The collection was drawn from those of Forkel and C. P. E. Bach . It included J. S. Bach autographs. Offered to D-Bds about 1832, it was not acquired until 1841, according to **Albrecht**.

2139   _____

> ["Inventare der Sammlung Poelchau."] In D-Bds, Catalog Mus. Ms. 41, 51, 56, 61, 131.
>
> Collection acquired by the library in 1841. **Albrecht.**

2140 _____

> "2. Literatur musicale, fonds Poelchau," in Berlin. "Catalogus librorum et manuscriptorum de re musica manuscriptae et impressae bibliothecae regiae berelinensis. . . . " Ms. in Fétis/Brussels Catalog no. 5171.
>
> > Catalog was compiled by Siegfried Dehn.

2141 _____

> *LITERATURE*
>
> Schulze, W. "Zur Entstehung und Bedeutung der Musikalien-Sammlung Georg Poelchau. Berlin, 1938."
>
> > Typescript at D-Bds, according to **Schaal** (1966), p. 146.

2142   Pohlenz, Christian August, 1790-1843

> *Verzeichniss der von dem verstorbenen Musik-direktor und Organist Aug. Pohlenz hinterlassenen ansehnlichen Sammlung von Musikalien und Büchern, welche vom 2. bis 10. October (1843) in Leipzig versteigert werden sollen.* Leipzig, 1843. 108 p. 2931 lots.
>
> > > > [D-Bds]
>
> **Folter**, no. 289.

2143   Pompadour, Jeanne Antoinette (Poisson), Marquise de, 1721-64

> *Catalogue des livres de la bibliothèque de feu Madame la marquise de Pompadour, Dame du Palais de la Reine.* Ed. Chez Jean-Th. Hérissant . . . et Jean-Thomas Hérissant. Paris, 1965. xvi, 404, lxxii p. \[US-Wc, -NYp, -NYp, -NYgr, compiler (pp. 381-99)]
>
> > "Musique," pp. 381-98; "concernant opéra et ballets," pp. 149-71.

Poniatowski, Jozef. *See under* **Hopkins, John Larkin**

2144   [Porcher,   ]

> PUTTICK & SIMPSON, AUCTIONEER, LONDON   CAT. NO. 353
>
> *Catalogue of the Musical Library of a Distinguished Professor, Deceased . . . Handel's Works . . . Psalm Tunes, Theoretical and Historical Works . . . Sold . . . February 4th, 1854.* [London], 1854. 14 p. 354 lots. Music, lots 1-341.   [GB-Lbl]

2145   Posonyi, Alexander

> COHEN, FIRM, BONN   CAT. NO. 98
>
> *Autographen-sammlung Alexander Posonyi in Wien. II. Musiker. Meist kostbare Briefe und Musikmanuskripte der berühmtesten Komponisten. Virtuosen und Musikschriftsteller nebst einer kleinen Auswahl von Musikdrucken und Werken zur Musikliteratur. . . .* Bonn: Cohen, 1900. 144 p. 1661 + lots.   [NL-DHgm, US-Mb]
>
> > Prices fixed.

Potocki Family (Lancut Castle, Poland). *See under* **Lubomirska, Izabella**

2146   Potter, Philip Cipriani Hambly, 1792-1871

> > **King**, p. 92, notes that the William Sterndale Bennett sale catalog mentions the sale of Potter's library "(probably a sound working collection)," but the catalog has not been located. Potter's and J. W. Joyce's instruments were sold by Puttick & Simpson in a sale 22 November 1881.

2147 Potts, Arthur

Sᴏᴛʜᴇʙʏ & Cᴏ., ᴀᴜᴄᴛɪᴏɴᴇᴇʀ, Lᴏɴᴅᴏɴ

Catalogue of Fine Illuminated Manuscripts, Valuable Printed Books . . . [etc.] *Works on Music . . . The Property of . . . Sold . . . the 26th of April, 1937. . . .* [London], 1937.

[Film at CRL]

"A Collection of Music Books," pp. 76-82, lots 371-403.

Powis, Earl of. *See* **Herbert, Edward Robert Henry, 5th Earl of**

2148 Prado, Samuel

Mʀ. Eᴠᴀɴs, ᴀᴜᴄᴛɪᴏɴᴇᴇʀ, Lᴏɴᴅᴏɴ

Catalogue of the Library and Music of the Late . . . to Which Is Added Another Collection, Also a Valuable Assemblage of Manuscripts . . . Sold . . . April 11, and Two Following Days . . . , 1839. [London], 1839. 40 p. 738 lots. Music, lots 261-79 (many more items, e.g., lot 270 = 16 volumes of overtures). [GB-Lbl]

Preller, Johann Gottlieb. *See under* **Mempell, Johann Nicolas**

2149 Pretlack, Ludwig, Freiherrn von, 1716-81

Jaenecke, Joachim. *Die Musikbibliothek des . . . (1716-81).* Neue Musikgeschichtliche Forschungen, 8. Wiesbaden: Breitkopf & Härtel, 1973. 330 p. [US-Wc]

Originally a Ph.D. diss., Frankfurt a.M. Summarized in *Mf* 26 (1973): 380. **Albrecht:** 1079 items; now at D-B.

Previte, P. E. *See* **Kirby, Percival Robson** (sale of 8 May 1972)

2150 Preyer, Gottfried von, 1807-1901

Gɪʟʜᴏғᴇʀ & Rᴀɴsᴄʜʙᴜʀɢ, ғɪʀᴍ, Vɪᴇɴɴᴀ   Cᴀᴛ. ɴᴏ. 67

. . . Musikwissenschaft. Geschichte und Theorie der Musik . . . Enthaltend die Bibliothek des k. k. Hof-und Domkapellmeisters. . . . Wien, 1902. 46 p. 1069 items.

Not examined; cited from *ZiMG* 3 (1901/02): 426.

2151 Preyre, Émile

Pᴀsᴄᴀʟʟᴀᴛ, Jᴜʟᴇs (C.-P.); A. Cʟᴀᴜᴅɪɴ (Lɪʙʀᴀɪʀᴇ), Mᴀʀsᴇɪʟʟᴇ

Catalogue des livres et partitions de musique composant la bibliothèque de . . . dont la vente aura lieu à Marseille . . . le 12 mai 1873. . . . Marseille, 1873. viii, 323 p. Music, pp. 9-38, lots 153-835. [GB-Lbl (Hirsch)]

2152 Prieger, Erich, 1849-1913

Pʀᴜssɪᴀ, Sᴛᴀᴀᴛsʙɪʙʟɪᴏᴛʜᴇᴋ, Bᴇʀʟɪɴ

Neue Erwerbungen der Königlichen Bibliothek zu Berlin. Beilage zu den Monatshefte für Musik-Geschichte, 35. [Leipzig, 1903.] 10 p. [g.a.]

Catalog of music autographs purchased from Artaria (**90**) by Prieger, then sold to D-Bds in 1901. Albrecht says ca. 3000 autograph leaves, mainly Haydn and Beethoven, plus Ms. copies and prints.

2153   **Prieger, Erich; Ludwig Scheibler**

M. LEMPERTZ, AUCTIONEER, COLOGNE

*Katalog der bedeutenden Musiksammlung aus dem Nachlasse Dr. Erich Prieger–Bonn . . .
Versteigerung: Dienstag, den 7. bis Freitag, den 10. November 1922 . . . durch M. Lempertz'
Buchhandlung und Antiquariat; Inhaber: P. Hanstein & Söhne, Bonn a. Rhein.* [III. T.: Dienstag
den 15. Juli 1924, Köln am Rhein.] [Bonn u. Köln, 1922-24.] 2 vols. Parts I & II in vol. 1.
84 p. 2282 lots. Part III (vol. 2), 42 p. 451 lots.   [US-NYp, -Wc, -NH, NL-Avb, GB-Lbl]

I. T., ". . . Werke aus älterer und neuerer Zeit zur Geschichte und Theorie der
Musik. II. T., Praktische Musik aller Art. . . . III. T., Musikerbriefe,
Handschriften, Musikalien. Gedruckte Musikalien (Sammlung Dr. Ludwig
Scheibler zur Geschichte der Klaviermusik des 19. Jahrhunderts)."

There is a note about the sale of the Artaria collection (by private treaty) to
Prieger in *MT* 39 (1898): 20, a longer notice about this Lempertz sale and its
rarities in *ZfMW* 5 (1922/23): 351-52, where it says Paul Hirsch "saved"
some items from the proceedings for his library ("und für Deutschland").
Folter, no. 290.

2154   **Prieger, Erich; Ludwig Scheibler**

M. LEMPERTZ, AUCTIONEER, COLOGNE

*Musiksammlung aus dem Nachlasse Dr. Erich Prieger, Bonn. . . . III. Teil, Musikerbriefe,
Handschriften, gedruckte Musikalien (Sammlung Dr. Ludwig Scheibler zu Geschichte der
Klaviermusik des 19. Jahrhunderts), u.a. . . . beschreibendes Verzeichnis von Georg Kinsky.
. . . Versteigerung Dienstag den 15. Juli 1924.* Köln am Rhein, 1924. 42 p. 451 lots.

[US-NYp, -Wc, -NH, NL-Avb, GB-Lbl]

Part 3 and volume 2 of preceding.

2155   **[Prieger, Erich]?**

J. A. STARGARDT, AUCTIONEER, MARBURG   CAT. NO. 510

Autographen. Auktion am 17. November 1953. . . . Marburg, 1953. 68 p. 314 lots (more items).

[US-NYgr]

Prieger's properties according to **Folter,** no. 292, and **Schaal**.

2156   **Priewe, Gustav**

*Portrait-Katalog zur Geschichte des Theaters und der Musik von Gustav Priewe in Seebad
Heringsdorf. . . .* Berlin, [n.d.]

Not located; cited in **Scheurleer** 1 (1923): 20.

2157   **Prileský-Ostrolícky Family**

Terrayová, M. JK. "Súpis Archívnych hudobných fondov na Slovenskú." *Hudobnovné Studie*
4 (1960): 197-328.

Not located; cited in **Albrecht**.

2158   **Pringsheim, Heinz,** 1882-1974

HANS SCHNEIDER, FIRM, TUTZING   CAT. NO. 190

Musikliteratur, darunter die Bibliothek Heinz Pringsheim. Tutzing: Schneider, 1975 [1974].
72 p. 695 lots.   [g.a]

Folter, no. 293.

2159   Prod'homme, Jacques Gabriel, 1871-1956
    Lucien Dorbon, firm, Paris   Cat. no. 639
Théâtre - Musique - Danse, livres provenant en majeur partie de la bibliothèque de. . . . Paris:
[n.p., 1958]. 80 p. 1625 lots (many more items, e.g., lots 1613-614 = 68 books on Wagner).
[compiler]

Folter, no. 294.

2160   Proelss, Johannes; Edmund Frank
    R. Levi, firm, Stuttgart   Antiq. Cat. no. 198
*. . . Werke aus Literatur, Theater, Musik, Kunst, Philosophie . . . aus dem Bibliotheken des
Hofschauspielers Edmund Frank, und des Schriftstellers Dr. Proelss.* Dagerloch, 1912.
74 p. 1543 lots.   [GB-Lbl (Hirsch)]
    Folter 2, no. 601.

2161   Prokesch von Osten, Anton, Grafen (Vater und Sohn, 1795-1876 and 1837-1919)
    Karl Ernest Henrici, auctioneer, Berlin   Cat. no. 74
*Autographen-Sammlung der Grafen von Prokesch-Osten (Vater und Sohn) . . . Versteigering
. . . 16. [-17.] Dezember 1921.* . . . Berlin, 1921. 115 p. 900 lots.   [US-NYgr, NL-Avb]
    "Musik, bildende u. darstellende Kunst," lots 1-183, include excellent
    Beethoven items. See note in *ZfMW* 4 (1921/22): 192.

2162   Proksch, Joseph, 1794-1864
    Hans P. Kraus, firm, Vienna   Ant.-Cat. no. 2
*Musikbibliothek Joseph Proksch Prag. Musikliteratur. Frühdrucke. Instrumental- und
Vokalmusik. Erstausausgaben.* Wien, [1934]. 88 p. 1717 lots.
[US-Wc, -CN, GB-Lbl; compiler]

Folter, no. 295.

2163   Proske, Karl, 1794-1861
    Bischöfliche Zentralbibliothek, Regensburg
Thematischer Katalog der Musikhandschriften, vol. 1: *Sammlung Proske,* by Gertraut
Haberkamp [u.a.]. München, 1989-90.   [g.a.]
    3 vols. (Kataloge bayerischer Musiksammlungen, 14/1-3.) Vol.1:
    *Manuskripte des 16. und 17. Jahrhunderts aus den Signaturen A.R., B, C,
    AN.* Vol. 2: *Manuskripte des 18. und 19. Jahrhunderts aus den Signaturen
    A.R., C, AN.* Vol. 3: *Mappenbibliothek.*

2164   _____

Literature
Weinmann, Karl. "Die Proske'sche Musikbibliothek in Regensburg." In *Festschrift zum 90.
Geburtstage . . . Rochus Freiherrn von Liliencron,* 386-403. Leipzig: Breitkopf & Härtel, 1910.
[US-BUu]

2165   _____

Weinmann, Karl. "Die Proske'sche Musikbibliothek in Regensburg." *KmJ* 24 (1911):
107-31.   [g.a.]
    "Komponisten-Verzeichnis der 'antiquitates Ratibonenses' und der Abteilung
    'Butsch' [i.e. Fidelis Butsch, antiquariat, Augsburg]," pp. 120-31.

2166 ⎯⎯⎯⎯⎯⎯

Schnargl, August. "Die Proske'sche Musiksammlung in der bischöflichen Zentralbibliothek zu Regensburg." *Oberpfälzer Dokumente der Musikgeschichte* 1 (1976): 11-30.　　　　[g.a.]

Prowse, Thomas. *See* anonymous sales 30 January 1868 and 1 September 1868

2167 **Prunières, Henri,** 1886-1942

?Liepmannssohn (Otto Haas?), firm, London?

"Catalogue des manuscrits italiens de cantates des XVIIIᵉ siècles de la bibliothèque de M. Henry Prunières à Paris." [N.p., n.d.] 8 p. Typescript.　　　　[US-NYp; GB-LRosenthal]

> Transferred to Otto Haas according to **Albrecht**, eventually sold to Madame de Chambure.

> → *See also under* **Rokseth, Yvonne**

2168 **Puckett, Newbell Niles,** 1898-1967

Doucette, Laurel. "An Introduction to the Puckett Collection of Ontario Folklore." *Canadian Folk Music* 3 (1975): 22-29.　　　　[g.a.]

> Includes a checklist of titles.

2169 **Pugno, Raoul,** 1852-1914

L. Carteret, auctioneer? Paris

. . . Bibliothèque Raoul Pugno. Beaux livres anciens et modernes, première et seconde parties. Ouvrages relatifs aux arts et aux artistes et ouvrages sur la théâtre, la musique et les musiciens; musique . . . vente après décès, du lundi 7 main au jeudi 10 mai 1917. . . . Paris, 1917. 121 p. 883, 21 lots.　　　　[US-NYp]

> **Folter**, no. 296.

2170 **Puy, Rouchon**

Ulysse. *La Musique et la librairie au Puy à la fin du XVIᵉ siècle.* Paris, 1909. 12 p.

> "Extrait du *Bulletin historique et philologique* 1908." Not located; cited from May & May antiquariat sale catalog no. 177, June 1989.

2171 **Puzzi, Signor**

Puttick & Simpson, auctioneer, London

Catalogue of a Valuable Music Library, Comprising . . . Theoretical & Practical Treatises . . . Important Manuscript Collections of Signor Puzzi . . . Also Musical Instruments . . . Sold August 21st, 1874. [London], 1874. 19 p. 423 + lots (many more items, e.g., lot 262, a vast collection of Mss.).　　　　[GB-Lbl]

Pymar, T. *See under* **Cerutti**

2172 **Raben, Otto Ludwig, Count,** 1730-91

Koudal, Jens Henrik. "The Music Discovered at Aalholm Manor: A Brief Introduction." *Fontes* 41 (1994): 270-78.　　　　[g.a.]

> Translated by Michael Talbot from a Danish-language article in *Caecilia: Aarbog . . .* (Aarhus Universitet, 1992-93).

2173   Rambert, Marie
SOTHEBY & CO., AUCTIONEER
[Sale of 3 June 1969 of Theatre and Ballet Items.]   [Film at CRL]
    Not examined.

2174   Rancken, Johann Oskar Immanuel, 1824-95
Förteckning öfver folksånger, melodier, sagar och äfventyr från det Svenska Österbotten, i
handskrift samlade af. . . . 2 vols. Nikolaistad/Wasa: F. W. Unggren, 1874-90. 68, 94 p.
                                                                      [US-CA, -AA, -U]

        Vol. 1: *Bih. till Redogörelse för Elementarlänoverket i Wasa,* 1873/74.
        Vol. 2: *Bih. till Program öfver Lyceum i Wasa,* 1889/90.

2175   Randall, John, 1715-99
MR. CHRISTIE, AUCTIONEER, LONDON
A Catalogue of the Valuable Library of Printed & MS. Music of the Late Dr. Randall, Deceased
. . . *Sold by Auction by Mr. Christie* . . . *June* . . . *1799.* [London], 1799. 12 p. 130 lots.
                                                       [US-NYp (partly priced), GB-Lbl]

    Folter, no. 297.

Randall, Richard.   *See* **Chichester, J. H. R.** (1863 sale)

2176   Rau, Arthur
A Brief List of Valuable Books, Manuscripts and Autographs Exhibited by . . . [of 130 Boulevard
Haussmann, Paris]. Paris, 1934. 16 p. no lotting.   [US-Wc (ML 152)]
        → *See also under* **Toulouse, Louis Alexandre**

Raucheisen, Michael.   *See* **Ivogün, Maria**

2177   Rauzzini, Venanzio Matteo, 1747-1810
MR. CHRISTIE, AUCTIONEER, LONDON
A Catalogue of the Very Valuable and Extensive Collection of Vocal and Instrumental Musick,
Manuscripts and Printed, of the Late . . . *Comprising Numerous Unpublished Works of This*
Much Admired Composer, and His Choice Musical Library [including] *Motetts and Rare*
Pieces by Durante, Leo, Pergolesi [et al.] . . . *Sold* . . . *March 6th, 1811, and Following Day.*
[London], 1811. 24 p. 237 + addenda of 45, 13 lots.   [US-NYp, -R]

        Music, except for final 13 lots. **King,** p. 91, says this is the second Rauzzini
        sale, the first conducted by a Mrs. Plura on 26 December 1810 at 2 Gay
        Street, Bath.

2178   Ravel, Maurice, 1875-1937
LITERATURE
Nectoux, Jean-Michel. "Maurice Ravel et sa bibliothèque musicale." *Fontes* 24 (1977): 199-206.
                                                                      [g.a.]

2179   Raveta, Guillaume
P. H. CARPENTIERS, AUCTIONEER, ANTWERP
Naemlyst van de boekken, musiek-werken, schriften uit de bibliotheek, naargelaten door . . .
Welke zullen verkogt worden 15 October 1827. . . . Antwerp, 1827. 15 p. 138 lots, mostly
music.   [B-BR; compiler (film)]

2180 **Razumovsky, Dmitri Vasil'yevich,** 1818-89
Kudriavtsev, I. M. *Sobraniya D. V. Razumovskovo i V. F. Odovevskovo arkhiv A. V. Razumovskovo opisaniya.* Moskva, 1960.

> A catalog of 170 manuscripts, biographical materials, papers, letters, etc., in the archive, according to *RILM*.

2181 **Read, C   J   (of Salisbury)**
PUTTICK & SIMPSON, AUCTIONEER, LONDON   CAT. NO. 2597B
Catalogue of An Extensive Collection of Music, Including the Library of . . . With Others, Comprising Instrumental Duets [etc.] *Full and Vocal Scores of Operas and Oratorios . . . Scarce Editions of Works by Early Composers . . . Sold . . . July the 27th, 1888.* 18 p. 345 lots.
[GB-Lbl]

> Read's lots not differentiated. Some Mss. **King**, p. 140, spells name "Reed."

2182 **Read, Keith M.**
LITERATURE
Hoogerwerf, Frank W. "Confederate Sheet Music at the Robert W. Woodruff Library, Emory University." *Notes* 34 (1977): 7-26.   [g.a.]

2183 **[Reade, C.   ; Ayrton, William]** [i.e., **Anonymous**]
PUTTICK & SIMPSON, AUCTIONEER, LONDON   CAT. NO. 83
Catalogue of a Valuable Miscellaneous Property, Comprising a Collection of Music, Including Some Choice Works of the Best Masters . . . Musical Instruments . . . Sold . . . July 26th, 1848. [London], 1848. 14 p. 219 lots. Music, lots 1-104, 133-219.   [GB-Lbl]

2184 **Reavy, Joseph M**
Reavy, Joseph M. *The Music of Corktown: The Reavy Collection of Irish-American Traditional Tunes.* Vol. 1. Philadelphia: author, 1979. 56 p.   [g.a.]

> Cited from *Music Index.*

2185 **Reay, Samuel**
PUTTICK & SIMPSON, AUCTIONEER, LONDON
Catalogue of Valuable Books from Various Sources, Including a Portion of the Musical Library of the Late . . . Proclamations and Autographs [not musical] *. . . Sold . . . June 25th, 1914.* [London], 1914. 27 p. 323 lots. Reay's properties, lots 164-210.   [NL-Avb]

2186 **Reay, Samuel (of Song School, Newark); Rev. W. Becher**
FRANK MURRAY, FIRM, DERBY   LIST NO. 225, PART 2
Clearance List . . . Old Music, a Very Fine Collection of the Original Editions in Full Score . . . Being the Musical Library of the Late . . . and Including Works from the Famous Musical Library of the Late Rev. W. Becher of Southwell (the Friend of Lord Byron). . . . Derby, 1907. 58 p. 2159 lots. Music, lots 1-297.   [US-NYgr]

2187 **Redern, Wilhelm Friedrich, Graf von**
LEO LIEPMANNSSOHN, FIRM, BERLIN   CAT. NO. 59
. . . Dramatische und dramaturgische Literatur, zum grössten Theile aus dem Besitz . . . Schauspieler Autographen. Berlin, 1887. 44 p. 824 lots.   [US-Wc]

2188 _____

LEO LIEPMANNSSOHN, FIRM, BERLIN   CAT. NO. 106

. . . Werke aus verschiedenen Fächern . . . zu grössten Theil aus den Nachlass des Grafen. . . .
Berlin, 1894. 50 p. 1052 lots.   [US-Wc]

     → *See also* sales by Leipmannssohn, no. 58, 1887, and no. 75 [-76], 1889,
under **Grell, Edward A.**

2189   **Redivivas, Carolina**

"Livsbrunn och tröstekälla' . . . Pa strövtag bland komponister och musiksamlare i Carolina
Rediviva handskrifts- och musik-avdelning. . . . " *Svenska dagbladet*, 11 June 1939, pp. ?

     Not examined; cited from *DaSML*.

2190   **Redl, Charles Arthur; [Godfrey J. G. Hochstatter;** et al.]

SOTHEBY, WILKINSON & HODGE, AUCTIONEER, LONDON

*Catalogue of the Libraries of . . . Comprising Early Works of Music . . . [etc.] . . . Sold 25th
August, 1881, and Three Following Days.* [London, 1881.] 87 p. 1667 p. Music, *inter alia.*

     [Film at CRL]

2191   **Redlich, Hans Ferdinand,** 1903-68

LANCASTER, ENGLAND, UNIVERSITY, LIBRARY

*Catalogue of the . . . Collection of Musical Books and Scores (Including Material on the
Second Viennese School . . . Cataloguing by Graham Royds).* Miscellaneous publications
series. Lancaster: University, 1976. xi, 117 p. 1659 items, including recordings.

     [US-Wc]

   Reed, C.   *See* **Read, C** (Puttick sale of 27 July 1888)

2192   **Reekes, John**

PUTTICK & SIMPSON, AUCTIONEER, LONDON   CAT. NO. 1887

*Catalogue of the Interesting, Curious and Valuable Collection of Musical Works of the Late
. . . With Others Comprising . . . Rare Treatises, Collection of Psalmodies, Scarce Sets of
Harpsichord Lessons . . . Original Autograph Score of Haydn's Third Notturno . . . Sold . . .
January 19, 1880.* [London], 1880. 21 p. 343 lots.   [GB-Lbl, US-CHua (priced)]

2193   **Reeves, Harold** (antiquarian)

SOTHEBY & CO., AUCTIONEER, LONDON   19-21 DECEMBER 1960

*Catalogue of Valuable Printed Books, Fine Bindings, Music, Autograph Letters and Portraits.
. . . The Autograph Full Score of Wagner's "Rienzi," and the Corrected Proofs of "Tristan
. . ." Autograph Notebooks and Relics of Fanny Burney . . . Property of . . . Wachope . . . Sold.
19th of December 1960 and Two Following Days.* London, 1960. 1st Day, 58 p. 197 lots,
music, 98- Wilkins's property, lots 135-36; Reeves's, lots 137-210; Wachope's, lots 282-97. Lot
178, "Well over 1000 ALS."   [Film at CRL]

2194 _____

MESSRS. HODGSON, & CO., AUCTIONEER, LONDON   CAT. No. 8 OF 1960/61

*A Catalogue of Books, Including Books from a Country House Library and Other Properties
. . . Music and Books on Music, the Property of Harold Reeves (Dec'd.), and Others . . . Sold
. . . May 18th, 1961.* London, 1961. 40 p. 643 lots. Music, lots 504-643. Reeves's properties,
lots 504-38.   [NL-Avb; compiler (Reeves's properties priced)]

2195 _____

MARLBOROUGH RARE BOOKS, LTD., FIRM, LONDON CAT. NO. 8
Autograph Letters and Documents of Famous Musicians. [A selection from the collection of Harold Reeves.] London, [n.d., 197-?]. 17 p. 174 + lots. [US-R]

2196 **Reger, Max,** 1873-1916
LITERATURE
Güntzel, Otto. "Das Max-Reger-Archiv in Meiningen, seine Geschichte und Bedeutung." In *Max Reger: Festschrift aus Anlass des 80. Geburtstages . . . 19. März 1953,* 85-90. Leipzig: Hofmeister, 1953. [g.a.]

2197 _____

Well, Philippine. "Das Reger-Archiv in Meiningen." *Musik und Gesellschaft* 11 (1961): 733-34.
[g.a.]
Collection donated by his wife, mostly his works, but also his "library."

2198 _____

Fröhlich, Hanna. "Die Max-Reger-Sammlung." In *Weiden in der Oberpfalz,* 161-66. München: Hoeppner, 1971.
Not located; cited from *RILM* 7:1428.

2199 **Régibo, Abel**
Catalogue d'une bibliothèque musicale et d'une collection d'antiquités . . . vente . . . September 1897. Renaix, 1897.
Not located; cited from **Hirt, Heyer, Boalch II.**

2200 **Reichardt, Johann Friedrich,** 1752-1814
Verzeichniss der von dem zu Giebichenstein bei Halle verstorbenen Herrn Kapellmeister Reichardt hinterlassenen Bücher und Musikalien, welche den 29sten April 1816 und in den darauf folgenden Tagen Nachmittags um 2 Uhr zu Halle an den meistbiethenden verkauft werden sollen. Halle, 1815. 110 p. [US-Wc, compiler]
Music books, pp. 14-19, lots 489-599; Scores, pp. 82-110, 570 lots (more items); R's compositions, pp. 96-98. **Folter,** no. 298.

2201 **Reichel, Bernard**
Matthey, Jean-Louis. *Fonds Musical Bernard Reichel.* Lausanne: Bibl. cantonale et universitaire, 1974. 101 p. ca. 400 items.
Thematic. Now at CH-LAcu. Cited from *RILM.*

2202 **Reid, John D.,** 1907-74
ARKANSAS ART CENTER, LITTLE ROCK
Catalog of the John D. Reid Collection of Early American Jazz. Compiled by Meredith McCoy and Barbara Parker, John D. Reid, advisor. Little Rock: Arkansas Arts Center, 1975. 112 p.
[US-Wc]

2203   Reid, John R., General, 1721-1807
EDINBURGH UNIVERSITY, LIBRARY, REID LIBRARY
Catalogue of Manuscripts, Printed Music and Books on Music up to 1850 in the Library of the Music Department . . . (Reid Library). Ed. Hans Gal. Edinburgh: Oliver and Boyd, 1941. xv, 78 p.   [US-Wc, -R, -BE, -NH, -MUu, -PSt]

> Given to the University in 1806, moved there in 1838, but the manuscript bequest is no longer available with which to identify Reid's library items.
> See **King**, p. 24, and **Albrecht**.   [GB-Lbl]

2204 _____

> LITERATURE
> Allan, Jean M. "The Reid Music Library, University of Edinburgh: Its Origins and Friends." *Library World* 51 (1948): 99-101.

2205   Reid, Robert
SOTHEBY, WILKINSON & HODGE, AUCTIONEER, LONDON
Catalogue of the Remaining Portion of the Library of G. Sharp . . . [and] the Late Robert Reid . . . Collections of Valuable Music, & Works on Music . . . Sold . . . 3rd of July, 1879. [London, 1879.] 84 p. 1510 lots.   [Film at CRL]

> Reid's musical properties, lots 1134-1382.

2206   Reiffenberg, Friedrich von
Kopp, Arthur. "Die Liedersammlung des Freiherrn Friedrich von Reiffenberg (1588). Zum erstenmal kritisch Untersucht." *Archiv f. d. Studium d. neuern Sprachen* 105 (1900): 265-95.
                                                                        [US-HOUr]

Reimann, Heinrich. *See under* **Eitner, Robert,** *and* **Rust, Friedrich Wilhelm**

2207   Reinecke, Karl Heinrich Carsten, 1824-1910
OSWALD WEIGEL, AUCTIONEER, LEIPZIG   AUK. CAT. NO. 49
Bibliothek Carl Reinecke, nebst Beiträgen anderer Herkunft, darunter Collectio Jóa. Linkii hymnologica . . . versteigert . . . 8.-12. Juni. . . . Leipzig, [n.d., 1914]. 124 p. 2009 lots. Music, lots 1-557, Theater, 559-1014a, Autographs, 1015-67.   [US-NYgr, -NYp, NL-DHgm]

> **Folter,** no. 299.
> → *See also* **Linke, Johannes**

2208   Reisig, J   H   ; R. W. Lelius de Thoer; H. Omeijer
CRAJENSCHOT GARTMAN, VERMANDEL EN ZOON AND SMIT
Catalogus eener pretiense collectie van de allervoornamste en meest moderne . . . printen . . . Een groote party muziek . . . nagelaten door de heeren . . . Al het welk verkocht . . . 9 den May 1794 . . . in de Brakke Grond. . . . A'dam, 1794. 18 p. 174 lots. Music, pp. 14-18 and *inter alia.*   [NL-Avb]

2209   Rellstab, Heinrich Friedrich Ludwig, 1799-1860
Verzeichniss aller gestochenen wie auch gedruckten und geschriebenen Musikalien. . . . Berlin: Rellstab, 1785.

> Not located.

2210 Remondini, Pier Costantino, 1829-93
LITERATURE
Tarrini, Maurizio. "Une Nouvelle Source pour l'histoire de l'orgue et de la musique sacrée en Italie au XIXème siècle: Les Archives de la Bibliothèque de Pier Constantine Remondini à Genoa." *Fontes* 38 (1991): 319-23. [g.a.]

2211 Repos, J B E
ANTONIN CHOSSONERY, AUCTIONEER, PARIS
. . . *Vente des ouvrages en nombre composant le fonds de commerce d'éditeur de musique, livres de chant romain, planches et clichés . . . liquidation de la Maison de Commerce de . . . vente . . . 24 [-] 25 Octobre 1882.* . . . Paris, 1882. [33] p. 189 lots. [NL-Avb]

2212 Resse, Pio, Conte
Catalogo di libri musicali raccolti dal conte . . . in Firenze. Parte prima. Firenze: Coi Tipi dell'arte della stampa, 1879. 72 p. 751 lots. Music, lots 460-702. [US-NYp, -CN]

2213 Revelstoke, Edward Charles Baring, 1st Lord Revelstoke
PUTTICK & SIMPSON, AUCTIONEER, LONDON   CAT. NO. 3407
A Catalogue of a Valuable Musical Library Formed by . . . Interesting and Important Lectures by Sir H. R. Bishop . . . in MS. [lots 1-70] . . . and a Portion of the Library of the Late Dryden [inter alia] . . . *Sold November 2nd.* . . . London, 1899. 327 lots. [GB-Lbl]

2214 Revelstoke, Louisa Emil Charlotte, Lady (wife of **Edward Charles Baring, First Lord Revelstoke**)
CHRISTIE'S, AUCTIONEER, LONDON
Valuable Autograph Letters, Historical Documents and Music Manuscripts . . . Sold . . . 16 October 1985. London, 1985. 243 lots. [US-NYgr]
> "The Revelstoke Collection Formerly at Althorp," lots 141-65A; "The Music Correspondence of Edwin Evans," lots 166-239.

2215 Rheda. Fürst zu Bentheim-Tecklenburgische Musikbibliothek
Domp, Joachim. *Studien zur Geschichte der Musik an westfälischen Adelshöfen im 18. Jarhrunderts.* Regensburg: Pustet, 1934. [US-Wc]
> Catalog of the library, pp. 14-34, has no special title. Vol. 1 of *Freiburger Studien zur Musikwissenschaft.* Now at D-MÜu.

2216 Rhodes, Willard, b. 1901
Hickerson, Joseph C., and Rae Korson. "The Willard Rhodes Collection of American Indian Music in the Archive of Folk Song [at US-Wc]." *Ethnomusicology* 13 (1969):196-304. [g.a.]

2217 Ribera, San Juan de
Robres Lluck, Ramón. "Obras impresas del siglo XVI en la biblioteca de San Juan de Ribera." *Anales del Seminario de Valencia* 6 (1966): 111-383. [Collection now at E-VAcp]
> Not examined; cited from **Benton 3**:52, no. 108, and a review in *Hispania sacra* 20, no. 40 (1967): 498-99.

2218   Ricasoli, Pietro Leopoldo, 1778-1850

Weaver, Robert Lamar. "Report on the Ricasoli Collection." In International Musicological Society, *Congress (14th: 1987): III, Free Papers*, 315-28.

> Now at University of Louisville. Assembled by Cavaliere Priore Pietro Leopoldo Ricasoli Zanchini Marsuppini and his wife, Lucrezia di Alessandro Rinuccini di Teresa Bardi.

2219   Rice, Helen

> The Helen Rice Memorial collection of chamber music belongs to the organization Amateur Chamber Music Players. Though kept in the Hartford Memorial Library it is a memorial only, not her library.

2220   Richbourg, John D.

LITERATURE

Steele, Suzanne. "From the Blues Archive: The John R. Richbourg Collection." *Living Blues* 70 (1986): 13-15.

Richter, Bernhard, Friedrich, 1850-1931.   *See* **Heuss, Alfred** (sale of 1935)

2221   [Richter, Hans, 1843-1916; et al.]

SOTHEBY & CO., AUCTIONEER, LONDON

Catalogue of Valuable Autograph Letters, Literary Manuscripts and Historical Documents . . . [Including] An Important Letter of Joseph Haydn . . . The Autograph of an Handel Overture; and the Signed Autograph Manuscript of Wagner's "Siegfried Idyll" . . . Sold . . . 27th Day of June, 1932. *[London, 1932.] 48 p. 198 lots.*   [Film at CRL]

2222   Ridder, J. Herman de; G. A. Fijnvandraat; et al.

J. H. DUNK, AUCTIONEER, ROTTERDAM

Catalogus van boeken, bouwkundige en andere plaatwerken enz. waarbij de bibliotheken nagelaten door de heeren . . . VIe afdeeling. Muziek, waarvan de verkooping . . . 8 December 1904 en volgende dagen. . . . Rotterdam, 1904.   [NL-Avb]

> Afdeeling VI, music, pp. 181-206, lots 5789-6667, but it is not clear whose properties they were.

2223   Riedl,

LITERATURE

Brednich, Rolf Wilhelm. "Flugschriften-sammlung Riedl im Deutschen Volksliedarchiv [Freiburg im Bresgau]." *Jahrbuch für Volksliedforschung* 17 (1972): 209-14.   [g.a.]

2224   Riehl, Heinrich Wilhelm von

ACKERMANN, FIRM, MUNICH   CAT. NO. 446

. . . Geschichte der Musik. Theaterwissenschaftliche Werke . . . Bibliothek Riehl. . . . München, 1898.

> Not located; cited from **Folter 2**, no. 630.

Riemann, Hugo.   *See under* **Müller-Reuter, Theodor**

2225   Riemenschneider, Albert, 1878-1950
BALDWIN-WALLACE COLLEGE, BEREA, OHIO
Emilie and Karl Riemenschneider Bach Library: Catalog. Ed. Sylvia W. Kenney. New York: Columbia University Press, 1960. xv, 195 p. 2537 nos.   [g.a.]
    Folter, no. 300.

2226   _____
Barber, Elinore. "Riemenschneider Bach Library Vault Holdings." *Bach* 1-3 (1970-72), whole issues.   [g.a.]

2227   _____
LITERATURE
Riemenschneider, Albert. "The Bach Library at Berea, Ohio." *Notes,* 1st ser., 8 (1940): 39-48.
                [g.a.]

2228   _____
Boyd, Charles Newell. *The Bach Library at Berea, Ohio.* Pittsburgh: author, 1937. 12 p.
                [US-Wc]

2229   _____
Boyd, Charles Newell. "Festival and Library Make Berea, Ohio an American Bach Center." *Diapason* 28 (February 1937): 18-19.   [g.a.]

2230   Riesenfeld, Hugo; Stefan Zweig
HEINRICH HINTERBERGER, FIRM, VIENNA   CAT. NO. 20
Interessante Autographen. . . . Wien, 1937. 100 p., 23 plates. 881 lots. Music, lots 1-590.
                [compiler]

    Folter, no. 301, notes that while Riesenfeld's properties are not here differentiated, they can be ascertained by comparing this and the Parke-Bernet auction in 1941 (**2231**).

2231   _____
PARKE-BERNET GALLERIES, AUCTIONEER, NEW YORK
Incunabula, Early and Late Manuscripts [etc. from Several Owners]. *Together with the Musical Autograph Letters and Manuscripts by the World's Greatest Composers, Assembled by the Late . . . Riesenfeld . . . Sale November 26 [-27] 1941.* New York, 1941. 145 p. 592 lots. Music throughout.   [US-CN, -PHu, compiler]
    Folter, no. 302.

2232   Rietz, Julius, 1812-77; **A. von Zahn**
R. VON ZAHN, AUCTIONEER, DRESDEN   ANTIQ. CAT. NO. 22
Auction zu Dresden der von Generalmusikdirektor Dr. Julius Rietz, Hofrath Dr. A. von Zahn in Dresden hinterlassenen Bibliotheken Musikalien-sammlung, sowie einiger werthvollen Kupferstiche in Glas und Rahmen an 29. April und den folgenden Tagen durch R. v. Zahn's Antiquariat. . . . [Dresden, 1877.] 104 p. 3040 lots, not continuously numbered. 324 lots, music literature; 1020 scores.   [US-Wc, -CHua, GB-Lbl (Hirsch)]

    Properties not differentiated. **Folter,** no. 303. **Schaal** (1966), p. 51, says 1878.

2233   _____

        GUSTAV SALOMON, FIRM   BÜCHER-AUK.
        [Katalog . . . Autographen Including Tonkünstler]. Dresden, 1883.   [US-NYp]
           Not examined.

2234   _____

        OTTO AUGUST SCHULZ, FIRM, LEIPZIG   AUTOGR.-CAT. NO. 15
        Verzeichnis einer kostbaren Sammlung von Autographen der berühmtesten Tonkünstler,
        Sänger, Schauspieler etc. . . . 3. T. aus den Nachlasse des . . . zu beziehen von . . . Schulz in
        Leipzig. . . . Leipzig-Reudnitz, 1884. 35 p. 555 lots.   [US-NYp, GB-Lbl (Hirsch)]
           Folter, no. 304. **Schaal** (1966), p. 51.

2235   _____

        LEO LIEPMANNSSOHN, FIRM, BERLIN   AUTOGR.-CAT. NO. 18
        Katalog einer hervorragenden Sammlung von Musiker-Autographen (Musikmanuskripte
        und sonstige Schriftstücke) . . . Zum grössten Teil aus den Nachlasse des . . . Versteigerung
        . . . 17. Oktober 1896. Berlin, 1896. 27 p. 228 lots.   [NL-R]
           Folter, no. 305.

2236   **Rigby, Dr. Edward**

        PUTTICK & SIMPSON, AUCTIONEER, LONDON   CAT. NO. 689
        A Catalogue of a Collection of Music, Including the Libraries of Frederick Perkins, Dr.
        Edward Rigby . . . Sold . . . July 17-19. . . . London, 1861. 790 lots.   [GB-Lbl]

2237   **Rimbault, Edward Francis,** 1816-76

        MESSRS. CHRISTIE & MANSON, AUCTIONEER, LONDON
        A Catalogue of the Very Extensive and Valuable Collection of Drawings in Water-Colours,
        Formed by . . . Also His Collection of Printed Music . . . Sold . . . December 13, 1837, and Two
        Following Days. . . . London, 1837. 28 p. 597 lots. Music, lots 565-97 (many more items).
        Rimbault, himself, purchased many lots!   [GB-Lc, -Bu]

2238   **[Rimbault, Edward Francis; Dickens (Charles?)]**

        PUTTICK & SIMPSON, AUCTIONEER, LONDON   CAT. NO. 506
        A Catalogue of Highly Interesting and Important Collections . . . Extremely Valuable and
        Curious Works . . . Interesting Manuscript Music . . . Valuable Full Scores of Operas . . . and
        Several Musical Instruments . . . Sold . . . August 24th, 1857, and Following Days. . . . London,
        1857. 39 p. 766 lots. Music, lots 1-710.   [GB-Lbl]
           P&S "Index" (see Preface) notes Dickens.

2239   [_____]

        [Lonsdale, R.?] *Catalogue of the Extensive Library of Dr. Rainbeau Which Messrs. Topsy, Turvy*
        & Co. Will Put Up for Public Competition on Saturday, October 1862. [London, 1862.] 10 p.

2240   _____

        [Lonsdale, R.?] *The "Rainbow" Catalog: A Facsimile Edition.* [N.p.]: Distant Press,
        1962. [5], 10 p.   [GB-Lbl (original); facsimiles, g.a.]
           A satirical catalog in facsimile with a preface by James Coover. **King** later
           included the spoof in his facsimile reprint of the 1877 Sotheby sale catalog
           (2241).

2241   _____

SOTHEBY, WILKINSON & HODGE, AUCTIONEER, LONDON

Catalogue of the Valuable Library of . . . Comprising . . . Ancient Music . . . Works of the Early English Poets and Dramatists . . . Miscellaneous Literature . . . Sold . . . the 31st of July, 1877, and Five Following Days. . . . [London]: J. Davy and Sons, [1877]. 159 p. 2259 lots.

[US-MB, -Wc, NYp, GB-Lbl; film at CRL]

> Reprinted in facsimile with an introduction by A. Hyatt King in the series Auction Catalogues of Music, 6 (Buren: F. Knuf, 1975). He does not note the preceding reprint of the "Rainbow" catalog. An overview of the auction appeared in *MT* (1877): 425-27.

2242   _____

Hiscock, W. G. "Christ Church Missing Books, II - Printed Music." *Times Literary Supplement,* 11 February 1939, p. 96.

> Sadly, it makes a strong case for thievery by Rimbault.

2243   _____

LITERATURE

Andrews, Richard. "Edward Francis Rimbault, 1816-76." *Fontes* 30 (1983): 30-34.   [g.a.]

2244   **Rinck, Johann Christian Heinrich,** 1770-1846

Noack, E. "Eine Briefsammlung aus der 1. Hälfte des 19. Jahrhunderts." *AfMW* 10 (1953): 323-37.

[g.a.]

> A gift from Rinck's uncle. List of letters, pp. 334-37. His library was bought by Lowell Mason (**1808**). Now at US-NH.

2245   _____

Fall, Henry Cutler. "A Critical-Bibliographical Study of the . . . Collection." M.A. thesis, Yale University, n.d. Various pagings, illus.

2246   **Rischel, Thorvald,** 1861-1939**; Frederik Birket-Smith,** 1880-1952

Torpp Larsson, Jytte. *Catalogue of the Rischel and Birket-Smith Collection of Guitar Music in the Royal Library of Copenhagen.* Compiled by Jytte Torpp Larsson, edited by Peter Danner. Columbus: Editions Orphée, 1989. iv, 263 p.   [US-Wc, -NH, -R, -NYp]

2247   **Ritter, August Gottfried,** 1811-85**; Johann Andre Grabau,** 1808-84

LIST & FRANCKE, FIRM, LEIPZIG   CAT. NO. 182

Verzeichniss von theoretischen Werken über Musik sowie von seltenen, älteren, praktischen Musikstücken und neueren Musikalien aus den nachgelassenen Sammlungen der Herren Prof. A. G. Ritter in Magdeburg und Johann Andr. Grabau in Leipzig. Leipzig, 1886. 102 p. 3194 lots.   [US-Wc, GB-Lbl, NL-DHgm, -Avb]

> **Folter,** no. 306.

2248   **Ritter, Frédéric Louis,** 1834-91

TUFTS COLLEGE, LIBRARY

Catalogue of the Musical Library of the Late. . . . [N.p., 189-?] 31 p. 878, 401 lots.

[US-PO, -Wc, -Bp, -BUu (copy)]

> Collection presented to Tufts by L. R. Metcalf. Some of it is also at US-PO.
> **Folter,** no. 307.

2249 **Rivers, Lady Martha** and **Sir Henry**

THOMAS KERSLAKE, FIRM, BRISTOL

Books from the Library of . . . and Various Others, Including Handel's Autograph Scores. . . .
Bristol, 1856.   [GB-BRp]

> Not examined. Originally the property of J. C. Smith, Handel's amanuensis,
> who willed the collection to Rivers ("I give to Lady Rivers all my music
> books") then acquired by Kerslake as "wastepaper" in 1851. Kerslake offers
> in this catalog to sell it *en bloc* for £45. The scores were purchased by
> Victor Schoelcher and offered to the British Museum, which declined to
> buy. They were ultimately sold to Chrysander for the Hamburg Staats- und
> Universitäts-Bibliothek. See: *Handel: A Celebration*, ed. Jacob Simon
> (London: National Portrait Gallery, 1986), 24, n. 4.
>
> Kerslake's catalog entry for the Handel scores is reprinted in Hans Dieter
> Clausen's *Händel's Direktionspartituren (Handexemplare),* Hamburger
> Beiträge für Musikwissenschaft, 7 (Hamburg: Verlag der Musikalien-
> handlung, 1972), 17-18.
>
> Not noted by **Folter**, **King**, or **Albrecht**.

2250 **Robert, Lord Clive,** d. 1774

ALBI ROSENTHAL, FIRM, LONDON   CAT. NO. 10

Rare Music [the music collection of Lord Clive of India (1725-74) and his family]. Oxford:
Rosenthal, 1948. 186 p. 5 plates. 186 lots.   [GB-LRosenthal]

> Clive's collection, pp. 1-8 (short-title entries). Engraved and manscript music,
> mostly 18th century.

2251 **Robert de Bourbon, Duke of Parma,** 1848-1907

Bohatta, Hanns. *Katalog der liturgischen Drucke des XV. und XVI. Jahrhunderts in der herzogl.*
Parma'schen Bibliothek in Schwarzau am Steinfeld, N.-Ö. Im Auftrage weiland Seiner
Königlichen Hoheit Herzog Robert von Parma. . . . 2 vols. Wien: [Druck von A. Holzhausen],
1909-10. 606 entries.   [US-Wc, -CA]

> Robert de Bourbon inherited the library of his grandfather Charles, Louis
> de Bourbon (**473**), a catalog of whose liturgical collection was published in
> Paris, 1878, with a supplement in 1884, listing in all 376 titles.
>
> After Robert's death, the collection was divided and appeared in two
> separate sales. See the following (**2252**).

2252 _____

L. GIRAUD-BADIN, FIRM, PARIS AND ULRICO HOEPLI, FIRM, MILAN

La Bibliothèque liturgique Bourbon-Parma . . . vente . . . 30 mai au mercredi 1ᵉʳ juin 1932.
[Milano: Tip. cav. U. Allegretti di S. Allegretti, 1932.] 39 p. 317 entries.   [US-Wc, -STu]

2253 _____

L. GIRAUD-BADIN, FIRM, PARIS

Livres de liturgie imprimés aux XVᵉ et XVIᵉ siècles faisant partie de la bibliothèque de Son
Altesse royale le duc Robert de Parme. Paris: Guraud-Badin [etc.], 1932. xi, 162 p. 345 entries.
                                                                                [US-CA, -NYp, -U, -AA, -BE]

> US-Wc says preface by Seymour de Ricci; Haas catalog 18, lot 15 says
> edited by him.

2254 Roberts, Rev. H   G
PUTTICK & SIMPSON, AUCTIONEER, LONDON   CAT. NO. 5704
Catalogue of Valuable Books, Including the Library of the Late . . . A Music Library Removed from Sussex . . . Sold February 8th, and Following Day. [London], 1922. 38 p. 525 lots.
[GB-Lbl]

"Library of music," lots 203-54 but many more items, e.g., lot 230 comprises some 120 volumes; lot 214, 20 volumes of overtures. Roberts' properties not explicitly identified.

2255 Roberts, John
LEIGH AND SOTHEBY, AUCTIONEER, LONDON
A Catalogue of the Very Select and Elegant Library of the Late . . . With His Book of Prints, and His Choice Collection of Music . . . Sold . . . March 17th, 1815, and Following Day. . . . [London, 1815.] 14 p. 351 lots. Music, lots 303-51.   [Film at CRL]

Robien, Christoph Paul.   *See under* **Bourblanc, Saturnin de**

2256 Robinson, John, of York
PUTTICK & SIMPSON, AUCTIONEER, LONDON   CAT. NO. 496
Catalogue of Very Important, Interesting, and Valuable Musical Properties, Including the Library of the Late . . . With Selections from Other Libraries, Numerous Costly Musical Instruments . . . Sold . . . June 16th, and . . . 18th, 1857. [London, 1857.] 34 p. 816 lots. Music, lots 1-641.   [GB-Lbl]

Robinson's musical library cannot be positively identified; his collection of excellent instruments is set out in lots 652-74.

2257 Rodeheaver, Homer Alvin, 1880-1955; **Ruthella Feaster Rodeheaver**
THE OLD MUSIC SHOP   LIST 75
[About 325 items from their collections were offered *en bloc* for $650 and $300 in this catalog, *Church Music.* Duplicates of items in the two collections were offered as lots 128-52.] Three Oaks, Michigan, 1990.

2258 Rodger, James, 1871-1952
RHODES UNIVERSITY, GRAHAMSTON, SOUTH AFRICA, LIBRARY
Catalogue [of the James Rodger Hymnological Collection]. Grahamstown: University Library, 1966. 21 leaves.   [US-Wc]

Rödelberger, C.   *See* **Schlatter, V**

2259 Röntgen, Julius; et al.
VAN HUFFEL, AUCTIONEER, UTRECHT
. . . Catalogus van eene belangrijke verzameling oude en nieuwe boeken . . . De muziekbibliotheek van wijlen Julius Röntgen . . . Verkooping 14-17 januari 1941. Utrecht, 1941. 83 p. 1575 lots. Music (R.'s), lots 1307-575.   [NL-Avb (interleaved with names and prices)]

2260 Roggenbach, P   W   ; S   Davies; "Un Amateur Inconnu"
VAN HEUGEL & EELTJES (J. VAN BAALEN ET FILS, AUCTIONEER, ROTTERDAM)
Catalogue d'une belle collection de livres, gravures, musique, objets divers, etc. délaisée par . . . Vente publique à Rotterdam . . . 9 Avril 1874 et jours suivants. . . . Rotterdam, 1874. 110 p. 3244 + 181 lots. Music, lots 2848-3135.   [NL-Avb (priced)]

2261 Rohlff, J
WOODROW, FIRM, NORWICH

> **King**, p. 135, reports a note in *Musical World* (1843), p. 402, and another in the *Norwich Mercury,* which indicate Woodrow sold Rohlff's music properties, 18 December 1843. Not verified.

2262 Rokseth, Yvonne, 1890-1948; **Henry Prunières,** 1886-1942
BROUDE BROS., FIRM, NEW YORK   CAT. NO. 3
Musical Literature, Musicology, Biography, Periodicals, Bibliography, Early Printed Books, Scholarly and Rare Music from the Libraries of. . . . New York, 1950. 49 p. 1749 lots.   [g.a.]

> Properties are not differentiated. **Folter**, no. 308.

2263 Rolandi, Ulderico, 1874-1951
. . . La collezione Rolandi di libretti d'opere musicali. [N.p., 1927.] 12 p., illus.   [US-Wc]

> "Estratto dalla rivista *Accademie e biblioteche*" 1 (1927): 46-57.

2264 _____

LITERATURE
Storia e vicende della collezione Rolandi di libretti per musica. Cagliari: Edizione della rivista "Sardegna," 1930. 16 p., illus.   [US-Wc]

2265 _____
"La biblioteca musicale Rolandi." *Accademie e biblioteche* 16 (1941/42): 242-43.   [g.a.]

2266 _____
"Unici, rari e curiosi nella biblioteca musicale Rolandi." *Accademie e biblioteche* 19 (1951): 118-24.   [g.a.]

2267 Roman, Johann Helmich, 1694-1758
Vretblad, Aake. "Johann Helmich Romans Bibliotek." *STMf* 35 (1953): 145-51.   [g.a.]

2268 _____
Bengtsson, Igmar. *Handskilar och notpikturer i Kungl. Musikaliska Akademiens Roman-samling. Handwriting and Musical Calligraphy of the Swedish Royal Academy of Music av . . . Bengtsson och Ruben Danielson.* Studia musicologica Upsaliensia. Uppsala: [Almquist & Wiksells boktr.], 1955. viii, 74 p., facs.   [US-Cu, -AA, -CHH, -BLu]

Rombouts, Dr.   *See under* **Plugge, P. C.**

2269 Rondinelli, Prof.   ; William Weeks
STAN. V. HENKELS, FIRM, PHILADELPHIA
Elegant Miscellaneous Books from the Library of William Weeks. . . . Also the Valuable Musical Library Formed by Professor Rondinelli . . . Sold . . . March 10th, 1902. Philadelphia, 1902. 20 p. 185 lots (not music; note at the end says Rondinelli's library was "To Be Sold Immediately After Lot 185," but that list has not been located).   [US-NYgr, -NYp]

2270 Rontani,   , Abbé
Catalogue des livres provenant de la bibliothèque musicale de l'abbé Rontani. . . . Paris, 1846.   [F-Pn]

> Not examined.

2271   **Rookwood, Mrs. A.** (formerly property of Dr. Curt Sluzewski)**; Richard Peyton; P. MacClellan;
W. D. Kearns**
SOTHEBY, PARKE-BERNET GALLERIES, AUCTIONEER, NEW YORK
*Catalogue of Valuable Manuscript and Printed Music, and Autograph Letters of Composers.
. . . Books on Musical Instruments. . . . The Richard Peyton Collection of Autograph Letters
and Photographs* [etc.] *. . . Sold 20th-21st November, 1978.* New York, 1978. 110 p. 482 lots.
[US-BUu]

> Rookwood's properties, lots 430-82; Peyton's, lots 403-22 (lot 415 over 100
> items!); MacClellan's, lots 113-73; Kearn's, lots 384-93 (more items, including
> ALS and Mss.).

2272   **Roothaan, A**
G. THEOD. BOM, & ZOON, AUCTIONEER, AMSTERDAM
*Catalogus uitgebreide en belangrijke verzameling muziekvoor piano, viool, violoncel, fluit
en orgel . . . zangmuziek . . . opera's, oratorien en kermuziek . . . verkooping . . . 12 en maandag
14 mei 1888. . . .* Amsterdam, 1888. 24 p. 569 lots. Music, lots 1-555.   [NL-Avb]

2273   **Roothan, Th. J. & Co., Amsterdam**
H. G. BOM, AUCTIONEER, AMSTERDAM
*Catalogus van eene groote collectie muziek voor zang en piano-forte, viool, fluit en verdere
instrumenten . . . afkonstig van de gerenommeerde muziek-bibliotheek van de heeren . . .
verkooping . . . 19 februari 1874. . . .* Amsterdam, 1874. 16 p. 491 lots.   [NL-Avb]

2274   **Rosati, Vincenzo**
LIBRERIA ROMANA, FIRM, ROME
Catalogo della biblioteca musicale appartenuta al distinto Professore. . . . Roma: Tip. Ed.
Romana, 1903. 48 p. 481 lots.   [US-NYgr]

2275   _____
LIST & FRANCKE, FIRM, LEIPZIG   ANT. CAT. NO. 360
*Musikliteratur. Musikalien. Theater und Tanz. Autographen von Musikern und Bühnen-
Künstlern, z. T. aus dem Nachlasse des. . . .* Leipzig, 1904. 44 p. 1051 lots.
[US-Wc, NL-Avb, GB-Lbl]

> Note in *ZiMG* 5 (1903/04): 344 says it continues Ant. Catalog no. 353.
> **Folter**, no. 309.

2276   **Rosbaud, Hans,** 1895-1962
Evans, Joan. "The Hans Rosbaud Library at Washington State University." *Notes* 41 (1984):
26-40.   [g.a.]

2277   **Rose, Kenneth David,** 1888-1960
Literature
Rose, Kenneth David. "The Story of a Music Collection." *Tennessee Historical Quarterly* 15
(1956): 356-63.   [g.a.]

> Sheet music, now at US-NAs.

2278 Rosenberg Family (Prague)
"Svenskt musikhistoriskt arkiv: reproduktions-sammlingen." *Svenskt musikhistoriskt arkiv, Bulletin* 2 (1967), leaves 7-9; 3 (1968), leaf 38; 6 (1970), leaves 35-36; 7 (1971), leaf 38.   [g.a.]

> New additions to the archive, and a list of music books owned by the Rosenberg family in Prague, brought to Sweden during the 30 Years War.

2279 Rosenbloom, Charles J
LITERATURE
Hunt, J. L. "Music in the Rosenbloom Collection of Hunt Library at Carnegie-Mellon University." *Notes* 33 (1977): 553-62.   [g.a.]

2280 Rosenthal, Bernard M
BERNARD QUARITCH, FIRM, LONDON   CAT. NO. 1088
Medieval Manuscript Leaves, Principally from the Rosenthal Collection. London, 1988. 97 p. Plates throughout.   [US-BUu]

> "Liturgy and Church Music," lots 30-55, pp. 37-57.

2281 Rossi, D Fr de
LITERATURE
Morelot, Stephen. "Notice sur les manuscrits relatifs à la musique, conservés dans la bibliothèque de M. le Commandeur de Rossi à Rome." *Revue de la musique religieuse, populaire et classique* 4 (1848): 81-88.   [US-Wc, -NYp, -AA, -MB]

2282 Rothschild, Carl, Freiherr von
LITERATURE
Berghoeffer, Christian. "Musikwissenschaftliche Büchersammlungen. Erworben durch die Freiherrlich C. v. Rothschild'sche Bibliothek in Frankfurt." *Frankfurter Zeitung* 44 (18 August 1900): 1-2.   [US-BUu (film)]

> Incorrectly in **Benton 2**:64, no. 86, as Boerghoeffer. Collection now at D-Fsm.

2283 Rouveroit,   , Baron de
Lamsoul, Charles. "Une Collection de musique de chambre du XIIIᵉ siècle." *Société archéologique de Namur, Annales* 42 (1936): 91-105.   [US-NYp]

2284 Rowe, Louis Thompson, 1855-1927
LITERATURE
Vlasto, Jill. "The Rowe Music Library [at King's College, Cambridge]." *MR* 12 (1951): 72-75.   [g.a.]

> "Almost exclusively the gift of one devoted anonymous member of the College. . . ." It began with the gift in 1928 (**King** says 1927) of Rowe's collection of 18th-century chamber music. Rowe's incunabula and non-musical rarities were sold by Hodgson in 1928 (**Benton 2**:167, no. 20).

The Rowfant Library. *See under* **Locker-Lampson, Frederick,** 1821-95

2285 Roy, Léo
Vézina-Demers, Micheline, and Claire Grégoire-Reid. *Catalogue des oeuvres musicales du fonds Léo Roy.* Québec: Atelier de musicographie, 1987. viii, 143 p., facs.   [US-BUu, -CA]

Rubin, Harold.   *See under* **Clarence, O. B.**

2286   **Rudolph, Johann Joseph Rainer, Erzherzog,** 1788-1831
"Sammlung von Musikstücken aus den Besitze Erzherzog Rudolphs, als Katalog geführt vom Jahre 1801 bis zum Juli 1819."

> Ms. in the Gesellschaft der Muskfreunde in Vienna where most of the collection went, though some of it, mostly his own manuscripts, stayed at CS-KRa. Discussed in Croll's book (**2289**).

2287   _____
"Katalog der Sammlung des Erzherzogs Rudolph."

> Ms. in the Gesellschaft der Musikfreunde, with no date. Ca. 200 p., according to Croll, listing some 336 works of Beethoven.

2288   _____
Vetterl, K. "Der musikalische Nachlass des Erzherzogs Rudolf in erzbischöflichen Archiv zu Kremsier." *ZfMW* 9 (1926/27): 168-79.   [g.a.]

2289   _____
Croll, Gerhard. "Die Musiksammlung des Erzherzogs Rudolph." In *Beethoven-Studien*, 51-55. Wien, 1970.   [g.a.]

> Reprints or discusses a number of inventories and 5 registers in A-Wgm, the first complete:
>
> 1) "Register über die Musikalien-Sammlung, welche von Seiner König. Hoheit dem Erzherzoge Rudolph in dreyzehnten Jahr Ihres Alters, im Jahre 1801 angefangen. . . . "
>
> 2) "Register der Partituren und Clavierauszüge," dated 17 April 1816.
>
> 3) "Verteiler" der Aufschluss über die Ordnung und Aufstellung der Musikalien gibt, "Wien, 17. April 1817."
>
> 4) "Register für Gesamtwerke und Zeitschriften," dated February 1818.
>
> 5) "Register der Musikstücke für Clavier und Harfe."

2290   _____
Brandenburg, Sieghard. "Die Beethovenhandschriften in der Musikalien-sammlung des Erzherzogs Rudolph." In *Zu Beethoven: Aufsätze und Dokumente*, 3 (Berlin: Neue Musik, 1988), 141-76.   [g.a.]

2291   **Rudorff, Ernst Friedrich Karl,** 1840-1916
Schwartz, Rudolf. "Jahresbericht und Mitteilung über die Erwerbung der Rudorffschen Sammlung." *Jahrbuch der Musikbibliothek Peters* 24 (1917): v-ix. Reprint, Vaduz: Kraus, 1965.
   [g.a.]

2292   _____
Reich, Nancy B. "The Rudorff Collection." *Notes* 31 (1974): 247-61.   [g.a.]

> From 1869 to 1910, head of the Piano Department at the Berlin Hochschüle, and a friend of Brahms whose letters to him were published in vol. 3 of the Brahms correspondence (Berlin, 1907), according to *Baker's Biographical Dictionary*. It remains a private library in Leipzig.

2293 **Ruge, Filippo,** 1725-67
"Catalogue de la collection symphonique établie par Filippo Ruge au Château de Seignelai."
Ms., ca. 1757. Thematic catalog at US-SFsc.

2294 _____
LaRue, Jan, and M. W. Colin. "The Ruge-Seignelay Catalogue." In *Elektronische Datenverarbeitung in der Musikwissenschaft,* ed. Harald Heckmann, 41-56. Regensburg, 1967.
[g.a.]

Ruggles-Brise, Dorothea, Lady. *See under* **Glen, John**

2295 **Ruperti, Friedrich**
LIST & FRANCKE, AUCTIONEER, LEIPZIG
Verzeichniss der hinterlassenen Bibliothek des Herrn Dr. Phil. Ruperti in Bremen . . . einer reichhaltigen Sammlung von Landkarten und Musikalien . . . am 20. April 1868 . . . versteigert werden. . . . Leipzig, 1868. 198 p. 5630 lots.   [D-W]
> **Folter,** no. 2:640A. Not examined.

2296 **Ruppeldt, Milos,** 1881-1943
Dvořák, Vladislaw. *Hudebná pozostalost' Milosa Ruppeldta v Univerzitnej kniznici v Bratislave.* Bratislava, 1967. 191 p.
> Not examined; cited from *RILM* 1:502 and **Folter,** no. 310. **Albrecht** says thematic catalog of the collection now at CS-BRu.

2297 **Russell, Raymond Anthony,** 1922-64; et al.
SOTHEBY & CO., AUCTIONEER, LONDON
Catalogue of Valuable Printed Books, Botanical Books and Drawings, Fine Bindings, Music, Autograph Letters, etc. . . . Including the Property of . . . Sir Richard Cotterell . . . Miss Edna H. Bahr [etc.] *. . . Extensive Musical Autograph MS. of Mozart, Letters of Bizet . . . Sold . . . the 9th December, 1957 and Two Following Days.* [London], 1957. 133 p. 729 lots. Music, lots 500-38.
> Russell's properties, lots 500-10; Mss. and ALS, lots 529-38; lot 538, holograph of Mozart's *Studies in Canon* from the **Fuchs** collection; lot 533, a Liszt holograph.

2298 **Russell, Ross**
LITERATURE
Lawn, Richard. "From Bird to Stravinsky to Schoenberg: The Ross Russell Collection." *Library Chronicle of the University of Texas at Austin* 25/26 (1984): 137-47.   [US-BUu]

2299 _____
Komara, Edward. "The Dial Recordings of Charlie Parker." In *The Bebop Revolution in Words and Music,* ed. Dave Oliphant, 79-104. Austin: Humanities Research Center, University of Texas, 1994.
[g.a.]
> Originally published in the *Library Chronicle of the University of Texas at Austin* 24, nos. 1-2.

2300   Rust, Friedrich Wilhelm, 1739-96; **Robert Eitner,** 1822-1905
LEO LIEPMANNSSOHN, FIRM, BERLIN   CAT. NO. 156
Antike und moderner Musik-theorie und Musikästhetik. Akustik . . . darunter Werke aus den
Bibliotheken von Fr. W. Rust und R. Eitner. . . . Berlin, [n.d., ca. 1906]. 47 p. 633 items.
[GB-Lbl, US-Wc, -R, NL-Avb, compiler]

> Properties are not differentiated. **Folter**, no. 311. See note in *ZiMG* 7
> (1905/06): 302.
>
>   → **Rust** properties also here *under* **Picquot & Cartier** (Liepmannssohn's
>   sale catalogs nos. 157, 167, and 169, **2117**)

2301   Rust, Friedrich Wilhelm; Robert Eitner; Julius Stockhausen, 1826-1906
LEO LIEPMANNSSOHN, FIRM, BERLIN   CAT. NO. 165
Musiker-Biographen aus den Sammlungen von. . . . Berlin, [n.d., 1907]. 93 p. 1715 lots.
[GB-Lbl, NL-Avb]

> Properties not differentiated. **Folter**, no. 312.

2302   Sacher, Paul, 1906-99
Lichtenhahn, Ernst. *Musikhandschriften aus der Sammlung Paul Sacher: Festschrift zu Paul*
Sachers siebzigstem Geburtstag, Verbindung mit Ernst Lichtenhahn und Tilman Seebass. . . .
Basel: Hoffmann-LaRoche, 1976. 197 p., facs.

2303   _____

Inventories of the Paul Sacher Foundation. Winterthur: Amadeus Verlag, 1988-.   [g.a.]

>   1. Sammlungen Paul Sacher, Antoinette Vischer, Margit Weber (1988)
>   2. Luciano Berio (1988)
>   3. Pierre Boulez (1988)
>   4. Anton Webern (1988/1994)
>   5. Igor Stravinsky (1989)
>   6. Bruno Maderna (1990)
>   7. Walther Geiser (1990)
>   8. Alberto Ginastera (1990)
>   9. Jean Binet (1990)
>   10. Frank Martin (1990)
>   11. Rudolf Kelterborn (1991)
>   12. Roman Haubenstock-Ramati (1991)
>   13. Conrad Beck (1992)
>   14. René Leibowitz (1995)

2304   _____

LITERATURE
Paul Sacher Stiftung [A guide and description of the collections]. [Basel]: Paul Sacher Stiftung,
1991. 36 p.   [g.a.]

2305   _____

Jans, Hans Jorg. *Komponisten des 20. Jahrhunderts in der Paul Sacher Stiftung.* Basel: Paul
Sacher Stiftung, 1986. 462 p., illus.   [g.a.]

> For the opening of the Paul Sacher Stiftung, 28 April 1986. Related exhibit,

April 25 to July 20 in the Kunstmuseum, Basel, entitled *Die Musik des 20. Jahrhunderts in der Paul Sacher Stiftung.*

2306 _____

Publications of the Paul Sacher Foundation. Winterthur: Amadeus Verlag, 1990-.   [g.a.]

2307 _____

Rich, Maria F. "Opera USA - Perspective: The Stravinsky Legacy." *Opera Quarterly* 3 (1985): 80-98.

2308 _____

Mitteilungen, Paul Sacher Stiftung, no. 1, January 1988-. Basel: Paul Sacher-Stiftung.   [g.a.]

2309 _____

Wilkins, Grover. "A Most Extraordinary Maestro." *Musical America* 108 (March 1988): 19-21.
[g.a.]

2310 Sachs, Johann Gabriel
LITERATURE
Vretblad, Aake. "Bidrag till friketstidens operarepertoar ur Johann Gabriel Sacks bibliotek." *StM* 32 (1950): 191-216.   [g.a.]
Now at S-Skma.

2311 Sackville, John Frederick, 3rd Duke of Dorset, 1745-99
LITERATURE
LaRue, Jan. "A Music Catalogue at Knole." *M&L* 38 (1957): 247-49.   [g.a.]

2312 Sacred Harmonic Society
Husk, W. H. *Catalogue of the Library of the Sacred Harmonic Society.* . . . London, 1863.

_____. *Supplement.* London, 1865.

2313 _____

[Husk, W. H.] *Catalogue of the Library of the Sacred Harmonic Society. A New Edition, Revised and Augmented.* London: The Society, 1872. 399 p. 2923 items.   [g.a.]
Benton 2:180, no. 63, notes an 1882 supplement. Not located. The collection now at GB-Lcm.

2314 _____

PUTTICK & SIMPSON, AUCTIONEER, LONDON   CAT. NO. 2139
Catalogue of the Valuable Stock of Orchestral Music of the . . . Full and Vocal Scores, Principal Singers' Copies, Chorus and Band Parts. . . . Also the Stock of Ernst Pauer's Lectures . . . One Hundred Copies of the Library Catalogue . . . a Few Interesting Music Relics, Including Handel's Pitchpipe . . . Framed Music Portraits, etc. . . . Sold November 28th, 1882.
[London], 1882. 13 p. 450 lots.   [GB-Lbl]

2315   _____; "A Bankrupt"

PUTTICK & SIMPSON, AUCTIONEER, LONDON   CAT. NO. 2146

Catalogue of an Extensive Assemblage of Music Property . . . A Collection of Music, Including the Residue of the Orchestral Library of the . . . Society . . . Works for Stringed Instruments . . . The Small Stock of a Bankrupt . . . Sold December 18th, 1882. 15 p. 400 lots.

[GB-Lbl]

Society's "residue," lots 217-353.

2316   _____

PUTTICK & SIMPSON, AUCTIONEER, LONDON   CAT. NO. 2674

Catalogue of the Extensive and Valuable Library of Music Belonging to the Late . . . Consisting of Vocal and Instrumental Parts and Scores . . . Large Number of Word Books . . . A Collection of Antique and Modern Music . . . Works on Musical History and Theory . . . Sold . . . July 8th, 1889. [London], 1889. 22 p. 400 lots (more items).   [GB-Lbl]

Society's properties, lots 304-88.

2317   **Saint-Saëns, Camille,** 1835-1921

JOSEPH NOURRY, LIBRAIRE, LYON

Catalogue des partitions, oeuvres musicale diverse, livres et autographes, dessins . . . provenant de la succession de Camille Saint-Saëns à qui ils ont appartenu . . . vente . . . 23 novembre. . . . Lyon, [n.d., 1926]. 3, 37 p. 264 lots. Music, lots 1-237.   [B-Br]

Folter, no. 315. **Blogie 2.**

2318   _____

LITERATURE

Bonnerot, Jean. "Saint-Saëns bibliophile." *Archives de la Société des Collectionneurs d'Ex-Libris* 40 (1933): [113]-16.

Folter, no. 315. Not examined.

2319   **Sale, John,** 1758-1827; **P. Taylor**

W. P. MUSGRAVE, AUCTIONEER, LONDON

A Catalogue of the Libraries of John Sale . . . and Mr. P. Taylor (both deceased) . . . Forming a Very Choice Collection of Ancient and Modern Vocal and Instrumental Music, Valuable Treatises on Every Branch of the Science . . . Sold . . . the 12th and 13th of May, 1828. [London]: Watson, 1828. 21 p. 291 lots. Music, lots 1-55, 63-238.   [GB-Lbl, US-BUu (film)]

King, pp. 28-29.

2320   **[Sale, John Bernard]**

PUTTICK & SIMPSON, AUCTIONEER, LONDON   CAT. NO. 481

Catalogue of a Large Collection of Music in All Classes. 10,000 Pieces of Modern Publications, Instrumental Music, etc. . . . Sold . . . March 28th, 1857. [London], 1857. 19 p. 600 lots. Music, lots 104-600.   [GB-Lbl]

→ *See also under* **Stone, William Henry**

Salisbury, Earl of.   *See* **Cecil, Robert, 1st Earl of Salisbury,** 1563-1612

2321   Salmreifferscheid, Monseigneur le Compte de
Catalogue raisonné des diverses curiosités du cabinet de . . . évèque de Tournay, composé d'une nombreuse collection d'histoire naturelle, de tableaux, d'estampes, de divers instruments et pièces de musique de differens maîtres. . . . Tournay: Imprimerie de Romain Varle, 1771. 108, 93, [4] p.   [I-BC, compiler (film)]

> In the second half (93 p.): "Table alphabetique des diverses pièces de musique . . . qui composant cette belle collection, tant en symphonies, ouvertures, quatuor, que nocturnes & trios," pp. 88-93 (many lots but no description or titles).

2322   Samazeuilh, Gustave, 1877-1967
MICHEL CASTAING, (EXP.); ADER & PICARD (C.-P.), PARIS
Autographes et documents musicaux avant appartenu à . . . vente . . . Hôtel Drouot . . . 15 December 1967. Paris, 1967. [20] p. 145 lots.

> **Folter**, no. 316. **Blogie 2.** Not examined.

2323   Samuel, Stuart M
SOTHEBY, WILKINSON & HODGE, AUCTIONEER, LONDON
Catalogue of the Valuable and Choice Library, the Property of. . . . Original Autograph Music by Bach, Meyerbeer, Paganini and Schubert . . . Sold . . . 1st of July, 1907. [London, 1907.] 29 p. 199 lots.   [Film at CRL]

> "Autograph MSS. of Schübert [*sic*]," lots 125-32.

2324   Sánchez Garza, Jesús
Stevenson, Robert. "Colección Jesús Sánchez Garza." In his *Renaissance and Baroque Musical Sources in the Americas,* 166-92. Washington: Organization of the American States, 1970.
                                                        [g.a.]

> Now at the Instituto Nacional de Bellas Artes, Mexico. According to Albrecht, a complete catalog is in preparation by María del Carmen Sordo Sodi.

2325   Sanderson, James, 1769-1841
MR. WATSON, AUCTIONEER, LONDON
A Catalogue of the Musical Library of the Late . . . for Many Years Conductor at Astley's Royal Amphitheatre, Including Various Compositions by the Most Eminent Masters . . . [Musical Instruments] . . . *Several Lots of Music Uncleared from the Sale in Hanway Street . . . Sold . . . 19th September 1832, and* [two] *Following Days.* . . . London, 1832. 20 p. 397 lots.
                                                        [US-NYp, compiler (copy)]

> Music and non-music items, lots 1-226, 236-374.

> The previous day, Watson auctioned off a library of Sanderson's which contained no music items.   [US-NYp, compiler (copy)]

2326   Sandys, William
BERNARD QUARITCH, FIRM, LONDON   CAT. NO. 20
A List of Rare Music, Books of Chess, Hunting, Falconry . . . Natural History [etc.]. London, 1874. 24 p.   [US-NYgr]

> "Old Music, Chiefly from the Library of the Late . . . ," lots 1-50.

2327 Sankey, R B

PUTTICK & SIMPSON, AUCTIONEER, LONDON   CAT. NO. 3912

Catalogue of Valuable Musical Properties, Including Pianofortes [etc.] *and a Library of Music of the Late . . . Sold 28 March 1905.* [London], 1905. 14 p. 269 lots.   [GB-Lbl]

Sankey's properties—not much of a collection—lots 215-69.

Santen, Jan von, 1849-96 (**Folter** says Santen-Kolff).   *See under* **Weiss, Edmund**

2328 Santini, Fortunato, 1778-1861

Most of the articles about this remarkable Italian bibliophile/composer/priest/copyist fall short of presenting all the facts of his life and work. Suffice it to say here that with access to most Rome libraries he spent about 50 years copying and transcribing music in those archives, both for his own library, which eventually numbered nearly 4000 manuscripts (as well as a thousand printed works) and for others. (See the list made for Vincent Novello in 1843, below.) He printed a catalog of his library in 1820. Meantime, numerous manuscript catalogs were prepared which found their way into libraries around the world—Brussels, Paris, Münster.

When he retired to a monastery his collection was first at the German College in Rome, then the Diocesan Museum at Münster in 1856 (US-Wc catalog card says 1862!), then finally, "after other adventures" (according to Lattes in his brief article in the *NG*), in the Episcopal Seminary in Münster. It went to the Münster University Library in 1923. About 500 volumes were destroyed during World War II.

In 1903 E. J. Dent visited the collection at the Seminary and wrote an article for the *MMR* 34, no. 397 (January 1904): 64-65, describing the shocking conditions in the room which housed the collection: "holes in the roof, broken shelves," a total lack of organization. "Between the pigeons, the mice and the weather, the filth in the room was indescribable . . . 60 years ago it was the most famous private musical library in Europe . . . [it] does exist, however, practically entire. . . . "

2329 _____

"Catalogo della musica antica, sacra e madrigalesca, che si trova in Roma via dell'anima no. 50, presso Fortunato Santini."

A Ms. in the Fétis collection, no. 5166 in that catalog, now at B-Br.

2330 _____

"Catalogo compendiato della musica . . . che si trova . . . presso Fortunato Santini [begun by G. Gaspari of Bologna]. Descrizione della libreria musicale . . . che trovasi . . . presso Fortunato Santini."

A Ms. in the Paris Conservatoire Library, noted by Rudolf Ewerhart in his article in *MGG* 11 (1963), cols. 1382-83. Ewerhart adds note ["aus den Nachlass Teschner"].

2331   _____

"Indice alfabetico della musica madrigalesca che si trova nella collezione musicale di Fortunato Santini."

> A Ms. in the Münster Bischöflichen Priester Seminar und Santini-Sammlung, no. 4447. Cited by Ewerhart in his *MGG* article.

2332   _____

"Indice generale della musica sacra e profana antica e moderna a 1, 2, 3, 4, 5, 6, 7, 8, 9, 12 e 16 v. molta della quale con stromenti che trovarsi nell' Archivio di Fortunato Santini."

> Another Ms. catalog in the Münster Priester Seminar, no. 4462. Kindler (**2357**) dates somewhere between 1820 and 1845, before the collection moved to Münster.

2333   _____

Santini, Fortunato, Abbate. *Catalogo della musica esistente presso Fortunato Santini in Roma nel palazzo de'principi Odescalchi incontro la chiesa de SS. XII. Apostoli.* Roma: P. Salviucci, 1820. 46 p. ca. 300 nos.   [GB-Lbl (Hirsch)]

> **Folter**, no. 318.

2334   _____

Santini, Fortunato, Abbate. "Select Catalogue of the Curious MSS. in the Library of the Abbate Santini . . . at Rome . . . Brought from Italy for Vincent Novello by Uvedale Price . . . 1843." 9 fols. British Museum Add. Ms. 33,240.   [GB-Lbl, compiler (film)]

> "Presented to the Library of the Musical Antiquarian Society by V. N. N. July 1844."

2335   _____

"Indice della musica sacra profana madrigalesca e da camera che si trova presso Fortunato Santini."

> A Ms. in the Münster Priester Seminar. Kindler (**2357**) dates 1845.

2336   _____

Wörmann, Wilhelm. "Katalog der Santini-Bibliothek . . . " [n.p., n.d.]. 3 vols. Typed.

> Noted by Kindler, by Ewerhart (**2344**), and in **Schaal** (1966), p. 123, but none give more information, and it has been impossible to locate the copy referred to.

2337   _____

Stasov, Vladimir Vasil'evich. "Abbat Santini i ego muzykal'naia kollektsia v Rome." *Biblioteka dlia Chtenniia* 3 (April 1853): 107-28.

> Also reprinted without the catalog in vol. 3 of his complete works (St. Petersburg, 1894), according to Vladimir Fédorov in his "V. V. Stasov chez l'abb. F. Santini à Rome." See **2353**.

2338   _____

Stasov, Vladimir Vasil'evich. *L'abbé Santini et sa collection musicale à Rome.* Florence: Impr. de F. Le Monnier, 1854. 70 p.   [US-Wc, -AA, -BE, -Bp, -CHH]

    "Extrait du Catalogue Santini," pp. 39-65. Ca. 200 numbers. **Folter**, no. 319.

    → *See also* a catalog of the Santini collection deposited by Stasov in the Leningrad Public Library in 1870 *here under* **Stasov, Vladimir Vasilevich**

2339   _____

Killing, Joseph. *Kirchenmusikalisches Schätze der Bibliothek des Abbate Fortunato Santini:* Vol. 1: *Das sechszehnte Jahrhundert.* . . . [Münster i. W.: Aschaffendorffische Buchdr., 1908.] 71 p.   [GB-Lbl (Hirsch); US-BUu]

    Diss. **Folter**, no. 320.

2340   _____

Killing, Joseph. *Kirchenmusikalische Schätze der Bibliothek des Abbate Fortunato Santini; ein Beitrag zur Geschichte der katholischen Kirchenmusik in Italien.* . . . Düsseldorf: L. Schwann, [1910]. 516 p. 640 nos.   [GB-Lbl (Hirsch), US-Wc, -BUu, CA, -Rd]

    Folter, no. 320. "Verzeichnis der in der Bibliothek Santini enthaltenen Druckwerke," pp. [455]-67. "Verzeichnis von Musikwerken die in der Santinischen Bibliothek als Handschriften enthalten sind," pp. [469]-516.

2341   _____

Hüntemann, Josef Albert. "Verzeichnis der italienischen Mess-Kompositionen aus der Bibliothek . . . Santini." In Heinrich Stute, *Studien über den Gebrauch der Instrumente in den italienischen Kirchenorchester des 18. Jahrhunderts,* 45-59. Quackenbrück: R. Kleinert, 1929.

                                [US-BUu, -BE, -CA, -AA, -CHH (film)]

    Diss., Münster, 1929. 450 items.

2342   _____

Fellerer, Karl Gustav. *Die musikalischen Schätze der Santinischen Sammlung: Führer durch die Ausstellung der Universitäts-Bibliothek Münster anlässlich des III. Westfälischen Musikfestes in Münster i. Westf. vom 15. bis 17. Juni 1929.* Münster i. Westf.: Westfälische Vereinsdruckerei, 1929. 32 p. 170 nos.   [US-Wc, -NYp]

    Folter, no. 321.

2343   _____

Killing, Joseph. "Verzeichnis der kirchenmusikalischen Werke der Santinischen Sammlung [Münster]." *KmJ* 26 (1931): 111-40; 27 (1932): 157-71; 28 (1933): 143-54; 29 (1934): 125-41; 30 (1935): 149-68.   [g.a.]

    Incomplete; to "Pu" only. **Folter**, no. 322.

2344   _____

Ewerhart, Rudolf. "Die Händel-Handschriften der Santini-Bibliothek in Münster." *Händel-Jahrbuch* 6 (1960): 111-50.   [g.a.]

    Folter, no. 322.

2345

Marx, Hans Joachim. "The Santini Collection." In *Handel Collections and Their History,* ed. Terence Best, 184-97. Oxford: Clarendon Press, 1993.   [g.a.]

> Appendix 1: "Documents in the Sale of the Santini Collection," purchased by the Diocese of Münster, pp. 191-93. Appendix 2: "Handel Manuscripts in D-Müs," pp. 195-97.

2346

LITERATURE

Marx, Hans Joachim. "Fortunato Santini." *MGG* 11 (1963), cols. 1382-83.

2347

Kandler, F. S. "Ueber den Musikzustand von Rom." *Allgemeine Musikzeitung* [zur Beförderung der theoretischen und praktischen Tonkunst]. Frankfurt a.M.? (1927/28), 411-.

> Not able to verify. Cited from *MGG,* article noted above.

2348

Dent, Edward Joseph. "The Library of Fortunato Santini." *MMR* 34, no. 397 (January 1904): 64-65.   [g.a.]

> See information at the head of these citations.

2349

Jansen, Heinz. "Die Musikbibliothek des Abbate Santini [nunmehr in der Universitäts-Bibliothek Münster]." *Hochland* 23 (1925/26): 762-65.

> **Folter**, no. 322. Not located.

2350

Smend, Friedrich. "Zur Kenntnis des Musikers Fortunato Santini." In *Westfälische Studien: Alois Bömer zum 60 Geburtstag,* 90-98. Leipzig, 1928.

> **Folter**, no. 322. Not located.

2351

Hüntemann, Josef Albert. "Die Messen der Santini-Bibliothek zu Münster i.W." Quackenbrücke: Gedruckt von R. Kleinert, 1928. vii, 72 p.   [US-CA, -U, -Rd.]

> Diss. **Folter**, no. 322.

2352

Fellerer, Karl Gustav. "Fortunato Santini als Sammler und Bearbeiter Handel'scher Werke." *Händel-Jahrbuch* 2 (1929): 25-40.   [g.a.]

> **Folter**, no. 322.

2353

Fédorov, Vladimir. "V. V. Stasov chez l'abb. F. Santini à Rome." In *Anthony van Hoboken: Festschrift zum 75. Geburtstag,* ed. Joseph Schmidt-Görg, 55-62. Mainz: B. Schott's Söhne, 1962.   [g.a.]

2354 _____

Ewerhart, Rudolf. "Die Bischöfliche Santini-Bibliothek." *Das schöne Münster* 35 (1962): ?
> **Folter**, no. 322, **Benton 2**:92, no. 205, and *MGG* 11, col. 1383, but not examined.

2355 _____

Watanabe, Keiichiro. "Santini-Bibliothek (Münster) no. Henderu Sakuhin no Hisshafu niokeru kopisuto no Kenkyu." *Ongaku gaku* 16 (1971): 325-62.
> Not examined; cited from *RILM* 1972, no. 3207.

2356 _____

Lattes, Sergio. "Santini, Fortunato." *NG* 16 (1980): 40.

2357 _____

Kindler, Klaus. "Zur problematik der Masi-Handschriften in der Santini-Sammlung in Münster (Westf.)." *Fontes* 31 (1984): 112-18.   [g.a.]

2358 Sapin, Léon

A. VOISIN (LIB.-EXP.), PARIS
Catalogue de la bibliothèque théâtrale de M. Léon Sapin, dont la vente aura lieu le 25, 26, 27, 28 février et 1ᵉʳ mars 1878. Deuxième partie: Opéra, opéra comique, lettérature musicale . . . chansonniers . . . documents manuscrits. . . . Paris, 1878. [5], 143 p. 1588 lots (many more items). Lot 1587, 15 vols.; lot 912, 19 parodies of operas.   [US-NYgr]
> First part contains no music.

2359 _____

ÉTIENNE CHARAVAY, AUCTIONEER, PARIS
Catalogue des lettres autographes et des documents historiques, composant la collection théâtral de M. . . . dont la vente . . . 11 mars 1878. . . . Paris, 1878. 43 p. 231 lots.
                                                                          [US-NYgr (priced)]
> "Compositeurs de musique," lots 25-45. Lot 39, Meyerbeer to Liszt about *Les Huguenots.*

2360 Sarasin, Lucas, 1730-1802

BASEL, UNIVERSITÄTSBIBLIOTHEK
"Katalog d. Luk. Sarasin Mus. Slg. (CH Bu: Handbibl. Kunst. d 119)."   [US-NYcg (film)]
> Ms., ca. 1500. Cited from **Brook**, 76, who says that some of the contents are included in Refardt's published catalog (Bern, 1957, **2361**), but not all. **Albrecht** notes.

2361 _____

Refardt, Edgar. *Thematischer Katalog des Instrumentalmusik des 18. Jahrhunderts in den Handschriften der Universitäts-bibliothek Basel.* Schweizerische musikforschende Gesellschaft, Publikationen, 6. Bern: P. Haupt, [1957]. 50 p.   [US-Nyp]
> Most of the collection from the library of Sarasin with additions from the Archives of the Basler Collegium and the music library of Charles Albert de Pury. Catalog (in Ms.) was completed by Refardt in 1928.

2362 _____; ? **Wirtz**
KARL ERNST HENRICI, AUCTIONEER, BERLIN   AUK. CAT. NO. 88
Autographen . . . Sammlung Sarasin. Sammlung Wirtz, und andere Beiträge aus Berliner Privat-Besitz . . . Versteigerung . . . 13. Mai 1924. . . . Berlin, 1924. 79 p. 470 lots.

[US-NYgr]

Properties are not differentiated.

2363 _____

LITERATURE
Nef, Karl. "Eine Basler Musikbibliothek aus der zweiten Hälfte des 18. Jahrhunderts." *ZiMG* 4 (1902/03): 385-89.   [g.a.]

2364 _____

Sondheimer, Robert. "Sinfonie aus dem 18. Jh. in den Basler Sammlungen Lucas Sarasin und Collegium Musicum." In *Bericht über die Musikwissenschaftlichen Kongress in Basel, 1925,* 321-25. Leipzig: Breitkopf & Härtel, 1925.   [g.a.]

2365 _____

Sondheimer, Robert. Idem. *Schweizerische musikforschende Gesellschaft, Bericht (1924),* 321-25.   [g.a.]

2366 Sauret, Elisabeth
Rust, Willy. *Autographes de musiciens célèbres.* Neuchâtel: Imp. centrale, [n.d.]. 119 p., illus, facs.   [GB-LReeves]
         The collection of Mrs. Harry Edward (née E. Sauret) now at CH-N.

2367 Sawyer, [Frank Joseph?], Dr.; John Tiplady Carrodus, 1836-95
WILLIAM REEVES, FIRM, LONDON   CAT. NO. 27
Rare and Interesting Items from the Libraries of the Late Dr. Sawyer (Early Organ Music, etc.) and J. T. Carrodus (Chamber Music, etc., See Items Starred Thus*). London, 1910. 48 p.

[US-NYp]

2368 Sayn-Wittgenstein, Moritz Casimir I, Graf von Berleburg
[Catalog of the Rheda Library.] In Joachim Domp, *Studien zur Geschichte der Musik an Westfälischen Adelshofen im 18. Jahrh.,* 7-34. Freiburger Studien zur Musikwissenschaft, 1. Regensburg: Pustet, 1934.   [US-BE]

2369 Scala, Francis
LeClair, Paul Joseph. "The Francis Scala Collection: Music in Washington D.C. at the Time of the Civil War." Thesis, Catholic University of America, 1973; Ann Arbor: University Microfilms, 1974. iii, 159 leaves, illus.   [g.a.]

2370 Scalvini, Guido, and **Carmen Asensio**
Pompilio, Angelo. "La collezione Scalvini dell' Isituto Nazional di Studi Verdiani. I: Catalogo degli spartiti per canto e pianoforte delle opere liriche complete con un saggio sui criteri di datazione edizioni Ricordi," *Studi Verdiani* 7 (1991): 111-88.
         Bought by the Institute (I-PAi) in 1974—ca. 427 scores, 100 miscellaneous volumes, 24 + manuscripts. Catalog, 381 items.

Schaake, G. *See* **Gerdes, H.**

2371 Schaden, Franz Michael von
"Verzeichnis der versteigerten Musicalien des Geheimrats und Regierungsdirektors . . . , 1791. Mit Angabe der Käufer."

> Ms. in Archiv Wallerstein, Dienerakten F. M. Schaden, III, 6, 32a, reprinted in Gertraut Haberkamp, *Thematischer Katalog der Musikhandschriften der Fürstlichen Oettingen-Wallerstein'schen Bibliothek, Schloss Harburg* (München: Henle, 1976), xxvi-xxx.

2372 Schang, F C
Visiting Cards of Violinists from the Collection of . . . With a Comment by Him. [N.p.]: Schang, [1975]. 80 p.   [US-Wc]

> Collections at US-NYcu.

2373 _____

Visiting Cards of Prima Donnas, from the Collection of . . . With Commentary by Him. New York: Vantage Press, 1977. 111 p.   [g.a.]

> Extracted from his *Visiting Cards of Celebrities,* 1971. First issued privately in 1973. This, therefore, is 2nd ed.

2374 Schatz, Albert, 1839-1910
Joseph Baer, & Co., firm, Frankfurt a.M.   Cat no. 575
Theater und Oper, zum Teil aus der Bibliothek des Herrn . . . in Rostock. Geschichte der Schauspielkunst - Die Bühnen einzelner Städte-Ballet - Theaterkostüme - Biographien von Schauspielern, Dramtikern und Komponisten. . . . Frankfurt a.M., [n.d., ca. 1910]. 162 p. 2425 lots.   [NL-Avb]

> Acquired by US-Wc. See below. According to **Albrecht,** 12,240 librettos sold to US-Wc in 1909. Sonneck (**2375**) says 1908.

2375 _____

U. S. Library of Congress, Music Division
Catalogue of Opera Librettos Printed Before 1800, prepared by Oscar George Theodore Sonneck. 2 vols. Washington, D.C.: Government Printing Office, 1914. Reprint, New York: Johnson Reprint Corp., 1968.   [g.a.]

> Pages 5-7, in German and English, Schatz writes about the origin and history of his collection.

2376 _____

Bonds, Mark Evan. "The Albert Schatz Opera Collection at the Library of Congress." *Notes* 44 (1988): 655-95.

2377 _____

Literature
Fawcett, Waldon. "Oscar G. T. Sonneck, Representative to International Conventions in Rome and London. Purchase of the Schatz Operatic Library. . . ." *Musical America* 14, no. 12 (1911): 3.
                                                                                                          [g.a.]

> Librettos.

2378 **Schaumburg, Georg**
Stobbe, auctioneer, Munich   No. 11
Theatergeschichte und Dramaturgie. Deutsche Literatur - Almanache - . . . Oper - Musik - Dramen - [etc.] Aus der Bibliothek . . . Versteigerung 22.6.1931. München, 1931. 48 p. 912 lots.

    Not located. Cited from **Folter**.

Schaumburg-Lippe, Philipp, Grafzur.   *See* **Lippe, Simon VI, Grafzur**

2379 **Scheepers, J F M**
J. L. Beijers, auctioneer, Utrecht
Catalogus van een zeer belangrijke verzmaeling fraaie en zeldsame boeken der 16e-18e eeuw . . . bibliotheek van wijlen . . . te Rotterdam . . . Tooneelspelen . . . Liedboeken . . . Verkooping . . . 6 en dinsdag 7 januari 1947. . . . Utrecht, 1947. 72 p. 676 lots. 51 lots, music.

    Auctions of songbooks, 6-7 January 1947 and 13-14 December 1949. Cited in **Vereeniging** . . . *Catalogus* 8:400.

Scheibler, Ludwig Adolf, 1848-1921.   *See under* **Prieger, Erich** (1922 sale)

2380 **Scheide, William H.,** b. 1914
The Scheide Library [articles about the library at Princeton University by Edwin Wolf, et al.]. Princeton University Library Chronicle 37, no. 2. Princeton University Press, 1976. 172 p., illus.   [g.a.]

2381 _____
Literature
Bryan, Mina R. "Portrait of a Bibliophile XVII: The Scheide Library." *Book Collector* 21 (1972): 489-502.   [g.a.]

2382 _____
"To a Near Centennial of Shared Bibliophily [the Olschkis and Rosenthals and Scheides]." In *Festschrift Albi Rosenthal,* ed. Rudolf Elvers, 259-64. Tutzing: H. Schneider, 1984.   [g.a.]

2383 **Schellenberg, Hermann,** 1816-62
List & Francke, firm, Leipzig   Cat. no. ?
Verzeichniss einer höchst werthvollen Sammlung von Werken aus der theoretischen und praktischen Musik, aus dem Nachlasse des Herrn Organisten . . . in Leipzig. Leipzig: List & Francke, 1862. 39 p.   [GB-LRosenthal, NL-Avb]

2384 **Schenker, Heinrich,** 1868-1935
Heinrich Hinterberger, firm, Vienna   Cat. no. 12
. . . Musik und Theater, enthaltend die Bibliothek des Herrn Dr. . . . Wien, [1936]. 32 p. 394 lots.   [NL-Avb, GB-Lbl (Hirsch 5844)]
    Folter, no. 323.

2385 **Scherer, Georg,** 1828-1909
Süddeutsches Antiquariat, Munich   Cat. no. 105
Bibliothek Georg Scherer. Vol. 1? Munich, 1909?   [US-NYgr]

2386 _____

SÜDDEUTSCHES ANTIQUARIAAT, MUNICH   CAT. NO. 112
Bibliothek Georg Scherer, vol. 4: *Theoretische und praktische Musik. Geistliches und weltlichen Lied. Theater und Theaterstücke.* München, 1909. 66 p. 1648 lots. Music, lots 1-912.   [GB-LBl (Hirsch 5896)]
   Folter, no. 657.

2387 Schermar, Egenolf von, [and son] **Anton von,** 1604-81
Gottwald Clytus. *Katalog der Musikalien in der Schermar-Bibliothek Ulm.* . . . Veröff. der Stadtbibliothek Ulm, 17. Wiesbaden: Harrassowitz, [1993]. 185 p. 239 items.   [US-NBu]

2388 _____

LITERATURE
Blessinger, Karl. *Studien zur Ulmer Musikgeschichte im 17. Jahrhundert.* Ulm: Buchdruckerei Dr. Karl Höhn, 1913.   [US-BE, -PHu]
   "Verzeichnis der Musikalien der Schermar'schen Bibliothek," pp. 72-73.

2389 Scheurleer, Daniel François, 1855-1927
Most of Scheurleer's collection of musical literature, instruments, and iconography were donated to the Gemeentemuseum in The Hague in 1935 and formed the basis of the extraordinary collection that exists there now. Much of that material is being made available in microform editions.

2390 _____

Scheurleer, Daniel François. *Catalogus der muziekbibliotheek en der verzameling van musikinstrumenten van.* . . . 's-Gravenhage: M. Nijhoff, 1885. 5, 290 p., illus.
                          [NL-DHgm, US-Wc, -Eu, -AA]

_____. *Vervolg.* Ibid., 1887. 109 p.   [NL-DHgm, US-AA]
   Superseded by catalog of 1893-1910, that by the catalog of 1923-25.
   See both below.

2391 _____

SCHILDERKUNDIG GENOOTSCHAP PULCHRI STUDIO
Catalogus der Tentoonstelling van muziekinstrumenten, prenten, photografiën en boeken daarop betrekking hebbende. October-November, 1893. Den Haag, 1893. 64 p. (small 8$^{vo.}$)
                                  [NL-DHgm]
   Could not be located elsewhere. The exhibition was prepared by the Pulchri
   Studio, according to Clemens von Gleich, head of the musical section at the
   Museum.

2392 _____

Catalogus der muziekbibliotheek van. . . . 's-Gravenhage: [Gedrukt bij Gebr. Giunta d'Albani], 1893. 6, 567 p., facs.   [NL-DHgm, US-Wc, -NYp, -CA, -AA]
   One of 120 examples, 20 on Holland paper. The latter were issued in 2 vols.,
   Deel I and II.

_____. *Catalogus . . . vervolg.* 's-Gravenhage: Gebr. Giunta d'Albani, 1903. [vii], 357 p.   [NL-DHgm, US-BUu]

_____. *Catalogus . . . 2. vervolg.* 's-Gravenhage: [Gedrukt bij Gebr. Giunta d'Albani],
1910. 4, 217 p.   [NL-DHgm, US-Wc, -NYp, -CA, -AA, -BUu]

       "Niet in den handel."

2393   _____

AMSTERDAM, HUYGENS COMMISSIE
*Catalogus van de Tentoonstelling ter herinnering aan den 300-jarigen geboortedag van
Constantijn Huygens.* s'Gravenhage: W. P. van Stockum & Zoon, 1896. xii, 146 p.

                                     [NL-DHgm, GB-Lbl]

       Published also, same year, by Mouton, in 's-Gravenhage, according to the
Gedenkboek for Scheurleer (**2398**).

2394   _____

*Eene Wooninge, in de welcke ghesien worden veelderhande gheschriften, boeken, printen
ende musicaale instrumenten.* ['s-Gravenhage, 1913.] 2 p., 36 plates, obl. 4°.

               [NL-DHgm, US-BE, -NYp, -AA, -Wc, GB-Lbl (Hirsch 420)]

       Photos of the house and collections of Scheurleer in The Hague, with
portraits. **Folter,** no. 324.

       The National Union Catalog cites another edition dated 1920 (2, 49 p.).

                                      [US-BUu, -STm]

2395   _____

Catalogus van de muziekwerken en de boeken over muziek. [3. uitg.] . . . s'Gravenhage:
M. Nijhoff, 1923-25. 3 vols., facs. 16,000 items.

                    [NL-DHgm, US-Wc, -AA, -NYp, -BE, -BUu (vol. 1)]

       Supersedes catalogs of 1885-87 and 1893-1910 (see above).

2396   _____

VAN STOCKUM, AUCTIONEER, THE HAGUE
Bibliothèque de feu m.-le dr. . . . vente publique . . . 12-16 decembre 1927. . . . La Haye: Van
Stockum (J. B. Kerling), 1927. 204 p.   [NL-DHgm, US-NYgr, -AA]

       No music items; literature only. **Folter,** no. 325.

2397   _____

Pulver, Jeffrey. "Dr. D. F. Scheurleer: His Writings and Collections." *MT* 55 (1914): 521-22.

                                             [g.a.]

2398   _____

Adler, Guido. "Ein Musikkatalog aus unserer Zeit." In *Gedenkboek aangeboden aan Dr. D. F.
Scheurleer op zijn 70ˢᵗᵉⁿ verjaardag: Bijdragen van vrienden en vereerders op het gebied der
muziek,* 39-41. 's-Gravenhage: M. Nijhoff, 1925.   [US-Wc, -NH, -CHua]

2399   _____

Sanders, Paul F. "Het Museum Scheurleer." *Muziek* 2 (1928): 312-19.   [NL-DHgm, US-NYp]

2400 _____

H ,W. "Van het Museum Scheurleer en van een voorgenomen belangwekkende Tentoonstelling." *Symphonia* (Hilversum) 14 (1931): 142 (only).

[NL-DHgm, US-Wc, compiler (copy)]

Noted in *ZfMW* 14 (1931/32): 56.

2401 _____

André, ? "Het Museum Scheurleer." *Symphonia* (Hilversum) 15 (1932): 108-09, illus.

[compiler (Xerox)]

_____. Idem. *Caecilia* 89 (1933): p. ?

Not examined; noted in *ZfMW* 15 (1932/33): 36.

2402 _____

Verveen, Arie, and Magda Klerk. "The Gemeentemuseum at the Hague." *Fontes* 21 (1974): 106-09.   [g.a.]

2403 _____

Gleich, Clemens von. *Haags Gemeentemuseum: Over het ontstaan van de muziekafdeling - Portret van de verzameling-Scheurleer.* 's-Gravenhage: Gemeentemuseum, 1985. 44 p., illus.

[g.a.]

2404   **Schicht, Johann Gottfried,** 1753-1823

Versteigerungs-katalog der von dem verstorbenen Herrn J. -G. Schicht, Canto an der Thomasschule zu Leipzig, hinterlassenen Musikaliensammlung welche als Anhang der Bücherauction vom 19ten November [i.e., Dezember] *zu Leipzig dem Meistbietenden gegen baare Bezahlung überlassen werden soll.* Leipzig, 1823. 56 p. 1336, 86 lots.   [D-Bds]

> **Folter**, no. 326, **Albrecht** (notes sale, not catalog). Cited from **Bobillier**, but not examined.

2405   **Schindler, Anton Felix,** 1795-1864

LITERATURE

Schmidt-Görg, Joseph. "Anton Schindlers musikalischer Nachlass im Beethoven-Archiv." *Sborník prací filosofické fakulty brnenske university* 14 (1965): 263-72.

> The collection of Beethoven's friend is partly at D-Bds, mostly at D-BNba.
> **Albrecht.**

2406   **Schirmer, Gustave,** 1864-1907

A Catalogue of the String Music Library of . . . , Kneisel Hall, Blue Hill, Maine. [Blue Hill, Me.?, 19-?] 12 p.   [US-Wc]

2407   **Schlatter, V ; E. A. Stüchelberg; C. Rödelberger; M. His**

L'ART ANCIEN/HAUS DER BÜCHER, ZÜRICH   VERST. NO. 8

Musik und Musikwissenschaft, sowie Autographen, speziell von Musikern . . . Versteigerung . . . 2. -3. Mai 1947. . . . Zürich, 1947. 65 p. 574 lots. Music, lots 1-107, including musicians' autographs.   [US-R]

2408   **[Schleinitz, Heinrich Conrad,** 1802-81]
LIST & FRANCKE, FIRM, LEIPZIG   CAT. NO. ?
Catalogue d'une très précieuse collection de manuscrits et lettres autographes. . . . Leipzig,
1882. 23, 3 p.   [US-Bp]
The Mss. are mostly music.

2409   **Schlesinger, Henry**
SOTHEBY & CO., AUCTIONEER, LONDON
*Catalogue of Valuable Printed Books, Illuminated and Other Manuscripts . . . With a Selected
Portion of the Schlesinger Collection of Musical Manuscripts . . . Sold 29th of June, 1925,
and Two Following Days.* [London, 1925.] 112 p. 789 lots.   [US-NYp]
Schlesinger's collection, lots 420-61 (many more items), including Mss. of
Beethoven, Liszt, Wagner, etc., mostly bought by Maggs.   [GB-Lbl]

2410   **Schlesinger, Henry; William Laffan; Franklin Mackay**
ANDERSON GALLERIES, AUCTIONEER, NEW YORK   CAT. NO. 2002
Important Historical Letters and Documents . . . [etc.] *Musical Manuscripts and Letters of
Noted Musicians from the Collection of the Late . . . Schlesinger . . . Sold . . . November
Thirtieth, 1925.* . . . New York, 1925. 48 p. 359 lots.   [US-NYgr, -NYp, -NH]
Schlesinger's Ms. and ALS, lots 183-268. Mackay 8873.

Schlesinger, Maurice Adolf, ca. 1800-71.   *See* **Stockhausen, Julius**

2411   **Schletterer, Hans Michael,** 1824-93
C. H. BECK, FIRM, NÖRDLINGEN   CAT. NO. 219
*Antiquarischer Katalog der C. -H. Beck'schen Buchhandlung . . . enthaltend den musikalischen
Teil der Bibliothek des Herrn Dr. H. -M. Schletterer in Augsburg.* Nördlingen, 1894. 169 p. 3825
lots.   [D-Bds]
Properties not differentiated. **Folter,** no. 327.

2412   ———
GEIGER & JEDELE, FIRM, STUTTGART   CAT. NO. 223
*Geschichte und Litteratur des Theaters, Dramaturgie, Tanz . . . (Bibliothèque des Kapellmeisters
Dr. Schletterer in Augsburg).* . . . Stuttgart, [1894]. 46 p. 1288 lots.
Folter, no. 328. Not examined.

Schlobitten Collection.   *See* **Abraham, Burggraf zu Dohna**
According to **Albrecht,** destroyed in World War II.

2413   **Schlösser, Rudolf,** 1867-1920
H. TREICHEL, FIRM, JENA   CAT. NO. 10
. . . Bibliothek Rudolf Schlösser. Deutsche und fremde Literatur, Theater, Kunst, Musik. . . .
Jena, 1941.
Not located. Cited from *ZfMW* 3 (1920/21): 448.

2414   Schlosser, Julius von

V. A. HECK, FIRM, VIENNA   LISTE NO. 237

Musikbibliothek Prof. Julius von Schlosser. Wien, [1962]. 62 p. 763 lots.

Not located. Cited from *IBAK*, 1962/63.

2415   [Schlosser, Louis and Adolf]

SOTHEBY, WILKINSON & HODGE, AUCTIONEER, LONDON

Catalogue of Autograph Letters, and Historical Documents, Including an Important Collection of Letters and Manuscripts of Musical Composers, Chiefly Addressed to . . . Sold . . . the 30th of April, 1914, and Following Day. [London, 1914.] 46 p. 482 lots.   [Film at CRL]

Schlossers's Ms. and ALS, lots 171-232.

2416   Schmidt, Franz, 1874-1939?

LITERATURE

Brosche, Günter. "Neuerwerbungen 1982 der Musiksammlung der Österreichischen Nationalbibliothek." *ÖmZ* 38 (1983): 266-67.   [g.a.]

2417   Schneider, Johann Friedrich, 1785 (6?)-1853

K. E. HENRICI, AUCTIONEER, BERLIN   AUK. CAT. NO. 15

Goetheautographen. Goethe in den Briefen . . . Briefe aus dem Weimarer Kreis . . . Musikerautographen aus den Nachlass . . . und anderem Besitz. Versteigerung . . . 19. Mai 1913. . . . Berlin, 1913. 64 p. 518 lots, illus. Music, lots 373-518.   [US-Wc, -NYgr, NL-Avb]

Folter, no. 329.

2418   _____

LITERATURE

Wege, Erich. "Friedrich-Schneider-Ausstellung anlässlich seines 100. Todestages." *Zentralbalatt für Bibliothekswesens* 68 (1954): 208-09.   [g.a.]

A display of Ms. scores and memorabilia from his library, part of which was bequeathed to D-DEl.

2419   Schneider, Sophie

MARTIN BRESLAUER, AUCTIONEER, BERLIN   CAT. NO. 21

Handschriften-Versteigerung am 29. und 30. April 1912. Autographen und Dokumente, die in Auftrage der Erben der Frau Sophie Schneider, Braunschweig-Wilhelmshöhe, versteigert werden. . . . Berlin, 1912. 64 p. 738 lots, illus. Music, lots 420-84a.   [US-Wc, -NYgr]

Not a large, but a rich, collection, including Beethoven, Mozart, and others' ALS and Mss. Sale noted in *MT* 53 (October 1912): 647.

2420   Schoelcher, Victor, 1804-93

"Catalogue chronological et raisonné [of Handel's works]."

Ms. bought in 1856; sold to D-Hs. A copy of Schoelcher's catalog from the Julian Marshall sale, part in English, part French is at GB-Lbl, R.M.18.b.2.

2421   _____

Clausen, Hans Dieter. "The Hamburg Collection [of Handel Directing Scores]." In *Handel Collections and Their History*, ed. Terence Best, 10-23. Oxford: Clarendon Press, 1993.   [g.a.]

Collection provenance: J. C. Smith, Lady Rivers, the dealer Kerslake, Victor Schoelcher; now at D-Hs.

2422　Schoenbaum, Camillo, b. 1925

"Collection C. Schoenbaum." [16th to19th-century Czech music collection, still private.] Ms. thematic catalog done by the owner, according to **Albrecht**. Ca. 200 double-staff incipits, compiled 1946-48. **Brook**, no. 1176.

2423　Schoenberg, Arnold, 1874-1951

Steuermann, Clara. "From the Archives: Schoenberg's Library Catalogue." *Journal of the Arnold Schoenberg Institute* 3, no. 2 (October 1979): 203-18.　　　　　　　[g.a.]

Collection is now at the Arnold Schoenberg Center, Vienna.

2424　——————

Simms, Bryan. "A Major Addition to the Schoenberg Collection at the Library of Congress." *Abstracts of Papers Read at the 46th Annual Meeting of the AMS* [and] *SMT, Denver, Colorado, 6-9 November 1980,* 32-33.　　　　　　　[g.a.]

2425　——————

Arnold Schoenberg Institute
Arnold Schoenberg Institute Archives Preliminary Catalog, by Kathryn P. Glennan, Jerry L. McBride and Wayne Shoaf. Los Angeles: Arnold Schoenberg Institute, University of Southern California, 1986. 3 vols.　　　　　　　[g.a.]

Vol. 1, Archival scores; reference scores (695+55 p.)

Vol. 2, Archival books; reference books (293+457 p.)

Vol. 3, Recordings; text manuscripts; photographs (234+52+338 p.)

2426　——————

Literature
Meggett, Joan, and R. Moritz. "The Schoenberg Legacy." *Notes* 31 (1974-75): 30-36.　　　[g.a.]

Ca. 6000 manuscript pages and a library of ca. 2000 books.

2427　Schönborn-Wiesentheid Library

Zobeley, Fritz. "Schönborn." *MGG* 12, cols. 26-29.

Includes an extensive bibliography of writings about the Schönborn collection, which is now at D-PO (see **Benton** 2:98, no. 229). The succession of owners in **2431**.

2428　——————

Schmitt, Max. "Verzeichnis der Musikalien in d. Grafl. von Schönbornschen Musikbibliothek, Wiesentheid."

Ms. in Wiesentheid. Cited from Zobeley (**2431**), but no date or Ms. number.

2429　——————

Zobeley, Fritz. "Werke Handels in der Gräfl. von Schönbornschen Musikbibliothek." *Händel-Jahrbuch* 4 (1931): 98-116.　　　　　　　[g.a.]

Partly thematic.

2430 _____

Rudolf F. E. von Schönborn . . . seine Musikpflege und seine Musiksammlung. Neujahrsblätter der Gesellschaft für fränkische Geschichte, 21. Würzburg: F. Schöningh, 1949. 100 p.

[US-NYp, -AA, -I, -CA]

Bibliography, pp. 92-96; "Das Repertoire . . . ," pp. 72-77.

2431 _____

Zobeley, Fritz, and Frohmut Dangel-Hofmann. *Die Musikalien der Grafen von Schönborn-Wiesentheid.* Vol. 1: *Das Repertoire des Grafen Rudolf Franz Erwein von Schönborn (1677-1754).* 2 vols. *Katalog.* Tutzing: Hans Schneider, 1967.   [g.a.]

Collected 1690-1740 by Rudolf Franz Erwein; 1738-1817 by his grandson, Hugo Damian; and 1776-1840 by his great-grandson, Franz Erwein. Vol. 1, no. 1: *Drucke aus den Jahren 1676 bis 1738*; no. 2, *Handschriften*; vol. 2, [no. 3]: *Der Notennachlas der Grafen Hugo Damien Erwein und Franz Erwein.* Thematic.

2432 _____

LITERATURE

Marigold, W. Gordon. [A review of the Zobeley catalog, above, and the Schönborn collection.] *Notes* 24 (1968): 715-16.   [g.a.]

2433 Scholes, Percy Alfred, 1877-1958

Kallmann, Helmut. "The Percy Scholes Collection: Nucleus for National Music Library." *Canadian Music Journal* 2, no. 3 (spring 1958): 42-45.

Despite the optimism, it was only Scholes's general collection that was acquired in 1957 by C-On. The Burney portion—Burney correspondence, Scholes's correspondence, and other music items—were once the property of James Marshall Osborn and are now at US-NH. See Laurence C. Witten, "Contemporary Collectors XXIII: James Marshall Osborn," *Book Collector,* winter 1959, 383-96.

2434 _____

LITERATURE

Calderisi, Maria. "An Unsung Treasure at the National Library of Canada: The Percy A. Scholes Collection." *Fontes* 41 (1994): 53-65.   [g.a.]

2435 Scholfield,   ; Dr. Thomas Carter

PUTTICK & SIMPSON, AUCTIONEER, LONDON   CAT. NO. 1906

Catalogue of a Scarce, Curious and Interesting Collection of Music, Comprising the Libraries of . . . and Others, Among Which Will Be Found Rare Compositions . . . Original Autograph Manuscripts . . . and the Disputed Handel-Smith MS. of "Amadigi" from Mr. Smee's Collection . . . Sold . . . 22 March 1880. [London, 1880.] 18 p. 313 lots.   [GB-Lbl, US-Wc]

Scholten, R. L.   *See* **Brugman, Johann B. H.** (sale of 18 June 1913)

2436 Scholz, K   W

FELIX DÖRFFEL, FIRM, DARMSTADT   CAT. NO. 40

Autographen. . . . Darmstadt, 1964. 40 lots.

Not located; cited from *IBAK.*

2437   **Schott, Bernhard,** 1748-1809

Federhofer, Hellmut. "Zwei Mainzer Sammlungen von Musiker-briefen des 19. Jahrhunderts." In *[Festschrift Prof. Adam Gottron . . . zum 75. Geburtstag am 11. Oktober 1964],* Mainzer Zeitschrift . . . Jg. 60/61 (1965/66), 1-33. Mainz, 1966.

> An alphabetical catalog. Collection now at D-MZs, bequest of Franz Schott.

2438   **Schramm, Paul** and **Dinny**

Palmer, Jill. "A Dutch-Austrian Duo: The Paul and Dinny Schramm Collection at the National Library of New Zealand." *Fontes* 39 (1992): 226-32.   [g.a.]

> Collection at NZ-Wt.

2439   **Schreker, Franz,** 1878-1934

VIENNA, NATIONALBIBLIOTHEK, MUSIKSAMMLUNG
Der Franz-Schreker-Fonds in der Musiksammlung . . . Katalog, ed. Friedrich C. Heller, with Hans Jancik and Lucia Vogel. Wien: Hollinek in Komm, 1975. xiii, 70 p.   [US-Wc]

> *Museion,* 3. Reihe no. 4.   [g.a.]

2440   **Schubert, Ferdinand**

LITERATURE
"Witteczek-Spaun'sche Schubert-Sammlung." In *Die Gesellschaft des österreichischen Kaiserstaates und ihr Conservatorium, . . .* by C. F. Pohl, 114-?. Wien: Braumüller, 1871.

Schucht, J.   *See under* **Kossmaly, Carl**

2441   **Schumann, Robert Alexander,** 1810-56; **Clara Schumann,** 1819-96

LEO LIEPMANNSSOHN, AUCTIONEER, BERLIN   VERST. NO. 60
Autographen von Musikern, Schriftstellern, Gelehrten . . . Schauspielern . . . versteigerung . . . 21. -22. November 1930. Berlin, 1930. 118 p. 833 lots.   [GB-Lbl]

> ". . . aus dem Besitz und mit Widmungen an Robert und Clara Schumann," lots 270-90. **Folter,** no. 331.

2442   **Schurig, Arthur, Dr.,** 1870-1929

PAUL ALICKE, FIRM, DRESDEN   ANTIQ. CAT. NO. 189
Bibliothek Dr. Arthur Schurig. Vol. 2: Musik und Theater (hierbei eine schöne Don Juan-Sammlung). . . . Dresden, [19-]. 551 lots.   [NL-Dhgm]

> Not examined.

2443   **[Schurmann,]**

MR. HODGSON, AUCTIONEER, LONDON
A Catalogue of a Large Collection of Miscellaneous Music . . . Instruments . . . Consisting of Operas, Oratorios, Overtures . . . [etc.] *Sold by Auction . . . October 30th, 1857.* London, 1857. 13 p. 340 lots.   [compiler]

> It is not clear whether this was a private collection or a dealer's stock.

2444   **Schwaan, Friedrich L.,** 1772-1845

KARL ERNST HENRICI, AUCTIONEER, BERLIN   VERST. 36
. . . Autographen. Music und Theater. Bildende Künstler . . . sowie Autographen aus den Nachlass des Musikmeisters Schwaan, Rostock . . . 9. Dezember 1916. Berlin, 1916. 80 p. Music, lots 719-932, vol. 2.   [US-NYp, NL-Avb]

Schwarzenberg, Ernst von, Prince-Bishop.   *See* **Philip Karl, Graf zu Oettingen-Wallerstein,**
section 3

2445   **Schwencke, Christian Friedrich Gottlieb,** 1767-1822
Index librorum ex omni scientia lectissimorum integritate et nitore insignium, quos collegit
C. F. T. Schwencke, per XXX annos et amplius in Joanneo, quod Hamburgi floret, cantor et
chori musici director. Publice vendentur in aedibus beati possessoris d. 25. augusti 1823.
Hamburgi: Typis Hermannianis, 1823. 130 p. 2252 + 163 + 38 lots.   [compiler]

> "Section secunda: De arte music scriptores," lots 2113-252 (many more
> items). Fétis/Brussels catalog no. 5176.

2446   _____

Verzeichniss der von dem verstorbenen Herrn Musikdirektor C. F. G. Schwencke hinterlassenen
Sammlung von Musikalien aus allen Fächern der Tonkunst, enthaltend sowohl die
sämmtlichen eigenen Werke des verstorbenen, als Partituren und Auszüge von früheren
und neueren Compositionen sowohl für Kirche als Theater, aller Zeiten und Nationen, nebst
einer besonders reichen Liedersammlung, Handschriften berühmter Tonsetzer, theoretischen
Schriften, und einer Folge von Bildnissen vieler Tonkünstler, welche am 30sten August und
folgende Tage im Kramer-Amthause . . . durch den Auctionarius J. J. Berndes öffentlich verkauft
werden soll. Hamburg: Hermann'sche Erben, 1824. viii, 79 p. 1432 + ca. 60 unnumbered items.
[GB-Lbl (Hirsch), US-R, compiler]

> "Original-Handschriften," lots 225-57, include 2 Bach Magnificats, the *Kunst*
> *der Fuge, Orgel-Büchlein,* the Christmas Cantata, etc.! Schwencke's works
> in Ms., lots 66-149; his copies and arrangements of others' works, lots 150-
> 224. **Folter**, no. 333.

Schwender, Gustav E.   *See under* **Stockhausen, Ernst von**

2447   **Scott, John (M.D., of Bedford Square)**
S. Leigh Sotheby & Co., auctioneer, London
Catalogue of the Valuable Collection of Most Esteemed Music, and Rare and Curious Musical
Works . . . Sold . . . June 19th, 1850. . . . [London, 1850.] 13 p. 203 lots. Scott's, lots 1-191.
[US-NYp; film at CRL]

2448   **Scrive, Charles (of Lille)**
Hourez (Exp.); Desante (C. -P.)
Catalogue de la riche collection d'objets d'arts, fayence, grès, porcelaines [etc.] *Livres et*
partitions de musique . . . vente . . . à Lille . . . 29 janvier 1872 et jours suivants. . . . [Lille],
1872. 48 p. 852 lots.   [F-Paa, F-Pn]

2449   **Scuderi, Francesco,** fl. 1560
Ongaro, Giulio M. "The Library of a Sixteenth-Century Music Teacher." *Journal of Musicology*
11 (1944): 357-75.   [g.a.]

> List of Scuderi's music [in English]. 366 pp. "Appendix: Inventory of Music
> Books Owned by Scuderi" [in Italian], p. 375. 23 music vols., "miniscule"
> says **Ongaro**, but still impressive, as he explains. List in Ms. at I-Vas, Sant'
> Uffizio, busta 15, processo 49.

2450   **Sedó y Guichard, Arturo**

Montaner, Joaquín. *La coleción teatral de don Arturo Sedó.* . . . Barcelona: Seix y Barral, 1951. 349 p., 8 plates.

> Collection now at Instituto del Teatro, Barcelona (E-Bit). Catalog not located.
> Cited from **Benton 3:**10, no. 13.

Segnitz, Eugen, 1862-1927.   *See* **Kipke, Carl**

2451   **Séguin, Armand,** 1768-1835

LEBLANC, LIBRARIE, AUCTIONEER, PARIS
Catalogue de la bibliothèque musicale de feu. . . . *Méthodes, solfèges, partitions et oeuvres divers. Manuscrits, imprimés ou gravés, la plupart fort rares . . . vente . . . 15 juin 1835 et jours suivants.* . . . Paris: Merlin, 1835. 39 p. 805 lots (many more items). Ms. vocal works, lots 97-239.   [US-NYp, -BE, NL-DHgm, Gb-Lbl]

2452   _____

GUSTAV FOCK BUCHHANDLUNG, LEIPZIG   ANT. CAT. NO. 624
Musik - Theater. Bücher und Zeitschriften aus dem Gebiete der historischen, theoretischen und praktischen Musik, sowie des Theaters, zum Teil aus dem Besitz von. . . . Leipzig, [1930]. 98 p. 2493 lots. Music, lots 1-2041.   [US-Wc, -NYp, -R, GB-Lbl (Hirsch), compiler]

> **Folter**, no. 334.

2453   _____

KARL MAX POPPE, FIRM, LEIPZIG   ANT. CAT. NO. 46
. . . *Musik -Theater.* . . . Leipzig, [ca. 1933].

> Lot 1953: "Aus dem Besitz des bekannten Musikschriftsteller A. Seidl stellten mit eine Sammlung von zus. ca. 200 Schriften u. Abhandlungen über Musik und Theater zusammen." A. Seidl.   [compiler]

Seiffert, Max, 1868-1948.   *See under* **Mempell, Johann Nicolaus**

2454   **Seitz, Alipius**

Münster, Robert. "Die Musik im Augustinerchorherrenstift Beuerberg von 1768 bis 1803 und der thematische Katalog des Chorherren Alipius Seitz." *KmJ* 54 (1970): 47-76.   [g.a.]

2455   **Seixas, Alexandre Metelo Napoles Lemos de**

A. H. OLIVEIRA, FIRM, LISBON
Primeira parte do catálogo da magnífica livraria do . . . cerca de 5000 escolhidas espécies bibliográficas . . . coleção de cancioneiros . . . venda . . . 15 de novembro de 1961 e dias seguintes. . . . Lisboa, 1961. 144 p. 1600 lots. Music, *inter alia.* 15 January 1962.   [NL-Avb]

> Cited from **Vereeniging.** . . . *Catalogus* 8:481.

2456   **Selander, N J T**

Förteckning öfver musikalier tillhöriga N. J. T. Selander den 1 Juli 1877. Stockholm, 1877. 48 p.

> Not located; cited from *DaSMl.*

2457   Selden-Goth, Gisela, 1884-1975

Literature

"A New Collection of Music Manuscripts in the United States." *MQ* 26 (1940): 175-85.   [g.a.]
Collection given to US-Wc.

2458   Selhof, Nicolas

Catalogue d'une très belle bibliothèque de livres curieux et rares, en toutes sortes de facultez et langues . . . auquel suit le catalogue d'une partie très considérérable de livres de musique, [tant Italiens que Français, Espagnols, Anglaise, Hollandais,] *ainsi qu'une collection de toutes sortes d'instruments deslaissez par feu M. Nicolas Selhof, libraire, lesquels seront vendus publiquement aux plus offrants mercredi 30 mai 1759 et jours suivants, dans la maison de la veuve d'Adrien Moetjens, libraire, dans Hofstraat.* La Haye: Chez la veuve d'Adrien Moetjens, 1759. 260 p. 2945 numbers.

> Last ten pages given to instruments (210). There is a lengthy discussion of this catalog and its important musical contents in the Vereeniging voor Noord-Nederlands Musikgeschiedenis, *Bouwsteenen* 3:114-17.

2459   _____

Reprint, with an introduction by A. Hyatt King. Auction Catalogs of Music, 1. Amsterdam: Frits Knuf, 1973. xii, 264 p.   [g.a.]

> "Reproduced from the unique copy in the Toonkunst-Bibliotheek, Amsterdam (Pressmark 205 D II)."

2460   _____

Literature

Becker, Georg. [An article about the Selhof collection.] *Le Guide musical,* 24 June 1878.

> Not examined; there are no U.S. locations for this issue.

2461   _____

[A lengthy discussion of the 1759 catalog and its important musical contents.] *Bouwsteenen* 3:114-17.

2462   Sellers, Ernest Orlando, b. 1869; **William P. Martin**

Daniel, A. H. "The Sellers-Martin Hymnal Collection [at US-NORts]: A Source for the History of Gospel Hymnody." Thesis, New Orleans Baptist Theological Seminary, 1970.

2463   Selvaggi, Gaspari

"Catalogue of Music Collected by Signor Gaspare Selvaggi of Naples and Presented to the British Museum by [Spencer Joshua Alwyne Compton] the [Second] Marquess of Northampton, P.R.S., April 1843." 35 fols. No numbering system.

[GB-Lbl, US-NYp, compiler (copy of -NYP)]

> Add. Ms. 14,249 at GB-Lbl, in the hand of Mrs. Maclean Clephane, sister of Margaret, Marchioness of Northampton, with pencil notes in the hand of Thomas Oliphant.

2464   _____

Biblioteca scelta di libri italiani di scienze, arti, e letteratura di G. S. Napoli: Nel Gabinett bibliografico e tipografico, 1830. 291 p. Not examined.   [US-BE]

> Another catalog of his library (Napoli: Stab. Tipografico, 1859, 304 p.) contained no music.   [US-Wc, -MSu]

2465 Sérieyx, Auguste, 1859-1949
Matthey, Jean-Louis. *Fonds musical Auguste Sérieyx.* Lausanne: Bibl. cantonale et universitaire, 1974. 124 p.

> Thematic catalog of the collection now at CH-LAcu. Not located; cited from *RILM.*

2466 Seroen, Berthe
LITERATURE
Sanders, Henriette. "Belangrijke nalatenschap tekent persoon en werk van legendarische zangeres; de bibliotheek van. . . ." *Mens en melodie* 38 (1983): 6-9.   [g.a.]

2467 Sevastopulo, M. Jean
SOTHEBY & CO., AUCTIONEER, LONDON
Catalogue of Valuable Printed Books, Music, Autograph Letters and Historical Documents, Comprising . . . Autograph Music or Letters of Debussy, Dvořák, Mendelssohn, Brahms [etc.] *. . . Sold . . . 23rd of May, 1960, and the Following Day. . . .* [London], 1960. 95 p. 542 lots. Music, lots 401-64.   [Film at CRL]

> Not a great many music lots but most are important, e.g., lots 415-27, all Debussy items including a holograph of a scene from *Pelléas* and a sizeable number of ALS.

Seydel, Martin [pseud. of **Hugo Martin**], 1871-1934.   *See under* **Heuss, Alfred Valentin** (1935 sale)

2468 Seydl, Josef Antonín, 1775-1837
Holeček, Jaroslav, comp. *J. A. Seydl decani Beronensis, operum artis musicae collectio: catalogus.* . . . Artis musicae antiquioris catalogorum series, 2. Pragae: Editio Supraphon, 1976, 1974. 201 p., facs. 585 nos.   [g.a.]

> Given by Seydl to Bezirksarchiv Beroun (CS-BER) in 1957.

2469 Seymour, Berkley; R. Harneise
A Catalogue of the Libraries of . . . Late Fellow of King's College and the Rev. Mr. R. Harneise, Late Fellow of Magdalen College, Deceased . . . Sold . . . at the Falcon-Inn in the Petty-Curry Cambridge . . . February 26, 1745-46. . . . The Day After the Sale of the Books Is Ended, There Will Be Sold a Curious Collection of Musick in 33 Volumes, Each Volume To Be Sold Separate . . . Catalogues to Be Had at All Coffee-Houses, at W. Thurlbourn's Bookseller, and at the Place of Sale. [London, 1745/46.]   [GB-Lbl]

> 33 lots of music, pp. 31-32, are indexed in **Coral,** p. 184, and discussed, p. 65.

2470 Shaftesbury, Anthony Ashley Cooper, 4th Earl of, 1711-71
[Ms. inventory of his Handel collection made in 1761 now at GB-Lbl, Add. Ms. 29,864, ff. 98-102.]   [g.a.]

> Winton Dean notes in *Handel: A Celebration,* ed. Jacob Simon (London: National Portrait Gallery, 1985), 22-24.

2471   Sharp, Granville, 1734-1813
"A Catalogue of the Manuscript and Instrumental Music in the Joint Collection of James, William, and Granville Sharp, London, 1859." Drexel Ms. 1022 at US-NYp.

[compiler (Xerox)]

> This implies that William and James were collectors, but **King**, p. 29, says Granville "seems to have shared his extensive library with his brothers James and William, though there is no evidence that they were active in building it up."

2472 _____

Holland, Jeanette B., and Jan LaRue. "The Sharp Manuscript, London 1759-ca. 1793: A Uniquely Annotated Music Catalogue." *Bulletin of the New York Public Library* 73 (1969): 147-66.

[g.a.]

> Illustrated, with a list of works.

2473 _____

Leigh & Sotheby, auctioneer, London
A Catalogue of the Extensive and Valuable Music, Printed and Manuscript of the Late Granville Sharp . . . Sold . . . February 7th, 1814, and Two Following Days. [London], 1814. 15 p.   539 lots.   [GB-Lbl, US-R, compiler (copy, names & prices)]
> **King**, pp. 29-30. **Albrecht.**

2474 _____

Puttick & Simpson, auctioneer, London   Cat. no. 2012
Catalogue of the Extensive Library of Music of the Late William Sharp (with Others), Comprising Fine Sets . . . Sold . . . April 25, 1881. . . . [London, 1881.]   15 p.   308 lots (many more items).   [GB-Lbl]
> Lot 169 = 80 Mss.

2475 _____

Literature
Crosby, Brian. "Durham Cathedral's Music Manuscripts." *MT* 105 (1974): 418-21.   [g.a.]
> The Sharp collection from Bamburgh Castle at GB-Drc.
> → *See* catalog here *under* **Halle, Philip**

2476 _____

Doyle, A. I. "Unfamiliar Libraries IV: The Bamburgh Library." *Book Collector* 8 (1959): 14-24.

[g.a.]

> → *See also under* **Halle, Philip**

2477   Sharpe, Mr. (of Knutsford); et al.
W. P. Musgrave, auctioneer, London
A Catalogue of the Well-Known Instruments, Late the Property of Mr. [Henry] Condell. . . . The Music Consists of . . . Works and Treatises, of the Most Distinguished Ancient and Modern Composers, Comprising the Collection of Mr. Sharpe of Knutsford . . . Sold March 30, 1825. . . . [London], 1825.   18 p.   183 lots. Music, lots 1-75, 88-183.

[GB-Lbl, compiler (film)]

Shaw-Hellier Collection.   *See under* **Hellier, Samuel,** 1736-84

2478   **Shedlock, John South; A Gentleman Who Has Ceased to Collect**
PUTTICK & SIMPSON, AUCTIONEER, LONDON   CAT. NO. 5337
A Catalogue of Valuable Books, Including the Musical Library of the Late. . . . A Choice Selection from the Library of a Gentleman . . . Sold . . . April 29th, 1919, and Following Day. . . . [London], 1919. 33 p. 640 lots.   [GB-Lbl]
    Shedlock's musical properties, lots 1-137 (many more items).

2479   **Shenk, Morris J., Dr.**
MUSICAL AMERICANA (HARRY DICHTER), FIRM, ATLANTIC CITY, N. J.   CAT. NO. 10
Songs and Music. Atlantic City, N. J., [n.d.]. Unnumbered pp. 380 + lots.   [US-R]
    "Presidential and Political Items . . . [lots 147-363] purchased by Dr. Morris J. Shenk."

2480   **Shield, William,** 1748-1829
W. P. MUSGRAVE, AUCTIONEER, LONDON
A Catalogue of the Music, Books, Instruments, Paintings, Engravings, &c. Late the Property of. . . . Excellent Violins, Tenors [etc.] *. . . Sold . . . 22nd of June, 1829.* [London], 1829. 23 p. 341 lots.   [GB-Lbl, compiler (film)]
    King, p. 29: ". . . 247 distinguished lots of music." **Albrecht.**

2481   **The "Shipton Hoard"**
    King, pp. 39-42, offers an amusing account of this supposed music collection, calls the announcement of its discovery "a hoax, the only musical one that appears to be known."

2482   **Shoubridge, James,** 1804-1872
PUTTICK & SIMPSON, AUCTIONEER, LONDON   CAT. NO. 1404
A Catalogue of the Antiquarian and Miscellaneous Musical Library of the Late. . . . Old Compositions in Manuscript, Collections of Scarce Harpsichord Solos, Duets, etc. . . . Also Numerous Musical Instruments . . . Sold . . . June 30th, 1873. [London], 1873. 31 p. 578 lots. Music, lots 1-468.   [GB-Lbl, US-NYp]

2483   **Sibelius, Jean,** 1865-1957
Jean Sibelius Kirjaston luettelo. . . . Catalogue of the Library of Jean Sibelius [at his home, Ainola, in Järvenpää]. Helsinki, 1973. 186 leaves. 2928 numbers.   [US-Wc, -I]

2484   **Sibley, Hiram W.**
UNIVERSITY OF ROCHESTER, N.Y., EASTMAN SCHOOL OF MUSIC, SIBLEY MUSICAL LIBRARY
Catalogue of the Sibley Musical Library Presented to the University of Rochester, by Hiram W. Sibley. Rochester, N.Y., 1906. 90 p.   [US-NYp, -R]

_____. *Supplement,* [no. 1]. Rochester, 1909.

2485 _____

LITERATURE

"A Library for Musical Research." *Musical Leader and Concert Goer* 14, no. 1 (1907): 18.

[g.a.]

2486   Sidney, R. C. (of Mortimer St., London)
W. P. MUSGRAVE, AUCTIONEER, LONDON
A Catalogue of Vocal and Instrumental Music . . . Sold April 25, 1827. . . . [London], 1827.

[GB-Lbl]

2487   Sieber, [probably either **Jean-Georges**, 1734-1822, or his son **Georges-Julian**, 1775-1834]
Catalogue de musique vocale et instrumentale appartenant à M. Seiber. . . . Paris, [n.d.]

Not located; cited from **Scheurleer** 1 (1923): 22.

2488   Sigismondo, Giuseppe, 1739-1826
Cafiero, Rosa. "Una biblioteca per la biblioteca: La collezione musicale di. . . ." *Quaderni della Rivista italiana di musicologia* 28 (1993): 299-367.   [g.a.]

> Appendice II, a list of Sigismondo's bequests and indications of which items appear in Gasparini and Gallo's *Catalogo delle opere musicali del Conservatorio di Musica* [and] *San Pietro a Majella di Napoli* (Parma, 1934; reprint, [Bologna]: Forni, [1988]), as part of the series *Bibliotheca musica Bononiensis,* Sez. I, 21).   [g.a.]

2489   Silva, Ivo da Cunha e
ARNALDO HENRIQUES DE (LIVRARIA) OLIVEIRA AND MANUEL DOS SANTOS   LEILÃO No. 89
Catálogo de duas magnificas livrarias: de laureado professor do conservatório, Ivo da Cunha e silva [and] *João da G. Telles de Lemos* [not a musician] *. . . venda . . . Lisboa . . . 30 de junho. . . .* Porto, 1941. 74 p. 1146 lots (all Cunha's).   [US-Cn]

> Telles de Lemos's part of the collection was held over for sale, no. 90.

2490   Silva, Luigi
UNIVERSITY OF NORTH CAROLINA, GREENSBORO, WALTER CLINTON JACKSON LIBRARY
Cello Music Collections in the Jackson Library . . . Pt. 1 - The Luigi Silva Collection. Compiled by Barbara B. Cassell and Clifton H. Karnes, III. . . . Greensboro: the University, 1978. xviii, [207] p. Ca. 2000 nos.   [g.a.]

> **Folter,** no. 337.

2491   Silverstolpe, Fredrik Samuel, 1769-1851
Mörner, Stellan. "Johan Wikmanson und die Brüder Silverstolpe." Diss., Stockholm, 1952.

> Collection described, pp. 410-48, according to Boer and Jonsson (**2492**).

2492 _____

Van Boer, Bertil H., Jr., and Leif Jonsson. "The Silverstolpe Music Collection in Rö, Uppland, Sweden: A Preliminary Catalogue." *Fontes* 29 (1982): 93-103.

_____. ["Additions".] Ibid., 30 (1983): 219-20.

> A detailed catalog will appear in *RISM*. Some Mss. of J. M. Kraus from the collection are now at S-Uu, according to **Albrecht**.

2493   Simon August, Graf und Edler zur Lippe-Detmold

Kettle [or Kittel?] J. F. "Verzeichniss derer, in der Musicalien Kammer des Hoch Reichs Gräfl. Schlosses zu Dtm. befindlichen Instrumente und Musicalien, geführt von Concertmaster I. F. Kittel, 1780." Reprinted in Joachim Domp, *Studien zur Geschichte der Musik am Westfälischen Adelshöfen im 18. Jahrhunderts,* 48-51. Freiburger Studien zur Musikwissenschaft, 1. Regensburg: Pustet, 1934.   [compiler (copy)]

2494   Simoni, Livia

Manni, Teresa Rogledi. "La biblioteca Livia Simoni." In *Il museo teatrale all Scala, 1931-1963,* 381-94. Milano, 1964.   [US-CA, -Cu, -LAu]

> Not examined. Cited from **Benton** 3:260, no. 190.

2495   Simoni, Renato, 1875-1952

LITERATURE

Vittadini, Stefano. "La biblioteca de Renato Simoni al Museo teatrale alla Scala." *Accademi e biblioteche d'Italia, Annali* 22 (1954): 579-80.

> Not examined; cited from **Benton** 3:206, no. 190.

2496   Sinclair, Florence May

PUTTICK & SIMPSON, AUCTIONEER, LONDON   CAT. NO. 5895

Catalogue of Musical Instruments . . . [etc.] *The Musical Library of the Late Miss . . . Sold October 4th., 1923.* [London], 1923. 10 p. 197 lots.   [GB-Lbl]

> Sinclair's music, lots 171-97, but many more items, e.g., lots 181 and 190, each comprise 20 volumes.

2497   Six van Vromade, J   W

VAN STOCKUM, AUCTIONEER, THE HAGUE

[Sale of songbooks in 3 auctions, 1925, 1926, 1930. Music is in Dl. 1, 1925.]   [NL-Avb]

> Not examined; cited from **Vereeniging.** . . . *Catalogus* 4:293.

2498   Skene, George, 1695-1756

Turbet, Richard. "The Music Collection of a Scottish Laird: George Skene of Skene, 1731." *Brio* 32 (1995): 24-27.   [g.a.]

> Catalog, pp. 25-27, drawn from a general "Catalogue of Books Belonging to . . . Aberdeen, June 14th, 1731" (GB-A Ms. 3175 v746).

2499   Skotak, Ondrej

Turková, Marie. "Sbírka hudebnin Ondreje Skotáka její tvurce." *Slezského musea,* ser. B 21 (1972): 78-87.

> Collection now at CS-OP. Not examined; cited from *RILM* 7:1489.

2500   Skraup, J   N

ISAK TAUSSIG, FIRM, PRAGUE   ANT. CAT. NO. 32

Werke über Musik-Theorie, Geschichte, Aesthetik, Gesangsschulen. Volkslieder. Geistliche Musik: Oratorien, Messen aus dem Nachlasse des. . . . Prag, [n.d.]. 32 p. 982 lots. [US-NYp]

2501 Sloane, Sir Hans, d. 1735
> *LITERATURE*
> Turner, Malcolm, and Arthur Searle. "The Music Collection of the British Library Reference Division." *Notes* 38 (1982): 499-549. [g.a.]
>> The collection, its organization, and services are largely based on the personal library of Sloane.

Sluzewski, Curt. *See under* **Rookwood, Mrs. A.** (sale of 20 November 1978)

2502 Smart, Sir George, 1776-1867; **Sir George Alexander,** 1813-87; **Anonymous**
> Mr. WATSON, AUCTIONEER, LONDON
> *A Catalogue of a Valuable Assemblage of Vocal and Instrumental Music, Including the Duplicates from the Library of Sir George Smart, the Library of Mr. Macfarren, and Other Collections . . . Sold April 18th, 1833, and Following Day.* [London], 1833. 15 p. 295 lots. Music, lots 1-281. [US-NYp, compiler]
>> **King,** pp. 53-54, 131. **Albrecht.**

2503 Smart, Sir George; Sir Andrew Barnard
> PUTTICK & SIMPSON, AUCTIONEER, LONDON   CAT. NO. 634
> *Catalogue of a Large Portion of Excellent, Curious and Valuable Musical Library of . . . Comprising a Large Number of Scores . . . by Eminent Composers . . . Also a Portion of the Musical Library of the Late Sir Andrew Barnard . . . Sold . . . June 28th, 1860, and Following Day.* [London, 1860.] 32 p. 632 lots. [GB-Lbl, US-Wc, -NYp]
>> **King,** pp. 53-54: "Smart kept together a very large quantity of sale catalogues . . . chiefly musical. . . . Many are now unique. Bound in 12 volumes, copiously annotated, they are now preserved in the British Museum."
>> → *See also under* **Callcott, John Wall** (sale of 5 July 1886)

2504 Smee, Frederick
> PUTTICK & SIMPSON, AUCTIONEER, LONDON   CAT. NO. 1878
> *. . . Catalogue of the Valuable Musical Library (Antiquarian and Miscellaneous) of the Late . . . Comprising English Church Music . . . Scarce Original Editions of Handel's Works . . .* [etc.] *Sold . . . 15th December 1879.* [London, 1879.] 396 lots. [GB-Lbl, US-CHua (priced)]
>> **King,** pp. 98-99.

2505 [Smith, Charles Britiffe]
> Mr. EVANS, AUCTIONEER, LONDON
>> [**King,** p. 38, notes Evans's sale, 27 May 1842, of Smith's properties, "the earliest known collector of autograph letters of musicians." However the Evans catalog of this date at GB-Lbl does not contain the Smith collection, nor has a catalog of it been identified!]

2506 Smith, Edward Orlebar, Rev.
> Mr. SOUTHGATE & Co., AUCTIONEER, LONDON   CAT. NO. 1684
>> There is a lengthy paragraph about the sale of Smith's musical collection on the "31st ult." at Southgate's shop in Fleet Street, in *Musical Standard* 4 (9 September 1865): 65. It notes a number of items sold, with prices fetched. The British Museum dates the sale on the 29th of May. Catalog not located to verify either.

2507   **Smith, George Townshend,** 1813-77

PUTTICK & SIMPSON, AUCTIONEER, LONDON   CAT. NO. 1706

Catalogue of the Interesting and Valuable Musical Library of the Late . . . Comprising . . . Old Manuscripts etc., Also of [various properties] *a Few Music Plates and Copyrights, Together With Numerous Valuable Musical Instruments . . . Sold . . . November 27th, 1877.* [London, 1877.] 18 p. 377 lots. Music, lots 1-279.   [GB-Lbl, US-CHua]

> **King**, p. 63.

Smith, J. C.   *See under* **[Markey]** (sale of 29 January 1858) *and* **Rivers, Lady Martha** (sale of 1856)

2508   **Smith, John Stafford,** 1750-1836

> **King**, p. 43: His collection passed to his daughter, was later sold in an anonymous sale, 24 April 1844, by "an ignorant auctioneer" [and was hopelessly scattered] . . . at an out of the way place in Gray's Inn Road. "The collection was thus dispersed almost without trace, and no copy of the catalogue has come to light." King draws his information from Husk's article in *Grove's Dictionary*, 3rd ed. (1935), p. 793, who says, in part: "the library, remarkably rich in ancient English manuscripts," was sold with "such books as were described at all being cataloged from the backs and heaped together in lots, each containing a dozen or more works. 578 volumes were so disposed of. . . . Smith's name did not appear on the catalogue; nothing was done to attract the attention of the musical world. . . ." **Albrecht** says a total of 2191 volumes were in the sale.
>
> Some items were acquired by Hamilton & Bird and 113 lots were listed in their catalog no. 10, 1844 (not seen). Some remained in the stock of Calkin & Budd and were sold with other collections at Puttick & Simpson sales of 27 August 1852 and 17 August 1853 (**2509, 2510**).

2509   _____

> PUTTICK & SIMPSON, AUCTIONEER, LONDON   CAT. NO. 292
>
> *Catalogue of the Third Portion of . . . the Stock of Messrs. Calkin & Budd . . . Including a Large Collection of Curious Books and MSS. Formerly in the Library of That Celebrated Antiquary, the Late . . . Sold . . . August 27 and Following Day, 1852.* [London, 1852.] 33 p. 721 lots. Music, lots 1-678.   [GB-Lbl]

2510   _____

> PUTTICK & SIMPSON, AUCTIONEER, LONDON   CAT. NO. 337
>
> *Catalogue of 1,900 Engraved Music Plates . . . Ancient and Modern Music . . . and Many Curious Books from the Library of . . . Sold . . . August 17, 1853. . . .* [London, 1853.] 30 p. 474 lots. Music, lots 1-417.   [GB-Lbl]

2511   _____

> *LITERATURE*
>
> M., H C . "John Stafford Smith's Library." *Musical Opinion* 26 (1902/03): 33.   [g.a.]

2512   Smith, Robert (of St. Paul's Church-Yard)

MR. WHITE, AUCTIONEER, LONDON

A Catalogue of the Musical Library of . . . Comprehending a Valuable Collection of the Works of the Most Eminent Masters of Italy, England, etc. . . . Some of the Identical Books Used by Mr. Handel, at His Oratorios, &c. . . . Sold . . . May the 18th 1813. [London, 1813.] 16 p. 276 lots.   [GB-Lbl, compiler (copy)]

> **King**, p. 26. Hirsch copy has Ms. note inside flyleaf: "The last sheets [? & ?] were published long after all the former part of the Catalogue and only distributed toward the close of the sale." It may be in Novello's hand since his name appears at the bottom of the title page.

2513   Smith, William Charles; Gerald Coke; Saul Starr; Fritz Busch

LITERATURE

Falconer, Joan O. "Music in the Lilly Library." *Notes* 29 (1972): 5-9.   [g.a.]

> Smith's and Coke's properties, Handeliana; Starr's, over 100,000 pieces of sheet music; Busch's, annotated scores.
>
> → *See also under* **Coke, Gerald** *and under* **Starr** (**2554**, about his record collection)

2514   Smits, Wilhelms

R. W. P. DE VRIES, FIRMA WEDDEPOHL, AMSTERDAM

Catalogus van eene uitmuntende verzameling geillustreerde pracht- en prentwerken, teekeningen, prenten . . . enz. Verscheidenheden en eene belangrijke collectie muziek, welke laatste nagelaten door . . . verkooping . . . 27 en 28 December 1870. . . . Te Amsterdam, 1870. 24 p. 447, 252 + lots. Music, final 250 + lots.   [NL-Avb]

2515   Smolian, Arthur, 1856-1911

KARL MAX POPPE, FIRM, LEIPZIG   LAGER CAT. NO. 2

Musik. Hierin die Bibliothek des verstorbenen Herrn Kapellmeisters und Musikkritikers Prof. Arthur Smolian. Leipzig: Druck von O. Bonde, [1912]. 63 p. 1738 lots.

[US-Wc, -NYp, NL-DHgm, compiler]

> **Folter**, no. 338.

Smyth, James.   *See* **Stone, William Henry** (1885 sale)

Snapper, Mrs. A. L.   *See* **Arundell, Dennis**

2516   Snoxell, William

PUTTICK & SIMPSON, AUCTIONEER, LONDON   CAT. NO. 1847

Catalogue of a Large Collection of Ancient and Modern Music, Including the Library of the Late . . . a Numerous Assemblage of Valuable Musical Instruments . . . Sold June 30th, 1879, and Following Day. [London, 1879.] 30 p. 718 lots. Music, lots 1-500.   [GB-Lbl]

2517   _____

PUTTICK & SIMPSON, AUCTIONEER, LONDON   CAT. NO. 1854

Catalogue of the Collection of Autographs and Manuscripts of the Late . . . Including Specimens of Eminent English Authors, Poets, and Musicians; the Original Autograph Will with Codicils of . . . Handel; Handel's Watch and an Inventory of His Effects Made by Executors after His Death; Also the "Handel Anvil;" Miscellaneous Autograph Letters . . . Sold . . . July 21st, 1879. . . . [London], 1879. 23 p. 134 lots. [US-CHua, GB-Lbl]

Excellent collection of musicians' ALS; many items in each of lots 1-80.

2518 **Society of British Musicians; A Distinguished Professor**
PUTTICK & SIMPSON, AUCTIONEER, LONDON CAT. NO. 888
Catalogue of the Library of Music of the Society . . . Numerous Full Scores . . . Concerted Instrumental Works . . . Also Musical Instruments . . . Sold December 5th, 1865, and Following Day. [London], 1865. 25 p. 653 lots. Music, lots 1-569. [GB-Lbl]

2519 **Söderman, Johann August,** 1832-76
L[indgren], A. "August Södermans manuskriptsamling." *Svensk Musiktidning* 8 (1888): 98-99, 107-09, 113-14, 122-24, 132-34, 138-39, 146-47; 9 (1889): 26-28, 34-36, 51-52, 59-60, 75-77, 82-83, 91-92. [g.a.]

2520 **Somerset, Charles, Sir,** ca. 1588-1665
Brennan, Michael G. "Sir Charles Somerset's Music Books (1622)." *M&L* 74 (1993): 501-18. [g.a.]

2521 **Somerset, Edward, 4th Earl of Worcester,** ca. 1550-1628 (father of preceding)
Brennan, in the article above, notes two manuscript inventories of music books in 1622: "A note of the Musick-bookes, and other things in the Presse, standing in the roome next to the Oulde Gallerie . . . 1622," supplemented by a second list, "A more particular Note of all the Authors and Setts contained in yᵉ aforesaide bookes." Both are transcribed in appendices to the Brennan essay.

2522 **Sonneck, Oscar George Theodore,** 1873-1928
"Library of O. G. Sonneck." [New York, 192- .]
Typescript with additions in ink at US-NYp. Two letters laid in concern the inventory and are dated 1929.

2523 _____
"A List of Books and Pamphlets [formerly owned] by Oscar G. Sonneck Received in the Library of Congress, February 2, 1929 . . . Selection of Books and Pamphlets on Music, Musical Scores, and Non-musical Works, Total ca. 880 Items." 59 leaves. [US-Wc]

2524 **Sonnleithner, Joseph von,** 1766-1835
Deutsch, Walter, and Gerlinde Hofer. *Die Volksmusiksammlung der Gesellschaft der Musikfreunde Wien. Sonnleithner-Sammlung.* Vol. 1. Schriften zur Volksmusik, 2. Wien: Schendl, 1969. 186 p. [US-Wc]
Albrecht: given to Hofbibliothek, now at A-Wn.

2525 _____
Deutsch, Walter. "Materialen aus Oberösterreich in der Sonnleithner-Sammlung des Jahres 1819." In *Beiträge zur Volksmusik in Oberösterreich,* 55-68. Schriften zur Volksmusik, 6. Wien: Schendl, 1982. 1511 nos.

Sonsfeldt Family.   *See* **Wittenhorst-Sonsfeldt, Friedrich Otto von,** 1678-1755

2526   **[Sotheby, S   ]**
S. LEIGH SOTHEBY, AUCTIONEER, LONDON
Catalogue of a Valuable Collection of Miscellaneous Books . . . Music, by Eminent Composers, Operas by Rossini, &c. . . . Sold . . . February 22, 1842. . . . [London, 1842.] 38 p. 1039 lots. Music, 298-318 et passim.   [Film at CRL]

> In truth, not much of a collection.

2527   **Sousberghe, Clerque de Wissocq, Vicomte de**
VYT, CAMILLE (EXP.), GHENT
. . . Catalogue de la bibliothèque musicale délaissée par feu le Vicomte de . . . La vente publique aura lieu le Mardi 28 février et le jour suivant . . . par le ministère de l'hussier L. van Waesberghe, sous la direction de Camille Vyt, libraire expert, en sa salle de ventes, rue des Régnesses, no. 1 . . . à Gand. Gand: Vyt, 1888. 47 p. 658 lots.   [NL-DHgm, US-CHua]

[Southgate, T. L.]   *See under* **Cummings, W. H.** (Reeves's catalog no. 8)

Spence, Sydney A.   *See under* **Hirsch, Paul**

2528   **Spencer, Frances G.**
LITERATURE
Samuel, Harold E. "Notes for Notes [announces gift of Spencer's collection of American printed music to US-wc]." *Notes* 23 (1967): 713-14.

2529   **Speyer, Edward,** 1839-1934
"Dotted Crochet." "Private Musical Collections. I. Mr. Edward Speyer." *MT* 47 (1906): 233-35, 314-16, 383-85.   [g.a.]

> Collection first formed by his father, Wilhelm. **Folter,** nos. 339-40 under
> Wilhelm. Ca. 500 items.

2530   _____
"Verzeichniss der Beethovenschriften in der Sammlung von Edward Speyer in Shenley bei London." *Beethoven-Jahrbuch* 2 (1909): 305-18.   [g.a.]

2531   _____
"The Speyer Collection." In *The Second Sunday Times Book Exhibition, November 12-16, 1934. Catalogue of the Loan Collection . . . ,* lots 1-54. [London: Sunday Times, 1934.]
                                                                                      [US-BUu]

> Whole catalog, 20 p., also includes properties from the Newman Flower
> collection (**894**). **Folter,** no. 339.

2532   _____
Speyer, Mrs. Edward. "Collection of Musical Autographs. Property of Edward Speyer. . . ." [N.p., n.d.] 144 leaves. 379 lots.

> Photocopy of a typescript Liepmannssohn catalog at US-WC with notes,
> proofreader's marks, etc. At end, the original typescript of the English
> language introduction to the catalog.

2533 _____

SOTHEBY & CO., AUCTIONEER, LONDON
Catalogue of Manuscripts, Printed Books, Autograph Letters, etc., Comprising . . . [the properties of various collectors]. *First Editions of Beethoven. Letters and Manuscripts of Musicians, etc.* . . . *Sold* . . . *the 24th of June, 1940, and Following Day.* [London, 1940.] 64 p. 564 lots. [Film at CRL]

Speyer's Beethoven, lots 367-418; Mss. & ALS, 419-52; other ALS scattered in lots 453-65.

King, p. 74, says the bulk of the collection had been purchased by Eisemann in 1935 and notes this Sotheby sale plus a second, 2 July 1940, in which only lots 489-503 were from the Speyer collection. But there were others; see **2534**.

2534 _____

SOTHEBY & CO., AUCTIONEER, LONDON
Catalogue of Valuable Printed Books, Illuminated and Other Manuscripts . . . *Important Letters and Manuscripts of Brahms, Mozart, Schubert, and Other Famous Composers* . . . *Will Be Sold* . . . *the 20th of April, 1943, and Following Day.* [London], 1943. 53 p., illus. [Film at CRL]

"Musical manuscripts and autograph letters of famous composers. Mostly from the celebrated collection of the late Edward Speyer," lots 406-22, pp. 50-53. Lots 394-405 were also musicians' ALS.

2535 _____

KENNETH MUMMERY, FIRM, BOURNEMOUTH   CAT. NO. 11
A Catalogue of Music. Bournemouth, 1957. 32 p. 687 lots. [compiler]

Speyer's properties, lots 127-256. **Folter**, no. 340.

→ *See also under* **Heyer, Wilhelm** (catalog by Unger, 1939)

2536 _____

LITERATURE
Einstein, Alfred. "Die Sammlung Speyer [Musikautographen]." *Philobiblon* 8 (1935): 155-60. [g.a.]

Folter, no. 340, and **Albrecht**.

2537   **Spiegel, Edgar, Edler von Thurnsee,** 1839-1908; **Freiherr von Friedrich Schwy-Koromla, Jr.**
CHRISTIAN M. NEBEHAY, FIRM, VIENNA   LISTE 60
Autographen. Wien, [1959]. 63 p. 657 lots. Mimeographed. [US-NYgr]

Musicians and composers, lots 435-524; singers and actors, 525-650.

Spiker, Samuel Heinrich.   *See under* **Anna Amalia** (Eitner catalog of Joachimsthal, 1884)

2538   **Spilbeeck, Désiré van**
GREFFIER JEAN DIRICKX, AUCTIONEER, ANTWERP
Catalogue des gravures, dessins, eaux-fortes, estampes et livres scientifiques, litteraires . . . *provenant de la collection de feu* . . . *vente* . . . *14 mai 1888, et jours suivants.* . . . Anvers: Impr. B. J. Mees, 1888. 100 p. Music, lots 302-60 ("richement reliées"). [B-Abm]

2539   Spinney, Robert; Dr. Austin (of Cork); [H. Jackson]
PUTTICK & SIMPSON, AUCTIONEER, LONDON   CAT. NO. 663
Catalogue of a Collection of Music, Including the Library of the Late Spinney . . . Capital Vocal Music, Works of Handel in Nearly Every Edition . . . Sold . . . February 4th and Following Day. . . . London, 1861. 821 lots.   [GB-Lbl]

2540   Spitta, Philipp, 1841-94
Wolff, Christoph. "From Berlin to Lódz: The Spitta Collection Resurfaces." *Notes* 46 (1989): 311-27.   [g.a.]
      Albrecht: collection now at D-Bhm.
      → *See also under* **Joachim, Josef** *and* **Kalbeck, Max**

2541   Spoellberch de Louvenjoud, Charles Victor, Vicomte de, 1836-1907
LITERATURE
Kobylanska, Krystyna. "Chopin w zbiorach Chantilly [now in Institut de France, Paris]." *Ruch muzyczny* 18 (1968): 13-14.

2542   Spohr, Ludwig, 1784-1859
GEORG H. WIGAND, FIRM, KASSEL
Verzeichnis der hinterlassenen musikalischen Bibliothek von Louis Spohr, welche entweder im ganzen oder einzeln bis zum 1. Juni 1860 verkauft werden soll. Cassel: Wigand, 1860. 26 p. 657 , 346 lots.
      Not located; cited from **Folter**, no. 341.

2543   _____
LEO LIEPMANNSSOHN, AUCTIONEER, BERLIN   VERST. [12]
Autographen-Sammlung enthaltend Musiker-briefe und Musik-Manuskripte aus dem Nachlasse des berühmter Komponisten . . . 15. und 16. Oktober 1894. Berlin: 1894. 80 p. 694 lots.   [GB-Lhaas]
      Folter, no. 341.

2544   _____
Glenewinkel, Hermann. "Verzeichnis des Musikalien Nachlasses von L. Spohr." *AfMW* 1 (1918/19): 432-36.   [g.a.]
      Includes items not in the Wigand sale (**2542**).

2545   Squier, Ephraim George, 1821-88
BANGS, MERWIN & CO., AUCTIONEER, NEW YORK
Catalogue of the Library of . . . Edited by J. Sabin. To Be Sold by Auctioner . . . April . . . 1876. . . . New York: C. C. Shelley, 1876. 377 p.   [US-NYp]

2546   Stade, Friedrich, 1844-1928
HEINRICH KERLER, FIRM, ULM   ANT. -CAT. NO. 74
Die Bibliothek des Musikdirektors und Organisten Herrn Stade zu Arnstadt i/Th. . . . Ulm, 1883. 14 p. 506 lots.   [GB-Lbl (Hirsch)]

2547 Stagemann, Max

H. & E. MEYER, FIRM, BERLIN   CAT. NO. 102

Musik und Theater. Breifnachlass von. . . . Berlin, [n.d.]. 168 lots.

Not located. Cited from Landré Antiquariat catalog no. 115, lot 36, December 1990.

2548 Stainer, Sir John, 1840-1901

Catalogue of English Song Books Forming a Portion of the Library of . . . , With Appendices of Foreign Song Books, Collections of Carols, Books on Bells, &c. London: printed for private circulation by Novello, Ewer and Co., 1891. Reprint, Boston: Longwood, 1977. 107 p. Ca. 1000 + nos.   [US-Bp, -Wc, -Pc, -PHu; Reprint, g.a.]

Not a sales catalog. Collection now at GB-Ob. **Folter**, no. 342.

→ *See under* **Cummings, W. H.** (sale, October 1919)

2549 _____

HODGSON & CO., AUCTIONEER, LONDON

A Catalogue of Interesting Early Manuscripts and Rare Black-Letter and 16th Century Books. . . . Also the Extensive Collection of Rare Old English Songbooks Formed by the Late . . . Sold . . . May 25th, 1932 and 2 Following Days. London, 1932. 82 p. 909 lots. Music, lots 588-853 (Stainer's) and lots 854-75.   [GB-Lbl, US-Wc]

King, p. 73, and **Albrecht**. The collection was purchased by Walter N. Harding and at his death was acquired by GB-Ob.

2550 _____

HODGSON & CO., AUCTIONEER, LONDON

A Catalogue of Valuable Books, Comprising . . . the Property of the Late Dr. J. F. Farrar. Also, Books on Music, Singing and Dancing from the Library of the Late . . . Sold . . . December 5th, 1934, and 2 Following Days. London, 1934. 62 p. 957 lots.

[GB-Lbl, US-Nyp, compiler (priced)]

Third day's sale, Stainer's properties, lots 636-768. **King**: residue from the 1932 sale (**2549**). **Albrecht** says Stainer's 19th-century hymnbooks are now at GB-Lbl.

Stainfurth, F.   *See under* **Vaughan, W. A.**

2551 Stanford, John Frederick

PUTTICK & SIMPSON, AUCTIONEER, LONDON   CAT. NO. 2030

Catalogue of a Large Collection of Instrumental Music, Including the Libraries of the Islington Musical Society, the Lynn Philharmonic Society, and That of the Late . . . Symphonies and Overtures . . . Standard Works . . . Choral Music . . . Sold . . . June 22th [sic] *1881.* [London, 1881.] 18 p. 492 lots.   [GB-Lbl]

Properties are not differentiated.

2552 Stanley, John, 1714-86

MR. CHRISTIE, AUCTIONEER, LONDON

A Catalogue of All the Capital Musical Instruments, Extensive and Valuable Collection of Manuscript and Other Music, by the Most Eminent Composers, Late the Property of . . . Sold . . . the 24th of June, 1786. . . . [London], 1786. 4 p. 92 lots. Music, lots 1-54.

[GB-Lbl, compiler (copy)]

2553   Starr, Dorothy

Gibbs, Jason. "Dorothy Starr Sheet Music Collection at S[an] F[rancisco] P[ublic] L[ibrary]." *MLA Newsletter* 8, no. 1 (fall 1993): 9-10.

> Estimated at 300,000 pieces!

2554   Starr, Frederick A., 1858-1963

Gillis, Frank J. "The Starr Collection of Recordings from the Congo (1906) in the Archives of Traditional Music, Indiana University." *Folklore and Folkmusic Archivist* 10, no. 3 (spring 1968): 49-62.   [g.a.]

> See **2513** for information about his music in the Lilly Library at Indiana University.

2555   Startz, Gotthardt

MATTH. LEMPERTZ, AUCTIONEER, AACHEN
Katalog der nachgelassenen Sammlung von Gemälden, Alterthümern und Musikalien des Herrn . . . Versteigerung in Aachen . . . October 1871. . . . Aachen, 1871. 13 p. 289 lots. Music, pp. 6-11 (155 lots, but many more items).   [NL-Dhrk]

2556   Stasov, Vladimir Vasilevich

Kollektsia rukopisnykh muzykal'nykh p'es, spisannykh v Rime v 1852-1854 godakh abbatom Santini iz raznykh muzykal'nykh arkhivov i prinesennkh v dar Biblioteke S. S. Stavosym. V kn: Otchet Publichnoi biblioteki za 1870 god. St. Petersburg, 1872.

> Ms.? Cited from **Koltypina** (1963), p. 50.

> → *See also* information under **Santini**

2557   _____

LITERATURE
Komarova, V. D. "Iz Stasovskago arkhiva. I. Vladimir Stasov v Italii (1851-1854)." In *Sbornik Puskinskago doma na 1923 god,* pp. ? Petrograd, 1922.

> Not located. Cited from **Fédorov**, p. 61:23.

2558   Steed, A   O   ; et al.

WILLIAM REEVES, FIRM, LONDON   CAT. NO. 9
Catalogue of Music and Musical Literature, Ancient and Modern . . . Music from Several Libraries Recently Purchased (Including That of the Late A. O. Steed and John Hiles, Carl Engel, and Others. . . . London, 1882-83. Part 2-3, pp. 30-82. No lotting.   [GB-LReeves]

2559   Steifel, E.

"Ulm II: Musikdrucke und Musikhandschrift der Schermar-Bibliothek." *MGG* 12, cols. 1045-46.   [g.a.]

2560   _____

Wiegandt, O. "Anton Schermar und seine Bibliothek in Ulmer Münster." *Schwäbische Heimat* 5 (1954): 159-.

> Not examined. Cited from **Benton 2**:108, no. 272.

2561   Stellfeld, Jean Auguste, 1881-1952

UNIVERSITY OF MICHIGAN LIBRARY
"Stellfeld Collection Checklist Classifications: ML & MT." Ann Arbor, 1954. 273 leaves. Typewritten.   [US-Wc (carbon copy)]

2562 _____

LITERATURE

Pols, André M. "Die Musikbibliothek Stellfeld in Antwerpen." *Philobiblon* 7 (1934): 367-70. Illus.
[g.a.]

2563 _____

Piscaer, Anny. "De bibliotheek Stellfeld." *Caecilia en de muziek* 93, no. 10 (1936): 199-207.
[g.a.]

2564 _____

Kerr, Jessica M. "The Stellfeld Library in Antwerp." *R. C. M. Magazine* 34 (July 1938): 53-56.
[g.a.]

2565 _____

Sutherland, Gordon A., Louise E. Cuyler, and Hans T. David. *The University of Michigan's Purchase of the Stellfeld Music Library.* [Washington, 1954.] 19 p.   [g.a.]
    Offprint from *Notes* 12 (1954): 41-57.

2566 _____

Wilson, B. E. "Something to Say About the Stellfeld Collection." *Notes* (University of Michigan Library) 1 (19 November 1954): 9-12.   [g.a.]

2567 **Stephen, J. Leslie** (piano maker, London)
HYMAN LEONARD, FIRM, LONDON   CAT. NO. 63
["Remarkable Collection of Printed and Manuscript Material Relating to the Construction of Pianos and Other Keyboard Instruments . . . Over One Thousand Items." Offered for sale en bloc by Hyman on the wrapper of his catalog 63, 1954.]
    No other information available. No list offered.

2568 **Stern, Julius,** 1820-83
HELMUT & ERNEST MEYER , AUCTIONEER, BERLIN   CAT. NO. 52
Autographen, Literatur: Naturwissenschaften, Kunst: Geschichte, sowie eine umfangreiche Musikersammlung . . . Versteigering 12. Juni, 1936. Berlin, 1936. 50 p. 761 lots. Music, lots 331-556.
    Folter, no. 343, says more than 900 autographs of musicians.

Stern, Ladt.   *See* **Herbert, Edward Robert Henry**

2569 **Sternfeld, Frederick William,** b. 1914
BLOOMSBURY BOOK AUCTIONS, LONDON
Catalogue of Printed Books, Music and Manuscripts . . . Sold . . . 18 December 1986. . . . London, 1986. Music, lots 1-93, pp. 3-14.   [compiler]

2570 **Steuermann, Edward,** 1892-1964
Dunsby, Jonathan Mark. "The Steuermann Collection." *Journal of the Arnold Schoenberg Institute* 2, no. 1 (October 1977): 63-71.   [g.a.]
    With a listing.

2571 Stevens, Richard John Samuel, 1757-1837

PUTTICK & SIMPSON, AUCTIONEER, LONDON CAT. NO. 1202

Catalogue of a Large and Varied Collection of Music, Including the . . . Musical Library of . . . [and a Stock of Musical Instruments, the Property of Thomas Kennedy] *. . . Sold . . . March 27, 1872.* [London, 1872.] 23 p. 708 lots. Music, lots 1-447. Stevens's music, lots 324-89.

[GB-Lbl]

> **King**, p. 58: much went to the Royal Academy of Music. It included a large number of catches and glees.

2572 Stevens, Wallace, 1879-1955

Stegman, Michael O. "Wallace Stevens and Music: A Discography of Stevens' Phonograph Record Collection." *Wallace Stevens Journal* 3, nos. 3/4 (1979): 79-97. [g.a.]

2573 Stiedry-Wagner, Erika; Fritz Stiedry

Dunsby, Jonathan Mark. "The Stiedry Collection." *Journal of the Arnold Schoenberg Institute* 1, no. 3 (June 1977): 152-69. [g.a.]

> With a catalog of the collection.

Stobler, Paul. *See* **Hobler, Paul**

2574 Stochove, Nicolas; Charles Heems

Terlinck, E. J. *Catalogue d'une belle collection de livres . . . suivi de tableaux, estampes . . . objets divers, musique et instruments, délaissés par feu. . . .* Bruges, [1812]. 2, 92 p. 1688 lots. Music, lots 1-107. [B-Gu]

2575 Stock, Walter Henry, 1905-93

King, A. Hyatt. "Walter Henry Stock, 1905-1993: An Appreciation." *Brio* 30 (1993): 61-62.

[g.a.]

2576 Stockhausen, Ernst von; Gustav E. Schwender

VON ZAHN & JAENSCH, FIRM, DRESDEN CAT. NO. 191

Musik. Hierin die Bibliotheken der Herren Ernst von Stockhausen und Gustav E. Schwender (Richard-Wagner Litteratur), sowie Bibliotheks-Dubletten. . . . Dresden, 1906. 74 p. 2333 lots.

> Wagner items, lots 927-1078. GB-Lbl (Hirsch 5901).

2577 Stockhausen, Julius, 1826-1906; **Carl Gottfried Wilhelm Taubert,** 1811-91; **Maurice Schlesinger,** 1798-1871

LEO LIEPMANNSSOHN, AUCTIONEER, BERLIN CAT. NO. 37

Katalog einer Autographen-Sammlung, bestehend aus wertvollen Musik-Manuskripten a. d. Nachlässen von Julius Stockhausen und Wilhelm Taubert und des Musikverlegers Maurice Schlesinger, Paris . . . sowie aus Autographen von Dichtern, Schriftstellern, Schauspielern, . . . Versteigerung am 4. und 5. November 1907. . . . Berlin, 1908. 120 p. 483 lots. Music, lots 1-287. [US-NYp, -Wc, -Bp, NL-Avb, GB-Lbl]

> According to Günther Mecklenberg's *Vom Autographen Sammeln* (Marburg: Stargardt, 1963), Schlesinger's collection included autographs from Meyerbeer's library. The sale is noted in *MT* 48 (1907): 786, with a list of some rarities sold and their prices. **Folter**, no. 344. [g.a.]

2578 Stockhausen, Julius, 1826-1906; **Louis Lüstner**
Leo Liepmannssohn, firm, Berlin   Cat. no. 196
Orchestermusik in Partituren, z. T. aus dem Besitz von J. Stockhausen und Louis Lüstner. . . .
Berlin, [n.d., 1916?]. 38 p. 765 lots.   [NL-Avb, GB-Lbl]
        Folter, no. 345.

2579 Stoelzer, Ernst Richard, 1864-1947
The Stoelzer Collection at Adelphi University: An Inventory. Gary E. Cantrell, supervising
editor; Madelein M. Hogan, compiler. . . . Garden City, N.Y.: Adelphi University Libraries, 1985.
73 p., illus. Music, pp. 26-73.   [g.a.]

Stokoe, John. *See* **Butler, George** (sale, 1853)

2580 Stolberg-Wernigerödische Bibliothek
        Partly responsible for the collection: Graf Wolfgang Ernst Stolberg and
        Graf Albrecht Stolberg-Wernigerode, 1886-.

2581 ──────────
        List & Francke, firm, Leipzig   Cat. no. 217
        Verzeichnis . . . Doubletten der Gräflich Stol'bergschen Bibliothek in Wernigerode.
        Kirchenmusik, Hymnologie. . . . Leipzig, 1890. 32 p. 884 lots.   [NL-Avb]

2582 ──────────
        "Catalogue of Music and Books on Music in the . . . Bibliothek." [1938?] 79
        leaves. Mimeographed from typescript.   [US-Wc]

            At head of title: Hart in Breslaus, Berlin Verlagsbuchhändler und Antiquar.
            Prepared in connection with an auction to be held 26-28 April 1938. "Kurze
            systematische übersicht der Bibliothek," 23 leaves laid in. No printed catalog
            found.

2583 ──────────
        Literature
        Eitner, Robert. "Stolberg-Wernigeroder Bibliothek im Harz." *Leipziger Allgemeine Musik Zeitung*
        3 (1868): 247, 253-54.
                Albrecht.
                → *See also under* **Voullième, Ernst**

2584 Stone, William Henry, 1830-99?; **James Smyth** (Bandmaster); **Harold Thomas**
        Puttick & Simpson, auctioneer, London   Cat. no. 2369
        Catalogue of a Large and Interesting Assemblage of Musical Properties, Including the
        Collections of . . . [musical instruments] *. . . Also the Very Extensive Library of Music, Comprising*
        a Large Number of Full Scores of Operas, Oratorios . . . &c. by Celebrated Composers. A
        Large Quantity of Valuable MS. Arrangements for Full Band . . . Sold November and Following
        Day, 1885. . . . [London], 1885. 12, 20 p. 357 lots. Music, 1st day, lots 301-57; 2nd day, 453
        lots.   [GB-Lbl]

2585   Stone, William Henry; John Bernard Sale, 1779-1856; **A Well-Known Amateur**
PUTTICK & SIMPSON, AUCTIONEER, LONDON   CAT. NO. 2399
Catalogue of an Extensive Collection of Ancient and Modern Music, the Properties of Dr. Stone, of Dean's Yard, the Late Mr. J. B. Sale, That of a Well-Known Amateur . . . Instrumental Works, String Solos, Duets [etc.] *Flute Music, Cathedral Services . . . Works on Music History and Theory, Scarce Treatises, a Few Manuscript Compositions . . . Sold March 22nd, 1886.* . . . [London], 1886. 21 p. 602 lots. Lots not differentiated.   [GB-Lbl]

2586   Stradivari, Antonio, 1644?-1737
Sacconi, Simone F. *Die Geheimnisse Stradivaris, mit dem Katalog des Stradivari-Nachlasses im Städtischen Museum "Ala Ponzone" von Cremona . . . Übersetzung aus dem Italienischen von Olga Adelmann. . . .* Fachbuchreihe Das Musikinstrument, 31. Frankfurt/Main: Verlag Das Musikinstrument, 1976. xx, 238 p.   [US-Wc]

2587   Strange, Harold
JOHANNESBURG, PUBLIC LIBRARY, STRANGE COLLECTION
Catalogue of Music in the Strange Collection of Africana [music composed by South Africans and music dealing with South Africa or South African events, no matter where published, vocal music with Afrikaans or Bantu words, and music published in South Africa]. Johannesburg, 1944. 118 p.   [US-Wc, -NYp]

—————————. *Supplement.* Johannesburg, 1945. 21 leaves.

2588   Stratton, George W., 1830-1901
N. H. WEST SWANZEY, STRATTON FREE LIBRARY AND ART GALLERY
Catalogue. [1st]-2nd ed., 1865, 1900. Boston: David Clapp & Son, 1885-[1900]. 2 vols., illus.   [US-Bp]

"A present to his native village. . . . "

2589   Strauch,
LIST & FRANCKE, FIRM, LEIPZIG   CAT. NO. ?
Verzeichniss einer werthvollen Sammlung von Werken aus der theoretischen und praktischen Musik, aus dem Nachlasse des Herrn Cantor Strauch in Ernsthal. Leipzig, 1863.   [GB-LHaas]

Not otherwise located.

2590   Strauss, Franz and Alice
LITERATURE
Ott, Alfons. "Documenta musicae domesticae Straussiana." In *Festschrift Dr. Franz Strauss,* 65-81. Tutzing: Hans Schneider, 1967.   [g.a.]

2591   Stravinsky, Igor, 1882-1971
Shepard, John. "The Stravinsky Nachlass: A Provisional Checklist of Music Manuscripts." *Notes* 40 (1984): 719-50.

Miscellaneous music materials, chiefly S's own works, once deposited at US-NYp, now in the Sacher Stiftung.

→ *See here also under* **Sacher, Paul**

2592 _____

LITERATURE

Rosenthal, Albi. "Die Stravinsky-Nachlass in der Paul Sacher Stiftung." In *Stravinsky: Sein Nachlass, sein Bild,* 19-22. Basel: Kunstmen, 1984.   [g.a.]

2593 Street, J P

PUTTICK & SIMPSON, AUCTIONEER, LONDON   CAT. NO. 224

Catalogue of the Musical Library of the Late. . . . Comprising Glees and Vocal Music, Sacred Music, Including Some Early and Rare Works. Handel's Works, Arnold's Edition, Complete; Purcell's Works, a Very Complete Collection, Several in MS., Also Musical Instruments . . . Sold August 14th, 1851. . . . [London], 1851. 16 p. 389 lots. Music, lots 1-148, 180-389.

[GB-Lbl, US-NYp]

King, p. 49. **Coral.**

2594 _____

PUTTICK & SIMPSON, AUCTIONEER, LONDON   CAT. NO. 972

Catalogue of Ancient and Modern Music . . . Handel's Works by Arnold, Psalms of David. . . [etc.] *. . . Sold February 21st and Following Day. . . .* [London], 1867. 831 lots.   [GB-Lbl]

2595 Streit, Sigismund

Bellermann, Heinrich. "Verzeichniss der grosstenteils von Sigismund Streit dem grauen Kloster geschenkten Musikalien." In Berlin, Gymnasium zum grauen Kloster, *Zur feier des Wohlthäterfestes im berlinischen Gymnasium zum grauen Kloster, Sonnabend, den 20 December, 1856 . . .* , 5-18. Berlin: Nauck'sche Buchdr., 1856.   [US-Wc, -NYp]

2596 Strickland, W H ; J W Matthew

PUTTICK & SIMPSON, AUCTIONEER, LONDON   CAT. NO. 4108

Catalogue of Musical Properties, Comprising . . . [Musical Instruments] *and a Small Library of Music, the Property of the Late W. H. Strickland and J. W. Matthew . . . Sold April 30th, 1907.* [London], 1907. 16 p. 331 lots. Music, lots 205-331.   [GB-Lbl]

"Small" libraries—and not very important: Strickland's lots 205-68; Matthew's 269-331.

2597 Strong, George Templeton, 1856-1948

Matthey, Jean-Louis. *George Templeton Strong: Inventaire du fonds musical.* Lausanne: Bibl. cantonale et universitaire, 1973. 134 p.   [g.a.]

Thematic.

Stüchelberg, E. A. *See* **Schlatter, V.**

2598 Stuart, John, 3rd Earl of Bute, 1713-92

Alm, Irene. *Catalog of Venetian Librettos at the University of California, Los Angeles.* University of California Publications. Catalogs and Bibliographies, 9. Berkeley: University of California Press, 1993. xxviii, 1053 p. 1215 items.   [g.a.]

The collection was once that of the Earl. Acquired by private treaty. Collections from his library sold by Sotheby's in 1785, 1794, and 1798 contained no music materials. Collection catalog now available on microfilm from Harvester Corp.

2599   Stumpff, Johann Andreas
PUTTICK & SIMPSON, AUCTIONEER, LONDON   CAT. NO. 19
Catalogue of the Musical Collections of the Late . . . Comprising Original Manuscripts of Mozart, Beethoven, &c. . . . Also the Stock in Trade [Musical Instruments] *. . . Sold . . . March 30th, 1847, and Following Day.* London, 1847. 13 p. 379 lots.   [GB-Lbl; compiler (Xerox)]

> An important collection: Mozart holographs ". . . purchased . . . of the widow of Mozart in 1811 for £350" (**King**, p. 46, thinks more likely from J. A. André!), lots 36-44, ten great string quartets, including 6 dedicated to Haydn. Other Mss. include 9 autographs of Beethoven, lots 67-73, others by Spohr and Cipriani Potter.
>
> **King**, in his *Mozart in Retrospect* (London: Oxford University Press, 1955), 81-88, provides fascinating aspects of Stumpff's acquisition of the manuscripts and subsequent attempts to dispose of them, even by raffle. King notes a letter from Stumpff to Ludwig Storch and published by Storch in 1857 where Stumpff says he paid £150 for the Mozart treasures, far less than he claims in Puttick's catalog.

2600 _____
Farrenc, Aristide. "Extrait du catalogue de vente del la bibliothèque de M. Bourret . . . 1735." *Revue de musique ancienne et moderne* 1 (1856): 559-60.   [NL-DHgm, D-Mbs, F-Pn]

> Includes a short list of the Mozart holographs in Stumpff's collection.

2601 _____
Kallir, Rudolf F. "A Beethoven Relic." *MR* 9 (1948): 173-78.   [g.a.]

> The same appeared in German in Kallir's *Autographen-sammler - Lebenslänglich* ([Zürich]: Atlantis, [1977]), 20-21, illustration and 113-17. See **1495**.

Stuttgarter Hofkapelle.   *See under* **Eberhard III,** 1628-57

2602   Succi, Emilia
. . . Catalogo con brevi cenni biografici e succinte descrizioni degli autografi e documenti di celebri o distinti musicisti posseduti da. . . . Bologna: Società tipografica già compositori, 1888. ix, 179 p. 886 lots.   [US-Wc, -NYp, -Bp]

> For the "Mostra Internazionale di Music" in Bologna, 1888. Now at I-Baf.

2603   Sullivan, Sir Arthur Seymour, 1842-1900
PUTTICK & SIMPSON, AUCTIONEER, LONDON   CAT. NO. 3510
Catalogue of Music, a Portion of the Library of the Late . . . Sold February 28th, 1901. [London], 1901. 13 p. 190 lots.   [GB-Lbl]

2604 _____
Allen, Alfred Reginald. *Sir Arthur Sullivan: Composer and Personage. . . .* In collaboration with Gale R. D'Luhy. New York: Pierpont Morgan Library, [1975]. xxviii, 215 p.   [g.a.]

> Catalog of an exhibition at US-NYpm.

2605   Suppan, Wolfgang
"Das Blasmusikarchiv Suppan auf der Pürgg/Steiermark." *Pannonische Forschungsstelle Oberschützen, Arbeitsberichte - Mitteilungen* 2 (September 1991): 111-20.

Suringar, Hugo.   *See under* **Hartog, Jacques**

Sussex, Duke of.   *See* **Augustus Frederick**

Swain, Rev. John.   *See* Anonymous section (sale of 15 March 1790)

2606   Swan, Alfred J., 1890-1970
Velimirović, Miloš Gottfried, "The Swan Music Collection." *Chapter and Verse* (University of Virginia Library) 5 (1977): 20-21.   [g.a.]
      Rare music scores and books.

2607   Swieten, Gottfried van, Baron
LITERATURE
Holschneider, Andreas. "Die musikalische Bibliothek. . . ." *Bericht über den internationalen Musikwissenschaftliche Kongress, Kassel, 1962,* 174-78. Kassel: Bärenreiter, 1963.   [g.a.]

2608   Sydney, John (of Hunton, Kent)
LEIGH AND SOTHEBY, AUCTIONEER, LONDON
A Catalogue of the Very Extensive Collection of Music, the Property of the Late . . . Oratorios and Operas . . . Instrumental and Pianoforte Music, Italian Operas, &c., &c. . . . Sold Monday, November 8, 1813, and Three Following Days. . . . [London, 1813.] 25 p. 741 lots.
[US-R, compiler]

2609   Sykes, Lady Mark Elizabeth
PUTTICK & SIMPSON, AUCTIONEER, LONDON   CAT. NO. 29
Remaining Library of the Late . . . Including an Extensive Assemblage of the Works of Handel, Including the Collected Works by Arnold; Musical Literature . . . Also Musical Instruments . . . Sold May 22, 1847. [London], 1847. 9 p. 245 lots.   [GB-Lbl]

2610   Synge, Edw__
MILLARD, AUCTIONEER, GLOUCESTER
[According to **Lugt** 10,967, an auction of 30 August 1825 containing music, books, etc. No other information is available; no catalog located.]

2611   Szirmay-Keczer, Anna
Hlawiczka, Karol. *Tánce polskie ze zbioru Anny Szirmay-Keczer przelom XVII i XVIII w.* Zródla do historii muzyki polskiej, 6. Warszawa, 1963.
      Collection now at CS-Mms. Not examined; cited from *RILM.*

2612   _____
Kresanek, J. "Die Sammlung Szirmay-Keczer." *Studia musicologica* 6 (1964): 39-66.

2613   Szymanowski, Karol, 1882-1937
LITERATURE
Pinkwart, Maciej. "Losy biblioteki Szymanowskiego." *Ruch muzyczny* 25 (1977): 17-18.   [g.a.]

2614 [Tabart,   ]
PUTTICK & SIMPSON, AUCTIONEER, LONDON   CAT. NO. 600
Catalogue of a Large Collection of Music, Including the Surplus Stock of an Eminent Publishing House; the Library of an Amateur Deceased [Tabart?], *etc. . . . Handel's Works . . . Works on Music History and Theory . . . Portraits of Musical Celebrities . . . Numerous Musical Instruments . . . Sold . . . November 11, 1859 and Following Day.* [London], 1859. 32 p. 860 lots. Music, lots 1-785.   [GB-Lbl]

2615 Tait, C. B.
Catalogue of the Tait Library, Edinburgh. Edinburgh: Alex. Laurie & Co., 1839. 15 p.
                                                                                        [US-CA]

2616 _____
TAIT & NISBET, AUCTIONEER, EDINBURGH
Catalogue of the Extensive and Valuable Private Library, the Original Manuscript in Burns' Handwriting of His Correspondence with George Thomson . . . Together with the Extensive Collection of Classical Music of the Late Mr. C. B. Tait [. . . Sold by Tait & Nisbet, 12 November and 4 following days, 1852]. [Edinburgh, 1852.] 63 p.   [GB-Lbl, US-CA]
        King says music, lots 1096-120 only.

2617 Talich, Václav, 1883-1961
Kuna, Milan. *Katalog pozustalosti národního umelecke Václava Talicha.* Beroun: Orkesní muzeum v Berouné, 1979. 156 p.
        Not located. Cited from *RILM.*

2618 Taneyev, Sergei Ivanovich, 1856-1915
Nauchnaya muzikal'naya Biblioteka imeni S. I. Taneyeva. [Moskva?], 1966.
        Collection at USSR-Mk since 1924 (*NG*-L: 796). Catalog not located.

Taparelli, R. *See* **Azeglio, Massimo Taparelli**

2619 Taphouse, Thomas William, 1838-1905
SOTHEBY, WILKINSON & HODGE, AUCTIONEER, LODON
Catalogue of the Valuable and Interesting Library, Consisting of Ancient and Modern Printed Music, Musical Manuscripts, and Collections of the Late . . . (Late Mayor of Oxford) . . . Sold . . . Monday the 3rd of July, 1905 and Following Day. . . . London: J. Davy & Sons, [1905]. 87 p. 876 lots.   [US-NYp, -Wc, -SM, GB-Lbl (Hirsch 480)]
        King, p. 71, and **Albrecht** say 123 lots were purchased by GB-LEc.

2620 _____
WILLIAM REEVES, FIRM, LONDON   CAT. NO. 124
. . . Music and Musical Literature, Ancient and Modern, Second-Hand. . . . Some Interesting Manuscripts and Other Items from the Recently Dispersed Taphouse Collection. London, 1905. 28 p.   [GB-LReeves]
        Noted in *ZiMG* 6 (1904/05): 488.

2621 _____

LITERATURE

"Dotted Crochet." "The Musical Library of. . . . " *MT* 45 (1904): 629-36.

[US-NYgr, GB-LReeves]

> With notes about his instrument collection and photographs.
>
> **Folter**, no. 346, notes, but not the two preceding catalogs. He does cite a 1906 catalog of the firm of Ellis whose title page claims that "The Books and Manuscripts . . . are mainly derived from the celebrated libraries of . . . Julian Marshall . . . and . . . Taphouse." Probably more from the former than the latter since Ellis's previous sale, no. 7, in 1905 included a "portion of the Marshall Collection."

2622 **Tappert, Wilhelm,** 1830-1907

BERLIN ?

Katalog der Spezialausstellung W. Tappert. Die Entwicklung der Notenschrift. Berlin, 1898.

> Not located. Cited from **Wolffheim** catalog 1, in item 340, described as "Kat. seiner Ausstellung. . . . "

2623 **Tardini, Vincenzo,** d. 1903

Roncaglia, Gino. "Intorno a una biblioteca musicale donata dall famiglia Tardini." *Accademia nazionale di scienze lettere ed arti di Modena, Atti e memorie . . .* ser. 6, 3 (1961): xxxi-xxxvi.

[compiler (Xerox)]

Tauber, Mrs. Diana Napier. *See under* **Kirby** (Sotheby sale of 16 April 1975)

Taubert, Wilhelm. *See under* **Stockhausen, Julius**

2624 **Taussig, Otto,** 1888-1969

Mühlhäuser, Siegfried. *Die Handschriften und Varia in Schubertiana-Sammlung Taussig in der Universitätsbiblithek Lund.* Quellenkatalog zur Musik-Geschichte, 17. Wilhelmshaven: Heinrichshofen, 1981. 203 p., plates. [g.a.]

2625 _____

LITERATURE

Orel, Alfred. "Schubertiana in Schweden." In *Musa - mens - musici: Im Gedanken an Walther Vetter,* 297-307. Leipzig: Verlag für Musik, 1969. [g.a.]

> In "Übersicht über die Schubertiana in Schweden," pp. 301-06, Orel locates several hundred Schubert items. Major collections are those at the Stiftelsen Musikulturens Främjande in Stockholm and Otto Taussig's in S-L (Lund) and in Malm. Some of Taussig's collections are also in Stockholm. Other "Kopiensammlungen" noted are those of Ebner, Kner, Schindler, Stadler, and Witteczek.

[Taylor, Mr .] *See under* **Grant, Miss** (sale, 22 July 1909)

2626 **Taylor, Colin**

LITERATURE

Smith, Barry. "The Colin Taylor Collection." *Jagger Journal* 10 (1989/90): 1-5.

> Not examined; cited from *MLA Newsletter* 5/6 (1991): 12.

2627 **Taylor, Edward,** 1784-1863 (Gresham Professor of Music)
PUTTICK & SIMPSON, AUCTIONEER, LONDON   CAT. NO. 789
Catalogue of the . . . Musical Library and Musical Instruments of the Late . . . Sold . . . December 3rd, 1863 and Two Following Days. . . . [London], 1863. 69 p. 1208 lots. Music, lots 1-1,148.   [US-NYp, GB-Lbl]
> **King,** p. 55, **Blogie, Albrecht.**

2628 _____
PUTTICK & SIMPSON, AUCTIONEER, LONDON   CAT. NO. 1389
Catalogue of a Collection of Ancient and Modern Music, Including the Library of a Professor . . . Rare Treatises, Old Manuscript Compositions . . . Also Musical Instruments . . . Sold April 29, 1873. [London], 1873. 26 p. 551 lots (many more items).   [GB-Lbl]
> "From the Collections of Dr. Burney . . . and Richard Clark," lots 183-220. "Orchestral Parts . . . from the Library of Edward Taylor," lots 221-327.

2629 _____
PUTTICK & SIMPSON, AUCTIONEER, LONDON   CAT. NO. 1412
Catalogue of a Collection of Miscellaneous Music, Comprising Many Scarce and Valuable Treatises on the History and Theory of Music . . . Also Musical Instruments . . . Sold . . . July 30th, 1873, and Following Day. London, 1873. 24 p. 535 lots.   [GB-Lbl]
> Music, lots 1-420, but many more items: an unusual number of opera scores and excellent collections of early treatises, manuscripts, association items, Benjamin Cooke's *Diary* "written while under the tuition of Dr. Pepusch," correspondence, and a few autographs—Gigli, Guglielmi, Neukomm, and others, interspersed.

2630 **Taylor, Isidore Justin Séverin, Baron,** 1789-1879
J. TECHENER, AUCTIONEER, PARIS
Catalogue de livres rare et précieux composant la première partie de la bibliothèque de . . . , dont la vente se fera . . . 17 Octobre 1848 et jours suivants . . . Ministère, Lenormant de Villeneuve. . . . Paris: J. Techener, 1848. xii, 511 p.   [US-NH, -CA, -NYp, -Cn]

2631 _____
J. TECHENER, AUCTIONEER, PARIS
Catalogue de livres anciens et modernes, rares et curieux sur les beaux-arts, la littérature . . . principalement sur l'art dramatique, provenant de la bibliothèque de m. le baron T***. 3 vols. Paris: J. Techener, 1876-77.   [US-BE]
> 2ᵉ partie, "Théâtre" . . . vente 10-13 April 1876 (iv, 136 p., 136 lots).

2632 _____
J. TECHENER, AUCTIONEER, PARIS
Catalogue de la bibliothèque dramatique de feu le Baron Taylor, dont la vent aura lieu du lundi 27 November au mercredi 13 Dec. 1893. Par M. Delestre. . . . Paris: Techener, 1893. xvi, 491 p.   [US-Wc, -NYp, -COu, -U, -CA]

2633   Taylor, John Bianchi, 1801-76

PUTTICK & SIMPSON, AUCTIONEER, LONDON   CAT. NO. 2072

Catalogue of a Large Collection of Music from the Libraries of Bianchi Taylor . . . the Liverpool Festival Choral Society, and Other Sources . . . Extensive Collection of Psalmodies . . . Organ Music . . . Works for Choral Societies . . . Scarce MSS., Some Autograph . . . Sold January 23rd, 1882. [London], 1882. 21 p. 434 lots.   [GB-Lbl]

Taylor, P.   *See* **Sale, John** (sale, 1828)

2634   Taylor, Colonel Thomas

S. LEIGH SOTHEBY & JOHN WILKINSON, AUCTIONEER, LONDON

Catalogue of the Library of the Late . . . Containing . . . a Collection of Modern Music, an Invaluable Series of the Libretti of the Most Popular Operas Ever Produced in 224 Volumes . . . Sold . . . 21st January, 1861. . . . [London, 1861.] 52 p. 934 lots. Music, lots 58-91, 538-59.

[Film at CRL]

2635   Taylor, William Lawrence, 1829-1910

UNIVERSITY OF ABERDEEN LIBRARY

. . . Catalogue of the Taylor Collection of Psalm Versions. Aberdeen University Studies, 85. Aberdeen: University Press, 1921. v, 307 p. Ca. 1700 vols.

[US-Wc, -BE, -AA, -CA]

> Collection of ca. 1700 hymnbooks (**Albrecht**) given to the school by William Dey. Catalog first printed in the *Aberdeen University Library Bulletin* from no. 3 to no. 23, here revised. **King,** p. 87.

2636   Tcherepnine, Alexandre, 1899-1977

RYUGINSHA, PUBLISHER, TOKYO

Modern Japanese Music: Catalogue of Collection Alexandre Tcherepnine. Tokyo, [193-?] 6 p., facs.   [US-Wc]

> **Folter,** no. 348, says [4] p., 34 nos.

2637   Tena, Vicente

LITERATURE

Siemens Hernández, Lothar. "El P. Vicente Tena y su tarea de recopilación del patrimonio musical valenciano." *Revista de musicologia* 8 (1985): 198.   [g.a.]

2638   Terby, Joseph

Catalogue de la belle et rare collection de musique religieuse, dramatique et instrumentale, délaissée par M. Joseph Terby, maître de chapelle de l'église primaire de Saint-Pierre à Louvain . . . vente . . . 24 octobre et jour suivant, 1860. Louvain: Cuelens, 1860. 50 p. 906 + 25 + 296 lots.   [B-Br]

2639   _____

Catalogue de la belle collection de violons italiens, arches de Tourte . . . vente . . . 17 juillett 1879. . . . [Louvain], 1879. 14 p.   [B-Br]

> Only a few instruments; principally literature for and about violins.

2640   Tereza Christina Maria, Empress Consort of Pedro II, Emperor of Brazil, 1822-89

Rio de Janeiro, Biblioteca nacional

Ediçōes raras de obras musicais, coleçao Teresa Cristina Maria. Rio de Janeiro: Biblioteca nacional, [1955]. 24 p. 88 items (rare!).   [US-BUu]

2641   Terry, Léonard, 1816-82

Liège, Conservatoire royal de musique, Bibliothèque

Catalogue de la bibliothèque du Conservatoire royal de musique. Fonds Terry, par Eugène Monseur. 3 vols. (to date; planned for 8). [Liège, 1959- .]

[US-NYp; US-Wc and -BUu have Pt. III]

I. Musique dramatiques.

II. Musique vocale.

III. Musique instrumentale.

2642   _____

Liège, Conservatoire royal de musique, Bibliothèque

Inventaire général des manuscrits anciens du Conservatoire . . . [by] *Maurice Barthelemy, Bibliothécaire.* Liége: DUP, 1977.   [B-Lc]

Includes 3 collections: 1. Réserve générale; 2. Fonds Debroux; 3. Fonds Terry. 768 of 894 numbers in the catalog are Terry's.

2643   _____

Liège, Conservatoire royal de musique

Catalogue des imprimés musicaux anciens . . . [by] *Maurice Barthélémy.* Liège: Mardaga, 1992. 219 p.

Contains collections of Léonard Terry, the Brigode de Kemlandt family, and that of Prof. De Glimes.

2644   _____

Literature

Auda, Antoine. "Léonard Terry, professeur, compositeur, chef d'orchestre et musicologue liégois." In International Society of Musicology, 1st Congress, Liège, *Compte rendu . . . ,* 73-75. Guilford: Billings, 1950.   [g.a.]

2645   _____

Wolf, Robert E. "Liège's Buried Treasure." *MQ* 41 (1955): 355-60.   [g.a.]

Describes Terry's Mss., etc. at B-Lc.

2646   _____

Monseur, Eugène. "Léonard Terry et sa bibliothèque." *La Vie wallone* (1956), 48-73.

Not located. Cited from **Benton 2**:24, no. 22, and *Fontes* 2 (1957).

2647   _____

Barthélemy, Maurice. "Le Fonds Terry de la Bibliothèque du Conservatoire Royal de Musique de Liège." *Fontes* 23 (1976): 124-26 ("Belgian Issue," ed. Bernard Huys).   [g.a.]

2648   **Teschner, Gustav Wilhelm,** 1800-83
LEO LIEPMANNSSOHN, BERLIN   CAT. NO. 34
. . . Catalog einer Sammlung von Schriften zur Gesangliteratur und einer reichen Auswahl von Gesangschulen, Solfeggien und Gesangscompositionen aus dem Nachlass des Professor. . . . Dresden/Berlin: [Liepmannssohn], 1884. 62 p. 1208 lots.   [US-Wc, NL-Avb]
> **Folter,** no. 349. **Schaal** (1966), p. 53.

2649   **Tessier, André,** 1886-1931
Ratouis de Limay, Paul. "Contribution à un fichier musical des archives photographiques des beaux-arts. . . . " *Revue de musicologie* 17 (1936): 161-78.   [g.a.]
> A collection of notes by Tessier about photographs in the Archives photographiques du Ministère des Beaux-Arts.

2650   **Tessier, Andrea; Marchese of *****
JACQUES ROSENTHAL, AUCTIONEER, MUNICH
The Tessier Library. Catalogue of the Splendid Collection of Books, Maps, Manuscripts, Bindings. The Property of the Chevalier Andrea Tessier and the Marchese of *** Days of Sale . . . May 21st [-23rd] 1900. [München, 1900.] 121 p., illus.   [US-Wcu]
> "Musique. Musik," lots 581-636 include Renaissance partbooks, treatises by Gaforius, Salinas, etc.

2651   **Thaddäus Wolfgang, Freiherr von Dürniz,** b. 1756
"Catalogue de musique - appartenante à Mons: le Baron: de Dürniz."
> Ms. of 977 titles. Nos. 1-822 with thematic incipits were reprinted in August Scharnagl's *Freiherr Thaddäus von Dürniz und seine Musikaliensammlung, mit Wiedergabe des handschriftlichen Katalogs,* Musikbibliographische Arbeiten, ed. Rudolf Elvers, 12 (Tutzing: Hans Schneider, 1992), 9-185.   [g.a.]

2652   **Thalberg, Sigismond,** 1812-71
DETKEN UND ROCHOLL, AUCTIONEER, NAPLES
Katalog der autographischen Sammlung . . . Nähere Auskunft zu Ertheilen sind bereit: Tie [!] *herren Detken und Rocholl, Buchhändler, Neapel. . . .* Neapel: Gedruckt bei der "Iride," 1872. 34 p. No lotting, ca. 600 items.   [US-Wc]
> **Folter,** no. 350. Nancy Reich in a review in *Fontes* (1979) notes an English-language version of the catalog, but that has not been located. The collection contained some Mss. from the Aloys Fuchs collection (**940**).

2653   _____
ST. GOAR, FIRM, FRANKFURT a.M.   ANT. CAT. NO. 44
Verzeichniss einer werthvollen Sammlung von seltenen älteren Musikstücken und neueren Musikalien sowie theoretischen Werken über Musik zum allergrössten Theile aus dem Nachlasse. . . . Frankfurt a.M.: Ludolph St. Goar, 1877. 28 p. 846 lots.
     [US-Wc (but missing March 1979)]
> **Folter,** no. 351; **Schaal** (1966), p. 53.

2654 _____

SIEGESMUND & VOLKENING, FIRM, LEIPZIG
Verzeichnis ausgewählte Musikalien. Vol. 1: *Piano-Musik.* Leipzig, 1879. 86 p.

> Not located. Cited from Kayser's *Bücherlexikon.*

2655 _____

LEO LIEPMANNSSOHN, AUCTIONEER, BERLIN
Katalog einer bedeutenden Sammlung von Musiker-Autographen seit Mitte des sechzehnten Jahrhunderts . . . nebst anhang von Autographen und Documenten verschiedenen Inhalts. . . . Versteigerung . . . 3-4 Dezember, 1886. Leipzig, 1886. 48 p. 485 lots. Thalberg's, lots 234-428.   [US-NYgr]

> **Folter**, no. 352.

2656 Thayer, Alexander Wheelock, 1817-97
C. F. LIBBIE & CO., AUCTIONEER, BOSTON
Auction Sale. . . . Part 1. Valuable Musical Collection of the Late . . . Including Many German Musical Serials, Rare American Music, Engraved by Paul Revere, Thos. Johnston and Others, Musical History and Biography, etc., etc. . . . Part 2. Music Books from the Library of [Thayer] *Together with Other Consignments.* Boston, 1898. 76 p 1111 lots.   [US-NYp, -SM, -PHu]

> Sale days, 8-9 February 1898. **Folter**, no. 353.

2657 _____

SOTHEBY, WILKINSON & HODGE, AUCTIONEER, LONDON
Catalogue of Important and Valuable Autograph Letters and Historical Documents, Comprising Letters and Documents Signed, of Beethoven, Mendelssohn [etc.] *and Including the Valuable Series of Interesting Musical Scores of Beethoven, Schubert, &c. Formed by the Late . . . Sold . . . 18th Day of February, 1899.* [London, 1899.] 34 p. 289 lots. Music, including Mss., lots 1-38.   [Film at CRL]

> **Folter**, no. 354. Reviews of the sale, with mentions of items sold and prices
> fetched appeared in both *Musical News* 16 (1899): 192, and in *MT* 40 (1899):
> 166.

2658 Thibault, Geneviève, Countess de Chambure, 1902-75
PIERRE BERÈS, (EXP.); ADER-TAJAN (C.-P.), PARIS
La Bibliothèque musicale de la Comtesse de Chambure . . . consacrée à la théorie musicale et aux arts du spectacle. Constituée au cours de plusiers décennies, cette célèbre collection c'est formée à partir de celles d'Henry Prunières, d'Alfred Cortot et d'autres grandes collections du monde entier . . . vente . . . 26 mai 1993. Paris, 1993.

> Cited from prospectus. Not examined.

2659 _____

LITERATURE
Thibault, Geneviève. "Les Collections privées de livres." In *Hinrichsen's Eleventh Music Book . . . ,* 145-47. London: Hinrichsen, 1961.   [g.a.]

> **Albrecht**: "A Special Catalogue of Unica May be Consulted at F-Pn."

2660   Thibaut, Anton Friedrich Justus, 1774-1840
Georg Reichard, auctioneer?, Heidelberg
Katalog der Bibliothek von . . . , welche vom 16ten November 1840 an, in Heidelberg öffentlich Versteigert werden soll. Heidelberg: Georg Reichard, 1840. 79 p. 1839 lots.

> **Folter**, no. 355. Collection, according to **Benton 2**:88, no. 191, now at D-Mbs.

2661   _____

Verzeichniss der von dem verstorbenen grossh. Badischen Prof. der Rechte und Geheimrathe . . . zu Heidelberg hinterlassenen Musikaliensammlung, welche aus ein ganzes ungetrennt Veräussert werden soll. Heidelberg, 1842.   [US-Wc, -NH, -GB-Lbl (Hirsch)]

> US-Wc says published by K. Groos; Hirsch catalog 4:1092 says Gross. Dealer? **Folter**, no. 356. **Albrecht**.

2662   Thierry-Poux, Olgar, b. 1838
Paris, Bibliothèque Nationale, Department des imprimés
Catalogue d'une collection musicale et d'ouvrages divers légués par. . . . [Paris], 1896. 59 p.
[US-NYp, -Wc]

2663   Thoinan, Ernest, 1827-94 (pen-name: **Antoine-Ernest Roquet**)
Roquet, Antoine-Ernest. *Catalogue de la bibliothèque de feu M. Ernest Thoinan.* Paris: Em. Paul, 1895. 32 p. 280 lots. Music, lots 45-129.   [US-R, NL-Avb]

2664   Thomas, Ambroise, 1811-96
Georges Andrieux, (Exp.), Paris
I. Manuscrits musicaux d'Ambroise Thomas . . . II. Précieux livres modernes . . . III. Bibliothèque Marcel Boulenger . . . IV. Livres anciens et romantiques, etc. [La vente aura lieu les 6, 8, 9 avril 1935]. Paris, [1935]. 87 p. 620 lots.   [GB-Lbl (Hirsch 5803)]

Thomas, Harold.   *See* **Stone, William Henry** (sale, 1885)

2665   Thomas, Isaiah, 1749-1831
Ford, Worthington C. . . . *The Isaiah Thomas Collection of Ballads.* Worcester, Mass.: American Antiquarian Society, 1924. 81 p.   [g.a.]

> Reprinted from the Society's *Proceedings* 33 (1924): 34-112.

[Thomas, J   ]   *See* **Hammond Jones, W. H.**

2666   Thomas, Theodore, 1835-1905
"Catalogue of the Musical Library of. . . . " 140 leaves. Ms.   [US-Cn, copy at BUu]

> Part donated to US-Cn, some to US-CU.

2667   Thompson, Thomas Payne, 1860-1924
Thompson, Donald Eugene. *A Bibliography of Louisiana Books and Pamphlets in the T. P. Thompson Collection of the University of Alabama. . . .* University of Alabama Studies, 2. University of Alabama, 1947. vii, 210 p.   [g.a.]

2668 Thulemeier, Friedrich Wilhelm von
BERLIN, JOACHIMSTHALSCHES GYMNASIUM, BIBLIOTHEK
Thematischer Katalog der von Thulemeier'schen Musikaliensammlung in der Bibliothek. . . .
Beilage zu den Monatsheften für Musikgeschichte 1898/99. Leipzig: Breitkopf & Härtel, 1899.
110 p.

> Preface signed by R. Eitner, but the catalog was prepared by R. Jacobs in
> 1860. The complete run of the *Monatshefte* was reprinted, Scarsdale, N.Y.:
> A. Schnase, 1960-62, and is g.a. The collection is now at D-Bds.

Thurn und Taxis Hofbibliothek, Regensburg. *See* **Alexander Ferdinand, Fürst zum Thurn
und Taxis**

2669 Tiedka, Jakob
ERNST MAX HACKE (PEER-BAEDEKER), FIRM, ?
Katalog 1. Bibliothek. . . . 1960.

> Not located or verified. Cited in *IBAK*.

2670 Tiersot, Julien, 1857-1936
GUSTAV LEGOUIX, FIRM, PARIS   CAT. NO. 18
Littérature musicale. Musique. Ouvrages sur la musique et les musiciens sur la chanson . . .
provenant en partie de la bibliothèque de M. . . . Paris, [n.d., 1937?]. 41 p. 664 lots.
[US-NYp, GB-Lbl (Hirsch 585)]

> **Folter,** no. 357 dates 1938.

2671 [Tiggers, Piet]
J. L. BEIJERS, AUCTIONEER, UTRECHT
Book Auction Sales, 23rd and 24th April 1970, Including the Ornithological Library of
the Late Dr. J. Bierman. Important Collections on Gastronomy, Dutch Topography and Music
[from the collection of Piet Tiggers] . . . [etc.]. Utrecht, 1970. 174 p. 2353 lots. Music, lots
2033-353.   [NL-Avb]

2672 Timbs, Mr. ; Another Amateur
W. P. MUSGRAVE, AUCTIONEER, LONDON
Catalogue of a Very Choice Collection of Vocal and Instrumental Music, Including the Libraries
of Mr. Timbs and Another Amateur . . . [Also Musical Instruments] . . . *Sold . . . the 28th of*
January, 1830. London, 1830. 12 p. 154 lots. Music, lots 1-57, 117-54 but ownership not
differentiated.   [GB-Lbl, US-NYp]

2673 Tirabassi, Antonio, 1882-1947
Biblioteca del Dott. Tirabassi . . . Bruxelles. Prima transcrizione inedita corretta, di opere
antichi. . . . [N.p.: n.d., 1937.] 42 fols.

> White on black photocopy is at US-Wc with "Ms. corrections by W.
> Rubsamen."

2674 ─────────
Tirabassi, Antonio. "Bibliothèque manuscrite du docteur Antonio Tirabassi." [N.p.: ca.
1950.] Typewritten. 13 fols.   [US-NYp]

> Note on US-NYp catalog card: "A catalog of transcriptions into modern
> notation (mainly of unpublished music) made by Tirabassi. Notice by
> Charles van den Borren, 2 leaves at end."

2675   Tobin, Robert L. B.
The Operatic Muse: An Exhibition of Works from the Robert L. B. Tobin Collection Honoring the 30th Anniversary Season of the Santa Fe Opera. San Antonio, Tex.: Marion Koogler McNay Art Museum, 1986. 39 p.   [g.a.]

2676 _____
Cunningham, James Goady. "A Catalog: The Robert L. B. Tobin Collection of Original Scene Designs, 1900-1940." *Dissertation Abstracts International* 52/08-A:2758. Ph.D. diss., Texas Tech University, 1991. 196 p. (leaves?)

Toerring-Jettenbach, Counts of.   *See under* **Wilhelm, Herzog von Bayern,** 1752-1837

2677   Toggenburg Family
Chini, Tarcisio, and Giuliano Tonini. *La raccolta di manoscritti e stampe musicali "Toggenburg" di Bolzano (secc. XVIII-XIX).* Cataloghi di fondi musicali italiani, 5. [Torino]: EDT/Musica, [1986]. xxxii, 307 p. plates.   [g.a.]

2678   Tokugawa Yorisada, Founder of the Nanki Music Library
Tokugawa formed the initial collection in the 1890s, opened the library in 1914. The Cummings collection was added in 1917 (one-half the sale items), followed by parts of the collections of Joseph Hollmann and Max Friedländer during the years 1917-20. In 1923 the Great Earthquake ruined the building; rescued materials were then stored at Keio University. In the late 1940s, Tokugawa sold the library to Kyubei Okhi, who hid it until 1964. McLean, in an article in *MT* 126 (1985): 665, under **Granville** disagrees, noting that Thurston Dart talked about it in the 1950s. In 1966 the Nanki Library was once again publicly re-established. See lengthy commentary by Albrecht and other related catalogs here *under* **Cummings, Hollmann, Handel, Granville,** and **Friedländer**.

2679 _____
NANKI-ONGAKU-BUNKO, TOKYO
Catalogue of the Nanki-Ongaku-Bunko (Musical Scores). Vol. 1. [Tokyo: Nanki Buno, Arabu], 1917. 36 p.   [US-NYp, -Bp, NL-DHgm]

2680 _____
TOKYO, UNIVERSITY, NANKI LIBRARY
Catalogue of the . . . Library . . . II. [i.e., 2nd ed.]. 2 vols. in 1. Tokyo, 1920.   [US-NYp]
Contents. [Vol. 1] Musical Scores (principally European composers).
[Vol. 2] Books on Music (principally English titles . . .).

2681 _____
TOKYO, UNIVERSITY, NANKI LIBRARY
Catalogue of the . . . Library. . . . Tokyo: Nanki Music Library, 1929-.   [US-Wc]
Contents. Pt. 1, Musicology (372 p.). Copy at US-AUS is dated 1925!

2682 _____

Murakami Yoshiyuki. *Nanki-Ongaku-Bunko* [Catalogue of the special public exhibition of the Nanki Music Library]. Tokyo: Yomiuri Shimbun, 1967. 159 p., illus.

Not examined; cited from *RILM*.

2683 _____

Nanki Ongaku Bunko. . . . *Catalogue of Rare Books and Notes: The Okhi Collection.* Tokyo: Nanki Music Library, 1970. 60 p.   [US-Wc]

2684   **Tolbecque, Auguste,** 1830-1919
GODILLON (C.-P.)
Catalogue des collections, livres faiences . . . instruments de musique de la bibliothèque musicale et de l'atelier de lutherie de musique . . . de Niort . . . la plus grande partie des objets mis en vente sont anciens. Niort: Fort-Faucault, 1922. 48 p. 318 unnumbered lots of music.

Sale date, 18 April 1922. **Folter**, no. 358. Not located.

2685   **Tollefsen, Carl H.,** 1882-1963
LITERATURE
Deyo, Felix. "Letters of Famous Musicians Recall a Brilliant Past [the collection of Carl H. Tollefsen]." *Musical America* 52, no. 2 (January 1932): 26, 28.   [g.a.]

Collection given to US-EDu, according to *Baker's*, but **Albrecht** says the large collection of string chamber music was purchased in 1969! No catalog located. Noted in *ZiMG* 14 (1931/32): 56.   [g.a.]

2686   **Torello, Anton,** 1884-1959
Mapes, Gordon. "Music Manuscripts in the Anton Torello Bequest." Typescript at US-PHci.

Not examined; cited from *RAMH*.

2687   **Torrefranca, Fausto,** 1883-1955
Rossi, Franco. *I manoscritti del Fondo Torrefranca del Conservatorio Benedetto Marcello. Catalogo per autori.* Historiae musicae cultores. Biblioteca, 45. Firenze: Leo S. Olschki, 1986. xv, 357 p.   [g.a.]

Thematic. 283 items.

2688 _____

Fabiano, Andrea. *Le stampe musicali antichi del fondo Torrefranca del Conservatorio Benedetto Marcello.* . . . 2 vols. Catalogo dei fondi storici della Biblioteca del Conservatorio . . . Venezia, 5. Historiae musicae cultores, 65 [cf. citation above!]. Firenze: L. S. Olschki, 1922. (xxiii, 773 p.)   [g.a.]

2689 _____

Negri, Emanuela. *Catalogo dei libretti del Conservatorio Benedetto Marcello. I.* Historiae musicae cultores. Biblioteca, 66. Firenze: Leo S. Olschki, 1994. xxii, 393 p.   [g.a.]

861 items of ca. 4200 in this, vol. 1, of the *Catalogo*—all so far issued.

2690   **Tottmann, Albert,** 1837-1917; et al.

List & Francke, firm, Leipzig   Ant. Cat. no. 466

Musikliteratur. Musikalien. Theater . . . Aus dem Besitz des . . . u.a. Leipzig, 1918. 90 p. 2742
lots.   [US-Wc, -NYgr, NL-DHgm, -Avb, GB-Lbl]

Properties not differentiated. **Folter,** no. 359.

2691   **Toulouse, Louis Alexandre, Comte de,** 1678-1737

The collection was originally put together for the Comte, who was the son
of Louis XIV (1643-1715) and Mme. de Montespan. It contained about 350
volumes of Mss., almost all in the hand of André Danican Philidor, Louis
XIV's music librarian, and some by Philidor's eldest son. The manuscripts
were supplemented by approximately 70 printed works. Most of the
manuscripts bear the inscription "copiez par l'ordre de son Altesse
Serenissime le comte de Toulouze par Philidor l'aîné . . . et par son fils aîné."

The collection passed to the Comte's son, then to his granddaughter, who
married the Duke of Orleans, thence to their son, King Louis Philippe (1773-
1850), and the collection went to the Palais Royal in Paris, stamped "Bibl.
du Roi."

Upon his death, the collection was dispersed in an 1852 sale (**2695**), the
greater part being purchased by William Hope, an Englishman living in
Paris. Fellowes hints in his *M&L* article in 1931 (**2694**) that Hope may have
served as Sir Frederick Ouseley's agent to purchase items for
St. Michael's College, Tenbury, but elsewhere he says that Hope died in
1855 and implies that Ouseley bought them at about that time.

Some 60 other manuscript volumes in the sale were secured by Crétain.
Surprisingly, they remained together until sold by an English book dealer,
Arthur Rau, in a 1935 catalog (Oboussier wrongly gives the date as 1934!).
These volumes were fortunately also secured for St. Michael's; ten volumes
of Lalande motets, for example, which had been split between Hope and
Crétain were thus finally reunited after nearly a hundred years.

Fellowes, in his *M&L* article, claims that the Comte's collection of
manuscripts was almost equal in value to that of the King at Versailles,
remnants of which constitute another Philidor collection in the Bibliothèque
Nationale. Still others, done for Louis XIV, were kept in the Conservatoire
in Paris, to be moved to the Bibliothèque Nationale's Departement de la
Musique when its new building opened in 1964.

The following citations, then, cover several Philidor collections: that of
Louis XIV, the Comte de Toulouse, King Louis Philippe (now at Versailles,
F-V), remnants in F-Pn, and the collections at St. Michael's, Tenbury (now
at the Bodleian Library, Oxford). The citations are set out chronologically
and not here separated into Catalogs and Literature.

2692   ⸻

"Catalogue de la collection faite par Philidor, garde de la musique de Louis XIV. MS. copié sur
celui de la Bibliothèque du Conservatoire de Paris."

In Fétis collection at B-Br.

2693 _____

Fétis, François Joseph. "Notice d'une collection manuscrite d'ancienne musique française, recueillie par Michel Danican Philidor en 1690." *Revue musicale* 25 (about 1827): 9-13.

[g.a.]

First notice of the Conservatoire collection.

2694 _____

5 large folio service books transcribed in 1691 by Philidor for Louis XIV's Chapel Royal were in a Puttick & Simpson auction of the library "of a Distinguished Professor," 23 June 1849. According to Fellowes's 1931 *M&L* article, "it is not known how [the set] found its way to the sale," but the books were purchased by Ouseley for St. Michael's.

2695 _____

A. L. POTIER, FIRM, PARIS
Catalogue de livres provenant des bibliothèques du feu roi Louis-Philippe dont la vente aura lieu le lundi 6 décembre 1852 et les vingt jours suivants . . . Bibliothèques du Palais-Royal et de Neuilly. Deuxième partie. . . . Paris: Potier, M. Defer, 1852.

This collection was acquired by Sir Frederick Ouseley and eventually became part of the library at Tenbury College. See **2691**.

2696 _____

Farrenc, Aristide. "Notice d'une collection manuscrite d'ancienne musique française, recueillis par Michel Danican Philidor, en 1690." *Revue de musique ancienne et moderne* (1856), 470-78.

Farrenc reprints Fétis's earlier notice of the Conservatoire collection (**2693**).

2697 _____

Gautier, Eugène. "À propos de la collection Philidor [at the Conservatoire]." In his *Un Musicien en vacances: Études et souvenirs*, 284-99. Paris: Leduc, 1873.   [US-MSu]

2698 _____

Weckerlin, J. B. "La Collection Philidor au Conservatoire de Musique de Paris [le catalogue de l'abbé Roze]." *La Chronique musicale* 4, no. 22 (1874): 159-65; no. 23: 223-25.   [US-NYp]

2699 _____

Wasielewski, W. J. von. "Die Collection Philidor." *VfMW* 1 (1885): 531-45.   [g.a.]

Describes the contents of the 59 Philidor volumes at the Conservatoire.

2700 _____

Weckerlin, Jean Baptiste. "La Collection Philidor." In his *Dernier musiciana,* 200-04. Paris: Garnier Frères, 1899.   [g.a.]

2701 _____

Ms. at St. Michael's College, Tenbury: "List of the contents of the 59 volumes of Philidor's manuscripts in the Conservatoire de Musique, Paris. Thirty-four volumes only are now extant. This list communicated to Dr. Fellowes by M. Leon Mathieu, secty to the Conservatoire . . . [with] letters . . . (on the subject of the Philidor collections and the library of the Comte de Toulouse) . . . 1930."

2702 _____

Fellowes, Edmund H. "The Philidor Manuscripts. Paris, Versailles, Tenbury." *M&L* 12 (1931): 116-29.   [g.a.]

2703 _____

Tessier, André. "Une Fonds musical de la bibliothèque de Louis XIV [à Versailles]: La Collection Philidor." *Revue musicale* 12 (1931): 259-302.

>   Published separately, 1931.

2704 _____

Tessier, André. "Un Catalogue de la bibliothèque de la musique du Roi [à Versailles]." *Revue de musicologie* 15 (1931): 106-17, 172-89.   [g.a.]

>   Tessier comments on inventories of 1765 and 1780 but does not reprint them.

2705 _____

ST. MICHAEL'S COLLEGE, TENBURY, ENGLAND
Fellowes, Edmund H., comp. *The Catalogue of Manuscripts in the Library of. . . .* Paris: Éditions de l'Oiseau-Lyre, 1934. 319 p., illus., facs.   [g.a.]

>   Mss. from the library of Rev. Sir F. A. Gore Ouseley.

>   "Printed Books from the Toulouse Collection," pp. 34-39; "Extract from the catalogue [by A. L. Potier] of the Louis-Philippe sale in Paris, December 1852," pp. 40-48.

>   The 59 volumes from the sale by Arthur Rau in 1934 (or 1935, as the catalog is dated; see **2706**) were acquired too late to be included in this catalog.

2706 _____

ARTHUR RAU, FIRM, PARIS   CAT. NO. 5
Musique ancienne. Paris, Octobre 1935. 177 p., illus. 671 lots.   [compiler]

>   Philidor items are not identified in the catalog, and it may well be that Rau sold those 59 volumes to Ouseley before issuing the catalog. The Lalande items, for example, referred to in **2691**, are not included in Rau's list.

2707 _____

ARTHUR RAU, FIRM, PARIS
"The Music Library [at St. Michael's College, Tenbury]." In M. F. Alderson's and H. C. Colles's *History of St. Michael's College*, 78-101. London: Society for Promoting Christian Knowledge, 1943.   [g.a.]

2708 _____

Oboussier, Philippe. "Couperin Motets at Tenbury." *Proceedings of the Royal Musical Association* 98 (1971/72): 17-29.   [g.a.]

>   Inventories of Mss. 1432-36 (5 part-books) and Ms. 1437.

2709 _____

Thomas, Orlan Earl. "Music for Double-Reed Ensembles from the Seventeenth and Eighteenth Centuries: 'Collection Philidor.'" Ph.D. diss., University of Rochester, 1973.   [g.a.]

2710 _____

Sandman, Susan Goertzet. "Wind Band Music of 17th Century France: The Philidor Collection."
Ph.D. diss., Stanford University, 1974.   [g.a.]

> The collection at Versailles, F-V.

2711 _____

Sᴏᴛʜᴇʙʏ's, ᴀᴜᴄᴛɪᴏɴᴇᴇʀ, Lᴏɴᴅᴏɴ
*Catalogue of the Highly Important Toulouse-Philidor Collection of Manuscripts and Printed
Music and Other Valuable Manuscripts and Printed Books, the Property of St. Michael's
College, Tenbury Wells . . . Sold . . . 26 Juin 1978. . . .* London: Sotheby's, 1978.   [g.a.]

2712 _____

Pɪᴇʀʀᴇ Bᴇ̀ʀᴇs (Exp.), Pᴀʀɪs
*Livres de musique du Comte de Toulouse. Cantates, motets, opéras, ballets, partitions gravées
ou imprimés . . . Manuscrits de Philidor ayant appartenu à Louis Alexandre de Bourbon,
Comte de Toulouse, d'un des sept enfants de Louis XIV . . . et en dernier lieu, au Saint
Michael's College, Tenbury . . . vente du 30 novembre 1978.* Unnumbered, cols.,
illus., plates. 85 lots.   [compiler]

> Immense bibliographical details provided. At end: "Fers de Armoires du
> Conte de Toulouse," [2] p., 11 illus.

_____. *Complément au catalogue. . . . Autographes musicaux. Manuscrits et lettres de
Debussy, Liszt, . . . etc.* Paris, 1978. [8] p., illus. lots A-P.   [compiler]

2713 _____

Carroll, Charles Michael. "The Toulouse-Philidor Collection: A Suite in Four Parts." *College
Music Symposium* 19 (1979): 60-66.   [g.a.]

2714 _____

Massip, Catherine. "La Collection musicale Toulouse-Philidor à Bibliothèque nationale." *Bulletin
de la Bibliothèque Nationale* (1979), 147-57.   [g.a.]

2715 _____

Waquet, Françoise. "Philidor l'aîné, ordinaire de la musique du roy et garde de tous les livres de
sa bibliothèque de musique." *Revue de musicologie* 66 (1980): 203-14.   [g.a.]

2716 _____

Milsom, John. "Bläsermusik aus der Philidor-Sammlung. I Pifferi." Orpheus ORP 0 701 [recording].
Reviewed in *Early Music* 10 (1982): 283.   [g.a.]

2717 _____

Massip, Catherine. "La Collection musicale Toulouse-Philidor à la bibliothèque nationale."
Fontes 30 (1983): 184-207.

> The manuscripts were prepared by copyists mainly around the years 1703-
> 06 according to the author, who describes the present collection by means
> of an inventory and a concordance with earlier catalogs.

2718 _____
Searle Arthur. "Salerooms." *Early Music* 12 (1984): 529, 531.   [g.a.]

Describes items from the Toulouse-Philidor collection that appeared in Sotheby's London sale 10 May 1984.

2719 _____
Ward Jones, Peter A. "The Fate of the Music Collection of St. Michael's College, Tenbury." *Brio* 27 (1990): 48-49.   [g.a.]

2720 **Trauterman, Georg,** 1828-91; et al.
LIST & FRANCKE, FIRM, LEIPZIG   ANT.-VERZ. NO. 230
Musikwissenschaft. Theoretische Werke über Musik, ältere praktische Musikstücke und neuere Musikalien, aus dem Nachlasse des Herrn . . . und Anderen. . . . Leipzig, 1892. 94 p. 3142 lots.
[NL-DHgm, -Avb, US-NYgr]

Folter, no. 360.

2721 **Trémont,   , Baron de**
"Catalogue de la musique de M. le Baron de T . . . avec une table des matières."
Ms. ca. 1800. 198 p. Gr.-8°. Not examined. Cited from Lengfeld catalog no. 36, lot 176. Fetched 36 marks.

Trend, John Brand, 1877-1958.   *See under* **Dent, Edward Joseph**

Trimnell, Thomas Tallis (?)   *See* **Hammond Jones**

2722 **Trolda, Emilián,** 1871-1949
Buchner, Alexander. *Hudební spírka Emiliána Troldy. Musical Collection of. . . .* [Sborník Národního musea v Praze, 8-A, Historický, 1.] Praha: Nákl. Národního musea v Praze . . . 1954. 132 p. 520 nos.   [US-Wc]

Thematic. Collection at CS-Pnm.

2723 **Tross,**
Notice de quelques livres rares et précieux, cantiques et chansonniers du XVIᵉ siècle, musique ancienne. . . . Paris: [Tross?], 1866.

Dealer's catalog or private collection? Not located. Noted in Lengfeld's catalog no. 36, lot 112; in **Wolffheim** 1:344; and in **Scheurleer** 1 (1923): 22. None provides full name.

2724 **Tucher von Simmelsdorf, Christian Karl; Gottlieb, Freiherr von,** 1798-1877
THEODOR ACKERMANN, FIRM, MUNICH
[Verzeichnis hinterlassene Bibliothek.] München: Ackermann, 1877. 883 lots.

Not located. Cited from *MfM* (1877). Library now at D-LM (**Albrecht**).

2725   Türk, Daniel Gottlob, 1750-1813
J. CH. LIPPERT, AUCTIONEER, HALLE
Verzeichniss der musikalischen und anderen Bücher, so wie auch der gedruckten und geschriebenen Musikalien des seligen professor der Musik und Universitäts-Musik-Direktor Dr. Türk, welche zu Halle und der Saale den 13. Januar 1817 und folgenden Tage . . . meistbietend versteigert werden sollen. . . . Halle, 1816. 72 p. Music, pp. 1-47, 622 lots.
[GB-Lbl (Hirsch), compiler (copy)]
    Folter, no. 361, and **Wolffheim** 1:321.

2726 _____
    [Reprint]: *Catalogue of the Music Library of Daniel Gottlob Türk Sold in Halle, 13 Januar 1817.* With an introduction by A. Hyatt King. Auction Catalogs of Music, 3. Amsterdam: Frits Knuf, 1973. xi, 74 p.   [g.a.]
    Reproduced from the Hirsch copy (**2725**).

2727   Tunstall, John; A Well-Known Music Critic
PUTTICK & SIMPSON, AUCTIONEER, LONDON   CAT. NO. 3950
Catalogue of Musical Instruments . . . Also a Large Quantity of Ancient and Modern Music . . . Autographs, Manuscripts, Engravings, etc., Including the Library of the Late . . . and That of a Well-Known Music Critic . . . Sold August 29th, 1905. [London], 1905. 16 p. 323 lots. Music, lots 170-323.   [GB-Lbl]
    Tunstall's properties, lots 170-202 (many items).

2728   [Turner, T ; Mr. Sikes (of Gloucester)]
PUTTICK & SIMPSON, AUTIONEER, LONDON   CAT. NO. 194
Catalogue of a Collection of Music, Comprising the Works of the Best Composers, Glees and Other Vocal Music, Modern Operas . . . Theoretical and Perceptive Works [Property of Turner?] *. . . Also Musical Instruments . . . Including the Collection of the Late Mr. Sikes . . . Sold February 4th, 1851.* [London], 1851. 12 p. 290 lots. Music, lots 1-200.   [GB-Lbl]
    Sale was advertised in *MT* 4 (1850): 124, as scheduled for "about the third week in January."

2729   [Turpin, ; H. Phillips]
PUTTICK & SIMPSON, AUCTIONEER, LONDON   CAT. NO. 437
Catalogue of a Large and Valuable Collection of Music . . . Valuable Assemblage of Instrumental Music . . . Large Collection of Flute Music . . . [Also] *Musical Instruments . . . Sold January 9th, 1856, and Following Day. . . .* [London], 1856. 21 p. 574 lots. Music, lots 1-517.   [GB-Lbl]

2730   Tuyll van Serooskerian (or **Serookerken?), Hendrik Otto Raimond, Baron von,** 1915-
CREYGHTON, FIRM, UTRECHT
Catalogue . . . Collection of Music Books . . . Mainly Referring to the Organ, in Possession of. . . . Utrecht: Creyghton, 1955.
    Not located. Cited from publisher's advertisement. Published?
    → *See also under* **Gresnirere**

2731   Uhrovec Collection
Mózi, Alexander. "Hajdúske tance z Uhroveckej zbierky piesní a tancov z roku 1730." *Hudobný archív* 2 (1977): 123-97.

Collection now at CS-Mms. Not examined; cited from *RILM*.

2732   _____

LITERATURE
Gajdos, Vsevlad. "Historicky o uhroveckej zbierke." *Slobenská hudba* 9 (1965): 299-302.

Not examined. Cited from *RILM*.

2733   Ulex, Oskar; Sammlung C**; Sammlung Holleben**
KARL ERNST HENRICI, AUCTIONEER, BERLIN   VERST. 120
Autographen, Literatur und Wissenschaft, Goethe und Schiller, Musik und Kunst, Geschichte und Politik . . . Versteigerung . . . 27. [-28.] Mai 1927. . . . Berlin, 1927. 166 p. illus. 937 lots.
[NL-Avb]

"Musik, Theater, bildende Kunst," lots 504-691.

Underwood, R.   *See under* **Bates, F. W.**

2734   Unger, Andreas, d. 1657
LITERATURE
Braun, Werner. "Mitteldeutsche Quellen der Musiksammlung Gotthold in Königsberg." *Musik des Ostens* 5 (1969): 84-86.   [g.a.]

2735   Unger, Max, 1883-1959
Beethovens Handschrift. . . . Veröffentlichungen des Beethovenhauses in Bonn . . . , 4. Bonn: Verlag des Beethovenhauses, 1926. 32 p., facs.   [US-Wc, -NYp]

2736   _____
Eine Schweizer Beethovensammlung: Katalog. Schriften der Corona, 24. Zürich: Verlag der Corona, [1939]. 235 p.   [US-Wc]

2737   Urban, W   (of Greiz); et al.
LIST & FRANCKE, AUCTIONEER, LEIPZIG
Verzeichnis einer reichhaltige Büchersammlung aus den Bibliothek der Herren Musikdirektor W. Urban in Greiz, Dr. a. Winckler-Atkinson in Dresden, u.s. Versteigerung 9 November u. f. T. Leipzig, 1896. 75 p. 2574 lots. Music, lots 2050-297.   [US-NYp]

Folter, no. 362. Properties not differentiated.

2738   Vadé, Jean Joseph, 1719-57
E. MAILLET, AUCTIONEER, PARIS
*Catalogue de la bibliothèque théâtrale et musicale de Vadé, Carmouche et Vieillot; 30,000 pièces de théâtre, 250 partitions, environ 500 volumes de poésies, 600 volumes de chansons, littérature et bibliographie . . . vente aura lieu à Paris . . . 14 [-17] juin 1887. . . .*Paris: E. Maillet, 1887. viii, 119 p. 990 lots. Music, lots 780-990, et passim.
[US-NYp, -NYgr (priced), -BE, GB-Lbl (Hirsch)]

Preface signed George d'Heylli (i.e., Antoine Edmond Poinsot). **Folter,** no. 363.

2739   Valdruche, Eugène, d. 1913?

H. Leclerc, auctioneer? Paris

Bibliothèque de feu . . . Livres anciens et modernes. Ouvrages et recueils de calligraphie, sténographie, ouvrages sur la musique et la danse (méthodes, partitions ouvrages en tous genres) . . . vente du 8 au 13 décembre 1913 par Gaston Charpentier et André Desvouges. . . . Paris, 1913. 219 p. Music, pp. 82-141, lots 432-826.   [UN-NYp]

2740   Vanbianchi, Carlo, b. 1862

Autografi di musicisti, commediografi e artisti, presentati all' Esposizione Nazionale d'Arte Teatrale in Milano. . . . Milano: Pirola, 1894. 21 p.

Not located. Cited from **Bobillier, Pag,** and *Jahrbuch Peters* (1895).

2741   Vanéechout,

Lavigne (Exp. = Libraire), Paris

Catalogue de la bibliothèque musicale de M. . . . Partitions, musique religieuse, musique instrumentale. Traités et méthodes . . . vente . . . 7 avril 1865. . . . Paris, 1865. 8 p. 116 lots.
                  [NL-DHgm (some prices in Ms.)]

2742   Van Hal, F

Jos. Fievez, firm, Brussels

[Catalogue de la bibliothèque . . . vente 6 avril 1900. . . .] Bruxelles, 1900. 39 + 1 p. 1020 + 12 lots. Music, *inter alia.*   [US-NYgr]

2743   Van Porys, Georges, 1902-72

Claude et André Faure Coulet, (Exp.), Paris

Succession de Madame Agnes van Porys, livres anciens et modernes . . . partitions anciens, précieux manuscrits et lettres, autographes littéraires et musicaus . . . vente . . . 7-8 mars 1979. Paris, 1979. 131 p. 603 lots. Music, lots 300-603 and *inter alia.*   [US-NYgr]
     Folter, no. 364.

2744   Vanselow, Albert

J. A. Stargardt, firm, Marburg   Cat. no. 573

Autographensammlung. . . . Marburg, 1965. 70 p. 386 lots. 14 plates.
     "III. Musik," lots 229-306.

2745   Van Vactor, David, b. 1906

Bayne, Pauline S., H. Stuart Garrett, Rebecca C. Smeltzer, Marsha M. Michie. *The David Van Vactor Collection: A Catalog.* Knoxville: University of Tennessee Libraries, 1993. 344 p.   [g.a.]

935 recordings, more than 1800 books and scores.

2746   Van Vechten, Carl, 1900-64

Fisk University Library, Nashville, Tenn.

Selected Items from the George Gershwin Memorial Collection of Music and Musical Literature. Nashville, [1947?].   [g.a.]

Gift of Van Vechten to Fisk University.

2747 [**Vasconcellos, Joaquim Antonio da Fonsca de,** 1849-1936]
Catalogue des livres rares composant la bibliothèque musicale d'un amateur. Porto: [Typ. de A. J. de Sousa & irmao], 1898. 193 p. 1567 lots (many more items).

[US-Wc, -NYp, -CHua NL-DHgm, GB-Lbl]

Some items are ex-libris O. Jahn. **Folter**, no. 365.

2748 [_____]
LEO LIEPMANNSSOHN, FIRM, BERLIN   CAT. NO. 144
. . . *Spanische und portugiesische Werke über Musik, Liturgie, Theater und Tanz. Ouvrages espagnols et portugais, relatifs à la musique.* . . . *Grosstehtheils aus der Bibliothek von* . . . *Hervorragende Seltenheiten.* . . . [Greifswald: H. Adler], 1900. 28 p. 291 lots.   [US-Wc]

2749 **Vatke,   , Frau Prof.**
"Verzeichnis der von Frau Prof. Vatke für die Königl. Bibliothek angekauften Autographe, Musikalien, Bücher, etc." 1879.

D-Bds, Cat. Mus. Ms. 119. Cited by **Schaal** (1966), 106.

2750 [**Vaughan, Charles   **]
PUTTICK & SIMPSON, AUCTIONEER, LONDON   CAT. NO. 1143
Catalogue of a Collection of Ancient and Modern Music from Various Private Libraries . . . *Antiquarian Music* . . . *Also Important Musical Instruments* . . . *Sold July 30th, 1869.* [London], 1869. 23 p. 587 lots. Music, lots 1-459.   [GB-Lbl]

2751 **Vaughan, Thomas,** d. 1843
MR. FLETCHER, AUCTIONEER, LONDON
Catalogue of the Extensive and Valuable Musical Library of the Late . . . *Early Treatises by Salinas, Ornithoparcus, Gafforius, Morley* [etc.] *and Valuable Cathedral Music* . . . *Also* . . . *Musical Instruments* . . . *Sold* . . . *June 27th, 1843, and Two Following Days.* [London], 1843. 34 p. 948 lots.   [GB-Lb, US-NYp, compiler]

> **King**, p. 92, says only the Harding copy, now at GB-Ob, exists, but that is not true. Another is at US-NYp, with Edward Rimbault's markings. The compiler's priced copy includes still other marginalia.

2752 **Vaughan, W. A.; F. Stainforth; W. T. Brooke; S. W. Christopher; John Dobson (of Richmond); R. H. Love;** et al.
CHARLES HIGHAM, FIRM, LONDON
Bibliotheca Hymnologica. A Priced Catalogue [compiled by Mr. W. T. Brooke] *of a Very Rich and Varied Collection of Hymnals, Psalms,* [Books on] *Hymnology, Church Psalmody and Music, Including Selections from the Libraries of.* . . . London: Charles Higham, 1890. 98 p. 1792 lots.   [US-NYgr]

> → *See also* separate catalog under **Dobson**.

2753 **Vautier, Félix Abel,** 1794-1863
. . . *Catalogue des livres rares et précieux composant la bibliothèque de feu* . . . , *dont la vente* . . . *à Caen* . . . *les 16, 17, 18, 19, 20 et 21 novembre, 1863.* Caen: Le Gost-Clérisse . . . , 1863. 184 p.   [US-Wc]

> "Extrait du catalogue général." Music collection now at F-Lym.

2754   Veer, Pieter van der (of Rotterdam)
Land, J. P. N. "Catalogus van allerley musijk met hare poyse 't welk te Rotterdam bij . . . [1701]."
Reprinted in *Tijdschrift der Vereeniging voor Muziekgeschiedenis* 4 (1894): 36-48.   [g.a.]
> Original catalog is at NL-DHgm.

2755   Venturi, Antonio
Meylan, Raymond. "La Collection Antonio Venturi, Montecatini-Terme (Pistoia)." *Fontes* 5 (1958): 31-44.   [g.a.]
> Italian manuscripts from the late 18th century.

2756   Venua, Frédéric Marc Antoine, b. 1788; **A Well-Known Professor**
PUTTICK & SIMPSON, AUCTIONEER, LONDON   CAT. NO. 858
Catalogue of an Extensive and Valuable Collection of Music, Including the Library of . . . , and the Library of a Well-Known Professor . . . Works of Ancient and Modern Composers . . . History, Theory and Biography of Music . . . Numerous Full Scores . . . Also Musical Instruments . . . Sold . . . April 12th, 1865. [London], 1865. 32 p. 716 lots. Music, lots 1-573.
[US-NYp (poor condition), GB-Lbl]
> **Coral** says some properties of Joseph Warren were included in the sale,
> but they are not identified in the catalog.

2757   Verchaly, André, 1903-76
H. BARON, FIRM, LONDON   CAT. NO. 111
Musical Literature, Including a Portion of the Library of. . . . London, 1977. 39 p. 989 lots.
[compiler]
> Properties not differentiated. **Folter**, no. 366.

2758   Verhulst, Johann J. H.; et al.
W. P. VAN STOCKUM, & FILS, AUCTIONEER, DEN HAAG
Catalogue d'une belle collection de livres de manuscrits et de documents historiques de gravures et de dessins . . . Bibliothèque musical de feu . . . [etc.] dont la vente . . . 23 janvier au 1 février 1892. . . . La Haye, 1892. 200 p. 3685, 364 + lots. Music, lots 3374-633.   [NL-Avb]

2759   Vervoitte, Charles Joseph, 1822-84
SAGOT, AUCTIONEER, PARIS
Catalogue des livres anciens et modernes, partitions musique religieuse composant la bibliothèque musicale de feu . . . vente . . . 5-9 février 1887. . . . Paris: Sagot, 1887. 63 p. 1027 lots.
[US-R, -NYp, NL-DHgm]
> **Folter**, no. 367.

2760   Vesper, Oliver Morse, 1845-1911; **? Hughes; ? Dow**
OAKLAND FREE LIBRARY
. . . Vesper Collection of Church Music: Finding List and Rules for Use. Oakland: [Enquirer Pub. Co.], 1914.
> Not examined; cited from *NUC*.

2761   _____
OAKLAND PUBLIC LIBRARY
Sacred and Secular Music List, Including the Vesper, Hughes, and Dow Gifts. . . . Oakland: Public Library, 1937.
[US-Wc]

2762   Victor, Count von Wimpffen, Wien, b. 1834

Christian M. Nebehay, firm, Vienna   Liste 29

. . . *Autographen*. . . . Wien, [n.d., 195-?] 20 p. 133 lots.   [US-NYgr]

"III. Komponisten und Musiker," lots 72-85—an excellent group.

2763   Vidal, Louis Antoine, 1820-91

Lavigne (Exp.); Charles Pillet (C.-P.)

Catalogue de la collection musical et des instruments de musique, provenant du cabinet de feu . . . , ancien premier violon de la chapelle de Charles X et de Louis-Philippe . . . vente . . . Hôtel Drouot . . . 6 février 1868. . . . Paris, 1868. 14 p. 102, 23 lots. Music, lots 1-102.

[NL-DHgm]

Folter, no. 368, under Jean-Joseph Vidal. Also in **Blogie** and **Fétis.**

→ *See also* catalogs and literature about Louis-Philippe's library here *under* **Toulouse, Louis Alexandre.**

Vieillot, L.   *See under* **Vadé, Jean Joseph**

Vila Viçosa.   *See under* **João IV, King of Portugal**

2764   Vincent, Alexandre Joseph Hydulphe, 1797-1868

Adolph Labitte, auctioneer, Paris

Catalogue des livres composant la bibliothèque de feu . . . membre de l'institut . . . la vente . . . 20 novembre 1871 [et 22 avril 1872 et jours suivants]. . . . 2 vols. Paris: Labitte, 1871-72. iv, 124; vi, 88 p.

[US-Wc, -NYp, -NYp, -CHua, -NH; also US-Ygr (with prices), GB-Lbl (Hirsch 483)]

Vol. 1: "Musique ancienne et moderne," 1634 lots. Vol. 2: "Science mathématiques; musique ancienne et moderne. . . ." **Folter,** no. 369.

2765   Vincent, G. Robert

Michigan State University, East Lansing

Dictionary Catalog of the G. Robert Vincent Voice Library at. . . . Ed. Leonard E. Cluley and Pamela N. Engelbrecht. Boston: G. K. Hall, 1975. vii, 677 p.   [US-Wc]

2766   Viner, William L

Catalogue of [his] *Musical Library. Sold March 21st, 1866.* Boston, 1866. 16 p.

A priced copy at US-Bp, the only known location. Cited from its *Catalogue*; not examined.

2767   Viñes, Ricardo, 1875-1943

Pierre Berès, firm, New York and Paris   Spec. List 62

Music and Musical Literature Including Books on Musical History, Early Theoretical Texts, Reference Works and the Extensive Collection Formed by the Eminent Spanish Guitarist and Composer. . . . New York: Berès, [194-?]. [28] p. 516 lots.   [compiler]

Item 452, "Spanish and South American Manuscripts," contains 68 Mss.!
Folter, no. 370, dates 1950.

2768 _____

Autographes musicaux: I. Manuscrits et lettres de compositeurs. II. Manuscrits et correspondence de Paul Dukas. III. Partitions et lettres provenant de Ricardo Viñes . . . vente à Paris le 20 juin 1977. [Paris: Drouot Rive Gauche, 1977?] Unpaged, [95 p.] 179 lots, plates.
[US-NYgr, -Wc]

> Magnificent Bach materials.

2769 Viollet-Leduc, Emmanuel Louis Nicolas, 1781-1857
J. FLOT (LIBRAIRE), PARIS
Catalogue des livres composant la bibliothèque de M. . . . Chansons, fabliaux, contes en vers et en prose. . . . Paris: Chez J. Flot, Libraire, 1847. 252 p. [US-NYgr]
> Chansons, many with music, pp. 1-55.

2770 _____

Méray, Antony. *Bibliographie des chansons, fabliaux, contes . . . ayant fait partie de la collection de M. . . . Nouv. éd., d'un avant-propos par M. Antony Méray. . . .* Paris: Claudin, 1859. xxii, 252, 30 p. [US-Wc, -CLwr, -CHH, NL-Avb]

2771 Vizentini, Albert
MAURICE (C.-P.) DELESTRE; JULES MARTIN (LIBR.), PARIS
Catalogue de livres anciens et modernes de littérature et d'historie. Collection d'ouvrages sur le théâtre et la musique, dont la vente . . . Hôtel des Commisaires - Priseurs, Rue Drouot. . . . Paris: Jules Martin, Libraire, 1892. 47 p. 624 lots. [US-R]
> Collector's name in Ms. on wrapper at US-R. That copy has buyers and prices which, according to a note, are in the hand of Arthur Pougin.

Vletter, W. C. de.   *See* De Vletter, W. C.

Vogel, Emil.   *See under* Kretzschmar, Hermann (Liepmannssohn sale catalog nos. 213-14)

Vogler, G. F.   *See under* F***, C. A.

2772 Vogler, Georg Joseph, Abt, 1749-1814
Verzeichniss der von dem als Theoretiker und Compositeur in der Tonkunst berühmten dahier verstorbenen . . . Abt G. J. Vogler nachgelassenen, grösstentheils noch nicht bekannten praktischen und theoretischen, im Manuscript vorhandenen Werke, sowie seiner im Druck erschienen und mehrerer fremden Musikalien . . . auf den 29ten September dieses Jahres . . . versteigert werden. Darmstadt, 1814. [4], 25 p. ca. 350 lots. [US-NH, -CHua (film)]
> **Folter,** no. 371.

2773 Vogt, Gustave [1781-1870?]
Friedland, Bea. "Gustave Vogt's Souvenir Album of Music Autographs. . . ." *Notes* 31 (1974): 262-73. [g.a.]
> Collection is at US-NYpm.

2774 Vogüé, Jacques Joseph François de, 1740-87

J. B. CAPEL, AUCTIONEER, DIJON

Catalogue de la musique et des instrumens dépendans de la succession de m. de Vogüé, évêque de Dijon, dont la vente commencers, au Palais épiscopal de la même ville, le mercredi 21 novembre 1787, heure de deux de relevée, & jours suivans. Dijon: J. B. Capel, 1787. 24 p. Music, lots 1-111.   [US-Wc, compiler]

2775 Volkmann, Robert, 1815-83

GILHOFER & RANSCHBURG, FIRM, VIENNA   CAT. NO. 83

Musik. Geschichte und Theorie. Praktische Musik. Portraits, Autographen, z. T. aus dem Nachlasse des . . . Vorrätig auf den Lager von Gilhofer und Ranschburg. Wien, [n.d., 1906]. 152 p. 3174 lots.   [US-Wc, NL-Avb, GB-Lbl]

    Folter, no. 372. Some indications of provenance.

Vollmöller, Karl. *See* **Löwis, August von**

2776 Volontè, Francesco

LITERATURE

Busnelli, Mariella. "Il fondo Volontè nell'Archivio della Veneranda Fabbrica del duomo di Milano." *Rivista internazionale di musica sacra* 7 (1986): 196-201.

    Not examined. Cited from *RILM*.

2777 Vondenhoff, Eleanore and **Bruno**

Gustav Mahler Dokumentation: Sammlung Eleanore Vondenhoff. Materialen zu Leben und Werk. Instituts für Österreichische Musikdokumentation, Publikationen, ed. Franz Grasberger, 4. Tutzing: Hans Schneider, 1978. xxii, 675 p., port.   [g.a.]

2778 Voullième, Ernst; Fürstl. Stollbergschen Bibliothek zu Wernigerode

MARTIN BRESLAUER, FIRM, BERLIN   NO. 49

. . . Bücher über Bücher . . . z. T. aus dem Besitz des Herrn Prof. Dr. . . . nebst Beiträgen aus der Fürst zu Stolberg-Wernigerodeschen Bibliothek, deren Bestände, die 120,000 Bände umfassen. . . . Berlin, 1932.   [US-NYgr]

    Not examined. Cited from a note about the sale in *ZfMW* 14 (1931/32): 432.

Vreedenburg, Max. *See under* **Cronheim, Paul**

2779 de Vries, H

VAN MARLE & DE SILLE, AUCTIONEER, KIJKDAGEN (NOTARIUS = J. A. MOLENAAR)

Catalogus van een belangrijke verzameling boeken en prenten . . . taal- en letterkunde, topographie . . . benevens de muziekbibliotheek van wijlen den heer . . . Organist der groote kerk te Rotterdam . . . 30 Sept., 1 [-3] Oct. . . . 7 Oct. 1929. . . . Kijkdagen, 1929. 96 p. 2078 lots. Music, lots 1936-2001.   [NL-DHgm]

2780 Wackerbarth, Athanasius Francis Diedrich, 1813-84

Lagerberg, Anders. "Katalog öfver A. D. Wackerbarths donerade samling af musikalier . . . Poträifades 1927 bl. framlidne öfverbibl. a. Anderssons papper."

    Ms. in Uppsala, Universitets Bibliotek, no. K. 82a. Cited by Lindberg (**2781**), p. 113.

2781 _____

LITERATURE

Lindberg, Folke. "Om Wackerbarthska Musiksamlingen i Uppsala universitets bibliotek." *STMf* 28 (1946): 113-19. [g.a.]

2782   Wälterlin, Oskar; Willem de Boer

HELLMUT SCHUMANN, FIRM, ZÜRICH   CAT. NO. 461

Bibliotheken Dr. Oskar Wälterlin, Schauspielhaus Zürich [und] *Willem de Boer, Konzertmeister. . . .* Zürich, [1964]. 80 p. 1632 lots. [US-NYgr]

Folter.

2783   Wagener, Richard (Prof., Marburg)

In 1864 and 1874 part of the collection went to D-Bds. Remainder was bought by B-Bc in 1902, but the most valuable items appeared in Boerner's sale of 1913 (**2784**). So much of it was purchased by Wotquenne (**2903**) that the Hirsch copy of the Boerner sale catalog bears on the spine the legend "Auction Wagener-Wotquenne, 1913," though Wotquenne's name does not appear in the catalog (and Wagener's only rarely!).

2784 _____

C. G. BOERNER, AUCTIONEER, LEIPZIG   AUK. CAT. NO. 114

Katalog einer wertvollen Bibliothek von Musikbüchern des XV. bis XVIII. Jahrhunderts. Versteigerung Mittwoch, den 2. und Donnerstag, den 3. April 1913. . . . Leipzig: Poeschel & Trepte, 1913. 140 p., illus. 624 lots. [US-Wc, -NYp, NL-Avb, -DHgm, GB-Lbl]

Sale noted in *ZiMG* 15 (1913/14): 224.

2785 _____

C. G. BOERNER, AUCTIONEER, LEIPZIG   LAGER-CAT. 27

. . . Musikbücher aus der Sammlung Wagener-Giessen. Leipzig: Boerner, [1914]. 47 p. 269 lots.
[GB-Lbl (Hirsch 484), NL-DHgm, -Avb, compiler]

Albrecht: Many of the Mss. were acquired by D-Bds, D-Ngm, G-Lbl (Hirsch), and US-AA. **Albrecht** also says a reprint of the catalog is in preparation, but it has not been located.

Includes an essay on lot no. 1, "Eine deutsche Lidersammlung des XVIII Jahrhunderts," pp. [1-3], by Max Friedländer.

2786 _____

Schaal, Richard. "Zur Musiksammeln von Richard Wagener. Dokumente über Handschriften-Schenkungen an die Berliner Staatsbibliothek." *Mozart-Jahrbuch* 16 (1970): 387-90. [g.a.]

2787   Wagner, Richard, 1813-83

Westernhagen, Curt von. *Richard Wagners Dresdener Bibliothek, 1842-1849: Neue Dokumente zur Geschichte seines Schaffens. . . .* Wiesbaden: Brockhaus, 1966. 116 p., ports.

[US-Wc, -NYp, compiler]

Catalog of the library, pp. 84-110. **Folter**, no. 373.

2788 _____

Kleemeier, Fr. J. "Richard Wagner als Bücherliebhaber." In *Zeitschrift für Bücherfreunde* 1 (1909/10): 248-51.   [g.a.]

    Folter, nos. 373 and 771 ("Über Notizen von Wagners Buchbinder Senfft").

Walcott, Mackenzie. *See* **Hipkins, A. J.**

2789 **Waldburg-Zeil, Georg von, Graf zu Zeil und Trauchburg**

[A manuscript thematic catalog of the collection, Fürstlich Waldburg-Zeil'sches Gesamtarchiv: "Musikalienkatalog" (1767-ca. 1786).]

    Brook, no. 1380.

2790 **Waldstein Family**

Rutová, Milada. *Valdstejnská hudební sbírka v Doksech: Das Waldsteiner Musikarchiv aus Schloss Doksy (Doza) . . . recenzoval Emil Hradečký.* Sborník Národního muzea v Praze, Rada A., Historie, 28. Praha: Narodní Muzeum v Praze v nakladetelstvi Orbis, 1976, 173-227. Illus.

[US-PHu]

    Previously a dissertation, Prague, 1971.

2791 **Walkden, John,** d. 1808

No catalog known. **King**, pp. 16-17, quotes a report that Walkden was passionately fond of Handel's music, of which he possessed a sufficient quantity to make a sale of six days. . . . "It is a thousand pities that no record of such a big sale . . . can now be traced." It is curious that the recent engrossing collection of essays edited by Terence Best, *Handel Collections and Their History* (Oxford: Clarendon Press, 1993) contains no mention of the name Walkden in the general index!

2792 **Walker, Daniel**

MR. SQUIBB, OF SAVILLE ROW, AUCTIONEER, LONDON

A Catalog of a Very Singular Collection of Musical and Physical Instruments . . . Printed and Manuscript Music . . . [Musical Instruments] . . . Property of the Late Mr. . . . Sold . . . the 21st of June, 1810 and Following Day. [London], 1810. 8 p. 121 lots. Music, *inter alia.* [US-R]

    King, p. 93.

2793 **Wallraf, Franz Ferdinand,** d. 1824

COLOGNE, UNIVERSITÄT, UNIVERSITÄTS- UND STADTBIBLIOTHEK

Katalog der in der . . . vorhandenen Musikdrucke des 16., 17., und 18. Jahrhunderts, von Willi Kahl. Beiträge zur rheinischen Musikgeschichte, 27. Köln: Arno Volk-Verlag, 1958. v, 20 p.

[g.a.]

    "Die Musikdrucke aus der Sammlung Wallraf . . . ," pp. 17-20, nos. 92-118.

2794 **Walmisley, Thomas Attwood,** 1814-56; **John Hingston**

PUTTICK & SIMPSON, AUCTIONEER, LONDON   CAT. NO. 812

Catalogue of a Collection of Music from the Library of the Late Walmisley, and the Library of Musical History, Theory, etc. of a Well-Known Collector [Hingston] *. . . Also Musical Instruments . . . Sold . . . May 18th, 1864, and Following Day. . . .* [London, 1864.] 26 + 2 p. 584 + A-Y lots. Music, excepting 412-501. Hingston's, lots 191-367.   [US-NYp, GB-Lbl]

2795   _____; et al.

PUTTICK & SIMPSON, AUCTIONEER, LONDON   CAT. NO. 965

Catalogue of a Large and Interesting Collection of Valuable Music from the Libraries of Several Distinguished Amateurs and Professionals . . . Historical and Theoretical Treatises . . . Scarce Works . . . Modern Music . . . Also Musical Instruments . . . Sold January 11th, 1867, and Following Day. [London], 1867. 32 p. 817 lots. Music, lots 1-773.   [GB-Lbl]

Ward, Rev. Arthur Robert.   *See* **Goss, Roger**

2796   [**Warren, Joseph,** 1804-81]

MR. FLETCHER, AUCTIONEER, LONDON

Catalogue of a Valuable Collection of Vocal and Instrumental Music . . . Early Madrigals, Motetts, Glees; Walsh's Editions . . . Rare Early Treatises . . . Rare Works for the Organ . . . Sold . . . May 31. . . . London, 1841.   [GB-Ob (Harding Collection)]

2797   _____

PUTTICK & SIMPSON, AUCTIONEER, LONDON   CAT. NO. 793

Catalogue of a Large Collection of Music. Valuable Full Scores of Operas and Oratorios. Modern Vocal Music . . . Also Musical Instruments . . . Sold Jan. 9th and Jan. 11th, 1864. . . . [London], 1864. 21 p. 544 lots. Music, lots 1-474.   [GB-Lbl]

> Though **King**, pp. 56-57, does not identify this as a sale of Warren's properties, it is listed as such in the typewritten index to early Puttick sales now at GB-Lbl (see discussion in **Coover 2**, p. 3, n. 1). **King** calls the 1872 sale the first Warren sale. Clearly, it was not. See his frequent notes about Warren, the sales, and Warren's huge collection of sale catalogs, pp. 42, 56-58, 70, 91n, 91-92, 98-99, 132-34.
>
> Smaller portions of the collections were also consigned, anonymously, to Puttick sales of 4 July 1864 and 12 April 1865, but are not noted by King.

2798   _____

PUTTICK & SIMPSON, AUCTIONEER, LONDON   CAT. NO. 1295

Catalogue of a Valuable Collection of Ancient and Modern Music, Including a Selection from the Library of . . . , Comprising Rare Antiquarian Treatises. . . . Also Musical Instruments . . . Sold February 23rd, 1872. [London], 1872. 19 p. 561 lots. Music, lots 1-527.
    [GB-Lbl, US-NYp]

> In the British Museum's *Catalogue of English Book Sales (1676-1900)* (*see under* **Pollard/Munby** in the Bibliography), this is considered the first Warren sale; to **King** it is the second, but if one takes into account the Fletcher sale of 1841 (as King does) and the two anonymous consignments to sales in 1864 and 1865, this is Warren sale number 4.
>
> Warren's properties here, lots 99-149, include lot 118, "Purcell. The works of entirely . . . autograph . . . In all 42 compositions, many of them now unknown. 1680."

2799   _____

PUTTICK & SIMPSON, AUCTIONEER, LONDON   CAT. NO. 1316

Catalogue of a Collection of Ancient and Modern Music, Including a Further Selection from the Library of. . . . Works on the History and Theory of Music. . . . Manuscript Compositions in the Autographs of Beethoven, Mozart [etc.] *. . . Musical Instruments . . . Sold . . . May 23rd,*

1872. . . . [London], 1872. 17 p. 356 lots. Music, lots 1-276.   [GB-Lbl, US-NYp]

> Warren's properties, lots 77-177, comprise many autograph compositions including one by Beethoven once the property of Stumpff (**2604**) and another by Mozart.

2800 ————

PUTTICK & SIMPSON, AUCTIONEER, LONDON   CAT. NO. 1326
Catalogue of a Large Assemblage of Ancient and Modern Music . . . Including a Further Selection from the Library of. . . . The Remaining Copies of Handel's "Messiah," Executed in Facsimile for the Sacred Harmonic Society . . . Also Numerous Musical Instruments Including the Collections of General Oliver and the Late F. W. Bates . . . Sold . . . June 28th and 29th, 1872. . . . [London], 1872. 32 p. 717 lots. Music, lots 1-571.   [GB-Lbl]

2801   **Warren, Joseph; F. X. Jelinek**

PUTTICK & SIMPSON, AUCTIONEER, LONDON   CAT. NO. 2008
Catalogue of the Valuable Musical and General Library, Autographs, Manuscripts, etc., of the Late . . . Comprising . . . Early Versions of the Psalms . . . Rare Theoretical Treatises, Fine Old English and Italian Manuscripts [lots 1-43]*, Some Probably Unpublished; Musical Autograph Letters and Biographical Sketches, Two Autograph Compositions of Mozart, the Property of the Late F. X. Jelinek . . . Sold . . . April 8th, 1881. . . .* [London], 1881. 21 p. 310 lots.   [GB-Lbl]

> Mozart manuscripts, lots 226-27. Lot 37, autograph letters, "Biographies chiefly written for the 'Biographical Dictionary of Musicians' by Sainsbury"—dozens of them.

2802 ————

PUTTICK & SIMPSON, AUCTIONEER, LONDON   CAT. NO. 2034
Catalogue of a Collection of Books on History, Theory and Practice [Property of Carl Engel]*; Also the Residue* [part 8] *of Warren's Library, Without Reserve . . . Sold . . . July 7. . . .* London, 1881. 433 lots.   [GB-Lbl]

> Warren's properties, lots 345-433; manuscripts, lots 345-78. Not a memorable sale.
>
> → *See also under* **Engel, Carl**

2803   **Warren, Samuel Prowse,** 1841-1915

ANDERSON GALLERIES, AUCTIONEER, NEW YORK   CAT. NO. 7737
. . . Catalogue of the Musical Library of the Late . . . and in a Separate Alphabet a Collection of Americana and Valuable Miscellaneous Books from Other Sources. To Be Sold October 26 and 27, 1916. . . . New York, [1916]. 61 p. 604 lots.
    [US-NYp, -NYgr, -NH, US-NYp and -Wc copies priced]
> Warren's properties, lots 1-475. **Folter**, no. 374, **McKay**.

2804   **Warren Horne, Edmund Thomas,** ca. 1730-94?

LEIGH & SOTHEBY, AUCTIONEER, LONDON
A Catalogue of the Vocal and Instrumental Music in Scores of . . . Carefully Collected by Himself, Containing Masses, Motetts, Psalms, Madrigals [etc.] *with Tallis's Hymn, in 40 Parts— Likewise Concertos, Sonatas* [etc.] *Most from the Middle of the Sixteenth Century to the Present Time . . . Sold . . . May 16, 1797. . . .* [London, 1797.] 8 p. 157 lots. Music (with many Mss.), lots 35-157.   [Film at CRL]

> **King**, pp. 60, 94.

2805 Warren Horne; J. C. Davis
Leigh & Sotheby, auctioneer, London
A Catalogue of the Entire Reserved Part of Vocal and Instrumental Music in Score of. . . . To Which Is Added the Manuscript and Printed Music . . . of J. C. Davis, Esq (Lately Deceased) . . . Likewise His Musical Instruments . . . Sold . . . January 8, 1810, and Two Following Days. [London, 1810.] 12 p. 315 lots. Music, lots 1-308. [US-R, film at CRL]
King, pp. 20-21.

2806 Warrington, James, 1841-1915
"Library became legendary." First collection removed to Hartford Theological Seminary in 1902 is now in the Pitts Theology Library at Emory University, Atlanta. A second, smaller collection, indexes, ledgers, and papers are in the Barbour Library at Pittsburgh Theological Seminary, according to *Amerigrove,* 4:480. Noted also briefly by Sonneck in his "Nordamerikanische Musikbibliotheken," *SiMG* 5 (1903-04): 329-35.

A note in *The Hymn* 42, no. 1 (1991), n. 1, cites "The Warrington-Pratt-Soule Collection of Hymnody" as part of the *Research Libraries Group Great Collections Microfilming Project, Phase Two.* No further information.

2807 _____
Warrington, James. *Short Titles of Books, Relating to or Illustrating the History and Practice of Psalmody in the United States, 1620-1820.* . . . Philadelphia: privately printed, 1898. 96 numbered leaves. [US-NY (film)]

In fact, includes other titles published 1821-96. Reprint, Bibliographia tripotampoloitana, 1 (Pittsburgh: Clifford E. Barbour Library, [1970]). Also reprinted in Burt Franklin Bibliography and Reference Series, 438 (New York: B. Franklin, [1971]). [both reprints g.a.]

2808 _____
Literature
Lowens, Irving. "The Warrington Collection: A Research Adventure at Case Memorial Library." In his *Music and Musicians in Early America*, 272-78. New York: Norton, 1964. [g.a.]

Previously published in the *Bulletin* of the Hartford Seminary Foundation, 12 (1952).

2809 _____
"Warrington - Pratt - Soule Collection Sold." *The Hymn* 28 (1977): 24 (only). [g.a.]

2810 Washington, Anne Blackburn (wife of George Washington's nephew)
Literature
Heintze, James R. "Music of the Washington Family: A Little-Known Collection." *MQ* 56 (1970): 288-93. [g.a.]

The collection is now at George Washington Masonic Museum, Alexandria, Virginia.

2811   Wassenaer, Unico Wilhelm, Count, 1692-1766

Gosse, Pierre Frédric. *Catalogue d'une bibliothèque . . . ainsi qu'une collection de musique . . . recueille . . . par . . . Messire Jacob Jan, Comte & Seigneur Banneret de Wassenaer . . . lesquels seront vendus publiquement . . . le mardi 9 Decembre 1788 . . .* A La Haye, 1788.

[g.a.]

> Two pages from this catalog containing 44 lots of music are reproduced in Albert Dunning's *Count Unico Wilhelm van Wassanaer: The Pergolesi-Riccioti Puzzle Solved* (Buren: Frits Knuf, 1980), 23, but no copy of the complete catalog located.

2812   Waters, Mrs. Frank; et al.

SOTHEBY & CO., AUCTIONEER, LONDON

Catalogue of Valuable Printed Books, Autograph Letters and Historical Documents . . . Property of . . . Lord Wharton . . . [etc.] Letters and MSS. of Hans Anderson, Goethe, Grieg, Jenny Lind, Mendelssohn and Sullivan, the Property of Mrs. Frank Waters, Great-Granddaughter of Jenny Lind. Letters and MSS. of Liszt and Other Musicians . . . the 20th of June, 1955 and the Following Two Days. [London], 1955. 115 p. 782 lots.   [Film at CRL]

> Lots 581-648, items associated with Jenny Lind.

2813   Watson, Henry, 1846-1911

B., John E. "A Munificent Gift." *Musical News* 17 (1899): 441-42.   [g.a.]

> With a lengthy list of rarities.

2814   _____

Russell, John F. *List of Compositions for the Pianoforte in the Henry Watson Music Library.* Manchester Public Libraries Music Lists, 1. Manchester, 1912. 71 p.   [US-NYp]

2815   _____

Russell, John F. *List of Chamber Music in the Henry Watson Music Library.* Manchester Public Libraries Music Lists, 2. Manchester, 1913. vi, 143 p.

[US-NYp, -BP, -Wc]

2816   _____

Nicholson, F. B. *List of Songs, Duets, and Vocal Methods in the Henry Watson Music Library.* Manchester Public Library Music Lists, 3. Manchester, 1913. 294 p.   [US-NYp]

2817   _____

Cartledge, J. A. *List of Glees, Madrigals, Part-Songs, etc., in the Henry Watson Music Library.* Manchester Public Library Music Lists, 4. Manchester, 1913. 197 p.   [US-NYp, -BP, -Wc]

2818   _____

Russell, John F. *List of Compositions for the Organ and Harmonium in the Henry Watson Music Library.* Manchester Public Library Music Lists, 5. Manchester, 1913. 54 p.

2819 _____

MANCHESTER PUBLIC LIBRARIES, HENRY WATSON MUSIC LIBRARY
Duck, L. W. *The Henry Watson Music Library: A Survey of Its Resources.* [2nd ed. Manchester],
1964. 14 p.   [US-Wc]

    First edition, 1961, not located.

2820 _____

Anon. "Henry Watson Music Library: MSS. [prints] Available in Microform." *Fontes* 13 (1966):
167-71.   [g.a.]

    Part 1: Orchestral, 87 items, 1730-1810.

2821 _____

Walker, Arthur D. *George Frideric Handel: The Newman Flower Collection in the Henry
Watson Music Library: A Catalogue.* . . . Manchester: Public Libraries, 1972. xiii, 134 p.
                                                                                        [g.a.]

    In his essay on the Aylesford collection of Handeliana in *Handel
    Collections and Their History* (see Bibliography), John Roberts says
    "Without question the most important repository [of Handel Mss.] is the
    Central Public Library in Manchester, which purchased Flower's Collection.
    . . ." It is odd that there is no separate essay about Fowler's collection in the
    group of essays.

2822 _____

LITERATURE
"The Music Library at Manchester." *Musical News* 30 (1906): 597.   [g.a.]

2823 _____

MANCHESTER ROYAL COLLEGE OF MUSIC
"Henry Watson. The Man. The Books. The Instruments." *MT* 50 (1909): 365-72.   [g.a.]

2824 _____

Russell, John F. "Manchester: Henry Watson Music Library." *Hinrichsen's Musical Year Book,*
4-5 (1947-48): 248-53.   [g.a.]

2825 _____

Duke, Leonard. "The Henry Watson Music Library." *MT* 93 (1952): 155-59.   [g.a.]

2826 _____

Ring, Layton. "Some Observations on the Contents of the Henry Watson Music Library."
Consort 9 (1952): 23-26.   [g.a.]

2827 _____

Duck, L. W. "The Henry Watson Music Library." *Library World* 63 (December 1961): 132-36.
                                                                                        [g.a.]

2828 _____

Duck, L. W. "Handel: Early Printed Editions in the Henry Watson Music Library." *Manchester
Review* 12 (1972-73): 73-81.   [g.a.]

2829 Wauvermans de Francquen

Raspé, Paul. "Le Souvenir de la Malibran au Conservatoire Royal de Musique de Bruxelles." *Cahiers Ivan Tourguéniev, Pauline Viardot, Maria Malibran* 11 (1987): 114-24.

A report on a forthcoming inventory of the bequest, with "an overview of works by Malibran and the Garcias" in the library (*RILM*).

2830 Webb, John (of Paris)

MESSRS. CHRISTIE & MANSON, AUCTIONEER, LONDON
Catalogue of the Collection of Violins, Printed Music, &c. of . . . , Deceased . . . Sold by Auction by . . . at Their Great Room . . . February 1, 1849. London, 1849. 8 p. 177 lots. Music, lots 1-110.

[compiler]

2831 Webbe, Samuel, Sr., 1740-1816

MR. WHITE, AUCTIONEER, LONDON
The Late Mr. Webbe's Library of Books, Collection of Music, and Unpublished MSS. A Catalogue of the Entire and Valuable Library of Books, and Collection of Music . . . Sold July 4th, 1816. . . . [London, 1816.] 16 p. 144 lots.

[US-Cn and compiler have copy of US-Wc catalog]

King, p. 26: includes 36 lots of Webbe's own unpublished Mss.

2832 Weber, Carl Maria von, 1786-1826

LITERATURE
Bartlitz, Eveline. "Reicher Bestand an Werken und Dokumenten: Die Weberiana-Sammlung der Deutschen Staatsbibliothek." *Musik und Gesellschaft* 36 (1986): 581-82. [g.a.]

2833 Weber, Gottfried, 1779-1839

Verzeichnis der von . . . nachgelassenen musikalischen Bibliothek bestehend aus einer reichen Sammlung von Musikalien aelterer und neuerer Zeit, theoretischen Werken, musikalisches Schriften . . . musikalischen Instrumenten. . . . Darmstadt: [Gedruckt J. J. Schmitt], 1842. 31 p. Ca. 1000 items. [US-NH]

Folter, no. 375. Not examined.

2834 Weber, Helen C

"Catalogo di una parte della musica di H. C. W."

A 4° Ms., ca. 30 leaves, listed by Otto Haas in his catalog no. 27, lot 44. Not examined. Is it the catalog of a collection or a works list?

2835 Weckerlin, Jean Baptiste Théodore, 1821-1910

Catalogue de la bibliothèque musicale de M. . . . bibliothécaire du Conservatoire National de Musique de Paris. Paris: Impr. Moret, 1908. ii, 86 p. [US-NYcu, -NYp (fiche copy)]

Folter, no. 376.

2836 _____

C. G. BOERNER, AUCTIONEER, LEIPZIG   AUK. CAT. NO. 98
Katalog der Musikbibliothek des Herrn . . . Lehrenbibliothekar des Conservatoire National de Musique de Paris. Musik, Tanz, Theater. Leipzig: Boerner, 1910. xvi, 172 p. 118 lots.

[Other copies are at US-Nyp, -Wc, -NH, -BP (priced), and NL-Avb]

Folter, no. 377. Noted in *ZiMG* 11 (1909/10): 202. The copy of the catalog, Hirsch 485, at GB-Lbl is a "Vorausgabe," no. 14 of an edition of 50.

2837 _____

KARL MAX POPPE, FIRM, LEIPZIG   CAT. NO. 1
Lager-katalog . . . Historische, theoreoretische und praktische Musik, zum grossten Teile aus der Bibliothek des Herrn. . . . Leipzig, 1911. 25 p. 588 lots.   [NL-DHgm]

Wegg, William.   *See* **Angel, Alfred** (sale, 24 November 1876)

2838   **Weiser, Severin Josef,** 1683-1756; **Antonin Sigisbert Krimer,** ca. 1700-70; **Antonín Jan Krimer,** 1740-97
Malý, František. "Blízkovická hudebni sbirke." *Časopis Moravského Musea* 70 (1985): 201-10.
    Cited from *RILM* (1985), p. 57.

2839   **Weiss, Edmund,** 1837-1917?; **Jan von Santen, Kolff**
LEO LIEPMANNSSOHN, AUCTIONEER, LEIPZIG   CAT. NO. 45
Autographen. Versteigerung, zum Teil aus den Sammlungen Edm. Weiss, München, am 28. und 29. November 1919. Leipzig, 1919. 64 p. 693 lots. Music, lots 407-693.   [US-Wc]
    ZfMW 2 (1919/20): 128, rich in music Mss.

2840   **Weisstein, Gotthilf,** 1852-1907
. . . Katalog der Bücher von. . . . Edited by F. von Zobelitz. [Für die Gesellschaft der Bibliophilen. . . .] 2 vols. [Leipzig], 1913.   [US-Wc, -NH, -I, -PHu, -Blu]
    Rich in theater materials, and vol. 2 includes much about opera.

2841   **Weitzmann, Carl Friedrich,** 1808-80
Catalog der hinterlassenen musikalischen Bibliothek von. . . . Berlin, 1881. 164 p. 1271 lots.   [US-CN, -Wc]

    Folter, no. 378.

2842 _____

R. DAMKÖHLER, FIRM, BERLIN   CAT. NO. 4
Musik. Zum Theil der Bibliothek des Prof. . . . enthaltend Geschichte, Theorie und Musikalien. Nachtrag. Berlin, [ca. 1880]. 37 p. 1187 lots.   [GB-Lbl (Hirsch 597) (2)]

2843   **Wenzel, Ernst Ferdinand,** 1808-80; **Emil Wilhelm Robert Naumann**
LIST & FRANCKE, FIRM, LEIPZIG   CAT. NO. 150
Verzeichniss der . . . bibliotheken der Herren . . . Versteigert am 25. April 1881. Leipzig: List & Francke, 1881. 56 p. 2070 lots.   [GB-Lbl, NL-DHgm, -Avb]
    Folter, no. 380.

2844   **Wertitsch, Hans P**
Angermüller, Rudolph. "Mozartiana aus der Sammlung Hans Wertitsch." *Mitteilungen der Internationalen Stiftung Mozarteum* 34, nos. 1-4 (July 1986): 65-92.   [g.a.]
    Donation of a collection of manuscript and engraved works, etc., from the estate of Franz Andrä Wagner, the administrator of the estate of Carl Mozart (1784-1858). "The collection's centerpiece of a catalogue of Carl Mozart's estate . . ." (*RILM*).

2845 _____

H[ilmar], E[rnst]. "Die Schubert-Autographe der Sammlung . . . : Katalog." In *Schubert durch die Brille: Mitteilungen 13 des Internationales Franz Schubert Institut*, 3-42. 1994.

2846 _____

Brosche, Günter. *Beiträge zur musikalischen Quellenkunde: Katalog der Sammlung Hans Wertitsch in der Musiksammlung der Österreichischen Nationalbibliothek.* . . . Publikationen des Instituts für Österreichische Musikdokumentation, 15. Tutzing: Hans Schneider, 1989. xiv, 522 p. [g.a.]

2847 Wesley, Charles, 1757-1834; **A Lady Deceased**
MR. PHILLIPS, AUCTIONEER, LONDON
A Catalogue of the Musical Library of the Late . . . Full Scores, Arrangements, and Orchestral Parts of Oratorios, Cathedral Manuscripts . . . Also a Harpsichord by Burkat Shudi, Which Belonged to Handel . . . Sold . . . 13th Day of July, 1835. London, 1835. 12 p. 200 lots.
[compiler]

"Original compositions in MS. of . . . Wesley," lots 112-58. "Property of a Lady Deceased," lots 166-80.

2848 West, Col.; A Lady of Rank
MR. WATSON, AT THE MART, AUCTIONEER, LONDON
Catalogue of an Assemblage of Vocal and Instrumental Music, Including the Library of the Late Colonel West, and a Portion of the Collection of a Lady of Rank . . . Also Instruments . . . Sold . . . May 7th, 1834, and Following Day. London, 1834. 12 p. 276 lots. Music, lots 1-214, 238-76. [compiler]

Lot 26, "Arnold's Compleat Psalmodist, scarce [etc.]" Lots 150-69, Handel oratorios, Walsh editions, large paper copies; lot 176, Arnold's edition of Handel's works, 38 vols.

2849 Westbrook, William Joseph; William Henry Monk; Joseph Haydn; Bourne Dando; et al.
PUTTICK & SIMPSON, AUCTIONEER, LONDON   CAT. NO. 3029
Musical Libraries of the Late . . . Full Scores, Treatises, Manuscripts, etc. . . . October 31st. . . . London, 1894.

Westbrook's lots, 111-27; Dando's, 320-79; Monk's, 64-110.

2850 Western Amateur Glee Club
PUTTICK & SIMPSON, AUCTIONEER, LONDON   CAT. NO. 687
Catalogue of a Collection of Music, Including the Library of the . . . Vocal and Instrumental Works of the Best Composers . . . Warren's Collection of Glees, the Original MSS., Including Many Unpublished Compositions . . . Set of Dr. Arnold's Edition . . . Sold . . . July 8th, 1861. 14 p. 348 lots. [GB-Lbl]

2851 Westphal, Johann Christoph, 1773-1828
Verzeichnis der von dem verstorbenen Herrn . . . hinterlassenen Bücher- und Musikaliensammlung. Hamburg: Gedruckt bei A. F. Künpel, 1830. 52 p. 1673, 30 + lots.

Not located; cited from **Folter,** no. 381. Sale, November 11 and following days (by which firm?).

2852 Westphal, Johann Jakob Heinrich, 1756-1825
Suchalla, Ernst. *Carl Philipp Emanuel Bach im Spiegel seiner Zeit: Die Dokumentsammlung . . . Westphals.* Hildesheim: Olms, 1993. 325 p. [g.a.]

> Westphal's collection consists of everything he could find about Bach, copied into a book to preserve them, now published.

2853 Westrow, A.
FRIEDLÄNDER & SOHN, AUCTIONEER, BERLIN
Katalog der von A. Westrow hinterlassenen aus gezeichneten Sammlung von Werken über theoretische Musik und Musikalien . . . versteigert 18 April 1853. Berlin: Friedländer & Sohn, 1853. 21 p. 779 lots. [GB-LRosenthal]

2854 Weyse, Christophe Ernst Friedrich, 1774-1842
Petersen, Carl S. *Det kongelige Biblioteks Haandskrift-samling. . . .* København: Nielsen & Lydicke, 1942. 48 p. [US-NH, -I, -BE, -Eu]

> Collection bequeathed to Dk-Kk (**Albrecht**).

2855 Whitaker, Edward; John Crookshanks; Charles Grimes; Thomas Howard
T. OSBORNE, AUCTIONEER, LONDON
A Catalogue of a Choice and Valuable Collection of Books, Chosen Out of Fifteen Libraries Lately Purchased: Particularly the Libraries of . . . [Including] *Musick-Books, Both in Print and Manuscript . . . Sold Very Cheap . . . 14th Day of November* [1737]. [London], 1737. 162 p. 5964 lots. [GB-L]

> 20 music lots are indexed in **Coral**; owner not identified.

2856 White, Eric Walter, 1905-85; **Allen Barlow;** et al.
SOTHEBY, PARKE BERNET & CO., AUCTIONEER, LONDON
Music. Catalogue of Important Musical Instruments, Printed and Manuscript Music . . . the Property of Eric Walter White . . . Allen Barlow . . . Royal Society of Musicians of Great Britain . . . Mrs. Barbara Box . . . Sold . . . 11th of May 1977. London, 1977. 157 p. Lavish illus. 504 lots. Music, lots 1-300. [Film at CRL]

2857 White, H
Catalogue of a Collection of Music. . . . 1846.

> Further information wanting. Cited from Otto Haas catalog no. 29, lot 33, which says "priced catalogue," but does not provide dealer or date.

2858 White, John Griswold
Thomas James Holmes and Gordon W. Thayer. *English Ballads and Songs in the John G. White Collection of Folk-lore and Orientalia of the Cleveland Public Library, and in the Library of Western Reserve University: Being a List of the Collections of English, Scottish and Anglo-American Ballads, Traditional Songs, Rhymes, Carols, Political Ballads and Songs, and Critical Material Concerning Them. . . .* Cleveland: Library Club, 1931. 4, 85 p. [US-Wc]

2859 White, Robert
Hunt, Christopher. "Scottish Ballads and Music in the Robert White Collection in the University Library, Newcastle upon Tyne." *Bibliotheck* (Glasgow) 5 (1968): 128-41.

2860   **Whittall, Gertrude Clark,** 1867-1965
U. S. Library of Congress, Music Division
Waters, Edward N. *Autograph Musical Scores and Autograph Letters in the Whittall Foundation Collection. . . .* Washington: Government Printing Office, 1951. 17 p.
[g.a.]

2861   **[Wiede, Alfred]**
Hans Schneider, firm, Tutzing   Cat. no. 188
Robert Schumann: Manuskripte - Briefe - Schumaniniana. . . . Tutzing, [1974.] 247 p. 256 lots.
[g.a.]

> The lots are magnificently described but there is no mention of Wiede anywhere, the sort of information about provenance that Schneider catalogs often include. According to **Albrecht**, the collection was preserved by Wiede's grandson, Alfred Ancot. After his death Schneider acquired about half of the collection. The Mss. are also listed in Wolfgang Boetticher's *Robert Schumann: Einführung . . .* , Veröffentlichung der deutschen Robert-Schumann-Gesellschaft (Berlin: Bernhard Hahnefeld Verlag, [1941]), 622-40.

2862   **Wighton, Andrew John,** 1804-66
Literature
Willsher, H. M. "The Wighton Collection of National Music." *Review of the Activities of the Dundee Public Libraries* 2 (July 1948): 12-13.   [GB-Lbl]

> **King**, p. 56. Now available in database form running on BIBL software (announced in *Brio,* February 1995).

2863   **Wilhelm, Herzog in Bayern,** 1752-1837**; Counts of Toerring-Jettenbach; Fugger Family**
Haberkamp, Gertraut, and Barbara Zuber. *Die Musikhandschriften Herzog Wilhelms in Bayern, der Grafen zu Toerring-Jettenbach und der Fürstem Fuggere von Babenhausen: Thematischer Katalog. Geschichte und Inhalt der drei Musiksammlungen, Robert Münster.* Katalog bayerischer Musiksammlungen, 13. München: G. Henle, 1988. x1, 195 p.   [g.a.]

Wilhelm von Redern, Graf.   *See* **Redern, Wilhelm Friedrich**

Wilkins, E. H.   *See under* **Lane, Capt. J. J.**

2864   **Wille, J**
J. L. Beyers, auctioneer?

> Volume 8 of the **Vereeniging** . . . *Catalogus,* without title statement or collation, notes four sales of songbooks from Wille's collection: 23 March and 26-27 April 1961, 27-28 February, and 29-30 May 1962. Not examined.

2865   **Willems, Alphonse**
Catalogue de livres anciens . . . provenant de la bibliothèque de feu. . . . Paris, 1914.
[NL-DHgm]

> Not examined. Cited from **Scheurleer** 1 (1923): 13.

2866 Willems, Leonard
INTERNATIONAL ANTIQUARIAAT, AUCTIONEER?

> Volume 8 of the **Vereeniging** . . . *Catalogus* notes, without title statement
> or collation, a sale of songbooks (with p & n) on 10 January 1939. Not
> examined.

2867 Willett, Ralph; John Hingston, d. 1683
PUTTICK & SIMPSON, AUCTIONEER, LONDON   CAT. NO. 567
Catalogue of Miscellaneous Music (Partly from the Celebrated Library of Ralph Willett) . . .
Handel's Works, in Full Score . . . Publications of the Musical Antiquarian, and Motett
Societies . . . Original Unpublished Manuscripts of the Late Charles Dibdin, and of the Late
Sir H. R. Bishop. . . . Also Musical Instruments . . . Sold . . . March 24th, 1659, and Following
Day. London, 1859. 30 p. 819 lots. Music, 750 lots.   [GB-Lbl]

2868 William V, Prince of Orange, 1748-1806
Smet, Monique de. *La Musique à cour de Guillaume V, Prince d'Orange (1748-1806), d'après*
les archives de la Maison Royale des Pays-Bas. Vereeniging voor Nederlandse Musiek-
geschiedenis, Muziekhistorische monografie, 4. Utrecht: Oosthoek's Uitgeversmaatschappij,
1973. vii, 282 p., illus.   [g.a.]

Williams, Justice.   *See* **Anonymous** (sale by Thomas Thorpe, 1847)

2869 Williams, George Ebenezer, d. 1819
MR. WHITE, AUCTIONEER, LONDON
A Catalogue of an Extensive and Valuable Collection of Music Books, Comprising the Work
of Ancient and Modern Composers in Great Variety, Vocal and Instrumental . . . Part of Which
Were the Property of . . . and Several Eminent Professors (Deceased) . . . Sold . . . 7th of June
1820, and Two Following Days. [London, 1820.] 28 p. 610 lots.   [GB-Lbl; film at US-BUu]

2870 Williams, William Warwick, 1846-1915
PUTTICK & SIMPSON, AUCTIONEER, LONDON   CAT. NO. 1808
Catalogue of the Very Valuable and Extensive Library of Music of the Late . . . Rare Autographs
and MSS., Early Printed Works . . . Original Documents [about the] *Concerts of Ancient Music*
. . . Also Musical Instruments . . . Sold February 24th, 1879, and Following Day. 37 p. 739
lots. Music, lots 1-605.   [GB-Lbl]

2871 Williams Wynn, Watkins, Sir, 4th Baronet, 1749-89
Picker, Martin. "Handeliana in the Rutgers University Library." *Journal of the Rutgers University*
Library 29, no. 1 (1965): 1.   [g.a.]

> The collection was first described by Charles Burney in his book on the
> Handel Commemoration, *An Account of the Musical Performances in*
> *Westminster Abbey, and the Pantheon, May 26th, 28th . . .* [etc.] (London
> & Dublin [etc.], 1785; reprint, 1964), 45. Some of the collection went to GB-
> BENcoke.
>
> **Albrecht. King**, pp. 16-17. Not mentioned in **Best**.

2872   **Willmott, Ellen Ann,** 1860?-1934
MESSRS. SOTHEBY & CO., AUCTIONEER, LONDON
Catalogue of Valuable Books and Manuscripts on Botany, Music and General Subjects
Selected from the Library at Warley Place, Essex, the Property of . . . Sold . . . 1st April, 1935,
and Two Following Days. . . . [London, 1935.] 68 p., illus.   [US-Wc; film at CRL]

> Part 2, musical library, pp. 40-68, lots 352-575. Lots 556-75. Autograph Mss.
> and letters of musicians. **Albrecht. King**, pp. 71, 96.

2873   _____
ELLIS, FIRM, LONDON   No. 324
Rare Old Music, Including Many Pieces of the 17th and 18th Centuries, Purchases from the
Late Miss Willmott's Collection, etc. London, 1935. [23] p. 124 lots.   [compiler]

Wilsing, Friedrich August.   *See under* **Mempell, Johann Nikolaus**

2874   **Wilson, Sir Giffin**
PUTTICK & SIMPSON, AUCTIONEER, LONDON   CAT. NO. 109
Catalogue of the Very Select Musical Library of the Late. . . . Valuable Full Scores, Complete
Copy of Arnold's Edition of Handel, on Large Paper; Theoretical Works; Also Musical
Instruments . . . Sold March 23rd, 1849. [London], 1849. 14 p. 953 lots. Music, lots 1-243,
276-953.   [US-NYp, GB-Lbl]

> Rich in harp music. **King**, pp. 94, 96. **Coral.**

2875   **[Wilson, Robert, Sir]**
PUTTICK & SIMPSON, AUCTIONEER, LONDON   CAT. NO. 1157
Catalogue of an Extensive Collection of Music, Rare Antiquarian Works, a Few Curious
MSS. . . . Sold . . . November 16-17. . . . London, 1869. 1257 lots.   [GB-Lbl]

2876   **Wilson, William (of the Minories, F.S.A.)**
SOTHEBY & SON, AUCTIONEER, LONDON
A Catalogue of the Choice and Valuable Library of the Late. . . . Together with a Most
Extensive Collection of Music and Works on Music . . . Sold . . . January 23rd 1833, and Three
Following Days. [London, 1833.] 40 p. 1334 lots. Music, lots 1288-333.   [Film at CRL]

Winckler-Atkinson, A.   *See under* **Urban, W.**

2877   **Winterfeld, Carl Georg August Vivigens von,** 1784-1852
R. FRIEDLÄNDER & SOHN, AUCTIONEER, BERLIN
. . . Carl von Winterfeld's weil. königl. obertribunalsrath musikalische Bibliothek welche
durch den königl. Commissarius in öffentlicher Auction versteigert werden . . . am 15, Juni
1857 und den folgenden Tagen. . . . Berlin: Druck von A. Bahn & Comp., [1857]. 20 p. 785 lots.
   [US-Wc, GB-Lbl]

> **Folter**, no. 382. **Albrecht** credits this catalog to Brenet (née **Bobillier**). The
> catalog is reproduced as the *Anhang* to Bernhard Stockmann's Ph.D. diss.,
> "Carl von Winterfeld" (University of Kiel, 1958).

Wissocq de Sousberghe.   *See* **Sousberghe, Clerque de Wissocq**

2878   Withers, George, 1847-1931

PUTTICK & SIMPSON, AUCTIONEER, LONDON   CAT. NO. 6971

Catalogue of the Valuable Collection of Old and Modern Italian, French, English and Other Violins [etc.] . . . *The Reference Library of Books on the Violin . . . Portraits . . . Paganini Relics . . . Autograph Letters, &c. . . . Sold May 12th, 1932 and Following Day.* [London], 1932. 20 p. 386 lots, plates. Music, lots 1-177, 213-338.   [US-NYp, -R, GB-Lbl]

> Paganini letters, lots 271-76. Withers was a dealer in musical instruments but the reference library could be called a private collection.

2879   Witmark, Isidore, 1871-1941

COLUMBIA UNIVERSITY, LIBRARY, ISIDORE WITMARK COLLECTION

Catalog of the . . . Collection of Autographed Books and Musical Scores. . . . New York: Columbia University Libraries, 1942. 76 p. Ca. 400 nos.   [g.a.]

> Notes on the scores prepared by Richard S. Angell. **Folter**, no. 383.

2880   Wittelsbach Family

MUNICH, BAYERISCHES NATIONAL-MUSEUM

Denkmale und Erinnerungen des Hauses Witelsbacher im. . . . Bayerisches Nationalmuseum, Kataloge, 11. München, 1909. vii, 268 p., illus, plates.   [US-Wc, -NYp, -CA]

2881   _____

MUNICH, BAYERISCHE STAATSBIBLIOTHEK

Leidinger, Georg, ed. *Katalog der Wittelsbacher-Ausstellung im Fürstensaale. . . .* München: A. Huber, 1911. 39 p.   [US-NH, GB-Lbl]

2882   _____

Wallner, Bertha Antonia. "Die Musikalien in der Wittelsbacher-Ausstellung der Kg. Hof- und Staats-bibliothek zu München." *ZIMG* 13 (1911/12): 82-92.   [g.a.]

> Noted in *ZfMW* 2 (1919/20): 302n. Wallner uses the numbers in Leidinger's catalog (**2881**).

2883   _____

LITERATURE

Einstein, Alfred. "Italienische Musiker am Hofe der Neuberger Wittelsbacher, 1614-1716." *SIMG* 9 (1908): 336-424.   [g.a.]

> Noted in *ZIMG* 9 (1907/08): 296.

2884   Wittenhorst-Sonsfeldt, Friedrich Otto von, 1678-1755

"Notenkatalog des Herrn Generalmajor Frey Herrn vons Sonsfeldt." Reprinted in Joachim Domp's *Studien zur Geschichte der Musik an westfälischen Adelshöfen.* Freiburger Studien zur Musikwissenschaft, 1:124-27. Regensburg: F. Pustet, 1934.   [US-NYp]

2885   _____

"Der Sonsfeldt-Katalog [thematic] MS. [facsimile]." In Deutsche Musikgeschichtliches Archiv, *Katalog der Filmsammlung,* ed. Jürgen Kinderman, nos. 20-21, 142-78. Kassel: Bärenreiter, 1992.

> The last two pages are a supplied composer index. The collection was bequeathed to Freiherr von Fürstenberg-Herdringen. "Located for a long time at D-Pa, it was returned to the Schloss Herdringen in 1970" (**Albrecht**).

2886   Wittgenstein, Karl

LITERATURE

Flindell, E. F. "Ursprung und Geschichte der Sammlung Wittgenstein im 19. Jahrhunderts." *Mf* 22 (1968): 298-314.   [g.a.]

> Flindell claims, among other things, that this Wittgenstein acquired certain Brahms manuscripts for his collection, but Bozarth in *Notes* 40 (1983): 241n, reports that they were assembled instead by Jerome Stonborough! Ultimately Stonborough's collection went to US-Wc. Some autographs were obtained by US-NYp from Paul Wittgenstein, according to **Albrecht**.

2887   Wittgenstein Family

LITERATURE

Unger, W. "Die Beethoven Handschriften der Familie Wittgenstein in Wien." *Neues Beethoven-Jahrbuch* 7 (1937): 155-70.   [g.a.]

2888   Witvogel, Gerard Frederik, ca. 1669-1746

ARENT RAMPEN, FIRM?, AMSTERDAM

Catalogus van een uitmuntende verzameling van een groote extra fraije gedrukte Partye Exemplaren van nieuw Musicq; Van de beroemste Meesters, Benevens De fyne kopere gesnedene Platen Van dien compleet . . . verkogt zullen werden 13 October 1746. Amsterdam: Arent Rampen, 1746. 28 p. Lotted in separate sections.   [NL-DHgm]

2889   _____

"De nalatenschap van G. F. Witvogel, 1746." *Tijdschrift der Vereeniging voor nederlandse muziekgeschiedenis* 9 (1914): 245-49.   [g.a.]

> Summary of the 1746 catalog (**2888**), ". . . bijeengebracht door Dr. D. F. Scheurleer." **Folter**, no. 384, cites this article but not the 1746 catalog.

2890   Wolbe, Eugen

SOTHEBY PARKE BERNET & CO., AUCTIONEER, LONDON

Catalogue of Important Musical Manuscripts, Autograph Letters of Composers and Musicians, Printed Music and Books on Music and Musical Instruments, Including Schumann, Schubert, Rossini, and Others' Autograph Scores . . . Sold . . . 23rd November, 1977. London, 1977. 61 p. 300 lots.   [Film at CRL]

> From the collection "of the late Prof. Eugen Wolbe," lots 192-300. Mostly autographs, ALS, and a few holographs.

2891   Wolf, Hugo, 1860-1903

Werner, Heinrich. *Hugo Wolf und der Wiener akademische Wagner-verein, mit Briefen des Meister an angehörige des Vereines und diesem nahestehende Personlichkeiten. . . .* Deutsche Musikbucherei, 60. Regensburg: G. Bosse, [1926].   157 (i.e., 163) p., facs.

[US-Wc]

> "Katalog der vom Wagner-verein übernommenen Privat-bibliothek Hugo Wolf's," pp. 145-56. 200 nos., including ca. 80 music items. **Folter**, no. 385.

Wolf, R. F.   *See under* **Caraman-Chinay** (sale of 14 June 1976)

2892   **[Wolf, Sándor],** b. 1871
Csatkai, André, and Ernst Fritz Schmid. *Joseph Haydn: Katalog der Gedächtnisausstellung in Eisenstadt, 1932, zur Feier der 200 jährigen Wiederkehr seines Geburtsjahres.* [Eisenstadt: Im Selbstverlag der Sammlung Sándor Wolf, 1932.] 15, [3] p., illus., facs.   [US-Wc]
> Catalog of the Haydn exhibition, including Wolf's collection.

2893   _____

> *LITERATURE*
> Csatkai, André. "Aus dem Haydnzimmer der Wolfsammlung." *Burgenländische Heimatblätter* 1 (1932): 31-35.

2894   **Wolffheim, Werner Joachim,** 1877-1930
Kurzes Verzeichnis der Tabulatur-drucke in der Bibliothek Dr. Werner Wolffheim für Martin Bresaluer zum 16 Dezember 1921 zusammengestellt. [Berlin-Steglitz: Druck der Officina Serpentis, 1921.] [8] p. 29 items.   [US-Wc, GB-Lbl (Hirsch 489)]
> Only 20 examples printed. **Folter**, no. 386.

2895   _____

> MARTIN BRESLAUER, AND LEO LIEPMANNSSOHN, FIRMS, BERLIN
> *Versteigerung der Musikbibliothek des Herrn Dr. . . . Versteigerung: Mittwoch, den 13. Juni bis Sonnabend den 16. Juni 1928 . . . [Montag, den 3. Juni bis Sonnabend, den 7. Juni 1929. . . . Berlin, 1928-19.]* 4 vols. in 2.   [g.a.]
>> Contents of each volume set out in **Folter**, no. 387.
>> → *See also* **Albrecht**

2896   _____

> MAGGS BROS., FIRM, LONDON   CAT. NO. 512
> *Music, Early Books, Manuscripts, Portraits and Autographs. . . .* London, 1928. 300 p., 42 plates. Ca. 600 lots.
>> According to **Folter,** no. 388, most lots had been acquired by Maggs at the earlier Wolffheim sale.
>> → *See also under* **Friedländer, Max** (Liepmannssohn catalog nos. 237 and 238, each of which contained much material of Wolffheim provenance)

2897   _____

> L'ART ANCIEN, S.A., FIRM, ZÜRICH   BULLETIN 17
> *Incunabula, Early Illustrated Books, Music, Medicine and Natural Sciences.* Zürich, 1929. 400 lots.
>> The editor of *ZfMW* 11 (1928/29): 608, says nos. 244-312, music, included many rare treatises, the first appearance, in part, of materials from the Wolffheim collection.

2898   _____

> *LITERATURE*
> Huth. "Versteigerung einer Kostbaren Musikbibliothek." *Der Auftakt* 8 (1927?): 7.   [g.a.]

2899 _____

"Versteigerung der Musikbibliothek Dr. Werner Wolffheim." *Zeitschrift für Musik* 95 (1928): 439-40. [g.a.]

2900 _____

Steinhard, Erich. "Musiksammlung Wolffheim." *ZfMW* 11 (1929): 605-06. [g.a.]

2901 Woolhouse, Wesley S. B., 1809-93
PUTTICK & SIMPSON, AUCTIONEER, LONDON   CAT. NO. 2960
Catalogue of a Collection of Valuable Instruments. . . . Also the Library of Music of the Late . . . Sold October the 24th, 1893 . . . and Following Day. [London, 1893.] 30 p. 632 lots. Music, lots 321-632. Woolhouse properties, lots 321-622. [GB-Lbl]

> A later mixed Puttick sale of 6 December 1893 contained mostly instruments and two holographs, but they may or may not have belonged to Woolhouse.

2902 Worp, J (organist, Matinikerk, Groningen)
G. THEOD. BOM & ZOON, AUCTIONEER, AMSTERDAM
Catalogus der uitgelreide muziekbibliotheek, nagelaten door . . . Theorie, methodes . . . zangmuziek . . . oper'a en oratorien . . . tonneel, instrumenten, enz. De verkooping . . . 23 [-26] Januari 1892. Amsterdam, 1892. 23 p. 442 lots. [NL-Avb]

2903 Wotquenne, Alfred, 1867-1939
C. G. BOERNER, AUCTIONEER, LEIPZIG   AUK. NO. 114
Katalog einer wertvollen Bibliothek von Musikbüchern des XV. bis XVIII. Jahrhunderts . . . versteigerung . . . 2-3 April, 1913. . . . Leipzig, 1913. 140 p. 624 lots. [US-WC, -NYp, GB-Lbl]

> **Folter,** no. 389. **Albrecht:** "many items obtained from the Wagener library" (**2783**).

2904 [Wright, J   ]
PUTTICK & SIMPSON, AUCTIONEER, LONDON   CAT. NO. 537
Catalogue of a Large and Valuable Collection of Music, Comprising a Large Portion of the Well Selected Library of a Late Distinguished Member of the Madrigal Society . . . Also Musical Instruments . . . Sold April 27, 1858. [London], 1858. 20 p. 497 lots. Music, lots 1-492. [GB-Lbl]

2905 Wrocki, Edward
Szarlett, Bernard. *Nieznany skarb w Polsce, zbiory muzyczne Edwards Wrockiego, napisal Bernard Szarlett.* Warszawa, 1929. 7, [1] p., illus. [US-Wc]

> Added title page: *Un trésor inconnu en Pologne, collection musicale Ëduard Wrocki.*

2906 _____

. . . Z doli i niedoli moich zbiorów muzycznych. Warszawa: [Zaklady drukarskie F. Wyszynski i s-ka], 1937. 30, [2] p., illus, facs. [US-Wc]

> Added title-page: *L'Essor et le sort d'une collection musicale.*

2907 **Wurzbach, Constantin Ritter von Tannenberg,** 1818-93
GILHOFER & RANSCHBURG, FIRM, VIENNA   CAT. NO. 67
Theoretische und praktische Musik. Sammlung Gottfried von Preyer . . . Nebst einem Anhange: Theatralia. Geschichte und Wesen des Theaters. Schauspielkunst. Zum Theile aus dem Nachlasse des Herrn Dr. Constantin Ritter von Wurzbach. . . . Wien, [1902]. 46 p. 1069 lots.
Not located; cited from **Folter**, no. 813.

2908 **Wustrow, A.**
R. FRIEDLÄNDER, & SOHN, AUCTIONEER, BERLIN
Catalog der von A. Wustrow . . . hinterlassenen ausgezeichniete Sammlung von Werken über theoretische Musik und Musikalien, welche am 18. April 1853 . . . versteigert werden sollen. . . . Berlin, [1853]. 21 p. 779 lots.   [GB-Lbl (Hirsch 492.6)]

2909 **Yaffe, Selomoh**
Gorali, Moshe. "Arkiyyon haq-qompozitor Selomoh Yafeh [Archives of the composer Shelomo Yaffe]." *Tatzlil* 9 (1977): 150-55.   [g.a.]
Given to the Haifa Music Museum and AMLI Library. Gorali lists compositions from 1953-76.

2910 **[Yates, Rev.   ]**
PUTTICK & SIMPSON, AUCTIONEER, LONDON   CAT. NO. 1100
Catalogue of Ancient and Modern Music . . . Full and Vocal Scores . . . Instrumental Music . . . Musical Instruments . . . Sold March 24th, 1869, and Following Day. [London], 1869. 31 p. 1125 lots. Music, lots 1-958.   [GB-Lbl]

2911 **Young, Bernard A.** and **Morris N.**
"The Young Collection of American Popular Music. Index." [Princeton, N.J.: Princeton Microfilm Corp., 197-?]
The collection is supposed to be available on microfilm, and an announcement also notes a "hard-copy index." Not examined.

2912 _____
LITERATURE
Lubrano, John and Jude. "American Popular Music, 1795-1920." *AB Bookman's Weekly* 76, no. 24 (9 December 1985): 4267, 4272-90.   [g.a.]

Young, W. *See under* **Novello, Vincent**

2913 **Young, William** (of Standlich)
MR. PRESTAGE, AUCTIONEER, STANDLICH
A Catalogue of the Large and Well-Chosen Library of Books of . . . (Who Is Going Abroad), Together with His Curious Manuscript Musick, Prints and Drawings . . . Sold . . . at Standlich Near Salisbury . . . the 23rd of July 1764, and the Seven Following Days (Sunday Excepted). [Standlich, 1764.] 52 p. 1163 lots. Music, lots 121-49 (but many more items). Lot 149, "Artazerse Musica del Leonardo Vinci, MSS."   [GB-Lbl]
King, pp. 18-19.

2914   [Ysaÿe, Eugène, 1858-1931]

Alb. de Tavernier (Libraire-Exp.), Antwerp

Catalogue d'une importante collection de musique . . . dont la vente publique . . . le 19 juin 1934 . . . par le ministère de . . . J. van Damme. . . . [Antwerp, 1934.] 20 p. 329 lots.

[GB-Lbl (Hirsch no. 5820)]

The copy in the Hirsch collection at GB-Lbl contains letters to Paul Hirsch regarding purchases.

2915   Zacheis, Les

Literature

Gillis, Frank J. "The Les Zachei Jazz Collection." *Resound* 4, no. 2 (April 1985): 4-6.   [g.a.]

Collection given to Indiana University Archives of Traditional Music.

Zahn, A.   *See* **Rietz, Julius**

2916   Zambeccari,

Frati, Lodovico. "Un impresario teatrale del settecento e la sua biblioteca." *RMI* 18 (1911): 6-26.

[g.a.]

Also printed in his *Studi e notizie reguardanti la storia della musica . . . ,* 183-203. Reprint, Bologna: Forni, [1976].

2917   Zavertal, Ladislao, 1849-1942

Farmer, Henry George. *New Mozartiana: The Mozart Relics in the Zavertal Collection at the University of Glasgow . . . by . . . Farmer . . . and Herbert Smith. . . .* Glasgow: Jackson, Son and Company, 1935. ix, 157 p., plates.   [US-Wc, -NYp, -CHuas, -BE, -BP]

Reprint, New York: AMS Press, 1979. Collection formed by Venceslao Hugo Zavertal (d. 1899).

2918   Zborowsky, Nicolas

Maurice Bridel, firm, Lausanne

Danse, ancienne et moderne. Théâtre. Musique. (Bibliothèque de M . . .). Hors sér., 1. Lausanne: Bridel, 1950. 62 p. 519 lots.   [US-NYgr]

2919   Zellner, John

McGee's Closet, firm, Omaha, Nebraska

Collector's Lifetime Accumulation of Sheet Music. Parts 1-. [Omaha?, 199-?-   ].

All published? American sheet music. Reserve prices indicated. Compiler has Part 5, 16 p., 340 lots.

2920   Zelter, Carl Friedrich, 1758-1823

"Verzeichnis seiner Bibliothek [nach Zelters eigener Hanschrift copiert]." 69 p.

A manuscript alphabetical catalog from about 1810 or 1820, sold by Liepmannssohn in his catalog no. 210, lot 183. Collection now at J-Tn (M 01/80.Ms.), according to **Beisswenger.**

2921   Zenettis, Leopold von
Maier, Elisabeth. "Der Nachlass Leopold v. Zenettis in der Musiksammlung der Österreichischen Nationalbibliothek." *Bruckner-Studien: Festgabe der Österreichischen Akademie der Wissenschaften zum 150. Geburtstag von A. B.,* 53-79. Wien: Akademie der Wissenschaft, 1975.
[g.a.]

2922   Zeune-Spitta Sammlung
LEO LIEPMANNSSOHN, AUCTIONEER, BERLIN
Briefe und Urkunden von Fürsten, Staats- und Kriegsmännern, Dichtern, Gelehretn und Künstlern. Versteigert am 23-25 November 1908 durch J. A. Stargardt. . . . Berlin, 1908. 113 p. 1489 lots, illus.   [US-NYgr]
"Musiker, Schauspieler und bildende Künstler," lots 1252-489. Includes several dozen Chopin letters.

2923   Ziehrer, C   M
Schönherr, Max. *Inventar des C. M. Ziehrer-Archives in der Musiksammlung und Theatersammlung der Österreichische Nationalbibliothek in Wien.* Wien, 1969. xxix, 355 p.
Not examined; cited from *RILM.*

2924   Zilevicius, Jouzas
LITERATURE
Braun, Joachim. "Two Unique Baltic Music Collections." *Journal of Baltic Studies* 14 (1983): 85-88.
Not examined; cited from *RILM.*

2925   Zimbalist, Efrem, 1890-1985
PARKE-BERNET GALLERIES, AUCTIONEER, NEW YORK
First Editions of English and American Authors: Library of Efrem Zimbalist, Sold by His Order . . . November 15 and 16. . . . New York, 1939. 71 p. 382 lots.   [US-Wc, -NYp]
Folter, no. 390. Lot no. 5, a 16th-century Antiphonary.

2926   Zingarelli, Niccolò, 1752-1837
Catalogo della musica lasciata dal maestro . . . e che ora si trova presso il suo cameriere Benedetto Vita. [Naples: Benedetto Vita, 1837?] 8 p. Ca. 250 nos.   [US-Wc]
Folter, no. 391.

2927   Zitterbart, Herbert
Schmalz, Robert. "The Zitterbart Collection: A Legacy Unevaluated." *College Music Symposium* 19 (fall 1979): 77-88.   [g.a.]

2928   Zoeller, Carli, 1840-89; **W. Winterbottom**
PUTTICK & SIMPSON, AUCTIONEER, LONDON
Valuable Library of Music and Books on the History and Theory of Music Belonging to the Late . . . Mostly in Good Bindings; Also a Collection of Works in Score of the Composers of English Church Music . . . the Orchestral Arrangements in Manuscripts [probably unpublished] *. . . Belonging to . . . Winterbottom . . . Sold 5 December 1889.* [London], 1889. 358 lots.
[Not at GB-LBL; at GB-Cu]
Zoeller's properties, lots 135-335—an excellent collection.

Zopf, Hermann, 1826-83.   *See* **Hummel, Johann Nepomuk**

2929   **Zulehner, Carl,** ca. 1770-1841
*Verzeichniss der geschriebener und gedruckten Musikalien aus dem Nachlasse des . . .
bestehend in Kirchenmusiken, Opern, Vaudevilles, etc. in Partitur, Sing- und Instrumenten-
stimmen und in Klavier-auszügen, welches vom 4 Juli 1842 und folgende Tage . . . versteigert
werden.* Mainz, 1842. 44 p. Ca. 900 nos.   [US-Wc]
    Folter, no. 392.

Zumsteeg, Adolf.   *See* **Köstlin, Heinrich Ad.**

Zur Lippe, Simon VI, Graf.   *See* **Lippe, Simon VI, Graf zur**

2930   **Zweers, H   A   ; J   A   Frentrop**
    G. THEOD. BOM & ZOON, AUCTIONEER, AMSTERDAM
*Catalogus eener uitgebreide en belangrijke verameling muziek. Oude italiaansche violen
. . . nagelaten door . . . H. A. Zweers, Muziekhandelaar, te Amsterdam en J. A. Frentrop,
Muziekhandelaar, te's Hage . . . 21 . . . 22 Maart 1887. . . .* Amsterdam, 1887. 26 p. 668
lots. Music, lots 1-644.   [NL-Avb]

2931   **[Zweig, Stefan,** 1881-1942]
    HEINRICH HINTERBERGER, FIRM, VIENNA   CAT. NO. 9
*Original-Manuskripte deutscher Dichter und Denker. Musikalische Meister-Handschriften
deutsche und ausländischer Komponisten. Eine berühmte Sammlung repräsentativer
Handschriften* [aus dem Besitz Stefan Zweig]. Vol. 1. Wien, [n.d., 1936?] 80 p., 59 plates,
facs. 304 lots.   [US-NYgr]
    "Musikalische Meisterhandschriften," lots 232-304—holographs by Bach,
    Beethoven, Brahms, Boccherini, Chopin, etc.
    Folter, no. 838. "Probably [with catalog 20] constitute the most complete list
    of Zweig's collection that was ever published," according to Zohn (**2943**).

2932   _____
    ADOLF WEIGEL, FIRM, LEIPZIG   CAT. NO. 142
Romantica [und Teile aus Stefan Zweigs Autographen-Sammlung]. Leipzig, 1936. ? p. 1317
lots.   [NL-Avb dated [1935]
    Half-title: "20 Mozart-Manuskripte." **Folter,** no. 839.

2933   _____
    HEINRICH HINTERBERGER, FIRM, VIENNA   CAT. NO. 18
Autographen und historische Dokumente [zum Teil aus der Sammlung Stefan Zweig]. *Im
Nachtrag einige interessante Autographen von Schweizer Dichtern und Gelehrten.* Wien,
[1937]. 48 p. 316 lots.   [NL-Avb]
    Folter, no. 841.

2934   _____
    HEINRICH HINTERBERGER, FIRM, VIENNA   CAT. NO. 20
*Interessante Autographen. I. Musiker. II. Dichter, Schriftsteller . . . III. Nachtrag . . . Aus zwei
bekannten Sammlung* [Stefan Zweig, II. Teil und Hugo Reisenfeld?]. Wien, 1937. 100 p. 881
lots. Music, lots 1-590.   [NL-DHgm, US-NYgr]
    Folter, no. 840.

2935 _____

"Autographs from the Collection of the Heirs of Stefan Zweig (Deposited on Loan)." In British Museum, *Mozart in the British Museum*, 27. London: British Museum, 1968.   [g.a.]

> Originally published in 1956.

2936 _____

King, A. Hyatt. *A Mozart Legacy: Aspects of the British Library Collections.* London: British Library Reference Division, 1984. 110 p.   [g.a.]

> List of manuscripts, pp. 92-95.

2937 _____

[Searle, Arthur.] *75 Musical and Literary Autographs from the Stefan Zweig Collection.* British Library Exhibition Notes. London: British Library, 1986. [8] p.   [g.a.]

2938 _____

Chesser, Richard, ed. *Stefan Zweig Series of Concerts, Lectures and Exhibitions, April-May 1987.* London: British Library, 1987. 40 p., illus.

> A list of Zweig's collection, over 200 literary and music manuscripts donated to GB-Lbl, May 1986, with an essay on the collector and his music autographs by Oliver W. Neighbour, pp. 9-13, and another by Albi Rosenthal, "Aspects of Autograph Collecting, Past and Present."

2939 _____

LITERATURE

Zweig, Stefan. "Meine Autographen-Sammlung." *Philobiblon* 3 (1930): 279-89.   [g.a.]

2940 _____

Wolbe, Eugen. "Stefan Zweig als Autographensammler. Zum 50. Geburtstag." *Kunstwanderer* 13 (November 1931): 32-33.

2941 _____

Zweig, Stefan. "Sinn und Schönheit der Autographen." *Philobiblon* 8 (1935). 14 p.   [g.a.]

> Separately printed, Wien [etc.]: Reichner, 1935. **Albrecht.**

2942 _____

Ecker, Karl. "Die Sammlung Stefan Zweig." In *Die Österreichische Nationalbibliothek: Festschrift,* ed. Josef Bick, 321-30. Wien: Bauer, 1948.

> Not examined; cited from Zohn (**2943**).

2943 _____

Zohn, Harry. "Stefan Zweig as a Collector of Manuscripts." *German Quarterly* 25 (1952): 182-91.   [g.a.]

> **Folter.**

2944 _____

Thommen-Girard, Georg. "Stefan Zweig als Autographen-Sammler." *Antiquariat* (Wien) 10 (1954): 205-08.   [g.a.]

> **Folter.**

2945 _____

Jonas, Oswald. "Eine private Brahms-Sammlung und ihre Bedeutung." In *Bericht über den internationale musikwissenschaftlichen Kongress, Kassel, 1962,* 212-15. Kassel: Bärenreiter, 1963.   [g.a.]

2946 _____

Neighbour, Oliver W. "The Stefan Zweig Collection." *MT* 77 (1986): 331-32.

2947 _____

Tyson, Alan. "Problems in Three Mozart Autographs in the Zweig Collection." In *Sundry Sorts of Music Books . . . Essays Presented to O. W. Neighbour,* 248-55. London: British Library, 1993.   [g.a.]

Section 2

Unnamed Collections
(arranged chronologically)

2948   **1699 (2 November)**
"A Private Gentleman"
R. MEERS AND M. RAWLINS, FIRM, LONDON?
An Excellent Collection of Italian, English, and French Musick, Both Vocal and Instrumental, Printed and Prick'ed; Likewise a Choice Collection of Church Music, Adapted for Cathedral Churches, Being Collected by a Private Gentleman, a Great Judge in That Noble Science; and Are Now to Be Exposed to Sale at Half the Rates As They Were Formerly Valued . . .

> A newspaper advertisment quoted in Michael Tilmouth's "Calendar of References to Music in Newspapers published in London and the Provinces (1660-1719)," *Research Chronicle of the Royal Musical Association* 1 (1961). No catalog located. Not in **Coral**.

2949   **1700 (16 November)**
"A Gentleman Lately Deceased"
HENRY PLAYFORD, FIRM, LONDON
A Choice Collection of Valuable Books of Musick, Being Part of the Study of a Gentleman, Lately Deceased . . .

> As the preceding, an advertisement quoted by Tilmouth. The same sale was also advertised for 17 May 1701. No catalog located.

2950   **1714 (25-26 May)**
"A Gentleman"
A Catalogue of Vocal and Instrumental Music; Being a Compleat Collection of the Best Italian Masters, &c., Which Will Be Sold by Auction, At Covent Garden Coffee House . . .

> Like the two preceding citations, an advertisement quoted by Tilmouth, with an addendum: The music has been "collected by a Gentleman in his Travels abroad" and was "all printed at Amsterdam." No catalog located.

2951 1730

Anonymous

PREVOST & CO., FIRM, LONDON

Catalogo de' libri Italiano e Spanuoli. . . . London: Prevost and Comp., in the Strand, 1730.

[copy at Worcester College, Cambridge]

24 music lots are indexed by **Coral**, p. 164.

2952 1741 (9-13 October)

[B , Ph. ; E V]

FREDRIK BOUCQUET, FIRM?

Catalogus insignium & rarissimorum in omni scientiarum genere. Librorum . . . prent-boeken . . . Alles nagelaten door . . . Bonefacius van der Haar . . . Waar agter een Appendix van Regtsgeleerde en andere boeken, musiek-boeken, en rarieteyten . . . verkogt . . . 9 October 1741 en volgende daagen. . . . 's-Gravenhage, 1741. 2, 124 p. 2979 lots.   [NL-Avb]

> **Lugt**, p. 545: 102 music items. "Appendix. Van eenige Regtsgeleerde en andere boeken als mede van een schoone partye musiek boeken, nagelaten door de Heeren Ph. B. en E. V. . . ."

2953 1757 (14 November)

Anonymous

ANDREAS LANDT, AUCTIONEER, COPENHAGEN

Fortegnelse paa endeel gode . . . Bøger, item adskillige rare og curieuse Kaaberstykker og Musicalia, som mandagen den 14 Nov. . . . offentlig auction i Madam Lindströms Gaard . . . Betolingen sheer til studiosus Andreas Landt paa auctionsstaedet. . . . Kiøbenhavn: Trykt hos Andreas Hartvig Godiche, 1757. 80 p. "Musicalia," pp. 74-76, 67 lots (but many more items).

[Dk-Kk]

2954 1764 (10 September)

Anonymous

ANDREAS LANDT, AUCTIONEER, COPENHAGEN

Fortegnelse paa endeel gode . . . bøger . . . samt nogle musicalia af adskillige berómmelige moend, som maandagen d. 10 Septemb . . . og folgende dage med auction . . . i Mad. Linströms Gaard . . . betales imod Annamelse til Andreas Landt. . . . Kiøbenhavn: Trykt hos Andreas Hartvig Godiche, 1764. 102 p. "Musicalia," p. 102, 17 lots (but more items).   [Dk-Kk]

2955 1773 (3-? December)

M****

HERISSANT, AUCTIONEER, PARIS

Notice des livres du cabinet de M****, dont la vente se fera dans une des salles des Grand Augustins, le vendredi 3 décembre 1773 . . . et jours suivans . . . Elle consiste en livres rares, curieux et estampes . . . et d'un très grand nombre d'oeuvres de musique, des plus célèbres auteurs, tant de France qu'étrangers, gravé, imprimées et manuscrites. A Paris: Chez Herissant, [1773]. 140 p.   [F-Tlm (FA 15142(10))]

> In the regular part of the catalog, there are 36 lots devoted to music books.
> 43 lots at the end comprise "Catalogue de musiques, françaises, italiennes, allemandes, anglois & autres, &c. des plus celebres auteurs . . . [scores]."

2956   1774 (22 November)
Anonymous

P. FR. DIDOT, FIRM, PARIS

Notice de livres, de musique et d'estampes provenant d'une bibliothèque, dont la vente . . . 22
novembre 1774, en une des salles des Grand Augustins. [A Paris: chez P. Fr. Didot, 1774.]
8 p. "Musique gravée," pp. 6-7 (29 lots).   [F-Tlm (FA 15144 (16)) priced]

> At end of music, "L'on vendra au commencement beaucoup de musique
> imprimée & manuscrite."

2957   1776 (14-? October)
Anonymous

C. KRIBBER, A. V. PADDENBURG; JO. V. SCHOONHOVEN & COMP., AUCTIONEER, UTRECHT?

Catalogue fait sur un plan nouveau, systématique & raisonnée, d'une bibliothèque de
littérature, particuliérement d'histoire & de poésie; d'environ XIX mille volumes . . . dont la
vente se sera à Utrecht, le 14 octobre 1776 & les jours suivans, par les Srs. . . . 2 vols. [n.p.,
Utrecht?], 1986. "Musique," vol. 1, pp. 265-70, lots 2734-805.   [US-NYgr]

2958   1776 (25-? November)
Anonymous

JUNGE, BOGHANDLER, COPENHAGEN

Fortegnelse paa endeel gode . . . Bøger i adskillige sprog og bidenskaber, samt nogle musicalia,
som mandagen den 25 November . . . og folgende dage ved offentlig auction . . . hos boghandler
Junge. . . . Kiøbenhavn: Trykt hos Morten Hallager, 1776. 104 p. "Musicalia," p. 78, 17 lots, but
more items.   [DK-Kk]

2959   1789 (11-? August)
Anonymous

KÖSTER, AUCTIONEER, HAMBURG

Verzeichniss auserlesener theologischer, juristischer . . . Bücher . . . nebst einigen Musikalien
und Kupferstichen welche am 11 August und folgende Tage . . . durch den Auctionator Hrn.
Köster, auf dem Einbeckischen Hause öffentlich verkauft werden sollen. Hamburg: Gedruckt
bey Nicolaus Conrad Wörmer, 1789. 80 p. Music, pp. 61-80, 395 lots.   [Compiler (copy)]

2960   1789 (30-? September)
Anonymous

HOFRATH HERTEL, AUCTIONEER, SCHWERIN

Verzeichnis einer Sammlung juristischer, medizinischer, historischer . . . Bücher in allerley
Sprachen, nebst einigen Musikalien und Landcharten, welche den 30. Septbr. und folgende
Tage 1789 zu Schwerin in dem Hause des . . . Hofrath Hertel . . . verkauft werden sollen.
Schwerin, 1789. 47 p. Music, pp. 3-5, lots 1-87.   [Compiler (copy)]

2961   1790 (15 March ?)
Anonymous

JOHN DREWRY, AUCTIONEER, LONDON

A Catalogue of Books Containing Many Thousand Volumes in the Several Branches of Science
and Literature, in Which Is Included the Library of . . . John Swain . . . to Which Is Added a
Catalogue of Modern Music, That Will Be Sold Exceeding Cheap for Ready Money . . . the

15th of March, 1790 . . . and Will Continue on Sale to the End of the Year. . . . [London], 1790. 103 p. 3100 items. Music, lots 2980-3100.

Music at 30% under the original price. Indexed in **Munby/Coral**. Title page information furnished by D. J. McKitterick at GB-CU; shelf number Munby d.136[4].

2962   1790 (5 July)
Anonymous

Catalogus von Kupferstichen und Musicalien welche den 5ten Jul. 1790 in loco convitorii hieselbst gegen baare Bezahlung in Neue 2/3tel an den Meistbietenden öffentlich verkauft werden sollen. Rostock: Gedruckt mit Müllers Schriften, 1790. 24 p. 167, 181, 4 lots. Music, pp. 13-14, 181 lots.   [compiler (copy)]

2963   1791

Anonymous

G. & T. BOOTH, FIRM, NORWICH
Books and Music . . . Norwich, This Day, 1791. . . . Norwich, 1791.

[GB-Cu (Munby Collection)]

Appears as a manuscript addendum to **Pollard/List**.

2964   1792 (3-7 December)
Anonymous

ROOS, GERBRAUD & JOHANNES WEEGE, AUCTIONEER, AMSTERDAM
Catalogus van een . . . schoone verzameling . . . boeken . . . nevens een groote en keurige verzameling muziek werkenen instrumenten en fraaye rariteiten . . . tekeningen . . . verkogt . . . 3 December 1792, en volgende dagen, ten Huize van Johannes Weege. . . . Te Amsterdam, 1792. 80, 66 p. 4170 lots.   [NL-Apk (some names and prices in Ms.)]

"Muziek-werken," pp. 2-9 of second part, 331 lots (many more items).

2965   1793

Anonymous

JAMES LACKINGTON, FIRM, LONDON
Lackington's Catalogue for 1793, Consisting of Above One Hundred Thousand Volumes . . . Including Many Valuable Libraries Late Purchased . . . Scarce Old and Valuable Books . . . Selling at . . . Prices Which Are Printed in the Catalogue . . . Not an Hour's Credit Will Be Given to Any Person. . . . London, 1793. 576 p. 19,517 lots.

"Music, treatises on music, and psalmodies, etc.," lots 6604-836.

"Second volume . . . will be ready in February."

2966   1796 (9-11 May)
"A Gentleman"

GRAHAM & PHILLIPS, AUCTIONEER, LONDON
A Catalogue of All of the Elegant Household Furniture . . . Porcelaine . . . Plate . . . Library of Select Books . . . Violin by Stainer . . . [Printed Music] *. . .* [Sold] *at His House . . . Leicester Fields . . . May the 9th, and Two Following Days. . . .* [London, 1796.] 24 p., 115, 109, 99 + lots. "Printed music," not well-described. "Second Day's Sale," lots 11-22 (over 50 items in parcels).   [compiler (copy)]

At GB-Lbl, interleaved with names and prices and additional offerings.

2967   18 ? (19-20 February)
Anonymous

THOMAS & SONS, AUCTIONEER, PHILADELPHIA

Sale of a Private Library . . . Catalogue of a Library of Choice Books . . . Elegantly Bound
. . . Also a Large Number of Bound Volumes of Well-Selected Music for Pianoforte, Violin, &c.
. . . Sold . . . February 19th and 20th . . . at the Auction Rooms, 139 & 141 S. Fourth St. . . .
[Philadelphia?: Printed at 5th and Chestnut, 18—?] 22 p. 545 lots. Music, lots 360-418.

[US-NYp]

2968   18 ? (28 May)
Anonymous

GEORGE A. LEAVITT & CO., AUCTIONEER, NEW YORK

Catalogue of a Private Library of Musical Works, Anthems, Operas, Cathedral Services,
Scores . . . the Most Valuable Library of Works Relating to Music Ever Offered [!]. *The Whole*
To Be Sold at Auction at the Clinton Hall Sale Room, Astor Place . . . May 21st [struck
through, changed to "28"]. [New York, 18—?] 22 p. 590 lots.

> Drexel copy at US-NYp includes some marginal prices. Date changed on
> wrappers by hand.

2969   1804 (5-6 December)
"A Gentleman, Deceased"

MR. KING, JR., AUCTIONEER, LONDON

A Catalogue of a Small Library of Books, Musical Instruments and Music, of a Gentleman
Deceased . . . the Music Comprises . . . Works of Mozart, Handel, Pleyel [etc.] *. . . Sold . . .*
Dec. 5th, 1804 and Following Day. . . . [London], 1804. 14 p. 244 lots.   [GB-Lbl, NL-Apk]

> Not examined; cited by **Lugt**, no. 6872, who says it includes 96 lots of music
> and musical instruments.

2970   1805 (28 February - 4 March)
Anonymous

H. GARTMAN, W. VERMANDEL EN ZOON, J. W. SMIT, AUCTIONEER, AMSTERDAM

Catalogus van eene verzameling gekleurde en ongekleurde teekeningen en printen . . . [etc.]
Modern muziek en muziek instrumenten . . . verkocht . . . den 28 February, 1, 2, en 4 Maart
1805. . . . Te Amsterdam . . . 1805. 2, 68 p. 1157 + 40 lots.

> "Musiekwerken en instrumenten," pp. 54-68. 166 music lots but many
> more items. **Lugt**, no. 6898. At library of the Rijksmuseum, Amsterdam.

2971   1805 (25-? November)
Anonymous

J. C. HANSEN, AUCTIONEER, COLOGNE

Verzeichnis auserlesener meist ganz sauber gehaltener historisch-politisch-diplomatisch-
[etc.] *Bücher . . . wie auch Musikalien . . . den 25. November 1805 . . . und folgende Tage . . .*
verkauft. . . . [Köln], 1805. 380 p. 4193 lots.   [D-KNu]

> Not examined; **Lugt**, no. 7008, says 3995 lots of music.

2972   1812 (18 December)
Anonymous

MR. STEWART, FIRM, LONDON

A Catalogue of the Works of Handel . . . Many of His Most Celebrated Compositions in Parts,
So That a Family May Sit Round Their Fire-side, and . . . Enjoy . . . the Plates of All Handel's

Celebrated Oratorios, and a Collection of Scarce Music . . . Sold . . . December 18th . . .
(Without Reserve) . . . At His Great Room, No. 194, Piccadilly. . . . [London], 1812. 8 p. 136
lots.   [compiler]

> Handel's works comprise lot 41, 57 titles; the oratorio plates, lots
> 81-103. Items in lot 41 each bear a fixed price. Lot 42, a small paper copy
> of the works was sold *en bloc* for £70. All other lots were individually
> auctioned.

2973   1813 (18 February)
Anonymous

Mr. White, auctioneer, London
Musical Library, Instruments, &c. A Catalogue of a Fine Collection of Music Books. A Valuable
Amati . . . Handel's Works [etc.] *Sold . . . February 18th, 1813.* [London], 1813. 8 p. 186
lots. Music, lots 1-116, 128-86.   [GB-Lbl (with n & p)]

2974   1813 (27-28 April)
"A Professor of Music"

Mr. White, auctioneer, London
A Catalogue of a Most Complete, Scarce and Valuable Collection of Music, Being the
Duplicates of the Library of a Professor of Music, Collected by Him at a Great Expence . . . and
Valuable Instruments . . . Sold April the 27th, 1813, and Following Day. [London], 1813.
16 p. 401 lots. Music, lots 1-302, 310-401.   [GB-Lbl (with n & p)]

2975   1816 (23-24 May)
Anonymous

Mr. White, auctioneer, London
A Catalogue of a Collection of Music, Consisting of a Very Fine Set of Handel's Works,
Complete . . . and Other Articles . . . Also a Valuable Pair of French Horns . . . &c., &c. . . . Sold
May 23rd, 1816, and Following Day. London, 1816. 12 p. 316 lots. Music, all but 2 lots.
                                            [Us-Wc (with n & p); -Cn (xerox copy)]

2976   1820 (8 June)
Anonymous

Mr. White, auctioneer, London
A Catalogue of an Extensive and Valuable Collection of Music Books . . . in Great Variety
. . . Also a Fine Toned Violin . . . Sold . . . 8th June, 1820, and Two Following Days. [London,
1820.] 28 p. 610 lots.   [US-BUu (film)]

2977   1821 (12 December)
"Several Persons, Deceased"

Mr. White, auctioneer, London
Catalogue of the Reserved Part of the Music Books, Printed & Manuscript of Several Persons,
Deceased . . . Sold . . . December 12, 1821. [London, 1821.] 16 p. 277 lots.
                                                      [GB-Lbl, US-BUu (film)]

2978   **1822 (15-17 May)**
"An Eminent Professor, Recently Deceased"
Mr. W. P. Musgrave, auctioneer, London
A Catalogue of a Very Valuable and Extensive Library of Vocal and Instrumental Music, Chiefly the Property of an Eminent Professor, Recently Deceased . . . Including a Curious and Unique Collection of Italian Operas in Full Score . . . Procured by a Nobleman on the Continent at Great Expense . . . [Instruments] . . . Sold May 15, 1822, and Two Following Days. [London], 1822. 23 p. 426 lots. Music books, lots 65-77; Italian and French operas, many in manuscript, lots 170-241.   [GB-Lbl, US-BUu (film)]

2979   **1822 (3-4 July)**
"An Amateur Residing in the Country"
W. P. Musgrave, auctioneer, London
A Catalogue of a Very Complete and Extensive Library of Vocal and Instrumental Music . . . With a Choice Collection of English Operas . . . [Musical Instruments] . . . and Some Valuable Treatises, the Property of an Amateur Residing in the Country, Recently Deceased . . . Sold . . . July 3rd, 1822, and Following Day. [London], 1822. 16 p. 272 lots. Music, lots 1-49, 54-272.   [GB-Lbl; compiler (film)]

> A manuscript note on the title page of the GB-Lbl copy says "A Gentleman in Leicestershire, Deceased."

2980   **1823 (10-11 July)**
Anonymous
W. P. Musgrave, auctioneer, London
Vocal and Instrumental Music, Instruments, Treatises and Books. A Catalogue of An Extensive and Valuable Library of Vocal and Instrumental Music (To Be Disposed of under Peculiar Circumstances,) . . . Likewise a Number of Excellent [Instruments] . . . Sold July 10th, 1823, and Following Day. [London, 1823.] 16 p. 258 lots. Music, lots 1-73, 92-358.
                [GB-Lbl; compiler (film)]

2981   **1826 (1-2 May)**
Anonymous
W. P. Musgrave, auctioneer, London
A Catalogue of Vocal and Instrumental Music . . . [Musical Instruments] . . . Sold . . . the 1st & 2nd of May, 1826. [London], 1826. 21 p. 259 lots. Music lots 1-202.   [GB-Lbl; compiler (film)]

2982   **1826 (13 December)**
Anonymous
W. P. Musgrave, auctioneer, London
A Catalogue of a Choice Collection of Vocal and Instrumental Music . . . Many Hundred Engraved Plates . . . a Large Consignment of Roman Strings . . . Likewise, [Musical Instruments] . . . Sold December 13th, 1826. [London], 1826. 20 p. 290 lots. Music and plates, lots, 1-241.
                [GB-Lbl; compiler (film)]

2983   **1827 (17 March)**
Anonymous
W. P. Musgrave, auctioneer, London
A Catalogue of a Very Extensive and Highly Valuable Collection of Vocal and Instrumental Music . . . Also [Musical Instruments] . . . Sold . . . 17th of March, 1827. . . . 31 p. 426 lots. Music, lots 1-390.   [GB-Lbl; compiler (film)]

2984   1827 (14 December)
Anonymous

W. P. MUSGRAVE, AUCTIONEER, LONDON

A Catalogue of a Choice Collection of Modern Vocal and Instrumental Music . . . [Also Musical Instruments] . . . *Sold . . . the 14th of December, 1827. . . .* [London], 1827. 10 p. 134 lots. Music, lots 1-50, 62-124.   [GB-Lbl; compiler (film)]

2985   1829 (13 May)
Anonymous

ANTON VON HAYKUL, AUCTIONEER, VIENNA

Verzeichnis in- und ausländischer Kupferstiche, Werke, Landkarten und Musikalien . . . welche vom 13th May [in Ms.] *angefangen im Bürgerspital Nr. 1100 . . . versteigert werden.* Wien: Gedruckt bey Anton v. Haykul, 1829. 37 p. 2714 lots.   [NL-DHrk, A-Wal]

"Gestochene in- und ausländische Musikalien," lots 969-1606.

2986   [1829] (6-? August)
Anonymous

W. P. MUSGRAVE, AUCTIONEER, LONDON

Music Books, Instruments, Paintings . . . A Catalogue of a Very Choice Collection of Modern Vocal and Instrumental Music . . . and a Small Library of Books . . . Sold . . . 6th of August, and Following Days. . . . [London, n.d., probably 1829.] 16 p. 258 lots.   [GB-Lbl; compiler (film)]

Lugt, no. 12116.

2987   1829 (26 September)
Anonymous

W. P. MUSGRAVE, AUCTIONEER, LONDON

A Catalogue of a Miscellaneous Assemblage of Books, Music, Violins, Flutes [etc.] . . . *Sold . . . 26th of September, 1829.* [London, 1829.] 8 p. 141 lots. Music, lots 1-69, 81-141.

[GB-Lbl; compiler (film)]

2988   1830 (5-9 March)
Anonymous

WHEATLEY & ADLAND, AUCTIONEER, LONDON

Catalogue of a Miscellaneous Collection of Books . . . a Very Curious Collection of Scarce Early English Music . . . Sold . . . March 5, 1830, and Four Following Days (Sunday Excepted). . . . [London], 1830. 46 p. 1332 lots.   [GB-Lbl]

Music, lots 1298-1325 but many more items — e.g., lots 1312 was a fine collection of Italian madrigals for 5 voices: 12 works by Soriano, Anerio, Pietro Paulo, Rota, Virchi, and others. All the parts were bound in 5 volumes and fetched £1/3!

2989   1830 (1-2 November)
Anonymous

W. P. MUSGRAVE, AUCTIONEER, LONDON

Catalogue of a Choice Collection of Vocal and Instrumental Music . . . [Also Musical Instruments] . . . *Sold . . . the 11th of November, 1830 and Following Day. . . .* [London], 1830. 14 p. 239 lots. Music, lots 1-191.   [US-NYp]

2990   **1831 (10-13 May)**
"A Professor - A Gentleman - A Dealer"
MR. WATSON (LATE WITH MR. MUSGRAVE), AUCTIONEER, LONDON
A Catalogue of a Choice Collection of Modern Music . . . Duplicates of a Professor, the
Library of a Gentleman, Removed into the Country, and a Portion of the Stock in Trade of a
Dealer . . . Vocal and Instrumental Compositions . . . [Also Musical Instruments] *. . . Sold . . .*
the 10th of May, 1831, and Three Following Days. . . . [London], 1831. 22 p. 400 lots. Music,
lots 1-259, 269-375.   [US-NYp (some n & p)]

2991   **1831 (18-19 August)**
"A Celebrated Amateur"
MR. WATSON, AUCTIONEER, LONDON
Catalogue of a Choice Collection of Vocal and Instrumental Music, Including the Duplicates
of a Celebrated . . . [Also Musical Instruments] *. . . Sold 18th of August, 1831 and Following*
Day. . . . [London], 1831. 12 p. 259 lots. Music, lots 1-203, 226-259.
                                                       [US-NYp (some n & p); compiler]

2992   **1831 (28-29 September)**
Anonymous
MR. WATSON, AUCTIONEER, LONDON
A Catalogue of a Choice Collection of Modern Music . . . [Also Musical Instruments] *. . . Sold*
28th September 1831, and Following Day. [London], 1831. 14 p.   322 lots.   Music, lots
1-88, 98-253, 275-322.   [US-NYp; compiler]

2993   **1833 (3 December)**
Anonymous
MR. WATSON, AUCTIONEER, LONDON
Catalogue of a Collection of Musical Property . . . Sold . . . December 3rd, 1833. London,
1833. 7 p.   [US-NYp; compiler]
> 158 lots, mainly good antiquarian books and music: lot 107, holograph of a
> Pleyel symphony; lots 59-60, Carissimi works in Ms.; lot 118, Viotti
> holograph.

2994   **1834 (5 July)**
Anonymous
MR. WATSON, AUCTIONEER, LONDON
Catalogue of a Collection of Vocal and Instrumental Music . . . Opera di Paisiello, 29 vols.
[etc.] *. . .* [Also Musical Instruments] *. . . Sold . . . at Mr. Stanley's Rooms . . . July 5th, 1834.*
London, 1834. 8 p. 188 lots. Music, lots 1-170.   [GB-Lbl; compiler]

2995   **1834 (23-24 September)**
Anonymous
MR. WATSON, AUCTIONEER, LONDON
Catalogue of a Collection of Vocal and Instrumental Music, Including Very Fine Copies of
. . . Oratorio Songs, 10 Volumes . . . Opera di Paisiello, 29 Volumes . . . [Also Musical Instruments]
. . . Sold . . . At the Mart . . . Sept. 23rd, 1834 and Following Day. London, 1834. 12 p. 270
lots. Music, lots 1-206, 227-70.   [GB-Lbl; compiler]
> Contents very similar to those in Watson's July 5 sale (**2994**).

2996   1835 (11 March)
"A Professional Gentleman Lately Deceased"
Mr. Watson, auctioneer, London
Catalogue of a Quantity of Vocal and Instrumental Music, by Modern Composers, [Also Musical Instruments, etc.] . . . *Sold . . . At The Mart . . . March the 11th, 1835.* London, 1835. 8 p. 171 lots. Music, lots 1-94, 132-71.   [GB-Lbl; compiler]

2997   1835 (10-11 December)
A Gentleman, Deceased
Mr. Watson, auctioneer, London
A Catalogue of a Collection of Vocal and Instrumental Music, Including the Library of . . . a . . . Collection of Music for the Harp and Pianoforte . . . [Also Musical Instruments] . . . *Sold . . . at the Mart . . . December 10th, 1835, and Following Day.* London, 1835. 20 p. 380 lots. Music, lots 1-309, 319-80.   [GB-Lbl; compiler]

2998   1836 (18-19 February)
"Two Eminent Professors"
Mr. Watson, auctioneer, London
Catalogue of a Vocal and Instrumental Music, Including Portions of the Libraries of . . . [Also Musical Instruments] . . . *Sold . . . February 18th, 1836, and Following Days.* London, 1836. 16 p. 346 lots. Music, lots 1-260, 279-346.   [GB-Lbl; compiler]

2999   1837 (3-5 October)
Anonymous
S. de Grebber, auctioneer, Amsterdam
Catalogus van eene zeer groote en extra fraaije verzameling van muziek, soowel instrumentale als vocale, als opera-partitiën . . . gevolgd van muzikale instrumenten . . . verkocht . . . den 3den October 1837 en daaropvolgende dagen. . . . Amsterdam, 1837. 50 p. 2330 lots.
[NL-Avb]

3000   1837 (17, 20 November)
"Two Libraries"
Mr. Watson, auctioneer, London
A Catalogue of New Vocal and Instrumental Music, a Number of Engraved Music Plates, Together with Two Libraries . . . [Also Musical Instruments] . . . *Sold Friday 17th, and Monday 20th November, 1837.* London, 1837. 8 p. 200 lots.   [GB-Lbl; compiler]

3001   1839 (16-22 December)
"A Gentleman Removed from the Country"
Messrs. Southgate, auctioneer, London
Catalogue of the Valuable Property of a Gentleman, Removed from the Country . . . Books . . . Engravings . . . Collection of Music, Instrumental and Vocal . . . Sold December 16th, 1839, and 6 Following Days. . . . London, 1839. 50 p. 1243 [i.e., 1423] lots.   [GB-Lbl]
        Music, 6th day's sale, lots 1280-[1423].

3002   1841 (3 June)
"A Gentleman"
S. Leigh Sotheby, auctioneer, London
Catalogue of the Very Select and Valuable Library of A Gentleman, in Which Are . . . to Which Is Added, Another Collection of Books . . . Sold . . . June 3rd, 1841, and Two Following Days. . . . [London], 1841. 40 p. 854 lots. Music, lots 844-54 (over a hundred items). [GB-Lbl; film at CRL]

3003   **1843 (24-27 July)**
Anonymous
Mr. McCalla, auctioneer, London
An Extensive and Valuable Collection of Music, &c., &c. A Catalogue of a Genuine Collection of Vocal and Instrumental Music . . . Piano-fortes . . . Sold . . . at the Auction Mart . . . July 24, and 3 Following Days. . . . [London, 1843.] 23 p. 855 lots.   [compiler]

3004   **1844 (31 January - 4 February)**
"Two Gentlemen, Deceased"
S. Leigh, Sotheby & Co., auctioneer, London
Catalogue of a Miscellaneous Collection of Books . . . a Small Collection of Sacred and Other Music; With Some Musical Instruments . . . Sold . . . January 31st, 1844, and Four Following Days. . . . [London, 1844.] 66 p.   [Film at CRL]

> Music, lots 1657-706, plus a few song collections, passim.

3005   **1845 (28 March)**
"Two Well-Known Amateurs, Deceased"
Mr. Fletcher, auctioneer, London
Catalogue of a Collection of Classical Music, Comprising the Musical Libraries of Two Well-Known Amateurs, Deceased; Including a Valuable Selection of the Most Esteemed Productions of the Ancient and Modern Masters . . . Works on the Theory, by Hummel, Reicha, Choron, Kollmann, &c. A Small Collection of Valuable Modern Music . . . Sold . . . March 28, 1845. [London, 1845.] 9 p. 207 lots.   [GB-Ob; compiler]

> "Italian operas, full scores, MSS., fine copies . . . in vellum," lots 1-6.

3006   **1845 (24 June)**
"Several Private Gentlemen"
Mr. Fletcher, auctioneer, London
Catalogue of a Collection of Music, Vocal and Instrumental . . . Also Numerous Musical Instruments (the Property of . . .) Sold . . . June 24th, 1845. [London, 1845.] 8 p. 184 lots. Music, lots 1-118.   [GB-Ob; compiler]

3007   **1846 (23 January)**
"A Gentleman, Deceased"
Mr. Fletcher, auctioneer, London
Musical Library of . . . Instrumental Music, Pianoforte Music, Operas, Vocal Music . . . Full Scores, Also Several Musical Instruments. . . . [London, 1846.] 170 lots.   [GB-Ob]

3008   **1847**
Anonymous [in a sale including properties of Justice Williams]
Thomas Thorpe, auctioneer, London
Part 2 for 1847. A Catalogue of Very Choice, Curious and Valuable Books . . . from the Libraries of Justice Williams [et al., not music] *Original Manuscript Music in the Autographs of the Celebrated Matthew Locke, Dr. Blow, and Christopher Gibbons, Including a Splendid Volume Presented by Locke to King Charles II . . . for Ready Money Only. . . .* London, 1847. 190 p. 2778 lots.

> Gibbon's holograph, lot 1346; Locke's, lots 2042-47, and songs, 2491-96; other music, mostly manuscript, lots 2163-66. Examined Harrison Horblit's copy.

3009   1847 (26-29 April)
Anonymous

MESSRS. WINSTANLEY, AUCTIONEER, LONDON

. . . A Catalogue of Nearly the Whole of the Excellent Furniture . . . and Other Articles of Taste . . . the Valuable Library of Music . . . a Fine Copy of Marcellos' Psalms . . . [etc.] *Sold . . . the 26th of April 1847, and Three Following Days. . . .* London, 1847. 39 p. 637 lots. Music, lots 84-174.   [GB-Lbl]

3010   1847 (30 August)
"A Gentleman"

S. LEIGH SOTHEBY & CO., AUCTIONEER, LONDON

Catalogue of a Small Collection of Engravings . . . Together with Valuable Musical Works, the Property of a Gentleman . . . Sold . . . August 30th, 1847. . . . [London, 1847.] 9 p. 98 lots. Music, lots 32-51.   [Film at CRL]

3011   1847 (9-11 December)
"A Gentleman"

S. LEIGH SOTHEBY & CO., AUCTIONEER, LONDON

Catalogue of a Valuable Assemblage of Fine Books . . . Together with the Choice Music Library . . . [Which] *Contains Many Valuable and Interesting Volumes of Madrigals, Motetts, &c., in Manuscript from the Collections of the Late Mr. Bartleman, Mr. Parker, and Others . . . Sold . . . December 9th, 1847, and Two Following Days. . . .* [London, 1847.] 57 p. 988 lots. Music, lots 305-452.   [Film at CRL]

1847 (17 December)
"A Distinguished Professor."   *See* **Gauntlett, Henry John** *in section 1*

3012   1848
Anonymous

THOMAS THORPE, FIRM, LONDON

Part II for 1848. Catalogue of a Very Choice, Interesting and Valuable Collection of Books, Manuscripts, and Portraits . . . the Property of Frederick, Earl of Bessborough. . . . A Curious Collection of Music, Printed and Manuscript, Some in the Autograph of Matthew Locke, Blow, Jordan, and Other Eminent Composers . . . for Ready Money Only. . . . London, 1848. 81 p. 2244 lots, priced.

> Music, lots 1931-57. Locke holographs, lots 1933-36, but many pieces.
> Examined Harrison Horblit's copy.

3013   1852 (7 June)
Anonymous

MESSRS. ROBINS, AUCTIONEER, LONDON

A Catalogue of Vocal and Instrumental Music, Ancient and Modern Music . . . Overtures, Arias, Ballads, Duets [etc.]; *Also a Scarce Collection of* [252!] *Italian Opera Books with English Translations, from the Year 1723 to the Present . . . Sold . . . the 7th Day of June, 1852.* London, 1852. 34 p.   [compiler]

> Not consecutively lotted: overtures, 25 lots; the 252 librettos in 21 lots, pp. 2-9; ballet books, 14 items, lot 22; 226 titles of soprano, tenor and bass songs "with orchestral parts and conductor's copy," pp. 10-19; 69 lots of duets "with orchestral parts and conductor's copy," pp. 20-22; etc., etc.

3014   1853
"M***"

J. -F. DELION, FIRM, PARIS
Catalogue le livres la plupart relatifs à la dramatique, provenant de la bibliothèque de M***. . . . Paris, 1853. 65 p. 614 lots.   [NL-DHgm]

3015   1853 (11 February)
"A Gentleman"

PUTTICK & SIMPSON, AUCTIONEER, LONDON   CAT. NO. 312
Catalogue of the Musical Library of a . . . Comprising Ancient and Modern Compositions . . . History and Theoretical Works . . . Also a Miscellaneous Collection, Including Many Modern Publications . . . Several Original Manuscript Compositions, Some of Which Are Valuable Copyrights, Together with Musical Instruments . . . Sold . . . February 11th, 1853. [London], 1853. 14 p. 310 lots. Music, lots 1-272.   [GB-Lbl]

3016   1854
F*, C A and G F Vogler**

Verzeichniss der werthvollen Bibliothek des Herrn Musikdirektor C. A. F. in Sainte-Marie-aux-Mines, und einer interessanten Sammlung von Musikalien für Pianoforte mit und ohne Begleitung, sowie einiger noch ungedruckten kirchenmusikalien Compositionen vom Abt G. J. Vogler. Frankfurt a.M., 1854. 32 p. + pp. 419-26 (parts of 2 catalogs issued as one). 648 lots + lots 8380-530.   [US-Wc]

F's and Vogler's properties mixed up. Many Mss.

3017   1854 (18 February)
Anonymous

J. SACRÉ, FIRM, BRUSSELS   CAT. NO. 181
181ᵐᵉ catalogue d'une superbe collection de livres anciens et modernes . . . dont la vente publique aura lieu samedi 18 février 1854. . . . Bruxelles: Imp. de J. Sacré, 1854. 15 p. 366 lots. Music, *inter alia*.   [B-Br, compiler (film)]

1855 (14-16 June)
"A Distinguished Amateur."   *See* **Bishop, Sir Henry Rowley**

1856 (25 June)
"A Distinguished Collector."   *See under* **[Hole, Captain A.]** (Puttick & Simpson catalog no. 453)

3018   1857 (15-? April)
Anonymous

J. A. STARGARDT, AUCTIONEER, BERLIN
Verzeichniss einer werthvollen und hymnologischen Bibliothek, welche am Freitag, den 15. April 1859, und folgende Tage . . . versteigert werden sollen. . . . Berlin, [1859]. 38 p. 781 lots.
                                                                 [GB-Lbl (Hirsch)]

3019   1857 (2 May)
"A Late Distinguished Professor"; Clark, Richard; and "A Well-Known Amateur"
PUTTICK & SIMPSON, AUCTIONEER, LONDON   CAT. NO. 487
A Large and Interesting Collection of Music, Comprising a Selection from the Library of the Late Clark [lots 87-153], *Instrumental and Miscellaneous Music from the Library of a Late Distinguished Professor; Very Valuable and Extensive Collection of Glees from the Library of a Well-Known Amateur; Instruments . . . Sold May 2. . . .* London, 1857. 538 lots.   [GB-Lbl]

1857 (24 August)
Anonymous.   *See* Puttick & Simpson sale of this date *under* **Rimbault, Edward Francis**

3020   **1858 (29 January)**
"A Distinguished Amateur [Markey?]; John Christopher Smith; Bernard Granville
PUTTICK & SIMPSON, AUCTIONEER, LONDON   CAT. NO. 526
Very Important Collection of a Distinguished Amateur; and Important Series of Handel's Works Written by J. C. Smith for Bernard Granville [lot 183] *; . . . Other Interesting Manuscripts from the Library of J. C. Smith* [lots 188-200] *. . . Sold January 1.* . . . London, 1858. 477 lots.
[GB-Lbl]

See lengthy annotation describing this and related sales in **Coover 2**, pp. 164-70.

3021   **1859 (12 August)**
"Deceased Amateur"; et al.
PUTTICK & SIMPSON, AUCTIONEER, LONDON   CAT. NO. 594
Catalogue of a Large Collection of Miscellaneous Music, Vocal and Instrumental; Works on the History and Theory of Music . . . Manuscript Full Scores Entirely in the Autograph of Haydn . . . Musical Instruments . . . Sold . . . August 12th, 1859. [London], 1859. 22 p. 484 lots. Music, lots 1-400. Manuscripts, lots 86-99.   [GB-Lbl]

3022   **1859 (11 November)**
"A Deceased Amateur"; et al.
PUTTICK & SIMPSON, AUCTIONEER, LONDON   CAT. NO. 594
Miscellaneous Music . . . Manuscript Full Scores Entirely in the Autograph of Haydn; an Autograph of Beethoven ["his 32nd Sonata for Pianoforte and Violin, lot 389"] *. . . Also Instruments . . . Sold . . . November 11.* . . . London, 1859. 860 lots.   [GB-Lbl]

1860 (24-26 April)
"An Amateur, Deceased."   *See* Puttick & Simpson sale of this date *under* **Forbes, Henry**

3023   **1860 (25 June)**
Anonymous
ÉDOUARD TER BRUGGEN, FIRM, ANTWERP
Catalogue d'une belle collection de tableaux, anciens et modernes de bons maitres flamands et français, gravures, musique de chant et d'orchestre. Partitions de Messes, oratorios, musique sacrée et opéras . . . Méthodes et musique anglaise . . . vente publique aura lieu Édouard ter Bruggen . . . 25 juin 1860. . . . Anvers, 1860. 60 p. 501 lots.   [B-Abm]
Lugt, no. 25670.

3024   **1860 (28-29 August)**
Anonymous
PUTTICK & SIMPSON, AUCTIONEER, LONDON   CAT. NO. 643
Catalogue of a Small and Select Musical Library . . . Also . . . Musical Instruments . . . the Stock of Mr. Maucotel . . . Sold . . . August 28th, 1860, and Following Day. [London], 1860. 21 p.
[GB-Lbl]

On Harrison Horblit's and the Hirsch copies of this catalog, the printed "28" has been struck through, replaced with a "3." The Puttick & Simpson "Index" also indicates that the sale was moved to August 3-4.

3025   1862 (6-7 January)
"A Well-Known Collector; A Provincial Music Seller"; Various Private Collectors
PUTTICK & SIMPSON, AUCTIONEER, LONDON   CAT. NO. 7
Catalogue of the Musical Library of a Well-Known Collector, Together With the Stock of a Provincial Music Seller, and Selections from Various Collections Also Musical Instruments . . . Sold January 6th, 1862, and Following Day. [London], 1862.   [GB-Lbl]

3026   1863
Anonymous
A. ASHER, & CO., FIRM, BERLIN   CAT. NO. 74
Catalogue d'une belle collection de musique ancienne, en vente chez. . . . Berlin, 1863.
26 p. 267 lots.   [US-NYp]

3027   1863 (29-30 April)
"An Amateur"
PUTTICK & SIMPSON, AUCTIONEER, LONDON   CAT. NO. 761
Catalogue of a Large Collection of Music, Including the Library of an Amateur, and the Foreign Stock of an Eminent Publishing House . . . Also Instruments . . . Sold April 29th, 1863 and Following Day. [London], 1863. 26 p. 681 lots. Music, lots 1-636.   [GB-Lbl]

3028   1864 (8 April)
Anonymous [Lady Eyre?; Thomas Oliphant?]
PUTTICK & SIMPSON, AUCTIONEER, LONDON   CAT. NO. 805
Catalogue of a Collection of Music . . . Early and Rare Works . . . History and Theory . . . Also Musical Instruments . . . Sold . . . April 8th, 1864. [London], 1864. 22 p. 47 lots. Music, lots 1-356.   [GB-Lbl]

1864 (22 August)
"A Professor."   *See* sale of this date *under* **Whittingham**

3029   1865 (23-27 October)
Anonymous
Cooley, J. E. *Catalogue of an Extensive Private Library of Choice Books . . . Bibliography, French Literature, and the History and Science of Music . . . Sold . . . at the "Trade-sale Rooms . . . New York"; October 23, 1865, and 4 Following Days.* Philadelphia: Collins, 1865. 81 p. 1976 lots. Music, lots 1494-976.   [US-NYp]
          "Introduction" written by Joseph Sabin.

3030   1865 (25 November)
Anonymous
SOTHEBY, WILKINSON & HODGE AUCTIONEER, LONDON
Catalogue of a Unique Collection of Political Ballads, Plays, Opera, Libretti, Music . . . [Above Two Thousand Opera Libretti, Plays, Ballets, &c.] *. . . Sold . . . the 25th Day of November, 1865. . . .* [London, 1865.] 25 p. 252 lots.   [Film at CRL]

3031   **1866 (3 May)**
Anonymous

TROSS (LIBRAIRE), PARIS

Notice des quelques livres rares et précieux. Catalogue et chansonniers des XVIᵉ siècle.
Musique ancienne . . . Dont la vente . . . 3 mai 1866 . . . Maison Silvestre. . . . Paris, 1866.
12 p. 47 lots (but many more items).   [GB-Lbl]

3032   **1867 (8 January)**
Anonymous

J. A. STARGARDT, AUCTIONEER, BERLIN

Verzeichniss einer werthvollen Sammlung von musikalischen, hymnologischer und liturgischer
Werken. Volksliedern, Dichtungen, Manuscripten, Autographen, etc., welche am . . . 8. Januar
1867 . . . versteigert werden. Berlin, [1867]. 23 p. 632 lots.   [GB-Lbl]

3033   **1868 (7-9 July)**
Anonymous

PUTTICK & SIMPSON, AUCTIONEER, LONDON   CAT. NO. 1068

Catalogue of a Valuable Collection of Rare and Curious Books, Scriptures, Liturgical Works,
Specimens of Early Typography . . . Antique Music, Including Manuscripts of the XI., XII. and
XIII Centuries, Rare Treatises, Airs and Songs. . . . [London], 1868. 93 p. 998 lots.   [GB-Lbl]

3034   **1868 (23-24 July)**
Anonymous

PUTTICK & SIMPSON, AUCTIONEER, LONDON   CAT. NO. 1071

Catalogue of a Collection of Ancient and Modern Music. Rare Antiquarian Music, Theoretical
Treatises, etc., Also Musical Instruments. . . . [London], 1868. 26 p. 745 lots. Music, lots 1-636.
                                                                                        [GB-Lbl]

3035   **1868 (1-2 September)**
"Several Eminent Professors"

PUTTICK & SIMPSON, AUCTIONEER, LONDON   CAT. NO. 1082

Catalogue of a Large Collection of Ancient and Modern Music . . . Selections from the
Libraries of . . . with the Remaining Printed Stock of the Late T. Prowse . . . Sold . . . September
1[-2], 1868. [London, 1868.] 30 p. 947 lots. Music, lots 1-839.   [GB-Lbl]

3036   **1869 (19-20 February)**
Anonymous

PUTTICK & SIMPSON, AUCTIONEER, LONDON   CAT. NO. 1107

Catalogue of a Large Collection of Ancient and Modern Music of Every Kind . . . [Also]
Musical Instruments . . . Sold April 19th and Following Day, 1869. . . . [London], 1869.
40 p. 1127 lots.   [GB-Lbl]

> The buyers include some very important collectors, the sale of whose
> collections show up in *section 1* of this book, one of whom was **F. J. Fétis**.

3037   **1869 (September)**
Anonymous

KIRCHOFF & WIGAND, FIRM, LEIPZIG   CAT. NO. 252

Antiquarisches Bücherlager: Musikwissenschaft, Musikalien. Leipzig . . . New York: F. W.
Christern, 1869. 88 p. 1785 lots.   [US-NYp]

3038   187?
Anonymous
FRANZ HANKE, FIRM ZÜRICH   CAT. NO. 97
Musikalien und Musikwissenschaft. Nebst einem Anhang werthvoller Werke aus verschiedenen Fächern der Literatur. . . . Zürich, [187-]. 209 p.   [US-Cn]

3039   1870 (28 February)
Anonymous
PUTTICK & SIMPSON, AUCTIONEER, LONDON   CAT. NO. 1176
Catalogue of a Collection of Valuable Music, Rare Antique Various Treatises and Works on the Theory of Music; Full Scores of Operas, Oratorios . . . Also Musical Instruments . . . Sold February 28th, 1870. [London], 1870. 18 p. 492 lots. Music, lots 1-433.   [GB-Lbl]

3040   1870 (25 June)
Anonymous
PUTTICK & SIMPSON, AUCTIONEER, LONDON   CAT. NO. 1197
Catalogue of a Valuable Collection of Antiquarian Music . . . History, Theory, and Biography of Music, Many of Great Interest and Rarity . . . Instrumental Works . . . Full and Vocal Scores . . . Also Musical Instruments . . . Sold June 25th, 1870. [London], 1870. 18 p. 453 lots. Music, lots 1-374.   [GB-Lbl]

3041   1871
Anonymous
LIST & FRANCKE, FIRM, LEIPZIG   CAT. NO. 92
Verzeichnis einer werthvollen Sammlung neuerer Musikalien und theoretische Werke über Musik, sowie einer Anzahl älterer praktischer Musikstücke. . . . Leipzig, 1871. 35 p. 1392 lots (prices fixed).   [GB-Lbl (Hirsch)]

3042   1871 (26-27 June)
Anonymous (with G. Corsby's stock)
PUTTICK & SIMPSON, AUCTIONEER, LONDON   CAT. NO. 1230
Catalogue of a Collection of Miscellaneous Music . . . Scores . . . Scarce Music Treatises . . . Also . . . Musical Instruments . . . Sold June 26th, 1871 and Following Day. . . . [London], 1871. 21 p. 637 lots. Music, lots 1-441.   [GB-Lbl]

3043   1871 (28 July)
"A Professor"
PUTTICK & SIMPSON, AUCTIONEER, LONDON   CAT. NO. 1261
Catalogue of a Collection of Ancient and Modern Music, Including the Library of a Professor and Comprising Valuable Musical Treatises, Full Scores . . . Instrumental Music . . . Also Musical Instruments . . . Sold July 28th, 1871. [London], 1871. 20 p. 536 lots. Music, lots 1-475.   [GB-Lbl]

3044   1871 (31 October)
Anonymous
ADOLPHE LABITTE, FIRM, PARIS
Notice sur de livres sur la musique. Partitions musicales . . . la vente . . . 31 octobre 1871. . . . Paris, 1871. 16 p. 148 lots.   [US-NYgr]

3045   1871 (27 November)
"A Professor"

PUTTICK & SIMPSON, AUCTIONEER, LONDON   CAT. NO. 1278

Catalogue of the Music Library of a Professor, With Other Properties . . . Full Scores . . . Rare
Antique Works . . . Also Musical Instruments . . . Sold November 27th, 1871. [London], 1871.
17 p. 468 lots. Music, lots 1-428.   [GB-Lbl]

3046   1871 (11-13 December)
Anonymous

VAN ROSSUM, AUCTIONEER, AMSTERDAM

[Catalogue of musical instruments and music.] Amsterdam, 1871. 35 p. 1001 lots. [NL-Avb]

  Not examined; cited by **Lugt**, no. 32765.

3047   1871 (18 December)
Anonymous

PUTTICK & SIMPSON, AUCTIONEER, LONDON   CAT. NO. 1283

Catalogue of an Interesting Collection of Music . . . Comprising Valuable and Rare Treatises,
Orchestral, Pianoforte and Vocal Compositions. Scores of Operas, Oratorios and Masses . . .
Also Valuable Musical Instruments . . . Sold . . . December 18th, 1871. [London], 1871.
17 p. 486 lots. Music, lots 1-437.   [GB-Lbl]

3048   1871 (28 December)
Anonymous

LEGOUIX, FIRM, PARIS (C.-P., PAUL RAIN)

[Catalog.] Paris, 1871. 13 p. 89 lots.   [B-Br]

  Not examined; cited in **Blogie 2**.

3049   1872 (26 April)
Anonymous

PUTTICK & SIMPSON, AUCTIONEER, LONDON   CAT. NO. 1310

Catalogue of a Collection of Music, Comprising Rare Antiquarian Works . . . Also Musical
Instruments . . . Sold . . . April 26th, 1872. . . . [London], 1872. 18 p. 484 lots. Music, lots 1-439.
    [GB-Lbl]

3050   1872 (19-20 June)
Anonymous

VAN ROSSUM, AUCTIONEER, AMSTERDAM

[Catalog: porcel., ant., instr. & liv., musique. div.] Amsterdam, 1872. 27 p. 613 lots.
    [NL-Avb]

  Not examined; cited by **Lugt**, no. 33309.

3051   1872 (12 July)
[A Gentleman]

SOTHEBY, WILKINSON & HODGE, AUCTIONEER, LONDON

Catalogue of a Choice Collection of Manuscript Music, Autograph Letters, Documents, &c.,
&c. . . . Comprising Compositions, Entirely Autograph, by Handel, Bach, Mozart . . . Sold . . .
12th Day of July 1872. 18 p. 325 lots.   [GB-Lbl, US-NYp; film at CRL]

  "Mozart and Beethoven autograph MSS.," lots 310-20.

3052   **1872 (28 October)**
"An Eminent Professor"

PUTTICK & SIMPSON, AUCTIONEER, LONDON   CAT. NO. 1345

Catalogue of a Valuable Collection of Music, Including the Library of an Eminent Professor, Comprising Compositions in the Autograph of Celebrated Composers, Letters of Musical Celebrities and Miscellaneous Music . . . Also Musical Instruments . . . Sold . . . October 28th, 1872. [London], 1872. 24 p. 419 lots. Music, lots 1-358.   [GB-Lbl]

> Autograph music, lots 189-226.

3053   **1872 (25-28 November)**
Anonymous

J. L. BEIJERS & LOUIS ROOTHAN, AUCTIONEER, UTRECHT

Catalogus van eene belangrijke verzameling muziekwerken. Boeken over muziek en muziekinstrumenten . . . verkooping . . . 25 November 1872 en twee volgende dagen . . . van den Notaris E. P. Temminck. . . . Utrecht: J. L. Beijers, [1872]. 52 p. 1265 lots. Music, all lots except 1210-28.   [NL-Avb]

3054   **1873 (3-7 March)**
Anonymous

J. BOULLAND (=C. P.); LEGOUIX (ASSISTÉ)

Catalogue de musique ancienne et moderne. Ouvrages théoriques. Ouvrages et écrits sur la musique . . . vente . . . (Maison Silvestre) . . . Mars 1873. . . . Paris, 1873. 42 p.   [I-Mc; compiler (copy)]

3055   **1873 (29 April)**
"A Recently Deceased Professor" (and Edward Taylor)

PUTTICK & SIMPSON, AUCTIONEER, LONDON   CAT. NO. 1389

Ancient and Modern Music, Including the Library of a Recently Deceased Professor . . . Full Scores of Operas and Oratorios, Rare Treatises, Old Manuscript Compositions . . . Also Musical Instruments . . . Sold April 19, 1873. . . . London, 1873. 451 lots.   [GB-Lbl]

> Lots 182-220, items once in the collections of Burney and Richard Clark, included lot 198, songs by James Hook, in holograph; lot 199, glees, etc. by Robert Cooke, in holograph. Taylor's properties were orchestral parts from his library. Lots 1-65, multiple copies from dealer's stock.

1873 (30 July)
"A Professor." *See under* **Taylor, Edward** *in section 1, . . . Ancient and Modern Music, Including the Library of a Professor. . . .*

3056   **1874**
Anonymous

OTTO'SCHE BUCHHANDLUNG, FIRM, ERFURT   CAT. NO. 172

Verzeichnis Nr. 172 des antiquarischen BücherLagers der . . . Philosophie . . . Pädagogik. Anhang: Bücher über Musik. . . . Erfurt, 1874. 15 [20] p.   [GB-Lbl (Hirsch)]

3057   **1874 (23-25 February)**
["A Well-Known Amateur"]

SOTHEBY, WILKINSON & HODGE, AUCTIONEER, LONDON

Catalogue of a Valuable Collection of Rare and Early Music, and Works on Music, the Property of . . . Comprising the Productions of Eminent English and Foreign Composers . . . Sold . . . 23rd February, 1874, and Two Following Days. [London, 1874.] 80 p. 1157 lots. Music, lots 1-101.   [Film at CRL]

3058   1874 (29 May)
"A Musician, Deceased"
PUTTICK & SIMPSON, AUCTIONEER, LONDON
Catalogue of the Library of a Musician, Deceased . . . Handel's Works, Theoretical Treatises,
Psalmodies, etc. . . . Prints Relating to Handel and Vauxhall, Also Musical Instruments . . .
Sold May 29th, 1874. London, 1874. 16 p. 343 lots. Music, lots 1-266.   [GB-Lbl]

3059   1875 (3-5 November)
Anonymous
G. THEOD BOM, AUCTIONEER, AMSTERDAM
Notitie van Oostersche Wapens en andere Indische Zaken . . . goud- en zilverwerk . . .
schilderijen, muziek, muziek-instrumenten, enz. . . . verkocht . . . op 3-5 November 1875. . . .
Amsterdam, 1875. 43 p.   [NL-DHrk]
          Section 1, "Muziek," pp. 31-40 (222 lots).

3060   1876 (28 April)
"A Professor"
PUTTICK & SIMPSON, AUCTIONEER, LONDON   (NO CAT. NO.)
Catalogue of the Library of . . . , Together with Miscellaneous Collections from Various
Sources, Also a Valuable Assemblage of Musical Instruments . . . Sold April 28, 1876. [London],
1876. 16 p. 485 lots. Music, lots 1-427.   [GB-Lbl]

3061   1877 (3-12 April)
Anonymous
G. THEOD. BOM, AUCTIONEER, AMSTERDAM
Catalogus van uitgebreide verzamelingen . . . Boeken, kostbare pracht- en plaatwerken . . .
[etc.] *Muziek en muziek-instrumenten . . . nagelaten door verschillende geachte en voorname*
overleden liefhebbers . . . verkocht . . . 3 April 1877 en volgende dagen. . . . Amsterdam,
1877. 268, 30 p. 5447 + 76 lots. Music, pp. 248-52 (103 lots).   [NL-Avb]
          Lugt, no. 37303.

3062   1877 (30 April)
"A Gentleman"
PUTTICK & SIMPSON, AUCTIONEER, LONDON   CAT. NO. 1662
Catalogue of a Valuable and Extensive Collection of Music, Including the Library of . . . ,
Comprising Rare Sets of Violin Duets [etc,]*, Curious Manuscripts and Autograph Letters . . .*
Also Musical Instruments . . . Sold . . . April 30, 1877, and Following Day. [London], 1877.
34 p. 757 lots. Music, lots 1-707.   [GB-Lbl]

          "Rare sets of trios for 2 vlns. and Vllo.," lots 104-16 (but many more items).
          "MS. music, autographs, etc.," lots 498-540. Buyers: Cummings and
          Compton.

3063   1877 (25 May)
"A Professor"
PUTTICK & SIMPSON, AUCTIONEER, LONDON   CAT. NO. 1669
Catalogue of the Music Library of . . . , Also of Numerous Popular Editions of Operas and
Other Publications, Modern Sheet Music, etc., Also of Important Musical Instruments . . . Sold
. . . May 25th, 1877. [London], 1877. 15 p. 455 lots. Music, lots 1-371.   [GB-Lbl]

3064   **1877 (25 October)**
"A Professor"
PUTTICK & SIMPSON, AUCTIONEER, LONDON   CAT. NO. 1697
Catalogue of an Interesting Collection of Music . . . Original Editions of Handel's Operas,
German Operas by Composers of Mozart's Period, Benda, Hiller [et al. . . .] *from the Library of*
. . . Standard Editions of Operas, Oratorios, &c. . . . Also Musical Instruments . . . Sold . . .
October 25th, 1877. London, 1877. 15 p. 397 lots.   [GB-Lbl]

3065   **1877 (12-14 December)**
"An Organist, Deceased"; "A Roman Catholic Priest"
PUTTICK & SIMPSON, AUCTIONEER, LONDON   CAT. NO. 1712
Catalogue of Miscellaneous Books, Including the Library of an Organist . . . Also, the Library
of a . . . Priest, Removed from Gloucester . . . Sold . . . December 12th, 1877, and Two Following
Days. London, 1877. 68 p. 1085 lots.   [GB-Lbl]
        Music interspersed; many more items.

3066   **1878 (27 February)**
"A Gentleman (Removed from Lancashire)"
PUTTICK & SIMPSON, AUCTIONEER, LONDON   CAT. NO. 1728
Catalogue of a Valuable Library of Music, the Property of . . . Operas and Oratorios, Well
Bound, Scarce and Curious Treatises, Original Editions of Sir H. R. Bishop's Works, etc. Also
Musical Instruments . . . Sold February 27th, 1878. London, 1878. 12 p. 298 lots. Music, lots
1-228.   [GB-Lbl]

3067   **1878 (24-25 June)**
"A Distinguished Professor"
PUTTICK & SIMPSON, AUCTIONEER, LONDON   CAT. NO. 1759
Catalogue of the Valuable Library of Music of . . . Useful Works on Music; Also Musical
Instruments . . . Sold June 24th, 1878, and Following Day. London, 1878. 27 p. 641 lots. Music,
lots 1-544.   [GB-Lbl]

3068   **1880 (17 February)**
"An Amateur"
PUTTICK & SIMPSON, AUCTIONEER, LONDON   CAT. NO. 1896
A Very Capital Collection of Instrumental Music from the Library of . . . ; Full Scores of
Symphonies and Other Works; A Selection of Flute Music; Valuable Mechanical Curiosities
. . . Musical Instruments . . . Sold . . . February 17, 1880. London, 1880. 16 p. 376 lots. Music,
lots 1-242.   [GB-Lbl]

3069   **1880 (24 May)**
"A Distinguished Professor"
PUTTICK & SIMPSON, AUCTIONEER, LONDON   CAT. NO. 1923
Catalogue of the Valuable Instrumental and General Musical Literature of . . . , Including the
Best Editions of String Duets, Trios, Quartettes, Quintetts, etc. . . . Old Violin Sets, Flute Solos,
Duets and Trios . . . Early Editions of Scarce and Curious Works . . . Sold May 24, 1880.
London, 1880. 14 p. 313 lots.   [GB-Lbl]

3070   **1880 (21 June)**
"A Distinguished Professor, Resident in the Provinces"
PUTTICK & SIMPSON, AUCTIONEER, LONDON   CAT. NO. 1932
*Catalogue of a Valuable Collection of Music . . . Full Scores and Orchestral Parts . . . Best
Folio Editions of Operas, Oratorios, and Cantatas, from the Library of . . . Sold . . . June 21,
1880.* London, 1880. 13 p. 363 lots.   [GB-Lbl]

3071   **1880 (19 July)**
"A Well-Known Amateur"
PUTTICK & SIMPSON, AUCTIONEER, LONDON   CAT. NO. 1942
*Large and Interesting Library of Music from the Collection of a . . . Concerted Music, Sets of
Parts, Italian and Other Old MSS. (some probably unpublished), Autograph Letters . . . Sold
. . . July 29th. . . .* London, 1880. 414 lots.   [GB-Lbl]

3072   **1880 (11 November)**
"An Amateur"
PUTTICK & SIMPSON, AUCTIONEER, LONDON   CAT. NO. 1967
*Choice Collection of Autographs, Principally of Musical, Dramatic, and Literary Celebrities,
the Property of . . . ; A Series of Papers in Connection with the "King's Concerts of Ancient
Music" . . . a Large Parcel in a Trunk . . .* [also offered in sales of 18 August 1879 and 10
February 1881] *. . . Sold . . . 11th November. . . .* 202 lots.   [GB-Lbl]

3073   **1881**
"Un Amateur parisien"
CHARAVAY, FIRM, PARIS
*Catalogue d'une curieuse collection de lettres autographes de célébrités des XVIIIe et XIXe
siècles, écrivains, artistes, hommes d'état et compositeurs de musique, composant le cabinet
d' . . . .* Paris, 1881. 38 p. 250 lots.   [US-Bp]
> Music, lots 21-22, 57, 168-250.

3074   **1881 (10-11 February)**
"A Collector"
PUTTICK & SIMPSON, AUCTIONEER, LONDON   CAT. NO. 1991
*Catalogue of a Portion of the Library of the Late H. N. Clifton, of Islington . . . Also, Rare and
Curious Books, MSS., Autographs, etc. (from the library of a Collector) . . . Sold . . . February
10th, 1881, and Following Day.* London, 1881. 42 p. 700 lots.   [GB-Lbl]
> "Collector's" library, including music and liturgy, lots 561-649, comprising
> some manuscripts from the Dutchess of Hamilton. Autographs, mostly
> music, lots 620-30, but many items in each lot.

3075   **1881 (30 June)**
F***
LABITTE, FIRM, PARIS
*Catalogue de livres sur la musique, de partitions musicales gravées et manuscrits et
d'autographes de musiciens, de la bibliothèque de M. de F*** . . . vente . . . le jeudi 30 juin
1881. . . .* Paris: Labitte, [1881 or 82?]. 32 p. 346 lots. Autographs, lots 249-346.
                                                                          [NL-Avb (Fv 272^d)]
> Lot 341 alone consists of 460 autographs of 19th-century composers! In
> **Bobillier** and **Scheurleer** 1 (1923):13.

3076   **1882 (3 April)**
"A Gentleman"; Henry Leslie's Choir
PUTTICK & SIMPSON, AUCTIONEER, LONDON   CAT. NO. 2090
Catalogue of a Large Collection of Ancient and Modern Music, Including a Number of
Historical and Theoretical Treatises . . . Sold . . . April 3, 1882. London, 1882. 21 p. 445 lots.
[GB-Lbl]

"Gentleman's" properties, lots 1-142.

3077   **1882 (28 April)**
"A Foreign Collector"
PUTTICK & SIMPSON, AUCTIONEER, LONDON   CAT. NO. 2094
Collection of Extremely Rare and Precious Books and Manuscripts (the Property of a . . .),
Choice Illuminated and Other Manuscripts, a Large Number of Rare Printed Missals,
Breviaries, Books of Hours, Many Important Musical works . . . Sold . . . April 28th. . . . 412 lots.
[A GB-Lbl]

3078   **1882 (13 May)**
F***
É. CHARAVAY, FIRM, PARIS
Catalogue d'une intéressant collection d'autographes de compositeurs de musique, composant
le cabinet de feu M. de F***, et comprenant la partition originale du Christophe Colomb de
Félicien David. La vente . . . 13 mai 1882. . . . Paris, 1882. 16 p. 127 lots.   [US-NYgr]

In Ms. on copy at US-NYgr, "ons-Colombe."

3079   **1882 (7 June)**
Anonymous
DARIO GIUSEPPE ROSSI, FIRM, ROME   CAT. NO. 22
Catalogo di una scelta e preziosa raccolta di opere antichi attinenti alla musica. Vendita
unica . . . 7 giugno 1882. Roma: Rossi, 1882. 23 p. 150 lots.   [US-NYgr]

1882 (23 June)
"A Deceased Professor."   *See under* **Plumb, J. B.,** *section 1*

3080   **1882 (27 November)**
"A Distinguished Musician"
PUTTICK & SIMPSON, AUCTIONEER, LONDON   CAT. NO. 1882
Catalogue of the Extensive Library of . . . Comprising Valuable Full Scores, Operas, Oratorios,
Masses, Cantatas . . . Vocal Scores . . . Organ Music . . . Autograph and Other Manuscript
Compositions . . . a Number of Works on Music . . . Sold November 27th, 1882. London,
1882. 23 p. 529 lots.   [GB-Lbl]

Buyers included Taphouse, Cummings, Novello, Robinson, Matthews, and
others.

3081   **1883 (22 December)**
G., A.
Catalogue de livres anciens et modernes sur la musique. Collection importante composant la
bibliothèque de. . . . Paris: Martin, 1883. 12 p. 104, 94 lots.   [US-Bp]

3082 **1883 (18 June)**
"Un Cabinet connu"
É[TIENNE?] CHARAVAY, AUCTIONEER, PARIS
Catalogue d'une intéressant collection d'autographes provenant d'un cabinet connu . . . la
vente . . . 18 juin 1883. Paris, 1883. 22 p. 178 lots.   [US-NYgr]

   Music items throughout: Berlioz, Boieldieu, Chopin, Rossini, Verdi, etc.

3083 **1883 (17 July)**
"A Well-Known Collector"
SOTHEBY, WILKINSON & HODGE, AUCTIONEER, LONDON
Catalogue of a Choice Collection of Autograph Music and Autograph Letters of Musicians,
the Property of . . . Sold . . . the 17th Day of July, 1883. . . . [London, 1883.] 31 p. 325 lots.
                                                       [GB-Lbl; film at CRL]

   Excellent ALS.

3084 **1884 (23 January)**
"A Distinguished Professor"; "A Music-Seller"
PUTTICK & SIMPSON, AUCTIONEER, LONDON   CAT. NO. 2231
Catalogue of Ancient and Modern Music, Including Full Scores of Works by Franz Schubert
(Some Unpublished), Operas, Oratorios, Masses . . . Theoretical and Practical Treatises, etc.,
from the Library of . . . Stock of a Music-Seller . . . Sold January 23, 1884. London, 1884.
17 p. 395 lots.   [GB-Lbl]

      Some manuscripts bought by Ouseley.

3085 **1884 (16 June)**
Anonymous
ÉTIENNE CHARAVAY, AUCTIONEER, PARIS
Catalogue d'une précieuse collection d'autographes de compositeurs de musique, comprenant
des pièces de Bach, Mozart, Gluck, Rousseau, Rameau, Cimarosa, Beethoven, Haydn, Weber
. . . etc. La vente . . . 16 juin 1884. Paris, 1884. 26 p. 185 lots.   [US-NYgr]

       1884 (June 25)
"An Amateur." *See under* **Hullah, John Pyke,** *section 1*
PUTTICK & SIMPSON, AUCTIONEER, LONDON   CAT. NO. 2273

3086 **1884 (29 July)**
"A Well-Known Collector, Residing Abroad"
PUTTICK & SIMPSON, AUCTIONEER, LONDON   CAT. NO. 2283
Catalogue of a Valuable Library of Music, the Property of . . . Antiquarian Works on the
History and Theory of Music . . . Full Scores . . . Early Manuscripts . . . Instrumental Music
. . . a Few Lots of Popular Sheet Music . . . Sold July 29, 1884. London, 1884. 20 p. 437 lots.
                                                                        [GB-Lbl]

      Taphouse was a heavy buyer.

3087 **1884 (11 November)**
Anonymous
SOTHEBY WILKINSON & HODGE, AUCTIONEER, LONDON
Catalogue of Madrigals, Music, Books and Autographs, Principally Relative to and

Illustrative of the Drama and Music in Italy, France and England . . . the Autographs Include
. . . Grétry, Rossini, Verdi, Meyerbeer, Méhul, Haydn, Mozart, Paër, Wagner [etc.] *. . . Sold . . .*
the 11th Day of November, 1884. London, 1884. 24 p. 303 lots.   [GB-Lbl; film at CRL]

    Buyers included Cummings, Osborne, Squire, Matthews, and others.

3088   **1884 (1 December)**

Anonymous

GABRIEL CHARAVAY, FIRM, PARIS

Catalogue d'un precieuse collection de lettres autographes de compositeurs de musique . . .
et contenant une important série de chartes sur la musique, depuis le XIVe siècle . . . vente . . .
11 Décembre 1885. . . . Paris: Maison Gabriel Charavay, 1885.   [US-Wc]

1885 (19 May)

"A Collector."   *See under* **Lemann, H. B.** *in section 1*

3089   **1886**

"Distincto philologo e dilletante"

Arthur da Silva, Francisco. *Catálogo de livros que pertenceram a um . . . musica, theatro,*
pedagogia, philosophia . . . [etc.]. Lisboa: Typ. da Viuva Sousa Neves, 1886. 79 p.   [P-Ln]

3090   **1886 (July 5)**

["A Gentleman Retiring"]; Robert S. Callcott

PUTTICK & SIMPSON, AUCTIONEER, LONDON   CAT. NO. 2431

Effects of the Late Callcott Consisting of the Library of Music [lots 39-80] *from the Libraries of*
John Wall Callcott [and others] *. . . Sold . . . July 5th. . . .* 250 lots.   [GB-Lbl]

    Property of "A Gentleman retiring from the profession," lots 89-250.

3091   **1886 (October 14)**

"A Well-Known Amateur"

PUTTICK & SIMPSON, AUCTIONEER, LONDON   CAT. NO. 2444

A Valuable Library of Music, Comprising Scarce Treatises on History and Theory, Old Organ
and Harpsichord Lessons, Cathedral Services, Anthems, Psalmodies, Manuscript Music, etc.
[from the collection of a Well-Known Amateur] *. . . Sold . . . October 14th. . . .* 401 lots.

[GB-Lbl]

3092   **1887 (25 May)**

"A Distinguished Amateur"; A Choral Society

PUTTICK & SIMPSON, AUCTIONEER, LONDON   CAT. NO. 2498

Catalogue of an Extensive Library of Music (the Property of . . .), Including Full and Vocal
Scores . . . a Large Selection of Flute Music . . . Part Music, the Property of a Choral Society
. . . Valuable Theoretical and Practical Treatises, Works on Musical History . . . Scarce and
Curious Early Works, Psalm and Hymn Tune Books, Manuscripts . . . Sold . . . May 25th, 1887.
[London], 1887. 21 p. 426 lots.   [GB-Lbl]

3093   **1889**

"Eines bedeutenden Musikforschers"

JOSEPH BAER & CIE., FIRM, FRANKFURT A.M.   CAT. NO. 248

. . . Musik. Theater. Volkslieder. (Enthaltend die Bibliothek eines bedeutenden Musikforschers).
Frankfurt a.M., 1889. 65 p. 1273 lots.   [NL-DHgm]

3094   1890 (26-27 March)
"Een zeer geacht Pastoor"
H. G. BOM, AUCTIONEER, AMSTERDAM
Catalogus eener belangrijke roomsch katholieke bibliotheek, nagelaten door . . . eene kostbare verzameling plaatwerken . . . Muziek en muziek-instrumenten . . . Verkooping . . . 27 Maart, en volgenden dag. . . . Amsterdam: H. G. Bom, 1890. 39 p. 744 lots. Music, lots 364-444.   [NL-Avb]

3095   1890 (5-7 May)
"B***, Comte de"
EUGÈNE (EXP.) CHARAVAY; GEORGES BOUAARD (C.-P.), PARIS
Collection de la Comte de B*** . . . Dessins . . . Autographes et manuscrits de musique . . . lettres autographes . . . vente 5 [-7] mai 1890. Paris, 1890. 104 p. 784 lots. Music, lots 1-353.
[US-Wc (priced)]

Includes autographs of Mozart's K. 52 and 53, a Gluck ALS, Beethoven holographs of *Für Elise* and the op. 133 *Grosse Fuge!*

3096   1896 (7-8 May)
"Wohlbekannten Sammler"
LEO LIEPMANNSSOHN, AUCTIONEER, BERLIN   AUK. CAT. NO. 16
Katalog einer schönen Autographen-Sammlung zum grössten Theile aus dem Besitze eines wolhbekannten Sammlers . . . Musiker (Briefe und Musikmanuskripte). Versteigerung 7. Mai 1896 und folgenden Tage. Berlin, 1896. 87 p. 1172 lots.   [GB-LRosenthal]

This was the I. Abtheilung; the second (14 October 1896) contained no music.

3097   1897
Anonymous
ELLIS AND ELVEY, FIRM, LONDON   CAT. NO. 85
Spring Catalogue of Choice Books and Manuscripts, Including a Remarkable Collection of Rare Books upon Music (General and Historical, Vocal and Instrumental). On Sale. . . . London, [1897]. 74 p., illus. 618 lots. Music, lots 381-618.   [US-NYgr (priced)]

3098   1897 (8 February)
Anonymous
BANGS, FIRM, NEW YORK
Catalogue of an Important and Valuable Collection of Autograph Letters, Documents, Play Bills and Portraits Relating to Music and the Drama. New York: Bangs, 1897. 47 p. 911 lots.
[US-NY, -NYp]

3099   1897 (30 March)
"An Amateur" (with William Henry Edwards and Thomas Baker)
PUTTICK & SIMPSON, AUCTIONEER, LONDON   CAT. NO. 3220
Catalogue of Grand and Cottage Pianofortes, Organs . . . Violins, Violas, Violoncellos and Double Basses, Including the Collections of the Late . . . Also a Library of Music . . . Collected by an Amateur . . . Sold March the 30th, 1897. [London], 1897. 16 p. 357 lots. Amateur's music, lots 267-357.   [GB-Lbl]

3100   **1898 (3 May)**
"Amateur bien-connu"

J. L. Beijers, (Libraire-Exp.), Utrecht

Catalogue d'une collection importante de partitions et de pièces de musique, de livres sur l'histoire et la théorie de la musique, de livres sur le théâtre . . . provenant de la succession d'un amateur bien-connu, dont la vente . . . 3 mai 1898. . . . Utrecht, 1898.   [NL-Avb]

3101   **1898 (22 December)**
"A Gentleman"

Sotheby, Wilkinson & Hodge, auctioneer, London

Catalogue of Books and Manuscripts, Including the Library of Mrs. Torrens [no music] *. . . the Property of a Gentleman Consisting Chiefly of Scarce Musical Treatises and Songs . . . Sold . . . 22nd of December, 1898.* [London, 1898.] 73 p. 873 lots. Music, lots 358, 523-24, 764-84, et passim.   [Film at CRL]

3102   **19 ? (19-20 February)**
Anonymous

Thomas & Sons, auctioneer, New York

Catalogue of a Library of Choice Books . . . Also . . . Bound Volumes of . . . Music . . . To Be Sold . . . February 19 and 20th. . . . [New York, n.d.] 22 p. 545 lots. Music, lots 360-419.

   [US-NYp]

3103   **1901 (4-? March; 10-11 June); 1902 (20 January)**
"Bekannten Privatbesitz"

Leo Liepmannssohn, auctioneer, Berlin   Auk. Cat. nos. 27, 29, 30

Katalog einer schönen Autographen-Sammlung aus . . . Versteigerung . . . 4 März 1901 und folgenden Tage . . . [10.-11. Juni, 1909 und 20. Jan. 1902]. 3 vols. Berlin, 1901-02. (67, 57, 32 p.) 782, 708, 232 lots.   [GB-LRosenthal]

3104   **1903 (25-26 March)**
Anonymous

Bangs, auctioneer, New York

Catalogue of a Library . . . Ballad Literature and Songs, and a Large and Interesting Collection of Music, Music Literature . . . Sold . . . March 25th and 26th, 1903. New York: Bangs, 1903. 39 p. 608 lots.   [US-Wc, -NH, -NYp, -NYgr]

     Music, throughout—*mostly* up to lot 474.

3105   **1903 (3-6 June)**
["Various (Several) Collectors"]

Sotheby & Co., auctioneer, London

Catalogue of Books and Manuscripts . . . Property . . . of [Various (Several) Collectors] *. . . Collection of Musical Manuscripts . . .* [etc.] *Sold 3rd of June, 1903 and Three Following Days. . . .* London, 1903. 130 p. 1595 lots. Music Mss., lots 278-312.   [NL-Avb]

3106   **1905?**
Anonymous

Chiswick Press, firm, London

Catalogue of a Unique and Extremely Important Collection of Autograph Letters and Manuscripts of the World's Greatest Composers. . . . London: Chiswick Press, [1905?].

   [GB-Lbl]

3107   1905?

Anonymous

RICHARD ZEUNE, FIRM, WEIMAR   CAT. NO. 20

Belle Collection de lettres autographes de célèbres artistes. Verzeichniss von Autographen berühmter Künstler (Musiker - Sänger und Schauspieler - Maler [etc.] *).* . . . Weimar: Zeune, [n.d., ca. 1905]. 16 p. 309 lots.   [US-NYgr]

3108   1906 (10 May)

"A Dramatic Author"

MERWIN-CLAYTON SALES CO., FIRM, NEW YORK

The Library of a Dramatic Author and Critic . . . Including . . . Portraits, Prints, etc., Relating to Opera, Dancing, and the Ballet. New York: Merwin, 1906. 91 p. 938 lots.   [US-Bp]

3109   1906 (29-30 October)

Anonymous (a private collection?)

GILHOFER & RANSCHBURG, AUCTIONEER, VIENNA   AUK. CAT. NO. 21

Katalog einer besonders hervorragenden Sammlung von Autographen berühmte Dichter und Schriftsteller. Briefen und Manuskripten Musikern und Komponisten . . . [etc.] *Versteigerung . . . 29.* [30.] *Oktober 1906.* Wien, 1906. 68 p. 878 lots.   [US-NYgr]

    Musiker und Komponisten, lots 1-370 (Liszt, Mozart, Schubert, et al.).

3110   1908 (6 May)

"M*, Compositeur et Chef d'orchestre"**

PAUL, EM., ET FILS ET GUILLEMIN, FIRM, PARIS

*Catalogue de la bibliothèque de feu M*** . . . livres anciens et modernes. Ouvrages sur la musique. Partitions très bien reliées . . . vente . . . 6 mai 1908.* Paris, 1908. 24 p. 189 lots. Music, lots 98-189 (many more items).   [NL-Avb]

3111   1909?

Anonymous

LEO LIEPMANNSSOHN, FIRM, BERLIN   CAT. NO. 174

Musiker-Autographen, darunter viele eigenhändige Musikmanuskripte. . . . Berlin, [n.d.]. 137 p. 2337 lots. Illus.   [NL-AVb]

3112   1909?

Anonymous

LEO LIEPMANNSSOHN, FIRM, BERLIN   CAT. NO. 175

. . . enthaltend eine Anzahl seltener älterer Werke aus allen Gebieten der Musikliteratur . . . darunter eine kostbare Sammlung gedruckter und handschriftlicher Lauten- und Orgel-Tabulaturen. Berlin, [1909?]. 66 p. 224 lots.   [US-Wc, -MB, NL-AVb]

1909 (21-22 May)

"C*, Baron von."**   *See* Liepmannssohn Autogr.-Verst. no. 39 *under* **Bovet, Alfred**

3113   1910

Anonymous

G. C. BOERNER, FIRM, LIEPZIG   CAT. NO. 16

Musik. Autographen, Manuskripte, Partituren, Bücher . . . [aus einer sehr bekannten und berühmten Sammlung, deren Besitzer sich nunmehr engültig von diesen Sammelgebiet]. Leipzig,

1910. 94 p., illus. 456 lots (many more items).   [US-Wc, -NYgr]

> Splendid collection of Mss. and ALS by Beethoven, Handel, Haydn, Marschner, et al.—many for each.

3114 1910
"A Well-Known Conductor"; Lesley Alexander

WILLIAM REEVES, FIRM, LONDON   CAT. N.S. NO. 23

. . . A Large Selection of Full Scores, from the Library of a Well-Known Conductor of Works by Raff, Reger, Berlioz . . . [etc., etc.] a Selection of Chamber Music . . . Being a Portion of the Library of the Late . . . Alexander. London, 1910. 40 p. No lotting.   [US-Wc]

3115 1910 (24-25 January)
Anonymous

KARL ERNST HENRICI, AUCTIONEER, BERLIN   AUK. CAT. NO. 1

. . . Autographen, Ansichten, Porträts und Original-Silhouetten . . . Musikerautographen, darunter: Bach, Gluck, Haydn, etc. Versteigerung . . . 24. & 25. January 1910. Berlin, 1910. 79 p., 8 plates, illus. 529 lots.   [US-NYgr]

> Music autographs, lots 415-529; lot 517 was Wagner's *Gesammelte Schriften* with his manuscript corrections.

1911
Anonymous [i.e., Alex. M. Cohn].   *See* Pearson sale of 1911 *under* **Cohn** *in section 1*

3116 1912 (? February)
"An Amateur"

ALPHONSE PICARD, ET FILS, LIBRAIRE, PARIS   CAT. NO. 186

Catalogue mensuel de livres anciens et moderns . . . collection d'ouvrages de Wagner, sur Wagner et la musique en général, provenant d'un amateur. . . . Paris, 1912. 45 p. 1072 lots. Wagner items, lots 1-678.   [NL-Avb]

3117 1916 (11-12 February)
"L., L. (of Berlin)"

KARL ERNST HENRICI, FIRM, BERLIN   CAT. NO. 29

Autographen, darunter Briefe aus dem Nachlass des Herrn . . . ein süddeutsche Autographen-Sammlung, sowie eine Auswahl Briefe Giacomo Meyerbeer worunter ungedruckte Wagnerbriefe aus früher Zeit. Berlin, 1916. 96 p. 732 lots.

3118 1917 (29 November)
Anonymous; [J. Pearson]

PUTTICK & SIMPSON, AUCTIONEER, LONDON   CAT. NO. 5179

Catalogue of a Highly Important Collection of Original Musical Manuscripts and Autographs of the Great Masters and Composers, Including Arne, Bach, Beethoven, Bellini [etc.] Also a Manuscript Antiphonarium on Vellum by Nicolas Jarry, the First Spanish Printed Book Containing Music . . . Sold November 29th, 1917. London, 1917. 28 p. 142 lots.   [GB-Lbl]

> A curious catalog but one with splendid annotations, most of which may have been written by the dealer J. Pearson for his sale of Meyer-Cohn items, without naming them, in 1911. (See under **Cohn, Alex. M.** in *section 1*; Puttick's does not name him, either.) See lengthy annotation in **Coover 2** along with a comparison of Pearson's expected prices with those actually fetched at this auction.

1919 (29-30 April)
"A Gentleman (Who Has Ceased to Collect)."   *See under* **Shedlock, John South,** *section 1*

3119   **1921 (30-31 May)**
"Ein bekannter Sammler"
LEO LIEPMANNSSOHN, AUCTIONEER, BERLIN   AUTOGR. VERST. NO. 46
Autographen z. T. aus dem Besitz eines . . . versteigert durch dem beedigten und öffentlich angestellten
Versteigerer Werner Haehnel . . . 30. [-31.] *Mai 1921.* Berlin, 1921. 84 p. 808 lots.   [US-NYp, -Wc]
> "Musiker," lots 1-306, includes autograph of Beethoven's second piano
> concerto. Otto Kinkeldey's copy of the catalog at US-NYp has "dealer's
> estimates" in the margins.

3120   **1922 (February 8)**
"A Musical Library Removed from Sussex"
PUTTICK & SIMPSON, AUCTIONEER, LONDON   CAT. NO. 5704
Valuable Books, Including the Library of the Late Rev. Roberts [non-music]; *Also a Musical*
Library Removed from Sussex [lots 203-54, but many more items] . . . *Sold . . . February 8th.*
. . . 525 lots.   [GB-Lbl]
> Lot 203, about 120 volumes; lot 214, 20 volumes of overtures.

3121   **1924 (13 May)**
Anonymous
VANDER EECKEN AND NOWE (NOTAIRES)
Catalogue de la bibliothèque musicale qui sera vendue . . . le Mardi 13 mai 1924 . . . le vente
comprend: 1°) 579 partitions de chant et piano; 2°) 610 partitions orchestrales; 3°) 1041
morceaux d'orchestre; 4°) 1074 volumes de littérature musicale [etc.]. Gand, 1924. 88 p. 2729
lots.   [B-Br, compiler (film)]
> A private collection? Poorly cataloged.

3122   **1925**
"A Collection Privately Purchased"
MESSRS. ELLIS, FIRM, LONDON
A Catalogue of Books of and Relating To Music, Including Many Rarities from a Collection
Privately Purchased, on Sale. . . . London, 1925. 49 p. 307 lots.   [US-NYgr, compiler]
> "Catalogue 233 [i.e., No. 25 of Music Series]."

3123   **1927 (8-9 June)**
"*"**
POSECH, AUCTIONEER, BERLIN   VERST. NO. 1
*Autographen Sammlung ***, und Beiträge aus anderen Besitz. Historische und literarische*
Autographen. Musiker, Schauspieler und bildende Künstler. Versteigerung . . . 8. [-9.] *Juni*
1927. . . . Berlin, 1927. 116 p., illus. 1266 lots.   [US-NYgr]
> "Musiker, Schauspieler, Künstler," lots 1119-266. Lot 1205, Mozart
> holograph of the violin sonata, K. 454.

3124   **1930 (28-29 April)**
Anonymous
Catalogue d'une important bibliothèque . . . Livres sur la musique en général et spécialement
sur Wagner. . . . Paris: Libr. R. Simonson, 1930.
> Not located; cited from *Jahrbuch Peters*, 1930.

3125 1931?
"B*"**
Gustav Legouix, firm, Paris   Cat. no. 15
Oeuvres vocales en partitions d'orchestre. Éditions originales. Anciennes editions de 17ᵉ -
18ᵉ - 19ᵉ siècles, provenant de la bibliothèque de Monsieur. . . . Paris, [n.d., 1931?]. 29 p. 364
lots.   [GB-Lbl (Hirsch)]

      Noted in *ZfMW* 13 (1930/31): 586.

3126 1931 (19 December)
"B . . . (Geigenvirtuosen)"
Helmut and Ernst Meyer, firm, Berlin   Verst. Cat. no. 21
. . . *Paganini Sammlung von original Porträts und Studienblättern nach dem Leben, aus dem*
Besitz des verstorbenen Geigenvirtuosen B . . . *19 Dezember 1931.* . . . Berlin, 1931. 56 p., 25
plates (mostly caricatures of Paganini). 28 lots.   [US-NYgr, NL-DHgm, GB-Lbl (Hirsch)]

      Noted in *ZfMW* 14 (1931/32): 192.

3127 1932 (21 November)
"Zwei Sammlungen aus rheinischen Besitz"
M. Lengfeld'sche, Buchhandlung, Cologne   Cat. no. 42
Autographen von geistlichen Persönlichkeiten, Dichtern . . . *und Musikern. Zwei Sammlung*
aus rheinischen Besitz, beschreibendes Verzeichnis von Dr. Georg Kinsky . . . *Versteigerung*
. . . *21. November 1932.* Köln a.Rh., 1932. 95 p., 15 plates. 571 lots.   [NL-Avb, compiler]

      "Musik und bildende Kunst," lots 323-571.

3128 1934 (28-30 May)
"A Private Collector Resident in Germany"
Sotheby & Co., auctioneer, London
Catalogue of Highly Important Autograph Letters and Literary Manuscripts . . . *Including the*
Property of G. C. Taylor [and others] . . . *Sold* . . . *28th Day of May and Two Following Days.*
. . . [London, 1934.] 94 p. 628 lots.   [Film at CRL]

      "Musical manuscripts, property of a private collector resident in Germany,"
      lots 387-94 but many more items (e.g., lot 393 = 26 ALS).

3129 1934 (19 June)
Anonymous
Alb. de (Exp.) Tavernier, Antwerp
Catalogue d'une important e collection de musique. Traité divers, musique ancienne en
éditions de l'époque, musique moderne, oeuvres symphoniques, dont la vente publique . . . *19*
juin 1934. Anvers, 1934. 20 p. 329 lots.   [B-Br, compiler (film)]

      "Oeuvres symphoniques," lots 118-329.

1937
"Zwei bekannten Sammlungen."   *See under* **Zweig, Stefan** *in section 1*

3130 1937 (13 December)
Anonymous
Luigi Lubrano, firm
[Music.] [N.p.], 1937.   [NL-Avb]

      Not examined; cited from **Vereeniging** . . . *Catalogus.*

3131   1937 (13 December)
"Um distinto bibliófilo"

A. H. DE OLIVEIRA, FIRM, LISBON

Catálogo duma preciosa e seleccionada biblioteca . . . Japão - China - India . . . Cancioneiros clássicos . . . venda . . . de 13 Dezembro de 1937 e seguintes no. . . . Lisboa: Livraria Manuel dos Santos, 1937. 105 p. 1217 lots. Music *inter alia.*   [NL-Avb]

3132   Anonymous

ALB. DE (LIB.-EXPERT) TAVERNIER, ANTWERP

Ville d'anvers, Saal Lamorniere . . . Catalogue d'un importante collection de livres anciens et modernes de tous genres. Musique: musique de chambre. Oeuvres symphoniques avec matériel d'orchestre . . . vente publique . . . 28 janvier 1942 et deux jours suivants. . . . Antwerp, 1942. 28 p. 1095 lots. 267 lots, music.   [NL-Avb]

3133   1949 (7 May)
Anonymous

L'ART ANCIEN, FIRM, ZÜRICH; HAUS DER BÜCHER, FIRM, BASEL

Autographen und Stammbücher aus bedeutenden Privatsammlungen, dabei wertvolle Musik-Manuskripte und umfangreiche Brieffolgen . . . 7. Mai 1949. . . . Zürich: L'Art Ancien; Basel: Haus der Bücher, 1949. 42 p., illus. 370 lots.   [US-NYgr]

Music throughout. Liszt Mss., lots 206-13.

3134   1949 (26 January)
"Aus zwei schweizerische Musiksammlungen"

L'ART ANCIEN, FIRM, ZÜRICH; HAUS DER BÜCHER, FIRM, BASEL

Auktion XVI. Autographen, dabei Beiträge aus . . . 26. November 1949. . . . Zürich: L'Art Ancien; Basel: Haus der Bücher, 1949. 44 p., illus. 330 lots.   [US-NYgr]

Music throughout. Mendelssohn Mss., lots 192-99.

3135   1959 (9-10 June)
Anonymous

L'ART ANCIEN, FIRM, ZÜRICH; HAUS DER BÜCHER, FIRM, BASEL

Aukton XXXI. Eine umfangreiche Bibliothek aus altem Zürcher Familienbesitz . . . Musik und Musikwissenschaft. eine bedeutende Sammlung . . . aus den Besitz eines Musiker und zweier Musikgelehrter . . . Versteigerung . . . 9. [-10.] Juni 1959. Zürich; Basel, 1959. 144 p., illus. 1385 lots.   [US-NYgr]

"V., Musik," lots 246-710a but many more items (e.g., lots 365, ca. 30 vols. of the DTÖ).

3136   1960 (12-13 January)

J. L. BEIJERS, ANTIQUARIAT, UTRECHT

Book Auction Sale . . . the Second Portion of the ***S [in Ms., Kramers] *Collection. **M* [in Ms., Amsterdam] *and Books, Prints and Periodicals . . . Songbooks. . . .* Utrecht, 1960. 204 p. 2174 lots. 84 songbooks, *inter alia.*   [NL-Avb]

3137   **1962 (22-24 March)**
Anonymous
PAUL VAN DER PERRE (LIB. -EXP.)
Importante bibliothèque: Musique et musicologie. Ouvrages variés, anciens et modernes.
Éditions originals . . . Vente publique . . . 22 [-24] mars 1962. Bruxelles, 1962. 141 p. 1336
lots. Music, lots 1-657.   [B-Br, NL-Avb, US-NYgr, compiler]

3138   **1964 (2 June)**
"Amateur"
ÉTIENNE ADER (C.-P.)
Ouvrages sur le musique provenant de la bibliothèque d'un amateur. Vente . . . Hôtel drouot
. . . 2 juin 1964. 17 p. 126 lots.   [US-NYgr]

3139   **1966 (16 May)**
Anonymous
DR. ERNST HAUSWEDELL, AUCTIONEER, HAMBURG   AUK. CAT NO. 146
Musik - Autographen - Noten - Bücher versteigerung in Hamburg . . . 16., 17. Mai . . . [und] 22.
Mai 1966. Hamburg, 1966. 68 p. 728 lots.   [NL-Avb]

3140   **1967 (16-17 October)**
"A Lady"
SOTHEBY & CO., AUCTIONEER, LONDON
Catalogue of a Distinguished Collection of Early Medical Books and Books on Music, the
Property of . . . Sold . . . 16th [-17th] October, 1967. 87 p., illus. 448 lots. Music, lots 372-448.
                                                                              [g.a.]

3141   **1970 (9 June)**
Anonymous
J. A. STARGARDT, AUCTIONEER, MARBURG
Musik-Autographen. Eine Privatsammlung. Auktion am 9. Juni 1970. Marburg, 1970.
56 p., plates. 162 lots.   [US-NYgr]
        Includes Mss. of Ravel, Liszt, Mozart, Fauré, Chausson, and others.

3142   **1970 (28 November)**
Anonymous
GALERIE EMILE RELECOM, BRUSSELLS
Livres en tous genres, dont de nombreux ouvrages de musicologie - Partitions musicales . . .
[Sold] *28 Novembre 1970.* Bruxelles, 1970. 10 p. 401 lots.   [NL-Avb]

3143   **[1971]**
"A Private Collection"
CREYGHTON, FIRM, BILTHOVEN
Catalogue of a Private Collection [chamber music from the eighteenth and early nineteenth
centuries]. Bilthoven, [1971]. 97 p., illus.   [compiler]

3144   **1972**
"A Musicologist"
CREYGHTON, FIRM, BILTHOVEN   LIST 138
Antiquarian Works from the Library of. . . . Bilthoven, 1972. [12] p. 129 lots.   [g.a.]

3145 1979

"A Scholar's Music Library"

RICHARD MACNUTT, FIRM, TUNBRIDGE WELLS   CAT. NO. 109

Music, Theatre and Ballet: [a scholar's music library]. Tunbridge Wells, [1979]. [62] p. 317 lots.   [g.a.]

3146 1978?

"A Private Collection"

WR MUSIC LITERATURE, FIRM, FAIRBANKS, ALASKA

Sale of a Private Collection: Music, Books, Scores, Periodicals. Fairbanks, [n.d., 198?]. 31 p. 530 lots.

3147 1983

"A Scholar"

J & J LUBRANO, FIRM, GREAT BARRINGTON, MASS.   CAT. NO. 12

A Scholar's Music Library [with emphasis on the medieval, renaissance, and baroque periods]. South Lee, Mass., [1983]. 53 p. [923] lots (sections separately lotted).   [g.a.]

3148 1985

Anonymous

Henze-Döhring, Sabine. "Eine Libretti-Sammlung in der Musikgeschichtliches Abteilung des Deutschen Historischen Instituts in Rom." *Mf* 38 (1985): 202-03.

Section 3

The Migration of Private Collections
(arranged chronologically)

The following list attempts primarily to establish the present location (mainly institutionalized) of what were private music collections. For these collectors, I have tried to provide the fullest possible names and birth and death dates. But that has not always been easy. It would require more than a lifetime to run to earth such information for a "Burtron," a "Stradlett," or an "Unvergoff" who surface in secondary sources in phrases such as "The Burtron Bequest," "The Gift of Sradlett," or "Bequeathed by Unvergoff." If the gifts, sales, and bequests are those from persons with more usual names—Smith, Jones, or Williams—the puzzle is past all solution.

I have pursued data more avidly for some collectors than others, persuaded partly by the size and importance of their collections. It did not seem proper for me to ask my colleagues in many institutions to plow laboriously through dusty, ancient deeds of gift (if such exist) for facts about the likes of the Burtrons, Stradletts and the Unvergoffs; their constrisions probably do not warrant such an imposition—or at least I have so surmised. I have tried to see as much of the literature cited in section 1 as possible, but to endeavor to see at first hand the myriad collections here noted was, of course, unthinkable.

Many collectors whose collections appeared in sale catalogs or other such lists and which are set out in section 1 of this work are absent from this section. If the collections were dispersed—by sale, neglect, or whatever method—and their present whereabouts remain unknown, they will not appear here.

Their *whence*abouts remain a major concern of section 1; their *where*abouts that of this section. Annotations in the two sections must therefore contain some overlapping.

Despite the monumental works by Albrecht, Krummel, Folter, Davies, King, Penney, and the many others in the list of secondary sources upon which this compilation massively depends—and despite this determined effort to cumulate their information—many collections undoubtedly will have been missed, a number perhaps more deserving of inclusion than many of uncertain merit which are included here.

And, of course, every day, in some part of the world, someone gives their collection to an institution, or an institution purchases one brought to the market. As with the other sections of this book I have tried to keep this as complete through 1995 as possible.

3149   **Abbado, Marcello**

     At I-PCcon. **Benton 3**:235, no. 275.

3150   **Aber, Alice Larson**

     Early 19th-century harp music at US-BE. *Amerigrove.*

3151   **Abraham, Burggraf zu Dohna (Saxony),** b. 1579

     Elizabethan music prints at D-Schlobitten. Entry in *section 1.*

3152   **Adams, Mrs. John Quincy,** 1775-1852

     Music books at US-Wsi. *RAMH.*

3153   **Adler, Guido,** 1855-1941

     Library purchased in 1948 by US-ATS. Entries in *section 1.*

3154   **Agosti, Arrigo** and **Egle**

     Ca. 5000 recordings donated to Teatro municipale di Reggio Emilia. Entry in *section 1.*

3155   **Aguilera de Heredia, Sebastian,** 1565-1627

     Sale, in 1892, of rare Spanish treatises and music to GB-Lbl. *Grove 5.*

3156   **Aiblinger, Johann Kaspar,** 1779-1867

     At D-Mbn.

3157   **Aiguillon, ducs d'**

     Collection now at F-AG. Entries in *section 1.*

3158   **Albert, Duke of Prussia,** 1490-1568

     Collection in Königsberg, Staats- und Universitäts-Bibliothek. *Grove 3.*

3159   **Albert, Friedrich August, King of Saxony,** 1828-1902

     4000 volumes and 300 cases from the Royal Library acquired in 1896 by D-Dlb. **Albrecht.**

3160   **Albert I, Prince of Monaco,** 1848-1922

     At F-NI. *NG-L,* p. 741.

3161   **Albrecht, Henry F.,** d. 1875

     Scores, books and autographs collected in Europe between 1854 and 1858 bought by Joseph Drexel and were nucleus of his library given to US-NYp. Entries in *section 1* under **Albrecht** and **Drexel.**

3162   **Albrecht, Jan,** b. 1919

     Collection part of Primrose International Viola Archive at US-PRV.

3163   **Aldrich, Henry,** 1648-1710
        8000 items, printed and manuscript, of Tudor and Stuart music given to
        GB-Och in 1710. Entry in *section 1*.

3164   **Aldrich, Richard,** 1863-1937
        Books, including ca. 100 dated before 1800, donated to US-CA in 1986.
        Entry in *section 1*.

3165   **Ales, Oreste**
        Collection given in 1929 to I-MAC. **Benton 3**:198, no. 173.

3166   **Alexander, Ferdinand, Fürst,** 1704-73
        At D-Rtt. Entries in *section 1*.

3167   **Alfonso de Bourbon y Braganza**
        At E-Mam. Entry in *section 1*.

3168   **Algarotti, Nikola Udina**
        3000 manuscript and printed works received in 1935 by YU-Zh. *NG*-L,
        p. 795.

3169   **Allan, Erskine**
        Bequest to GB-Cus in 1897. **Penney**.

3170   **Allen, Alfred Reginald,** b. 1905
        Gilbert and Sullivan materials at US-NYpm. Entry in *section 1* under **Sullivan**.

3171   **Allen, Sir Hugh**
        Bequest to GB-Ouf. **Davies**; *Grove 5*.

3172   **Alsbach, Johan Adam,** 1873-1961
        The music publisher's collection of 13,000 Dutch compositions ended up
        at NL-Ad. Auction catalog in *section 1*.

3173   **Alströmer, Patrick A., Baron,** 1733-1804
        Books on music and 18th-century works in S-Skma. Entries in *section 1*.

3174   **Altemps, Giovanni Angelo, Duke of Gallese**
        Collection originating in 16th century now at I-Rvat. **Benton 3**:347.

3175   **Altieri, Paolo**
        Collection now at I-NT. Entry in *section 1*.

3176   **Ambrogio, Aldo**
        At I-PCcon. **Benton 3**:235, no. 275.

3177   **Ambros, August Wilhelm,** 1816-76
Now at A-Wn. Entry in *section 1.*

3178   **Ambrosini, Raimondo,** d. 1914
Manuscripts, incunabula, early editions, mostly Bolognese now at I-Bam.
Entry in *section 1.*

3179   **Amerbach, Bonifacius,** 1495-1562
Now at CH-BU. *NG*-L, p. 793.

3180   **Ammende, Dietrich,** b. 1901
Now at D-Mbn. **Münster.**

3181   **Amplonius de Berka,** fl. 1400
Now at D-EF. Entry in *section 1.*

3182   **Anderson, Muriel V.**
Collection related to Jenny Lind at US-NH. **Samuel.**

3183   **André, Johann Anton,** 1755-1842
Institutionalized collections at D-Bds and D-FUl. *Section 1.*

3184   **Anglès, Higini,** 1888-1969
Acquired by E-Bc in 1971.

Anhalt Zerbst, Princes of.   *See* **Johann IV, Fürst zu Anhalt-Zerbst**

3185   **Anna Amalia, Duchess of Saxe-Weimar,** 1739-1807
Ca. 2000 volumes at D-WRz. **Albrecht.**

3186   **Anna Amalia, Princess of Prussia,** 1723-87
On her death, acquired by the Joachimsthal Gymnasium in Berlin, then sent
to D-Bds. After World War II most went to D-Bim; some volumes back in
D-B. Entries in *section 1.*

3187   **Anrooy, Peter van,** 1879-1954
At NL-DHgm. **Gleich.**

Ansbach, Margrave of.   *See* **Friedrich Georg, Markgraf von Ansbach,** 1557-1603

3188   **Anton, Karl (of Mannheim)**
Nachlass and catalog at D-DS. **Beisswenger.**

3189   **Apel, Willi,** 1893-1988
Materials regarding pianoforte and violin music, at US-BLu. Entry in
section 1.

3190 **Aragon, Corona de**

The archive of the Aragonese crown — ca. 100 manuscripts on music from monasteries. *NG*-L, p. 787.

3191 **Archibald, Mary Mellish**

Canadian folk music at C-SAu. Entries in *section 1.*

3192 **Areu, Manuel**

Zarzuela collection at US-ALBu. Entry in *section 1.*

3193 **Arms, Fanny**

7000 items of popular music at US-COu. **Bradley**.

3194 **Arnold, Franck Thomas,** 1861-1940

17th- to 18th-century chamber music at GB-Cu. Part now at GB-Cpl and GB-CDu. Entries in *section 1.*

3195 **Artaria, Karl August,** 1855-1919

Went to D-Bds in 1901. Entries in *section 1.*

3196 **Asenjo y Barbieri, Francisco,** 1823-94

4000 volumes of materials for a history of Spanish music at E-Mn. Entry in *section 1.*

3197 **Atholl,** [possibly **James Stewart-Murray, Duke of**, 1879-1957]

Bequest to GB-P of ca. 1000 scores and books of early Scottish music. **Penney**, p. 506.

3198 **Atkins, Sir Isaac,** 1897-1950

Part books were donated to GB-WO. **Penney**, p. 709.

3199 **Attl, Vojmer**

A collection of ca. 800 opera and symphonic harp parts at US-Los Angeles Public Library. *Amerigrove.*

3200 **Aubry, Pierre,** 1874-1910

Library is now at F-Pim. **Albrecht**.

3201 **August II, Duke of Braunschweig-Lüneburg,** 1579-1666

Now part of D-W. **Albrecht**.

3202 **Auguste Friederike, Consort of Friedrich Ludwig, Archduke of Mecklenburg-Schwerin,** 1776-1871

Now at D-SWl. Entries in *section 1.*

3203 **Avé-Lallemont, Luise**

Now at D-LEu. Entry in *section 1.*

3204   Ayer, Edward E.

> Collection of American hymnals at US-Cn. *RAMH*.

3205   Aylward, Theodore, ca. 1730-1801

> English sacred and organ music at GB-CDp. **Davies**; **King**, p. 82.

3206   Bach, Carl Philipp Emanuel

> Part of his collection at D-Ha. Many entries in *section 1*.

3207   Bachelet, Théodore

> Printed music and manuscripts, 16th-19th centuries; sacred music, 18th-century operas and cantatas, now at F-R. **Albrecht**.

3208   Bachmann, Edwin

> 10,000 volumes, ALS and manuscripts acquired in 1958 by US-AUS. Entry in *section 1*.

3209   Bacigalupi, Remo

> 6000 early vocal music recordings at US-BE. *RAMH*.

3210   Baden, J.

> Song collection at Dk-Kk. Entry in *section 1*.

3211   Bäumker, Wilhelm, 1842-1905

> German Catholic song at D-KNu. Entry in *section 1*.

3212   Bagford, John, 1650 or 51-1716

> Early printed music at GB-Lbl. Entries in *section 1*.

3213   Baker, Thomas

> 50 volumes of 18th-century printed music at Hampshire County Library, Winchester, Hants.

3214   Balaton, ?

> Collection at H-KE. Entry in *section 1*.

3215   Balbour, Lucius H.

> His father's collection of late acoustic and early electric recordings at US-NH. *Amerigrove*.

3216   Baldi-Papini Family [Ubualdo, 1907- ?]

> Gift to I-PS. *NG*-L, p. 777.

3217   Balfour, Arthur James, 1st Earl of, 1848-1930

> **King** says he acquired Handel materials from Julian Marshall (**1785**), which then went to GB-En in 1938. **Albrecht**.

3218   Banér, Gustaf Adam, 1624-81
Collection at Sk-U. Entry in *section 1*.

3219   Bang, Maria, 1879-1940
Paganiniana now at US-Wc. See entry under **Paganini.**

3220   Baralli, Raffaelo
Collection now at I-Lc. **Benton 3**:195-96, no. 167.

3221   Barbier, Jules, 1822-1901
Collection "Recently deposited" at F-Po. *NG*-L, p. 741.

Barbieri, Francisco Asenjo, 1823-94.   *See* **Asenjo y Barbieri, Francisco**

3222   Barbirolli, Sir John, 1899-1970
Conducting scores presented by his widow in 1971 to GB-Lbl. Entry in *section 1*.

3223   Barbosa Machado, Diego, 1681-1772
Printed scores now at BR-Rn. Entries in *section 1*.

3224   Barjarel, ?
At F-C.

3225   Barker, Chester
Vocal scores at US-STu. *Amerigrove.*

3226   Barker, John
Collection of part books at GB-LF. **Penney,** p. 358.

3227   Barlow, Robert
1954 gift of sheet music, vocal scores, recordings helped establish the American Musical Theater Collection at US-NH. *Amerigrove.*

3228   Barnekow, Christian, 1837-1913
18th-century instrumental music bequest to S-L. **Albrecht** says other portions at DK-Kv and DK-KM(m).

3229   Baroni-Cavalcabò, Mrs. Julie
Given the collection of Felix Xaver Wolfgang Mozart, 1791-1844, which she bequeathed to A-Sm and A-Sd. Entry in *section 1*.

Barrett-Lennard, 1818-99.   *See* **Lennard, Henry Barrett,** 1818-99

3230   Barry, C. A.
At GB-Lbl. **Davies**.

3231 **Bartók, Béla,** 1881-1945

Southeastern European folk music, including manuscripts of his collections and studies, deposited in 1942 at US-NYcu. Some also in
H-BA(mi). *NG*-L, p. 768.

3232 **Basevi, Abramo,** 1818-85

Given to I-Fc. Entry in *section 1*.

3233 **Bass,** [probably **Iris**]

Opera scores and first and early editions at US-NYp.

3234 **Bates, Edward**

The Puttick & Simpson auction of his library in 1867 comprised many works
formerly his father's, Joah Bates, most bought by James Hook (**1362**). In
the sale of Hook's library in 1874, most bought by A. H. Mann (**1757**),
some of which are now at various institutions. See entries in *section 1*
under **Mann, Edward** and **Joah Bates,** and **Hook**.

3235 **Bates, Lucy**

Dance collection at US-TA. *RAMH*.

Batková, Tekla. *See under* **Seydl** *in section 1*

3236 **Baudry, ?**

Orchestral parts to 560 operas at F-R. **Benton 3**:119, no. 144.

3237 **Baughman, Roland**

Notable collection of Berlioz items at US-NYcu. Entry in *section 1*.

3238 **Baumann, Ludwig,** b. 1866

At D-KA. **Benton 2**:75, no. 138.

3239 **Baumgartner, August,** 1814-62

At D-Mbn. **Münster**.

3240 **Bax, Arnold (Edward Trevor),** 1813-1953

Benton 2:158 and *NG*-L, p. 769, say at EIR-C. **Davies** says GB-Lbl.

3241 **Beard, Harry R.**

Materials related to British stage at GB-Lva. *NG*-L, p. 765.

3242 **Bech, Terence R.**

Music research collection at US-BLu. Entry in *section 1*.

3243 **Becker, Carl Ferdinand,** 1804-77

Now at D-LEm. Entry in *section 1*.

3244   **Becker, Georg,** 1834-1928
        1500 rarities acquired by F-LYm. Entry in *section 1*.

3245   **Becker, Georg Horst**
        Pianoforte arrangements at D-Fmi. **Benton 2**:63, no. 85.

3246   **Becker, Karl E.**
        German folk song collection at US-Wc. Entry in *section 1*.

3247   **Belden, Louis**
        Ca. 13,000 78 rpm jazz recordings at US-TC. *RAMH*.

3248   **Bell, Joseph** and **Max**
        Collection of over 150,000 recordings at US-SYa. *RAMH*.

3249   **Bellamy, Rev. Dr.**
        Bequest to GB-Ouf, nucleus of its collection. Entry in *section 1*.

3250   **Beneke, Paul Victor Mendelssohn,** d. 1944
        Given to Margaret Deneke, who put it on loan to GB-Ob, about 1950. **King**,
        p. 147.

3251   **Benson, L.**
        AT GB-Lbl. **Davies**; *Grove 5*. **Benton 2**:180, no. 63, says items also at
        GB-Lcm.

3252   **Benson, Louis Fitzgerald,** 1855-1930
        9,000 volumes of American hymnology at US-PRs; some materials at US-
        PHphs. **Albrecht**.

3253   **Bentheim-Techlenburg, Graf zu**
        With that of Graf Bentheim of Burgsteinfurt, on deposit at D-MH and
        D-MÜu. Thematic catalog in *section 1*.

3254   **Bentinck, Count**
        Collection in the Castle Archives in Amerongen, Holland. Catalog at NL-
        Uim. **Albrecht**.

3255   **Benvenuti, Giacomo,** 1885-1943
        Collection acquired by I-Mc in 1951. *NG*-L, p. 774.

3256   **Berger, Kenneth Walter,** b. 1924
        Materials on band music at US-MSu. *Amerigrove*.

3257   Berggreen, Andreas Peter, 1801-80

Folksongs in Deutsches Voksliedarchiv. Entry in *section 1*.

3258   Bernini, [?**Giuseppe**, 1834-1922]

At I-Ls. **Benton 2**:197, no. 170.

3259   Bertarelli, Achille

I-Mcon collection based on his library. 11,000 illustrations of musicians and theatrical personages. Entry in *section 1*.

3260   Berwald Family

The family archive donated in 1969 to S-Skma. *NG*-L, p. 792.

3261   Besseler, Heinrich, 1900-69

Bequest to D-LEm. *NG*-L, p. 746.

3262   Best, C. W.

Collection of autographs, a bequest in 1948 to US-OB. Entry in *section 1*.

3263   Betti, Adolfo, 1873-1950

Chamber music at US-AUS. Entry in *section 1*.

3264   Bickford, Vahdah Olcott, 1885-1980

Collection of guitar music given to California State University, Northridge. Entries in *section 1*.

3265   Bird, Frederic M., 1838-1908

Library of hymnology now at US-NYts. *Amerigrove*.

Birkat-Smith, Frederick, 1880-1952. *See entry under* **Rischel** *in section 1*

3266   Birnbaum, Eduard

Cantorial music of the 19th century at US-Clhc. Entry in *section 1*.

3267   Bischoff, Ferdinand, 1826-1915

17th-century guitar and lute tabulatures and 18th-century editions at A-Gk (h). Entry in *section 1*.

3268   Blaze, François Henri Joseph, called **Castil-Blaze,** 1784-1857

Part of his library now at F-A. **Albrecht**.

3269   Bliss, Mildred

Bequest to US-CA, 1969. Entry in *section 1*.

3270   **Bliss-Herter Families**

> Gift of autograph letters to US-NYp.

3271   **Blom, Eric,** 1888-1959

> Collection now at GB-Lwcm. **Davies**.

3272   **Blome, Count of Salzau**

> 300 prints and manuscripts of the 19th century at D-KIl. *NG*-L, p. 754.

3273   **Blunt, Janet Heatley,** 1859-1950

> Folk material now at GB-Lcs. Entry in *section 1*.

3274   **Bodmer, Hans Conrad Ferdinand,** 1891-1956

> Bequest to D-BNba. Entries in *section 1*.

3275   **Böhme, Franz-Magnus,** 1827-1898

> Some of the collection now at D-WRh. Entries at *section 1*.

3276   **Boers, Jan Conradus,** 1812-96

> Now at NL-DHgm. Entries in *section 1*.

3277   **Boghen,** [perhaps **Carlo Felice**, 1869-1945]

> Collection given to I-Fc. **Benton 3**:182, no. 129.

3278   **Bohn, Emil,** 1839-1909

> Part of collection at PL-WRu.

3279   **Boije of Gennäs Family**

> Guitar music at S-Skma; donated in 1924. *NG*-L, p. 792.

3280   **Boissy,** [probably **Louis de**, 1694-1758]

> Theatrical material at F-AIXm. *NG*-L, p. 737.

3281   **Bok, Mary Louise Curtis,** 1876-1970

> Gift to US-PHci included letters and manuscripts of Wagner, once Lady Burrell's. Many items sold at auction in 1982. Entries in *section 1* under **Burrell, Mary**.

3282   **Bokemeyer, Heinrich,** 1679-1751

> According to Folter, most of the library came from Georg Österreich (1664-1735). The library was acquired by J. N. Forkel, and in 1819 it passed to Kgl. Institut für Kirchenmusik in Berlin, eventually to D-B and D-Bds. Entries in *section 1* under **Bokemeyer** and **Forkel**.

3283   **Bonamici, Diomede,** 1823-1912

Livorno collector's 6000 librettos sold to I-Fm in 1904. (**Benton** says 10,000!) Entry in *section 1*.

3284   **Bonaventure, Jules**

Collection at F-C. Entry in *section 1* under **Laurens, Jean Joseph**.

3285   **Bonavia, F** [probably **Feruccio**, 1877-1950]

Now at GB-Lbbc. *Grove 5*, p. 188.

3286   **Bonime, Josef**

Collection at US-PRV. *Amerigrove*.

3287   **Boot, Henry**

"Palm Court Collection" now at GB-Y. **Penney 4**.

3288   **Booth, ?**

Collection of Catholic liturgical music at GB-LVp. **Penney**, p. 364.

3289   **Borghese, Paolo, Principe,** 1845-1920

Collection dispersed in 1892. Many items acquired by F-Pc, I-Rac, GB-Lbl. Entries in *section 1*.

3290   **Botkin, Benjamin Albert,** 1901-75

Southern folksong materials collected in the 1920s now at US-LIu. **Benton** 1:145, no. 201. Materials on folk music and jazz of the 1930s with related recordings and some oral history tapes at US-LIhs. *RAMH*.

3291   **Bottée de Toulmon, Auguste,** 1797-1850

Now at F-Pn. **Albrecht**.

3292   **Bottini, Mariana Andreozzi, Marchese,** 1802-58

Now at I-LI. **Benton 3**:196-97, no. 169.

3293   **Boucher, Anthony**

Ca. 2000 recordings of the "Golden Age of Opera" at US-SB. *Amerigrove*.

3294   **Boulanger, Nadia,** 1887-1979

Ca. 2000 items, mainly scores, including autograph manuscripts, are at F-Pn, as is her collection of correspondence. At F-LYc are another ca. 15,000 scores, 1000 volumes of books and journals. Entries in *section 1*.

3295   **Boult, Sir Adrian,** 1889-1983

Orchestral parts to GB-Lbbc; scores to GB-Lcm. **Davies**.

3296   Boulton, Laura, 1899-1988

> Traditional and liturgical music (10,000 field recordings) at US-NYcu. **Benton** **1**:171, no. 258.

3297   Bourbon (Royal Family: Amadeo di Savoia, 1845-90**; Isabel Francisca de Bourbon y Asis; José Eugenio de Baviera y Bourbon)**

> Given to E-Mc. *NG*-L, p. 789.

3298   Bourne, Thomas William, d. 1949

> Collection of 18th-century editions of Handel given to GB-Ob in 1947. **Penney**, p. 465.

3299   Bover, Felix

> Ca. 400 psalters at CH-N. Entry in *section 1.*

3300   Boyd, Charles N., 1875-1937

> Pittsburgh organist and scholar's material on Pittsburgh music bought in 1938 by Us-Pc.

3301   Braathen, Sverre O.

> Circus band scores and literature are at US-NO. *RAMH.*

3302   Bradley, Carol June, b. 1937

> Oral interview tapes and papers relating to American music librarianship at US-BUu.

Bragança, House of.   *See under* **João IV** *in section 1*

3303   Brahms, Johannes, 1833-97

> Bequeathed to A-Wgm. Entries in *section 1.*

3304   Brandt-Buys, Hans, 1905-59

> At NL-Uim. *NG*-L, p. 781.

3305   Breitkopf, Johann Gottlieb Immanuel, 1719-94

> Some now at D-DS. Entries in *section 1.*

3306   Brewsaugh, V. G.

> Memorial music collection given by Frank Mannheimer to Emporia State University, Kansas. **Bradley.**

3307   Briccialdi, Giulio

> At I-TE. **Benton 3**:266, no. 361.

3308   Bridge, Sir Frederick, 1844-1924

> At GB-Ctc. **Davies.** Entry in *section 1.*

3309 **Bridges, ?**
Bequest to GB-Ouf. *Grove 5.*

3310 **Bridgewater, Francis, 6th Earl of,** 1736-1803
Collection begun by Sir Thomas Egerton (**3538**). Now at US-SM.

3311 **Brigode de Kemlandt Family**
Music now at B-Lc. See under **Terry, Léonard** in *section 1.*

3312 **Bristow, George Frederick,** 1825-98
Manuscripts acquired in 1948 by US-NYp.

3313 **Britton, Thomas,** 1644-1714 (the "Small-Coal Man")
Some items at GB-LBl, -Ob; US-CA, -NYp. Entry in *section 1.*

Britwell Court Library. *See* **Christie-Miller, William Henry**

3314 **Broadwood, Lucy Ethelred,** 1858-1929
Manuscript folksongs at GB-Lcs. **Davies.**

3315 **Brochet, L[ouis?]**
Theatrical materials at F-AU. **Benton 3**:67, no. 18.

3316 **Brock, Robert Alonzo,** 1839-1914
Early American music and 19th-century American sheet music related to the American Southeast at US-SM. *RAMH.*

3317 **Brodin, Linus**
Collection now at S-KA.

3318 **Brodsky, Adolph,** 1851-1929
Archive at GB-Royal Northern College of Music. Entry in *section 1.*

3319 **Brooks, Elmer**
Pictures and photographs of musicians who performed with the Minneapolis Symphony at US-MSp. *RAMH.*

Brose, David. *See here under* **Lumpkin, Ben Gray**

3320 **Brossard, Sebastien de,** 1655-1730
His manuscript collection given to Louis XV, the basis of the collection at F-Pn. Entries in *section 1.*

3321 **Brossmer, Alfred Erwin**
Bequest at D-FRu. **Benton 2**:64, no. 89.

3322   **Brotherton, Edward Allen, Baron Brotherton of Wakefield,** 1856-1930
Part of music library now at GB-LEbc. **Albrecht.**

3323   **Brown, Allen Augustus,** 1835-1916
Given to US-Bp in 1874. Entries in *section 1.*

3324   **Brown, Mary Elizabeth (Adams),** 1842-1918
Collection of musicians' portraits at US-NYmm.

3325   **Browne, John,** 1608-91
Manuscript instrumental music now at GB-Och. Entries in *section 1.*

3326   **Browning, Oscar**
Schubertiana and Schumaniana in a bequest to GB-Hastings Public Library.
Penney, p. 209.

3327   **Brucken Fock, Gerard von,** 1859-1935
At NL-DHgm. **Gleich.**

3328   **Bruning, Harry F.**
American sheet music at US-PRV. *Amerigrove.*

3329   **Brunnings, Florence E.**
1115 collections of folksongs in private library in Massachusetts. Entry in
section 1.

3330   **Brunswick (Brunsvik) Family**
Beethoven materials now at CS-BRsa. Entry in *section 1.*

3331   **Buchanan, Annabel Morris,** 1889-
Religious tunebooks and manuscripts at US-CHH. Entry in *section 1.*

3332   **Buck, William**
Scottish bagpipe music at US-BE. *Amerigrove.*

3333   **Bückens, Ernst,** 1884-1949
Acquired by D-KNu in 1950. Entry in *section 1.*

3334   **Bülck, Rudolf,** 1880-1954
Collection at D-KIu. **Benton 2**:79, no. 151.

3335   **Bülow, [?Hans Guido von,** 1830-94]
Bequest to D-MEIr. **Benton 2**:140-96.

3336   **Bukofzer, Manfred,** 1910-55
At US-BE. *RAMH.*

3337   Bullard, Ernest E.

Published music, 1883-1940, plus theater music, ca. 1900, at US-U of Connecticut. *RAMH*.

3338   Bunting, Edward, 1773-1843

Manuscript collection of Irish folk melodies at Queen's University, Belfast. Entry in *section 1*.

3339   Burchuk, David and **Rhoda**

Large collection of chamber music parts in private collection, US-SSburchuk. **Benton 1**:226, no. 396.

Burdick, D. C.   *See here under* **Stetson, Mrs. E. G.**

3340   Burgis, Peter

Australiana collection of 30,000 recordings, plus library at AUS-CAnl. **Benton 4**:28, no. 15.

3341   Burgundy, Dukes of

Manuscripts at B-BR. See literature under "Burgundy" in *NG*.

3342   Burney, Charles, 1726-1814

Some books and treatises at GB-Lbl; letters and notebooks at US-NH. See lengthy annotations in *section 1*.

3343   Burrage, ?

Collection of film music and dance band arrangements and recordings at US-Laramie, University of Wyoming. **Bradley**.

3344   Burrell, Mary (Banks), d. 1898

Wagner letters and manuscripts were bought by Mary Louise Curtis Bok, then given to US-PHci. Entry under **Burrell** in *section 1*.

3345   Burrill, Roger H[olmes, b. 1909]

Ca. 14,000 pieces of sheet music, ca. 1790-1960 at US-HA.

3346   Burrows, Benjamin

Ca. 100 manuscripts and photographs of songs and chamber music at Leicester University. **Penney**, p. 353.

3347   Busch, Fritz, 1890-1951

Collection at US-BLu. Entries in *section 1*.

3348   Busoni, Ferruccio, 1866-1924

Portions now at D-B and in the Galston-Busoni Archive at US-KN. See under **Galston** and **Busoni** in *section 1*.

3349 **Bute, John Stuart, 3rd Earl of Bute,** 1713-92

Collection of 1215 librettos, mostly Venetian imprints, now at US-LAuc.

3350 **Butler, Pierce,** 1866-1939

18th- to 19th-century operas at US-PHu. *Amerigrove.*

3351 **Butler, Samuel,** 1835-1902

38 printed items, mostly Handel, at GB-Cjc.

3352 **Butterworth, George S. K.**

Folksong manuscripts at GB-Lcs. **Davies**.

3353 **Buzzard, Joe, Jr.**

Hillbilly song recordings at US-BO. *Amerigrove.*

3354 **Byrd, Frederick M.,** 1838-1908

Hymnology collection donated in 1880 by Henry Day to US-NYts. *Amerigrove.*

3355 **Calvet, Esprit Claude François,** 1728-1810

An 1810 bequest to F-A. **Benton 2**:68, no. 21.

3356 **Calvör, Calvin,** 1650-1725

Private library at D-CZ. Entry in *section 1.*

3357 **Camm, John B. M.**

The Bournemouth library's collection is based on Camm's 1912 bequest of a large number of 19th-century full scores, especially those of Dvořák. Entry in *section 1.*

3358 **Campori, Giuseppe Marchesi,** 1821-87

Collection of manuscripts, 15th-19th centuries, now at I-MOe. Entries in *section 1.*

3359 **Canal, Lorenzo**

Collection at I-Vnm, according to **Benton 3**:280. (But see below.)

3360 **Canal, Pietro,** 1807-83

Collection — by some describers numbering 20,000 items — acquired in 1927 by I-Vnm. Entries in *section 1.*

3361 **Canals, José**

Collection at E-Bit. *NG*-L, p. 788.

3362   **Candia, Mario di,** 1810-83

>   "Fonds Mario," a collection of 17th- and 18th-century vocal music at I-Rsc. **Benton 3**:252, no. 316.

3363   **Capanna, Alessandro,** 1814-92

>   Ca. 1000 manuscripts and many prints at I-Bsf. **Benton 3**:155, no. 45.

3364   **Capdevilla Roviro, Felipe**

>   Manuscripts, etc., from the 12th-16th centuries in collection in Fondo Capdevilla in Barcelona. Entry in *section 1*.

3365   **Capece Minutolo Family**

>   Several hundred manuscript volumes given to I-Nc in 1970. **Albrecht.**

3366   **Capes, S. J.**

>   Pianoforte music given by widow of George J. Openhym (**440**) at US-NH. Entry in *section 1*.

3367   **Carlo, Alberto, King of Sardinia,** 1798-1849

>   Manuscripts from his private library now part of I-Tr. Entry in *section 1*.

3368   **Carminati, Constantino** and **Alessandro**

>   In I-Vmc. Entry in *section 1*.

3369   **Carotti, V.** [or **Caroti, Vittoria?**]

>   4000 librettos, 17th-19th centuries, at I-Rsc. **Benton 3**:252, no. 316.

3370   **Carpenthier-Morphy, Madame T. le**

>   Received in 1911 by US-Cn. *Amerigrove.*

3371   **Carreño, Teresa,** 1853-1917

>   Library now at US-PO. *Amerigrove.*

3372   **Carrera, Valentino**

>   17th-20th century opera and ballet librettos at I-Tci. *NG*-L, p. 779.

3373   **Carreras y Dagas, Juan,** 1828-1900

>   Collection at E-Bc. Entry in *section 1*.

3374   **Carvalhaes, Manoel Pereira Peixoto d'Almeida,** 1856-1922

>   Over 21,000 opera, oratorio, and cantata librettos at I-Rsc. Entry in *section 1*.

3375   **Carvalho, Abrahãode,** 1891-1970

>   Collection of 19,000 items, including many rare books and scores, was bought by Brazilian government, now at BR-Rn. **Albrecht.**

3376   Carvalho Monteiro, Antonio Augusto de
  The collection noted in the entry in *section 1* (**457**) "could not be traced" by **Albrecht**.

3377   Cary, Mary Flagler, 1901-67
  All given to US-NYpm. Entries in *section 1*.

3378   Casamorata, L [perhaps Luigi Ferdinando, 1807-81]
  Collected at I-Fc. **Benton 3**:182, no. 129.

3379   Casanate, Girolamo, Cardinal, 1620-1700
  Library founded in 1698 passed to the state in 1873 and is now at I-Rc. *NG*-L, p. 778; **Benton 3**:249, no. 309.

3380   Castelfranchi, Cesare
  At I-Li. **Benton 3**:193, no. 162.

3381   Cederhamn, ?
  Collection at S-Skma, according to Johansson article [under **Alströmer** in *section 1*]. Auction list of "Bibliothecam Cederhamniana," Uppsala, 1771, at S-Sk.

3382   Censi, Carlo
  At I-PCcon. **Benton 3**:235, no. 275.

3383   Cernkovic, Rudolph
  At US-Pct. Entry in *section 1*.

3384   Cerwuetelli, Giuseppe
  At I-TE. **Benton 3**:266, no. 361.

3385   Cesari, Gaetano, 1870-1934
  Given to the city, I-CR, by his widow in 1934. Entry in *section 1*.

3386   Chaillez-Richer, ?
  Classical pianoforte music, received in 1961 at F-Pim. **Benton 3**:112, no. 121.

3387   Champagne, Claude, 1891-1965
  Correspondence now in C-On. Entry in *section 1*.

Chandos, Duke of.   *See* **Brydges, James, 1st Duke of Chandos,** 1674-1744

Chandos, Leigh, 1st Baron of Stoneleigh, 1791-1850.   *See here under* **Leigh, Lord, of Stoneleigh**

3388   Chappell, William, 1809-88

Folksong manuscripts went to GB-Lcs. **Davies**. Entry in *section 1*.

3389   Charles, Louis de Bourbon, Duke of Parma, 1799-1883

Entry in *section 1*. Inherited by his grandson Robert de Bourbon (**473**).

3390   Chase, Theodore

816 bound volumes, including 400 operas, mostly from the 1860s, at US-Bh. *RAMH*.

3391   Checcacci, Felice

Collection at I-LI. **Benton 3**:193, no. 162.

3392   Chelle, W.

Manuscript treatises at GB-Lambeth Palace. **Davies**.

3393   Chigi Family

Bought by Italian government in 1918, donated to I-Rvat in 1923. Some materials donated to I-Sac in 1847. Entries in *section 1*.

3394   Chilesotti, Oscar, 1848-1916

Now at I-BDG. **Albrecht**.

3395   Chiti, Girolamo, 1681-1759

He gave his collection to Cardinal Corsini. See many entries under that name in *section 1*. Collection is now at I-Rli.

3396   Christie-Miller, William Henry, 1789-1848

In a 1919 sale, ca. 160 items from this Britwell Court library were acquired by US-SM, particularly English madrigals.

3397   Christoff, Boris, b. 1918 [**Baker's** says b. 1914]

Private library in Rome, I-Rchristoff. **Sartori**.

3398   Chrysander, Karl Franz Friedrich, 1826-1901

Largest part, Handel conducting scores, at D-Hs. Entry in *section 1*.

3399   Chujoy, Anatole, b. 1894

Memorial dance collection of composers' manuscripts now at US-CIu. *Amerigrove*.

3400   Chybinski, Adolf, 1880-1952

Collection at PL-Pu. *NG*-L, p. 783.

3401   **Cicogna, Emanuele Antonio,** 1759-1868
Collection in I-Vmc. Entries in *section 1.*

3402   **Cini, Giorgio, Fondazione**
At I-Vgc. Entry in *section 1.*

3403   **Clam-Gallas, Count Christian,** 1771-1839
Now at CS-Pnm. **Albrecht**.

3404   **Clapisson, Louis,** 1808-66
Bequest to F-Bo. *NG*-L, p. 738.

3405   **Clark, Keith C.**
Hymnology collection now at CBN University in Virginia Beach. *Amerigrove*.

3406   **Clark, William Andrews, Jr.,** 1877-1934
Bequest of 750 scores in 1934 to US-LAp. *Amerigrove*.

3407   **Clarke, Herbert L.,** 1867-1945
Band-related memorabilia at US-U. **Benton 1**:235, no. 424.

3408   **Class, Peter**
1300 first and early editions acquired from Willy Solomon now at US-RIVu. *Amerigrove*.

3409   **Claude, ?**
Chamber music at F-AU. **Benton 3**:67, no. 18.

3410   **Claudius, Carl August,** 1855-1931
Ca. 2000 prints and some liturgical manuscripts in his collection in Copenhagen.

3411   **Clayton, Rev. J. B.**
1200 hymnals and tunebooks included in George Stebbins Memorial Collection at US-Wca. *RAMH*.

3412   **Clemens Franz von Paula, Herzog in Bayern,** 1722-70
In D-Mbn. **Münster**.

3413   **Clive, Robert, Lord,** 1725-74
Sold by Rosenthal in 1948; 50 volumes to US-BE. Entry in *section 1.*

3414   **Closson, Ernest,** 1870-1950
Private library now at B-M. **Benton 2**:24, no. 27.

3415   Coates, Eric
Collection at Nottinghamshire County Library. **Penney 4**.

3416   Cobb, G. F.
Collection given to GB-Lva by his widow. *Grove 3*.

3417   Cobbett, Walter William, 1847-1937
Albrecht says purchased by C-TU in 1960. *Grove 5* says it went to Cobbett Free Library of British Chamber Music (Society of Women Musicians), London.

3418   Coci, Claire, d. 1978
Collection of organ music, books, etc., left to Gettysburg College, Pennsylvania, by her family.

3419   Cockx, Mr. (of Antwerp)
Collection, including printed works by Phalèse, acquired in 1886 by GB-Lbl. *Grove 5*.

3420   Coe, Saide Knowland
1600 scores, 400 pieces of sheet music, 572 piano rolls at US-Eu. Entry in *section 1*.

3421   Cohan, George Michael, 1878-1942
At US-NYmc. **Bradley**.

3422   Cohen, Harriet
Autograph manuscripts of Sir Arnold Bax given to GB-Lbl. Entry in *section 1*. **Penney 4** says recordings are at GB-Lam.

3423   Cohn, Alexander Meyer, 1853-1904
Now at D-Bim. Entry in *section 1*.

3424   Coirault, Patrice
Folk songs with the Weckerlin collection at F-Pn. Entry in *section 1*.

3425   Coke, Gerald E., 1907-90
Purchased part of the Handel collection of Anthony Ashley Cooper, 4th Earl of Shaftesbury. The collections also include that of William C. Smith. Now at GB-BLl. Entry in *section 1*.

3426   Coles, T. H., Rev. Dr.
Small "but interesting" collection of old English organ music at GB-Celc. *Grove 5*.

3427   **Colin, Eugène,** 1879-1965
Now at B-Bc. Entry in *section 1*.

3428   **Collalto Family**
Now at CS-Bm. Entry in *section 1*.

3429   **Colles, Henry Cope,** 1879-1943
Went to GB-LRoyal School of Church Music and GB-Ckc. Entry in *section 1*.

3430   **Collins, Walter S.,** 1924-97
Collection of college songbooks now at US-BO.

3431   **Colloredo Family**
Now at CS-KRa. Entry in *section 1*.

3432   **Colón, Fernando,** 1488-1539
Surviving portions now at E-Sco. Entries in *section 1*.

3433   **Comden, Betty**, and **Adolph Green Collection**
At US-NYmc. **Bradley**.

3434   **Commer, Franz,** 1813-87
Now at D-Bds. Entries in *section 1*.

3435   **Compagnoni-Maresfaschi** (family?)
Recent acquisitions from the library now at I-Rc. *NG*-L, p. 778.

Connick, Harris D. H.   *See* **Addenda**, p. 572

3436   **Conole, Frances R.**
65,000 discs and 2000 tapes of singing and opera at US-BI. *Amerigrove*.

3437   **Console, ?**
Collection at I-Fc. **Benton 3**:182, no. 129.

3438   **Contarini, Marco,** 1631-89
17th-century Venetian opera scores willed by descendents to I-Vnm. Entry in *section 1*.

3439   **Conti Castelli, Sebastiano, Marchese**
Collection in I-Bc. Entry in *section 1*.

3440   Contin di Castelseprio

Bequest to I-Vc. Entry in *section 1*.

3441   Cooper, Anthony Ashley, 4th Earl of Shaftesbury, 1711-71

Collection at GB-Lbl. Entry in *section 1*.

3442   Cooper, Gerald Melbourne, 1892-1947

Gave library to E. J. Dent (**563**, *section 1*), who gave it to GB-Lwcm; smaller portions to GB-Cfm and GB-Cpl. **King**, p. 75, and **Albrecht**.

3443   Coopersmith, Jacob Maurice, 1903-68

Papers related to Handel studies at US-AA. Library, with much Handeliana, at US-CP. *Amerigrove*.

3444   Coover, James B., b. 1925

6000 music antiquarian catalogs plus several hundred catalogs of private music collections and related materials at US-BUu. Entry in *section 1*.

3445   Cornelius, Peter, 1824-74

Bequest to D-MZs. **Benton 2**:85, no. 177.

3446   Corner, Musco [*sic*]

Collection of papers at GB-Lam. **Penney 4**.

3447   Cornewall Family (of Moscas Court, Hereforshire)

See entry in *section 1*.

3448   Corniani-d'Algarotti, Conte, of Treviso, 1767-

Opera and oratorio librettos, 16th-18th centuries, now at I-Mb. *NG*-L, p. 774.

3449   Cornick, Harris D. H.

5000 18th-19th century scores in 1950 to US-BE. *Amerigrove*.

3450   Corning, Bly

According to **Krummel**, some 30,000 items were acquired by US-AAc.

3451   Corsini, T.

Collection at I-Fc. **Benton 3**:182, no. 129.

3452   Corsini Family

Bequest to I-Rli in 1883. Entries in *section 1*.

3453   Corte ?

Bequest in 1970, scores and musicology, at F-AU. **Benton 3**:67, no. 18.

3454   Corte, Andrea Della, 1883-1968
>   Collection acquired in 1968 by I-Tci. **Benton 3**:67, no. 18.

3455   Corte-Callier, Gaetano, La
>   Collection I-ME. Entry in *section 1*. *NG*-L, p. 773.

3456   Cortot, Alfred, 1877-1962
>   Portions now at US-NYp, US-Cn, US-LEX, and US-BE (327 full scores and
>   300 18th-century librettos). Entries in *section 1*.

3457   Cosin, John, Bishop of Durham, d. 1672
>   Donation in 1635 to GB-Cp of 17th-century church music. **King,** pp. 8-9.

3458   Cotarelo y Mori, Emilio, 1857-1936
>   Collection at E-Bit. **Benton 3**:10, no. 13.

3459   Cowan, Alexander, d. 1929
>   Donated ca. 1000 volumes rich in materials on Scottish music history in
>   1929 to GB-En. **King,** p. 87.

3460   Cowden Clarke, Mary (Novello), 1809-98
>   Collection of Vincent Novello's daughter now at GB-LEbc. See *section 1*
>   under **Novello**.

3461   Cowell, Sidney Robertson
>   Archive of California folk music at US-BE. *Amerigrove*.

3462   Craig, Edward Gordon
>   Collection at F-Pa. *NG*-L, p. 741.

Crandall, Marjorie Lyle.   *See under* **Harwell, Richard Barksdale** *in section 1*

3463   Crawford, J. R.
>   Theater collection at US-NH. Entry in *section 1*.

Critchlow, Barbara N.   *See* **Addenda**, p. 572

3464   Croft, Marcella
>   Opera scores at US-RIVu. *Amerigrove*.

Crosby Brown, Mary   *See under* **Brown, Mary Elizabeth (Adams)**

3465   Cross, Percy (Siddell Library, Manchester)
>   At GB-Lbbc. *Grove 5*.

3466   Crotch, William 1775-1847

Some of Crotch's materials were donated by members of the family of Arthur Henry Mann **(1757-60)** to GB-NW in 1941. Entries in *section 1*.

3467   Croy, [probably **Emmanuel**, 1718-84] **Duc de**

Collection at F-VAL.

3468   Cruz, Ivo, 1901-85

Collection at P-Ln. *NG*-L, p. 786.

3469   Cudworth, Charles, 1908-77

LP recordings of Baroque and 17th-19th century music donated to GB-CWolfson collection. **Penney**, p. 112.

3470   Cummings, William Hayman, 1831-1915

Some volumes are at US-Wc, but the bulk of it is at J-Tn. Entries in *section 1*.

3471   Cunningham, G. D.

Organ music, autographs, glees and instrumental music donated to GB-Lbl, according to **Penney**, p. 542; also items at GB-Lam, according to **Benton 2**:179, no. 62.

3472   Curran, Elma Hege

Donated collection to Moravian Music Foundation, Winston-Salem. Entry in *section 1*.

3473   Curtis, Ford E. and **Harriet R.**

Theater collection, some 750,000 items, at US-Pu. *RAMH*.

3474   Dahlgren, Valdemar

Now part of the Folkrörelsernas Arkiv för Värmland, Karlstadt, Sweden.

3475   Dalley-Scarlett, Robert, 1887-1959

Collection at AUS-Sml. Entries in *section 1*.

3476   Da Motta, José Vianna, 1868-1948

Collection at P-Leg. *NG*-L, p. 786.

3477   Dance, Stanley Peter, b. 1932

6000 photographs of black musicians given to US-NH. **Samuel**.

3478   Daniel, Oliver, 1911-90

20th-century materials at US-Pu. *Amerigrove*.

3479   **Dannreuther, Edward,** 1844-1905

Portion at GB-Lcm; 1200 sets of string quartet parts at US-PO. *Amerigrove.*

3480   **Dart, Thurston,** 1921-71

Library acquired by GB-Lkc. **Albrecht.**

3481   **David, Hans Theodore,** 1902-67

1900 books and music at US-BER. Entry in *section 1.*

3482   **De Baum, ?**

Collection of American sheet music at US-AU. **Bradley.**

3483   **DeBellis, Frank V.,** d. 1968

1000 books, 5000 early editions of music, 500 manuscripts, and 20,000 early recordings now at US-SFsc. Entry in *section 1.*

3484   **Debroux, Joseph**

Violin music in B-Lc. See under **Terry, Leonard** in *section 1.*

3485   **De Courcy, Geraldine**

Paganini collection now at US-AA. **Albrecht.**

3486   **De Geer, Charles,** 1730-78

Music library, including much plectral music, bought by S-N in 1904; previously at Finspäng. **Albrecht,** under **Greer, Louis de,** 1622-95, says some items remain at Leufsta, S-LB.

3487   **Dehn, Siegfried Wilhelm,** 1799-1858

Many items now at D-Bds; 66 volumes of theoretical works acquired by Lowell Mason (**4116**) now at US-NH.

3488   **Delany, William, Music Shop**

Collection of popular songs at US-BU. **Bradley.**

3489   **Del Bello, ?**

Collection given to I-Fc. **Benton 3**:182, no. 129.

3490   **De Lerma, Dominique-René,** b. 1928

Collection related to black music at US-BAMorgan State College. *Amerigrove.*

Delle Sedie, Enrico.   *See* **Sedie, Enrico delle,** 1822-1907

3491   **Deneke, Margaret**

Inherited collection of Paul Victor Benecke Mendelssohn, then deposited it at GB-Ob. See entry under **Paul Mendelssohn** in *section 1.*

3492   Densmore, Frances, 1867-1957

>   4000 cylinders of Indian music transferred in 1948 from US-Wsi to US-Wc. *Amerigrove*.

3493   Dent, Edward Joseph, 1876-1957

>   Included the collection of Gerald M. Cooper. Went mainly to GB-Lwcm; other portions to GB-LSadler's Wells Theatre; some to GB-Cfm; papers to GB-Ckc; transcriptions to GB-Cpl. Entries in *section 1* under **Dent** and **Cooper**.

3494   Dermota, Edward Joseph, 1856-1957

>   Collection at A-Wn.

3495   Destinn, Emmy, 1878-1930

>   Private bequest to CS-Pu. Entry in *section 1*.

3496   Deutsch, Otto Erich, 1883-1967

>   Now at A-Smi. Entry in *section 1*.

3497   De Vincent, Sam [elsewhere **Di Vincent**]

>   Illustrated American sheet music at US-Wsi. Entry in *section 1*.

3498   De Windt, Clara

>   Collection of American music donated to US-CA. **Albrecht.**

3499   Dichter, Harry, 1900-77

>   Original collection of 3300 sheet music items at US-U, expanded by materials from Millie Emory. *Amerigrove*. Other portions mainly to US-PHf. Contents of Dichter's *Musical Americana, Catalogue 10*, now owned by Morris J. Sheak, Oakland, California.

3500   Diehl, Katherine Smith

>   77 hymnals donated to US-AUS. Entry in *section 1*.

3501   Dielman, Louis H [probably **Henry,** 1864-1959]

>   American imprints at US-BAhs. Entry in *section 1*.

3502   Ditterich, Richard von, 1869-1918

>   At D-Mbn. **Benton 2**:89, no. 192.

3503   Doane, George W.

>   Presented by his wife in 1918 to US-NYp. *Grove 5*.

3504   Dobrée, Thomas, 1810-95

>   Ca. 100 items in an 1895 bequest to F-Nd. Entry in *section 1*.

3505   **Döbereiner, Christian,** 1874-1961
         At D-Mbn. **Benton 2**:89, no. 192.

3506   **Doerring,** [probably **Karl Heinrich,** 1834-1916]
         Bequest to D-Bmm. *NG*-L, p. 744.

3507   **Døving, Carl,** 1867-1937
         Norwegian hymnology collection at US-St. Paul, Minnesota, Luther Theological Seminary. *RAMH.*

3508   **Dolmetsch, Arnold,** 1858-1940
         Collection now his son Carl's (b. 1911) at Haslemere. Catalog at Haslemere and at GB-Lbl. Entry in *section 1.*

3509   **Donaldson, John**
         At GB-Er. *NG*-L, p. 761.

3510   **Donini, Idino**
         At I-TE. **Benton 3**:266, no. 361.

3511   **Dopper, Cornelis,** 1870-1939
         At NL-DHgm. **Gleich**.

3512   **Dordević, Vladimir R.,** 1869-1938
         Ethnomusicological collection at YU-Bma. **Benton 5**:199, no. 3.

3513   **Dore, William,** 1844-95
         Part books donated to GB-WO. **Penney**, p. 709.

       Doria-Pamphilj Family.   *See* **Pamphilj, Benedetto, Cardinal**

3514   **Douay, Georges**
         At F-Pa. *NG*-L, p. 741.

3515   **Douglas, Charles Winfred,** 1867-1944
         Hymnology and liturgical music now at US-Wca. Entry in *section 1.*

3516   **Downes, Olin,** 1886-1955
         Personal library now at US-TA. Papers, correspondence and clippings at US-ATS. *Amerigrove.*

3517   **Downs, Joseph**
         Manuscript collection at US-WIN. *RAMH.*

3518   **Draeseke, Felix,** 1835-1913
         "Some manuscripts" at DODlb. *NG*-L, p. 744.

3519   Dragonetti, Domenico, 1763-1846

Donated 182 opera scores in manuscript to GB-Lbl; other items to Vincent Novello (**4215**) (now at GB-Cfm) and to Ouseley (**4249**) (now at GB-T). **King**, pp. 43-44.

3520   Dreer, Ferdinand Julius, 1812-1902

Collection of ALS now at US-PHhs. **Albrecht**.

3521   Drexel, Joseph Wilhelm, 1833-88

Bought scores and autographs from Henry F. Albrecht (**710**) now at US-NYp. Entries in *section 1*.

3522   Drinker, Henry Sandwith, 1880-1965; **Sophie Hutchinson Drinker,** 1888-1968

Music collection deposited in 1965 in US-Nsc. *Amerigrove*.

3523   Driscoll, James Francis, 1875-1959

83,000 titles of American music acquired, much of it about Boston and Massachusetts, by US-Cn; part gift, part purchase. Entry in *section 1*.

3524   Drysdale, [F. Learmont, b. 1866]

At GB-Gu. **Benton 2**:173, no. 42.

3525   Du Bus, François [1669-1710?]

Italian opera libretto collection now at B-Gu. Entry in *section 1*.

3526   Dudley, Bayard Turner Gross

4450 scores, programs, and books at US-Univ. of Houston, Texas.

3527   Düben, Freiherr Anders von, 1673-1738

Donated over 1500 17th-century manuscripts in S-Uu. Entry in *section 1*. *NG*-L, p. 793.

3528   Dumba, Nicolaus, 1830-1900

Rich Schubert collection now at A-Wn and A-Wgm. **Albrecht**.

3529   Dumont, Frank

1500 minstrel and music hall items acquired in 1923 by US-BU. *RAMH*.

3530   Durazzo, Giacomo, 1717-94

A detailed account of how the collection came to I-Tn. **Albrecht**.

→ *See also article under* **Foà** *in section 1*

Duvernoy.   *See* Le Blanc-Duvernoy. Collection at F-Au.

3531   Dzialynski, Adam Titus, 1795-1861

At PL-KO. **Albrecht**.

Earl of Aylesford.   *See* **Finch, Charles Wightwick**

Earls of Sefton.   *See* **Sefton, Charles William Molyneux,** 1748-95 *and* **Sefton, William Philip Molyneux,** 1772-1838

3532   **Ebart, Paul von**

> Collection now at D-Cl. *NG*-L, p. 750.

3533   **Edberg, Albert**

> Now at Svenskt musikhistoriskt arkiv. See details in *section 1.*

3534   **Edelberg, David**

> Handeliana collection now at C-Mm.

3535   **Edison, Thomas Alva,** 1847-1931

> Collection later acquired by Bly Corning (**3450**).

3536   **Edwards, Frederick George,** 1853-1909

> Library of the former editor of the *MT*, including many Mendelssohn autographs acquired by GB-Lbl in 1934. Entries in *section 1.*

3537   **Edwards, Julian**

> 800 vocal and instrumental pieces acquired in 1914 by US-NYp. Entries in *section 1.*

3538   **Egerton, Sir Thomas,** 1540-1617

> Collection he began passed to 6th Earl of Bridgewater; left by him to George Granville Leveson-Gower, later purchased in its entirety by Henry Huntington (**3861**) in 1917. Now at US-SM.

3539   **Ehrenfels, Normann von**

> At YU-OSm. **Benton 5**:227, no. 66.

3540   **Eichheim, ?**

> Music collection at US-Santa Barbara, California, Public Library. **Bradley.**

3541   **Einstein, Alfred,** 1880-1952

> Ca. 3000 items related to his work on Italian madrigals and Mozart now at US-BE; early treatises and other music at US-Nsc. Entries in *section 1.*

3542   **Eisner-Eisenhof, Angelo Franz Victor, Baron von,** b. 1857

> Donated his collected of music and music literature to I-Milan La Scala. Some of it exhibited in the *Austellung anlässlich der Centenarfeier Domenico Cimarosa* (Vienna: Verlag des comités, 1901). See *RMI* 28:357.

3543   **Elizaveta Alexeyevna, Empress of Russia,** 1779-1826

> Scores now at USSR-Lit, according to **Albrecht.**

3544   Ella, John, 1802-88

Collection first at Victoria and Albert Museum, now at GB-Lcm, according to *Grove 5*.

3545   Ellingson, Ter

Collection of field tapes at US-Blu.

3546   Ellis, [? Alexander John, 1814-90]

Bequest to GB-Ouf. **Benton 2**:185, no. 89.

3547   Ellis, Bruce T.

800 pieces of sheet music, 1850-80, at US-ALBu. *RAMH*.

3548   Elson, Louis Charles, 1848-1920

9000 items purchased in 1924 by US-BU. Entry in *section 1*.

3549   Elvey, George, Sir, d. 1893

Bequeathed on permanent loan to GB-Lu. **Benton 2; Davies;** *NG*-L, p. 765.

3550   Emerick, Albert G., b. 1817

Theoretical works at US-PHlc. *Amerigrove*.

3551   Emory, Millie

Sheet music added to the Dichter collection at US-U. *Amerigrove*.

3552   Engel, Lehman, 1910-82

Collection of 1000 scores, 3000 books and recordings at Millsaps College, Jackson, Mississippi. *Amerigrove*.

3553   Engelhart, Hinrich Christoph, 1694-1765

Early 18th-century works at S-L. *NG*-L, p. 791; **Albrecht**.

3554   Engelke, Bernhard, 1884-1950

At D-KIl. *NG*-L, p. 754.

3555   Engländer, Richard, 1889-1966

Mozart collection at A-Smi. **Benton 2**:10, no. 35.

3556   Enthoven, Gabrielle, d. 1950

Gift to the Theatre Reference Section at GB-Lva. *NG*-L, p. 765.

3557   Erlebach, Philipp Heinrich, 1667-1714

Collection now at D-RUl. Entries in *section 1*.

3558   Erwein, Franz, 1776-1840

Collection at D-WD. Entry in *section 1* under **Schönborn-Wiesentheid**.

3559   **Erwein, Hugo Damien, Graf,** 1738-1817

Collection at D-WD. Entry in *section 1* under **Schönborn-Wiesentheid**.

3560   **Estação, Achille,** 1524-81

Bequeathed to I-Rv, 1581. **Benton 3**:251, no. 314.

3561   **Este, House of** (9th-19th century)

Now at I-Moe and includes library of the **Obizzi Family**. See details in *section 1*.

3562   **Esterházy Family**

Now at H-Bn. See details in *section 1*.

3563   **Euing, William,** 1788-1874

Now at GB-Ge. See annotations in *section 1*.

3564   **Evans, Edwin, Jr.,** 1874-1945

Sold in 1947 to GB-Lwcm. **King**, p. 76.

3565   **Evelyn, John,** 1620-1706

Manuscript catalog at GB-Och. Entries in *section 1*.

3566   **Fabre, François-Xavier, Baron,** 1766-1837

1825 gift to F-Mov. **Benton 3**:97, no. 93.

3567   **Fairbank, Janet,** 1903-47

Ca. 1500 modern American songs, some in manuscript, given to US-Cn. Entry in *section 1*.

3568   **Falchi, Stanislao**

At I-TE. **Benton 3**:266, no. 361.

3569   **Falck, Martin,** 1888-1914

Bequest to D-LEb. *NG*-L, p. 746.

3570   **Falicon, [Pierre?], Count of**

Bequest to F-NI. *NG*-L, p. 741.

3571   **Falle, Philip,** 1656-1742

Now at GB-DRu. **King**, p. 15.

3572   **Fallén, Carl Fredrik,** 1764-1830

Now at S-Skma. **Albrecht**.

3573   **Faltin, Friedrich Richard,** 1835-1918

At SF-HY. *NG*-L, p. 736.

3574   Fanan, Giorgio

Private library. Entry in *section 1*.

3575   Fane, John, 11th Earl of Westmoreland, known as **Lord Burghersh,** 1784-1859

Some of his collection went to GB-Lam before a Puttick & Simpson sale of 1887. Entries in *section 1*.

3576   Fantoni, Gabriel, 1833-1890?

Part at I-Vlmc, another portion at I-Vmc. Entries in *section 1*.

3577   Farber, Norma

100 songs, 20th-century holographs, copies of holographs and copyists' manuscripts at US-Bc. *RAMH*.

3578   Farmer, Henry George, 1882-1965

Three gifts to GB-Gu: oriental music; old Scottish music in 1950; 19th-20th century Scottish composers in 1941-50. **Albrecht**.

3579   Fassati, ?

Gift to I-Raf. **Benton 3**:244, no. 303.

3580   Fassmann, Auguste

Bequest to D-MEIr. **Benton 2**:140, no. 96.

3581   Ferguson, ?

At GB-Gu. **Benton 2**:173, no. 42.

3582   Ferguson, Donald Nivison, 1882-1985

Library of books, tunebooks, etc., now at US-MSu. *Amerigrove*.

3583   Ferguson, Virginia, b. ca. 1870

Sheet music, tunebooks, hymnals, books and journals at MacMurray College, Jacksonville, Illinois. *RAMH*.

Fernández de Hijar, José Rafael Fadrique, 12th duque de, fl. 1848.   *See under* **Hijar**

3584   Ferrand, G[abriel, 1864-1935?]

Ca. 15,000 operatic 78 rpm recordings to F-Pim. **Benton 3**:112, no. 121.

3585   Ferroud, [Pierre Octave, 1900-36?]

Bequest to F-Bo. *NG*-L, p. 738.

3586   **Fétis, François Joseph,** 1784-1871

Contained portions of the libraries of Pierre Libri, Gaspari, and LaFage. Collection, sold in 1872, now at B-BR. Entries in *section 1.*

3587   **Fibiger, August**

At CS-BA. Entry in *section 1.*

3588   **Ficker, Rudolf von,** 1886-1954

At D-Mms. **Benton 2**:91, no. 199.

3589   **Fiedler, Arthur,** 1894-1979

1000 scores, 2200 opera scores, papers, and letters at US-BU. *Amerigrove.*

3590   **Field, Harold**

9000 items of sheet music, 1865-1950, at US-St. Paul, Minnesota Public Library. *RAMH.*

3591   **Fife, Austin E.** and **Alta**

Collection of Mormon American folklore materials on tapes, recordings, other sources at US-Logan, Utah State University. *RAMH.*

3592   **Figus-Bystrý, Viliam**

At CS-Mms. Entries in *section 1.*

3593   **Filmer Family, Baronetcy**

Collection of lute and keyboard manuscripts and early editions sold to US-NH, 1946. Entries in *section 1.*

3594   **Finch, Charles Wightwick, 8th Earl of Aylesford,** 1851-1924

Part of the collection at GB-Lbl; another portion at GB-Mp. Lengthy annotation in *section 1.*

3595   **Finney, Theodore M.,** 1902-78

Early editions of 17th-18th century music and American and English popular ballads and hymnbooks, part at US-Ps, part at US-Pu. **Benton 1**:344-45, no. 203-04.

3596   **Finzi, Gerard,** 1901-56

Mainly 18th-century music acquired in 1966 at GB-SA. **Penney 4** says at GB-R, and includes part of Parry's library. Entries in *section 1.*

3597   **Fischoff, Joseph,** 1804-57

At D-Bds, acquired in 1859. Entries in *section 1.*

3598   **Fisher, Sidney Thomson,** b. 1908

Manuscript and printed 18th-century flute music at C-TU. **Albrecht.**

3599   Fitch, Lorraine Noel Finley
> 1000 scores and books at US-R. *RAMH*.

3600   Fitzalan, Henry, 12th Earl of Arundel, d. 1580
> Commenced what became the Nonesuch Library. See entries under **Lumley, John, Baron,** 1534?-1609, *section 1.*

3601   Fitzgerald, Gerald, Lord
> Collection at GB-Lbl. Entry in *section 1.*

3602   Fitzwilliam, Richard, 7th Viscount, 1745-1816
> Manuscripts and printed editions, much French baroque music, at GB-Cfm, bequeathed 1816. Entries in *section 1.*

3603   Flade, Ernst, b. 1884
> At D-Bds. *NG*-L, p. 743.

3604   Flanders, Helen Hartness, 1898-1972
> 3500 field recordings of ballads, collected 1930-50, at US-MB. Entries in *section 1* and detailed summary in *RAMH*.

3605   Fleisher, Edwin Adler, 1877-1959
> Orchestral and chamber music collection at US-PHf. Entries in *section 1.*

3606   Fleisher, Oskar, 1856-1933
> Notation examples, 10th-16th centuries, bought in 1935 by US-R. *Amerigrove*.

3607   Flörsheim, G. (of Basle)
> Present owner of the autograph collection formed by Louis Koch, 1862-1930. Entries in *section 1.*

3608   Flower, Sir (Walter) Newman, 1879-1964
> Now at GB-Mp. Entries in *section 1.*

3609   Foà, Mauro
> Partly the collection of the Durazzo family, according to **Albrecht**. Given to I-Tn, 1927. Entries in *section 1.*

3610   Foley, B. W. [Bernice Williams, b. 1902?]
> Donated oratorio collection to US-CIu. *Grove 5.*

3611   Fontane, [Theodor, 1819-98?]
> Bequeathed to D-Bmm. *NG*-L, p. 744.

3612   Forbes-Leith, William, 1833-1921
> At GB-A. **Penney**.

3613   Forde, William

> The "Forde-Pigott Collection," over 4000 volumes, received in 1910 by EIR-Da. *NG*-L.

3614   Forkel, Johann Nikolaus, 1749-1818

> Collection eventually acquired by D-B and D-Bds. See annotations in *section 1*.

3615   Forrest, William

> Tudor masses now at GB-Ob. **Davies**.

3616   Fouché d'Otrante, Duke Paul Athanase, 1801-86

> Collection went to S-Skma in 1858. **Albrecht**.

3617   Fox-Strangeways, Arthur Henry, 1859-1948

> Sold to GB-LBbc in 1947 but some to GB-Lwcm. **Albrecht**.

3618   Fraenkel, Gottfried Samuel, b. 1901

> Over 800 first and early editions, including decorative music title pages at US-U. **Benton 1**:235, no. 424.

Francesco II d'Este, Duke of Modena.   *See under* **Este, House of**, *section 1*

3619   Francis, Deffret

> Collection of 18th-19th centuries, including scores, at University College of Swansea Library. **Penney**.

3620   Francisci, Miloslav

> At CS-Mms. Entry in *section 1*.

3621   Francisco de Paula Antonio de Bourbon

> At E-Mn. *NG*-L, p. 789.

3622   Frank, Ernst, 1847-89

> In D-Mbn. See *section 1*, annotation.

3623   Franz, Robert, 1815-92

> At D-HAmi. *NG*-L, p. 746.

3624   Franz II, 1768-1835; **Franz Joseph,** 1848-1916, **Emperors of Austria**

> Collection sold to A-Wn in 1936, but see history in annotation in *section 1*. **Albrecht**.

3625   Freiser, Julienne

> At D-Mmb. **Benton 2**:91, no. 201.

3626   **Friedländer, Max,** 1852-1934

        Sale 1929. Much of the collection now at J-Tn. See annotations in *section 1.*

3627   **Friedrich, Georg, Markgraf von Ansbach,** 1557-1603

        Librettos and opera scores went from Ansbacher Hofkapell to D-AN and D-ERu. **Benton 2**:44, no. 9; *NG-L*, p. 751.

3628   **Friedrich II, Herzog von Sachsen-Gotha,** 1732-72

        Now at D-GOl. **Albrecht.**

3629   **Friedrich Emil August, Prince of Schleswig-Holstein Noer,** 1800-65

        At D-KIL. *NG-L*, p. 754.

3630   **Frimmel, August**

        At D-BNms. **Benton 2**:52, no. 44.

3631   **Frost, Maurice,** d. 1961

        Collection to Royal School of Church Music, Addiscombe, Surrey, according to **King**, p. 85. **Penney 4** says hymnology collection went to GB-Lcm.

3632   **Fryklund, Lars Axel Daniel,** 1879-1965

        10,000 music manuscripts and editions, and some 800 instruments. Part at S-Skma, others at S-Sm. *NG-L*. Entries in *section 1.*

3633   **Fuchs, Aloys,** 1799-1853

        A huge and immensely valuable collection widely dispersed over many years into various institutions and through various sales. See lengthy annotations and many entries in *section 1.*

3634   **Fuchs, Carl** [probably **Carl Dorius Johann,** 1838-1922]

        Bequest at D-SWl. *NG-L*, p. 747.

3635   **Fuchs, Carl** [probably 1836-1920]

        To US-Cn in 1891. *Grove 5* 50:209.

3636   **Fuchs, Julius**

        At US-Cn. **Benton 1**:104-05, no. 94.

3637   **Fürstenberg, Joachim Egon, Fürst zu,** b. 1923

        3000 manuscripts of 18th-19th century symphonies and operas at D-DO. **Albrecht**; **Benton 2**:58, no. 63.

3638   **Fürstenberg, Prince [?]**

        Collection at CS-KRik. **Benton 5**:43.

3639 Fugger Family

The library begun by Johann Jakob (1516-75) and Raimund (1528-69) mostly survives at D-Mbs, A-Wn, and D-Af. Many entries in *section 1.*

3640 Fuld, James J., b. 1916

800 pieces of sheet music, ca. 1850-1900, donated to US-WM.

3641 Fulford, F H

Collection of chamber music donated to GB-LEbc. **Penney,** p 350.

3642 Fuller-Maitland, John Alexander, 1856-1936

Collection of some 7000 items including scores and manuscripts bequeathed by the critic of *The Times* in 1936 to GB-LA (according to **Penney,** p. 344; **King**; and *NG*-L, p. 176. **Albrecht** says loaned to GB-LVu while **Benton 2**:176 says at GB-LVp!)

3643 Fumi, [?Vincelslao, 1823-80]

Given to I-Fc.

3644 Gabrilowitsch, Ossip, 1878-1936

Pianoforte and orchestral scores given to US-NYp, ca. 1940. *Grove 5.*

3645 Gänge, ?

At D-KImi. **Benton 2**:78, no. 149.

3646 Galeazzi, Francesco, 1758-1819

Approximately 150 manuscripts and 25 early editions purchased in 1972 from descendents are now at US-NH. *Amerigrove.*

3647 Gallo, Vincenzo and **Antonio**

Collection at I-BAR. Entry in *section 1.*

3648 Galston, Gottfried, 1879-1950; **Galston-Busoni Archive**

Now at US-KN. Entry in *section 1.*

3649 Gambalunga, Alessandro

Given to I-RIM in 1619. *NL*-L, p. 777.

3650 Gansevoort, Anna Maria

Collection at US-Wc.

3651 Gardiner, George B.

Folksong collections now at GB-Gm and GB-Lcs. Entry in *section 1.*

3652 Gardiner, H. Balfour

Folk music at GB-Lcs. **Davies.**

3653   **Gardiner, William,** 1770-1853

> Music library, including almost complete 19th-century edition of Handel, at Goldsmith Library, Leicester. **Penney**, p. 355.

3654   **Gardner, Isabella Stewart,** 1840-1924

> "Letters, manuscript scores and memorabilia" at US-Bgm.

3655   **Garrett, Robert,** b. 1875

> Early sacred music at US-PRu. *Amerigrove.*

3656   **Gas, José,** d. 1713

> Collection at E-G. *NG-*L, p. 788.

3657   **Gaspari, Gaetano,** 1807-61

> Part of his collection now at I-Bc. Entries in *section 1.*

3658   **Gatti, Luigi**

> Library included in that of Giuseppe Greggiata now at I-OS. **Benton 3**:221, no. 232.

3659   **Gatty, R[eginald?] A.**

> Folksongs at GB-Lcs. **Davies**; *NG-*L, p. 765.

    Geer, Charles, 1730-78.   *See* **De Geer, Charles**

3660   **Gehring, Franz Edward,** 1838-84

> Some items now at D-Mbs, still others at D-BN, according to *NG-*L, p. 750. Entries in *section 1.*

3661   **Gehrkens, Karl Wilson,** 1882-1975

> Private library at US-OB. *Amerigrove.*

3662   **Geigy-Hagenbach, Karl,** d. 1949

> Manuscript collection now at CH-Bu. Entries in *section 1.*

3663   **Genet, Edmond Charles,** 1763-1834

> Sheet music at US-Wc. **Krummel 2.**

3664   **George, Collins**

> 4500 recordings at Oakland University, Rochester, Michigan. **Bradley.**

3665   **George, Robert Olney**

> Over 2000 jazz recordings donated to US-BLu. Entry in *section 1.*

3666   Gerber, Ernst Ludwig, 1746-1819

Library was bought by A-Wgm, though some of it was also acquired by André. See annotations in *section 1*.

3667   Germinet-Vinot, Gabriel

Collection went to F-Pa. *NG*-L, p. 741.

3668   Gershwin, George, 1898-1937

A Memorial Collection consisting of his personal library presented to Fisk University of Carl Van Vechten in 1944. Catalog in *section 1*. Items also at US-NYmc. **Bradley**.

3669   Gherardeschi Family (Filippo Maria, 1738-1808; **Domenica,** 1733-1800; **Giuseppe,** 1759-1815)

Collection given to I-PS. *NG*-L, p. 777.

3670   Giani, Romualdo

Gift to I-PIN. **Benton 2**:236, no. 278.

3671   Giedde, Wilhelm Hans Rudolf Rosenkrantz, 1756-1816

Acquired by DK-Kk in 1903. Entries in *section 1*.

3672   Gigliucci, [Valeria, Contessa - Clara Novello's daughter?]

Gift to I-Raf. **Benton 3**:244.

3673   Gilchrist, Anne Geddes

Bequest to GB-Les. Entry in *section 1*.

Gimo House and Collection.   *See* **Lefebure, Jean,** 1736-1805

3674   Giordano, Renzo

The combined **Foà** -**Giordano** collection is at I-Tn. Entries under both names in *section 1*.

3675   Giustiniani, Alvise, Conte, 1909-62

Collection of 200 late 18th-century editions donated in 1949 to I-Vc. Entry in *section 1*.

3676   Glaser, Alexander

At PL-GD. **Benton 5**:127, no. 5.

3677   Gleason, Frederick Grant, 1848-1903

Collection at US-Cn. Entry in *section 1*.

3678   Glen, John, 1833-1904

Collection purchased by Lady Ruggles-Brise, who gave it to GB-En in 1927. Entry in *section 1*.

3679   **Goethe, Johann Wolfgang von,** 1749-1832

Collection of 18th to 19th-century music, prints, and manuscripts, at D-WRgs. **Benton 3**:148, no. 134.

3680   **Goetz, Mrs. Angelina (Levy)**

Mainly full scores, according to Davies, presented to GB-Lcm in 1904. Entry in *section 1*.

3681   **Goldmark, Rubin,** 1872-1936

Autographs, letters and memorabilia at US-NYp. Entry in *section 1*.

3682   **Goldovsky, Boris,** b. 1908

Collection at US-Eu. *Amerigrove*.

3683   **Goldstein, Kenneth S.,** b. 1927

3000 books and 4500 recordings related to folklore at US-HAT. *RAMH*.

3684   —————

Over 3000 American song broadsides now at Center for Popular Music at Middle Tennessee State University, Murfreesboro, Tennessee.

3685   **Golinelli, Stefano,** 1818-91

At I-Bsf. **Benton 3**:155, no. 45.

3686   **Gonzaga Family**

Family and court archives now at I-MAa. **Benton 3**:199, no. 175.

3687   **Goodkind, Herbert K.**

Collection of materials related to the violin at US-OB. Entries in *section 1*.

3688   **Goodson, Richard,** 1655-1718

Bequest of books to GB-Ouf, manuscript and printed music to GB-Och. Entries in *section 1*.

3689   **Goodwin, George**

Sheet music at US-NYp. **Krummel 2**.

3690   **Gordon, J   B**

About 400 vocal scores given to GB-Sadler's Wells Theatre. **Davies**; *Grove 5*.

3691   **Gordon, Jacques,** 1845-1948

2000 string and chamber music items at US-R. Entry in *section 1*.

3692   **Gordon, Robert W.**

225,000 pages of transcripts from various folklorists' works now at US-Wc. *RAMH*.

3693   **Gorke, Manfred,** 1897-1956
>   Collection at D-LEb. **Benton 2**:136, no. 82. Entry in *section 1*.

3694   **Gorokhoff,** [probably **Ivan T.]**
>   Collection of choral music at US-Bp. *Amerigrove*.

3695   **Gostling, William,** ca. 1652-1733
>   According to **Davies**, many 17th-century choirbooks from the 1777 sale of
>   his library ended up at GB-Y. Sale catalog in *section 1*.

3696   **Gotthold, Friedrich August,** 1778-1858
>   Before World War II it was in USSR-KA. Catalogs in *section 1*.

3697   **Gottschalk, Louis Moreau,** 1829-69
>   Manuscripts at US-NYp (a collection of his own?). *Grove 5*.

3698   **Goujet, [Claude-Pierre,** 1697-1767?]
>   16th-century music at F-V. **Benton 3**:134, no. 179.

3699   **Graham, G** [probably **George Farquhar,** 1789-1867]
>   Some materials included in Stillie (**4561**) bequest to GB-Gu. *NG*-L, p. 762.

3700   **Grainger, Percy Aldridge,** 1892-1961
>   Now at AUS-NLwm. Small portion at GB-Lcs; band library at US-NH. Entries
>   in *section 1*.

3701   **Granville Family (Bernard,** 1709-75; **John (Dewes); Capt. Bernard)**
>   37 Handel manuscripts acquired at the March 1912 Granville sale. Catalog
>   in *section 1*.

3702   **Grasnick, Friedrich August**
>   Bought most of Aloys Fuchs collection. The Fuchs-Grasnick collection
>   now in D-Bds. Entries in *section 1* under both **Fuchs**; **Grasnick**.

3703   **Gratz, Simon,** 1840-1925
>   Ca. 2000 ALS of musicians now in US-PHhs. **Albrecht**.

3704   **Gray, Thomas,** 1716-71
>   Italian opera manuscripts to Mr. Lewis of Farmington, Connecticut. See
>   subsequent migrations in *section 1* annotation under **Gray**.

3705   **Great Britain - Kings and Rulers**
>   "Kings Music Library" now at GB-Lbl. Entries in *section 1*.

3706   **Greatorex, Thomas,** 1758-1831

"Famous" 67 volumes of J. C. Smith copies of Handel's works bought by Barrett-Lennard (**1667**) were presented to GB-Cfm. Entries in *section 1*.

Green, Adolph.   *See* **Comden, Betty,** and **Adolf Green** collection at US-NYmc

3707   **Green Collection of American Sheet Music**

At US-G. *RAMH*.

3708   **Greenway, George Lauder,** 1904-81

9000 rare operatic and vocal recordings at US-NYp. *Amerigrove*.

3709   **Greggiati, Giuseppe, Canon,** 1793-1866

Benton says the music formerly at the Capitolo di S. Barbara di Mantova was sold to Greggiati in 1850 who subsequently bequeathed it to the Milan Conservatorio. Most other sources, including a 1983 catalog by Claudio Sartori, locate the collection at I-OS. Entries in *section 1*.

3710   **Greissle, Felix,** 1894-1982

Collection at US-LAusc. Entry in *section 1*.

3711   **Grenier-Haynl**

Collection of 19th-century scores at F-CF, according to **Benton 3**:80, 51.

3712   **Gresham, ?**

17th to 19th-century manuscripts and printed music at GB-Lgc. **Penney**, p. 370; **Davies**. There is an entry under **Gresham** (this one?) in *section 1*.

3713   **Grétry, André Ernest Modeste,** 1741-1813

At B-Lc. **Benton 2**:24, no. 22.

3714   **Grieg, Edvard Hagerup,** 1843-1907

At N-Bo. Entries in *section 1*.

3715   **Grieg, Gavin,** 1856-1914

Manuscript collection of folk music at GB-A. Entry in *section 1*.

3716   **Griffin, Ralph,** 1854-1942

Main donations to GB-Cfm from 1925 onwards; some to GB-Ob and GB-Lbl. **King**, p. 83.

3717   **Grillparzer, Franz,** 1791-1872

Collection at A-Wst. **Benton 2**:16, no. 59. Entry in *section 1*.

3718   **Groenland, Peter,** 1761-1825

Collection acquired in 1834 by DK-Kk.

3719   **Grove, Sir George,** 1820-1900
          Now at GB-Lcm. **Benton 2**:180, no. 63.

3720   **Gruenberg, Louis,** 1844-1964
          Collection at US-Nyp.

3721   **Grumman, Ellsworth**
          First and early editions of Beethoven pianoforte sonatas at US-NH.
          Amerigrove.

3722   **Grundmann, Herbert,** b. 1902
          In D-BNba. Entry in *section 1.*

3723   **Guerra, [?Antonio,** 1810-46]
          Collection at I-Ls. **Benton 3**:197, no. 170.

3724   **Guerra, María Luisa,** b. 1870
          At E-Bit. **Benton 3**:10, no. 13.

3725   **Guilhomet, ?**
          Modern music, especially Russian, at F-MLN. **Benton 3**:97, no. 92.

3726   **Guilmant, Alexandre,** 1837-1911
          Organ music at F-Pim. *NG*-L, p. 742.

3727   **Guion, David W.**
          Collection of manuscripts at US-Wc; other books, recordings, reproductions
          of Mss., and correspondence at US-WC. **Bradley**; *RAMH.*

3728   **Gulbenkian Foundation (Calouste Sarkis Gulbenkian)**
          EIRE-C received a bequest of scores and recordings from the Foundation's
          collection. *NG*-L, p. 769.

3729   **Gurlitt, Willibald,** 1889-1963
          Bequest to D-FRms. **Benton 2**:64, no. 88.

3730   **Gustavus II Adolphus, King of Sweden,** 1594-1632
          At S-Uu. *NG*-L, p. 793.

3731   **Gutman, Monroe C.**
          Music textbooks at US-CA. *Amerigrove.*

3732   Haas, Alma, d. 1932
> Bequest to GB-Lu. *NG*-L, p. 765.

3733   Haberl, Franz Xaver, 1840-1910
> Some holdings given to Proske-Bibliothek (D-Rp, *section 1*). **Albrecht**.

3734   Hacker, Fr_____ X.
> Bequest to D-DIN. **Benton 2**:57, no. 62.

3735   Hackley, Emma Azalia, 1867-1922
> Black music, dance, and drama collection at US-Dp. Entry in *section 1*.

3736   Haenschen, Gustave, b. 1889
> 50,000 radio orchestral. Collection at US-I.

3737   Hagedorn, R.
> Bequest to D-LEm. **Benton 2**:139, no. 89.

3738   Hagen, Sophie Albert Emil, 1842-1929
> Acquired by DK-Kk. **Albrecht**.

3739   Hale, Philip, 1854-1934
> Early music treatises at US-Nf, according to *Amerigrove*. **Albrecht** says collection now at US-Nsc. Entry in *section 1*.

3740   Hall, James S.
> Handel collection (published 18th-century editions and some manuscripts) at US-PRu. Entry in *section 1*.

3741   Hall, Townley
> At EIR-Dtc. *NG*-L, p. 770.

3742   Hallardt, Johan Fredrik, 1726-94
> Purchased in 1795 by S-Skma. *NG*-L, p. 792.

3743   Halle, Philip, 1656-1742
> Collection at GB-Drc. Entry in *section 1*.

3744   Halliwell-Phillipps, James Orchard, 1820-89
> 3000 items, not all music but many ballads, given to GB-Mch. Entries in *section 1*.

3745   Hamilton, Emma, Lady, ca. 1765-1815
> The collection was held by W. Gardner Waterman but presented to US-NH by Mrs. Edward Harkness in 1931. **Albrecht**.

3746   Hammond, Henry Edward Denison, 1866-1918
> Folk materials at GB-Lcs. *NG*-L, p. 765.

3747   Hammond, Thomas, d. 1662
> Acquired by Rev. Osborne Wight (**4713**), then bequeathed to GB-Ob, with some items going to GB-Lbl and GB-Och. **Albrecht**. The Bodleian collection discussed in *section 1*.

3748   Handschin, Jacques, 1886-1955
> Bequest to D-ERms. **Benton 2**:61, no. 77.

3749   Hanford, Charles B., 1859-1926
> Part books, orchestral music, and other scores for plays and operas at US-WS. *RAMH*.

3750   Hansson, Per Wilhelm
> Collection at S-Smf. Entry in *section 1*.

3751   Haraszti, Emil, 1885-1959
> Liszt biographical material went to F-Pim in 1965. Entry in *section 1*. **Benton 3**:112, no. 121.

3752   Harding, Albert A., 1880-1958
> Band-related music and other materials at US-U.

3753   Harding, Walter N. H., 1883-1973
> "One of the finest collections [of American music] in the USA." **Albrecht**. Given to GB-Ob. Entries in *section 1*.

3754   Harkness, Mrs. Edward
> Presented to the collection of Lady Emma Hamilton to US-NH in 1931.

3755   Harley, Edward, 2nd Earl of Oxford, 1689-1741
> Manuscripts sold by Lady Harley to GB-Lbl in 1753. Entry in *section 1*.

3756   Harline, Leigh
> Collection at US-Clu. **Bradley**.

3757   Harmsworth, Robert Leicester, Sir, 1878-1937
> Collection of early music books and psalters from a Sotheby sale in 1946 now at US-WS. *Amerigrove*. Sale catalog in *section 1*.

3758   Harris, Caleb Fiske, 1818-81
> Collection of sheet music at US-PROu commenced by Albert G. Greene. Includes songsters and sheet music. Entry in *section 1*.

3759 Harris, George W.
Hymnal collection at US-I. Entry in *section 1*.

3760 Harris, William James, 6th Earl of Malmesbury
Private collection in Basingstoke.

3761 Hart, George [1839-91?]
Printed music and musical literature collection in GB-Lbl along with a catalog dated 1903. Entry in *section 1*.

3762 Hartenstein, [? Carl, b. 1863]
Collection at D-WRiv. **Benton 2**:148-49, no. 135.

3763 Hartmann, A[rthur, 1881-1956?]
Orchestral music and manuscripts at US-R. *Grove 5*.

3764 Hartmann, P
Bequest to A-SH. **Benton 2**:12, no. 44.

3765 Harty, Hamilton, Sir, 1879-1941
Personal library and autograph manuscript scores at Queen's University, Belfast. **Penney**, p.518; **Davies**.

3766 Hartzler, J   D
2750 volumes of early American church and instructional music deposited at US-GO.

3767 Harvard, Lawrence
At GB-Ckc. **Davies**.

3768 Harwell, Richard Barksdale
Sheet music collection at US-U, including Confederate imprints. Entry in *section 1*.

3769 Harwood, Basil, 1859-1949
Music, including early editions, bequeathed to GB-BRp. **Penney**, p. 11; *NG*-L, p. 759.

3770 Hatzi, James
Collection of violin music (2000 violin works, 600 orchestral scores) at US-Mc. *RAMH*.

3771 Hauber, Johann Michael, 1778-1843
Large portion went to D-Mds in 1821, a smaller group to D-Rp in 1824. Entries in *section 1*.

3772 **Hauptmann, Gerhardt,** [?1862-1946]

Collection bequeathed to D-Bmm. *NG-L*, p. 744.

3773 **Hauser, Franz,** 1794-1870

Collection now in D-Bds and D-DS. Entry in *section 1*.

3774 **Haverlin, Carl**

Nearly complete sets of first editions of Beethoven, Chopin, Wagner, et al., plus letters and manuscripts at US-NYbm. Entry in *section 1* under **BMI**.

3775 **Hawkins, James** (organist at Ely Cathedral, 1682-1739)

Manuscripts from Ely Cathedral deposited in 1970 at GB-Cu (his collection, or his works?). Entry in *section 1*.

3776 **Hawkins, Sir John,** 1719-89

Much of his collection that was not destroyed by fire or left to his sons John Sidney (**1207**) was bequeathed to GB-Lbl. Entries in *section 1*.

3777 **Hawkins, Micah,** 1777-1825

Manuscripts at US-NH, -Wc, -NYhs. *Amerigrove*.

3778 **Hazen, Robert M.,** b. 1948

Brass band photographs and ephemera at National Museum of American History, Washington, D. C.

3779 **Heartman, ?**

African-American collection acquired in 1950 by Texas Southern University, Houston.

3780 **Heath, John Benjamin**

Collection of letters of early 19th-century singers and 18th to 19th-century opera composers at US-CA. Entry in *section 1*.

3781 **Heather William,** ca. 1563-1627

Bequeathed to GB-Ouf. Entry in *section 1*.

3782 **Heberden, ?**

Bequest to GB-Ouf. *Grove 5*, p. 192. **Penney**, p. 466, spells Herberden!

3783 **Hedley, Arthur,** 1905-69

Chopin collection at Museo de Chopin, La Cartuja, Valldemosa, Mallorca, Spain. **Albrecht**.

3784 **Heine, Heinrich,** 1797-1856

Most at D-DÜl. Entry in *section 1*.

3785   **Heineman, Dannie N.,** 1872-1962

Music of the Heinemann Foundation at US-Wc; books and manuscripts given in 1962 to US-NYpm. *Amerigrove.* Entries in *section 1.*

3786   **Heinrichs, ?**

Bequest to D-Kl. **Benton 2**:77, no. 143.

3787   **Heiss, H[ermann?,** b. 1897]

At D-DS. *NG*-L, p. 751.

3788   **Helfert, Vladimír,** 1886-1945

At CS-Bm. **Benton 5**:35, no. 21.

3789   **Hellier, Samuel,** 1737-84

At GB-Bu. Entries in *section 1.*

3790   **Hellmuth, Max**

At D-Cl. **Benton 2**:55, no. 55.

3791   **Helm, Everett Burton,** 1913-99

Early editions of 18th and 19th-century scores, especially French, at US-ALBu (scores and art songs; -CAh (printed scores); -Chu (3000 items from library); -LOu (part of working library); -U (800 scores, mainly Brazilian). See Index to **Benton 2**.

3792   **Helmore, Thomas,** 1811-90

Collection of liturgical and music books, constituting part of the Plainsong and Medieval Music Society's library, dispersed in sales. See *section 1* entries under both.

3793   **Helwig, Carl**

Florida-interest recordings and jazz at US-TA. *RAMH.*

3794   **Henderson, John Murdoch**

966 volumes of Scottish music to GB-En; other Scottish works to Aberdeen City Library. **Penney** 1:1, 2:422; *NG*-L, p. 761.

3795   **Henkel, Heinrich,** 1822-99

His daughter bequeathed much of the collection to D-FUl; other parts went to Frankfurt and to US-Wc. See Wolf article in *section 1* for excellent description of the breakup of the collection.

3796   **Henry, Sam**

Collection of Irish songs to Belfast Public Libraires. **Penney**, p. 26.

3797   **Henry IV, King of France,** 1553-1610

Library originally at College de la Trinité, now at F-LYm. **Benton 3**:93.

3798   **Henschel, Ernst**

Collection of programs at GB-Lbl. Entry in *section 1.*

3799   **Her, ?**

18th-19th century German librettos at D-Mbs. *NG*-L, p. 755.

3800   **Herbst, Johannes,** 1735-1812

Collection now at US-WS. Entries in *section 1.*

Heredia.   *See* **Aguilera de Heredia, Sebastian,** 1565-1627

3801   **Heron-Allen, Edward,** 1861-1943

Collection acquired by GB-Lcm; some given to GB-Ouf. Many entries in *section 1.*

3802   **Hertzberg, Harry**

Collection at San Antonio Public Library. *Amerigrove.* Entry in *section 1.*

3803   **Hertzmann, Erich,** 1882-1963

Beethoven manuscripts at US-BE, according to catalog issued by the University, but *Amerigrove* says at US-NYcu! See entry in *section 1.*

3804   **Herwart Family (Hans Heinrich; Johann Heinrich,** 1520-83)

Collection now at D-Mbs. Entries in *section 1.*

3805   **Hess, ?**

Collection of viola and chamber music at Toledo-Lucas County Public Library. **Bradley.**

3806   **Heth, Charlotte Anne Wilson,** b. 1937

Field recordings of Cherokee music at US-Lau. *Amerigrove.*

3807   **Heubner, Dr.**

At D-WGp. *NG*-L, p. 748.

3808   **Hevingham-Root, Laurie**

Recordings and scores at AUS-CAnl. Entry in *section 1.*

3809   **Hewitt, Helen,** 1900-77

Renaissance items at US-DN. *Amerigrove.*

3810   **Heyse, Paul,** 1830-1914

At D-Mbn. **Münster.**

Heyther, William, ca. 1563-1627.   *See* **Heather, William**

3811   Hibberd, Isaac Lloyd

Library at US-DN includes many 18th-century French and English stage works. *Amerigrove*.

3812   Higgin, A., Dean

1624 bequest to GB-RI. **Benton 2**:186, no. 88.

3813   Hijar, Duque de (in Epila) or? **Fernández de Hijar, José Rafael Fadrique, 12th duque de,** fl. 1848

Collection at E-Bim. **Benton 3**:11.

3814   Hijman, Julius, [perhaps 1901-69]

Collection at NL-DHK. *NG*-L, p. 781.

3815   Hill, Arthur Frederick, 1860-1940

Some portraits of musicians at GB-Lcm. Some items in Sotheby sale in 1947 acquired for GB-Lbl. Entry in *section 1*.

3816   Hill, Grant L.

Collection of 120,000 20th-century items at US-TC. *Amerigrove*.

3817   Hill, William E., 1886-1962

Theater collection, "several hundred thousand items," including music materials at US-DAp. *RAMH*.

3818   Hiller, Lejaren A., 1924-94

Over 2500 books, scores, manuscripts, recordings, and correspondence now at US-BUu.

3819   Hilton, Arthur

Collection at NZ-Wt.

3820   Hirsch, Paul, 1881-1951

At GB-Lbl. Many entries in *section 1*.

3821   Hirschberg, ?

Librettos at D-Bu. **Benton 2**:120, no. 15.

3822   Hitzig, [perhaps **Wilhelm,** b. 1876]

Bequeathed to D-Bmm. *NG*-L, p. 744. Entry in *section 1* under **Breitkopf**.

3823   Hoboken, Anthony von, 1887-1983

Donated to A-Wn. Detailed annotations with entries in *section 1*.

3824   Hodges, Edward, 1796-1867

At US-Wc. Entries in *section 1*.

3825   **Hoffman, Frederick J.**
> Donated to US-CIu. *Grove 5.*

3826   **Hoguet, [Michael Françoise,** 1793-1871]
> Collection bequeathed to D-Bmm. **Benton 2**:121, no. 19.

3827   **Hohenlohe-Jagstberg, Fürst**
> Private library in D-HL. **Benton 2**:68, no. 106.

3828   **Hohenlohe-Langenburg, Fürst**
> Small collection at D-LB. **Albrecht**.

3829   **Hohenzollern, House of**
> Court library at D-SI. Collection now at D-Bds. Entries in *section 1.*

3830   **Hohn, Maia Bang**
> Paganiniana at US-Wc. Entry in *section 1.*

3831   **Hol, Richard**
> At NL-DHgm. **Gleich**. Entry in *section 1.*

3832   **Holcman, Jan,** b. 1922
> Collection of historical pianoforte recordings at US-NYp. *Amerigrove.*

3833   **Hollenfeltz, ?**
> Collection now at B-Bc. Entry in *section 1.*

3834   **Hollier, Laetitia,** d. 1871
> Gift to GB-Lgc. Entry in *section 1.*

3835   **Hollmann, Joseph**
> Collection now at J-Tn. Entry in *section 1* under **Tokugawa**.

3836   **Holmes, Augusta Mary Anne,** 1847-1903
> 19th-century music at F-V. Entry in *section 1.*

3837   **Holt, Roland**
> Collection of American theater materials, 1881-1931, including clippings, photographs, librettos, and books at US-CHua. *RAMH.*

3838   **Homolka, E   E**
> At CS-Pnm. *NG*-L, p. 735.

3839   **Honywood, Michael**
> Partbooks at Wren Library, Lincoln Cathedral. Entries in *section 1.*

3840 Hook, James, 1746-1827

Some of his manuscripts acquired in Puttick & Simpson sale of 1874 are now at GB-Cu.

→ *See also under* **Arthur Henry Mann**, part of whose library was purchased at this same sale. Entries in *section 1*.

3841 Hopkinson, Cecil, 1898-1977

Donated Berlioz materials to GB-En in 1952, Verdi materials in 1969. Entries in *section 1*.

3842 Hopkinson, Francis, 1737-91

Almost all at US-PHu. **Benton 1**:199, no. 335.

3843 Horenstein, [Jascha? 1898-1973]

Bequeathed books on music to Royal Northern College of Music, Manchester. **Penney**, p. 546.

3844 Horn, Adam

Collection at S-Skma, according to Johnson article under **Alströmer** in *section 1*. Auction on 19 February 1778; catalog at S-Sk.

3845 Hornik, Andreas, 1864-1917

Now at CS-Pnm. **Albrecht**.

3846 Horowitz, Vladimir, 1903-89, and **Wanda,** 1908-98

Gifts to US-NH began in 1986. **Samuel**.

3847 Horsley, William, 1774-1858

Collection at GB-Ob. **Penney 4**. Entry in *section 1*.

3848 Howes, Frank Stewart, 1891-1974

Collection at GB-Ouf.

3849 Hrdina, František

Choir archive once owned by CS-BSk now at CS-SSR. *NG*-L; **Benton 5**, p. 44.

3850 Huber, William, Jr.

13,000 items of organ music presented to US-CU in 1919, the rest to US-Wc. *Grove 5*.

3851 Huberman, Bronislaw, 1882-1947

Donated to Central Library, Tel Aviv. **Albrecht**.

3852 Hueber, Peter, 1766-1843

Nachlass in D-Mbs. Entry in *section 1*.

3853 **Huger, Melvina**

Anthems and sacred songs given to US-Dp. *Grove 5*.

3854 **Hughes-Hughes, Augustus,** 1857-1942

Some items at GB-Lcm. *NG*-L, p. 765. Entry in *section 1*.

3855 **Hulka, K.**

At CS-Pnm. *NG*-L, p. 735.

3856 **Hulthem, Charles van,** 1764-1832

Collection bought by Belgian government in 1837, nucleus of B-Br. Entry in *section 1*.

3857 **Humperdinck, Engelbert,** 1854-1921

Nachlass in Frankfurt. See entry in *section 1*.

3858 **Huneker, James Gibbons,** 1857-1921

Acquired in the 1920s by US-NYp. *Grove 5*.

3859 **Hunt, Arthur Billings,** 1890-1967

A gift from Alfred C. Berol permitted purchase of Hunt's collection of 30,000 items of American sheet music by US-NYp. His personal library is also there. Other American sheet music went to US-NYcu. Some hymnology books went to Macalester College, St. Paul, Minnesota. Entry in *section 1*.

3860 **Hunterian, ?**

At GB-Gu. **Benton 2**:173, no. 42.

3861 **Huntington, Henry Edwards,** 1850-1927

Approximately 5500 items of music, principally from the collections of Thomas Egerton (1917, **3538**), the **Britwell Court Library** (sales, 1916-17, see *section 1*), and **Huth** (sales, 1911-20, *section 1*), now at US-SM.

3862 **Huth, Alfred Henry,** 1815-78

Some manuscripts and printed books bequeathed to GB-Lbl, songsheets to US-SM. Entries in *section 1*.

3863 **Idelsohn, Abraham Zebi,** 1882-1938

Collection at IL-J. Entry in *section 1*.

3864 **Ingersoll, Janet T.**

Gospel music collection at US-LOs. *Amerigrove*.

3865 **Inglis, Alexander Wood,** d. 1929

Bequest of ca. 740 items of English and Scottish music of the 18th and early 19th centuries to GB-En in 1929. **King**, p. 87; **Penney**, p. 422.

3866   Inguimbert, Malachie de, Bishop of Carpentras, 1683-1757

Founded the collection at F-C; opened in 1747. *NG*-L, p. 739.

3867   Ireland, John, 1879-48

67 volumes of manuscript copies of Handel, which were acquired by Henry Barret-Lennard (**1667**, *section 1*) and from him by GB-Cfm in 1902.

3868   Isenberg, ? , Fürst

Private library in Birstein, Germany. At D-BIR. **Albrecht**.

3869   Israel, Fanny and **Julius**

European and American illustrated editions at US-R. *Amerigrove*.

3870   Ivaldi, Filippo, 1874-1943

Bequest to I-Bl in 1969. **Benton 3**:153, no. 42.

3871   Jachimecki, Zdzislaw

At PL-Kpwm. **Benton 5**:137, no. 17.

3872   Jackson, George Pullen, 1874-1953

At US-LAuc. Entry in *section 1*.

3873   Jackson, John

In 1703, on the death of Samuel Pepys, he acquired a "life interest" in Pepys's library, which later went to GB-Cmc in 1724. **King**, p. 145.

3874   Jacobi, Erwin Ruben, 1909-78

At CH-Zz. Entry in *section 1*.

3875   Jacobi, Samuel

At D-Dlb. Entry in *section 1*.

3876   Jacobsthal, Gustav, 1845-1912

At F-Sim. Entry in *section 1*.

3877   Jaëll, Marie, 1846-1925

At F-Sn. Entry in *section 1*.

3878   Jahant, Charles

Signed photographs of opera starts at US-Wc. Entry in *section 1*.

3879   Jahn, Otto, 1813-69

At D-Bds; some at D-BNu. Entry in *section 1*.

3880   **James, Arthur, 1st Earl of Balfour,** d. 1930

Printed Handel scores and librettos in 1876 from Julian Marshall, then in 1930 to GB-En. *Grove 5.* Entries in *section 1.*

3881   **James, Harry** and **Grace,** 1916-83

Ca 10,000 recordings and catalogs to US-RIVu. *Amerigrove.*

3882   **Jan, Karl von,** 1836-99

Library was absorbed by the Rothschild Bibliothek in Frankfurt (D-F). *ZiMG* 1 (1899/1900): 307.

3883   **Jarvis, Charles**

Printed music at US-PHci. **Bradley.**

3884   **Jefferson, Thomas,** 1743-1826

Library now at US-Wc. Some musical materials in the Monticello Music collection at US-CHua. Entries in *section 1.*

3885   **Jenkins, Jean**

Collection of field recordings at the Horniman Museum and Gardens Library. **Penney 4.**

3886   **Jenks, Francis H.,** 1838-94

19th-century scores, 1000 printed and manuscript items formerly at US-MFi now at US-MFiT. *RAMH.*

3887   **Jennens, Charles,** d. 1773

Greatest of all collectors of Handel's works passed to his relative, the Earl of Aylesford [Finch, Heneage] in 1773. Later at auction by Sotheby in 1918 (see under **Finch, Charles Wightwick**). Part went to GB-Lbl, part to dealer, Harold Reeves. From him to Newman Flower, thence to GB-Mp. See sales under **Flower** in *section 1.*

3888   **Jennings, J. W., Mrs.**

Medieval manuscripts and early printed music at US-Wc. *Amerigrove.*

3889   **Jeppesen, Knud,** 1892-1974

At DK-A. Entry in *section 1.*

3890   **Jerkowitz, Joseph**

Collection at D-Mbs. Entry in *section 1.*

3891   **Jessye, Eva A.**

African-American music materials at US-AA. Entry in *section 1.*

3892   **Jimmerthal, Hermann**

Donated to D-LÜh. *NG*-L, p. 754.

3893   **Joachim, Joseph,** 1831-1907

Now at D-Bhm. Entry in *section 1*.

3894   **João IV, King of Portugal,** 1604-56

At P-VV. Entries in *section 1*.

3895   **Joffe, Judah A.**

Recordings from the acoustic era at US-NYcu. *Amerigrove*.

3896   **Johann IV, Fürst zu Anhalt-Zerbst**

At D-ORB. Entry in *section 1*.

3897   **Johnson, ?**

At EIR-C. **Benton 2**, no. 158.

3898   **Johnson, Eldridge Reeves,** 1867-1945

50 phonographs, 50 cylinder recordings, and 12,000 78 rpm records at US-DOV. Entry in *section 1*.

3899   **Johnson, Frances Hall**

Program collection (principally Hartford, Connecticut concerts), mid-19th- early 20th century, at Hartford Seminary Foundation. *RAMH*.

3900   **Johnson, Harold E.**

Jean Sibelius collection at US-Butler University. Entry in *section 1*.

3901   **Johnson, James Weldon,** 1871-1938

Editions, recordings and holographs of music by black composers at US-NH. Entry in *section 1*.

3902   **Johnson, Travis**

Early American songbooks at US-Wc. *Amerigrove*.

3903   **Joly, Jasper,** d. 1892

23,500 volumes of music in 1863 to EIR-Dn. **Benton 2**:159, no. 4.

3904   **Jonas, Oswald,** 1897-1978

Memorial Collection, including the Heinrich Schenker Archive, at US-RIVu. Entries in *section 1*.

3905   **Jones, Fern Patterson**

Memorial Music Library at US-BERr. *Amerigrove*.

3906   **Josef von Lessberg, Freiherr**

Collection received at D-DT in 1855. *NG*-L, p. 751.

3907   **Joseffy, Rafael,** 1852-1915

Collections of 200 manuscripts and 2000 editions of 19th-century pianoforte music with Joseffy's annotations at US-U. Entry in *section 1.*

3908   **Juana, Princess of Austria,** 1535-73

Collection at E-Mah. Entries in *section 1.*

3909   **Julian, John, Rev.,** d. 1913

Hymns and psalms given to GB-Lbl in 1949. **King**, p. 85.

3910   **Jumentier, Bernard,** 1749-1829

18th-19th century scores to F-SQ. **Benton 3**:122, no. 149.

3911   **Kahl, Willi,** 1893-1962

At D-BOCHmi. **Benton 2**:52, no. 42.

3912   **Kalisch, Alfred,** 1863-1933

Vocal scores at GB-Lam. Davies says at GB-Lcm.

3913   **Kalliwoda, Johann Wenzel,** 1801-66; **Wilhelm Dunstan Kalliwoda,** 1827-93

At D-KA. *NG*-L, p. 753.

3914   **Kammerer, ?**

At D-Rs. *NG*-L, p. 757.

3915   **Kapp, Jack**

Cartoons for the recording industry at US-Wc. Entry in *section 1.*

3916   **Karl von Steiermark, Erzherzog von Innerösterreich,** 1540-90; **Ferdinand II, Erzherzog,** 1578-1637

Collection in the Grazer Habsburgerhof. Entries in *section 1.*

3917   **Kastner, Jean Georges,** 1810-67

At D-Bds. *NG*-L, p. 743.

3918   **Katz, Erich**

Collection of recorder music at US-BO.

3919   **Katzman, Henry M[anners],** b. 1912

Manuscripts and early editions of Gershwin, Irving Berlin, Kern, et al., at US-Lu. Entry in *section 1.*

3920   **Keating, George T.,** 1892-196-?

Gifts to US-STu in 1950. Sold collection of 19th-20th century vocal recordings to Laurence Witten II, who gave it in turn to US-NH. *Amerigrove.* Entry in *section 1.*

3921   Keepers, W. Lloyd, 1886?-1978

Collection eventually came to US-LAu. *Amerigrove.*

3922   Keffer, Edward J., 1862-1933

Early American music given to the Musical Fund Society of Philadelphia, then transferred to US-PHf in 1932. **Benton 1**:192, no. 319. See entry under **Dielman** in *section 1.*

3923   Keith, Edward D.

5000 published and manuscript hymnals or psalters at US-NORts. **Bradley**.

3924   Keller, Ludwig

At D-KA. **Benton 2**:75, no. 138.

3925   Keller, Max, 1770-1855

At D-Mbn. Entry in *section 1.*

3926   Kemble, Frances Anne [Fanny], 1809-93

Some items at GB-H, others at US-PHu. **Penney**, p. 283.

3927   Kemble, John Philip, 1757-1823

Collection given to the 6th Duke of Devonshire, eventually acquired by US-SM. Entries in *section 1* under **Huntington**.

3928   Kennedy, Peter

Folksong recordings at GB-Lcs. *NG*-L, p. 765.

3929   Kennedy-Fraser, Marjorie

Gaelic song recordings at GB-Eu. **Benton 2**:171, no. 35.

3930   Kerner, [?Justinus, 1786-1862]

Bequest to D-MB. **Benton 2**:86, no. 180.

3931   Kerveguen, Count G.

Bequest to F-Dc in 1895. **Albrecht**.

3932   Kestner, Hermann, 1810-90, and **August**

Collections at D-HVsa and D-HVkm. Entries in *section 1.*

3933   Kidson, Frank, 1855-1926

9000 items of early English music and folksongs, most to GB-Gm, some by bequest in 1926 to GB-LEc. Entry in *section 1.* **Albrecht**; **Penney**, p. 237; *NG*-L, p. 761—do not all agree.

3934   Kiesewetter, Raphael Georg, 1773-1850

Most went to A-Wn; some at D-DS. Entry in *section 1.*

3935   **Kimpton, G.**

Orchestral music collection at GB-Lam. **Davies**.

3936   **King, Florence Rich**

Organ music at US-Bp. *Grove 5*, p. 208.

3937   **Kinscella, Hazel Gertrude**

American music, including early tune books, hymnals, autographs, photographs, and MacDowell items at US-WAU. **Benton 1**:223, no. 393.

3938   **Kippenberg, Anton** and **Katherina**

Now at D-DÜK. Entries in *section 1*.

3939   **Kircher, Robert Alfred,** 1889-1946

Bequest to D-SWl. *NG*-L, p. 747.

3940   **Kirkpatrick, Ralph,** 1911-84

Collection of Scarlatti at US-NH. Entry in *section 1*.

3941   **Kirnberger, Johann Philipp,** 1721-83

A collection of Bach manuscripts, etc., now at D-Bds. *NG*-L, p. 336.

3942   **Klanert, K.**

At D-HAu. *Grove 5*.

3943   **Klein, August**

Collection at D-BNms. **Benton 2**:52, no. 44.

3944   **Klein, Christian Benjamin,** 1754-1825

Collection at D-BNms and D-BNu. Entries in *section 1*.

3945   **Klemperer, Otto,** 1885-1973

Scores, parts and archive at GB-Lam. **Penney**, p. 542.

3946   **Klingemann, Karl,** 1798-1862

Most of collection now at D-BNba. Entries in *section 1*.

3947   **Klughart, August,** 1847-1902

Bequest from his estate at D-DEl. *NG*-L, p. 744.

3948   **Knappertsbusch, Hans,** 1888-1965

At D-MB. **Benton 2**:91, no. 201.

3949   **Knophius, Georges**

162 volumes of madrigals and motetts at PL-GD. **Benton 5**:127, no. 5.

3950   Knote, Heinrich

At D-Mmb. **Benton 2**:91, no. 201.

3951   Knudtzen, N. H.

Beethoven literature at N-Oum. *NG*-L, p. 782.

3952   Koch, Fred R.

Collection part of the Mary Flagler Cary collection (**458**) now at US-NYpm. Entry under **Koch** in *section 1*.

3953   Koch, Louis, 1862-1930

Catalog of the autograph collection entered in *section 1*, but it is now owned privately by G. Flörsheim.

3954   Koczalsk, Raoul von

Bequest in 1975 to D-Bim, transferred to D-BB. *NG*-L, p. 750.

3955   Kodály, Zoltán, 1882-1967

Ca. 100,000 Hungarian folksongs and related materials gathered with Bartók, now at H-Ba and H-Bami. *NG*-L, p. 768.

3956   Köchel, Ludwig, Ritter von, 1800-77

Now at A-Wgm. **Benton 2**:14, no. 48.

3957   Koehler, ?

Collection of band, orchestra, and chamber music scores at US-Toledo-Lucas County Library.

3958   Köhler, Louis, 1820-86

Acquired in 1935 by USSR-KA. **Albrecht**.

3959   Kolisch, Rudolf, 1896-1978

At US-CA. Entry in *section 1*.

3960   Kolovrat-Krakovský [family?]

At CS-Pnm. Entry in *section 1*.

3961   Koudelka, Joseph, Freiherr von, 1773-1850

First acquired by A. W. Thayer, and then with his library presented to US-Bp by Joshua Bates. Entries under each in *section 1*.

3962   Koussevitzky, Serge, 1874-1951

Archive of his "Nachlass" at US-Bp. *Amerigrove*.

3963   Kozma, Tibor, 1909-76

2500 operas scores at US-BLu. *RAMH*.

3964   Kraft, Ernst, Prince Graf von Oettingen-Wallerstein

Now at D-HR. Many entries in *section 1*.

3965   Kraus, Friedrich

Late 17th- early 18th-century chamber, orchestral, and vocal works now at S-L. **Albrecht**.

3966   Kraus, Hans Peter, 1907-88

Donated 4000 librettos to US-AUS. *Amerigrove*.

3967   Krauss, Karl August

Collection in D-SPlb.

3968   Krehbiel, Henry Edward, 1854-1923

Acquired in the 1920s by US-NYp, excepting the "9 volumes of opera airs made for Thomas Gray." See sale under **Gray** in *section 1*. Krehbiel's folksong collection at US-R. **Benton 1**:179, nos. 284 and 214, no. 370.

3969   Kreisler, Fritz, 1875-1962

Brahms and Chausson manuscripts at US-Wc. Entries in *section 1*.

3970   Krejcí, Josef

845 items at CS-SO. **Benton 5**:61, no. 96.

3971   Krohn, Ernst C., 1888-1975

8500 volumes, 3000 pieces of sheet music now at US-SLug. Entry in *section 1*.

3972   Kruse, Georg Richard, 1856-1944

At D-DT. *NG*-L, p. 751.

3973   Kubelík, Jan, 1880-1940

Collection at CS-Pu. *Grove 5*.

3974   Kuckei, Max, b. 1898

Bequest to D-KIl in 1970. *NG*-L, p. 754.

3975   Kuhac, Franjo Ksaver

Musicological collection at YU-Zda. **Benton 5**:248, no. 110.

3976   Kuhnle, Wesley, 1898-1962

Archive in historic tunings and temperament, plus personal library, at US-LONcs. Entry in *section 1*.

3977   **Kunst, Jaap,** 1891-1960
At NL-AEC. *NG*-L, p. 780.

3978   **Kuntz, Rosamond E.** and **Emile**
New Orleans history collection, including Gottschalk memorabilia, at US-NORtu.

3979   **Kursh, Maurice**
Gift of 8500-plus songs, 1800-1950, to US-SFp. *RAMH*.

3980   **Kurth, Richard A.**
Compositions and arrangements [his alone?] at US-WS. *Amerigrove*.

3981   **Kurtz, Andrew George (of Liverpool),** d. 1895
Some materials bequeathed to GB-Lbl. Entry in *section 1*.

3982   **Labat, Jean-Baptiste,** 1802-75
At F-MON. **Benton 3**:96, no. 90.

3983   **Lachner, Franz,** 1803-90
At D-Mbs. *NG*-L, p. 755.

3984   **LaCorte-Cailler, Gaetano**
At I-ME. **Benton 3**:201, no. 182.

3985   **Lacroix, [Antoine,** 1756-1806?]
18th-century works at F-MON. **Benton 3**:96, no. 90.

3986   **Lago, Dr.**
E-SCu includes the library of the Doctor. Entry in *section 1*.

3987   **Lambert, Alexander,** 1862-1929
ALS, manuscripts and photographs given to US-NYp. *Amerigrove*.

3988   **Lambert, Constant,** 1905-51
Orchestral music to GB-Lbbc. **Davies**.

3989   **Lambertini, Michel'angelo,** 1862-1920
At P-Lc. Entries in *section 1*.

3990   **Landau, Horace de, Baron,** 1824-1903
Some items in a Sotheby sale in 1949 went to US-Wc. According to **Davies**, "selected manuscripts and early editions" are at GB-Lbl. In 1945, some items given to I-Fn by Horace Finlay. Entries in *section 1*.

3991   Landauer, Mrs. Bella Clara, 1874-1968

   Some sheet music from her collection at US-NYhs; also 1500 items at the U.S. National Air and Space Museum in Washington. Entries in *section 1*.

Landon, Robbins, H. C. *See here under* **Robbins Landon, H. C.**

3992   Landsberg, Ludwig, 1807-58

   Part is at B-BR; another portion at D-Bds. Entries in *section 1*.

3993   Lang, Nikolaus, 1772-1837

   Michael Haydn copies at D-Mbn. Entry in *section 1*.

3994   Lang, Ossian

   Collection of 1000 songs at US-BU. **Bradley**.

3995   Lange, Henry R.

   Historical collection of musical instruments and books at US-STu. **Bradley**.

3996   Langenus, Gustave, 1883-1957

   Clarinet literature collection at US-OB. *Amerigrove*.

3997   Lannoy, Heinrich Edoard Joseph, Freiherr von, 1787-1853

   Now at A-Wn and A-Gk(h), but see annotation in *section 1*.

3998   Larcher, ?

   At F-MR. **Benton 3**:96, no. 89.

3999   LaRoche, R. A.

   The Drexel collection, foundation at US-NYp comprised in part of union of LaRoche's and H. F. Albrecht's libraries. See entries in *section 1*.

4000   Larpent, John, 1741-1824

   Italian manuscript plays and librettos now at US-SM. Entry in *section 1*.

4001   Lassus, Augé de.

   Collection at F-SQ. **Benton 3**:122, no. 149.

4002   Laude, ?

   19th-century chamber music at D-Hs. **Benton 2**:70, no. 114.

4003   Laurens, Jean-Joseph Bonaventure, 1801-90; **Jules Bonaventure Laurens**

   At F-C. Entries in *section 1*.

4004   Lauri, Tommaso

   Donated to I-MAC. **Benton 3**:198, no. 173.

4005   Lavoisier, Marie Anne Pierette Paulze, 1758-1836

   Collection at US-I. Entry in *section 1*.

4006   Lawrence, Marjorie, 1909-79

Music, programs, letters, etc., now at US-CAD. *Amerigrove.*

4007   Layton, Alvin G.

2400 early 20th-century theater and salon orchestra arrangements in the Alvin G. Layton Theater Music collection in the American Music Research Center at US-BO.

4008   Leahy, ?

Collection of American sheet music at US-BU. **Bradley.**

4009   Lean, Vincent Stuckey

At GB-BRp. Entry in *section 1.*

4010   Leather, Ella Mary

Folklore at GB-Lcs. *NG*-L, p. 765.

4011   Le Beau, Luise Adolphe, 1850-1927

Bequest of Modinhas to D-Mbs. Entry in *section 1.*

4012   Leberman, Walter, 1910-84

Collection part of Primrose International Viola Archive at US-PRV.

4013   Le Blanc-Duvernoy [family?]

At F-AU. Entry in *section 1.*

4014   Lefebure, Jean, 1736-1805

His collection of manuscripts at Gimo Castle given to S-Uu by Gustaf Brun in 1951. Entry in *section 1.*

4015   Lefranc de Pompignan

Formerly at F-TLc, now at F-TLm. *NG*-L, p. 742.

4016   Lehman, Robert Owen

Partly from the Cortot collection; part given to US-NYpm, part on deposit since 1972. Entry in *section 1.*

4017   Lehmann, ?

6000 folksong books at D-KIl. *NG*-L, p. 754.

4018   Leibl, Carl, 1764-1870

At D-KNd. Entry in *section 1.*

4019   Leichtentritt, Hugo, 1874-1951

At US-SLC. Entry in *section 1.*

4020   **Leigh, Lord, of Stoneleigh, Warwickshire,** [probably **Chandos Leigh, 1st Baron**, 1791-1850]

17th and 18th-century printed music acquired in late 18th century by GB-Ooc. **Penney**, p. 485.

4021   **Leining, House of**

Small collection of pre-1800 editions includes materials from Abbey of Amorbach, now at D-AB. Entry in *section 1*.

Leith, Forbes.   *See* **Forbes-Leith, William,** 1833-1921

4022   **Lennard, Henry Barrett,** 1818-99

67 volumes of Handel manuscripts, once property of Greatorex (**1113**, s*ection 1*), then John Ireland. Presented by Francis Barrett-Lennard to GB-Cfm in 1902. Entry under **Lennard** in *section 1*.

4023   **Leonard, Hazel B.**

Anthems and sacred songs at US-Dp. *Grove 5.*

4024   **Levi, Hermann,** 1839-1900

At D-Mbs. **Münster**.

4025   **Levy, Hal**

5000 pieces of popular sheet music, 600 song folios, books, and 15,000 issues of popular music magazines, plus lecture tapes at US-LAu. *RAMH.*

4026   **Levy, Lester Stern,** 1896-1989

30,000 pieces of American sheet music at US-BAuc; some at US-U. Entries in *section 1*.

4027   **Lewalter,** [probably **Johann,** b. 1862]

Bequest to D-Kl. **Benton 2**:77, no. 143.

4028   **Liebeskind, Josef,** 1866-1916

At CH-BEl. Entries in *section 1*.

4029   **Liechtenstein-Katelkorn, Karl, Prince of Olomouc,** 1624-95

Collection at CS-KRa. Entry in *section 1*.

Lifar, Serge, 1905- .   *See under* **Diaghileff, Sergei** *and under* **Kochno, Boris** *in section 1*

4030   **Lineback, Harold T.**

Private collection of autograph scores of violin concertos, etc., in St. Louis.

4031   **Linek, J. I.**

At CS-BA. **Benton 5**:27, no. 1.

4032   Liszt, Franz, 1811-86

Collections at H-Bl and H-Bn. Entries in *section 1*.

4033   Littleton, Alfred Henry, 1845-1914

Early music treatises now at GB-Lu; portions in sales. Entries in *section 1*.

4034   Liviabelli [in some sources **Liviabella**], **Lino,** 1902-64

Bequest toH-Bl in 1968. **Benton 3**:152, no. 42.

4035   Lloyd, ?

Collection of harp music at EIR-C. *NG*-L, p. 769.

4036   Lloyd, A. L.

Collection of ethnomusicological and folk materials now at Goldsmith's College Library, London.

4037   Lob, Otto

Acquired by US-Cn in 1892. **Benton 1**:104, no. 94.

4038   Lobkowitz, Prince Joseph Franz (Maximilian), 1772-1816

At CS-Pnm. Entries in *section 1*.

4039   Locker-Lampson, Frederick [The Rowfant Library]

Some autographs now at US-NYp. Entry in *section 1*.

4040   Lockspeiser, Edward, 1905-73

Acquired in 1973 by GB-Lau. Emphasis on Ravel and Debussy. **Penney**, p. 346; *NG*-L, p. 762.

4041   Lockwood, Normand, b. 1906

Archive at US-BO. Entry in *section 1*.

4042   Loebell, J. W., 1786-1863

At D-Bl. **Benton 2**:51, no. 40.

4043   Löwenhielm, Carl Gustav, Count, 1790-1858

Small chamber music collection at S-KA. *NG*-L, p. 791.

4044   Löwenstein-Wertheim-Freudenberg, Hubertus, Graf zu, b. 1906

At D-WERl. Entry in *section 1*.

4045   **Lomax, Alan,** b. 1915
Recordings at GB-Lcs. *NG*-L, p. 765.

4046   **Long, François**
Now in possession of sister, Mme. Henry Gouin, Abbey de Royaumont, France, it includes some books from Debussy's library with his annotations. **Albrecht**.

4047   **Longe, Francis,** 1748-1812
Collection of librettos at Us-Wc. Entry in *section 1*.

4048   **López-Calo, José,** b. 1922
Ca. 3000 volumes in a private collection in Salamanca. **Albrecht**.

4049   **Lorenz, Edward Simon**
Hymnals and scrapbooks donated to US-BIRu. Entry in *section 1*.

4050   **Lortzing, Karl**
At D-DT. **Benton 2**:56, no. 59.

4051   **Lotter, J. J.** [probably **Johann Jakob,** 1683-1738, and **Johann Jakob,** 1726-1804]
Collection at NL-At. *NG*-L, p. 780.

4052   **Louise, Caroline**
At D-RUl. **Benton 2**:144, no. 117.

4053   **Lowens, Irving,** 1916-83, and **Margery**
Early American sacred music to US-B. 1000 tunebooks moved to US-WS. Songster collection transferred to US-WOa. *Amerigrove*. Entry in *section 1* under **Warrington**.

4054   **Lubomirska, Izabella,** 1736-1816
Founded the collection later owned by the Potocky Family (**1417**) at PL-LA. Entry in *section 1*.

4055   **Lucca, Francesco,** 1802-72
At I-Mr, acquired 1888. *NG*-L, p. 774.

4056   **Lucchesi-Palli, Eduardo, Count,** 1784-1847
NG-L says 60,000 volumes; *Grove 3* says 40,000 volumes, 26,000 on theatre and opera history form an independent section of I-Nn. Entry in *section 1*.

4057   **Luconi, Albert**
Collection of woodwind music at US-AA. *Amerigrove*.

4058   **Ludwig, Friedrich,** 1872-1930
At D-Gs. **Benton 2**:67, no. 102.

4059   Ludwig I, König von Bayern, 1786-1868

At D-Mbs. **Münster**.

4060   Ludwig I von Hessenberg-Darmstadt

Collection at D-DS. *NG-L*, p. 751.

4061   Ludwig II, König von Bayern, 1845-86

At D-Mbs. **Münster**.

4062   Lumley, John, Baron, 1534?-1609

Lumley's library at Nonesuch "seems to have been dispersed." **Albrecht**; "Many passing to the Crown" (Milsom). Entries in *section 1*.

4063   Lumpkin, Ben Gray, b. 1901

Recorded folksong collection of ca. 1500 items at US-BO. Entry in *section 1*.

4064   Lunsford, Bascom Lamar

Folksong collection at US-OX. Entry in *section 1*.

4065   MacBean, William Munro, 1852-1924

Collection rich in Stuart and Jacobite songs at GB-A. Entry in *section 1*.

4066   McConathy, Osbourne

The school and folk songs and 800 volumes of music teaching songs he received from Luther Whiting Mason (see *section 1*) he gave to Silver, Burdett Co. From there the collection went to US-Wc. Entry in *section 1*.

4067   McCormack, John Count, 1884-1945

Bequest to EIR-Duc in 1945. **Benton 2**:160, no. 9.

4068   MacCunn, [Hasmish, 1868-1916?]

At GB-Bu. *British Music Yearbook*.

4069   McCutchan, Robert Guy, b. 1877

650 18th-19th century American tunebooks and hymnology at US-CLAc. Entry in *section 1*.

4070   McDaniel, David

800 volumes, 10,000 recordings, 300 cylinders at US-San Jose, California, Public Library. *RAMH*.

4071   McDevitt, Josephine A., and **Edith A. Wright**

5192 pieces of early American music bought in 1950 by US-PHf. **Albrecht**.

4072   MacDougall, Hamilton Crawford, 1858-1945

3000 hymnals and psalters are at US-PROu. *Amerigrove*.

4073   **MacDowell, Edward Alexander,** 1860-1908
At US-NYcu. *Amerigrove.*

4074   **McEwen, [John B.,** 1868-1924?]
At GB-Gu. *British Music Yearbook.*

4075   **MacKay-Smith, Alexander**
1000 items of European chamber music and instrumental tutors at US-CHua. *Amerigrove.*

4076   **Mackinlay, Thomas** (publisher)
Some of his collection of letters are at GB-Lbl. Entry in *section 1.*

4077   **Mackworth, Herbert, Sir,** 1737-91
After Mackworth's death, acquired by Bonner Morgan, then to GB-CDp. Entry in *section 1.*

4078   **McLellan, Charles W.**
Lincoln collection at US-PROu. **Benton 1**:208, no. 359.

4079   **Magnin, Charles,** 1793-1862
Autograph collection at F-SA. **Benton 3**:122, no. 150.

4080   **Magnis, Franz Anton, Count,** 1772-1848
At Stráznice, Czech Republic. Entry in *section 1.*

4081   **Main, Herbert Platt,** 1839-1925
3000 English and American hymnals and gospel songs received by US-Cn in 1906. *Amerigrove.*

4082   **Mainardi, Della Corna,** [probably **Enrico,** b. 1897]
Received by I-CR from the widow in 1970. *NG-L,* p. 772.

4083   **Maîtrise de Siffrein**
12th-13th century sacred music at F-C. **Benton 3**:76, no. 43.

4084   **Maldeghem, Robert Julien van,** 1810-93
Part of his collection at F-Pc. Entries in *section 1.*

4085   **Malherbe, Charles Théodore,** 1853-1911
Bequest to F-Pc. Entry in *section 1.*

4086   **Malipiero, [Gian Francesco,** 1882-1973?]
At I-Vgc. **Benton 3**:283, no. 408.

Malmesbury, Earls of.   *See* **Legh, Elizabeth,** 1695-1734

4087 Mandell, Eric, b. 1802

> Collection of Jewish music at US-PHgc (formerly US-PHem). Entry in *section 1*.

4088 Manetti, ?

> Bequest to I-Fc. **Benton 3**:182, no. 129.

4089 Mann, Arthur Henry, 1850-1929

> Collection distributed to several libraries. Handel and Handeliana to GB-Ckc; hymn and psalm books to Church House, Westminster; 10 volumes of autographs of James Hook to GB-Cu; William Crotch collection with manuscript notes to Norwich Public Library. See entries and annotations in *section 1*.

4090 Manners, Charles, 1857-1935

> 2900 volumes of opera scores with conductors' annotations at GB-Gm. *NG*-L, p. 761. **Penney 4** says 4000 volumes!

4091 Mansfeldt, Hugo

> At US-BE. Entry in *section 1*.

4092 Manskopf, Friedrich Nicolas, 1869-1928

> Now at D-F. Entry in *section 1*.

4093 Margaretha of Austria, Regent of the Netherlands, 1480-1530

> At B-BR. *NG*-L, p. 730.

4094 Margherita di Savoia, Queen

> At I-Rsc. **Benton 3**:251-52, no. 316.

4095 Maria Anna, Electress, Consort of Maximilian III, Joseph, 1728-97

> At D-Mbs. Entry in *section 1*.

4096 Maria Antonia Walpurgis, Electress of Bavaria, 1724-80

> Manuscript catalog of her library is at D-Mbs. **Albrecht**.

4097 Maria Leopoldine of Austria, 1797-1826

> Wife of Pedro I, Emperor of Brazil, "formed nucleus of music section of BR-Rn." **Albrecht**.

4098 Maria Theresia, Empress of Austria, 1717-80

> Founded I-Mb. *NG*-L, p. 774.

4099 Marie Louise, Empress, Consort of Napoleon I, 1791-1847

> Music library at I-PAc. *NG*-L, p. 776.

4100 Mario, Giovanni Matteo, Conte di Candia, 1810-83

> Rome, Biblioteca di St. Cecilia. Entry in *section 1*.

4101   Mariotti, ?
> At I-Fc. **Benton 3**:182, no. 129.

4102   Marr, Robert A.
> Collection of 481 volumes rich in Scottish music history given to GB-Ep. **Penney 4**.

4103   Marsh, Narcissus, Archibishop, 1638-1713
> Bequest to EIR-Dm in 1713. Entries in *section 1*.

4104   Marshall, Julian, 1836-1903
> Collection divided but some manuscripts are at GB-Lbl, others—through James Balfour—went to GB-En. Many entries in *section 1*.

4105   Marshall-Hall, George William Lewis, 1862-1915
> Collection in Grainger Museum, University of Melbourne, Australia. Entry in *section 1*.

4106   Martellini, ?
> At I-Fc. **Benton 3**:182, no. 129.

4107   Martin, ?
> Collection at US-BER. Described by **Bradley**, p. 166.

4108   Martin, John B.
> Orchestral collection at US-Dp. *Grove 5*.

4109   Martin, L.
> Ca. 200 works at F-ANN. *NG-L*, p. 738.

4110   Martin, William P.
> Along with **Ernest Orlando Sellers**, a collection of Baptist and gospel hymnody given to US-NORts. Entry in *section 1*.

4111   Martinengo, Leopardo, Count
> At I-Vc. Entry in *section 1*.

4112   Martini, Padre Giovanni Battista, 1706-84
> Library was divided after his death between I-Bc, I-Bsf, and A-Wn. Entry in *section 1*.

4113   Martorell y Fivaller, Marquesas de
> 1300 numbers from 18th and early 19th centuries in some 249 volumes bought by Us-Wc. Entry in *section 1*.

4114   Marucelli, Francesco, 1625-1713
> At I-Fm. *NG-L*, p. 772.

4115   **Marx, Joseph,** d. 1964

At A-Wn. Entry in *section 1.*

4116   **Mason, Lowell,** 1792-1872

Ca. 11,000 items given to US-NH in 1873, many bought from the Rinck collection (**2244**). Entry in *section 1.*

4117   **Mason, Luther Whiting,** 1828-96

Ca. 700 books, school and folk songs went from Mason to Osbourne McConathy, eventually to US-Wc. Entry in *section 1.*

4118   **Masseangeli, Masseangelo,** 1809-78

Collection of autographs given to I-Baf. Entry in *section 1.*

4119   **Massey, Edward Stocks**

Music library now at GB-Burnley, Central Public Library. Entry in *section 1.*

4120   **Massimo, Leone, Fürst**

Manuscripts and autographs at I-Rassimo. Entry in *section 1.*

4121   **Masson, Paul Marie,** 1882-1954

Acquired by F-Pim in 1959. **Benton 3**:111, no. 121.

4122   **Mathias, James**

Bequest in 1782 to GB-Lbm. *NG*-L, p. 763.

4123   **Mattei, Saverio,** 1742-95

I-Nc founded in 1791 with a donation from him. *NG*-L, p. 775.

4124   **Mattei, Stanislao,** 1750-1825

Some items at I-Bc, also 200 autographs at I-Bsf. Entry in *section 1.*

4125   **Mattei-Gentili, Guido**

Ca. 1000 manuscripts and 3000 printed works at I-RIM. *NG*-L, p. 777.

4126   **Mattern, David E.**

Collection at US-AA. *Amerigrove.*

4127   **Matthei, Karl**

At D-FRms. **Benton 2**:64, no. 88.

4128   **Mattheson, Johann,** 1681-1764

Collection at D-Hs (lost during World War II). Entries in *section 1.*

4129   **Matthew, James E.,** d. 1910

Much of his collection, through sale by Liepmannssohn, ended up in the collection of **Paul Hirsch**, then later at GB-Lbl. Many entries in *section 1*.

4130   **Mauersberger, Rudolf**

At D-Dlb. *NG-L*, p. 744.

4131   **Maule, James, 4th Earl of Panmure**; **Harie Maule**

Collection of the two brothers now at GB-En. Entry in *section 1*.

4132   **Maximilian II, King of Bavaria,** 1811-64

At D-Mbs and D-Mbn. Entries in *section 1*.

4133   **Maximilian III, Joseph, Elector of Bavaria,** 1727-77

At D-Msa. Entry in *section 1*.

4134   **May, Henry** [d.? ca. 1680]

Donated to GB-Cpc in 1642/43? **King**, p. 145.

4135   **Mayr, Johann Simon,** 1763-1845

Most of the music in I-BGc belonged to him. *Grove 3*.

4136   **Mazarin, Cardinal Jules,** 1602-61

Gifts to College de la Trinité, now F-LYm, also to F-Pm. **Benton 3**:93, no. 81 and *NG-L*, p. 741.

4137   **Mazer, Johann,** 1790-1847

3000 rarities and manuscripts given to S-Skma in 1847. Entry in *section 1*.

4138   **Mearns,** [probably **James**, author of early Latin hymnaries]

Hymnological collection, over 2000 items, now at GB-Gu. **Penney**, p. 238.

4139   **Mecklenburg-Schwerin, House of**

Ducal library divided between D-ROu and D-SWl. Entries in *section 1*.

4140   **Medinaceli, Duques de**

" . . . finest private collection of Spanish music . . . " **Albrecht**. Now at E-Mmc. Entries in *section 1*.

4141   **Mees, Arthur,** 1850-1923

Gift to US-NYp in 1920s. *Grove 5*.

4142   **Mees, John Henry,** b. 1852

Bequest to GB-Ouf. **Davies**.

4143   **Méjanes, Jean Baptiste Marie Piquet, Marqui de,** 1729-86

Collection at F-AIXm. Entry in *section 1*.

4144   Mellor, Charles C., 1836-1909

500 volumes at US-Pc. *RAMH*.

4145   Meltzer, Charles Henry, 1873-1936

Collection of musicians' autographs, 19th-20th century at US-College of Charleston. *RAMH*.

4146   Mempell, Johann Nicolaus, and **Johann Gottlieb Preller**

Manuscripts passed from Mempell-Preller collection through later collections of Friedrich Eduard Wilsing and Max Seiffert, eventually to D-LEm and D-B. Entry in *section 1* only under **Mempell**.

4147   Mendel, Bernardo

Opera scores given to US-BLu. Entries in *section 1*.

4148   Mendelssohn, Paul Victor Benecke, 1868-1944

Grandson of Felix. Collection augmented after Paul's death by Margaret Deneke, inheritor, who deposited it at GB-Ob ca. 1950. Entry in *section 1*.

4149   Mendelssohn-Bartholdy, Ernst von

Composer's grandson. Library to D-Bds in 1908; ca. 700 family letters to US-NYp in 1970. Entry in *section 1*.

4150   Mendelssohn-Bartholdy, Felix, 1809-47

Most papers at GB-Ob, but some of the family letters were acquired by US-NYp in 1970; still other items are at D-Bds and in Leipzig. See entries in *section 1*.

4151   Mertius, ? (of Kiel)

At D-KImi. **Benton 2**:78, no. 149.

4152   Merz, Karl [1836-90?]

13,000-volume collection served as foundation of music collection at US-Pc. Entry in *section 1*.

4153   Metcalf, Frank J., 1865-1945

Hymnology collection at US-BU; an additional 800 items at US-WOa. *Amerigrove*.

4154   Mettenleiter, Johann Georg, 1822-68

Some holdings bequeathed to Proske-Bibliothek (**1877**, *section 1*) now at D-Rp. *Grove 3*.

4155   Mettetal, Jerome, 1925-77

Collection of opera materials: correspondence, scores, books, recordings, programs at US-St. Peter, Minnesota, Gustavus Adolphus College. *RAMH*.

4156   **Meyerbeer, Giacomo,** 1791-1864
Bequest to D-Bds. Entry in *section 1.*

4157   **Meyerstein, Edward Henry William,** d. 1952
"Distinguished" autographs bequeathed to GB-Lbl. Entry in *section 1.*

4158   **Michael, Jakob**
Jewish music and books given to IL-J in 1966. 10,000 printed works and 15,000 manuscripts of Jewish liturgical music. **Albrecht.**

4159   **Mikorey, Franz,** 1873-1947
Holographs of Cornelius, Ludwig Thuille, and Josef Reiter given to D-Mbn.

4160   **Milanés, John** (English ambassador to Madrid)
Gift of chamber music in 1952 to E-Mc. *NG*-L, p. 789.

4161   **Miles, Napier**
At GB-BRu.

4162   **Miller, Dayton Clarence,** 1866-1941
Collection bequeathed to US-Wc in 1941. Entry in *section 1.*

4163   **Miller zu Aichholz, Victor** and **Olga von**
Brahms items donated to Kammerhof-museum, Gmunden. Entry in *section 1.*

4164   **Misligowsky, Carl**
At Fürstlichen Oettingen-Wallersteinschen Bibliothek, Schloss Harburg. Entry in *section 1.*

4165   **Möller, H[einrich,** 1876-1958?]
At D-WRl. *NG*-L, p. 748.

4166   **Moeran,** [probably **Ernest John,** 1894-1950]
Irish folk music given to EIR-Dtc. *NG*-L, p. 770.

4167   **Mörike, Hermine**
At D-Mmb. **Benton 2**:91, no. 201.

4168   **Mörner, Marianne,** 1895-1977
At S-Skma. Entry in *section 1.*

4169   **Moffat, Alfred Edward,** 1866-1950
Many Moffat materials from Otto Haas's catalog no. 20 in 1944 were purchased by US-Wc. **King.** Some also at US-Nf. Entries in *section 1.*

4170   **Moldenhauer, Hans,** 1906-87
Manuscripts Italian and English composers to US-Eu; R. Strauss and Reger to D-Mbs; 18th-19th century Viennese composers to A-Wst; estate of Hans Rosbaud to US-Wash. St. U.; Americana to US-CA. Many entries in *section 1.*

4171   **Mompou, Frederic,** 1893-1987
Collection left to Centro de documentación musical.

4172   **Moorland, Jesse E.**
Collection of Negro life and history, including music at US-Whu. *RAMH.*

4173   **Mooser, Robert Aloys,** 1876-1969
Ca. 2000 volumes now at CH-Gpu. **Albrecht.**

4174   **Moreno Gil de Borja, José Maria**
Bequeathed dance music to E-Mc. *NG-L,* p. 789.

4175   **Morgan, R. Bonner**
17th-18th century music collected by Sir Herbert Mackworth (**1740**) at Gnoll Castle, 1766-90, given by Morgan to GB-CDp. Entry in *section 1.*

4176   **Morini,** [perhaps **Ferdinando,** 1791-1879]
Gift to I-Fc. **Benton 3**:182, no. 129.

4177   **Morrow, Irving F.**
5500 items, including 1500 opera scores, at US-BE. *RAMH.*

4178   **Mozart, Carl** [Wolfgang's son], d. 1858
Gave a collection of Mozartiana to A-Sm. See ÖmZ, 10:252.

4179   **Mozart, Felix Xaver Wolfgang,** 1791-1844
Collection given by him to Mrs. Baroni-Cavacabo, who in turn bequeathed it to A-Sm. Entry in *section 1.*

4180   **Mozart, Leopold,** 1719-87
Bequest to D-Ahk. *NG-L,* p. 749.

4181   **Mozart, Wolfgang Amadeus,** 1756-91
At D-W and A-Sm. Entry in *section 1.*

4182   **Mühlfeld, Christoph**
Bequest to D-MEIr. **Benton 2**:140, no. 96.

4183   Müller, Joseph, 1877-1939

Paganiniana sheet music and 500 portraits from his collection are at US-NYp. "Star-Spangled Banner" collection (200 items) sold to US-Wc. Entries in *section 1*.

4184   Mure, Sir William [of Rowallen Castle], 1594-1657

At GB-Eu. *NG*-L, p. 761.

4185   Murphy, William H.

Orchestral music collection at US-Dp. *Grove 5*.

4186   Murray, Charles Fairfax

At GB-Cfm. *NG*-L, p. 759.

4187   Myddleton-Biddulph, Thomas

The Chirk Castle collection, mainly 17th-century English church music, bought by US-NYp in 1970.

4188   Nachod, Hans, 1885-1958

His Schoenberg collection is at US-DN. Entries in *section 1*.

4189   Nan Kivell, Rex de Charambac

At AUS-CAnl. Entry in *section 1*.

4190   Napoleon I, Emperor of France, 1769-1821

Collection at F-AJ. *NG*-L, p. 737.

4191   Naue, Johann Friedrich, 1787-1858

Part of collection sold to D-Bds, 1824-25.

4192   Neal, Heinrich

Bequest to D-F. **Benton 2**:63-64, no. 86.

4193   Nedbal, Oskar, 1874-1930

At CS-Pnm. Entry in *section 1*.

4194   Negri, Corrado Pavesi

At I-PCcon. **Benton 3**:237-275.

4195   Nejedlý, Zdenek

Now at CS-Pnm. Entry in *section 1*.

4196   Newman, Eldridge

Purchased by GB-Lbbc. *Grove 5*.

4197   Newman, William Stein, 1912-2000

His Beethoven collection now at the Center for Beethoven Studies, San José, California. His collection of about 3100 keyboard sonatas by 720 composers now at US-CHH. Entries in *section 1*.

4198   Newmarch, Rosa, 1857-1940

At GB-LSadler's Wells Theatre. *Grove 5.*

4199   Nicholl, Horace Wadham, 1848-1922

Manuscripts acquired in 1922 by US-NYp. *Grove 5.*

4200   Nichols, Arthur H.; Margaret Homer Nichols Shurcliff

Campanology collection at US-Ba. *Amerigrove.*

4201   Nichols, Ernest Loring ("Red"), 1905-65

Jazz records given to US-Lu. *Amerigrove.*

4202   Nicholson, Sir Sydney Hugo, 1875-1947

Collection at Royal School of Church Music, Addington. **Penney,** p. 585.

4203   Nicodé, Jean Louis, 1853-1919

At D-Dlb. *NG-L,* p. 744.

4204   Nicolai, Otto, 1810-49

81 volumes of his large collection acquired by D-Bds. **Albrecht.**

4205   Nicoletti, ?

Collection given to I-Raf. **Benton 3**:244, no. 303.

4206   Niecks, Friedrich, 1845-1924

Scottish music at GB-Ep. **Penney,** p. 212.

4207   Niessen, Carl, 1898-1969

History of theater collection now at US-Wc. Entry in *section 1.*

4208   Niles, Edward Abbé, 1894-1963

Bequest of 24,000 items of sheet music, some previously the property of Bella Landauer (**1612**), to US-Hw. *Amerigrove.*

4209   Nilson, Kristina, 1843-1921

Pianoforte scores at S-Skma. *Grove 5.*

Noble, George, Count Plunkett.   *See under* **Plunkett, George Noble, Count,** b. 1851

Noer, Prince von.   *See* **Friedrich Emil August, Prince of Schleswig-Holstein Noer,** 1800-65

4210 **Nötzoldt, Fritz,** b. 1908

> At Deutsche Volksliederarchiv, Freiburg i. Br. Entry in *section 1.*

4211 **Nolen, W. W.**

> 7200 pieces of sheet music and 51 bound volumes acquired in 1923 by US-BU. *RAMH.*

Nonesuch Library. *See section 1 under* **Lumley, John, Baron,** 1534?-1609

4212 **Noseda, Gustavo Adolfo,** 1837-66

> 10,253 items deposited in I-MC in 1899. Entries in *section 1.*

4213 **Nostitz-Rieneck, Erwin, Count**

> Now at CS-Pdobrovského. Entry in *section 1.*

4214 **Notopoulos, James Anastasioa**

> Traditional music from Yugoslavia, Greece, Africa, and Iran at US-CA. *Amerigrove.*

4215 **Novello, Vincent,** 1781-1861

> Gifts in the 1840s to GB-Lbl; some also to GB-Cfm; others to GB-Lcm. Entries in *section 1.*
>
> → *See also under* **Cowden Clarke, Mary,** 1809-98

4216 **Novello & Co.**

> At GB-Lcm and some scores on permanent loan to GB-LSadler's Wells Theatre. Entry in *section 1.*

4217 **Nowacki, Henryk**

> 400 volumes at PL-Lk. **Benton 5**:143, no. 25.

4218 **Nuitter, Charles Louis Etienne,** 1828-99

> At F-Po. *NG*-L, p. 741.

4219 **Nutter, Charles Sumner,** b. 1842

> Hymnology collection at US-Bu. *Amerigrove.*

4220 **Nydahl, Rudolf**

> Autographs of Mozart, Beethoven, et al., at S-Smf. Entries in *section 1.*

4221 **Oakeley, Herbert Stanley,** 1830-1903

> At GB-Er. *NG*-L, p. 761. *Grove 5* says d. 1891.

4222 **Oberhoffer, Emil Johnson,** 1867-1933

> Donation to US-MSp. *Grove 5.*

Obizzi Family.   *See under* **Este, House of**, *section 1*

4223   **Odoevski, Vladimir Federovich, Prince,** 1804-69
　　　　Now at USSR-Mk, donated by his widow. Entry in *section 1*.

4224   **Örtel, Friedrich Benedikt**
　　　　At Sächsischen Hof- und Justizrates. Entry in *section 1*.

4225   **Österreich, Georg,** 1664-1735
　　　　Most of his library sold to Henrich Bokemeyer (**294**, *section 1*), then acquired
　　　　by J. N. Forkel (**913**, *section 1*), eventually to D-B and D-Bds.

4226   **Oetting, C d'**
　　　　At CS-K and D-HR. Entry in *section 1*.

4227   **Oettingen-Baldern, Count Franz Wilhelm von,** d. 1798
　　　　6000 sacred and secular works at CS-K. **Benton 5**:36, no. 27.

4228   **Oettingen-Wallerstein, Fürst**
　　　　Until 1948 in Maihingen, now at D-HR. See entry in *section 1* for cross
　　　　references to portions of the collection elsewhere.

4229   **Ogle, Cuthbert**
　　　　Now at US-WGc. Entry in *section 1*.

4230   **Okhi, Kyubei**
　　　　Present owner of Nanki Music Library in Tokyo formed by **Yorisada
　　　　Tokugawa**. Entries under his name in *section 1*.

4231   **Oldman, Cecil Bernard,** 1894-1969
　　　　Some printed music at Gb-Lbl. Some presented by his widow to A-Sm in
　　　　1974. Entries in *section 1*.

4232   **Olivier, François,** 1907-48
　　　　Acquired in 1965 by CH-LAcu. Entry in *section 1*.

4233   **Olney, Marguerite**
　　　　Joint collector with Helen Hartness Flanders in her ballad collection at US-
　　　　MB. See under **Flanders** in *section 1*.

4234   **Olschki, Leo Samuel,** 1861-1940
　　　　17th-century sacred partbooks bought in 1940 by US-R. *Amerigrove*.

4235   **Openhym, George J.**
　　　　European recordings at US-NH. Entry in *section 1* under **Capes**.

4236   Opochinsky, David and **Fanny**
Manuscripts at US-NH. **Samuel**.

4237   Opperman, Kalmen
Clarinet music at US-Hhc. **Bradley**.

Oranje-Nassau, House of.   *See* **William V, Prince of Orange**

4238   Ord, Boris
At GB-Ckc. **Penney**, p. 93.

4239   Orel, Alfred, 1889-1967
At A-Smi. *NG*-L, p. 727.

4240   Orsini, Alessandro, 1832-90
At I-Rsc. *NG*-L, p. 778.

4241   Ortmann, Otto Rudolph, 1889-1979
At US-BApi. *Amerigrove*.

4242   Osborn, James Marshall, 1906-76**; Marie-Louise**
Important collection including notebooks and manuscripts of Charles
Burney now at US-NH. Given in the 1970s. Entries in *section 1*.

4243   Ossolinski, Jozef Maksymilian, 1748-1826
At P-WRzno. Entries in *section 1*.

4244   Oster, Ernst F.
Large collection of Schenker writings in manuscript at US-NYp. *Amerigrove*.

4245   Otho I, King of Greece, 1815-67
Now at D-Mbs. Entry in *section 1*.

d'Otrante, P. A.   *See* **Fouch d'Otrante, Duke Paul Athanase**

4246   Ottheinrich, Kurfürsten von Neuberg
At D-NBsb. Entries in *section 1*.

4247   Otto, König von Griechenland, 1815-67
At D-Mbn.

4248   Ottoboni, Pietro, Cardinal, 1667-1740
At GB-Mp. Entries in *section 1*.

4249   Ouseley, Sir Frederick Arthur Gore, 1825-89

Once at GB-T, now somewhat dispersed through sales. The transfers and provenance are described under both his name and **Toulouse** in *section 1.*

4250   Owen, John Dale

Early jazz recordings to US-NEij. *Amerigrove:* on deposit from US-MAu. *RAMH.*

4251   Oxenstierna, Gustaf Göran Gabriel, Count

Printed and manuscript operas, arias, and ensembles, 1700-1858, were given to S-SkmA in 1860. **Albrecht.**

4252   Pacher, Alois, 1822-84

At D-Mbn. **Münster.**

4253   Pachta, Jan Josef, Count, 1756-1834

Half of his archive was given by the Umélecká Beseda to CS-Pnm. **Albrecht.**

4254   Pacini, Giovanni

Collection at I-PEA. **Benton 3**:233, no. 271.

4255   Paderewski, Ignace Jan, 1860-1941

Switzerland properties now at PL-Kdp. **Benton 5**:139, no. 21.

4256   Padilla, ?

Bequest to D-Bdso. *NG*-L, p. 744.

4257   Päuler, Bernhard

Collection under administration of CH-Zz. *NG*-L, p. 794.

4258   Paganini, Nicolò, 1782-1840

The collection was considerably dispersed, much of it to Maia Bang Hohn (see under **Hohn**, *section 1*), elsewhere through sales. Hohn's collection was eventually secured by US-Wc.

→ *See also under* **Paganini** *in section 1*

4259   Pagliara, [probably **Rocco E.,** 1856-1914]

At I-Ria. **Benton 3**:253, no. 321.

4260   Paine, Silas K.

Collection was merged with J. Warrington's and W. S. Pratt's at US-Hm; now divided between US-ATu and US-Ps.

→ *See also under* **Warrington**, *section 1.* **Krummel,** *Bibliography Handbook.*

4261   Pamphilj, Benedetto, Cardinal, 1653-1730; later **Cardinal Giuseppe Doria**

Now a private collection at I-Rdp. Many entries in *section 1.*

4262   **Paris, Pierre-Adrien**

Rich library, including opera material, at F-B. **Benton 3**:70, no. 27.

4263   **Parker, Mrs. C. T. M.**

Library formed basis of collection at US-Oa. *Amerigrove.*

4264   **Parker, Rev. John**

Manuscripts, including Continental madrigals, at GB-Lbl. **King**, p. 25.

4265   **Parry, Charles Hubert Hastings,** 1848-1918

At GB-Lcm. **Benton 2**:180, no. 63.

4266   **Parry, Milman**

Collection of oral literature and Afro-American preaching and blues now at US-CA. Entry in *section 1.*

4267   **Pasqualini,** [perhaps **Marc'Antonio**, 1614-91]

At I-Rsc. **Benton 3**:252, no. 316.

4268   **Pasta, Giuditta,** 1797-1865

Over 500 letters and documents at US-NYp. Entry in *section 1.*

4269   **Pastori, Clelia**

Library at I-VEaf. **Benton 3**:423.

4270   **Pastrić, Ivan**

568 items established Biblioteca Pastrizia in 1706 at YU-Snb. Entry in *section 1.*

4271   **Patti, Adelina,** 1843-1919

Pianoforte works at S-Skma. *Grove 5*, p. 205.

4272   **Patzak, Julius,** 1898-1974

31 manuscripts from his collection at D-Mbs. **Münster.**

4273   **Pavlovna, Archduchess Maria,** 1786-1859

At D-WRz. *NG-L*, p. 740.

4274   **Peach, Robert W.,** d. 1936

4400 tunebooks and hymnals at US-WOa. *RAMH.*

4275   **Pearsall, Robert Lucas De,** 1795-1856

At CH-E. Entry in *section 1.*

4276   **Pearson, Alfred K.**

Collection of 78 rpm discs, 1925-45, at US-BOW. *Amerigrove.*

4277   Pech, J.

Acquired by US-NYcu in 1913. *Grove 5.*

4278   Pedrell, Felipe, 1841-1922

Manuscripts at E-Bc. Entry in *section 1.*

4279   Pena Costa, Joaquín, 1873-1944

6000 volumes including a Wagneriana collection to E-Bc. **Benton 3**:9.

4280   Pendlebury, Richard, 1880-1902

Gave collection to GB-Cfm. Was transferred to University Music School, 1925-26, now in library that bears his name, GB-Cpl. **King**, p. 83.

4281   Pepys, Samuel, 1633-1703

"Life interest," manuscripts, and printed music given to John Jackson in 1703, went intact to GB-Cmc in 1724. **King**, p. 145; **Albrecht;** *NG-*L, p. 259. Entry in *section 1.*

4282   Perabo, Johann Ernest, 1845-1920

ALS and music given to Mrs. E. Perry Warren in 1904, given by her to GB-Lbl in 1928. **Albrecht**.

4283   Percheron, Achille Remy, 1797-1969

Collection rich in chansonniers now at US-NYp. Entry in *section 1.*

4284   Peter I, Emperor of Russia, 1672-1725

Collection the basis of manuscript and rare book division of USSR-Lan. *NG-*L, p. 795.

4285   Peters-Marquart, Franz

Bequest to D-Cl. **Benton 2**: 255.

4286   Petrie, George, 1789-1866

Irish folk music to EIR-Dtc.

4287   Petter, Gustav, 1828-68

His autograph collection contained items from the Fuchs collection (**940**, *section 1*). After Gustave's death it went to his brother Theodor. Some items from what is called the Fuchs-Petter collection are now at F-Pc, A-Wgm, and in the Heyer collection (**1278**, *section 1*). **Schaal** (1966), p. 49.

4288   Peyrou, Pierre Alexandre du

At CH-N, including J.-J. Rousseau's autographs.

4289   Pfatteicher, Carl F.

Collection on the history of church music at US-PHu. **Bradley**.

4290   **Pfitzner, Hans,** 1869-1949

At A-Wn. 70 holographs at D-Mbs (Münster); others (his works?) at D-Mbn. Entries in *section 1*.

Philidor Collection.   *See under* **Toulouse, Louis Alexandre** *in section 1*

4291   **Philip Karl, Graf zu Oettingen-Wallerstein**

Collection purchased by Ernst von Schwarzenberg between 1805 and 1808 and is now at CS-K. Entry in *section 1*.

4292   **Philipp I, Duke of Pomerania-Wolgast,** 1515-60

Collection now at D-GRu. Entry in *section 1*.

4293   **Piancastelli, Carlo**

Went to I-FOc in 1937. Entries in *section 1*.

4294   **Piatti, Alfredo Carlo,** 1822-1901

At I-BGi. **Benton 3**:149, no. 33.

4295   **Picchi Family**

18th- and early 19th-century manuscript works at I-Fc. **Benton 3**:182, no. 129.

4296   **Picken, Laurence**

At GB-Ckc. **Penney**.

4297   **Pickering, Thomas**

Some of his excellent collection was purchased at the sale of Oliphant's (**2032**, *section 1*) library, 24-25 April 1873.

4298   **Pigott, John Edward**

In 1910 the EIR-Da received the combined [William] Forde-Pigott collection, over 400 airs.

→ *See also under* **Forde**. *NG*-L, pp. 769-70.

4299   **Piper, Edwin Ford,** 1871-1939

Ballads, folksongs and materials related to Chautauqua movement at US-IO. Entries in *section 1*.

4300   **Piron,** [probably **Alexis,** 1689-1773]

Collection at B-Bc. **Benton 2**:22, no. 15.

4301   **Pisani, Baron Pietro** and **Antonio**

Gift of manuscripts to I-PLcon. Entry in *section 1*.

4302   **Pitt, Percy,** 1870-1932

Bought by GB-Lbbc. *Grove 5*, p. 188.

Pitti Palace.   *See* **Palazzo Pitti**

4303   **Pittschau, ?**
Bequest to D-Bdso. *NG*-L, p. 744.

4304   **Plamenac, Dragan,** 1895-1983
Large collection acquired by US-NH in 1975. Entry in *section 1*.

4305   **Plant, Fred** and **Rose**
35,000 photographs plus correspondence with composers at US-NH.
Samuel.

4306   **Platzman, Robert** and **Eva**
Recordings at US-Lu. *Amerigrove*.

4307   **Playford, John,** 1623-86, and **Henry**
Entry in *section 1*.

4308   **Plimpton, George Arthur,** 1885-1936
Early liturgical manuscripts including Greek hymns and antiphons at US-NYcub. *Amerigrove*.

4309   **Plowden Family (Charles Hood Chichele; Charles Chichele;** and **Harriet Chichele)**
Bequest in 1907 to GB-Lbl of holographs of Mozart's Ten Great Quartets and Beethoven's autograph manuscript of the First Violin Sonata. Entry in *section 1*.

4310   **Plunkett, George Noble, Count,** b. 1851
Ca. 400 volumes to EIR-Dn in 1942. *NG*-L, p. 769.

4311   **Poach, Peter**
Italian madrigals at D-Z. *NG*-L, p. 748.

4312   **Podleská-Batková, Tekle,** 1764-1852
Now at CS-BER. **Albrecht**.

4313   **Pölchau, Georg Johann Daniel,** 1773-1836
Collection drawn from Forkel and C. P. E. Bach to D-Bds in 1841. Entries in *section 1*.

4314   **Pohl, Jan,** 1861-1914
1993 items now at CS-Pnm. **Albrecht**.

4315   **Politz, Karl Heirnch Ludwig,** 1772-1838
Chamber and vocal music, 1750-1820, now at D-LEm. *NG*-L, p. 746.

4316   Polo, [perhaps Enrico]

Given by his daughter in 1954 to I-Mc. **Benton 3**:207, no. 192.

4317   Potocki Family (Lancut Castle, Poland)

Collection founded by Lubomirska (**1717**, *section 1*) in 1780.

4318   Pougin, François-Auguste-Arthur, 1834-1921

3000 items on French opera and theater now at US-R. **Albrecht**.

4319   Powell, Maud, 1868-1920

At US-Dp. *Grove* 5:210-11.

4320   Pozzi, Antonio

Bequest in 1845 to I-Bsf. **Benton 3**:154, no. 45.

4321   Prandau, Counts

Score collection at YU-OSm. **Benton 5:**227, no. 66.

4322   Pratt, Waldo Selden, 1857-1939

The collections of Pratt, Silas K. Paine (**4260**); James Warrington (**2806**, *section 1*), were merged at US-Hm, now divided between US-ATu and US-Ps. **Krummel**, *Bibliography Handbook*.

4323   Preller, Johann Gottlieb

See under **Mempell, Johann Nicolaus** in *section 1*. The Mempell-Preller library went through the later collections of Daniel Friedrich Edward Wilsing and Max Seiffert (entries in *section 1*), eventually to D-LEm and D-B.

4324   Prendergast, H.

Church music at GB-Lam. *NG*-L, p. 764.

4325   Preske, ?

19th-century chamber music at D-Hs. **Benton 2:**70, no. 114.

4326   Preston, John A.

Collection of 19th-century letters of musicians at US-Bc. *Amerigrove*.

4327   Pretlack, Ludwig Freiherrn von, 1716-81

1079 18th-century works acquired by D-B in 1975. Entry in *section 1*.

4328   Prieger, Erich, 1849-1913

Mostly autograph manuscripts acquired from Artaria (**89**), now at D-Bds. Entries for each in *section 1*.

4329   Prileský-Ostrolícky Family

Now at CS-Mnm. Entry in *section 1*.

4330   Primrose, William, 1903-82

Viola library founded in 1977 at US-PRV.

4331   Proske, Karl, 1794-1861

Absorbed bequests from Karl Weinmann, Franz Xaver Haberl, Johann Georg Mettenleiter, and Franz Witt (**2163**). Proske's collection bequeathed to D-Rp. Entries in *section 1.*

4332   Prout, Ebenezer, 1835-1909

Collection bought by EIR-Dtc in 1909. *NG*-L, p. 770.

4333   Puliti, [perhaps **Leto,** 1818-75]

Collection at I-Fc. **Benton 3:**183, no. 129.

4334   Quinn, John Kirker

4022 recordings and "important early jazz" at US-U. *RAMH.*

4335   Radcliff, Thomas

Collection of popular 20th-century sheet music at US-LAu. *RAMH.*

4336   Radiciotti, Giuseppe, 1858-1931

Bequest to I-MAC. **Benton 3:**198, no. 173.

4337   Rainbow, Bernarr, Dr., b. 1914

Several thousand items on the history of music education at GB-Lu; another small collection donated to Kingston Polytechnic, Surrey. **Penney,** p. 318 and 380.

4338   Randle, William

Several thousand early jazz and rhythm and blues recordings at US-BOW. *Amerigrove.*

4339   Rappaport, Eda Rothstein

Collection at US-NYcu. **Bradley.**

4340   Rau, Arthur

Sale 1934; many items to GB-T, now mainly at F-Pn. See under both **Rau** and **Toulouse** in *section 1.*

4341   Raugel, Félix, 1881-1975

Organ literature at US-OB. *Amerigrove.*

4342   Ravanello, Oreste

Bequest to I-Pca. **Benton 3:**222, no. 233.

4343 **Rawlinson, Richard,** 1690-1755

Sold in 1755 to GB-Ouf, then in 1893 to GB-Ob. *Grove 5*, p. 373.

4344 **Razumovsky, Andrey Kyrillovich, Prince,** 1752-1836

2500 works now at USSR-Kan. *NG*-L, p. 795.

4345 **Razumovsky, Dmitry Vasil'evich,** 1818-89

At USSR-Ml. Entry in *section 1*.

4346 **Read, Keith M.**

Confederate sheet music at US-ATeu. Entry in *section 1*.

4347 **Redlich, Hans Ferdinand,** 1903-68

At GB-Lau. **Penney**.

4348 **Reed, Edward Bliss,** 1872-1940

Carol collection at US-NH. *Amerigrove*.

4349 **Reger, Max,** 1873-1916

Bequest to D-MEIr. Entry in *section 1*.

4350 **Reichel, Bernard**

Now at CH-LAcu. Entry in *section 1*.

4351 **Reid, John D.,** 1907-74

American jazz collection at Arkansas Art Center, Little Rock. Entry in *section 1*.

4352 **Reid, John R., Gen.,** 1721-1807

"Noteworthy as the earliest known library of music formed in Scotland . . . no list of the bequest [to GB-Er in 1806] has survived." Collection acquired from daughter in 1838. (**King**, p. 24, says now at GB-Eu.) Entry in *section 1*.

4353 **Reinach, Théodore,** 1860-1928

17th- and 18th-century works at F-Pim. *NG*-L, p. 742.

4354 **Reiner, Fritz,** 1888-1963

Scores and books at US-Eu. *Amerigrove*.

4355 **Reinhold, Otto**

At D-Dlb. *NG*-L, p. 744.

4356 **Requien, Esprit, Dr.**

Autograph collection at F-A. **Benton 3**:68, no. 21.

4357   **Resse, Pio, Conte**
      751 items bought by US-Cn in 1889. Entry in *section 1*.

4358   **Rheinberger, Joseph Gabriel,** 1839-1901
      At D-Mbs. *NG*-L, p. 755.

4359   **Rhodes, Willard,** b. 1901
      American Indian folksong at US-Wc. Entry in *section 1*.

4360   **Ribera, San Juan de**
      Now at E-VAcp. Entry in *section 1*.

4361   **Ricasoli, Pietro Leopoldo,** 1778-1850
      Now at US-LOu. Entry in *section 1*.

4362   **Rich, Blanche Browning**
      Collection of Edison recordings, cylinders and discs, 1903-23, at US-Logan, Utah State University. *RAMH*.

4363   **Richbourg, John D.**
      In Blues Archive at University of Mississippi. Entry in *section 1*.

4364   **Richelieu, [Armand Jean de Plessis, duc de,** 1585-1642?]
      Gifts to Collège de la Trinité now at F-LYm. **Benton 3:**93, no. 81.

4365   **Richter, Ján Jozef,** 18th-century organist
      Collection, once the choir archive at CS-BSk, now at CS-Mms. **Benton 5:**44, no. 53.

4366   **Ridenour, Harry E.**
      Folksong collection at US-BERr. *Amerigrove*.

4367   **Riedl,**
      Collection in Deutschen Volksliedarchiv, Freiburg in Bresgau. Entry in *section 1*.

4368   **Riemenschneider, Albert,** 1878-1950
      Now at US-BER. Entries in *section 1*.

4369   **Ries, Ferdinand,** 1784-1838
      At GB-Lam and GB-Lcm. *NG*-L, p. 764.

4370   **Ries, Franz,** 1847-1932
      At GB-Lam. **Benton 2:**177, no. 62.

4371   Rignani, ?

18th-century operas and oratorios at I-MC. *NG*-L, p. 775.

4372   Rimbault, Edward Francis, 1816-76

Some items in sale of his collection in 1877 are now at US-NYp. **Albrecht**.

4373   Rinck, Johann Christian Heinrich, 1770-1846

Collection, rich in contemporary manuscript copies from sources close to early composers, was purchased by Lowell Mason (**1808**) in 1852 and is now at US-NH. Entry in *section 1*.

Ring, Stanley. *See here under* **Willson, Meredith**

4374   Rischel, Thorvald, 1861-1939; **Frederik Birket-Smith,** 1880-1952

Collection now at DK-Kk. Entry in *section 1*.

4375   Riseley, George

Bequest to GB-BRp in 1930. **Penney**, p. 11.

4376   Ritter, Frédéric Louis, 1834-91

His library of 1500 books and 500 scores bought by Albert Metcalf and given to US-MED; some are at US-PO. Entry in *section 1*.

4377   Robbins Landon, H. C., b. 1926

Some materials on Haydn and his contemporaries now at GB-CDp. **Penney**, p. 4.

4378   Robinson, Carol

Music collection at US-TA. *Amerigrove*.

4379   Rodger, James, 1871-1952

Hymnology collection at Rhodes University, South Africa. Entry in *section 1*.

4380   Rohde, [perhaps **Achim,** b. 1936]

Bequest to D-Nst. **Benton 2:**95, no. 218.

4381   Rohloff, E [probably **Ernst**]

At D-SWl. *NG*-L, p. 747.

4382   Rolandi, Ulderico, 1874-1951

35,000 libretti to I-Vgc and some items at I-MAC. **Benton 3:**282, no. 408. Entry in *section 1*.

4383   Roman, Johann Helmich, 1694-1758

Now at S-Skma. Entry in *section 1*.

4384   Romberg, Sigmund, 1887-1951
4500 volumes of operas now at US-BE. *Amerigrove.*

4385   Ronald, Landon, Sir, 1873-1938
Library purchased by GB-Lbbc. **Davies**.

4386   Rondel, August, 1858-1934
Now at F-Pa. *NG*-L, p. 741.

4387   Root, George Frederick, 1820-95
Music library at US-CN. *RAMH.*

4388   Rosa, Carl, 1842-89
Operas now at GB-LVp and GB-Lcm. *NG*-L, p. 762.

4389   Rosbaud, Hans, 1895-1962
His estate sold by Moldenhauer to Washington State University. Entry in *section 1.*

4390   Rose, Gloria, 1933-74
Transcriptions of 17th-century Italian works now at GB-Bu. *NG*-L, p. 758.

4391   Rose, Kenneth David, 1888-1960
10,000 items of sheet music to US-NAs. Entry in *section 1.*

4392   Rosenberg Family (Prague)
Collection at S-Sm. Entry in *section 1.*

4393   Rosenbloom, Charles J.
Now at US-Pc and US-NH. Entry in *section 1.*

4394   Rosenthal, Harold
Opera programs and press cuttings at GB-Ob. **Penney 4**.

4395   Rospigliosi Family
Bequest to I-PS. *NG*-L, p. 777.

4396   Rossiter, John P.
12,000 items of band music to US-MSp. *Notes, Supplement* 25 (1952): 20.

4397   Roth, Stephan
Italian madrigals, etc. at D-Z. *NG*-L, p. 748.

4398   Rothschild, Carl, Freiherr von
At D-Fsm. Entry in *section 1.*

4399   **Rothschild, Edouard de, Baron**
        Private library in Paris. **Albrecht**.

4400   **Rothschild, James de, Baron,** 1844-81
        Collection given by his son to F-Pn in 1933. **Albrecht**.

4401   **Rottmanner, Eduard,** 1809-43
        At D-Mbn.

4402   **Rouché, Jacques,** b. 1862
        Collection "recently deposited" at F-Po. *NG*-L, p. 741.

4403   **Rowe, Louis Thompson,** 1855-1927
        Bequest in 1927 to GB-Ckc. Entry in *section 1*.

        Rowfant Library.   *See under* **Locker-Lempson, Frederick**

4404   **Rowland, G.**
        Collection of oboe music at GB-York County Central Museum. **Penney**.

        Royal Family.   *See* **Great Britain - Kings and Rulers** *in section 1*

4405   **Rubinovitch, ?**
        Collection of 5000 opera recordings at Royal College of Music, Manchester.
        Penney 4.

4406   **Rubinstein, Anton,** 1829-84, and **Nikolay,** 1835-81
        At USSR-Mk. *NG*-L, p. 796.

        Rudolf, Franz Erwein, Graf zu Schönborn-Wiesentheid.   *See under* **Schönborn, Rudolf
        Franz Erwein von, Graf,** 1672-1754

4407   **Rudolph, Johann Joseph Rainer, Erzherzog,** 1788-1831
        Part at A-Wgm; some at CS-KRa. Entries in *section 1*.

4408   **Rudorff, Ernst Friedrich Karl,** 1840-1916
        At D-LEm. Entries in *section 1*.

4409   **Ruge, [Filippo,** 1725-67?]
        Manuscript thematic catalog and collection at US-SFsc. Entries in
        section 1.

        Ruggles-Brise, Dorothea, Lady.   *See under* **Glen, John**

4410   **Ruppeldt, Milos,** 1881-1943
        Now at CS-BRu. Entry in *section 1*.

4411   **Russell,** [probably **Henry,** 1812-1900]

Collection of 1100 Victorian songs at GB-BRp. Acquired 1968. *NG*-L, p. 759.

4412   **Russell, Ross**

Papers and jazz collection at US-AUS. Entry in *section 1*.

4413   **Rust, Friedrich Wilhelm,** 1739-96

At D-HAmi. Entry in *section 1*.

4414   **Sabater, Juan María Thomás,** 18th century

Basis of the collection at E-PAp. **Benton 3:**36, no. 75.

4415   **Sabatier,** [**Ernest,** fl. 1880?]

18th- and 19th-century operas at F-NS. *NG*-L, p. 741.

4416   **Sacerdote, Giacomo**

Bequest to I-Tci. **Benton 3:**268, no. 367.

4417   **Sacher, Paul,** b. 1906

Private collection at the Paul Sacher Foundation. Entries in *section 1*.

4418   **Sachs, Curt,** 1881-1959

Part of his library now at US-NBu. *Amerigrove*.

4419   **Sachs, Johann Gabriel**

Now at S-Skma. Entry in *section 1*.

4420   **Sackville, John Frederick, 3rd Duke of Dorset**, 1745-99

At Knole Castle. Entry in *section 1*.

Salisbury, Earl of.   *See* **Cecil, Robert, 1st Earl of,** 1563-1612

4421   **Sampaio Ribeiro, Mario Luis de,** 1898-1966 (or 7)

Now at P-Ln. *NG*-L, p. 786.

4422   **Sánchez Garza, Jesús**

Now at Instituto de Bellas Artes, Mexico. Entry in *section 1*.

4423   **Sandberger, Adolf,** 1864-1943

At D-Mbs. **Benton 2:**89, no. 191.

4424   **Sandherr, Charles**

Ca. 1500 volumes on history and theory acquired by F-CO, 1876-85. **Albrecht**.

4425   **Sandvik, Ole Mark,** 1875-1976

Gave his printed music collection to N-Ou in 1924. Works on history and theory are at N-Oum. **Albrecht**.

4426   **Sandvik, Paul,** 1847-1936

Library given to Folkebibliotek, Hamar, Norway. **Albrecht**.

4427   **Santangelo, Nicola (of Naples)**

At I-Ra. *NG*-L, p. 777.

4428   **Santini, Fortunato,** 1778-1861

Most of the collection at D-MÜs; some manuscripts at I-Bsf, others in Aiblinger *Nachlass* at D-Mbn. Entries in *section 1*.

4429   **Sarasin, Lucas,** 1730-1802

At CH-Bu. Entries in *section 1*.

4430   **Sargent, Sir Malcom,** 1895-1967

Orchestral music at GB-Lcm. **Davies**.

4431   **Sauret, Elisabeth (Mrs. Harry Edwards)**

At CH-N. Entry in *section 1*.

4432   **Saxe-Coburg, Dukes of**

The ducal library is now at D-Cl. **Albrecht**.

4433   **Sayn-Wittgenstein, Moritz Casimir I, Graf von Berleburg**

Still a private library at D-BE. Entry in *section 1*.

4434   **Sbarbi,** [probably **Sbarbi y Osuna, José Maria,** 1834-1910]

18th-century church music at E-Mm.

4435   **Scalvini, Giulio** and **Carmen Asensio**

Now at I-PAi. Entry in *section 1*.

4436   **Schaden, Franz Michael von**

Collection at D-HR. Entry in *section 1*.

4437   **Schafhäutl, Karl Emil von,** 1803-90

Ca. 300 manuscripts, 476 printed works at D-Mbs. **Münster**.

4438   **Schang, Frederick C.**

1500 calling cards of composers now at US-NYcu. Entry in *section 1*.

4439   **Schatz, Albert,** 1839-1910

At US-Wc. Entries in *section 1*.

4440   Scheide, William H., b. 1914

At US-PRu. Entries in *section 1.*

4441   Schelling, Ernest, 1876-1939

Several manuscripts from his library are at US-NYpm. *Amerigrove.*

4442   Schenker, Heinrich, 1868-1935

Materials included in the **Oswald Jonas** Memorial Collection at US-RIVu. *Amerigrove.* Entries in *section 1.*

4443   Scherber, [Paul Friedrich]

Bequest to D-Nst. **Benton 2:**95, no. 218.

4444   Schermar, Egenolf von (and son, **Anton**)

Now at D-Usch. Entries in *section 1.*

4445   Scheurleer, Daniel François, 1855-1927

Songbooks at NL-DHK; bulk of the collection the basis of that at NL-DHgm. Entries in *section 1.*

4446   Schick, Philippine

At D-Mmb. **Benton 2:**91, no. 201.

4447   Schiedermair, Ludwig, 1876-1957

Early printed works at D-BNms. *NG*-L, p. 750.

4448   Schiller, ?

Bequest to D-MB. **Benton 2:**86, no. 180.

4449   Schindler, Anton Felix, 1795-1864

Divided between D-BNba and D-Bds (acquired in 1843). *NG*-L, p. 743. Entry in *section 1.*

4450   Schlecht, Raimund, 1811-91

Collection now at D-Es. **Albrecht.**

4451   Schlesinger, Johann

870 copies from 1700 to 1835 at CS-SO. **Benton 5:**61, no. 96.

4452   Schmid, Joseph, 1868-1945

At D-Mbs. **Münster.**

4453   Schmidt, Franz, 1874-1939

At A-Wgm. Entry in *section 1.*

4454 Schmidt, Max

Now at US-PHf. *Amerigrove.*

4455 Schmitz, E. Robert, 1889-1949

Given by his daughter Mrs. Monique Ludec to US-NH. **Samuel.**

4456 Schneider, [Johann?] Friedrich, 1785 (or 6)-1853

Bequest to D-DEl. *NG*-L, p. 744. Entry in *section 1.*

4457 Schoelcher, Victor, 1804-93

Manuscripts of Handel bought in 1856 from Thomas Kerslake, the bookseller, were acquired by businessmen in Hamburg in 1868, later, in 1875, given to D-Hs. Some other Handel items acquired by F-Pc in 1873. **Albrecht.** Entry in *section 1.*

4458 Schoenbaum, Camillo, b. 1925

Still a private collection. According to **Brook,** no. 1176, a thematic catalog exists. **Albrecht.** Entry in *section 1.*

4459 Schoenberg, Arnold, 1874-1951

Ca. 6000 manuscript pages and a library of ca. 2000 volumes, formerly at US-LAs, moved in 1998 to A-Wsc; other material at US-Wc. Entries in *section 1.*

4460 Schönborn, Rudolf Franz, Graf von (in Pommersfelden)

A private library. Entry in *section 1.*

4461 Schönborn-Wiesentheid, Graf zu

Collection begun by Rudolf Franz Erwein, Graf von Schönborn (1677-1754), now at D-PO. Entries in *section 1.*

4462 Schöpflin, Jean-Daniel

Part of the foundation of F-Sm in 1765. **Benton 3:**125.

4463 Schoettle, Gustave

Purchased in 1919 by US-MSp. **Bradley.**

4464 Scholes, Percy Alfred, 1877-1959

General collection now at C-On. Burney portion now at US-NH. Entry in *section 1.*

4465 Schott, Bernhard, 1748-1809

Bequest to D-MZs. Entry in *section 1.*

4466 Schramm, Paul and **Dinny**

Collection at NZ-Wt. Entry in *section 1.*

4467   **Schramm,** [probably **Willi,** b. 1884]
Bequest to D-DT. *NG*-L, p. 751.

4468   **Schreker, Franz,** 1878-1934
At A-Wn. Entry in *section 1.*

4469   **Schrüber, ?**
Collection at D-HS, rich in Handel items. **Benton 2:**70, no. 114.

4470   **Schubert, Ferdinand,** 1794-1859
He inherited the literary estate of his brother Franz, now called the "Witteczek-Apaun'sche Schubert-Sammlung" at A-Wgm. Entry in *section 1.*

4471   **Schumer, Harry G.,** d. 1971
Former librarian at the Metropolitan Opera; collection bought by US-NYp in 1975. **Albrecht.**

4472   **Schwarzenberg, Ernst von**
Purchased collection from Philip Karl, Graf zu Oettingen-Wallerstein; now at CS-K. See under **Philip Karl** in *section 1.*

4473   **Schwarzenberg, Maria Eleonora,** 1747-97
At CS-K. **Benton 5:**36, no. 27.

4474   **Schwarzwald, Henryk**
At PL-GD. **Benton 5:**127, no. 5.

4475   **Scott, Charles Kennedy**
Madrigal collection in the Central Music Library, Westminster. **Davies.**

4476   **Scott, F. G.**
Collection of song manuscripts bequeathed to GB-Gm. **Penney,** p. 237.

4477   **Scott, Marion Margaret,** d. 1955
Notable Haydn collection given to GB-Cu in 1953. *NG*-L, p. 759; **Benton 2:**165, no. 13.

4478   **Sedie, Enrico Delle,** 1822-1907
At I-Li. *NG*-L, p. 773.

4479   **Sedo Peris-Mencheta, Juan**
At E-Bc, acquired in 1969. *NG*-L, p. 787.

4480 **Sedo y Guichard, Arturo**
At E-Bit. Entry in *section 1*.

4481 **Sefton, Charles William Molyneux, [1st] Earl of**, 1748-95, and **William Philip**, 1772-1838
Pianoforte and chamber music at GB-LVp. *NG*-L, p. 762.

4482 **Séguir, Jean-François**
At F-NS. **Benton 3**:102, no. 105.

4483 **Seidl, Anton,** 1850-98
Personal library including musical autographs acquired 1905 by US-NYcu.
Amerigrove.

4484 **Seiffert, Max,** 1868-1948
With Friedrich Edward Wilsing owned some of the collection formed by J. N. Mempell and J. G. Preller. See under **Mempell** in *section 1*. Now at D-LEm and D-B.

4485 **Seitz, Alipius**
Collection now at D-BG. Entry in *section 1*.

4486 **Selden-Goth, Gisela,** 1884-1975
Now at US-Wc. Entry in *section 1*.

4487 **Sellers, Ernest Orlando,** b. 1869
With William P. Martin, a collection of Baptist and gospel hymnody at US-NORts. Entry in *section 1*.

4488 **Selvaggi, Gaspari**
Collection given by Spencer Joshua Alwyne Compton, 2nd Marquis of Northampton to GB-Lbl. Entries in *section 1*.

4489 **Sérieyx, Auguste,** 1865-1949
At CH-LAcu. Entry in *section 1*.

Servera, Bartolomé March, b. 1917. *See in section 1 under* **Medinaceli**

4490 **Seuffter, Johanna**
Bequest to D-KNh. **Benton 2**:80, no. 156.

4491 **Seydl, Josef Antonín,** 1775-1837
At CS-BER. Entries in *section 1*.

4492 **Seymour, John Laurence,** b. 1893
600 volumes of works on opera at US-CLac. *Amerigrove*.

Shaftesbury, 4th Earl of.   *See* **Cooper, Anthony Ashley**

4493   **Shapiro, Elliott,** 1896-1956
Large collection of sheet music acquired by US-NYp. **Albrecht.**

4494   **Sharp, Cecil,** 1859-1924
Manuscripts at GB-Drc and GB-CClc. Folksong collection went to GB-Lcs in 1924.

4495   **Sharp Family, Bamburgh Castle,** 1644-1772
Collection transferred in 1958 on indefinite loan to GB-DrC. Entries in *section 1.*

Shaw-Hellier Collection.   *See under* **Hellier, Samuel,** 1736-84

4496   **Sheard, ?**
General music library at GB-Gm. *Grove 5.*

"The Shipton Hoard."   *See entry in section 1*

4497   **Shirk, William A.**
1165 recordings, including many early vocal pieces at US-U. *RAMH.*

4498   **Shurcliff, Margaret Homer Nichols**
Collection of campanology now at US-Ba. *Amerigrove.*

4499   **Sibley, Hiram W.**
At US-R. Entries in *section 1.*

4500   **Siddell, F. W.**
Orchestral hire library at GB-Lbbc. **Davies.**

4501   **Siegel, Daniel** and **Ruth**
Sheet music at US-WM. *RAMH.*

4502   **Sigismondo, Giuseppe,** 1739-1826
Collection bequeathed to I-Nc. Entry in *section 1.*

4503   **Silva, Luigi**
Now at US-GRB. Entry in *section 1.*

4504   **Silverstope, Fredrik Samuel,** 1769-1851
Bequest in 1852 to S-Uu. Entry in *section 1.*

4505   **Silvestri, ?**
Rich collection of libretti given to F-Po. **Benton** 3:109, no. 115.

4506   Silvestri, Counts

The collections at I-RVI is based on theirs and Abbé Gnocchi's library, 1835-36. **Benton 3:**258, no. 336.

4507   Simoni, Livia

At I-Ms. Entry in *section 1.*

4508   Simoni, Renato, 1875-1952

Collection to I-Ms in 1954. **Benton 3:**205-06, no. 190.

4509   Simpson, A. Carson, 1895-1965

Opera collection at US-Pu. *RAMH.*

4510   Sinderem, Howard van

Gift of ALS in 1929 to US-NYp. *Amerigrove.*

4511   Singer, Godfrey F.

Collection of recorded music at US-Pu. **Bradley**.

4512   Skene, George, 1695-1756

Collection probably at GB-A. Entry in *section 1.*

4513   Skotak, Ondrej, 1817-91

At CS-OP. Entry in *section 1.*

4514   Sloane, Sir Hans, d. 1735

Now at GB-Lbl. Entry in *section 1.*

4515   Smart, George, Sir, 1776-1867

"Paper and journals" to GB-Lbl. Entries in *section 1.*

Smith, Alexander Mackay, b. 1903.   *See under* **Mackay-Smith, Alexander**

4516   Smith, John Christopher, the Younger, 1712-95

Presented many Handel autographs to King George III. Now at GB-Lbl. **King**, pp. 36, 107.

→ *See also* a Puttick & Simpson sale, 29 January 1958, under **A Dinstinguished Amateur**

4517   Smith, William Charles

His library now incorporated in the Gerald Coke collection (**527**). Entry in *section 1.*

4518   Soler Francisco, ca. 1625-88

Bequest (of his library or just his own compositions?) to E-G. *NG*-L, p. 788.

4519   Solms-Lich, Fürst

> Collection including the library of Fürstin Henriette (1780-1835) now at D-LCH. **Albrecht**.

4520   Sonneck, Oscar George Theodore, 1873-1928

> Most at US-Wc; part of personal library at US-R. Entry in *section 1*.

4521   Sonnleithner, Joseph von, 1766-1835

> Bequest to A-Wn. Entry in *section 1*.

4522   Sonsfeldt Family

> Part at CS-KRik in Fürstenberg collection. Entry in *section 1* under both.

4523   Sour, Robert B.

> "Music of the Theatre" collection (12,000 songs) at US-PRu. *Amerigrove*.

4524   Spadoni, Giovanni

> Donated to I-MAC. **Benton 3:**198, no. 173.

4525   Spain, Helen Knox

> Music and theater programs from New York and Atlanta, 1905-30, at Atlanta, Georgia, Historical Society.

4526   Spanke, [? Hans, 1884-1944]

> Bequest to D-Hmi. **Benton 2:**69, no. 112.

4527   Spaun, Josef, Freiherr von, 1788-1865

> The "Spaun-Witteczek Schubert Collection" is at A-Wgm. *Grove 5:*162.

4528   Spencer, Frances G.

> 30,000 items of American printed sheet music, songsters, and light opera at US-WC. Entry in *section 1*.

4529   Spencer, Mrs. Kay

> Now at US-WC. **Krummel**.

4530   Sperrin-Johnson, J. C.

> Estate of chamber and folk music received 1949 by EIR-C. *NG*-L, p. 769.

4531   Spiering, Theodore, 1871-1925

> At US-Dp. *Grove 5:*210.

4532   Spingarn, Arthur Barnett, 1878-1971

> 2000 pieces of sheet music by black composers at US-Whu. *Amerigrove*.

4533   **Spitta, Philipp,** 1841-94
>   At D-Bhm. Entry in *section 1*.

4534   **Spoellberch de Louvenjoud, Charles Victor, Vicomte de,** 1836-1907
>   Collection at F-Pi. Entry in *section 1*.

4535   **Spohr, Louis,** 1784-1859
>   Bequeathed to D-Kl. **Benton 2:**77, no. 143.

4536   **Spontini, Gaspare,** 1774-1851
>   Bequeathed to F-Bo. *NG-L*, p. 738.

4537   **Sporr, Karl**
>   Folk music collection now at Svensk Visarkiv, Stockholm.

4538   **Spurgeon, Charles Haddon,** 1834-92
>   Hymnology collection at William Jewett College, Liberty, Missouri. *Amerigrove*.

4539   **Spy, Walter,** 1868-1953
>   2600 pieces of early 20th-century sheet music donated to US-Converse College, Spartanburg, South Carolina. *RAMH*.

4540   **Squire, William Barclay,** 1855-1927
>   At GB-Lcm. *NG-L*, p. 765.

4541   **Srb, Josef,** 1836-1904
>   At CS-Pnm. **Albrecht**.

4542   **Staehle, ?**
>   Collection bequeathed to D-Kl. **Benton 2:**77, no. 143.

4543   **Stainer, Sir John,** 1840-1910
>   The English song books from his collection were purchased in 1932 by Walter Harding and are now at GB-Ob, the hymnbooks at GB-Lbl. (Extensive description in **King**, pp. 73, 82, and elsewhere.) Entries under both in *section 1*.

4544   **Stambler, Benedict**
>   3000 Jewish folk and cantorial recordings at US-NYp.

4545   **Stanford, Sir Charles Villiers,** 1852-1924
>   At GB-Lcm. **Benton 2:**180, no. 63.

4546   **Stanton, Royal B.**
>   Hymnals at US-LAu. *Amerigrove*.

4547   Starr, Dorothy

        Sheet music collection at US-SFp. Entry in *section 1*.

4548   Starr, Frederick A., 1858-1963

        Congo recordings at US-BLu. Entry in *section 1*.

4549   Starr, Saul

        Over 100,000 items of American sheet music, some bought, some donated by Bernardo Mendel (**4147**), now at US-BLl. **Albrecht**; *Amerigrove*.

4550   Stearns, Marshall Winslow

        Jazz collection transferred to US-BNu. *Amerigrove*.

4551   Stebbins, George C., 1846-1945

        Memorial collection of gospel-song materials organized by the Rev. J. B. Clayton at US-Wca. *RAMH*.

4552   Steffani, Agostino, 1654-1728

        In Propoganda-Archive, Rome.

4553   Stein Collection

        T'ang dynasty manuscripts at GB-Lbl. *NG*-L, p. 764.

4554   Stellfeld, Jean Auguste, 1881-1952

        Ca. 10,000 items, ca. 1600-pre-1800 sold to US-AA. Entries in *section 1*.

4555   Stetson, Mrs. E. G. and **D. C. Burdick**

        2500 theater programs, many for Chicago productions, presented to US-U by Alyene Westall Prehn. *RAMH*.

4556   Steuermann, Eduard, 1892-1964

        At US-LAs. Entry in *section 1*.

4557   Stevens, Richard John Samuel, 1757-1837

        Much of the collection acquired in 1872 by GB-Lam; diaries and other archives are at GB-Cpl. **Albrecht**; **Penney**, p. 542. Entry in *section 1*.

4558   Stevens, William Bacon, 1815-87

        30,000 religious books, mostly liturgical works formerly in the Protestant Episcopal Church in Philadelphia, Pennsylvania, now at South Bend, Indiana, University of Notre Dame.

4559   Stiedry-Wagner, Erika, and **Fritz Stiedry,** 1883-1968

        Bequest to US-LAs. Entry in *section 1*.

4560 **Stiehl, Heinrich,** 1829-86
Bequest of 16th-century works to D-LÜh. *NG*-L, p. 754.

4561 **Stillie, Thomas L.,** d. 1883
Bequest (chiefly operas) to GB-Gu. **Penney,** p. 238.

4562 **Stock, Frederick A.,** 1872-1942
Acquired by US-CU in 1941. *Grove* 5:210.

4563 **Stock, Walter Henry,** 1905-93
At GB-Lam. Entry in *section 1*.

4564 **Stoelzer, Ernst Richard,** 1864-1947
At Adelphi University. Entry in *section 1*.

4565 **Stolberg-Wernigerödische Bibliothek**
Collection at D-WER. Entries in *section 1*.

4566 **Stolze, H. W.,** d. 1863
At D-Celle, Kirchenministeriat-Bibliothek. *Grove* 5:174.

4567 **Stonborough, Jerome**
Acquired Brahms manuscripts from Wilhelm His in 1927. Usually—and wrongly—considered part of the Wittgenstein collection. The collection was sold to US-Wc by Stonborough's heirs in the 1940s. See George S. Bozarth, "The First Generation of Brahms Manuscript Collectors," in *section 1* under Wittgenstein (**2886**).

4568 **Stone, Jacob**
18th-century manuscript scores (Purcell, Croft, Handel, et al.) presented to EIRE-Dm in 1924. *NG*-L, p. 769.

4569 **Stradivari, Antonio,** d. 1737
Nachlass at Museo "Ala Ponzone," Cremona. Entry in *section 1*.

4570 **Strange, Harold**
Collection of Africana at Johannesburg, South Africa, Public Library. Entries in *section 1*.

4571 **Stratton, George W.,** 1830-1901
At Stratton Free Library and Art Gallery, W. Swanzey, N.H. Entry in *section 1*.

4572 **Straube, Karl,** 1873-1950
Bequest to D-LEb. *NG*-L, p. 746.

4573   Stravinsky, Igor, 1882-1971

> Most now in the Paul Sacher Stiftung in Basel. Entries in *section 1*. Some 200 piano editions at US-U. *RAMH*.

4574   Streit, Sigismund

> At D-Bgk. Entry in *section 1*.

4575   Strohl, Joseph P.

> East European recording labels and artists at US-SB. *Amerigrove*.

4576   Strong, George Templeton, 1856-1948

> At CH-LAcu. Entry in *section 1*.

4577   Strugnell, Alan

> Jazz LPs collection at London Borough Council, Morden. **Penney 4**.

4578   Stuart, John, 3rd Earl of Bute, 1713-92

> Collection of 1215 librettos, mostly Venetian imprints, now at US-LAuc. Entry in *section 1*.

4579   Stupple, David

> Ca. 1000 rhythm and blues 45-rpm recordings at US-BOW. *Amerigrove*.

"Stuttgarter Hofkapelle."   *See entry in section 1*

4580   Subirá, José, 1882-1979

> The Centre de Documentació Musical, Barcelona, was built on his library.

4581   Succi, Emilia

> At I-Baf. Entry in *section 1*.

4582   Swan, Alfred J., 1890-1970

> At US-CHua. Entry in *section 1*.

4583   Sylvester, Stephen A.

> Sheet music, acoustic recordings, books, and journals at US-HOUr. *RAMH*.

4584   Szigeti, Joseph, 1892-1973

> 200 manuscripts, 2000 editions of music at US-U. *Amerigrove*.

4585   Szirmay-Keczer, Anna

> At CS-Mms. Entries in *section 1*.

4586   Taddei, [? Antonio]

> Collection of 4500 opera librettos plus letters of Jommelli at US-BE. **Bradley**.

4587   **Taneyev, Sergei Ivanovich,** 1856-1915
Music theory collection acquired in 1924 by USSR-Mk. Entry in *section 1.*

4588   **Taphouse, Thomas William,** 1838-1945
123 of 876 lots in the Sotheby sale of 3 July 1905 went to GB-LEc. Entry in *section 1.*

4589   **Tappert, Wilhelm,** 1830-1907
At D-Bds. Entry in *section 1.*

4590   **Tardieu,** [probably **André, Premier,** 1876-1945]
Bequest to F-NI. *NG*-L, p. 741.

4591   **Tardini, Vincenzo,** d. 1903
Library acquired in the 1960s by I-MOa. Entry in *section 1.*

4592   **Taubert, Carl Gottfried Wilhelm,** 1811-91
Bequest to D-Bdso. Entry in *section 1* under **Stockhausen, Julius.** *NG*-L, p. 744.

4593   **Taussig, Otto,** 1888-1969
At S-L and elsewhere. See long annotation under entry in *section 1.*

4594   **Taut, Kurt,** 1888-1939
Bequest to D-LEm. **Benton 2:**139, no. 89.

4595   **Taylor, Archer**
10,000 volumes and tapes at US-ATS. *Amerigrove.*

4596   **Taylor, Edward,** 1784-1863
Some of the collection at GB-Lgc. Most sold in 1863. **Albrecht**; **King,** p. 55.

4597   **Taylor, William Lawrence,** 1829-1910
Ca. 1700 hymnbooks bequeathed in 1910 to GB-A. Entry in *section 1.*

4598   **Tereza Christina Maria, Empress Consort of Pedro II, Emperor of Brazil,** 1822-89
Her royal library, the foundation of the music section of the Biblioteca Nacional, São Paulo, Brazil. Entry in *section 1.*

4599   **Terry, Charles Sanford,** 1864-1936
Bach collection donated in 1937 to GB-Lcm; on loan to GB-Ouf. **King,** p. 146.

4600   **Terry, Léonard,** 1816-82
At B-Lc. Entries in *section 1*.

4601   **Thayer, Alexander Wheelock,** 1817-97
100 volumes donated to US-Bp. **Benton 2:**86, no. 51.

4602   **Thibault, Geneviève, Comtesse de Chambure,** 1902-75
Entries in *section 1*.

4603   **Thibaut, Anton Friedrich Justus,** 1774-1840
At D-Mbs. Entries in *section 1*.

4604   **Thierry-Poux, Olgar,** b. 1838
Bequest to F-Pn. Entry in *section 1*.

4605   **Thilman, Johann Paul**
At D-Dlb. *NG*-L, p. 744.

4606   **Thin, James**
7500 items of hymnology at GB-Enc. **Penney**, p. 214.

4607   **Thomas, Arthur Goring,** 1850-92
At GB-Lcm. **Benton 2:**180, no. 63.

4608   **Thomas, Isaiah,** 1749-1831
Collection of ballads at US-WOa. Entry in *section 1*.

4609   **Thomas, Theodore,** 1825-1905
Part donated to US-Cn, some to US-CU. Entry in *section 1*.

4610   **Thompson, Sir Herbert,** 1859-1944
At Gb-LEbc. **Penney**, p. 350.

4611   **Thompson, T. P.**
New Orleans materials at US-UN. *RAMH*.

4612   **Thomson, Virgil,** 1896-1989
Library now at US-BApi and US-NH, with some also at US-KC. *Amerigrove*.

4613   **Thuille, Ludwig,** 1861-1907
At D-Mmb. **Benton 2:**91, no. 201.

4614   **Thulemeier, Friedrich Wilhelm von**
At D-Bds. Entry in *section 1*.

4615 Thurn und Taxis, Princes

A private library but available to scholars at D-Rtt. See in *section 1* under **Alexander Ferdinand, Fürst zum Thurn und Taxis**.

4616 Thysius, Johan, 1621-53

17th-century lute music collection at NL-Lu. *NG-L*, p. 781.

4617 Tichenor, Trebor Jay

Private collection of ragtime sheet music, piano rolls, trade publications, etc. *RAMH*.

4618 Tinney, Charles H.

Circus items at US-NO. *Amerigrove*.

4619 Tobin, Robert L. B.

Entries in *section 1*.

4620 Törring-Seefeld, Anton von, Count, 1725-1812

Collection supposedly lost but part of a thematic catalog is at D-Mbs. See under **Wilhelm, Herzog in Bayern** in *section 1*. **Albrecht**.

4621 Tokugawa, Yorisada

At J-Tn. Entries in *section 1*.

4622 Tollefsen, Carl H., 1882-1963

4000 items of string chamber music acquired by US-EDu in 1969. (**Albrecht** says purchased, others say a gift; *Amerigrove* does not indicate.) Entry in *section 1*.

4623 Torchi, Luigi, 1858-1920

At I-Bc. *NG-L*, p. 771.

4624 Torello, Anton, 1884-1959

Music for contrabass in manuscript at US-PHci. Entry in *section 1*.

4625 Torrefranca, Fausto, 1883-1955

At I-Vc. Entry in *section 1*.

4626 Toulouse, Louis Alexandre, Comte de, 1678-1737

At one time at GB-T; later F-Pc. Many entries in *section 1*.

4627 Tovey, Sir Donald Francis, 1875-1940

Bequeathed to GB-Er in 1940. **King**, p. 88.

4628   Trefusis, Lady Mary

> At Royal School of Church Music, Addington. **Davies**.

4629   Trend, John Brand, 1887-1958

> Transcriptions of Spanish music at GB-Cpl.   See under **Dent, Edward Joseph** in *section 1*.

4630   Tretzsch, Rudolph, 1905-81

> Collection part of Primrose International Viola Archive at US-PRV.

4631   Trolda, Emilián, 1871-1949

> At CS-Pnm. Entry in *section 1*.

4632   Tronchi, Aurelio

> Bequest to I-PCcon. **Bequest 3:**235, no. 275.

4633   Tucher von Simmelsdorf, Christian Karl Gottlieb, Freiherr von, 1798-1877

> At D-LM. Entry in *section 1*.

4634   Turnbull, Robert

> At GB-Gm. **Benton 2:**174, no. 43.

4635   Turnovsky, Fred

> Collection at NZ-Wt. *Fontes* 39 (1922): 226n.

4636   Tuthill, Burnet Corwin, 1888-1982

> 2000 manuscripts and printed editions of clarinet music at US-BP. *Amerigrove*.

4637   Tyson, Alan, 1926-2000

> Private collection in London, GB-LTyson. **Albrecht**.

4638   Udbye, Odd, d. 1960

> At N-Oum. *NG*-L, p. 782.

4639   Uhrovec Collection

> Songs and dances of the year 1730 at CS-Mms. Entries in *section 1*.

4640   Unger, Max

> Acquired in 1961 by D-BNba. Entry in *section 1*.

4641   Uphagen, Jan

> At PL-GD. **Benton 5:**127, no. 5.

4642   Upton, George Putnam, 1834-1919

> Donated by his widow in 1920 to US-Cn. **Benton 1:**104, no. 95.

4643   Urspruch, Anton, 1850-1907
> Bequeathed to D-F. **Benton 2:**63, no. 86.

4644   Ursprung, Otto, 1879-1960
> Bequeathed to D-Mms. **Benton 2:**91, no. 199.

4645   Valle, Anselmo Gonzalez del'
> At E-Bim. *NG*-L, p. 788.

4646   Valva, Fred D.
> 139 boxes of scores for silent-film accompaniments now at US-PRV. *RAMH.*

4647   Van Vactor, David, b. 1906
> 935 recordings, more than 1800 books and scores at US-KN. Entry in *section 1.*

4648   Van Vechten, Carl, 1880-1964
> Gershwin collection at US-NA. Entry in *section 1.*

4649   Vatielli, Francesco, 1876-1946
> At I-Bc. *NG*-L, p. 771.

4650   Vatke, Frau Prof.
> At D-Bds. Entry in *section 1.*

4651   Vautier, Félix Abel, 1794-1863
> 19th-century scores at F-LYm. Entry in *section 1.*

4652   Venturi, Antonio
> At Montecatini-Terme, Pistoia. Entry in *section 1.*

4653   Verhulst, Johannes, 1816-91
> At NL-DHgm. Entry in *section 1.*

4654   Vernon,   , Lord
> Ca. 500 pieces of Italian music given to GB-Lbl. *Grove 5.*

4655   Vesper, O   M
> Gift of 375 anthems basis of collection at US-Oa. *Amerigrove.*

4656   Vessella, Alessandro, 1860-1929
> At I-Ria. **Benton 3:**253, no. 321.

Vianna da Motta, José, 1868-1948.   *See* **Da Motta, José Vianna**

Vila Viçosa.   *See under* **João IV, King of Portugal**

4657   Vincent, Alexandre Joseph Hydulphe, 1797-1868
At F-MEL. Entry in *section 1.*

4658   Vincent, G. Robert
Voice collection at Michigan State University, East Lansing. Entry in *section 1.*

4659   Vitry, Henry
Works on music theater at F-MIR. **Benton 2**:96, no. 89.

4660   Vogeleis, Martin, Abbé, 1861-1930
Bequeathed to F-SEL in 1930. **Benton 3**:123, no. 152.

4661   Vogt, Gustave, 1781-1870
Some pieces in autograph at US-NYpm. Entry in *section 1.*

4662   Volckmar, [Wilhelm Valentin, 1812-87?]
Bequeathed to D-Kl. **Benton 2**:77, no. 143.

4663   Volkmann, Robert, 1815-83
At D-Dlb. Entry in *section 1.*

4664   Vollmer,
Bequeathed to D-Bmm. *NG*-L, p. 744.

4665   Volontè, Francesco
At I-Mcap(d). Entry in *section 1.*

4666   Voormolen, Alexander, b. 1895
At NL-DHgm. (Gleich in Grasberger Festschrift)

4667   Vose, Edwin
1200 pieces of sheet music and 3000 recordings at US-CA. *Amerigrove.*

4668   Voss-Buch, Carl Otto Friedrich von, Count
Collection, including 250 volumes of manuscripts, given to D-Bds in 1851.
Albrecht.

4669   Voto, Alfred de
Piano works at US-BRc. *Amerigrove.*

4670   Wackerbarth, Athanasius Francis Diedrich, 1813-84
At S-Uu. Entries in *section 1.*

4671   Wagener, Richard

> Donation to D-Bds, including 45 autograph manuscripts; rest of collection bought by B-Bc in 1902. Entries in *section 1*.

4672   Wagner, Eugene

> 16th-17th century church music to F-Sm. **Benton 3**:125, no. 156.

4673   Wagner, Franz Andrä (administrator of the estate of Carl Mozart)

> Donated to A-Sm by Hans P. Wertitsch. See *section 1* under **Wertitsch**.

4674   Wagner, Rudolf

> A bequest to D-Mms; also to D-Nst. **Benton 2**:91, no. 199.

4675   Waldburg-Zeil, Georg von, Graf zu Zeil und Trauchburg

> Thematic catalog of the collection, 1767-ca. 1786, at Fürstlich Waldburg-Zeil'sches Gesamtarchiv. Brook (**379**); **Albrecht**. Entry in *section 1*.

4676   Waldstein, Ferdinand, Count, 1762-1823

> Now at CS-Pnm and CS-MH. Entry in *section 1*.

4677   Waley, S   W

> At GB-Lcm. *Grove 5*:186.

4678   Walker, Ernest, 1870-1949

> Bequeathed to GB-Ouf. **Penney**, p. 464.

4679   Walker-Hill, Helen

> Collection of music by African-American women composers at US-BO.

4680   Wallenstein, Alfred, 1898-1983

> Performance library of radio station WOR now at US-CP. *Amerigrove*.

4681   Wallfisch, Ernst, 1920-79

> Collection a part of Primrose International Viola Archive at US-PRV.

4682   Wallraf, Franz Ferdinand, d. 1824

> Acquired in 1824 by D-KNu. Entry in *section 1*.

4683   Ward, John Milton, b. 1917

> Ethnomusicological materials deposited at US-CA. *Amerigrove*.

4684   Warner, Frank and **Anne**

> Private collection of traditional folksongs and related books, correspondence, photos, and ephemera. *RAMH*.

4685   Warrington, James, 1841-1915
"Legendary library." Collection merged with that of Silas K. Paine and W. S. Pratt at US-HM purchased in 1975 by US-ATet. About 8800 titles in the collection. Entry in *section 1*.

4686   Warshaw, Isadore
Business Americana, including music-related materials at US-Wsi. *RAMH.*

4687   Washington Family
Now at US-ALX. Entry in *section 1*.

4688   Watson, Henry, 1846-1911
Gave 16,700 volumes to GB-Mp in 1902 and added to it until his death. Entries in *section 1*.

4689   Wauvermans de Francquen
Bequeathed to B-Bc. Entry in *section 1*.

4690   Weber, Carl Maria von, 1786-1826
Bequeathed to D-Bds. Entry in *section 1*.

4691   Weckerlin, Jean Baptiste Théodore, 1821-1910**; Patrice Coirault**
At F-Pn. Entry in *section 1*.

4692   Weinmann, Alexander, b. 1901, and **Ignaz,** 1897-1976
Joint collection now at US-DMu.

4693   Weinmann, Karl, 1873-1929
Some holdings bequeathed to Proske Bibliothek, D-Rp.

4694   Weiss, Paul
Beethoveniana to GB-Er. **Penney,** p. 315.

4695   Weiss, W   H
At GB-Cpl. *NG*-L, p. 759.

4696   Wellesz, Egon, 1885-1974
Byzantine study materials at US-Bm. *Amerigrove.*

4697   Wendell, Evert J.
Sheet music at US-CAh. *RAMH.*

4698   Wenster, Emanuel, 1785-1856
Given to S-L, 1832-56.

4699 **Werdenstein, Johann George von** (16th century)

Manuscripts and printed works given in 1594 through Wilhelm, Herzog von Bayern (**2863**). In D-Mbn.

4700 **Werner, Arno,** 1865-1955

At D-HAu and D-WRh. *NG*-L, pp. 746 and 748. **Benton 2**:148, no. 135, says another bequest to D-WRiv!

4701 **Werner, Benedict**

Bequest to D-FS in 1827. **Benton 2**:65, no. 90.

4702 **Wertitsch, Hans P.**

Donated from the estate of Franz André Wagner materials of Carl Mozart (1784-1858) to A-Sm in 1986. Entries in *section 1*.

4703 **Westmoreland, [? Francis William Henry, 12th Earl of,** 1825-91]

At GB-Lam. **Benton 2**:180, no. 62.

4704 **Weyse, Christoph Ernst Friedrich,** 1774-1842

Bequeathed to DK-Kk. Entry in *section 1*.

4705 **White, E. H.**

At GB-Lcs. **Benton 2**:181, no. 69.

4706 **White, John G.**

Ballads and songs at US-CLp and US-CLwr. Entry in *section 1*.

4707 **White, Robert**

Scottish ballads and songs at GB-NTp. Entry in *section 1*.

4708 **Whiteman, Paul,** 1890-1967

3500 original volumes and arrangements, 2000 pieces of sheet music at US-WI.

4709 **Whittaker, W   G**

At GB-Gu. *NG*-L, p. 762.

4710 **Whittall, Gertrude Clark,** 1867-1965

At US-Wc. Entry in *section 1*.

4711 **Whitworth, ?**

Bequest of organ music to Sheffield Library. **Penney 4**.

4712 **Wiel, Taddeo,** 1849-1920

Bequeathed to I-Vc. *NG*-L, p. 780.

Wiesentheid.   *See under* **Schönborn-Wiesentheid**

4713   **Wight, Osborne, Rev.,** d. 1800

Acquired collection of Thomas Hammond (d. 1662; **1168**, *section 1*), also items from the Philip Hayes collection (**1215**, *section 1*). Presented materials to GB-Ob, others to GB-Lbl and GB-Och. **Albrecht**; **Penney**, p. 465.

4714   **Wighton, Andrew John,** 1804-66

At GB-DU. Entry in *section 1*.

4715   **Wilkins, Edward Raymond Sanger,** 1891-1971

Sheet music at US-CAh. *RAMH.*

4716   **William V, Herzog von Bavaria**

Collection at D-Mbs. **Benton 2**:88, no. 191.

4717   **William V, Prince of Orange,** 1748-1806

At "Maison Royale des Pays-Bas," NL-DHa. Entry in *section 1*.

4718   **Williams Wynn, Watkins, Sir, 4th Baronet,** 1749-89

Some of his collection now at US-NBu. Entry in *section 1*.

4719   **Wilsing, Friedrich Eduard**

Manuscripts from collections of J. N. Mempell and Max Seiffert eventually went to D-LEm and D-B.   See under **Mempell** in *section 1*.

4720   **Wilson, Earl**

Sold 1,000 orchestral scores and part to US-LAu. *Amerigrove.*

4721   **Wilson, Meredith**

Over 250,000 sheet music items, cylinder and 78 rpm recordings now at US-LAu.

4722   **Wilt, Henry C.**

Collection at US-SE. **Bradley**.

4723   **Wimmer, Archabbat Boniface,** 1809-87

Left his library to US-LT. **Benton 1**:142, no. 194.

4724   **Windsor, J   M**

At GB-Lcm. *Grove 5*, p. 186.

4725   **Windt, Clara de**

Sheet music at US-CAh. *RAMH.*

4726   **Winterfeld, Carl Georg August Vivigens von,** 1784-1852

His sons gave 110 volumes to D-Bds in 1885; rest of library dispersed at sale. Entry in *section 1.*

4727   **Witmark, Isidore,** 1871-1941

Manuscript scores and letters to American publishers from song composers at US-NYcu. Entry in *section 1.*

4728   **Witt, Franz Xaver,** 1834-88

Bequeathed in part to Proske Bibliothek (D-Rp; **2163** in *section 1*).

Witteczek-Spaun'sche Schubert-Sammlung.   *See under* **Schubert, Ferdinand**

4729   **Wittelsbach Family**

Part of collection at D-Mbn, part at D-Mbs. Entries in *section 1.*

4730   **Witten, Laurence C.**

Annual gifts, plus rare 19th-20th century vocal recordings from the George Keating and Albert Wolf collections to US-NH. *Amerigrove.*

4731   **Wittenhorst-Sonsfeldt, Friedrich Otto von,** 1678-1755

Collection bequeathed to Freiherr von Fürstenberg-Herdringen and located for a long time at D-Pa. It was eventually returned to Schloss Herdringen in 1970. **Albrecht.** Entry in *section 1.*

4732   **Wittgenstein, Paul,** 1887-1961

Some autograph manuscripts to US-NYp. Entry in *section 1* under **Wittgenstein, Karl**.

4733   **Wohlberg, Max,** b. 1909

Materials from his library. including 600 volumes of Yiddish and Hebrew songs and books at US-NYjts. *RAMH.*

4734   **Wolf, Heinrich**

At DNBsb. *NG*-L, p. 756.

4735   **Wolff Bequest**

To D-Bdso. **Benton 2**:120, no. 14.

4736   **Wolffheim, Werner Joachim,** 1877-1930

US-Cn bought some 17th-18th century scores at famous sale in 1929. Entries in *section 1.*

4737   **Wolhowe, Fred**

Private collection presented to Luther College, Decorah, Iowa (*RAMH*) includes 40,000 pieces of sheet music, 6000 dance band orchestrations, folios, catalogs, and 25,000 78 rpm discs of popular, folk, and classical music, 1900-45.

4738   Wollong, Ernst
>   At D-RUl. **Benton 2**:144, no. 117.

4739   Wollonz, Caroline Louise and **Ernst**
>   At D-RUl. *NG*-L, p. 747.

4740   Wolstenholme, William
>   Scores and original manuscripts (his own?) at Blackburn District Central
>   Library (UK). **Penney**, p. 341.

4741   Wood, Sir Henry Joseph, 1869-1944
>   Library acquired by GB-Lam, 1938; some autographs went to GB-Lbl.
>   **Penney**, p. 542; **Albrecht**.

4742   Woodbury, Isaac Baker, 1819-58
>   60,000 pieces of sheet music plus tunebooks and hymnals at US-KC.
>   *Amerigrove*.

4743   Wooldridge, Warren
>   American recordings at US-Lu. *Amerigrove*.

4744   Wright, Edith A.
>   American sheet music sold to US-PHf. **Benton 1**:193, no. 319.

4745   Würthmann, Friedrich, ca. 1807-64
>   At D-Mbs. **Münster**.

4746   Wurlitzer, Helen V. B. and **Rudolph H.,** 1873-1948
>   Chamber music donated to US-CIu. *Amerigrove*.

4747   Wurzbach, Constantin, Ritter von Tannenberg, 1818-93
>   Large portion at A-Wst. Entry in *section 1*.

4748   Wyman, ?
>   Ballad collection at US-New London, Connecticut, Connecticut College.
>   **Bradley**.

4749   Yaffe, Selomoh
>   Donated to IL-Hml. Entry in *section 1*.

4750   Yoder, Don
>   Religious tunebook collection to US-CHH. *Amerigrove*.

4751   Young, Bernard A. and **Morris N.**
>   At US-PRu. Entries in *section 1*.

4752 **Yusopov, Nikolai Borisovich,** 1827-91
Collection now in USSR-Lsc. **Albrecht**.

4753 **Zacheis, Les**
Jazz collection given to US-B. Entry in *section 1*.

4754 **Zavertal, Venceslao Hugo,** d. 1899; **Ladislao,** 1849-1942
Collection donated to GB-Gu in 1934 by son, Ladislao. Entry in *section 1*.

4755 **Zeller, K.**
Religious works at D-HAu. *Grove 5*:173.

4756 **Zelter, Carl Friedrich,** 1758-1823
Bequeathed to D-DÜK. *NG*-L, p. 751.

4757 **Zenettis, Leopold von**
At A-Wn. Entry in *section 1*.

4758 **Zeyringer, Franz,** 1920-
Collection a part of the Primrose International Viola Archive at US-PRV.

4759 **Ziehrer, C M**
At A-Wn. Entry in *section 1*.

4760 **Zirner, Ludwig**
450 opera scores and related materials now at US-U. *RAMH*.

4761 **Zweers, Bernard,** 1854-1924
At NL-DHgm. **Gleich**.

4762 **Zweig, Stefan**
Bequeathed to GB-Lbl. Entries in *section 1*.

ADDENDA

Some of these are simply oversights, but most result from a second scanning of the principal secondary sources noted earlier in this book. A number of collections mentioned by **Benton**, **Bradley**, *RAMH*, and others seemed at first study unworthy of inclusion. A second run-through raised second thoughts and a decision to err on the side of including too many rather than too few. For many such items, the size, caliber, and character of the collections remain obscure. Many others are principally collections of recordings or popular music not thought to be important at first. Now, perhaps they belong.

And, of course, since the initial compilation of section 3, bequests and inheritance of estates by libraries have taken place and need to be recorded. Whatever their quality or importance, all here are fully analyzed in the over-all Index.

4763   Allanson, Clifford A.

A private collection: 15,000 music items, 1850-1970, plus hymnals, popular orchestrations, recordings, including 600 wax cylinders and 5000 78s. *RAMH*.

4764   Berdes, Jane L.

46,000 items, many bearing on the *ospedali* of Vienna, now at US-DMu.

4765   Callaerts, Joseph

At B-Ak according to **Benton**.

4766   Connick, Harris D. H.

Part of a 9000-item opera score collection now at US-CU. **Bradley.**

4767   Day, Henry

Collection of hymnology, linguistics and ecclesiastical law was donated in 1908 to US-NYts.

4768   Dye, William Seddinger

Posters of Philadelphia musical events and those in other venues, 1836-1900 now at US-UP. *RAMH*.

4769   Ettel, Mrs. Michael F.

Private collection of popular sheet music, 1820-60, 1200 with lithographed wrappers. *RAMH*.

4770   Evans, David H. and **Cheryl T.**

Private collection of 30,000 recordings, including 200 cylinders, several thousand 78s, mostly popular, folk, country, rock and roll. Several thousand LPs of the same character. See *RAMH*, no. 1442, for details.

4771   Haden, Walter Darrell

Huge private collection of recordings of popular, country, classical and ethnic music on 78s, 45s, LPs, and transcriptions, plus sheet music and songbooks, including hymnals, gospel and country and western folios. *RAMH.*

4772   Hesbacher, Peters

Private collection of 42,000 disc recordings ". . . comprising a complete collection of single discs on the *Billboard* magazine weekly charts. . . . " *RAMH.*

4773   Horton, Zilphia

Private folk music collection, including social-protest songs and recordings, now at US-Nashville, Tennessee, State Library and Archives.

4774   Jasen, David A.

Private collection of popular American music, including 10,000 items of sheet music; 2500 78 rpm ragtime discs; 1500 piano rolls, biographical materials, catalogs, books, and journals. Entries in *section 1.*

4775   Kennis, W. -J. -J.

Now at B-Ak, according to **Benton**.

4776   Kienzel, Wilhelm, 1857-1941

A bequest to A-Wst, according to **Benton 2**:59.

4777   Kierney, Paul

Private collection of recordings: 3000 78s, 1825-35, 50 cylinders, mostly jazz, ethnic, and country music. *RAMH.*

4778   Kincaid, William, 1895-1967

Library of flute music now at US-PHci.

4779   Krummel, Donald W., b. 1929

Private collection of research materials on music printing, publishing, and publishers' plate numbers; also 5000 items of sheet music.

4780   Marchot, ?

Now at B-Bc, according to **Benton 2**:15.

4781   Mare, Frank

Private collection of 5500 78 rpm discs of American country music and rural blues. *RAMH.*

4782 Mayfield, Lyle and **Doris**

Private collection of Illinois folk music, recordings, and textual materials. *RAMH*.

4783 Merrill, William Stetson

Collection of 83,000 items many relating to Boston and Massachusetts musical activities now at US-CN. *RAMH*.

4784 Mikhashoff, Yvar, 1941-93

1300 recordings, 77 posters, over a thousand scores of New Music, now at US-BUu. Inventory in progress.

4785 Millöcker, Karl, 1842-99

A bequest to A-Wst, according to **Benton 2**:59.

4786 Montbéliard, George

Collection now at (?) F-MD. Entry in *section 1*.

4787 Montgomery, Michael

Private collection of 2000 U.S. piano rolls, mainly popular, plus related collections of piano-roll catalogs, and a sheet music collection. *RAMH*.

4788 Müller, Adolf, 1801-86

A bequest to A-Wst. Entry in *section 1*.

4789 Onegin, Sigrid

Opera scores, annotated, and art songs at US-Sweet Briar, Virginia, Sweet Briar College. *RAMH*.

4790 Powell, Reuben

Private collection including that of Robert O. Hyland of early country music on tape, hundreds of hours of festivals, broadcasts, and transcriptions from 78 rpm discs. Will go to Berea College, Kentucky, according to *RAMH*.

4791 Schlick, Lawrence A.

Private collection of early catalogs from record companies, and early recordings, including 5000 cylinders. *RAMH*.

4792 Spiker, Samuel Heinrich

Part of the former library at the Joachimsthalsches Gymnasium, now at D-Bds. NG 10:743.

4793 Strauss, Johann

Bequest to A-Wst, according to **Benton 2**:59.

4794   Suppé, Franz von, 1820-95

> Bequest to A-Wst, according to **Benton** 2:59.

4795   Westphal, J. J. H.

> Collection now at B-Bc, includes many works by Bach's sons. Entry in *section 1.*

4796   Wolfe, Charles

> Private collection of materials mostly related to country and traditional music. *RAMH.*

Section 4

Private Collections Now in Institutions
(arranged by RISM sigla)

Not included here are collections in libraries and archives which center on a collector's personal effects—his or her manuscripts, compositions, correspondence, programs of performances of the collector's works, photographs, reviews, recordings, personal papers, household accounts, and other such accumulated materials. In the United States, many collections like these can be located in some Sources cited (pp. xxv-xxxviii), more especially in *RAMH* and the Benton directories. The following is a typical description (paraphrased): "Miss Global Singer's collection, including x linear feet of her correspondence with x, xx, and xxx (with an inventory); press clippings, books, memorabilia, scrapbooks of her career, pictures and portraits, miscellaneous sheet music, etc."

Miss Singer was not, in the sense of this book, a true "collector," but a performer with a normal performer's ego. The same criteria rule out the collection of 10,000 vocal and violin-music editions used by a teacher of violin and coach of vocal ensembles in a U.S. university collection. And the collection of John Cage manuscripts is now at Northwestern University!

All of these names appear in the general Index and will lead the user to citations describing the nature of the collections deposited.

Because many collections now reside in institutions which do not appear in lists arranged by official RISM sigla, the following have been "invented." They follow RISM criteria, and are proceeded by an asterisk (*).

*AUS-Mg	Melbourne, Grainger Museum
*A-Wsc	Wien, Arnold Schönberg Center
*BR-Sa	São Paulo, Biblioteca nacional
*CS-Pd	Prague, Dobrovského narodní muzeum
*D-CEk	Celle, Kirchenministeriat-Bibliothek
*D-Ds	Dresden, Sächsischen Hof- und Justizrates
*D-Gm	Gmunden, Kammerhof-Museum
*D-Ko	Königsberg, Staats- und Universitäts-Bibliothek
*D-Sc	Schlobitten Castle

*E-B	Barcelona, Centre de documentación musical
*EIR-Bep	Belfast Public Libraries
*EIR-Beq	Belfast, Queen's University
*GB-A	Addington, Royal School of Church Music
*GB-Ad	Addiscombe, Surrey, Royal School of Church Music
*GB-Bu	Burnely, Central Public Library
*GB-C	Wolfson Cambridge, Wolfson Collection
*GB-Ha	Hastings Area Library
*GB-K	Knole Castle
*GB-LEg	Leicester, Goldsmith Library
*GB-LEu	Leicester, University of
*GB-Lg	London, Goldsmith's College
*GB-Lh	London, Horniman Museum
*GB-Lrsc	London, Royal School of Church Music
*GB-Mm	London, Borough of Merton, Morden District Library
*GB-LSa	London, Sadler's Wells Theatre
*GB-Nt	Nottinghamshire County Library
*GB-SH	Sheffield, Central Library
*I-Rp	Rome, Propaganda-Archive
*I-PSm	Pistoia, Montecatini-Terme
*N-H	Hamar, Folkebibliotek
*US-ATh	Atlanta, Georgia, Historical Society
*US-BAm	Baltimore, Maryland, Morgan State College
*US-BLU	Blue Hill, Maine, Kneisel Hall
*US-CHC	Charleston, South Carolina, College of
*US-D	Decorah, Iowa, Luther College
*US-EL	East Lansing, Michigan, Michigan State University
*US-EM	Emporia, Kansas, Emporia State University
*US-GAa	Garden City, New York, Adelphi University
*US-GBc	Gettysburg, Pennsylvania, Gettysburg College
*US-G	Mayfield, Greenfield, Illinois, private collection
*US-Hss	Hartford, Connecticut, Hartford Seminary Foundation
*US-HOU	Houston, Texas, Houston University
*US-HOUt	Houston, Texas, Texas Southern University
*US-Jm	Jackson, Mississippi, Millsaps College
*US-Law	Laramie, Wyoming, University of Wyoming
*US-LI	Liberty, Missouri, William Jewell College
*US-LIa	Little Rock, Arkansas, Art Center
*US-Log	Logan, Utah, Utah State University
*US-MUR	Murfreesboro, Tennessee, Middle Tennessee State University
*US-Nc	New London, Connecticut, Connecticut College
*US-NTC	Northridge, California, California State University Northridge
*US-Ro	Rochester, Michigan, Oakland University
*US-SPAm	St. Paul, Minnesota, Macalester College
*US-SPAp	St. Paul, Minnesota, Public Library
*US-SPE	St. Peter, Minnesota, Gustavus Adolphus College
*US-SAp	San Antonio, Texas, Public Library
*US-SBp	Santa Barbara, California, Public Library
*US-SOb	South Bend, Indiana, University of Notre Dame
*US-SPc	Spartanburg, South Carolina, Converse College

*US-Tl Toledo, Ohio, Toledo-Lucas County Library
*US-UNm University, Mississippi, University of Mississippi, Blues Archive
*US-VB Virginia Beach, Virginia, CBN University
*US-Wn Washington, D.C., National Museum of American History
*US-WSa West Swanzey, New Hampshire, Stratton Free Library and Art Gallery

AUSTRIA

A-Gk (h) **Graz, Hochschule (ehem. Akademie) für Musik und Darstellende Kunst und Landesmusikschule**
    Bischoff, Ferdinand
    Lannoy, Henrich Edoard Joseph, Freiherr von

A-Sd **Salzburg, Dom-Musikarchiv**
    Baroni-Cavalcabò, Mrs. Julie

A-Sm **Salzburg, Mozarteum, Bibliotheca Mozartiana**
    Baroni-Cavalcabò, Mrs. Julie
    Mozart, Carl
    Mozart, Wolfgang Amadeus
    Oldman, Cecil Bernard
    Wagner, Franz Andrä
    Wertitsch, Hans P.

A-Smi **Salzburg, Musikwissenschaftliches Institut der Universität**
    Deutsch, Otto Erich
    Engländer, Richard
    Orel, Alfred

A-SH **Solbad Hall, Franziskaner-Kloster Solbad Hall in Tyrol, Archiv und Bibliothek**
    Hartmann, P.

A-Wgm **Wien, Gesellschaft der Musikfreunde**
    Brahms, Johannes
    Dumba, Nicolaus
    Gerber, Ernst Ludwig
    Petter, Gustav
    Rudolph, Johann Rainer, Erzherzog
    Schmidt, Franz
    Schubert, Ferdinand
    Spaun, Josef, Freiherr von

A-Wn **Wien, Österreichische Nationalbibliothek. Musiksammlung**
    Ambros, August Wilhelm
    Dermota, Edward Joseph
    Dumba, Nicolaus
    Franz II, 1768-1835, and Franz Joseph, 1848-1916, Emperors of Austria
    Fugger Family

Hoboken, Anthony von
Kiesewetter, Raphael Georg
Lannoy, Heinrich Edoard Joseph, Freiherr von
Martini, Padre Giovanni Battista
Marx, Joseph
Schreker, Franz
Sonnleithner, Joseph von
Zenettis, Leopold von
Ziehrer, C. M.

*A-Wsc   **Wien, Arnold Schönberg Center**
Schoenberg, Arnold

A-Wst   **Wien, Stadtbibliothek, Musiksammlung**
Grillparzer, Franz
Kienzel, Wilhelm
Millöcker, Karl
Müller, Adolf
Strauss, Johann
Suppé, Franz von
Wurzbach, Constantin, Ritter von Tannenberg

AUSTRALIA

AUS-CAnl   **Canberra, National Library of Australia**
Burgis, Peter
Hevingham-Root, Laurie
Nan Kivell, Rex de Charambac

*AUS-Mg   **Melbourne, Grainger Museum**
Marshall-Hall, George William Louis

AUS-NLwm   **Nedlands, Wigmore Music Library, University of Western Australia**
Grainger, Percy Aldridge

AUS-Sml   **Sidney, Fisher Library, University of Sydney**
Dalley-Scarlett, Robert

BELGIQUE

B-Ak   **Antwerp, O. L. Vrouw-Kathedraal, Archief**
Callaerts, Joseph
Kennis, W. J. J.

B-Bc   **Brussels, Conservatoire Royal de Musique, Bibliothèque**
Colin, Eugène
Hollenfeltz, ?
Marchot, ?
Piron [probably Alexis]
Wagener, Richard
Wauvermans de Francquen
Westphal, J. J. H.

B-BR   **Brussels, Bibliothèque Royale Albert 1ᵉʳ**
Burgundy, Dukes of
Coussemaker, Edward deFétis, François-Joseph
Hulthem, Charles von
Landsberg, Ludwig
Margaretha of Austria

B-Gu   **Ghent, Rijksuniversiteit, Centrale Bibliothek**
Du Bus, François

B-Lc   **Liège, Conservatoire Royal de Musique, Bibliothèque**
Brigode de Kemlandt Family
Debroux, Joseph
Grètry, André Ernest Modeste
Terry, Léonard

B-M   **Mons, Conservatoire Royal de Musique, Bibliothèque**
Closson, Ernest

BRAZIL

BR-Rn   **Rio de Janeiro, Biblioteca Nacional**
Barbosa Machado, Diego
Carvalho, Abrahãode

*BR-Sa   **São Paulo, Biblioteca Nacional**
Tereza Christina Maria, Empress, Consort of Pedro II

CANADA

C-Mm   **Montreal, McGill University, Redpath Library**
Edelberg, David

C-On   **Ottawa, National Library of Canada**
Champagne, Claude
Scholes, Percy Alfred

C-Sau   **Sackville, Mount Allison University Library**
Archibald, Mary Mellish

C-TU   **Toronto, University of Toronto, Edward Johnson Music Library**
Cobbett, Walter William
Fisher, Sidney Thomson

SWITZERLAND

CH-BSacher   **Basel, private collection of Paul Sacher**
Stravinsky, Igor

CH-Bu   **Burgdorf, Stadtbibliothek**
Amerbach, Bonifacius
Geigy-Hagenbach, Karl
Sarasin, Lucas

CH-E   **Einsiedeln, Kloster, Musikbibliothek**
Pearsall, Robert Lucas de

CH-Gpu   **Genève, Bibliothèque publique et universitaire**
Mooser, Robert Aloys

CH-LAcu   **Lausanne, Bibliothèque cantonale et universitaire**
Olivier, Francois
Reichel, Bernard
Sérieyx, Auguste
Strong, George Templeton

CH-N   **Neuchâtel, Bibliothèque publique de la Ville**
Bover, Felix
Peyrou, Pierre Alexandre du
Sauret, Elisabeth (Mrs. Harry Edwards)

CH-Zz   **Zürich, Zentralbibliothek, Kantons-, Stadt- und Universitätsbibliothek**
Jacobi, Erwin Ruben
Päuler, Bernhard

CZECHOSLOVAKIA (now Czech Republic, Slovakia)

CS-BA   **Bakov nach Jizerou, Pobocka Okresního archivu v Mladé Boleslavi**
Fibiger, August
Linek, J. I.

CS-BER   **Beroun, Okresní archív**
Podleská-Batková, Tekla
Seydl, Josef Antonin

CS-Bm   **Brno, Moravské múzeum, Ústav dejin hudby**
Collalto Family
Helfert, Vladimir

CS-BRsa   **Bratislava, Státný slovenský ústredný archív**
Brunswick (Brunsvik) Family

CS-BRu   **Bratislava, Univerzitná kniznica**
Ruppeldt, Milos

CS-K   **Ceský Krumlov, Státní archív Trebon**
Oetting, C. d'
Oettingen-Baldern, Count Franz Wilhelm von
Philip Karl, Graf zu Oettingen-Wallerstein
Schwarzenberg, Ernst von
Schwarzenberg, Maria Eleonora

CS-KRa   **Kroměříž, Státni zámek a zahrady**
              Colloredo Family
              Liechtenstein-Kastelkorn, Karl, Prince of Olomouc
              Rudolph, Johann Rainer, Erzherzog

CS-KRik   **Krikovlát, Zámecká Knihovna**
              Fürstenberg, Prince [?]
              Sonsfeldt Family

CS-MH   **Mnichovo Hradiste, Mestské muzeum**
              Waldstein, Ferdinand, Count

CS-Mms   **Martin, Matica Slovenská, Literárny archiv**
              Figus, Bystrý, Viliam
              Francise, Miloslav
              Hrdina, Frantisek
              Richter, Ján Jozef
              Szirmay-Keczer, Anna
              Uhrovec Collection

CS-Mnm   **Martin, Slovenské národné múzeum, archív**
              Prileský-Ostrolícky Family

CS-OP   **Opava, Slezské múzeum**
              Skotak, Ondrej

* **CS-Pd**   **Pdoborovského, Narodní muzeum, Dobrovského (Nostická) knihovna**
              Nostits-Rieneck Erwin, Count

CS-Pnm   **Praha, Národni muzeum hudební oddelení**
              Clam-Gallas, Count Christian
              Homolka, E. E.
              Hornik, Andreas
              Hulka, K.
              Kolovrat-Krakovský [Family?]
              Lobkowitz, Prince Joseph Franz (Maximilian)
              Nedbal, Oskar
              Nejedlý, Zdenek
              Pachta, Jan Josef, Count
              Pohl, Jan
              Srb, Josef
              Trolda, Emilián
              Waldstein, Ferdinand, Count

CS-Pu   **Praha, Státní knihovna CSR**
              Destinn, Emmy
              Kubelík, Jan

CS-SO   **Sokolov, Státní archív**
              Krejci, Josef
              Schlesinger, Johann

GERMANY

D-AB   **Augsburg, Verlagsarchiv Böhm & Sohn**
Leining, House of

D-Ahk   **Augsburg, Heilig-Kreuz-Kirche, Dominikanerkloster, Bibliothek**
Mozart, Leopold

D-Af   **Augsburg, Staats- und Stadtbibliothek**
Fugger Family archive

D-AN   **Ansbach, Regierungsbibliothek**
Friedrich, Georg, Markgraf von Ansbach
Leeuwen Boomkamp, ?

D-BB   **Benediktbeuern, Pfarrkirche, Bibliothek**
Koczalsk, Raoul von

D-BE   **Berleburg, Fürstlich Sayn- Wittgenstein-berleburgsche Bibliothek**
Sayn-Wittgenstein, Moritz Casimir I, Graf von Berleburg

D-B   **Berlin, Staatsbibliothek (Stiftung Preussischer Kulturbesitz)**
Anna Amalia, Princess of Prussia
Bokemeyer, Henrich
Busoni, Ferruccio
Forkel, Johann Nikolaus
Mempell, Johann Nicolaus
Österreich, Georg
Preller, Johann Gottlieb
Pretlack, Ludwig Freiherrn von
Seiffert, Max
Wilsing, Friedrich Eduard

D-Bds   **Berlin, Deutsche Staatsbibliothek**
Anna Amalia, Princess of Prussia
André, Johann Anton
Artaria, Karl August
Bokemeyer, Heinrich
Commer, Franz
Fischoff, Joseph
Flade, Ernst
Forkel, Johann Nikolaus
Grasnick, Friedrich August
Hauber, Johann Michael
Hauser, Franz
Jahn, Otto
Kastner, Jean Georges
Kirnberger, Johann Philipp
Landsberg, Ludwig
Menselssohn-Bartholdy, Felix

Meyerbeer, Giacomo
Naue, Johann Friedrich
Nicolai, Otto
Pölchau, Ernest [?] and Georg
Schindler, Anton Felix
Spiker, Samuel Heinrich
Tappert, Wilhelm
Thulemeier, Friedrich Wilhelm von
Vatke, ? , Frau Prof.
Voss-Buch, Carl Otto Friedrich von, Count
Wagener, Richard
Weber, Carl Maria von
Winterfeld, Carl George August Vivigens von

D-Bdso   **Berlin, Bibliothek der deutschen Staatsoper**
Padilla, ?
Pittschau, ?
Taubert, Carl Gottfried Wilhelm
Wolff Bequest

D-Bgk   **Berlin, Bibliothek der Streit'schen Stiftung (Berlinisches Gymnasium zum Grauen Kloster)**
Streit, Sigismond

D-Bmm   **Berlin, Märkisches Museum, Bibliothek**
Doerring [probably Karl Heinrich]
Fontane [Theodore]
Hauptmann, Gerhardt
Hitzig [perhaps Wilhelm]
Hoguet [Michael Francoise?]
Vollmer, ?

D-BN   **Berlin, Nikolaikirche, Bibliothek**
Gehring, Franz Edward

D-Bhm   **Berlin, Staatliche Hochschule für Musik und darstellende Musik**
Joachim, Joseph
Spitta, Philipp

D-BG   **Beuerberg über Wolfratshausen, Stiftskirche, Bibliothek**
Seitz, Alipius

D-BI   **Bielefeld, Städtisches Ratsgymnasium, Bibliothek**
Loebell, J. W.

D-BIR   **Birstein über Wächtersbach, Fürst von Isenburgisches Archiv und Schlossbibliothek**
Isenberg, ? , Fürst

D-BNba **Bonn, Wissenschaftliche Beethovenarchiv**
Bodmer, Hans Conrad Ferdinand
Grundmann, Herbert
Klingemann, Karl
Schindler, Anton Felix
Unger, Max

D-BNms **Bonn, Musikwissenschaftliches Seminar der Universität**
Frimmel, August
Klein, August
Schiedermaier, Ludwig

D-BNu **Bonn, Universitätsbibliothek**
Jahn, Otto
Klein, Christian Benjamin

D-BOCHmi **Bochum, Musikwissenschaftliches Institut der Ruhr-Universität**
Kahl, Walli

D-Bu **Büdingen, Fürstlich Ysenburg- und Büdingsches Archiv und Schlossbibliothek**
Kirschberg, ?

＊**D-CEk** **Celle, Kirchenministeriat-Bibliothek**
Syolze, H. W.

D-Cl **Coburg, Landesbibliothek**
Ebart, Paul von
Hellmuth, Max
Peters-Marquart, Franz
Saxe-Coburg, Dukes of

D-CZ **Clausthal-Zellerfeld, Kirchenbibliothek (Calvörsche Bibliothek)**
Calvör, Calvin

D-DEl **Dessau, Universitäts- und Landesbibliothek Sachasen-Anhalt**
Klughart, August
Schneider, [Johann?] Friedrich

D-DIN **Dinkelsbühl, Bibliothek des Katholischen Pfarramts St. Georg**
Hacker, Fr. X

D-DS **Darmstadt, Hessische Landes- und Hochschulbibliothek**
Anton, Karl (of Mannheim)
Breitkopf, Johann Gottlieb Immanuel
Hauser, Franz
Heiss, H[ermann?]
Kiesewetter, Raphael Georg
Ludwig I von Hessenberg-Darmstadt

D-DT **Detmold, Lippische Landesbibliothek**
Josef von Lessberg, Freiherr

Kruse, Georg Richard
Lortzing, Karl
Schramm [probably Willi]

D-DO   **Donaueschingen, Fürstlich Fürstenbergische Hofbibliothek**
Fürstenberg, Joachim, Egon, Fürst zu

*D-Ds   **Dresden, Sächsischen Hof- und Justizrates**
Örtel, Friedrich Benedeikt

D-Dlb   **Dresden, Sächische Landesbibliothek**
Albert, Friedrich August, King of Saxony
Jacobi, Samuel
Mauersberger, Rudolf
Nicodé, Jean Louis
Reinhold, Otto
Thilman, Johann Paul
Volkmann, Robert

D-DÜK   **Düsseldorf, Goethe-Museum (Kippenberg Stiftung)**
Kippenberg, Anton and Katherine
Zelter, Carl Friedrich

D-DÜl   **Düsseldorf, Universitätsbibliothek**
Heine, Heinrich

D-EF   **Erfurt, Wissenschaftliche Allgemeinbibliothek**
Amplonius de Berka, fl. 1400

D-ERms   **Erlangen, Musikwissenschaftliches Institut der Universität**
Handschin, Jacques

D-ERu   **Erlangen, Universitätsbibliothek**
Friedrich, Georg, Markgraf von Ansbach

D-Es   **Essen, Musikbücherei der Stadtbücherei**
Schlecht, Raimund

D-F   **Frankfurt a.M., Stadt- und Universitätsbibliothek, Musik-und Theater-Abteilung**
    Manskopfisches Museum
Jan, Karl von
Manskopf, Friedrich Nicolas
Neal, Heinrich
Urspruch, Anton

D-Fmi   **Frankfurt a.M., Musikwissenschaftliches Institut der Johann-Wolfgang-von-Goethe**
    Universität
Becker, Georg Horst

D-FRms   **Freiburg i.B., Musikwissenschaftliche Seminar der Universität**
Gurlitt, Willibald
Matthei, Karl

D-FRu   **Freiburg i.B., Universitätsbibliothek**
Brossmer, Alfred Erwin

D-FRva   **Frieburg i.B., Deutsches Volksliedarchiv**
Nötzoldt, Fritz
Riedl, ?

D-FS   **Freising, Dombibliothek**
Werner, Benedict

D-Fsm   **Frankfurt a.M., Bibliothek für neuere Sprachen und Musik**
Rothschild, Carl, Freiherr von
Neal, Heinrich
Urspruch, Anton

D-Fmi   **Frankfurt a.M., Musikwissenschaftliche Institut der Johann-Wolfgang-von-Goethe Universität**
Becker, Georg Horst

D-FUl   **Fulda, Hessische Landesbibliothek**
André, Johann Anton

∗ D-Gm   **Gmunden, Kammerhof-Museum**
Miller Zu Aichholz, Victor and Olga von

D-GOl   **Gotha, Forschungsbibliothek**
Friedrich II, Herzog von Sachsen-Gotha

D-GRu   **Greifswald, Universitätsbibliothek**
Philipp I, Duke of Pomerania

D-Gs   **Göttingen, Niedersächische Staats- und Universitätsbibliothek**
Ludwig, Friedrich

D-Ha   **Hamburg, Staatsarchiv**
Bach, Karl Philip Emanuel

D-HAmi   **Halle/Salle, Sektion Germanistik und Kunstwissenschaften der Martin-Luther-Universität**
Franz, Robert
Rust, Friedrich Wilhelm

D-HAu   **Halle, Salle, Universitäts- und Landesbibliothek Sachsen-Anhalt, Musiksammlung**
Klanert, K.
Werner, Arno
Zeller, K.

D-HL   **Haltenbergstetten, Schloss über Niederstetten**
Hohenlohe-Jagstberg, Fürst

D-Hmi   **Hamburg, Musikwissenschaftliches Institut der Universität**
Spanke, [Hans?]

D-HR   **Harburg über Donauwörth, Fürstlich Oettingen-Wallerstein'sche Bibliothek,**
            Schloss Harburg
Kraft, Ernst, Prince Graf von Oettingen-Wallerstein
Oetting, C. d'
Oettingen-Wallerstein, Fürst
Schaden, Franz Michael von

D-Hs   **Hamburg, Staats- und Universitätsbibliothek, Musikabteilung**
Chrysander, Karl Franz Friedrich
Laude, ?
Mattheson, Johann (lost in WW II)
Preske, ?
Schoelcher, Victor
Schrüber

D-HVsa   **Hannover, Staatsarchiv**
Kestner, Hermann

D-KA   **Karlsruhe, Badische Landesbibliothek, Musikabteilung**
Baumann, Ludwig
Kalliwoda, Johann Wenzel and Wilhelm Dunstan
Keller, Ludwig

D-Kl   **Kassel, Murhard'sche Bibliothek**
Heinrichs, ?
Lewalter, [probably Johann]
Spohr, Louis
Staehle, ?
Volckmar, [Wilhelm Valentin]

D-Kll   **Kiel, Schleswig-Holsteinische Landesbibliothek**
Blome, Count of Salzau
Engelke, Bernhard
Friedrich Emil August, Prince of Schleswig-Holstein
Noer
Kuckei, Max
Lehmann, ?

D-KImi **Kiel, Musikwissenschaftliches Institut der Universität**
Gänge, ?
Mertuis, ? [of Kiel]

D-KIu **Kiel, Universitätsbibliothek**
Bülck, Rudolf

D-KNd **Köln, Erzbischöfliche Diözesanbibliothek**
Leibl, Carl

D-KNh **Köln, Staatliche Hochschule für Musik**
Seuffter, Johanna

D-KNu **Köln, Universitäts- und Stadtbibliothek**
Bäumker, Wilhelm
Bückens, Ernest
Wallraf, Franz Ferdinand

*__D-Ko__ **Königsberg, Staats und Universitäts-Bibliothek**
Albert, Duke of Prussia, 1490-1568

D-LB **Langenburg, Fürstlich Hohenlohe-Langenburg'sche Schlossbibliothek**
Hohenlohe-Langenburg, Fürst

D-LCH **Lich, Kreis Giessen**
Solms-Lich, Fürst

D-LEb **Leipzig, Bach-Archiv**
Falck, Martin
Gorke, Manfred
Straube, Karl

D-LEm **Leipzig, Musikbibliothek der Stadt**
Becker, Varl Ferdinand
Besseler, Heinrich
Hagedorn, R.
Mempell, Johann Nicolaus
Politz, Karl Heinrich Ludwig
Preller, Johann Gottlieb
Rudorff, Ernst Friedrich Karl
Seiffert, Max
Taut, Kurt
Wilsing, Daniel Friedrich Edward

D-LEu **Leipzig, Universitätsbibliothek der Karl-Marz-Universität**
Avé-Lallemont, Luise

D-LM **Leitheim über Donauworth, Schlossbibliothek**
Tucher von Simmelsdorf, Christian Karl Gottlieb, Freiherr von

D-LÜh   **Lübeck, Bibliothek der Hansestadt Lübeck**
　　　　　　Jimmerthal, Hermann
　　　　　　Stiehl, Heinrich

D-MZs   **Mainz, Stadtbibliothek**
　　　　　　Cornelius, Peter
　　　　　　Schott, Bernhard

D-MH   **Mannheim, Wissenschafliche Stadtbibliothek**
　　　　　　Bentheim-Techlenburh, Graf zu

D-MB   **Marbach, Schiller-National Museum, Deutsche Literaturarchiv**
　　　　　　Kerner, [Justinus?]
　　　　　　Knappertsbusch, Hans
　　　　　　Schiller ?

D-MEIr   **Meiningen, Staatliche Museen mit Reger-Archiv**
　　　　　　Bülow, [Hans Guido von?]
　　　　　　Fassmann, Auguste
　　　　　　Mühlfeld, Christoph
　　　　　　Reger, Max

D-Mbn   **München, Bibliothek der Bayerische Nationalmuseum**
　　　　　　Aiblinger, Johann Kaspar
　　　　　　Ammende, Dietrich
　　　　　　Baumgartner, August
　　　　　　Clemens Franz von Paula, Herzog in Bayern
　　　　　　Ditterich, Richard von
　　　　　　Döbereiner, Christian
　　　　　　Frank, Ernst
　　　　　　Heyse, Paul
　　　　　　Keller, Max
　　　　　　Lang, Nikolaus
　　　　　　Maximilian II, King of Bavaria
　　　　　　Mikory, Franz
　　　　　　Otto, König von Griechenland
　　　　　　Pacher, Alois
　　　　　　Rottmanner, Eduard
　　　　　　Santini, Fortunato
　　　　　　Werdenstein, Johannes Georg von
　　　　　　Wittelsbacher Family

D-Mbs   **München, Bayerische Staatsbibliothek**
　　　　　　Fugger Family
　　　　　　Gehring, Franz Edward
　　　　　　Her, ?
　　　　　　Herwart Family
　　　　　　Hueber, Peter
　　　　　　Jerkowitz, Joseph
　　　　　　Lachner, Franz

Le Beau, Luise Adolphe
Levi, Hermann
Ludwig I, König von Bayern
Ludwig II, König von Bayern
Maria Anna, Electress, Consort of Maximilian III Joseph
Maria Antonia Walpurgis, Electress of Bavaria
Maximilian II, König von Bayern
Moldenhauer, Hans
Otho I, König von Griechenland
Patzak, Julius
Pfitzner, Hans
Rheinberger, Joseph Gabriel
Sandberger, Adolf
Schafhäutl, Karl Emil von
Thibaut, Anton Friedrich Justus
Wilhelm V, Herzog von Bayern
Wittelsbacher Family
Würthmann, Friedrich

D-Mmb   **München, Städtische Musikbibliothek**
Freiser, Julienne
Knote, Heinrich
Mörike, Hermine
Schick, Philippine
Thuille, Ludwig

D-Mms   **München, Musikwissenschaftliches Institut der Universität**
Fischer, Rudolf von
Ursprung, Otto
Wagner, Rudolf

D-Msa   **München, Staatsarchiv**
Maximilian III Joseph, Elector of Bavaria

D-MÜu   **Münster, Universitätsbibliothek**
Bentheim-Techlenburg, Graf zu

D-MÜs   **Münster, Santini-Bibliothek**
Santini, Fortunato

D-NBsb   **Neuburg/Donau, Staatliche Bibliothek**
Ottheinrich, Kurfürsten von Neuburg
Wolf, Heinrich

D-Nst   **Nürnberg, Stadtbibliothek**
Rohde, [perhaps Ernst]
Scherber, [Paul Friedrich]
Wagner, Rudolf

D-ORB   **Oranienbaum, Historisches Hausarchiv**
Johann IV, Fürst zu Anhalt-Zerbst

D-Pa   **Paderborn, Erzbischöfliche Akademisch Bibliothek**
                Wittenhorst-Sonsfeldt, Friedrich Otto von

D-PO   **Pössneck, Kreiskirchenamt**
                Schönborn-Wiesentheid, Graf zu

D-Rp   **Regensburg, Bischöfliche Zentralbibliothek**
                Haberl, Franz Xaver
                Hauber, Johann Michael
                Mettenleiter, Johann George
                Witt, Franz Xaver

D-Rtt   **Regensburg, Fürst Thurn und Taxis Hofbibliothek**
                Alexander, Ferdinand, Fürst
                Thurn und Taxis, Princess

D-Rs   **Regensburg, Staatliche Bibliothek**
                Kammerer, ?

D-ROu   **Rostock, Universitätsbibliothek**
                Mecklenburg-Schwerin, House of

DRUl   **Rudolstadt, Staatsarchiv**
                Erlebach, Philip Heinrich
                Louise, Caroline
                Wollong [or z?], Ernst
                Wollonz, Caroline Louise and Ernst

D-Sc   **Schlobitten Castle**
                Abraham, Burggraf zu Dohna

D-SI   **Sigmaringen, Fürstlich Hohenzollernsche Hofbibliothek**
                Hohenzollern, House of

D-SPlb   **Speyer, Pfälzische Landesbibliothek**
                Krauss, Karl August

D-SWl   **Schwerin, Wissenschaftliche Allgemeinbibliothek**
                Auguste Friederike, Consort
                Fuchs, Carl [probably Carl Dorius Johann]
                Kircher, Robert Alfred
                Mecklenburg-Schwerin, House of
                Rohloff, Ulderico

D-Usch   **Ulm, Von Schermar'sche Familienstiftung**
                Schermar, Egenolf von (and son, Anton)

D-WD   **Wiesentheid, Musiksammlung des Grafen von Schönborn-Wiesentheid**
                Erwein, Franz
                Erwein, Hugo Damien, Graf

D-W   **Wolfenbüttel, Herzog-August-Bibliothek**
                    August II, Duke of Braunschweig-Lüneburg
                    Mozart, Wolfgang Amadeus

D-WRgs   **Weimar, Goethe-Schiller-Archiv**
                    Goethe, Johann Wolfgang von

D-WRh   **Weimar, Bibliothek der Franz-Liszt-Hochschule**
                    Böhme, Franz-Magnus
                    Werner, Arno

D-WRiv   **Weimar, Institut für Volksmusik Forschung**
                    Hartenstein, [Carl?]
                    Werner, Arno

D-WRl   **Weimar, Staatsarchiv**
                    Möller, Heinrich

D-WRz   **Weimar, Zentralbibliothek der deutschen Klassik**
                    Anna Amalia, Duchess of Saxe-Weimar
                    Pavlovna, Archduchess Maria

D-WER   **Wernigerode, Heimatmuseum**
                    Stollberg-Wernigerödische Bibliothek

D-WERl   **Wertheim/Main, Evangelisches Pfarramt, Kirchenbibliothek**
                    Löwenstein-Wertheim-Freudenberg, Hubertus, Graf zu

D-WGp   **Wittenberg, Evangelisches Predigerseminar**
                    Heubner, Dr.

D-Z   **Zwickau, Ratsschulbibliothek**
                    Poach, Peter
                    Roth, Stephan

DENMARK

DK-A   **Aarhus, Statsbiliotek**
                    Jeppeseon, Knud

DK-Kk   **København, Kongelige Bibliotek**
                    Baden, J.
                    Giedde, Wilhelm Hans Rudolf Rosenkrantz
                    Groenland, Peter
                    Hagen, Sophie Albert Emil
                    Weyse, Christop Ernst Fredrich

DK-Kv   **København, Universitets Musikvidenskabelige Institut**
                    Barnekow, Christian

DK-KM(m)   **København, Musikhistorisk Museum**
                    Barnekow, Christian

ESPAÑA

*E-B   **Barcelona, Centro de documentación musical**
                   Subirá, José

E-Bc   **Barcelona, Biblioteca de Catalunya**
                   Anglès, Higini
                   Carreras y Dagas, Juan
                   Pedrell, Felipe
                   Pena Costa, Joaquín
                   Sedo Peris-Mencheta, Juan

E-Bim   **Barcelona, Instituto Español de Musicologia**
                   Hijar, Duque de
                   Valle, Anselmo Gonzalez del'

E-Bit   **Barcelona, Instituto del Teatro**
                   Canals, José
                   Cotarelo y Mori, Emilio
                   Guerra, María Luisa
                   Sedo y Guichard, Arthuro

E-G   **Gerona, Archivo musical de la Catedral**
                   Gas, José
                   Soler, Francisco

E-Mah   **Madrid, Archivo historico nacional**
                   Juana, Princess of Austria

E-Mam   **Madrid, Biblioteca musical circulante**
                   Alfonso de Bourbon y Braganza

E-Mc   **Madrid, Conservatorio Superior de Musica**
                   Bourbon (Royal Family)
                   Milanés, John
                   Moreno Gil de Borja, José Maria

E-Mm   **Madrid, Biblioteca Municipal**
                   Sbarbi, [probably Sbarbi y Osuna, José Maria]

E-Mmc   **Madrid, Biblioteca de la Casa Ducal de Medinaceli**
                   Medinaceli, Duques de

E-Mn   **Madrid, Biblioteca nacional**
                   Asenjo y Barbieri, Francisco
                   Francisco de Paula Antonio de Bourbon

E-PAp   **Palma de Mallorca, Biblioteca provincial**
                   Sabater, Juan María Thomás

E-SCu **Santiago de Compostela, Universidad**
Lago, Dr. ?

E-Sco **Sevilla, Archivo capitular de la Catedral**
Colón, Fernando

E-VAcp **Valencia, Colegio y capilla de Corpus Christi**
Ribera, San Juan de

EIRE (IRELAND)

* **EIR-Bep** **Belfast, Public Libraries**
Henry, Sam

* **EIR-Beq** **Belfast, Queen's University**
Hacker, Fr. X.
Harty, Sir Hamilton

EIR-C **Cork, University College, Music Library**
Bax, Arnold (Edward Trevor)
Gulbenkian
Johnson, ?
Lloyd, ?
Sperrin-Johnson, J. C.

EIR-Da **Dublin, Royal Irish Academy**
Forde, William

EIR-Dm **Dublin, Archbishop Marsh's Library**
Stone, Jacob

EIR-Dn **Dublin, National Library and Museum of Ireland**
Joly, Jasper
Plunkett, George Noble, Count

EIR-Dtc **Dublin, Trinity College Library**
Hall, Townley
Moeran, [probably Ernest John]
Petrie, George
Prout, Ebenezer

EIR-Duc **Dublin, University College, Music Library**
McCormack, John Count

FRANCE

F-A **Avignon, Bibliothèque du Musée Calvet**
Blaze, François Henri Joseph
Calvet, Esprit Claude François
Requiem, Dr. Esprit

F-AG   **Agen, Archives départementales**
Aiuguillon, ducs d'

F-AIXm   **Aix-en-Provence, Bibliothèque municipale**
Boissy, [probably Louis de, 1694-1758]
Méjanes, Jean Baptiste Marie Piquet, Marquis de

F-AJ   **Ajaccio, Bibliothèque municipale**
Napoleon I, Emperor of France

F-ANN   **Annecy, Bibliothèque municipale**
Martin, L.

F-AU   **Auxerre, Bibliothèque municipale**
Brochet, L[ouis?]
Claude, ?
Leblanc-Duvernoy [Family?]

F-B   **Besançon, Bibliothèque municipale**
Paris, Pierre-Adrien

F-Bo   **Bordeaux, Bibliothèque municipale**
Clapisson, Louis
Ferroud, [Pierre Octave]
Spontini, Gaspare

F-C   **Carpentras, Bibliothèque Inguimbertine et Musée de Carpentras**
Barjarel, ?
Bonaventure, Jules
Inguimbert, Malachie de, Bishop of Carpentras
Laurens, Jean-Joseph Bonaventure and Jules Bonaventure
Maîtrise de Siffrein

F-CF   **Clermont-Ferrand, Bibliothèque municipale et universitaire**
Grenier-Haynl

F-CO   **Colmar, Bibliothèque municipale**
Sandherr, Charles

F-Dc   **Dijon, École nationale de musique et d'art dramatique**
Kerveguen, Count G.

F-LYc   **Lyon, Conservatoire national de musique**
Boulanger, Nadia

F-LYm   **Lyon, Bibliothèque municipale**
Becker, George
Henry IV, King of France
Louis XIII, King of France
Mazarin, Cardinal

Richelieu, [Armand Jean de Plessis, duc de]
Vautier, Félix Abel

F-MIR   **Mirecourt, Bibliothèque municipale**
Larcher, ?
Vitry, Henry

F-MD   **Montbéliard, Bibliothèque municipale**
Montbéliard, George

F-MEL   **Melun, Bibliothèque municipale**
Vincent, Alexandre Joseph Hydulphe

F-MLN   **Montluçon, Bibliothèque municipale**
Guilhomet, ?

F-MON   **Montauban, Bibliothèque municipale**
Labat, Jean-Baptiste
Lacroix, [Antoine]

F-Mov   **Montpellier, Bibliothèque de la ville et du Musée Fabre**
Fabre, François-Xavier, Baron

F-Nd   **Nantes, Bibliothèque du Musée Dobrée**
Dobrée, Thomas

F-NI   **Nice, Bibliothèque municipale**
Albert I, Prince of Monaco
Falicon, [Pierre?]
Tardieu, [probably André, Premier]

F-NS   **Nîmes, Bibliothèque municipale**
Séguir, Jean-Francois

F-Pa   **Paris, Bibliothèque de l'Arsenal**
Craig, Edward Gordon
Douay, Georges
Germinet-Vinot, Gabriel
Rondel, August

F-Pc   **Paris, Conservatoire national de musique et de Déclamation, Bibliothèque, Fonds Blancheton**
Blancheton, Pierre Philibert
Borghese, Paolo, Principe
Boulanger, Nadia
Maldeghem, Robert Julius von
Malherbe, Charles Théodore
Petter, Gustav
Schoelcher, Victor
Toulouse, Louis Alexandre, Comte de

F-Pi   **Paris, Bibliothèque de l'Institut de France**
Spoellberch de Louvenjoud, Charles Victor, Vicomte de

F-Pim   **Paris, Institut de musicologie de l'Université**
Aubry, Pierre
Chaillez-Richer, ?
Ferrand, G[abriel]
Guilmant, Alexandre
Haraszti, Emil
Masson, Paul Marie
Reinach, Théodore

F-Pm   **Paris, Bibliothèque Mazarin**
Mazarin, Cardinal

F-Pn   **Paris, Bibliothèque nationale**
Bottée de Toulmon, Auguste
Brossard, Sebastian de
Boulanger, Nadia
Coirault, Patrice
Rothschild, James de, Baron
Thierry-Poux, Olgar
Weckerlin, Jean Baptiste Théodore

F-Po   **Paris, Bibliothèque Musée de l'Opéra**
Barbier, Jules
Maré, Rolf de
Nuitter, Charles Louis Étienne
Rouché, Jacques
Silvestri, ?

F-R   **Rouen, Bibliothèque municipale**
Baudry, ?
Bachelet, Théodore

F-SQ   **Saint-Quentin, Bibliothèque municipale**
Jumentier, Bernard
Lassus, Augé de

F-SA   **Salins, Bibliothèque municipale**
Magnin, Charles

F-SEL   **Sélestat, Bibliothèque municipale**
Vogeleis, Martin, Abbé

F-Sm   **Strasbourg, Archives et bibliothèque de la ville**
Schöpflin, Jean Daniel
Wagner, Eugene

F-Sim   **Strasbourg, Institut de musicologie de l'Université**
Jacobsthal, Gustav

F-Sn   **Strasbourg, Bibliothèque national et universitaire**
Jaëll, Marie

F-TLc   **Toulouse, Bibliothèque du Conservatoire**
Lefranc de Pompignan

F-TLm   **Toulouse, Bibliothèque municipale**
Lefranc de Pompignan

F-V   **Versailles, Bibliothèque municipale**
Goujet, [Vlaude-Pierre]
Homes, Augusta Mary Anne

F-VAL   **Valenciennes, Bibliothèque municipale**
Croy, [probably Emmanuel], Duc de

GREAT BRITAIN

GB-A   **Aberdeen, University Library, King's College**
Forbes-Leith, William
MacBean, William Munro
Skene, George
Taylor, William Lawrence

*GB-A   **Addington, Royal School of Church Music**
Trefusis, Lady Mary

*GB-Ad   **Addiscombe, Surrey, Royal School of Church Music**
Frost, Maurice

GB-Bu   **Birmingham, University Music Library; Barber Institute of Fine Arts**
Hellier, Samuel
Hunterian, ?
MacCunn, [Hamish]
Rose, Gloria

GB-BLl
Coke, Gerald

GB-BO   **Bournemouth, Central Library**
Camm, John B. M.

GB-BRp   **Bristol, Public Libraries, Central Library**
Harwood, Basil
Lean, Vincent Stuckey
Riseley, George
Russell, [probably Henry]

GB-BRu   **Bristol, University Library**
Miles, Napier

*GB-Bu	**Burnley, Central Public Library** Massey, Edward Stocks
GB-CClc	**Cambridge, Clare College Library** Sharp, Cecil
GB-Cfm	**Cambridge, Fitzwilliam Museum** Cooper, Gerald Melbourne Dragonetti, Domenico Fitzwilliam, Richard, 7th Viscount Griffin, Ralph Ireland, John Lennard, Henry Barrett Murray, Charles Fairfax Novello, Vincent Pendlebury, Richard
GB-Cjc	**Cambridge, St. John's College** Butler, Samuel
GB-Ckc	**Cambridge, King's College, Rowe Music Library** Colles, Henry Cope Dent, Edward Joseph Harvard, Lawrence Mann, Arthur Henry Ord, Boris Picken, Laurence Rowe, Louis Thompson
GB-Cmc	**Cambridge, Magdalene College** Jackson, John Pepys, Samuel
GB-Cp	**Cambridge, Peterhouse Library** Cosin, John, Bishop of Durham
GB-Cpc	**Cambridge, Pembroke College Library** May, Henry
GB-Cpl	**Cambridge, Pendlebury Library** Arnold, Thomas Cooper, Gerald Melbourne Dent, Edward Joseph Pendlebury, Richard Trend, John Brand Weiss, W. H.
GB-Ctc	**Cambridge, Trinity College Library** Bridge, Sir Frederick

GB-Cu   **Cambridge, University Library**
         Arnold, Franck Thomas
         Hawkins, James (of Ely Cathedral)
         Hook, James
         Mann, Arthur Henry
         Scott, Marion Margaret

GB-Cus   **Cambridge, Cambridge Union Society**
         Allan, Erskine

GB-CDp   **Cardiff, Public Library**
         Aylward, Theodore
         Landon, H. C. Robbins
         Mackworth, Sir Henry
         Morgan, R. Bonner

GB-CDu   **Cardiff, University College of South Wales**
         Arnold, Franck Thomas

GB-Drc   **Durham, Cathedral Library**
         Halle, Philip
         Sharp, Cecil
         Sharp Family

GB-DRu   **Durham, University Library**
         Falle, Philip

GB-DU   **Dundee, Public Libraries**
         Wighton, Andrew John

GB-En   **Edinburgh, National Library**
         Balfour, Arthur James, 1st Earl of
         Cowan, Alexander
         Glen, John
         Henderson, John Murdoch
         Hopkinson, Cecil
         Marshall, Julian
         Maule, James

GB-Enc   **Edinburgh, New College Library**
         Thin, James

GB-Ep   **Edinburgh, Public Library, Central Public Library**
         Marr, Robert A.
         Niecks, Friedrich

GB-Er   **Edinburgh, Signet Library**
         Donaldson, John
         Oakeley, Herbert Stanley

Reid, John R.
Tovey, Donald Francis
Weiss, Paul

GB-Eu   **Edinburgh, University Library**
Kennedy-Fraser, Marjorie
Mure, Sir William
Reid, John R.

GB-Ge   **Glasgow, Euing Music Library**
Euing, William

GB-Gm   **Glasgow, Mitchell Library**
Gardiner, George B.
Kidson, Frank
Manners, Charles
Scott, F. G.
Turnbull, Robert

GB-Gu   **Glasgow, University Library**
Drysdale, ? F. Learmont
Farmer, Henry George
Ferguson, ?
Graham, [probably George Farquhar]
Hunterian, ?
McEwen, [John B.]
Mearns, [probably James]
Stillie, Thomas L.
Whittaker, W. G.
Zavertal, Vences lao Hugo and Ladislao

GB-H   **Hereford, Cathedral Library**
Kemble, Frances Anne [Fanny]

* GB-Ha   **Hastings Area Libraries**
Browning, Oscar

* GB-K   **Knole Castle**
Sackville, John Frederick, 3rd Duke of Dorset

GB-LA   **Lancaster, District Central Library**
Fuller-Maitland, John Alexander

GB-Lau   **Lancaster, University Library**
Lockspeiser, Edward
Redlich, Hans Ferdinand

GB-LEbc   **Leeds, Brotherton Collection, University of Leeds**
Brotherton, Edward Allen, Baron Brotherton of Wakefield
Cowden Clarke, Mary (Novello)
Fulford, F. H.

GB-LEc   **Leeds, Leeds Public Library**
Kidson, Frank
Taphouse, Thomas William

** **GB-LEq**   **Leicester, Goldsmith Library**
Gardiner, William

GB-LF   **Lichfield, Cathedral Library**
Barker, John

GB-LVp   **Liverpool, Public Libraries, Central Library**
Booth, ?
Fuller-Maitland, John Alexander
Rosa, Carl
Sefton, Charles William Molyneux, [1st] Earl of

GB-Lvu   **Liverpool, University Music Department**
Fuller-Maitland, John Alexander

GB-Lam   **London, Royal Academy of Music**
Cohen, Harriett (recordings)
Corner, Musco
Cunningham, G. D.
Fane, Joseph, 11th Earl of Westmoreland, known as Lord Burghesh
Kalisch, Alfred
Kimpton, G.
Klemperer, Otto
Prendergast, H.
Ries, Ferdinand
Stock, Walter Henry
Westmoreland, [Francis William Henry], 12th Earl of
Wood, Sir Henry Joseph

GB-Lbbc   **London, BBC Music Library**
Bonavia, F [probably Feruccio]
Boult, Sir Adrian
Cross, Percy
Fox-Strangeways, Arthur Henry
Lambert, Constant
Newman, Eldridge
Pitt, Percy
Ronald, Sir Landon
Siddell, F. W.

GB-Lbl   **London, British Library**
Aquilera de Heredia, Sebastian
Bagford, John
Barbirolli, Sir John
Barry, C. A.
Bax, Arnold (Edward Trevor)
Benson, L.
Borghese, Paolo, principe

Britton, Thomas
Burney, Charles
Cockx, Mr. (of Antwerp)
Cohen, Harriett
Cunningham, G. D.
Dolmetsch, Arnold
Dragonetti, Domenico
Edwards, Frederick George
Finch, Charles Wightwick, 8th Earl of Aylesford
Fitzgerald, Gerald, Lord
Griffin, Ralph
Hammond, Thomas
Harley, Edward, 2nd Earl of Oxford
Hart, George
Hawkins, Sir John
Hayes, Philip
Henschel, Ernst
Hirsch, Paul
Huth, Alfred Henry
Jennens, Charles
Julian, Rev. John
"King's Music Library"
Kurtz, Anrew George
Landau, Horace, Baron de
Mackinlay, Thomas
Marshall, Julian
Mathias, James
Matthew, James E.
Meyerstein, Edward Henry William
Oldman, Cecil Bernard
Parker, Rev. John
Perabo, Johann Ernst
Plowden Family
Selvaggi, Gaspari
Sloane, Sir Hans
Smart, Sir George
Smith, John Christopher, the Younger
Stein Collection
Vernon, ?
Wight, Rev. Osborne
Wood, Sir Henry Joseph
Zweig, Stefan

GB-Lcm   **London, Royal College of Music**
Benson, L.
Boult, Sir Adrian
Ella, John
Frost, Maurice
Goetz, Mrs. Angelina (Levy)
Heron-Allen, Edward

Hill, Arthur Frederick
Hughes-Hughes, Augustus
Kalisch, Alfred (!)
Novello, Vincent
Novello & Co.
Parry, Charles Hubert Hastings
Ries, Ferdinand
Sargent, Sir Malcolm
Squire, William Barclay
Stanford, Sir Charles Villiers
Terry, Charles Sanford
Thomas, Arthur Goring
Waley, S. W.
Windsor, J. M.

GB-Lwcm   **London, Central Music Library, Westminster**
Blom, Eric
Cooper, Gerald Melbourne
Dent, Edward Joseph
Evans, Edwin, Jr.
Fox-Strangeways, Arthur Henry
Scott, Charles Kennedy

GB-Lcs   **London, Vaughan Williams Memorial Library**
Blunt, Janet Heatley
Broadwood, Lucy Ethelred
Butterworth, George S. K.
Chappell, William
Gatty, R[eginald] A.
Gardiner, George
Gardiner, H. Balfour
Grainger, Percy Aldridge
Hammond, Henry Edward Denison
Kennedy, Peter
Leather, Ella Mary
Lomax, Alan
Sharp, Cecil
White, E. H.

*GB-Lg   **London, Goldsmith's College**
Lloyd, A. L.

GB-Lgc   **London, Guildhall Library**
Gresham, ?
Hollier, Laetitia
Taylor, Edward

*GB-Lh   **London, Horniman Museum**
Jenkins, Jean

GB-Lkc   **London, King's College Library**
Dart, Thurston

GB-Llp   **London, Lambeth Palace**
Chelle, W.

*GB-Lrsc   **London, Royal School of Church Music**
Colles, Henry Cope

*GB-LSa   **London, Sadler's Wells Theatre**
Gordon, J. B.
Newmarch, Rosa
Novello & Co.

*GB-Mm   **London, Borough of Merton, Morden District Library**
Strugnell, Alan

GB-LTyson   **London** (private collection)
Tyson, Alan

GB-Lu   **London, University of London Music Library**
Elvey, Sir George
Haas, Alma
Littleton, Alfred Henry
Rainbow, Bernaar

GB-Lva   **London, Victoria & Albert Museum**
Beard, Harry R.
Cobb, G. F.
Enthoven, Gabrielle

GB-Mch   **Manchester, Chetham's Library**
Halliwell-Phillipps, James Orchard

GB-Mcm   **Manchester, Royal Northern College of Music**
Brodsky, Adolph
Horenstein, ?

GB-Mp   **Manchester, Central Public Library (Henry Watson Music Library)**
Finch, Charles Wightwick, 8th Earl of Aylesford
Flower, Sir (Walter) Newman
Jennens, Charles
Ottoboni, Pietro, Cardinal
Watson, Henry

GB-NW   **Norwich, Central Library**
Crotch, William

*GB-Nt   **Nottinghamshire, County Library**
Coates, Eric

GB-Ob   **Oxford, Bodleian Library**
               Beneke, Paul Victor Mendelssohn
               Bourne, Thomas William
               Britton, Thomas
               Deneke, Margaret
               Forrest, William
               Griffin, Ralph
               Hammond, Thomas
               Harding, Walter N. H.
               Horsley, William
               Rawlinson, Richard
               Rosenthal, Harold
               Wight, Rev. Osborne

GB-Och   **Oxford, Christ Church**
               Aldrich, Henry
               Browne, John
               Evelyn, John
               Goodson, Richard
               Hammond, Thomas
               Hayes, Philip
               Wight, Rev. Osborne

GB-Ouf   **Oxford, University, Faculty of Music Library**
               Allen, Sir Hugh
               Bellamy, Rev. Dr.
               Bridges, ?
               Ellis, [Alexander John?]
               Heather, William
               Heberden, ? [or Herberden, as Penney says?]
               Heron-Allen, Edward
               Howes, Frank Stewart
               Mees, John Henry
               Rawlinson, Richard
               Terry, Charles Sanford
               Walker, Ernest

GB-P   **Perth, Sandeman Public Library**
               Atholl, [possibly James Stewart-Murray, Duke of]

GB-R   **Reading, University Music Library**
               Finzi, Gerard

GB-RI   **Ripon, Cathedral Library**
               Higgin, A., Dean

GB-SA   **St. Andrews, University Library**
               Finzi, Gerard

*GB-SH   **Sheffield Central Library**
Whitworth, ?

GB-SWu   **Swansea, University College**
Deffret, Francis

GB-T   **Tenbury, St. Michael's College Library** (now at Bodleian Library, Oxford)
Dragonetti, Domenico
Rau, Arthur
Toulouse, Louis Alexandre, Comte de

GB-WO   **Worcester, Cathedral Library**
Atkins, Sir Isaac
Dore, William

GB-Y   **York, Minster Library**
Boot, Henry
Bostling, William

HUNGARY

H-BA (mi)   **Budapest, Magyar Tudományos Akadémia Zenetudományi Intezet Könyvtára**
Bartók, Béla
Kodály, Zoltán

H-Bl   **Budapest, Liszt Ferenc Zenemúvszeti Foiskola Könytára**
Liszt, Franz
Liviabelli [or Liviabella], Lino

H-Bn   **Budapest, Országos Széchényi Könyvtár**
Esterhazy Family
Liszt, Franz

H-KE   **Keszthely, Helikon Kastélymúzeum**
Balaton, ?

ITALY

I-BAR   **Barletta, Biblioteca comunale Sabino Loffredo, Teatro comunale G. Curci**
Gallo, Vincezo and Antonio

I-BDG   **Bassano del Grappa, Biblioteca civica**
Chilesotti, Oscar

I-BGc   **Bergamo, Biblioteca civica**
Mayr, Johann Simon

I-Bgi   **Bergamo, Civico Istituto musicale "G. Donizetti"**
Piatti, Alfredo Carlo

I-Baf   **Bologna, Archivio dell' Accademia filarmonica**
Masseangeli, Masseangelo
Succi, Emilia

I-Bam   **Bologna, Biblioteca Raimond Abrosini**
Ambrosini, Raimondo

I-Bc   **Bologna, Civico museo bibliografico musicale**
Conti Castelli, Sebastiano, Marchese
Gaspari, Gaetano
Martini, Padre Giovanni Battista
Torchi, Luigi
Vatielli, Francesco

I-Bl   **Bologna, Conservatorio di musica G. B. Martini**
Ivaldi, Filippo
Liviabelli, Lino

I-Bsf   **Bologna, Archivio del Convento di San Francisco**
Capanna, Alessandro
Golinelli, Stefano
Martini, Padre Giovanni Battista
Mattei, Stanislao
Pozzi, Antonio
Santini, Fortunato

I-CR   **Cremona, Biblioteca Statale**
Cesari, Gaetano

I-CRp   **Cremona, Museo "Ala Ponzone"**
Stravidari, Antonio

I-Fc   **Firenze, Conservatorio di musica Luigi Cherubini**
Basevi, Abramo
Boghen, [perhaps Carlo Felica, 1869-1945]
Casamorata, L. [perhaps Luigi]
Console, ?
Corsini
Fumi, [Vincelslao?]
Manetti, ?
Mariotti, ?
Martinelli, ?
Morini, [perhaps Ferdinando]
Picchi Family
Puliti, [perhaps Leto]

I-Fm   **Firenze, Biblioteca Marucceliana**
Bonamici, Diomeded
Maruccelli, Francesco

I-Fn   **Firenze, Biblioteca Nazionale Centrale**
Landau, Horace de, Baron

I-FOc **Forli, Biblioteca civica "Aurelio Saffi"**
    Piancastelli, Carlo

I-Lc **Lucca, Biblioteca capitolare Feliniana & Archivio Arcivescoville del Duomo (San Martno)**
    Baralli, Raffaello

I-Li **Lucca, Istituto musicale**
    Bottini, Mariana Andreozzi, Marchese
    Castelfranchi, Cesare
    Checcacci, Felice
    Sedie, Enrico Delle

I-Ls **Lucca, Biblioteca del seminario vescovile**
    Bernini, [Giuseppe]
    Guerra, [Antonio?]

I-MAC **Macerata, Biblioteca comunale Mozzi-Borgetti**
    Ales, Oreste
    Lauri, Tommaso
    Radiciotti, Giuseppe
    Rolandi, Ulderico
    Spadoni, Giovanni

I-MAa **Mantova, Archivio di stato**
    Gonzaga Family

I-ME **Messina, Biblioteca universitaria governativa**
    La Corte-Callier, Gaetano

I-Mb **Milano, Biblioteca nazionale Braidense**
    Corniani-d'Algarotti, Conte, of Treviso
    Maria Theresia, Empress of Austria

I-Mc **Milano, Biblioteca del Conservatorio "Giuseppe Verdi"**
    Benvenuti, Giacomo
    Noseda, Gustavo Adolfo
    Polo, [perhaps Enrico]

I-Mcap(d) **Milano, Cappella musicale del Duomo**
    Volontè, Francesco

I-Mcom **Milano, Biblioteca comunale**
    Bertarelli, Achille

I-Mr **Milano, Ricordi (Casa Editrice)**
    Lucca, Francesco

I-Ms   **Milano, Biblioteca teatrale Livia Simoni, Museo teatrale Alla Scala**
                  Eisner-Eisendorf, Angelo Franz
                  Simoni, Livia
                  Simoni, Renato
                  Victor, Baron von

I-MOa   **Modena, Accademia nazionale di scienze lettere ed arti**
                  Tardini, Vincenzo

I-MOe   **Modena, Biblioteca Estense**
                  Campori, Giuseppe Marchesi
                  Este, House of

I-Nc   **Napoli, Biblioteca del Conservatorio di Musica S. Pietro a Maiella**
                  Capece Minutolo Family
                  Mattei, Saverio
                  Sigismondo, Giuseppe

I-Nn   **Napoli, Biblioteca nazionale**
                  Lucchesi-Pallo, Ferdinando, Count

I-NT   **Noto, Biblioteca comunale**
                  Altieri, Paolo

I-OS   **Ostiglia, Fondazione Greggiati**
                  Gatti, Luigi
                  Greggiata, Giuseppe, Canon

I-Pca   **Padova, Archivio musicale privata della Veneranda Arca del Santo**
                  Ravanello, Oreste

I-PLcon   **Palermo, Biblioteca del Conservatorio "V. Bellini"**
                  Pisani, Baron, Pietro, and Antonio

I-PAc   **Parma, Sezione musicale dell Biblioteca Palatina presso il Conservatorio "Arrigo Boito"**
                  Marie Louise, Empress, Consort of Napoleon I

I-PAi   **Parma, Instituto di studi Verdiani**
                  Scalvini, Giulio and Carmen Asensio

I-PEA   **Pescia, Biblioteca comunale Carlo Magnani**
                  Pacini, Giovanni

I-PCcon   **Piacenza, Biblioteca del Conservatorio di music "G. Nicolini"**
                  Abbado, Marcello
                  Ambrogio, Aldo
                  Censi, Carlo
                  Negri, Corrado Pavesi
                  Tronchi, Aurelio

I-PIN   **Pinerolo, Biblioteca comunale Camillo Alliaudi**
         Giani, Romualdo

***I-PSm**   **Pistoia, Montecatini-Terme**
         Venturi, Antonio

I-PS   **Pistoia, Archivio capitolare della Cattedrale**
         Baldi-Papini Family
         Gherardeschi Family
         Rospigliosi Family

I-REt   **Reggio-Emilia, Teatro municipale**
         Agosti, Arrigo and Egle

I-RIM   **Rimini, Biblioteca civica "Gambalunga"**
         Gambalunga, Alessandro
         Mattei-Gentili, Giudo

I-Rac   **Roma, Conservatorio di musica Santa Cecilia**
         Borghese, Paolo, Principe

I-Raf   **Roma, Biblioteca dell'Accademia Filarmonico Romana**
         Fassati, ?
         Gigliucci, [Valeria, Countess]
         Nicoletti, ?

I-Rc   **Roma, Biblioteca Casanatense**
         Casanate, Girolamo, Cardinal
         Compagnoni-Maresfaschi Family

I-Rchristoff   **Rome, Biblioteca privata Boris Christoff**
         Christoff, Boris

I-Rdp   **Roma, Archivio Doria Pamphilj**
         Pamphilj, Benedetto, Cardinal

I-Ria   **Roma, Biblioteca dell'Istituto di Archeologia e Storia dell'Arte**
         Pagliara, [probably Rocco E.]
         Vessella, Alessandro

I-Rli   **Roma, Biblioteca dell Accademi nazionale dei Lincei e Corsiniana**
         Chiti, Girolamo
         Corsini Family

***I-Rp**   **Roma, Propoganda-Archive**
         Steffani, Agostino

I-Rsc **Roma, Biblioteca musicale governative del Conservatorio di Santa Cecilia**
Candia, Mario di
Carotti, V.
Carvalhaes, Manoel Pereira Peixoto d'Almeida
Mario, Giovanni Matteo, Conte di Candia
Margherita di Savoia
Orsini, Alessandro
Pasqualini, [perhaps Marc'Antonio]

I-Rv **Roma, Biblioteca Vallicelliana**
Estação, Achille

I-Rvat **Roma, Biblioteca Apostolica Vaticana**
Altemps, Giovanni Angelo, Duke of Gallese
Chigi Family

I-RVI **Rovigo, Accademia e biblioteca dei Concordi**
Silvestri, Count

I-Sac **Siena, Biblioteca dell'Addademia musicale Chigiana**
Chigi Family

I-TE **Terni, Istuituto musicale "G. Briccialdi"**
Briccialdi, Giulio
Cerwuettelli, Giuseppe
Donini, Idino

I-Tci **Torino, Biblioteca civica musicale "A. della Corte"**
Carrera, Valentino
Corte, Andrea Della
Sacerdote, Giacomo

I-Tn **Torino, Biblioteca nazionale universitaria**
Durazzo, Giacomo
Foà, Mauro
Giordano, Renzo

I-Tr **Torino, Biblioteca reale**
Carlo, Alberto, King of Sardinia

I-Vc **Venezia, Biblioteca del Conservatorio "Benedetto Marcello"**
Contin di Castelsprio
Giustiniani, Alvise, Conte
Martinengo, Leopardo, Conte
Pascoluto, Alessandro
Torrefranca, Fausto
Wiel, Taddeo

I-Vgc	**Venezia, Biblioteca e istituto di lettere, musica e teatro della Fondazione "Giorgio Cini"**
	Cini, Giorgio, Fondazione
	Malipiero, [Gian Francesco]
	Rolandi, Ulderico
I-Vmc	**Venezia, Museo civica Correr, Biblioteca d'arte e storia veneziana**
	Carminati, Constantino and Alessandro
	Cicogna, Emanuel Antonipo
	Fantoni, Gabriel
I-Vnm	**Venezia, Biblioteca nazionale Marciana**
	Canal, Lorenzo
	Canal, Pietro
	Contarini, Marco
I-VEaf	**Verona, Biblioteca dell' Accademia filarmonica**
	Pastori, Clelia
I-Vlmc	**Vicenza, Biblioteca Sebastiano Rumor, Museu Civico**
	Fantoni, Gabriel

ISRAEL

IL-Hml	**Haifa, Haifa Museum and AMLI Library**
	Yaffe, Selomoh
IL-J	**Jerusalem, Jewish National & University Library**
	Idelsohn, Abraham Zeli
IL-T	**Tel Aviv, Central Library**
	Huberman, Bronislaw

JAPAN

J-Tn	**Tokyo, Okhi Collection, Nanki Music Library**
	Cummings, William Hayman
	Friedländer, Max
	Hallmann, Joseph
	Okhi, Kyubei
	Tokugawa, Rorisada

NORWAY

N-Bo	**Bergen, Offentlige Bibliotek**
	Grieg, Edvard Hagerup
*N-H	**Hamar, Folkebibliotek**
	Sandvik, Paul
N-Ou	**Oslo, Universitetsbibliotek**
	Sandvik, Ole Mark

N-Oum   **Oslo, Universitetsbibliothek, Norsk Musiksamling**
Knudtzen, N. H.
Sandvik, Ole Mark
Udbye, Odd

NEDERLAND

NL-AN   **Amerongen, Archief van het Kasteel der Graven Bentinck**
Bentinck, Count

NL-Ad   **Amsterdam, Stichting Donemus**
Alsbach, Johan Adam

NL-AEC   **Amsterdam, Ethnomusicologisch Centrum**
Kunst, Jaap

NL-At   **Amsterdam, Toonkunst Bibliotheek**
Lotter, J. J., [probably Johann Jakob]

NL-DHa   **Den Haag, Koninklijk Huisarchief**
William V, Prince of Orange

NL-DHgm   **Den Haag, Gemeente Museum**
Anrooy, Peter van
Boers, Jan Conradus
Brucken Frock, Gerard von
Dopper, Corneli
Hol, Richard
Scheurleer, Daniel Francois
Verhulst, Johannes
Voormolen, Alexander
Zweers, Bernard

NL-DHK   **Den Haag, Koninklijke Bibliotheek**
Hijman, Julius
Scheurleer, Daniel Francois

NL-Lu   **Leiden, Universiteisbibliotheek**
Thysius, Johan

NL-Uim   **Utrecht, Institut voor muziekwetenschap der Rijksuniversiteit**

NEW ZEALAND

NZ-Wt   **Wellington, Alexander Turnbull Library**
Schramm, Paul and Pinny
Turnovsky, Fred

POLAND

PL-GD   **Gdansk, Biblioteka Gdańska Polskiej Akademii Nauk**
     Glaser, Alexander
     Knophius, Georges
     Schwarzwald, Henryk
     Uphagen, Jan

PL-KO   **Kornik, Bibliotec Kórnicka Polskiej Akademii Nauk**
     Dzialnynski, Adam Titus

PL-Kdp   **Kraków, Ósrodek Dokumentacii Życia i Twórczósci L. J. Paderewskiego**
     Paderewski, Ignace Jan

PL-Kwpwm   **Kraków, Biblioteka Polskiego Wydawnictwa Muzycznego**
     Jachimecki, Zdzislaw

PL-LA   **Lańcut, Muzeum-Zamek**
     Lubomirska, Izabella

PL-Lk   **Lublin, Biblioteka Uniwersytecka Katolickiego Uniwersytetu Lubelskiego**
     Nowacki, Henryk

PL-Pu   **Poznan, Biblioteka Glówna Uniwersytetu im A. Mickiewicza**
     Chybinski, Adolf

PL-WRu   **Biblioteka Uniwersytecke, Oddzial Zbiorów Muzycznych**
     Bohn, Emil

P-WRzno   **Wrocklaw, Polska Akademia Nauk, Zaklad Narodowy im Ossolinskichm Biblioteka**
     Ossolinski, Josef Maksymilian

PORTUGAL

P-Lc   **Lisbon, Conservatorio nacional**
     Lambertini, Michel'angelo

P-Leg   **Lisbon, Fundaçao Calouste Gulbenkian**
     Da Motta, José Vianna

P-Ln   **Lisbon, Biblioteca nacional de Lisboa**
     Cruz, Ivo
     Sampaio Ribeiro, Mario Luis de

P-VV   **Vila Viçosa, Casa de Bragança, Museu-Biblioteca, Paço Ducal**
     João IV, King of Portugal

SOUTH AFRICA

     Johannesburg, Public Library
     Strange, Harold

SWEDEN

S-KA   **Karlstad, Stifts- och Läroverksbiblioteket**
Brodin, Linus
Löwenhielm, Carl Gustav

S-LB   **Leufstra Bruk, Stifts- och Landesbiblioteket Institut**
De Geer, Charles

S-L   **Lund, Universitetsbiblioteket**
Barnekow, Christian
Engelhart, Hinrich Christoph
Kraus, Friedrich
Taussig, Otto
Wenster, Emanuel

S-N   **Norrköping, Stadsbiblioteket**
De Geer, Charles

S-Sk   **Stockholm, Kungliga Biblioteket**
Cederhamn, ?

S-Skma   **Stockholm, Kungliga Musikaliska Adademiens Bibliotek**
Alströmer, Patrick A., Baron
Berwald Family
Boije of Gennäs Family
Cederhamm, ?
Edberg, Albert
Fallén, Carl Fredrik
Fouché d'Otrante, Duke Paul Athanese
Fryklund, Daniel
Hallardt, Johan Fredrik
Horn, Adam
Mazer, Johann
Mörner, Marianne
Nilson, Kristina
Oxenstierna, Gustaf Göran Gabriel, Count
Patti, Adelina
Roman, Johann Heinrich
Sachs, Johann Gabriel

S-Sm   **Stockholm, Musikhistoriska Museet**
Fryklund, Daniel
Rosenberg Family (Prague)

S-Smf   **Stockholm, Stiftelsen Musikkulturens Främjande**
Hanson, Per Wilhelm
Nydahl, Rudolf

S-Ssv   **Stockholm, Svensk Visarkiv**
Sporr, Karl

S-Uu   **Uppsala, Universitetsbiblioteket**
Düben, Freiherr Anders von
Gustavus II Adolphus, King of Sweden
Lefebure, Jean
Silverstope, Fredrik Samuel
Wackenbarth, Athanasius Francis Diedrich

UNITED STATES

US-AA   **Ann Arbor, University of Michigan**
Coopersmith, Jacob Maurice
De Courcy, Geraldine
Jessye, Eva A.
Luconi, Albert
Mattern, David E.
Stellfeld, Jean Auguste

US-AAc   **Ann Arbor, University of Michigan, William L. Clements Library**
Corning, Ely
Ellis, Bruce T.

US-ALBu   **Albuquerque, University of New Mexico**
Areu, Manuel
Helm, Everett Burton

US-ALX   **Alexandria, Virginia, George Washington Masonic Museum**
Washington Family

US-Atet   **Atlanta, Georgia, Emory University, Pitts Theology Library**
Paine, Silas K.
Pratt, W. S.
Warrington, James

US-ATeu   **Atlanta, Georgia, Emory University Library**
Read, Keith M.

* **US-ATh**   **Atlanta, Georgia, Historical Society**
Spain, Helen Knox

US-ATS   **Athens, University of Georgia Libraries**
Adler, Guido
Downes, Olin
Taylor, Archer

US-AU   **Aurora, New York, Wells College Library**
De Baum, ?

US-AUS   **Austin, University of Texas**
Bachmann, Edwin
Betti, Adolfo
Diehl, Katherine Smith
Kraus, Hans Peter
Russell, Ross

US-BAhs   **Baltimore, Maryland, Enoch Pratt Free Library**
Dielman, Louis H. [probably Henry]

*US-BAm   **Baltimore, Maryland, Morgan State College**
De Lerma, Dominique-René

US-BApi   **Baltimore, Maryland, Peabody Conservatory of Music**
Ortmann, Otto Rudolph
Thomson, Virgil

US-BE   **Berkeley, University of California**
Aber, Alice Larson
Bacigalupi, Remo
Buck, William
Bukofzer, Manfred
Clive, Robert, Lod
Cornick, Harris D. H.
Cortot, Alfred
Cowell, Sidney Robertson
Einstein, Alfred
Hertzman, Erich
Mansfeldt, Hugo
Morrow, Irving F.
Romberg, Sigmund
Taddei, [Antonio?]

US-Ba   **Boston, Massachusetts, Boston Athenaeum Library**
Nichols, Arthur H.
Shurcliff, Margaret Homer Nichols

US-Bc   **Boston, Massachusetts, New England Conservatory of Music**
Faber, Norma
Preston, John A.

US-Bgm   **Boston, Massachusetts, Isabella Stewart Gardiner Museum-Library**
Gardiner, Isabella Stewart

US-Bh   **Boston, Massachusetts, Harvard Musical Association**
Chase, Theodore

US-Bm   **Boston, Boston University, Mugar Memorial Library**
Wellesz, Egon

US-Bp   **Boston, Massachusetts, Public Library**
Brown, Allen Augustus
Gorokoff, [probably Ivan T.]
Koudelka, Joseph, Freiherr von
Thayer, Alexander Wheelock
Tuthill, Burnet Corwin

US-BER   **Beria, Ohio, Baldwin-Wallace College, Riemenschneider Bach Institute Library**
David, Hans Theodore
Martin, ?
Riemenschneider, Albert

US-BERr   **Beria, Ohio, Baldwin-Wallace College Conservatory**
Jones, Fern Patterson
Ridenour, Harry E.

US-BI   **Binghamton, University of, New York, William Mitchell Music Collection**
Conole, Frances B.

US-BIRu   **Birmingham, Alabama, Samford University, Davis Library**
Lorenz, Edward Simon

US-BLl   **Bloomington, Indiana University, Lilly Library**
Starr, Paul

US-BLu   **Bloomington, Indiana University, School of Music Library**
Apel, Willi
Beck, Terence R.
Busch, Fritz
Ellingson, Ter
George, Robert Olney
Kozma, Tibor
Mendel, Bernardo
Starr, Frederick A.

*US-BLU   **Blue Hill, Maine, Kneisel Hall**
Schirmer, George

US-BO   **Boulder, University of Colorado**
Buzzard, Joe, Jr.
Collins, Walter S.
Katz, Erich
Layton, Alvin G.
Lockwood, Normand
Lumpkin, Ben Gray
Walker-Hill, Helen

US-BOW   **Bowling Green, Ohio, Bowling Green State University**
Randle, William
Stupple, David

US-BRc   **Brooklyn, New York, Brooklyn College Music Library**
Voto, Alfred de

US-BU   **Buffalo, New York, Buffalo & Erie County Library**
Delany, William, Music Shop
Dumont, Frank
Elson, Louis Charles
Fiedler, Arthur
Lang, Ossian
Leahy, ?
Metcalf, Frank J.
Nolen, W. W.
Nutter, Charles Sumner

US-BUu   **Buffalo, New York, S.U.N.Y. at Buffalo**
Bradley, Carol June
Chowaniec, Mark
Coover, James B.
Cornelissen, Arnold
Gearhart, Livingston
Hiller, Lejaren A.
Mikhashoff, Yvar
Perry, J. Warren
Sapp, Allen
Smit, Leo
Williams, Jan
Wolf, Anton

US-CA   **Cambridge, Massachusetts, Harvard University, Eda Kuhn Loeb Music Library**
Aldrich, Richard
Bliss, Mildred
Britton, Thomas
De Windt, Clara
Gutman, Monroe C.
Heath, John Benjamin
Kolisch, Rudolf
Moldenhauer, Hans
Notopoulos, James Anastasioa
Parry, Milman
Vose, Edwin
Ward, John Milton

US-CAh   **Cambridge, Massachusetts, Harvard University, Houghton Library**
Helm, Everett Burton
Wendell, Evert J.
Wilkins, Raymond Sanger
Windt, Clara de

US-CAD   **Carbondale, Southern Illinois University**
Lawrence, Marjorie

US-CHH   **Chapel Hill, University of North Carolina**
Buchanan, Annabel Morris
Newman, William Stein
Yoder, Don

*US-CHc   **Charleston, South Carolina, College of Charleston**
Meltzer, Charles Henry

US-CHua   **Charlottesville, University of Virginia**
Holt, Roland
MacKay-Smith, Alexander
Swan, Alfred J.

US-Cn   **Chicago, Illinois, Newberry Library**
Ayer, Edward E.
Carpentheir-Morphy, Madame T. le
Cortot, Alfred
Driscoll, James Francis
Fairbank, Janet
Fuchs, Carl
Fuchs, Julius
Gleason, Frederick Grant
Lob, Otto
Main, Hubert Platt
Merrill, William Stetson
Resse, Pio, Conte
Thomas, Theodore
Upton, George Putnam
Wolffheim, Werner Joachim

US-CU   **Chicago, University of Chicago, Joseph Regenstein Library**
Connick, Harris (D. H.)
Huber, William, Jr.
Stock, Frederick A.
Thomas, Theodore

US-CIhc   **Cincinnati, Ohio, Hebrew Union College**
Birnbaum, Edward

US-CIu   **Cincinnati, Ohio, University of Cincinnati College-Conservatory of Music**
Chujoy, Anatole
Foley, B. W.
Harline, Leigh
Helm, Everett Burton
Hoffman, Frederick J.
Wurlitzer, Helen V. B. and Rudolph H.

US-CLAc   **Claremont, California,   Claremont College, Honnold Library**
McCutcheon, Robert Guy
Seymour, John Laurence

US-CLwr   **Cleveland, Ohio, Cleveland Public Library**
White, John G.

US-CLp   **Cleveland, Ohio, Case Western Reserve University**
White, John G.

US-COu   **Columbus, Ohio State University**
             Arms, Fanny

US-DAp   **Dallas, Texas, Dallas Public Library**
             Hill, William B.

US-DEC   **Decorah, Iowa, Luther College**
             Wolhowe, Fred

US-DN   **Denton, North Texas State University**
             Hewitt, Helen
             Hibberd, Isaac Lloyd
             Nachod, Hans

US-Dp   **Detroit, Michigan, Detroit Public Library**
             Hackley, Emma Azalia
             Huger, Melvina
             Leonard, Hazel B.
             Martin, John B.
             Murphy, William H.
             Spiering, Theodore

US-DOV   **Dover, Delaware State Museum**
             Johnson, Eldridge Reeves

US-DMu   **Durham, North Carolina, Duke University**
             Berdes, Jane L.
             Ricasoli, Pietro Leopoldo

US-EDu   **Edwardsville, University of Illinois**
             Autenreich, Max
             Tollefsen, Carl H.

US-EL   **East Lansing, Michigan State University**
             Vincent, G. Robert

＊**US-EM**   **Emporia, Kansas, Emporia State University**
             Brewsaugh, V. G.

US-Eu   **Evanston, Illinois, Northwestern University**
             Coe, Sadie Howland
             Moldenhauer, Hans
             Reiner, Fritz

US-FI   **Fitchburg, Massachusetts, Public Library and State College**
             Jenks, Francis H.

US-GAa   **Garden City, New York, Adelphi University**
             Stoelzer, Ernst Richard

*US-GBc   **Gettysburg, Pennsylvania, Gettysburg College**
Coci, Claire

*US-G   **Mayfield Greenfield, Illinois, Mayfield private collection**
Mayfield, Lyle and Doris

US-GO   **Goshen, Indiana, Goshen College**
Hartzler, J. D.

US-GRB   **Greensboro, University of North Carolina**
Silva, Luigi

US-HA   **Hanover, New Hampshire, Dartmouth College**
Burrill, Roger H[olmes?]

US-HAT   **Hattiesburg, University of Southern Mississippi**
Goldstein, Kenneth S.

US-Hhc   **West Hartford, Connecticut, Hart College of Music**
Opperman, Kalmen

*US-Has   **Hartford, Connecticut, Hartford Seminary Foundation**
Johnson, Frances Hall

US-Hw   **Hartford, Connecticut, Trinity College**
Niles, Edward, Abbé

US-HOU   **Houston, Texas, University of Houston**
Dudley, Beyard Turner Grocs

US-HOUr   **Houston, Texas, Rice University**
Sylvester, Stephen A.

US-HOUt   **Houston, Texas Southern University**
Heartman, ?

US-I   **Ithaca, New York, Cornell University**
Haenschen, Gustave
Harris, George
Lavoisier, Marie Anne Pierette Paulze

*US-Jm   **Jackson, Mississippi, Millsaps College**
Engel, Lehman

US-KC   **Kansas City, University of Missouri - Kansas City**
Thomson, Virgil
Woodbury, Isaac Baker

US-KN   **Knoxville, University of Tennessee**
Busoni, Ferruccio
Galston, Gottfried
Van Vactor, David

US-Law   **Laramie, University of Wyoming**
                Burrage, ?

US-LT   **Latrobe, Pennsylvania, St. Vincent College and Archabbey**
                Wimmer, Archabbat Boniface

US-Lu   **Lawrence, University of Kansas Libraries**
                Katzman, Henry Manners
                Nichols, Ernest Loring ("Red")
                Platzman, Robert and Eva
                Wooldridge, Warren

US-LEX   **Lexington, University of Kentucky**
                Cortot, Alfred

*US-LI   **Liberty, Missouri, William Jewell College**
                Spurgeon, Charles Haddon

*US-LIa   **Little Rock, Arkansas Art Center**
                Reid, John D.

US-LIu   **Lincoln, University of Nebraska**
                Botkin, Benjamin Albert

*US-LOg   **Logan, Utah State University**
                Fife, Austin E. and Alta
                Rich, Blanche Browning

US-LONcs   **Long Beach, California State University**
                Kuhnle, Wesley

US-LAp   **Los Angeles, Public Library**
                Attl, Vojmer
                Clark, William Andrews, Jr.

US-LAs   **Los Angeles, Schoenberg Institute** (now at **A-Wsc**)
                Schoenberg, Arnold
                Steuermann, Eduard
                Stiedry-Wagner, Erika, and Fritz Stiedry

US-LAu   **Los Angeles, University of California, Music Library**
                Heth, Charlotte Anne Wilson
                Ring, Stanley
                Stanton, Royal B.
                Wilson, Earl
                Willson, Meredith

US-LAuc   **Los Angeles, University of California, Clark Memorial Library**
                Jackson, George Pullen
                Stuart, John, 3rd Earl of Bute

US-LAusc   **Los Angeles, University of Southern California**
Greissle, Felix

US-LOs   **Louisville, Kentucky, Southern Baptist Theological Seminary**
Ingersoll, Janet T.

US-LOu   **Louisville, Kentucky, University of Louisville**
Helm, Everett Burton
Ricasoli, Pietro Leopoldo

US-MAu   **Madison, University of Wisconsin**
Owen, John Dale

US-MED   **Medford, Massachusetts, Tufts University Library**
Metcalf, Albert
Ritter, Frédéric Louis

US-MB   **Middlebury, Vermont, Middlebury College**
Flanders, Helen Hartness
Olney, Marguerite

US-Mc   **Milwaukee, Wisconsin Conservatory of Music**
Hatzi, James

US-MSp   **Minneapolis, Minnesota, Public Library**
Brooks, Elmer
Oberhoffer, Emil Johnson
Rossiter, John P.
Schoettle, Gustave

US-MSu   **Minneapolis, University of Minnesota Music Library**
Berger, Kenneth Walter
Ferguson, Donald Nivison

US-NA   **Nashville, Tennessee, Fisk University**
Gershwin, George
Van Vechten, Carl

US-NAs   **Nashville, Tennessee, State Library and Archives**
Norton, Zilphia
Rose, Kenneth David

US-NBu   **New Brunswick, Rutgers - State University of New Jersey**
Sachs, Curt
Williams Wynn, Watkins, Sir, 4th Baronet

US-NH   **New Haven, Connecticut, Yale University**
Anderson, Muriel V.
Balbour, Lucius H.
Barlow, Robert

Burney, Charles
Capes, S. J.
Crawford, J. R.
Dance, Stanley Peter
Dehn, Siegfried Wilhelm
Filmer Family, Baronetcy
Galeazzi, Francesco
Grainger, Percy Aldridge
Grumman, Ellsworth
Hamilton, Emma, Lady
Harkness, Mrs. Edward
Hawkins, Micah
Johnson, James Welson
Horowitz, Vladimir and Wanda
Keating, George
Kirkpatrick, Ralph
Mason, Lowell
Rinck, Johann Christian Heinrich
Openhym, George J.
Opochinsky, David and Fanny
Osborn, James MarshallPlamenac, Dragan
Plant, Fred and Rose
Reed, Edward Bliss
Rosenbloom, Charles J.
Schmitz, E. Robert
Thomson, Virgil
Witten, Laurence C.
Wolf, Albert

*US-NL   **New London, Connecticut College**
Wyman, ?

US-NORts   **New Orleans, Louisiana, Baptist Theological Seminary**
Keith, Edward D.
Martin, William F.
Sellers, Ernest Orlando

US-NORtu   **New Orleans, Louisiana, Tulane University**
Kuntz, Rosamond E. and Emile

US-NEij   **Newark, Rutgers - State University of New Jersey**
Owen, John Dale

US-NO   **Normal, Illinois State University**
Braathen, Sverre O.
Tinney, Charles H.

US-Nf   **Northampton, Massachusetts, Forbes Library**
Moffat, Alfred Edward

US-Nsc   **Northampton, Massachusetts, Smith College**
Drinker, Henry Sandwith

Einstein, Alfred
Hale, Philip

*US-NTc   **Northridge, California State University**
Bickford, Vahdah Olcott

US-NYcu   **New York, Columbia University Music Library**
Bartók, Béla
Baughman, Roland
Boulton, Laura
Hertzman Erich
Hunt, Arthur Billings
Joffe, Judah A.
MacDowell, Edward Alexander
Peck, J.
Rappaport, Eda Rothstein
Schang, Frederick C.
Seidl, Anton
Witmark, Isidore

US-NYcub   **New York, Columbia University, Butler Library**
Plimpton, George Arthur

US-NYbm   **New York, Carl Haverlin/BMI Archives**
Haverlin, Carl

US-NYjts   **New York, Jewish Theological Seminary**
Wohlberg, Max

US-NYmm   **New York, Metropolitan Museum of Art**
Brown, Mary Elizabeth (Adams)

US-NYmc   **New York, Museum of the City of New York**
Cohan, George Michael
Comden, Betty
Green, Adolph
Gershwin, George

US-NYhs   **New York, Historical Society**
Hawkins, Micah
Landauer, Mrs. Bella Clara

US-NYp   **New York Public Library**
Bass, [probably Iris]
Bliss-Herter Families
Bristow, George Frederick
Britton, Thomas
Cortot, Alfred
Doane, George W.
Drexel, Joseph Wilhelm
Edwards, Julian

Gabrilowitsch, Ossip
Goodwin, George
Gottschalk, Louis Moreau
Greenway, George Lauder
Holcman, Jan
Huneker, James Gibbons
Hunt, Arthur Billings
Krehbiel, Henry Edward
Lambert, Alexander
LaRoche, R. A.
Locker-Lampson, Frederick
Mendelssohn-Bartholdy, Felix
Myddleton-Biddulph, Thomas
Nicholl, Horace Wadham
Oster, Ernst F.
Percheron, Achille Remy
Schumer, Harry G.
Shapiro, Elliott
Sinderem, Howard van
Stambler, Benedict
Wittgenstein, Paul

US-NYpm   **New York, Pierpont Morgan Library**
Allen, Alfred Reginald
Byrd, Frederick M.
Cary, Mary Flagler
Heinemann, Dannie N
Koch, Fred R.
Lehman, Robert O.
Schelling, Ernest
Vogt, Gustave

US-NYts   **New York, Union Theological Seminary**
Byrd, Frederick M.
Day, Henry

US-Oa   **Oakland, California, Public Library**
Parker, Mrs. C. T. M.
Vesper, O. M.

US-OB   **Oberlin, Ohio, Oberlin College Conservatory of Music**
Best, C. W.
Gehrkens, Karl Wilson
Langenus, Gustave
Raugel, Félix

US-OX   **Oxford, Ohio, Miami University**
Lunsford, Bascom Lamar

US-PHci   **Philadelphia, Pennsylvania, Curtis Institute of Music**
Bok, Mary Louise Curtis
Burrell, Mary (Banks)

Jarvis, Charles
Kincaid, William
Torello, Anton

US-PHf   **Philadelphia, Pennsylvania, Free Library of Philadelphia**
Dichter, Harry
Fleisher, Edwin Adler
Keffer, Edward J.
McDevitt, Josephine A.
Schmidt, Max
Wright, Edith A.

US-PHgc   (formerly US-PHem) **Philadelphia, Pennsylvania, Gratz College**
Mandell, Eric

US-PHhs   **Philadelphia, Historical Society of Pennsylvania**
Dreer, Ferdinand Julius
Gratz, Simon

US-PHphs   **Philadelphia, Pennsylvania, Presbyterian Historical Society**
Benson, Louis Fitzgerald

US-PHu   **Philadelphia, University of Pennsylvania**
Albrecht, Otto E.
Butler, Pierce
Hopkinson, Francis
Kemble, Frances Anne [Fanny]
Pfatteicher, Carl F.

US-Pc   **Pittsburgh, Pennsylvania, Carnegie Library of Pittsburgh**
Boyd, Charles N.
Mellor, Charles C.
Merz, Karl
Rosenbloom, Charles J.

US-Pct   **Pittsburgh, Pennsylvania, Carnegie-Mellon University**
Cernkovic, Rudolph

US-Ps   **Pittsburgh, Pennsylvania, Pittsburgh Theological Seminary**
Finney, Theodore M.
Paine, Silas K.
Pratt, W. S.
Warrington, J.

US-Pu   **Pittsburgh, Pennsylvania, University of Pittsburgh, Theodore M. Finney Music Library**
Curtis, Ford E. and Harriet R.
Daniel, Oliver
Finney, Theodore M.
Simpson, A. Carson
Singer, Godfrey F.

US-PO   **Poughkeepsie, New York, Vassar College, George Sherman Dickinson Music Library**
Carreño, Teresa
Dannreuther, Edward
Ritter, Frédéric Louis

US-PRs   **Princeton, New Jersey, Princeton Theological Seminary**
Benson, Louis Fitzgerald

US-PRu   **Princeton, New Jersey, Princeton University**
Hall, James S.
Scheide, William H.
Young, Bernard A. and Morris H.

US-PROu   **Providence, Rhode Island, Brown University**
Harris, Caleb Fiske
MacDougall, Hamilton Crawford
McLellan, Charles W.

US-PRV   **Provo, Utah, Brigham Young University**
Albrecht, Jan
Bonime, Josef
Bruning, Harry F.
Garrett, Robert
Leberman, Walter
Primrose, William
Tretzsch, Rudolph
Valva, Fred D.
Wallfisch, Ernst
Zeyringer, Franz

US-RIVu   **Riverside, University of California**
Class, Peter
Croft, Marcella
James, Harry and Grace
Jonas, Oswald
Schenker, Heinrich

US-R   **Rochester, New York, Eastman School of Music, University of Rochester, Sibley Music Library**
Fitch, Lorraine Noel Finley
Fleisher, Oskar
Gordon, Jacques
Hartmann, A[rthur]
Israel, Fanny and Julius
Krehbiel, Henry Edward
Olschki, Leo Samuel
Pougin, Francois-Auguste-Arthur
Sibley, Hiram W.
Sonneck, Oscar George Theodore

*US-Ro	**Rochester, Michigan, Oakland University**
	George, Collins
US-SLC	**Salt Lake City, University of Utah**
	Leichtentritt, Hugo
US-SFp	**San Francisco, California, Public Library**
	Kursh, Maurice
	Starr, Dorothy
US-SFsc	**San Francisco, California, San Francisco State University**
	De Bellis, Frank W.
	Ruge, [Filippo]
US-SLug	**Saint Louis, Missouri, Washington University**
	Krohn, Ernst C.
*US-SPAm	**Saint Paul, Minnesota, Macalester College**
	Hunt, Arthur Billings
*US-SPAp	**Saint Paul, Minnesota, Public Library**
	Field, Howard
*US-SP	**Saint Peter, Minnesota, Gustavus Adolphus College**
	Hertzberg, Harry
US-SM	**San Marino, California, Henry E. Huntington Library**
	Bridgewater, Francis, 6th Earl of
	Brock, Robert Alonzo
	Christie-Miller, William Henry
	Egerton, Sir Thomas
	Huntington, Henry Edwards
	Huth, Alfred H.
	Kemble, John Philip
	Larpent, John
US-SB	**Santa Barbara, University of California**
	Boucher, Anthony
	Strohl, Joseph P.
*US-SBp	**Santa Barbara, California, Public Library**
	Eichheim, ?
US-SE	**Selinsgrove, Pennsylvania, Susquehanna University**
	Wilt, Henry C.
*US-SOb	**South Bend, Indiana, University of Notre Dame**
	Stevens, William Bacon
*US-SPc	**Spartanburg, South Carolina, Converse College**
	Spy, Walter

US-SPma   **Spokane, Washington, Moldenhauer Archive**
Moldenhauer, Hans

US-STu   **Stanford, California, Stanford University**
Barker, Chester
Keating, George T.
Lange, Henry R.

US-TA   **Tallahassee, Florida State University**
Bates, Lucy
Downes, Olin
Helwig, Carl
Robinson, Carol

*US-Tl   **Toledo, Ohio, Toledo-Lucas County Library**
Hess, ?
Koehler, ?

US-TC   **Tucson, University of Arizona**
Belden, Louis
Hill, Grant L.

US-UN   **University, University of Alabama**
Thompson, T. P.

US-UNm   **University, University of Mississippi**
Goldstein, Kenneth S.

US-U   **Urbana, University of Illinois**
Bullard, Ernest E.
Clarke, Herbert L.
Dichter, Harry
Emory, Millie
Fraenkel, Gottfried Samuel
Harding, Albert A.
Harwell, Richard Barksdale
Helm, Everett Burton
Joseffy, Rafael
Levy, Lester Stern
Quinn, John Kirker
Shirk, William A.
Stetson, Mrs. E. G., and D. C. Burdick Collection
Szigeti, Joseph
Zirner, Ludwig

*US-UKrummel **Urbana, Illinois, private collection**
Krummel, Donald W.

US-UP   **University Park, Pennsylvania State University**
Dye, William Seddinger

US-VB   **Virginia Beach, Virginia, CBN University**
Clark, Keith C.

US-WC   **Waco, Texas, Baylor University**
Spencer, Frances G.
Spencer, Mrs. Kay

US-Whu   **Washington, D.C., Howard University**
Spingarn, Arthur B.

US-WM   **Waltham, Massachusetts, Brandeis University**
De Koven, Reginald

US-Wc   **Washington, Library of Congress**
Bang, Maria
Becker, Karl E.
Cummings, William Hayman
Densmore, Frances
Gansevoort, Anna Maria
Genet, Edmond Charles
Gordon, Robert W.
Hawkins, Micah
Heineman, Dannie N.
Henkel, Heinrich
Hodges, Edward
Hohn, Maia Bang
Huber, William, Jr.
Jahant, Charles
Jefferson, Thomas
Jennings, Mrs. J. W.
Johnson, Travis
Kapp, Jack
Kreisler, Fritz
Landau, Horace de, Baron
Longe, Francis
McConathy, Osbourne
Mason, Luther Whiting
Martorell y Fivaller, Marquesas de
Miller, Dayton Clarence
Moffat, Alfred Edward
Müller, Joseph
Niessen, Carl
Paganini, Nicolò
Rhodes, Willard
Schatz, Albert
Schoenberg, Arnold
Selden-Goth, Gisela
Sonneck, Oscar George Theodore
Stonborough, Jerome
Whittall, Gertrude Clark

US-Wca   **Washington, Washington Cathedral Library**
Clayton, Rev. J. B
Douglas, Charles Winfred
Stebbins, George C.

US-Wsi   **Washington, Smithsonian Institution**
Adams, Mrs. John Quincy
Devincent, Sam [or Daniel?]
Warshaw, Isadore

*US-WSc   **West Swanzey, New Hampshire, Stratton Free Library and Art Gallery**
Stratton, George W.

US-WGc   **Williamsburg, Virginia, College of William and Mary**
Ogle, Cuthberg

US-WI   **Williamstown, Massachusetts, Williams College Library**
Whiteman, Paul

US-WS   **Winston-Salem, North Carolina, Moravian Music Foundation**
Hanford, Charles B.
Harmsworth, Sir Robert Leicester
Herbst, Johannes
Kurth, Richard A.
Lowens, Irving and Margery

US-WIN   **Winterthur, Delaware, Henry Francis Du Pont Winterthur Museum Library**
Downs, Joseph

US-WOa   **Worcester, Massachusetts, American Antiquarian Society**
Lowens, Irving and Margery
Metcalf, Frank J.
Peach, Robert W.
Thomas, Isaiah

RUSSIA (formerly **USSR**)

USSR-KA   **Kaliningrad, Oblastaia biblioteka**
Gotthold, Friedrich August
Köhler, Louis

USSR-Kan   **Kiev, Biblioteka Gosudarstvennoi konservatorii P. I. Caikovskogo**
Raovsky, Andrey Kyrillovich, Prince

USSR-Lan   **Leningrad, Biblioteka Akademii nauk SSSR**
Peter I, Emperor of Russia

USSR-Lit   **Leningrad, Nauchnaia biblioteka Gosudarstvennogo instituta teatra muzyki i kinematografii**
Elizaveta Alexeyevna, Empress of Russia

USSR-Lsc **Leningrad, Gosudarstvennaia publichnaia biblioteka im. Saltykova-Shchedrina**
Yusopov, Nikolai Borisovich

USSR-Mk **Moscow, Nauchna a muzykal'naia biblioteka im. S. I. Taneeva, Gosudarstvennaia konservatoriia im. P. I. Chaikovskogo**
Odoevski, Vladimir Federovich, Prince
Rubinstein, Anton, and Nikolay
Taneyev, Sergey Ivanovich

USSR-Ml **Moscow, Gosudarstvennaia bibliotek SSSR im. V. I. Lenina**
Razumovsky, Dmitry Vasil'evich

YUGOSLAVIA, CROATIA

YU-Bma **Belgrade, Muzička Akademija**
Dordević, Vladimir R.

YU-OSm **Osijek, Muzej slavonije**
Ehrenfels, Normann von
Prandau, Count

YU-Snb **Split, Nadbiskupso sjemenište**
Pastrić, Ivan

YU-Zda **Zagreb, Državni arhiv hrvatske**
Kuhac, Franjo Ksaver

YU-Zh **Zagreb, Hrvatski glazbeni zavod**
Algarotti, Nikola Udina

Section 5

Vendors of Collections

Some firms issued catalogs under a variety of names, the most prolific of these, of course, Sotheby's—S. Leigh Sotheby; Sotheby & Son, Mr. Sotheby, Sotheby, Wilkinson & Hodge — as well as other forms. This firm was by no means unique. I have tried to gather all the variants such vendors used under a single rubric, e.g., "Sotheby," supplying *see* references from the variants to those rubrics. Where the variants are minimal I have simply listed them as they appear on the catalogs, e.g., see "Beijers," "Weigel," et al.

The numbers refer to item numbers elsewhere in this book.

1476, 1478, 1509, 1515, 1559, 1600-01, 1660, 1664-65, 1673, 1718-19, 1731, 1739, 1757, 1767-69, 1777-78, 1819, 1834, 1841, 1888-89, 1916-19, 1921, 1923, 1931, 1954, 1956, 1960, 1971, 1998-2000, 2011, 2032-34, 2038, 2088, 2102, 2115, 2129, 2136, 2144, 2146, 2171, 2181, 2183, 2185, 2192, 2213, 2236, 2238, 2254, 2256, 2314-16, 2320, 2327, 2435, 2474, 2478, 2482, 2496, 2503-04, 2507, 2508-10, 2516-18, 2539, 2551, 2571, 2584-85, 2593-94, 2596, 2599, 2603, 2609, 2614, 2627-29, 2633, 2694, 2727-29, 2750, 2756, 2794-95, 2797-2802, 2849-50, 2867, 2870, 2874-75, 2878, 2901, 2904, 2910, 2928, 3015, 3019-22, 3024-25, 3027-28, 3033-36, 3039-40, 3042-43, 3045, 3047, 3049, 3052, 3055, 3058, 3060, 3062-72, 3074, 3076-77, 3080, 3084, 3086, 3090-92, 3099, 3118, 3120

Quaritch, Bernard, London   472, 625, 774, 2280, 2326

Rampen, Arent, Amsterdam   2888

Rau, Arthur, Paris   2706-07

Reed, Alexander, London   1043

Reeves, Harold, Claygate, Surrey   623, 860-62, 1792

Reeves, Harold, London   765, 861, 2097-98

Reeves, William, London   598, 775, 1142, 1788, 2367, 2558, 2620, 3114

Reichard, Georg, Heidelberg   2660

Reichmann, Alois, Vienna   1118

Relecom, Emile, Brussels   834, 3142

Ricke, Walter, Munich   1585

Ricordi, Edizione, Milan   2370

Robins, Messrs., London   3013

Robins, George, London   707

Roos, C. F., G. de Vries, W. Engelberts, Amsterdam   358

Roos, Gerbraud & Johannes Weege, Amsterdam   2964

Rosenthal, Albi, London   515, 651, 2250

Rosenthal, Jacques, Munich   2650

Rosenthal, Ludwig   713

Rossberg'schen Buchhandlung, Leipzig   1587

Rossi, Dario Giuseppe, Rome   1854, 3079

Rossum, van, Amsterdam   3046, 3050

Sacré, J., Brussels   3017

Sagot, Paris   2759

St. Goar, Frankfurt a.M.   2653

Salomon, Gustav, Dresden   1059, 2233

Sanders & Co., Oxford   676

Sapin, Paris   893

La Scala Autographs, Hopewell, N.J.   427

Schletter'sche Buchhandlung, Breslau   1926

Schneider, Hans, Tutzing and München   13, 53, 284, 336, 637, 680, 778, 784, 1034-35, 1150, 1165, 1176, 1228, 1407, 1412, 1467, 1576, 1776, 1887, 1934, 1979, 2158, 2861

Schultze (Auktions-Secretaire), Schwerin (?)   867

Section 6

Lists, Catalogs, and Inventories
(prepared before 1850)

This chronology inevitably omits many such documents, because their dates and accessibility cannot always be determined, even when their existence is mentioned in the literature—often repeatedly. Some famous collections inventoried at some time before 1850* fall into this category—e.g., those of Pepys (1633-1703), Sigismondo (1739-1826), Pamphilj (1653-1730), and even Mozart—all of whose collections are covered by post-1850 catalogs and cognate literature. But where are the earlier registers and lists?

Dates refer to date of list; numbers refer to entries in *section 1*.

Date	*Collector*	*No.*
1467	House of Este, [also 1625]	791
ca. 1530	Fernando Colón	540, 542-43
1544	Kürfursten von Neuburg Ottheinrich, [also 1556]	2051, 2053-54
1555	Georg Montbéliard	1915
1556	Ottheinrich [also 1544]	2052
1557	Heklar Joachim II	1448
1566	Fugger Family [also 1580, 1655]	985
1569	Eberhard III	747
1572	Karl von Steiermark [also 1577]	1499-1500
1577	Karl von Steiermark [also 1572]	1498
1580	Fugger Family [also 1566, 1655]	986
1582	von Brandenburg Johann George	1461
1586	Herwart Family	1268
1596	John Lumley [also 1609]	1726
1609	John Lumley [also 1596]	1726

*A cut-off date chosen because the mid-19th century saw the beginnings of the rapid rise of a newly rich mercantile class. With that rise came vast increases in the numbers of sales and literature associated with collectors and collections.

Date	*Collector*	*No.*
1622	Sir Charles and Edward Somerset	2520-21
ca. 1625	Karl von Neisse, Erzherzog von Hapsburg	1502
1625	House of Este, [also 1467]	790
1649	João IV, King of Portugal	1449-50, 1456
1655	Fugger Family [also 1566, 1580]	987
1667	Jean-Baptiste de Dandeleu	638-39
ca. 1680	Constantin Huygens [also 1688]	1397
1682	William Heather [also 1690]	1221-22
1685	Harie Maule	1835-36
1687	John Evelyn	822
1688	Constantin Huygens, [also 1680]	1398-99
1690	William Heather, [also 1682]	1223
	John Playford, [also 1691]	2132
1691	John Playford, [also 1690]	2133
1704, 1705	Gottfried Finger	868-69
1705	Marcus Meibom	1850
1708	Leendert van Beke	220
1709	Anthony Ashley Cooper, 4th Earl of Shaftesbury	561
1711	Robert Orme	2041
1714	Thomas Britton	371
1719/20	Arthur George Leigh	1660
1721	Esterházy Family [also 1737-38, 1740, 1759, 1784, 1806]	804
1724	Sebastian de Brossard	382
1727	Samuel Moreland	1920
1729	Frederick Ashfield	98
	Nicolai Francesco Haym	1216
1730	anonymous	2951
1731	George Skene	2498
1735	? Bourret (of Neuchâtel) [also 1841]	317-18
1737	Edward Whitaker, et al	2855
1737-38	Esterházy Family [also 1721, 1740, 1759, 1784, 1806]	804
1738	Johann Albert Fabricius	824
1740	Le Gendre D'Arminy	644
	Esterházy family [also 1721, 1737-38, 1759, 1806]	804
	Jon. Col. John Mercer	1873
	Johann Christoph Pepusch	2103
1741	[B , Ph. ; E V]	2952
	Ger. Koen.	1549
1742	Johann Sebastian Bach [also 1750]	133
1743	Francisco Lopez Duliz [De Liz]	739-40
1745	Ernst Kraft, Graf von Oettingen-Wallerstein [also 1765]	1568
1745/46	Berkley Seymour and R. Harneise	2469
1746	Gerard Frederik Witvogel	2888-89
1747	Rev. David Comarque	544-45
1748	Lorenzo Corsini [also 1751, 1754, 1756, 1757]	574
1749	? Denielle	657
1749	Cornelis Claesz	505

Date	*Collector*	*No.*
1750	Johann Sebastian Bach [also 1742]	127
	Richard Graham, et al.	1084
	"Several Gentlemen"	148
1751	Lorenzo Corsini, [also 1748, 1754, 1756, 1757]	575
	Jos. Antoine Crozat	617
ca. 1753	Edward Harley	1180
1754	Lorenzo Corsini [also 1748, 1751, 1756, 1757]	576
ca. 1755	Aberdeen Musical Society	3
1756	Lorenzo Corsini [also 1748, 1751, 1754, 1757]	577
1757	anonymous	2953
	Lorenzo Corsini [also 1748, 1751, 1754, 1756]	579
1759	H. Constapel [also 1760, 1771]	553
	Esterházy Family [also 1721, 1737-38, 1740, 1784, 1806]	804
	Nicolas Selhof	2458-59
	Granville Sharp [also 1793, 1814]	2471
1760	H. Constapel [also 1759, 1771]	551
	George Frideric Handel	1170
1761	Anthony Ashley Cooper, 4th Earl of Shaftesbury [also 1709]	561-62
1762	J. van Doorn and Antoni van Heurn	701
1763	Charles De Geer	652-53
	Ephraim Kelner	1508
1764	anonymous	2954
	Chigi Family [also 1795]	479
	Johann Mattheson	1823-24
	William Young (of Standlich)	2913
1765	Ernst Graf von Oettingen-Wallerstein Kraft [also 1745]	1569
	Pietro Antonio Locatelli	1701
	Jeanne Antoinette Pompadour	2143
1766	House of Hohenzollern [also 1768]	1344
1767-ca. 1786	Georg von Waldburg-Zeil	2789
1768	Patrick A. Alströmer	40
	House of Hohenzollern [also 1766]	1343
ca. 1770	Lord Clive Robert	2250
1770	Charles Burney, [also 1814]	408
	Christoph Daniel Ebeling	745
1771	H. Constapel, [also 1759, 1760]	552
	Mons. le Comte de Salmreifferscheid	2321
1772	Alexander Ferdinand, Fürst [also 1784, 1786, 1790, 1795, 1838]	30
1773	M***	2955
	Merkman, Vve P. [née Leeuwarden]	1875
1774	anonymous	2956
1776	anonymous	2957-58
1777	William Gostling, and Son	1076-77
1779	William Boyce, the Elder [also 1824]	330

Date	*Collector*	*No.*
ca. 1780	Compte d'Ogny	2024-25
1780	Franz Xaver Fürall	978
	Graf und Edler zur Lippe-Detmold Simon August	2493
1781	William Maserer	1807
1783	Princess of Prussia Anna Amalia [also 1787, 1800]	62-63
	Rev. Thomas Crofts (of Peterborough)	613
	Gideon de Gast	1024-25
1784	Fürst Alexander Ferdinand [also 1772, 1786, 1790, 1795, 1838]	30
	Esterházy Family [also 1721, 1737-38, 1740, 1759, 1806]	804
1785	Heinrich Friedrich Ludwig Rellstab	2209
1786	Fürst Alexander Ferdinand [also 1772, 1784, 1790, 1795, 1838]	27, 30
	John Stanley	2552
1787	Carl Friedrich Abel	1
	Richard Aldrich	25
	Princess of Prussia Anna Amalia [also 1783, 1800]	64
	Richard Goodson, the younger	1069-70
	Jacques Joseph Francois de Vogüe	2774
1788	Georg Andreas Henkel	1242
	Unico Wilhelm Wassenaer, Count	2811
1789	Rev. Mr. Airson	17
	anonymous	2959-60
	Carl Philipp Emanuel Bach [also 1790, 1805]	119
	Paolo Fabbrini	823
1790	Fürst Alexander Ferdinand [also 1772, 1784, 1786, 1795, 1838]	30
	anonymous	2961-62
	Carl Philip Emanuel Bach [also 1789, 1805]	139-40, 143
	Broek (Cornelis van den) Cornelisz	376
	Collegium Musicum "Audi et Tace," Leeuwarden	537
1791	anonymous	2963
	Ove Schjeldberg Bull	400
	Jacob Hemett	1240
	Ernst Kraft, Graf von Oettingen-Wallerstein [also 1745, 1765]	1570, 1574
	Franz Michael von Schaden	2371
1792	anonymous	2964
1793	anonymous	2965
	Granville Sharp [also 1759, 1814]	2472
1794	Louis Gautier, Jr.	1028
	J. H. Reisig	2208
1795	Fürst Alexander Ferdinand [also 1772, 1784, 1786, 1790, 1838]	26
	Chigi Family [also 1764]	480
	Paul Hobler [perhaps John Paul]	1326

Date	*Collector*	*No.*
1796	John Brooke, of Leicester	380
	John Wall Callcott [also 1805, 1819]	419
	"A Gentleman"	2966
1797	Dorothea Graumann	1103
1798	Thomas Bever	247
	William Hayes	1215
1799	Dr. Samuel Howard	1373
ca. 1800	Anna Amalia, Princess of Prussia [also 1783, 1787]	65
	Joseph Haydn [also ca. 1804]	1212
	? Trémont, Baron de	2721
1801	J. F. Euler	820
1802	Mr. Balham	160
	F. Fiers, and Hyacinthe de Grave	850
1803	Samuel Arnold	86
	Auguste Friederike, Consort of Friedrich Ludwig	106
	Smith Barry	175
	Ignaz Franz von Beecke	203
	Maximilian III Joseph, Elector of Bavaria	1839
ca. 1804	Haydn Joseph [also ca. 1800]	1211
1804	J[ac] Baden	149
	J. C. W. de Daehne	631
	"A Gentleman, Deceased"	2969
	Ernst Ludwig Gerber	1037-38
	Alipius Seitz	2454
1805	anonymous	2970-71
	Carl Philipp Emanuel Bach [also 1789, 1790]	122
	John Wall Callcott [also 1796, 1819]	419
1806	Esterházy Family [also 1721, 1737-38, 1740, 1759, 1784]	804, 807
	Johann Joseph Rainer Rudolph, Erzherzog [also 1816, 1817, 1818, 1819]	2289
1807	James Bartleman [also 1816, 1822]	178
	Nicolas Findeisen	867
	Fürst Hohenlohe-Langenburg	3828
	August Leduc, firm	1648
1808	J. H. Colizzi	535
1809	François Hippolyte Barthélemon	177
	Count Jan Rudolph Chotek	491
	William Kitchiner [also 1827, 1838]	1531
	Johann Christian Kittel	1535
1810 (or 20)	Carl Friedrich Zelter	65
1810	Count Christian Clam-Gallas	3403
	Charles Greville	1129
	Daniel Walker	2792
1811	Balle [Nic Edinger]	161
	Henry Compton	549
	Venanzio Matteo Rauzzini	2177

Date	*Collector*	*No.*
1812	anonymous	2972
	Ijsbrand von Hamelsveld	1166
	Nicolas Stochove	2574
1813	J. G. Flack	882
	Rev. John Parker	2087
	"A Professor of Music"	2974
	Robert Smith (of St. Paul's Church-Yard)	2512
	John Sydney (of Hunton, Kent)	2608
1814	Charles Burney [also 1770]	405, 407
	D. Pasquale Caracciolo, Marchese di Arena	441
	John Baptist Malchair	1750
	Granville Sharp [also 1759, 1793]	2473
	George Joseph Vogler, Abt	2772
1815	Johann Friedrich Reichardt	2200
	John Roberts	862, 866
1816	anonymous	2975
	John Bacon	147
	James Bartleman [also 1807, 1822]	180
	Johann Baptist Cramer [also 1835]	607
	H. W. Dean	647
	Richard Fitzwilliam, 7th Viscount	880-81
	Dr. Henry Harington (of Bath)	1179
	James Horsfall [also 1817]	1369
	Frank Östergren	936
	Johann Joseph Rainer Rudolph, Erzherzog [also 1806, 1817, 1818, 1819]	2289
	Daniel Gottlob Türk	2725-26
	Samuel Webbe, Sr.	2831
1817	James Horsfall [also 1816]	1369-70
	Johann Joseph Rainer Rudolph, Erzherzog [also 1806, 1816, 1818, 1819]	2289
1818	John Carter	451
	Johann Joseph Rainer Rudolph, Erzherzog [also 1806, 1816, 1817, 1819]	2289
1819	Francesco Bianchi	249
	Sir Patrick Blake	269
	John Wall Callcott [also 1796, 1805]	419
	Johann Nikolaus Forkel	913
	Johann Joseph Rainer Rudolph, Erzherzog [also 1806, 1816, 1817, 1818]	2286
1820	anonymous	2976
	Joseph Gwilt	1147
	Fortunato Santini, Abbate [also 1843, 1845]	2333
	George Ebenezer Williams	2869
1821	Giuseppe Naldi	1968
	"Several Persons, Deceased"	2977
1822	"An Amateur, Residing in the Country"	2979
	"An Eminent Professor, Recently Deceased"	2978

Date	*Collector*	*No.*
	James Bartleman [also 1807, 1816]	180
	Henry Hinckley	1297
1823	anonymous	2980
	William Dowding	706
	Rev. Dr. Monkhouse	190
	Johann Gottfried Schicht	2404
	Christian Friedrich Schwencke [also 1824]	2445
1824	William Boyce, the elder [also 1779]	331
	Johann Andreas Göpel	1057
	John Gunn	1146
	Edward Jones, Bard y hrenin [also 1825]	1474
	Maas [probably Johann Gebhard Ehrenreich]	1735
	Christian Friedrich Schwencke [also 1823]	2446
1825	Dr. ? Jameson (of Cheltenham)	1427
	Edward Jones, Bard y hrenin [also 1824]	1475
	William Knyvett	1544
	Mr. Sharpe (of Knutsford)	2477
	Edw. Synge	2610
1826	anonymous	2981-82
	Caspar Siegfried Gaehler	1005
	T. Jones (of Nottingham)	1477
1827	anonymous	2983-84
	Ludwig van Beethoven	204-10, 214, 216
	Duke of York Frederick Augustus	926
	Carl Joseph Hammer	1167
	William Kitchiner [also 1809, 1838]	1532
	Guillaume Raveta	2179
	R. C. Sidney (of Mortimer St.)	2486
1828	John Flaxman	885
	John Bernard Sale and P. Taylor	2319-20
1829	anonymous	2986-87
	(C. de) L. F. Fouw	918
	Aloys Fuchs [also 1841, 1848, 1850]	941-50
	Joseph Major	1749
	William Shield	2480
1830	anonymous	2988-89
	Ayrton, probably William [also 1849]	112
	Mathew Cooke and B. Jacobs	558-59
	John Feltham Danneley	642
	William Edward Heather	1225
	Gaspari Selvaggi [also 1843]	2464
	Mr. Timbs	2672
	Johann Christoph Westphal	2851
1831	anonymous	2992
	"A Celebrated Amateur"	2991
	J. Coggins (late of Piccadilly)	518
	Burford George Henry Gibsone	1043
	George Edward Griffith	1134

Date	*Collector*	*No.*
	? Heath, et al.	1237
	Rev. Osias Thurston Linley	1689
	Henry Llewellyn	1697
	"A Professor - A Gentleman - A Dealer"	2990
1832	Muzio Clementi	513
	Thomas Greatorex	1114-15
	Stephen Groombridge	1137
	John Sidney Hawkins [also 1843]	1207-09
	? Holbrooke	1350
	Joseph Jerkowitz	1444
	Georg Johann Daniel Pölchau	2138-40
	James Sanderson	2325
1833	Thomas Alcock	23
	anonymous	2993
	Pio Cianchettini	500
	William Hawes	1204
	J. C. Nightingale	1984
	Sir George Smart	2502-03
	William Wilson (of the Minories, F.S.A.)	2876
1834	anonymous	2994-95
	Jean Bernard	238
	James Jennings	1441
	Col. ? West; and "A Lady of Rank"	2848
1835	Johann Baptist Cramer [also 1816]	607
	James Kent and Vincent Novello	1510
	James Paddon (organist of Exeter Cathedral)	2070
	"A Professional Gentleman Lately Deceased"	2996
	Armand Séguin	2451
	Charles Wesley	2847
1836-37	Charles von Hulthem	1382
1836	? Bêche	194
	Marie Anne Pierretee Paulze Lavoisier	1643
	"Two Eminent Professors"	2998
1837	anonymous	2999
	Edward Francis Rimbault	2237-43
	"Two Libraries"	3000
	Niccolò Zingarelli	2926
1838	Fürst Alexander Ferdinand [also 1772, 1784, 1786, 1790, 1795]	28
	William Kitchiner [also 1809, 1827]	1533
	William Young Ottley	2056
	René Charles Guilbert Pixérécourt	2130
	Samuel Prado	2148
1839	"A Gentleman Removed from the Country"	3001
	Ludwig Samuel Dietrich Mutzenbecker	1959
	C. B. Tait, auctioneer, Edinburgh	2615
1840	S. M. Boer	287
	Adalbert Gyrowetz	1149

Date	Collector	No.
	Henry Hase	1191
	Anton Friedrich Justus Thibaut [also 1842]	2660-61
1841	André, publishers	56-57
	? Bourret (Neuchâtel) [also 1735!]	319
	Aloys Fuchs [also 1829, 1848, 1850]	941-50
	"A Gentleman"	3002
	Thomas Hill	1294
	Joseph Warren	2796
1842	Lovell Adamson	6
	James Orchard Halliwell-Phillips	1159
	James Hook	1361
	Rev. Christian Ignatius Labrobe	1636
	Charles Britiffe Smith	2505
	S. Sotheby	2526
	Anton Friedrich Justus Thibaut [also 1840]	2660-61
	Gottfried Weber	2834
	Carl Zulehner	2929
1843	anonymous	3003
	Carl Ferdinand Becker [also 1846]	196-97
	John Sidney Hawkins [also 1832]	1207-09
	Thomas Hawkins	1210
	Abbate Santini, Fortunato [also 1820, 1845]	2334
	Gaspari Selvaggi [also 1830]	2463
	Thomas Vaughan	2751
1844	Docteur Bibliophobus	251
	Benjamin Heywood Bright [also 1845]	369-70
	Calvert	424
	Gerald Melbourne Cooper, Ernest Augustus Kellner, and [John] Fawcett	563
	François Cramer	606-08
	Dr. Gratiano (of San Marco)	1102
	Felix Xaver Wolfgang Mozart	1933
	John Stafford Smith	2508
	"Two Gentlemen, Deceased"	3004
1844/45	Augustus Frederick, Duke of Sussex [also 1845, 1846]	108
1845	Adolph Joseph Louis Alizard	35
	Augustus Frederick, Duke of Sussex and Dr. Southey [also 1846]	109
	Benjamin Bright [also 1844]	369-70
	Benjamin Cooke	557, 2538
	Julius Kötschau	1556
	Barhan J. Livius	1696
	Erasmus Madox	1742
	Fortunato Santini, Abbate	2335
	"Several Private Gentlemen"	3006
	"Two Well-known Amateurs, Deceased"	3005
1846	Augustus Frederick, Duke of Sussex [also 1845]	110

Date	*Collector*	*No.*
	Carl Ferdinand Becker [also 1843]	196-97
	Domenico Dragonetti	707-09
	Gottfried Wilhelm Fink	870
	Louis Gantter [also 1847]	1015
	"A Gentleman, Deceased"	3007
	Thomas Mackinlay (publisher)	1738-39
	H. White	2857
1847	anonymous	3008-09
	? Binfield (of Reading)	258
	John Capel	438
	Comtesse de Cordelia Castellane (Greffulhe)	463
	Neville Butler Challoner [also 1849]	470-?
	Louis Gantter [also 1846]	1016
	Henry John Gauntlett [also 1849]	1026-27
	"A Gentleman"	3010-11
	Enoch Hawkins	1205
	Raphael Georg Kiesewetter	1521-22
	William Mason	1812
	Jean Baptiste Charles Mathieu	1821
	Ignaz Moscheles	1923
	Johann Andreas Stumpff	2599-2600
	Lady Mark Elizabeth Sykes	2609
	Emmanuel Louis Nicolas Viollet-Leduc	2769-70
1848	anonymous	3012
	Tim Essex	789
	Aloys Fuchs [also 1829, 1841, 1850]	941-50
	Charles Hatchett	1193-94
	Charles Hodges	1336
	T. F. Millar and [Mrs. Stevens]	1889
	Samuel Picart	2115
	C. Reade	2183
	Isidore Justin Séverin Taylor, Baron	2630-32
1849	William Ayrton	113
	Neville Butler Challoner [also 1847]	470-?
	L. Ganz	1017
	Henry John Gauntlett [also 1847]	1026-27
	John Webb (of Paris)	2830
	Sir Giffin Wilson	2874
1850	Adolphus Frederick, Duke of Cambridge	9-10
	Aloys Fuchs [also 1829, 1841, 1848]	941-50

Index

Numbers refer to item numbers, *not* pages. The siglum "H" indicates holographs in that item. See more, below, under *autographs*.